introduction to psychology

FIFTH EDITION

INTRODUCTION

FIFTH EDITION

TO PSYCHOLOGY

Ernest R. Hilgard
Stanford University

Richard C. Atkinson
Stanford University

Rita L. Atkinson
Stanford University

 HARCOURT BRACE JOVANOVICH, INC.

New York   Chicago   San Francisco   Atlanta

ISBN: 0-15-543647-3

Library of Congress Catalog Card Number: 72-141606

Printed in the United States of America

Acknowledgments and Copyrights

Tables

3-1 Sigel, I. E. The attainment of concepts. In M. L. Hoffman and L. W. Hoffman (eds.), *Review of child development research,* Vol. I. New York: Russell Sage Foundation, 1964. 3-2 Data from Erikson, E. H. *Identity: youth and crisis,* Norton (1968), p. 94, copyright © 1968 by W. W. Norton & Company, Inc. And from Erikson, E. H., *Childhood and society,* 2nd edition, Norton (1963), p. 274, copyright © 1950, 1963 by W. W. Norton & Company, Inc. By permission of W. W. Norton & Company, Inc., The Hogarth Press Ltd., and Faber and Faber Ltd. 3-3 From *Patterns of child rearing* by Robert R. Sears, Eleanor E. Maccoby, and Harry Levin. Adaptation of Table D-7, "Relationship Between Children's Feeding Problems and the Training Practices of Their Parents." New York: Harper & Row, 1957. 3-4 From *Patterns of child rearing* by Robert R. Sears, Eleanor E. Maccoby, and Harry Levin. Adaptation of Table X-4, "High Conscience: Relationship to the Mother's Warmth and Her Use of Withdrawal of Love." New York: Harper &

Row, 1957. 3-5 Hilgard, J. R. *Personality and hypnosis.* Chicago: The University of Chicago Press, 1970. Data from Table 33, p. 191, and Table 34, p. 192. Copyright © 1970 by The University of Chicago. All rights reserved. 3-6 Kohlberg, L. The development of children's orientations toward a moral order: L. Sequence in the development of moral thought. *Vita Humana,* 6: 11–33, 1963. By permission of S. Karger Basel and the author.

4-1 Condensed from *The American teenager* by H. H. Remmers and D. H. Radler, copyright © 1957 by H. H. Remmers; reprinted by permission of the publishers, The Bobbs-Merrill Company, Inc. 4-2 McCord, W., McCord, J., and Zola, I. K. *Origins of crime.* New York: Columbia University Press, 1959, p. 77. 4-3 Rosenberg, M. *Society and the adolescent self-image.* Princeton, N. J.: Princeton University Press, 1965. 4-4 Webster, H., Freedman, M. B., and Heist, P. Personality change in college students. In W. Sanford (ed.), *The American college.* New

York: Wiley, 1962. 4-5 Rosenberg, M. *Society and the adolescent self-image.* Princeton, N. J.: Princeton University Press, 1965. 4-8 Lehman, H. C. *Age and achievement,* Figure 129, p. 255. Princeton, N. J.: Princeton University Press, 1953. Copyright © 1953 by the American Philosophical Society.

5-1 Adapted from Table 1, "Some Approximate Detection Threshold Values," from "Contemporary psychophysics" by Eugene Galanter, from *New directions in psychology* by Roger Brown, E. Galanter, E. H. Hess, and G. Mandler. Copyright © 1962 by Holt, Rinehart and Winston, Inc. Reprinted by permission of Holt, Rinehart and Winston, Inc.

6-1 Soal, S. G., and Bateman, F. *Modern experiments in telepathy.* New Haven, Conn.: Yale University Press, 1954. Reprinted by permission of Yale University Press and Faber and Faber Ltd. (London) from *Modern experiments in telepathy.*

continued on page 626

Part 1: Charlotte Brooks, LOOK magazine ©;
Part 3: *Equivocation.* 1964. Benjamin Frazier Cunningham.
Collection of the Museum of Modern Art, New York. Larry Aldrich Foundation Fund;
Part 4: Dr. Leo Ganz; Part 5: National Education Association—Carl Purcell;
Part 6: The Bettmann Archive; Part 7: Wayne Miller—Magnum Photos;
Part 8: Marc Riboud—Magnum Photos

Art on the following pages by David K. Stone:
30, 32, 34, 35, 40, 41, 44, 47, 112, 127, 131, 139, 155, 190, 210, 258, 261, 298, 434

Art on page 275 by Anna Makowska

All other art by Bertrick Associate Artists, Inc.

preface

There is an old story concerning a peasant housewife whose blanket kept unraveling at one end, and who kept knitting on an equivalent amount at the other end. After all the material had changed, was it the same blanket? A similar question may be asked of a textbook going into a fifth edition, with each edition thoroughly revised. Is it still the same textbook? The reply in each case is a conditional "yes," for both blanket and book serve the same purposes today that they served in the past, and there is continuity in the midst of change. The purpose of this book has always been to introduce contemporary psychology to the beginning student, in full recognition that between editions both psychology and the student change. As a simple quantitative idea of the amount of change that occurs in psychology, we can note that 40 percent of the fourth edition references were new over the third edition, and that fifth edition references are 50 percent new over the fourth.

Students come to the first course in psychology for a variety of reasons, but few of them are motivated primarily to know what psychologists are doing in psychology. They want to know what is pertinent to their own lives, and to the problems of society. A new awareness of social ills—racial strife, war, poverty, overpopulation, pollution of the environment, social injustice—has brought increasing numbers of students to courses in behavioral and social sciences; and they want the subject matter to be made relevant to these larger issues. We have attempted to write primarily for the student, but in such a way as to satisfy the critical psychologist as well.

In the fourth edition we presented issues close to the students' lives in a chapter on "States of awareness"; this chapter is continued in this edition (Chapter 7), with an expanded treatment of the drug problem and a new section on meditation. The fifth edition also treats the large social issues in a new chapter on "Psychology and society" (Chapter 23), which acknowledges that psychologists must change their emphases and join with people from other fields if social problems are to yield to scientific study.

Each instructor designs his course in view of his students, his course objectives, and the available time. We tried to treat as much of psychology as can be covered in a book of reasonable length; even if all chapters are not assigned, the students will at least have them for reference, and the instructor need not feel that he has short-changed them if he has not completely "covered the ground." For a short introductory course we recommend that the instructor treat a few chapters fully. Proposed below are two 16-chapter alternatives, one for a course with a biological and experimental emphasis, the other for a course with a personal and social emphasis. These are, of course, only illustrative of other possible combinations. Some instructors prefer to depart from the chapter order in the text. By providing a few transitions, they find that this works out satisfactorily.

A 16-chapter version:
Biological and Experimental Emphasis

1. Psychology as a behavioral science (Chapter 1)
2. The behaving organism (Chapter 2)
3. Sensory processes (Chapter 5)
4. Perception (Chapter 6)
5. States of awareness (Chapter 7)
6. Learning and conditioning (Chapter 8)
7. Memory (Chapter 9)
8. Optimizing learning (Chapter 10)
9. Language and thought (Chapter 11)
10. Physiological background of motivation (Chapter 12)
11. Human motivation (Chapter 13)
12. Affect and emotion (Chapter 14)
13. Ability testing and intelligence (Chapter 15)
14. Behavior genetics (Chapter 16)
15. Theories of personality (Chapter 17)
16. Personality assessment (Chapter 18)

A 16-chapter version:
Personal and Social Emphasis

1. Psychology as a behavioral science (Chapter 1)
2. Infancy and childhood (Chapter 3)
3. Adolescence and adulthood (Chapter 4)
4. States of awareness (Chapter 7)
5. Learning and conditioning (Chapter 8)
6. Memory (Chapter 9)
7. Language and thought (Chapter 11)
8. Human motivation (Chapter 13)
9. Affect and emotion (Chapter 14)
10. Ability testing and intelligence (Chapter 15)
11. Personality assessment (Chapter 18)
12. Conflict and adjustment (Chapter 19)
13. Behavior disorders (Chapter 20)
14. Psychotherapy and related techniques (Chapter 21)
15. Social psychology (Chapter 22)
16. Psychology and society (Chapter 23)

The chapters continue to be grouped into parts, but a change in the order of the parts places the unit on motivation and emotion after that on learning and thinking. The new order permits learning concepts to be used more comfortably in the discussion of acquired motives, and the transition to the section on individuality and personality is now somewhat smoother.

Critical discussions have again been included because they help to show that psychologists do not always agree and that advances often come out of the reexamination of previously accepted facts and theories. The openness of these discussions permits the instructor to disagree with text interpretations without discrediting either the text authors or himself. The suggestions for further reading at the end of each chapter refer to material of an advanced nature that the student would not be expected to read as part of regular assignments, but the sources are there for those who may wish to investigate a topic of interest more extensively. We have retained the explicit documentation of statements made in the text through citation of sources, because we believe that psychology has not yet reached that stage in which declarative statements can be made dogmatically and anonymously. Most assertions have to be qualified by the context in which they have arisen, and this context is often best indicated by citing a source. Statements such as "Emotions disrupt learning," or "Women change their attitudes more readily than men," may be true in some contexts, but if one questions the statement, he should be able to find where it originated, who asserted it, and what the circumstances were.

Changes of substance have been made throughout the book to reflect advances in psychology. The two chapters on development from early infancy through adolescence and adulthood, placed early in the book as a preview of psychology in the context of human problems, have been brought up-to-date with new material on early childhood and the importance of early experiences in both animals and man. The treatment of sensory processes takes into account the increasing interest in signal detectability theory and includes an exposition of ROC curves. The problems of recurrent inhibition in visual perception are considered. The material on learning has been extensively rewritten. The chapter on management of learning now emphasizes optimization procedures (and the chapter is accordingly renamed "Optimizing learning"). New models of short- and long-term memory are discussed and evaluated, and computer models of information processing are freshly examined. Psycholinguistics is discussed more extensively, with attention given to the distinction between surface and deep structure in language. And the approximations to language by animals, especially the sign language experiments with chimpanzees, are treated.

The sections on ability, personality, and social interaction have been reorganized, and many topics have been enriched by new material. The distinction between "fluid" and "crystallized" intelligence is brought out in the discussion of ability testing. The personality chapters have been extensively rewritten to include discussion of the specificity theories of social behavior theorists and the many new studies proceeding from experimental approaches to personality. In the discussion of psychotherapy, the development of sensitivity and encounter groups is considered, in a context of theory. The social psychology chapter has been revised to take account of developments in experimental social psychology, including the "risky-shift" as a consequence of group discussion and experimental studies of techniques for inoculation against persuasive communications. To illustrate that social psychology must not be merely a laboratory science but must deal with actual social life, we have included an interpretation of voting behavior in the 1968 presidential election.

The final chapter on "Psychology and society" has replaced the one entitled "Psychology as a profession" in the fourth edition. The purpose of an introductory course should not be so much to enlist those who wish to be trained as psychologists as to alert students from many fields of interest to the possibilities open to a new generation of problem-solvers.

The statistics chapter now appears as an appendix. In our view a competent statistics chapter may be too difficult to master in the time commonly allotted to a text chapter, but ought to be included for those who wish to cover it. The statistical methods presented in the first chapter make it possible to understand the tabular material and statistics presented in the text.

Our debts of gratitude to those who have helped with the preparation of the book continue to mount. Those who contributed to earlier editions have had a continuing influence. In the preparation of this edition critical reviews of fourth edition chapters or of drafts of present chapters (or both) have been prepared by:

Harry Beilin, City University of New York, Graduate Center
Thomas G. Bever, Rockefeller University
Arthur H. Brayfield, Claremont Graduate School
Jonathan L. Freedman, Columbia University
Bert F. Green, Johns Hopkins University
John M. Grossberg, San Diego State College
Richard M. Held, Massachusetts Institute of Technology
Jerry Hirsch, University of Illinois
David L. LaBerge, University of Minnesota
Thomas K. Landauer, Bell Laboratories
Brendan A. Maher, Brandeis University
Edward J. Murray, University of Miami
Allen Newell, Carnegie-Mellon University

Irwin G. Sarason, University of Washington
Richard F. Thompson, University of California, Irvine

Acknowledgments of permissions to use copyrighted material appear in a list beginning on the copyright page. We are grateful for these permissions, for without them it would be impossible to produce a book of this kind.

As usual, we have been ably assisted by our secretaries, Nadine Cline, Myrna E. Valdez, and Carolyn B. Young, and by the efficient staff of our publisher.

Stanford University

Ernest R. Hilgard
Richard C. Atkinson
Rita L. Atkinson

contents

III PERCEPTUAL PROCESSES

IV LEARNING AND THINKING

VI INDIVIDUALITY AND PERSONALITY

VII CONFLICT, ADJUSTMENT, AND MENTAL HEALTH

VIII SOCIAL BEHAVIOR

PART ONE

THE SCIENCE OF PSYCHOLOGY

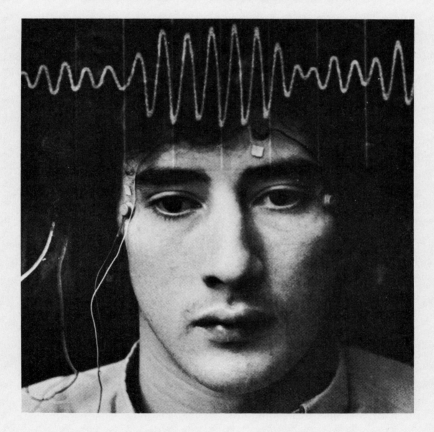

CHAPTER 1. psychology as a behavioral science

CHAPTER 2. the behaving organism

psychology as a behavioral science

1

MAN HAS ALWAYS SOUGHT TO UNDERSTAND himself and the world around him. When he discovered occurrences beyond his comprehension, he at first tended to attribute them to divine intervention or to some sort of magic, perhaps practiced upon him by his enemies. The roots of science took hold when he started to find an order in natural occurrences that made them comprehensible—when, for example, he found that he could control his food supply by domesticating animals or by planting crops.

The physical and biological sciences were the first to be developed because the basic concept of *orderliness* is readily observed in the movements of the stars, the turning of the seasons, and the cyclic changes in trees and plants. Man could observe these changes, think about them, and use the knowledge acquired for his own purposes (as in navigation or in storing food against the winter); at the same time man did not change his conception of himself very strikingly. This capacity to keep some distance from the facts of observation—not to be too much influenced by personal preferences or prejudices—is the essence of objectivity, the dispassionate search for understanding that science embodies.

It was more difficult for man to take a scientific view of himself. By the time he was ready to do so—following the Renaissance, when other sciences were being developed—the prevailing philosophical and theological conceptions were powerful deterrents against man's viewing himself with the same kind of objectivity that he used in studying other natural occurrences. The study of mental activity—the province of a scientific psychology—did not get seriously under way until the latter half of the nineteenth century.

A natural science of man, which would include psychology, awaited Darwin's theory of evolution. Man's affiliation with animals, by the fact that he also was a mammal and a primate, was too obvious to have escaped the notice of early philosophers. Man has to eat and sleep and reproduce his kind as other animals do; he is subject to many of the same diseases and is fed and poisoned by many of the same substances. But man's special place in the world was saved by positing something else—a higher nature—that was not shared with the animals. Descartes (1596–1620) made this distinction explicit by sharply separating man's bodily characteristics, which he shared with the lower animals, from his mental characteristics, which were his alone. This resolution of the problem of man's place in nature permitted Descartes, who was a mathematician and a scientist, to carry on experimentation with animals without conflict with ecclesiastical authorities. Darwin (1809–82) exploded this distinction with his theory of evolution, which placed man squarely inside the realm of biology. If man was to be conceived as continuous with the lower animals, it was understood that a natural science of man, including his adaptive behavior, must be possible. Psychology, as we know it, is a post-Darwinian science.

Behavior, mind, and the brain

The doctrine of evolution encompasses both the evolution of bodily structures and the evolution of behavior that adapts the organism to its environment. The basic notion of "survival of the fittest" places emphasis upon those adjustments to the environment that permit some organisms to win out in competition with others and hence to pass on, through hereditary mechanisms, those qualities that gave them an advantage. When applied to man, evolutionary theory has to account for those features of human behavior that have given man his unique position in the animal kingdom: his capacity to invent and use tools and machinery to modify his environment; his capacity to use language, and with its help to store, retrieve, and make use of information; his ability to plan and thus both protect himself from dangers and enlarge the scope of his existence. The problem of man's being continuous with other animals and yet unique is with us in the post-Darwinian period as it was before, though it is now viewed in a new light.

Behavior

Behavior, strictly speaking, refers to those activities of an organism (whether a lower animal or man) that can be observed. A child eats breakfast, rides a bicycle, talks, blushes, laughs, and cries. All these verbs describe forms of behavior. Observations of behavior may be made unaided, as in watching a child at play, or they may be aided with instruments, as in giving a lie-detection test. Psychology seeks through objective observations to find orderliness in all behavior (setting aside, for the time being, the question of defining what constitutes "mental" behavior) and thus seeks to be like other sciences.

The position that behavior, as strictly defined

Ivan P. Pavlov

John B. Watson

Fig. **1-1 Three scientists important in the history of behaviorism** Pavlov was a Russian physiologist and Nobel Prize winner whose experiments on conditioned reflexes helped promote an objective science of brain and behavior. Watson was an American psychologist who made behaviorism a popular position; he adopted Pavlov's conditioned reflex as a tool to study processes that had been considered to be open to study only through introspection. Skinner is a contemporary American psychologist who has held to the behaviorist position, extending it in important ways to the study of verbal behavior, programed learning, and psychotherapy.

B. F. Skinner

above, is the subject matter of psychology was advanced in 1913 by John B. Watson (1878–1958), an American psychologist (Watson, 1913).[1] Prior to that time psychology had been defined as the study of mental experiences, and reliance for data

[1]Throughout this book the reader will find references, cited by author and date, that document or expand on the statements made here. Detailed publishing information on these studies appears in the bibliographical list at the end of the book. This list also serves as an index to the pages on which the citations appear.

had been placed very largely upon self-observation in the form of introspection. But introspection could not be used with lower animals, infants, or disturbed adults. Watson felt that psychology could free itself and enlarge its scope by making behavior its subject matter.

In order for psychology to become a science, Watson said, its data must be open to public inspection like the data of any other science. When a rat runs a maze you can take a motion picture of its movements, and any competent person can check your statement about the order in which it entered the blind alleys. As long as you study what the animal or person *does,* then you can have an *objective* science distinct from the *subjective* science to which introspection limits you. Behavior is public; consciousness is private. According to Watson, science should deal with public facts.

Behaviorism, as Watson's position came to be called, has been very influential in the half-century or so since it was announced. Although many correctives have been introduced, as we shall see, behaviorism is still strong in American psychology today, particularly through the work of a Harvard psychologist, B. F. Skinner (1904–), and his many followers (Skinner, 1969).

One consequence of behaviorism has been a continuous development of *comparative psychology,* that is, the study of the behavior of lower organisms from an evolutionary point of view. The study of lower organisms has many advantages. Their lives can be controlled in the laboratory from the moment of birth. In those organisms with a short life span, it is possible to study inheritance through several generations. Brain surgery, possible in human subjects only under special conditions of illness or injury, may be undertaken more readily. Although caution is always needed in applying the results of animal experimentation to man, study of lower animals contributes to knowledge in psychology just as it does in biology and medicine.

Another consequence of behaviorism was the favoring of a *stimulus-response psychology,* or S-R psychology, as it is commonly designated. S-R psychology, based on the model of the physiological reflex, antedated behaviorism but was readily incorporated into it. A typical reflex, such as pupillary constriction in the presence of a bright light or a knee jerk in response to a tap on the tendon, is a relatively direct *response* (movement) to a *stimulus* (the occasion for the response). The Russian physiologist Pavlov (1849–1936) introduced the notion of a learned reflex, a *conditioned reflex,* whereby a response becomes attached to a novel stimulus that did not previously evoke it (Pavlov, 1927). The concept of stimulus and response, then, provided an explanation for habit formation and learning and fitted well into the

behaviorist's desire for some analytical unit that could account for behavior. If the stimuli responsible for behavior can be identified, then the behavior can be predicted and, through conditioning, brought under control.

We thus need to distinguish among several consequences of the rise of behaviorism. One of these, the emphasis upon objective methods in psychological science, is of enduring significance and may outlast the other consequences. A second, an emphasis upon the comparative approach to psychology, is also of continuing importance, although for a time it may have led to an overemphasis upon animal studies and to some neglect of human problems. The third consequence, an emphasis upon a strictly S-R psychology, has recently come under attack as being too narrow to encompass the richness of psychological data; the issues of controversy between S-R psychology and other approaches to psychology are matters of contemporary debate.

Conscious processes, awareness, and mental activity

Each of us knows what it feels like to be hungry, to have a headache, to sense the burn of a finger. Each of us knows what it feels like to be praised or reproved. Each is aware of his own anger and fear, excitement and fatigue; no one else has full access to this awareness. An individual's perceptions of his world, his memories, his dreams, his pleasures and pains belong to a private world, the world of his own *consciousness,* accessible to self-observation, or *introspection.* By conscious experience we mean simply those events of which the person experiencing them is fully aware. We may learn from external signs that a man is suffering pain and we may even arrive at a satisfactory judgment of its intensity, but the conscious process—the actual awareness of the pain—is his alone.

What is the place of conscious processes in a scientific psychology? The behaviorist's answer to this question is a clear one. He either denies the facts of consciousness altogether, or he considers these facts to be poor materials with which to construct a science of psychology and thus ignores

Science News Service

Menninger Foundation

Wolfgang Köhler   Edward C. Tolman   Jean Piaget

Fig. **1-2 Psychologists important in the development of cognitive psychology** Köhler, a German psychologist who migrated to America in the Hitler era, called the attention of American psychologists to *insightful* learning, as opposed to the more mechanical forms of learning implied in the prevalent S-R psychology. Tolman, an American psychologist sympathetic to Köhler's position, extended behaviorism to include cognitive processes. Piaget is a Swiss psychologist and logician whose studies of children's thinking have done much to encourage contemporary cognitive psychology.

them. Edward C. Tolman (1886–1959), a broad-minded behaviorist, said that "raw feels" (by which he meant facts that could be uncovered by introspection) were materials for the artist, not for the scientist. In being so outspoken against consciousness the early behaviorist was reacting against a view that considered psychology to be concerned with the facts of consciousness and nothing else. He was able to show that good and useful studies could be made ignoring these facts, and in this reaction against consciousness as the *only* topic of study he tended to ignore consciousness entirely.

The facts of awareness and mental activity are too self-evident to be dismissed in cavalier fashion, and they have come back into psychology by two ways: through "verbal reports," acceptable to a behaviorist, and through the methods of contemporary cognitive psychology.

An introspective report is made in words, and words are behavior. They are produced by movements of the human organism and can be recorded on magnetic tape so that they are open to objective study. Hence the strict behaviorist can accept verbal reports as valid behavioral data. From the standpoint of the behaviorist we have access to the

private world of the subject, to mental activity, only as an *inference* from his verbal reports, but the making of inferences from data is permissible in an objective science.[2] The inclusion of verbal report as a form of acceptable behavior has permitted the behaviorist to study dreams, hallucinations, and other "subjective" phenomena, without violating his commitment to objectivity.

Although the behaviorist's program is formally defensible, by denying the reality of subjective experiences and insisting upon inferences from verbal behavior instead of accepting the data of experience, the behaviorist introduces some artificiality into the study of mental activity. Contemporary *cognitive psychology* (a psychology of "knowing") is less restrictive and recognizes that awareness may provide data for psychology. The

[2]Our observations almost always include inferences that go beyond the data given. If you see a man waving his hand on a street corner in New York, you *observe* merely the hand-waving, though you may *infer* that he is trying to hail a taxicab. You may be wrong: he may be trying to catch a friend's attention or he may be making a meaningless drunken gesture. Inferences are always somewhat uncertain; the scientific task is to see that the inferences from data are made in such a manner as to ensure a high probability of accuracy.

cognitive psychologist accepts mental activity as he finds it. He wishes to use objective methods of verifying his findings through repetition or systematic variation of conditions, but he does not insist on the analogy of the reflex arc that is used in S-R psychology. He may use other analogies, such as that of a computer, which, rather than "responding" to the input, *processes* the information received and issues an output based on this complex processing. He finds he must deal with pattern recognition, distortions in the perception of reality, and distinctions between attention and inattention.

To study many of the cognitive processes in detail one must carefully examine how they appear to the experiencing person. The position of the cognitive psychologists, expressed very simply, is that a great variety of cognitive processes exist, and if we are to have a complete psychological science we have some obligation to study them as they present themselves in awareness.

Unconscious processes

A difficult problem is raised when we infer the presence of *unconscious processes.* No difficulty would arise were this term applied to the "nonconscious" physiological processes, such as the circulation of the blood or the reflex constriction of the pupil of the eye. Difficulties do arise when by unconscious processes we mean thoughts, wishes, and fears of which the person is unaware but which still influence his behavior.

Sigmund Freud (1856–1939), the founder of psychoanalysis, brought unconscious processes strongly to the attention of psychologists (Freud, 1933). Freud believed that the unacceptable (forbidden, punished) wishes of childhood are driven out of awareness and become part of an active unconscious where they remain influential. The active unconscious, according to Freud, presses to find expression in dreams, slips of speech, unconscious mannerisms, and symptoms of neurotic illness, as well as through socially approved behavior such as artistic, literary, or scientific activity.

Although Freud's views are controversial, it is possible to accept unconscious processes as legitimate inferences from behavior without subscribing fully to psychoanalysis. Most psychologists grant that we can infer unconscious motives from speech, gestures, and other behavioral signs. For example, if a person acts in a conceited manner it may be that he is actually boasting in order to conceal an *unconscious* fear of being thought inferior. Because no sharp distinction exists between conscious and unconscious, it would perhaps be better to speak of degrees of awareness. For example, we may be only dimly aware of the clock's striking, yet be able later to count the strokes; we may catch ourselves humming a tune we did not know we had started to hum. The conceited person is not wholly unaware of his need to hide his fears; he may simply be unaware of the extent to which he "covers up." Unconscious processes are always inferred rather than directly observed, but this does not forbid including them within psychological science.

The role of the brain

Overt behavior is obviously regulated by the brain and nervous system; conscious and unconscious processes are also the products of the action of the brain and nervous system. An interesting question to consider is whether psychology might be merely the study of the action of the brain. A broad field of study, sometimes referred to as *biobehavioral* science, is just that—it attempts to relate behavior to what happens in the brain and nervous system.

It has been found that there are centers deep in the brain (in a part of the brain, old from an evolutionary standpoint, called the *hypothalamus*) that appear to produce the equivalent of pleasure or pain when electrically stimulated (Olds, 1969). Psychologists not only participated in the original experiments in which this discovery was made, but have since carried out a number of experiments to determine how similar the responses to electrical stimulation are to the effects of external pain or food reward. For example, studies have been made of the reaction to conflict when a thirsty rat receives an electric shock on its snout as it attempts to drink. The rat at once approaches the water and withdraws from it, assuming a characteristic posture.

Fig. **1-3** **Conflict between thirst and pain in the rat**   A rat that has learned to drink from the spout (left) is given an unpleasant stimulation through the electrode implanted in its brain when it approaches the spout.

This produces the typical conflict position shown: the rat's neck is stretched out toward the water, but it is ready to back away because of the threatened shock. The conflict between thirst and the pain produced by brain stimulation is indistinguishable from that between thirst and the pain produced by an external electric shock.

Martin Iger

When the shock is received through an implanted electrode in the brain, the rat behaves just as if the shock had been received on its snout (see Figure 1-3). Thus it appears that the shock through the electrode is equivalent to external stimulation.

Comparable studies of human brain function can be made when it is necessary to operate on the brain of a human patient in order to relieve some sort of disturbance. It has been found that stimulation of some parts of the brain produces movements such as the flexing of a finger, while stimulation of other parts may produce sensory effects ("It feels as if my finger just moved"). Stimulation of still other parts may activate memories of past events. There can be no doubt about the intimate relationship between brain activity and behavior and experience.

Although, in principle, all psychological events are represented in some manner by the activity of the brain, it is not feasible to study them exclusively in that manner. The brain is both too complex and too inaccessible for such study; in many cases it is more practicable to study antecedent conditions and their consequences for behavior, without concern for what goes on inside the organism. This is sometimes called the "black box" view; that is, while it is recognized that the brain and nervous system carry on complex activities out of view (in the "black box"), the science of psychology is concerned with what goes into the box and what comes out, and not necessarily with what happens inside. This does not imply that there is no division of labor: some psychologists are concerned primarily with neurophysiological events, the operations of the "black box"; others study regularities of behavior independent of the neurophysiological correlates. In the day-to-day work of the psychologist this division serves quite well.

By raising the question of whether psychology can be thought of as the study of the activity of the brain, we have raised an old philosophical problem, that of the relationship between mind and body. The historical answers to the mind-body problem were given by philosophers who had other problems to solve about the nature of man and his destiny. Although their answers were not proposed to satisfy psychologists, it is worthwhile to review some of the classical positions on this problem.

CRITICAL DISCUSSION[3]

The mind-body problem

The clearest answers were formulated either as dualisms or monisms. The *dualistic* answer is most prevalent in our ordinary thought about mind and body. Because mind and body are different, the problem to be resolved is how to characterize the interaction between an immaterial mind and a material body. A typical common-sense view is that the body takes orders from the mind, and the bodily condition in turn limits what the mind can do. This sensible view is more or less implied in what we call *psychosomatic medicine,* in which bodily illnesses are considered in some instances to be brought about by mental disturbances. The expression "sound mind in sound body" implies such an interaction. Historical figures who held such views include the philosophers Descartes and Locke (1623–1704), and, in modern times, the psychologist James (1842–1910). This view, however, has many difficulties, particularly if we accept the principle of the conservation of energy. If mind is not material, it is difficult to see how it can be a cause of energy changes such as occur in willed movements.

Those who are troubled by the difficulties in the interaction view tend to adopt a *monistic* answer, which says that the basic substance of the universe is of one kind, not two. If this substance is neutral, it may be viewed from two aspects: one mental, the other material. This *double-aspect* theory originated with the philosopher Spinoza (1632–77). We can consider thought from the viewpoint of the mental activity or from the viewpoint of the functioning of the brain. In modern dream research, for example, evidence that the person is dreaming comes through physiological processes that are electrically recorded; the person is then awakened and asked to tell about the content of his dream (Stoyva and Kamiya, 1968). Here the investigator shifts his inquiry from the brain activity to the mental activity, with an assumption that these are two ways of getting at a common underlying process. This modern version of a Spinoza-like theory is sometimes called a *double-language* theory, in which one talks either the language of observable events (physiology and behavior) or the language of mental activities (private experience, intentions, and the like). A double-language position of this kind permits the investigator to carry on his scientific enterprises without committing himself to a fixed position on some of the larger and more controversial philosophical problems.

The family of behavioral sciences

To study human behavior meaningfully, we have to go beyond what happens to an isolated person and consider the institutional arrangements under which man lives: the family, communities, and larger societies, with their complex interrelationships. Because the problems of these arrangements are much too varied to be understood from any single standpoint, a number of different fields of inquiry have developed: history, anthropology, economics, geography, political science, sociology, and other specialties. These, taken together, are known as the *behavioral* or *social sciences.* Earlier the term "social science" was the more inclusive one, with behavioral science restricted to those fields that focused more particularly on individual

[3]Critical discussions are introduced from time to time, especially to point up controversial issues in contemporary psychology. They may be omitted at the discretion of the instructor.

behavior (anthropology, psychology, and sociology), but as all fields have become more alike in their use of empirical data and have become more like other sciences in their use of rigorous methods, the terms "behavioral science" and "social science" have come to be used interchangeably.

Just as there are divisions of labor among the specialties within psychology, so are there divisions of labor among and within the other behavioral sciences. As methods of study became more sophisticated and tools of inquiry more refined, it was inevitable that specialization should proceed in this manner, but there is a price to pay for such specialization. What is lost is a common attack on important human problems. This now has to come about from some new act of synthesis or integration in which the results obtained from the divergent and specialized approaches are brought back together.

Basic and applied aspects of the behavioral sciences

All sciences have two foci of interest. *Basic science,* the first focus of interest, has as its goal the understanding of natural phenomena. The scientist investigating these basic phenomena proceeds by analysis to find some order that links his observations, and he seeks explanations that are simple and elegant and that cover as wide a range of phenomena as possible. His purpose, intellectual and esthetic in character, rather than practical, is to satisfy curiosity about nature. This does not mean that his results will not have practical consequences, but only that they are not to be judged by their practicality, and he should not be asked to justify what he does in terms of any immediate benefits to society. Thus the behavioral scientist who studies how bees communicate with one another is not trying to improve the honey industry; the archeologist who tries to find out how man lived thousands of years ago is not trying to solve contemporary community problems.

The second focus of interest is that of *applied science,* having the practical goal of improving the human condition by discovering something that can be put to human use. This aim has been particularly evident in the biological and physical sciences, which have made enormous contributions to agriculture, medicine, and our material economy. Although there are misuses of scientific advance, these should not be charged to the scientific method itself; atomic fission can be used to provide inexpensive power to serve human needs as well as to produce destructive weapons.

These two aspects, the basic and the applied, are at work in the behavioral sciences. These sciences seek to develop their facts and theories in an orderly way so that they may take their places among other sciences contributing to a general understanding of man and his place in nature; they seek also to find ways of designing human arrangements that will alleviate suffering and increase human well-being and the quality of life.

The broad province of contemporary psychology

We may define psychology as *the science that studies behavior and mental activity.* However, the activities of scientists in any field of endeavor do not arise solely from the definition of the field but depend upon a complex social history. Hence we understand psychology better by looking at some of the things psychologists actually do. We may begin by considering some of the fields of specialization within psychology.

About half of those who have advanced degrees in psychology work in colleges and universities; many others work in the government and in private agencies—in business, industry, clinics, and guidance centers. Those who practice privately, offering their services to the public for a fee, represent only a small minority. Within their various work locations, psychologists do a great variety of things, depending upon their fields of specialization.

TABLE 1-1 FIELDS OF SPECIALIZATION WITHIN PSYCHOLOGY	
AREA OF COMPETENCE	PERCENTAGE
Clinical	37%
Counseling/Guidance	11
School	6
Educational	9
Experimental	12
Social	5
Developmental	3
Personality	3
Industrial/Personnel	8
Psychometrics	2
Engineering	2
General and "Others"	2
Total: percent	100%
number reporting	19,027

Source: Jones (1969). Based on replies to a questionnaire from the National Science Foundation.

One estimate of the proportion of psychologists who classify themselves in each of a number of specialties is found in Table 1-1. The fields of specialization are described below.

Experimental psychologists

The field of basic experimental psychology, devoted to research in the principles of psychology as they apply to man or to organisms in general, is best supported in our institutions of higher learning. Experimental psychology encompasses work with animals (comparative psychology), including biobehavioral studies in physiological psychology (interaction of brain and behavior, effects of drugs and hormones). With human subjects it includes work on sensory and perceptual problems, on learning and memory, and on motivation and emotion. Experimental psychology is a laboratory science in the strict sense, using precision instruments and seeking refinements of control and measurement.

Clinical and counseling psychologists

The greatest number of psychologists are involved in *clinical psychology*. The typical clinical psychologist gives care or treatment in an agency—a mental hospital, an institution for the mentally subnormal, a prison, a juvenile court, a mental-health clinic, or a university medical school. He may also practice privately, alone or in association with other professional colleagues. His affiliations with the medical profession, especially psychiatry, are close. This affiliation draws the clinical psychologist largely to hospitals and clinics.

Psychological service for normal people, whose problems are typically those of minor difficulties in social adjustment or a need for vocational and educational guidance, is given by advisement and guidance workers known as *counseling psychologists*. The differences between the counselor and the clinical psychologist are not sharp, for the counselor has to be alert to the person who seems merely upset about a superficial problem but who is deeply disturbed. The counselor refers such a person to clinical services, confining himself to problems not classified as mental illness. Clinical and counseling psychologists together account for almost half the psychologists in Table 1-1.

Developmental, personality, and social psychologists

There is a good deal of overlap among those who are defined as developmental psychologists, personality psychologists, and social psychologists. The reason for this overlap is not hard to find: the *development* of the human individual takes place in the context of other persons, at first the parents and immediate family, later the playmates and school companions. Behavior in the presence of other people, and influenced through interaction with them, defines *social psychology*. To the extent that personality, as we know it, is both a social and developmental product, the province of *personality psychology* overlaps both of the other categories.

Social psychology is concerned, in addition, with

the behavior of groups of people. Social psychologists are perhaps best known for their work in public opinion and attitude surveys, audience measurement, and market research. The survey method is now widely used for a variety of purposes by newspapers, magazines, radio and television networks, as well as by agencies of the government, such as the Bureau of the Census, the Department of Agriculture, and the Department of Labor.[4]

Social psychology, like other specializations within psychology, has both its basic and its applied aspects. As a basic science it is concerned with the investigation of such problems as the influence of the culture upon personality development, social motives leading to competition and cooperation, the change in an individual's behavior when in the presence of others, the nature of conflict, and the occasions that arouse aggressive behavior or lead to acts of violence. As an applied science, social psychology is concerned with the methods of changing group behavior and of ameliorating intergroup tensions (including international conflicts). In this concern, social psychologists join with other behavioral scientists in seeking to work for the benefit of the underprivileged and to improve intergroup relations of all kinds at community, state, and national levels.

Industrial and managerial psychologists

An industrial society makes available many goods that add to the comforts and satisfactions of living, but it also creates a number of problems. Modern technologies make warfare more destructive and more frightening; misuse of technology pollutes the air and the water, uses up natural resources, and may drastically change the values according to which men regulate their lives. Many of these problems are being brought to the attention of the public and are causing such strong reactions that some perceive this as a revolutionary era—not necessarily a violent revolution in the political sense, but one that will force our institutions to adapt to the changes associated with a postindustrial society.

Industrial and managerial psychologists are deeply involved with these problems. At one level they serve the technological process much as engineers do, being concerned with human factors in industry, such as personnel problems, employee morale, and the design of complex machines so that errors by the human operator are minimized. At another level, however, they are concerned with the larger problems of an industrial civilization. Here they join social psychologists and other scientists in planning for the future with shared concern over the use of resources, the pollution of the environment, overcrowding, and other influences on the quality of life.

Educational and school psychologists

The public schools provide a wide range of opportunities for psychologists—teachers have to be trained, methods and materials provided, and children with special problems served. A specialty within psychology has developed around the central problems of the schools—learning, problem-solving, motivation, and social participation—because these problems all require psychological understanding for their solution. The *educational psychologist* makes research on these problems his primary concern, and he tends to work in a school of education where teachers and school administrators are trained. The *school psychologist* usually works in a local school system, where he serves the children, teachers, and administrators by bringing psychological knowledge to bear on the actual operation of the school. His responsibilities commonly include administering and interpreting tests, participating in remedial or guidance functions, and working with teachers and parents to determine the source of a child's behavior problems in the classroom.

---

[4]The survey method is so widespread in the behavioral sciences that it belongs to economics, political science, and sociology, as well as to psychology. The fact that psychologists engage in various kinds of specialized activities does not imply that they have exclusive claims on these activities. The boundaries between the various fields within the behavioral sciences are arbitrary.

Methodologists

With the development of modern methods of experimentation and treatment of data—symbolized by the high-speed computer—problems of research design, statistics, and computation have become so complex that the methodologist has become a specialist. Whenever any large-scale research enterprise is undertaken, at least one statistical expert is needed, and often many more.

Statisticians in psychology were formerly associated chiefly with test construction and the interpretation of test results, but their duties are now much wider. As experts in sampling theory they may be called upon to design a systematic procedure by which people are to be located for questioning in a survey of public opinion or of voting behavior. As experts in experimental design they may be asked to help research psychologists arrange their procedures for gathering and analyzing data.

Methods of psychology

Above all else, the aim of science is to provide new and useful information in the form of verifiable data, that is, data obtained under conditions such that other qualified people can make similar observations and obtain the same results. This task calls for orderliness and precision in uncovering relationships and in communicating them to others. The scientific ideal is not always reached, but as a science becomes better established it rests upon a larger body of relationships that can be taken for granted because they have been validated so often.

Methods of the experimental laboratory

The experimental method is applicable to problems of behavioral science outside the conventional laboratory as well as inside it. Thus it is possible to conduct experiments in economics to investigate the effects of different taxation methods by trying them out on separate but similar communities. The experimental method is a matter of logic, not of location. Even so, most experimentation takes place in special laboratories, chiefly because the control of conditions commonly requires special equipment that is best housed and used in one place. The laboratory is generally located in a university or a research institute of some kind, where it is accessible to scientists who work on a variety of topics.

The distinguishing characteristic of a laboratory is that it is a place where conditions can be carefully controlled and measurements taken, so that regular ("lawful") relationships among variables can be discovered. By a variable we mean something that can occur with different values. For example, in an experiment seeking to discover the relationship between learning ability and age, both learning ability and age can have different values, learning being either slower or faster and the learner being either younger or older. To the extent that learning ability changes systematically with increasing age, we can discover an orderly, or lawful, relationship between them. In this case learning ability and age are the variables.

The ability to *control the variables* is what distinguishes the experimental method from other methods of observation. If the experimenter seeks to discover whether learning ability depends upon age, he can control the age variable by selecting groups of children of different ages. If he then sets the same learning task for each group, such as memorizing a sequence of numbers, he can determine whether the older children do indeed master the task more rapidly than the younger ones. In this situation the various age levels are the *antecedent* conditions; the learning performances are the *results* of these conditions (among others). We call the antecedent condition the *independent variable* because it is independent of what the subject does; the variable that changes as a result of the change in the antecedent condition, and that represents a consequence of the subject's behavior, is called the *dependent variable*. The distinction between the two kinds of variables will become clearer in the following discussion of an actual experiment.

Sometimes experiments are designed to study relationships that are known to follow a general pattern, but for some purposes it is important to know the relationships with greater precision. For example, everybody knows that to place your hand in ice water for a long time will be painful, but if a psychologist is interested in the physiological accompaniments of the pain experienced, he needs to know the relationship more precisely than this. In one series of experiments, in which the blood pressure rises associated with pain were to be studied, the first step was to see how pain would mount with water of different temperatures. Again, we know that very cold water will be more painful than water that is less cold, but without experimentation we do not know how much difference a few degrees in temperature will make. Subjects were taught to report pain on a numerical scale, with 10 a critical level at which they very much wished to terminate the pain. Figure 1-4 shows the pain reported by subjects whose hands were placed in circulating cold water for forty seconds at different temperatures. As expected, the colder the water, the more rapidly the pain rose. In this case the temperature of the water is an *independent variable,* and the reported pain is a *dependent variable,* because the experimenter controlled the water temperature but the reported pain was an outcome of the experiment. The experimenter then went on to show that the blood pressure rise associated with pain also depended upon temperature. In that part of the experiment (not shown in Figure 1-4) temperature was again the independent variable, but blood pressure became the dependent variable (Hilgard, 1969).

The degree of control possible in the laboratory makes a laboratory experiment the preferred scientific method when it can be used appropriately. The precision instruments with which psychological laboratories are equipped are usually necessary to control the experiment and to obtain exact data. The experimenter may need to produce colors of known wavelengths in studies of vision, or sounds of known frequency in studies of audi-

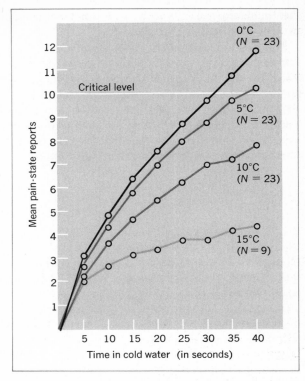

Fig. **1-4 Water temperature and reported pain** Regardless of water temperature, pain rises with the length of time the hand and forearm are kept in the circulating cold water; the colder the water, however, the more rapid the rise in pain. In this experiment *both* temperature and time in water are independent variables, under control of the experimenter, while reported pain is the dependent variable. (After Hilgard, 1969)

tion. It may be necessary to expose a pattern in an aperture of a viewing screen for a fraction of a second. Thus, apparatus to control stimuli is often required. In measuring responses the psychologist may also need precision instruments. Time can be measured in thousandths of a second, and physiological activity can be studied by means of slight electrical currents amplified from the muscles or from the brain. For this reason the psychological laboratory has its audiometers, photometers, oscilloscopes, electronic timers, electroencephalographs, and computers.

The value of an experiment is not determined, however, by the amount of apparatus used. If the logic of experimentation requires precision apparatus, then such apparatus is used; if it does not, then good experimentation can be done by means of pencil-and-paper procedures.

Moreover, for psychology to develop as a science it is not essential that all its problems be brought into the laboratory. Some other sciences, such as geology and astronomy, are experimental only to a very limited extent. Having recognized the great value of the laboratory approach, without establishing its claims as exclusive, we may turn now to some other methods used in psychological investigations.

Field observations

In the early stages of a science it is necessary to explore the ground, to become familiar with the relationships that will later become the subject of more precise study. Careful observation of animal and human behavior (including the study of our own conscious processes) is the starting point of psychology. Observation of chimpanzees in their native environment of Africa may well tell us things about their social organization that will help us conduct our laboratory investigations (Figure 1-5). Study of nonliterate tribes will help us see the ranges of variation in human institutions, which would go unrecognized if we confined our study to men and women of our own culture. Motion pictures of a newborn baby reveal the details of movement patterns shortly after birth. Such observations of naturally occurring phenomena gradually become experiments as the conditions of observation are standardized through laboratory controls.

In making field observations of naturally occurring behavior there is a danger of substituting anecdotes for genuine observation, and interpretations for descriptions. Thus we may be tempted to say that an animal known to have been without food is "looking for food" when all we have observed is heightened activity. Investigators must be trained to observe and record accurately in order to avoid projecting their own wishes or biases into what they report. Properly used, naturalistic observations in the field can be important not only in the early stages of a science but also in the later stages, as correctives to incomplete theories.

Photo by Eric Hamburg

Fig. **1-5** **Chimpanzees observed in their natural habitat** Such naturalistic studies tell more about social behavior than strictly experimental studies can. For example, grooming behavior, as shown in the picture, is a common form of social contact among chimpanzees in the wild.

Survey method

The *survey* is one of the most widely used methods in the social sciences. It has the advantage that the questions that are asked can be pertinent to genuine problems, and the replies can be obtained from the persons affected by the problems. An adequate survey requires a carefully pretested questionnaire to serve as the basis for data gathering, a group of interviewers trained in its use, a carefully designed sample to assure that the respondents are representative of the population that the survey is intended to study, and appropriate methods of data analysis and reporting so that the results of the survey are properly interpreted. The survey is a method of field observation, but a refined and disciplined one.

Test method

The *test* has an important place in contemporary psychology as an instrument of research. It is used to measure all kinds of abilities, interests, attitudes, and accomplishments. By means of tests, large quantities of data can be obtained from people in factories or hospitals or schools, with a minimum of disturbance of their living routines and without elaborate laboratory equipment. Test construction and use are, however, no simple matters, involving as they do many steps of item preparation, scaling, and establishing of norms. Later chapters will explore the problems of testing in some detail.

Case histories and longitudinal studies

Psychologists are often interested in the individual. For that reason scientific biographies, known as *case histories,* become important sources of data. There can of course be case histories of institutions or groups of people as well.

Most case histories are prepared by *reconstructing the biography* of a person according to remembered events and records. Reconstruction is necessary because the person's earlier history often does not become a matter of interest until he develops some sort of problem; at such a time an understanding of the past is thought to be important to understanding his present behavior. The retrospective method has the disadvantage of distortions of events or of oversights, but it is often the only method available.

A second method is the *longitudinal study.* This type of study follows an individual through time, with measurements made at periodic intervals. Thus the biography (or case history) is constructed from contemporary observations made according to a plan by the investigator. The advantage of the longitudinal study is that it does not depend upon the memories of those interviewed at a later date; the disadvantage is that a large amount of data has to be collected from many people in the hope that a few of the data will eventually show the characteristics of particular interest to the investigator—perhaps unusual creative abilities or some forms of mental disturbance. Because tests may also be administered periodically, the longitudinal method sometimes combines the test method with that of the case study.

Measurement in psychology

Whatever methods psychologists use, sooner or later they find it necessary to make statements about *amounts* or *quantities.* Variables have to be assessed in some clear manner, so that investigations can be repeated and confirmed by others. Occasionally variables can be grouped into *classes* or *categories,* as in separating boys and girls for the study of sex differences. Sometimes the variables are subject to ordinary *physical measurement:* for example, the temperature of the water and time in the water (Figure 1-4), or height or weight or age. Sometimes variables have to be *scaled* in a manner that places the values in some sort of order: for example, from least preferred to most preferred. Usually, for purposes of precise communication, *numbers* are assigned to objects or events; then we can say that we are dealing with *quantitative values.* We may speak of *measurement* in a general sense whenever we have assigned numerical values to independent and dependent variables, or indeed to any variables with a systematically studied relationship.[5]

Experimental design

When an investigator plans his experiments, he has in mind the ways in which he will gather his data and how he will treat the data in order to discover the relationships involved and make inferences from what he finds. The expression *exper-*

[5]The discussion of measurement and statistics in this chapter is designed to give the student a general introduction to the problems involved in order to make it somewhat easier to understand the tables and charts in the chapters that follow. A more thorough discussion of statistics in psychology is provided in the Appendix.

imental design is used to describe any of the more formal patterns according to which experiments are planned. The same design might be used for an experiment in vision, one in learning, and perhaps one in psychotherapy. The total plan includes more than the design, for it involves the substance of the particular experiment.

The designs that are most easily understood are those in which the investigator manipulates one variable (the independent variable) and studies its effects on another variable (the dependent variable). The ideal is to hold everything else constant so that one arrives at an assertion of the form "With everything else constant, when X increases, Y also increases." Or, in other cases, "When X increases, Y decreases." Note that almost any content can fit into this kind of study: the loudness that is reported as related to the energy of the sound stimulus, the rate of learning as related to the age of the learner, the fear of snakes as related to the prior experience with snakes. The method of *graphical representation* is a convenient one to use, with the independent variable plotted on the horizontal axis (the abscissa) and the dependent variable plotted on the vertical axis (the ordinate). As we shall see later, some kinds of psychological theory attempt to predict what forms such curves will take. The orderly relation between the variables can be stated more precisely by fitting a mathematical expression to the relationship. In other words, we are interested in more than the fact that when X increases, Y also increases; we want to know what the precise relationship is.

Sometimes an experiment focuses only on the influence of a single condition, which can be either present or absent. (Such a condition is simply a variable with only two values, one representing its presence, the other its absence.) In this case the experimental design commonly calls for an *experimental* group in which the condition is present and a *control* group in which the condition is absent. The results of such an experiment are presented in Figure 1-6. It is clear that the experimental group had a higher percentage of correct responses than the control group, the differences becoming more marked as the experiment proceeded.

In some instances it is necessary to investigate

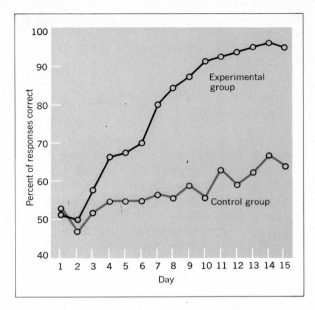

Fig. **1-6 Experimental and control groups** The response called for was a discrimination between a circle and a triangle; the experimental animals had been reared in cages with circles and triangles on the walls, the control animals had not. (After Gibson and Walk, 1956)

the simultaneous effects of several variables. Suppose, for example, that you are studying plant growth and wish to study the effects of moisture, temperature, and illumination. You could hold two of these variables constant and study the effect of the third, but a little reflection will show how limited this design would be: unless *favorable* levels of the other variables were chosen, the plant would not live, and the experiment could not be performed at all; but *how* favorable they would have to be cannot be determined in advance. A better procedure would be to vary moisture, temperature, and illumination in different combinations. Then the effect of one variable would be studied not against a *constant* value of other variables, but against an *array* of other values. Many behavioral science problems have this multivariable character; school performance, for example, is affected by the child's native ability, his diet, his family background, the facilities of his school, the skill of his teacher, and so on. The statistical problems of such a *multivariate design* are more complex than those of a design involving changes in only one independent variable at a time, but the yield in information is often greater for the same amount of experimental effort.

Correlation as an alternative to experimentation

Sometimes strict experimental control is not possible. For example, the experimenter who is interested in the human brain is not free to remove portions at will, as he does with lower animals; but when brain damage occurs through disease, injury, or gunshot wounds, he can study how parts of the brain are related to corresponding behavior. For instance, a relationship may be found between the extent of damage at the back of the brain and the amount of difficulty in seeing. This method of assembling correspondences, without experimental control over them, is known as *correlation*.

When large masses of data are available, the method of correlation is often the best available one for discovering relationships. Suppose we have records of the high school grades of students entering college. The best way to find out the relation between high school grades and freshmen grades in college is to *correlate* them, that is, to find out if those who did well in high school generally do well in college, and vice versa. Measurement in correlation studies is provided by the *coefficient of correlation,* signified by the letter *r,* which expresses the degree of relationship.

A distinction between experimental and correlational methods is in order. In an experimental study, as we have said, one variable (the independent variable) is systematically manipulated to determine its effect on some other variable (the dependent variable). Similar cause-effect relationships cannot always be inferred from correlational studies. The fallacy of interpreting correlations as implying cause and effect is best illustrated with a few examples. The softness of the asphalt in the streets of a city may correlate with the number of sunstroke cases, but this does not mean that the asphalt when soft gives off some kind of poison that sends people to hospitals. We understand the cause in this example—a hot sun both softens the asphalt and produces sunstroke. Another example, which is frequently used as an illustration, is the high positive correlation obtained for the number of storks seen nesting in English villages and the number of child births recorded in the same communities. We shall leave it to the reader's ingenuity to figure out possible reasons for such a correlation, without postulating a cause-effect relation between babies and storks. These examples provide sufficient warning against giving a causal interpretation to a correlation. When two variables are correlated, variation in one may *possibly* be the cause of variation in the other, but in the absence of evidence no such conclusion is justified.

Interpreting statistical measures

Because the tabular material from psychological studies generally includes a few statistical assertions, it is well to be familiar with the most common of these so that the reports will appear less baffling.

The most common statistic is the *mean,* or *arithmetic average,* which is merely the sum of the measures divided by their number. In experiments designed with a control group there are often two means to be compared, a mean for the sample of subjects run under the experimental condition and a mean for the sample of subjects run under the control condition. The difference between these two means is, of course, what interests us. If the difference is large, as in Figure 1-6, we are satisfied to accept the difference at its face value. But what if the difference is small? What if our measures are somewhat crude and subject to error? What if a few extreme cases in one of the groups are producing whatever difference is observed? These are problems that statisticians solve for us by producing tests of the *significance of a difference.* What "significance" means in this context is how *trustworthy* the difference is (not how important it is). Stated otherwise, these statistical tests tell us whether a difference observed in one experiment is likely to occur again if the experiment is repeated, or if, instead, the observed difference was due to chance factors and is not reproducible.

The significance of a difference between two means is commonly stated by a statistic known as the *t*-test (devised by a statistician who wrote under the name of Student), which is then interpreted according to how probable it is that the result is in the direction indicated. A higher *t* means a more trustworthy difference. The degree of trustworthiness is assigned a probability value (usually stated as a *p*-value). The difference is significant when the probability is less than 5 in 100 ($p < .05$) that the observed difference between the means might have occurred even if the populations from which the samples of experimental and control subjects came were identical. If the difference is *not* significant, that is, if *p* is greater than .05 ($p > .05$), then the obtained difference will be attributed to sampling or measurement errors. The significance statement protects us against accepting differences obtained in experiments that are in fact indecisive.

Understanding and interpreting a coefficient of correlation

The relationships expressed by a coefficient of correlation will become clearer if we look at a diagram of actual test results (Figure 1-7). Forty-nine subjects were given a test of their susceptibility to hypnosis on two separate days. Each tally in the diagram represents the *combined* score of one subject on the two tests. Thus two subjects made scores of 1 on both days, and two other subjects made scores of 13 on both days. But one subject (see the lower right-hand portion of the diagram) made a score of 11 on the first test but only 5 on the second one.

If all subjects had repeated their original scores on the second day, all the tallies would have fallen in the diagonal shaded squares, and the correlation would have been $r = +1.00$. Enough fall to either side, however, so that in this case the correlation drops to $r = +.86$. The interpretation of the coefficient of correlation requires a few words of explanation. Here are some rules of thumb:

1. A correlation of $r = +1.00$ means a perfect *positive* relationship (a one-to-one correspondence) between two variables. If weight corresponded exactly to height, so that you could precisely state

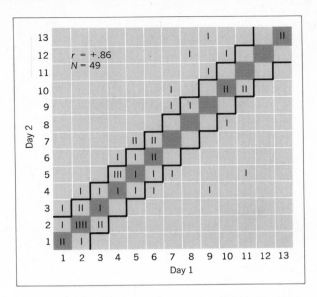

Fig. 1-7 A scatter diagram illustrating correlation Each tally indicates the combined scores of one subject on two separate days of testing hypnotic susceptibility. Tallies in the shaded area indicate identical scores on both tests; those between the solid lines indicate a difference of no more than one point between the two scores. The correlation of $r = +.86$ means that the performances were fairly consistent on the two days. (After Hilgard, 1961)

a person's weight if you knew his height, then height and weight would be perfectly correlated. (The circumference of a circle and its diameter are perfectly correlated, but the perimeter of a triangle and its height are not.) When the correlation is positive, the plus sign is often omitted.

2. A correlation of $r = -1.00$ means a perfect *negative* relationship. For example, if the price of a used car decreased as its age increased, so that one could precisely specify the price if the age were known, then the relation between the car's age and price would be expressed by a correlation of $r = -1.00$.

3. A correlation of $r = .00$ signifies no relation. Thus one would expect a zero correlation between the number of freckles on a person's face and his score on an intelligence test. Knowing the value of one variable in no way helps predict the value of the other variable.

4. A correlation between $r = .00$ and either $+1.00$ or -1.00 indicates an imperfect rela-

tionship. The *degree of relationship* is specified by the extent to which the value of the correlation approaches 1.00, plus or minus. Negative and positive correlations of the same size represent the same degree of relationship.

5. A correlation is *not* a percent, so a correlation of $r = .25$ cannot be interpreted as being half as great as one of $r = .50$. The relationship expressed by a correlation coefficient varies more nearly with its *square*. Thus a correlation of $r = .70$ (note that $.70^2 = .49$) expresses nearly double the relationship of $r = .50$ (note that $.50^2 = .25$). It helps to have some idea of the sizes of correlations commonly reported: (a) a correlation of $r = .50$ between the height of a parent and the adult height of a child of that parent; (b) correlations of about .40 between scholastic aptitude tests and freshman grades in college; (c) correlations of about $r = .75$ between grades in the first semester of the freshman year and those in the second semester.

6. Some supplementary information is needed to indicate whether or not a given correlation is *statistically significant.* This is the same problem met in determining whether a difference between two means is significant. For example, if too few cases have been studied, a few extreme cases might produce a high correlation, whereas none actually exists in the total population. Hence statisticians have developed formulas for stating the significance of a correlation, those correlations being most dependable that are both high and based on a large number of cases. Again a *p*-value can be assigned, stating the likelihood, or probability, that a correlation of the reported size would be observed if none existed in the population from which the studied sample was drawn.

Developmental and interactive explanations

Because of its advances in method and measurement, psychology is able to assemble data from its investigations in a form that makes these data convincing as descriptions of behavior and mental activity. As in the case of any science, however, the results of research are interpreted in accordance with theory, and, of course, the theories themselves pose problems for research.

In the past, psychological theories were often expressed as comprehensive systems, competing with one another. Thus behaviorism was at first a "school" of psychology, competing with the prevailing introspectionism, or "structuralism." Another broad system is that of psychoanalysis. Still another, originating in Germany about the time that behaviorism was getting started in the United States, was known as Gestalt psychology. The word "Gestalt" means "pattern" or "configuration," and this "school" emphasized the importance of wholes over parts. It provided some of the background for contemporary cognitive psychology. The importance of such comprehensive all-embracing systems has declined, however, as psychologists

have come to recognize that adherence to any one "school" leads either to the disregard of some of the data of psychology or to a warping of relationships in order to make all the data fit a preconceived pattern.

We shall be able to get along with a minimum of system in this book because so many of the references will be to concrete, factual relationships. When there are important alternative ways of formulating an explanation, particularly if the alternatives are a source of controversy, they will be pointed out. Two prevailing modes of explanation in psychology recur enough for attention to be called to them at this point. One of them is *developmental,* the other *interactive.*

A developmental explanation stresses the historical roots of present behavior, focusing on individual experiences as the person grows and learns. This mode of explanation has its origins in "association psychology," which generally tried to explain what happens in the present according to associations built up in the past. Modern S-R psychology, because of its strong emphasis upon learning, is very largely a developmental psychology. Psychoanalysis, with its emphasis upon early childhood, also favors such explanations.

An interactive explanation deals with the arousal and control of behavior in the present, according to the motives and needs that are currently active, the stimuli that are perceived, and the possibilities of action that are open. Gestalt theory and forms of cognitive theory related to it have been emphatic in stressing present "configurations" or "contexts" as determiners of behavior and experience. All psychological theories must be concerned with present behavior as well as with residues from the past. All must deal, for example, with the way individuals resolve conflicts, since the conflicting tendencies are simultaneously present no matter what their origins may have been.

The two modes of explanation, developmental and interactive, belong together, because development always provides the potential that is capitalized on in the present. It is a matter of convenience to stress at some points explanations that are largely developmental, at other points explanations that are largely interactive, but one explanation need never exclude the other. It is important to keep both aspects in mind in order to avoid explaining too much according to the past or too much according to the present. For example, when we learn that delinquent youths have alcoholic fathers more often than nondelinquent youths, we should not be tempted to adopt the developmental explanation that a particular youth is delinquent *because* he had an alcoholic father. The fact is that he becomes a delinquent because he shows some inadequacy *at the present time* in relation to specific temptations and opportunities for delinquent acts. It is this inadequacy that must be understood for what it is now, if it is to be corrected. It may help us to understand this present inadequacy if we know both what kind of early history produces delinquent boys and what neighborhoods and other social contexts encourage delinquent behavior in the present. It is not illogical to accept both a developmental and an interactive explanation at the same time.

Summary

1. Psychology is defined as the science that studies *behavior* and *mental activity.* While some psychologists (behaviorists) believe that mental activity is always an inference from behavior, other psychologists (cognitive psychologists) accept some forms of mental activity present in conscious experience, or awareness, as sources of primary data for psychological science.

2. In practice, psychologists are interested in overt movements, conscious processes, and unconscious processes. Unconscious processes are not directly observable, but have to be inferred from either overt behavior or conscious experience.

3. Psychology, like other *behavioral sciences,* has overlapping interests with many neighboring sciences, chiefly with biology and the social sciences. Many promising opportunities for studies and application lie in areas where psychology blends with other sciences.

4. Of the numerous specializations that help to indicate psychology's broad province, *clinical psychology* and the related *counseling psychology* account for almost half the psychologists. *Experimental psychology,* concerned with the problems of the psychological laboratory, comes next. Other specialities include *developmental, personality,* and *social psychology; industrial* and *managerial psychology; educational* and *school psychology.* Some psychologists are chiefly *methodologists,* whose expertise is primarily in mathematics, statistics, and computation.

5. Among the methods of psychology as a science the *methods of the experimental laboratory* are preferred where they are applicable. These methods have the advantage that variables can be brought under control through the aid of laboratory apparatus, and precise measurements can be made, both of the *independent variables,* the values of which the experimenter sets, and the *dependent variables,* which take on different values depending upon the outcome of the experiment. The logic of experimentation is not limited to the formal laboratory, however, and experiments can be carried out in the community and other social contexts.

6. Other methods include *field observations,* the *survey* method, the *test* method, *case histories,* and *longitudinal studies.*

7. Measurement in psychology requires arranging observations in such a manner that numerical values can be assigned to the resulting data. One approach is through *experimental design,* in which experiments are so arranged that changes in the dependent variable can be studied in relation to changes in the independent variable (or to several variables at once). If the independent variable is either present or absent, *the control group method* is appropriate; then the experimenter compares what happens in a given setting when the variable is present and when it is absent. Any differences in *means* can be tested for *significance* by appropriate statistical tests.

8. Another approach to measurement is by way of *correlation.* When the experimenter does not have control of the independent variable, but has to take things as he finds them, he can make widely ranging observations and then study how one variable changes as another one changes. This method is commonly used with scores from psychological tests. A correlation between X and Y tells how a change in X is related to a change in Y. If the relation is one-to-one, then the correlation is either $r = +1.00$ or $r = -1.00$; correlations between zero and ±1.00 represent imperfect relationships. A correlation can also be tested for *significance,* a high correlation based on a large number of cases being more significant than a lower one or an equal one based on fewer cases.

9. Two modes of explanation occur frequently within psychology. These are *developmental* explanations and *interactive* explanations. Developmental explanations attempt to account for present behavior on the basis of what has gone before, relying on the *history* of the present behavior. Interactive explanations are contemporary and nonhistorical, trying to account for behavior on the basis of current stimuli, mental activity, bodily processes, aroused conflicting tendencies, and so on. The two kinds of explanation are not contradictory because the past provides the potentiality for response in the present. It is occasionally convenient, however, to emphasize one kind of explanation over the other; often a full account requires propositions reflecting both explanations.

Suggestions for further reading

The topical interests and theories of any contemporary science can often be understood best according to their history. Four useful books are Boring, *A history of experimental psychology* (2nd ed., 1950), Murphy, *Historical introduction to modern psychology* (rev. ed., 1949), Herrnstein and Boring, *A sourcebook in the history of psychology* (1965), and Watson, *The great psychologists: From Aristotle to Freud* (2nd ed., 1968).

For the larger systems of theory that have influenced contemporary psychology, the standard text is Woodworth and Sheehan, *Contemporary schools of psychology* (3rd ed., 1964). A more recent discussion is Krantz, *Schools of psychology: A symposium* (1969).

The relation of psychology to the other behavioral or social sciences may be found in National Academy of Sciences/Social Science Research Council, *Behavioral and social sciences: Outlook and needs* (1969), and in Clark and Miller (eds.), *Psychology: Behavioral and social science survey* (1970).

For a concise description of the specialty areas in psychology, with information about training to become a psychologist, see American Psychological Association, *A career in psychology* (1970).

For the methods of psychology, see Sidowski (ed.), *Experimental methods and instrumentation in psychology* (1966), and Underwood, *Experimental psychology* (2nd ed., 1966). For an overview of the tactics and strategies involved in psychological research, see Helson and Bevan, *Contemporary approaches to psychology* (1967). Rosenthal, *Experimental effects in behavioral research* (1966), calls attention to some of the special hazards in psychological research.

the behaving organism 2

MAN IS A FLESH-AND-BLOOD ORGANISM related to other organisms through an evolutionary history. Man's habits, thoughts, and aspirations are centered in his brain and nervous system, and whenever we study him we study something he does or expresses through his bodily processes.

The emphasis in this chapter will be upon the evolution of man's nervous system; by discovering how the nervous system in the lower animals has evolved we will learn a good deal about the significance of the various nervous structures for the behavior of man. The nervous system and the related structures of sense organs, muscles, and glands provide for man's responsiveness to the environment and his immediate adjustment to it; they also provide for the storing up of experiences and the development of habits and attitudes that make the past serve the present and the future.

Again we confront the distinction between present interactions and developmental history; the nervous system is important in whichever viewpoint we are emphasizing.

The areas of behavior in which we can hope to achieve enlightenment through the study of bodily processes (particularly the action of the brain) are: first, sensory discrimination, because the brain makes use of the information that comes to it by way of the senses; second, regulatory, need-serving, and emotion-laden behavior (eating and sleeping, fighting, escaping, sexual behavior), the impulsive processes that we share with the rest of the animal world; third, the processes of learning, language, thought, appreciation, and creativity, which at best establish man's high place in the evolutionary scheme; and, finally, those aspects of individual differences in ability, temperament, and style of life, which we call "personality." In each of these areas we are interested both in normal functioning and in what happens when the bodily processes go awry.

Many aspects of behavior cannot be fully understood without considering the underlying neurophysiological correlates. This chapter gives only a brief overview of neurophysiology; its aim is to provide enough basic information so that discussions in later chapters of the relation between neurophysiological events and psychological processes will be more meaningful. Students with a background in biology will find much of the material familiar to them.

Integration within the organism

The word "organism" implies organization. The body is not only a collection of cells but an arrangement of cells as organs and organ systems. The psychologist is interested in knowing how the bodily machinery works, for he is concerned with the skilled acts of which the individual is capable, the hierarchical nature of controls that permits voluntary acts to be carried out smoothly with the cooperation of involuntary reflexes, the effects of emotional arousal, and the manner in which information is retained. However mind and body are conceived, it is through the body that mental activity finds its expression. The character of the body as a unitary organism is determined by the manner in which parts fit together so that the whole operates with reasonable smoothness.

Integration through skeleton and muscles

What does the psychologist need to know about the skeleton and the related structures of muscles and tendons that tie it together and make it operate? The answer depends upon his purposes. If, for example, the psychologist becomes interested in the limits of possible human performance, he may wish to know about the maximum weight a muscle can support, or about the maximum speed with which it can contract, or about the effects of practice upon it. If he is interested in muscular fatigue, he may wish to learn something about the chemical by-products of muscular action. Of course, we cannot go into such details here; we will merely call attention to the importance of the skeleton and the muscles as mechanical integrators of the body.

The body operates as an effective machine partly because of the way in which it is constructed around a jointed skeleton of rigid bones. This *mechanical integration* makes possible the maintenance of posture, locomotion, skilled action, facial expression, and speech.

When a muscle contracts, it commonly produces a movement at the joints, as in walking or lifting. But if the joint is prevented from moving, the muscle may still contract. In an alert but quiet state the muscles are bombarded by an irregular barrage of nervous impulses that maintain a normal amount of contraction called *muscle tone*. The tone of muscles varies with the condition of the individual: an energetic, athletic person tends to have high tone; a weak, listless person low tone. If tone is reduced too far, the person collapses; if tone is too high, his movements are disturbed, as in the condition known as *spastic paralysis*. Spastic paralysis, with muscle tone so high that smooth movement is impossible, is often a result of birth injury.

Although muscle tone is maintained automatically through reflex mechanisms, we can increase the tension in our muscles voluntarily, as in "making a muscle" without moving the arm. Some people habitually tense their muscles and are unable to relax. Such a high-tension state is fatiguing and may carry with it signs of mild personality disturbance. The voluntary increase of muscular tension, without movement, comes about through increasing the tension of *antagonistic muscles*. Such muscles are arranged in pairs; the contraction of one member of the pair tends to stretch the other member of the pair. The biceps of the upper arm is a *flexor* muscle, bending the arm at the elbow, while the triceps is an *extensor* muscle, antagonistic to the biceps and by contraction straightening the arm at the elbow. The nervous control of muscles is such that when one of a pair of antagonists contracts, the other ordinarily relaxes. This principle, known as *reciprocal innervation,* is important in the free movements of, say, walking along and swinging the arms. When we move muscles voluntarily, we can either take advantage of this reciprocal relationship to produce free movement or contract both antagonists at once and raise tension as in the case of "isometric" exercises.

Reciprocal innervation demonstrates a principle that is important to the organization of bodily controls: the interplay between *facilitation* (leading to increased activity) and *inhibition* (leading to decreased activity). The balance of these two processes enables us to coordinate action, to maintain appropriate levels of alertness and emotion, and in many other ways to manage our affairs more smoothly.

Integration via the blood stream

A second system that maintains the body as a smoothly operating machine is the circulatory system: the heart, the blood vessels, and the other closely related structures that feed into the system. Because the system contributes to integration by sending chemical substances throughout the body, we may think of it as *chemical* in its action, supplementing the mechanical integration of muscles and joints.

The blood stream carries certain special substances called *hormones,* a word derived from the Greek root meaning "activators." The glands of internal secretion (the *endocrine,* or *ductless,* glands) discharge hormones directly into the blood stream, affecting growth, behavior, and personality. These glands are distinguished from the *duct* glands, such as tear glands or salivary glands, which secrete their products on the surface of the body or into the body cavities but not into the blood stream. Seven endocrine glands (some occurring in pairs) produce hormones, the actions of which are fairly well understood, although new evidence about their activity is still being collected:

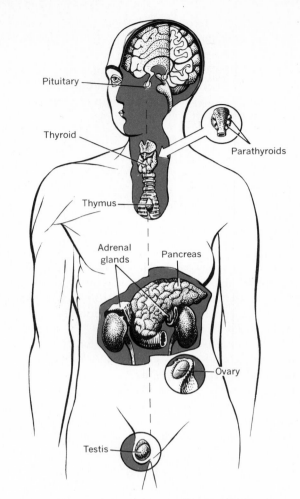

Fig. **2-1 The endocrine glands** The left side of the illustration includes one of the pair of glands characteristic of the male (testes), and the right side one of the pair of glands characteristic of the female (ovaries). Since the parathyroids are not visible in the frontal view, they are shown from the back in the separate drawing. (After Simpson and Beck, 1969)

(1) the thyroid gland, (2) the parathyroids, (3) the thymus, (4) the pancreas, (5) the adrenal glands, (6) the sex glands, or gonads (ovaries in the female and testes in the male), and (7) the pituitary gland. In Figure 2-1 their locations are pictured in a schematized human body; their functions are summarized briefly in Table 2-1.

As one illustration of the relevance of the endocrine glands to psychology we may consider the

TABLE 2-1	SOME TYPICAL FUNCTIONS OF THE ENDOCRINE GLANDS
GLAND	ACTIVITIES REGULATED
Pituitary—anterior	Growth (dwarfism, giantism); as "master gland" influences secretions of thyroid, pancreas, adrenal glands, and gonads.
—posterior	Water metabolism, etc.
Thyroid	Metabolic rate, hence activity and fatigue; body weight.
Thymus	Important in regulation of the lymphoid system, and in the development of immune reactions of the body.
Parathyroid	Calcium metabolism; maintenance of normal excitability of the nervous system.
Pancreas	Via insulin, controls sugar metabolism; excess insulin leads to state of shock.
Adrenal—cortex	Secretes life-maintaining regulators; control of salt and carbohydrate metabolism; may be important in mental illness.
—medulla	Active in emotion through the effects of epinephrine and norepinephrine.
Gonads*	Secondary sex characteristics distinguishing the male and female at maturity; maintenance of a functional condition in male and female reproductive organs.

*As glands of internal secretion; to be distinguished from their reproductive functions.

role of the *adrenal* glands. These glands have two major parts, each secreting its own hormones. The *medulla* of the glands secretes *epinephrine* (also known as adrenalin) and *norepinephrine* (noradrenalin). The *cortex* of the gland secretes a number of hormonal products collectively called *adrenocortical* hormones.

The adrenal medulla is active in emotion. Secretion of the hormone epinephrine produces many of the symptoms found in excited emotion: tremor in the striate muscles increases; smooth muscles relax; the blood distribution of the body changes; the liver releases blood sugar into the blood and thereby makes available a ready supply of energy; blood pressure increases; blood clots more quickly in case of injury. The discovery of norepinephrine, another secretion of the adrenal medulla, has furthered knowledge of the action of the adrenal glands. Epinephrine and norepinephrine occasionally produce similar consequences and occasionally opposite ones. Whereas epinephrine may dilate blood vessels, norepinephrine constricts them. As yet no simple formula can describe their interrelated actions.

The adrenocortical hormones are so important

to the maintenance of life that destruction of the adrenal cortex invariably produces death unless the missing hormones are continuously replaced from outside—a very difficult process. These life-maintaining regulators, which control salt and carbohydrate metabolism, have been identified as complex chemical substances known as *steroids*. The steroids have become useful agents for the treatment of many health disturbances, such as shock, allergy, and arthritis. Their possible role in mental disturbance is suggested by the occasional appearance of symptoms similar to those of mental illness among mentally normal patients being treated with adrenal steroids, such as cortisone.

Neural integration

The nervous system controls the muscles as they make use of the skeletal apparatus; it controls the beating of the heart, respiration, and circulation of the blood; it regulates the secretions of the glands. Therefore this third system, the *neural mechanism,* rules over the mechanical and chemical integrators that we have just considered. Because it possesses a nervous system, the organism is capable of complex and modifiable action, of learning as a result of experience, and of increased adaptability to variety in the environment. So important is the nervous system that most of the remainder of this chapter will be devoted to it.

Evolution of the nervous system

We need not concern ourselves here with the details of evolutionary theory, which belong to the science of biology. The basic assumptions, since Darwin, are that living organisms are not all alike and that some of the variations among them are more adaptive than others. An adaptive variation gives the organism a competitive advantage in the environment in which it finds itself (or perhaps helps it to seek a more favorable environment). Thus as a result of protective coloration, the white polar bear is less visible against the snow of its natural habitat, and the brown bear less visible in the dark woods where it lives. Among man's nearest relatives, the primates, there has been a striking change in the size of the jaw relative to the size of the brain. As man's ancestors came to use tools to hunt game and to fight enemies, the size of the jaw became less important than the size of the brain; hence the course of evolution of man capitalized on variations that made him craftier of mind rather than stronger of tooth.

Both adaptive and maladaptive (unfavorable) variations are transmitted by heredity, and differences become accentuated through time as organisms continue to vary and to adapt to their special environments, the successful ones surviving, the unsuccessful ones dying off. Modern genetic theory has helped show how variation and selection can occur not only by way of mutations but by way of shifts in the available hereditary determiners (genes) as populations of individuals become isolated from one another. In time, as species develop that can no longer mate successfully with one another, families of organisms develop along branching lines. The branching lines along which man has developed include, far back, the earliest vertebrate, but specialization continued through the mammalian line and the primate line until now

the genus to which man belongs contains only one species, *Homo sapiens.* The so-called races of man are all variants of the one species.

Because of our interest in behavior, the aspect of evolution that is of primary importance for us to consider here is the evolution of the brain and nervous system, those parts of the body that interpret the sensory inputs from the environment, coordinate the organism's responses, and, in general, serve memory and thought.

Nerve net and synaptic nervous system

One-celled animals, such as the amoeba, get along without a nervous system. The cell body is responsive to stimulation, so that the amoeba moves about, avoids noxious stimuli, engulfs food. There must be some sort of conduction within the cell body, for movement often takes place at a distance from the point of stimulation. The sponge is a multicellular organism without a nervous system; its cells conduct impulses individually. Muscle fibers have already evolved in the sponge, so we have here the beginning of muscular contraction but without a nerve supply to the muscles. Some coordination is provided by one cell's influencing a neighboring cell, but the influence is not by way of any connecting nerve fibers.

The real beginning of a nervous system is the *nerve net* such as is found in coelenterates like the polyps. Here individual specialized cells, called *neurons,* are spread rather evenly through the outer layers of the body. When any part of the nerve net is stimulated, impulses diffuse from that point and produce local contraction of muscles in the areas where the neurons are activated. Nothing very complex is controlled by such a nervous system.

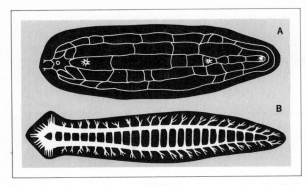

Fig. **2-2 Nerve net and ladder nervous system in flatworms** In some flatworms (A) the nervous system is still of the simple net type, while others (B) show the beginning of a central nervous system in the ladder-like structure of cords with a concentration of cell bodies at the head end, constituting a primitive brain. (After Simpson and Beck, 1965)

A characteristic of the nerve net is that impulses can travel in either direction. Modern research on coelenterates has shown that there is some differential responsiveness based on the number of nervous impulses per second reaching a particular muscle, and that there is some facilitation when impulses converge at a junction between nerve cells. Even with these additions, the processes are relatively simple.

Some flatworms (planaria) show a further stage in the evolution of the nervous system; in these the nerves form a ladder-like system much more like that of man. In this type of nervous system the neurons are arranged in bundles called *nerve cords* (a kind of primitive spinal cord), and the cell bodies of the neurons are concentrated in the head to form something similar to a brain (Figure 2-2). This nervous system is of the *polarized synaptic* variety. A *synapse* is a junction between neurons. A polarized synapse is a junction at which there is conduction of the impulse in only one direction; it is characteristic of all higher nervous systems.[1] The cells making up the eyes at the front end of the flatworm are connected to the collection of neurons that we may call a brain; this pattern is continued in higher forms.

[1]Higher organisms may display residues of earlier forms. The human intestine, for example, contains a nerve net in its wall.

Beyond the primitive synaptic nervous system of the flatworms the lines of evolution divide between invertebrates, such as insects, and vertebrates. Since man is of the latter category, the development of the vertebrate nervous system, and particularly the vertebrate brain, is of primary interest to us here.

Basic units of the nervous system

The specialized cells called *neurons* are basic units of the nervous system. It is important that we understand them, for they probably hold the secrets of learning and memory and mental functioning generally. We know their role in the transmission and coordination of nervous impulses, but their more complex functioning in learning, emotion, and thought remains to be unraveled.

Nerves and synapses. Each neuron is a living cell with a nucleus and other parts common to all cells. As a specialized structure it consists of three main parts: the *cell body,* containing the nucleus; the *dendrites,* the many short fibers projecting from the cell body that receive activity from adjacent cells; and the *axon,* a long fiber extending away from one side of the cell body that transmits activity to other neurons or to muscles and glands (see Figure 2-3). Nerve impulses normally move in one direction—from the dendrites, through the cell body, and along the axon to the dendrites or cell body of the next neuron, or to a muscle or gland. While all neurons have these general features, they vary greatly in their dimensions and construction. A neuron in the spinal cord may have an axon 2 or 3 feet in length, but some neurons in the brain may cover only a few thousandths of an inch with all their parts. Closely interwoven among the neurons are a large number of cells, called *glia* cells, which until recently were considered to serve only a nutritive and supportive function. New evidence suggests that the glia cells may be actively involved in the metabolic processes related to neural activity, but their exact role is as yet unknown.

A nerve is not a simple fiber, but a bundle of

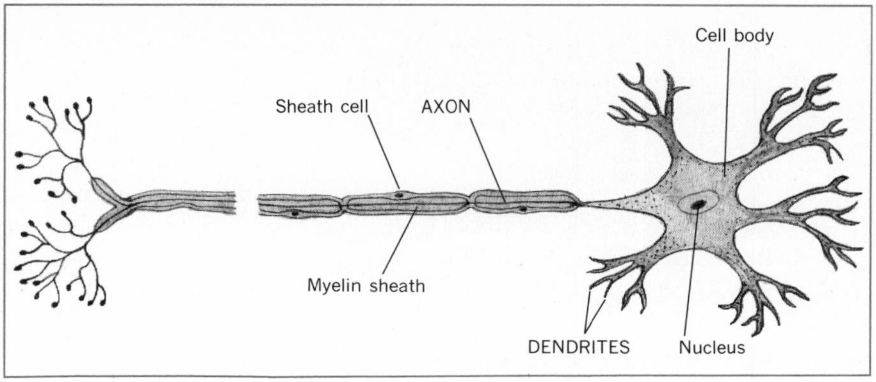

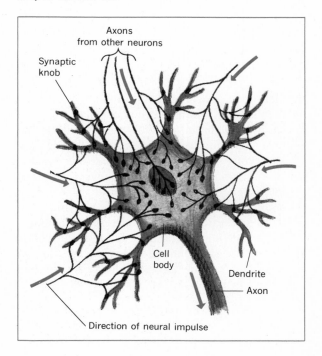

Fig. 2-3 A nerve cell An idealized diagram of a motor neuron. Stimulation of the dendrites activates a neural impulse that travels the length of the neuron to the end of the axon. The myelin sheath covers the axons of some, but not all, neurons; it serves to increase the speed of nerve conduction.

elongated dendrites or axons belonging to hundreds of neurons. The axons from a great many neurons (perhaps about 1000) may make synaptic junctions with the dendrites and cell body of a single neuron. The synapse is not a direct connection; there is always a slight physical separation across which the nervous impulse is transmitted by a chemical intermediary.

Transmission of neural impulses. The movement of a neural impulse along a nerve is not strictly comparable to the flow of an electric current through a wire. Electricity travels at the speed of light (186,300 miles per second), while a nerve impulse in the human body may travel anywhere from 2 to 200 miles an hour, depending upon the diameter of the axon and a number of other factors. The analogy to a fuse has sometimes been used: when a fuse is lighted, one part of the fuse lights the next part, the impulse being regenerated along the way. The details of neural transmission are much more complex than this. The process is electrochemical. The thin membrane that holds together the protoplasm of the cell is not equally permeable to the different types of electrically charged ions that normally float in the protoplasm of the cell and in the liquid that surrounds it. In its normal or resting state the protoplasm of the nerve cell is negatively charged with respect to the surrounding fluid; the internal potential is approximately 70 millivolts negative with respect to the outside.

We can conceive of the nerve cell as a tiny polarized battery, with the inside of the cell as the negative pole and the outside of the membrane as the positive pole. When the axon of a nerve cell is stimulated, the electric potential of the pro-

Fig. 2-4 Synapses at the cell body of a neuron Many different axons, each of which branches repeatedly, synapse on the dendrites and cell body of a single motor neuron. Each branch of an axon terminates in a swelling called a synaptic knob. Inside each synaptic knob are numerous synaptic vesicles containing the chemical intermediary that transmits the nerve impulse across the synapse to the dendrite or cell body of the next cell.

toplasm inside that part of the axon is lowered below its normal 70 millivolts. If this reduction in potential, or *depolarization,* is large enough, an abrupt change in the permeability of the cell membrane takes place that allows sodium (Na+) ions from outside the membrane to flow rapidly into the cell, and a smaller number of internal potassium (K+) ions to flow out (see Figure 2-5). This interchange results in a voltage difference between the depolarized region and the adjacent protoplasm; the next segment of the axon is thereby depolarized enough to cause its membrane permeability to break down, and the process is repeated. In this way a pulse of voltage breakdown, or *action potential,* is propagated along the axon. Because the nerve impulse is generated anew at each stage of its progress, no energy is lost during transmission; the nerve impulse is as strong when it reaches its destination as it was when it left the generating neuron.

Some nerve fibers have an insulating sheath called a *myelin sheath;* such fibers are known as *myelinated* fibers. The sheath is interrupted every 2 millimeters or so by constrictions called nodes, where the myelin sheath is very thin or absent. Because conduction jumps along the fiber from node to node, it is much more rapid in myelinated fibers than in nonmyelinated fibers. The myelin sheath was a late development in evolution and is characteristic of the nervous systems of higher animals. The fact that the formation of the myelin sheath of many of the nerve fibers in the brain is not completed until some time after birth suggests that the slow maturation of some of the infant's sensory and motor functions may be related to the gradual process of myelination.

Synaptic transmission. The synaptic junction between neurons is of tremendous importance because it is there that switching of impulses takes place, making possible facilitation, inhibition, coordination, and integration of impulses through the way in which groups of neurons act together. A single neuron transmits an impulse, or "fires," when the impulses reaching it become strong enough. Because its axon does not transmit at all prior to this, the neuron has been said to follow

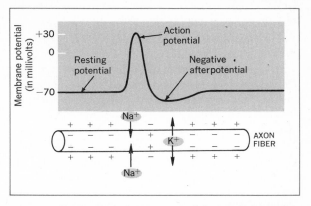

Fig. **2-5 Electrochemical basis of the nervous impulse** Transmission of the nervous impulse is made possible by an interchange of charged particles, or ions, through the membrane of the nerve fiber. The inward movement of the sodium (Na+) ions gives rise to the initial large, positive "spike" of the action potential; the outward flow of the potassium (K+) ions then restores the resting potential.

an "all-or-none" principle of action. The neuron fires in a single brief and transient burst and then is temporarily inactive (in what is called a *refractory phase*) for a few thousandths of a second. The size of the action potential is constant, and once started it travels all the way down the axon to the synapses. But the decision of the neuron to fire or not fire depends upon *graded* potentials (potentials that are not all-or-none but can be any size) in the dendrites or cell body. These graded potentials are induced by stimulation at the synapses by other neurons, the size of the graded potential varying with the amount and kind of incoming activity. When the graded potential becomes sufficiently large, it generates enough depolarization in the cell body to trigger the all-or-none action potential that then travels down the axon. If the graded potential does not reach the discharge threshold of the action potential, no activity occurs. Thompson (1967) has likened the occurrence of the graded potentials in the nerve cell to a decision-making process. The neuron considers all incoming activity and, depending on the amount and kind of this activity, decides to fire or not fire.

Since the size of the action potential is constant—that is, it does not vary with the strength of the stimulus—how is information concerning stimulus strength conveyed? The answer is that a strong stimulus will (1) cause the individual neuron to fire more frequently and (2) excite more neurons than a weaker stimulus.

It is now fairly well established that synaptic transmission occurs by means of chemical "transmitters" that are released when the action potential reaches the end of the axon. Several of these chemicals have been identified, although no one knows yet how many more there are or exactly which synapses involve which transmitter. The chemicals act on the dendrites and cell body of a neuron to produce the graded synaptic potentials. To complicate matters further, there appear to be two basic types of synaptic transmission: excitation and inhibition. Release of the chemical transmitter from the axon at an excitatory synapse produces a small graded shift in the cell membrane potential of the receiving neuron that is in the same direction as the action potential. When this depolarization is large enough, the cell fires an all-or-none action potential down its own axon to influence other cells.

The inhibitory synapse works in an analogous but opposite manner. Release of the chemical transmitter produces a small graded shift in the receiving neuron that is *opposite* in direction to the action potential. During this brief period it is considerably more difficult for excitatory synapses to fire the neuron. Remember that any one neuron may synapse with dendrites from many other neurons. Some of these synapses may be excitatory and some inhibitory. It is the constant interplay of excitation and inhibition that determines the likelihood that a given neuron will fire an all-or-none action potential at any particular point in time. These complex synaptic processes may help to account for the fine adjustments that must occur in learning, memory, and thought.

The chemical changes take place on a minute scale. The energy involved in firing a neuron is something like a billionth of a watt; with 10 billion neurons in the human brain, and assuming every neuron is active simultaneously (which is hardly likely), the whole brain can operate on a power supply of about 10 watts. This is a remarkably low energy requirement for such a complex operating mechanism.

Evolution of the vertebrate brain

The general characteristics of the brain reveal a common pattern throughout the vertebrate series beginning with primitive fishes and moving through the reptiles; the development of the brains of birds and mammals follows somewhat different directions from this common background. The basic pattern is that of a single hollow cord made up of partially interconnected neurons running along the back of the body, with various more complicated areas of interconnections forming enlargements at the forward (head) end. There are, in most primitive brains, three such enlargements, the *forebrain, midbrain,* and *hindbrain,* and these three are still identifiable in man.

The structure of the main parts of a primitive vertebrate brain helps us to understand the pattern upon which the much more complex human brain is built. A schematic representation of a dogfish brain is shown in Figure 2-6. At this stage the *forebrain* consists of the *olfactory bulb,* connected

Fig. 2-6 A primitive vertebrate brain The basic structure of a tube with various bends, folds, and outpouchings is clearly visible in this schematic drawing of the dogfish brain. The three main portions (forebrain, midbrain, hindbrain) are distinguishable, but a "between-brain" (thalamus and hypothalamus) is also present, and the hindbrain has developed a cerebellum distinguishable from the medulla. The forebrain and midbrain are paired structures (see Figure 2-7). (After Simpson and Beck, 1969)

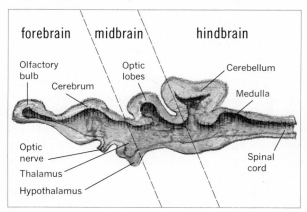

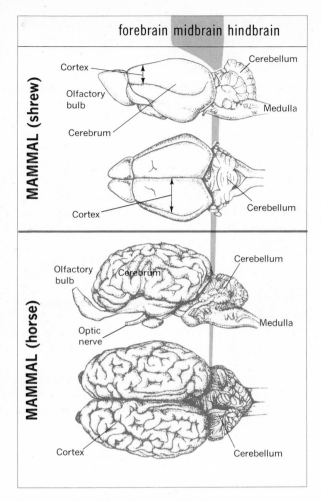

MAMMAL (shrew)

forebrain | midbrain | hindbrain

Cortex
Olfactory bulb
Cerebrum
Cerebellum
Medulla

Cortex
Cerebellum

MAMMAL (horse)

Olfactory bulb
Cerebrum
Cerebellum
Optic nerve
Medulla

Cortex
Cerebellum

Fig. 2-7 Development of the forebrain in vertebrate evolution The cortex is still small and unconvoluted in the shrew, a primitive mammal; the convoluted surface of the horse cerebrum is made up entirely of cortex. Side and top views are shown. (After Simpson and Beck, 1969)

with the sense organs of smell; the *cerebrum,* chiefly at this stage a "nose brain," using the information coming from the sense of smell to guide the behavior of the fish; the *thalamus,* a way station for impulses coming up from the spinal cord and down from the cerebrum; and the *hypothalamus,* concerned with many of the internal regulatory processes. The *midbrain* consists chiefly of the *optic lobes,* connected with the eyes and regulating be-

havior by way of stimuli affecting the eyes. The *hindbrain* includes the *cerebellum,* controlling balance and muscular coordination, among other things, and the *medulla,* the enlargement of the spinal cord that is important in maintaining the vital functions, such as respiration and circulation of the blood.

The evolution of the brain structures is related, of course, to the kinds of lives the various organisms lead. Fishes, which rely heavily on their chemical senses to detect food, have large olfactory lobes; birds, with their complex flight patterns, have highly developed cerebellums. As mammals developed their more complex sensory systems and came to rely more on learning, memory, and problem-solving, a new brain developed in the form of an out-pouching, or cover, over the cerebrum; it is called the "neocortex" ("new cortex") or simply the *cerebral cortex,* as we know it in higher forms, including man.

The changes in proportionate size of the forebrain and midbrain are shown in Figure 2-7. The cerebral cortex has become highly wrinkled, or *convoluted,* so that its actual surface area is far greater than it would be were it a smooth covering of the surface of the brain.

Hierarchical organization of the human brain

The human brain consists essentially of the structures of the primitive vertebrate brain, preserved in similar anatomical relations but modified in detail, plus the enormously developed cerebral cortex built upon the older brain. It helps to think of the human brain as composed of three concentric layers: (1) a primitive central core, (2) an old brain (the *limbic system*) evolved upon this core, and (3) an outer layer of new brain (the *cerebrum*) evolved upon the second layer. Figure 2-8 shows how these layers fit together. All three layers are, of course, interconnected in a complex fashion, and a new layer cannot evolve without changing the conduction of impulses to and from the earlier and more central layers of the brain. A more detailed cross section of the human brain may be seen in Figure 2-9.

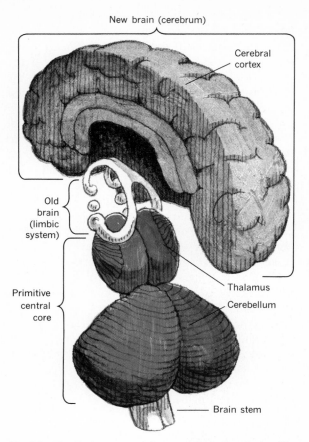

New brain (cerebrum)

Cerebral cortex

Old brain (limbic system)

Primitive central core

Thalamus

Cerebellum

Brain stem

Fig. **2-8 The three concentric layers of the human brain** The primitive core and the old brain are shown in their entirety, but the left cerebral hemisphere of the new brain has been removed. The cerebellum of the primitive core controls balance and muscular coordination; the thalamus serves as a switchboard for messages coming from the sense organs; the hypothalamus (not shown but located in front of the thalamus) regulates endocrine activity and such life-maintaining processes as metabolism and temperature control. The limbic system, or old brain, is concerned with emotion and sequential activity. The cerebral cortex, an outer layer of cells covering the cerebrum, is the center of higher mental processes, where sensations are registered, voluntary actions initiated, decisions made, and memories stored.

The central core. The central core includes parts of the hindbrain, midbrain, thalamus, and hypothalamus, that is, much of the *brain stem,* or stalk, upon which the other brain structures are attached. It functions in such life-maintaining processes as respiration and metabolism, the regulation of endocrine gland activity, and the maintenance of *homeostasis.* The term "homeostasis" refers to the general level of functioning characteristic of the healthly organism, such as a normal body temperature, a standard concentration of salt in the blood, and normal heart rate and blood pressure. Under stress the usual equilibrium is disturbed, and processes are set into motion to correct the disequilibrium and return the body to the normal level of functioning. Thus if we are too warm we perspire and if we are too cool we shiver—both processes tending to restore the normal temperature. Working like a thermostat that controls temperature, *homeostats* in the body detect changes in various systems and correct the balance. These control mechanisms, the details of which are unknown, are located in the hypothalamus, near the midline of the ventricles (hollow portions) at the center of the brain. The homeostats are conceived as structures sensitive to chemical and other changes that represent a feedback from the rest of the body.

Their action is closely related to that of the neighboring *reticular formation,* a collection of neurons with short connections to other neurons lying in the brain stem, forming a structure about the size of the little finger. Most of the incoming and outgoing nerve impulses pass through the reticular formation either directly or by means of *collaterals,* which are smaller branches off the main nerve. The reticular formation controls the state of arousal of the organism, as in changing from sleep to waking, or from diffuse awareness to alert attention. According to Wooldridge (1968) the reticular formation acts as a "consciousness switch," turning consciousness on or off by sending suitable signals to the parts of the brain involved in conscious processes. When an electric current of a certain voltage is sent through electrodes implanted in the reticular formation of a cat or dog, sleep is produced; stimulation by a current with a more rapidly changing wave form always awakens the sleeping animal. Lesions in the reticular formation will produce permanent coma. The effects of general anesthesia result from the deactivation of the neurons of the reticular formation. A stimulus, such as a loud sound or a pin prick to the skin, will produce electrical activity in the appropriate regions of the brain as clearly when

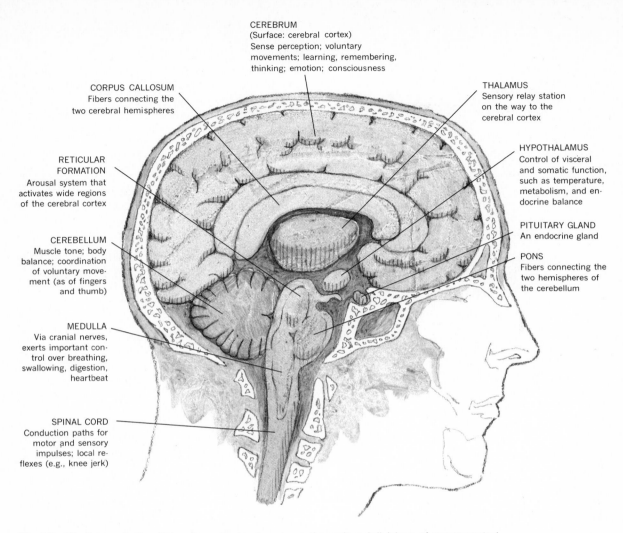

CEREBRUM
(Surface: cerebral cortex)
Sense perception; voluntary
movements; learning, remembering,
thinking; emotion; consciousness

CORPUS CALLOSUM
Fibers connecting the
two cerebral hemispheres

THALAMUS
Sensory relay station
on the way to the
cerebral cortex

**RETICULAR
FORMATION**
Arousal system that
activates wide regions
of the cerebral cortex

HYPOTHALAMUS
Control of visceral
and somatic function,
such as temperature,
metabolism, and en-
docrine balance

CEREBELLUM
Muscle tone; body
balance; coordination
of voluntary move-
ment (as of fingers
and thumb)

PITUITARY GLAND
An endocrine gland

PONS
Fibers connecting the
two hemispheres of
the cerebellum

MEDULLA
Via cranial nerves,
exerts important con-
trol over breathing,
swallowing, digestion,
heartbeat

SPINAL CORD
Conduction paths for
motor and sensory
impulses; local re-
flexes (e.g., knee jerk)

Fig. **2-9 The human brain** This schematic drawing shows the main subdivisions of man's central nervous system and their functions. (Only the upper portion of the spinal cord, which is also part of the central nervous system, is shown here.)

a person is anesthesized as when he is conscious and alert. But he is unaware of these actions because under the influence of the drug the reticular formation fails to send to the cortex the additional signals needed to turn on the state of consciousness. Thus we see how important this central core of the brain is for the life-maintaining functions.

Much of the information about the homeostats and the reticular formation is quite recent, and the developments provide an exciting field of inquiry in contemporary neurophysiology and physiological psychology. An example of research in this area is an experiment on the control of perspiration as a result of temperature change in the region of the hypothalamus (Benzinger, 1961). The investigator placed a thermocouple (a heat-measuring instrument) on the eardrum in order to measure temperature as near as possible to the hypothala-

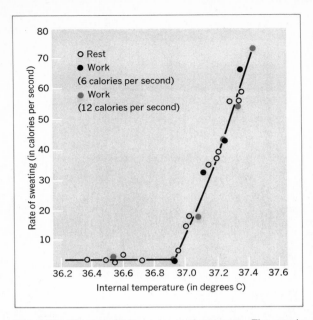

Fig. **2-10 The hypothalamus as a thermostat** The graph shows the relation between internal temperature and heat dissipation by sweating. A thermocouple giving a precise temperature measurement was placed on the eardrum to be near the hypothalamus; heat loss was measured by a calorimeter in which the subject worked or rested. (After Benzinger, 1961)

mus, where the "thermostat," or "homeostat," is located. He then placed the subject in a calorimeter, where heat loss from the body could be measured to indicate the amount of perspiration. The subject's body (internal) temperature was changed by control of the external temperature and by the subject's exertion. A very clear relationship was found between the internal temperature and the rate of sweating (Figure 2-10). The sharp break in the curve is at 36.9°C (98.4°F). It is as if the thermostat were set for this temperature. Below it no sweating occurred; above it sweating began. A change in temperature of .01°C was enough to increase the dissipation of heat through sweating by a measurable amount.

The old brain, or limbic system. Around this central core, lying along the innermost edge of the cerebral hemispheres, are parts of the brain that serve somewhat more complex functions. These structures are now commonly referred to as the *limbic system.* Because the system is related to some of the internal controls that occur in digestion and circulation, it has sometimes been called the *visceral brain.* But it has other "higher" functions also, as in some aspects of memory. Pribram (1969a) suggests that if all the data are combined, we would find that the limbic system is concerned with *sequential activities,* that is, with activities that proceed for some time and involve a number of movements before they are completed. These include the activities of feeding, attacking, fleeing from danger, mating—kinds of activities that have often been called "instinctive" because they are so characteristic of the members of a species. Milner (1966) has shown dramatically that human patients with lesions in parts of the limbic system are particularly helpless in carrying out an intended sequence of actions; a small distraction makes them forget what they have set out to do. The evidence from experiments with both lower animals and humans suggests that the limbic system builds upon the homeostatic mechanisms, regulating the dispositions of the organism to engage in sequences of activities related to the basic adaptive functions.

Finally, we reach the outer core, or cerebral cortex. This portion of the brain is so important in behavior that it will be given separate treatment in the next section.

Treating the brain as three concentric structures—a central core, an old brain, and an outer core—must not lead us to think of these interrelated structures as being independent. We might use the analogy of a bank of interrelated computers. Each has specialized functions, but they still work together to produce the most effective result. Similarly, the analysis of information coming from the senses requires one kind of computation and decision process, for which the cortex is well adapted, differing from that which controls a sequence of activities (limbic system). The finer adjustments of the muscles (as in writing or in playing a musical instrument) require another kind of control system, in this case mediated by the cerebellum. All these activities are ordered into complex subordinate and superordinate systems that maintain the integrity of the organism.

The brain is a very complex structure, and great ingenuity has been required to discover how it operates. The information already given, and that to follow, has been derived from painstaking research over the years. We may note six methods that psychologists, in conjunction with neurophysiologists and neuroanatomists, use to study the brain.

1. Study of the evolution of the brain. By comparative study we find that parts of man's brain are very similar to parts of the brains of lower animals. The parallels in structure found between man's brain and simpler brains lead us to infer similar functions, which need to be verified by further investigation. Another way to study the evolution of the brain is through observation of its embryological development, for in its early stages of development the brain of the human embryo reveals its relation to the brains of organisms lower in the evolutionary scale.

2. Study through disease, injury, or extirpation. Some forms of tumor and disease injure circumscribed areas of brain tissue. Similarly, gunshot wounds and other accidents may injure specific parts of the brain or spinal cord. By noting the symptoms produced by the injury (paralysis, loss of sensation, or other disturbances), it is often possible to infer what role a given part of the brain serves.

Instead of waiting for disease or accident, it is possible to perform systematic *extirpation* experiments to determine by surgical removal of parts of the brain what kinds of defects are produced by their loss. Surgery of this kind is done primarily upon animals, although surgeons have performed extirpations of parts of the human brain when they expected the operation to benefit the patient.

3. Study of nerve degeneration. When an area of the brain is destroyed, nerves connecting with the area may degenerate. The pathways of these connecting fibers, which in a normal brain would be lost in a mass of other fibers, can therefore be traced through microscopic study.

4. Study through stimulation. Stimulating parts of the brain with mild electrical currents produces effects on behavior. Surgical patients with their brain surfaces exposed under local anesthetics have assisted in such studies by reporting their experiences when different points are stimulated. Some rather satisfactory "maps" of the cortex have resulted from these studies.

More recently, experimenters with animals have used permanently implanted electrodes to produce repeated stimulation of a local part of the brain (Figure 2-11). Studies done with the aid of such electrodes help determine where sensory effects occur in the brain, and where various types of muscular activity are controlled.

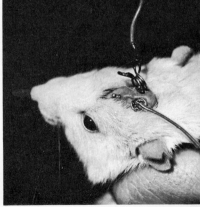

Fig. **2-11 Electrodes implanted in the brain A.** Rat being weighed before operation to determine the proper dose of anesthetic. **B.** Anesthetized rat under the stereotaxic instrument, which implants the electrodes through tiny holes in the skull. **C.** Insertion of screws that help to anchor dental cement to skull. **D.** Electrodes are cemented and connected to pins that project from the cement.

Courtesy N. E. Miller; photos by Martin Iger

A

B

C

D

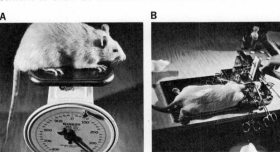
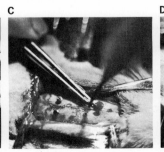

5. Study of electrical effects of nervous action. When neural action takes place, slight electrical currents are always produced. By inserting electrodes at appropriate places, connected in turn to measuring devices, one can detect whether impulses starting at, say, the ear reach the part of the brain where the electrodes are inserted.

The brain as a whole also produces rhythmical electrical discharges. The record of these total brain discharges, known as an electroencephalogram (EEG), plays its part in the study of central nervous activity. For example, if a particular kind of stimulation gives rise to changes in the rhythmic discharges picked up from one part of the brain and does not affect those discharges from another part, we can assume that the stimulation affected that particular region (see Figure 2-12).

A more recent method of brain study, made possible by the development of the modern computer, is the study of *evoked potentials*. This method averages a large number of EEG

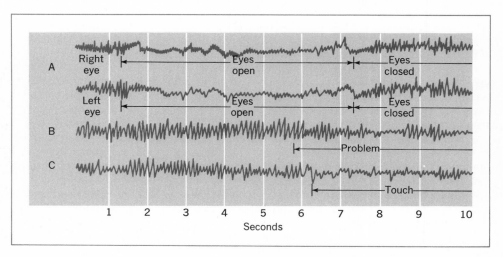

Fig. 2-12 Electrical action of the brain Through electrodes attached to the outside of the skull, the electroencephalograph measures the pattern of electrical activity within the brain. When the brain is at rest, the basic pattern is a large-amplitude "alpha" wave of about 10 cycles per second, as shown in the extreme left column of A and the first six columns of B and C. When the brain responds to sensory inputs, such as vision or touch, or when it is engaged by a mental problem, the alpha waves give way to irregular waves that are higher in frequency and lower in amplitude. (After Eccles, 1958)

The cerebral cortex in man

The two large hemispheres at the top of the human brain represent man's "new brain." The convoluted layer of gray matter that covers them—the cerebral cortex—controls man's most distinctively human behavior. Of the approximately 12 billion neurons in the human brain, 9 billion are in the cerebral cortex.

Our clearest knowledge of the cortex has to do with those functions that are related to specific areas of the brain. We speak of these as the *localized functions,* the ones that can be mapped; the places where they appear on a map of the cortex

are called *projection areas.* Some areas of the cortex when stimulated electrically will produce known and specifiable kinds of *motor responses* (those involving motion or activity in parts of the body) or *sensory effects* (those involving sensation, feeling, awareness).

When tumors exert pressure on these projection areas, there are disturbances in the responses. When, through disease or injury, these areas are destroyed, the same functions are altered or obliterated. Yet we would be making an error in logic if we assumed that these functions are *controlled* records, each of which represents the response to a given type of stimulus. Thus the random EEG activity is averaged out, and the more uniform consequences of stimulation can be detected, consequences that would ordinarily be lost in the complex EEG pattern. An example is given in Figure 2-13.

These methods are merely noted here; later chapters will give more specific indications of how results obtained by these methods further our psychological understanding.

6. Study of single neuron activity. The development of extremely refined microelectrodes (about one thousandth of a millimeter in size) has made it possible to record the nerve impulse from a single neuron. This new technique, which permits the investigator to study the behavior of a single nerve cell while the organism is being exposed to different stimuli, may uncover information that could not be obtained by recording greater electrical discharges.

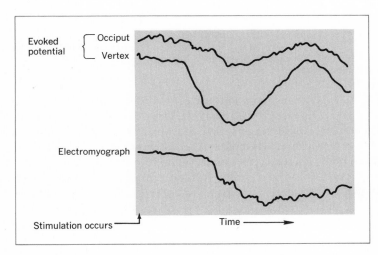

Fig. 2-13 Visually evoked potential from the human cortex Visually evoked potential precedes muscular response to the evoking stimulus. The curves are obtained by averaging 100 of these responses with the aid of a computer, the responses being time-locked to the moment of stimulation so that random activity is averaged out and only events related in time to the stimulus show. The top curves (evoked potential) represent responses from the occiput (rear of the head) and from the vertex (top of the head), corrected for visual responses occurring when no movement is called for. The bottom curve (electromyograph) is from the responding muscle, and shows that there is a delay between the time that the cortex responds to the light and the time that the movement (a flexion of the foot) begins. (After Vaughan and others, 1965)

by these areas alone. Even though an area is essential to a function, it may not be sufficient to control that function.

Before examining some illustrations of localization of function, we need a few landmarks by which to describe areas of the *cerebral hemispheres.* The two hemispheres are symmetrical, one on the right and one on the left, with a deep division between them, running from front to rear. So our first classification is the division into *right* and *left hemispheres.* For the most part, functions of the right side of the body are controlled by the left hemisphere and functions of the left side by the right hemisphere. Each hemisphere is divided into

four *lobes:* the *frontal* lobe, the *parietal* lobe, the *occipital* lobe, and the *temporal* lobe. The landmarks dividing these lobes are shown in Figure 2-14. The frontal lobe is separated from the parietal lobe by the *central fissure,* running down from the part of the cerebrum near the top of the head sideways toward the ears. The division between the parietal lobe and the occipital lobe is not as clear-cut; it suffices for our purpose to know that the parietal lobe is at the top of the brain, behind the central fissure, while the occipital lobe is at the rear of the brain. The temporal lobe is well set off by a deep fissure at the side of the brain, the *lateral fissure.*

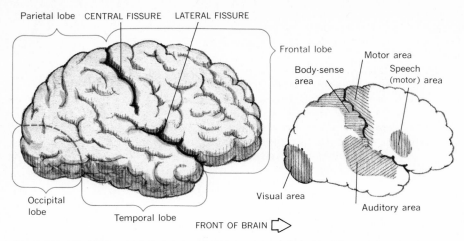

Parietal lobe   CENTRAL FISSURE   LATERAL FISSURE

Frontal lobe

Body-sense area

Motor area

Speech (motor) area

Occipital lobe

Temporal lobe

FRONT OF BRAIN ⟹

Visual area

Auditory area

Fig. **2-14   Localization of function in the human cortex**   Left: the lobes of the cerebral hemispheres and the landmarks separating them. Right: the projection areas.

Cortical areas and their functions

The motor area. The motor area, which controls all movements of the body, lies just in front of the central fissure, half of the body being represented by each side. When stimulated electrically, parts of the motor area cause movements in the extremities, and when these parts are injured, the same extremities are paralyzed. The body is represented in approximately upside-down form, movement of the toes being mediated by the part near the top of the head, and tongue and mouth movements by the part near the bottom of the area toward the side of the brain (Figure 2-15). Movements on the right side of the body originate through stimulation of the motor area of the left hemisphere, movements on the left side through stimulation of the right hemisphere.

The body-sense area. In the parietal lobes, separated from the motor area by the central fissure, lies an area that if stimulated electrically gives rise to sensory experiences, as though a part of the body were being touched or moved. The lower extremities of the body are represented high on the area of the opposite hemisphere; the face, low.

It seems to be a general rule that the amount of cortex corresponding to a particular region of the body surface is directly proportional to the sensitivity and use of that region. We can see from Figure 2-15 that the area devoted to the hands and fingers, for example, is much larger than that devoted to the feet and toes. Among four-footed mammals, we may note that the dog has only a small amount of cortical tissue representing the forepaws whereas the raccoon, which makes extensive use of its forepaws in exploring and manipulating its environment, has a much larger representative cortical area, including regions for the separate fingers of the forepaw (Welker, Johnson, and Pubols, 1964).

Disease or injury in the body-sense area produces disturbances of sensory processes but seldom produces complete absence of sensation (*anesthesia*). The injured person may lose the ability to tell the positions of his arms or hands when his eyes are closed or to recognize objects by touch. While he may still be able to detect extremes of temperature, he may be at a loss to judge finer gradations of warmth and coolness.

The visual area. At the very back of each cerebral hemisphere, in the part of the occipital lobe known as the *striate area,* lie centers important in vision.

New knowledge of the functioning of the visual cortex has come through studies of the electrical responses of single cells in the cortex, chiefly in

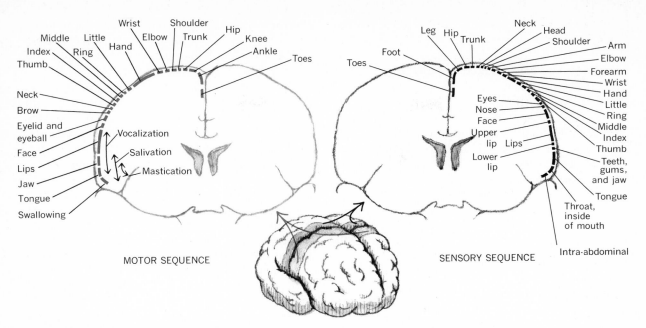

MOTOR SEQUENCE

SENSORY SEQUENCE

Fig. 2-15 **Localization of function within the motor and sensory areas** Two cross sections through the cerebrum are indicated: one for the motor cortex (in brown) and the other for the sensory cortex (in black). The various functions are represented in mirror image in both hemispheres, but in the figure only one side is labeled. (After Penfield and Rasmussen, 1950)

cats, either unrestrained and mobile or lightly anesthetized (Hubel and Wiesel, 1965). When spots of light, or slits of light, are presented in different positions in the cat's visual field, the response from cells within the visual cortex differs in orderly ways. For example, some cells will respond to a light slit that is horizontal but not to slits that differ from the horizontal by as much as 45 degrees; other cells will respond only to vertical slits of light. It appears that the sensory system is organized to perceive aspects of form and movement, and not simply points of light. We will have more to say about this intriguing area of research when perception is discussed in Chapter 6.

The auditory area. An area for audition is found on the surface of the temporal lobes at the sides of the hemispheres. There is some spatial distribution, one part being sensitive to high tones and a different part sensitive to low tones. Both ears are totally represented in the auditory areas on both sides, so that the loss of one temporal lobe has very little effect upon hearing.

The relation between the auditory projection area and behavior is illustrated by an experiment in which monkeys with electrodes implanted in their auditory cortex were trained to press a key in response to a tone. When the tone was turned on, the animal required approximately 200 milliseconds to respond. Later, however, when direct electrical stimulation of the auditory cortex was substituted for the tone, the response time was 185 milliseconds; the 15-millisecond difference between responses to acoustic and cortical stimulation presumably reflects the time required for the nerve impulse to reach the auditory cortex. The fact that recordings of action potentials in the auditory cortex also show a 15-millisecond delay following onset of the tone supports this assumption (Miller, Moody, and Stebbins, 1969).

The speech area. One of the very earliest findings in localization is still under dispute. As early as 1861 the neurologist Paul Broca examined the brain of a patient with speech loss and found damage in an area on the side of the left hemisphere. This area, known as "Broca's speech area," has been assigned the functions of motor speech, that is, control of the tongue and jaws in speaking. The conventional interpretation is that the area is located in the left hemisphere of right-handed people (those whose left hemisphere is dominant), while it is found in the right hemisphere of left-handed people (those whose right hemisphere is dominant).

Speech is far too complex to be localized in this simple manner, and psychological disorders of speech and language have defied simple classification and therefore precise localization. In a careful study of ten left-handed people, half with lesions on the right sides of their brains and half with lesions on the left sides, all but one showed disturbances of speech; this one had a lesion on the right side, which, according to convention, should cause more severe disturbance for a left-handed person (Humphrey and Zangwill, 1952).

The association areas. The many large areas of the cerebral cortex that are not directly concerned with sensorimotor processes have been called *association areas*. They are distinguished from the primary projection areas in that they integrate phenomena arising from the stimulation of more than one sense and function in learning, memory, and thinking. This assumption was based largely on our ignorance of the actual functions of these areas, as well as on the fact that the amount of association area increases dramatically as we ascend the phylogenetic scale from the rat, which has virtually none, to man, in whom these areas comprise almost three-fourths of the cerebral cortex.

Although our knowledge about the association areas is still fragmentary, recent research makes it clear that a number of different functions are involved. The *frontal association areas* (those parts of the frontal lobes anterior to the motor area) appear to play an important role in the thought processes required for problem-solving. In monkeys, for example, the ability to solve a delayed-response problem is destroyed by lesions in the frontal lobes. In this kind of problem food is placed in one of two cups while the monkey watches, and the cups are covered with identical objects. An opaque screen is then placed between the monkey and the cups; after a specified time (anywhere from five to sixty seconds) the screen is removed and the monkey is allowed to choose one of the cups. Normal monkeys can "remember" the correct cup after delays of several minutes, but monkeys with frontal lobe lesions cannot solve the problem if the delay is more than a second or so (French and Harlow, 1962). This delayed response deficit following brain lesions is unique to the frontal cortex; it does not occur if lesions are made in other regions of the cortex.

Human beings who have suffered damage to the frontal lobes can perform normally on many intellectual tasks, but they do show a deficit similar to that of the monkeys when delay is involved or when it is necessary to shift frequently from one method of working on a problem to another method (Milner, 1964).

The *posterior association areas* are located among the various primary sensory areas and appear to consist of sub-areas, each serving a particular sense. For example, the lower portion of the temporal lobe is related to visual perception. Lesions in this area produce deficits in the ability to recognize and discriminate different forms. The lesion does not cause loss of visual acuity as would be true of a lesion in the primary visual area of the occipital lobe; the individual "sees" the forms and can trace the outline with his finger but cannot identify the shape or distinguish it from a different form. Pribram (1969a) has suggested that the function of this part of the temporal lobe is to organize the information coming in through the primary visual area.

Several areas, also in the temporal lobes, are concerned with the symbolic use of speech. Damage to tissue in these areas does not interfere with the motor production of speech but results in certain types of speech problems (called *aphasias*), in which the individual has trouble recalling words or naming objects, or sometimes has difficulty understanding what is said to him. Electrical stimulation of these areas in epileptic patients undergoing brain surgery has produced some interesting results. When epileptic seizures cannot be satisfactorily controlled by drugs, removal of brain tissue in the spot where the epileptic disturbance is focused sometimes has beneficial results. To be certain that removal of the focal area will not interfere with important behavioral functions, the surgeon carefully "maps" the surrounding region by electrical stimulation while the patient is under local anesthesia. When the electrode is placed in one of these symbolic speech areas, the patient may be temporarily unable to name common objects. For example, when shown a picture of a foot one patient said "Oh, I know what that is. That is what you put in your shoes." After withdrawal of the electrode he said "foot." A little later he was unable to name the picture of a tree, although he knew what it was, naming it properly as soon as the stimulus was turned off. The patient can speak effectively but for some reason cannot locate words that normally would come easily to him (Penfield and Roberts, 1959).

Even more puzzling is the fact that very vivid memories can be elicited by electrical stimulation of some of the association areas in the temporal lobes. The experiences relived by the patient when the electrical stimulus is applied appear to be real events from the past, such as recollections of a childhood scene or a tune once heard played by an orchestra and only vaguely remembered. The tune can be "turned on" or "turned off" through electrical stimulation. These recalled events are always much more vivid than ordinary memories; it is as if the electrical current had started a film-strip on which were registered the details of a past event that the patient had long since forgotten (Penfield and Roberts, 1959). These results are intriguing, but their interpretation is baffling. Is the memory of this experience really localized in this small spot? When the spot is surgically removed it is no longer possible to secure the effect formerly produced by stimulating that spot. But the excision does not destroy the subject's ability to tell what the tune sounded like when the spot was earlier stimulated. Evidently other parts of the brain are involved in the total memory experience.

These various results may seem confusing, but one thing that is clear is that the association areas play a role in many kinds of complex responses. Although the functions of the association areas are still not well understood, it appears that these areas provide a major part of the organizing and controlling activities necessary to coordinate the overall activity of the nervous system. In a way, they appear to act as an "executive process," monitoring and governing the flow of information in the total system; if they are knocked out, the system can still function but with less precision and organization.

The autonomic nervous system

The outgoing nerves, running from the central nervous system to the response mechanisms, can be classified into two groups: those running to the striate muscles and those running to smooth muscles and glands. Those going to the striate muscles are usually grouped with the central nervous system, while those going to smooth muscles and glands are grouped together as the *autonomic nervous system*. An anatomical basis for the distinction is that the nerve fibers of the autonomic system always have a junction with another neuron (a synapse) *outside* the brain or spinal cord on the way to a smooth muscle or gland, while such outside synapses are not found for nerves running to striate muscle. The autonomic nervous system derives its name from the fact that many of the activities it controls are "autonomous" or "self-regulating" activities, such as digestion and circulation, which go on even when a person is asleep or unconscious.

The autonomic system has two divisions often antagonistic in their action. These are the *sympathetic* and the *parasympathetic* divisions.

The sympathetic division

On either side of the spinal column, closely connected with it through the spinal nerves, lie

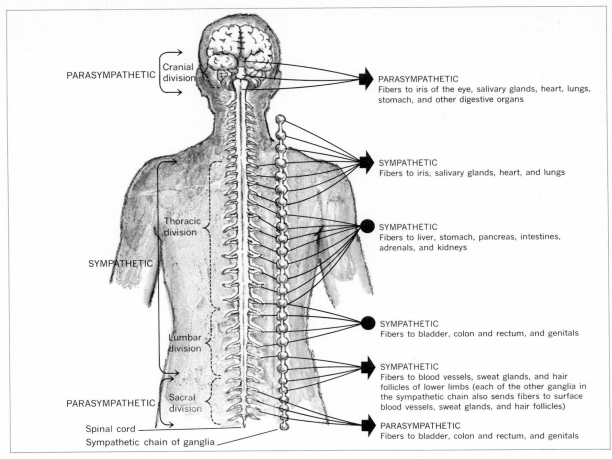

PARASYMPATHETIC   Cranial division

PARASYMPATHETIC
Fibers to iris of the eye, salivary glands, heart, lungs, stomach, and other digestive organs

SYMPATHETIC
Fibers to iris, salivary glands, heart, and lungs

Thoracic division

SYMPATHETIC
Fibers to liver, stomach, pancreas, intestines, adrenals, and kidneys

SYMPATHETIC

SYMPATHETIC
Fibers to bladder, colon and rectum, and genitals

Lumbar division

SYMPATHETIC
Fibers to blood vessels, sweat glands, and hair follicles of lower limbs (each of the other ganglia in the sympathetic chain also sends fibers to surface blood vessels, sweat glands, and hair follicles)

PARASYMPATHETIC   Sacral division

PARASYMPATHETIC
Fibers to bladder, colon and rectum, and genitals

Spinal cord
Sympathetic chain of ganglia

Fig. **2-16 The autonomic nervous system** The diagram represents only one-half of the system, which is duplicated on the other side of the spinal cord. The *sympathetic* system is characterized by chains of ganglia on either side of the cord and by other large ganglia (represented by large circles). The *parasympathetic* system has its ganglia (not shown) nearer the organs stimulated, so that it acts in a piecemeal fashion.

chains of nerve fibers and masses of cell bodies (*ganglia*) from which fibers extend to the various visceral organs. These chains are known as the *sympathetic chains*. The fibers coming from the spinal cord to the sympathetic chains originate in the thoracic and lumbar portions of the spine, between the cervical (neck) and the sacral (lower spine) regions. All the fibers and ganglia together constitute the *sympathetic division* of the autonomic system (Figure 2-16).

The sympathetic division tends to act as a unit. In emotional excitement it simultaneously speeds up the heart and dilates the arteries of the muscles and heart, while constricting those of the skin and digestive organs; its action leads also to perspiration and to secretion of epinephrine. In fact, the responses to epinephrine (see p. 27) and to the action of the sympathetic system are very much alike, and these chemical and neural actions support each other in strong emotion.

The parasympathetic division

The parasympathetic division falls into two parts, some of its fibers originating in the cranial region, above those of the sympathetic system, and others originating in the sacral region, below those of the sympathetic system.

Unlike the sympathetic system, the parasympathetic system tends to act in a piecemeal fashion, affecting one organ at a time. If the sympathetic system is thought of as dominant in violent and excited activity, the parasympathetic system may be thought of as dominant in quiescence. It participates in digestion and, in general, maintains the functions that conserve and protect bodily resources. (It is worth noting that there is no parasympathetic connection to the adrenal gland, which is dominant in excitement.)

Competition and cooperation between the divisions

When both sympathetic and parasympathetic fibers are connected to the same muscle or gland, they usually act in opposite manners. Thus the sympathetic system speeds the heart rate, the parasympathetic system slows it; the sympathetic system inhibits digestive processes, the parasympathetic system facilitates them. A list of the functions of the two systems is given in Table 2-2.

There are some exceptions to the principle that the two systems are antagonistic. Both divisions may be active at once, and in some cases they act together in sequence. Although the sympathetic system is usually dominant in fear and excitement, a not uncommon parasympathetic symptom in extreme emotion is the involuntary discharge of the bladder or bowels. Another example is the complete sex act in the male, which requires erection (parasympathetic) followed by ejaculation (sympathetic). Thus, while the two divisions are often antagonistic, they interact in complex ways, and their interaction is not yet fully understood.

TABLE 2-2   FUNCTIONS OF THE TWO DIVISIONS OF THE AUTONOMIC NERVOUS SYSTEM

ORGAN	SYMPATHETIC FUNCTION	PARASYMPATHETIC FUNCTION
Heart	Acceleration	Inhibition
Blood vessels In skin In striate muscle In heart In abdominal viscera	Constriction Dilation, constriction Dilation Constriction	None None Constriction None
Pupil of eye	Dilation	Constriction
Tear glands	(Possibly a secretory function)	Secretion
Sweat glands	Secretion	None
Hair on skin	Hairs erected	None
Adrenal glands	Secretion	None
Liver	Sugar liberated	None
Salivary glands	(Possibly a secretory function)	Secretion
Stomach	Inhibition of secretion and peristalsis (some excitation)	Secretion, peristalsis (some inhibition)
Intestines	Inhibition	Increased tone and motility
Rectum	Inhibition	Feces expelled
Bladder	Inhibition	Urine expelled
Genital organs (male)	Ejaculation	Erection

Thus far we have considered both the finer features of integrated nervous action (neuron, nervous impulse, synapse) and some gross aspects of anatomical localization of function. Now we shall consider some further aspects of integrated action as represented in reflex patterns and in responsiveness to under- and overstimulation.

The reflex pattern

The basic pattern of stimulation by the environment and response to stimulation is that of the *reflex circuit.* Irritability and contractibility are primitive properties of protoplasm, as found in single-celled organisms, but when nervous systems develop, response to stimulation becomes divided into the processes of *reception of stimuli, transmission and integration of nervous impulses,* and *activation of muscles and glands.* Specialized *receptors* convert the energy from the environment into nervous impulses; the nerves and central nervous system provide the *connectors;* the nervous impulses are converted back into action by the *effectors.*

	TABLE 2-3 MAN'S RECEPTORS	
BODILY ORGAN OR TISSUE	LOCATION OF SENSITIVE PORTION	SENSORY EXPERIENCE OR DISCRIMINATION
Eye	Retina	Black, white, color; visual perception of objects, space, motion
Inner ear	Cochlea	Tones, noises; speech, music; location of sounds in space
	Saccule, utricle	Static position of the body in reference to gravity; accelerated motion
	Semicircular canals	Rotation of the head
Nose	Olfactory epithelium (in upper part of right and left nasal cavities)	Smell
	Sensitive nerve endings (in membranes of nose)	Irritation
Tongue, mouth, and throat	Taste buds (on surface and edges of tongue; in lesser numbers, in other tissues of mouth and throat)	Sweet, salt, sour, bitter
Skin	Various end organs (organs and nerve endings of differential sensitivity, distributed unevenly through the superficial and deeper layers of the skin)	Light touch, deep pressure, warmth, coolness, pain
Internal organs	Various	Pain from distention (also, in some parts of some organs, touch, warmth, coolness, pressure)
Muscles, tendons, and joints	Muscle spindles (stimulated by stretching of muscle)	Position and movement of parts of the body
	Endings in tendons (stimulated when muscles contract)	
	Pressure-sensitive end organs in tissues around joints	

The truly simple reflex is a convenient fiction. It would represent a simple receptor that, when activated, would transmit impulses through a single neuron to a waiting muscle. Actual reflexes involve the stimulation of numerous nerve fibers, which in turn make junctions with other neurons, often supplemented by bursts of impulses coming from other sources, and resulting in impulses transmitted along numerous fibers before reaching a muscle or gland, or several muscles and glands. Some reflexes operate in a relatively mechanical manner, despite these complications of the simple reflex circuit. Thus a tap on the patellar tendon will ordinarily produce a knee jerk; light flashed into the eye will be followed by constriction of the pupil. Even in these cases, however, other processes may accentuate (facilitate) or diminish (inhibit) the response. For example, one way of obtaining a more pronounced knee jerk is for the subject to grip his hands together just before the tendon is tapped. Evidently what is happening in the leg is affected by what is happening elsewhere. When we consider more complex processes, such as memory and imagination, the notion of a reflex is maintained with greater difficulty, yet it is convenient to assume that the same principles can be applied.

Receptors. A receptor is an energy-converter, what the engineer calls a *transducer.* That is, it converts energy from the environment into chemical processes that in turn produce electrochemical nervous impulses (Loewenstein, 1960).

Man's equipment of *receptors* is very inadequately indicated by the traditional five senses. Not only do some of these (for example, touch) break down into several senses, but receptors related to bodily position and to muscular movements are totally unaccounted for in the traditional scheme. A catalogue of human receptors and their functions is given in Table 2-3.

Effectors. The *effectors,* which carry out the responses to stimuli, are the muscles and the glands. They mediate the smooth-muscle and glandular responses within the body as well as responses to the environment.

Connectors. Between the receptors and the effectors lie the *connectors,* or what we call "the nervous system." These may be grouped into three classes:

1. Incoming, or *afferent,* nerves. The receptors all over the body are connected to nerve fibers that carry impulses to the central nervous system. A nerve is a bundle of individual nerve fibers.

2. *Centers.* The internal connections and interconnections of nerve cells, made across their endings at *synapses,* occur chiefly within the brain and spinal cord, although some junctions occur between neurons (synapses) outside the brain and spinal cord in collections of nerve cells, or *ganglia.* We may group all these complex switching places together as *central processes,* or, simply, *centers.*

3. Outgoing, or *efferent,* nerves. From the centers, nerve fibers lead out, again through bundles called nerves, to connect with effectors. (It is easy to recall which nerves are called *a*fferent and which

Fig. 2-17 **Three-neuron reflex arc** Diagram illustrates how nerve impulses from a sense organ in the skin reach a skeletal muscle by a three-neuron arc at the level of entrance to the spinal cord. Awareness of this automatic reflex occurs because impulses also reach the cerebral hemisphere by way of an ascending tract. Arrows indicate the direction of nerve impulses. The H-shaped portion is gray matter at the center of the spinal cord, consisting largely of cell bodies and their interconnections.

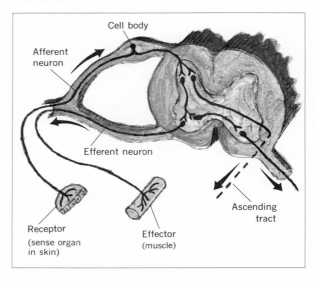

*e*fferent by remembering that *e*fferent nerves are connected with *e*ffectors.)

Until recently it had been assumed that afferent nerves were sensory nerves and efferent nerves motor nerves; that is, that afferent nerves served purposes of signaling changes at the sense organ, and efferent nerves served purposes of movement and secretion. It is now known, however, that the efferent fibers also regulate the amount of sensory input, thereby selectively allowing more or fewer afferent impulses to be transmitted. As many as one-third of the fibers in the *efferent* ventral roots to muscles serve this purpose of regulating the *afferent* impulses from muscle receptors. Similar efferent modification of afferent processes has been reported for the visual and auditory mechanisms in the brain.

Stimulation

The simple reflex as the unit of behavior tends to picture the organism as passive, waiting like a calculating machine to be stimulated from without. If nothing triggers a reflex, nothing happens. This is not, of course, a true picture of a living organism. Many reflex mechanisms are kept active by internal sources of stimulation—circulatory, respiratory, digestive, postural. Any new stimulus is received into a stream of activity, so reflex activity always takes place in a context. Some of this context can be described according to general levels of stimulation, varying between understimulation and overstimulation.

It was pointed out earlier that the body tends to preserve a normal state of equilibrium, or homeostasis, from which behavior departs in response to stimulation. Once there is effort or change of any sort, homeostasis is temporarily disturbed, and mechanisms are aroused that tend to restore it. Despite the importance of homeostasis and the stresses that are implied when it is upset, the normal life of the organism is not one of quiescence, but one of action.

The fact that a healthy organism seeks stimulation and activity is evident to anyone who has watched children and animals at play. As adults we know that solitary confinement is the cruelest form of punishment, reducing as it does opportunities for physical stimulation and eliminating social stimulation and response.

Our level of activity can vacillate between complete quiescence and an overactive, stressful level. In the normal cycle of sleep and wakefulness, the vacillation is between moderate limits of quiet and action. The harmful effects of extreme overactivity are obvious (exhaustion, collapse), but extreme inactivity can also have serious consequences.

Understimulation. Experiments have shown that even a relatively short period of inactivity will disturb the adaptive responses of a person. In one such experiment, college students were paid to remain in bed in isolated cubicles for two to three days under conditions of very restricted stimulation. Not only were the rooms free of pictures and other centers of interest, but the students wore special cuffs to reduce the stimulation from their own movements as they lay quietly in bed. They were interrupted occasionally for psychological testing. During the isolation period, scores on a number of intelligence test items decreased markedly. Some disturbances in perception were noted as the students left the cubicles. Occasionally during the period of isolation, hallucinations appeared, not dissimilar to those found in some cases of mental illness (Doane and others, 1959).

These experiments show in rather striking fashion that the normal level of psychological functioning depends upon active participation with the environment. Workers in mental hospitals have found that some gains are produced merely by keeping patients active, as in sports and hobbies. Some minimum level of active stimulation and response is necessary for normal functioning.

Overstimulation: stress. When conditions place the organism under great strain, the homeostatic mechanisms no longer operate smoothly; if the stresses continue, the organism may suffer injury, even as a consequence of its own efforts to meet the stress. Agents and events that can place the organism under stress include infections, nervous strain, physical injury, excessive heat or cold, and muscular fatigue.

Conditions of modern life place some people under stress for long periods of time. A number of investigators have been concerned with a response pattern that develops under such conditions. The physiological changes that occur when the body tries to adapt to stress may lead to "diseases of adaptation" (Selye, 1956). Of particular interest psychologically are the *psychosomatic disorders,* in which psychological stress in the form of worry or anxiety may produce tension states resulting in such conditions as ulcers or high blood pressure. We will have more to say about such disorders in Chapter 20.

Optimal levels of functioning. Between the understimulation that is harmful to human functioning and the stress conditions that produce disease and exhaustion, there is a wide range within which normal functioning goes on. Man can live an active life or a sedentary life and still be healthy.

W. B. Cannon, who introduced the notion of homeostasis, is often misunderstood as proposing that the condition of homeostasis represents the optimal level of activity. On the contrary, he stated the position that homeostasis merely protects the body so that a person can go about his enterprises, motivated by goals unrelated to maintaining the equilibrium of processes within the body. According to Cannon, bodily homeostasis liberates the nervous system

from the necessity of paying routine attention to the management of the details of bare existence. Without homeostatic devices we should be in constant danger of disaster, unless we were always on the alert to correct voluntarily what normally is corrected automatically. With homeostatic devices, however, that keep essential bodily processes steady, we as individuals are free from such slavery—free to enter into agreeable relations with our fellows, to enjoy beautiful things, to explore and understand the wonders of the world about us, to develop new ideas and interests, and to work and play untrammeled by anxieties concerning our bodily affairs [Cannon, 1939, p. 323].

Homeostasis, then, does not define the appropriate level of human functioning; it is merely a protective device. Among man's highest attainments are those that homeostasis permits him to accomplish without his giving thought to the condition of his body.

Summary

1. The human body is a complex sensitive and responding organism, capable of functioning harmoniously because of its mechanical structure of bones and muscles, its blood stream that carries hormones, and its nervous system that rules over all the rest.

2. Among the mechanisms that permit fine muscular coordination are those of *reciprocal innervation,* whereby the interaction of *antagonistic muscles* is provided for, and the slight but constant action in resting muscles that yields *muscle tone.*

3. The *endocrine glands* secrete *hormones* into the blood stream and are important to aspects of behavior concerned with emotion, motivation, and personality. Among those most relevant to behavior are the *pituitary, thyroid,* and *adrenal glands,* and the *gonads,* but the *parathyroids, thymus,* and *pancreas* are also important.

4. Because of its intimate relationship to behavior, the evolution of the *brain* and *nervous system* is of primary interest. One-celled animals react directly to the environment, without a specialized nervous system; even a multicellular animal such as a sponge has no nerves. The beginning of the nervous system is seen in the *nerve net* found in coelenterates like the polyps. This is a network of nerve cells called *neurons.* Muscles contract locally where the nerves are stimulated; conduction spreads

in all directions from the point of stimulation. In the flatworms (planaria) we find the beginnings of the kind of nervous system found in higher forms. The nerve net is combined with a *polarized synaptic* nervous system, in which conduction is in one direction only across the synapse, the junction between neurons. Some flatworms have a ladder-type nervous system with nerve cords and a primitive brain.

5. The nervous system is composed of cells called *neurons.* They receive stimulation by way of their *dendrites* and *cell body* and transmit impulses via their *axons.* Two types of propagation of the nerve impulse are of importance: that along nerve fibers and that across the synaptic junction between the neurons. Propagation along fibers is by way of an electrochemical process involving the interchange of sodium and potassium ions through the cell membrane, which generates the *action potential;* the conduction is much more rapid for myelinated fibers. The activation of a neuron across a synapse is also by way of a chemical intermediary; the chemicals act on the dendrites and cell body of the receiving neuron to produce *graded synaptic potentials* that, when large enough, discharge the all-or-none action potential. Two types of synaptic transmission, *excitation* and *inhibition,* interact to determine whether or not a neuron will fire.

6. The vertebrate brain evolved about a single hollow cord of nerves running along the back of the body, with some enlargements at the forward (head) end. The three enlargements became the *forebrain, midbrain,* and *hindbrain,* connecting in turn with the *spinal cord.* This basic pattern is preserved in man's brain.

7. Even a primitive vertebrate such as the dogfish has developed specialized parts of the forebrain, such as the *olfactory bulb, cerebrum, thalamus,* and *hypothalamus.* The midbrain consists at this stage chiefly of *optic lobes* connected with the visual apparatus. The hindbrain includes the *cerebellum* and *medulla.*

8. The most notable change in the brain in higher vertebrate forms is the development of the new brain, the *cerebral cortex,* the large convoluted surface of the brain that is about all one sees when he looks at the brain of a higher animal, such as that of a horse or dog or human being. The midbrain has decreased a great deal in relative size.

9. The human brain is composed of three concentric layers: a *primitive core,* an *old brain* evolved upon this core, and a third or outer layer of *new brain,* evolved in turn upon the second layer.

    a. The primitive core within the *brain stem* serves life-maintaining processes such as respiration and metabolism and keeps the level of body functioning near a steady equilibrium state through *homeostatic* processes. These homeostatic processes operate by way of *homeostats* within the hypothalamus, analogous to thermostats in maintaining constant temperature. An activating system, the *reticular formation,* lies within the brain stem and helps control waking and sleeping, alertness and attention.

    b. At the next level, lying along the innermost edge of the cerebral hemispheres, are structures that make up the older or more primitive cortex, now referred to as the *limbic system.* These structures regulate the *sequential* activities, such as feeding, attacking, fleeing from danger, mating—essential activities that include interaction with the environment and take place in sequences somewhat spread out in time.

    c. Finally, the outer core of new brain, the *cerebral cortex,* controls discrimination, choice, learning, and thinking—the "higher mental processes," the most flexible, least stereotyped aspects of behavior. The *projection areas* represent specific sensory inputs or centers for control of specific movements; the remainder of the new brain consists of *association areas.*

10. The *autonomic nervous system* is made up of two parts, a *sympathetic* and a *parasympathetic* division. Because its fibers mediate the action of the smooth muscles and of the glands, the autonomic system is particularly important in emotional reactions. The sympathetic division is usually involved in excited action and the parasympathetic in quiescent states, but the antagonism between the two divisions is not universal; they do cooperate in complex ways.

11. In considering the way in which the nervous system works, psychologists find it convenient to build upon the notion of the *reflex circuit,* beginning with the stimulation of a sensitive organ (*receptor*), where the energy of the stimulus is converted into a *nervous impulse* (or a chain of such impulses) that travels to the spinal cord and brain via incoming (*afferent*) nerves; switching and integration take place in *centers* of the nervous system; then impulses are propagated along outgoing (*efferent*) nerves to the responding organs, muscles, and glands (*effectors*). The notion of a simple reflex is a convenient fiction, but the pattern of the reflex circuit does permit discussion of action in terms of input from the environment, central coordination and elaboration, and output in the form of response.

12. Studies of the consequences of under- and overstimulation show the radical effects of extreme departure from the equilibrium state of homeostasis. Understimulation may produce in adult human beings extreme symptoms of loss of adaptive response and the development of hallucinations. Overstimulation, in the form of continued stress, may lead to disease. But the normally functioning organism has enough protective devices to allow it to engage in widely varied activities without threatening its survival.

Suggestions for further reading

For a general introduction to neurology and neuroanatomy, see Stevens, *Neurophysiology: A primer* (1966), or Ochs, *Elements of neurophysiology* (1965). A careful account of the methods and results of electrostimulation as a means of studying brain function is that of Sheer, *Electrical stimulation of the brain* (1961).

For physiological psychology in general, see Morgan, *Physiological psychology* (3rd ed., 1965), Thompson, *Foundations of physiological psychology* (1967), and Grossman, *A textbook of physiological psychology* (1967). Landauer, in *Readings in physiological psychology* (1967), republished many of the more important papers of the last few years, which already are considered "classics" in the field.

A speculative account relating neurophysiology to psychological problems is Pribram (ed.), *On the biology of learning* (1969b).

PART TWO

GROWTH AND DEVELOPMENT

infancy and childhood 3

THE HUMAN INFANT IS HELPLESS FOR A longer time than any other mammal. If we consider only man's nearest relatives in the animal world, a scale of dependency can be made from the comparatively primitive lemur through the more highly evolved primates to man. The newborn lemur can move about by himself within a few hours; the monkey is dependent for a few days or weeks; the infant chimpanzee remains with his mother three to six months. The human infant is dependent for a number of years. Despite (or because of) this slow start a human being has had a highly diversified background by the time he becomes an adult. He is subjected to a long period of learning and interaction with others before he is fully "on his own."

The nature of an individual's early experience is of psychological interest for a number of reasons. Most of the behavior and personality traits characteristic of an adult are dependent upon events and influences in his childhood, particularly those that occur during the early years of life. In order to understand the psychological processes of the adult—his perceptions, patterns of thinking, motives, emotions, conflicts, and ways of coping with conflicts—we must have some knowledge of how these processes originate and develop. To formulate a comprehensive theory of visual perception, for example, it is essential to know what the newborn infant perceives and how his perceptions change as he matures.

From a practical standpoint, knowledge of the

way in which an individual is shaped by his early experiences permits us to be wiser in our child-rearing practices. Many of the problems that confront society today—aggression, alienation, drug abuse, suicide, and mental illness—could perhaps be averted if we had a better understanding of how parental behavior and attitudes affect the child, how some of these problems originate, and how they might be dealt with at an early age.

The developmental viewpoint

We have distinguished the developmental and interactive viewpoints in a general way; the developmental point of view emphasizes the historical antecedents of behavior, while the interactive approach focuses on those factors currently influencing behavior. What can be learned from taking the developmental viewpoint should become clearer as we study the development of the human infant in relation to some more general aspects of biological development.

Why we study development

Any topic in psychology can be studied both in its basic science aspects and in its applied aspects. The development of the human organism is interesting as a basic scientific problem, but it is of course a practical problem for parents, educators, and others responsible for the management of human lives. The main assumption of the developmental viewpoint is that there is a continuity from the past to the present, so that the present can be understood in terms of its history; this is so obvious that it would not elicit much theoretical interest in development if it were not for some controversial aspects of this continuity. One controversy concerns the possibility of *critical periods* in development, during which both favorable and unfavorable outcomes have lasting and almost irreversible consequences.

The concept of critical periods originated in the study of embryological development. As the embryo grows, the various organ systems develop in a fixed time sequence, each system having its critical period during which it is maximally sensitive to growth stimulation and maximally vulnerable to disruptive factors. If the organ system does not develop normally during its critical period, it does not get a second chance, because the focus of growth shifts to other systems. Thus, if the mother contracts German measles during the first three months of pregnancy, the effect on the embryo depends on the exact time of infection. The infant may be born blind, deaf, deformed, or brain-damaged, depending upon which organ system was in its critical phase of development at the time of the infection.

It is possible that there are critical periods in the psychological development of the child as there are critical periods in embryological development. For example, it has been hypothesized that a person's basic trust in other people is a characteristic developed in the first year of life through the warmth and affection of those who care for him (Erikson, 1963). If this hypothesis is true, and the child who lacks such early affectionate care grows up to be inadequate and mistrustful in social relationships, then the first few months of life would represent a critical period with respect to the development of basic trust.

Another controversy centers on the possibility that growth proceeds in definable *stages,* so that behavior and personality become somewhat restructured as growth proceeds. The shifts in interest with the onset of adolescence would be one of the familiar aspects of such restructuring, but there are others that are less obvious. The concepts of critical periods and of stages suggest that there are aspects of the developmental process that are inherent in growth and not the result solely of learning. The issue between inherent growth aspects, or *maturation,* and the influence of experience, or *learning,* is one that has to be faced in many areas of psychology.

Patterns of maturation and development

The concept of *maturation* assumes that the timing and patterning of changes, beyond birth, are relatively independent of experience and go on despite wide variations in the environment, as long as these variations occur within limits favorable to survival and growth. Some birds reared in isolation, so that they never hear the song characteristic of their species, are still able to reproduce it properly at the appropriate stage of development. Thus we can reasonably say that singing in some species of birds is controlled largely by maturation rather than by learning.

Development of the human fetus goes on in the uniform environment of the mother's body according to a relatively fixed time schedule. Fetal behavior, such as turning and kicking, also follows an orderly sequence, depending upon the growth

David Linton

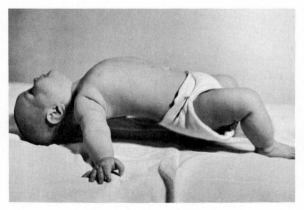

stages of the fetus. Infants who are born prematurely and kept alive in an incubator develop at much the same rate as infants remaining in the uterus full term. The regularity of development before birth provides a clear picture of what is meant by maturation, for growth occurs in an orderly and predictable way.

In postnatal maturation many kinds of behavior follow orderly sequences little affected by environmental influences, provided only that the environment is sufficiently favorable to support the necessary growth. Such sequences are found in standing, walking, using hands and fingers, and talking. For example, every infant goes through such regular sequences of crawling and creeping before he walks upright that a uniform growth pattern is evidently responsible for the behavior.

Maturation of structure continues into adult life. Some of the growth changes at adolescence are internally regulated in a sequence not unlike the regulation of fetal development. To the extent that adolescent behavior corresponds to bodily changes, maturational principles apply. The changes associated with aging also go on at their own fixed rates, relatively independent of experience. While maturation is a lifelong process, its nature is most readily understood through observing infants and young children, in whom behavioral changes dependent upon growth are rapid and distinct.

Long before learning to walk, the infant goes

Fig. 3-1 Muscular activity of babies at the rolling stage This six-month-old baby discovers movements that prepare him for further development and lead to his ability to walk later on.

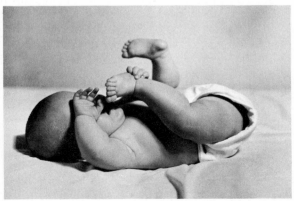

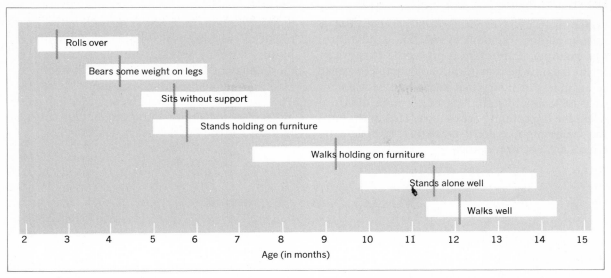

Fig. **3-2** **Babies develop at different rates** Although development is orderly, some infants reach each stage ahead of others. The left end of the bar indicates the age by which 25 percent of infants have achieved the stated performance, whereas the right end gives the age by which 90 percent have accomplished the behavior. The vertical mark on each bar gives the age by which 50 percent have achieved it. (After Frankenburg and Dodds, 1967)

through a number of movement stages related to this later and more complex behavior. An early form of "locomotion" is rolling over (Figure 3-1). Again this regularity of sequence suggests that a growth process determines the order of behavior. The alternative conclusion would be that all parents go through a training ritual that leads to this uniformity of performance from one child to another. We know, of course, that *all* parents do nothing of the sort.

Not all children go through the sequence at the same rate; in general, the *order* in which they go from one stage to the next is more alike from infant to infant than the *age* at which they reach each stage. An idea of the range of variation from child to child is given in Figure 3-2, which shows the age zones within which infants reached a stated level of performance. Some infants are more than four or five months ahead of others in reaching the stage of standing alone or walking.

Further evidence of the influence of maturation comes from experiments in which the environment is either restricted or enriched. If environmental variations produce little difference in the rate of

change of behavior, then it becomes clearer that the process is determined by growth *within* rather than by influence from *without*.

Observations on the effects of restriction of movement have been made with human infants. Until recently it was the custom in Russia and some of the Balkan countries to *swaddle* an infant—to wrap him up to the neck in long, narrow bands of cloth, thereby completely restricting his movements. The rationale behind this procedure was to keep him warm and to prevent him from scratching or hurting himself. When investigators compared the development of a group of infants who had been swaddled until one year of age with that of a group who had not, they found that although the former children displayed poor muscular coordination when first released from the swaddling clothes, they caught up with the nonswaddled children after only a brief period of practice. There was obviously no permanent impairment (Orlansky, 1949).

These and related observations indicate that motor development is largely a matter of maturation rather than learning. It depends primarily upon the growth of neural and muscular tissue rather than upon experience or practice. But a certain minimal amount of practice is necessary. For example, if an infant is prevented from walking at the time he is maturationally ready (because of an illness or injury that keeps him bedridden), then he learns to walk with much more difficulty when the opportunity arises later. This is evidence for something like a critical period, although the effects are not irreversible.

The practical importance of recognizing the influence of maturation lies in the relation of maturation to the effects of training at different ages. Maturation may provide a readiness to learn, but most behavior depends upon *both* maturation and learning. Language provides a useful illustration. The child learns to talk only when he has grown old enough to learn (maturation), but the language he learns is the one he hears (learning).

Effects of early experience

As we have said, behaviors that depend upon maturation appear at the appropriate times regardless of environmental conditions, provided the environment is not seriously deficient. But conditions of severe deprivation or unusual stimulation can affect the rate at which development takes place and can have serious psychological consequences in later years. We will look first at some studies involving restricted or deprived environments and then examine the effects of unusual stimulation.

Early deprivation

Even though the development of a sensory system may be largely due to maturation, a certain amount of stimulation is necessary for it to function properly. Infant rhesus monkeys were reared in total darkness from birth to the age of three months except for a brief period each day when they were exposed to light while wearing translucent, plastic goggles. The goggles permitted only diffuse, unpatterned light to reach the eyes.[1] When the monkeys were first exposed to light without goggles, they showed serious deficiencies in visual behavior. They could not follow moving objects with their eyes, did not blink when threatened by

a blow to the face, nor put out their arms when being moved rapidly toward a wall. All these behaviors improved with continued exposure to light, however, so that by the end of several weeks the dark-reared monkeys were performing as well as normal monkeys. In fact, in most instances they acquired the responses more quickly than normal monkeys. For example, following a moving object with the eyes occurs at anywhere from four to twenty-eight days of age for animals reared in light; the dark-reared monkeys showed this response between the fourth and twelfth day of exposure to a normal visual environment (Riesen, 1965). This study provides evidence for the importance of both maturation and learning. Fully adequate use of vision depends upon neuromuscular growth continuing after birth as well as on practice in the use of vision. The dark-reared monkeys required experience in light before they could develop the proper response; but the fact that they required so much less experience than newborn monkeys indicates the role of maturation.

In another experiment, dogs reared in confined quarters (so that they did not have an opportunity to explore the environment) were perfectly healthy, but in some respects they appeared stupid (Scott, 1968). For one thing, they seemed quite insensitive to pain. They did not respond to a pin prick or to having their tail stepped on. Time after time, they would investigate a lighted match by putting their nose into the flame. Whatever the felt experience may have been to the dog, certainly the pain

[1]Earlier studies found that animals reared in total darkness suffered some degeneration of nerve cells in the eyes; a small amount of diffuse light through plastic goggles is sufficient for normal neurological development of the eyes yet does not provide experience with visual patterns.

stimulus did not evoke the avoidance responses found in normal dogs. Subsequent studies with dogs and other animals have led to the conclusion that restriction or deprivation of stimulation generally produces animals that in later life do not learn new tasks as quickly as their normal counterparts.

Enriched environments

Suppose instead of a restricted or deprived environment we provide an organism with an unusual amount of stimulation. What will be the psychological effects? Young gerbils (small mouse-like rodents) housed together in a large cage equipped with various kinds of toys are significantly different after thirty days from gerbils kept singly in small, bare cages (see Figure 3-3). They perform better on learning tasks; their brains weigh more and show a higher concentration of some of the chemicals associated with learning (Rosenzweig and Bennett, 1970).

Human infants also benefit from an enriched or more stimulating environment, even in the first weeks after birth. A study by White (1969) demonstrates the effect of early stimulation upon *visually directed reaching*—a visual-motor response that develops in clearly specified maturational steps. A month-old baby lying on his back will stare at an attractive object held above him but will make no attempt to reach for it. By two months he will swipe at it but be far off target. By four months he will alternate glances between his raised hand and the object, gradually narrowing the gap between. By five months he will make accurate contact with the object, thus achieving visually directed reaching.

Although this response of the infant is basically maturational, its rate of development can be accelerated. White enriched the environment of a group of month-old infants in a state hospital by (1) increasing the amount of handling, (2) providing a view of ward activities by placing the infants on their stomachs with the crib liners removed for several periods each day, (3) replacing the white crib sheets and liners with patterned ones, and (4) hanging an elaborate ornament featuring contrasting colors and forms over the cribs. Infants receiving this kind of treatment succeeded in visually directed reaching at an average age of three and a half months as contrasted with five months for a control group of infants reared in the relatively unstimulating conditions of regular hospital routine. Interestingly enough, the enriched-environment infants were delayed in one aspect of their development; they did not begin visually studying their hands until around two months, as contrasted with a month and a half for the control

M. R. Rosenzweig

Fig. **3-3 An enriched environment** Animals raised together in this cage, which provides a complex and enriched environment, show better learning ability and have better developed brains than gerbils reared singly in bare cages (Rosenzweig and Bennett, 1970).

infants. With virtually nothing else to look at, the control infants discovered their hands earlier than either the experimental infants or babies raised in their own homes.

It is important to note, however, that increased stimulation will not result in accelerated development unless the infant is maturationally ready. In fact, too much stimulation provided too early may be upsetting. This appeared to be the case in White's study: during the first five weeks of the experiment, infants in the enriched group spent less time looking at their surroundings (seeming to ignore the ornament and patterned bumpers) and engaged in much more crying than did the control infants. It may be that a month-old infant is actually distressed by being surrounded by so much stimulation to which he is unable to respond. White (1969) reported a subsequent study supporting this. Providing infants with only a simple but colorful object mounted on the crib rails for the first two months of life and then introducing more complex ornaments seemed to provide the optimal development. These infants showed no signs of unusual distress, were consistently attentive to their surroundings, and achieved visually directed reaching at *less* than three months. Thus we see the importance of providing stimulation appropriate to the degree of maturation.

Early stress

A curious effect of early experience upon emotional responsiveness, and development generally, has been reported, based on experiments with white rats. The experimenter subjected one group of young rats to mild electric shock that lasted for three minutes once a day, expecting to produce some abnormalities in behavior later on. As controls he had two other groups of young rats. One group was handled as the experimental rats were, but without shock (that is, they were placed in the shock apparatus for three minutes each day with the current turned off). The other group was left in the nest and not disturbed. The result of the experiment was unexpected: the later behavior of the shocked rats was not distinguishable from that of the rats that were handled but not shocked; it was the undisturbed rats that showed the abnormalities. They were particularly timid when placed in a new environment, crouching in the corner rather than exploring the open cage. Other lines of evidence show that rats exposed to mild stress as infants (being shocked or removed from the nest) develop more rapidly in many respects, opening their eyes sooner, gaining weight more rapidly, growing larger. Later, under stress, these animals were found to have a more rapid response from the adrenal glands than the nonhandled ones. Thus mild stress in infancy produced profound changes in development, reflected in changes of the regulatory systems within the body as well as in overt behavior (Levine and Mullins, 1966).

We may well ask whether there is comparable evidence in human growth for the effects of stressful experiences in early infancy. One might investigate effects on adult height, since the animals in the experiments showed pronounced changes in size as a result of infantile stress. Two investigators set out to find what evidence they could for the correlation of stress in infancy and adult height in men (Landauer and Whiting, 1964). They used as their source of information the Human Relations Area Files at Yale University—a collection of data on many nonliterate cultures gathered by anthropologists over a period of years. Evidence on both infant care and adult size exists for many cultures in these records. Landauer and Whiting found eighty cultures for which the evidence seemed adequate, and then they proceeded to classify these cultures separately for (1) stressful treatment of infant boys and (2) adult male size. The stressful events that were selected for study were *piercing* (piercing the nose, lips, or ear to receive an ornament; circumcision, inoculation, scarification, or cauterization) and *molding* (stretching the arms or legs or shaping the head, usually for the sake of some preferred appearance). The somewhat surprising result was that the males stressed in infancy averaged 2.7 inches taller as adults than those not so stressed.

This finding is in accordance with the animal studies, but it is, of course, subject to some reservations. The authors themselves looked for confounding factors (such as different racial stock, different amounts of available food, or different climates) but were not able to find any alternative explanations. The Spartan explanation—that in those cultures that treat their infants harshly only the fittest and strongest survive—cannot be completely ruled out, for these practices may have gone on for many generations. A supplementary finding is that the adult stature appears to be affected when the stress occurs within the first two years rather than later in childhood. It may be that the first two years are a "critical period" for the stresses affecting physical size.

Early stimulation and later development

These diverse studies suggest that early experiences are important for both animals and man in providing the background for coping with the environment when they are older. The implications for child-rearing practices are not firm, but they suggest that a certain amount of fondling and stimulation is important for development, and that neglect may be more harmful than a mild degree of stress. The parents who are so proud of the "good baby" who lies quietly in the crib may not be giving to that baby what is best for him. The importance of a stimulating environment in the first two years of life is illustrated by a classic study by Skeels and Dye (1939).

A group of orphaned children whose development at the age of nineteen months was so retarded that adoption was out of the question was transferred to an institution for the mentally retarded. In this institution, in contrast to the overcrowded orphanage, each child was placed in the care of an older, mildly retarded girl who served as a mother surrogate, spending great amounts of time playing with the child, talking to him, and training him. In addition, the living quarters were spacious and well equipped with toys. As soon as the children could walk they began to attend a nursery school where additional play materials and stimulation were provided. After a period of four years this experimental group showed an average gain in intelligence of 32 I.Q. points; a control group that remained in the orphanage showed a loss of 21 points. After twenty-one years a follow-up study

(Skeels, 1966) showed that the experimental group was still superior to the control group. Most of the experimental group had completed high school (a third had gone to college), were self-supporting, and had married and produced children of normal intelligence. Most of the control group, on the other hand, had completed less than the third grade and either remained institutionalized or did not earn enough to be self-supporting.

The results of these studies indicate the remarkable improvement in development that can be brought about by providing a stimulating environment at an optimal age (generally considered to be under two or three years of age). Similar results from other studies have encouraged those concerned with education of culturally disadvantaged children to attempt to enrich the child's environment in the preschool years. The realization that such children were already so seriously behind in intellectual development when they entered kindergarten that they were doomed to be dropouts or at the least underachievers prompted the federal government to sponsor the Head Start program, which provides a variety of preschool experiences.

Enrichment programs of all kinds have been explored, varying from short, intensive classes the summer before the child enters school to more

Fig. **3-4 Early intellective training** Program involving a long-term relationship between a child and adult at the Harlem Research Center. The program, aimed at providing intellective training for children two and three years of age, is based on the assumption that the early acquisition of certain concepts will provide the child with a head start so that he can more profitably interact with his environment.

Courtesy F. H. Palmer

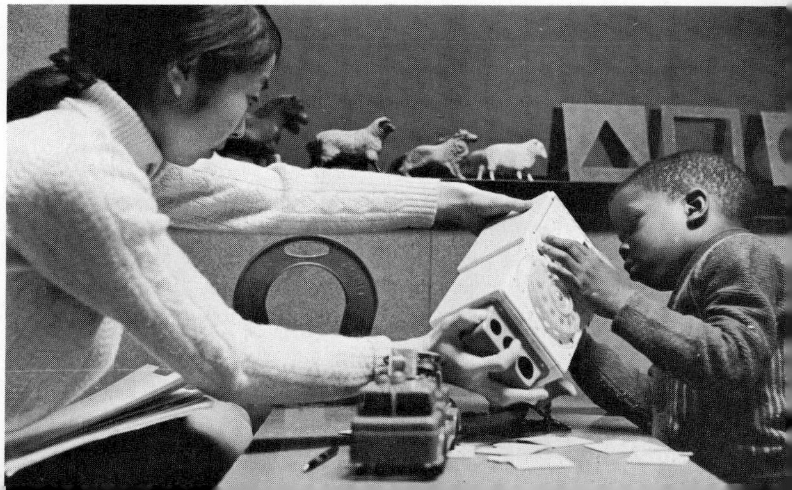

long-term attempts to work with both the mother and the child in the home, starting shortly after birth. In general, the results of short-term enrichment programs have been disappointing. A three- or four-week summer school program that emphasizes training in language skills and ability to label and classify objects does result in improved performance when the child enters first grade the following fall. The gains in performance, however, appear to be short-lived; frequently by the following year the children who have received preschool training are no better off than those who did not. More substantial effects have been attained when the program starts earlier and actively involves the mother as well as the child. In one such study (Miller, 1969) three and four year olds from low-income families (most of whose mothers were black and worked as domestic help) spent an hour a day in classes that emphasized learning concepts of color, shape, size, time, number, and part-whole relationships. In addition, the mothers of some of the children were seen once a week and helped with such skills as reading to the child, playing counting games, and meal planning; they were taught the importance of health care and the use of positive reward instead of punishment in working with their children. The children whose mothers were actively involved in the program showed much greater and longer-lasting gains in ability than the other children in the group. An additional interesting fact was the effect on the younger siblings of the children whose mothers were involved in the program. These siblings when tested were markedly superior to the siblings of those children whose parents had not been involved. Thus, the mother appears to be a crucial agent in providing intellectual stimulation for her child.

Stages in development

Another issue to be faced in assessing the continuities between early and later life is whether there are definable stages through which the individual goes as he grows up, with their special problems to be surmounted. Perhaps psychological development does not proceed at a steady rate but is instead somewhat steplike, as one stage is left and another entered. We identify crude stages of this sort as a matter of common practice when we distinguish between successive periods such as infancy, childhood, adolescence, and adulthood.

There is a close relationship between critical periods and stages, but the two concepts are not identical. The critical period principle assumes that at a given stage of development certain experiences are unusually important. If they are lacking, development will be stunted later; failures at this period can be made up, if at all, only with great difficulty. The notion of stages is related in that a failure to deal adequately with the developmental problems at a particular stage may hinder development at a subsequent stage, but the effects are not irreversible. The organism may progress normally through definable stages in development even though an ability that fails to develop at its "normal" stage may be attained later. Thus, an individual may proceed through adolescence normally, regardless of whether he has been taught to read as a child, and he can still learn to read as an adult. Learning to read is not dependent upon a critical period. What is critical, and what is stage-related, can be determined only by study.

Stages in cognitive development

The one who has done the most to make the stage concept plausible in human development is the Swiss psychologist Jean Piaget. He has been interested for many years in the development of children, focusing primarily on their cognitive, or intellectual, development. Although his work has been known to American psychologists for four decades, it has recently been receiving renewed attention. The main stages of intellectual development according to Piaget are presented in somewhat simplified form in Table 3-1.

TABLE 3-1   PIAGET'S STAGES OF INTELLECTUAL DEVELOPMENT

STAGE	APPROXIMATE AGES	CHARACTERIZATION
I. Sensorimotor period	Birth to 2 years	Infant differentiates himself from objects; seeks stimulation, and makes interesting spectacles last; prior to language, meanings defined by manipulations, so that object remains "the same object" with changes in location and point of view.
II. Preoperational thought period Preoperational phase	2–4	Child egocentric, unable to take viewpoint of other people; classifies by single salient features: if A is like B in one respect, must be like B in other respects.
Intuitive phase	4–7	Is now able to think in terms of classes, to see relationships, to handle number concepts, but is "intuitive" because he may be unaware of his classification. Gradual development of *conservation* in this order: mass (age 5), weight (age 6), and volume (age 7).*
III. Period of concrete operations	7–11	Able now to use logical operations such as *reversibility* (in arithmetic), *classification* (organizing objects into hierarchies of classes), and *seriation* (organizing objects into ordered series, such as increasing size).
IV. Period of formal operations	11–15	Final steps toward abstract thinking and conceptualization; capable of hypothesis-testing.

*Ages for 50 percent passing, according to Kooistra (1963). The ages given by Piaget and Inhelder (1941) are generally higher.

Source: After Piaget, modified from Sigel (1964).

Noting the close interplay between action and perception in infants, Piaget designated the first two years as a *sensorimotor* period. One consequence of the infant's manipulations and of his "playing" with the environment is what is called *object-attainment,* that is, the awareness that an object, seen from different angles, is an enduring something, the "same" object that it was before. For example, once the infant has learned to hold a bottle and nurse from it, if the bottle is presented in reversed position, he will try to suck the glass bottom. Later, however, when he recognizes the bottle for what it is as an enduring object, he will turn it around in order to suck on the nipple. Other evidence that the infant has formed an object concept comes when he searches for hidden or lost objects. At five months if a ball is placed beneath a blanket, the infant acts as if the ball no longer exists; at eight months he will lift the blanket to look for it. These events, so much taken for granted, in Piaget's hands have become a source of developmental principles.

The kinds of evidence that Piaget and his co-workers have used in studying thought problems of children in a slightly later stage, the *intuitive phase of preoperational thought,* can be illustrated by the development of what he calls *conservation,* approximately during the ages from five to seven. As adults we take the conservation principle for granted: the amount (mass) of a substance is not changed when its shape is changed or when it is divided into parts; the total weight of a set of objects will remain the same no matter how they are packaged together; and liquids do not change volume by being moved from a container of one shape to that of another. But for children the attainment of these concepts is an aspect of intellectual growth requiring several years.

In a study of the conservation of mass, a child is given some plastic clay to make into a ball equal

Harbrace Photos

Fig. 3-5 Concept of conservation A four year old acknowledges that the two balls of clay are the same size. But when one ball is rolled into a long thin shape, he says that it has more clay. Not until he is a year older will he state that the two different shapes contain the same amount of clay.

to another ball of the material; he declares them to be "the same." Now, leaving one for reference, the other is rolled out into a long sausage shape. If the child is about four years old, he does not consider the two objects to contain the same amount of clay: to him the longer one contains more (Figure 3-5). Not until the age of five years can we expect half the children to have reached the stage in which the clay in five balls made from one larger one is perceived to be the same amount of clay as that in the original large ball (Piaget, 1970).

The same kind of experiment can be used to study the conservation of weight and volume. For example, the child who knows that equal things will balance on a scale (he can test this with the two balls to begin with) is then asked whether the sausage-shaped form will keep the scale arm straight out the way the original ball did. Conservation of weight is a harder concept to perceive than conservation of mass, and it comes about a year later in development. In the experiment with volume, the child first sees that equal-sized balls will raise the water level in a graduated cylinder an equal amount. When asked whether the sausage shape will raise the water a like amount the child doubts it until still older—typically another year.

We may ask: Are the sequences that are found in the attainment of conservation a result of inherent development (maturation) rather than prior experience? Can training speed up the transition to a higher stage? Although the answers to such questions cannot be given with assurance at this time, many kinds of evidence bear upon the answers. The evidence in answer to the first of these two questions is consistent, coming as it does from many studies that show the *sequences* of stages to be similar to those that Piaget describes (conservation of mass, weight, and volume, in that order). Answers to the second question come from the effort to train children in the concepts of a later stage of development when they have not quite reached that stage according to tests.

Some experiments by Smedslund (1961) are instructive in this respect. In the first place, he was able to show that children who had not yet attained the principle of conservation of mass were able to acquire it through training, especially if taught in the presence of conflict. For example, when the plastic clay was rolled into an elongated shape (to make it appear longer), some of it was at the same time removed (to make it appear smaller). This made the child reflect on what was happening, and he was thus able to learn the principle of conservation. Of interest from the viewpoint of the developmental significance of stages of learning, children who had acquired a conservation concept naturally, rather than by training, held on to it against challenging experimental conditions, in which, for example, the experimenter removed a bit of clay without their seeing it. When they said that the two pieces should weigh alike (by balancing on a scale) and he proved they no longer weighed alike (by demonstrating this on the scale), those who had come by the conservation of weight naturally said that some must have fallen on the floor, while those who had been trained experimentally went back to their nonconservation explanations.

Taken together, these experiments bring conservation into line with other experiments on maturation, showing that special training is effective temporarily, but the child tends to revert to the developmental level that has been gradually acquired over time. Thus Piaget's theory may be interpreted as coherent with a maturational viewpoint. Before a child can progress from one stage to another, not only must appropriate learning take place, but certain processes related to internal (maturational) changes must also occur. Piaget's work gives support to the notion that restructuring goes on at certain periods in development, interrupting a mere steady accumulation of changes; this is the essence of a stage theory.

Psychosexual and psychosocial stages

Another type of stage theory was proposed by Sigmund Freud. In some respects it is a more comprehensive theory than Piaget's because it is concerned with the whole personality in its emotional and motivational aspects; it is like Piaget's, however, in assuming clearly definable stages.

Freud considered the childhood stages as having to do with deriving pleasure from different zones of the body at different ages, leading up to the gratifications of adult sexuality. By using a very broad definition of sexuality, these stages became known as *psychosexual* stages. The chief ones are *oral* (gratification through stimulation of the lips and mouth region, as in nursing or thumbsucking), *anal* (gratification through withholding and expelling feces), *phallic* (gratification through fondling the sex organs), *Oedipal* (a sexual desire for the parent of the opposite sex that is said to be concurrent with the phallic phase), *latent* (in which sexual interests are no longer active, so that the child of elementary-school age turns his interests to the environment), and, finally, *genital* (at which point normal heterosexual interests arise). Each of the earlier stages is normally outgrown, but in the event of arrested development ("fixation"), some of the problems associated with an earlier stage persist beyond their normal time; in this respect the theory is also a critical period theory. This classification of stages, while it has been influential, is not generally accepted by psychologists as a precise statement of development, whatever partial truths there may be within it.

A later psychoanalyst, Erikson (1963), has proposed another way of looking at stages of development. He describes a progression of *psychosocial* stages in which the child faces a wider range of human relationships as he grows up and has specific problems to solve at each of these stages. Again, as with Freud's theory, how well the child solves his problems at any one stage may determine how adequate a person he will become later and how well he will be able to cope with new problems as they arise.

Erikson's psychosocial stages of development are listed in Table 3-2. There is enough plausibility to the issues raised within Erikson's stages to make his scheme a useful one in calling attention to problems of social development. It lacks, however, the rigor of a strictly scientific delineation of stages, and its appeal must be thought of as speculative until more precise evidence in support of it is forthcoming.

The evidence on stages of development and on critical periods in human development is far from

TABLE 3-2   EIGHT STAGES OF PSYCHOSOCIAL DEVELOPMENT

STAGES (AGES ARE APPROXIMATE)	PSYCHOSOCIAL CRISES	RADIUS OF SIGNIFICANT RELATIONS	PSYCHOSOCIAL MODALITIES	FAVORABLE OUTCOME
I. Birth through first year	Trust vs. mistrust	Maternal person	To get To give in return	Drive and hope
II. Second year	Autonomy vs. shame, doubt	Parental persons	To hold (on) To let (go)	Self-control and willpower
III. Third year through fifth year	Initiative vs. guilt	Basic family	To make (going after) To "make like" (playing)	Direction and purpose
IV. Sixth to onset of puberty	Industry vs. inferiority	Neighborhood; school	To make things (competing) To make things together	Method and competence
V. Adolescence	Identity and repudiation vs. identity diffusion	Peer groups and outgroups; models of leadership	To be oneself (or not to be) To share being oneself	Devotion and fidelity
VI. Early adulthood	Intimacy and solidarity vs. isolation	Partners in friendship, sex, competition, cooperation	To lose and find oneself in another	Affiliation and love
VII. Young and middle adulthood	Generativity vs. self-absorption	Divided labor and shared household	To make be To take care of	Production and care
VIII. Later adulthood	Integrity vs. despair	"Mankind" "My Kind"	To be, through having been To face not being	Renunciation and wisdom

Source: Erikson (1963); slightly modified from original.

conclusive. Overlapping of one "stage" with another seems to be more common than a sharp transition, and usually a deficiency from an earlier period can be corrected later. Thus, while it is doubtless advantageous to learn to read early in life, people do learn to read as adults, some going on to careers as writers and scholars. The evidence favoring critical periods and stages is interesting, however, and the issues involved are important enough to deserve investigation.

Personality development in early childhood

We now turn from more general issues of development to some specific ones concerned with child-care practices, particularly as they affect personality and social behavior. Different peoples use different child-care practices, and even within one country the many social groups may raise their children in different ways. We wish to discover how these practices mold the child's personality and prepare him for life in society.

Early socialization

Cultural influences begin at birth; from the very first day of life we begin to civilize the child. Among the important early social influences are those concerned with feeding and with toilet training.

Psychological accompaniments of feeding. One has only to observe the angry cries and wild thrashing of an infant waiting for his bottle to realize how painful the sensation of hunger must be for him. How the feeding situation is handled will determine to a great extent the infant's attitudes toward the world around him. If his hunger is satisfied without undue delay and frustration, he learns that those who care for him are trustworthy and that his own actions (crying) can have some effect in alleviating his discomfort. If, on the other hand, his cries of hunger do not bring relief, he may resort to other forms of behavior, such as head-banging or rocking, to provide distracting stimulation. He may eventually become apathetic in all his responses when he learns that there is nothing he can do to solve his problem. The infant's first social contact occurs while he is being fed. If the experience is a pleasant one, he learns to associate his mother with satisfaction and relaxation. If not, then the mother becomes associated with continued tension and frustration.

Whether the infant is breast or bottle fed appears to make little difference as long as the feeding situation provides a warm, close contact between mother and child. If the bottle-fed baby is held closely and provided with the sight of his mother's face and her voice talking or singing to him (as opposed to feeding from a bottle propped up in the crib), then he appears to thrive as well as the baby who is breast fed. The nature of the mother-child interaction seems to be the crucial factor. Regardless of the method of feeding, the mother who is tense or uncomfortable in the situation can transmit these feelings to her baby. In one study it was shown that the degree of tension in the baby during feeding (as measured by heart rate and muscle tension) closely correlated with the same measures on the mother; when the mother was at ease and relaxed so was the baby. This was true for both bottle- and breast-fed babies (Kulka, 1968).

Toilet training. Toilet training may often constitute the child's first experience with discipline. He has to learn appropriate responses to two compelling biological drives and to perform these responses only in the right places. To the child, society's restrictions concerning the time and place of eliminatory functions may seem quite meaningless, and he conforms only to please his parents.

Maturational readiness plays an important role in toilet training. Before the training can proceed without difficulty, the youngster must be mature enough to control his sphincter muscles and to communicate his need. Most child experts recommend delaying toilet training until eighteen to twenty months. Efforts to train too early are usually unsuccessful and may make the child dimly aware that he is not living up to his parents' expectations; the parent, too, may experience a sense of disappointment and failure that may be communicated to the child. The textbook used to train nurses for the state-run nursery schools in the Soviet Union gives detailed procedures for training the child beginning at three or four months. But reports indicate that Russian children on the average are not fully trained until about eighteen months (Chandler, Lourie, and Peters, 1968). The use of early methods apparently "trains" the nurse, in the sense that she becomes alert to the child's signs and may manage to catch his elimination products in a potty. Actual control, however, does not occur until the child is maturationally ready. From the standpoint of efficiency early attempts at toilet training seem unwarranted.

The processes of infant care and child rearing are incompletely described by feeding schedules, disciplinary practices, and the like, because much depends on the nature of the interaction between the helpless and sensitive infant and the available adult caretakers. Attitudes of acceptance and warmth (or of rejection and coldness) may be communicated no matter what specific training methods are used. Hence we turn now to consider the development of social attachments, intimately related to methods of handling the child.

Development of social attachments

A careful study of normal infants investigated the development of attachment to the mother, attachments to other persons, and fear of strangers (Schaffer and Emerson, 1964). While there were some individual differences, specific attachments to the mother and to other persons began at about seven months, and fear of strangers developed a little later, with usually about a month between the showing of attachment and the onset of fear (Figure 3-6).

Other lines of evidence also show that differentiation between those who are strange and those who are familiar begins during the second half of the first year. For example, the infant tends to smile at a strange face between the ages of two and six months, but thereafter, as detection of strangers begins, the smiling tends to be confined to those who are familiar. A three-stage theory has been proposed for the development of attachments

(Schaffer and Emerson, 1964). In the first stage the infant seeks stimulation of any kind from the environment, whether or not it is social. In the second stage he begins to find people the most interesting and satisfying agents in the environment and seeks closeness to them, without expressing much preference among them. Finally, he narrows his interests to selected people; at this stage his reactions are truly social.

It was formerly thought that the beginning of social attachment came about because the mother, as a source of food, met the infant's needs, reduced tensions, and hence was satisfying. It is now felt, however, that attachment may have relatively little to do with the mother as a source of food; the study mentioned above indicated that attachments to the mother were commonly accompanied by attachments to others, usually, but not exclusively, the father. Observations of animals also confirm this interpretation. Some species of animals, such as young ducklings, feed themselves from birth, yet they follow their mothers around closely and spend a great deal of time in contact with their mothers; the comfort they derive from the mother cannot come from the mother's role in feeding.

More dramatic are some experiments with young

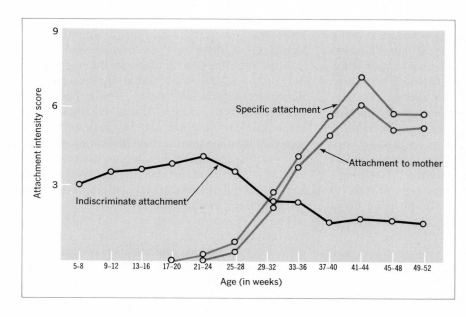

Fig. **3-6 The development of attachments during the first year of life** Attachment was measured by the amount of protest made by the infant when separated from the person to whom he was then close. Attachments are indiscriminate during the first six months or so, then become specific to recognized persons, with a peak at seven months. As specific attachments develop, indiscriminate ones weaken. (After Schaffer and Emerson, 1964)

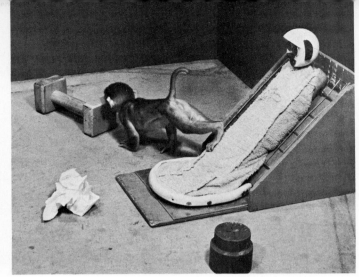

Fig. **3-7** **A monkey's response to an artificial mother** Left: Although fed via the wire "mother," the infant spends more time with the terry-cloth mother. Right: The inert "mother" is a safe base from which to explore the world.

monkeys reared in isolation from their true mothers but permitted to feed from and cling to artificial mothers (Harlow and Harlow, 1966; Harlow and Suomi, 1970). Two "laboratory mothers" were provided with arrangements permitting the young monkeys to obtain milk by sucking. Both "mothers" were immobile and, although they had torsos, heads, and faces, they did not much resemble monkey mothers (see Figure 3-7). One of the laboratory mothers was constructed of wire. The other, covered with soft terry cloth, was more "cuddly" than the wire model.

The experiment sought to determine whether the "mother" that was always the source of food would be the one to which the young monkey would cling. The results were dramatic: no matter which mother was the source of food, the infant monkey spent its time clinging to the terry-cloth "cuddly" mother. This purely passive but soft-contact mother served as a source of security for the monkey. For example, when the infant monkey was placed in a strange environment in which it showed great signs of fear, the fear was allayed if the infant could make contact with the cloth mother. While holding on to it with one hand or foot, the monkey was willing to explore objects that were otherwise too terrifying to approach.

Although contact with an artificial mother provides an important aspect of "mothering," it is not sufficient to produce satisfactory development. Inadequate experience with other monkeys (particularly other young monkeys) during the first six months of life produces various types of bizarre behavior in adult life. Monkeys raised in this sort of early isolation rarely engage in positive interactions with other monkeys later on and are very difficult to mate. When females without early social contact are successfully mated after considerable effort, they make poor mothers, tending to neglect or abuse their infants. The effects of isolation during the first six months of life on social behavior in adulthood are so striking that these early months would seem to constitute a critical period for the development of social attachments. Regardless of the amount of exposure to other monkeys that occurs during the intervening years, these early-isolates never develop normal social behavior (Sackett, 1967).

Effects of parent-child separation

Once a monkey has established a relationship with a real mother, the effects of separation are impressive. In one study infant monkeys were separated from their mothers for a period of four weeks when they were five months old. During the first day or so of separation the infants were very agitated; they slept hardly at all, paced back and forth, sucked their fingers, and handled their genitals and other parts of the body. By the third day there was another striking change in behavior. Each infant monkey sat hunched over, almost in a ball, rarely moving. The few responses made were very slow; little response was made to other infant monkeys, and there was no play activity at all. This state of depression lasted for almost a week, after which there was some return to normal behavior. When the mothers returned, the infants spent much time clinging to them whereas normal monkeys by the age of five months are becoming more independent (Kaufman and Rosenblum, 1967). With repeated separations from the mother, there was no indication that the infant monkeys learned to adjust to the situation. On the contrary, each successive separation produced more disturbed behavior. Even a year after the final separation, which occurred when the monkeys were eight months old, these monkeys were noticeably more fearful in their reactions than normal monkeys (Mitchell and others, 1967).

A striking parallel has been observed in the behavior of human children who for various reasons were separated from their parents and placed in hospitals or residential nurseries before the age of two. Like that of the infant monkey, the human child's initial response of agitation, crying, and other signs of distress soon gave way to withdrawn and apathetic behavior. For some children this depression was accompanied by retardation in physical development, loss of weight, and physical illness. Children for whom the separation was prolonged eventually appeared to make a superficial adjustment but tended to be indifferent to people, showing no real affection or interest in anyone (Bowlby, 1960).

If the separation is not too long, and if the child receives adequate substitute mothering, the effects may not be permanent. Maas (1963) studied twenty adults who, as children, had been separated from their parents and sent to small residential nurseries in the country to escape the bombing of London during the Second World War. He found that most

In some countries, such as Russia and Israel, mothers are encouraged to work while their children are cared for in state-run institutions. On the collective farms, or *Kibbutzim*, of Israel, for example, the children are cared for from earliest infancy by professional caretakers in houses separate from those of the parents. Practices differ somewhat from one Kibbutz to another, but the following arrangement is typical.

During the first year of life the mother provides the major portion of the feeding and care of her infant, although the infant is still housed in the communal nursery. After the first year the mother works full time and sees her child mainly during the evening and on Saturdays. This combination of institutional and maternal care, sometimes called *intermittent mothering*, has been closely studied to determine if these children differ from those raised in single-family homes. Because earlier studies had shown that children raised in orphanages were markedly retarded in development, those responsible for setting up communal child-care centers were especially concerned with providing a warm relationship with a mother-substitute as well as sufficient intellectual stimulation to prevent retardation. They realized that adequate physical care was not enough to produce a healthy child. Consequently, the caretakers received special training in all areas of child development.

Reports from those who have observed life among Kibbutz children indicate that the approach to such areas as toilet training and self-care is warm and permissive, and independence is encouraged. They note that Kibbutz-raised children seem to develop early a feeling of group concern and identification, supporting their group against others and excluding others from play. The fact that discipline and training are handled primarily

of them were getting along satisfactorily in their adult roles, although those separated from home when under one year of age seemed to show somewhat more personality disturbance.

Language and socialization

The socialization of the child is greatly facilitated by his comprehension of language. Through the use of words he learns to control other people, he learns taboos and social distinctions, and he acquires a tool that permits him to think and reflect. Learning to talk reveals another aspect of development that can be understood only in the light of the interplay of biological potentialities and the molding effect of culture. Biological development (maturation) accounts for the ability to talk; the culture (the language heard) accounts for what the child actually says. All children regardless of race or nationality emit the same speech sounds initially. The babbling of a Chinese infant cannot be distinguished from the babbling of a Russian or English infant (Atkinson, MacWhinney, and Stoel, 1970). But as the child develops, his vocalizations become increasingly like those of the adults in his environment. A discussion of how language is acquired is taken up in Chapter 11; at this point only a few comments will be made about the development of speech and the factors that influence its development.

The average child says his first word (usually a noun) by the time he is a year old, although he is able to comprehend words long before he can utter them. By age two he has a fair-sized vocabulary of nouns, adjectives, and verbs, but the period of greatest vocabulary increase is between the ages of two and four, during which time pronouns and connectives are added. By the time he is six the average child has acquired a vocabulary of some seven to eight thousand words and has mastered most of the grammatical constructions of his native language.

Some variables that influence speech development are sex (girls tend to speak earlier and more skillfully than boys), number of siblings (single children acquire language earlier than those with siblings close in age), and social class (children of middle-class parents develop language ability ear-

by the caretaker, so that the child's daily visits with his parents involve mostly pleasurable activities, is assumed to do much to reduce parent-child conflicts (Rabkin and Rabkin, 1969).

Actual studies of Kibbutz children have yielded conflicting results. One study indicated that the Kibbutz children are somewhat retarded in mental development when compared to children growing up in noncollective rural settlements (Rabin, 1965). A more recent study found that the Kibbutz children were equal in motor and mental development to Israeli children raised in private homes, and both groups were superior to Israeli children reared in institutions. Abilities such as walking and eye-hand coordination (which are presumably more dependent upon maturation) showed little difference among the three groups. Language ability and fine motor coordination, on the other hand, were superior in the Kibbutz and private-home children as compared to the institutionalized children (Kohen-Raz, 1968). When Kibbutz-raised seventeen and eighteen year olds were questioned about their feelings concerning Kibbutz life, the majority of them expressed satisfaction with communal living. The girls, however, regretted the fact that they had not spent more time with their parents as children and expressed a desire to care for their own children more than their parents had cared for them (Rabin, 1968a).

One potential advantage of the Kibbutz is that it is possible to keep records of the various training methods used, so as to determine which are most effective in the long run. To the extent that this can be accomplished, it should be possible to identify more accurately the important factors in an effective child-rearing program.

lier than those of working-class parents). The delayed language development of working-class children has been attributed to the fact that middle-class mothers spend more time talking to their children than do working-class mothers, thus providing more stimulation for the child's vocalizations. Another possibility is that the vocalizations heard by the working-class child are less distinctive than those provided to the middle-class child. Kagan (1968) found little difference between middle- and working-class homes in the amount of time the mother vocalized to her infant, but a significant difference in the distinctiveness of the vocalizations. For example, the middle-class infant is apt to be lying in his crib in a quiet room when the mother enters and speaks to him, thus providing a distinctive dialogue. The working-class infant, on the other hand, may be lying on the sofa in a one-room apartment surrounded by talkative siblings, with the noise of television in the background. In this situation whatever the mother says to the infant is apt to be lost in a background of other sounds and is not likely to elicit the infant's attention. In addition, many of the infant's vocalizations are not likely to be noticed by anyone nor are they likely to elicit a response. The fact that infants cared for in institutions are retarded in language development as compared with children raised in a single family may be attributed to some of the same factors.

Disciplinary practices and later behavior

In order to raise a child who obeys the demands of the society in which he grows up and who internalizes these values so that he becomes a self-controlling person, parents find it necessary to exert control in the form of discipline, approving some kinds of behavior, disapproving others. Discipline may take various forms, and it is not simply a matter of choosing between rewards and punishments. Again, such matters as parental affection and warmth in the training process may be as important as the particular kinds of discipline used.

One classification of discipline techniques groups together the *love-oriented techniques* (praise as reward, withdrawal of love as punishment) and the

TABLE 3-3 CHILDREN'S FEEDING PROBLEMS AND THE TRAINING PRACTICES OF THEIR PARENTS	
TRAINING PRACTICES OF PARENTS	PERCENTAGE OF CHILDREN HAVING FEEDING PROBLEMS
Extent of use of physical punishment:	
Rarely or never used	17%
Occasionally to fairly often	20
Regularly used	36
Mother's affectional warmth toward child:	
Exceptionally warm	11%
Warm and quite warm	19
Matter-of-fact	22
Cold, some hostility	35

Source: Sears, Maccoby, and Levin (1957).

object-oriented techniques (tangible rewards, deprivation of privileges, physical punishment) (Sears, Maccoby, and Levin, 1957). Which of these is favored in child training makes a difference in the kind of child that results.

If we think first of effectiveness in producing socially conforming behavior, such as good eating habits, we find that those mothers who report the regular use of physical punishment have more feeding problems with their young children than those who use punishment rarely or occasionally; in turn, those mothers who show affectionate warmth toward their children have fewer feeding problems than those who tend to be cold and hostile. Some findings are shown in Table 3-3.

If, instead of looking at the behavior itself, we consider self-control or a developed conscience in the child, we also find a relationship to the kind of training the parents have given. The children rated highest on conscience were those whose mothers were not only relatively warm but used withdrawal of love as a means of control (Table 3-4).

Other studies have shown that parents who discipline by means of physical punishment tend to raise children who are low in self-esteem (Coopersmith, 1967), aggressive (Eron and others, 1963), and unfriendly (Becker and others, 1962). The relationship to aggression is interesting; boys whose parents physically punish aggressive responses tend to inhibit aggression in the home but show increased aggression in other situations, such as in school. In essence, by using physical punishment as a discipline technique the parents are providing an aggressive model for their children to imitate (Bandura and Walters, 1963).

It is evident that home training is an important factor in the socialization of the child. The subtleties are such that it is difficult to give cookbook recommendations as to how parents should treat children, but some of the preferred directions are sufficiently apparent from the results of research. Whatever the method is, it should be used with consistency and firmness. Punitive methods, especially if used erratically, appear to be notably unsuccessful, whereas love-oriented techniques, including affectional warmth but also withdrawal

TABLE 3-4 CONSCIENCE OF CHILD AS RELATED TO MOTHER'S WARMTH	
PRACTICES OF MOTHER	PERCENTAGE OF CHILDREN RATED HIGH ON CONSCIENCE
Mother relatively warm and uses withdrawal of love fairly often	42%
Mother relatively warm and uses little or no withdrawal of love	24
Mother relatively cold and uses little or no withdrawal of love	25
Mother relatively cold and uses withdrawal of love fairly often	18

Source: Sears, Maccoby, and Levin (1957).

of love to enforce conformity, appear to be successful in producing not only desirable behavior but the kind of conscience that internalizes control.

The process of identification

The child has to establish his place in the society of people about him and eventually must take his place as a man or a woman. Very important to him in finding his place are the members of his own family: mother, father, brothers, and sisters.

Because parents are the dominant figures and the primary sources of both satisfactions and prohibitions, the child's attitudes toward them are mixtures of wishes to please and wishes to protest. In our culture a period characterized by defiant or *negativistic* behavior often takes place between the ages of two and three. It may be that with his new-found freedom of locomotion and with the increase of manipulative skills, the child asserts his individuality and tests his powers by his refusals to respond to parental requests. His favorite word becomes "No!" The negativistic stage is not an inevitable one; it is not found in all children. It is common, however, and parents and teachers should be prepared for it.

Although a kind of tug of war between children and parents goes on, the children exhibiting occasional negativism and defiance, the long-run influence of parents is that of models, or *identification figures,* for the children to copy. The process of identification is an important one in the development of personality.

Sex-role identification

Each culture sets certain approved ways in which men and women are expected to behave; these may be called the *sex-role standards* for that culture. The role that the boy will eventually play in society is that of a man, and the man he knows best is his father. Similarly, the girl learns the woman's role from her mother. Both mother and father, through their attitudes toward themselves and one another, help the child of either sex to acquire an appropriate role.

The play activities of boys and girls gradually diverge, especially after the age of five years. By that age they are aware that their roles in society differ, and they begin to try out in play the roles

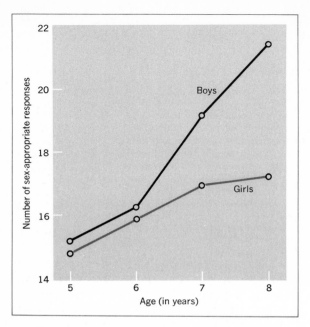

Fig. **3-8 Sex-typing in young children** When a choice is given between two toys (one masculine and the other feminine), the number of sex-appropriate responses increases with age for both boys and girls. Note that boys consistently make more of these responses than do girls, although the difference is very small at ages five and six. (Data from DeLucia, 1963)

With increasing age both girls and boys make increasingly more sex-appropriate choices (see Figure 3-8), but boys consistently make more of them than do girls (DeLucia, 1963).

The taboos against effeminate behavior for boys, although somewhat less stringent now than in the past, are still fairly strong in our culture. Learning how to be masculine seems to be more a matter of avoiding any behavior regarded as "sissyish" rather than being positively taught masculine behavior. When kindergarten boys were individually permitted to play with a group of attractive feminine toys and unattractive neutral toys, most of them avoided the feminine toys, spending their time with the unattractive and dilapidated neutral toys. The presence of an adult increased avoidance of the feminine toys, while observation of another boy playing with the feminine toys reduced avoidance. Observing a girl play with the feminine toys brought no change in behavior (Kobasigawa, Arakaki, and Awiguni, 1966).

Although research findings indicate similar trends for girls, avoidance seems much less important in their sex-role behavior. In our society it is becoming increasingly acceptable for girls to wear pants and to participate in games and activities that have been traditionally considered masculine.

The development of identification would seem to be straightforward enough. The child knows his or her sex and imitates the like-sexed parent. This sex-appropriate behavior is rewarded and sex-inappropriate behavior is punished. The only problems would seem to occur when there has been some interference with this process, because the appropriate parent is either inadequate or missing through divorce or death. When, however, careful studies investigate the development of identification, the situation does not turn out to be as simple as this account would suggest.

It is usually supposed that the parent the child models himself after is the one who is nurturant, that is, responsive to the needs of the child. Because this is commonly the mother early in life, the girl can continue this modeling of her, but the boy must shift to his father later on. Evidence does show that boys tend to imitate and identify more

that they will assume someday in fact. The individual gradually comes to see himself as appropriately masculine or feminine; this self-perception is called his *sex-role identity*. For the young child it is based on his perception of himself as similar to the like-sexed parent and as capable of adopting the games and activities encouraged for his sex.

One method for measuring sex-typed behavior in young children involves having the child choose between pictures of various toys and play activities. Toys such as a doll carriage and dishes are classified as feminine, while a dump truck and tools are classified as masculine. Examples of neutral toys (appropriate to either sex) are a wading pool and roller skates. Studies using this method indicate that even as early as three years boys begin to prefer sex-appropriate toys. Many girls show an early preference for masculine toys and games; in kindergarten more girls show a preference for masculine toys than boys do for feminine toys.

with fathers who are nurturant and that boys who score high on a test of masculinity tend to have a warmer and more affectionate relationship with their fathers than boys who score low (Mussen and Distler, 1960).

Which parent is the more dominant and more powerful in controlling rewards and punishments can also have an effect. The more interaction a boy has with a powerful and nurturant father, the greater will be his assimilation of the masculine role. In families where the mother is dominant, problems may occur in the development of an appropriate masculine sex-role in boys. For girls, however, parental dominance has little relation to their sex-role preferences or to their similarity to their mothers; the mother's warmth and self-confidence seem to be more important factors (Hetherington and Frankie, 1967). To the extent that both parents are seen as nurturant, powerful, and competent, the child will identify to some extent with both, although the strongest identification will be with the parent of the same sex.

In summary, the circumstances producing identification include: (1) perceiving the like-sexed model as supportive; (2) perceiving the model as exercising power (in the case of boys), commanding love, and being competent in valued areas; and (3) finding some objective basis, such as appearance, for being similar to the model. An inadequate parent can fail as a model according to (1) or (2), in which case (3) will produce a poor self-identity.

Personal (non-sex-role) identification

Many personal qualities are not strongly sex-typed, such as enthusiasm, sense of humor, personal warmth; and many moral qualities, such as integrity and considerateness, are shared by both men and women. The child may thus learn and imitate qualities of *either* parent in these areas without violating the adoption of an appropriate sex standard of behavior. That is, there are many areas of life in which a male and a female can act similarly without going against any cultural taboos.

Personality, temperament, and attitudes toward work and play can come from either parent, even for the fully masculine boy or the fully feminine girl. A mother's standards of housekeeping may be reflected in the son's work, even though he models after his father and enters his profession; a daughter, gracefully accepting the woman's role in imitation of her mother, may still tell a story the way her father does. Not much is known in detail about these subordinate aspects of identification because of the unresolved puzzles in respect to sex-typing. Yet it takes little reflection or observation of one's friends to see the importance

TABLE 3-5   NON-SEX-ROLE IDENTIFICATIONS OF UNIVERSITY STUDENTS WITH THEIR PARENTS

REPORTED SIMILARITY	MALE STUDENTS (N = 115)		FEMALE STUDENTS (N = 72)	
	TEMPERA-MENT	RECREATIONAL INTERESTS	TEMPERA-MENT	RECREATIONAL INTERESTS
To father only	47%	44%	29%	31%
To both parents	19	11	33	25
To mother only	30	25	35	33
To neither parent	3	18	3	10
Not ascertained	1	2	—	1
Total	100%	100%	100%	100%

Source: J. R. Hilgard (1970).

University students give many indications of resemblance to the parent of the opposite sex in temperament and recreational interests, in which sex-typing is of little importance.

of both parents in determining how a boy or girl will develop.

University students who were interviewed about their behavioral similarities to their parents in temperament and in recreational interests frequently reported similarity to the parent of the opposite sex. A fourth or more of the boys thought that they resembled their mothers in these respects, and a similar proportion of the girls thought they resembled their fathers; many reported resemblances to both parents (Table 3-5). That identifications are present is evident from the relatively few who felt they resembled neither parent. It is clear that considering identification only in terms of sex roles is an incomplete way of viewing the influences of parents upon children.

Identification with siblings and peers. Although the parents are the primary identification figures, siblings and peers are also important influences in the development of an identity. A child comes to conceive of himself as someone distinctive and valuable (or, on the contrary, someone inadequate) through his relations with brothers and sisters and age mates outside the home. It will be recalled that in his discussion of psychosocial development (Table 3-2) Erikson noted the gradually enlarging radius of significant relations, from the parents to the immediate family, to the neighborhood, and beyond.

Birth order affects the ease with which a child finds a place for himself. One study of children in large families identified three personality roles that showed a relation to birth order; these were the responsible child (often the first born), the sociable, well-liked child (often second), and the spoiled child (often the youngest) (Bossard and Ball, 1955).

First-born or only children differ significantly from other children; several factors tend to make their position in the family unique. Parents have more time and attention to devote to a single child; they may be more protective and cautious in caring for him; the single child has only adult models to copy and adult standards of conduct and achievement to emulate, while later-born children have siblings with which to identify; the single child

does not have to fight for his rights or compete with older siblings. Research findings indicate that these factors do have an effect. For example, first-born or only children tend on the average to score higher on intelligence and ability tests, to be more likely to attend college, and more likely to achieve eminence. Among finalists for the National Merit Scholarship from two-child families, there are twice as many first-born as second-born. Among finalists from three-child families there are as many first-born as second- and third-born combined (Nichols, 1968). First-born or only children have also been found to be more conscientious, less aggressive, and higher in self-esteem than later-born children (Altus, 1966). As can be seen in Figure 3-9, they are less likely to engage in dangerous sports.

In addition to order of birth, the sex of the other siblings relates to the child's interests and behavior; girls with older brothers are likely to be more masculine (tomboyish) than girls with older sisters. Similarly, boys with older sisters are less aggressive than boys with older brothers. The growing child learns from the siblings as well as the parents.

In trying to retain his share of attention from parents, a child often shows jealousy of brothers

Fig. **3-9 Birth order and participation in dangerous sports** The graph shows the proportion of male undergraduates who play dangerous sports (football, rugby, soccer) in relation to their birth order. Note that the first-born is less likely to engage in a dangerous sport than later-borns. The same study found no relationship between birth order and participation in nondangerous team sports such as baseball or crew. (Data from Nisbett, 1968)

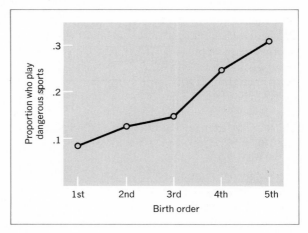

and sisters, especially at the time of the birth of a sibling. The phrase *sibling rivalry* has been used to describe this condition and its resulting behavior. Apparently when the age difference is two to four years, the birth of a sibling is most threatening to the older child. Before two years his perception of himself is still diffuse enough that the appearance of a rival does not disturb him; when he is older than four he is already somewhat independent and hence less threatened. Parents may minimize rivalry by preparing the older child for the birth of the baby and by taking care that the new baby does not completely absorb their affection. But some signs of sibling rivalry are almost inevitable in our competitive culture.

Racial identification. The process of self-identification may be disrupted by the child's discovery of racial or ethnic differences, particularly for children who are members of a minority group. Awareness of racial differences is evidenced by children as young as three years of age. White nursery school boys in a doll-play situation tend to attribute more undesirable characteristics (stupid, bad, mean) to dark-skinned dolls, and this trend increases between the ages two to five (Ammons, 1960). This hostility may be less an expression of prejudice acquired from parents than a disturbed reaction by some children who are in the process of forming their own identity to individuals who differ physically from themselves.

Many black children seem to accept the prevailing Negro stereotypes and to depreciate their own race. Figure 3-10 shows the responses of some 250 black children between the ages of three and seven when presented with dolls that were identical except for skin color and given a series of instructions including "Give me the colored doll," "Give me the doll that looks like you," and "Give me the doll you like best." The majority of black children at each age level indicated a preference for the white doll and a rejection of the brown doll. Even though many of the three year olds could correctly identify the colored and white dolls, only a third selected the brown doll as looking like themselves (Clark and Clark, 1947). Some of the lighter-skinned children may have had

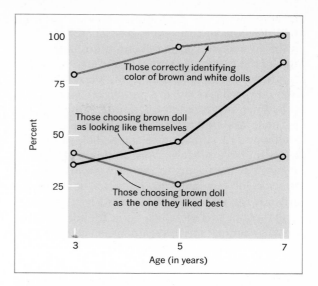

Fig. 3-10 Doll preference among black children Black children were presented dolls that were identical except for skin color and asked a series of questions. Even though they could correctly identify the colors, the majority at each age level indicated a preference for white dolls. (Data, by permission, from Clark and Clark, 1947)

difficulty deciding which doll was appropriate, but the difference between the two percentages also seems to reflect the black child's unwillingness to identify himself with a darker skin color. Several investigators have noted the emotionality with which some black children respond to questions about racial identification. By age seven most of the children correctly identified themselves, suggesting that they had ceased trying to escape a realistic self-identification. But even at this age the majority of the children selected the white doll as the one they liked best.

That the black child's rejection of his own race relates to the degree of discrimination in the community is indicated by a study comparing racial attitudes of black and white preschoolers in the North and the South. The children were shown pictures of black and white youngsters and asked which they would like to be and which they would prefer as playmates. Of the four groups studied—two in the North and two in the South—the southern black children made the fewest choices of pictures of children of their own race (Morland, 1966).

Concern for the black child's lack of positive identification with his race has led to programs designed to create pride in himself through awareness of the black man's history and heritage. Such programs, based on the concept "black is beautiful," may well give rise to a pattern of identification quite different from those found in earlier studies.

There are indications that the critical social problem of racial prejudice can be helped by integrated nursery schools. Work in this area has just begun, but the results so far seem promising. The directors of one such project noted that friction between the two races disappeared by the middle of the school year, at which point friendships were based on mutual interests rather than color; by this time there was no difference in the amount of time the children spent interacting with members of their own race as opposed to that spent with the other (Stevenson, 1967).

Moral development

An important aspect of identification with parents involves the child's taking over their standards of conduct, so that he learns how to react to other people according to accepted standards of what is good and proper and to resist the temptation to transgress the rules of acceptable behavior. Many studies have been directed to the investigation of the moral development of children. Because of conceptual difficulties, however, widespread agreement has not yet been reached and some uncertainties persist. Piaget, whose scheme for intellectual development was presented earlier (p. 63), has proposed some stages in moral development; these stages have provided the background for later work. For example, Kohlberg (1963) distinguished six stages of moral reasoning, classified them into three levels, and studied their development between ages seven and sixteen. The stages are given in Table 3-6, with illustrative behavior at each stage. These illustrations have to do with motivation for moral action; other dimensions of morality could have been listed, as, for example, the basis for respecting human life or the basis for respecting social morality.

Kohlberg claims that conduct earlier in life is controlled according to the principles of the earlier stages, later according to the more mature principles. In Figure 3-11 the statements made by children when commenting on various acts of morality have been combined to reflect the three levels of Table 3-6. We see that at the age of seven nearly all statements are at Level I; by age thirteen more than half the statements are at Level II; at age sixteen the Level II statements continue at a high level, but more Level III statements appear, and those from Level I continue to drop off.

TABLE 3-6 STAGES IN THE DEVELOPMENT OF MORAL CHARACTER	
STAGE	ILLUSTRATIVE BEHAVIOR
Level I. Premoral	
Stage 1. Punishment and obedience orientation	Obeys rules in order to avoid punishment
Stage 2. Naive instrumental hedonism	Conforms to obtain rewards, to have favors returned
Level II. Morality of conventional role-conformity	
Stage 3. "Good-boy" morality of maintaining good relations, approval of others	Conforms to avoid disapproval, dislike by others
Stage 4. Authority maintaining morality	Conforms to avoid censure by legitimate authorities, with resultant guilt
Level III. Morality of self-accepted moral principles	
Stage 5. Morality of contract, of individual rights, and of democratically accepted law	Conforms to maintain the respect of the impartial spectator judging in terms of community welfare
Stage 6. Morality of individual principles of conscience	Conforms to avoid self-condemnation
Source: Kohlberg (1963).	

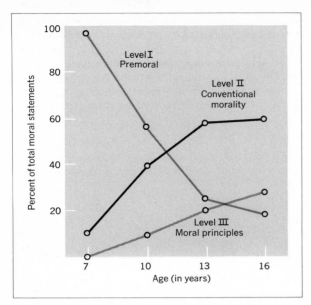

Fig. **3-11** **Moral development** Age changes in moral statements according to three levels of moral development. (Data from Kohlberg, 1963)

cepting the norms of the culture as he becomes old enough both to have the necessary experiences and to make the necessary discriminations, or (2) that the developmental process has large *maturational* components, so that the stages are more nearly spontaneous products of development, each stage arising from the one before. Kohlberg (1964) accepts the second of these interpretations because he believes that each stage depends upon the earlier one. When the statements of any one child are studied, it is found that if most of his moral statements come from one stage, the rest of the statements will usually come from the neighboring stages. When an effort is made to move the child ahead, it is found that he can more readily learn moral reasoning one level above his stage than two levels above it (Turiel, 1966).

Supporting the viewpoint that moral development is the result of social learning, Bandura and McDonald (1963) have shown that when children are exposed to adult models who express moral judgments counter to the children's orientation, the children modify their judgments in the direction of the models' and will maintain these altered judgments in new situations where adult models are absent.

The two chief interpretations of these data are (1) that the development of moral reasoning is a result of *social learning,* the child gradually ac-

To say that the "child is father of the man" is to imply that the adult personality will reflect the characteristics of the child. This conjecture is subject to direct study. We have already noted some results of early experience as bearing upon adult height (p. 60).

Some direct data comparing child and adult characteristics come from an investigation by Kagan and Moss (1962). During the years from 1929 to 1939, a number of children were studied at the Fels Research Institute, Yellow Springs, Ohio, and careful records were kept from birth through adolescence. Of these children, seventy-one were brought back for interviews and ratings as young adults, in the age range of twenty to thirty years.

Correlations were arrived at between ratings in the various age ranges—the years from birth to age 3, from 3 to 6, from 6 to 10, from 10 to 14, and early adulthood. While some continuities were found from the earliest years on, the most striking findings showed how predictive the ages six to ten were for the young adult years. Representative findings are summarized in Figure 3-12.

The various behaviors are arranged in the figure according to the heights of the correlations for males, although the correlations for females are shown also. Both males and females show relatively high correlations for intellectual achievement as demonstrated in the early school years and in early adult life, and for sex-typed activity. Spontaneity of behavior shows moderate correlations for both sexes. Apparently, the cultural pressures on boys and girls are similar in these respects. For the other items the sex differences

CRITICAL DISCUSSION

Durability of personality as continuous from childhood

are striking. It is fairly clear that the overt expression of anger is less controlled in boys than in girls, while girls are freer to continue their passive and dependent behavior from childhood.

The fact that there are a number of significant correlations between behavior in the early school years (ages six to ten) and in early adult life strengthens the conviction that early socializing experiences in school and among peers are important for further development. Kagan and Moss believe that the sex-role identification plays a major part in this development.

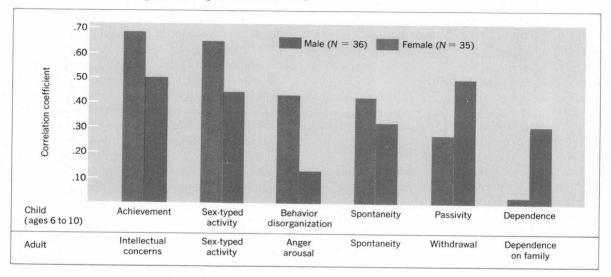

Fig. 3-12 **Correlation between child and adult behavior** Subjects were rated on various psychological dimensions during childhood and again in early adulthood. The bars indicate the correlation between the measures, and thus the degree to which adult behavior can be predicted from childhood ratings. (After Kagan and Moss, 1962)

Summary

1. The course of development in man, as in other organisms, is shaped by *maturation* and *learning*. Development through maturation proceeds at its own rate, relatively independent of the environment, although an essential minimum of environmental stimulation and support is needed. Some evidence suggests that there may be *critical periods* in development when the organism is most plastic and ready to acquire some of the behavior essential for optimal development later.

2. Conditions of severe deprivation or unusual stimulation can affect the rate at which development takes place. Animals deprived of stimulation at an early age are poorer learners as adults than normal animals; an enriched environment produces better learning ability as well as increased brain size. Studies with human infants, however, point to the fact that increased stimulation will not result in accelerated development unless the infant is maturationally ready.

3. An unsolved problem of development is whether it is essentially *continuous* or consists of a series of definable *stages*. Among the theories stressing stages, one of the better substantiated is that of Piaget. Piaget describes stages in cognitive, or intellectual, growth, moving from the sensorimotor period through the period of preoperational thought to the period of concrete operations and finally to the period of formal operations. The psychosexual stages of Freud and the psychosocial stages of Erikson are attempts to place the whole personality development in the context of a theory of stages. Critical periods and stages are still to some extent controversial.

4. Personality development of the child is influenced by early feeding and toilet training practices, which require that he conform to the demands of a culture. The accompaniments of feeding may be psychologically as important as nutrition; the need for appropriate body contact has been dramatically illustrated by experiments using monkeys with artificial mothers. They support the results of studies that indicate that human children separated at an early age from their mothers show signs of disturbance.

5. The gradual development of language provides a tool for social interaction. It serves purposes of status and power that go beyond mere communication. The delayed language development of working-class children may be due to the fact that the vocalizations heard by them are not distinctive.

6. Disciplinary practices are important not only in the control of specific behavior, but in the development of conscience and later social conduct. Emphasis on physical punishment has been shown to have undesirable consequences.

7. The process of identification is a crucial factor in personality development. Some distinctions can be made between *sex-role identification,* in which modeling after the like-sexed parent is central, and *personal (non-sex-role) identification,* in which temperament and other traits are learned from both parents and from siblings and peers. Other factors, such as birth order and racial group membership, also affect how the individual perceives himself.

Suggestions for further reading

Of the many textbooks on child development the following are representative: Mussen, Conger, and Kagan, *Child development and personality* (3rd ed., 1969); Stone and Church, *Childhood and adolescence* (2nd ed., 1968); Johnson and Medinnus, *Child psychology* (2nd ed., 1969). A useful short paperback is Mussen, *The psychological development of the child* (1963). For historical background see Kessen, *The child* (1965).

More advanced treatments may be found in Mussen (ed.), *Carmichael's manual of child psychology* (3rd ed., 1970); Goslin (ed.), *Handbook of socialization theory and research* (1969); Baldwin, *Theories of child development* (1967); Endler, Boulter, and Osser (eds.), *Contemporary issues in developmental psychology* (1968); Janis (ed.), *Personality: Dynamics, development, and assessment* (1969).

Research relevant to Piaget's theory is presented in Elkind and Flavell (eds.), *Studies in cognitive development: Essays in honor of Jean Piaget* (1969). Papers concerned with the effects of preschool education may be found in Hess and Bear (eds.), *Early education* (1968).

adolescence and adulthood 4

ALTHOUGH ADJUSTMENT TO CONTINUAL change is characteristic of human growth, adolescence constitutes the period of most striking and far-reaching change. It is during this time that one must make the transition from childhood to adult life. The success with which the individual copes with the demands and problems of adolescence will determine to a large extent the person he is as an adult.

The problems faced by the adolescent are many, and in different periods of history they have taken different forms. In the United States—and indeed in much of the world—the past few years have witnessed an adolescent revolt against the conventionalities of contemporary society, largely in those affluent societies where the very technological advances that have made life more comfortable somehow detract from its meaning for the individual. These influences, combined with international unrest, have led to various forms of protest —unconventional dress, rejection of traditional attitudes toward work and study, dropping out, the search for highly personal experiences through drugs or meditation, and occasionally violent confrontation with the "Establishment." Although the particular expression of adolescent protest is tied to events of the time, some universals lie beneath it. During childhood, the individual's values are largely those of his parents, but as he grows up he must decide who he is and what his values are. Exposed to a diversity of situations, people, and ideas, he may discover discrepancies between his earlier attitudes and their application to the world as it has changed since his parents' youth. He finds too that there is a discrepancy between what he has been taught is right and how people actually behave. He then must face the uncomfortable task of evaluating for himself.

The adolescent's problems are complicated by the fact that his status is ambiguous—he is treated as a child in some ways and as an adult in others. Adults are frequently reluctant to recognize his maturity. When he wants to use the family car or take a trip on his own they may tell him he is too young. When he regresses to childlike or irresponsible behavior they tell him to grow up. The transition from childhood to adulthood is difficult in societies such as ours, where the status of the adolescent is undefined. Many nonliterate societies signalize the importance of the transition to sexual maturity by initiation ceremonies through which the adolescent is inducted into adulthood. Anthropologists have described such ceremonies in societies all over the world, in places as remote from one another as Africa, Indonesia, Polynesia, and South America. Although these rites of initiation often force the adolescent to undergo ordeals of starvation, sleeplessness, and pain, once the initiation is over he is honored by new status and responsibilities. The more gradual transition to adult life in our society may have advantages, but it also produces in the adolescent a period of conflict and vacillation between dependence and independence. Such vestigial remains of ceremonial introduction into adult life as are seen in the confirmation ceremonies of some religious groups, the "coming out" parties of debutantes, and the fraternity initiation form no sharp break with the past, nor do they confer the status of full adulthood.

The adolescent period is only a phase in the course of growth, and it is a mistake to emphasize too sharply its discontinuities with other phases. There is a certain amount of mythology about adolescence, so that parents wait in fear and trembling for their teen-age children to show the expected defiance and rebellion; when some issue comes up they say to themselves "Here it is!" and perhaps make more of the incident than they should. For many adolescents the transition to adult life proceeds smoothly; for others, the problems and conflicts have a long history, and troubles in adolescence are but further manifestations of earlier troubles.

Bodily changes during adolescence

Everyone is aware of the striking changes that take place in the body during adolescence. Changes take place in *primary sex characteristics,* that is, in the reproductive organs. Modifications also occur in the *secondary sex characteristics,* those physical features distinguishing a mature man from a mature woman in ways not directly related to the sexual apparatus. Some of these modifications, such as the development of the breasts, appear only in girls; some, such as the marked change in voice and the growth of a beard, appear only in boys; others, such as the appearance of pubic hair, are common to both boys and girls. In addition to the more obvious developments there are widespread internal changes of which we are less aware: blood pressure and heart rate increase, the weight of the heart doubles, metabolic rate decreases, and oil and sweat glands become more active. The physical changes of adolescence are of psychological interest because of the behavioral changes that accompany them—changes in attitudes, in emotional responsiveness, and in social behavior.

The definition of adolescence

The period of adolescence is difficult to specify with precision because the developments that lead to sexual maturity occur gradually. Roughly, adolescence extends from *pubescence* to late teens when physical growth is relatively complete. Pubescence refers to a period of about two years during which physical changes occur that culminate in *puberty;* pubic hair appears, there is a marked spurt in physical growth, and the primary and secondary sex characteristics gradually mature. Puberty, the climax of pubescence, is marked by menstruation in girls and by the appearance of live sperm cells in the urine of boys.

There has been a trend over the last 150 years for both boys and girls to mature earlier. The average age for menstruation, for example, has dropped from 17 in 1830 to 12.6 in 1960, and indications are that this downward trend is continuing (Tanner, 1970). Improved nutrition appears to be the major factor. But while physical maturation is occurring earlier, the assumption of the adult role is being delayed in most Western societies. A few generations ago adolescence scarcely existed. Many teen-agers worked fourteen hours a day and went from childhood to the responsibilities of adulthood with little time for transition. With a decrease in the need for unskilled workers and an increase in the length of apprenticeship required to enter a profession, the interval between sexual maturity and adult status has become longer. Such symbols of maturity as financial independence from parents and completion of school are now achieved at later ages. This discrepancy between physical maturity and psychological maturity in our society has fostered an adolescent subculture, which we will discuss later in this chapter.

The growth pattern

In infancy the child grows very rapidly in height, so that half the adult height is reached between the ages of two and three. Then the rate of growth slows until another spurt occurs that signifies the beginning of pubescence. Figure 4-1 shows the rate of growth in height and weight from birth to age nineteen. As can be seen, boys and girls average the same size until around age eleven, when the girls suddenly spurt ahead in both height and weight. They maintain this advantage for about two years, at which point the boys forge ahead and maintain a height and weight advantage for the rest of their lives. This period of growth inversion reflects the fact that girls mature two years earlier on the average than boys.

The difference in onset of the growth spurt is shown more clearly in Figure 4-2, which plots annual gains in height and weight for both boys and girls. In general, youngsters begin their growth spurt two years prior to puberty, and the year just before puberty is known as the *age of maximum growth*. In girls, for example, menstruation occurs at the apex of the growth-rate curve, after which

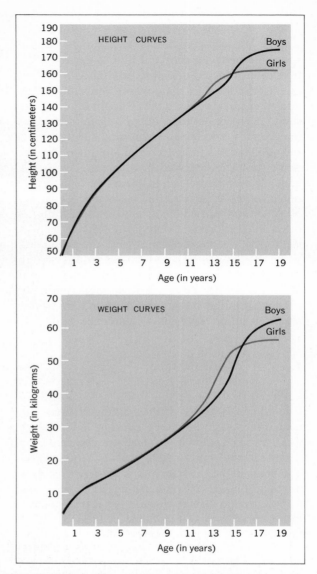

Fig. **4-1 Growth curves** Height and weight curves for the first 19 years (1 centimeter = .3937 inches; 1 kilogram = 2.2 pounds). The beginning of puberty at an earlier age for girls is reflected in the years between 11 and 14, when their height and weight exceed that of boys. (After Tanner, Whitehouse, and Takaishi, 1966)

the rate of increase slows down until adult height is reached at about nineteen. Eighty-three percent of girls will grow less than 4 inches after the onset of menstruation (Fried and Smith, 1962). A similar

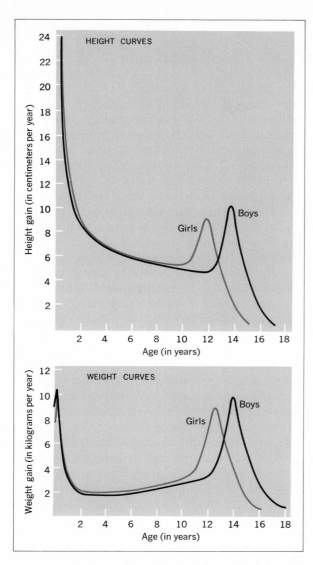

HEIGHT CURVES

Boys

Girls

Age (in years)

Height gain (in centimeters per year)

WEIGHT CURVES

Boys

Girls

Age (in years)

Weight gain (in kilograms per year)

Fig. **4-2 Annual gains in height and weight** Note that the peak period comes earlier for girls than for boys. (After Tanner, Whitehouse, and Takaishi, 1966)

growth pattern is seen in boys, although, because of the later onset of the growth spurt, maximum height may not be reached until age twenty-one or twenty-two.

The maximum growth rate is achieved by girls at twelve and by boys at fourteen years. This difference in rate of physical development is most striking in seventh- or eighth-grade classrooms,

where one can find quite mature young ladies seated alongside a group of male children. But while girls as a group mature earlier than boys as a group, there are large individual differences in the age of maximum growth. Figure 4-3 shows that the ages of maximum growth extend over the years from ten to eighteen, with considerable overlap between boys and girls. Two-thirds of the girls achieve their maximum growth within a year before or after the age of twelve; two-thirds of the boys achieve their maximum growth within a year before or after the age of fourteen. But the overlap cannot be ignored; some girls will mature *later* than some boys.

The question is often asked whether the early maturer tends to grow taller than the late maturer. The answer is that the time of onset of puberty shows very little relationship to adult height. There is, however, a high correlation between prepubescent height and adult height; the best time to estimate adult height is before the pubescent growth spurt begins.

The time of maximum growth rate has come to be accepted as a convenient index of maturing, but the process of reaching adulthood is much more complex than this. For example, the fact that a

Fig. **4-3 Age of maximum growth rate** The age at which height increment was most rapid was determined for each boy and for each girl; these results were then plotted to make the figure. (Data are approximate, from various determinations)

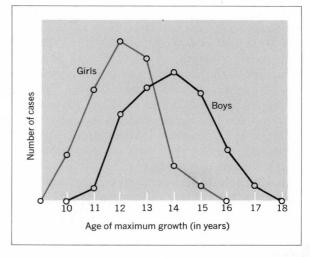

Girls

Boys

Number of cases

Age of maximum growth (in years)

girl has menstruated does not necessarily indicate that she has become fertile. Most girls menstruate before their ovaries can produce ripe eggs, and although pregnancy is certainly possible in the late teens, the period from age twenty to thirty is the time of greatest fertility. Even less is known about when actual fertility begins for boys, since a large number of spermatozoa must be present for conception to take place.

Early and late maturers

Growth curves for height indicate that not all adolescents follow the same pattern of growth. As a result of differing growth patterns a boy once relatively tall may find himself short by comparison to friends; a girl once considered small may find herself unusually tall for her age. Too much may be expected of those adolescents who mature early, while anxiety may be created among those who mature late and are left behind by their companions.

Late-maturing boys face a particularly difficult adjustment because of the importance of strength and physical prowess in their peer activities. During the period when they are shorter and less sturdy than their classmates they may lose out on practice of game skills, so that they may never catch up with the early maturers who take the lead in physical activities. Studies have shown that boys who mature late tend to have poorer self-concepts and to be more concerned about their social acceptance than early maturers. They are less popular with their classmates and tend to engage in relatively immature, attention-seeking behavior; they are more talkative, restless, bossy, and aggressive (Mussen and Jones, 1958). The late maturers also tend to feel rebellious toward their parents, have strong dependency needs, and feel rejected and dominated by their peers. The early maturers, on the other hand, appear to be more self-confident, independent, and capable of playing an adult role in interpersonal relationships. Few of them feel rejected, dominated, or rebellious toward their families (Mussen and Jones, 1957). Some of these personality differences between early and late maturers persist into adulthood, long after the physical differences have disappeared (Jones, 1957).

There is evidence that part of the difference in adjustment between early- and late-maturing boys may be attributed to cultural factors. Americans tend to emphasize independence and competition and equate physical strength and large size with masculinity. When a boy looks physically mature he is more apt to be treated as an adult and will enjoy some of the privileges of adulthood earlier than his slower-maturing classmates. He is consequently more likely to become self-assured and independent. Italians, on the other hand, place less emphasis on physical size and strength in evaluating a man, and Italian families tend to encourage their children's dependency, showering them with warmth and affection and doing little to stimulate the development of independence. When early-maturing Italian boys were compared with late maturers little difference was found in their behavior and self-attitudes (Mussen and Bouterline-Young, 1968).

But among a group of Italian-American boys (boys whose parents were native-born Italians living in this country), the late-maturing boys showed some of the same problems characteristic of American boys who mature late. They seemed to have acquired American attitudes toward growth and maturity and reacted to their slow physical development, as did the American late maturers, by feeling that others did not like or respect them. Thus, cultural attitudes concerning physical size and strength and the desirability of independence are important in determining how acceleration or retardation in physical maturation may affect an individual's personality.

The effects of rate of maturation on personality are less striking for girls. Some early-maturing girls may be at a disadvantage because they are too "grown-up" for their age groups in the late elementary grades, but by the junior high school years the early maturers tend to have more prestige among their classmates and to take leadership in school activities. At this stage, the late-maturing girls, like the boys, may have less adequate self-concepts and poorer relations with their parents and peers (Weatherly, 1964). Because the physical requirements for femininity in our society are more ambiguous than those for masculinity (petiteness, for example, is more acceptable for girls than smallness is for boys), it is not surprising that rate of maturation is less important in influencing personality development in girls.

Adolescent growth rates may vary in another way: the body does not grow as a unit, and the growth of one part may be out of step with that of another. The arms and legs may shoot out in apparent disregard for the rest of the body. The nose and chin may suddenly become more prominent facial features. Metabolism has to adjust to rapid growth, and a new glandular balance has to be reached. The relative sizes of different bodily tissues at different periods, plotted in Figure 4-4, show most rapid fluctuation during the early teens. No wonder there are occasional disturbances in the balance of physiological processes within the body as these shifts take place. Adolescent acne is a common symptom of these internal disharmonies.

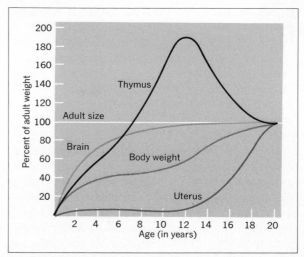

Fig. 4-4 **Uneven growth rates of different body tissues** The growth of different parts of the body expressed as a percentage of their adult weight. The brain approaches adult size very early; tissues related to reproduction (uterus) wait until later for rapid growth. Note that at 12 years the thymus is almost twice its adult weight. (After Jackson, 1928)

The role of the adolescent

When the adolescent becomes a problem to his parents, the school, or the community, it is usually because he has become a problem to himself. The transition from childhood to adulthood brings with it both the strains accompanying physical growth and the conflict associated with adopting the social behavior transitional to adulthood in our culture. At a time of very rapid change in values, moreover, the "generation gap" may be genuine, so that the adolescent, as an adult, will refuse to accept the adult values of other generations.

Sexual development and the adolescent role

The bodily changes that accompany sexual maturing are a source of pride as well as embarrassment for the adolescent. How comfortable he feels about his new physique depends to a large extent upon the attitudes toward sexual development conveyed by his parents and the school. Parental attitudes of secrecy and taboo concerning the sexual functions cannot fail to generate feelings of anxiety among their teen-age offspring. The recent expansion of sexual education programs in schools to include films and discussions on human growth and sexual development as early as the upper elementary grades has done much to help youngsters accept their physical maturation as a source of interest and pride rather than embarrassment and concern.

The newly intensified sexual urges that accompany puberty are not easily handled. Despite what appears to be something of a sexual revolution in our society, the attitude is still one of taboo on sexual relations before marriage. Since the circumstances of modern life lead to the postponement of marriage for several years beyond the attainment of sexual maturity, the adolescent must find a satisfactory way of coping with his sexual desires in the interim.

The adolescent's decision regarding his sexual behavior may be a more difficult one today than it was twenty years ago. The continual bombardment by sexual stimuli in magazines, TV, and movies, the availability of birth control pills, and the more liberal attitude toward premarital sexual experience expressed by some segments of society, all give the newly matured youngster more freedom of choice and, at the same time, produce more conflict than he would have experienced two decades ago.

It should be pointed out that the problem of control of sexual impulses is quite different for adolescent boys than for girls. In boys the biological urge is highly specific, aroused by a variety of external stimuli, and aimed at rapid discharge of tension in orgasm. Although some adolescent girls may experience sexual impulses in the same way as boys, sexual desire for many is less intense and less specific; it is a diffuse feeling not clearly differentiated from other feelings such as romantic yearnings, maternal impulses, or any strong emotion. This difference is exemplified in the dating situation—the girl is quite happy with the sensations engendered by hugging and kissing, whereas for the boy such pleasures may be only a means to an end. For the girl sexual feelings are closely tied to feelings of love; whereas for the boy, initially, sexual impulses are quite separate from such feelings.

There is a theory that the "storm and stress" of adolescence is due more to cultural conflicts arising from sexual restrictions than to biological development. This theory receives support from studies of nonliterate cultures in which greater sexual freedom is permitted. In these more permissive cultures adolescence is relatively uneventful, and the transition from childhood to adulthood is reported to be smoother than in ours. The Trobriad Islanders, for instance, are tolerant of premarital sexual relationships. Sexual experimentation goes on freely among preadolescents, and an easy transition from childhood to adulthood ensues (Malinowski, 1929). Anthropological studies of several New Guinea and Samoan groups indicate that the period of adolescence is easier in the tribes that have less restrictive sex taboos (Mead, 1935).

To examine one aspect of a culture apart from its other aspects may be misleading, however, for cultures that permit greater sexual freedom than ours may also permit greater freedom for the adolescent in other ways. The adolescent may be relieved of "stress and strain" in problems of wider scope as well as in sexual problems.

Just as sexual restrictions vary from one culture to another, they also vary in the subcultures of a complex society such as ours. The Kinsey report, for example, indicates that in American society young men from lower educational and occupational levels are more likely to find sexual outlets in actual intercourse than are those from upper educational and social levels, who are more likely to find their outlets in masturbation and petting to climax (Kinsey, Pomeroy, and Martin, 1948). Although the years since this report was published have seen some lessening of class differences in sexual behavior (largely through the influence of the mass media), some differences still remain.

Among those who accept the cultural taboos, any form of sexual interest or sexual fantasy brings with it feelings of apprehension. Under these circumstances sex becomes a source of adolescent conflict, even though biological demands alone would not make such conflict inevitable.

Emancipation from home

Emancipation from parental authority and from emotional dependence upon parents begins in childhood, but the process of emancipation is greatly accelerated during adolescence. In order to function effectively as an adult, the adolescent must begin to detach himself from his family and develop some independence in his behavior, his emotions, and his values and beliefs. Clearly, the ease of transition to fuller independence in later adolescence depends to a great extent upon the attitudes parents take during the preceding years. Some parents who have insisted upon close supervision of the child in his early years attempt to continue their control through his adolescence. As a result the child is likely to continue his childish dependence and obedience through adolescence, and never fully mature as an adult.

Studies have shown that a "democratic family" (in which the child is allowed a fair degree of autonomy, is included in important decisions, and is controlled primarily by verbal discipline) produces an adolescent who is self-reliant and effective. He feels free to disagree with his parents but usually has a warm relationship with them. On the other hand, the "authoritarian family" (in which rules are set without consulting the children, autonomy is limited, and discipline is predominantly physical) produces an adolescent who is less poised and effective. He tends to be compliant on the surface but is rebellious and impulsive underneath; his view of morality makes acceptable whatever one can get away with (Douvan and Adelson, 1966).

Most family conflicts during adolescence center around the adolescent's desiring more freedom than the parents think he is ready for, or, on the other hand, the youngster's unwillingness to assume some of the responsibilities that the parents feel should accompany increased maturity and independence. The parent is ambivalent because, although he knows the adolescent must learn to stand on his own feet, he still wants to protect him from the unpleasant realities of existence, to keep him from getting hurt when his decisions are poor ones. The adolescent is ambivalent because, although he wants to be a free agent, he does not always want to give up the security and lack of responsibility that go with continued dependence.

Table 4-1 lists some parent-child conflicts as reported by high school boys and girls in a nation-wide survey. On the whole, there is no evidence of very high parent-child conflict; for no specific problem did more than one in five high school students voice a complaint about their parents. But the areas of conflict reported are of interest. Many of the problems concern restrictions on grown-up behavior (dates, use of the family car, use of money); in these areas, as in others, the teen-ager sees the parents as treating him too much like a child. The differences in replies of boys and girls represent in part a sex-typing in our culture: the boy is troubled about having a car and about spending the money he earns, while the girl is troubled about her freedom in choosing friends, about strictness concerning dates, and about favoritism (which, one may guess, she feels is demonstrated in her brother's greater freedom). Concealed in the figures may be the fact of the girl's earlier maturing, so that her desire for dates in the ninth grade may produce parental opposition, while a ninth-grade boy may not yet care very much about dating.

Several recent studies have indicated that the rebellion and defiance of parental authority thought to be "characteristic" of adolescence is much more of a problem for boys than it is for girls. When questioned about their relationship with their family, the majority of the girls interviewed described their family life as pleasant and harmonious; there were few indications of conflict, and the girls generally felt that parental rules were fair and lenient (Douvan and Adelson, 1966). Girls may have less of a problem in this area than boys

TABLE 4-1 THE "PARENT PROBLEM" AS SEEN BY HIGH SCHOOL STUDENTS

PROBLEM	PERCENTAGE OF STUDENTS WHO ACKNOWLEDGE PROBLEM*		
	BOYS	GIRLS	TOTAL
Afraid to tell parents what I've done wrong	18%	19%	19%
Parents too strict about my going out at night	16	19	18
Parents too strict about family car	24	9	16
Family always worried about money	15	15	15
Parents too strict about dating	8	17	13
Parents interfere in my choice of friends	10	15	13
Parents nag about studying	16	10	13
Parents hate to admit I'm sometimes right	13	13	13
Parents too strict about dates on school nights	10	13	12
Wish parents would treat me like a grown-up	10	14	12
Parents interfere with spending money I earn	15	7	11
Parents play favorites	8	12	10

* The percentages are not additive, because one student may make several complaints.

Source: Remmers and Radler (1957).

for a number of reasons: (1) girls tend to be more compliant than boys at all ages, largely because of social expectations as to how a girl should behave and possibly because of some innate differences; (2) as noted earlier, girls have a more diffuse and less intense sex drive during adolescence than boys and hence may feel less need to rebel in situations concerning sexual behavior; and (3) because boys are expected in our society to be independent and masterful, they must, of necessity, show some rebellion against parental control to demonstrate these qualities.

The adolescent subculture

If the adolescent can find secure relationships with others of his own age, he is freer to emancipate himself from home ties. The support and values of his contemporaries help in making the transition from parental control to individual autonomy. Adolescents place great importance upon being accepted by their own group.

The need for the security that comes from the group leads to the formation of in-groups, such as gangs among boys and cliques among girls. Members of an in-group feel especially close to others within the group and are very much aware of the distinction between "in" and "out," between those who belong and those who do not. Here again, however, we notice sex differences. The boy uses the gang to help him in his quest for autonomy, to give him support in his rebellion against parental authority. The girl tends to use the clique as a means of finding close personal friendships. Girls during the middle teens seem more interested in, and perhaps are more capable of forming, an intimate relationship with one or two best friends. Boys tend toward more casual group relationships. In either case, relations with peers help the adolescent to prepare for adult love and friendship and to bridge the transition from dependence on parental standards to the formation of his own. To some extent the peer group takes over the parental function of controlling behavior; for example, petulance or self-centeredness that might be overlooked by the parents may not be tolerated by one's peers.

Parents are sometimes disturbed by their offspring's apparent slavish adherence to peer standards, but in actuality the adolescent relies on his companions' values mainly on less important issues. One study found that high school girls tended to comply with their peers on issues the peers considered important (such as which of two dresses to buy) and to comply with their parents on issues the parents considered important (such as which of two part-time jobs to take). But the more important the girl *herself* felt the issue to be, the more apt she was to rely on her parents' judgment (Brittain, 1968).

Juvenile delinquency

Enough adolescents engage in antisocial behavior to make juvenile delinquency a major social problem, and apparently an increasingly grave one (Figure 4-5). Fifteen to nineteen year olds commit more than half of the serious crimes in the United States today; the greatest number of people arrested for rape, assault, and robbery are age eighteen, for burglary age fifteen, and for auto theft age sixteen. The circumstances that lead adolescents into antisocial behavior, if understood, can

Fig. **4-5 Increase in juvenile arrests** The number of arrests of those under 18 has more than doubled in the period from 1960 to 1970, while arrests of those 18 and older have shown only a slight increase. (Data from Federal Bureau of Investigation)

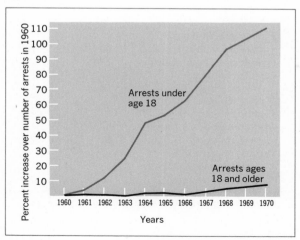

TABLE 4-2 PARENTAL DISCIPLINE AND LATER CRIME CONVICTIONS AND INCARCERATION		
TYPE OF DISCIPLINE EMPLOYED BY PARENTS	PERCENTAGE OF BOYS CONVICTED OF CRIMES	PERCENTAGE OF BOYS SENTENCED TO PENAL INSTITUTIONS
Punitive ($N = 14$)	21%	7%
Love oriented ($N = 60$)	27	5
Erratic ($N = 41$)	49	19
Lax ($N = 52$)	50	19

Source: McCord, McCord, and Zola (1959).

Families living in an area where social conditions fostered delinquency were observed by social workers over a period of two or more years. The table presents the percentage of boys later convicted of crimes and incarcerated, in relation to the type of discipline employed by the parents.

throw light on the more general problem of adolescent development.

A certain amount of what adults would call delinquent behavior is normal during the course of childhood and adolescence. Youngsters may be tempted at times to take money from their mother's purse or to pocket a toy from a store counter. Teen-age gangs may indulge in pranks that destroy property or border on delinquency in other ways. Such indiscretions are usually not serious, and most children develop the proper controls and inhibitions without intervention by the authorities. Among more pervasive delinquent behavior it is customary to distinguish between two types: *social delinquency* and *individual delinquency*. Social delinquency expresses itself in gang behavior in which large numbers of young people conform to a neighborhood pattern that may include car stealing, fighting, sexual indulgences, the use of illegal drugs, or other forms of behavior frowned upon by society. Such behavior may not be deviant in the subculture to which the adolescent belongs. Individual delinquency, in contrast, crops up anywhere, in "good" families and neighborhoods as well as "bad" ones, and can best be understood as an attempt by the young person to solve some sort of problem of his own.

Social delinquency is a symptom of broader problems that are currently acute in American society: the alienation of many adolescents, particularly those in minority and low-income groups, from our culture and institutions, and their inability to find jobs because of lack of the appropriate skills. Children from lower-class homes are ill-prepared to meet the demands of the schools, which tend to value middle-class standards. Those who encounter a great deal of frustration and humiliation in their attempts to meet scholastic standards may draw together in groups to express their defiance. They may drop out of school and, failing to find employment, turn to theft and acts of violence in their boredom, resentment, and desire for the material affluence so enticingly depicted by the mass media. Their gang confers the status denied them through other avenues to success. That desire for status is a crucial factor is indicated by a study showing that youngsters with strong, positive self-concepts are immune to delinquency even though they reside in high-delinquency areas (Lively, Dinitz, and Reckless, 1962). Poverty, broken homes, cruelty and rejection by parents all add to the complex forces that induce high delinquency rates in slum areas.

Individual delinquency, not associated with bad neighborhoods or cultural conflict, is in some ways more puzzling. The part that the subtle influence of child-rearing practices plays is suggested by data pertaining to the influence of childhood discipline on later aggression and crime (Table 4-2). The fact that the tendency toward delinquent careers starts early has been pointed out in several studies in which delinquent or criminal careers have been foreshadowed between the ages of six and ten (Glueck and Glueck, 1964).[1]

[1]The type of personality that tends toward criminal careers will be considered in the discussion of psychopathic behavior in Chapter 20.

Self-perception, ideals, and values

If the adolescent is to achieve any consistency in his social behavior, he has to formulate certain standards of conduct. He must decide what kind of person he wants to be and ascertain for himself what things are worthwhile. Such standards are known as *ideals* or *values*. When he becomes independent of home, will he continue to accept the standards that his parents approve? In making himself acceptable to his peers, does he have to do everything they urge or dare him to do? He must choose whether to conform or defy, whether to respect conventional taboos or to see what he can "get by" with, whether to seek immediate pleasures or to work toward distant goals. He arrives at an image of the ideal self he would like to become and then judges himself according to this ideal.

The adolescent does not always find it easy to attain stable standards and guiding values. Although he has incorporated his parents' values into many of his own basic values, times have changed since his parents' youth. As mentioned earlier, the younger generation faces some problems the older generation did not have to face, such as drugs, the pill, greater exposure to sexually arousing stimuli via the mass media, and, in later adolescence, the decision whether to fight in a war for which one may feel no moral commitment. The young person of today must make decisions in areas where his parents' standards may be obsolete.

CRITICAL
DISCUSSION

Adolescent
social protest

In their search for a sense of identity and a set of values consistent with this identity, some older adolescents find themselves questioning not only the standards of their parents but also the goals and values of society itself. Such adolescents have been designated by various names—"rebels," "radicals," "activists," and "protestors."

We cannot touch upon the many factors that have contributed to this state of dissension, but it is informative to look at several deviant life styles adopted by young people in an attempt to develop their own identity. It should be kept in mind, however, that even in this age of dissent only a small group seriously questions or protests against the values of society. Most young people strive to fit into society and to achieve the adult role.

Activists. These are the young people who have rejected many of society's values and are determined to demonstrate, and in some cases even to advocate revolution, in order to change or abolish those institutions that conflict with their ethics. They feel compelled to speak out on issues they view as morally wrong, and in their rejection of authority they are willing to use civil disobedience and risk arrest to attain their goals.

When university students active in protest movements were asked to check a list of adjectives that described their ideal selves, the items that differentiated them from a representative cross section of students were "imaginative," "free," and "not hung up." The adjectives that distinguished the cross-section group were "ambitious," "foresightful," "orderly," and "conventional" (Smith, 1968). When asked to provide solutions to a series of stories that posed a moral dilemma, the activists were more likely to respond on the basis of self-accepted moral principles, while the cross-section group tended to respond according to the morality of conventional role-conformity (see Table 3-6, p. 78).

Studies at several universities indicate that student activists come from families of greater economic, educational, and social status than the average student. Since their parents tend to be politically liberal, the radical position of the offspring cannot be viewed as rebellion against parental authority. Student activists describe their relations with their parents as close and affectionate; the parents were rational and permissive in their approach to childrearing, placing less emphasis on prohibitions and punishments (Block, Haan, and Smith, 1968).

Alienated youth. These young people also reject the traditional values of society but

TABLE 4-3   RELATION BETWEEN PARENTAL INTEREST AND THE ADOLESCENT'S SELF-ESTEEM

ADOLESCENT'S SELF-ESTEEM	PARENTAL INTEREST	
	NO EVIDENCE OF LACK OF INTEREST	SOME EVIDENCE OF LACK OF INTEREST
High	49%	29%
Medium	25	26
Low	26	45
Total percentage	100%	100%
	N = 945	N = 241

Source: Rosenberg (1965).

Percentage of adolescents with high, medium, and low self-esteem in relation to the degree of parental interest.

The desire of the adolescent to amount to something, to do what adults do, but on his own initiative, leads to an uncertain relationship to adult models. He wants to be like the adults he knows and at the same time break away from them. As he struggles for a satisfying self-image, parental influences are strongly in evidence despite his conflicts with them. For example, in a study of high school juniors and seniors, parental interest (as shown by interest in the adolescent's friends and school work, and in dinner conversations) was found to be associated with high self-esteem; lack of interest, with low self-esteem (Table 4-3).

Finding a set of values by which to regulate conduct is a crucial task for a young person—a task made even more difficult today because the

differ from the activists in their pessimism that protesting will produce any change. They have no use for long-range goals or commitment; instead they escape from society by "dropping out." Concerned with the creation of experiences, with immediate gratification, such young people frequently resort to "consciousness-expanding" drugs.

The alienated youth tends to be estranged from his parents as well as from society; his ideological views are not extentions of his parents' views but instead are formed in rebellion against parental attitudes. Fathers of alienated male college students are described by their sons as cold, withdrawn men who are concerned with success and status and are little involved in relationships with their offspring. The alienated youth rejects at the same time the values of his parents and those of society (Keniston, 1966).

Conservatists. These are young people who are active in extreme conservative movements. They accept the traditional American values and authority structure; they want to maintain the status quo or even to return to a period of greater individualism. Many have been influenced by the individualistic philosophy of Ayn Rand (1964). Studies of the background of these students suggest that their parents were authoritarian, somewhat lacking in warmth in their child-rearing practices, and apt to place a high value on achievements and "goodness." Schiff (1966) distinguishes between those youngsters whose conservative commitment is an extension of the ideological views of their parents, and those who converted to conservatism in late adolescence. This conversion appears to be less an ideological commitment than an attempt to find comfort in the status and structure of the conservative movement—to escape the anxiety created by a world of changing values by adhering to the old traditions.

The three types of life style described above are, of course, not the only ones adopted by adolescents in our society. Many young people try to promote change not by rebelling against society's values but by working within the existing institutions—contributing their efforts to such agencies as Vista and the Peace Corps, for example. Because there are as yet little data on the background and attitudes of these young people, they were not included in our discussion.

As in all attempts to classify individuals according to types, there are probably as many young people who do not fit neatly into these categories as those who do.

TABLE 4-4	ATTITUDE CHANGE DURING COLLEGE		
STUDENTS BY MAJOR AREA	PERCENTAGE OF "NO" RESPONSES TO MEDICARE QUESTION		
	END OF FRESHMAN YEAR	END OF JUNIOR YEAR	PERCENT CHANGE
Engineering (men)	29%	42%	+13%
Mathematics (men)	19	11	− 8
Humanities (women)	39	26	−13
Humanities (men)	38	22	−16
Source: Webster, Freedman, and Heist (1962).			

Responses of National Merit Scholars attending a wide variety of colleges to the question, "Should the government provide medical and dental care for citizens who cannot afford such services?" All except the engineering majors shifted toward a more liberal attitude after three years of college. The engineers became significantly more conservative. Whether this change in opposite directions is due to the kinds of students who enter the different programs or to variations in the influence of the different curricula is difficult to determine.

values of society itself are in a state of flux. With increased education, values change, usually becoming more liberal, less ethnocentric, and more tolerant of diversity (see Table 4-4). The importance of education, rather than simply increasing age, in producing a change of values is indicated by a study that compared students who voluntarily withdrew from college with those who remained in school. The groups were initially matched in terms of intelligence and scores on a test of ethnic prejudice. Over a period of two years the students who remained in college showed a significant decrease in prejudice, while those who withdrew did not (Plant, 1958).

What the adolescent values and the way in which he sees himself are, of course, the results of many background factors that determine what he has experienced and what he expects of himself. Some of the influences are a result of the social and economic background in which he has grown up. A high value on education and self-respect is associated with higher socioeconomic status, and a high value on manual skill and toughness is associated with the lower classes (Table 4-5). It should be noted, however, that even among those of the lowest class, the number who stress being a good student is equal to that of those who value being tough; all members of a class should not be characterized by certain values because of some differences in percentages between classes.

TABLE 4-5	SOCIAL CLASS AND SELF-VALUES AMONG ADOLESCENT BOYS			
HOW IMPORTANT IS IT TO YOU TO BE . . ."	SOCIAL CLASS OF RESPONDENT			
	HIGH (N = 31)	HIGH MIDDLE (N = 295)	LOW MIDDLE (N = 164)	LOW (N = 54)
a good student?	71%	56%	51%	39%
well-respected, looked up to by others?	46	30	21	16
tough, not afraid to fight?	15	25	28	39
good at working with your hands?	17	28	32	53
Source: Rosenberg (1965).				

Percentage of adolescent boys who answer "very important" to the questions in the left-hand column, in relation to their social class.

The adult years

The early adult years are for most men and women the years of greatest energy and productivity. The adjustment problems of young adults, as distinct from those of adolescents, are often decisions of choice (vocation, marriage, family size) rather than problems of emotional conflict and insecurity. This does not mean that young adults do not have such personal difficulties, for choices stir up any problems of dependency and insecurity that remain unresolved from the preceding years.

The community gives young adults access to many areas of life that permit significant participation. A careful study of where people of different ages go in their daily lives and what they do when they get there, shows clearly that it is the young adults who have the widest range of participation of any age group (Figure 4-6). The adolescents have not yet achieved that full access, and restrictions come again with advancing age (Barker and Barker, 1963).

Fig. **4-6   Range of behavioral settings in which different age groups are performers**   Two studies of small towns, one in the midwestern United States and the other in England, show that adults are active participants in a wider range of behavioral settings than any other age group. (After Barker and Barker, 1963)

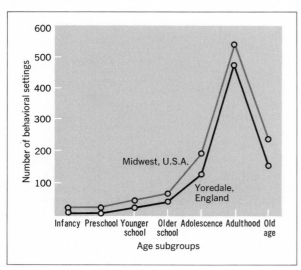

Most older people look back upon young adulthood as their period of greatest happiness (Table 4-6). In the studies cited, women often reported satisfaction in housekeeping and raising their children; men, while also referring to happy family life, mentioned interest in their work during those years. It is worth noting that in the Iowa group studied, two-thirds of those who had not been married selected the childhood years as the time of greatest happiness, while only a third of the married ones chose the years of childhood and youth in preference to the years of early adult life (Landis, 1942).

For many men and women life becomes somewhat stabilized during the early adult years. Satisfactory adjustments in these years occur when the preparation for a career has been successfully accomplished, when marriage has led to the establishment of a home, and when children are finding their places in school. Friendships are established with congenial families; opportunities are found for participating in the civic life of the community; and there is enough energy to enjoy what leisure remains. But this picture of the young family settled in the community is, unfortunately, not the only picture; in fact, it is perhaps a rare one.

Each of the areas of satisfaction is also an area or risk. Vocational adjustment is not easy, military service may delay fulfilling a plan, and many young adults face from time to time the demoralization of unemployment. The young wife who wishes to devote herself to her children finds that she must go to work in order to supplement the meager income of her husband, or, conversely, the wife who wishes to continue to work finds her children a burden and an interference. Marriage begun with romantic enthusiasm may end in the divorce court. Prolonged illnesses may upset well-laid plans. The young man who pictured himself as a contented husband and father may find himself a disgruntled bachelor, a divorced man, or a widower. The young woman similarly may end up single, divorced, or widowed.

There are no sharp transitions from young

TABLE 4-6 YEARS THAT APPEARED HAPPIEST IN RETROSPECT		
"HAPPIEST" YEARS	RESIDENT IN NEW YORK*	RESIDENT IN IOWA†
Childhood (5 to 15 years)	15%	11%
Youth (15 to 25 years)	19	19
Young adulthood (25 to 45 years)	49	51
Middle age (45 to 60 years)	12	6
Later life (60 and up)	5	5
Undecided	0	8
Total percentage	100%	100%
Number of persons reporting	370	450

*Source: Morgan (1937). Respondents were from ages 70 to 90.
†Source: Landis (1942). Respondents were from ages 65 to 98.

adulthood to middle age, but the ages of forty-five to sixty-five bring a number of shifts. Often the individual reaches something of a plateau in vocational accomplishment: either he has arrived (or is well on the way) or he must content himself with a station in life that is likely to persist with little advancement. The woman's life is changed by her menopause, which marks the end of her child-bearing years. By the age of fifty half the parents have seen the departure of the last child from the home. Future orientation becomes more difficult as awareness gradually comes that life is more than half over. The sharp increase in suicide rate in the forty to fifty age group reflects some of these problems.

The years of later maturity are commonly thought of as beginning around age sixty-five or seventy, when those in employed positions face retirement, often with reduced income and other attendant dislocations. The proportion of retired people in the population is steadily increasing because of longer life expectancy (see Table 4-7).

We tend now to think of old age as setting in when there is a general decline in abilities, restriction of activities, often the abandonment of independent living. Some people, even of advanced years, really never reach this stage, for they remain active and independent until overtaken by death.

Each of these periods in life has its attendant problems. Instead of considering the whole gamut of adjustments that people make, we shall illustrate some of the characteristics of adult life by considering a few specimen topics: adjustment to the sex role of being a man or a woman, marital happiness, productive work, and successful aging.

Masculine and feminine roles

In the adult years we find the culmination of the differences between the sexes that have resulted in part from biological differentiation and in part from the roles assigned the sexes in our culture.

Because the sexes are physiologically unlike, it would be easy to infer that as adults the differences in behavior between them correspond simply to their different biological organizations. Actually the situation is more complex. Whether it is the man or the woman who wears lace, long hair, or brightly colored clothes depends upon the styles current at the time. A series of historical accidents determined that until recently men became bank clerks and women became cashiers in stores; men, telegraph operators, and women, telephone operators. Now, as women are increasingly taking over some of the jobs men alone formerly held, the problem becomes one of determining whether the

TABLE 4-7 LIFE EXPECTANCY IN 1900 AND 1966 (UNITED STATES)		
AGE	NUMBER OF YEARS OF LIFE REMAINING	
	1900	1966
Birth	49.2	70.1
1	55.2	70.8
5	55.0	67.1
25	39.1	48.0
65	11.9	14.6

Source: U. S. Department of Health, Education, and Welfare.

Average number of years of life remaining at specified ages in the years 1900 and 1966. Women have gained more than men; in 1900 they lived two years longer than men on the average, whereas now they live seven years longer.

behavioral distinctions between men and women are to be attributed to biological differences or to cultural influences.

Studies of cultures very unlike our own dramatically reveal the wide range of possibilities in the behavior of the two sexes. Reports on sex roles in three New Guinea tribes illustrate well how these roles differ in various cultures (Mead, 1949).

1. In a mountain-dwelling tribe known as the Arapesh, men and women were found to be more alike than those in our culture. Their similarity lay in their passivity, gentleness, mildness, and domesticity—traits predominantly "feminine" in our culture. Men and women shared the care of the children and other home duties with less division of labor than that with which we are familiar.

2. Among a river-dwelling people called the Mundugumor, men and women also were more nearly alike than those in our culture. But the Mundugumor similarity was "masculine." Both sexes tended to be ruthless, aggressive, and violent.

3. The lake-dwelling Tchambuli offer the most dramatic contrast to our culture. Although the sexes had dissimilar roles, as ours do, the pattern was largely reversed. The Tchambuli woman was the aggressive partner, the manager of business affairs. The man was emotionally responsive to the feelings of his children, and he was subordinate to and dependent upon his mate. The psychological reversal was so real that the Tchambuli interpreted it as biologically natural—even to the extent that the man went into confinement and suffered while his wife had the baby.

What these contrasting cultures tell us is that sex roles are subject to a number of different patternings. The difference does not mean that anatomical and physiological differences between the sexes have nothing to do with behavior, but it does mean that culture has to be taken into account.

It is certainly true that the division of labor between the sexes commonly found in nonliterate cultures is determined in part by physical differences between men and women. Study of 224 tribes throughout the world shows that, in general, men gravitate toward work requiring muscular strength (warfare, metalworking, hunting, mining and quarrying, boat-building). Women tend toward occupations centering around the home and children (basketry, gathering fruits and nuts, water-carrying, grain-grinding, pottery-making, and clothes manufacture and repair) (Murdock, 1937). The task of bearing and nursing children provides a biological reason for keeping women at home; man's greater muscular strength makes possible his participation in more strenuous activities. Once the division of labor is established, however, complex regulation by social pressure sets in, and familiar ways of doing things are enforced by taboo, ritual, superstition, prejudice, and other forms of social control. After the patterns have been set, members of one sex may do exclusively what members of the other sex could do equally well.

Among Western societies the distinction between tasks that are feminine and those that are masculine has become increasingly blurred. Women are now seen as mail carriers, bus drivers, and construction workers. Men may be interior decorators, clothes designers, or hair stylists. But in terms of recognized achievements, women still tend to fall far behind men. Although women have become increasingly more numerous in professions that were previously predominantly male—for example, medicine, law, politics, and the sciences—the number of women achieving eminence in these fields is slight. This discrepancy cannot be attributed to differences in ability; ability tests show no significant differences between males and females. Instead, we must look for differences in cultural expectations of the sexual roles. Our culture offers men more opportunities for achievement, so that in spite of equal ability the man tends to be more encouraged than the woman. Society also exerts greater pressure in motivating the man toward achievement. All men, for example, are expected to earn a living, for which marriage provides an added incentive; women, on the other hand, often expect a professional career to be ended by marriage and child rearing. Many women are torn between their professional ambitions and the feeling that the successful rearing of children is an essential aspect of womanhood. To achieve both requires an unusual amount of dedication and work. What our culture expects of men and women is more important in determining sexual roles than any differences in abilities.

Marital happiness

As we follow the development of the child through adolescence into adult life, we may naturally inquire as to his or her suitability for marriage and the likelihood of making a happy marriage. The increasing divorce rate is only one indication of the amount of unhappiness in marriage, for many unhappy marriages do not end in divorce. We may well ask what factors in early life make one person better suited for marriage than another.

Studies comparing the backgrounds of those who are happily married and those who are not show that the factors most predictive of marital happiness have their origins in early childhood: the happiness of the parents' marriage, lack of conflict with either parent, attachment to the parents, and the attractiveness of the opposite-sexed parent. Any of these factors increases the likelihood of a happy marriage when the child grows up (Burgess and Wallin, 1953). In essence, parents provide a model for spouses and parents-to-be. Children reared in a family in which the marriage is functioning effectively not only have a model to emulate but also develop confidence that success in marriage is possible.

The best single predictor of marital happiness is happiness in childhood. Those who remember their childhoods as being happy report greater marital happiness than those whose childhoods are remembered as less happy. Conversely, emotional disturbance in childhood tends to be correlated with unsatisfactory marital adjustment (Pond, Ryle, and Hamilton, 1963).

There is some indication that the background and personality of the husband are more important than those of the wife in determining marital success. Marriage usually creates more of a change in life style for women than it does for men. The man continues in his career; the woman must make a transition from the relative independence of single life to the demands, responsibilities, and restraints required of a wife and mother. The more stable the husband, the more capable he is of being supportive and helpful in his wife's adjustment to her new role (Barry, 1970).

Even for people whose backgrounds predict a successful marriage, the early months of marriage impose a number of adjustment problems. The birth of the first child before a couple has learned to adjust to one another may severely strain the marriage. Illness during pregnancy, financial worries, and the frustration of being tied down by the care of an infant often make living together even more difficult. For these reasons it is not surprising that the length of time before the birth of the first child is an important factor in a marriage's success. The divorce rate is markedly higher for those couples who conceive immediately after marriage than for those who wait several months to a year (Christensen, 1966). The divorce rate is even higher for those who conceive before marriage, but in this case, of course, a number of additional factors contribute to marital discontent.

Other variables that show a relationship with a happy marriage are age (divorce rate is higher for those who marry before the age of twenty-one), similarity of educational and socioeconomic status, ability to communicate with one another, and a democratic approach to decision-making and the sharing of responsibility (Blood and Wolfe, 1968).

When the wife is clearly dominant, difficulty in social and sexual adjustment usually ensues. The same is true, but to a lesser extent, when the husband is extremely dominant. More important than who dominates is whether the wife and husband agree on the question of equality. When divorced and married couples were asked about their attitudes concerning equality in decision-making, the married couples showed more agreement than did divorced couples. Divorced women tended to believe strongly in the equality of wives, whereas divorced men believed in male dominance (Jacobson, 1952).

Much debate centers on whether happy marriages are based on similarity of interests and temperament ("like attracts like") or on the fact that the two partners complement rather than replicate one another ("opposites attract"). There are studies that support each viewpoint, so no conclusive answer can be given. It is clear that many different patterns of marital relations function satisfactorily, but the following elements seem to be common to the various patterns: (1) mutual respect—each partner finds some important quality or ability to respect in the other; the greater the number of areas of respect, the more satisfactory the marriage; (2) tolerance—the ability to accept one another's shortcomings; and (3) the ability to agree on common goals and to work toward such goals (Lederer and Jackson, 1968).

Productive work

As we shall see in later chapters, self-esteem and mental health often are influenced by seeing onself as a productive person. The years in school and in career preparation come to fruition in the work-life of the adult, and we may well inquire into the changes in physical and mental ability throughout the life span, and when the most productive work can be expected.

So far as physical strength and agility are concerned, there is obviously some slowing down with age. But exercise appears to be the crucial factor. Some active seventy year olds are as strong and physically fit as some men in their thirties who are engaged in sedentary occupations. As would be

expected, the reaction times of elderly subjects are slower than those of young athletes. When elderly subjects are compared with young nonathletes, however, no significant difference in speed of response is found (Botwinick and Thompson, 1968).

More complex skills, involving mental ability rather than muscular speed and precision, can be retained well into the sixties and seventies. A study of chess masters showed that they reached their peaks in tournament play in the thirties and that there was little decline until the fifties. The chess master Blackburne in nine exhibitions between the ages of seventy-six and seventy-nine played an average of twenty-one games at each exhibition and won 86 percent of the games played. Although he had declined in ability, as measured against the performance of other champions, it is evident that the amount of residual ability was of a high order (Buttenwieser, 1935). The retention of abilities of this kind makes many people doubt the wisdom of setting fixed ages for retirement.

It is still of interest to ask: From which years can we expect man's best work? The answer is important in case our culture is prolonging dependency by continuing students' education too long, when they ought to be producing on their own.

Performers who depend upon strength, speed,

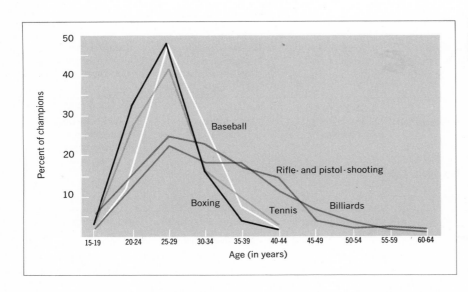

Fig. **4-7 How old are champions?** Ages at which championships have been won in sports. (After Lehman, 1938)

or precision of movement tend to reach their peaks of skill in the years from twenty-five to twenty-nine. Since we assume that champion performers are always well trained and eager to do their best, a study of the ages at which the championship is reached furnishes useful evidence of age as an

TABLE 4-8 AGE OF MAXIMUM RATE OF VERY SUPERIOR CONTRIBUTIONS				
GENERAL FIELD OF CREATIVE WORK	AGE AT TIME OF MAXIMUM RATE OF CONTRIBUTION			
	25–29	30–34	35–39	40–44
Physical sciences, mathematics, inventions	Chemistry	Mathematics Physics Electronics Practical inventions Surgical techniques	Geology Astronomy	
Biological sciences and medicine		Botany Classical descriptions of disease	Bacteriology Physiology Pathology Medical discoveries	
		Genetics Entomology Psychology		
Philosophy, education, and social sciences		Economics and political science		
			Logic Ethics Esthetics "General philosophy" Educational theory and practice	Metaphysics
			Social philosophy	
Musical compositions	Instrumental selections	Vocal solos Symphonies	Chamber music Nonsymphonic orchestral music Grand opera	Cantatas Light opera and musical comedy
Literary compositions	Lyrics and ballads (German) Odes Elegies Pastoral poetry Narrative poetry Sonnets Lyric poetry	Satiric poetry Short stories Comedies	Tragedies "Most influential books"	Novels "Best books" Best sellers Miscellaneous prose writings
Painting and sculpture		Oil paintings	American sculpture	Modern architecture
Source: Lehman (1953).				

element in skill. The ages at which championships were won in a number of sports are plotted in Figure 4-7. The sports that make less demand upon stamina and more upon precision (rifle- and pistol-shooting, billiards) do not show the rapid falling off with age characteristic of the more strenuous sports, such as tennis, baseball, and boxing. The leisure-time interests of adults correspond in part to these age changes in skill: as adults grow older, they turn to sports that can be played at a pace suited to their age.

But what about productive efforts in science, literature, and the arts? When are men at their best in creative work? The results of a large-scale study are summarized in Table 4-8. Here we find the ages at which men tend most frequently to make superior contributions to the fields specified in the table. The data were obtained by going to bibliographies and historical summaries of the various fields and by getting the cooperation of experts in sorting out the superior from the pedestrian performances. By then finding out the age of each man at the time of his discovery or most creative work, it is possible to chart the most productive years in each of the fields. In this way one can avoid the bias that comes from looking either for very young producers or very aged ones. For most of the fields the age of maximum productivity is between thirty and forty; for a few it is earlier, for a few later. Within each field, productivity begins before thirty and continues after forty; a generalized curve for the fields of science, mathematics, and invention is plotted in Figure 4-8. Although distinguished contributions are made throughout life, the rapid rise to the peak of productivity and the gradual decline thereafter are striking.

Eminent scientists, whether they achieve eminence early or late in life, continue to be productive throughout their lives, so that a relationship can be established between eminence and productivity. In the sciences and such other fields as music, general books, and linguistics, between one-third and two-thirds of the material is produced by only 10 percent of those active in the respective field (Dennis, 1955). These data raise fascinating but elusive problems. Do very productive people have

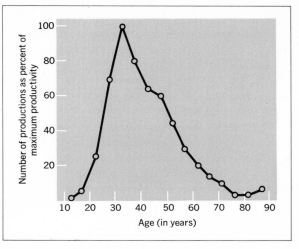

Fig. **4-8 Ages at which superior works were produced** This figure shows the ages at which 933 scientists, mathematicians, and inventors produced 1359 superior contributions. (After Lehman, 1953)

a better chance to hit upon something important? Do people who happen to achieve eminence early become motivated to remain productive? Further research is needed to obtain answers to these questions. We do know that people who are productive early are more likely than the less productive to continue to create in their later years, regardless of whether they attain eminence (Dennis, 1954a, 1954b).

Two major lessons can be learned from these data on the productivity of creative persons. The first is that the early adult years are important ones; it would probably be a good idea to place able people on their own at the youngest feasible age. The second is that some means should be found for continuing the creativity of those who show early promise. Equally impressive as the early age at which major contributions are made is the very rapid fall-off in contributions beginning, as shown in Figure 4-8, immediately beyond the high peak in the early thirties. It may be that society's rewards for early success are antithetical to creative work, as the contributor shifts to "better" jobs with loss of continuity of effort, takes on administrative duties, and meets excessive demands for lecturing away from his desk or laboratory.

Successful aging

Some changes with age are inevitable; successful aging does not mean retaining youth, but achieving satisfaction in the later years through wise choices. There are two main theories of how successful aging is achieved. The one stresses *activity,* the other *disengagement.*

The activity theory operates on the assumption that society often forces retirement when a person is still energetic and capable of productive participation in the life of the community. Hence he should make plans for his retirement, so that he can turn to other interests and find ways in which to see himself as continuing to be significant. The extreme of this idea is that a person wishes "to die with his boots on," that is, while still in the midst of things. This theory can of course be modified to take into account the lessened energies of older people; plans are proposed, for example, for "partial retirement," in which the person remains active on a part-time basis. This is familiar in university circles, where the emeritus professor, no longer conducting classes, commonly continues his research and writing.

The disengagement theory assumes that as a person gets older he views himself differently and can make a good adjustment through a gradual withdrawal from active participation and responsibility. This withdrawal is not forced upon him, but is at least in part a matter of his own choosing (Cummings and others, 1960). Instead of being preoccupied with what he is doing or achieving now, the disengaged person is content to reflect upon what he was and what he accomplished in the past.

Indications that disengagement is not merely a response to lessened capacity for social interaction, and to society's isolation of the older person, come from some studies of changes during the ages of forty to sixty-five. Gross measures of social competence show no changes over these years that can be associated directly with age (Havighurst, 1957). Careful personality studies, however, show that significant personality changes associated with age take place within these years, particularly as they

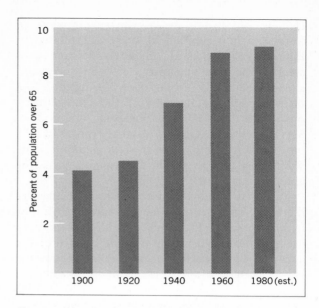

Fig. **4-9 The aged in the United States** The percentage of the total population aged 65 or over has more than doubled in the last half-century, though the trend shows signs of slackening. (U. S. Bureau of the Census)

bear on the image of the self and outlook for the future (Neugarten and others, 1964). It appears, then, that processes leading toward disengagement may start as early as the forties, even though full social competency is maintained during the next twenty or more years.

The problems of the later years of life have many facets. The person who has suffered a heart attack or some other debilitating illness is often demoralized by the experience, and he may require a period of psychological as well as physical rehabilitation. Loneliness owing to death of family members, children's moving away, or the inability to travel has to be confronted. Various activity centers for older people are being developed to meet these needs. The present scale of the problem is aggravated by the fact that the proportion of older people in the population is progressively increasing (Figure 4-9). With more research and inventiveness being directed toward the solution of these problems, it is certain that sound new policies can be proposed.

Summary

1. Changes during *pubescence* bring the greatest modifications in physiological processes during the lifetime of the individual. These changes differ between boys and girls, but there are similarities in the pattern of changes both undergo. Girls begin the puberal changes earlier and on the average reach maturity about two years before boys, but because of individual differences some boys go through puberal changes earlier than some girls.

2. The different rates of bodily growth have their psychological consequences. The adjustment problems of the late-maturing boy are aggravated by his falling behind his classmates in size and physical prowess. Early-maturing boys have many advantages in terms of self-confidence and capability. Cultural attitudes influence the effect that rate of maturing has on personality. For girls, rate of maturation is less important, although the advantage is still with the early maturer.

3. Specific adolescent problems arise in the areas of sex emancipation from home, relation to age mates, and arriving at standards of value. The peer culture becomes very important and is to some extent a distinctive subculture.

4. Adolescent conflicts may result in juvenile delinquency. *Individual delinquency,* based on personal problems, is distinguished from *social delinquency,* expressed in gang behavior.

5. The problems of adolescence do not end with the attainment of adulthood. But the problems of early adult life are more often those of vocational and marital choice rather than emotional conflict and insecurity.

6. *Sex roles* become differentiated in adult life. Studies of nonliterate cultures show that the differences depend only in part upon the biological roles of the two sexes; cultural arrangements and expectations determine many of the differences that we find.

7. Studies of marital happiness point up the fact of continuity of development, because the important predictors of marital happiness originate in childhood: the happiness of the child, the happiness of parents, and affectionate relations with parents and siblings. Once married, the important elements in a satisfactory relationship are mutual respect, tolerance, and agreement on common goals.

8. The years of greatest proficiency and productivity are those between the ages of twenty and forty. For some individuals, however, productivity may continue until late in life; those who are highly productive early in their careers are most likely to continue to be so.

9. Increased longevity creates new problems for those who pass the retirement age. There appears to be an important choice between *activity* and *disengagement* as approaches to successful aging.

Suggestions for further reading

There are a number of textbooks on adolescent psychology, such as Douvan and Adelson, *The adolescent experience* (1966), Adams, *Understanding adolescence* (1968), and Horrocks, *The psychology of adolescence* (3rd ed., 1969).

For many ways of viewing the adolescent, see Muuss, *Theories of adolescence* (1962). A useful book of readings on adolescent psychology is Grinder (ed.), *Studies in adolescence* (1963). *Carmichael's manual of child psychology* (3rd ed., 1970) edited by Mussen has considerable material relevant to adolescence; see especially Tanner's chapter on growth in adolescence.

For some of the problems of aging, see Neugarten and others, *Personality in middle and late life* (1964), and Williams and others, *Processes of aging* (1963).

PERCEPTUAL PROCESSES

sensory processes

ALL ORGANISMS DISCRIMINATE among stimuli that impinge upon them by way of sensitive tissues, which in the higher organisms take the form of sense organs. The senses are the input channels for information about the world. They enable us to appreciate the sights, sounds, and odors that surround us—to savor the taste of a vintage wine or to enjoy the tingle of a cold shower. They also are essential to our very survival in that they enable us to detect changes in the environment.

To understand behavior we need to know something of how the sensory mechanisms are constructed and how they mediate the sensations of light, sound, touch, taste, and the like. But perception goes beyond the discrimination of single stimuli; the human organism must be able to interpret and react to patterns of stimuli. He must be able to extract information from the array of stimulation provided by the environment. In this chapter we will consider the role of the specific sense organs in perceiving. In the next chapter we will turn to the factors involved in our perception of objects and events.

There are two different, but closely related approaches to the study of sensory processes. One approach emphasizes basic research. Its aim is to discover what aspects of the environment the sense organs respond to, how they register this information, and how it is conveyed to the brain. Such knowledge is a first step in the understanding of human thought and behavior.

The second approach to the study of sensory processes is concerned with more practical, or applied, problems. As our technology becomes increasingly complex it depends more and more upon accurate perceptual discriminations by human beings. The radar operator must be able to detect brief visual blips on his radar screen that indicate the approach of aircraft. The sonar operator must learn to discriminate between echoes returning from a whale or school of fish and those from a submarine. The pilot has to monitor an elaborate panel of instruments and make appropriate adjustments. The astronaut must make countless complex discriminations under conditions of weightlessness and acceleration that alter his normal functioning. The applied approach to research on sensory processes seeks to determine man's ability to discriminate and interpret sensory stimuli so that his capabilities can be matched to the task requirements.

Both the basic and the practical approach to an analysis of sensory mechanisms have contributed much to our understanding of these phenomena.

Some general characteristics of the senses

Absolute thresholds

A certain minimum of sense-organ stimulation is required before any sensory experience will be evoked. For example, a spot of light in a dark room must reach some measurable intensity before it can be distinguished from darkness, and a sound emitted in a soundproof room must reach a certain intensity level before it can be heard. The minimum physical energy necessary to activate a given sensory system is known as the *absolute threshold*. One method for determining the absolute threshold is simply to present the subject with a stimulus of given intensity and ask whether or not he detects it; on the next trial a different stimulus intensity is used, and so on, through a wide range of intensities. When such a procedure is used, the term "absolute threshold" is somewhat inappropriate because the investigator does not arrive at a *single* intensity value below which the subject never detects the stimulus and above which he always reports detecting it. Instead, there is a range of intensities over which the physical energy of the stimulus gradually moves from having no effect to having a partial effect (that is, it sometimes detected and sometimes not) to having a complete effect.

This region of partial effect is illustrated in Figure 5-1. The curve depicted in the figure is called a *psychophysical function* because it expresses the relationship between a "psychological"

variable (the experience of perceiving the stimulus) and a "physical" variable (the intensity of the stimulus). It plots the percentage of times the subject says, "Yes, I detect a stimulus," against a measure of the physical energy of the stimulus. Whenever the stimulus is below an energy level equal to three units the subject almost never re-

Fig. **5-1 Psychophysical function** Plotted on the ordinate is the percentage of times the subject responds "Yes, I detect the stimulus"; on the abscissa is the measure of the physical energy of the signal. Psychophysical functions can be obtained for any sensory modality; when vision is involved the function is sometimes called the "frequency-of-seeing curve."

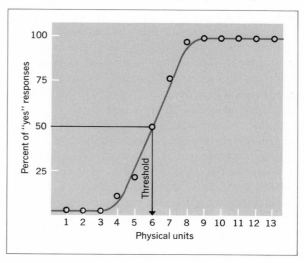

TABLE 5-1	SOME APPROXIMATE VALUES FOR ABSOLUTE THRESHOLDS
SENSE MODALITY	THRESHOLD
Vision	A candle flame seen at 30 miles on a dark, clear night
Hearing	The tick of a watch under quiet conditions at 20 feet
Taste	One teaspoon of sugar in two gallons of water
Smell	One drop of perfume diffused into the entire volume of a six-room apartment
Touch	Wing of a fly falling on your cheek from a distance of 1 centimeter

Source: Galanter (1962).

ports the presence of a stimulus, whereas above nine units he almost always reports it. Between three and nine units the relative frequency of reporting the presence of a stimulus gradually increases.

How do we define the threshold for a particular stimulus dimension when the performance can be characterized by a psychophysical function of the type presented in Figure 5-1? Is it the point where the subject's curve first appears to break away from zero (in this case at about three physical units) or where it finally appears to reach 100 percent responding (in this case at about nine units)? Obviously, the definition of a threshold must be somewhat arbitrary. On the basis of certain theoretical considerations, psychologists have agreed to define the *absolute threshold* as that value at which the stimulus is perceived 50 percent of the time. Thus, for the data displayed in Figure 5-1, the absolute threshold would be at six units.

Table 5-1 presents some estimates of absolute thresholds for various sense modalities in terms of physical measures that are intuitively meaningful. Of course, the absolute threshold varies considerably from one individual to the next. And the threshold for a particular individual will also vary from time to time, depending on his physical condition, his motivational state, and the conditions under which the observations are made.

Difference thresholds

In the same manner that a certain minimum amount of stimulation is required to evoke a sensory experience, there must also be a certain magnitude of difference between two stimuli before one can be distinguished from the other. The minimum amount of stimulation necessary to tell two stimuli apart is known as the *difference threshold*. Two reds must differ by some finite amount before they can be discriminated from each other; two tones must differ in intensity by a measurable amount before one can be heard as louder than the other. Thus, thresholds are identified at the transitions between no experience and some experience (the absolute threshold) and between no difference and some difference (the difference threshold).

Like the absolute threshold, the difference threshold is defined as a statistical quantity. It is the amount of change in physical energy necessary for a subject to detect a difference between two stimuli 50 percent of the time. Psychologists frequently use the term *just noticeable difference* (j.n.d.) to refer to this amount of change.

One remarkable feature of the human organism and, for that matter, of most animals, is that the difference threshold tends to be a constant fraction of the stimulus intensity. To illustrate, suppose we estimate the difference threshold for a subject judging weights. If he is given a 100-gram weight we note that his difference threshold is 2 grams; that is, the 100-gram weight must be compared to a weight of at least 102 grams in order for him to detect a j.n.d. about 50 percent of the time. Similarly, if we give him a 200-gram weight the difference threshold is 4 grams. For a 400-gram weight, the difference threshold is 8 grams; and for an 800-gram weight, the difference threshold is 16 grams. Note that the difference threshold relative to the weight being judged is constant:

$$\frac{2}{100} = \frac{4}{200} = \frac{8}{400} = \frac{16}{800} = .02$$

The above observation is known as *Weber's law*, named after Ernst Weber, who first pointed out the relationship in 1846. Stated mathematically, if I is the amount of stimulation taken as a referent, and ΔI is the increase in stimulation necessary for a j.n.d., then:

$$\frac{\Delta I}{I} = k$$

where k is a constant that does not depend on I. The quantity k is called *Weber's constant*. In our example, $k = .02$.

We may observe the operation of Weber's law in everyday experience: a twenty-minute increase in air-travel time from Los Angeles to San Francisco may be detected as a "just noticeable difference," but a similar increase in travel time from San Francisco to London may not; an increase of five dollars in the cost of a shirt is quite noticeable, whereas a similar increase in the cost of a suit may be of little concern.

Table 5-2 presents values of Weber's constant for various sense modalities. The tremendous range in values reflects the fact that some sensory systems are much more responsive to changes in the physical environment than are others.

It is interesting to conjecture about the aspects of the sensory system that make Weber's law hold, and many theories have been proposed. We shall not discuss these theories here, but the research initiated by them has made it clear that matters are more complex than indicated by Weber's law. Weber's law holds fairly well in the middle range

of sensory dimensions but is somewhat in error at the extremes, particularly at very low levels of stimulation.

While Weber's law applied only to thresholds, it was early extended by Fechner (1860) to the development of scales for measuring sensory experiences. By summing successive j.n.d.'s, he developed a scale for measuring how far a given stimulus was above threshold; this procedure in turn permitted him to measure the psychological distance between any two stimuli. His formulation of the relationship, commonly called the *Weber-Fechner law,* holds that the sensory experience bears a logarithmic relationship to the intensity of the physical stimulus. Modern workers in the study of sense distances have modified his law somewhat in order to fit empirical results more closely (Stevens, 1966). Relationships of this kind have proved useful, for example, to telephone engineers in specifying scales for loudness and pitch. They have also been used to scale complex stimulus dimensions such as consumer attitudes toward prices (Webb, 1961), stock market analyses (Osborne, 1959), and court penalties for crimes (Stevens, 1966).

Sensory adaptation

Although thresholds are always changing, their changes are not entirely haphazard. One consistent type of change, found within several senses, is called *sensory adaptation.* It refers to the reduction in sensitivity to stimulation as stimulation persists through time, and to the increase in sensitivity with lack of stimulation. It is a familiar phenomenon in vision, smell, and temperature, though not limited to these senses. When we have been in sunlight, our eyes become much less sensitive, so that if we enter a dimly lighted room we cannot see the objects about us until our eyes have become adapted. A person working in a fish market or a paint store soon becomes unaware of the odors around him. A room that feels hot to someone coming in from the cold may feel cold to someone who just had a hot bath.

The range of sensory adaptation can in some

[continued on page 112]

TABLE 5-2 WEBER'S CONSTANT	
SENSE MODALITY	WEBER'S CONSTANT
Pitch of a tone	1/333
Deep pressure, from skin and subcutaneous tissue	1/80
Visual brightness	1/60
Lifted weights	1/50
Loudness of a tone	1/10
Cutaneous pressure	1/7
Taste for saline solution	1/5
Source: Data are approximate, from various determinations.	

Approximate values of Weber's constant for various sensory discriminations. The smaller the fraction, the greater the differential sensitivity.

The problem of establishing thresholds involves some complications that can be illustrated by considering the following experiment. Suppose we wanted to determine the likelihood that a subject will detect a particular weak auditory signal. An experiment could be set up involving a series of trials, each initiated with a warning light followed by the auditory signal. The subject would be asked to indicate on each trial whether he heard the signal. Suppose that on one hundred such trials the subject reported hearing the signal sixty-two times. How should this result be interpreted? On each trial precisely the same signal is presented, and the subject's responses presumably tell us something about his ability to detect it. But if the subject knows the same tone will be presented on each trial, what prevents him from always saying "yes"? Obviously nothing, but we assume that he is honest and trying to do as good a job as possible. The task of detecting very weak signals is difficult, however, and even a conscientious subject will often be uncertain whether to respond yes or no on a given trial. Further, motives and expectations can influence our judgments; even the most reliable subject may unconsciously tend toward yes answers to impress the experimenter with his acuity.

To deal with this problem *catch trials*, on which there is no signal, can be introduced to see what the subject will do. The following results are typical of a subject's performance in an experiment involving several hundred trials, 10 percent of which are randomly selected as catch trials.

	Response	
	Yes	No
Signal trial	.89	.11
Catch trial	.52	.48

Each entry in the table represents the proportion of times the subject answered yes or no when the signal was or was not presented. For example, on 89 percent of the trials on which a signal was presented, the subject said, "yes, there was a signal." We refer to these correct responses as *hits*. When the subject says "yes, there was a signal" on a trial when the signal was not presented, the response is called a *false alarm*. In the example, the probability of a hit was .89 and the probability of a false alarm was .52.

What interpretation can be given to the fact that the subject falsely reported hearing the signal on 52 percent of the catch trials? We might conclude that the subject is careless or inattentive except for the fact that these results are typical of data obtained with dedicated, highly trained subjects. Even under the best of conditions subjects make false alarms. The answer to the question of how to interpret false alarms appears when some additional observations are made. Suppose that the subject is tested for several days, with the same signal used but with the percentage of catch trials varied from day to day. Results from such an experiment, in which the number of catch trials ranged from 10 percent to 90 percent, are given in the table in Figure 5-2. These data show that hits and false alarms both change as the proportion of catch trials to signal trials is manipulated. As the proportion of catch trials increases, the subject becomes aware of this fact (either consciously or unconsciously) and biases his judgments in favor of more "no" responses. Put another way, his *expectation* of a large number of catch trials causes him to inhibit "yes" responses, which leads to a decrease in both hits and false alarms.

Obviously, there is no fixed probability that the subject will detect a given intensity signal; the probability varies as the proportion of catch trials is manipulated. At first glance this is a discouraging picture, and one may question whether a simple measure can be devised to describe the subject's sensitivity level for a particular signal. Fortunately, recent developments have provided a clever answer. It involves plotting the hit and false alarm probabilities, as is done in the left graph in Figure 5-2. Note, for example, that the point farthest to the right is for data obtained when 10 percent of the trials were catch trials; referring to the table, the hit rate plotted on the ordinate is .89, and the false alarm

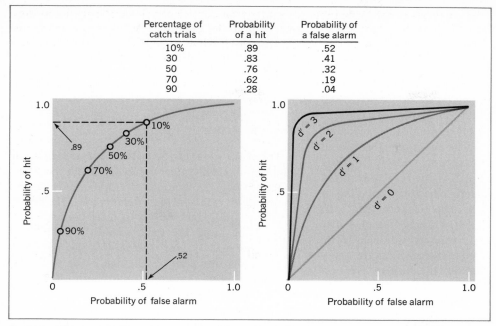

Percentage of catch trials	Probability of a hit	Probability of a false alarm
10%	.89	.52
30	.83	.41
50	.76	.32
70	.62	.19
90	.28	.04

Fig. **5-2** **ROC curves** The table presents data on the relationship between hits and false alarms as the percentage of catch trials is increased. The left figure plots these same data in the form of an ROC curve. The right figure presents ROC curves for several different values of d'. The more intense the signal, the higher the value of d'; the actual d' value for the data in the table is 1.18.

rate on the abscissa is .52. When all five points are plotted an orderly picture emerges. The points all fall on a symmetric bow-shaped curve. If we ran still other experiments with the same signal but different percentages of catch trials, the hit and false alarm probabilities would differ from those in the table but would fall somewhere on the curve. This curve is called the *receiver-operating-characteristic curve,* or more simply the ROC curve. The term "ROC" describes the fact that the curve measures the operating, or sensitivity, characteristics of a person receiving signals.

The points that are plotted in the left figure are for a certain signal intensity. When a stronger signal is used in the trials, the ROC curve arches higher; when the signal is weaker, the ROC curve is closer to the diagonal line. Thus, the degree of bowedness of the ROC curve is related to the intensity of the signal, and a measure of it gives the subject's sensitivity level to the signal. The measure used to define the bowedness of the ROC curve is called d'. The right-hand graph in Figure 5-2 gives several ROC curves for d', ranging from 0 through 3.

Thus, hit and false alarm rates can be converted into a d' value that is a psychological dimension measuring the subject's sensitivity level for a particular signal. Manipulating the percentage of catch trials, or any of a number of other variables, will affect hits and false alarms for a fixed signal, but the proportions will generally fall on the ROC curve defined by a particular d' value. Theoretical work based on this method for measuring sensitivity is called *signal detectability theory* (Green and Swets, 1966). Even in a simple task like signal detection, performance is not just a function of the signal intensity but depends on the experience, motives, and expectations of the subject. Signal detectability theory permits one to separate out these factors and obtain a relatively pure measure of the sensory process. This measure, d', characterizes the sensory capacities of a subject, independent of nonsensory variables that influence his judgments.

cases be quite large. For example, the longer the eye is in total darkness, the more sensitive it is to visual stimuli. As a rough indication of the magnitude of the adaptation effect, the eye in its most sensitive state (after a long period in total darkness) will respond to a stimulus 1/100,000 as intense as that required when the eye is least sensitive (after a sustained exposure to bright light).

The visual sense

Each of the sense organs responds to a particular type of physical energy. The eye is sensitive to that portion of the electromagnetic energy traveling through space that we call light. It is convenient to think of electromagnetic energy as traveling in waves, with wavelengths (the distance from one crest of a wave to the next) varying tremendously from the shortest cosmic rays (10 trillionths of an inch) to long radio waves that may measure many miles. The wavelengths that the human eye perceives as light extend only from about 380 millimicrons ($m\mu$) to about 780 $m\mu$. Since a millimicron is one millionth of a millimeter, it is clear that visible energy is but a very small section of the total electromagnetic spectrum.

Sir Isaac Newton discovered more than three hundred years ago that when sunlight passes through a prism it breaks into a band of varicolored light such as we see in a rainbow. The colors correspond to wavelengths, the red end of the rainbow being produced by the longer waves and the violet end by the short waves. The prism spreads the light waves out by bending the short wavelengths more than the long ones. A band produced by sunlight passing through a prism is described as a *solar spectrum* (see Figure 5-10). The eye can be injured by infrared rays just beyond the red end of the spectrum and by ultraviolet rays at the other end, although these rays are not perceived as light.

The eye will respond to other forms of stimulation than light waves. Pressure on the eyeball or the passing of an electric current through the head will produce the sensation of light. These observations point up the fact that light is actually a quality produced in the eye when it is stimulated. The visible portion of the electromagnetic spectrum is called "light" because it is what usually produces that sensation.

The human eye

The main parts of the human eye are shown in Figure 5-3. Light enters the eye through the transparent *cornea*, the amount of light being regulated by the *pupil;* the *lens* then focuses the light on the sensitive surface, the *retina*. Constriction and dilation of the pupil are under control of the autonomic nervous system (see p. 45): the parasympathetic division controls the change in pupil size as a function of changes in illumination (in much the same way as we increase the shutter opening of a camera to admit more light on a dark day and decrease the opening under conditions of bright illumination). The sympathetic division acts to dilate the pupil under conditions of strong emotion, either pleasant or unpleasant. Even under conditions of mild emotional arousal or interest, systematic changes in pupil size can be detected

Fig. **5-3 A cross section of the left human eye** The size of the pupil is regulated by the iris, the diaphragm that gives the eye its color. The shape of the lens is regulated by the ciliary muscles. The external muscles that move the eye are not shown.

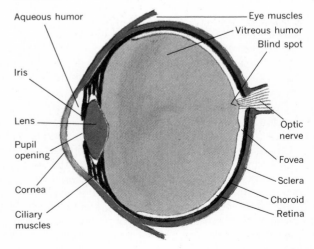

Aqueous humor
Iris
Lens
Pupil opening
Cornea
Ciliary muscles
Eye muscles
Vitreous humor
Blind spot
Optic nerve
Fovea
Sclera
Choroid
Retina

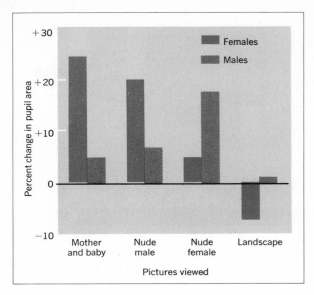

Fig. **5-4 Changes in pupil size as a response to pictures** Changes in pupil size were recorded on film and later measured. The figure shows the percentage of increase or decrease in pupil area in response to various pictures for both male and female subjects. The amount of light entering the eye was constant for all pictures. The sexes differ quite markedly with regard to the interest value of these particular pictures. A later study showed that homosexuals could be distinguished from normal males on the basis of pupillary responses to pictures of female pinups. (Data from Hess and Polt, 1960)

by means of sensitive photographic equipment (Figure 5-4).

The retina, the light-sensitive surface at the back of the eye, is composed of three main layers: (1) the *rods* and *cones,* the photosensitive cells that convert light energy into nerve impulses; (2) the *bipolar cells,* which make synaptic connections with the rods and cones; and (3) the *ganglion cells,* the fibers of which form the optic nerve (Figure 5-5). Strangely enough, the rods and cones form the *bottom* layer of the retina. The eye is a very imperfect optical system. The light waves not only have to pass through the lens and liquids that fill the eyeball, none of which is a perfect transmitter of light, but they have to penetrate the network of blood vessels and the bipolar and ganglion cells that lie on the inside of the eye before reaching the photoreceptors where light is converted into nervous impulses (note "direction of light" arrow

in Figure 5-5). Even when the light finally reaches the rods and cones it has to strike them at an angle because the photosensitive area of these cells is pointed toward the back of the eye rather than the front. From the standpoint of efficient optics it is surprising that we can see as well as we do.

If you stare at a homogeneous background, such as a blue sky, it is possible to see the movement of blood through the retinal blood vessels that lie in front of the rods and cones. The blood vessel walls can be seen as pairs of narrow lines in the periphery of our vision, and the disk-shaped objects that appear to move between these lines are the tiny platelets of the blood as it flows through the vessel.

The most sensitive portion of the eye in normal daylight vision is a small part of the retina called the *fovea.* Not far from the fovea is an insensitive

Fig. **5-5 Rods and cones and their connections** Shown here are the main layers of the retina: rods and cones, bipolar cells, and ganglion cells. The bipolar cells receive impulses from one or more rods or cones and transmit the impulses to the nerve fibers, whose cell bodies are shown as the ganglion cells. In A is a typical arrangement of several rods connected by one "mop" bipolar cell, in B an arrangement of one cone attached to a single "midget" bipolar cell, while in C some (but not all) of the more complex patterns are shown. Integration across the retina is accomplished by horizontal cells connecting rods and cones, and by internal association cells at the ganglion cell level, as well as by the mop bipolar cells. (After Polyak, 1941)

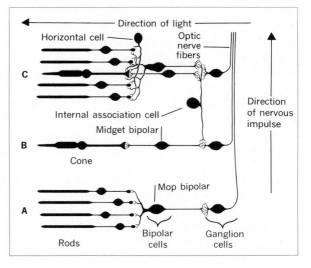

Fig. **5-6 Locating the blind spot**

A. With the right eye closed, stare at the upper right cross. Move the book back and forth about 1 foot from the eye. When the black circle on the left disappears, it is projected on the blind spot.

B. With the right eye closed, stare at the lower right cross. Move the book back and forth again. When the white space falls in the blind spot, the black line appears to be continuous. This phenomenon helps us to understand why we are not ordinarily aware of the blind spot.

area, called the *blind spot,* where the nerve fibers from the ganglion cells of the retina come together to form the *optic nerve.* Although we are not normally aware of the blind spot, its existence can easily be demonstrated, as is shown in Figure 5-6.

Figure 5-7 shows the optic nerve fibers leading from each eye to the cortical areas where vision is represented (the *occipital lobes*). Notice that some of the fibers go to the occipital lobe of the corresponding cerebral hemisphere (that is, from the right eye to the right cerebral hemisphere and from the left eye to the left hemisphere), whereas other fibers cross over at a junction called the *optic chiasma* and go to the opposite hemisphere. Fibers from the right sides of both eyes go to the right hemisphere of the cerebral cortex, and fibers from the left sides of both eyes go to the left hemisphere. Consequently, damage to the occipital lobe of one hemisphere (say, the left) will result in blind areas in *both* eyes (the left sides of both eyes). This fact is sometimes helpful in pinpointing the location of a cerebral tumor or injury.

Rods and cones

The retinal cells of special interest are the photoreceptors, the cylindrical rods and the more bulbous cones. The cones are active only in daylight vision. They permit us to see both *achromatic colors* (white, black, and the intermediate grays) and *chromatic colors* (red, green, blue, etc.). The rods function mainly in vision under reduced illumination (at twilight or night) and permit us to see only achromatic colors. Although the rods respond differently to different wavelengths, they transmit colors only as various shades of gray. The two types of photoreceptors differ in much the same way that color film differs from black and white film. Black and white film is more sensitive than color film and can produce a picture even under conditions of dim illumination. Color film requires much more intense light for proper operation.

More than 6 million cones and 100 million rods are distributed, somewhat unevenly, throughout the retina. The fovea contains only cones—some

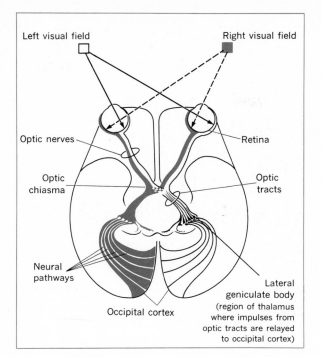

Fig. **5-7 Visual pathways** Light waves from objects in the right visual field fall on the left half of each retina; light waves from the left visual field impinge on the right half of each retina. The optic nerve bundles from each eye meet at the optic chiasma, where the nerve fibers from the inner, nasal half of the retina cross over and go to opposite sides of the brain. Thus stimuli impinging on the right side of each retina are transmitted to the occipital cortex of the right cerebral hemisphere, and stimuli impinging on the left side of each retina are transmitted to the left cerebral hemisphere. In terms of the visual field this means that objects in the right visual field are projected to the left cerebral hemisphere, while objects in the left visual field are projected to the right hemisphere.

50,000 of them packed together in an area smaller than a square millimeter. Outside the fovea are both rods and cones, with the cones decreasing in number from the center of the retina to the periphery. The rods are connected in groups, each of which has one neuron running to the optic nerve. The cones in the periphery of the retina are grouped together in units along with the rods, but each of the cones in the fovea has its own "private wire" to the brain (see Figure 5-5). Our vision is more acute when light waves strike the fovea, because the nonconverging "private line" does not

mix signals. It is for this reason that we turn our head to look directly at an object when we want to see it clearly. Under dim illumination, however, when the cones are not operative, we can more easily detect a faint stimulus, such as a dim star, if we do not look directly at it but let its image fall just outside the foveal region.

Although the rods will respond to a much dimmer stimulus than will the cones, the image they give is less clear. At night objects have indistinct outlines and lack much of the detail that is seen in daylight. When we remember that rods are grouped in their connections to bipolar and ganglion cells, we can realize why this would be the case. Because signals from many rods converge on a single optic nerve fiber, interpretation by the brain is less specific than it would be for the "private wire" cone cells in the fovea. In daylight the rods in the periphery of the retina serve as a warning system. When we see something colorless in the periphery of our field of vision, we quickly shift

Fig. **5-8 Visibility curves** There are two visibility functions, one for cones and the other for rods. The rods are far more sensitive than the cones throughout most of the spectrum, except at the red end, where they are about equally sensitive. Note that the cones are maximally sensitive (555 mμ) in the greenish-yellow range, whereas the rods respond maximally (511 mμ) in the bluish-green band.

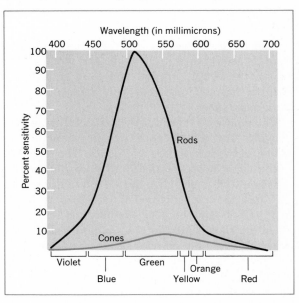

our eyes so that the image falls on the fovea, where we have maximum acuity.

Another difference between vision under high and low illumination is in the perceived brightness of different wavelengths at some fixed intensity. Cones are most responsive to wavelengths in the greenish-yellow part of the spectrum, while rods, although still giving only achromatic vision, are more sensitive to blue-green wavelengths (Figure 5-8). Thus in daylight yellow appears brighter, while at twilight (when the visual system begins shifting from cone to rod vision) blue appears brighter. A yellow flower and a blue one may appear equally bright in daylight, but as night approaches the blue flower appears brighter while the yellow one begins to appear darker.

Dark adaptation

The transition from day to night vision takes place gradually as daylight diminishes. At twilight both the cones and rods are operating but neither with full effectiveness. That is why motorists find driving hazardous at dusk. A sudden change from conditions of light to dark, or vice versa, is even more difficult to adjust to. It takes several minutes for the eye to shift from dim light to brightness, and even longer to adjust from bright light to darkness. We have all experienced the difficulty of finding our way to an empty seat when entering a dark theater. After a few minutes your eyes become accustomed to the dark, and you are able to see the people around you even though the lighting has not changed. You have undergone *dark adaptation.*

The course of dark adaptation (see Figure 5-9) provides further evidence for the difference in action between the rods and cones. The first part of the curve shows that the cones gradually become sensitive to fainter lights, but after five minutes in the dark their sensitivity has increased as much as it will, as measured by the absolute threshold. Then the rods continue to adapt and become appreciably more sensitive for about a half-hour. The sensitivity of the dark-adapted eye depends upon the wavelength of the light; it is much more sensitive to lights with wavelengths in the blue-green

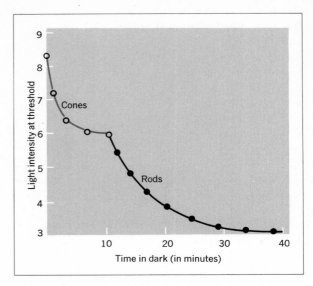

Fig. **5-9 The course of dark adaptation** The subject looks at a bright light until the retina has become light adapted. When he is then placed in darkness he becomes increasingly sensitive to fainter test flashes as the retina gradually becomes dark adapted. The curve shows the minimum light intensity for the test flash to be seen. The unfilled data points indicate at which points the color of the test flash was clearly visible; the filled data points indicate when the test flash appeared colorless. Note the sharp break in the curve at about 10 minutes, which is called the rod-cone break. By changing the color of the light flash or the area of the retina tested, it can be shown that the first part of the curve describes adaptation of the cones, and the second, adaptation of the rods. (Data are approximate, from various determinations)

region than to the longer wavelengths in the red region. This fact has had an important practical implication for individuals who must work in a darkened room or shift quickly from conditions of light to dark, such as a photographer, x-ray technician, or a ship's navigator on night duty. Wearing red goggles or working in a room illuminated by red light greatly reduces the time required for dark adaptation. Since red light stimulates the cones but not the rods, the rods remain in a state of dark adaptation. The person can see well enough to work under conditions of red light and still be almost completely dark adapted when it becomes necessary to go into the dark.

The process of dark adaptation is largely a matter of chemical changes in the rods. A reddish substance called *rhodopsin,* extracted from the rods in the retina, bleaches to yellow when exposed to daylight. Furthermore, it is bleached by lights of different wavelengths in a manner that corresponds to the sensitivity of the dark-adapted eye to these wavelengths. Rhodopsin appears to be the intermediary between light entering the eye and the activity of the sensory nerves that leads to seeing. When rhodopsin is stimulated by light, it decomposes into several substances, and this chemical reaction initiates the nerve impulse. The breakdown products change spontaneously back into rhodopsin under all light conditions, but the rate of change is much faster under dim illumination. In the dark, rhodopsin continues to build up so that the dark-adapted eye is much more sensitive to light than an eye that is continuously exposed to light.

One of the break-down products in the rhodopsin cycle is a form of vitamin A; a deficiency of vitamin A in the diet will prevent the rod cells from synthesizing sufficient rhodopsin and thus produces what is called *night blindness.* Rats, whose retinas consist almost entirely of rods, will show an increasing loss of visual sensitivity when fed on a diet deficient in vitamin A and will become permanently blind if so deprived for as long as ten months (Dowling, 1966). The person on a well-balanced diet, however, gets sufficient vitamin A to keep his rods functioning at peak performance; going on a carrot binge will not increase the sensitivity of his night vision.

Color

For the human subject the color spectrum fades into invisibility at the red end and at the violet end (Figure 5-10).[1] We are able to see, however, some vivid colors that do not exist in the spectrum at all; they do not correspond to any single wavelength but can be produced by mixing wavelengths. These are the purples redder than the violet end of the spectrum and the red that looks "purest" to most normal eyes. The reddest part of

[1] A useful mnemonic for remembering the order of colors on the spectrum involves the coined name "ROY G. BIV," which is a list of the first letters of the colors: *r*ed, *o*range, *y*ellow, *g*reen, *b*lue, *i*ndigo, and *v*iolet.

the solar spectrum looks a little yellowish to the human eye.

An interesting relationship exists among colors. If the spectral colors are wrapped in their natural order around the circumference of a circle, allowing room between the red and violet ends of the spectrum for the purples and reds not found on the spectrum, the colors opposite each other on the circle will be *complementary.* That is, if lights of these colors are mixed in proper proportions, they disappear to a neutral gray. Figure 5-11 presents such a color circle, with specimen complementary colors. For convenience in remembering the positions, we usually name the main complementary pairs as blue-yellow and red-green, although the yellow complementary to blue is slightly orange, and the green complementary to red is really a blue-green (see Figure 5-10).

Those familiar with painting will object to naming yellow and blue as complementaries, because those pigments when mixed give green, not gray. We are talking here about mixing *lights,* not pigments. The principles of mixture in the two cases are not contradictory, though the explanation of the difference is somewhat involved. The mixture of lights is an *additive* mixture, while the mixture of pigments is a *subtractive* mixture because of the way in which pigments selectively absorb some of the light. Light is the source of all color, and pigments are simply reflectors or absorbers of color. They achieve their color by absorbing, or subtracting, certain parts of the spectrum and reflecting the parts that remain. For example, the pigment in the chlorophyll of plants absorbs most of the purple, blue, and red wavelengths of light; the green that remains is reflected back to the eye, so we see most vegetation as various shades of green. Black pigment absorbs all wavelengths and reflects none; white pigment reflects equally all the colors of light. Additive mixtures may be studied in the laboratory by the use of colored lights or the color wheel; subtractive mixtures by light through colored filters (see Figure 5-12).

Some of the colors on the color circle appear to us to be more elementary than others; that is, they appear to be composed of a single hue. These elementary colors are called *psychological primaries,* and usually four primary colors are named: *red, yellow, green,* and *blue.* Between them are "secondary" colors, in which the primary components are still identifiable: orange between red and yellow, yellow-greens between yellow and green, blue-greens between green and blue, and purples and violets between blue and red. Another set of primaries is called *color-mixture primaries.* Any three widely spaced colors on the spectrum can be used to provide all the other colors by additive mixture. The three colors usually chosen are a *red,* a *green,* and a *blue.* For this purpose, the red and green that are chosen should yield yellow when mixed.

Psychological dimensions of color

Light waves can be precisely described through the measurement of wavelengths and amplitude (the height of the wave). But when man tries to describe what he sees, he must resort to using three somewhat inexact dimensions: hue, brightness, and saturation. *Hue* refers to the name of the color. The circumference of the color circle provides the scale along which the hues can be placed in order. There the hues follow the order of shortest to the longest visible wavelength.

Another dimension along which colors can be scaled is *brightness.* The achromatic colors have only the dimension of brightness from very dark (black) to very bright (white). The physical basis of brightness is primarily the energy of the light source, which corresponds to the amplitude of the wave. But brightness also depends to some extent upon wavelength. Yellow, for example, appears slightly brighter than certain red and blue wavelengths, even when all three have equal amplitudes.

A third dimension along which colors can be scaled is *saturation,* which refers to the apparent purity of the color. Highly saturated colors appear to be pure hues, without any gray, while colors of low saturation appear close to gray. The primary physical correlate of saturation is the complexity of the light wave. A light wave composed of only one or a few different wavelengths will produce the most highly saturated color. Light waves composed of many components result in colors of low saturation. However, as colors of a single wavelength become brighter (merge into white) or darker (merge into black) they begin to lose the apparent purity of their hues; a reduction in their saturation is concomitant with the change in brightness.

The color solid

The relationship between the three dimensions of hue, brightness, and saturation will become clearer if we look at the color solid (Figure 5-13), which represents all three simultaneously. The dimension of hue is represented by points around the circumference; saturation, by points along the radius, going from a pure or highly saturated color on the outside to a gray or unsaturated color in the center; and brightness, by points along the vertical axis going toward black at the bottom and toward white at the top. (The color plate does not show the actual gradations of gray going from black to white along the central axis.) You can see that the reds and purples become pink as light gray is added; the oranges and yellows become variations of brown as they become less saturated. On any vertical half-slice taken through the center of the solid, all the colors are the same hue (wavelength) but vary in brightness and saturation.

The color solid helps in our understanding of the relationship between brightness and saturation. The most highly saturated colors are of medium brightness. The color solid tapers to a point at both top and bottom. Consequently, as colors increase or decrease in brightness from the medial circumference, they become less saturated, approaching at the extremes either black or white, which are by definition without hue and therefore of zero saturation.

Color blindness

We may conveniently think of the normal eye as discriminating three pairs of colors: light-dark and the complementaries yellow-blue and red-green. All other combinations can be derived from these. Color blindness may show as a deficiency in one or two of these systems, the light-dark system remaining intact if the person can see at all. The person with normal vision is called a *trichromat*. If a person lacks one system but has use of the two others, he is called a *dichromat*. A dichromat is partially colorblind. Finally, if only the light-dark system remains, the person is a *monochromat* and totally colorblind.

By far the most common form of color blindness is red-green blindness, with the blue-yellow and light-dark systems intact. This deficiency affects some 7 percent of men but less than 1 percent of women. Total color blindness, in which the person sees merely black, white, and gray, is extremely rare; yellow-blue blindness, in which red-green discrimination is preserved, is rarer still.

Many colorblind persons are unaware of their defect because they are able to make such skillful use of their remaining color discrimination, combining it with the learned colors of familiar objects. Because our color vocabulary is not clear for unsaturated colors, the colorblind person can make some mistakes on these troublesome colors without being noticed.

Many tests are available for the detection of color blindness. They usually require the subject to read a figure composed of colored dots on a background of other colored dots (Figure 5-14). The colors are chosen so as to confuse subjects who have the various forms of color deficiency.

Is there any way of telling what color the colorblind person actually sees? We can be sure of the colors that look alike to him because he will confuse them when, for example, he attempts to sort out colored yarns. But we can go further than that, thanks to a few cases of people who are colorblind in only one eye (Hsia and Graham, 1965). We know that for the red-green blind, blues and yellows look very much the same as they do to those with normal eyes, and these, in combination with gray, are all that he sees. He has other words in his color vocabulary, however, so that he will call "green" the yellow of low saturation (that is, a grayish yellow) that he sees when he looks at

a lawn, and he will call "red" the grayish yellow that he sees when he looks at a fire engine.

Afterimages and color contrast

If you stare at a *red* circle and then look at a plain gray surface, you are likely to see a *green* circle on it; that is, you experience a *negative afterimage*. It is negative because green is the complementary color of red. Not all afterimages are in the complementary color—after staring at a very bright light you are likely to see a whole succession of colors—but seeing the complementary color is very common.

Complementary colors can also serve to enhance each other. When two complementary colors occur side by side, each color appears more highly saturated than it would when placed next to a noncomplementary color. This effect, termed *simultaneous contrast,* is one reason for making pennants of such complementary pairs as red and green and yellow and blue.

The facts of vision are enormously complex, and until our knowledge is more precise we must be prepared for exceptions to many of our generalizations. It was mentioned above that the afterimage need not always be in the complementary color. Another exception is worth noting. Usually dark surroundings make a light area seem lighter, and light surroundings make the enclosed area seem darker. But under some conditions there is what is called a *spreading effect,* so that dark areas make neighboring portions appear darker and light areas make neighboring portions appear lighter. We lack explanations of these seemingly contradictory effects, and they set problems for future investigators. Spreading effect, afterimage, and a contrast phenomenon are illustrated in Figures 5-15 through 5-17.

Theories of color vision

Exactly how the photoreceptors of the retina manage to send a different message to the brain for each of the many colors in the spectrum has been a question that has puzzled scientists for many years. Each attempt to explain how the eye sees color has taken as its starting point one of the three sets of facts about color that we have just discussed: color mixture, color contrast and afterimages, and color blindness.

One of the earliest theories of color vision—proposed by Thomas Young, an English physicist, in 1802 and modified by the German physiologist Hermann von Helmholtz a half-century later—was based on the fact that three colors are sufficient to produce all the colors in the spectrum. The Young-Helmholtz theory proposes three different kinds of color receptors, each maximally sensitive to a different wavelength (one sensitive to red wavelengths, one to blue, and one to green). All other colors are somehow produced by a combined stimulation of these receptors. Yellow is produced when red and green receptors are stimulated simultaneously. White is produced when all three receptors are stimulated simultaneously. The modern form of this theory attempts to link three kinds of cones (or three kinds of cone substances) with the three colors.

One of the chief difficulties with the Young-Helmholtz theory has been its inability to explain some of the facts of color blindness. If yellow is produced by activity in red and green receptors, how is it that a person with red-green color blindness has no difficulty seeing yellow? Another color theory, formulated by Ewald Hering in 1870, attempted to solve this problem. Hering felt that the Young-Helmholtz theory did not adequately reflect visual experience. He based his theory on the *psychological primaries* rather than the color-mixing primaries and argued that yellow is as basic a color as red, blue, or green. It does not appear to be a mixture of other colors, as orange appears to be a mixture of red and yellow, or purple a mixture of red and blue.

Hering was impressed with the facts of *color contrast* and *afterimages,* by the appearance of red-green and blue-yellow as pairs in so many circumstances. He proposed that there were three types of cones. One type responded to degrees of brightness, the black-white continuum. The other two types were color cones; one provided the basis for red-green perception and the other for blue-

yellow. Each receptor was assumed to function in two ways. One color of the pair was produced when the receptor was in a building-up phase (*anabolic*), and the other appeared when the receptor was in a tearing-down phase (*catabolic*). The two phases cannot occur at the same time in a given receptor; when a yellow-blue cone is stimulated it responds either with yellow or blue. It cannot react both ways simultaneously. That is why, according to the theory, we never see a red-green or a blue-yellow, whereas it is possible to see a reddish blue or greenish yellow. When stimulation is withdrawn, as in the afterimage experiment, the contrasting color appears because the anabolic-catabolic process is reversed. When we look at a blue circle and then transfer our gaze to a white sheet of paper, a yellow circle appears when the catabolic process takes over (see Figure 5-16). Hering's theory has become known as the *opponent-process theory*. In its modern form this theory assumes that the opponent processes take place not in the cones but in coding mechanisms further toward the brain in the optic system.

Recent developments suggest that both theories may be partially correct. MacNichol (1964), using a procedure called *microspectrophotometry,* was able to direct different wavelengths of light through single cones in the human retina and analyze the energy transmitted by means of a computer. He identified three kinds of light-sensitive pigments in the cones: one type primarily sensitive to wavelengths in the blue band, one sensitive to green, and a third sensitive to yellow. Although the third cone type had its peak sensitivity at 577 mμ (which is yellow), these cones were also sensitive to the longer wavelengths (up to 650 mμ) of the yellowish-red part of the spectrum. These measurements appear to support the Young-Helmholtz theory, although it is not clear whether the three cone types should be called blue, green, and yellow, or blue, green, and red.

At the same time, recordings taken with microelectrodes give evidence of an "on" and "off" type of process in bipolar cells and in cells of the lateral geniculate body—that portion of the thalamus where visual impulses are relayed to the visual cortex (see Figure 5-7). Some cells respond with

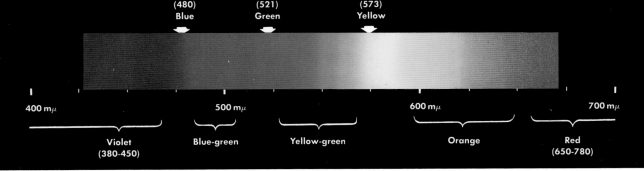

Fig. **5-10** **The solar spectrum** The colors are in the order of the rainbow, as seen when sunlight is sent through a prism.

Fig. **5-11** **A color circle showing complementary colors** The colors opposite each other, if in proper proportions, will mix on a color wheel to yield the neutral gray at the center. Wavelengths are indicated around the circle in mμ. Note that the spectral colors lie in their natural order on the circle, but their spacing is not uniform by wavelength. The circle also includes the nonspectral reds and purples.

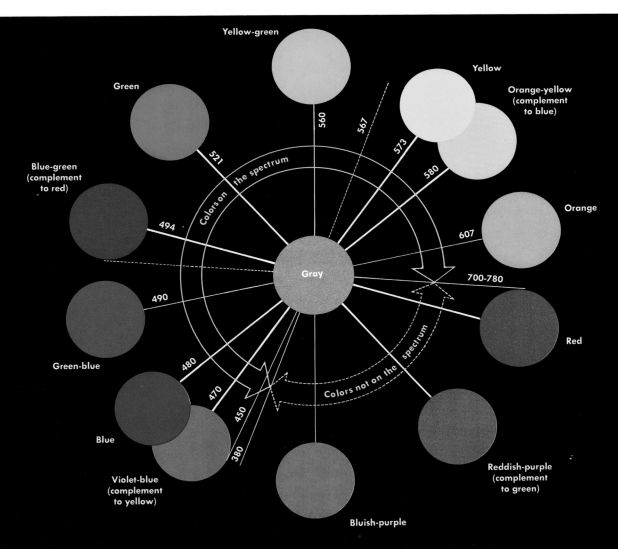

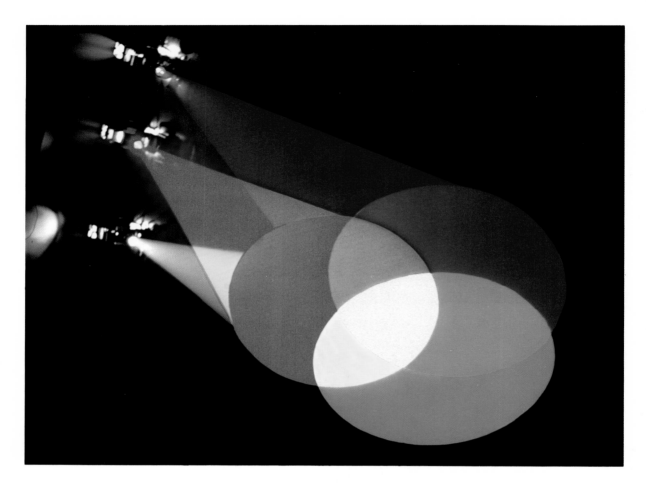

Fig. **5-12 Additive and subtractive color mixtures** Additive color mixture (illustrated by the top figure) takes place when lights are mixed or when sectors of colored papers are mixed by rotation on a color wheel. Red and green lights combine to give yellow, green and bluish-purple to give blue, and so on. The three colors overlap in the center to give white. Mixture of any two of the colors produces the complement of the third, as shown in the triangular portions.

Subtractive color mixture (illustrated by the bottom figure) takes place when pigments are mixed or when light is transmitted through colored filters placed one over another. Usually, blue-green and yellow will mix to give green, and complementary colors will reduce to black, as in the example given. Unlike an additive mixture, one cannot always tell from the color of the components what color will result. For example, blue and green will commonly yield blue-green by subtractive mixture, but with some filters they may yield red. Note that in the diagram the triangular portions are the original complementary colors used in the additive mixture, but here they appear as a result of subtractive mixture. (Fritz Goro for LIFE Magazine, © Time Inc.)

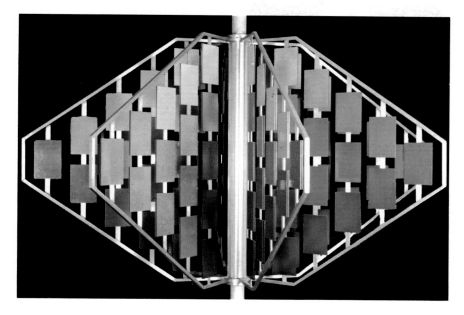

Fig. **5-13 The color solid** The three dimensions of color can be represented on a double cone: hue is represented by points around the circumference, saturation by points along the radius, and brightness by points on the vertical axis. A vertical slice from the color solid shows differences in saturation and brightness of a single hue. (Harbrace photo)

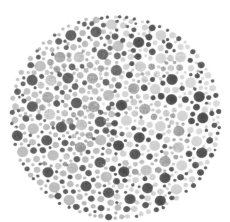

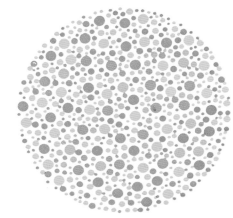

Fig. **5-14 Tests for color blindness** Two plates from the Dvorine Pseudo-Isochromatic series of color-blindness tests. In the left-hand plate, those with certain kinds of red-green blindness see only the number 5; others see only the 9; still others, no number at all. Those with normal vision see 95.

Similarly, in the plate at right, the person with normal vision sees the number 28, whereas those with red-green blindness see no number at all. (After I. Dvorine, Dvorine Pseudo-Isochromatic Plates, 1953, reproduced by permission of the author)

Fig. **5-15 The spreading effect** The same red is used throughout the strip. But the red with black looks darker than the red with white. (After Evans, 1948)

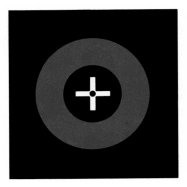  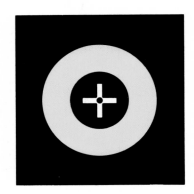

Fig. **5-16 Negative afterimages** Look steadily for about 20 seconds at the dot inside the blue circle; then transfer your gaze to the dot inside the gray rectangle. Now do the same with the dot inside the yellow circle. What do you see? (After Evans, 1948)

Fig. **5-17 Simultaneous contrast** Note the darkening effect on the gray patch when it is against white; the same patch of gray against black looks much lighter. A gray patch against a colored background tends to take on the complementary hue; the effect is much increased if a piece of thin tissue paper is placed over the colors. With colors that are approximately complementary (as in the red and green patches), there is an enhancement through contrast. For this reason, pennants are often red and green or yellow and blue.

a burst of impulses when stimulated by short wavelengths but are inhibited (respond as "off" cells) during illumination with long wavelengths, showing a burst of firing when stimulation ceases. Other cells are active when stimulated by long wavelengths and inhibited by short wavelengths. These results indicate an opponent-process of some kind operating not in the cones themselves, but further along in the pathway from the eye to the brain (DeValois and Jacobs, 1968).

At this point of scientific development it appears that color vision is a two-stage process: the retina contains pigments that respond differentially to the lights of three different colors; these responses are encoded into two-color on-off signals by cells further along in the optic system for transmission to the higher visual centers. A final theory of color vision may be a modification of this two-stage theory, or it may be an entirely different formulation based on future research. The interesting feature is that two theories, those of Hering and Young-Helmholtz, proposed over a century ago, have had to wait until recent technological developments (microspectrophotometry and single-neuron recording) could provide verification of their propositions.

Neural processing of visual information

Research on neural activity during visual stimulation suggests that much of the information transmitted to the brain is concerned with differences and changes in the environment. Because the rods and cones of the human eye are so minute and difficult to isolate for study, much of this research has been done with lower organisms. The horseshoe crab is a particularly good subject because one of its eyes is composed of over 800 individual receptor cells, each with its own lens and nerve fiber going directly to the brain. An electrode can be placed on a single fiber and its response to light stimulation measured. It has been shown that different light intensities cause the fiber to fire at different frequencies, indicating that intensity information is conveyed to the brain by the rate of nerve firings.

If a light is projected onto a single receptor, causing its fiber to begin firing, and a neighboring receptor is then stimulated, the original fiber will begin to fire at a slower rate. The activation of the second receptor is inhibiting the first. This inhibitory effect is exerted mutually among the receptors so that each inhibits, and is inhibited by, its neighbor. The impulse from each receptor flows out its optic nerve, but part of the impulse is diverted into horizontal nerve cells and flows to neighboring retinal units to affect them negatively (Ratliff, 1965). This mechanism, called *recurrent inhibition,* has interesting consequences. Suppose that both receptor units A and B are stimulated with a light. Now if we also stimulate C, it will inhibit B; B will fire less frequently and consequently will have less of an inhibitory effect on A. Thus, even though the light intensity on B is the same, B will have less of an inhibitory effect on A if B itself is more inhibited by C. By extending this type of argument it can be shown that a system with recurrent inhibition will display a burst of neural impulses in the optic nerve when a light is first turned on; but after the light has been on for a while inhibition will gradually build up, and the nerve activity will drop back to approximately its resting level. When the light is turned off, the receptors will fire less rapidly, but the inhibitory effects still remain for a brief period; thus the neural activity in the optic fibers will drop far below the resting level and then gradually return to it as the inhibitory effects dissipate. In general, any change in intensity—either up or down—will have a like effect on the activity of the fibers. An increase in intensity will result in a temporary increase in neural activity, after which it returns almost to its resting level; a decrease in intensity causes a temporary decrease in activity and a subsequent return to the resting level.

A system with recurrent inhibition has the ability to transmit information about changes in the environment while suppressing information about parts of the environment that are steady and unchanging. We can see that such a system has adaptive value for the organism; attention to changing aspects of its surroundings is important for survival.

The phenomenon of recurrent inhibition can be demonstrated in the human visual system. Look at Figure 5-18A. Cover one eye and stare with the other at the dot in the middle. You will notice that the blurred, light-colored disc soon fades and disappears. Close the seeing eye for a few seconds and then open it; the disc will reappear and then fade again. If you fixate the dot until the disc fades and then shift your gaze to the X, you will find that the disc reappears, and it will reappear each time you shift your eyes between the dot and the X.

If you try doing the same thing with Figure 5-18B, the disc will not disappear. Although you think you are fixating the dot steadily, your eyes are constantly making little oscillating movements. These minute oscillations, of which we are unaware although they occur continually, cause light from the stimulus to strike different retinal receptors from one moment to the next. When you are looking at the edge of something and the eye shifts from one side of the edge to the other, the receptors perceive a change in intensity. The intensity changes that occur with eye oscillations allow the receptors to continue firing at a high rate, and the disc remains visible. The same thing happens when you fixate the dot in Figure 5-18A, but because the gradient of intensity of the blurred disc is more gradual, the eye movements produce a smaller change in intensity on the receptors viewing the edge of the blurred disc. The changes in intensity are so small that little neural

Fig. **5-18 Recurrent inhibition** If you stare at the dot in A, the light-colored disk will disappear; this illustrates the fact that the eye principally responds to discontinuities in the environment and not to gradual changes. Shifting your gaze to the X will cause the disc to reappear. The sharp-edged disk in B will not disappear no matter how long you fixate the dot; this is a consequence of involuntary eye movements. (After Cornsweet, 1969)

T. N. Cornsweet

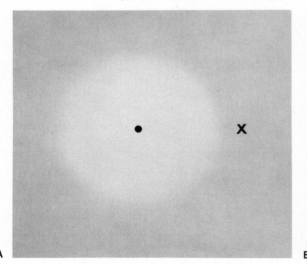

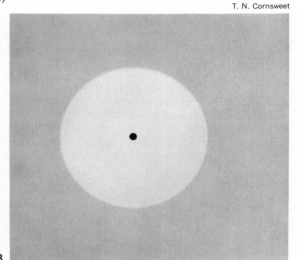

A

B

The auditory sense

While the eye responds to electromagnetic energy, the ear is sensitive to mechanical energy—to *pressure changes* among the molecules in the at-

mosphere. When an object, such as a tuning fork, vibrates it causes successive waves of compression and expansion among the air molecules sur-

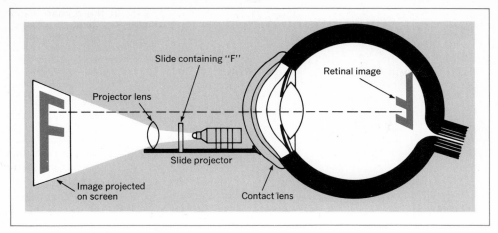

Fig. **5-19** **Stabilized image** A set-up to demonstrate that without movement of the eye in relation to a scene, the scene disappears. A tiny projector mounted on a contact lens is worn over the subject's cornea. With each minute movement of the eyeball, the lens and projector also move so that the projected image always falls on the same area of the retina. After a few seconds the image will fade and then disappear. (After Cornsweet, 1969)

excitation occurs in the receptors and the disc fades out. Closing and opening your eye causes marked changes in intensity and so does moving your eye to stare at the X.

What would happen if we could immobilize the eye so that its normal oscillations did not occur? It is impossible to hold the eye steady, but several devices have been developed to eliminate the movement of the image on the retina. One way is by means of a tiny slide projector mounted on a contact lens attached to the cornea, as diagrammed in Figure 5-19. The slide is projected onto a screen, and the eye wearing the lens looks at the image. Since the lens and projector move with the eye, the image presented to the retina is stabilized; that is, the retinal image impinges on the same retinal receptors regardless of eye movements. When the projector is first turned on, the subject sees the projected figure with normal, or slightly better than normal, visual acuity. Within a few seconds, however, the image begins to fade and within a minute disappears altogether (Cornsweet, 1969). This phenomenon is not an artifact caused by the attachment of the projector to the eye, because if the image that has disappeared is flickered, or moved on the retina, it immediately reappears.

From the research on recurrent inhibition and stabilized retinal images we can conclude that changes in illumination on receptors are necessary for us to see things. Without changes in intensity everything disappears. Our ability to see stationary objects depends on a visual system that responds to changes in illumination and an eye that transforms a fixed image into changing stimulation on the retina.

rounding it. The sound waves generated by the vibration of molecules (in air, water, or some other medium) are the stimuli for hearing. Unlike light, sound cannot travel except through a medium; a ringing bell suspended in a vacuum jar cannot be heard when the air is pumped out.

Sound waves can be graphically represented as *sine functions*. Figure 5-20 shows how the cycles of the sine wave represent the successive compression and expansion of the air as the sound wave moves along. The two main characteristics of such a wave are its *frequency* and its *amplitude*. Fre-

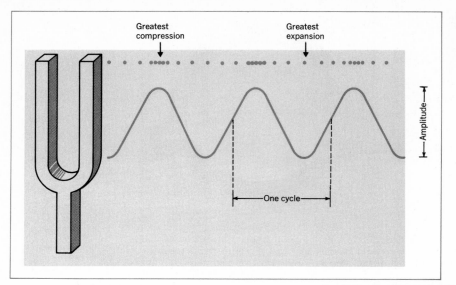

Fig. **5-20 Sound wave** As the tuning fork vibrates it produces successive waves of compression and expansion of the air that can be represented by a sine wave.

quency refers to number of vibrations per second, that is, the number of times per second that the whole wave is repeated. Amplitude refers to the amount of compression and expansion, as represented by the amount by which the curve is displaced above or below the baseline.

Pitch and loudness

The psychological correlate of frequency is *pitch:* the higher the vibration frequency, the higher the perceived pitch. The amplitude of the sound wave determines the intensity with which sound pressure strikes the eardrum. The psychological correlate of intensity is *loudness:* the greater the intensity, the louder the tone (provided pitch remains constant).

The range of frequencies that we can hear runs from about 20 to 20,000 cycles per second (abbreviated cps).[2] Reference points on this range are provided by the piano, which produces frequencies from roughly 30 cps to 5000 cps. The range of frequencies that can be heard is not the same for all organisms; for example, dog-calling whistles

[2]Note that light waves were specified in terms of the length of the wave, whereas sound waves are described on the basis of the number of waves per unit of time. In more technical literature the term "hertz" (abbreviated Hz) is often used in place of cps.

Fig. **5-21 Decibel scale** The loudness of various common sounds scaled in decibels. The take-off blast of the Saturn V moon rocket, measured at the launching pad, is approximately 180 db. For laboratory rats, prolonged exposure to 150 db causes death.

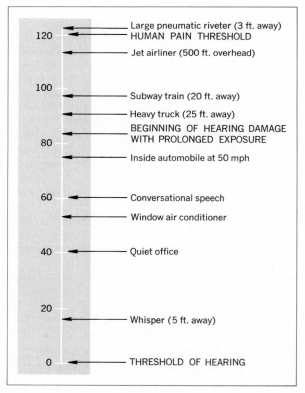

make use of tones too high for the human ear to hear.

We all know the difference between a loud and a soft sound, but assigning scale values to intensity is not so easy. Scientists from the Bell Telephone Laboratories have contributed to the measurement of sound intensity by formulating a convenient unit by which to convert the physical pressures at the eardrum into an understandable scale. The unit is called a *decibel* (one-tenth of a *bel,* named in honor of Alexander Graham Bell). A rough idea of what the decibel measures is given in the scale of familiar sounds shown in Figure 5-21. Zero decibels is arbitrarily set as the absolute threshold for hearing a 1000 cps tone. At about 120 decibels sound intensity becomes painful; the loudness of normal conversation is about midway between these extremes at 60 decibels.

As mentioned earlier, human beings are only sensitive to tones between about 20 and 20,000 cps. Moreover, the absolute threshold for hearing varies with the frequency of the source (Figure 5-22). Tones in the range from 800 to 6000 cps require less than 10 decibels to reach threshold, whereas tones less than 100 cps or greater than 15,000 cps require 40 decibels or more to reach threshold.

Complex tones and noise

Just as the colors we see are seldom pure hues produced by a single wavelength of light, so the sounds we hear are seldom pure tones represented by a sound wave of a single frequency. Even the musical note produced by striking middle C on the piano has, in addition to its fundamental tone of 256 cps, *overtones,* which are multiples of that frequency. The overtones result from the fact that the piano wire not only vibrates as a whole, producing a fundamental tone of 256 cps, but also vibrates in halves, thirds, quarters, fifths, and so on, with each partial vibration producing its own frequency.

The sounds of one musical instrument differ from those of another in the number of overtones produced and in the way in which the construction of the instrument enhances (resonates) certain overtones and deadens others. This characteristic

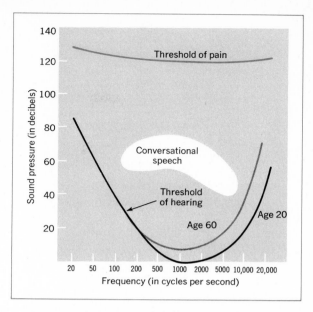

Fig. **5-22 Threshold of hearing** The curve across the top is the threshold of pain. The convex curves below are the thresholds of hearing for age 20 and age 60. Note that with increase in age, hearing is primarily affected in the range of frequencies above 500 cps. (Data are approximate, from various determinations)

quality of a musical tone is called *timbre.* It is the timbre of a tone that tells us whether it is being played by a piano or a clarinet.[3] Instead of the regular sound wave pictured at the top of Figure 5-23, a tone from any instrument has a complex wave form, preserving only the peaks and troughs that help to define the fundamental pitch.

If one compares the dimensions of tone with those of color, the following correspondences hold approximately:

Dimensions of color	Dimensions of tone
Hue ⟷	*Pitch*
Brightness ⟷	*Loudness*
Saturation ⟷	*Timbre*

Hue and pitch are functions of wave frequency; brightness and loudness are functions of ampli-

---

[3]If all overtones are eliminated by the use of sound filters, it is difficult to determine what instrument is being played.

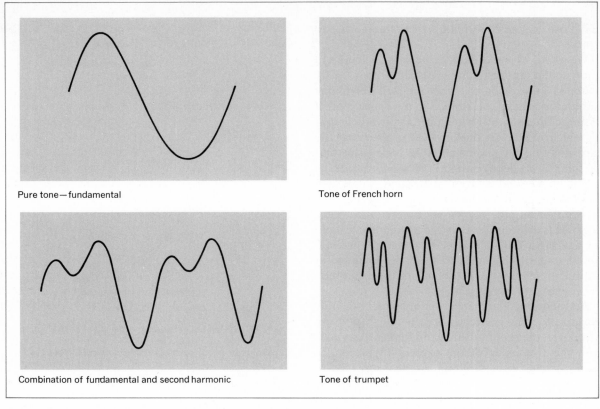

Pure tone—fundamental

Tone of French horn

Combination of fundamental and second harmonic

Tone of trumpet

Fig. **5-23** **The wave forms of complex tones** Each illustration is of the tone of A above middle C (440 cps).

tude; saturation is a result of mixture, just as timbre is. But these are only analogies and are limited as all analogies are.

What happens when two tones are sounded together? They do not lose their identity as colors do when mixed, but they may lead to a fusion that is heard as *consonant* (pleasant) or as *dissonant* (unpleasant). The two tones create a third tone based on the difference in their frequencies. This *difference tone* may or may not harmonize with the fundamental tones that are sounded; for this reason some combinations of tones are preferred to others. Musical harmony depends in part on the interaction between fundamental tones, overtones, and difference tones, which combine to make up the complex tonal stimulus.

A *noise* is a sound that is composed of many frequencies not in harmonious relation to one another. Acoustical experts sometimes speak of

"white noise" when referring to a noise composed of all frequencies in the sound spectrum at roughly the same energy level; it is analogous to white light, which is composed of all frequencies in the light spectrum. The sound of a hissing steam radiator approximates the sound of white noise.

A noise with energy concentrated in certain frequency bands may have a characteristic pitch. For example, we may legitimately use the musical term "bass" to characterize the sound of a drum, even though a drum is more noisy than tonal. Speech sounds make simultaneous use of tonal qualities and noise qualities: *vowels* are tonal, and *consonants* are noisy.

The human ear

The external ear connects with an auditory canal leading to the eardrum, a movable diaphragm

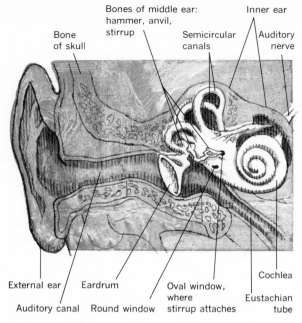

Bone
of skull

Bones of middle ear:
hammer, anvil,
stirrup

Inner ear

Semicircular
canals

Auditory
nerve

Cochlea

External ear

Eardrum

Oval window,
where
stirrup attaches

Eustachian
tube

Auditory canal   Round window

Fig. **5-24   A cross section of the ear**   This drawing shows the general structure of the ear. For the detailed neural connections, see Fig. 5-25.

activated by sound waves entering the ear (Figure 5-24). On the inner side of the diaphragm is a cavity housing the bony transmitters of the *middle ear* (three small bones called the hammer, anvil, and stirrup). The hammer is attached firmly to the eardrum, and the stirrup to another membrane, the *oval window.* The oval window conducts the sounds to the *cochlea,* the auditory portion of the

inner ear. Because the oval window is much smaller than the eardrum, small movements at the eardrum are condensed into a magnified pressure on the oval window.

Pressure at the oval window sets into motion the fluid inside the cochlea. This pressure is relieved at the *round window* at the other end of the fluid-filled channel that runs through the cochlea. Pressure changes in the fluid displace the *basilar membrane* in the cochlea, upon which the *organ of Corti* rests, and this displacement stimulates the sensitive elements in the *hair cells* of the organ of Corti, which are connected with the auditory nerve (Figure 5-25).

The pathways of the auditory nerves resemble those of the optic nerves (see Figure 5-7) in that nerve fibers from each ear travel to both cerebral hemispheres (terminating in the temporal lobes). Thus, destruction of one temporal lobe will not cause complete deafness in either ear.

Theories of hearing

As noted above, sound waves traveling through the fluid of the cochlea cause the basilar membrane to vibrate, thus activating the hair cells; these cells are connected to the nerve fibers of the auditory nerve. But how does a structure as small as the organ of Corti (less than the size of a pea) enable us to differentiate thousands of different tones? What are the mechanisms that provide for discriminations in pitch and loudness?

Fig. **5-25   Receptors for hearing**   The figure on the right is a cross section through the snail-shaped cochlea, shown on the left. The true auditory receptors lie in the organ of Corti, which rests upon the basilar membrane. Deflection of the basilar membrane activates the hair cells and produces impulses in the auditory nerve.

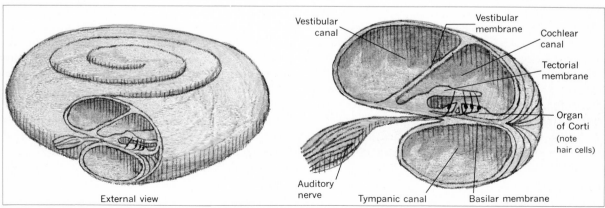

Vestibular
canal

Vestibular
membrane

Cochlear
canal

Tectorial
membrane

Organ
of Corti
(note
hair cells)

Auditory
nerve

Tympanic canal

Basilar membrane

External view

Loudness appears to be determined by the total number of fibers firing and by the activation of certain high threshold fibers, nerve fibers that require considerable bending of the hair cells in order to be stimulated (Thompson, 1967). Pitch is a more complicated matter. The two major theories of pitch discrimination are the *place theory* and the *frequency theory*. The place theory assumes that the frequency of a tone is indicated by the region of the basilar membrane that is maximally displaced by the sound wave. Von Békésy tested this theory in a series of precise experiments for which he was awarded the Nobel Prize in 1961. Using guinea pigs he cut tiny holes in the cochlea and observed the basilar membrane with a microscope as the ear was being stimulated by tones of different frequencies. He discovered that high frequency tones maximally displaced the narrow end of the basilar membrane near the oval window; tones of intermediate frequency caused displacement further toward the other end of the basilar membrane. Unfortunately for the consistency of the theory, however, low tones activated the entire membrane with roughly equal displacement. This result, plus the fact that tones of intermediate frequency displace a fairly broad area of the membrane, makes it unlikely that differential displacement of the basilar membrane is sufficient to fully explain our ability to discriminate pitch at low frequencies.

This leads us to the other major theory of hearing—the *frequency theory*—which assumes that the cochlea acts like a microphone and the auditory nerve like a telephone wire. According to this theory, pitch is determined by the frequency of impulses traveling up the auditory nerve. The greater the frequency, the higher the pitch. Studies have shown that for tones of up to about 4000 cps the electrical response of the auditory nerve does track the frequency of the tone. Thus a tone of 500 cps produces 500 evoked responses per second in the nerve, a tone of 2000 produces 2000 responses, and so on. Since an individual neuron can conduct only about 1000 impulses per second, the ability of the auditory nerve to track frequencies above this point up to 4000 cps has to be explained in terms

of a *volley principle* (Wever, 1949). This principle assumes that the different groups of fibers fire in turn, in a sort of squad system. Different squads fire at each compression of the sound wave. One group may fire at the first compression, remain in a refractory phase while another group discharges, and then be ready to fire again at the third compression. Thus, although no one fiber responds at each compression, all respond synchronously with the frequency of the sound wave. For a 2000 cps tone there would be a spurt of activity in the auditory nerve every five ten-thousandths of a second, with different groups of neurons firing each time. Pitch at intermediate frequencies depends upon the firing frequency of the volleys, not that of the individual nerve fibers. However, even with the volley principle the auditory nerve would not be able to match frequencies above 4000 cps.

As was the case with theories of color vision, an ultimate explanation of pitch discrimination will probably include some aspects of both theories. Both the place of excitation on the basilar membrane and the frequency of nerve response appear to be involved in transmitting information about the frequency of a tone. Place seems to be important for high frequencies (above 4000 cps), while synchronous discharge in nerve fibers is important for the lower frequencies.

More precise coding of auditory information takes place in the auditory pathways closer to the brain and in the auditory cortex itself. An auditory nerve fiber makes synaptic connections with at least four other neurons on its way to the auditory cortex. At each of these levels, neurons can be found that fire at the onset of a tone, or decrease their firing when a tone is turned on, or discharge continuously to a maintained tone (Thompson, 1967). In addition, as we ascend from the auditory nerve to the auditory cortex, the range of frequencies to which a particular cell will respond becomes increasingly narrow. Thus coding of information becomes more precise as the cortex is approached. An ultimate theory of hearing will undoubtedly have to take into account neural codes based on many different types of cell response patterns at each synaptic level of the auditory system.

Other senses

Man's senses other than vision and audition are important for his survival, but they lack the richness of patterning and organization that have led men to call sight and hearing the "higher senses." Our symbolic experiences are expressed largely in visual and auditory terms. Our spoken language is to be *heard;* our written language is to be *seen.* Musical notation permits music to be read or played on an instrument. Except for Braille (the raised form of printing that permits the blind to read) we do not have any comparable symbolic coding of odors, tastes, or touches.

Smell

From an evolutionary viewpoint, smell is one of the most primitive and most important of the senses. The sense organ for smell has a position of prominence in the head appropriate to a sense intended to guide behavior. Smell has a more direct route to the brain than any other sense. The receptors high in the nose, in the *olfactory epithelium* of each nasal cavity, are connected without synapse directly to the olfactory bulbs of the brain, lying just below the frontal lobes. The olfactory bulbs are in turn connected with the olfactory cortex on the inside of the temporal lobes and extend to the neighboring cortex; the exact neural connections are still a matter of some uncertainty. In fishes the olfactory cortex makes up the entire cerebral hemispheres. In the dog, the olfactory cortex represents about one-third of the area of the side of the brain, as contrasted with one-twentieth of this area in man.

The nature of the olfactory stimulus has been the source of a great deal of speculation. Some theorists assume that smell is caused by a chemical reaction between the odorous substance and the receptor (Davies, 1962), while others assume there is a kind of radiation activity, such as the differential absorption of infrared radiant energy corresponding to the gas being smelled (Wright, 1964). The whole matter is far from settled and remains a promising field for research.

Taste

We know that the primary taste qualities are *sweet, sour, salt,* and *bitter.* Every other taste experience is contributed by fusions of these qualities and other senses. Smell, texture, temperature, and sometimes pain (judging from the pleasure some diners derive from highly spiced Mexican food) all contribute to the sensations we experience when we taste a food. When we drink a glass of lemonade we enjoy its odor and its coolness by senses other than taste; the taste sense provides only for its sweet-sour-bitter components. With our nostrils clamped tight, we cannot distinguish between the taste of a raw apple and a raw potato.

The taste receptors are found in the *taste buds* on the edges and toward the back of the tongue; a few are located elsewhere in the soft palate, the pharynx, and the larynx. It is known that the number of taste buds decreases with age, so that older people are less sensitive to taste than children. Some taste buds at the tip of the tongue react only to sweet, salt, or sour, while others react to some or all of these in combination. In general, sensitivity to sweet is greatest at the tip of the tongue, to salt on the tip and the sides, to sour on the sides, and to bitter on the back.

Each of the approximately ten thousand taste buds in the human adult has fifteen to twenty taste cells arranged in budlike form on its tip, much like the segments of an orange. These taste cells are continuously reproducing themselves at the rate of a complete turnover for each taste bud every seven days. Consequently, the taste cells we kill when we scald our tongue with a cup of hot coffee provide no cause for concern; they are quickly replenished. Recordings from microelectrodes implanted in single cells show that even the individual cells vary in their response to the four basic taste stimuli; that is, some cells may respond only to sugar and salt while others on the same taste bud may respond only to salt and acids, and so forth.

The initial step in the taste process is a chemical one. It appears that stimulation by a taste solution

The general agreement that taste qualities include only sweet, salt, sour, and bitter led initially to a search for taste buds that mediated these qualities. This rather simple notion that the experienced quality would be closely related to underlying physiology goes back to the doctrine of *specific nerve energies* formulated early in the nineteenth century by Sir Charles Bell and Johannes Müller. This doctrine states that we are aware of the state of our nerves, rather than of external stimuli: that is, any stimulation of the eye gives rise to experiences of light, and of the taste buds, to experiences of taste. It was thus simple to infer that some taste buds should produce the experience of sweet, others of salt, sour, or bitter.

We now know that there is not a specific receptor for each of the taste qualities; although some receptor cells may respond only to a certain chemical, others respond to several of the primary tastes. Advances in electrophysiology have made it possible to record the nerve impulses from a single taste nerve fiber (isolated from the bundles of such fibers that make up a nerve). As a solution, such as salt, increases in concentration there is a corresponding increase in the number of impulses fired by the nerve fiber. Other taste substances will also produce impulses in the same fiber but at different thresholds. In the rat, for example, thresholds based on the minimum concentration of the substance that can be detected may be arranged in order from low to high for the following substances: quinine, hydrochloric acid, sodium chloride, potassium chloride, and sucrose. That is, the rat's taste mechanism reacts most readily to quinine (bitter) and is least sensitive to sucrose (sweet).

Since impulses in the taste nerve fiber taken alone do not indicate which of several substances was applied to the tongue, how are we to account for the fact that different substances do taste differently? The answer must lie in some sort of code, which takes into account the frequency of stimulation in neighboring fibers and the relative amounts of parallel activity in units that happen to be more sensitive to one kind of stimulation than to another (Pfaffmann, 1964). Something similar to the doctrine of specific nerve energies is still appropriate, but it must not misguide us into oversimplified theories of the relationship of phenomenal experience to what goes on in our nervous systems.

depolarizes the taste cell and a weak bond is formed between the ion or molecule of the taste substance and the molecular structure of the taste-cell surface. This depolarization in turn excites the nerve fibers and gives rise to a nerve impulse. It is hypothesized that differences in the configuration of the cell surface account for the selective absorption of a particular chemical (Beidler, 1961).

In contrast to the exclusive nerve tracts for audition, vision, and olfaction (the auditory, optic, and olfactory nerves), sensations from the taste buds are carried to the central nervous system by three different cranial nerves (the facial, glossopharyngeal, and vagus nerves), which also carry nerve fibers related to other functions such as chewing, swallowing, tactile sensation, and movement of the tongue. The area of the cortex where taste is represented lies behind the central fissure at the lower part of the side of the brain.

Other animals differ from man in the receptivity of their taste buds, as determined by measurement of impulses from the taste nerve fibers as well as behavioral evidence of ability to discriminate among taste substances. Cats and chickens, for example, appear to have no taste receptors that respond to sweet, whereas dogs, rats, pigs, and most other vertebrates do. This fact explains the observation of pet owners that dogs are usually fond of desserts, while cats generally ignore them.

The skin sensations

The familiar sense of touch is not one sensation but at least four: *touch, pain, warm,* and *cold*—all of which are felt through distinct kinds of sensitive spots on the skin surface. If the skin is explored with appropriate instruments (fine hairs, needle points, heated or cooled pointed hammers), it is found that these sensitive spots are unevenly distributed. The separate sensitive spots are not equally numerous nor are they found at the same locations. On most parts of the skin the relative frequencies are, in descending order: pain spots, touch spots, cold spots, and warm spots. All other skin sensations that we commonly describe, such as itch, tickle, quick-pricking pains, and dull long-lasting pains, are considered to be variations of the four basic sensations. An itching sensation, for example, can be produced by stimulating pain spots by a light, repeated needle prick; tickle is experienced when adjacent touch spots on the skin are touched lightly in rapid succession.

The precise receptors for the various skin sensations have been the subject of much study and dispute. At one time histologists identified a number of quite different nerve-end structures in the skin, each of which was thought to be the specific receptor for one of the four sensations. Psychology texts of some twenty years ago contained detailed drawings of these cutaneous receptors. Subsequent studies, however, failed to substantiate such claims: when investigators "mapped" cold, warm, touch, and pain spots on their own skin, excised the underlying tissue, and examined it microscopically, there was no consistent relationship between the type of sensation experienced and the type of underlying nerve-end structures. About all that can be stated with some degree of certainty is that (1) nerve fibers at the base of hair follicles serve as receptors for touch or light pressure (but they are not the only receptors, since the lips, which are hairless, are quite sensitive to pressure), and (2) free nerve-endings that terminate in the epidermis (as opposed to those nerves that end in certain encapsulated structures) are involved in pain reception.

In everyday experiences the four sensations are usually mingled; we seldom feel pain without touch, or warm or cold without touch. Stimulation by extreme heat or cold activates the pain receptors too, usually at about the point where the thermal

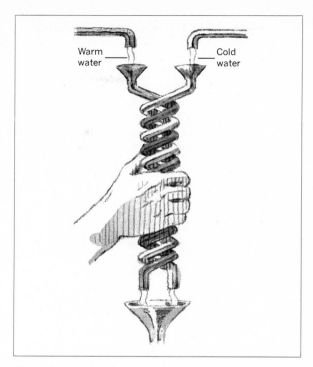

Fig. **5-26** **"Hot" as simultaneous stimulation of warm and cold spots** When cold water (0–5°C) is circulated through one coil and warm water (40–44°C) through another intertwining coil, the subject experiences a hot, burning sensation on grasping the coils. This experiment demonstrates that the sensation of "hot" is produced by the simultaneous stimulation of warm and cold spots in the skin.

stimulation begins to produce destructive changes in the tissue surrounding the pain receptors.

Temperature. The thermometer scale is continuous—it is not divided into a part called "cold" and another part called "warm." Yet our skin senses are so divided. The experiences of "warm" and "cold" depend upon a *level of adaptation*, this level providing a kind of zero point. A very simple experiment demonstrates this. Prepare three pails of water, one containing ice water, one containing hot water, and one containing water at room temperature. Then place your right hand in the hot water and your left hand in the ice water, and leave them there for a few minutes. Now plunge both hands into the water at room temperature. To the left hand, the water feels warm; to the right hand, it feels cool.

This experience is familiar. Another fact, however, is unlikely to be discovered without special experimentation. The experience of "hot" is distinct from the experience of "warm"; it results from the simultaneous stimulation of warm and cold spots. This can be demonstrated with a device that allows two streams of water to be passed through intertwined alternate coils (Figure 5-26). If cold water passes through both coils they of course feel cold when grasped with one hand. If warm water passes through both they feel warm. But when cold water circulates through one set of coils and warm water through the other, the coils feel *hot*. This is not the way the experience of "hot" is usually produced, but it is the way the receptors respond. Cold spots have two thresholds. They respond to stimuli of low temperature, do not respond to stimuli of intermediate temperature, but respond again to stimuli of high temperature. High temperatures, then, activate *both* warm and cold spots, and the felt experience of "hot" depends upon this double effect.

Kinesthesis

Our ordinary vocabulary lacks a word for the sensory system that informs us of the position and movement of parts of the body. In technical language this is *kinesthesis*—the muscle, tendon, and joint sense. Position and movement are detected by sense organs in the joints, while sense organs in the muscles and tendons tell us whether a muscle is stretched or contracted and help to adjust muscular tension to the load upon it.

Without kinesthesis we would have great difficulty in maintaining posture, in walking and climbing, and in controlling voluntary movements such as reaching, grasping, and manipulating. Whenever we act, we first make somewhat tentative movements and then adjust them according to their environmental effects. If something turns out to be heavier than expected, we brace ourselves and lift with greater effort. If we slip or stumble as we walk, we promptly make corrective movements. The kinesthetic sense gives us a feedback

from the environment that keeps telling us how things are going. We take this sense for granted until a foot "goes to sleep" and we realize how strange it is to walk without any information as to the foot's contact with the floor.

Equilibratory senses

Cooperating with kinesthesis are the *equilibratory senses,* which deal with total body position in relation to gravity and with motion of the body as a whole. The relation of bodily parts to one another and to external objects is the responsibility of kinesthesis; the orientation of the body in space is the responsibility of the equilibratory senses.

The sense organs for equilibrium, located in the inner ear, are a series of cavities extending from the cochlea. There are two systems: the *semicircular canals* and the *vestibular sacs.*

The three semicircular canals, each roughly perpendicular to the others, lie in three planes, so that bodily rotation in any one of the planes will have maximum effect on one of the canals and rotation at an angle to the planes will affect more than one. The canals are filled with a fluid that moves when the head rotates and exerts pressure on hair cells similar to those of the organ of Corti. Displacement of these hair cells by the movement of the fluid stimulates a nonauditory branch of the auditory nerve. When rotation is slow and of moderate amount, the chief consequence is information that we are moving. When it is more extreme we experience dizziness and nausea.

The vestibular sacs, between the base of the semicircular canals and the cochlea, provide for our perception of bodily position when the body is at rest. They respond to the tilt or position of the head and do not require rotation to be stimulated. The receptors again are hair cells that protrude into a gelatinous mass containing small crystals called *otoliths* (literally, "ear stones"). The normal pressure of the otoliths on the hair cells gives us the sense of upright position, and any distortion tells us that the head is tilted.

The equilibratory senses also signal accelerated motion in a straight line, but sometimes they produce illusions that distort the true path of motion. These illusions occur in flying, because of changes in speed and the banking and climbing of the plane. For example, when a plane is increasing its speed gradually, a blindfolded subject may feel sure that the plane is climbing; if its speed is decreasing gradually, he may feel equally sure that it is diving. Under conditions of poor visibility a flyer does better to trust his instruments than his equilibratory senses.

Summary

1. All sense experiences have their *thresholds* (both *absolute* and *difference* thresholds). Weber's law expresses the fact that difference thresholds tend to be a constant fraction of the stimulus intensity. Thresholds fluctuate, as illustrated by *sensory adaptation*—the modified sensitivity (altered threshold) after prolonged exposure to a stimulus or in the absence of stimulation.

2. Some of the main features of the *visual sense:*
a. The eye receives light waves by way of the *cornea, pupil, lens,* and *retina.* The actual receptors are the *rods* and *cones* of the retina. The cones, concentrated in the *fovea* but scattered throughout the retina, mediate experiences of both black and white and hue (*chromatic* colors). The rods, in the periphery of the eye, mediate experiences only of black and white (the *achromatic* colors). In night vision only the rods function.
b. The distinctive roles of the rods and cones can be inferred from *dark adaptation,* in which the cones reach their maximum sensitivity in about five minutes, while the rods continue to become increasingly sensitive for about half an hour.
c. The *chromatic colors* can be arranged around a color circle, following the order of wavelengths (the order seen in the rainbow or solar spectrum) but allowing space for the nonspectral purples and reds. When properly spaced, the colors opposite each other are *complementaries.* When complementary colors are mixed as lights (additive mixture), they cancel each other and result in a neutral gray. Although four *psychological primaries* can be identified (red, yellow, green, blue), three *color primaries* (red, green, and blue) are enough to produce the range of hues by additive mixture. The chief dimensions of color are *hue, brightness,* and *saturation,* which can be represented on the color solid.
d. *Afterimage* and *contrast effects* emphasize the pairing of colors, for very often (though not always) the withdrawal of stimulation of one hue produces the complementary hue, and the contrast effect is maximum between complementaries.
e. *Color blindness* also calls attention to color pairs as well as to the primacy of certain colors. The most common form, red-green blindness (a form of *dichromatism*), is much more frequently found among men than among women. Total color blindness (*monochromatism*) is rare, and yellow-blue blindness, the alternate form of dichromatism, is rarer still.
f. *Color theories* take these facts as their starting points and attempt to give them physiological explanation. The Young-Helmholtz theory begins with color mixture; the Hering theory starts with afterimages and contrast. Recent research indicates that both theories are partially correct; color vision may be a two-stage process involving three kinds of color responses from receptors in the retina that are encoded into two-color, on-off signals by cells further along in the optic system.

3. Some of the facts and principles arising from study of the *auditory sense:*
a. The chief dimensions of auditory experience are *pitch,* correlated with the

frequency of vibration of the sound waves that constitute the stimulus, and *loudness*, correlated with the *amplitude* of these waves. The absolute threshold for hearing depends on the frequency of the tone; very low- or very high-pitched tones must be more intense to be heard than tones in the middle range of frequencies.

b. Most tones are not pure, that is, composed of only a single frequency. Musical instruments may be differentiated by the *timbre* of their tones, a quality that depends on the *overtones* and other impurities differing from one instrument to another. Complex sounds composed of many frequencies not in harmonious relation to one another are called *noise.*

c. The auditory apparatus consists of the *external ear*, leading by way of the auditory canal to the *eardrum*, giving access to the *middle ear.* The bones of the middle ear transmit the sound waves to the *oval window*, leading to *the inner ear.* The *cochlea* houses the receptors of the inner ear, sensitive hair cells buried in the *basilar membrane*. Wave motion in the fluid of the inner ear agitates these hair cells, which in turn activate the auditory nerve.

d. Theories attempting to give a physiological explanation of pitch are the *place theory*, which emphasizes the place on the basilar membrane where a particular frequency produces its maximum effect, and the *frequency theory*, which assumes that pitch is determined by the frequency of impulses traveling up the auditory nerve. Evidence indicates that the place theory applies to high frequencies, while synchronous discharge is important for the lower frequencies. More precise coding takes place in the auditory pathways closer to the brain and in the auditory cortex.

4. The other senses, important as they are, do not enter as much into man's symbolic behavior, so they are thought of as "lower senses." They include *smell, taste,* the four *skin sensations* (touch, pain, warm, cold), *kinesthesis* (muscle, tendon, and joint sense), and the *equilibratory senses.*

Suggestions for further reading

For a general introduction to the various senses, see Mueller, *Sensory psychology* (1965), and Forgus, *Perception* (1966). A useful reference work is Sidowski (ed.), *Experimental methods and instrumentation in psychology* (1966), which contains several chapters on the psychology of sensation.

There are many sources on visual perception, including Graham and others, *Vision and visual perception* (1965), Gregory, *Eye and brain* (1966), and Haber (ed.), *Contemporary theory and research in visual perception* (1968). A readable and attractively illustrated treatment of vision is Mueller and Rudolph, *Light and vision* (1966), one of a series of books published by *Life* magazine.

Among the same *Life* series is Stevens and Warshofsky, *Sound and hearing* (1965). More advanced treatments of audition may be found in *Experiments in hearing* (1960) and *Sensory inhibition* (1967) by Békésy, the leading contemporary investigator of the physiological basis of hearing, who was awarded a Nobel Prize in 1961 for his contributions.

A survey of mathematical theories in sensory psychology is found in the *Handbook of mathematical psychology*, vol. I (1963) and vol. III (1965), edited by Luce, Bush, and Galanter. See also Swets, *Signal detection and recognition by human observers* (1964), and Green and Swets, *Signal detection theory and psychophysics* (1966).

perception 6

LIFE GOES ON IN A WORLD OF OBJECTS AND people. Were the individual not sensitive and responsive to his environment, he would be unable to satisfy his needs, communicate with his fellows, or enjoy his surroundings. The individual learns to know his world through the data that come to him by way of his sense organs, but what he perceives depends also on what he brings along with him from his past experiences and what his present needs and wishes are as he faces the world. Thus, like all the other topics of psychology, perception has its developmental as well as its inter-

active aspects; perception depends upon more than the stimuli now impinging upon sense organs.

The objects of which we are aware are usually sources of multiple stimuli and are embedded in surroundings providing additional stimuli. We see signs or pictures instead of spots of light; we hear words or music instead of single pure tones. We react to *patterns* of stimuli, usually with little awareness of the parts composing the pattern. The colors and sizes of figures in the individual pieces of a jigsaw puzzle often look entirely different from the way they look when composing the whole picture. An oil painting of a landscape, viewed close up, may appear to be a meaningless collection of daubs of paint. The total impression from organized stimuli has properties not predictable from the parts in isolation.

All experiences of objects and events take place within a framework of space and time. Vision and audition provide the most complex patterns of these perceptual experiences. Vision is our preferred spatial sense, giving us variegated patterns of form and color in three dimensions, but it is also a good time sense because we see succession, movement, and change. Audition is a spatial sense also, though its spatial patterns are much more limited than those of vision; it is primarily a time sense, for its main patterns are those of succession, change, and rhythm. Because of vision's preeminence as a spatial sense, most of our discussion of perception will focus on visual processes. Of course many perceptual experiences depend on the operation of several senses at once; then the prominence of one sense over another becomes a matter for study.

Object perception and perceptual constancies

If you look around the room and ask yourself what you see, your answer is likely to be, "a room full of people and objects." You may pick out specific people or objects instead of making such a general statement, but you are not likely to report that you see a mosaic of light and shadow. Perception is oriented toward things rather than toward the sensory qualities that describe them. Detached sensory qualities ("blueness," "redness") can be perceived, but they are usually perceived as the qualities of objects. You see the yellow flowers or the soft pillow or the hot radiator, not "yellowness," "softness," or "hotness."

Object constancy

Our perceptual experiences are not isolated; they build a world of identifiable things. Objects endure, so that you meet the same object over and over again. When you turn your head away, you think of the objects as remaining where you saw them. An object that has been constituted perceptually as a permanent and stable thing is perceived as such, regardless of the illumination on it, the position from which it is viewed, or the distance at which it appears. The tendency to see an object as of normal color regardless of light and shadow is called *color constancy* and *brightness constancy*. The tendency to see it as of standard shape regardless of the viewing angle is called *shape con-*

stancy. The tendency to see it as of measurable size regardless of distance is called *size constancy*. Finally, the fact that objects retain their "same" positions, even as we move about, is known as *location constancy*. The word "constancy" is an exaggeration, but it dramatizes our relatively stable perception of objects.

Brightness and color constancy

Brightness constancy is primarily due to the fact that the brightness of an object is judged in relation to its surroundings. The amount of light reflected by a piece of black velvet in bright sunlight is greater than that reflected by a piece of white velvet in the shade. But the *percentage* of available light reflected by an object (its relative brightness) is the same regardless of the degree of illumination; that is, a piece of white velvet will reflect a certain percentage of the light striking it regardless of the intensity of the light. Constancy breaks down when the object and its surroundings do not receive illumination from the same source, or when the individual incorrectly perceives the relationship between the light reflected by the object and that reflected by the object's surroundings.

Similar considerations apply for color constancy. We tend to see familiar objects as retaining their original color under a variety of lighting conditions—even when illuminated by colored light, provided there are sufficient contrasts and shadows. The owner of a blue car sees it as blue whether he is looking at it in bright sunlight, in dim illumination, or under a yellow street light. He is relying on "memory color," which is one factor contributing to color constancy. Information concerning the nature of the illumination and the color of surrounding objects are also clues to color constancy. When these clues are eliminated, color constancy diminishes or disappears. If you look at a ripe tomato through a narrow tube so that you do not know the nature of the object or the source and kind of illumination, the tomato will appear to be blue or brown or any of a number of other colors, depending upon the color of the light being shone on it. Without the clues that make color constancy possible we see the color of objects according to the wavelength of light being reflected to the eye.

Shape and size constancy

When a door swings open toward us, its rectangular shape goes through a series of distortions. It becomes a trapezoid, with the edge toward us looking wider than the hinged edge; then the trapezoid grows thinner, until all we can see is a vertical line the thickness of the door. We can readily distinguish these changes, but what we *perceive* is an unchanging door swinging on its hinges. The fact that the door does not seem to change its shape is called *shape constancy*. We see the top of a glass bottle as round whether we view it from the side or from the top.

Size constancy refers to the fact that as an object is moved farther away we tend to correct for distance and still see it as more or less normal in size. Hold a quarter a foot in front of your eyes and then move it out to arm's length. Does it appear to get smaller? Not noticeably so. Yet the retinal image of the quarter 12 inches away is half the size of the image of the quarter when it is 24 inches from the eye (see Figure 6-1). It certainly does not appear to reduce to half its size as we move it to arm's length.

When we see an object at a distance, we might conceivably judge its size in one of three ways:

1. *Perspective size.* We might judge it according to the geometry of perspective, seeing it as smaller the farther away it is, the size inversely proportional to distance. This size would correspond to the size of the image on the retina.

2. *Object size.* If object constancy were perfect, we might judge an object by its known (measurable) size and hence not see it any smaller at a distance.

3. *Compromise between perspective size and object size.* We might compromise and see the object smaller at a distance, but not as much smaller as the geometry of perspective indicates.

Fig. **6-1** **Object size and retinal image** This figure illustrates the geometric relationship between the physical size of an object and the size of its retinal projection. Arrow A and arrow B represent objects of the same size, but one is twice as far from the eye's lens as the other. As a result the image projected on the retina by A is approximately half as large as that projected by B. The object represented by arrow C is smaller than A but closer to the eye; note that arrows A and C produce the same-size retinal image.

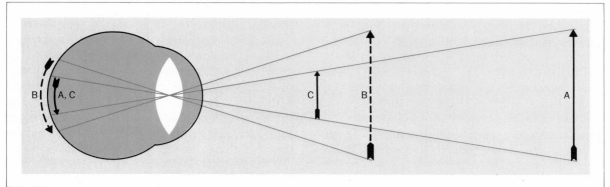

Of the three alternatives described, the last one is usually correct. Our size perceptions represent compromises between perspective size and object size. How well size constancy operates depends upon the presence of distance cues and upon our familiarity with the object. The more information available as to the distance of the object, the more the perceived size approaches the actual size. As distance cues are eliminated, the perceived size approaches the size of the retinal image, unless the object is familiar. Familiarity with an object enables us to judge its appropriate size, even in the absence of depth cues.

Size constancy develops largely as the result of experience. Although research indicates that infants as young as eight weeks possess some degree of size constancy for objects 3 to 9 feet away (Bower, 1966), size constancy for more distant objects appears to develop with increasing age. Figure 6-2 shows the results of an experiment comparing the performance of eight year olds and adults in judging the size of objects at different distances. At 10 feet both children and adults show close to perfect size constancy; that is, their judgment of size agrees with the physical size of the object. With increasing observation distances the children show increasingly less size constancy (their size estimates are closely related to the size of the retinal image), while the adults' judgments of size remain quite accurate (Zeigler and Leibowitz, 1957).

These results are consistent with observations of the behavior of young children. A three year old watching cars on a roadway below a lookout point will see the cars as miniatures and often insist that they cannot be full size. He may even beg for them as toys. His size constancy is not yet developed for this new viewing angle. Adult size constancy commonly breaks down also when objects are viewed from a height, but the adult makes an intellectual correction that the young child does not make.

The effect of limited experience on the development of size constancy is further illustrated by an incident concerning a pygmy who was taken for the first time from his home in the forest into open country. When he spotted a herd of buffalo

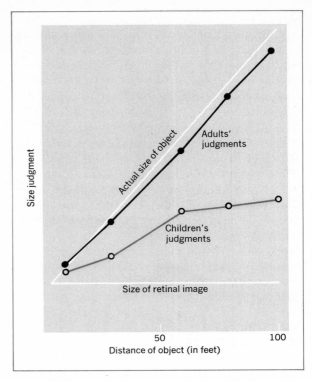

Fig. **6-2 Size perception and age** Adults and eight-year-old children viewed objects at distances ranging from 10 to 100 feet. The physical sizes of the objects were adjusted at the various distances so that the image projected on the retina was always the same size. The horizontal line indicates the size of the retinal image (which is constant for all distances), and the diagonal line the size of the physical object (which increases with distance). Note that adults make fairly accurate size judgments no matter how distant the object. The judgments of children, however, appear to be increasingly influenced by the size of the retinal image as the object is placed farther away. (Data from Zeigler and Leibowitz, 1957)

grazing several miles away the pygmy asked what kind of "insects" they were. He refused to accept the fact that they were buffalo, and actually larger in size than the forest buffalo with which he was familiar. As the car in which he was traveling approached the animals the pygmy became alarmed because the animals appeared to be growing in size; he suspected that he was the victim of some sort of magic. Later he perceived a boat with several men in it sailing some distance from the shore of a lake as a scrap of wood floating on the water. Just as the small child's limited experience with viewing objects from a great height causes him to err in his perceptions, the pygmy's inexperience with distance viewing on a horizontal plane created similar misperceptions (Turnbull, 1961).

Location constancy

Our world has perceptual stability for us because we perceive objects as enduring, as being the same as when we last looked. We also perceive these objects in a setting that remains essentially fixed, despite the fact that we see a kaleidoscopic world that sends us a myriad of changing impressions as we move about in it. We take for granted the stability of our perceptual world, but it too depends upon past experience.

The role of learning in location constancy has been demonstrated by some interesting experiments that rearrange the visual environment by the use of special glasses. In a classic study conducted more than seventy-five years ago, Stratton fitted himself with lenses that not only inverted the visual field so that he saw the world upside-down, but also reversed it so that objects perceived on the left were actually on the right and vice versa. Stratton reports that at first the world seemed to lose its stability:

> When I moved my head or body so that my sight swept over the scene, the movement was not felt to be solely in the observer, as in normal vision, but was referred both to the observer and to objects beyond. . . . I did not feel as if I were visually ranging over a set of motionless objects, but the whole field of things swept and swung before my eyes [Stratton, 1897, p. 342].

After a few days this swinging or swirling sensation decreased, indicating some restoration of location constancy. Another sign of regained location constancy was that a fire was again heard to crackle in the fireplace where it was seen, a harmony of location that was at first lost because only the eyes, and not the ears, were perceiving in reverse. Although the distortion provided by the lenses made even the simplest task extremely difficult and laborious, Stratton found that as the experiment progressed he became more skillful in dealing with his mixed-up perceptual world. He bumped into

objects less frequently and was able to perform such tasks as washing himself and eating, which initially had been very difficult. When the glasses were removed some adjustment was required before the old visual-motor habits were regained.

Experiments similar to Stratton's have been repeated with comparable results (Snyder and Pronko, 1952; Kohler, 1962). Human subjects have shown a remarkable ability to adjust to a visually rearranged world. What factors are involved in this adjustment? Is there a change in visual perception so that the location of objects is seen more accurately despite the displaced retinal image? Or is there a change in body position sense—in the awareness of where one part of the body is with respect to the rest?

An experiment by Rock and Harris (1967) sheds some light on the answers to these questions. The subject was asked to point under a table to one of five targets at the other end of the table (Figure 6-3). During the first part of the experiment the glass surface of the table was covered

Fig. **6-3** **Visual displacement** An apparatus for testing displaced vision. There are five targets, and the goggles are selected so that the visual field is displaced to the right by about 4 inches (the distance between adjacent targets). A cover can be placed over the table top when desired, to prevent the subject from seeing where he is pointing. The biteboard ensures that the head remains steady throughout the experiment. The experimenter instructs the subject to point to targets one at a time and then measures the discrepancy between where the finger is pointing and the target. (After Rock and Harris, 1967)

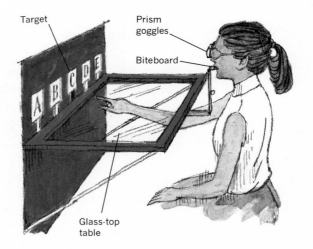

Target

Prism goggles

Biteboard

Glass-top table

with a black cloth so that the subject could see the targets but not his hand beneath the glass. Even so, he was able to point to the targets accurately. These data provided a baseline with which to compare later responses. During the next phase the subject wore prism goggles that displaced his vision so that objects appeared to be 4 inches to the right of their actual location. The cloth was removed, and he practiced pointing to the center target. At

first the prisms caused him to miss the target, but he quickly became quite accurate. In the third part of the experiment the goggles were removed and the subject was tested both with his adapted hand (the one he had used to practice pointing at the targets with the goggles on) and with the other hand. On tests with the adapted hand the subject showed a shift in pointing that was consistent with the extent of visual displacement provided by the

CRITICAL
DISCUSSION

**Sensorimotor
feedback in
perception**

Several experiments have indicated the importance of feedback from the muscles and motor parts of the nervous system in learning to adjust to visual rearrangement (Held, 1965). If a subject wearing distorting lenses is allowed to move freely, he gradually makes adjustment for the distortion. Another subject wearing the same lenses but whose movements are passive (for example, he is pushed in a wheelchair instead of walking) achieves virtually no adaptation. Both subjects encounter the same visual stimuli, but one is able to correlate his movements with the sensory information from his eyes while the other is not.

Held offers experimental evidence to support the proposition that the development of normal space and pattern perception in the young organism also requires active movement on the part of the perceiver. Kittens were reared in the dark with their mother and litter mates; their only exposure to visual stimulation occurred when they were placed in the apparatus shown in Figure 6-4 for three hours each day. One kitten could move more or less normally; his gross movements were transmitted by a system of gears and pulleys to a second kitten who was transported in a gondola. Both kittens received essentially

Fig. **6-4 Apparatus for determining effect of active vs. passive movements on spatial orientation** The gross movements of the "active" kitten, which moves about more or less freely, are transmitted by means of the chain and bar to the "passive" kitten, which is conveyed in a gondola. Both kittens are reared in the dark, except for their daily experience in the apparatus, and are subsequently tested for visual-motor coordination.

Photo by Ted Polumbaum; courtesy of *Life*

goggles. With the other hand, however, there was little or no adaptive shift. It appears that adaptation to the visual distortion involved a change in the position sense of the adapted arm rather than a change in visual perception. If the subject had learned to *perceive* the target in a new location, we would have expected him to point to that place with either hand.

It is not clear to what extent these results can be generalized to apply to experiments such as Stratton's, which involved much more radical distortion of the visual scene and in which the subject could move about more freely than in the laboratory situation. Nevertheless, it seems likely that the adaptation that occurred as Stratton learned to coordinate his movements with the rearranged visual world was in part due to a change in the position sense of his limbs.

the same visual stimulation because the pattern on the walls and the center post of the apparatus was unvarying. Eight pairs of kittens were raised in this manner. After an average of thirty hours in the apparatus the active member of each pair showed normal behavior in a series of visual tests: it blinked at an approaching object, put up its paws to avoid collision when carried toward a surface, and avoided the deep side of a visual cliff (see Figure 6-16). The passive kittens, on the other hand, failed to show this type of behavior; only after being allowed to run freely for several days did they develop appropriate behavior.

In an extension of this study a blindfold was placed over one eye of each kitten during its daily exposure, and the blindfolds and training conditions were shifted so that each kitten had an "active" and a "passive" eye. That is, one eye viewed the scene while each kitten was actively moving about; the other eye viewed the same scene while the kitten was being passively conveyed in the gondola. In subsequent visual tests the active eye responded normally, whereas the passive eye showed the same lack of appropriate response displayed by the passive kittens in the earlier experiment. The sensory feedback accompanying active movement appears to play a vital role in the development of visual-motor control in the young, as well as in the adjustment to changes in the visual environment as an adult.

A subsequent study with infant monkeys has shown that *both* perceptual experience and behavioral experience are necessary for accurate visual-motor coordination. The information provided by watching the response proved to be important. Infant monkeys were raised from birth in an apparatus with a wide collar that prevented them from seeing their hands and arms. The animals could move their hands and arms freely and were trained to reach for objects they could not see. After thirty-five days (past the age at which normal monkeys have developed good eye-hand coordination) the monkeys were removed from the apparatus and tested for visually guided reaching by presentation of their nursing bottle. Their aim was very inaccurate at first but improved with practice. An interesting sidelight was the infant monkey's fascination with watching its hand when it first came into view; initially the monkey ignored the bottle in favor of studying this strange appendage it had never seen before (Held and Bauer, 1967).

The experiments relating muscular adjustments to visual perception raise interesting questions for perceptual theory. The important point is that visual perception is not a passive (photographic-like) registration of the environment but involves integration of visual and nonvisual activity. One theory proposes that spatial perception requires "outflow" information derived from motor pathways as well as "inflow" information from the visual system (Festinger and Cannon, 1965); another theory, the sensory-tonic field theory, suggests that the perception of visual objects involves the total organism and not merely the stimulation of the retina and other visual areas (Werner and Wapner, 1952).

The perceptual constancies imply organization within perception. In a more analytical vein, let us attempt to isolate principles of perception that help to explain how objects are organized and perceived.

Figure and ground

Geometrical patterns are always seen against a background and thus appear to be like objects, with contours and boundaries. *Figure-ground* organization is basic to stimulus patterning. Patterns do not have to contain identifiable objects to be structured as figure and ground. Patterns of black and white and many wallpaper designs are perceived as figure-ground relationships, and very often figure and ground are reversible. In Figure 6-5 note that the part that is seen as *figure* seems more solid and well defined and tends to appear slightly in front of the background, even though you know it is printed on the surface of the page. You seem to look through the spaces in and around the figure to a uniform background behind, whether the background is in white (or a light color) or black (or a dark color). Figure 6-6 shows a somewhat different kind of reversible figure and ground effect.

Fig. **6-6 Ambiguous figure-ground effects** An ambiguous drawing that can be seen either as an attractive young woman ("the wife") or as an old hag (facetiously referred to as "the mother-in-law").

As we shall note in the next section, studies of what people see when cataracts are removed and they suddenly recover from a lifetime of blindness show that the figure-ground organization is present even when other features of perception are missing. Adults seeing for the first time have no difficulty in seeing a *something* as a figure on a background, although they are unable to identify familiar forms by sight.

We can perceive a figure-ground relationship through senses other than vision. We may hear the song of a bird against a background of other outdoor noises; the melody played by the violin stands out against the harmonies of the rest of the orchestra. Some of the factors that determine what is perceived as figure against ground will be considered in the discussion of selective attention later in the chapter.

Fig. **6-5 Reversible figure and ground** Note that either the light portions or the dark portions can be perceived as figures against a background.

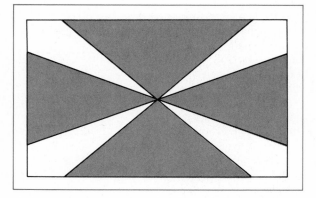

Perceptual grouping and patterning

Even simple patterns of lines and dots fall into ordered relationships when we look at them. In the top part of Figure 6-7 we tend to see three *pairs* of lines, with an *extra* line at the right. But notice that we could have seen three pairs beginning at the right and an extra line at the left. The slight modification shown in the lower part of the figure causes us to do just that. These tendencies to *structure* what we see are very compelling; what we see in figures seems to be forced upon us by the patterns of stimulation. The properties of wholes affect the ways in which parts are perceived. For that reason we may say that the whole is different from the sum of its parts—a favorite slogan of Gestalt psychology.

Perceptual hypotheses

Figure 6-8 shows a classic example of a reversible figure, the Necker cube. Study the figure and you will see that your perception changes. While looking at the cube you will find that the tinted face sometimes appears as the front of the figure and sometimes as the back. Once you have observed the cube change perspective, it will jump back and forth between the two perspectives with-

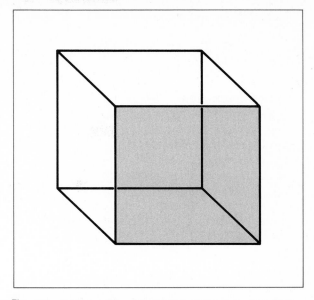

Fig. **6-8 Necker cube** An illusion devised by the Swiss naturalist L. A. Necker in 1832. Note that the tinted surface can appear as either the front or the rear surface of a transparent cube.

out any effort on your part. In fact, you will probably find it impossible to maintain a steady fixation of only one aspect.

Reversible figures such as the Necker cube point up the fact that our perceptions are not a static mirroring of visual stimuli. Perceiving is an active searching for the best interpretation of sensory information—an interpretation that includes our knowledge of object characteristics. According to Gregory (1966) a perceived object is a *hypothesis* suggested by the sensory data. The pattern of the Necker cube contains no clue as to which of two alternative hypotheses is correct, so the visual system entertains first one then the other hypothesis and never settles for an answer. This same testing of perceptual hypotheses goes on during normal perception, but usually a single correct solution presents itself. The problem arises with the cube because it is a three-dimensional object represented on a two-dimensional surface. If we were to see it in three-dimensional form we would know immediately which hypothesis to choose.

Fig. **6-7 Patterning and perceptual structuring**

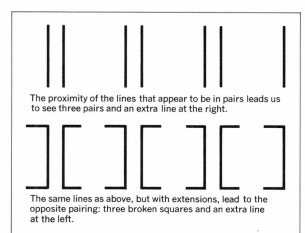

The proximity of the lines that appear to be in pairs leads us to see three pairs and an extra line at the right.

The same lines as above, but with extensions, lead to the opposite pairing: three broken squares and an extra line at the left.

Visual illusions

Sometimes we select a perceptual hypothesis that is incorrect; in this case we experience an illusion. Visual illusions have long intrigued psychologists; by studying the instances where perceptions were misleading they hoped to gain information about how perception works.

Geometrical illusions have been studied for many years, but their explanations are still not fully agreed upon. Some illusions are based on *relative size* in contrast with surroundings (Figure 6-9A). Others can be understood if we suppose the figures to be projected in the third dimension (Figure 6-9, B and C). If the lines in B and C were

Philip Clark From *Scientific American*

Fig. **6-10 An illusion involving perspective** The two rectangles superimposed on the photograph are precisely the same size. However, because we know that the railroad ties are all the same length, the rectangle that is farthest away is unconsciously enlarged. In fact, if the rectangles were real objects lying between the tracks, we would correctly judge the more distant one to be larger.

Fig. **6-9**

A. Illusion based on relative size The center circles are the same size, but the one to the left looks larger.

B. and C. Illusions based on intersecting lines The horizontal lines in B and C are parallel.

D. Ponzo illusion The two horizontal lines are the same length, but the upper one appears longer.

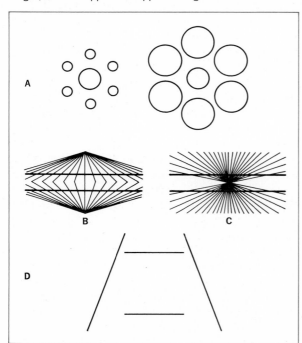

drawn on the surface of a solid double cone, or represented by a system of wires meeting at the horizon, they would have to be curved in order to be parallel as viewed. Because we tend to view these figures as though they were perspective drawings, we see the parallel lines as bent. In this case our tendency to "constancy" misleads us.

Figure 6-9D, the Ponzo illusion, can be better understood if we look at the photograph in Figure 6-10. The illusion can be thought of as a flat projection of three-dimensional space, with the vertical lines converging in the distance, as in the picture of the railroad tracks. We know from experience that the distant railroad ties are the same size as the nearest ones, even though the retinal image they give is much smaller. If real objects were lying between the tracks, the upper rectangle in the picture would be perceived as more distant. Because the brain tries to compensate for the expected shrinkage of images with distance (even though in this case there is no shrinkage for which to compensate), we see the upper rectangle as larger.

The fact that the Ponzo illusion increases in magnitude between childhood and adulthood suggests that the illusion depends upon learning to use linear perspective cues in two-dimensional drawings (Parrish, Lundy, and Leibowitz, 1968). Some of the problems of seeing three-dimensional forms on a two-dimensional surface are illustrated by the "impossible figure" (Figure 6-11). Incompatible depth information is given to the eye, and the brain cannot decide how to interpret it.

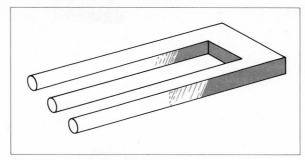

Fig. 6-11 An impossible figure This drawing appears as a "U" at the bottom, but has three prongs at the top.

Movement perception

Events are organized in time as well as in space; the pattern of a melody is an organization in time, just as a geometrical figure is an organization in space. When we perceive movement, we sense action in space taking place over time. We usually explain the perception of movement according to the stimulation of successive parts of the sensory surface. Trace a path on the skin and you feel movement as successive sensory receptors are stimulated. It seems reasonable to infer that a similar stimulation takes place on the retina. When an image moves across our line of vision it produces a pattern of successive stimulation of the rods and cones, and we perceive movement. The explanation is not this simple, however. It is possible for a pattern of successive stimulation to occur on the retina without any perception of motion. When you turn your head to look around the room, images move across the retina, yet objects in the room appear stationary. You are well aware that it is your head that is moving and not the room. The same thing occurs when you hold your head steady and move your eyes; objects in the room do not appear to move. Some higher cerebral process apparently integrates the information from the retinal stimulation and the kinesthetic information from your head, neck, and eye muscles to tell you that your head or eyes are moving and not the room.

It is also possible to perceive motion without a successive pattern of stimulation; we will now consider some examples of this kind of *apparent motion*.

Apparent motion

Autokinetic effect. If you stare at a single spot of light in a completely dark room, after a few seconds the light will appear to move about in an erratic manner—sometimes oscillating back and forth, sometimes swooping off in one direction. This apparent movement of a stationary light is known as the *autokinetic effect*. The phenomenon has been the subject of a great deal of experimentation, but there is still no certain explanation. What is clear is that the autokinetic effect occurs only in a visually impoverished environment where there is no frame of reference against which to determine that the light spot is stationary. When other lights are introduced or the room is lightened, the effect disappears. Pilots during night flights are particularly susceptible to the autokinetic effect; they sometimes line up a distant beacon with the edge of a windshield or some other frame of reference to avoid the effect.

Stroboscopic motion. Another kind of apparent motion, familiar to us as the basis for films, is known as *stroboscopic motion*. This illusion of motion is created when separated stimuli, not in motion, are presented in succession. Each frame of a film is slightly different from the preceding one, but if the frames are presented rapidly enough, the pictures blend into smooth motion.

A simpler form of stroboscopic motion, known as the *phi phenomenon,* has been studied extensively in the laboratory. One arrangement is diagramed in Figure 6-12. The four lights can be turned on and off in any order. When one light blinks on and then off, followed shortly by another, there is the illusion of a single light moving from the position of the first to the position of the second. The apparent movement is clearly seen as occurring through the empty space between the two lights. When the four lights of Figure 6-12 flash on and off in proper sequence, you see a rotating circle, but the diameter of the circle is less than that of a circle that would actually pass through the four lights. Whatever "attracts" the light to the position of the next light operates also to "attract" it toward the center of the circle, thereby making the circle smaller. The two tendencies result in the

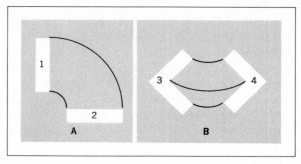

Fig. 6-13 Special cases of phi movement If a light is flashed on and off behind opening 1 in a screen and a moment later behind opening 2, then it appears as though a single bar of light is moving in an arc between the two positions in the plane of the paper. If a light is flashed on and off behind opening 3 and an instant later behind 4, then the motion is seen in the third dimension as if the figure were flipping over (like turning a page in a book) as it moves across.

Fig. 6-12 The phi phenomenon In a dark room if one of these four lights blinks on and off, followed shortly by another, there is the illusion of a single light moving from the first position to the second. When all four lights flash on and off in rapid sequence, it appears that a single light is traveling in a circle, but the perceived size of the circle is smaller (indicated by the dashed lines) than would be the case if the lights were actually rotating. (After Brown and Voth, 1937)

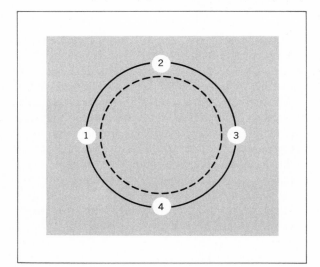

compromise that is seen as a circle too small to pass through the actual position of the lights.

Even though the phi phenomenon is illusory, it tends to preserve the perceptual structure that would be possible in real motion. For example, in Figure 6-13A the perceived motion is through an arc but in the plane of the paper, while in Figure 6-13B the motion is seen in the third dimension, the figure turning over as it moves across.

Real motion

These examples of apparent motion demonstrate that the perception of motion does not depend solely on real physical movement of stimuli in the environment. We can see apparent motion when there is no real motion at all. The perception of real motion is even more complex; it depends upon relations between objects within the visual field. Whenever there is movement, the brain has to decide what is moving and what is stationary with respect to some frame of reference.

Some early experiments have shown that when the only information we have about movement is visual, we tend to assume that large objects are stationary and smaller objects are moving. If a subject views a spot of light within a frame or against a screen background and the frame is moved while the spot remains stationary, he will perceive the spot as moving. Regardless of whether the spot or the frame is actually moved, the subject will always report that it is the spot that is moving against the background. This type of *induced movement* is experienced when we look at the moon through a thin cover of moving clouds. In a clear sky the moon appears to be stationary. When framed by the moving clouds the moon will appear to race across the sky, while the clouds appear stationary.

When we are walking or running, the decision about what aspect of our surroundings is moving is less of a problem because sensations from our limbs inform us of our motion along the ground. When we are transported, as in a car, train, or plane, our principal source of information is visual. Under these conditions we are more susceptible to illusions of induced movement. We are not always certain whether it is our railroad car that is moving or the one on the next track. Illusions of this kind are so frequent in air travel (particularly during night flights when it is difficult to establish a frame of reference) that pilots tend to trust their instruments rather than their perceptions. An even greater problem is faced by astronauts attempting to land a spacecraft on the moon; in the unfamiliar conditions of space the size, distance, and velocity of objects may be misjudged when evaluated on the basis of man's perceptual experiences on earth.

Depth perception

Our study of perception would be incomplete without considering the problems of perceiving the third dimension, that is, distance and depth. The retina is essentially a two-dimensional surface. How, then, is it possible to perceive things as filling a space of three dimensions?

Stereoscopic vision

Many of the facts of vision can be treated by considering phenomena that can be registered with only one eye. A man with vision in only one eye can have most of the visual experiences of a man using two eyes. He sees colors, forms, and space relationships, including third-dimensional configurations. We might suppose that two eyes have evolved merely to give man a "spare" in case of injury, just as he has two kidneys although one is enough.

A man with vision in both eyes does have one advantage over a man with vision in one eye: his total visual field is larger, so that he can see more at once, and he has the benefit of stereoscopic vision. In *stereoscopic vision* the two eyes cooperate to yield the experience of solidity and distance. That the experience does indeed depend upon the cooperation of the two eyes is clear enough from the effects that can be produced with a *stereoscope*. In this device two flat pictures, presented one before each eye, combine to yield an experience of depth very different from that received from a single flat picture. The depth appears real, as though the objects pictured were actually set up on a stage or in their true relations of depth and distance.

Stereoscopic experience differs from the experience of the third dimension in flat pictures because of *retinal disparity*.[1] Since our eyes are separated in our head, the left eye does not get exactly the same view as the right eye; the stereoscopic effect results from the combination of these slightly different pictures in one view. You can easily demonstrate retinal disparity for yourself. With one eye closed hold a pencil about a foot in front of you and line it up with some vertical edge on the opposite wall. Open that eye and close the other. The pencil will appear to have moved a considerable distance from its original alignment. If you line up the pencil with both eyes open and then close each eye alternately, you can determine

[1]Sometimes referred to as *binocular disparity*.

which is your dominant eye; that is, if the pencil shifts when you close the right eye, your right eye is dominant (which is usually the case with right-handed individuals).

The facts of stereoscopic vision are clear enough, but just how the process works is not so clear. Because of the way in which the nerve fibers from the eyes are separated in passing to the brain (see Figure 5-7, p. 115), the combination cannot take place in the eyes. The images from the two eyes must somehow be combined in the brain, probably at the level of the visual cortex.

Monocular cues to distance

Although having two eyes helps us to perceive depth and distance, we are by no means restricted to binocular effects for this perception. If you close one eye some precision is lost, but there is much left to go on.

An artist is able to give depth to his picture because he can make use of the many *monocular cues* that tell us the distance of objects. Except for those cues that depend upon movement, the artist can use all of the following cues.

Superposition of objects. If one object appears to cut off the view of another, the presumption is strong that the first object is nearer (Figure 6-14A).

Perspective. When you look down a railroad track, the rails appear to converge in the distance.

Most of us have been taught how to prepare perspective drawings making use of the fact that parallel lines apparently come together at the horizon. This geometry of perspective, or *linear perspective,* is one of the familiar signs of distance. Other facts of perspective are conveyed in many subtle ways, not all immediately evident. *Decreasing size* with distance is, of course, related to the geometry of perspective, so that the telegraph poles alongside the railroad track appear to grow smaller in the distance, just as the track becomes narrower. Even a series of scattered circles of different sizes may be viewed as spheres of the same size at varying distances (Figure 6-14B). Another hint of perspective is *height in the horizontal plane.* As we look along a flat plane, objects farther away appear to be higher, so that we can create the impression of depth for objects of the same size by placing them at different heights (Figure 6-14C). Even for irregular surfaces, such as a rocky desert or the waving surface of the ocean, there is a *gradient of texture* with distance, so that the "grain" becomes finer as distance becomes greater. This is also a form of perspective (Figure 6-14D). Finally, *aerial perspective* ("the purple of distance") produces changes in brightness and saturation of distant objects, some changes in hue, and a blurring of detail.

Light and shadow. Light and shadow help to define the contours of three-dimensional objects. One curious consequence of the prevalence of light

Fig. **6-14** **Visual distance perception** Several types of cues used in the perception of distance are shown here.

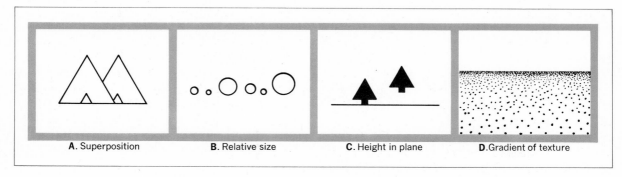

A. Superposition   **B.** Relative size   **C.** Height in plane   **D.** Gradient of texture

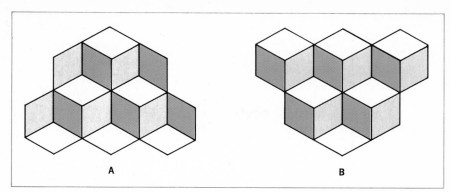

Fig. **6-15 Effect of light and shadow** Turn the book upside-down. Note the transformation when the pictures are inverted. (After Kahn, 1943)

A   B

sources from above is that convex and concave surfaces are sometimes reversed when a photograph is turned upside-down. It is difficult to believe that Figure 6-15A is 6-15B upside-down.

Movement. If you move in one direction, distant objects at the side appear to move with you, while near objects appear to move in the opposite direction. The relative movement provides a basis for judging distance. In attempting to judge distance, a person will often move his head back and forth even though he is unaware of the reason for doing so. He gets the same kind of advantage that retinal disparity provides in stereoscopic vision.

The role of learning in perception

Nativist and empiricist viewpoints

The phenomena of perceptual organization, movement and depth perception, and the various constancies lend themselves to simple and convincing experimental demonstrations, so that by now there is general agreement over what the subject perceives. Disagreements remain, however, over how to *explain* what happens. One of the traditional problems of visual perception has been the question of whether our abilities to perceive the spatial aspects of our environment are learned or innate. This is the age-old nature-nurture problem and its investigation with relation to perception began with the philosophers of the seventeenth and eighteenth centuries.

The *nativists* (Descartes, Kant) argued that we are born with the ability to perceive the way we do. The *empiricists* (Berkeley, Locke) maintained that we learn to perceive as we do through experience with objects in the world about us.

Among the early sensory psychologists, Hering and Helmholtz (whose theories of color vision were discussed in Chapter 5) held opposing views. Hering pointed to the fact of retinal disparity as evidence for the view that our eyes are innately designed to perceive depth; he developed a theory of distance vision based on the fact that each eye registers a different image. Helmholtz argued that visual perceptions were too variable (for example, reversible figure, p. 143) to be explained on the basis of fixed receptor mechanisms and must therefore be learned.

Most contemporary psychologists believe that a fruitful integration of these two viewpoints is possible. No one today really doubts that practice and experience affect perception. The question is whether we are born with some ability to perceive objects and space in our environment or whether these abilities are completely learned. Let us examine some of the areas of research that yield information on the role of learning in perception.

Effects of restored vision

As far back as the seventeenth century Locke quotes a letter received by him from Molyneux, in which the problem is posed:

> Suppose a man *born* blind, and now adult, taught by his *touch* to distinguish between a cube and a sphere of the same metal, and nighly of the same bigness, so as to tell, when he felt one and the other, which is the cube, which the sphere. Suppose that the cube and the sphere placed on a table, and the blind man be made to see . . . [could he] now distinguish and tell which is the globe, which the cube? [Locke, 1690]

Locke, supporting the empiricist viewpoint, concluded that he could not.

A partial answer to this question is provided by studies of individuals who were blind from birth with cataracts on both eyes and whose vision was restored by surgical means when they were adult (Senden, 1960). When the bandages are removed for the first time from the eyes of such a patient, he is confused by the bewildering array of visual stimuli. He is able, however, to distinguish figure from ground (apparently perceiving figure-ground relationships in much the same way as normally sighted people do), to fixate figures, scan them, and follow moving figures with his eyes. These abilities then appear to be innate. He cannot identify from sight alone objects very familiar from the sense of touch, such as faces, knives, and keys. He cannot distinguish a triangle from a square without counting the number of corners or tracing the outline with a finger. He cannot tell which of two uneven sticks is longer without feeling them, although he may report that the two sticks look somehow different. It often takes several weeks of training for such patients to learn to identify simple objects well from sight, and even after identification has been learned in a specific situation, the patient shows little evidence of generalization or perceptual constancy. A white triangle may not be recognized when it is turned over to its red side, or when viewed under altered illumination, or when turned upside-down. His poor performance cannot be attributed to difficulty in discriminating colors; the restored-vision patient can distinguish between colors (although he does not at first know

which name to attach to which color) long before he can distinguish between shapes.

These studies of previously blind adults who are suddenly able to see for the first time, suggest that our perceptions develop gradually from primitive visual experiences in which figure-ground relationships and color predominate, becoming more accurate and more detailed with practice. They cannot, however, be taken as conclusive evidence of the innate visual ability of the infant; we do not know what deteriorative changes may have occurred over the years the adult subject was blind, nor do we know what compensating skills this adult may have developed to overcome his handicap.

Visual deprivation with animals

In an attempt to provide a more controlled situation similar to restored vision in human subjects, animals have been raised in various degrees of darkness and then tested for visual ability. Earlier investigators who reared infant chimpanzees in total darkness until they were sixteen months old found serious perceptual deficiencies when the animals were tested upon first exposure to light. But these chimpanzees were later discovered to have defective retinas. Apparently a certain amount of light stimulation is necessary for normal anatomical development of the visual system. Without any light stimulation, nerve cells in the retina and the visual cortex begin to atrophy. This fact is interesting in itself, but it does not tell us much about the role of learning in perceptual development.

Later studies made use of translucent goggles so that the animals received light stimulation, but of a diffuse, unpatterned form. Studies have been carried out with monkeys, chimpanzees, and kittens wearing translucent goggles from birth to anywhere from one to three months of age. The results showed that although some simple perceptual abilities were unimpaired, more complex visual activity was seriously affected. The visually deprived animals did almost as well as normal animals in distinguishing differences in color, brightness, and size, and they could readily discriminate between a disc with horizontal stripes and one with vertical stripes. However, their visual acuity was poor, and they could not perform such tasks as following a moving object with their eyes, discriminating forms (a circle from a square or triangle), perceiving depth, and distinguishing between a moving and a nonmoving stimulus (Riesen, 1965). After experience with patterned light, the visually deprived animals caught up with the normal animals—in a matter of days or weeks, depending upon the particular task.

The results of the visual deprivation studies lead to the not too surprising conclusion that both maturation and experience are important in the development of visual abilities. Animals that have been deprived of patterned light react very much like newborn animals in their visual abilities when first exposed to light. This fact indicates the importance of experience. On the other hand, once exposed to patterned light, the visually deprived animals learn various visual skills more rapidly than newborn animals, thus pointing up the contribution of maturation.

Perception in newborns

If the human infant could tell us what the world looks like to him, many of our questions concerning the development of perception might be answered. Since he cannot, experimenters have had to stretch their ingenuity to try to measure his visual abilities. One method uses a head-turning response. The infant reclines in an infant-seat, with his head between two foam rubber pads. A slight turn of the head against either pad activates a microswitch that records the response. In one study with six week olds, the infant was rewarded by the smiling, peekaboo appearance of the experimenter every time he turned his head in the presence of a 12-inch cube. After the infant has learned to respond faithfully to the cube in order to obtain the peekaboo reward, he is then tested to see how he responds to other objects of different size, shape, or distance away. For example, after learning to respond to a 30-centimeter cube at a distance of 1 meter, he can then be tested with a 30-centimeter cube placed 3 meters away, a 90-centimeter cube at 1 meter, and a 90-centimeter cube at 3 meters.

We assume that the cube that elicits the most frequent head-turning appears to the infant to be most similar to the 30-centimeter cube at 1 meter. If the infant does not perceive distance and has not developed size constancy, then the 90-centimeter cube placed 3 meters away should appear most similar to the original stimulus; it is three times the height of the original stimulus but also three times the distance away, so it casts the same-size retinal image. The results showed that this stimulus received the *least* number of responses of the three (Bower, 1966). Apparently the infants were responding on the basis of real size and distance rather than retinal size. The results from this and other studies indicate that by the age of eight weeks human infants have some capability for distance discrimination, size constancy, and shape constancy, although these abilities improve with age.

One area of perception in infants that has been thoroughly investigated is the perception of height, which is a special case of distance perception. The apparatus shown in Figure 6-16 has been used with human infants and a wide variety of infant animals in an attempt to determine whether the ability to perceive and avoid a brink is innate or must be learned by the experience of falling off and getting hurt. Most parents, mindful of the caution they exercise to keep their offspring from falling out of the crib or down the stairs, would assume that the ability to appreciate height is something the child must learn. But observation of the human infant's susceptibility to such accidents does not tell us whether he is unable to discriminate depth or whether he can indeed respond to depth cues but lacks the motor control to keep from falling.

Gibson and Walk (1960) tested how thirty-six infants, ranging in age from six to fourteen months, responded when placed on the center board of the visual cliff. The mother called to the child from the cliff side and the shallow side successively. Almost all the infants crawled off on the shallow side but refused to crawl on the deep side. Their dependence on vision was demonstrated by the fact that they frequently peered through the glass on the deep side and then backed away. Some of the infants patted the glass with their hands but still

William Vandivert from *Scientific American*

Fig. **6-16 The "visual cliff"** Infants and young animals show an ability to perceive depth as soon as they can move about. The visual cliff consists of two surfaces, both displaying the same pattern, which are covered by a sheet of thick glass. One surface is directly under the glass; the other is dropped several feet. When placed on the center board shown in the photo, the infant refuses to cross the "deep" side, although he will readily move off the board onto the "shallow" side. (After Gibson and Walk, 1960)

remained unassured that it was solid and refused to cross.

Since the infants could not be tested until they were old enough to crawl, the experiment does not prove that depth perception is present at birth. The results of studies with other organisms, however, indicate that depth perception is present at least as soon as the animal is able to locomote. Chickens tested when less than twenty-four hours old never made a mistake by stepping off on the deep side. Goats and lambs placed on the center board as soon as they could stand (some only a day old) always chose the shallow side. When placed on the deep side such animals characteristically froze in a state of immobility. Rats, who respond more to smell and to tactile cues from their whiskers than to visual cues, will move off the center board on either side provided they can feel the glass with their whiskers. If the center board is raised several inches so that the glass is out of reach of their whiskers and they are forced to rely on visual cues, they will consistently descend on the shallow side. Kittens also possess whiskers, but they seem to respond more to visual cues and will invariably choose the shallow side when they are old enough to be tested, at about four weeks of age.

Experiments designed to isolate the specific visual depth cues to which the organism responds on the visual cliff have yielded contradictory results; it seems, however, that monocular cues are sufficient. Infants who wore eye patches on one eye discriminated as well as those with binocular vision (Walk, 1968).

Organization in the visual cortex

Some of the most interesting research bearing on the question of innate perceptual abilities has involved microelectrode techniques. Recordings were obtained from single nerve cells in the visual cortex of the cat while the cat's eyes were stimulated with light patterns projected on a screen. Unlike nerve cells in the retina and optic nerve, it was found that most cells in the visual cortex do not respond when stimulated by large or diffuse spots of light. Instead, these cortical cells seem to be highly organized in terms of the kinds of stimuli to which they will respond. Some cells will fire only when a slit or narrow rectangle of light is presented in a particular orientation—for example, horizontal or vertical. Other cells respond to the *movement* of a light slit and sometimes only when the movement is in a particular direction. Still other cells respond to more complex stimuli, such as angles or corners (Hubel and Wiesel, 1965). This study shows that some abstract stimulus qualities appear to be coded by single nerve cells; to some extent, then, the perception of visual forms is built into the structure and organization of the cells in the cortex. But we cannot jump from this fact to the conclusion that the perception of angles, corners, and edges is innately determined. Even though we possess a visual cortex that is innately organized to perceive certain kinds of form and motion, we still may have to learn how to use such equipment.

Attention and perception

Selective attention

Our perceptions are selective. We do not react equally to all the stimuli impinging upon us; instead we focus upon a few. This perceptual focusing is called *attention*. Through attentive processes we keep in focus selected stimuli and resist distracting stimuli.

Even as you sit reading this, stop for a moment, close your eyes, and attend to the various stimuli affecting you. Notice, for example, the tightness of the heel of your left shoe, the pressure of clothing on your neck or shoulders, the sounds coming from outside the room. We are constantly bombarded by stimuli to which we do not attend. In fact, our brains would be quite overloaded if we had to attend to every stimulus present in our environment. Somehow, our system selects for attention those stimuli that are pertinent and ignores the rest until such time as a change in a particular stimulus makes it important for us to notice it.

There is evidence, however, that stimuli to which we are not actively attending still register in some form in our perceptual system, even though we may not recognize them at the time. Consider what takes place during a cocktail party. Out of the complex volume of sound generated by the wavelengths of many voices taken together, we are able to listen to one voice. Although we may think we are not attending to the other voices, let someone in the far corner of the room mention our name and we are immediately aware of it; apparently our system monitors the other voices for relevant stimuli without our being aware of such activity.

The cocktail party situation raises two interesting questions: (1) How are we able to focus attention on one conversation out of the many that surround us? and (2) how much do we register of the conversations to which we are not attending? Some of the cues that enable us to concentrate on one voice in a babel of many are the directions of the sound, lip movements of the speaker, and the particular voice characteristics of the speaker (whether the voice is male or female, its speed, and intonation). Even if all these cues are eliminated, by recording two messages spoken by the same speaker and playing them on the same magnetic tape, it is still possible to distinguish the messages. The task is a difficult one requiring intense concentration, but most subjects can separate the two messages, apparently by relying on the grammatical and semantic content of the spoken material for cues. In the absence of appropriate grammatical cues, however, the task of separating two simultaneous messages by the same speaker becomes impossible.

Information about how much we register from conversations to which we are not attending is provided by an experimental situation similar to the cocktail party. Two different spoken messages are presented to the subject by means of earphones, one to the right ear and the other to the left. The subject has no difficulty in listening to either speech at will, rejecting the unwanted one; and he can switch his attention back and forth from one speech to the other. If we ask him to repeat aloud the speech presented to the right ear, he can do it fairly well even though the message is continuous; his words are slightly delayed behind those of the message to which he is listening. His voice tends to have a monotonous quality, however, with no inflection, and at the end of the passage he may have little idea of what it was all about, particularly if the material is difficult. What about the other message, the one to which he was not attending? How much information does the unattending ear assimilate? The answer depends upon a number of factors, including the difficulty of the two messages. If the attended message is a familiar nursery rhyme, then the subject will recall a fair amount of the message to the unattended ear. With more difficult material, however, the subject usually can recall nothing of the verbal content of the unattended message and will not even be certain whether it was in English or German. He is aware of certain general characteristics: whether the message was speech rather than a pure tone, whether the voice was male or female, and, for many subjects, whether their own name was mentioned.

If the subject is interrupted during his repetition of the message to the attending ear and asked quickly what was just presented to the other ear, there does appear to be some temporary memory for the message not attended (Norman, 1969). This is similar to the situation in which someone to whom you are not listening asks you a question; your immediate response is "What did you say?" but before the question is repeated you suddenly realized what was asked.

Studies of this kind have led to the conclusion that the nervous system must have some kind of register where incoming sensory information is temporarily stored in a rather crude and unanalyzed form. Of all the stimuli that bombard our senses, only those that our higher mental processes tell us are relevant to the psychological processes going on at the moment are selected for attention. Some sort of attention mechanism selects for further processing those sensory inputs that seem most important or pertinent. Certain classes of sensory inputs, such as the sound of one's name, can be expected to have a permanently high level of pertinence, but most will fluctuate depending upon the ongoing events in the central nervous system (Norman, 1969).

Determinants of stimulus selection

What factors determine which of many competing stimuli will gain our attention? The characteristics of the stimulus are important as are our own internal needs, expectancies, and past experience. The advertiser is concerned with discovering these factors so that he can direct attention to his product. Some of the physical properties of the stimulus that are important in gaining attention are *intensity, size, contrast,* and *movement.*

Certain internal variables, such as motives and expectations, are equally important in determining which stimulus attracts our attention. The advertiser counts on an appeal to the male sex drives when he uses pictures of scantily clad females to advertise everything from carpets to automobile tires. In a culture where hunger is a more generally unsatisfied drive than sex, pictures of food might prove to be a more powerful attention-getter.

Individuals vary greatly in their responses to the same stimuli because of habitual or momentary interests that prepare them for certain kinds of stimuli. The naturalist will hear sounds in the woods that the ordinary picnicker would miss because of his different habits of attention. A mother will hear her baby's cry above the conversation of a living room full of people. These two illustrations represent abiding interests. Sometimes momentary interest controls attention. When you page through a book looking for a particular diagram, what you see depends on what you are looking for. Only pages with illustrations cause you to hesitate; others you ignore. Emotional states, especially moods, may affect the ways in which attention is directed. In a hostile mood, personal comments are noticed that might go unremarked in a more friendly mood.

Physiological correlates of attention

When a stimulus attracts our attention, we usually perform certain body movements that enhance our reception of the stimulation. If it is a visual stimulus we turn our head in the proper direction, our eyes turn so that the image falls on the fovea, our pupils dilate momentarily to allow more light to enter the eye, and the lens muscles work to bring the image clearly into focus. If the stimulus is auditory we may cup our hands behind our ears or turn one ear in the direction of the sound, keeping the rest of our movements very still so as to enhance the reception of a faint auditory stimulus. These body movements are accompanied by certain characteristic internal physiological

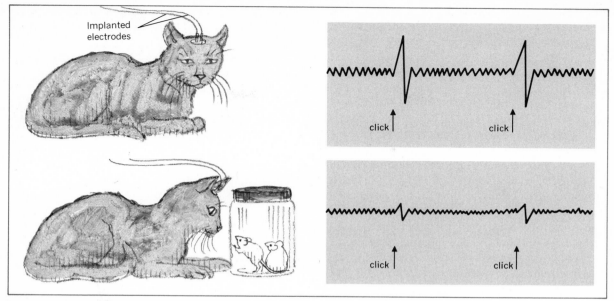

Fig. **6-17   Tuning out a stimulus**   The sound of a click produces a marked increase in electrical activity in the auditory cortex of the cat. When a jar of mice is placed in front of the cat the neural response to the click practically disappears, indicating that the auditory response is suppressed or tuned out when attention is directed elsewhere. (After Hernández-Peón, Scherrer, and Jouvet, 1956)

changes. The physiological reactions that occur in response to changes in stimulation in the environment form such a consistent pattern that they have been called the *orienting reflex* and have been studied extensively by psychologists.

The orienting reflex occurs in both man and animals in response to even minimal changes in the stimulus environment. The physiological accompaniments of attention, in addition to the body movements mentioned above, include dilation of the blood vessels in the head, constriction of the peripheral blood vessels, certain changes in the gross electrical responses of the brain (EEG), and changes in muscle tone, heart rate, and respiration. These responses serve the dual function of (1) facilitating the reception of stimulation and (2) preparing the organism to respond quickly in case action is needed. We can see why such a reflex is extremely valuable for self-preservation.

The facilitating effect of the orienting reflex on sensory reception can be demonstrated in the laboratory. The arousal of the reflex by a loud tone will increase visual sensitivity, making it possible for the subject to see a light that was too faint to be detected before the arousal. The orienting reflex habituates over time, however. With repeated presentation of the sound the reflex gradually diminishes; the visual threshold is raised to its previous level, and the same light intensity no longer evokes a response (Sokolov, 1963). Any change in the stimulus, or the introduction of a new stimulus, will reactivate the orienting reflex in its original strength.

Studies of electrical activity in specific areas of the cerebral cortex give us some idea of how the brain may operate to focus attention selectively. In one study electrical activity in the auditory cortex of the cat was measured by means of permanently implanted electrodes. When a click was sounded at regular intervals, the recording from the auditory cortex appeared as illustrated in the upper portion of Figure 6-17. Each click is accompanied by an increase in electrical activity in the auditory cortex. When a glass jar containing mice is placed in front of the cat, the neural response to the click practically disappears, indicating that when the cat's attention is focused on something else, the auditory response is suppressed. Removal of the mice produced a return of the pronounced electrical response to the clicks (Hernández-Peón, Scherrer, and Jouvet, 1956). Other attention-getting stimuli, such as fish odors or a shock to the forepaw, produced similar results.[2]

It appears that when one sensory channel is engaged, information from other channels may be suppressed or filtered out so that at any given moment only certain sensory impulses reach the brain. According to our earlier formulation, the sensory impulses selected for attention would be those most pertinent to the ongoing psychological processes of the organism. Some evidence indicates that the *reticular formation* (a region of the brain stem where impulses from all the sense modalities converge, see p. 34) is the control center where much of this screening takes place (Hernández-Peón, 1961).

Needs and values

What a person perceives and how he perceives it may be determined to some extent by his needs and personal values. The value an individual places on an object may affect such direct impressions as those of size. For example, children from poorer homes tend to overestimate the size of coins more than do children from well-to-do homes (Bruner and Goodman, 1947). The following experiment attempted to subject this process to direct laboratory control.

The experiment involved both an experimental and a control group of nursery school children. Children in the experimental group learned to turn a crank in order to receive a poker chip. When a child inserted the poker chip in a slot, he automatically received a piece of candy. The conjecture was that the candy would enhance the value of the poker chip and that this increased value would result in overestimation of size, as in the coin experiments. The size estimates were obtained by having each child adjust a variable spot of light so that it appeared equal to the poker chip when viewed from a few feet away. Both control and experimental subjects overestimated the size by 5 or 6 percent in a pretest, but after ten days of rewarded learning with poker chips the experimental group increased its overestimation to 13 percent. During the same period the overestimation of the control group had not increased significantly.

As further evidence of the importance of learning, the values of the experimental group underwent extinction through nonreward. Then the size estimation returned to its previous level. After reinstatement of the value of the poker chip through reconditioning, the size was again markedly overestimated (Lambert, Solomon, and Watson, 1949).

Extrasensory perception

If there are so many influences upon perception other than those coming from the presented stimuli, are there perhaps perceptions that require no sense-organ stimulation whatsoever? The answer to this question is the source of a current controversy within psychology over the status of *extrasensory perception* (ESP). Although some psychologists believe that the evidence for the existence of certain forms of ESP is now incontrovertible (for example, Rhine and Brier, 1968; Forwald, 1961; McConnell, 1969), most remain unconvinced.

The phenomena under discussion are of two main kinds:

1. Extrasensory perception (ESP)
   a. Telepathy, or thought transference from one person to another.
   b. Clairvoyance, or the perception of objects or events not influencing the senses (e.g.,

[2]For a more complete review of this work and some criticisms of it, see Horn (1965).

stating the number and suit of a card that is in a sealed envelope).

c. Precognition, or the perception of a future event.

2. Psychokinesis (PK), whereby a mental operation affects a material body or an energy system (e.g., wishing for a number affects what number comes up in the throw of dice).

Experimenters investigating these problems work in accordance with the usual rules of science and generally disavow any connection between their work and spiritualism, supernaturalism, and other occult doctrines. Yet the phenomena with which they deal are so extraordinary and so similar to the superstitious beliefs of nonliterate people that many scientists reject even the legitimacy of their inquiries. Such a priori judgments are out of place in science; the real question is whether the empirical evidence is acceptable by ordinary scientific standards. Many psychologists who are not convinced are nevertheless ready to accept evidence that they find satisfactory. For example, the possibility of some sort of influence from one brain to another, other than by way of the sense organs, would not be inconceivable within the present framework of science were the facts of telepathy to be established in an orderly fashion. Some of the other phenomena, such as precognition, are more difficult to find believable, but if the evidence were firm, previous beliefs would have to yield to the facts.

The case for ESP is based largely on experiments in card-guessing, in which, under various conditions, the subject attempts to guess the symbols on cards randomly arranged in packs. The usual ESP pack consists of 25 cards having 5 symbols, so that a chance performance would be 5 hits per pack. Even very successful subjects seldom reach as high a level as 7 hits, but they may score above 5 often enough to meet acceptable standards of statistical significance. If the experimenter, or "sender," thinks of the symbol at the time the subject makes his record, the experiment is one on telepathy; if the experimenter does not perceive the card at all (it may be face down on the table before him or sealed in an envelope), then the experiment is one on the subject's clairvoyance.

TABLE 6-1 RESULTS OF TELEPATHY AND CLAIRVOYANCE TRIALS WITH ONE SUBJECT*		
CHRONOLOGICAL ORDER OF SUCCESSIVE GROUPS OF 200 TRIALS	HITS PER 200 TRIALS (EXPECTED = 40)	
	TELEPATHY TRIALS	CLAIRVOYANCE TRIALS
1945	65	51
	58	42
	62	29
	58	47
	60	38
1947	54	35
	55	36
	65	31
1948	39	38
	56	43
1949	49	40
	51	37
	33	42
Total hits	707	509
Expected hits	520	520
Difference	+187	−11
Hits per 25 trials	6.8	4.9

* Each group of 200 trials consisted of alternating blocks of 50 telepathy and 50 clairvoyance trials.

Source: Soal and Bateman (1954).

The kind of evidence used in support of the non-chance nature of the findings can be illustrated by the successive runs of one "sensitive" subject, Mrs. Gloria Stewart, studied in England over a long period (Table 6-1). If the evidence is viewed in the same spirit as that from any other experiment, it would be clear that Mrs. Stewart responded above chance on the telepathy trials but not on the clairvoyance ones. This fact also meets certain objections about card arrangements sometimes voiced against such experiments, for her chance performance on the clairvoyance trials shows that above-chance scores are not an inevitable result possibly related to the method of shuffling the cards. The telepathy results are above the expected level in 11 of the 13 runs of 200 trials, and the average scoring level of 6.8 hits (instead of 5) per pack of 25 is well above chance.

The complaint has been voiced that ESP results are not subject to systematic variation through ordinary experimental control. This also is not an entirely fair criticism. For example, some order effects are reported, in which early trials are more successful than later ones (McConnell, 1968), and there is reported evidence that an attitude favorable to ESP, noted in advance, leads to positive results, while an unfavorable attitude leads to scoring below chance levels (Schmeidler and McConnell, 1958).

Empirical findings that meet ordinary statistical standards are offered in support of ESP and PK. Why, then, do the results not become a part of established psychological science? Many arguments have been used against the work, but they usually boil down to a few, such as the following: (1) the fact that many claims of extraordinary

CRITICAL DISCUSSION

Why many psychologists find ESP experiments unconvincing

We may expand a little upon the objections that psychologists have to the ESP and PK experiments and to *psi*, the special ability attributed to the "sensitive" subject.

1. General skepticism about extraordinary phenomena. Throughout history there have always been reports of strange happenings, ghosts, poltergeists (noisy spirits who engage in throwing things about), dreams foretelling the future. The continuing appearance of these stories does not make them true. Painstaking investigation by the U. S. Air Force has yielded no "flying saucers"; no one has ever trapped the Loch Ness monster. A famous medium is a case in point. Eusapia Palladino was able to make a table move and produce other effects, such as tapping sounds, by the aid of "spirits." Investigated repeatedly between 1890 and 1910, she managed to convince many distinguished scientists of her powers. On several occasions, however, she was caught in deceptive trickery, and the results were published. Even so, believers continued to support her genuineness, as some do today (Jastrow, 1935). When those most convinced about ESP are also convinced about already disproven phenomena, their testimony carries less weight than if they were more critical.

2. Problems of statistical inference. A major contribution of ESP research to psychology may turn out to be the attention it has drawn to the circumstances that make a scientific finding believable. It is commonly supposed that tests of statistical significance are sufficient guarantees of objectivity, and hence a satisfactory statistical outcome should lead to acceptance of a hypothesis as plausible. This turns out not to be the case in ESP experiments, and it is probably not the case in other experiments either. Statistical tests merely tell us how well measurement seems to establish something that is already plausible; if it is not plausible, we search for some confounding variable that may have produced the nonchance result.

In this regard let us consider an experiment performed in Rhine's Duke University laboratory (Rhine, 1942). He was trying to determine whether a subject might, through some combination of ESP and PK, influence the positions of cards in a mechanical shuffler. In all, fifty persons wrote down their predictions of the orders in which cards would come out of a mechanical shuffler ten days later. The experiment was carefully performed, and in a total of over fifty thousand trials the results were at chance level—just 11 hits in excess of expectation. But was this plausible result accepted? No—further statistical analyses were made. Two more of these, based on the division of the trials into segments, failed to yield nonchance results. Finally, a fourth analysis, based on a complex effect called a "covariance of salience ratio," gave a nonchance effect, with odds of 625 to 1 in its favor. When belief in bizarre effects is carried this far, it is no wonder that the unconvinced scientist begins to question the statistics, even though all the computations are accurate.

phenomena in the past have turned out to be false when investigated; (2) certain problems in statistical inference that arise when very large numbers of trials are used to establish the significance of small differences; (3) the failure of improved methods to yield better results than crude methods; and (4) a general lack of orderliness in the phenomena, without which rational theorizing cannot replace the current highly speculative theories.

These arguments are not, in fact, decisive, and it is desirable to keep an open mind about issues that permit empirical demonstration, as the ESP phenomena do. At the same time it should be clear that the reservations of the majority of psychologists are based on more than stubborn prejudice. The critical discussion below is provided for those who might care to look a little further into these issues.

3. Failure of improved methods to increase the yield. In most scientific fields, the assay from the ore becomes richer as the methods become more refined. But the reverse trend is found in ESP experiments; it is almost a truism in research in the fields of telepathy and clairvoyance that the poorer the conditions, the better the results. In the early days of the Duke University experiments subjects yielding high ESP scores were rather common. As the experiments have become better controlled, however, the number of high-scoring subjects has diminished. PK studies have shown a similar decrease in significant results with improved experimental control (Girden, 1962).

4. Lack of systematic consistency in the phenomena. Sensitive subjects in the Rhine laboratory appear to be equally successful at clairvoyance and telepathy, but the English subjects appear to be good at telepathy and not at clairvoyance. Other peculiarities emerge. In a famous series of experiments in England, one subject gave no evidence of either telepathy or clairvoyance when scored in the usual way against the target card. Instead he was shown to be successful in *precognition telepathy*, that is, in guessing what was *going to be* on the experimenter's mind on the next trial. He was unsuccessful in clairvoyance, no matter how he was scored (Soal and Bateman, 1954). Why, the skeptic asks, does the direct telepathy fail with this subject in favor of something far more mysterious than the telepathic success of Mrs. Stewart?

Because the *psi* ability does not follow ordinary rules, explanations of its operation can be produced with the greatest of freedom. It need not be affected in any ordinary way by space or time, so that success over great distances is accepted as a sign of its extraordinary power rather than something to cause a search for artifacts. Similarly, the precognition experiments are merely evidence to the ESP proponents that it is as easy to read what is *about* to be on someone else's mind as what is on it now. The PK effects, which require the results of card sorting or dice rolling to be produced by mental effort ("mind over matter"), are nevertheless said to occur without any transfer of physical energy, thus presumably violating the usual belief in the conservation of energy. But in any experimental work *some* aspects of time and space have to be respected. Unless some restraint is shown, one might invent any number of hypotheses: the subject was sometimes perceiving the cards in reverse order, sometimes in a place-skipping order, and so on. With such hypotheses no significant test could be applied.

The believer in *psi* is impatient with this kind of criticism. He says that more is asked of him than of other experimenters. In fact, we do ask more. To demonstrate something highly implausible requires better evidence than to demonstrate something plausible. Supporting evidence for the plausible finding comes from many directions, whereas the implausible one must hang upon a slender thread of evidence until systematic relationships are found that tie it firmly to what is known.

Summary

1. We mainly perceive things, and we perceive these environmental objects as stable and enduring. The stability of perceived objects depends upon various *constancies:* color and brightness constancy, shape constancy, size constancy, and location constancy. Size perception usually represents a compromise between perspective size and object size. The greater the number of distance cues available, the more the perceived size approaches object size. As environmental cues are reduced, perception approaches perspective size (that is, it corresponds to the size indicated by the retinal image).

2. The basic organization of visual perception appears to be that of *figure* and *ground,* so that we recognize patterns as figures against a background whether or not the patterns are familiar. Reversible figures illustrate the fact that perception involves an active search for the best interpretation of sensory information rather than a static mirroring of visual stimuli.

3. Visual illusions are incorrect perceptual hypotheses. Some are based on *size contrasts* with the surroundings, whereas others are created when we try to interpret figures on a two-dimensional surface as if they were three dimensional.

4. Movement perception depends upon the integration of signals from the *retina* with kinesthetic information from the head, neck, and eye muscles. Perception of *apparent motion,* as in the *autokinetic effect* and *phi phenomenon,* has not yet been completely explained. Perception of real motion depends upon the relation between objects within the visual field. When vision alone is operating, we tend to assume that large objects are stationary while smaller ones are moving.

5. Visual depth is perceived binocularly with the help of *stereoscopic vision,* the fusion of the slightly unlike images of the two eyes. Depth is perceived monocularly with the aid of a number of cues: *superposition* of objects, *perspective* (whether geometric or given through relative size, height in the frontal plane, gradients of texture, or aerial perspective), *movement,* and *light* and *shadow.*

6. Both learning and innate factors contribute to our abilities to perceive aspects of our environment. Perception of figure-ground relationships, color, and depth appears to be largely innate; form perception, although based upon an innate organization of cortical cells that respond selectively to specific features of the stimulus, must still be built up through experience.

7. Perception is *selective,* so that at any moment in time we *attend* to only part of the influx of sensory stimulation. Stimuli to which we are not actively attending may be registered temporarily in the nervous system, but they are not selected for attention unless deemed pertinent. Factors that favor attention to one stimulus in preference to another reside in its physical properties (intensity, size, contrast, movement) and in the habitual and momentary interest of the individual. What an individual perceives and how he perceives it is determined to some extent by his needs and personal values.

8. The *orienting reflex* is a pattern of physiological reactions that correlate with attention. These reactions facilitate the reception of stimuli and prepare the organism for action.

9. *Extrasensory perception* (ESP) in its various forms (telepathy, clairvoyance, precognition) and *psychokinesis* (PK), the influencing of physical events by mental operations, are areas of controversy in psychology. There are many reasons for reserving judgment on these phenomena, but an a priori condemnation of the experiments is unjustified. The experiments raise interesting issues about the criteria by which scientific credibility is established.

Suggestions for further reading

Textbooks covering the kinds of problems dealt with in this chapter include: Dember, *The psychology of perception* (1960); Graham and others, *Vision and visual perception* (1965); Hochberg, *Perception* (1964); and Forgus, *Perception* (1966). Allport's *Theories of perception and the concept of structure* (1955) is valuable for its review and critical analysis of the major theories of perception. A collection of papers on vision may be found in Haber (ed.), *Contemporary theory and research in visual perception* (1968b).

An excellent introduction to the psychology of seeing, with emphasis on illusions, movement perception, perspective, and related topics, is Gregory, *Eye and brain* (1966); this book also discusses some of the perceptual problems man may experience as he moves into outer space and explores alien planets.

Problems of attention, perceptual coding, and visual search are discussed in Neisser, *Cognitive psychology* (1967), and in Haber (ed.), *Information-processing approaches to visual perception* (1969). See also Gibson, *Principles of perceptual learning and development* (1969), which brings together theories of perceptual learning and reviews the facts of perceptual development.

For a review and criticism of extrasensory perception experiments, see Hansel, *ESP: A scientific evaluation* (1966). A review more favorable toward extrasensory perception is McConnell, *ESP and credibility in science* (1969).

states of awareness

BY STUDYING THE PERCEPTION OF THE WORLD through our senses—the substance of the two preceding chapters—we have already gained much information on the conditions of awareness in the normal waking state. But some problems of consciousness remain to be discussed, particularly the special problems connected with distorted, clouded, or even expanded awareness (ranging from sleep to ecstatic experiences).

At one time psychology was thought to be the study of consciousness, and consciousness was accepted as open to immediate observation. If you drop a brick on your toe you know whether or not it hurts, and you can specify where the pain is felt. Similarly, if you look at a bright light and then close your eyes you will see a succession of colored images, and you can describe them as you see

them. The question of whether there are "facts of consciousness" in this sense can be answered readily enough: of course there are. But another question has proved more difficult to answer: What is the status of consciousness as subject matter for a *scientific* psychology?

The objection to accepting consciousness as subject matter for science lies in a rejection of the dualism between mind and body, the belief that there are both physical facts and mental facts, following different "laws" of energy interchange. As was pointed out earlier (Chapter 1, p. 9), one way of combating this objection is to deny any fundamental dualism, but to accept the convenience of a double language, the language of mental activities (private experiences, intentions, and so on) on the one hand, and the language of physics and physiology, on the other. Thus when one describes a dream according to its content, the one language is used; when dreaming is described according to brain waves or eye movements, the other language is used.

Modern behaviorists freely accept a subject's verbal reports as behavior; his words recorded on electromagnetic tape can be counted and sorted as any other behavioral product. Thus the psychologist, in order to go about his business, does not have to take a strong stand on the scientific value of the study of consciousness. He uses what-

ever data help him to understand what is going on; if these data come from the answers his subjects give to his questions, he finds ways to justify the use of these answers.

Once we become interested in exploring the facts of consciousness, or awareness, our attention is directed to different *states of awareness,* of which two states—waking and sleeping—are the most familiar. It turns out, however, that these states are by no means simple ones, and within them various kinds of alterations can occur.

Varieties of waking states

The normal waking consciousness, in which we can report accurately what is happening in the environment about us, is but one of several states of waking awareness. Others include fatigue, delirium, intoxication, and ecstasy. Most people believe that they know what the normal waking state consists of and only the other states are interesting or puzzling. In fact, the ordinary waking state may be the most puzzling of all, but we are less troubled by it because it is so familiar.

The complexity of normal waking consciousness

Waking consciousness is not itself a single, simple state. We may be attentive or inattentive; we may be looking, listening, talking, or planning—or perhaps all of these at once. When we are listening to what a spokesman is saying, we may also be preparing our reply; and even while articulating the reply we may be thinking of further arguments to use. We have long known, however, that when we try to do too many things at once they tend to interfere with one another. A man may not find it difficult to talk while driving a car along a busy highway, but his conversation may give way as the traffic gets snarled. We noted in the discussion of the "cocktail party phenomenon" (p. 153) our remarkable ability to focus attention on one conversation out of many and to switch attention from one conversation to another. Although we can

attend fully to only one message at a time, some information registers from a second message.

The planning function that goes on, even while we are talking, has been commented upon by Miller, Galanter, and Pribram (1960). They note that during almost all of our waking consciousness we talk to ourselves about our plans—a kind of silent commentary on what is going on. ("How long shall I talk to Jim before having a word with Jane?" "Shall I take another helping?" "Is this worth writing in my notebook?" "Will there be time to get to the library after class?") Plans to stop activities now engaged in, to enter others, to accept or refuse invitations, to drift or to schedule—this stream of self-talk, beyond listening and speaking, is part of waking consciousness. Some writers of the stream-of-consciousness school, such as Gertrude Stein, James Joyce, and Virginia Woolf, have attempted to capture self-talk as a literary device.

Not all waking states are alert. Sometimes we find ourselves or others just staring—not examining anything, but looking rather blankly at nothing at all. We know the difference between our minds being very active and being almost free of thought; hypnotized subjects often report that they can sit for a time with their minds practically blank, passively waiting for something to be suggested to them. Observation of newborn babies indicates that alert and inert states begin very early in life.

Babies in the first five days of life tend to be mostly asleep, except when distressed or eating; in these states they pay little attention to sights and sounds about them. But in these first days there are also occasional quiet alert states, in which their eyes are wide open and their eyeballs are "bright" and appear to focus on objects. At this age these states last for a short time (the longest being seven minutes), and the total of the alert inactive periods does not exceed thirty minutes in a 24-hour period. Only during these alert inactive periods will the newborn baby turn his head and eyes to follow a visual object or turn toward a source of sound (Wolff, 1966).

The readiness for new stimuli, sometimes called a state of *vigilance,* can be tested in the adult by responses to the occasional appearance of a stimulus on a screen or to some change in a regularly appearing sound or other stimulus. Mackworth (1950) used a clock with a pointer that jumped regularly once a second, but at rare intervals the pointer gave a jump of double the length. The subject had to pay close attention in order to report these double jumps by pressing a key when they occurred. He found that a subject could do quite well for half an hour, but tended to make many more errors when set to work for a longer period. Mackworth found that he could reduce errors by reporting to the subject that he had responded correctly when he had, or by saying "You missed one there" when he had failed, or even by calling him over the telephone and asking him to do better.

Studies of vigilance have shown that there are many techniques by which subjects can be kept alert, and indeed we use such techniques on ourselves all the time. To keep from falling back into states of vacant staring we keep orienting ourselves to our tasks, reminding ourselves where we are and what time it is; we squirm, scratch, adjust clothing, tap with our fingers, chew a pencil. These are not mere nervous habits to discharge tension; they keep us from going to sleep, from becoming inattentive. Recent physiological studies suggest that these techniques serve to keep the reticular formation active (see p. 34).

Modifications of waking consciousness

The familiar waking consciousness can be subjected to various degrees of distortion by excessive fatigue or sleep loss, by disease, or by drugs. Some changes, occurring outside the experimental laboratory, provide examples of these extremes.

Fatigue and exhaustion. Hard muscular exertion produces a number of readily recognizable physiological changes, accompanied by subjective experiences of weariness, pain, and desire to rest or sleep. The ability to continue at work is reduced, and the quality of work suffers. If the fatigue process has not gone too far, recovery is rapid, and with rest the work can be resumed with satisfactory performance. More profound changes take place

Fig. **7-1 Vigilance after loss of sleep** The subject can perform well for a short time after considerable sleep loss, but how long he can do well depends on how long he has been without sleep. The baseline represents errors in the task when there has been no sleep loss. (After Williams, Lubin, and Goodnow, 1959)

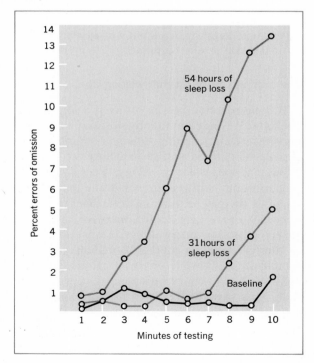

if exertion leads to exhaustion. In the cases of fatigue and exhaustion we are concerned with the results of actual physical work; many of the symptoms of listlessness may have other causes that are of psychosomatic or neurotic origin.

Quite a few experiments have been concerned with the debilitating effects of sleep loss. The most usual finding is that the sleep-deprived subject can pull himself together for a satisfactory performance on tasks of short duration, but that a long-continued task suffers more interference. For instance, on one test little loss of vigilance was shown for the first 7 minutes of testing following a 31-hour sleep loss, but after that, errors set in; following 54 hours of sleep loss the good performance was sustained for only 2 minutes (Figure 7-1).

Delirium. In its extreme form *delirium* is most often found in connection with alcoholism, but a confusional state with hallucinations and delusions may accompany high fever or affect patients who have undergone surgery. *Hallucinations* are sense-like perceptions that have a minimum of support from external stimuli, like the pink elephants seen in the hallucinations of some alcoholics. *Delusions* are faulty thought systems, in which sense percep-

tion may be accurate but events misinterpreted, as when a nurse is seen as planning to poison a patient, or visitors seen as enemy agents. This type of distorted awareness is also associated with mental illness (see Chapter 20).

Ecstasy. It must not be supposed that all altered awareness is a symptom of derangement. Some of the temporary distortions of consciousness under hypnosis and drugs are described as extremely pleasant by those who happen to experience them. Then there are the experiences of heightened illumination and joy, or *ecstasy,* as in religious mysticism, which defy categorization. William James (1902) called mystical experiences "noetic but ineffable," by which he meant that the mystic had a sense of gaining knowledge (noetic aspect), but the experience was essentially indescribable and therefore not communicable (ineffable aspect). Experiences short of ecstasy, but with somewhat similar meanings for those who have them, have been called *peak experiences* by Maslow (1959; see p. 331 of this text). These sustaining experiences are said to enrich life's meaning and are cherished by those who have them.

Sleeping and dreaming

The state that is most commonly contrasted with waking is sleeping, because it is a state of greatly lessened awareness and activity. Biologically, it is a restorative state. Like the waking state, however, it is not simple. Sleep does not come about simply when the bodily processes resulting from waking activities require it, for whatever the condition of the body a person can choose either to sleep or to remain awake. Sleep is not altogether unconscious, for upon waking, dreams can be recalled. It is not entirely quiescent, because some people walk in their sleep. It is not entirely insensitive, because a mother can be awakened by the cry of her baby. It is not altogether planless, because some people can set themselves to wake up at a

given time and do so. Still, sleep is the most obvious change in conscious state; most of us experience the transitions between the two states (sleep and waking) at least twice a day.

Sleep rhythms and depth of sleep

The newborn baby tends to alternate rather frequently between sleeping and waking; gradually one period of sleep is lengthened, and eventually the night-day rhythm is established (Figure 7-2).

Human adults establish a rhythm of sleep and waking that persists in part through internal regulation. Some travelers, for example, find it very hard to adapt to the new time schedules that jet

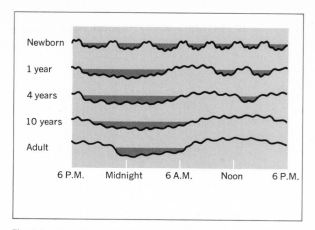

Fig. **7-2 Development of the sleep pattern** The shaded areas represent periods of sleep. Note that the newborn's short cycles of sleep and wakefulness gradually become the single night-day cycle of the adult. The minor fluctuations in each curve represent secondary cycles of activation that last 50 to 60 minutes in the infant and gradually lengthen to 80 to 90 minutes in the adult. (After Kleitman, 1963)

travel can produce within a few hours; the "jet lag," as it has come to be called, may persist for several days before they adjust to new bedtime and rising hours. An interesting experiment on adult

sleep rhythms was performed some years ago by the leading authority on sleep, Nathaniel Kleitman, and his associate (Kleitman, 1939). They set up temporary "housekeeping" for a month in the uniform illumination and temperature conditions of Mammoth Cave, Kentucky, and attempted to adapt to a 28-hour day, 19 hours under artificial illumination and 9 hours in the dark. By good fortune the two men differed sufficiently in their adaptation for the results to be highly instructive; one of them adapted to the new schedule in such a way that his daily temperature changes, when averaged for the last three weeks in the cave, showed the six peaks characteristic of the six lengthened (28-hour) days of the week; the other continued to have the seven peaks characteristic of his precave rhythm (Figure 7-3). Related experiments, under free conditions, have tended to show natural rhythms that are predominantly somewhat longer than 24 hours, but the pressures of environmental events tend to obscure these rhythms in favor of the 24-hour one (Aschoff, 1965).

Biological clocks. The rhythms of sleep and waking in man raise a number of questions about

Fig. **7-3 Physiological adaptation of two subjects to a changed length of day** The two men lived for one month on a 28-hour schedule in Mammoth Cave. The results are for the last three weeks in the cave. Subject *K* continued to have seven peaks of temperature corresponding to the days of the week (based on the 24-hour day). Subject *R* had adapted to the new schedule of six days, each of 28 hours. The dark bands are the hours spent in bed, mostly in sleeping. (After Kleitman, 1939)

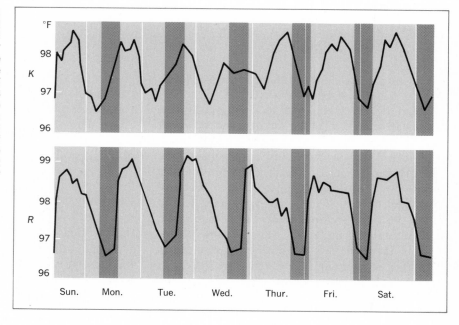

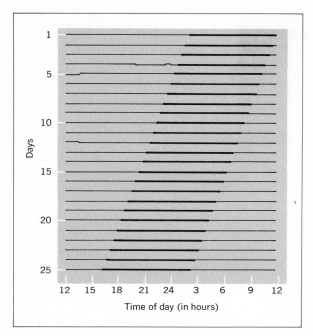

Fig. **7-4 Internally regulated daily activity rhythm** Activity of one flying squirrel in continuous darkness at uniform temperature. The dark lines represent activity; the thin lines, quiescence. Note that each day the activity begins a little sooner than that the day before, but the daily change is remarkably uniform. (After DeCoursey, 1960)

the extent to which control is external or internal. External control through changes in light and dark and temperature, including seasonal changes, can readily be demonstrated, but there are also internal controls, which are regulated by the hypothalamus in higher mammals. Evidence of internal control has come from experiments with flying squirrels; these animals were placed in living cages with revolving wheels, allowing their periods of activity to be measured. The flying squirrel, like other rodents, tends to have a cycle of high activity at night alternating with quiescence in the day. When the caged squirrel was kept continuously in the dark, its alternation of activity and quiescence continued to approximate a 24-hour cycle. Although the internal clock may run a little slow or fast, it is remarkably constant for any one animal, as shown in Figure 7-4. The activity cycle for this animal began a few minutes earlier each day, but if light and dark were again alternated, so that

darkness began at the same time each day, the onset of the activity rhythm would soon become adjusted to exactly a 24-hour period.

That man has internal regulating mechanisms has been shown in other experiments. For example, when investigators were kept in a room with no external signs by which to judge the passing of time, they were still able to report the time of day to within a few minutes, even after eighty-six hours for one of the subjects (MacLeod and Roff, 1936). Still, if time is interpreted according to watches that are set to run an hour slow or fast per day (under conditions in which external light does not give time clues), bodily processes eventually follow the new rhythm, though some processes do so after a short time while others may take a week or more. Bodily temperature rhythms, for example, adjust more readily than water excretion (Lobban, 1965).

Because of the speed of modern travel and the need to adjust to new time zones, the internally and externally controlled rhythms take on increasing interest.

Stages of sleep. One scale of depth of sleep is provided by evidence recorded from the scalp on the *electroencephalogram* (EEG), a method of studying the electrical activity of the brain (see p. 38). The EEG indicates four stages of sleep, as shown in Figure 7-5.

When subjects are wakened from sleep by noises of graded intensity, the ease of waking does not always correspond to the EEG stage. In general, a sleep continuum runs through these four stages, and it is easier to arouse a person from Stages 1 and 2 than from 3 and 4. But something else happens in Stage 1. It is only in this stage that dreaming occurs, a state that is usually accompanied by rapid eye movements (REMs). During the period of rapid eye movements in Stage 1 sleep, it is very difficult to arouse the sleeping subject (Figure 7-6). This dreaming state is sometimes known as "paradoxical sleep," because the subject is near to being awake by one criterion (EEG) but hard to arouse by another (REMs).

How much time is spent in each of the sleep stages? Studies show that this varies from person

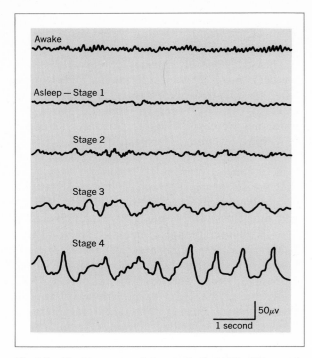

Fig. **7-5** **The four stages of sleep, as indicated by EEG records**
Stage 1 sleep is characterized by low voltage and relatively
fast patterns of change; Stage 2 is recognizable by the presence of sleep spindles, with some complex responses with a
low-voltage background; Stages 3 and 4 are identified by slow
waves known as delta waves. These distinctions are unimportant to the nontechnical reader; the main point is that the
expert is able to recognize changes. (After Dement and Kleitman, 1957)

ological states succeeding each other every day—
wakefulness, non-REM (NREM) sleep, and REM
sleep.

New knowledge about dreams and dreaming

The investigation of dreams and dreaming
opened up by the new psychophysiological
methods has given us the answers to some age-old
questions, but many new questions have also
arisen. To illustrate these findings, questions will
be stated and the present answers summarized.

**Is Stage 1-REM a satisfactory indicator that a
subject is dreaming?** Occasionally a subject awakened from NREM sleep reports a dream, but it
is usually more like "thoughts" than a dream, or
more like the images that sometimes occur in the
initial onset of sleep (without REMs). Monroe and

Fig. **7-6** **Sound intensity requisite for arousal from sleep** The
subject was asked to press a key attached to a finger when
he heard a loud sound. It is interesting that this response
can be made at all depths of sleep and is more frequent to
louder sounds at all stages. The impressive finding in this
experiment is that it is difficult to waken the subject at Stage
1 when this stage is accompanied by rapid eye movements
(REMs). (After Williams, 1967)

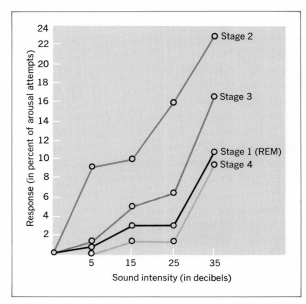

to person, but for any one person the sleep pattern
is often consistent night after night. Rough percentages for the four stages are: Stage 1, 25 percent; Stage 2, 50 percent; Stages 3 and 4, 25 percent of the night (Williams, Agnew, and Webb,
1964). The distribution is not even throughout the
night. Little dreaming occurs during the first hour;
Stages 3 and 4 are mostly concentrated in the first
few hours; Stage 2 is more evenly distributed
throughout the night; and most dreaming (Stage
1-REM sleep) occurs in the last third of the night.

The most important distinction in sleep analysis
has come to be the one between Stage 1-REM
sleep and the remaining sleep, so much so that
workers in the field now think of three main physi-

The discovery that most dreaming occurs in Stage 1-REM sleep has greatly increased the study of dreaming: investigators no longer need to wait for the subject's recall in the morning nor take the chance of waking him when there has been no dreaming.

CRITICAL DISCUSSION

Three states of the organism: wakefulness, NREM sleep, and REM sleep

The additional information about Stage 1-REM sleep as a result of experiments with animals and newborn babies has opened up new territories of exploration not just related to dreaming. REM sleep and NREM sleep are different in more respects than just the occurrence of rapid eye movements. Some of the physiological processes that are related to one another in the normal waking state appear to be "uncoupled" during REM sleep. The brain seems to be very active, as shown by circulatory changes and a rise in temperature; at the same time postural muscles are very relaxed and lose their tonus, so that the *electromyogram* (EMG), a measure of muscular activity, is about as satisfactory an indicator of REM sleep as the eye movements themselves. Still, some muscles escape from this inhibition occasionally, and a good deal of spontaneous twitching of the muscles associated with locomotion takes place. The notion that a dog that kicks while sleeping in front of the fire is dreaming that he is chasing a cat may not be so far-fetched. Apparently the brain is so active during REM sleep that, despite the general inhibition of the postural muscles, some of this activity spills over into jerky movements of the limb muscles (Dement, 1965). Although autonomic activity, such as the galvanic skin response (GSR), is depressed in REM sleep, the activity is heightened during the supposedly deeper phase of sleep in Stage 4, providing another paradox about depth of sleep.

The connection between REM sleep and dreaming, and between the physiological experiments and psychological interpretations of the nature of dreams, is complicated by the prominence of REM sleep in lower animals and in the very young, even in premature infants (Figure 7-7). The prevalence of REM sleep early in life suggests that very primitive processes must be associated with REMs. By analogy, it is not surprising that the dreams associated with REMs later in life may be manifestations of illogical primitive impulses.

Fig. **7-7** **Decrease in REM time with increasing age** The color portions show the ranges of means from different studies. REM time is highest through infancy and early childhood but does not decrease significantly after the elementary-school years. (Data from Kales, 1968)

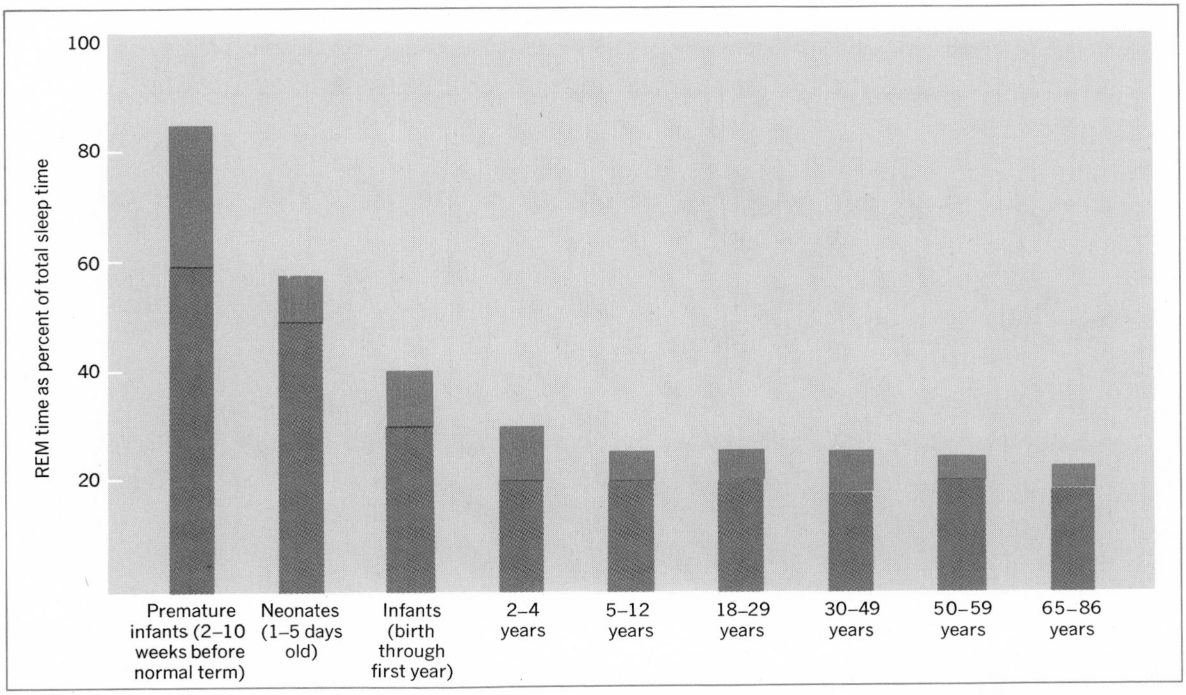

others (1965) collected "dream" reports from both REM and NREM sleep and then had judges attempt to determine what kind of sleep had produced each report. The judges were successful in better than 90 percent of the cases in determining which dreams had in fact been produced under REM conditions; there is little doubt that they are more "dreamlike" than those produced under NREM conditions. Because dreams are reported in about 80 percent of awakenings from Stage 1-REM, the association of dreaming with that stage is obviously close.

Do eye movements reflect the content of the dream? Here we are on more difficult grounds. *Occasionally* the eye movements correspond quite well to events reported in the dream (Figure 7-8), but this is by no means universal. It cannot be generally assumed that eye movements reflect what is being hallucinated in the dream. It is doubtful that the REM states of very young infants are accompanied by dreams, for dreams, as we know them, depend upon remembered perceptions, even though they may be organized in novel or bizarre ways.

Does everyone dream? Although many people do not recall dreams in the morning, "recallers" and "nonrecallers" appear to dream equally often, if we accept the REM-sleep evidence (Goodenough and others, 1959). It is of interest that the nonrecallers also have difficulty in recall when awakened at night, just following a REM period. Nonrecallers in everyday life tend to recall fewer dreams in the laboratory, and shorter ones than the recallers (Lewis and others, 1966). On the whole, the evidence is that everyone dreams.

Can the sleeper react to the environment without awakening? Williams, Morlock, and Morlock (1966), in an experiment in the series illustrated by Figure 7-6, showed that subjects could discriminate auditory signals during sleep better during Stage 1-sleep onset and Stage 2 than during Stage 1-REM phases. Such results bear on the possibility of sleep learning, because material read to the

Fig. **7-8 Rapid eye movement and dream imagery correspondence**   The eye movement record (ROC, LOC—referring to electrode positions for right and left movements) showed a regular sequence of 26 eye movements alternating to the right and to the left. Following this sequence the subject was awakened (at the arrow in the figure). He reported that just before being aroused he had dreamed that he was watching a ping pong game between two friends. He had been standing at the side of the table so that he looked back and forth to follow the ball during a lengthy volley. (After Dement, 1967)

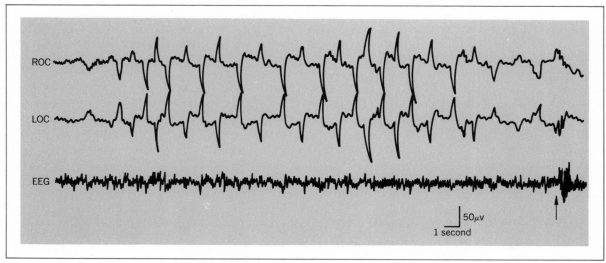

learner while asleep (often from a tape recorder) must be responded to if it is to be learned. Many claims have been made for learning during sleep, but laboratory substantiation is lacking (Emmons and Simon, 1956; Hoskovec and Cooper, 1967). Signals that occur during REM sleep may be incorporated into the dream rather than awaken the dreamer. Thus Berger (1963) showed that spoken names presented during REM sleep were incorporated into dream events. Subjects taught to respond posthypnotically to a verbal signal (for example, to scratch the nose, or to turn a pillow) carried out the instructions even though the signal was given during REM sleep (Cobb and others, 1965). Thus the state of sleep is by no means a completely inert one.

Do sleeptalking and sleepwalking take place in REM sleep? It has been found that sleeptalking occurs primarily during NREM sleep and probably not in relation to ordinary dreaming (Kamiya, 1961; Rechtschaffen, Goodenough, and Shapiro, 1962). Essentially the same applies for sleepwalking (Jacobson and Kales, 1967). Subjects usually forget what they did while sleepwalking, and the dreams they remember in the morning bear no resemblance to what they did while walking about.

Although sleeptalking does not appear to be related to dreams under normal circumstances, it can be used as a method for studying dream content. Through posthypnotic suggestions planted in the waking state it is possible to instruct the subject to talk about his dream *while it is occurring,* without awakening, and to sleep comfortably and silently when the dream is over (Arkin, Hastey, and Reiser, 1966). The dream recalled in the morning may be a fragmentary version of the full dream reported while it was happening.

Dream theories

Man has long been puzzled by his dreams. Because a person does not feel responsible for his dreams, he is likely to think of them as being in some manner informative, perhaps even prophetic, so that dream interpretation has had a long history.

Freud's theory. The most influential theory of dreams in the last half-century has been that of Freud, the founder of psychoanalysis. Freud announced his theory in *The interpretation of dreams* (1900), a book that he considered to be his most important work. He believed that unconscious impulses were responsible for the dream, and that the aim of the dream was the gratification of some drive (in the older terminology that he used, the fulfillment of a wish). The real meaning of the dream, called its *latent content,* is not directly expressed, but is instead dramatized in disguised form. The remembered content of the dream, in this disguised form, is its *manifest content.* According to Freud, the dreamer constructs the dream by representing the impulse-provoked ideas in acceptable form, commonly as visual imagery. The manifest content derives from the thoughts of the previous day (the *day residues,* as Freud called them), combined with thoughts and emotions from the past.

Freud's theory holds that the work of dream construction occurs through the mechanisms of condensation, displacement, and symbolization. *Condensation* refers to the combining of ideas into more abbreviated form, so that a single word or figure may have multiple meanings in the dream. *Displacement* permits one thing to stand for another, as one part of the body may stand for a different part. *Symbolization* is the more general term for representing ideas or events by something else. These may be private symbols, related to the individual experience of the dreamer, or more universal symbols, of which the sexual symbols are the best known. Since to Freud much of the impulsive life centers around sexual wishes, and sex has certain taboos associated with it, the symbolization of the sexual organs is to be expected: the male organ is represented by a snake or other long or pointed objects; the female organ is more often represented by some sort of container, such as a box, basket, or vessel.

Freud thought that the dream was the guardian of sleep because it got rid of unfulfilled impulses, which might otherwise disturb the sleep. The disguise was necessary so that the disturbing impulses would not be brought to the attention of the dreamer. If the raw meaning of the dream were open to the dreamer, the impulses would often be found to be intolerable, and he would wake up. The dream does often fail in its work; for instance, the dreamer sometimes awakens frightened, possibly because of anxiety aroused in the dream. In his later writings Freud acknowledged these failures of the dream work (Freud, 1933).

Alternative theories about dreaming. Freud's theory did not go unchallenged by his psychoanalytic followers and others who studied dreams without the benefit of physiology. Erikson (1954) felt that the dream revealed much more than disguised wish fulfillment, and that its manifest content was worth taking seriously. French and Fromm (1964) showed that a series of dreams could be interpreted as repeated attempts by the dreamer to solve his problems. Hall (1953) had earlier shown that sometimes the same thoughts that appeared in "disguised" form also appeared in "plain" form in the same dream. This led him to suggest that the so-called dream disguise was no disguise at all, but merely a form of metaphor—a literary device within the dream.

The Freudian theory has been put under considerable strain by the more recent studies of REMs and dreaming, although not all the evidence contradicts the theory. If one of the purposes of the dream is to protect sleep, this purpose should be reflected in some sort of "need to dream." To test this possibility, Dement (1960) introduced the method of depriving a subject of his normal quota of dreams by arousing him whenever dreaming began, as indicated by the appearance of REMs. He applied this method for several nights and was able to reduce the amount of dreaming by about 70 percent. This dream deprivation produced some sort of deficit, for when the subject was allowed to sleep freely, for several nights he dreamt much more than usual, perhaps 40 to 80 percent more than he did before deprivation. Controls were run, of course, to see that this was not merely a matter of having lost sleep through so many arousals during the night; when the same number of arousals were made from NREM sleep, no such increase in dreaming occurred on later nights. The fact that it is more difficult to awaken the subject from Stage 1-REM sleep than from Stage 1-NREM sleep is also coherent with the sleep-guardianship theory. Finally, the occurrence of penile erections in some 80 percent of REM states (Fisher, Gross, and Zuch, 1965) gives support to Freud's contention that many dreams are sexual in origin.

Still, many results from the physiological studies cast doubt on the Freudian theory. The prevalence of REM states in very young infants (including premature ones), and in animals low in the phyletic scale, makes it unlikely that the adaptive purpose of the REM state, whatever it may be, corresponds to the Freudian theory of the adaptive nature of dreams. A great deal of new information is now forthcoming on the effects of drugs, prolonged sleep, and sleep disturbances in various conditions of illness.

The controversies over the interpretation of dreams have a greater chance of being resolved now that the new methods of investigation permit samples of dreams under controlled conditions and more detailed reports of the dreams themselves. It is to Freud's credit that he made dreams a subject of modern scientific inquiry; it remains for others to build new theories based on sounder knowledge than was available to him.

Hypnosis as an altered state of awareness

The word "hypnosis" is derived from the Greek word for sleep (*hypnos*), and the metaphor of sleep is commonly used in inducing the hypnotic trance. Pavlov, the famous Russian physiologist (see p. 5), became interested in sleep and hypnosis during his later years; he conceived of hypnosis as a partial sleep. Now that EEG evidence is available, we can say with some assurance that hypnosis is not ordinary sleep, for the EEG of the hypnotic state is that of waking, not that of any of the four recognized stages of sleep. Whether it can be interpreted as some special kind of partial sleep is at present an open question.

Hypnotic induction

In order to hypnotize a willing and cooperative subject (the only kind who can be hypnotized under most circumstances), the hypnotist creates the conditions for entering hypnosis by any of a number of methods that relax the subject, exercise his imagination, and lead him to relinquish some control to the hypnotist and to accept some reality distortion. A common method is for the hypnotist to ask the subject to fix his eyes upon some small target, such as a thumbtack on the wall, concentrate on the target, detach his thoughts from other things, and gradually become relaxed or sleepy. The suggestion of sleep is a convenient one because it is familiar as being a relaxed state, out of touch with ordinary environmental demands. But it is a metaphor, and the subject is in fact told that he will not really go to sleep. The subject continues to listen to the hypnotist and, if susceptible, finds it easy and congenial to do what the hypnotist suggests and to experience what he invites the subject to experience.

In its modern form, hypnosis does not involve authoritarian commands by the hypnotist; with a little training the subject can hypnotize himself, using what he has learned from the hypnotist. In other words, the subject enters the hypnotic state when the conditions are right; the hypnotist merely helps set these conditions. The transition from the waking state to the hypnotic state takes a little time, but with practice this time tends to be shortened. With special procedures, such as observing others being hypnotized, the subject can learn to go somewhat more deeply into hypnosis.

Characteristics of the hypnotic state

The hypnotic state or trance recognized today is essentially as it was described to be in the nineteenth-century heyday of hypnosis. Some of its characteristics, as shown by subjects who illustrate a high degree of susceptibility, are the following:

1. *The planning function subsides.* The subject, deeply hypnotized, does not like to initiate activity; he waits for the hypnotist to tell him what to do.

2. *Attention is redistributed.* While attention is always selective, under hypnosis it becomes more selective than usual. If the hypnotist tells the subject to listen to his voice only, the subject will not then pay any attention to other voices in the room.

3. *Reality testing is reduced and reality distortion accepted.* Ordinarily one checks up on things to see that he is awake, oriented in space and time, not suffering from illusions, and so on. Under hypnosis one may uncritically accept hallucinated experiences (petting the imaginary rabbit in his lap) or other distortions that would usually be rejected.

4. *Suggestibility is increased.* Of course one has to accept suggestions in order to be hypnotized at all, but the question is whether normal suggestibility is *increased* under hypnosis. This is a matter of some dispute, but careful studies do find an increase in suggestibility, though perhaps less than might be supposed from the common identification of hypnosis with heightened suggestibility (Hilgard and Tart, 1966).

5. *The hypnotized subject readily enacts unusual roles.* When told to adopt a role, such as being someone other than himself, the hypnotized subject will commonly do so and will carry out complex activities related to that role. This includes re-enacting his own behavior at a much younger age (as in hypnotic age regression). There may be something of an actor in each of us, and the permissiveness of the hypnotic situation, in which ordinary restraints on behavior are set aside, makes this role-behavior congenial. Impressed by this kind of behavior, Sarbin (1956) has formulated a role-enactment theory of hypnosis, affirming that those who become hypnotized have a high order of role-enactment ability and have attitudes appropriate to role-enactment.

6. *Posthypnotic amnesia is often present.* Some susceptible hypnotic subjects react to the suggestion that they will forget events within hypnosis after they are aroused from it, until a prearranged signal is given by the hypnotist. Following such instructions they will forget all or most of what

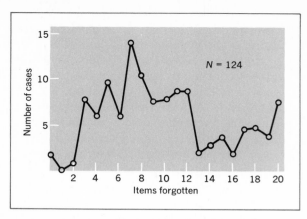

Fig. 7-9 Distribution of posthypnotic amnesia The scores are plotted according to items forgotten, with a possible of 20 items. Those who forget 0–13 of the 20 items are not very amnesic, but those who forget from 14 to 20 appear not only to be amnesic but to represent a special group of the more hypnotizable. Because this special group represents about one-fourth of the subjects, it is sometimes said that only about one-fourth of the population should be considered adequately hypnotizable, although most others show some hypnotic effects. (After Hilgard and others, 1961)

transpired during the hypnotic session. When the release signal is given, the memories are restored. How the extent of forgetting varies from person to person in a college population is shown in Figure 7-9. Most subjects forget a few of the things they did within hypnosis, just as they forget what

they have done in ordinary psychological experiments. But some are extremely forgetful following the suggestion that they will not "remember," and it is these we think of as demonstrating posthypnotic amnesia.

The hypnotic state resists precise definition, but the behaviors of hypnotized subjects, of which the above six are representative, are sufficiently consistent to serve as an approximate definition of the state.

Who can be hypnotized?

There is no disagreement that some people can be hypnotized more readily than others, but there is uncertainty whether some persons can be hypnotized at all, even given the most favorable circumstances. Occasional reports have been given of heroic attempts in which the same person underwent hypnotic induction for hundreds of trials until hypnosis was finally achieved. The record, a case report by Vogt in the last century, was six hundred trials. Under ordinary circumstances, a person's hypnotizability can be determined quite well from the first attempt to hypnotize him.

The availability of scales for measuring susceptibility to hypnosis permits more precise statements about the distribution of hypnotizability than were

TABLE 7-1	ITEMS OF THE STANFORD HYPNOTIC SUSCEPTIBILITY SCALE, FORM A
SUGGESTED BEHAVIOR	CRITERION OF PASSING (YIELDING SCORE OF +)
1. Postural sway	Falls without forcing
2. Eye closure	Closes eyes without forcing
3. Hand lowering (left)	Lowers at least six inches by end of 10 seconds
4. Immobilization (right arm)	Arm rises less than one inch in 10 seconds
5. Finger lock	Incomplete separation of fingers at end of 10 seconds
6. Arm rigidity (left arm)	Less than two inches of arm bending in 10 seconds
7. Hands moving together	Hands at least as close as six inches after 10 seconds
8. Verbal inhibition (name)	Name unspoken in 10 seconds
9. Hallucination (fly)	Any movement, grimacing, acknowledgment of effect
10. Eye catalepsy	Eyes remain closed at end of 10 seconds
11. Posthypnotic (changes chairs)	Any partial movement response
12. Amnesia test	Three or fewer items recalled

Source: Weitzenhoffer and Hilgard (1959).

formerly possible. The scales that have been found most satisfactory are based on the performances given by a subject following a standard form of hypnotic induction: the subject who responds most frequently like a hypnotized person is scored as most susceptible. The items of one such scale are listed in Table 7-1.

The relative success of such scales is illustrated by a study in which twenty-five subjects were chosen to represent the range of hypnotic susceptibility as measured by the scale described in Table 7-1. The individuals were hypnotized repeatedly until it was quite clear that they had yielded about all they could in the way of hypnotic responsiveness. Their carefully estimated hypnotic susceptibility at the end correlated $r = .75$ with their initial measure of susceptibility (Shor, Orne, and O'Connell, 1966). Hypnosis is thus shown to be a relatively stable ability, although with specially devised techniques of training some improvement is possible, especially for those who show at least slight initial susceptibility (Sachs and Anderson, 1967).

The exact percentage of people who can be hypnotized has been variously estimated by different authorities, but the development of standardized measures now permits more precise statements. Scores from 533 university students are shown in Figure 7-10. The distribution of scores shows that most students are only moderately susceptible. Those who scored 4 or less reacted only to suggestions that are readily responded to without a prior attempt to induce hypnosis: falling in response to the suggestion of swaying backward from a standing position, closing the eyes after staring at a target while being told that one is getting sleepy and one's eyes are closing, lowering an outstretched arm when the suggestion is that it is getting heavy, or moving the outstretched arms together or apart. Sometimes these mild responses are accompanied by some sensation of being in the hypnotic state, but usually this feeling is experienced only by those who make scores of 5 to 12. Within this range, those scoring higher are generally more deeply hypnotized; the full range of hypnotic phenomena is given only by those few who score near the top of the scale. A rough figure

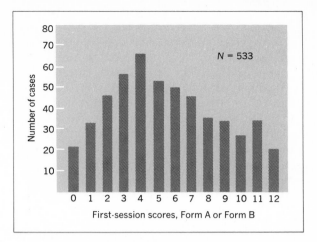

Fig. 7-10 Distribution of first-session scores, Form A or Form B When experiencing a hypnotic induction for the first time, a few subjects do everything expected of a well-hypnotized person (score of 12 on the scale), but most yield only a few of the responses tested. Those with scores of 8 to 12 are sufficiently hypnotizable to give most of the responses characteristic of the deeply hypnotized. They represent about one quarter of the population. (After Hilgard, 1965)

is that about one-fourth of randomly selected university students achieve a quite satisfactory hypnotic state, which includes such phenomena as posthypnotic amnesia. Fewer than this, perhaps 5 to 10 percent, can accomplish more advanced phenomena, such as posthypnotic visual hallucinations with the eyes open (Hilgard, 1965).

Despite the consistency with which subjects differ in their responses to hypnotic susceptibility tests, it is surprisingly difficult to determine just what kinds of people are more susceptible and what kinds less susceptible. Most studies have found either no correlations or very low ones with personality characteristics. Hypnotic-like experiences outside hypnosis are somewhat predictive of hypnotic susceptibility; favorable attitudes toward hypnosis have sometimes been found helpful; ideational interests are more favorable than highly competitive athletic ones (though many athletes are hypnotizable). The correlations reported in many studies are disappointingly small (Hilgard, 1965), but a picture of the hypnotizable person begins to emerge from test and interview data.

The hypnotizable person is one who has rich

subjective experiences in which he can become deeply involved. He reaches out for new experiences and thus welcomes the opportunity to become hypnotized. He is interested in the life of the mind, rather than being chiefly interested in competitive muscular performances. He is willing to accept impulses from within and is not afraid to relinquish reality testing for a time. He does not appear to be a weak or dependent person; evidence indicates that more troubled, withdrawn, or neurotic individuals do not generally make as good subjects as normal outgoing individuals.

How do these special characteristics related to hypnotic susceptibility come about? Interviews with hundreds of subjects, before and after induction of hypnosis, have pointed to the importance of early childhood experiences. Experiences of a particular kind appear to either generate or maintain the abilities that enter into hypnotizability (J. R. Hilgard, 1970). A capacity to become deeply involved in imaginative experiences derives from parents who are themselves deeply involved in

such areas as reading, music, religion, or the esthetic appreciation of nature. Another experience leading to hypnotizability is rather severe punishment in childhood. The conjecture is that a history of punishment may produce hypnotizability in either (or both) of two ways: first, through instilling a habit of automatic and unquestioned obedience; second, through a tendency to escape the harassment by moving off into a realm of imagination, thus practicing the dissociations that are later to be used in hypnosis.

These effects of childhood experiences have been inferred from the accounts by university students of their own experiences. Direct studies of children and their parents have not yet been carried very far. It is known, however, that children are much more highly hypnotizable than adults, so that a contagious influence from parents that maintains the ability would suffice to produce a hypnotizable adult. Correlational analysis of the relationship of the hypnotizability of children to that of their parents (a correlation that would be expected from

Most investigators of hypnosis would find nothing unacceptable in the foregoing account of hypnosis, except perhaps for minor aspects of terminology or emphasis. This does not mean that the field is free of controversy. Several investigators have wittingly or unwittingly led readers to doubt the reality of hypnosis. This comes about in part because hypnosis lends itself to extreme statements, and those who claim too much for hypnosis are just as much its scientific enemies as those who claim too little. We may briefly consider the views of four men who have left strong doubts about hypnosis in the minds of their readers—Sutcliffe, Orne, Sarbin, and Barber.

Sutcliffe, himself an able hypnotist and investigator of scientific hypnosis, has made a point of distinguishing between the "credulous" and "skeptical" views of hypnotic phenomena (Sutcliffe, 1961). Sutcliffe showed, for example, that subjects who reported no pain after hypnotic suggestion continued to give the physiological responses normally associated with pain. The skeptical view is that the physiological responses are the dependable ones; the hypnotic subject must therefore be deluding himself that he does not feel pain—even though he is willing to have an impacted tooth extracted or an arm amputated under hypnosis. Sutcliffe's findings are indeed puzzling, but they do not discredit the phenomena of hypnosis.

Orne, also an active investigator of hypnosis and a practicing hypnotherapist, has emphasized that many of the responses of the hypnotized subject depend upon what he thinks the hypnotist expects, the "demand characteristics" of the situation (Orne, 1962). This view gives the impression that there is a faked quality about hypnotic performances. But of course all hypnotic performances have within them the quality of response to suggestion; Orne is not denying this but is merely trying to specify what is inherent in

the point of view of the transmission of parental involvements) has not yielded clear results; in the only reported study a significant correlation was found between the hypnotizability of fathers and sons, but not between that of fathers and daughters or between that of mothers and children of either sex (Morgan, Davert, and Hilgard, 1970).

The significance of hypnosis research

Interest in hypnosis has fluctuated over the years, in part because of its use as an entertainment technique and its associations with the occult and mysterious. When it is permitted to take its place as a legitimate field of scientific inquiry, along with dreams, drug states, and other altered states of awareness, its potential usefulness within scientific psychology is easy to demonstrate. Recent years have seen a resurgence of interest in hypnosis from this point of view, and there are now scientific societies devoted to sharing experiences in its study and journals in which the results of experimental and clinical studies are reported. Both the British Medical Association and the American Medical Association have passed resolutions on the desirability of teaching hypnotic techniques in medical schools (Marcuse, 1964).

Within experimental psychology, hypnosis permits the study of some of the important problems of planning, self-control, and the circumstances in which control is relinquished. Hypnosis provides a method of reintroducing the study of voluntary and involuntary action, which has been somewhat neglected in recent experimental psychology. The features of the hypnotic state itself and of responsiveness to suggestions provide topics of interest not only for understanding hypnosis but for understanding broader aspects of the modification and control of behavior.

These uses of hypnosis—for the study of the state itself and its correlates, or as a control method in connection with other problems—qualify as essentially basic science uses. There are also direct hypnosis and what is imposed by the tradition in which the hypnotist works. He is not a disbeliever in the reality of hypnosis, but he is easily misinterpreted to be.

Sarbin's interpretation of hypnosis as role-enactment has been mentioned earlier (p. 173). The expression he uses gives the impression that he thinks of hypnosis as some sort of sham behavior. Actually, Sarbin does not believe this. For him the difference between someone who is hypnotizable and someone who is not is a matter of the degree to which the subject can lose himself in the role the hypnotist suggests; it is *not* just a matter of voluntary cooperation with the hypnotist (Sarbin, 1956; Sarbin and Andersen, 1967).

Of the investigators mentioned, Barber is the one who is most outspoken in denying the separateness of hypnotic phenomena from other psychological phenomena (Barber, 1969); he particularly objects to conceiving of hypnosis as a special "state." His main point is that most of the things that susceptible hypnotic subjects can do *after* hypnotic induction can be done *without* induction. Thus "waking suggestibility," as it is often called, is for him really the same as hypnotic susceptibility, provided the motivational circumstances are made the same. The individual differences and the age differences in hypnotic susceptibility that he finds are essentially the same as those found by others. Other investigators also find a high correlation between responsiveness in the waking state and that after hypnotic induction. The argument centers on both the relatively small increases in suggestibility produced by induction and the subjective characteristics of the established hypnotic state. These differences remain to be resolved.

Some genuine issues exist, but when the arguments are carefully examined no challenge to the legitimacy of hypnosis as a field of scientific inquiry has been made.

applications of hypnosis, as in dentistry, obstetrics, and psychotherapy.

A growing use of hypnosis in dentistry and obstetrics is based on two practical features of hypnosis: (1) it is a relaxed state and can be used to reduce anxiety; (2) it is possible to relieve pain through suggested anesthesia or analgesia. There are many other medical and surgical situations, such as the treatment of burns, in which the control of pain and discomfort is important. Burns that cover large areas of the body are often corrected by transplanting skin from other parts of the patient's body. To preserve the original circulation while the transplanting goes on may require, for example, immobilizing an arm that is attached to an ankle by way of a skin flap. The discomfort of retaining this awkward position may be relieved through hypnosis. Kelsey and Barron (1958) report a case in which an awkward posture in connection with a skin graft was maintained for three weeks with the help of hypnosis; the subject reported no discomfort at the time or after freedom of move-ment was eventually restored. Intractable pains, as in terminal cancer, may also be relieved by hypnosis. Thus one of the large areas of usefulness of hypnosis is in the relief of pain or of the anxieties associated with anticipated pain.

Hypnosis also plays several roles in psychotherapy. If it is used to provide relief of symptoms or control of behavior (as in directly suggested relief of pain or giving up cigarettes) through direct posthypnotic suggestion, then the therapeutic result belongs directly to the hypnotic technique. More often, however, hypnosis is used as an aid to other kinds of psychotherapy, such as those that are described in Chapter 21.

As our scientific knowledge of hypnosis increases, its practical applications will be better understood and managed. With the attention being given to its phenomena in recent years, we may expect increased scientific use of hypnosis and its gradual dissociation from entertainment and pseudoscience.

Meditation and self-induced alterations of consciousness

Because man can think and dream, he can transcend the everyday world and contemplate visions of ideal or unthought-of worlds. Through past ages men have isolated themselves on mountain tops, fasted, indulged in special exercises, or in other ways sought out experiences of novelty and depth; often this quest had religious significance, like the search of religious mystics for a reality that lies beneath and beyond the world as we know it. Many contemporary men of the Western world, dissatisfied with what they see as a corruption of life through material interests and an ever-encroaching technology, have turned to some of the practices of the Eastern religions in the hope of finding a new set of values.

Experimental meditation

It is possible to study what happens in meditation by inviting those without any special back-ground to participate in the kinds of exercises recommended by those practicing *yoga,* based on Hindu philosophy, or *Zen,* deriving from Chinese and Japanese Buddhism. Their experiences are then studied in the same manner as any other experiences of psychological interest.

Typically the exercises call for relaxation and controlled breathing, usually in a sitting or kneeling position on the floor, perhaps supported in part by cushions; the position must be conducive to relaxation without inducing sleep. In yoga the eyes may be closed, but in Zen they are kept open. There are many variations on what the meditator is trying to do, but the following is a representative statement:

> The radical approach begins with the resolve to do nothing, to think nothing, to make no effort of one's own, to relax completely and let go one's mind and body . . . stepping out of the stream of ever-changing ideas and feelings which your mind is,

watch the onrush of the stream. Refuse to be submerged in the current. Changing the metaphor, it may be said, watch your ideas, feelings and wishes fly across the firmament like a flock of birds. Let them fly freely. Just keep a watch. Don't allow the birds to carry you off into the clouds [Chaudhuri, 1965, pp. 30–31].

Two experimental reports can illustrate the findings from studies addressed to the results of the early stages in practiced meditation. In the first of these a subject sat in an armchair in a pleasant, carpeted room viewing a blue vase 10 inches high on a simple brown end table against the opposite wall, 8 feet before him. He was given the following instructions (quoted in part):

> The purpose of these sessions is to learn about concentration. Your aim is to concentrate on the blue vase. By concentration I do not mean analyzing the different parts of the vase, or thinking a series of thoughts about the vase, or associating ideas to the vase, but rather, trying to see the vase as it exists in itself, without any connections to other things. Exclude all other thoughts or feelings or sounds or body sensations . . . . [Deikman, 1963, p. 330].

After the session began, a number of sounds were presented by tape recorder in order to test the subject's ability to avoid being distracted by them. The meditation on the first day was five minutes, ten minutes on the second day, and fifteen minutes for each of the remaining sessions of the total of twelve spread over three weeks; a few sessions were spontaneously extended to as much as thirty-three minutes at the request of the subject. The most common effects were: (1) an altered, more intense perception of the vase; (2) some time-shortening, particularly in retrospect; (3) conflicting perceptions, as of the vase at once filling the visual field and not filling it; agitation, at once disturbing and pleasurable; (4) decreasing effectiveness of the external stimuli (both less distraction and eventually less conscious registration); (5) a pleasurable state, the experience of which was reported as valuable and rewarding.

In another experiment, practice sessions were designed according to a Zen program. Forty-five-minute practices, followed by short interviews, were held each weekday for a two-week period (Maupin, 1965). Twenty-eight subjects, who responded to a campus newspaper advertisement offering instruction in Zen meditation, served as the sample for the study of individual differences in response. The central instruction called for concentration on breathing:

> While you are sitting let your breath become relaxed and natural. Let it set its own pace and depth if you can. Then focus your attention on your own breathing: the movements of your belly, not your nose or throat. Do not allow extraneous thoughts or stimuli to pull your attention away from your breathing. This may be hard to do at first, but keep directing

TABLE 7-2   FREQUENCY OF RESPONSE PATTERNS TO ZEN MEDITATION

		PATTERNS (GREATER RESPONSIVENESS IN COLUMNS TO THE RIGHT)					
CLASSIFICATION	NUMBER OF SUBJECTS	DIZZINESS, FOGGINESS	RELAXATION, CALMNESS	PLEASANT BODILY SENSATIONS	VIVID BREATHING SENSATIONS	CONCENTRATION, DETACHMENT	TOTAL PATTERNS PER SUBJECT
High responders	6	0	2	3	4	6	2.5
Moderate responders	10	2	3	8	5	0	1.8
Low responders	12	6	8	0	0	0	1.2
Total	28	8	13	11	9	6	1.7

Source: Maupin (1965).

your attention back to it. Turn everything else aside if it comes up [Maupin, 1965, p. 140].

The responses reported in the interviews were judged by two raters. A "high-response" group was selected as having at least one experience described as extreme detachment: a deeply satisfying state of consciousness in which the meditator exhibits a "nonstriving" attitude and is able to take a calmly detached view of any thoughts or feelings that happen to emerge. The patterns as found among the twenty-eight subjects are summarized in Table 7-2. For the low responders, dizziness, fogginess, relaxation, and calmness were occasionally reported, but nothing else; the moderate responders were more frequently aware of an intensification of bodily sensations and of sensations associated with breathing; the high responders did not report dizziness or fogginess but gave all other responses, especially those described as detachment. A tolerance for unrealistic experience, prior to the meditation exercises, appeared to predict the higher responses to meditation. Because these conditions are similar to those favoring hypnosis, it is not unreasonable to suppose that the experiences are related, although detailed studies of the relationship are not available.

Subjective control of physiological processes

It is well known that some of those who practice yoga in India may gain remarkable control over certain physiological processes not ordinarily under voluntary control, such as heart rate and smooth-muscle responses (Wenger and Bagchi, 1961; Wenger, Bagchi, and Anand, 1961). Until recently it was assumed that they were able to do this only as a result of long-continued and disciplined exercise, but now laboratory methods permit at least some of the effects to be readily produced in randomly selected subjects.

One type of control is that over the EEG alpha rhythm. The *alpha rhythm* is a regular response of about 10 cycles per second that is often found in the subject sitting quietly with his eyes closed. The response commonly becomes irregular (desynchronized) when the subject opens his eyes or when he uses his mind alertly, as in mental arithmetic. By using special equipment attached to the electroencephalograph, it is possible to convert the presence of alpha to a tone that the subject can hear; when alpha is absent the tone is turned off. Thus the subject can tell, by listening for the tone, whether the alpha rhythm is being recorded from his scalp. He uses this information, or "feedback," to "learn" to maintain the alpha with his eyes open, or to turn it off when it appears. Many subjects can do this after perhaps only thirty minutes of practice. Their reports on how they do it are very similar to those given by meditating subjects. That is, the "alpha on" condition is very much like the calm and detached state that the better meditators achieve (Nowlis and Kamiya, 1970).

Corresponding "feedback" methods can be used for the control of other responses, such as blood distribution to the fingers. Because the methods are quite new, it is at present not clear just how far such control can go.

Effects of drugs

Drugs have been used from ancient times to poison or to cure, to relieve pain, to produce sleep or hallucinations. Some familiar ones, such as caffeine and alcohol, have become so accepted in Western culture that we scarcely think of them as drugs; others, thought to be addictive or dangerous, such as the opium derivatives, have been subject to severe legal restrictions. Many other drugs are at present popular and are causing a great deal of controversy—legal, moral, and medical.

Caffeine and alcohol

Coffee is a stimulant, owing to its content of caffeine; alcoholic beverages are depressants,

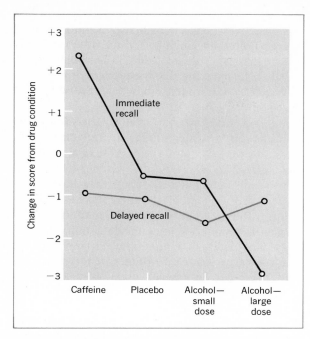

Fig. **7-11** **Effects of caffeine, placebo, and two concentrations of alcohol on immediate and delayed recall** Although immediate recall was facilitated by caffeine and depressed by alcohol in the large dose, delayed recall of a story told in the drug session about 20 minutes earlier did not appear to be affected. The small dose of alcohol, adjusted in amount for the body area of the subject, was the equivalent of the alcohol in two martinis; the large dose, the equivalent of four martinis. ($N = 14$ for each treatment.) (Data from Nash, 1962)

owing to the ethyl alcohol they contain. Their psychological effects depend upon the amounts that are used, and such effects are subject to experimental study. But studies of stimulants and depressants are difficult to make because of the expectations of the subject and the possibility that he is responding to suggestion rather than to the chemical substances. Experimenters use a *placebo* to control for these effects of suggestion. A placebo is an inert substance that the subject cannot distinguish from the real thing (decaffeinated coffee is an example). Because the subject believes he has taken a familiar substance he expects familiar effects; for example, if coffee keeps him awake he may expect to be kept awake by the beverage he has just drunk. In one experiment, caffeine and alcohol were given in pungent grape-colored

drinks; in that case, the placebo consisted of the same drink without caffeine or alcohol. Specimen results for the effects on memory of caffeine, placebo, and two concentrations of alcohol are shown in Figure 7-11. Caffeine commonly facilitated performance above placebo; mild doses of alcohol had rather slight effect, but the heavy dose was deleterious to performances in some of the psychological tests (Nash, 1962).

Hallucination-producing and consciousness-expanding drugs

An upsurge of interest in *psychoactive drugs*—drugs that affect man's behavior and consciousness—began in the 1950s. First in importance were the *tranquilizers,* which reduced anxiety and made otherwise disturbed persons more serene. One of these, reserpine, had been known for years in India; it is a derivative of a plant known as Indian snake root or rauwolfia. Soon many other tranquilizers came on the market, initially only for use in mental hospitals, but presently widely used by the general public on a physician's prescription. Then came the *energizers,* which tended to overcome fatigue and lassitude; these drugs tried to improve upon caffeine, which had long been serving as a stimulant in coffee. Finally, there appeared a group of drugs called at first *psychotomimetic,* because they appeared to mimic in the normal the states of mentally ill (psychotic) persons; among these was a drug known as LSD-25 (lysergic acid diethylamide). Although this parallelism with mental illness has not been found to be very close, the fact that this family of drugs produced extreme alterations of consciousness opened a whole new history of drug use. It is that history with which we are concerned here.

Drugs such as LSD are put to three main uses. The first is best described as self-indulgence, in which the drugs are used for "thrills" or "kicks," as alcohol is used for intoxication. This kind of use is assumed to be dangerous because drugs taken in this way have tended in past history to cause injury: (1) they may have dangerous side-effects; (2) they may be habit-forming, leading to addiction; and (3) they are usually taken in the company of alienated and nonconforming people, who, in defying law and convention, commonly get the user into trouble with the police.

A second use is in connection with psychotherapy, that is, in the treatment of mental or emotional disturbance. This use is, of course, to be encouraged if the research findings recommend it. There are some reports of generally therapeutic effects in cases of mild neurotic disturbances (Aaronson and Osmond, 1970).

The third use is for philosophical or religious benefits or for hoped-for enhanced creativity by serious-minded people who believe in this method of achieving valued ends. This use is in some ways the most controversial, because it treads upon issues of value that go beyond ordinary legal conventions with respect to the use of drugs. Those who favor this use commonly refer to the drugs as *psychedelic,* literally "mind-manifesting," because of their subjective, perception-modifying aspects. The so-called psychedelic experience commonly consists of visual hallucinations, either of unstructured colors or of a kind of visual pageantry; sometimes the person feels as if he is moving out from his body or is watching his body from a distance; sometimes he experiences a sense of awe or grandeur that gives him a feeling of well-being, with little communicable content. The experiences are not always pleasant. The particular experiences received seem to depend in part upon the expectations aroused in preparation for the experience.

Marijuana. Marijuana is derived from hemp; another name for it is hashish, and popular slang in the United States calls it "pot" or "grass." The leaves of the marijuana plant may be smoked or chewed to induce a general excitement or euphoria. Its psychological importance is reflected in the name hashish, which has the same root as *assassin;* years ago the hashish-indulging Moslems, fortified by the drug, killed the Christian leaders of the Crusades.

In the United States many young people have taken to marijuana as other generations took to alcohol; the legal restrictions appear to be no more inhibiting than those of the prohibition days were to the use of alcohol. One estimate is that 30 to 35 percent of students in major universities on the East and West coasts tried marijuana at least once (in the 1960s), although half of them stopped after the single trial (Abelson, 1968). Most users receive the drug by smoking the dried leaves of the plant.

Carefully controlled studies of the effects of marijuana are rare. In one of these, nine healthy young men who had not previously used marijuana volunteered to participate in an experiment; their reactions were compared with those of eight habitual users (Weil, Zinberg, and Nelson, 1968). In this laboratory setting it was found that the physiological and psychological effects reached a maximum within one half-hour of the smoking inhalation, were diminished after one hour, and appeared to be completely dissipated after three hours. The contrasts between the responses of the new users and those of the regular users were somewhat surprising. None of those using marijuana for the first time had any of the strong subjective experiences associated with the drug, even with a strong dose; the regular users had the expected experiences associated with becoming "high" on the drug. Two possible explanations are offered: the first, a psychological one, is that the effects are associated with expectations, which are not aroused in the neutral setting of the laboratory for the new users; the second, a physiological explanation, is that, contrary to the effects of many other drugs, there may be some sensitization, so that smaller doses later on produce greater effects. Another curious finding was that performances on tests of various motor and associative skills showed impairment for the inexperienced subjects but not for the experienced ones, even though the latter thought they were doing poorly on the tests. The physiological changes for both groups (heart rate, dilation of blood vessels of the eye) were mild; there was no change in pupil size as commonly reported.

On the whole, the dangers of marijuana tend to be exaggerated by the popular press, and the penalties associated with its use have tended to be excessive by comparison, for example, with those for the use of alcohol. Marijuana is not thought to be physiologically addicting. The company that is kept by marijuana users is more significant than the physiological effects. Most of those who indulge by smoking receive such small quantities of the drug that they experience only the initial effects of euphoria (Rubin, 1969).

The chronic, heavy use of marijuana, like the chronic and heavy use of alcohol, may have additional dangers. Little is known about how much distortion of perception, reflexes, and judgment, as caused by the drug, will, for example, prevent the safe handling of an automobile.

LSD. Although LSD was initially the most widely used of the psychedelic, or "mind-manifesting," drugs, the widespread knowledge of its dangers has apparently reduced its use to some extent. One problem with LSD (or "acid," as it is popularly called by its users) is that its effects are highly individual and unpredictable. Some users have vivid hallucinatory experiences of colors and sounds, while others have mystical or semireligious experiences. An adverse reaction (a "bad trip," in the language of the user) may occur in persons who have taken the drug once or one hundred times. This disturbance is often severe enough for the person to seek professional help, so that by now psychiatric hospitals have had a great deal of experience with adverse LSD reactions. In many cases a tranquilizing drug (particularly chlorpromazine) proves helpful in counteracting the drug (Ungerleider, 1969).

Amphetamine. The amphetamines include dexedrine sulfate (known as "speed") and methamphetamine (sometimes abbreviated "meth"). These powerful stimulants produce restlessness, irritability, anxiety, and exaggerated heart rates, including some heart irregularities. They are addicting because tolerance develops and increasing doses are required to produce effects; moreover, withdrawal symptoms appear when use of the drug ceases. Severe psychological disturbances and brain damage have been reported following use of amphetamines.

The difference between cautious and incautious uses of dangerous and powerful drugs is illustrated by studies using mild doses of drugs in combination. A combination of a tranquilizer (meproba-

mate) with an energizer (amphetamine) produced entirely good effects in small doses—600 mg meprobamate with 10 mg amphetamine; 400 mg meprobamate with 5 mg amphetamine. The favorable results, especially with the smaller dosage, were that the student subjects became more enthusiastic, friendly, work-oriented, and decisive, and simultaneously less depressed, apathetic, and nervous (Cameron, Specht, and Wendt, 1967).

Other drugs. Other drugs used for their psychological effects include mescaline, or peyote (from a variety of the cactus plant), psilocybin (a synthetic form of the drug contained in the Mexican hallucination-producing mushroom), and, of course, the opium derivatives, such as morphine, codeine, and heroin, long known to be dangerously addictive.

Many drugs have some consequences in common with other drugs, but other consequences that are not shared. In a careful comparison of the effects of LSD, mescaline, and psilocybin, for example, Sjoberg and Hollister (1965) found that LSD and mescaline (but not psilocybin) lead to about the same increase in responsiveness to a set of suggestions as a standard set of hypnosis-inducing instructions. These results confirm other observations that the effects of drugs often depend upon the person's preparation and expectancies, for the drug state often appears to be highly suggestible.

The social psychology of drug use

The widespread use of drugs, especially among the young, has led to many conjectures about the influences leading to the practice. The use of drugs for "kicks" or "defiance" or "sociability" is not unlike an earlier generation's use of alcohol in the prohibition era. More puzzling, perhaps, is the serious use of drugs in the hope of expanding consciousness and finding through a quasi-mystical experience a deeper meaning of life. The ordinary alternatives of realistic problem-solving (choosing among alternatives, or inventing new ones to overcome difficulties) and of committed effort to make one's desires come true are abandoned in favor of drugs or reorienting devices such as meditation or emotional encounters. The deep appeal of personal reorientation as a quick way to cut through personal and social problems has had a long history in America; one type of "positive thinking" has succeeded another (Meyer, 1965). But the promises have commonly been unfulfilled, just as the promises of enlightenment through drugs have often led to tragedy.

Summary

1. Although there is considerable interest in the study of altered states of awareness, careful examination of the normal *waking consciousness* shows it to be complex too. Our ability to register some information from two conversations heard at the same time indicates that waking consciousness is not a single, simple state. Another "split" in waking consciousness is the planning function, a sort of silent talking to oneself that goes on even as we are engaged in listening and overt talking. Attention tends to shift, and alert (vigilant) states may be followed by less alert ones. This process begins in early infancy; the newborn infant orients to sound or pursues with his head and eyes a visual object only in the alert state, which endures but a few minutes per day in the first few days of life. Later in life we maintain alertness by all sorts of devices of fidgeting and irrelevant responding that prevent our drifting off into vacant staring or sleep.

2. Sleep, a familiar altered state of awareness, is particularly interesting because of the fact of dreaming. Studies using the electroencephalogram (EEG) and the study of rapid eye movements (REMs) during sleep have now shown two main kinds of sleep: (1) that at EEG-Stage 1, accompanied by REMs, and (2) the remainder, occurring within all four EEG stages of sleep, which may be called nonrapid-eye-movement (NREM) sleep. It is during REM sleep that the characteristic dreaming takes place. Numerous studies have been made using this method of detecting when the subject is dreaming to study the frequency and duration of dreams. Studies have also been made of the reactivity of the dreamer to outside influences and of such spontaneous behaviors as sleeptalking and sleepwalking, which seem not to be related directly to REM sleep.

3. Freud's dream theory holds that dreams express unfulfilled wishes in disguised form; the purpose of the dream (and of the disguise) is to protect sleep. The new physiological studies are coherent with this theory in that it is very difficult to waken a sleeper while dreaming, and the need for dreams is shown by the dream-deprivation studies.

4. Hypnosis, though sometimes identified as a partial sleep, yields an EEG pattern unlike sleep. At present there are no clear physiological indicators by which to define the state. Highly susceptible hypnotic subjects exhibit phenomena that are sufficiently similar to enable the hypnotic state to be characterized by some of the things they do.

5. People vary in their susceptibility to hypnosis; about one-fourth of college students are able to experience relatively satisfactory hypnotic states upon their first hypnotic induction. Efforts to find out why some people are more readily hypnotizable than others have not proved conclusive. Normal, outgoing subjects are more likely to be susceptible than troubled, anxious, or withdrawn ones. But at the present time nobody is able to say prior to attempted hypnosis whether a given person is hypnotizable.

6. New interest in modifications of consciousness has led some in the Western world to adopt meditation practices associated with yoga or Zen Buddhism. These practices have been studied under conditions of experimental meditation, with many subjects reporting a kind of pleasurable detachment as a result of the assigned exercises. Methods of controlling normally involuntary processes have been developed using a "feedback" method, in which the subject's electrical responses are converted into auditory signals that he can learn to control. The consequence is that some of the physiological changes associated with meditative states can be achieved fairly quickly.

7. Drugs have long been used to affect consciousness. Some drugs, such as caffeine and alcohol, are in such wide use that the fact that they are drugs is sometimes overlooked. Experimental studies of caffeine show it to be a satisfactory stimulant, improving some performances, such as immediate recall. Alcohol in small doses has little effect on these performances, but in large doses it reduces immediate recall and interferes with other skilled performances.

8. Drugs tend to be used either for the gratification that the drug state is supposed to bring (thus leading to addiction) or for some beneficial results in psychotherapy or personality orientation that the drug experience is supposed to enhance, as in psychiatric or religious and philosophical contexts. Advances in biochemistry and pharmacology have brought a whole new set of drugs into existence to join the familiar ones. Among these are the *tranquilizers,* the *energizers,* the *psychotomimetics* and the *psychedelics.*

9. The results of the use of marijuana, LSD, amphetamines, and other widely used drugs vary in the symptoms produced and in the dangers consequent upon their use. The particular experiences received seem to depend in part upon one's expectations about the effect of the drug.

Suggestions for further reading

The problems of awareness, including subliminal processes, are treated in Eriksen (ed.), *Behavior and awareness* (1962). For some additional information on the complexity of waking experience, see Singer, *Daydreaming: An introduction to the experimental study of inner experience* (1966). For a set of readings covering the topics of this chapter (including meditation), see Tart (ed.), *Altered states of consciousness* (1969). For a later study of the physiological effects of meditation, see Wallace, "Physiological effects of transcendential meditation," in *Science* (1970).

The literature on sleep and dreams is expanding rapidly. Three useful books are Kleitman, *Sleep and wakefulness* (1963), Luce and Segal, *Sleep* (1966), and Kales (ed.), *Sleep: Physiology and pathology* (1969). For a review of the relation of physiological studies to the functional interpretation of dreaming, see Madow and Snow (eds.), *The psychodynamic implications of the physiological studies on dreams* (1970).

For night-day and other rhythms in man and in animals and plants, see Richter, *Biological clocks in medicine and psychiatry* (1965), and Bünning, *The physiological clock* (2nd ed., 1967).

Recent books on hypnosis include Barber, *Hypnosis, a scientific approach* (1969), E. R. Hilgard, *The experience of hypnosis* (1968a), J. R. Hilgard, *Personality and hypnosis* (1970), and Shor and Orne (eds.), *The nature of hypnosis* (1965).

The drug problems of the recent decades are covered in Nowlis, *Drugs on the college campus* (1968), and in a two-volume work: Blum and others, *Society and drugs,* vol. I, and *Students and drugs,* vol. II (1969). The issues surrounding one of the widely controversial drugs are discussed in E. Goode (ed.), *Marijuana* (1969).

PART FOUR

LEARNING AND THINKING

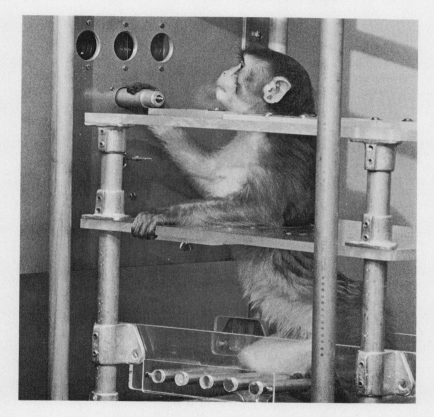

learning and conditioning 8

T HE PRECEDING CHAPTERS HAVE INCLUDED numerous examples of learning. We noted how children learn to identify with their parents, increase their vocabularies, acquire social motives, and perceive the environment. In presenting these examples, however, no attempt was made to provide a detailed analysis of the learning process. In view of its importance in understanding human behavior we now turn to an examination of the methods used to study learning and to some of the theories that have been proposed to explain the process.

Learning may be defined as a *relatively permanent change in behavior that occurs as the result of practice.* Not all changes in behavior can be explained as learning, and hence our definition has to be qualified to exclude them. The phrase *relatively permanent* excludes changes in behavior that result from temporary or transient conditions such as fatigue, the influence of drugs, or adaptation. By specifying that learning is the result of *practice* we exclude behavioral changes that are due to maturation, disease, or physical damage. Learning could be defined more simply as profiting from experience, were it not that some learning does not "profit" the learner: useless and often harmful habits are learned just as useful ones are.

The goal of an applied psychology of learning is to develop effective methods for optimizing the learning process. The more we know about the fundamentals of learning, the more soundly we can make recommendations for practice. But the scientific understanding of learning has a wider scope. Not only does it help us to understand the most evident kinds of learning, such as school learning; it also bears upon the fundamental problems of individual development, motivation, social behavior, and personality.

Because learning is basic to an analysis of behavior, a number of controversies within theoretical psychology revolve about it. Some psychologists who prefer to emphasize stimulus-response relationships interpret learning as *habit formation,* by which they mean *associative learning*—that is, acquiring a connection between a stimulus and response that did not exist before. Thus naming of objects in English depends upon a set of *verbal habits* according to which, for example, certain objects made of wood and graphite serve as stimuli for the associated response of "pencil." Riding a bicycle illustrates a set of *sensorimotor habits* appropriate to that complex stimulus. It is possible to go beyond these obvious habits and interpret *all* learned behavior as habit formation, including habitual attitudes, habitual ways of thinking, habitual emotional expression. According to this interpretation all our learning is associative learning: we learn only habits.

Other psychologists, not convinced that it is most profitable to treat all learning as habit formation, are impressed by the role of perception and understanding in learning; in a more technical vocabulary, they are concerned with the role of *cognitive processes.* Examples of cognitive processes are our ability to follow maps over routes we have never taken before and to reason our way to conclusions previously unfamiliar to us. In the end, have we learned something new, or have we merely exercised old habits? To be sure, we have used old habits, and herein arises disagreement among psychologists. Some psychologists are satisfied that this type of learning can be explained on the basis of habit formation, while others believe that more complex processes are involved. We shall return to this problem after examining the case for learning both as an associative process and as a cognitive process.

Within the concept of associative learning three sources of data about habits and the principles governing them can be distinguished: *classical conditioning, operant conditioning,* and *multiple-response learning.*

Classical conditioning

Pavlov's experiments

The study of associative learning can be carried on in the *conditioned-response* experiment. This experiment was originated by the Russian physiologist and Nobel Prize winner Ivan Pavlov. While studying the relatively automatic reflexes associated with digestion, Pavlov noticed that the flow of saliva in the mouth of the dog was influenced not only by food placed in the dog's mouth but also by the sight of food. He interpreted the flow of saliva to food placed in the mouth as an unlearned response, or, as he called it, an *uncondi-*

tioned response. But surely, he thought, the response to the *sight* of food has to be learned. Hence this is a learned or *conditioned response.* Pavlov experimented to find out how conditioned responses are formed. He taught the dog to salivate to various signals, such as the onset of a light or the sound of a metronome, thereby proving to his satisfaction that a new stimulus-response association could be formed in the laboratory.

Under Pavlov's method a dog is prepared for experimentation by having a minor operation performed on its cheek so that part of the salivary gland is exposed to the surface. A capsule attached

Fig. **8-1 Classical-conditioning apparatus** Arrangements used by Pavlov in classical salivary conditioning. The apparatus permits a light (as the conditioned stimulus) to appear in the window, and the delivery of meat powder (as the unconditioned stimulus) to the food bowl. (After Yerkes and Morgulis, 1909)

to the cheek measures salivary flow. The dog is brought to the soundproof laboratory on several occasions and is placed in a harness on a table where the experiment is to be conducted. This preliminary training is needed so that the animal will stand quietly in the harness once the actual experiment gets underway. The laboratory is so arranged that meat powder can be delivered to a pan in front of the dog by remote control. Salivation is recorded automatically. The experimenter can view the animal through a glass panel, but the dog is alone in the experimental room, isolated from extraneous sights and noises (see Figure 8-1).

A light (the *conditioned stimulus*) is turned on. The dog may make some slight movements, but it does not salivate in response to the light. After a few seconds, the meat powder (*unconditioned stimulus*) is delivered; the dog is hungry and eats. The recording device registers copious salivation. A few more trials are given in which the light is always followed by the meat, the meat by salivation. This following of the conditioned stimulus by the unconditioned stimulus and response is called *reinforcement*. After several reinforcements the dog salivates when the light is turned on, even though food may not follow. When this happens, a *conditioned response* has been established.

The usual order of events (conditioned stimulus—unconditioned stimulus—response) can best

be remembered if the conditioned stimulus is thought of as a *signal* that the unconditioned stimulus is about to appear; in the foregoing example the light is a signal that food is coming. The conditioned response may be considered a simple habit because (1) an association is demonstrated to exist between a stimulus and a response, and (2) this association is a learned one.

With this introduction we are ready for a definition of the process of *classical conditioning* as it is represented by the model of Pavlov's experiment. (We shall presently describe another variety of conditioning, called *operant conditioning;* hence the adjective "classical" is applied to Pavlov's experiment.) Classical conditioning may be defined as the formation of an association between a conditioned stimulus and a response through the repeated presentation of the conditioned stimulus in a controlled relationship with an unconditioned stimulus that originally elicits that response. The original response to the unconditioned stimulus is called an *unconditioned response;* the learned response to the conditioned stimulus is called a *conditioned response.*

The arrangement described in this definition is diagramed in Figure 8-2. Because the conditioned response resembles the unconditioned response, classical conditioning is sometimes referred to as learning through *stimulus substitution,* the condi-

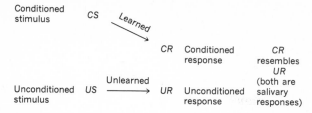

Conditioned
stimulus CS Learned

CR Conditioned
response

CR
resembles
UR
(both are
salivary
responses)

Unlearned
Unconditioned US UR Unconditioned
stimulus response

Fig. 8-2 A diagram of classical conditioning The association between the unconditioned stimulus and the unconditioned response exists at the start of the experiment and does not have to be learned. The association between the conditioned stimulus and the conditioned response is a learned one. It arises through the pairing of the conditioned and unconditioned stimuli followed by the unconditioned response. The conditioned response resembles the unconditioned one (though they need not be identical).

tioned stimulus eventually "substituting" for the unconditioned one in eliciting the response.

Laws of classical conditioning

Because classical conditioning represents an extremely simple form of learning, it has been regarded by many psychologists as an appropriate starting point for the investigation of the learning process. Variations of Pavlov's techniques have been used with many different organisms (ranging from flatworms to human subjects) and with responses other than salivation in an attempt to discover, under the controlled conditions of the laboratory, the laws that govern learning. We will now consider some of the laws that characterize classical conditioning.

Acquisition. Each paired presentation of the conditioned stimulus (CS) and the unconditioned stimulus (US) is called a *trial,* and the period during which the organism is learning the association between the CS and the US is the *acquisition* stage of conditioning. The time interval between the CS and the US may be varied. In *simultaneous conditioning* the CS begins a fraction of a second or so before the onset of the US and continues along with it until the response occurs. In *delayed conditioning* the CS begins several seconds or more before the onset of the US and then continues with

it until the response. And in *trace conditioning* the CS is presented first and then removed before the US starts (only a "neural trace" of the CS remains to be conditioned). These three situations are illustrated in Figure 8-3. In delayed and trace conditioning the investigator can look for the conditioned response on every trial because there is sufficient time for it to appear before the presentation of the US. Thus if salivation occurs before the delivery of food, we consider it a conditioned response to the light. In simultaneous conditioning the conditioned response does not have time to appear before the presentation of the US, and it is necessary to include test trials—trials on which the US is omitted—to determine whether

Fig. 8-3 Temporal relations in conditioning Inflections stand for stimulus onsets; deflections represent terminations. The advantage of the delay and trace methods is that the experimenter can measure the strength of the conditioned response on every trial and not use test trials as is necessary in simultaneous conditioning.

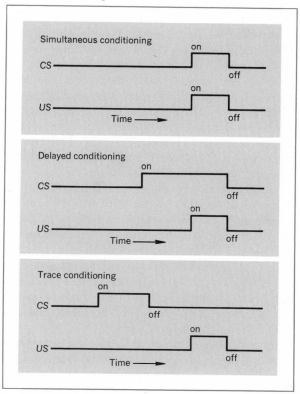

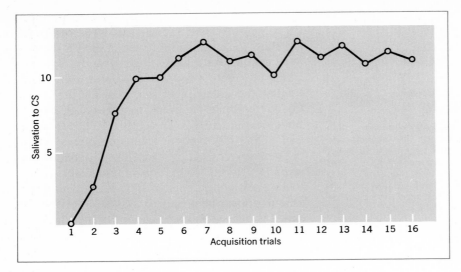

Fig. **8-4 Acquisition of a conditioned response** The curve depicts the acquisition phase of an experiment employing the trace-conditioning procedure. Drops of salivation to the conditioned stimulus (prior to the onset of the US) are plotted on the ordinate and trials on the abscissa. The conditioned response gradually increases over trials and approaches an asymptotic level of about 11 to 12 drops of salivation. (Data from Pavlov, 1927)

conditioning actually has occurred. If salivation occurs to the CS when it is presented alone, we consider that conditioning has occurred. Delayed-conditioning experiments designed to investigate the most effective CS-US time interval indicate that presenting the CS about .5 seconds before the US usually produces the fastest learning.

With repeated paired presentations of the CS and US the conditioned response appears with increasingly greater strength and regularity. We call the procedure of pairing the CS and US *reinforcement* because any tendency for the conditioned response to appear is facilitated by the presence of the unconditioned stimulus and the response to it. Figure 8-4 shows the dog's acquisition of the salivary response to the conditioned stimulus of a light. By the third trial the animal is responding to the CS with seven drops of saliva. By the seventh trial the amount of saliva secreted has leveled off and continues (with minor fluctuations) at about the same strength for the next nine trials (Pavlov, 1927). This stable level of responding is called the *asymptote* of the learning curve; further acquisition trials will not result in any greater strength of responding.

The number of drops of saliva secreted is one measure of the strength of conditioning in Pavlov's experiment. A number of quantitative measures may be used to demonstrate that one method of

conditioning is more successful than another, or that one subject conditions more readily than another. Some of these measures are given below:

1. Amplitude of conditioned response. (Drops of saliva, extent of muscular movement, and so on.)

2. Latency of conditioned response. (Promptness with which the conditioned response follows the onset of the conditioned stimulus.)

3. Number of trials to a criterion of conditioning. (Number of reinforcements needed before the first detectable conditioned response appears or before some other criterion is met, for example, before the first five conditioned responses have been given.)

4. Probability of conditioned responses. (Percentage of trials in which a detectable conditioned response appears. Even after considerable conditioning has been demonstrated, conditioned responses are not necessarily elicited on every presentation of the conditioned stimulus.)

Extinction. If the unconditioned stimulus is repeatedly omitted, so that there is no reinforcement, the conditioned response gradually diminishes. Repetition of the conditioned stimulus without reinforcement is called *extinction,* and its effect on the animal's performance is shown in Figure 8-5.

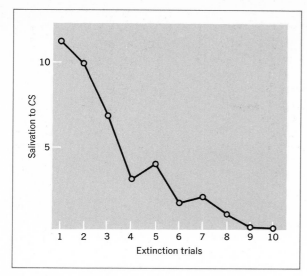

Fig. 8-5 Extinction of a conditioned response The conditioned response gradually decreases when food reinforcement is no longer paired with the conditioned stimulus. (Data from Pavlov, 1927)

Notice that on the fourth nonreinforced trial the amount of salivation has decreased to about three drops; by the ninth extinction trial the CS is eliciting no salivation at all (Pavlov, 1927).

Spontaneous recovery. Extinction does not actually destroy the conditioned response, for following a period of rest the conditioned response may partially recover, even though no reinforcements have intervened. This return of the conditioned response without reinforcement is called *spontaneous recovery* and is illustrated in Figure 8-6. The phenomenon of spontaneous recovery supports the idea that extinction involves some sort of inhibition or suppression of the conditioned response, rather than a forgetting or permanent disappearance of the response.

Additional examples of classical conditioning

Before going further in our discussion of classical conditioning it might be well to consider a few more examples of the basic procedure. A wide variety of responses (ones we would not ordinarily consider capable of being learned) have been successfully conditioned both with animals and human subjects. In one study with rats an insulin reaction was conditioned (Sawry, Conger, and Turrell, 1956). Insulin is a hormone that controls the blood-sugar level; a manufactured form of insulin is used in treating diabetics. An overdose of this hormone causes a severe physiological reaction known as *insulin shock,* which is often accompanied by unconsciousness. In the experiment the rats were exposed to a bright light and at the same time injected with an overdose of insulin. The bright light and the hypodermic needle served as the conditioned stimuli; the insulin was the un-

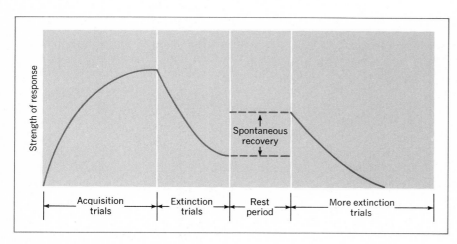

Fig. 8-6 Acquisition, extinction, and spontaneous recovery A schematic diagram of the course of acquisition, extinction, and spontaneous recovery. Within limits, the longer the rest period, the greater the degree of spontaneous recovery.

conditioned stimulus. After several pairings of the CS and US, a saline solution (which has no physiological effect) was substituted for the insulin. The animals continued to evidence a shock reaction that was almost indistinguishable from the reaction produced by insulin. We can thus say that the shock reaction had become a conditioned response.

We should note that in this experiment the conditioned response is not a single, easily measured response such as salivation, but a complex pattern of physiological and muscular responses that constitutes the insulin-shock reaction. A more quantitative physiological measure of conditioning was obtained in the following experiment using human subjects. When the human body is exposed to cold, one automatic reaction is the constriction of the small blood vessels close to the body surface—a reaction that serves to maintain body warmth. Although this is a reaction of which we are totally unaware, it can be conditioned. To do so a buzzer (CS) is sounded and at the same time the subject's left hand is immersed in a container of ice water (US). Since vasoconstriction of the left hand automatically results in some constriction of the blood vessels in the right hand, the degree of vasoconstriction can be accurately measured by means of an air-filled rubber tube placed around the subject's right hand. After a number of paired presentations of the buzzer and water immersion, vasoconstriction occurs in response to the buzzer alone (Menzies, 1937).

Generalization

When a conditioned response to a stimulus has been acquired, other similar stimuli will evoke the same response. If a dog learns to salivate to the sound of a tuning fork producing a tone of middle C, he will also salivate to higher or lower tones without further conditioning. The more nearly alike the new stimuli are to the original, the more completely they will substitute for it. This principle, called *generalization,* accounts for our ability to react to novel situations insofar as they are similar to familiar ones.

Careful study shows that the amount of generalization falls off in a systematic manner as the sec-

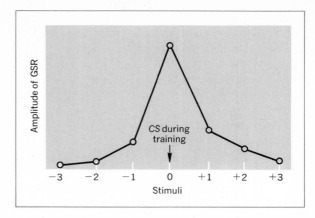

Fig. **8-7 Gradient of generalization** Stimulus 0 denotes the tone to which the galvanic skin response (GSR) was originally conditioned. Stimuli +1, +2, and +3 represent test tones of increasingly higher pitch; stimuli −1, −2, and −3 represent tones of lower pitch. Note that the amount of generalization decreases as the difference between the test tone and the training tone increases. (After Hovland, 1937)

ond stimulus becomes more and more dissimilar to the original conditioned stimulus. In a classic study with human subjects, Hovland (1937) conditioned a physiological measure of emotion, the galvanic skin response, or GSR, to a pure tone of a specific frequency (pitch), using mild shock as the US. After the GSR had been conditioned, the subject was tested with tones of higher and lower frequency than the original training tone. Figure 8-7 shows the results plotted in terms of the amplitude of the GSR versus test tones of varying frequencies. The high point of the curve represents the amplitude of the GSR to the original CS; the points to the left show the GSR amplitudes to tones lower than the CS, and those to the right the amplitudes to tones higher than the CS. As you can see, the GSR amplitude decreases as the tones become progressively more dissimilar to the CS in frequency. This plotted relationship is called the *gradient of generalization.*

Stimulus generalization need not be confined to a single sense modality. For example, with human subjects a GSR conditioned to the sound of a bell may also appear (although in a lesser amount) to the sight of a bell or to the spoken word "bell." The conditioning of a response to the meaning of a word (as opposed to the configuration or sound of a word) is called *semantic conditioning*. An interesting example of semantic conditioning and generalization is provided by the work of a Russian psychologist (Volkova, 1953). She used a modification of Pavlov's salivary-conditioning method in an experiment with young children. The US was cranberry purée delivered to the subject's mouth via a chute; the response was salivation. The CS was the Russian word for "good" pronounced aloud by the experimenter. After conditioning had been established, the experimenter tested for generalization by pronouncing some Russian sentences that could be construed as possessing a "good" meaning and some that could not. She found, for example, that the children would salivate to sentences like "The pioneer helps his comrade" and "Leningrad is a wonderful city," but not to ones like "The pupil was rude to the teacher" and "My friend is seriously ill."

Discrimination

A process complementary to that of generalization is *discrimination*. Whereas generalization is reaction to similarities, discrimination is reaction to differences. Conditioned discrimination is brought about through selective reinforcement and extinction, as shown in Figure 8-8. In the experiment illustrated (Baer and Fuhrer, 1968), two clearly different tones, CS_1 and CS_2, served as the discriminative stimuli. On some trials CS_1 was presented, followed by a mild electric shock; on other trials CS_2 occurred, not followed by shock. The two tones were presented equally often but in a random order. Initially the conditioned response (in this case, the GSR) occurred with about the same amplitude to the onset of both CS_1 and CS_2. During the course of the experiment, however,

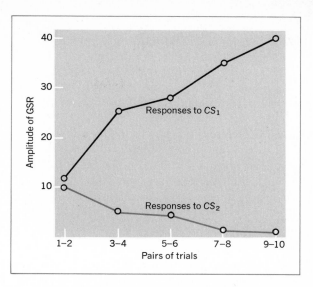

Fig. **8-8 The course of conditioned discrimination in man** The discriminative stimuli were two tones of clearly different pitch (CS_1 = 700 cps and CS_2 = 3500 cps). The unconditioned stimulus, an electric shock applied to the left forefinger, occurred only on trials when CS_1 was presented. The strength of the conditioned response, which in this case was the GSR, gradually increased following CS_1 and extinguished following CS_2. (After Baer and Fuhrer, 1968)

the amplitude of the conditioned response to CS_1 gradually increased, while the amplitude of the response to CS_2 decreased. Thus conditioned discrimination between CS_1 and CS_2 was demonstrated.

It is not difficult to illustrate the role of generalization and discrimination in ordinary behavior. When a young child has learned to say "bow-wow" to a dog, it is understandable that a similar stimulus, such as a sheep, might elicit the response "bow-wow." When a child first learns the name "Daddy," he may use it for all men. By differential reinforcement and extinction the response is finally narrowed to a single appropriate stimulus.

Operant conditioning

Operant conditioning is another approach to the study of habit formation. When you teach a dog a trick, such as playing dead or rolling over, it is very difficult to specify the unconditioned stimuli that could produce such behavior before conditioning. Actually, you "got him to do it" as best you could and *afterwards* rewarded him either with food or approval. The food or approval did not *produce* the behavior in the first place.

In Pavlov's experiment the conditioned salivation resembles the response elicited by the unconditioned (reinforcing) stimulus, but in operant training the behavior that is reinforced bears no resemblance to the behavior that is normally elicited by the reinforcing stimulus (that is, salivation is a dog's normal response to food but rolling over is not). Still, the learning that takes place corresponds in some respects to classical conditioning: it can be shown to exhibit such principles as extinction, spontaneous recovery, generalization, and discrimination.

Skinner's experiments

To describe this kind of conditioning, B. F. Skinner introduced the concept of *operant conditioning*. Operant conditioning supplements classical conditioning; many of the same principles apply to both. The arrangements for the experiments differ, however, as do some of the measures of the strength of conditioning.

Skinner proposed a distinction between two kinds of behavior, which he called *respondent* and *operant* behavior. Respondent behavior is directly under the control of a stimulus, as in the unconditioned responses of classical conditioning: the flow of saliva to food in the mouth, the constriction of the pupil to a flash of light on the eye, the knee jerk to a tap on the patellar tendon. The relation of operant behavior to stimulation is somewhat different. The behavior often appears to be emitted; that is, it appears to be spontaneous rather than a response to a specific stimulus. The gross movement of the limbs of a newborn baby can be classified as emitted behavior in this sense; most so-called voluntary behavior is emitted rather than respondent. A stimulus that controls operant behavior is called a *discriminative* stimulus. The ringing of a telephone is a discriminative stimulus; it tells you that the telephone is answerable, but it does not force you to answer. Even though the ringing telephone is compelling, the response to it is operant and not respondent behavior.

The word *operant* derives from the fact that the operant behavior "operates" on the environment to produce some effect.[1] Thus going to where the telephone is and raising the receiver are operant acts that lead to the telephone conversation.

To demonstrate operant conditioning in the laboratory, a rat is placed in a box of the sort diagramed in Figure 8-9, called a "Skinner box." Because the rat has been deprived of food for some specified period, it is assumed to be motivated by a hunger *drive*. (By "drive" we refer to the aroused condition of an organism that results from deprivation of some sort. The concepts of drive and motivation are treated more fully in Chapter 12.) The inside of the Skinner box is bare, except for the protruding bar with the food dish beneath it. A small light bulb above the bar can be lighted at the experimenter's discretion.

Left alone in the box, the rat moves about restlessly and by chance occasionally presses the bar. The rate at which it first pushes on the bar defines its preconditioned *operant level* of bar-pressing. Now the experimenter attaches the food magazine, so that every time the rat presses the bar a pellet of food falls into the dish. The rat eats and soon presses the bar again. The food *reinforces* bar-pressing, and a graph of the rate of bar-pressing plotted against time furnishes a record of the course of operant conditioning. If the food magazine is disconnected, so that pressing the bar no longer delivers food, the rate of bar-pressing will fall off. That is, the operant response undergoes *extinction* with nonreinforcement, just as a classical-conditioned response does.

The experimenter can set up a *discrimination* by presenting food only if the bar is pressed while the light is on. Thus the bar-press response is reinforced if the light is on, not reinforced if the response is made in the dark. This selective reinforcement leads to the rat's pressing the bar only in the presence of the light. In this example, the light serves as a *discriminative stimulus* that controls the occurrence of the bar-pressing response.

[1]For the same reason such behavior is sometimes called *instrumental* behavior; it produces effects just as a tool or other instrument does. Hence operant conditioning is also known as instrumental conditioning.

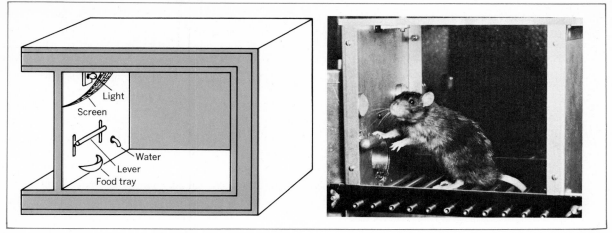

Fig. **8-9 Apparatus for operant conditioning** The diagram shows the interior arrangement of the box used in operant conditioning of the rat. The space behind the panel at the left contains additional apparatus. This box has been named a Skinner box after its developer. The photo shows an actual box in operation.

With this illustration before us, we are ready to consider the meaning of conditioned operant behavior. As indicated above, the behavior "operates" on the environment; the rat's bar-pressing *produces,* or *gains access* to, the food. In classical conditioning the animal is passive; it merely waits until the conditioned stimulus is presented and is followed by the unconditioned stimulus. In operant conditioning the animal has to be active; its behavior cannot be reinforced unless it does something.

Operant conditioning refers to increasing the probability of a response in a particular stimulus environment by following the response with *reinforcement.* Usually the reinforcement is something that can satisfy a drive, like a food pellet to satisfy hunger or water to satisfy thirst, but it need not be. *It is a reinforcing event if it strengthens the response that precedes it.*

A large part of human behavior may be classified as operant—turning a key in a lock, driving a car, writing a letter, carrying on a conversation. Such activities are not elicited by an unconditioned stimulus of the Pavlovian type. But once the behavior occurs it can be reinforced according to the principles of operant conditioning.

Measures of operant strength

Because the bar is always present in the Skinner box, the rat can respond to it as frequently or infrequently as he chooses. Hence *rate of response* is a useful measure of operant strength. The more frequently the response occurs during a given interval of time, the stronger it is. This measure cannot be used for classical conditioning because the response rate in that case depends upon how often the experimenter presents the conditioned stimulus.

The rate of response in operant conditioning is usually portrayed graphically by means of a *cumulative curve.* Figure 8-10 shows how a cumulative curve is obtained. The bar of the Skinner box is attached to a recording pen that rests on a slowly moving strip of paper. Each time the animal presses the bar the pen moves upward a short distance and then continues on its horizontal path. Because the paper moves at a fixed rate, the slope of the cumulative curve is a measure of response rate. A straight horizontal line indicates that the animal is not responding; a steep curve indicates a fast response rate. Figure 8-11A presents cumulative curves for two rats during acquisition of a

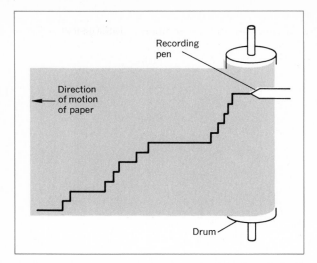

Fig. **8-10** **Cumulative recorder** The axis of the drum is fixed, and as the drum rotates, the recording paper moves right to left under the head of a writing pen. The pen is rigged so that it can only move upward, never downward. Each time the animal makes a response, the pen steps upward a fixed amount. When no responses are being made, the pen moves in a straight line across the paper. Thus the height of each step is the same, but the length of the horizontal line varies as a function of the time between responses. Since the paper is moving at a fixed rate, the slope of the cumulative curve indicates the response rate. When the animal is responding at a high rate the slope of the cumulative curve will be quite steep; when the animal is responding very slowly there will be hardly any slope at all.

bar-pressing response. Rat A had been deprived of food for thirty hours and rat B for ten hours. As indicated by the steepness of the curves, the hungrier rat responded much more rapidly.

Another measure of operant strength is the *total number of responses during extinction.* As Figure 8-11B illustrates, a single reinforcement can produce considerable strength according to this measure.[2]

Partial reinforcement

Operant conditioning shows a high degree of orderliness, or lawfulness. One illustration of this

[2]Note that the leveling off of these curves does not indicate an asymptotic level of responding as was true in Figure 8-4, but rather an absence of response. Here we are plotting cumulative number of responses against time rather than amplitude of response against trials.

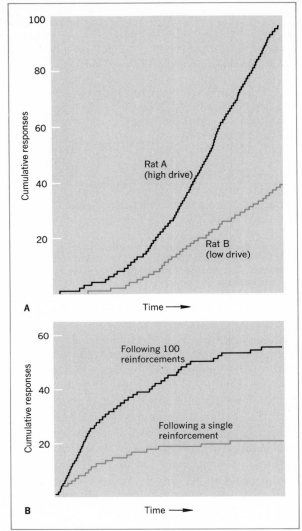

Fig. **8-11**

A. Cumulative curves during acquisition A comparison of the cumulative response curves for two rats during acquisition of a bar-pressing response. Rat A had been deprived of food for 30 hours and Rat B for 10 hours prior to the experiment. This difference in the drive level of the two rats is reflected in the rate of responding. (Data from Skinner, 1938)

B. Cumulative curves during extinction Curves of extinction of operant responses in the rat are plotted following a single reinforcement and following 100 reinforcements. The plot shows the cumulative number of bar-pressing responses; every response raises the height of the curve, and the curve levels off when responses cease. (Data from Skinner, 1938)

Partial reinforcement procedures are of particular interest because they represent the type of reinforcement regime under which most organisms operate in nature. In addition, on partial reinforcement schedules an animal's response rate tends to be extremely sensitive to changes in the stimulus environment (both internal and external); these procedures thus provide a natural barometer for assessing the effects of radiation, drugs, fatigue, and other variables on performance. In the early exploration of space, scientists frequently housed rats, pigeons, and other animals in the space capsule and placed them on a partial reinforcement schedule. By observing changes in response rate during actual flight, they were able to determine the effects of acceleration, weightlessness, and the like, on performance.

Many different reinforcement schedules have been studied, but basically they all can be categorized according to two dimensions: (1) the period between successive reinforcements is determined either by the number of intervening nonreinforced responses or by the elapsed time, and (2) the period between successive reinforcements is either regular or irregular. In terms of these two dimensions we can define the following four basic schedules.

1. **Fixed ratio** (FR). On this schedule reinforcement occurs after a fixed number of nonreinforced responses; if it occurs every 20 responses, for example, the ratio of nonreinforced to reinforced responses is 20 to 1.

2. **Fixed interval** (FI). Reinforcement follows the first response emitted after a fixed time period measured from the last reinforcement. For example, on a fixed-interval schedule of one minute, no further reinforcement will occur following a reinforced response until one minute has passed; once it has elapsed, the first response made will be reinforced.

3. **Variable ratio** (VR). Like the fixed-ratio schedule, reinforcement occurs after a specified number of nonreinforced responses. But for this schedule the number of responses intervening between reinforcements varies from one reinforcement to the next. For example, a 20-to-1 variable-ratio schedule might be produced by requiring that the number of intervening responses be randomly selected from the numbers 0 to 40; this schedule averages an interreinforcement ratio of 20 responses, but it has a wide range of values.

4. **Variable interval** (VI). In this schedule reinforcement occurs after a specified period of time that varies from one reinforcement to the next. A simple variable-interval schedule of one minute might be generated by randomly setting the time period between reinforcements in a range of values from 0 to 120 seconds; this schedule yields an average time period of one minute, but a given interval can range anywhere from zero seconds to two minutes.

These four reinforcement schedules produce characteristic modes of responding. On an FI schedule the animal's pattern of responding suggests that it is keeping careful track of time. Immediately after a reinforcement its rate of responding drops to near zero and then increases at an accelerating pace as the end of the interval approaches. On VI schedules the response rate does not fluctuate as much between reinforcements. This is to be expected, since the animal does not know when the interval will terminate; the animal responds at a fairly steady rate in order to receive reinforcement promptly whenever it becomes available.

In contrast to the interval schedules, both the fixed- and variable-ratio schedules tend to produce extremely rapid rates of responding. If the ratio is small, responding begins immediately after a reinforcement; when the ratio is **large** there may be a brief pause after each reinforcement, followed thereafter by **steady** bursts of responding. On ratio schedules the animal responds as though it knows that the next reinforcement depends upon its making a certain number of responses, and it bursts forth with them at as fast a rate as possible.

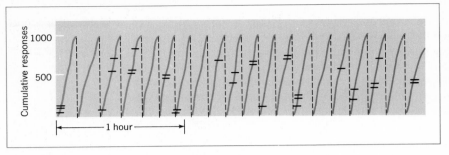

Fig. **8-12 Operant responses sustained by partial reinforcement** The curves record one pigeon's pecking responses, which were reinforced irregularly, but at an average interval of five minutes. The reinforcements are represented by horizontal dashes. Each of the sloping lines represents 1000 responses; the pen resets after each 1000.

orderliness is the behavior controlled by *partial reinforcement,* that is, behavior taking place when the response is reinforced only a fraction of the time it occurs.

In the typical experiment a pigeon learns to peck at a lighted disc mounted on the wall and receives access to a small quantity of grain as its reinforcement. Once this conditioned operant is established, the pigeon will continue to peck at a high and relatively uniform rate, even if it receives only an occasional reinforcement. The pigeon whose remarkably regular pecking is illustrated in Figure 8-12 was reinforced on the average of once every five minutes, that is, twelve times an hour; yet it pecked at a rate of some 6000 responses per hour.

The practical significance of partial reinforcement is very great. A child's mother is not always present to reward him for looking both ways before crossing the street. But the influences of reinforcements are such that they persist against many nonreinforcements. A long straight drive will keep a golfer at his game despite many balls lost in the rough.

Secondary reinforcement

Pavlov noted that once a dog had learned to respond to a conditioned stimulus in a highly dependable way, the conditioned stimulus could be used to reinforce a conditioned response to a new stimulus. Suppose the animal has learned to salivate to a tone as a conditioned stimulus. This is a first-order conditioned response. If a flashing light is then presented along with only the tone, the flashing light when presented alone will come

to elicit the conditioned response. Pavlov called this process *second-order conditioning.* The conditioned stimulus of first-order conditioning (tone) has become a *secondary reinforcer.* While second-order conditioning can be established in this manner within classical conditioning, it is more easily demonstrated within operant conditioning. The general principle, holding within both classical and operant conditioning, can be stated as follows: *any stimulus can be made reinforcing through association with a reinforcing event.*

The introduction of a minor variation in the typical operant-conditioning situation will demonstrate how secondary reinforcement works. When a rat in a Skinner box presses a lever, a tone comes on momentarily, followed shortly by a pellet of food. After the animal has been conditioned in this way, extinction is begun so that when the rat presses the lever, neither the tone nor the food appears. In time the animal virtually ceases to press the lever.

Now the tone is connected again, but without the food. When the animal discovers that pressing the lever turns on the tone, the rate of pressing markedly increases, overcoming the extinction, even though no food follows. The tone has acquired secondary reinforcing qualities. The total number of responses made with only the tone connected to the bar depends upon the frequency of tone-food pairings during acquisition. Thus the strength of the tone as a secondary reinforcer increases as a function of the number of times it was associated with the primary reinforcer, food.

A feature of secondary reinforcement that has important practical implications is its wide degree of generalization. The principle can be stated: *once established, a secondary reinforcer can strengthen responses other than the response used during its original establishment and can do so with drives other than the one prevailing during the original training.* We know from ordinary observation that such reinforcers as social approval can be effective over a wide range of behavior, but experimental evidence also supports the principle that secondary reinforcers have wide generality. In a study demonstrating this principle, the experimenter, using water-deprived rats, associated a tone with bar-pressing reinforced by water. When the rats were later deprived of food rather than water, the same tone evoked bar-pressing. If enough drive of any kind is present to instigate activity, a secondary reinforcer is effective, even though it derived its strength while another drive prevailed (Estes, 1949).

Secondary reinforcement greatly increases the range of possible conditioning. If everything we learned had to be followed by a primary reinforcer, the occasions for learning would be very much restricted. As it is, however, any habit once learned can have other habits built upon it. A verbal promise of food can reinforce behavior that would otherwise require the food itself; mere praise (without the promise of a primary reinforcer) itself becomes reinforcing.

Shaping behavior

As we noted earlier, classical conditioning is sometimes called the *method of stimulus substitution,* because the conditioned stimulus substitutes for the unconditioned stimulus in evoking the response appropriate to the unconditioned stimulus. The substitution principle fails, however, to account for *novelty* in behavior—for the learning of totally new responses. In contrast, operant conditioning plays an important role in eliciting novel behavior.

The experimenter can demonstrate how novel behavior is produced by operant conditioning. He takes advantage of random variations in the operant response, reinforcing only those responses that are in the desired direction. For example, he can make a pigeon hold its head high as it walks

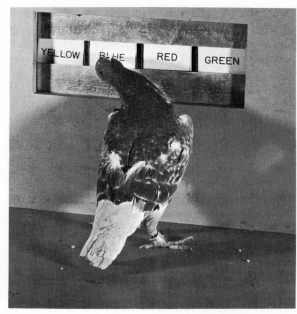

Yale Joel from *Life,* © Time, Inc.

Fig. **8-13 Shaping behavior** By reinforcing only the desired responses, the experimenter taught the pigeon to tap the correct sign when light of a certain color was turned on.

around, by reinforcing with grain at first when its head is at average height, then when slightly above average, and finally only when its neck is stretched high. Or if he wants to train a dog to press a buzzer with its nose, he can give a food reinforcement each time the animal approaches the area of the buzzer, requiring closer and closer approximations to the desired spot for each reinforcement until finally the dog's nose is touching the buzzer. This technique is called *shaping* the animal's behavior, reinforcing only responses that meet the experimenter's specifications and extinguishing all others (see Figure 8-13).

One psychologist and his wife, also a psychologist, developed a large-scale business teaching animals elaborate tricks and behavior routines by means of this shaping method. Using these relatively simple techniques, they and their staff trained thousands of animals of many species for television shows and commercials, country fairs, and various tourist attractions, such as the famous whale and porpoise shows at "Marine Studios" in Florida and

"Marineland of the Pacific" in California. For example, one popular show featured a pig called "Priscilla, the Fastidious Pig." Priscilla turned on the TV set, ate breakfast at a table, picked up dirty clothes and put them in a hamper, ran a vacuum cleaner over the floor, picked out her favorite food (from among foods competing with that of her sponsor!), and took part in a quiz program, answering questions from the audience by flashing lights indicating "Yes" or "No." She was not an unusually bright pig; in fact, because pigs grow so fast, a new "Priscilla" was trained every three

to five months. The ingenuity was not the pig's but the experimenters', who used operant conditioning and shaped the behavior to produce the desired result (Breland and Breland, 1966).

In all these training techniques the behavior is shaped by means of reinforcement that is contingent upon the proper response. The importance of reinforcement in strengthening behavior is demonstrated by what happens when we introduce *noncontingent reinforcement,* that is, reinforcement not contingent upon a specific response. In one experiment Skinner placed hungry pigeons in sep-

CRITICAL
DISCUSSION

**Operant
conditioning
of autonomic
responses**

Classical conditioning has traditionally been viewed as a "lower" form of involuntary learning involving glandular and visceral responses, whereas operant conditioning has been regarded as a "higher" form of voluntary learning involving responses of the skeletal muscles. In fact, it has been assumed by some that responses mediated by the autonomic nervous system could be learned only by classical conditioning, while those mediated by the central nervous system only operantly. This assumption has now been challenged by a series of studies indicating that it is possible to train animals to change their heart rate, blood pressure, and intestinal contractions by the proper application of operant techniques (Miller, 1969).

In one study (Miller and Banuazizi, 1968) rats were trained to modify two different visceral responses—heart rate and intestinal contraction. After a baseline of normal heart rate was established, one group of rats was rewarded for an increase in heart rate and another for a decrease. A shaping procedure was used so that initially any small increase or decrease above or below the baseline was rewarded; subsequently, progressively larger increases or decreases were needed to obtain reward. With this kind of training it was possible to slow a rat's heart rate, for example, from an initial 350 beats per minute to 230 within a relatively brief period of time. Similar procedures were used to train a third group of rats to increase intestinal contractions and a fourth group to decrease contractions.

Because visceral responses can be affected by tensing or moving skeletal muscles (for example, breathing slowly will decrease heart rate), it is possible that a subject, instead of learning a visceral response directly, may be learning a skeletal response that produces a visceral change. To control for this possibility the rats were given *curare,* a drug that temporarily paralyzes skeletal muscles without rendering the animal unconscious or affecting neural control of visceral responses. Since a paralyzed animal cannot be rewarded by food or drink, an unusual method of reward had to be used. This method consisted of electrical stimulation of certain "pleasure centers" in the rat's brain (see p. 37). Every time the rat produced a desired visceral change it received a brief electric current to a specific brain area where stimulation is known to have a reinforcing effect.

The results of this study are presented in Figure 8-14. One group of rats rewarded for increases in heart rate learned an increase, a second group rewarded for decreases learned a decrease, but neither of these groups showed a significant change in intestinal contractions. Conversely, a third group rewarded for increases in intestinal contraction showed an increase, and a fourth group rewarded for decreases in intestinal contraction showed

arate Skinner boxes and at random intervals turned on a light that was immediately followed by a food reinforcement. The effect on the behavior of the pigeons was quite amazing. Each bird tended to select and repeat whatever behavior it was engaged in at the time the reinforcement occurred. If one pigeon was pecking at its right wing just prior to reinforcement, this behavior tended to increase in frequency. The increased frequency made it more likely that this bit of behavior would occur about the time of the next food delivery, and so it would be reinforced again. Soon right-wing

pecking dominated the bird's behavior. Thus for each bird some particular act or mannerism gained dominance because it occurred at the time of reinforcement, regardless of the fact that the act was in no way instrumental in producing the reinforcement.

Skinner has noted the similarity between the pigeons' behavior and the superstitions people develop as the result of the chance occurrence of an act and a reinforcement together. The gambler who blows on the dice before throwing them and the baseball pitcher who habitually tugs at his cap

a decrease, but neither of these groups showed a change in heart rate. These results provide impressive evidence that visceral learning can be specific to an organ system; it is not the result of some general factor such as overall level of activation.

Similar work with human subjects suggests that they also can be trained to control visceral responses. If this is the case, the practical implications are enormous. Abnormal activities of the autonomic nervous system are important factors in heart disease, ulcers, and other ailments; if an individual could be taught to control his heart rate, intestinal contractions, or blood pressure, it would be a major step toward controlling these diseases.

Fig. **8-14 Operant conditioning of autonomic responses** Data from four groups of rats, each group rewarded for a different autonomic response. The left-hand figure plots rate of intestinal contractions for each group, and the right-hand figure plots heart rate. (After Miller and Banuazizi, 1968)

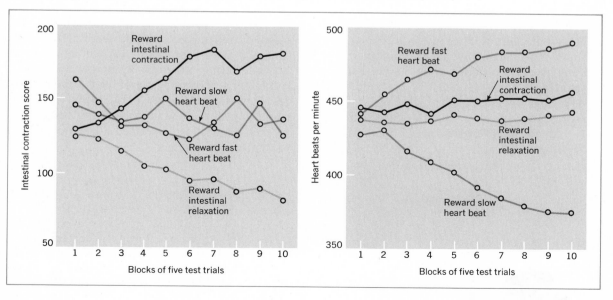

and shakes his left foot before pitching are reinforced often enough by a successful performance that the behavior is strengthened and becomes a part of their repertoire. They certainly are not successful every time. But, as we noted earlier, partial reinforcement is more resistant to extinction than continuous reinforcement.

Operant conditioning of human behavior

In the following experiment (Verplanck, 1955) a college student did not know that he was being experimented upon, and the experimenter thereby avoided the artificiality of many conditioning experiments. The experimenter carried on what appeared to be an informal conversation with the subject, but actually behaved according to a plan while he and the subject were talking together. The experimenter determined in advance to reinforce all statements of opinion made by the subject, such as sentences beginning "I think," "I believe," "It seems to me," and the like. The *reinforcement* was the experimenter's saying "You're right," "I agree," "That's so" after each statement of opinion. *Extinction* was carried out in another portion of the experiment by mere nonreinforcement—silence—following a statement of opinion.

Following verbal reinforcement, statements of opinion showed a marked increase in frequency; following extinction, they decreased. The experimenter controlled verbal behavior in this situation in much the same way as he controlled bar-pressing by a rat. In studies of this kind the subject may on some occasions begin to realize that the experimenter is actually manipulating his verbal behavior. There is some evidence, however, that verbal conditioning does occur without the subject's being consciously aware of the fact that his statements are being controlled by the rein-

forcement schedule of the experimenter (Rosenfeld and Baer, 1969).

Operant-conditioning principles have also been used to modify problem behavior in children. In one case nursery school teachers used social reinforcement to change the behavior of a three-year-old girl who was shy and withdrawn, spending most of her time crawling about the floor and resisting all attempts to encourage her to play or to join in group activities. On the assumption that getting the child to spend more time on her feet was the first step toward increasing participation in school activities, a reinforcement schedule was set up whereby the teachers gave attention to the child only when she was standing and ignored her completely the rest of the time. Careful recording of the child's minute-by-minute activity showed that she progressed from an initial rate of over 90 percent of the day on the floor to the point where after two weeks her behavior was indistinguishable from that of the other children in terms of talking, smiling, and use of the school equipment.

To determine whether the reinforcement schedule was the causative factor, the procedure was reversed so that only on-the-floor activity was reinforced. Within two days the child was again spending the majority of her time on the floor. Interestingly enough, she did not revert to her earlier behavior in other respects, but managed to play happily while sitting or crawling and continued to initiate contacts with the other children. A second reversal procedure (that is, again giving the child steady attention when she was on her feet and none when she was on the floor) reinstated her vigorous on-the-feet participation in school activities within a few hours, and her behavior in the days that followed seemed adequate in every way (Harris and others, 1965).

The principle of reinforcement

In our discussion of classical conditioning we used the term *reinforcement* to refer to the paired presentation of the unconditioned stimulus and the

conditioned stimulus. In operant conditioning reinforcement referred to the presentation of food following the occurrence of the desired response.

Put in other terms, in classical conditioning reinforcement *elicits* the response, and in operant conditioning reinforcement *follows* the response. Although the operation designated as reinforcement is quite different in the two situations, the result in both cases is an increase in the likelihood of the desired response. We can therefore define reinforcement as *any event the occurrence of which increases the probability that a stimulus will on subsequent occasions evoke a response.* We customarily distinguish between two types of reinforcers: *positive reinforcers* (such as food), which on being presented increase the probability of a response, and *negative reinforcers* (such as shock), which on being terminated increase response probability.[3]

Parameters of reinforcement

Psychologists have systematically investigated the effect of a number of reinforcement variables on the course of learning. Not surprisingly, the *amount of reinforcement* has been found to be an important parameter. Within limits the greater the amount of reinforcement, the more rapid the rate of learning. This relationship is illustrated by the following experiment (Clayton, 1964). The apparatus used was a T-maze, the simplest type of maze, consisting of a start box, straight runway, and a cross bar with a goal box at both ends (Figure 8-15). After the rat was placed in the start box, it ran to the *choice point,* where it had to decide between a right or left turn to reach the food placed in one of the goal boxes. In this experiment there were three groups of rats, the groups differing in the amount of food received for a correct turn: one group received four food pellets, another group two pellets, and a third group one pellet. Each rat ran four trials a day. The results in terms of proportion of correct responses per day are shown in Figure 8-16. Note that the group with the largest amount of reinforcement learned at the fastest rate, while the other two groups learned more slowly.

[3]These terms are synonymous with the terms "positive" and "negative incentives" used in the discussion of motivation in Chapter 12. Both are used interchangeably in psychological literature, but generally the word "reinforcer" is preferred to "incentive" in discussing learning.

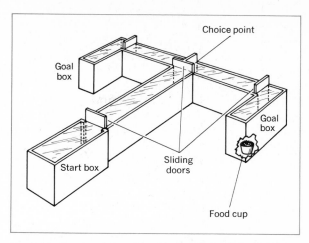

Fig. **8-15 T-maze** A maze used in the study of simple choice learning. The plexiglass covers on the start box and goal boxes are hinged so that the rat can be easily placed in or removed from the apparatus. The sliding doors (which usually are operated by a system of strings and pulleys from above) prevent the animal from retracing its path once it has made a choice. Note that the goal boxes are arranged so that the rat cannot see the food cup from the choice point.

Fig. **8-16 Amount of reinforcement** Acquisition curves for three groups of rats run in a T-maze experiment. The groups were distinguished by the number of food pellets a rat received when it entered the correct goal box. Half the animals were trained with the left side of the maze designated as the correct response, half with the right side as the correct response. (After Clayton, 1964)

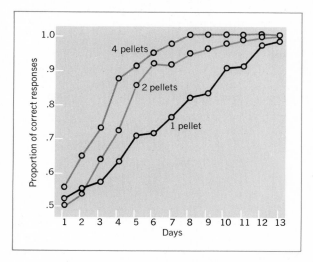

The curves start at about .5; since there are only two response choices, the animal should make the correct turn 50 percent of the time by chance alone prior to training.

The *delay of reinforcement* is another important parameter of reinforcement. A common assumption in training animals or young children has been that it is most effective to reward or punish the organism immediately after it responds. The spanking given by father when he returns home from work is less effective (other variables being equal) in reducing junior's aggressive behavior toward baby brother than punishment delivered immediately following or during the act.

The effectiveness of immediate reinforcement in a laboratory learning situation is demonstrated by the following experiment. The apparatus used was a T-maze having goal boxes equipped with food dispensers that could be set to delay the presentation of food pellets. One group of rats received their food immediately upon entering the

correct goal box (zero-second delay); another group was fed following a five-second delay; and a third group was delayed thirty seconds before receiving their food. Each rat was run ten trials per day. Figure 8-17 shows the proportion of correct responses over days for each of the three groups. The zero-second group and the five-second group both reached near perfect responding by the ninth day, but the zero-second group learned at a faster rate. The thirty-second-delay group was markedly inferior and never achieved better than 65 percent correct responses.

The nature of reinforcement

Why do reinforcing events increase the probability of a response? What is the nature of reinforcement? Why are some events effective reinforcers while others are not? These questions, which have been the subject of intense interest and debate among psychologists, are obviously closely related to the whole problem of motivation. The most prevalent hypothesis has been the *drive-reduction theory* of reinforcement. As we will see in Chapter 12, when an organism is in a state of physiological need (as the result of deprivation or some injury to the tissues), a concurrent state of tension exists, known as *drive*. Drive serves to energize the organism and to produce certain internal stimuli that are associated with the drive. An animal deprived of food exhibits restless activity, and the stimuli associated with the hunger drive (such as stomach contractions and low blood-sugar level) lead to food-seeking behavior. With the ingestion of food the hunger drive is reduced and the associated stimuli disappear. According to this theory, then, any event that is drive-reducing is reinforcing. All primary reinforcers are drive-reducing; secondary reinforcers are not drive-reducing in themselves but provide reinforcing effects by virtue of their previous association with primary reinforcers.

The drive-reduction theory of reinforcement does seem to be a reasonable explanation in many instances. Food, water, and shock termination (which reduce the drives of hunger, thirst, and pain) are among our most effective reinforcers.

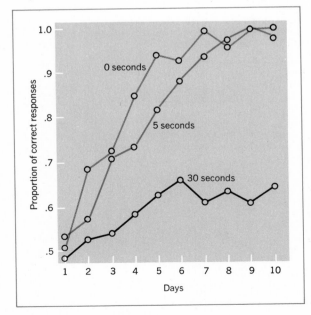

Fig. **8-17 Delay of reward** The figure shows acquisition curves for three groups of rats. The groups were distinguished by the time interval between entering the correct goal box and receiving a pellet of food. (Unpublished data from Atkinson)

And several studies have shown that learning does take place when drives are reduced by direct physiological intervention rather than by externally administered reinforcement. For example, Miller and Kessen (1952) provided a group of rats with stomach fistulas so that milk could be injected directly into the stomach. The rats were run in a simple T-maze, with milk introduced into the stomach for correct responses. Although learning was faster for another group of rats that received milk by mouth, the milk-injected rats also learned. In a related study food-deprived rabbits showed learning when the reinforcement was an intravenous injection of glucose that reduced the hunger drive by raising the blood-sugar level (Coppock and Chambers, 1954).

A number of experimental results, however, are difficult to explain on the basis of drive-reduction theory. Hungry rats will learn to press a bar or to choose the correct path in a maze when reinforced by a nonnutritive substance, such as saccharine; male rats will learn to jump a barrier to copulate with females in heat even though no ejaculation is permitted. In both instances no drive is reduced—in fact, one might consider the latter situation drive-increasing—yet learning to make the necessary movements to approach the incentive occurs. As we shall see in Chapter 12, animals as well as human subjects will learn in a variety of situations in which the only reinforcement is the opportunity to see or to explore a new environment or to manipulate novel objects.

Other theories have been proposed as alternatives to the drive-reduction concept of reinforcement. One viewpoint is that reinforcement is more a matter of the nature of the reinforcing activities than of the reinforcing stimuli (Premack, 1971). According to this view, if activities fall in the preferential order A-B-C-D, from low to high, then activity B can reinforce activity A, activity C can reinforce either A or B, and activity D can reinforce any one of the other three activities. Note that an activity can reinforce only certain of the other activities—those of lower preference, not those of higher preference. It is possible to use the eating of dessert to reinforce the eating of vegetables, but the reverse order has no reinforcing value. A good deal of experimental evidence with both animals and human subjects has given support to this position.

Still another viewpoint proposes that reinforcement is not essential for learning to occur. According to this theory, *temporal contiguity* between a stimulus and a response is the only necessary condition for learning. If a response occurs in the presence of a specific stimulus, then the S-R association is strengthened and the probability that the stimulus will evoke the same response on subsequent occasions is increased. Reinforcement, according to this position, is important in *motivating* the organism to perform the response, but it is not necessary for learning (Guthrie, 1952; Sheffield, 1965).

One area of research of great interest stems from the rather startling discovery that electrical stimulation of certain regions of the brain can be reinforcing. In 1953 Olds was investigating the reticular formation of the rat's brain (see p. 34) by means of microelectrodes. These tiny electrodes can be implanted permanently in specific brain areas without interfering with the rat's health or normal activity and, when connected with an electrical source, can supply stimulation of varying intensities. By accident an electrode was implanted in an area near the hypothalamus. Olds discovered that after he had delivered a mild current through the electrodes the animal repeatedly returned to the location in the cage where it had been when stimulated. Further stimulations at the same cage location caused the animal to spend most of its time there. Later Olds found that this same animal could be pulled to any spot in a maze by giving electrical stimulation after each response in the appropriate direction. And other animals with electrodes

CRITICAL DISCUSSION

Brain stimulation and reinforcement

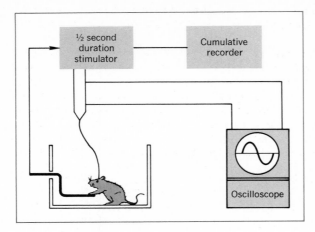

Fig. **8-18 Brain stimulation** The animal's bar-press delivers a 60-cycle current for one-half second, after which the animal must release and press again for more current. The animal's response rate is recorded on the cumulative recorder, and the experimenter can monitor the delivery of the current by means of the oscilloscope. Rats respond with rates up to 100 per minute with electrodes in the medial-forebrain region of the hypothalamus. (After Olds and Olds, 1965, by permission)

implanted in the same brain region learned to press a bar in a Skinner box to produce their own electrical stimulation (see Figure 8-18); each bar-press closed a circuit that automatically provided a brief current. These animals were bar-pressing at a phenomenal rate: a not unusual record would show an average of over 2000 responses an hour for fifteen or twenty hours, until the animal finally dropped from exhaustion (Olds and Olds, 1965).

Since the initial brain-stimulation discovery, experiments have been carried out using rats, cats, and monkeys in a wide variety of tasks, with microelectrodes implanted in many different areas of the brain and brain stem. The reinforcing effects of stimulation in certain areas (primarily the hypothalamus) are powerful: hungry rats will endure a more painful shock while crossing an electric grid to obtain brain stimulation than they will to obtain food (Olds and Sinclair, 1957); when given a choice between food or electric brain stimulation in a T-maze, rats that have been on a starvation diet for as long as ten days will invariably choose the path leading to stimulation (Spies, 1965). On the other hand, stimulation of some areas of the brain stem has been found to serve as a *negative* reinforcer; when the electrodes were moved to these different brain areas, rats that previously bar-pressed at a rapid rate to receive stimulation suddenly stopped responding and avoided the bar area entirely, indicating that the new stimulation was unpleasant.

Multiple-response learning

Thus far we have considered the strengthening or weakening of single identifiable responses. Although some of these responses are complex, they are still identifiable as unitary acts. But much of our learning consists of acquiring patterns or sequences of behaviors, as in learning athletic skills or in memorizing a poem. These patterns illustrate *multiple-response learning,* a kind of learning involving more than one identifiable act, with the order of events usually fixed by the demands of the situation. Psychologists have designed a number of laboratory tasks by which to study this kind of learning. Among them are mirror drawing, target tracking, and rote memorization. The first two tasks are forms of sensorimotor skill, and the last is largely verbal. Tasks such as these approximate

sented in the aperture of the memory drum, the subject tries to anticipate the response item; then the stimulus-response pair appears in the window until the next stimulus item is presented.

To illustrate the paired-associate procedure we shall briefly describe a study on second-language learning (Crothers and Suppes, 1967). The equipment used in this experiment was more elaborate than the typical memory drum, for reasons that will soon be obvious. The task was to learn the correct English translation for a list of spoken Russian words. The subject, who had no previous knowledge of Russian, wore a set of earphones while seated before a projection screen. A Russian word was pronounced over the earphones and, at the same time, three English words were projected onto the screen, one of which was the correct translation. The subject was required to press one of three buttons to indicate which word he thought was the correct translation. After he made his response the button corresponding to the correct answer lighted briefly. The subject studied the correct translation and, after a brief pause, the procedure was repeated with the next Russian word. After the entire list of Russian words had been run through, the experimenter rearranged the items in a new random order and again presented the list to the subject. Each run through the list constituted a new trial.

Two groups of subjects were used, one learning a list of fifteen words and the other a list of thirty. The proportion of correct responses over trials is plotted in Figure 8-24. Note that the shorter list

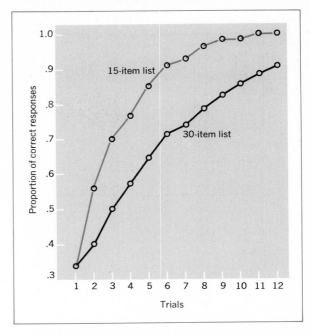

Fig. **8-24 Paired-associate learning curves** Proportion of correct anticipation responses over successive trials of a paired-associate learning experiment. Performance is at a chance level on the first trial but gradually improves over trials. The rate of learning is faster for the shorter list. (Data from Crothers and Suppes, 1967)

was learned more rapidly. These results are what one would expect. The more items that have to be mastered at one time, the slower the rate at which each individual item is learned.

[*continued on page 216*]

An important issue in learning theory concerns the way in which associations are formed. In the past it generally had been assumed that they were formed in a gradual fashion, with each reinforcement adding to the strength of a stimulus-response connection. Thus, if the strength of an association could be directly measured, the course of learning might be represented by a device like a light bulb controlled by a dimmer knob, with each reinforcement gradually increasing the brightness of the light. Because associative strength increases by small amounts, this is called the *incremental* position.

Estes (1960), Bower (1966), and others have challenged this view, arguing that in its most elementary form a stimulus-response association is acquired in an *all-or-none* fashion. Following the analogy between the incremental model and a dimmer knob, the all-or-none model can be represented by an on-off light switch that operates as follows. Initially the

CRITICAL
DISCUSSION

**All-or-none
versus
incremental
learning**

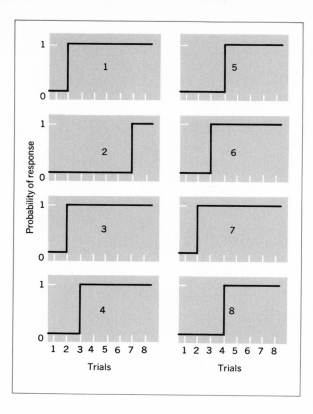

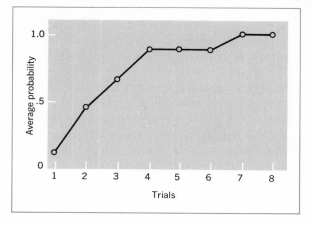

Fig. **8-25 All-or-none learning curves** The small graphs represent the probability of a response as a function of the number of reinforcements for eight hypothetical subjects. Because the curves for individual subjects jump to unity on different trials, the learning curve averaged over all eight subjects (plotted above) is a gradually increasing function. Thus, the average curve does not reflect the nature of the learning process for individual subjects.

switch is in the "unlearned" position; after each reinforcement there is some probability that the switch is turned from the "unlearned" to the "learned" position. Once the switch has been turned to the "learned" position, it remains there and the correct response is always given.

The assumptions of the all-or-none model are illustrated in Figure 8-25. Each of the small graphs represents the probability of a correct response as a function of the number of reinforcements for an individual subject. A subject begins at an initial level, and following each reinforcement there is some chance that his response probability will jump to 1. Because of the probabilistic nature of the process, different subjects learn on different trials; reinforcement was effective on trial 2 for subject 1, but not effective for subject 8 until trial 4. If data are averaged for a large group of subjects, all behaving in an all-or-none way, a curve representing the proportion of correct responses per trial would approximate a smooth increasing function. The larger graph in Figure 8-25 shows that even for our sample of eight subjects, the probability of a correct response averaged over these subjects is a gradually increasing function.

Figure 8-26 presents some predictions based on the all-or-none model for data from a large group of hypothetical subjects. In the figure we assume that all subjects start at an initial level of .5, and that the probability of reinforcement being effective on any trial is .1. The curve labeled $P(C_n)$ in the figure gives the proportion of correct responses per trial averaged over all subjects and is a smooth increasing function. Another prediction of the all-or-none model is indicated by the horizontal line labeled $P(C_n | E_{n-1})$. This line represents the probability that a correct response will occur, given that the subject made

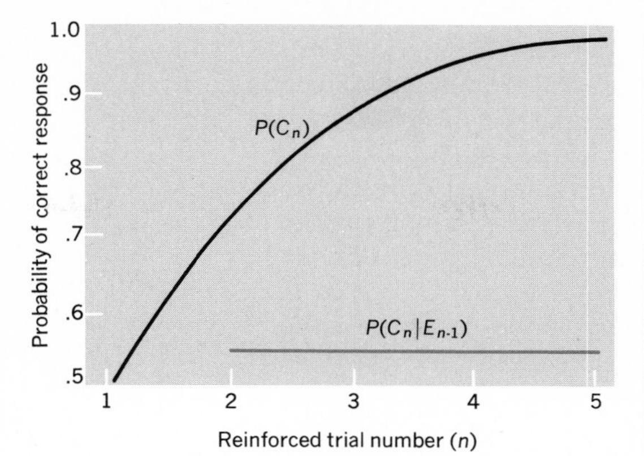

Fig. **8-26** **Predictions for all-or-none model** The curve marked $P(C_n)$ is the average probability of a correct response on trial n (where n represents any trial from 1 through 5). The curve labeled $P(C_n|E_{n-1})$ is the probability that a correct response will be made on trial n given an error on trial $n - 1$. Note that this curve does not show any improvement as a function of the number of previously reinforced trials.

an error on the preceding trial, and, as can be seen, is predicted by the all-or-none model to be constant.

The way to choose between two opposing theories is to find which one agrees better with experimental data. It happens that both the all-or-none model and the incremental model predict the same average course of learning, as represented by the $P(C_n)$ curve in Figure 8-26. But other predictions are quite different. For example, the incremental model predicts that the $P(C_n|E_{n-1})$ curve should be exactly like $P(C_n)$. This follows because according to the incremental model the probability of a correct response has been gradually increasing trial by trial, and the occurrence of an error on the preceding trial is not an indication of its strength; the whole record of reinforcements up to that trial is more important, and this record is that of a steadily rising curve of probability. For the all-or-none model, however, all errors (whether made on an early or late trial) occur in exactly the same unlearned state. The likelihood of learning on a trial following an error will not depend on how far along in the practice the trial is. That is why the $P(C_n|E_{n-1})$ curve is a horizontal line according to the all-or-none model. When an analysis is made to see whether the observed $P(C_n|E_{n-1})$ curve is that predicted by the incremental model or the all-or-none model, results very commonly favor the all-or-none assumption, although some experiments favor the incremental model (Atkinson, Bower, and Crothers, 1965; Restle and Greeno, 1970).

Estes (1964) has taken the position that all associations are formed in an all-or-none way, and that instances of apparent incremental change are simply cases of incomplete analysis. When a learning situation involves both the development of complex response units and the association of these units with an array of stimulus elements, then the probability of the total response may well change in a gradual incremental fashion over trials. Estes argues, however, that the apparent gradualness is due to the fact that the complex response depends upon numerous component stimulus-response associations, each being learned in an all-or-none fashion at different points in time; the observable process appears to be a gradually increasing one, but in fact it is an average of many unobservable component processes that are all-or-none.

It is too early to give a final evaluation of the controversy over all-or-none versus incremental learning. Recent research has certainly pointed out that much learning that psychologists previously regarded as incremental can be separated into component all-or-none processes. But this does not permit us to reject the possibility that some types of learning, in their most elementary form, are fundamentally incremental in nature.

Learning as a cognitive process

The kinds of learning that we have considered thus far all stress the organization of behavior into *habits,* or associations—learned stimulus-response sequences of greater or less complexity. In studying more complex forms of learning, more attention must be given to the roles of perception and knowledge, or *cognitive processes.* There is the possibility that emphasis upon habit formation may lead to too much concern for piecemeal activities and too little attention to organized relationships and meaning. In school, for example, the teacher impressed by habit formation may use rote memorization and drill excessively, without caring enough about whether the child organizes and understands what he learns.

Insight experiments

Partly in protest against too much study of the kinds of learning that involve stimulus-response associations, Wolfgang Köhler, a German psychologist who emigrated to the United States, performed some dramatic experiments with chimpanzees. At some point in working on a problem, chimpanzees appeared to grasp its inner rela-tionships through *insight;* that is, they solved the problem not through mere trial and error, but by perceiving the relationships essential to solution. The following experiment by Köhler is typical.

Sultan [Köhler's most intelligent chimpanzee] is squatting at the bars but cannot reach the fruit which lies outside by means of his only available short stick. A longer stick is deposited outside the bars, about two meters on one side of the object and parallel with the grating. It cannot be grasped with the hand, but it can be pulled within reach by means of the small stick. [See Figure 8-27 for an illustration of a similar multiple-stick problem.] Sultan tries to reach the fruit with the smaller of the two sticks. Not succeeding, he tears at a piece of wire that projects from the netting of his cage, but that too, is in vain. Then he gazes about him (there are always in the course of these tests some long pauses, during which the animals scrutinize the whole visible area). He suddenly picks up the little stick once more, goes up to the bars directly opposite to the long stick, scratches it towards him with the "auxiliary," seizes it, and goes with it to the point opposite the objective (the fruit), which he secures. From the moment that his eyes fall upon the long stick, his procedure forms one consecutive whole, without hiatus, and although

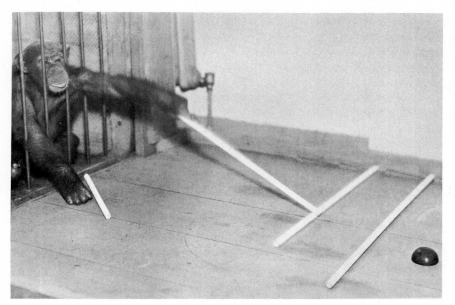

Fig. **8-27 A chimpanzee solving a multiple-stick problem** Using the shorter sticks, the chimpanzee pulls in a stick long enough to reach the piece of fruit. He has learned to solve this problem by understanding the relationship between the sticks and the piece of fruit.

Yerkes Regional Primate Center

the angling of the bigger stick by means of the smaller is an action that could be complete and distinct in itself, yet observation shows that it follows, quite suddenly, on an interval of hesitation and doubt—staring about—which undoubtedly has a relation to the final objective, and is immediately merged in the final action of the attainment of the end goal [Köhler, 1925, pp. 174–75].

A moderate degree of insight is so common in human learning that we tend to take it for granted. Occasionally insight comes dramatically, and then we have what has been appropriately called an "aha" experience. The solution of a problem becomes suddenly clear, as though a light had been turned on in the darkness. This experience usually comes with types of puzzles (or riddles) that make good parlor tricks, precisely because people enjoy the experience of insight when (and if) it comes. One illustration is furnished by the problem presented in Figure 8-28.

If we use the ordinary methods of problem-solving to deal with the problem of Figure 8-28, we may set up some sort of algebraic equation to determine, step by step, how far the bird flies on each trip. For example, we know that on the first trip the bird flies east at 80 mph while the train coming west toward it is traveling at 40 mph. It can be determined without too much difficulty that the bird will go twice as far as the train by the time they meet. Hence when they meet, the train will have gone 33 1/3 miles from its starting point while the bird has flown 66 2/3 miles. For the bird's return flight it will be necessary to take account of the movement of the first train during the time the bird flew the 66 2/3 miles. Then, knowing the rate of flight of the bird and of the train coming to meet it, the second trip can be computed just as the first one was. We continue these computations until the trains have met.

What is meant by solving this kind of problem with insight? Instead of trying to determine, first of all, how far the bird flies on each of its trips, we can take a different tack. The clue comes from the question: How long will the bird have been flying by the time the trains meet? When this question is answered, the rest of the solution comes quickly. If you now have the answer, having first been puzzled and then suddenly having "caught on," you know what the experience of insight is.

The variables that influence insight learning are not well understood but a few general remarks can be made.

1. *Insight depends upon the arrangement of the problem situation.* Appropriate past experience, while necessary, does not guarantee a solution. Insight will come easily only if the essentials for solution are arranged so that their relationships can be perceived. For example, a chimpanzee solves the stick problem more readily if the stick is on the same side of the cage as the food. He has more difficulty if he must turn away from the food to see the stick. Human beings can do much of their rearranging of a problem mentally; mental manipulations may at times go on subconsciously, and only when a solution has been found is the person suddenly aware of the fact that he had been thinking about the problem.

2. *Once a solution occurs with insight, it can be repeated promptly.* Gradual solution appears to be the rule in trial-and-error learning. Sudden solution is the rule in insight. Once the chimpanzee has used a stick for pulling in a banana, he will seek out a stick on the next occasion.

3. *A solution achieved with insight can be applied*

Fig. **8-28 The bird and the locomotives: an insight problem** Two locomotives, now 100 miles apart, are moving toward each other. The east-bound locomotive is traveling at the rate of 60 mph. The west-bound one is traveling at the rate of 40 mph. An energetic bird, starting from the east-bound locomotive, flies back and forth between the two locomotives, without stopping or losing any speed on the turns. The bird flies at the uniform rate of 80 mph. Problem: How far does the bird fly from the start to the moment that the two trains meet? The problem can be solved by those without mathematical training (see text).

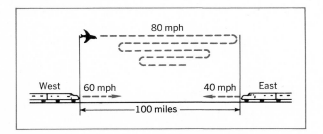

in new situations. What is learned in the insight experiment is not a specific movement habit, but a cognitive relationship between a means and an end. Hence one tool may be substituted for another. In Figure 8-28 boats could replace trains without confusing the solver of the problem.

An effective learner is a resourceful, adaptable person, able to use what he knows in new situations and to discover for himself solutions to problems that he has never faced before. Emphasis upon insightful learning, rather than upon rote learning or mechanical skills, encourages such problem-solving behavior.

Sign learning

It is possible that some learning classified as conditioned response may actually involve learning the signs of "what leads to what." This was the contention of Edward C. Tolman, who believed that much learning is *sign learning* (Tolman, 1948). A rat running through a complex maze may be developing a kind of map, or *cognitive representation,* of the maze instead of learning merely a sequence of left and right turns. If a familiar path is blocked, the animal can adopt another route based on this understanding of spatial relationships.

Sign learning may be defined as an acquired expectation that one stimulus will be followed by another in a particular situation. Note that what is acquired is an expectation (a cognitive representation) rather than a chained sequence of responses. Although the expectation may lead the animal to make a specific response, the response need not be completely stereotyped; that is, one response may be readily substituted for another, provided both lead to the same end point where the expected stimulus will be encountered. Thus a rat that has learned to run a maze to obtain food in the goal box will, if the maze is flooded with water, swim without error to the goal. The rat appears to have learned the location of the goal rather than a chain of specific stimulus-response connections.

Because what is learned is a set of expectations or a cognitive map of the environment rather than specific responses, sign learning classifies as learn-

There is a controversy among learning theorists over the question of whether learning in its most fundamental form is best understood in terms of stimulus-response *associations* (which conditioning theories imply) or *cognitive structures* (which sign-learning theories imply). The conflicting theories are too abstract to discuss here. For our purposes it is possible to view associative learning and cognitive learning as complementary, neither of which is complete in itself as an explanation but each helping to explain some of the features of learning that the other neglects or explains with greater difficulty.

A provisionally satisfactory position is that any given illustration of learning can be graded on a crude scale, with the most automatic kind of learning (explained best as conditioning) at the one end and the most rational (explained best as involving cognition) at the other. Such a scale is represented by the diagram of Figure 8-29. At the left are the habits learned automatically (that is, without awareness and with a minimum of understanding) by conditioning mechanisms. Learning to secrete gastric juice in our stomach when we see food before us illustrates such conditioning. Toward the right of the diagram are the tasks learned with full awareness but still in a somewhat conventional manner, such as using a map to select the route we will follow on a trip. At the extreme right fall tasks that require reasoning about concepts in complex relationships. Most learning falls somewhere between, as a kind of mixture of habit formation and understanding. Learning to operate a typewriter competently, for example, includes both the automatic habits of finger action as well as the insights involved in inserting carbon paper or in changing a ribbon.

ing with understanding rather than as conditioning.

Latent learning. Experiments on latent learning support the concept of cognitive representations. *Latent learning,* broadly conceived, refers to any learning that is not evidenced by behavior at the time of the learning. Typically, such learning goes on under low levels of drive or in the absence of reward. When drive is heightened or appropriate reinforcement appears, there is a sudden use of what has been previously learned.

In one experiment (Tolman and Honzik, 1930) three groups of rats were run daily in the maze diagramed in Figure 8-30. One group was given a food reinforcement when it reached the goal box at the end of the maze. A second group was allowed to explore the maze, but when the rats reached the goal box they were removed with no reinforcement. A third group was treated in the same way as the second group for the first ten days, and then given reinforcement for the remaining seven days. As we can see in Figure 8-30, all groups showed some learning in that they made fewer errors in reaching the goal box as the number of trials increased. But the reinforced group clearly learned more rapidly than the two nonreinforced groups. With the introduction of food on the eleventh day, however, the error scores of the third group dropped markedly and it was soon performing as well as, and even better than, the reinforced group. Evidently the rats were learning something about the spatial orientation of the maze prior to the time that they were rewarded. Tolman would claim that in this experiment the rat formulated a schematic representation of the maze that included information about dead ends and incorrect pathways as well as about the path that leads to the goal.

In theorizing about how rewards and punishments influence behavior, Tolman distinguished between *learning* and *performance*. In the latent-learning study the rat learned something about the spatial arrangement of the maze, but this learning was not evidenced in performance until reward motivated the animal to perform. Tolman would maintain that for learning, reward and punishment serve to convey information, to teach "what leads

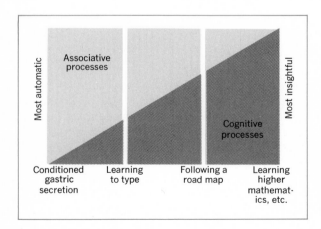

Fig. **8-29 Automatic vs. insightful learning** Hypothetical scaling of learning tasks according to degree of understanding involved. Most tasks involve a mixture of associative and cognitive learning.

This kind of "mixture" theory is considered too eclectic by many psychologists who would rather commit themselves to one or the other position and then attempt to "derive" the behavior that the opposing theorists find critical of the adopted position. In all likelihood, however, future learning theories will be characterized by a mixture of associative learning and cognitive organization.

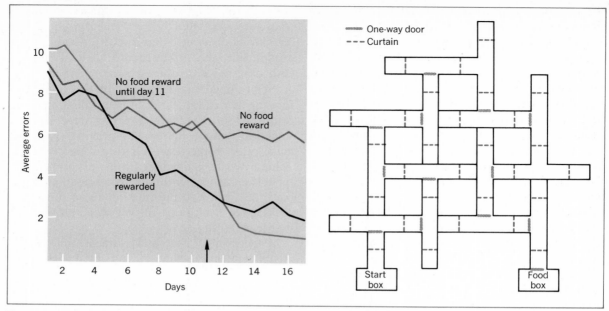

Fig. **8-30** **Latent learning in rats** Note that after reward is introduced on the eleventh day, the rats represented by the brown line perform as well as, and even a little better than, those regularly rewarded (black line). On the right is a diagram of the maze used in this study. (After Tolman and Honzik, 1930)

to what." They do not "stamp in" specific responses and eliminate others. In performance, on the other hand, rewards and punishments function (in conjunction with the schemata built up through past experience) to determine which of a repertoire of possible responses the subject decides to use. The response with the greatest expectation of reward will be made more quickly and efficiently.

Mathematical models of learning[4]

The experimental study of learning has progressed far enough that a number of psychologists have attempted to formulate theories of the learning process in the language of mathematics. In this, psychology repeats the history of other sciences that have become more mathematical as they have become more advanced in their theories and more precise in their measurements. While the details of mathematical theories of learning must be left for more advanced study, the student should know something of these developments if he is to be fully aware of contemporary trends within psychology.

One of the most significant efforts to use mathematics to describe learning was undertaken by William K. Estes and has come to be known as *stimulus sampling theory.*[5] It is appropriate that we consider this particular development in our discussion of mathematical models, since much of the current theoretical work in learning is based on it.

Stimulus sampling theory begins with some assumptions about the nature of the stimulus and the nature of associative learning. The stimulus is represented conceptually as a set of stimulus ele-

[4]This section may be regarded as optional by instructors, depending upon the mathematical preparation of the students.

[5]This theory was formalized in a series of important papers by Estes (1950, 1959), Estes and Burke (1953), and Estes and Suppes (1959). A survey of the theory can be found in Neimark and Estes (1967) and Atkinson and Estes (1963).

ments, and the effective stimulation on any trial is conceived of as a sample drawn from the total set of stimulus elements. In common-sense terms, we may think of the subject as paying attention to only part of the stimuli arrayed before him at any point in time; this limitation on his attentiveness to the stimulus situation is expressed theoretically in terms of a sample of stimulus elements from the total set. As an illustrative analogy we might think of a person looking into a hardware store window containing a wide variety of items. His attention may be drawn to a display of fishing tackle, and he may fail to note the adjacent array of kitchen utensils. Stimulus sampling theory supposes that at any moment in time only a sample of the possible stimuli impinging on the receptor system affects the individual.

On any trial of an experiment, each stimulus element is conditioned to exactly one response. As a first approximation Estes assumes (1) that all stimulus elements are equally likely to be sampled on a trial, and (2) that the probability of a particular response is equal to the proportion of stimulus elements in the sample conditioned to that response. For example, if ten elements are sampled and three are conditioned to the correct response, then its probability of occurrence will be 3/10. The Greek letter θ (theta) is used to designate the probability that any stimulus element will be sampled; it determines the *rate* at which learning will occur.

Estes assumes that the conditioning of individual stimulus elements occurs on an all-or-none basis, and that all elements sampled on a trial become conditioned to the reinforced response. Thus, over a series of reinforced trials the probability of a correct response increases as more and more elements are conditioned to it. If the number of elements in the stimulus set is small, then the probability of a correct response can appear to be all-or-none in character (p. 213), but if the stimulus set is large, the response probability is a gradually increasing function.

Beginning with these assumptions, the mathematical development of the theory is straightforward. The basic equation for the change in probability of a response from trial n to trial $n + 1$ of an experiment is

$$p_{n+1} = p_n + \theta(1 - p_n)$$

An equation of this type is known as a *difference equation* because it expresses the change in probability from one trial to the next. Put into words, it says that response probability on the next trial (denoted p_{n+1}) equals the probability on the previous trial (p_n) plus a proportion θ of the remaining possible increase (which is $1 - p_n$).

To see how this equation works, consider the case of a rat in a T-maze in which a right turn leads to food (the task described in reference to Figure 8-15). On the first trial ($n = 1$) the probability of a correct response is at chance level, and hence $p_1 = .50$. If the learning-rate parameter θ is known, then the difference equation can be used to compute the entire learning curve. For example, assume $\theta = .10$. Then substituting the trial number 1 for n in the difference equation yields

$$p_2 = p_1 + \theta(1 - p_1)$$

But $p_1 = .50$ and $\theta = .10$, hence

$$p_2 = .50 + .10(1 - .50)$$
$$= .55$$

Next substitute the trial number 2 in the original equation:

$$p_3 = p_2 + \theta(1 - p_2)$$

But p_2 has already been calculated to be .55, so

$$p_3 = .55 + .10(1 - .55)$$
$$= .595$$

Proceeding in this way for $n = 3$, $n = 4$, and successively higher values of n, the entire learning curve can be computed. These computations are presented in Table 8-1 for the first ten trials. As can be seen in column 3 of the table, the gain in probability from one trial to the next is always decreasing. This characteristic of learning functions is the reason that they are sometimes referred to as *curves of decreasing gains* (see p. 211).

It is possible by mathematical methods, which need not concern us here, to develop a mathematical expression for what happens when the difference equation is applied over and over again, beginning with the probability at trial 1 and ending

TABLE 8-1	THEORETICAL COMPUTATIONS	
n	p_n	$p_n - p_{n-1}$
1	.500	
2	.550	.050
3	.595	.045
4	.636	.041
5	.672	.036
6	.705	.033
7	.734	.029
8	.761	.027
9	.785	.024
10	.806	.021

Theoretical computations of the probability of a correct response for trials 1 through 10; computations based on $p_1 = .50$ and $\theta = .10$.

at any trial n. The equation that results is

$$p_n = 1 - (1 - p_1)(1 - \theta)^{n-1}$$

It describes an exponentially increasing function that starts out at p_1 and over trials approaches 1 as an asymptote. The rate of approach to the asymptote is determined by θ; the larger the value of θ, the faster the rate at which learning proceeds, as illustrated in Figure 8-31.

Let us now examine how the above equations can be used to predict the course of learning. Figure 8-32 presents observed data from a simple learning task in which the probability of a correct response is .50 on trial 1. Looking at the figure we see that on trial 2 the observed probability of a correct response has increased to .60 (see dotted lines on graph). Using the original difference equation with n set equal to 1 gives

$$p_2 = p_1 + \theta(1 - p_1)$$

We can now substitute the observed values for p_1 and p_2 to obtain

$$.60 = .50 + \theta(1 - .50)$$

Solving this equation provides us with an estimate of $\theta = .20$. Using this value of θ, predictions can now be generated for the entire learning curve. These predictions are represented by the smooth curve in the figure, and it is evident that the observed data points do indeed fall very close to

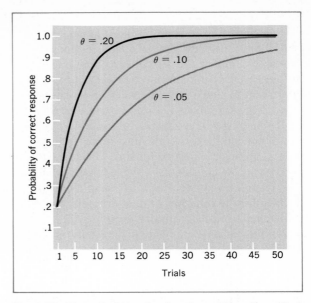

Fig. **8-31 Theoretical learning functions** Three theoretical curves are presented all with $p_1 = .20$, but with θ taking on the values .05, .10, and .20. Note that the larger the value of θ, the more rapidly the curve approaches asymptote.

the theoretical curve. Thus the equation derived from stimulus sampling theory proves to be a powerful tool for predicting the course of learning, given knowledge only about performance on the first two trials.

Fig. **8-32 Observed and predicted learning functions** Observed probabilities of a correct response are indicated by the dots, and the theoretical predictions are represented by the solid curve. (Unpublished data from G. H. Bower)

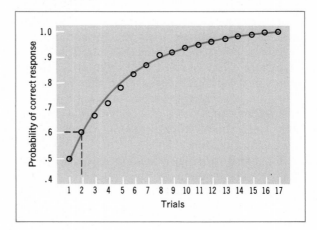

Only the early steps in model-building have been described for stimulus sampling theory. Many further steps have been taken in order to account for what happens in extinction, discrimination, generalization, and in various forms of multiple-response learning. Independent of these specific theoretical developments, the general notion of learning as a probabilistic process that can be described in mathematical terms has been taken up by so many investigators that it is likely to be one of the major trends in future developments of learning theory.

Summary

1. Pavlov's experiments on *classical conditioning* of the dog brought to light several principles useful in the understanding of habit formation. These include reinforcement, extinction, spontaneous recovery, generalization, and discrimination.

2. Skinner's experiments on *operant conditioning* have extended conditioning principles to kinds of responses that cannot be elicited by recognized unconditioned stimuli. Operant behavior acts upon the environment to produce or gain access to reinforcement and becomes strengthened by reinforcement.

3. Rate of responding is a useful measure of operant strength. *Partial reinforcement* illustrates the orderliness of operant behavior, since long and regular runs of responses can be sustained by occasional reinforcement. *Secondary reinforcement,* the fact that a stimulus associated with a reinforcing stimulus acquires reinforcing properties, increases the possible range of conditioning and explains the reward value of such incentives as social approval and money.

4. An animal trainer can *shape behavior* by reinforcing those variations in the operant response that meet his specifications and by extinguishing those that do not. Thus operant conditioning can account for the learning of novel behavior. Recent experiments have shown that some aspects of ordinary daily behavior can be brought under control through operant conditioning.

5. *Reinforcement* refers to any event the occurrence of which increases the probability that a stimulus will, on subsequent occasions, evoke a response. *Amount,* delay, and rate of reinforcement are important variables that affect learning. The *drive-reduction* hypothesis is one of several theories that have been proposed to explain the effects of reinforcement.

6. Conditioning is most directly applicable to single identifiable responses, but much habit formation is more complex than this. These more complex instances are classified as *multiple-response learning.* Two examples are sensorimotor skills (such as mirror drawing and pursuit learning) and rote memorization (including serial learning and paired-associate learning).

7. The experimenter plots the results of multiple-response learning in the form of *learning curves,* indicating changes in proficiency with practice. These curves usually show *decreasing gains* over trials. Shifts from lower-order to higher-order learning habits may result in a period of no improvement, called a *plateau.*

8. Emphasis within conditioning and multiple-response learning is upon the acquiring of movements or verbal habits. Some psychologists warn against an overemphasis upon the automatic nature of learning that comes from exclusive concern with stimulus-response associations. They stress instead situations in which understanding is prominent. Köhler's *insight* experiments pointed out how the arrangements of the problem make the solution easy or hard, and how a solution once achieved with insight can be repeated or applied to novel situations.

9. Tolman's *sign-learning* experiments also emphasize the role of understanding and the development of cognitive schemata. Results from an experiment on *latent learning* provide opposing evidence to theories that lay stress upon the acquisition of particular response sequences without taking into account the subject's *cognitive representation* of the relationships involved.

10. Something can be learned from each of these emphases. Learning goes on in part through *associative processes,* with little rational direction from the learner, and in part through *cognitive processes,* with which the learner perceives relationships and organizes knowledge.

11. As research on learning has become more precise, theorists have begun to develop *mathematical models* to provide a more detailed account of the learning process. The models are formulated in terms of certain basic assumptions, and then mathematical equations are derived from these assumptions and fitted to experimental data. If the equations fit the data well, the assumptions have greater plausibility than if they do not. Starting with rather simple assumptions, the models are gradually extended to cover more complex instances of learning. *Stimulus sampling theory* illustrates some of these developments.

Suggestions for further reading

Pavlov's *Conditioned reflexes* (1927) is the classic work on conditioned salivary reflexes in dogs. Skinner's *The behavior of organisms* (1938) is the corresponding statement on operant conditioning. The later developments in conditioning theory and experiment are reviewed in Kimble, *Hilgard and Marquis' conditioning and learning* (1961), Reynolds, *A primer of operant conditioning* (1968), Honig (ed.), *Operant behavior: Areas of research and application* (1966), and Kimble (ed.), *Foundations of conditioning and learning* (1967).

Cognitive theories also have their classics: Köhler's *The mentality of apes* (1925) describes the famous insight experiments with chimpanzees; Tolman's *Purposive behavior in animals and men* (1932) is the major statement of his cognitive (sign-learning) position.

The principal points of view toward learning, presented in their historical settings and with some typical experiments to which they have led, are summarized in Hilgard and Bower, *Theories of learning* (3rd ed., 1966). Relevant material is also available in Dixon and Horton (eds.), *Verbal behavior and general behavior theory* (1968), and in Glaser (ed.), *The nature of reinforcement* (1971).

For substantive approaches, emphasizing the contributions of the learning laboratory, there are a number of textbooks on learning, such as Deese and Hulse, *The psychology of learning* (3rd ed., 1967), and Logan, *Fundamentals of learning and motivation* (1970). A more advanced but easily readable treatment is presented in Estes, *Learning theory and mental development* (1970).

The literature on mathematical models for learning is growing rapidly. Elementary accounts of this work are presented in Atkinson, Bower, and Crothers, *An introduction to mathematical learning theory* (1965), Coombs, Dawes, and Tversky, *Mathematical psychology: An elementary introduction* (1970), and Restle and Greeno, *Introduction to mathematical psychology* (1970).

memory

9

ALL LEARNING IMPLIES RETAINING, FOR IF nothing were left over from previous experience, nothing would be learned. We think and reason largely with remembered facts; the very continuity of our self-perceptions depends upon the continuity of our memories. We are able to deal with the concept of time as no other animal can, relating the present to the past and making predictions about the future, because of the strength, flexibility, and availability of our memories.

One way of remembering is to recollect or *redintegrate* an event and the circumstances surrounding it, as when you remember going with a date to your first dance. The word *recollect* is from ordinary vocabulary; *redintegrate* is a technical word meaning to reintegrate or to reestablish an earlier experience on the basis of partial cues. For example, you redintegrate that first dance only if something "reminds" you of it. The stimuli to redintegration are in a literal sense souvenirs, remembrances or reminders of a total, personal experience that occurred at a given time in the past. In your recollection you conjure up the band playing the popular songs of that time, the cool breeze as you stepped outside, perhaps your aching feet when you finally got home. Such redintegrative memories are often quite detailed and complete, but they need not be. They are distinguished from other kinds of remembering because they reconstruct a past occasion from your personal autobiography, with its setting in time and place.

Many signs of earlier experience lack this reconstruction of the past. For example, you may *recall* a poem by reciting it, even if you do not remember the circumstances under which you learned it. You can remember how to ride a bicycle or sing a song without any direct reference to the past. Remembering through recall is easier to measure than the redintegration of earlier experiences, and it is the kind usually studied in the laboratory.

Another kind of remembering is the indication of memory merely by *recognizing* someone or something as familiar. "That tune is familiar. What is it?" "Someone I used to know had a copy of that picture on the wall, but I can't place it now." Finally, you may show that you once learned something by now *relearning* it more rapidly than you could if there were no retention of the earlier learning.

Redintegration, recall, recognition, and relearning all give evidence of memory, but each of these terms implies a different aspect of remembering.

Kinds of remembering

Redintegrative memory

Experimental psychologists have paid relatively little attention to redintegrative memory, partly because it is difficult to check details of the recovery of events in the personal past of the subject. A few studies have used hypnosis; one of these, for example, has shown that memories of schoolroom experiences at ages from seven to ten can be more accurately recovered by adults under hypnosis than in the waking state (Reiff and Scheerer, 1959). These memories—of other pupils in the class, of the teacher's name—were subject to confirmation.

Studies of testimony are concerned with the reinstatement of scenes witnessed in the past. A class may unexpectedly be made witness to a staged crime and then be asked to report what happened. The reports are often distorted, even when a student insists his recollections are vivid and dependable. One of the authors engaged in a staged argument with a workman who interrupted his lecture. The workman spoke with a German accent. Although the assistant who acted the part of the workman in this little drama had blond hair and dark brown eyes, a substantial proportion of the students reported confidently that they had seen his *blue* eyes—the color falsely inferred from his Nordic appearance and German accent. Such experiments have bearing on the reliability of witnesses in courtrooms.

More studies of personal memories have been carried on by those engaged in psychotherapy than by experimental psychologists. In psychoanalysis the recollection of childhood memories is one of the bases of treatment and cure. A curious problem, not yet fully understood, is posed by the paucity of very early memories, from that period in life when the child is having many exciting new experiences. This is the problem of "childhood amnesia," early noted by Freud. One conjecture is that the child perceives the world so differently from an adult that the adult's effort to remember what registered for the child fails because of this difference. It may be too that the storage of memories depends upon language development.

Recall

The kind of remembering most easily tested in the laboratory is active recall of some performance learned in the past. You may show that you remember how to ride a bicycle by climbing on one and riding away. You may show that you know Hamlet's soliloquy on death by reciting it. You are demonstrating that present performance is different from what it would be if there were no residue from the past. You ride the bicycle. If there were no residue from the past, you could not ride it.

To get a quantitative measure of recall in the laboratory, the investigator allows time to elapse after a subject has memorized some material, often by the paired-associate method described in Chapter 8 (p. 212). Then the subject returns to the laboratory and attempts to recall the response previously paired with each stimulus as it is presented. The percentage correct is called the *recall score*.

Recognition

When we recognize something, we acknowledge that it is familiar, that we have met it before. Recognition is a common experience, but it is a rather complex and, in a sense, mysterious process. The entire process takes place quite automatically. We meet someone and say, "I'm sure we have met before, though I cannot recall your name or just where or when it was."

We learn a little about recognition from faulty recognition, from a deceiving sense of familiarity. The French expression *déjà vu* ("previously seen") is often used to describe the sense of familiarity that is sometimes aroused in otherwise strange surroundings. So important and convincing was this experience that the Greek philosopher Plato made it part of the basis for his belief in a previous existence. What may happen is that a pattern of buildings along a street is actually somewhat like one seen in earlier experience, or that in a strangely familiar garden the scent of a flower permeating the air is one met on an earlier occasion but since forgotten. Then the present situation, though actually novel, seems vaguely familiar. This is a form of generalization from past experience.

The following experiment demonstrates how recognition is studied in the laboratory. The subjects looked through a deck of some 540 cards, on each of which was printed a common English word. The subjects were then given a series of test cards, each containing a word they had just seen plus a new word and were asked to identify which member of the pair was the "old word." They chose correctly on about 90 percent of the test pairs. When colored pictures were used instead of words, the recognition rate rose to 98 percent. Thus, pictures were easier to remember than printed words (Shepard, 1967).

Relearning

Another way to show that there is some residue from the past is to demonstrate that previously familiar material can be learned more rapidly than it could be learned if it were unfamiliar. Even though something may seem to be completely "forgotten," it may be easier to learn a second time because it was once learned in the past. A dramatic illustration of how this may occur is given by a study in which a child was read selections from Greek and then learned those same selections years later.

For three months the experimenter read the same three Greek selections every day to a boy about one year old. Each selection consisted of twenty lines of iambic hexameter material. At the end of three months another set of three selections was read daily for three months. The procedure was continued until twenty-one selections had been read.

The residual influence of this early experience was studied through memorization experiments conducted with the boy at 8, 14, and 18 years of age. He had not studied Greek in the meantime. At each of these ages he learned selected passages from the early experience along with equivalent but unfamiliar passages. The results indicated a substantial saving in learning the familiar material at age 8; about 30 percent fewer repetitions were required than for equivalent new material. By age 14, however, the saving was only 8 percent, and by 18 years no saving could be demonstrated. The main point is that there was demonstrable saving in learning more than five years after the original reading took place, even though the material to which the child had listened was classical Greek, a language that to him was without meaning (Burtt, 1941).

To use the relearning method in the laboratory, the experimenter proceeds as in the study of recall. After the initial learning he allows a time period to elapse over which retention is to be tested in a second learning. The subject, having previously learned by one of the standard methods well enough to meet some *criterion of mastery* (for example, one perfect recitation), learns the material again *to the same criterion*. If the second learning requires fewer trials than the first, we may express this saving as a percentage by using the formula:

Saving score =
$$100\left[\frac{\text{Original trials} - \text{Relearning trials}}{\text{Original trials}}\right]$$

As an example, suppose a subject is asked to learn a list of paired-associates to a criterion of one perfect trial. On initial learning he reaches this criterion on, say, the thirteenth trial—that is, on this trial he gives correct responses to all of the stimuli in the list for the first time. On relearning the same list a week later, he reaches the criterion on the fourth trial. Thus, on initial learning, twelve trials occurred before the criterion trial, and on relearning, three trials. Applying the formula, the saving score is

$$100\left[\frac{12-3}{12}\right] = 75\%$$

An example of the use of the saving score is illustrated in a classic study by Ebbinghaus (1885). Using himself as a subject, Ebbinghaus learned seven lists of nonsense syllables until he could make two errorless repetitions. After learning the first list he waited 20 minutes and then relearned the list again to two errorless repetitions. After learning the other lists he waited for longer intervals—1 hour, 9 hours, 1 day, 2 days, 6 days, and 31 days, respectively, before relearning each list. Figure 9-1 shows the amount retained from each list as indicated by saving scores. After 20 minutes the saving score was 60 percent, while after 31 days it was only 20 percent. This type of curve is called a *retention curve* because it shows the amount of learning retained as a function of time.

Varieties of memory processes

The processes underlying redintegration, recall, recognition, and relearning are not distinct. Each kind of memory, however, makes a somewhat different demand upon the subject, so that his retention of earlier learning might be detected by one method and not by another. For example, the retention of a past experience completely unavailable to redintegrative memory or to direct recall might be detected by recognition or relearning. Recognition is generally a more sensitive measure of memory than recall: when a picture of a person is presented, it is easier to *recognize* the person as familiar than to *recall* his name. In special circum-

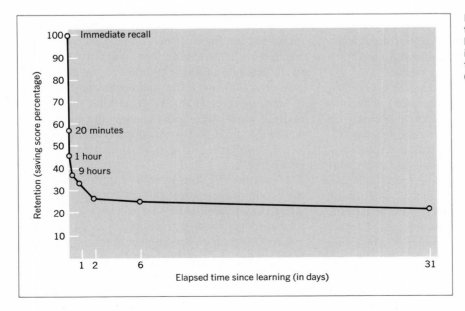

Fig. **9-1 Retention curve** Retention of lists of nonsense syllables was measured by relearning. The dependent variable is the saving score percentage. (After Ebbinghaus, 1885)

stances, however, recall may be easier. For example, we may on occasion correctly recall the spelling of a word, only to fail to recognize that it is correct.

There does seem to be an important difference between a memory dated in one's personal past and the kind of undated memory shown in, say, memory for a familiar vocabulary word. If one remembers having looked up an unusual word, then the memory is a recollection of a concrete experience, but most words are not tied in such

a way to personal history. In cases of amnesia it is usually the personal memories that are lost; the amnesia victim is still able to speak his familiar language, buy a theater ticket, count his change, and do many other things that indicate that his undated or impersonal memories are not lost. Recognition has some features of redintegration (having been experienced before), whereas recall can be automatic, without any personal reference whatever.

CRITICAL DISCUSSION

Eidetic images

Although most of us can occasionally retain visual impressions of things that we have seen, such impressions usually are vague and lacking in detail. Some individuals, however, are able to retain visual images that are almost photographic in clarity. They can glance briefly at a picture and when it is removed still "see" its image located, not in their heads, but somewhere in space before their eyes. They can maintain the image for as long as several minutes, scan it as it remains stationary in space, and describe it in far more detail than would be possible from memory alone. Such people are said to have a "photographic memory," or, to use the psychologist's term, *eidetic imagery.*

Eidetic imagery is relatively uncommon. Studies with children indicate that only about 5 percent report visual images that last for more than a half-minute and possess sharp detail. The existing evidence suggests that after adolescence the occurrence of eidetic individuals is even less frequent. In a typical procedure for investigating eidetic imagery, the experimenter places a richly detailed picture against an easel painted a neutral gray, gives the child thirty seconds to look at it, removes the picture, and then asks him to describe what he sees on the easel. Most children either report seeing nothing or describe fleeting afterimages of the picture. But some report images that are vivid and prolonged. When questioned they can provide a wealth of detail, such as the number of stripes on a cat's tail or the number of buttons on a jacket. These are details that the children often cannot provide upon questioning without first studying their eidetic image.

Studies with eidetic children indicate that a viewing time of three to five seconds is necessary to produce an image. The children report that when they do not look at the picture long enough, they do not have an image of parts of it, although they may remember what those parts contain. Exaggerated eye blinking or looking away from the easel usually makes the image disappear (Haber, 1969b).

One theory assumed that eidetic imagery served to improve the transfer of visual stimuli into memory. But evidence suggests that this is not the case. Eidetic children seem to have no better long-term memories than other children. In fact, if while looking at a picture an eidetic child is asked to name parts of it (or otherwise actively attend to the parts), he is unable to form an image. It appears that eidetic children retain information either in the form of an image or in the form of the more typical verbal memory, but they are unable to do both at the same time.

Other evidence indicates that eidetic imagery is visual in nature and not a function of memory. For example, when the eidetic child tries to transfer the image from the easel to another surface, it disappears when it reaches the edge of the easel. At the same time, the eidetic image is not an exact photographic reproduction. The image usually contains additions, omissions, and distortions of the stimulus picture in the same way that memories contain distortions of the original event. The aspects of the picture that are of principal interest to the child are the ones reproduced in greatest detail in the eidetic image.

229

The *storage* of information in memory and its *retention* over time are critical components of the memory process. Equally important, however, is the *retrieval* of information from the memory store. Our ability to retrieve a word or name from memory is so efficient that we are usually not aware of the process involved. Sometimes an item cannot be retrieved immediately, although we feel certain that we know it. For example, you may not recall offhand the name of your third grade teacher. But if you think for a while, trying out various possibilities, you probably will recall the name. In some cases the name may suddenly come to you out of the blue, long after you stopped thinking about it. Events of this kind suggest that an active search of the memory store is going on even though consciously we may not be aware of it.

Another interesting fact about memory is that we usually recognize immediately when something is new to us. For example, if shown a photograph of a person, we can generally decide whether we have seen the person before. If the photograph is of a familiar person that we cannot name right away, we can still predict accurately whether we could recall the name if given sufficient time.

Cues can often aid us in the retrieval of information. In one study in which subjects were asked to identify by surname photographs of relatively well-known persons, such cues as the first letter of the first name or the first letter of the surname facilitated recall. The subjects were also able to predict quite accurately upon first seeing each picture whether they would eventually be able to recall the correct name (Hopkins and Atkinson, 1968).

Tip-of-the-tongue phenomenon

The situation of feeling certain we know a specific name or word yet being unable to recall it immediately has been called the tip-of-the-tongue (TOT) state. The word seems to be on the tip of our tongue, and we may feel quite tormented until an active search of memory (dredging up and then discarding words that seem close but are not quite right) reveals the correct word.

In an experimental investigation of the TOT state Brown and McNeill (1966) demonstrated that the words that come to mind when one is searching for a particular word (called the "target word") have certain characteristics in common with the target word. In this study college students were read the definitions of words that are used infrequently in the English language. These were words like *cloaca, ambergris,* and *sampan,* some of which were in the recognition vocabulary of the subjects but not in their active vocabulary. Whenever a subject felt that he knew the word that was being defined but was unable to recall it immediately (a TOT state), he was asked a number of questions concerning the words he was thinking of in his attempt to arrive at the correct word.

The results of the study indicated that while a subject is in the TOT state, he has information about a number of characteristics of the target word, and the closer he is to successful recall the more accurate is his information. Although some of the words that came to mind could be classed as similar in *meaning* to the target word, the majority of words were similar in *sound.* For example, if the target word is *sampan,* then similar-sounding words would be *Saipan, Siam, Cheyenne, sarong,* and *sympoon,* whereas similar-meaning words would be *barge, houseboat,* and *junk.* An analysis of the similar-sounding words showed that while in a TOT state the subject can specify with a high degree of accuracy the number of syllables in the target word and its initial letter. He can also frequently state, although with less accuracy, the final sound or suffix and the syllable that receives the primary stress.

Thus retrieval is not a simple all-or-none process; we can forget certain characteristics of a word while still retaining other relevant information. Studies of this type have led to interesting speculations (some of which we will consider later) as to the manner in which information is stored in memory and subsequently retrieved.

The nature of forgetting

There are three traditional explanations of forgetting. Because the explanations are not contradictory, each may help us to understand the nature of what we remember and why we forget. The three are (1) *decay* through disuse, (2) *interference effects* (retroactive and proactive inhibition), and (3) *motivated forgetting.* No single explanation by itself can account for all the facts of forgetting; consequently a number of psychologists have argued for more complex theories of memory.

Decay through disuse

One of the oldest explanations of forgetting, and perhaps the one still most widely held by the layman, is that forgetting takes place simply through the passage of time. This explanation assumes that learning leaves a "trace" in the brain; the *memory trace* involves some sort of physical change that was not present prior to learning. With the passage of time the normal metabolic processes of the brain cause a fading or decay of the memory, so that traces of material once learned gradually disintegrate and eventually disappear altogether.

The experience of rapid fading of barely learned material lends credence to this view of forgetting. Even as you try to write down verbatim a definition given in a lecture you may find it fading away. Our forgetting of pictures or stories also suggests a process of fading with the passage of time. When first perceived, a picture may reveal a wealth of detail. But as time passes, the details are rapidly forgotten and only the main outlines are remembered.

Plausible as is the disuse, or organic-decay, theory of forgetting, no direct evidence supports it, and much evidence suggests that it is a dubious or at least incomplete explanation. The form of the retention curve can be accounted for on other grounds. There are many instances in which learning is retained over long intervals of time with no intervening practice. Most motor skills are not easily forgotten. We do not forget how to swim or drive a car even though we may not have used

these skills for many years. And some verbal material may be retained over long periods, while other material is forgotten. We may be able to recall quite accurately a poem we memorized in sixth grade yet be unable to remember the part in a play we learned as a high school senior. Why should the decay process affect the second material but not the first?

Another argument against the decay theory rests on the recovery of memories supposedly lost. People approaching senility often vividly recall events of their youth when they can barely remember the events of the day. Occasionally in delirium a patient speaks a foreign language unused since childhood. Unavailable memories have not necessarily "decayed."

Although a great deal of evidence seems to argue against a theory of passive decay, it cannot be denied that some forgetting may occur through the organic changes taking place in the nervous system with the passage of time. All we can be sure of is that this explanation does not account for all the facts about forgetting.

Interference effects

A second explanation of forgetting maintains that it is not so much the passage of time that determines the course of forgetting but what we do in the interval between learning and recall; new learning may interfere with material we have previously learned. A story told about Stanford University's first president illustrates this theory of interference. David Starr Jordan was an authority on fishes. As the president of a new university, he began to call the students by name, but every time he learned the name of a student he forgot the name of a fish. Hence, it is said, he gave up learning the names of students. Although the story lacks foundation in fact, it illustrates how new learning may interfere with the recall of old learning. The theory that the the new learning may interfere with the old is known as *retroactive inhibition.* A companion interference theory, based on the same

The use of the expression *memory trace* in the discussion on p. 231 requires a word of explanation. The memory trace is a *hypothetical construct;* it is not something known or something we can point to in the brain. It refers to whatever representation of an experience persists in the nervous system. When we say that a memory trace fades or that something else happens to it, all we are saying is that what emerges when we attempt recall is different from the experience that was originally registered.

The durability of memories implies that a stable change in brain structure may be involved. One hypothesis is that some sort of change takes place in the biochemical nature of the cell; more specifically it has been proposed that ribonucleic acid (RNA) might well be the complex molecule that serves as a chemical mediator for memory (Hydén, 1969).

It has been known for some time that deoxyribonucleic acid (DNA) is the substance that is primarily responsible for genetic inheritance; the genes are comprised chiefly of DNA, and the genetic code is literally written in a sequence of bases along the DNA molecule. In this rather unique package DNA crams the information needed to create a complete man—a man with blue eyes and a tendency to baldness, a man with a heart that can beat and a brain that can think. The genetic instructions contained on a single DNA molecule, if spelled out in English, would require the space of several 24-volume sets of the *Encyclopaedia Britannica.*

DNA never leaves the cell's nucleus but directs the cell's activities by manufacturing its own assistants to which it then delegates responsibilities. These assistants are various forms of RNA, which (after being produced in the nucleus) move out to the cytoplasm where they control cellular functions. Hydén reasoned that if DNA, which is exceptionally stable, encodes "racial memory," then perhaps RNA, which is known to be more malleable, could act to encode the organism's individual memories.

Three types of studies tentatively support this idea. In the first, chemicals are injected to block the formation of RNA. For example, mice that learned to avoid shock in a maze were injected after training with an antibiotic (puromycin) known to inhibit the synthesis of RNA. Their memory of the maze was completely destroyed (Flexner, 1967). The second type of study attempts to show that training produces a change in the RNA of specific nerve cells. For example, young rats were trained to balance on a thin, slanting wire in order to obtain food. Subsequently, the particular vestibular nerve cells involved in the

---

principles, maintains that prior learning may interfere with the learning and recall of new material. This aspect of the theory is called *proactive inhibition.*

Retroactive inhibition. Retroactive inhibition can easily be demonstrated by experiment. The subject learns a list of items such as nonsense syllables (list A), and then learns a second list (list B). After an interval he attempts to recall list A. If a control group (that has not learned list B) recalls list A better than the group that has learned the new list, we infer that the new learning has interfered with the recall of list A. The experimental arrangement can be diagrammed as follows:

Arrangement for testing retroactive inhibition			
	Phase 1	Phase 2	Phase 3
Experimental group	Learn A	Learn B	Recall A
Control group	Learn A	Rest or unrelated activity	Recall A

If the control group's recall of A is significantly better than the experimental group's recall of A, we attribute the difference to *retroactive inhibition;* the *later* learning of B interfered with the recall of the *earlier* learning of A.

act of balancing were analyzed microscopically. These nerve cells not only showed more RNA, but RNA of a significantly different composition than was found in the cells of control animals that had not received balance training. Thus a specific type of learning produced altered rates of RNA synthesis in the relevant cells (Hydén, 1967).

The third type of experiment implicating the role of RNA in memory is even more dramatic (McConnell and others, 1970). It involves training planaria (see Figure 2-2, p. 29), using classical-conditioning procedures. The planaria are housed in a trough of water; when a brief electrical current is passed through the water, the planaria respond with a vigorous muscular contraction. The onset of the shock is paired with the onset of a light. After repeated pairings, test trials with the light alone elicit the contraction response. The planaria, which had not previously responded to the light, now generate a muscular contraction when the light is turned on. A substance containing RNA is extracted from the bodies of the trained planaria and injected into untrained animals. The latter animals are then given the same classical-conditioning routine, along with a control group of untrained animals that are injected with RNA taken from untrained planaria. The results of these studies show that planaria injected with RNA extracted from previously trained planaria learn the conditioned response more rapidly than animals injected with RNA from untrained animals.

The results with planaria have been found difficult to repeat, but excitement over the role of RNA has been enhanced by experiments indicating that RNA injected from trained rats reproduces learned responses in untrained rats (Golub, and others, 1970). Some evidence also indicates that the RNA transfer effect is specific to the stimulus used in the learning task rather than simply a generalized improvement in learning (Jacobson and others, 1965). Unfortunately, efforts to replicate these experiments have not always been successful, and conclusions regarding transfer effects must be quite tentative.

If subsequent research verifies the hypothesis that learning is coded on the RNA molecule and is capable of transfer from one organism to another, the speculations from a science-fiction viewpoint are intriguing. For example, students in the distant future may be able to avoid the rigorous study involved in learning calculus by receiving their knowledge instead through an injection of RNA that was extracted from their mathematics instructor!

If recall is tested after an interval of rest, without interpolated activity, some forgetting of course occurs. Can this, too, be accounted for according to the theory of retroactive inhibition? Perhaps, but only if we think of the ordinary processes of waking life as corresponding in some respects to active learning between original learning and recall. This extension of the theory of retroactive inhibition can be tested by comparing retention after periods of sleep and waking. If waking activity interferes with recall, then retention should be better after sleep, when less intervening activity has occurred. As Figure 9-2 shows, it has been found that we do forget more when awake than when asleep. We lose a little during the first hour or two of sleep, but after that we forget very little more during the night (Jenkins and Dallenbach, 1924).

We may therefore accept the demonstration that retroactive inhibition occurs, not only when formal learning occurs between initial learning and recall but also when ordinary waking life intervenes. Retroactive inhibition has a secure place as one phenomenon of forgetting. Can we go even further and say that it is a *sufficient* theory of forgetting and that the passive-decay theory is thereby disproved?

It would be very difficult indeed to disprove a decay theory. The nearest we can come is to look for a state close to suspended animation, and then try to show that no forgetting occurs while the

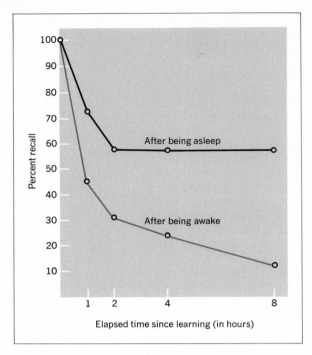

Fig. **9-2 Retroactive inhibition** The retention of information when the subject is either awake or asleep during the interval between initial learning and a subsequent test for recall. (Data from Jenkins and Dallenbach, 1924)

and then dropped little further over twenty-four hours (Minami and Dallenbach, 1946).

Proactive inhibition. Another kind of interference occurs when material that we have previously learned interferes with the recall of something newly learned. The following experimental arrangement may be compared with that used in the study of retroactive inhibition:

Arrangement for testing proactive inhibition			
	Phase 1	Phase 2	Phase 3
Experimental group	Learn A	Learn B	Recall B
Control group	Rest or unrelated activity	Learn B	Recall B

Experiments using the above design have demonstrated results similar to those found for retroactive inhibition; the control group does indeed recall better than the experimental group. The prior learning of the experimental group apparently interferes with their recall of list B.

Underwood (1957) has shown, by reviewing a large number of experiments on retention, that proactive inhibition plays an important role when "experienced" subjects are used in an experiment. As we can see from Figure 9-3, the more lists a subject has previously learned, the poorer his retention of the newly learned list. The size of the proactive effect is quite remarkable as demonstrated in a study that involved a long series of successive cycles of learning and recall. On each cycle a list of paired-associates was learned to a criterion of perfect recitation followed by recall of the list two days later. Immediately upon completion of the recall test a new learning-recall cycle was begun. Data were obtained on thirty-six successive cycles, each involving a new list of paired-associate items. Recall for the list in the initial cycle was about 70 percent, while the recall for the list in the last cycle was virtually zero (Postman, 1969).

Lest the reader become too discouraged and decide that it is fruitless to learn anything new,

learner is in that state. One of the more successful experimental attempts has been made with cockroaches.

The cockroach in this experiment learned to avoid a given corner of the cage; if it went there, it received an electric shock. The experimenters sought to find out whether it would remember what it had learned, and how its retention would be affected by its activity between the original learning and the test of retention. A very satisfactory rest condition was discovered. If the cockroach was placed in a dark, damp passageway, it would remain immobile for as long as twenty-four hours. Placed in a dry, lighted cage, it was very active. The results were similar to those obtained in the sleep experiments with humans. When activity intervened, forgetting occurred, with an increase in forgetting as the length of time since learning increased. When the cockroach was immobilized, its retention lessened over the first hour or two,

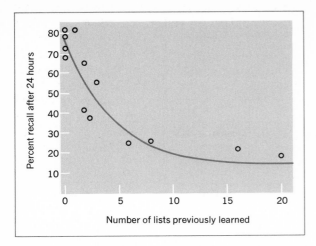

Fig. **9-3 Proactive inhibition** Each dot represents results from one experiment. For those experiments in which the subject had less previous experience in list-learning, the amount retained after an interval of a day was greater than in those in which the subject had learned many prior lists. (After Underwood, 1957)

we should hasten to point out that the effects of proactive inhibition (as well as retroactive inhibition) are much less striking when the material to be learned is meaningful as opposed to nonsense syllables. In addition, the further a person learns beyond the point of bare mastery, the less susceptible he is to interferences of either the proactive or retroactive type. Nevertheless, there is considerable evidence that much of the forgetting that takes place in our daily lives is the result of proactive and retroactive inhibition.

Motivated forgetting

The preceding explanations of forgetting emphasize that it is a matter either of physiological processes affecting the memory trace or of interference between new and old material. Neither theory gives much attention to a person's motives in remembering and forgetting. This omission is a serious one, for a complete theory of forgetting cannot ignore what the person is trying to do—both when he remembers and when he forgets.

Repression. According to the principle of repression, some of our memories become inaccessible to recall because of the way in which they relate to our personal problems. The inaccessibility is due neither to faded traces nor to disruptive learnings, for the memories are still there and can be revealed under appropriate conditions. The theory of repression holds that the memories are not recalled because their recall would in some way be unacceptable to the person—because of the anxiety that they would produce or the guilt that they might activate.

The nature of the forgetting that takes place in dramatic instances of amnesia aids in the understanding of repression. The amnesia victim does not forget everything. He uses a rich store of memories and habits to conduct his current activities. What he forgets are items of personal reference—his name, his family, his home address, his personal biography. The beginning of the amnesia can often be traced to some severe emotional shock that the individual suffered and from which the amnesia provides an escape.

Occasionally cases in psychotherapy give rather convincing evidence of repressed memories and recovery from the repression, of which the following is a striking, if unusual, illustration.

A 40 year old man came to a mental hospital with serious depression and haunting ideas about death. As a child he had lost his mother under traumatic circumstances. About the actual death he could remember only being awakened from sleep in order to be taken to the hospital some distance away. When he and his sisters arrived there, his mother was dead. The mother's death had been very disturbing to him, and it was evident to the therapist who treated him that some of his present symptoms dated from it. In order to help him recall specific events of that period, the therapist asked, among other questions, whether he recalled the time of night the events happened. He could not remember. That these memories were repressed is suggested by the information that came in a dream the night following this interview.

The patient dreamt that he saw two clocks. One was running and one had stopped. The one that was running said twenty minutes to three, and the one that had stopped said twenty minutes to five. He was mystified by the dream.

Because of the possibility that those clocks represented the repressed childhood memories, the man's older sister was located and asked about the circumstances of the mother's death. She said that they had been roused from sleep in their farmhouse about 2:30 A.M. and had driven to the distant hospital. When they arrived there about 4:30, their mother had just died.

Whether we accept the sister's version or the patient's, it is quite convincing that the times dreamed of were close to reality. Yet this memory was not consciously accessible to the patient, even when the therapist pressed him for it. But the probing by the supportive therapist in the midst of treatment may have facilitated the recall in the dream [Case courtesy of Josephine R. Hilgard].

Laboratory analogy of repression. Psychoanalytic studies suggest that repression is a very general phenomenon that occurs in the ordinary experiences of people who do not show striking symptoms of memory disturbance. If it is, it should be possible to demonstrate it experimentally, and a number of studies have attempted to do so.

A study by Glucksberg and King (1967) serves to illustrate the laboratory approach. In the first stage of the experiment subjects learned the list of A-B paired-associates shown in Table 9-1. You may recall from our discussion of the paired-associate method (p. 212) that on each trial, A is presented first, the subject tries to anticipate the appropriate B associate, and then the A-B pair is presented for study. After the A-B pairs had been learned to a criterion of one perfect trial through the list, the second stage of the experiment began. In this stage only the D words were presented, and electric shock was associated with some and not with others. In the third and final stage of the experiment the A nonsense syllables were presented again to test for retention of B. The words in the C column were never presented during the experiment, but previous studies had shown

TABLE 9-1 STIMULUS WORDS AND ASSOCIATIVE RESPONSES			
PAIRED-ASSOCIATE LIST		INFERRED CHAINED WORD	WORDS ASSOCIATED WITH SHOCK OR NO SHOCK
A	B	C	D
CEF	stem	flower	smell*
DAX	memory	mind	brain
YOV	soldier	army	navy
VUX	trouble	bad	good
WUB	wish	want	need
GEX	justice	peace	war*
JID	thief	steal	take
ZIL	ocean	water	drink
LAJ	command	order	disorder
MYV	fruit	apple	tree*

* D items paired with electric shock during the second phase of the experiment.

Source: Glucksberg and King (1967).

that the C words are implicit mediators linking the B and D words. That is, when the B word is presented most people tend to think of the C word, and thinking of C is likely to evoke the D word (for example, the word *stem* makes one think of *flower,* which in turn elicits *smell*).

Thus, if a subject learns the A-B pair CEF-*stem* and is later shown the D word *smell,* he will link *smell* with CEF-*stem* because flower is the word in his mind that mediates between the two. The results of the experiment showed that pairing shock with associates of memory items interferes with their subsequent recall. For example, when *smell, war,* and *tree* were the shocked D words, their associated A-B pairs were less likely to be recalled than were the other A-B pairs whose D words had not been associated with shock. In this laboratory demonstration, forgetting was clearly related to unpleasant associations.

Are memories permanent?

The explanations of forgetting that have been considered so far—decay of the memory trace, interference effects, and motivated forgetting— have different implications for the hypothesis that events once recorded in memory are never lost. The decay theory emphasizes actual erosion or physical loss of memories. The notion of motivated forgetting suggests that information is permanently stored in memory, but certain emotionally-toned events have made it inaccessible for retrieval. The interference hypothesis can be interpreted as supporting either position; interfering materials could actually destroy the memory trace, or they could leave the memory trace intact while building up some sort of inhibition or barrier to prevent its retrieval.

This distinction between loss of information versus inability to retrieve information has been called *trace-dependent* versus *cue-dependent* forgetting (Tulving and Madigan, 1970). Trace-dependent forgetting is caused by the actual decay of the memory trace. In cue-dependent forgetting, the information is stored in memory, but the critical cues that would allow it to be retrieved are lacking. The latter type of forgetting is most obvious in such instances as the TOT state, when a cue permits sudden access to a name or word previously unrecalled.

Failure to recall in most situations probably represents a combination of trace-dependent and cue-dependent forgetting. But the question of whether some memories are permanent has important theoretical as well as practical implications. Unfortunately, at this stage of investigation we have no conclusive answer. There is considerable evidence, however, that memories are much more permanently etched upon our brains than we might assume on the basis of everyday experience. When we make a concerted effort to remember a specific event, we frequently find that we can recall more than we had thought possible. The recovery of childhood memories under hypnosis is another example pointing to the permanent nature of memory.

Even more startling evidence comes from direct electrical stimulation of the brain of epileptic patients undergoing surgery (see p. 42). When epileptic seizures cannot be controlled by drugs removal of brain tissue in the area where the epileptic disturbance is focused sometimes has beneficial effects. To be certain that the removal of the focal area will not interfere with important func-

tions, the surgeon carefully "maps" the surrounding area by electrical stimulation while the patient is under local anesthesia; the patient is conscious and can describe his sensations as various points on the brain are electrically stimulated. When the electrode is placed in certain areas of the temporal lobes, vivid memories can be elicited. The patient reports a sudden "flashback" of some previous event complete with all the sensations experienced at that earlier time. The experiences relived appear to be real events from the past, such as recollections of a childhood scene or of an orchestra playing a tune that was only vaguely remembered. For example, one man saw himself in his childhood home laughing and talking with his cousins. The scene and sounds were as clear to him as they would have been at the time the event occurred.

These recalled events are far more vivid than ordinary memories; it is as if the electrical current had started a film strip on which were registered the details of a past event that the patient had long since forgotten. As long as the electrode is held in place the experience of the former day goes forward. When the electrode is removed, it stops abruptly (Penfield, 1969).

Interestingly enough, surgical removal of the area of the temporal lobe from which a recollection has been evoked does not destroy the individual's memory of that event. The reason may be that the information is actually stored in some other area of the brain and the sequence of nerve activity initiated by the stimulating electrode activates this remote location. Another possibility is that the brain contains multiple representations, or copies, of a remembered event, and the removal of tissue in a specific area of the brain simply destroys one copy.

Electrical-stimulation studies of this type on a large number of patients provide strong evidence for the hypothesis that many memories remain intact long after a person's ability to recall them has disappeared. What procedures other than electrical stimulation and hypnosis might be used to tap these hidden memories is an intriguing question.

Because no single explanation discussed so far provides an adequate account of forgetting, a number of theorists have argued for a two-process theory of memory. They propose that one type of storage mechanism is involved in remembering events just recently experienced and that a different type is involved in the recall of information that has received repeated attention. These two storage mechanisms have been labeled short-term memory (STM) and long-term memory (LTM). The difference between them is like the difference between recalling a telephone number you just looked up in the directory and recalling your own telephone number, which you have used repeatedly. Your own number is stored in long-term memory—as are memories of such items as your name, the words and grammar of the language, addition and multiplication tables, and important events in your life. Except for occasional mental blocking on a word or the name of an acquaintance, these memories are relatively permanent. In contrast, the telephone number you have just looked up, the definition the instructor has just given in class, and the name of a stranger to whom you have just been introduced remain with you in short-term memory only momentarily; unless you make a conscious effort to focus your attention on the information, it is quickly lost.

Figure 9-4 presents a retention curve obtained in a short-term memory experiment in which rehearsal (either covert or overt) was eliminated (Peterson and Peterson, 1959). The subjects attempted to recall a single trigram of three consonants (for example, XJR) after intervals of 3, 6, 9, 12, 15, or 18 seconds. The trigram was presented auditorily; during the next second a number was presented and the subject counted backward by 3's from that number until he received a signal to recall the trigram. This counting procedure prevented the subject from rehearsing the trigram. As the figure shows, recall after 18 seconds in this situation is practically zero. The rapidity of the memory loss when rehearsal is prevented is striking if these results are compared with the retention curve in Figure 9-1 (p. 228) for nonsense syllables learned with repeated practice.

Long- and short-term memory

A number of current theories postulate a distinction between LTM and STM (Broadbent, 1963; Norman and Rumelhart, 1970). Because the theories are similar in many respects, it will suffice to present a simplified version of one of them (Atkinson and Shiffrin, 1968; Atkinson and Wickens, 1971) to illustrate the basic ideas involved. Two storage mechanisms are postulated, one for short-term memory and the other for long-term memory; the interaction between the two memories is characterized by the flow chart in Figure 9-5. As indicated above, STM is viewed as a rapidly decaying system, whereas LTM is essentially a permanent store. In terms of our earlier distinction, STM is characterized by trace-dependent forgetting; the memory trace of items entering STM is subject to rapid decay. In contrast, LTM is characterized by cue-

Fig. 9-4 Retention curve for short-term memory When rehearsal is prevented, recall of information stored in short-term memory decays rapidly. (Data from Peterson and Peterson, 1959)

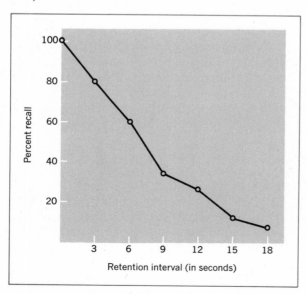

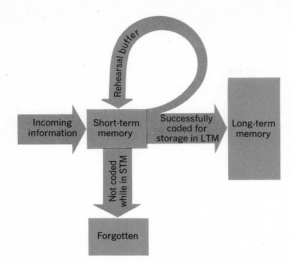

Fig. 9-5 Flow chart for a two-process theory of memory
Schematic representation of short-term and long-term storage mechanisms. All incoming sensory information enters STM, where it can be maintained by rehearsal and either successfully coded for storage in LTM or forgotten.

dependent forgetting; the information is permanently recorded in LTM, but the ability to retrieve it depends upon having the appropriate cues.

Incoming information is fed into STM and, if not attended to, begins to fade away. It is possible, however, to maintain selected information in STM by means of rehearsal. By rehearsing the information, the trace in STM is prevented from decaying—at least for a short period of time. Each decaying trace is, so to speak, reset by rehearsal, at which point it begins to decay again. But the necessity for rehearsal imposes a limit upon the number of items that can be maintained simultaneously in STM; if an item is not rehearsed frequently enough, it will fade away. The set of traces being maintained in STM at any one time is referred to as the *rehearsal buffer*. We can think of the rehearsal buffer as being like a box of fixed size that can hold only so many blocks. Each block represents a stimulus input. When new blocks are added to the box, old ones have to be removed to make room for them. The information coming into STM begins to decay rapidly unless the person regards it as particularly important, in which case it is entered into the rehearsal buffer. Information

is maintained in the rehearsal buffer until the individual feels that he knows it or until his attention is drawn to new information that must be entered into the buffer. Thus information is temporarily stored in STM via rehearsal until new incoming information replaces it. While information resides in STM it may be coded and transferred to long-term storage; if the information is allowed to decay in STM before such a transfer takes place, then it will be permanently lost.

In contrast, LTM is assumed to be virtually unlimited, so that any information transferred from STM to LTM will have a place for permanent storage. Even though the information is permanently stored, retrieval from LTM may fail because the cues needed to identify the information are incomplete. With incomplete cues a search of LTM may bring forth an incorrect recall or may fail to recover any appropriate information. The tip-of-the-tongue state is an example of a situation in which an individual has inadequate cues to find the desired information. He cannot recall the information immediately, but he may have enough cues to narrow down the area of search and retrieve some words that are similar in certain characteristics to the target word; these similar words may provide additional cues that enable him to eventually find the target word.

Long-term memory storage is analogous to a filing cabinet of large capacity. As any file clerk knows, it is one thing to toss items into various file drawers; it is a more difficult task to retrieve a desired item. For example, Mr. Johnson's letter to the city council complaining about possible pollution of the water supply may have been filed under "Johnson," "complaints," "sanitation," or "pollution." It is also possible that initially only part of the desired information was coded into long-term memory and complete retrieval is not possible.

The two-process theory of memory provides several reasons why forgetting may occur. Immediate recall may fail because subsequent inputs to STM have bumped out the information. Long-term recall may fail because the information was never transferred to LTM or because not enough cues are available at the time of attempted recall to locate the information in LTM. The student who complains that he "knew the material backwards and forwards" but could not recall it for the examination may simply have stared at the textbook with his mind on other things and never rehearsed the material so that it could be encoded into LTM. Or the material may be stored in LTM, but the examination questions did not provide sufficient cues to permit retrieval.

The theory sketched rather roughly above does an adequate job of accounting for much of the data on memory. Of particular interest are conjectures about the mechanism that allows information to be transferred from short-term to long-term memory. One conjecture is that the transfer involves a *coding process.* The information temporarily stored in STM is rehearsed and translated into smaller "chunks" of information that can be more readily stored in LTM. An example of such a coding process is a person's use of a *mnemonic* (any system of coding information to make it easier to remember) to facilitate recall. For example, the telephone number 149-1625 is hard to memorize on a single reading, but it can be easily remembered if it is coded as the successive squares of the numbers 1, 2, 3, 4, and 5.

How do our earlier explanations of forgetting fit into this conceptual scheme? Although the information stored in STM is a fairly faithful representation of the stimulus input, some decay is possible in this state before the information is encoded and transferred to LTM. But once coded and stored in LTM, the code is assumed to be relatively fixed over time and not susceptible to decay. However, if other items of information with similar codes are stored in LTM, we have difficulty retrieving the correct item upon recall. The phenomena of retroactive and proactive inhibition can demonstrate their effects in this manner.

Items of information that we use frequently may be coded in such a way that many different cues lead to them. In terms of our file-drawer analogy, they may be cross-indexed. Such items are thus readily available and require no searching. Or at times, when the recall of certain information is painful to us, we may instruct our "retrieval mechanism" to ignore the information; it is not lost, however, and can be retrieved once the need for repression is gone.

Physiological evidence for a two-process theory

Theories of the sort we have just described are frequently called *information-processing* models. Such models are highly schematized representations of the flow of information in the nervous system and do not venture into any of the physiological details. There is clearly a large gap between the study of complex behavior and that of neurophysiology, and many psychologists feel that the use of simplified diagrams to describe the flow of information from the initial stimulus input to the response output forms a useful bridge between the two.

In the case of the two-process theory of memory, however, some neurological data provide striking evidence for the theory. The evidence comes from patients who have undergone surgery for relief of epileptic seizures. If a lesion is made in a specific area deep in the temporal lobes (an area called the hippocampus), the patient then appears to be unable to successfully transfer new information from STM to LTM. Such patients have no trouble remembering skills and information learned prior to the operation, but they have serious difficulty with new learning. For example, in one case, several months after the operation the patient's family moved to a new house a few blocks away on the same street. A year later the patient still could not remember his new address (although he recalled the old one perfectly) nor could he find his way to the new home alone. He could not remember where things he continually used were kept, and he would read the same magazines over and over without finding their contents familiar. Some patients with hippocampal lesions consistently fail to recognize or learn the names of people they have met following surgery even though they may have talked with them countless times. In fact, if a person to whom they are talking walks out of the room for a few minutes, they may fail to recognize him on his return (Milner, 1966).

The postoperative defect in these cases does not

seem to be a deficiency in short-term memory per se. The patient can hold items, such as a series of digits, in memory if he concentrates upon repeating them. He can even carry out complicated mental arithmetic with speed and accuracy. But his rehearsal does not produce permanent learning. He can walk to the store for a newspaper if he keeps repeating verbally to himself where and why he is going. When he stops rehearsing he quickly forgets what he was supposed to do. The difficulty appears to lie in an inability to transfer new material from STM to LTM. The material can circulate in the short-term memory buffer but fails to be stamped into long-term memory.

There is increasing evidence that once new information is entered into LTM a period of time is required for it to consolidate and be firmly recorded in memory. This idea, which has been called *consolidation theory,* proposes that changes in the nervous system produced by learning are time dependent; that is, the memory trace must undergo a consolidation phase during which it is unstable and vulnerable to obliteration by interfering events. If the trace is in any way disrupted during this period, memory loss occurs. If no disruption takes place, then the trace consolidates and becomes a relatively permanent part of long-term memory, resistant to future destruction.

Some of the earliest evidence supporting the notion of consolidation comes from the observation that following a concussion or injury to the brain individuals usually have amnesia for events that occurred immediately prior to the accident. Depending upon the severity of the injury, the amnesia (called *retrograde amnesia* because it refers to memory loss before the accident) may cover a period from several minutes to more than an hour prior to the concussion (Russell and Nathan, 1964). For example, it is not unusual for individuals who suffer head injuries in automobile accidents to have no recollection of the events that caused the accident. These facts are consistent with the theory that neural activity must have an opportunity to consolidate for a period of time following an experience if permanent storage is to take place.

Retrograde amnesia can be produced in the laboratory by using electroconvulsive shock (ECS). A typical experiment is roughly as follows. An animal is trained on some learning task and shortly thereafter is given an ECS that produces temporary unconsciousness. The animal is then tested several days later to measure retention of the learned response; the crucial variable is the time between initial learning and administration of ECS. In one study rats were given ECS at intervals of either zero seconds, twenty seconds, thirty minutes, or one hour following the termination of a learning task. When the animals were tested the next day, it was found that retention of the learned response increased with the length of the interval between training and the administration of ECS; the animals with a zero-second interval showed virtually no retention, whereas animals with a one-hour interval showed almost perfect retention (Hudspeth, McGaugh, and Thompson, 1964).

Retrograde amnesia has been studied in a wide variety of organisms and produced by methods other than electroconvulsive shock. Although alternative explanations have been offered to account for the results of these experiments (Lewis, 1969), none of them have proved satisfactory. It seems increasingly clear that a period of consolidation is necessary for permanent storage of the memory trace (McGaugh and Herz, 1970).

Support for the idea that the storage process is time dependent also comes from studies in which certain drugs (such as strychnine, nicotine, caffeine, and amphetamine) given immediately following a learning trial appear to speed up the consolidation process. Animals so treated require fewer trials to reach a given learning criterion and make fewer errors overall. The assumption is that these drugs somehow accelerate the neurological processes in memory consolidation, but the mechanism by which they do this, possibly by increasing RNA synthesis, is not yet clear (McGaugh, 1970).

The whole course of learning and memory can be arbitrarily divided into three processes: *storing* the material, *retaining* it over a period of disuse, and *retrieving* it at the time of recall. At which of these three points can we most easily effect an improvement in memory? Improving our general ability for retentivity seems the least likely possibility for major improvement—unless we want to try to improve retention by injecting long periods of sleep or inactivity between fixation and recall, thereby reducing interference. But the circumstances surrounding the acts of storage and retrieval can certainly affect our memory. We shall consider some aspects of both of these processes.

Mental imagery and recall

If one is trying to memorize a poem or story, it often helps to visualize the action being described by forming a mental picture of the events. It is difficult to define *mental imagery,* but most people upon being questioned will readily agree that they can form mental pictures, although some find it easier than others and there are large individual differences in the vividness of the pictures and the amount of detail included. Case studies of people who have remarkable memories indicate that they often deal with new material by forming visual images. The case history of a Russian newspaper reporter with a phenomenal memory provides an example. When a sequence of digits was dictated to him, he would visualize the digits as written down on a piece of paper, usually in his own handwriting. To remember a long list of objects he would visualize the objects and arrange them in a row with their order preserved. He did this, for example, by taking an imaginary walk starting from Pushkin Square and going down Gorky Street. As he went along he would visualize each object at some point along the route. To recall the sequence, he would repeat his imaginary walk, reading off the objects that had been positioned along the way. In brief, his technique was to translate the verbal material into imaged objects and maintain their order by locating them against the background of a well-known route. With this technique he could memorize lists of more than one hundred digits, mathematical formulas, or musical motifs and recall them years later (Luria, 1968).

The kind of mental imagery we are talking about here is not the same as eidetic imagery (p. 229). Eidetic imagery involves looking at a picture and when it is removed being able literally to still see it projected somewhere before your eyes. Here the individual makes up his own images to help in the recall of material that may not be pictorial.

The effects of mental imagery can be investigated in the laboratory. In a typical task the subject is presented with a deck of one hundred cards, one at a time; each card is printed with an arbitrary pair of unrelated concrete nouns such as *dog-bicycle*. He is told that later he will be shown the first word of each pair and asked to recall the second. Subjects in one group are instructed to associate the two words on each card by imaging a visual scene in which they are interacting in some way. The instructions emphasize forming images that are bizarre or unusual and include as many details as possible. (For example, picturing a *dog* dressed in a clown's outfit, pedaling an old-fashioned *bicycle*.) Another group of subjects is given exactly the same learning task but simply told to study and rehearse the word pairs so that when tested later the first member will serve as a cue to recall the second. Both groups spend the same amount of time studying the material, but the group instructed to use imagery performs far better. In one experiment the imagery group showed 80 percent recall, while the control group remembered only 33 percent of the word pairs. The effectiveness of imagery may even be underestimated in this study, because interviews with the control subjects revealed some who were spontaneously using visual imagery to learn some of the pairs (Bower, 1970a).

As yet we know very little about the nature of mental imagery, but it undoubtedly plays an important role in many types of learning and problem-solving tasks. It may well be that as more is discovered about mental imagery, we will open up a cognitive resource that now is only sporadically and inadequately used by most individuals.

Organization and memory

The earlier discussion of retention curves implied that forgetting might be caused by the mere dropping out of items, so that retention was scored as the percentage of original material retained. But memory is not merely a collection of items, some of which escape with time. Memories are patterns of items, woven together by rules that impose varying degrees of *organization;* success in retention depends upon how much organization is present. When lists of words or other stimuli are studied, the greater the degree of organization that the learner can impose on the material, the better the subsequent recall (Mandler, 1969).

A dramatic illustration of the effect of organization on memory is provided in the following experiment (Bower, 1970b). The subjects were required to memorize four separate lists of words. For some subjects each of the word lists was presented on a slide in the form of a hierarchical tree, much like the example shown in Figure 9-6. The other subjects studied each of the lists for the same length of time, but the items in each list were arranged randomly on the presentation slide. When tested later, subjects recalled 65 percent of the words presented in a hierarchical organization, but only 19 percent of the same words presented in random arrangements. Further analysis of the data indicated that the subjects who were given the words in an organized form used the hierarchical arrangement as a retrieval scheme for generating recall.

Self-recitation during practice

Recall during practice usually takes the form of reciting to oneself. Such self-recitation increases the retention of the material being studied. Suppose, for example, a student has two hours to devote to the study of an assignment that he can read through in thirty minutes. Rereading the assignment four times is likely to be much less effective than reading it once and asking himself questions about the material he has read. He can then reread to clear up points that were unclear as he attempted to recall them. The generalization that it is efficient to spend a good fraction of study time in attempting recall is supported by experiments with laboratory learning as well as by experiments with school learning.

A well-known laboratory experiment dramatizes the value of self-recitation by showing that greatest efficiency in recall occurs when as much as 80 percent of the study time is devoted to active self-recitation (Gates, 1917). The materials used consisted of nonsense syllables and short biographies.

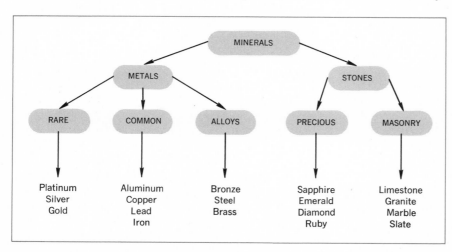

Fig. **9-6 Hierarchical organization** A list of words arranged in the form of a hierarchical tree. Trees of this sort have a simple construction rule; all items below a node are included in the class whose label is appended to the node. The same rule for constructing the tree also serves as an effective retrieval plan when a person is trying to remember the list of words. (After Bower, 1970b)

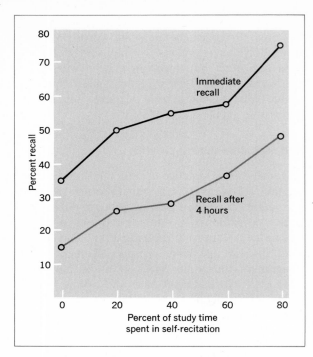

Fig. 9-7 Self-recitation during study Effects on retention of spending various proportions of study time in self-recitation rather than in silent study. Results are shown for tests given immediately and four hours after completing study. (Data from Gates, 1917)

The results for nonsense syllables are given in Figure 9-7. As you can see, for both immediate recall and recall after four hours the amount recalled is a steadily increasing function of the percentage of study time spent in self-recitation. Comparable results were found for the biographies. When similar experiments have been conducted with the learning of foreign language vocabularies, the kind of task often confronted in school, the self-recitation method proved superior to merely reading over the material.

One reason for the advantage of the self-recitation method in ordinary learning is that it forces the learner to define and select for himself what it is that he wishes to remember. In addition, recitation represents practice in the retrieval of information in the form likely to be demanded later on. That is, the learner tries to outline a history chapter or provide illustrations of operant conditioning as he may have to do on an examination. The rule is to begin an active process of recall early in a study period. Time spent in active recall, with the book closed, is time well spent.

Effects of overlearning on retention

Something to be long retained must be overlearned, that is, learned beyond the point of bare recall. A classic study by Krueger (1929) illustrates the advantage of overlearning. Three groups of subjects were required to memorize a list of nouns by the serial-anticipation method (p. 212); each group learned to a different degree of overlearning. For subjects in the group of zero-percent overlearning, practice was terminated at a criterion of one perfect recitation of the list. For the 50-percent overlearning group, practice was continued beyond the point of mastery for half as many trials as had been required to reach criterion; for the 100-percent overlearning group, the number of trials was doubled. The same list was then relearned from one to twenty-eight days later. The results of the experiment are shown in Figure 9-8, in which the dependent variable is the *saving score* on relearning (p. 228). The curves in Figure 9-8 indicate that the greater the degree of overlearning, the greater the retention at all time intervals. Further, the

Fig. 9-8 Effects of overlearning on retention Subjects learned a list of twelve nouns to three varying degrees of mastery and were then tested for retention at later points in time. Retention was measured as the saving score on subsequent relearning. (Data from Krueger, 1929)

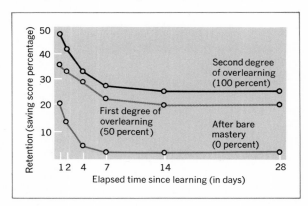

improvement in retention going from zero- to 50-percent overlearning is quite large, compared with a much smaller improvement going from 50- to 100-percent overlearning.

The retention of skills learned in childhood, even after years of disuse, is not so surprising when we consider the amount of overlearning involved in such skills as swimming, skating, or riding a bicycle. The skill is not learned only to bare mastery, but is repeated far beyond the point of original learning. Overlearning may not suffice to account for all the difference in retention between skills and information, but it is assuredly a strong contributing influence.

Summary

1. When we remember something we may show the marks of earlier memory in several ways. *Redintegrative memory,* or the recollection of a personal event, reconstructs a past occasion not only according to its content but also its setting in time and place. Such rich memories have been studied very little in the psychological laboratory. Much easier to test are *recognition,* requiring only a sense of familiarity, and recall, requiring a reinstatement of something learned in the past. A *saving in relearning* material previously mastered is another measure of prior learning.

2. *Cue-dependent forgetting* is most obvious in the *tip-of-the-tongue state:* a word is stored in memory, but the appropriate cues that would allow retrieval are lacking. *Trace-dependent forgetting,* on the other hand, is the result of actual decay of the *memory trace.* Studies of electrical stimulation of the brain in epileptic patients support the hypothesis that many memories are relatively permanent, with forgetting being of the cue-dependent type.

3. Traditional explanations of forgetting include: (1) *decay* through disuse, (2) *interference effects* (retroactive and proactive inhibition), and (3) *motivated forgetting.* These explanations are supplementary rather than contradictory, and each calls attention to important features of forgetting. Because no one of them can account for all the facts of forgetting, several two-process theories of forgetting have been proposed.

4. *Two-process theories* of forgetting distinguish between *short-term* and *long-term memory;* the former involves trace-dependent forgetting, and the latter involves cue-dependent forgetting. Information maintained in the *rehearsal buffer* is prevented from decaying in short-term memory and thus is more likely to be transferred to long-term memory. The results of retrograde-amnesia studies support the notion that a *consolidation* period is necessary following learning if the material is to be retained in long-term memory.

5. Significant improvements in memory come about primarily through more effective methods of storing and retrieving information. The use of *mental imagery, organizational schemes, self-recitation* during study, and *overlearning* beyond bare mastery will aid both the storage and retrieval processes.

Suggestions for further reading

The classic study that introduced the experimental analysis of memory is Ebbinghaus, *Memory* (1885; tr. 1913), now available in paperback (1964). A general survey of research on memory can be found in Adams, *Human memory* (1967), Deese and Hulse, *The psychology of learning* (3rd ed., 1967), and Jung, *Verbal learning* (1968). Studies on memory emphasizing an information-processing approach are described in Norman, *Memory and attention* (1969), in pertinent sections of Neisser, *Cognitive psychology* (1967), and in Kintsch, *Learning, memory and conceptual processes* (1970). *The machinery of the brain* (1963) by Wooldridge and *Memory* (rev. ed., 1964) by Hunter are two books available in paperback that offer lively reviews of many aspects of memory.

Also of interest is Whitty and Zangwill (eds.), *Amnesia* (1966), which presents papers dealing with various aspects of amnesia, and McGaugh and Herz (eds.), *Controversial issues in consolidation of the memory trace* (1970). See also Pribram (ed.), *On the biology of learning* (1969b), Byrne (ed.), *Molecular approaches to learning and memory* (1970), and Norman (ed.), *Models of memory* (1970).

optimizing learning

MOST OF THE PRINCIPLES OF LEARNING AND retention suggest practical applications, but it is seldom possible to move directly from general principles to applications. Usually it is necessary to take account of the setting, to try out the principles in practical contexts, and to make adjustments to fit the demands of special conditions. A drug may be found to kill the bacteria causing a given disease, but before this knowledge can be put to use, the dosage of the drug must be decided upon as well as the most appropriate way to administer it. In this chapter we shall examine some of the laboratory findings that bear upon the problems of efficient learning and that yield suggestions for the management of learning. We will be concerned with such issues as the manner in which learning one set of materials transfers to learning another, the importance of immediate information feedback, the optimal spacing of the learning sessions, and motivational and emotional factors that affect learning efficiency.

A great deal of society's energy is devoted to the management of learning—to instruction in schools, to job training in industry, and to teaching health and safety procedures to the community. The aim of an applied psychology of learning is to produce the highest quality of learning with the greatest possible efficiency. In recent years there have been many public discussions about the most effective methods for teaching reading, arithmetic, and social behavior. All these discussions concern the appropriate applications of the principles of learning in the field of instruction.

In the course of promoting learning, a number of teaching aids have been developed. Motion pictures, audio-visual tapes, and closed-circuit TV have become important adjuncts to instruction. A relative newcomer on the instructional scene is the so-called teaching machine. Although still largely in the developmental stage, such devices are worth considering because of the way in which they illustrate principles of learning.

Programed learning and automated instruction

One of the first teaching machines was developed almost fifty years ago by S. L. Pressey at Ohio State University (Pressey, 1926). While originally developed as a self-scoring machine for giving examinations, it was soon applied as a self-instructional device. The student read the question and chose his answer; he then pressed the button corresponding to this answer. If he was correct, the next question appeared in the slot; if he was incorrect, the original question remained until he pressed the right button. Because he knew he was right when the question moved, he had immediate information that told him which answer was correct, and he learned this while testing himself. The machine counted the number of errors that he made, so that his total score on the test could be read off as soon as he was finished.

Pressey's machine did not catch on, although a number of studies at that time showed it to be effective as a teaching device. A new forward push was given to the idea of automatic self-instruction by the publication of an important paper in 1954 by B. F. Skinner of Harvard University (Skinner, 1954), whose experiments on operant conditioning we studied earlier (pp. 195–204). Skinner and his students have developed several different models of machines; one inspired by Skinner's work is shown in Figure 10-1. The items to which the student makes his responses are presented in the form of statements with a fill-in blank. The student writes the appropriate word in the answer space, then moves a lever that exposes the correct answer beside his. After noting whether his response is correct he then moves the knob at the left to present the next item in the sequence.

Fig. **10-1 A Skinner-inspired machine** A statement with a fill-in blank is presented in the window at the left of the machine. The student writes the appropriate answer in the open space on the right-hand side. After being shown whether his response is correct he turns a knob on the left to proceed to the next item.

Will Rapport

Computer-assisted instruction (CAI)

Not all automated-instruction devices are restricted to the presentation of simple linear sequences of questions and answers. Some are far more versatile and make use of high-speed computers to keep track of the student's progress and to decide from moment to moment what should be done next in the instructional sequence. Figure 10-2 displays one of the student terminals of a computer-assisted instruction (CAI) system used for research purposes at Stanford University. Lo-

Fig. **10-2 Student station under computer control** An individual student's station in a computer-assisted instructional system.

cated at each student's station is a cathode-ray tube, a microfilm-display device, earphones, and a typewriter keyboard. Each of these devices is under computer control. The computer sends out instructions to the terminal to display a particular image on the microfilm projector—to write a message of text or construct a geometric figure on the cathode-ray tube—and simultaneously plays an auditory message. The student sees the visual display, hears the auditory message, and then is required to make a response. The student responds by operating the typewriter keyboard or by touching the surface of the cathode-ray tube with an electronic pencil. This response is fed back to the computer, where it is evaluated. If the student is correct the computer moves him on to the next instructional item; if he is incorrect the computer evaluates the type of error made and then branches him to appropriate remedial material. A complete record on each student is stored in the computer and is continually updated with each new response. The record is checked periodically to evaluate the student's rate of progress and to determine what particular difficulties he may be having. If he is making exceptionally good progress, he may be moved ahead in the lesson sequence, or branched out to special materials designed to enrich his understanding of the curriculum. If he is having difficulties, then he may be branched back to review earlier materials or to a remedial sequence.

In a very real sense, the computer-based instructional system simulates the human tutorial process. With such highly individualized instruction and completely flexible branching it is possible to adjust the instructional sequence to each student's particular needs and abilities.

So far CAI has had only limited development, but there is already enough experience and research to support the claim that it will have a broad range of application in the future. For example, CAI programs designed to teach reading and mathematics in the early grades have proved remarkably successful. Children receiving computer-based instruction made significant gains over comparable groups taught by traditional classroom methods (Atkinson and Wilson, 1969; Suppes and Morningstar, 1969).

One interesting result has to do with sex differences in reading performance. It is a common finding that girls as a group learn to read more rapidly than boys. Several explanations have been offered for this difference. It may be that the environment of the primary classroom, which is usually run by a female teacher, is more oriented toward the needs of girls. The fact that first-grade girls tend to be more mature physically than boys of the same age may also be important. Whatever the explanation, this sex difference in reading performance disappears with the CAI reading program; the boys progress through the curriculum as rapidly as the girls. Both sexes gain from CAI (as compared with a control group), but the boys show the greatest gains (Atkinson, 1968).

Instruction under computer control has also been used successfully at the college level. Students taught first-year Russian by computer performed significantly better on their final examinations than did a control group attending the regular Russian class. There were fewer dropouts in the CAI group, and more of these students elected to continue into the second year of Russian (Suppes and Morningstar, 1969).

Programing

The essence of learning by means of a teaching machine lies, of course, in the arrangement of the material to be learned. A body of material arranged so as to be most readily mastered is called a *program*.[1] The program is not intended as a review or testing device, as some older forms of testing machines or workbooks; it is intended to do the teaching, that is, to serve the purpose that textbooks and teachers do prior to an examination. Hence a program takes the place of a tutor for the student, and it leads him through a specific set of instructional materials designed and sequenced to optimize his learning of the information.

The basic unit of a program is called a *frame,* for it represents material that is exposed at one time. The frame may contain a question, a statement, or a problem to be solved; the frames introduce new material a little at a time and review old material as needed to make sure the student will remember it. The student is usually required to make a response to each frame. His response may be to fill in a blank with the correct word, to answer a question, to select one of a series of multiple-choice answers, or to list his solution to a problem. As soon as he has made his response, immediate feedback is given as to whether he was correct.

Samples of actual teaching programs are given in Figures 10-3 and 10-4. These examples illustrate two basic formats—the *linear* program and the *branching* program. In the linear program (Figure 10-3) the subject progresses along a single track from one frame to the next; each time he answers an item he moves on to the next regardless of whether his response was correct. In the branching program (Figure 10-4) the learner is given alternative answers from which to select; where he goes next depends on the one selected. If he chooses a wrong answer, his error is pointed out to him, and he is given help to avoid making that error again. If he has done very well on a number of questions, he may be given an opportunity to jump ahead, or, if he has made too many mistakes, he may retrace his steps or take an alternative route in an effort to clear up his difficulties.

Learning programs in a linear format do not need to be presented and sequenced by an automated device; therefore, for reasons of economy, they are often printed in textbook form.[2] In the *programed textbook* the answers to each frame usually are listed at the side of the page (see Figure 10-3). The student covers the answer column with a slider (strip of cardboard) and reads one frame at a time. After reading the frame he writes down his answer and then moves the slider down to uncover the appropriate answer and see if he was correct. He proceeds in the same way in the next frame, checking his answer to the frame before going on to the next.

If the program is complex and involves branching operations, it will usually require implementation by an automated device, and if the branching operations are very intricate, then implementation by a computer-based system. Some investigators have argued that all programs should be linear in form; others have argued for complex branching programs. Recent research makes it clear that the issue cannot be resolved in such a simple fashion. Some instructional materials can often be formulated quite nicely in a linear format, whereas other

[1]In discussions of CAI the terms *instructional program* and *teaching program* are often used, rather than simply the term *program,* to distinguish them from the *computer program,* which is a sequence of commands that controls the computer.

[2]The study guide designed to accompany this textbook contains chapter reviews written in the form of a linear program.

Sentence to be completed	Word to be supplied
1. The important parts of a flashlight are the battery and the bulb. When we "turn on" a flashlight, we close a switch which connects the battery with the ___.	bulb
2. When we turn on a flashlight, an electric current flows through the fine wire in the ___ and causes it to grow hot.	bulb
3. When the hot wire glows brightly, we say that it gives off or sends out heat and ___.	light
4. The fine wire in the bulb is called a filament. The bulb "lights up" when the filament is heated by the passage of a(n) ___ current.	electric
5. When a weak battery produces little current, the fine wire, or ___, does not get very hot.	filament
6. A filament which is *less* hot sends out or gives off ___ light.	less
7. "Emit" means "send out." The amount of light sent out, or "emitted," by a filament depends on how ___ the filament is.	hot
8. The higher the temperature of the filament the ___ the light emitted by it.	brighter, stronger
9. If a flashlight battery is weak, the ___ in the bulb may still glow, but with only a dull red color.	filament
10. The light from a very hot filament is colored yellow or white. The light from a filament which is not very hot is colored ___.	red
11. A blacksmith or other metal worker sometimes makes sure that a bar of iron is heated to a "cherry red" before hammering it into shape. He uses the ___ of the light emitted by the bar to tell how hot it is.	color
12. Both the color and the amount of light depend on the ___ of the emitting filament or bar.	temperature
13. An object which emits light because it is hot is called incandescent. A flashlight bulb is an incandescent source of ___.	light
14. A neon tube emits light but remains cool. It is, therefore, not an incandescent ___ of light.	source
15. A candle flame is hot. It is a(n) ___ source of light.	incandescent
16. The hot wick of a candle gives off small pieces or particles of carbon which burn in the flame. Before or while burning, the hot particles send out, or ___, light.	emit
17. A long candlewick produces a flame in which oxygen does not reach all the carbon particles. Without oxygen the particles cannot burn. Particles which do not burn rise above the flame as ___.	smoke

Sentence to be completed	Word to be supplied
18. We can show that there are particles of carbon in a candle flame, even when it is not smoking, by holding a piece of metal in the flame. The metal cools some of the particles before they burn, and the unburned carbon ___ collect on the metal as soot.	particles
19. The particles of carbon in soot or smoke no longer emit light because they are ___ than when they were in the flame.	cooler, colder
20. The reddish part of a candle flame has the same color as the filament in a flashlight with a weak battery. We might guess that the yellow or white parts of a candle flame are ___ than the reddish part.	hotter
21. "Putting out" an incandescent electric light means turning off the current so that the filament grows too ___ to emit light.	cold, cool
22. Setting fire to the wick of an oil lamp is called ___ the lamp.	lighting
23. The sun is our principal ___ of light, as well as of heat.	source
24. The sun is not only very bright but very hot. It is a powerful ___ source of light.	incandescent
25. Light is a form of energy. In "emitting light" an object changes, or "converts," one form of ___ into another.	energy
26. The electric energy supplied by the battery in a flashlight is converted to ___ and ___.	heat, light; light, heat
27. If we leave a flashlight on, all the energy stored in the battery will finally be changed or ___ into heat and light.	converted
28. The light from a candle flame comes from the ___ released by chemical changes as the candle burns.	energy
29. A nearly "dead" battery may make a flashlight bulb warm to the touch, but the filament may still not be hot enough to emit light—in other words, the filament will not be ___ at that temperature.	incandescent
30. Objects, such as a filament, carbon particles, or iron bars, become incandescent when heated to about 800 degrees Celsius. At that temperature they begin to ___.	emit light
31. When raised to any temperature above 800 degrees Celsius, an object such as an iron bar will emit light. Although the bar may melt or vaporize, its particles will be ___ no matter how hot they get.	incandescent
32. About 800 degrees Celsius is the lower limit of the temperature at which particles emit light. There is no upper limit of the ___ at which emission of light occurs.	temperature
33. Sunlight is ___ by very hot gases near the surface of the sun.	emitted
34. Complex changes similar to an atomic explosion generate the great heat which explains the ___ of light by the sun.	emission
35. Below about ___ degrees Celsius an object is not an incandescent source of light.	800

Fig. 10-3 Example of a linear program This is part of a program in high school physics. The student covers the answer column with a slider, reads one frame at a time, writes his answer in the blank, and then moves the slider to uncover the correct answer. Several programing techniques are illustrated by this set of frames. For example, technical terms are introduced slowly. The more familiar term "fine wire" in frame 2 is followed by a definition of the technical term "filament" in frame 4; "filament" is then asked for as a synonym in frame 5 and without a synonym in frame 9. Initially the student may be prompted to give the correct answer. In frame 25, for example, the response "energy" is easily evoked by the words "form of ___" because the expression "form of energy" is used earlier in the frame. The word "energy" appears in the next two frames and is finally asked for without a *prompt* in frame 28. Beginning with fairly simple facts the student is gradually led to an understanding of the topic. (After Skinner, 1968)

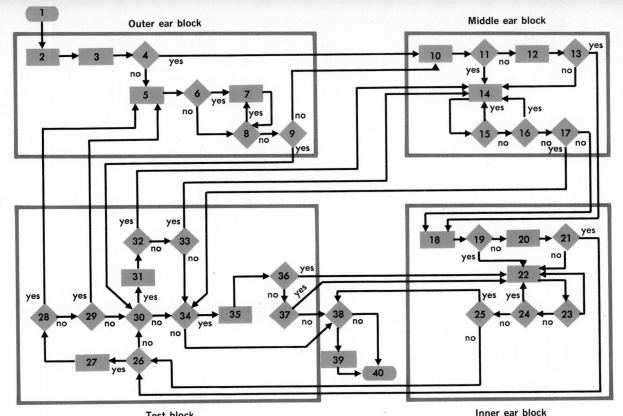

Outer ear block

Middle ear block

Test block

Inner ear block

KEY TO FLOW CHART

1. Student enters name on electric typewriter to start program
2. Introduction to procedures of computer-assisted instruction
3. Overview of outer ear
4. "Do you want to skip outer ear?"
5. Outer ear subprogram
6. Did student make ≥33% errors on pinna?
7. Remedial subprogram on pinna
8. "Do you want to cover pinna again?"
9. Did student come from Test Block (outer ear)?
10. First question on middle ear
11. Did student make ≥33% errors on pinna?
12. Overview of middle ear
13. "Do you want to skip middle ear?"
14. Middle ear subprogram
15. Did student make ≥50% errors on middle ear?
16. "Do you want to cover middle ear again?"

17. Did student come from Test Block (middle ear)?
18. First question on inner ear
19. Did student make ≥25% errors on the last time through middle ear subprogram?
20. Overview of inner ear and temporal bone
21. "Do you want to skip inner ear and temporal bone?"
22. Inner ear and temporal bone subprogram
23. Did student make ≥50% errors on inner ear and temporal bone?
24. "Do you want to cover inner ear and temporal bone again?"
25. Did student come from Test Block (inner ear and temporal bone)?
26. Did student skip outer ear subprogram?
27. Test on outer ear
28. Did student make ≥33% errors on outer ear test?

29. "Do you want to take outer ear subprogram?"
30. Did student skip middle ear subprogram?
31. Test on middle ear
32. Did student make ≥33% errors on middle ear test?
33. "Do you want to take middle ear subprogram?"
34. Did student skip inner ear and temporal bone subprogram?
35. Test on inner ear and temporal bone
36. Did student make ≥33% errors on inner ear and temporal bone test?
37. "Do you want to take inner ear and temporal bone subprogram?"
38. "Do you want to ask any questions?"
39. "Type your questions"
40. On with the course. Proceed to Chapter 2: "Detailed Anatomy of Ear"

Fig. 10-4 Flow chart for a CAI program The chart outlines the first part of an introductory course in audiology (the study of hearing) taught under computer control. The student attends class only one hour per week for lecture and orientation and spends as much additional time as necessary during the remainder of the week at the computer terminal. He communicates his answers by means of an electric typewriter connected with the computer. Each large block on the flow chart (marked in brown lines) represents a section of the course to be covered, plus a test section. Each small rectangle represents a series of instructional frames with related audio messages. The diamonds indicate choice points in the instructional sequence, where a decision is made as to what the student should do next, depending on the responses he made to the previous material. The large number of alternative paths between the initiation of the section at box 1 and its termination at box 40 indicates the flexibility of the program; it can accommodate both very fast and very slow learners, as well as those students who may have covered some of the material in previous courses. Thus each student can progress at his own pace. (From the Pennsylvania State University Computer-Assisted Instruction Laboratory)

subject matters virtually require a branching scheme. Undoubtedly, the successful programs of the future will utilize both linear and branching segments, the particular format adopted being a function of the nature of the material being taught.

As yet, not enough research has been done to prescribe a definite set of rules for developing a successful program. By and large the development of a good teaching program is still very much an art in the same sense as is writing a good textbook or preparing an effective lecture. One requisite for a person constructing a program is that he have in mind the *organization of knowledge,* both its *logical* organization (what has to be known before something else can be understood) and its *psychological* organization (how attention can be directed to significant parts, generalizations made from prior information, and so on). Because these tasks are elusive, programers conduct pilot tests of their programs.

The pilot testing is ordinarily done by trying the program out on one group of students, revising it to take care of the difficulties they experience, trying it on a second group, revising it again, and so on, until it seems to be adequate. This process of successive revisions and improvement of a program is important. It focuses attention on the individual learning process and helps the programer isolate for more careful analysis those aspects of the instructional sequence that cause particular difficulties.

Principles illustrated by programed instruction

What principles of learning does programed instruction illustrate? At least three seem to be particularly important.

1. *Active participation.* The learner is actively interacting with the curriculum materials by responding, practicing, and testing each step of what is to be mastered. The old adage "learning by doing" is well exemplified, in contrast to the passive learning that sometimes takes place during a classroom lecture.

2. *Information feedback.* The learner finds out with a minimal delay whether his response is correct, thus permitting immediate correction of an error. This type of feedback has been shown to be important in a range of tasks—from operant conditioning with animals, in which immediate reinforcement produces faster learning, to verbal learning studies with human subjects, in which knowledge of results provides similar benefits.

3. *Individualization of instruction.* The learner moves ahead at his own rate. The rapid learner progresses quickly through the material, while the slower learner moves less rapidly (often being diverted to a remedial program) until he too has mastered the basic concepts. Branching programs are particularly important in this regard because the learner moves through the material on a path that is designed to fit his aptitudes and abilities; essentially, each learner receives a course of instruction tailored to his particular needs.

Programed-learning devices have a value beyond their practical utility; namely, their contribution to psychological theory. There are already suggestions that individual differences between slow learners and rapid learners (as shown by other criteria) are reduced when programed materials are used; if this should turn out to be the case, it will contribute to our understanding of individual differences. Many principles from the theoretical analysis of learning in the laboratory are put to the test in programing: time interval in reinforcement, partial reinforcement, distribution of practice, reward versus punishment, generalization, and so on. The fact that most of the teaching devices provide an item-by-item response history of the learner presents a number of research possibilities. These response histories can be analyzed in great detail to determine where a student is having difficulties and the specific nature of the difficulties encountered. On the basis of such information the instructional program can be appropriately revised; in addition, this information helps to clarify the basic nature of the learning process involved. It may well be that new interpretations of learning that would not have been possible following more traditional avenues of research will arise from the work in programed learning.

The principal aim of CAI is to optimize the learning process. To do this we need a *theory of instruction* that sets forth rules concerning the most effective way of achieving knowledge or skill; these rules should be derivable from a more general view of learning. Thus, a distinction has to be made between a theory of learning and a theory of instruction. A theory of learning is concerned with *describing* or *explaining* learning. A theory of instruction is concerned with *prescribing* how learning can best be improved. Among other things, it should prescribe the most effective sequence in which to present instructional material and the nature and pacing of reinforcement.

As an example of the type of work that has been done to develop a theory of instruction, we will describe an optimization strategy for teaching spelling to grade-school children. This strategy is not very sophisticated, but it serves to illustrate an approach that can be used to attack more complex problems.

Suppose that we have a list of spelling words to be learned. On each trial the computer selects a word to be pronounced over the audio system, the student responds by typing the word, and the computer evaluates the student's answer. If the spelling is correct the computer types *C*; if incorrect, it types *X*, followed by the correct spelling. If a fixed number of trials is allocated for this type of instruction, how should they be used to maximize the amount of learning that will take place? Should each word be presented an equal number of times in a fixed order, or might other strategies be more effective (for example, one that takes into account the subject's trial-by-trial performance)?

If we assume that the learning process for this task can be adequately described by the all-or-none theory of learning presented earlier (p. 213), and there is evidence that this is the case, then the theory prescribes a specific procedure for carrying out instruction. The *optimal strategy* requires that a bank of counters be set up, one for each word in the list. To start, each word is presented once and a 1 or 0 is entered into its counter, depending upon whether the spelling is correct or incorrect. On all subsequent trials the strategy requires that we conform to the following two rules:

1. Present that word whose counter reads *lowest* among all the words. If more than one word is eligible, select randomly from among those eligible.
2. Whenever the word is presented again, add 1 if the subject's response is correct, but reset the counter to 0 on an error, regardless of what the previous count may have been.

The precise justification for this strategy is presented by Atkinson and Paulson (1971). It prescribes that words to which the learner has recently made an error should be repeated for study in preference to those for which a string of correct responses has occurred. But once a string of correct responses has been broken with an error, that word warrants the same likelihood of study as a word that was never correct; thus the history of information on a word prior to its last error is of no significance in this particular task. Even though this strategy is simple, it would be difficult to implement without the aid of a computer. A teacher working individually with a child might be able to employ the strategy by using flash cards, but it would be a tedious process; she certainly could not implement it on an individual basis for an entire class. Yet it has been shown that this strategy is more effective than one in which each of the words is presented equally often.

The above is an example of an extremely limited optimization strategy. Some strategies currently being tested attempt to optimize performance not only within a given day's session, but from one unit of the curriculum to the next. Still others try to determine whether the auditory or visual modality is best for presenting a particular type of problem to a particular student. The computer program for these strategies is arranged so that as it acquires information about the student, it can make increasingly better decisions on how to present the next unit of curriculum.

Transfer of learning

An important problem in the economy of learning is the extent to which the learning of one thing helps in the learning of something else. If every response we learned were specific to the situation in which it was learned, the amount of learning that would have to be crammed into a lifetime would be phenomenal. Fortunately, most learned behaviors are readily transferable, with some modification, to a number of different situations. We may have learned to drive in a car of specific make and vintage, but we can drive other cars with little difficulty even though there may be differences in the arrangement of the instrument panel or the drag of the clutch. In an emergency we could probably drive a truck or a bus without further training. The influence that learning one task may have on the subsequent learning of another is called *transfer of learning.*

The simplest experimental design for studying transfer of learning is as follows:

	Phase 1	Phase 2
Experimental group	Learn A	Learn B
Control group	Unrelated activity	Learn B

If the experimental group performs better than the control group on task B, then we can assume there has been *positive transfer* from the learning of A to B. If, on the other hand, the experimental group is inferior to the control group on task B, *negative transfer* has occurred.

We can think of numerous examples of negative transfer in everyday life. When we drive a car with automatic transmission after having been accustomed to one with a stick shift we may find ourselves depressing a nonexistent clutch pedal. When we change from a pedal-brake to a hand-brake bicycle we may still try to press back on the pedal when we have to stop quickly. And the transition from the American custom of driving on the right-hand side of the street to the British procedure of driving on the left is a difficult one for many American visitors to Great Britain. The original

habit is so overlearned that even after the individual has been driving successfully on the left for some time, he may revert to right-side driving when required to act quickly in an emergency.

Doctrine of formal discipline

The problem of transfer of learning has been historically of great concern to people working in education. For them it constitutes the very important practical question of how the school curricula should be arranged to ensure maximum positive transfer. Does learning algebra first help in the learning of geometry? Which of the sciences should be taught first to ensure maximum transfer to other scientific courses?

One of the earliest notions of transfer of learning, prevalent among educators around the turn of the century, maintained that the mind was composed of faculties that could be strengthened through exercise, much as one is able to strengthen one's muscles. This notion, known as the *doctrine of formal discipline,* was advanced in support of keeping in the high school curriculum such studies as Latin and Greek, the content of which is little used in everyday life. The argument that these subjects provided the discipline necessary to strengthen the mental faculties was presented in statements such as: "The study of Latin trains the reason, the powers of observation, comparison, and synthesis."

The doctrine of formal discipline has been largely discredited by experiments. Some transfer takes place, but it depends much less upon formal mental training than it does upon learning to use for a specific purpose the specific thing learned. For example, the study of Latin does indeed improve the understanding of English words, but only those with Latin roots. It does not improve the understanding of words of Anglo-Saxon origin. And the extent to which improvement occurs depends upon the way the Latin is taught: the gain in English vocabulary is much greater when the course is taught with emphasis on word derivation than when taught by more conventional methods.

Stimulus and response factors affecting transfer

When we compare a previously learned task with a new one in an attempt to determine what the transfer effects will be, we need to analyze both the stimulus and response variables in the two situations. If the task involves a specific stimulus-response pair (S_1-R_1), then we can conceive of transfer situations in which (1) the stimulus changes from the old task to the new while the response remains constant (first task, S_1-R_1: second task, S_2-R_1); (2) the response changes while the stimulus remains the same $(S_1-R_1: S_1-R_2)$; and (3) both change $(S_1-R_1 : S_2-R_2)$. This conceptualization has made it possible to bring together a number of diverse results, such as the negative transfer implied in retroactive inhibition, and positive transfer through generalization (Martin, 1965).

Stimulus changes. What will happen if we change the stimulus from the first to the second task but keep the response constant? In this case we are learning to give a familiar response to a new stimulus (S_2-R_1). An example would be learning the Spanish-English pair *amigo-friend* after having learned the French-English pair *ami-friend*. Studies have shown that learning to make an old response to a new stimulus generally results in positive transfer. And, as we would expect from the principle of stimulus generalization, the greater the similarity between the stimuli in the two situations, the more the positive transfer. In the above example the transfer would be quite easy because the stimuli *ami* and *amigo* are highly similar. We would expect somewhat less transfer with the French and Spanish equivalents for the English word "black" (*noir* and *negro*) and little if any transfer with the equivalents for "boy" (*garçon* and *muchacho*).

In most situations, however, even if the new stimuli are quite dissimilar to the old ones, when the responses remain the same we will still get some positive transfer. The practical meaning of this is that if we already have a response in our repertory of learned behavior, it is easier to attach it to a new stimulus than to learn both a new response and a new stimulus.

Response changes. What will happen if we change the response from the first to the second task but keep the stimulus constant (S_1-R_2)? The general finding for this situation is that learning a new response to an old stimulus results in negative transfer. But the experimental results are not clear-cut, and there appear to be a number of exceptions to this rule. If the responses in the two situations are clearly incompatible or antagonistic, then we have conflicting response tendencies and the transfer is negative. An example would be learning to "go" in response to a red light after having learned over many years of driving that red means "stop." The new response in this case would be difficult to learn and undoubtedly traffic accidents would soar were such a ruling to become part of the motor-vehicle code.

As the new response becomes more and more similar to the old one, negative transfer decreases. When the stimuli are identical and the responses similar but not identical we may get slight positive transfer.

General factors affecting transfer

Many examples of transfer are far too complex to be analyzed in terms of either stimulus or response similarity. In these cases more general factors operate to produce transfer between tasks that appear at first glance to be dissimilar.

Mediated transfer. Sometimes the learning of a new response to an old stimulus is facilitated by the presence of a previously learned intervening response that serves as a cue to mediate between the two tasks. Much of the advantage that human beings have over lower organisms in ease of learning results from the fact that we can use language as a mediating response.

The following experiment illustrates mediated transfer in a paired-associate learning task. The investigators selected a series of closely associated three-word chains after referring to a list that specifies the words most frequently associated with

TABLE 10-1 WORD LISTS FOR THE STUDY OF MEDIATED TRANSFER IN A PAIRED-ASSOCIATE LEARNING TASK							
GROUP I				GROUP II			
LIST 1		LIST 2		LIST 1		LIST 2	
STIMULUS	RESPONSE	STIMULUS	RESPONSE	STIMULUS	RESPONSE	STIMULUS	RESPONSE
CEF	stem	CEF	smell	CEF	stem	CEF	joy
DAX	memory	DAX	matter	DAX	memory	DAX	afraid
YOV	soldier	YOV	navy	YOV	soldier	YOV	cheese
VUX	trouble	VUX	good	VUX	trouble	VUX	music
WUB	wish	WUB	need	WUB	wish	WUB	table
GEX	justice	GEX	war	GEX	justice	GEX	house
JID	thief	JID	take	JID	thief	JID	sleep
ZIL	ocean	ZIL	drink	ZIL	ocean	ZIL	doctor
LAJ	command	LAJ	disorder	LAJ	command	LAJ	cabbage
MYV	fruit	MYV	red	MYV	fruit	MYV	hand

Source: Russell and Storms (1955).

By supplying your first association to the response words in List 1 you can probably guess most of the words from the Kent-Rosanoff List that mediated between the response words of List 1 and the response words of List 2 in Group I. In order they are: flower, mind, army, bad, want, peace, steal, water, order, and apple.

certain other words.[3] For example, by checking the list they determined that the word most frequently associated with *stem* was "flower," and the word most frequently given in response to *flower* was "smell." They hypothesized that because of these associations, subjects who had learned to respond with the word "stem" to the nonsense syllable CEF (CEF-*stem*) would learn the new stimulus-response pair CEF-*smell* more readily than subjects whose second pair was CEF-*joy*, because *joy* had no easy association to *stem*. The lists presented to the two groups of subjects are shown in Table 10-1. The results confirmed the experimenters' hypothesis: Group I learned their second list much faster than Group II. The chain of associations, for example, *stem-flower-smell,* mediated the transfer between List 1 and List 2 for Group I.

Learning to learn. Subjects who learn successive lists of nonsense syllables over a period of days are able to increase the speed with which they learn

subsequent lists. This positive transfer occurs even though there is no similarity between the lists. The subjects apparently learn a technique or an approach to the task that facilitates their performance on later tasks of the same sort. Positive transfer of this type is called "learning to learn."

Another example of learning to learn is provided by an experiment in which monkeys are presented with a series of discrimination problems. For each problem the animal is shown two objects, for example, a red triangle and a green circle, and is reinforced by food if it selects the correct object (see Figure 10-5). The position of the two objects is alternated in a random order from trial to trial so that sometimes the triangle is on the right and sometimes on the left. The animal must learn to ignore positional cues and select the correct object regardless of whether it appears on the right or the left. After the monkey has learned consistently to select the correct object, it is given a problem involving a different pair of objects.

In one experiment monkeys were each presented with a total of 344 such problems, each problem using a new and different pair of stimulus objects (Harlow, 1949). The learning curves over the first

[3]This list, known as the Kent-Rosanoff List, was compiled by obtaining associations to a large number of words from more than one thousand subjects and arranging the responses in order of frequency of occurrence to the test words.

Forward opaque screen

One-way vision screen

Stimulus tray

Fig. **10-5 Wisconsin General Test Apparatus** Apparatus used for discrimination training with monkeys. When the experimenter changes the stimulus objects, the forward opaque screen is lowered, blocking the monkey's view of the stimulus tray. (After Davenport, Chamove, and Harlow, 1970)

six trials for problems 10, 20, 150, and 300 are presented in Figure 10-6. All the curves begin at the 50-percent level; because on the first trial of each problem the objects are new, the animal must guess, and consequently will be correct half the time by chance. On the 10th problem the monkeys are making only about 75 percent correct choices by the sixth trial. On the 300th problem they are responding at the 98-percent level on the second trial. Whereas in the beginning the animals make little use of the information provided by the first trial, by the 300th problem they utilize this information to obtain almost perfect responding on

the second trial. That is, the monkeys now know that if the object they select on the first trial is rewarded they should pick the same object on the second trial regardless of its position; if the first trial choice is not rewarded they should select the other object on the second trial. The monkeys have learned how to learn or, to use the term proposed by Harlow, they have formed a *learning set* for this particular class of problems and can now proceed on the basis of "insight" as opposed to trial-and-error behavior.

Harlow and others have extensively investigated learning sets with monkeys and young children

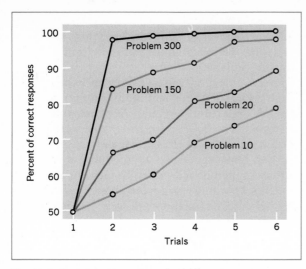

Fig. 10-6 Learning curves from the same subjects in a series of discrimination problems Plotted here is the probability of a correct response over the first six trials on the 10th, 20th, 150th, and 300th discrimination problem. (After Harlow, 1949)

(Levinson and Reese, 1963). Their findings indicate that the formation of learning sets occurs only after fairly extensive practice on a particular type of problem. If practice is discontinued too soon, there is little transfer to the next series of problems. The implications for education are significant: basic skills must be learned well before the learner proceeds to more complex ones. As we have seen, one of the advantages of programed instruction is that the learner is led through a graded series of related problems toward the development of principles and concepts.

Learning to learn is a general phenomenon that involves a number of different factors. One factor may be learning to relax in the experimental situation; another, to ignore irrelevant noises and other stimuli. Most important is learning to distinguish the relevant cues in the situation; for example, the monkey learns that the important cue is the quality (shape or color) of the object, not its position on the display board. In a sense this involves learning a principle. And as we shall see, learning principles, as opposed to specific responses, constitutes one of the chief ways in which learning transfers.

Transfer by mastering principles

One factor that makes transfer possible is the appropriate application to new situations of principles learned in old situations. The Wright brothers applied the principles they learned in flying kites to building an airplane. Principles of reasoning learned in logic are equally applicable in mathematics. The following experiment demonstrates the advantage of learning principles (Hendrickson and Schroeder, 1941).

Two groups of boys shot with rifles at a target submerged under water. Prior to the target practice the experimental group studied an explanation of the theory of refraction of light so that they understood the apparent displacement of objects viewed under water. The control group received no explanation. The experimental group learned to hit the target in about the same number of trials as the control group. However, after the boys had become proficient at hitting the target, the depth of the water was changed. Both groups showed positive transfer from the first to the second task, but the experimental group evidenced the greatest amount of transfer. Their knowledge of the principle of refraction enabled them to master the new task in significantly fewer trials than the control group.

Application to education

So far we have talked about transfer primarily in laboratory experiments and in situations where the stimulus and response changes can be specified. But a large number of studies on learning transfer have also been carried out in the classroom. What practical implications do they provide for the field of education?

It seems quite clear that the extent of transfer of an academic subject depends upon the method of teaching. As we mentioned earlier, Latin can be taught so as to improve understanding of English vocabulary. It is equally true that history can be taught in a manner that provides understanding of current political and economic problems, and arithmetic in a way that provides some positive transfer to the study of algebra. Teaching for transfer requires emphasizing the similarities between the current subject and the situations to which the new learning will transfer. If the two subject areas are similar in general principles or concepts rather than in stimuli and responses, then transfer depends upon the extent to which the principles and their broad application are stressed. Studies have shown, too, that principles transfer more readily when the student (1) has practiced the basic problem to a high degree of mastery and (2) has experience with a variety of similar problems to ensure generalization of the principle. If the two

he is presented with a wide variety of problems but does not have time to learn any one to a moderate degree of mastery, there will be little transfer (Postman, 1969).

Improvement in learning how to learn (in the sense of learning efficient study habits) provides another opportunity for transfer. One study demonstrated that college students who were taught certain principles of efficient memorization showed marked improvement in their ability to retain a variety of memorized materials as compared with students who simply practiced memorizing without any specific instructions (Bower, 1970b). Other

CRITICAL
DISCUSSION

Bilateral transfer and the cerebral hemispheres

Skills learned with one hand usually show some positive transfer to the other hand even though that hand has had no specific practice. If you learn to throw darts with the right hand, there is usually some positive transfer to the left hand. If you normally write with your right hand, you can also write with the left, although with much less skill. This transfer from one limb to the other is called *bilateral transfer*.

Recent studies have provided some interesting information concerning the neurological basis of bilateral transfer. You will recall from our discussion of the brain in Chapter 2 that the left hemisphere controls movements on the right side of the body, and the right hemisphere, those on the left. Communication between the two hemispheres takes place through a bundle of nerve fibers called the *corpus callosum* (see Figure 2-9).

Experiments have shown that under normal conditions when a task is learned by the right hand, information is stored not only by the hemisphere receiving sensory information from that hand (the left hemisphere) but also by the opposite hemisphere. The information crosses over by way of the corpus callosum and leaves some type of memory trace in the opposite hemisphere, thus providing the possibility for bilateral transfer of learning.

The role of the corpus callosum in conducting information between the two hemispheres has been studied in a series of experiments in which the corpus callosum fibers have been cut so that there is no connection between the two hemispheres. Animals surgically treated in this way are known as *split-brain* animals. In one study (Sperry, 1961), split-brain cats were trained to discriminate with the right paw between the tactile sensations of two different pedals. Pressing a pedal with raised horizontal lines was rewarded by food; pressing a pedal with raised vertical lines was not rewarded. The animals were prevented from seeing the pedals so that they received no visual cues (see Figure 10-7). After the discrimination had been well learned, the cats' discrimination with the left paw was tested. There was no transfer of training. The discrimination had to be learned all over again. Normal animals make the transfer to the untrained paw readily.

Split-brain cats can learn to make one discrimination with one paw and the opposite discrimination with the other paw with no apparent conflict. Normal animals would find this task difficult because the pedal-pushing response learned by one paw would transfer to the other, thus producing negative transfer.

To provide further proof that bilateral transfer takes place by means of the corpus callosum, normal cats were trained to make a tactile discrimination with one paw and then had the corpus callosum severed. When tested with the opposite paw following

studies have shown that introducing lessons on study skills in one high school course (teaching such skills as learning to use reference books, interpret charts, summarize, and outline) results not only in substantial gains in that specific course but these gains also transfer to other courses (Gagné, 1970).

Massed versus spaced learning

The spacing of learning sessions has received considerable experimental investigation. If you have a week in which to memorize the lines of a play or to learn a new motor skill but can only spend fourteen hours of that week in practice, what practice schedule would produce the greatest improvement? Should you practice two hours each day for a week, concentrate for a steady seven hours a day on the two days prior to the deadline, or adopt some intermediate schedule? The two

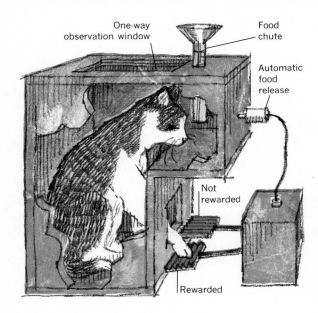

One-way observation window

Food chute

Automatic food release

Not rewarded

Rewarded

Fig. **10-7 Tactile discrimination apparatus** One pedal has a surface with raised horizontal lines (rewarded), and the other with raised vertical lines (not rewarded). The cat cannot see the pedals and makes its choice via tactile cues. During any part of the experiment the cat is permitted to use only its right or left paw. (After Sperry, 1961)

recovery from surgery, they showed good retention of the discrimination. The information had apparently been transferred from one hemisphere to the other prior to surgery.

Studies of human patients who have had their corpus callosum severed in an attempt to control intractable epileptic seizures show results similar to those obtained with split-brain animals. For example, if the patient (whose hands are screened from view) is given two objects simultaneously, one in each hand, and later is asked to retrieve these objects from a scrambled pile of items, each hand can search through the pile and find its own object. But one hand cannot find the object previously held by the other. In the process of searching, one hand may explore, identify, and then reject the item for which the other hand is searching. Each hemisphere appears to perceive as a separate unit unaware of the perceptual experience of the other (Sperry, 1968).

extremes represent, respectively, *spaced practice* (which implies rest intervals between sessions or trials) and *massed practice* (in which the practice sessions or trials are crowded together). The preponderance of experimental evidence indicates that for the same amount of practice, learning is better when practice is spaced rather than massed, although there are exceptions to this generalization. Let us first examine the evidence that spaced practice is advantageous.

We have already seen this principle demonstrated in (1) an experiment on mirror drawing (Figure 8-20, p. 210), in which greater gains were made with one trial per day than with all trials in one day, and (2) a target-tracking experiment (Figure 8-21, p. 211), in which a 45-second rest period between trials produced greater accuracy in following the target than did a 15-second period. Figure 10-8 also points to the efficacy of spaced practice: clearly, the longer intertrial interval produced the most rapid conditioning.

Several explanations have been offered for the

superiority of spaced practice. One of these is the consolidation theory (p. 241), which proposes that the changes produced in the nervous system by learning need time to consolidate, or "set," in order to be effectively stored in memory. If the physiological process that underlies learning is time dependent, then spaced practice would provide a better opportunity for these changes to take place than would massed practice.

An experiment by McGaugh and Hostetter provides additional support for consolidation theory. They argued that if the interferences of waking activity prevent the consolidation of what was learned, then material tested after a period of sleep should be better retained than material tested after waking, as had been found by other investigators (see p. 233). But they added another point to the argument: if sleep comes *after* a period of waking activity that is long enough to interrupt consolidation, it should not be of any benefit in retention; conversely, if waking activity follows a sleep period that is long enough to consolidate learning, then the waking activity should no longer be disruptive. Their results confirm these predictions (Figure 10-9), thus giving support to consolidation theory.

It should be kept in mind, however, that spaced practice is not always the most advantageous procedure. Some puzzling questions concerning massed and spaced practice have been studied in a long series of experiments by Underwood (1961). Usually spaced practice led to more rapid learning, but seldom in these experiments did it lead to better retention. Hence, the generalization that spaced practice is a favorable condition of learning has to be stated with caution, especially if it cannot be shown to have advantages for retention.

Other reservations about distribution of practice arise when more difficult materials are learned. In some kinds of difficult puzzles or other "thought" problems there seems to be an advantage in staying with the problem for a few massed trials at first, rather than spending a day or more between trials. This kind of learning calls for a varied attack, rather than a rote performance. It may be that massed practice leads to such variability, which is possibly an advantage in problem-solving but a disadvantage in rote memorization.

Fig. **10-8 Spaced practice in classical conditioning** The interval between trials was 9 seconds for the massed practice and 90 seconds for the spaced practice. The longer intertrial interval increased the likelihood of conditioned eyelid responses for a given number of reinforced trials. (Data from Spence, 1956)

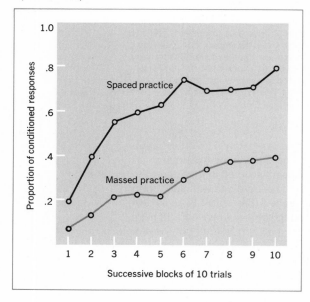

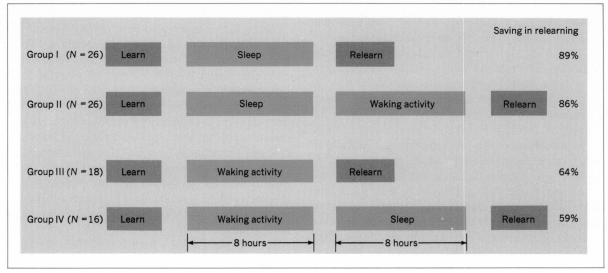

Fig. 10-9 **Evidence for a consolidation period in learning** When sleep follows immediately after learning, retention is high, regardless of whether the sleep is followed by waking activity before relearning. When learning is followed by waking activity, retention is less, regardless of whether sleep intervenes before the test of retention. The results show Group I to have a higher saving score (retention) than Group III, and Group II to have a higher score than Group IV, with equal elapsed time in each comparison. (Unpublished data from McGaugh and Hostetter)

In practical situations the distribution of study time depends upon a number of factors. If a fairly elaborate amount of preparation is required before the learning task can be started (gathering materials or equipment, organizing one's thoughts), then obviously much time is wasted in getting "warmed up" if the practice sessions are too brief. On the other hand, if the task requires considerable physical or mental exertion, then the rest periods provided by spaced practice allow for recovery. And with tasks that are particularly boring, spaced practice helps to maintain motivation.

Reward and punishment in the control of learning

Anyone who finds himself responsible for training or instruction, whether at home, in school, or industry, has to decide what motivational techniques to use. Through his position of responsibility he usually has access to both rewards and punishments, and part of his success will depend upon his skill in using them to encourage and guide the learning he wishes.

Intrinsic and extrinsic rewards

In choosing the goals that are to be set before the learner, it may be possible to select those *intrinsically* related to the task rather than those *extrinsically* related. The relation is *intrinsic* if it is natural or inevitable. For example, the boy who assembles a radio in order to communicate with a friend across town derives a satisfaction inherent in the task when he completes the instrument and finds that it works. The relation between a task and a goal is *extrinsic* if it is arbitrarily or artificially established. For example, a father may promise to buy his son a radio if he cuts the grass each week. The radio is an incentive extrinsically related to grass-cutting; there is no natural relationship between grass-cutting and the radio.

The distinction between intrinsic and extrinsic motivation is not clear-cut, and in most learning situations both types of motivation may be involved. A child learning to ride his new bicycle is usually intrinsically motivated by the pleasure he derives from mastering this new skill. But he may also be motivated by fear of derision from his peers if he does not succeed, which would be a form of extrinsic motivation.

Whenever possible, it is advantageous to use goals intrinsically related to the learning task. A child whose interest in music has been stimulated at an early age will persevere in practicing the piano longer than one whose motivation stems solely from promised rewards and threats of punishment. But even the intrinsically motivated child may require some extrinsic rewards at times when the drudgery involved in mastering technique outweighs the satisfactions of making music. In most cases, if the person who guides and controls the learning situation can capitalize on intrinsic motives, his battle is half won.

Although all that we know about the role of reinforcement in learning tells us that rewards are effective, extrinsic rewards—such as prizes for excellence—may have some objectionable by-products, two of which are worth specifying:

1. A reward planned by an adult (parent or teacher) and arbitrarily related to the activity is a kind of bribe. It leads to docility and deference to authority rather than to originality and self-initiated activity. It engenders in the child an attitude of "What do I get out of this?"—the activity becomes worthwhile only for the remuneration it brings in praise, attention, or financial gain. Some of the problems of cheating on examinations arise when desire for the external reward outweighs regard for the processes by which the reward is achieved.

2. Rewards are often competitive, so that while one or a few learners may be encouraged by the reward, many are doomed to frustration. If there is only one prize and many contestants, the problems of the losers must be faced. Is the gain to the winner worth the price in disappointment to the losers?

Controlling learning through punishment

Our folklore leads us to believe that punishment is an effective way of controlling learning. "Spare the rod and spoil the child" is not an isolated epigram. Social control by way of fines and imprisonment is sanctioned by all governments. Arguments have continued for many years over the relative advantages and disadvantages of kind treatment (emphasizing reward for good behavior) and stern treatment (emphasizing punishment for error). The preference has shifted slowly from punishment to reward, so that the paddle is used less today than formerly in home and school and the whipping post has disappeared from penal institutions.

It is worth asking whether this shift has come about solely on humanitarian grounds or whether punishment has been found less effective than reward. Evidence from psychological experiments indicates two important conclusions: (1) in many instances punishment is less effective than reward because it temporarily suppresses a response but does not weaken it; and (2) when punishment is effective it accomplishes its purpose by forcing the individual to select an alternative response that may then be rewarded.

The temporary effects of punishment are illustrated in a series of studies reviewed by Estes (1970). In one experiment two groups of rats learned a bar-pressing response to obtain a food reward. After the response had been well learned both groups were given extinction trials in which food was withheld. For the first few trials of extinction the rats in one group received an electric shock through the floor of the Skinner box every time they pressed the bar. During the remaining extinction trials no shock was administered; food was simply withheld. The results showed that although the punished rats did make fewer responses during the first stage of extinction, later they resumed their previous rate of bar-pressing and by the end of the experiment had made as many responses as the nonpunished animals. Punishment succeeded in temporarily suppressing the response but did not weaken it. As soon as punishment ceased, the response reappeared at full strength.

Other experiments have shown that the strength and duration of the suppression effect depends upon the intensity of the punishment and the degree of deprivation. Obviously, if the punishment is sufficiently severe and prolonged it may effectively stop a particular response, but the important point is that the response has only been suppressed, not unlearned; it may eventually reappear with the cessation of punishment if motivation becomes strong enough to overcome the aversive qualities of the punishment. In addition, severe punishment of a strongly motivated response (for example, intense shock every time an acutely hungry rat presses a bar for food) creates such conflict in the organism that grossly maladaptive behavior may result. As we shall see in Chapter 20, it is possible that a great deal of abnormal behavior is due to the repressive nature of punishment, for response tendencies are inhibited but remain active in indirect or disguised ways because they are not unlearned.

Pros and cons on the use of punishment. In addition to its suppressive effect, punishment may be an unsatisfactory means of controlling behavior for the following reasons:

1. The results of punishment, although they may include altered behavior, are not as predictable as the results of reward. Reward says: "Repeat what you have done." Punishment says: "Stop it!" Punishment by itself fails to tell you what to do. The organism may substitute an even more undesirable response for the punished one.

2. Punishment under some circumstances tends to fix the behavior rather than to eliminate it, perhaps as a consequence of the complex acquired motives (fear, anxiety) based on punishment. Punishing a child for bed-wetting, for example, often increases the frequency of the behavior.

3. The by-products of punishment may be unfortunate. Punishment often leads to dislike of the punishing person—whether parent, teacher, or employer—and to dislike of the activity that led to punishment.

These cautions about the use of punishment do not mean that punishment is never serviceable in learning and teaching. It may be useful for the following reasons:

1. Punishment can be an effective way of eliminating an undesirable response if alternative responses are available that are not punished or, better yet, that are rewarded. Rats that have learned to take the shorter of two paths to reach food in a goal box will quickly switch to the longer path if they are shocked in the shorter one. In fact, they will learn the new response more quickly than animals whose response of taking the shorter path is blocked by a newly placed barrier. In this case the temporary suppression produced by punishment provided the opportunity for the organism to learn a new response. Punishment was an effective means of redirecting behavior.

2. We have been talking so far about the difficulty of using punishment to eliminate an established response or habit. But punishment can be quite effective when all we want the organism to do is respond to a signal to avoid punishment. People learn to come in when they hear thunder, to seek shade when the heat of their skin tells them that additional sun may produce an uncomfortable sunburn, and so on. Avoiding a threatened punishment can be rewarding. The policeman is seldom a punishing person; he is more usually a symbol of *threatened* punishment. How does a policeman control us if he has never struck us with his stick or placed us under arrest? Our anxiety explains his control over us. If we drive too fast and see a police car in the rearview mirror, we become anxious lest we get a ticket, and feel reassured when we have slowed down and the police officer has driven past without stopping us. Our reward comes from the reduction in anxiety we feel as a result of conforming to the law. The threat of punishment is increased by occasional punishment; we drive more slowly on roads where we have been arrested or where we have seen others stopped by police.

3. Punishment may be informative. If the child handles electrical appliances and gets shocked, he may learn which connections are safe, which hazardous. A teacher's corrections on a student's paper are punishing (because they reduce the

grade received), but they are also informative about erroneous answers and thereby provide an occasion for learning if the student understands and corrects his errors. Informative punishment can redirect behavior so that the new behavior can be rewarded.

Parents are often puzzled about how much they should punish their children; yet most of them find that they resort to some sorts of deprivation if not to the actual inflicting of pain. The most effective use of punishment is the informative one, so that the child will know what is and is not allowed. Children occasionally "test the limits" to see what degree of unpermitted behavior they will be able to get by with. When they do, it is advisable to use discipline that is firm but not harsh and to administer it promptly and consistently. Nagging at the child for his nonconforming behavior may in the end be less humane than an immediate spanking. The child who is threatened with some kind of vague and postponed punishment ("What kind of person do you think you will grow up to be?") may suffer more severely than the child who pays a consistent penalty for infringement but afterward is always welcomed back into the family circle.

Anxiety and learning

The apprehensiveness and uneasiness engendered by school tasks are familiar to most of us. Examinations are threatening, and often a student does less well than he might have done had he not panicked during the examination. Young children occasionally develop school phobias; they may become nauseated every school morning yet escape all symptoms on Saturdays and Sundays. While these are extreme cases, most people carry some burden of anxiety. The following experiment gives some clues as to the effect of the individual's general anxiety level on his learning.

A large number of college students were given a questionnaire that asked each student about his subjective experiences in testing situations: uneasiness, accelerated heartbeat, perspiration, worry before and during a test session. On the basis of the answers to this questionnaire a high-anxious group and a low-anxious group were chosen.

The subjects received two types of instructions. Half of each group received "expected-to-finish" instructions: they were told the task would be easy enough to finish in the time allowed, and the instructions put pressure on them to finish. The other half of each group received "not-expected-to-finish" instructions: they were told that the task was too long to finish. (As it was, no one finished in the time allowed.) The "expected-to-finish" subjects fell behind what they thought they ought to be doing, while the "not-expected-to-finish" subjects had no need to worry because they had been told that nobody could finish.

The results for one of the tasks, which required the subjects to learn a code for substituting digits in place of geometrical symbols, are plotted in Figure 10-10. The conclusions that can be drawn from this experiment are (1) that low-anxious

Fig. **10-10 Anxiety and learning** Digit-symbol learning for low-anxious and high-anxious subjects under two sets of instructions. (Data from Sarason, Mandler, and Craighill, 1952)

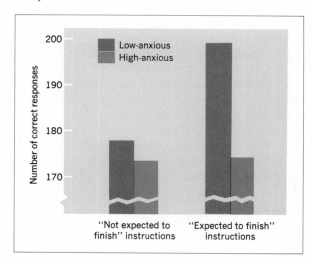

subjects generally do better than high-anxious subjects, and (2) that pressure to finish results in substantially improved scores for low-anxious subjects but not for high-anxious subjects (Sarason, Mandler, and Craighill, 1952).

The study reported above is but one of a number showing that anxiety level affects performance in learning tasks. These studies are so numerous that they have been the subject of several reviews (Sarason, 1960; Spence and Spence, 1966). In general, the findings have shown that high-anxious subjects learn a simple conditioned response (for example, an eye blink to an air puff) more rapidly than low-anxious subjects; on more complex learning tasks high-anxious subjects usually do less well than low-anxious subjects, although there are some exceptions which we will consider in a minute. Pressure of any kind—such as interrupting the task to report that the subject is doing poorly or giving ego-involving instruction implying that the task is an indication of intelligence—tends to depress the scores for high-anxious subjects but raises scores for low-anxious subjects.

Anxiety and competing responses

One explanation for the above results assumes that high anxiety does two things. It produces a high drive level (see p. 295) and at the same time arouses a number of responses that may interfere with learning—responses that are irrelevant to the task, such as autonomic responses or thoughts of worry and self-depreciation. Increasing the drive level in a classical-conditioning situation, in which a stimulus is associated with a single response, facilitates learning; response output varies directly with the strength of the drive. In more complex situations, such as paired-associate learning, in which each of a series of stimulus items may evoke a number of competing responses, increased drive level increases the strength of incorrect responses as well as that of the correct response and hence usually leads to poorer learning for high-anxious subjects. Because in most instances the correct response initially is weaker than one or more of the competing incorrect responses, the higher the drive level, the poorer the performance.

It is possible, however, to devise a paired-associate learning task for which the correct response is stronger than the possible incorrect responses. For example, in one study employing a list of paired-associates with high associative value (such as *tranquil-serene*) high-anxious subjects learned more rapidly than low-anxious subjects. When the stimulus words from the first list were paired with response words that had no easy association (such as *tranquil-verbose*) low-anxious subjects learned more rapidly than high-anxious subjects (Standish and Champion, 1960). Thus, when the response to be learned is clearly the dominant one, high-anxious subjects perform better than low-anxious subjects. When the correct response is not dominant, low-anxious subjects have the advantage. It is not the complexity of the task per se that determines the effect of anxiety on performance, but the relative strength of the correct and incorrect responses. Anxiety interferes with performance when the increased drive level energizes incompatible responses.

When stress is introduced in the form of noxious stimuli, ego-involving instructions, or reports of failure, the performance of high-anxious subjects becomes worse while that of low-anxious subjects usually improves. It is hypothesized that stress, in addition to increasing drive level, also elicits task-irrelevant responses in high-anxious subjects. Instructions that stress the importance of "doing well" appear to trigger irrelevant responses in high-anxious subjects, while for low-anxious subjects the effect is merely to increase attention to the task and hence improve performance. In a sense high-anxious subjects have a lower threshold for the arousal of anxiety than low-anxious subjects and tend to react to even mildly ego-involving instructions with a fear of failure that has a detrimental effect on performance (Spence and Spence, 1966).

Anxiety and academic performance

The effect of anxiety on the academic achievement of college students has been demonstrated by the following experiment (Spielberger, 1966). A group of high-anxious and a group of low-

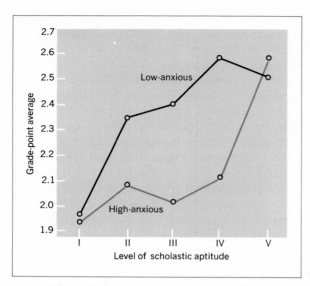

Fig. **10-11 Grade-point averages for high- and low-anxious college students** Students in the middle range of ability who score high on an anxiety questionnaire do less well scholastically than students of comparable ability who score low in anxiety. At the extremes of ability (Level I = lowest ability, V = highest ability), the degree of anxiety does not affect grade-point average. Ability level is measured by college entrance examination scores. (After Spielberger, 1966)

anxious freshmen were selected by means of a questionnaire. Both groups were subdivided into five levels of scholastic ability on the basis of their college entrance examination scores. The investigator then evaluated the joint effects of anxiety and scholastic ability on (1) the grade-point average at the end of the freshman year and (2) the dropout rate owing to academic failures by the end of the senior year. The grade-point averages for high- and low-anxious students of different ability levels are shown in Figure 10-11. In the broad middle range of ability, high-anxious students obtained poorer grades than low-anxious students. At the extremes of ability, anxiety had little effect on academic performance: the dull students did poorly regardless of their anxiety level; the most able students apparently were bright enough to overcome the detrimental effects of anxiety. In fact, there is some indication that at the highest level of ability anxiety may facilitate performance by providing increased motivation.

Analysis of dropouts owing to academic failure gives further evidence of the destructive effect of anxiety on academic performance. More than 20 percent of the high-anxious students selected for this study left college because of academic failure; less than 6 percent of the low-anxious students left for the same reason. We must conclude that some students who have the ability to obtain a college degree fail to do so because they are hampered by the effects of anxiety.

A follow-up study attempted to remedy this situation by providing group counseling for high-anxious students. All freshmen who scored high on the anxiety questionnaire were invited to participate in the experiment, and those who accepted were divided into two groups matched for college entrance examination scores and a number of other variables related to academic achievement. Students in one of the two groups met with a counselor (in small groups of six to eight students) for a series of about ten sessions. Many topics were discussed during the counseling sessions, ranging from personal problems to efficient study habits. Counseling for the second group was postponed until the next semester. At the end of the first semester a comparison of the grade-point average of the counseled group with that of the group that had not yet received counseling indicated that the program was quite successful. The degree of improvement was related to the frequency of attendance at the counseling sessions: those who attended frequently improved significantly more than those whose attendance was infrequent.

Concluding comments

Emotional attitudes and anxieties can have a profound effect on our learning efficiency. Personal problems unrelated to the learning situation may interfere with concentration and sap the energy required for effective work. A certain level of anxiety may facilitate performance by increasing motivation, but excessive concern over grades and test performance may be self-defeating. While no one can deny that in this day of specialization grades are important, the student who studies because he wants to improve his skills and widen his fund of information will be less anxious in a test situation than one whose sole concern is an extrinsic reward, the grade he obtains. The former knows he has achieved something of value and has progressed toward his goal regardless of his test grade; the latter feels that his efforts have been wasted should he not get the desired grade.

Summary

1. *Computer-assisted instruction* (CAI) is proving to be a valuable aid to learning. Curriculum material designed for CAI may be in the form of *linear programs,* in which the student progresses along a single track from one frame to the next, or *branching programs,* in which the material to be presented next depends upon the adequacy of the student's response to previous frames.

2. Programing makes use of three learning principles: active participation by the learner, immediate feedback, and rate of progress through the learning materials adjusted to individual differences.

3. The influence that learning one task has on the subsequent learning of another task is called *transfer of learning.* Learning to give a familiar response to a new stimulus generally results in *positive transfer,* whereas learning a new response to an old stimulus may result in *negative transfer,* especially if the two responses are antagonistic.

4. Other factors that produce transfer of learning include *mediating responses, learning to learn* (learning to relax in the situation, to ignore irrelevant stimuli, and to distinguish the relevant cues), and learning general *principles.*

5. In classroom situations transfer occurs best when there is a clearly designed effort on the teacher's part to emphasize similarities between the current subject and the situation to which the new learning will transfer, and to stress the application of principles.

6. In learning material *spaced practice* is usually more efficient than *massed practice* except for certain difficult problem-solving tasks. *Consolidation theory,* which assumes that changes produced in the nervous system by learning need time to "set," or consolidate, provides a plausible explanation for the superiority of spaced practice.

7. In attempting to guide the learning of another person, *reward* is generally favored over *punishment.* Reward strengthens the rewarded behavior, whereas punishment may not lead to unlearning of the punished behavior; instead, the behavior may be merely suppressed, reappearing again when the threat of punishment is removed or perhaps appearing in disguised form. Punishment may be effective, however, when it forces the individual to select an alternative response that can then be rewarded, or when it serves as an *informative cue* to avoid a certain response. Arbitrary rewards and punishments have some unfavorable consequences, in part because of the authoritarian control they often imply.

8. Subtle *emotional factors,* based on personal experiences of the individual, play a central role in learning. When college students are separated into *high-anxious* and *low-anxious* groups, the high-anxious subjects often perform better than the low-anxious ones in simple conditioning situations, but they do less well on complex tasks. Pressure on high-anxious students to do better may actually impede their performance, while such pressure spurs the low-anxious students to improve. High anxiety is also significantly related to lowered grade-point averages and dropout rates among college students.

Suggestions for further reading

Many of the standard experiments on economy in learning and transfer of learning are treated in Deese and Hulse, *The psychology of learning* (3rd ed., 1967), Gagné, *The conditions of learning* (2nd ed., 1970), and Ellis, *The transfer of learning* (1965). The relation of learning theory to problems of education and instruction is discussed from many points of view in Hilgard (ed.), *Theories of learning and instruction* (1964); see also Bruner, *Toward a theory of instruction* (1966), and Hilgard and Bower, *Theories of learning* (3rd ed., 1966).

Practical suggestions for the college student concerned with improving his study skills and exam-taking techniques may be found in Voeks, *On becoming an educated person* (3rd ed., 1970).

The literature on programed learning and computer-assisted instruction is rapidly expanding. Surveys of recent developments in programed learning are provided in Skinner, *The technology of teaching* (1968), and in Taber, Glaser, and Schaefer, *Learning and programmed instruction* (1965). Progress in the area of computerized learning is reviewed by Atkinson and Wilson (eds.) in *Computer-assisted instruction* (1969).

Punishment and aversive behavior (1969) by Campbell and Church (eds.) provides a survey of theories on the role of punishment in learning.

An excellent survey of research on anxiety in relation to learning is presented in Spielberger (ed.), *Anxiety and behavior* (1966). Some interesting observations on obstacles to learning (chiefly in the age range of seven to sixteen, but with a few cases at college level as well) are reported in Harris, *Emotional blocks to learning* (1961).

language and thought

11

MANY FORMS OF BEHAVIOR can be classified as thinking. We think as we woolgather while waiting for a bus. We think as we solve a problem in mathematics or write a poem or plan a trip. Much of our thinking is highly practical; we are more likely to think when we cannot operate by old habits alone, when thinking helps us to get where we want to go and do what we want to do. Thinking represents man's most complex form of behavior, his highest form of "mental activity," but it is not so different from the other activities he engages in that one must stand in awe of it. We proceed to study it as we do any other behavior, examining its antecedents (the conditions that facilitate and impede it) and its outcomes.

Thinking may be viewed as a cognitive process that is characterized by the use of *symbols* as "representations" of objects and events. When you eat an apple or walk across the room, you do not necessarily engage in thought (although of course you may), but if you try to make reference to the eating of something that is *not* present or to walking that is not now going on, then you must use a *symbolic* reference. Such a symbolic reference characterizes thought. Thought can deal with remembered, absent, or imagined objects and events (as well as with those that are currently impinging on the sensory system); because thought is symbolic, it can range more widely in its content than other kinds of activity. It incorporates present perceptions and activities into its topics, but it deals with their *meanings* in a way that goes beyond the present; hence thought reflects upon and elaborates what is given in perception and movement.

In this chapter we look first at the way symbols acquire their meanings and how they can be manipulated. Since language provides a rich source of symbols, we next consider the structure and acquisition of language. And finally some other complex cognitive processes are examined.

Symbols and meaning

A *symbol* is anything that stands for or refers to something other than itself. The word "book" is a symbol that stands for printed pages within a firm cover—the object called a book—but of course the symbol is not the book. We can think about the real books on the shelves and talk about them through the use of language symbols, one of which is the word "book." Words are thus important components of our *symbol system.*

Symbols are not limited to the familiar language of words. There are other symbolic languages, such as the language of logic or of mathematics. There are also many tangible symbols: a stop sign, a cross on a church, a musical note, a red flag, a paper dollar. Symbols always convey meaning through reference beyond themselves; that is, as symbols, they stand for something else. Of course we can talk about the symbols themselves. We can talk about the spelling of a word or the painting of a sign. When we do, we use symbols to refer to other symbols.

We think in symbols. Because verbal language is a rich symbolic process, much thinking goes on in terms of language. But it is possible to think without the aid of language. Some composers claim that they "hear" the music they are composing before they actually write it down or play it on an instrument. We could mentally visualize a dance routine, a series of tennis strokes, or some other athletic maneuver without resorting to language. But a large portion of our thinking is in linguistic terms.

A symbol conveys *meaning.* It provides information about some object or event to which it refers and thereby suggests appropriate action to the person who perceives it. Symbolic stimuli differ from stimuli in general in that the symbolic stimuli produce reactions appropriate to some stimulus *other than themselves.* The sign POISON alerts to danger, but the danger does not reside in the sign itself. A sign STOP arrests movement, without itself being a barricade or hazard. The fact that signs and words carry meaning is so familiar that it is a little surprising to find many theoretical disputes over what constitutes meaning, and over the relationship between the symbol and its meaning.

The problem of meaning would be less difficult if all symbols referred only to specific things or actions, such as names of objects (table, pencil) or specific directions (turn right, no parking). Such meanings are called *denotative;* they specify something to which you can point and are alike to all who can comprehend them. But there are other kinds of meaning, called *connotative,* which accompany the denotative meanings of many words; connotations are emotional, usually expressing some kind of evaluation or preference and varying from one person to another. The word "hippie" may refer to a specific group of nonconformists in our culture, but it adds the connotative meanings of being in tune with something ("hip") as well. Misunderstandings often arise because of the different connotations words have for different people.

In order to pin down connotative meanings more precisely, a method of measurement called the *semantic differential* has been developed (Snider and Osgood, 1969). The method is called "semantic" because it has to do with meaning, and "differential" because it provides several different dimensions of meaning. Despite individual differences in connotations, a fairly homogeneous group of people tend to have similar connotations for familiar words. For example, what distinctions in connotation do the words "good" and "nice" have for American college students? By using the semantic differential, it was found that "good" had slightly male overtones, and "nice" female ones. To express simple approval the nearly equivalent statements for the two sexes would be "He's a good man" and "She's a nice girl." It does not seem rational to assign sex overtones to simple words such as "good" and "nice," but connotative meanings are not strictly rational.

To determine the connotations of a word by the

semantic differential method, the subject is asked to rate the word according to a number of bipolar adjective pairs; an example is the pair "strong-weak." One member of the adjective pair is placed at one end of a seven-point scale, the other member at the opposite end. Then the subject indicates the direction and intensity of his judgment by rating the word under study at some point along this scale. Figure 11-1 illustrates the way such scale values were assigned by students judging the word "polite." Pooled judgments of two groups appear on the plot, and their interpretations of the meaning of "polite" turn out to be very much alike, even though the adjective pairs that are used have little to do with the denotative meaning of politeness.

Initially some fifty dimensions were used in determining the semantic differential for various words. But after analyzing a large number of English words, it was found that the connotative meaning of most words could be expressed in terms of three basic dimensions: an *evaluative* dimension (good-bad, clean-dirty, sacred-profane), a *potency* dimension (strong-weak, powerless-powerful, light-heavy), and an *activity* dimension (fast-slow, active-passive, sharp-dull). These three dimensions account for a good share of connotative meanings, with the evaluative factor carrying the most weight. Subsequent studies have found that these same dimensions characterize connotative meaning in a wide variety of languages, including Japanese, Finnish, and the Kannada dialect of India (Osgood, 1967).

The semantic differential has also proved to be a promising method for distinguishing between cultural groups. Figure 11-2 shows two examples from a number of words rated by Hopi, Zuñi, and Navajo Indians. Although anthropologists regard these three tribes as distinct cultures, the Hopi and Zuñi cultures are more similar to each other (both being classified as Western Pueblo) than they are to the Navajo. We can see this cultural similarity reflected in the semantic-differential profiles. Although there are exceptions, in most instances the connotative meanings given by the Zuñi and Hopi are closer together than are those given by the Navajo (Maclay and Ware, 1961).

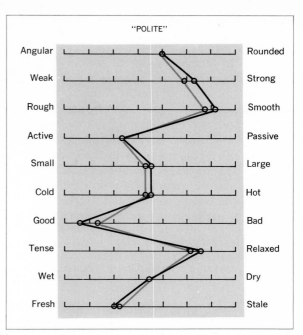

Fig. **11-1 Osgood's semantic differential** Profiles of ratings used in arriving at a semantic differential for measuring the connotative meaning of the word "polite." Median responses from two groups of 20 subjects each. (After Osgood, 1952)

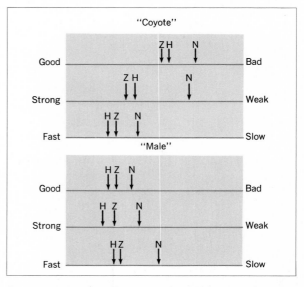

Fig. **11-2 Cultural differences reflected in the semantic differential** Two examples of word ratings made by Hopi (H), Zuñi (Z), and Navajo (N) Indians. Note that the connotative meanings given by the Zuñi and Hopi are closer together than are those given by the Navajo. (After Maclay and Ware, 1961)

Concept formation

When a symbol stands for a class of objects or events with common properties, we say that it refers to a concept. *Girls, holidays, vegetables,* and *round objects* are examples of concepts based on common elements; *equality, longer,* and *smoother* are concepts based on common relations. By means of concepts we are able to order and classify our environment. Most words (with the exception of proper nouns) represent concepts in that they refer not to a single object or event but to a class. "The house on the corner of 10th and Market Streets" specifies a particular object; the word "house"

Fig. 11-3 **Monkey solving the oddity problem** A monkey will learn to select the odd member of three objects if there is a bit of food or something else of interest in the well under it.

Harry Harlow

alone refers to a class of buildings that have certain features in common. Concepts possess varying degrees of generality: the concept symbolized by the word *building* is more general than the concept of a *house,* which in turn is more general than the concept of a *cottage.*

Man's superior position in the animal kingdom is based largely on his ability to use language and to learn concepts. But concepts can be learned without the use of language. Rats can learn the concept of triangularity: by being rewarded for selecting triangles of various shapes and sizes and not rewarded for responding to other geometrical forms, they can learn to respond consistently to triangles. Since the triangles vary in shape and size they are not responding to a specific object but to the concept of triangularity. Monkeys can learn the concept of "oddity" (see Figure 11-3). They can learn to select the odd stimulus object from a set of three objects, two of which are identical (Gunter, Feigenson, and Blakeslee, 1965). The stimuli vary from trial to trial, for example, two circles and a square on one trial and two squares and a triangle on the next, so that the animal is not responding to a specific object but is learning to abstract a common property—oddity—as the situation changes from trial to trial.

The learning of concepts utilizes the psychological processes of generalization and discrimination. In learning the concept of triangularity, a monkey generalizes the response initially to other geometrical forms, but since these responses are never rewarded they are extinguished, and it eventually narrows its discrimination to triangles. When a child is learning the concept *dog* he may generalize the term initially to include all small animals. He soon learns from his parents' corrections the instances when he is in error and gradually makes finer discriminations until his concept approximates our conventional conception of *dog.* He may refine the concept further and distinguish between "friendly or good dogs," whose wagging tails indicate that approach is safe, and "unfriendly or bad dogs," whose growls signify that avoidance is the best response; eventually he learns to distinguish among breeds.

Human beings, because of their language ability,

	Trial 1	Trial 2	Trial 3	Trial 4	Trial 5
	RELF	FARD	LETH	MOLP	LING
	FARD	PILT	MOLP	LETH	FARD
	LETH	RELF	FARD	LING	PILT
	LING	MOLP	PILT	RELF	MOLP
	MOLP	LING	LING	PILT	LETH
	PILT	LETH	RELF	FARD	RELF

Fig. 11-4 Concept formation These pictures were shown one at a time, starting on each trial from the top of the column and proceeding to the bottom. As each picture was shown, the subject tried to anticipate the nonsense word paired with it. After the subject made his response the experimenter called out the correct nonsense word, which is listed below each picture. On the first trial the subject had no way of knowing what word was paired with a picture, but over the course of several trials he gradually learned to anticipate correctly on all pictures. Note that none of the pictures are ever repeated, so it is not a question of learning a specific response to a specific stimulus, but rather learning a response to a concept. In this example the concept of face = RELF, building = LETH, tree = MOLP, circle = FARD, the number two = LING, and the number five = PILT. (After Heidbreder, 1947)

are able to deal with all sorts of concepts, from fairly concrete ones, such as *dog,* to highly abstract ones, such as *gravity, justice,* and *God.* The processes involved in forming these more abstract concepts are obviously too complex to be explained by a simple analysis, but the principles of generalization and discrimination still appear to play a major role.

What kinds of concepts are attained most readily? Studies by Heidbreder (1947) indicated that concrete characteristics are generally easier to conceive than the more abstract relationships of form and number. These studies used the paired-associate technique with the type of material illustrated in Figure 11-4. On each trial several stimuli were presented one at a time, and the subject was required to anticipate the response paired with each stimulus. The experimenter arbitrarily assigned a different nonsense word as the response for each concept. Thus, MOLP might refer to the object concept *tree,* FARD to the spatial concept of circular patterns, and PILT to the number concept of five objects. On the second trial *new* stimuli representing the same concepts were paired with the original responses. For example, Figure 11-4 shows six stimuli that might be presented on trial 1, a new set of six stimuli for trial 2, and so on. The experiment continued until the subject could give correct responses to all stimuli on a trial.

The results of a series of such experiments showed that object concepts (*shoe, book, bird*) were the easiest to learn, spatial forms the next easiest, and then numbers. Our thinking apparently tends to run to *objects* rather than to *abstractions.* We saw earlier in Piaget's stages of intellectual devel-opment (p. 62) that the child first learns object concepts and develops more abstract concepts only as he grows older. Interestingly enough, with certain types of brain damage the individual may lose his ability to deal with abstract concepts and can respond only in terms of concrete ideas. For example, he can use a key to open a door but is unable to demonstrate how to use the key unless the door is present. Or he can throw balls accurately into three boxes located at different distances from him but cannot state which box is nearest and which farthest or explain his procedure in aiming. This inability to think in abstract terms is so marked in certain types of brain damage that some of the tests designed to detect brain damage use performance on concept-learning tasks as a basis for diagnosis (for example, Goldstein and Scheerer, 1941).

Structure of language

Language serves two major functions: (1) it allows us to communicate with one another—if the speaker and listener share a common meaning of words—and (2) it provides a system of responses that facilitates our thinking and behavior. By supplying us with verbal symbols so that we can represent the past in the present, it allows us to profit from past experience. As we have seen, many of our verbal responses represent concepts and therefore can serve as stimuli for manipulating concepts. A kindergarten child might use his fingers to determine that there are twelve children in his classroom. A third-grader can arrive at the same answer more easily by noting that there are three tables with four children at each table and manipulating the verbal concept "three times four equals twelve."

Phonemes and morphemes

All languages are based on a certain number of elementary sounds called *phonemes.* The English language is composed of about forty-five phonemes, which correspond roughly to the different ways we pronounce the vowels and consonants of our alphabet. Some languages work with as few as fifteen phonemes, whereas others make use of as many as eighty-five. The smallest meaningful units in the structure of a language are called *morphemes.* Morphemes may be root words, prefixes, or suffixes and may consist of from two to six phonemes. The words *talk, rug,* and *strange* are single morphemes; *strangeness* consists of two morphemes, *strange* and *ness,* both of which have meaning (the suffix *ness* implies "being" or "having the quality of").

Although there are well over a hundred thousand morphemes in the English language, many more would be possible if each of the forty-five phonemes were used in every possible combination. But every language has certain restrictions on the way phonemes can be sequenced and combined. In English, for example, we seldom use more than two (and never more than three) consonants to begin a morpheme, and even then, only certain consonants can be combined in an initial cluster. We have words that start with *str* or *spl* but none beginning with *zb* or *vg* as is common in some Slavic languages. One function of the restrictions a language places on phoneme sequencing is to prevent errors of interpretation. If morphemes used all possible combinations of phonemes, then a change in a single phoneme would produce a new morpheme. A language based on such a system would be highly susceptible to communication errors. As it is, when we come across the typographical error *fwice* we know that an *fw* beginning is not permissible in English, so we guess at the nearest permissible morpheme (with help from the context of the sentence) and come up with *twice*. Studies have shown that nonsense words that follow the lawful sequence of phonemes (PRALL, THROOP) are easier to remember than nonsense words composed of unlawful sequences (TLIB, ZDRALL) (Brown and Hildum, 1956).

Phrase structure and rule learning

Just as rules govern the sequencing of phonemes, rules specify (1) how words are formed from morphemes (for example, add *s* to form the plural of nouns) and (2) how sentences are formed from words (for example, the subject precedes the verb). A sentence can be analyzed at a number of levels. The speech sounds can be analyzed and classified as phonemes. The phonemes can then be grouped into meaningful units as morphemes and words. And the words can be categorized into phrases to give structure to the sentence. Linguists have found it useful to describe a sentence by the organization of its various phrases. Such a description is called the *phrase structure* of the sentence.

Figure 11-5 shows the phrase structures of two sentences. The phrase-marking shows how the words are related to one another and what role each plays in the sentence. The location of pauses is also fixed by the phrase structure. In reading aloud the first sentence we normally would say (*the dog*) (*chased*) (*the ball*) rather than (*the*) (*dog chased*) (*the ball*) or (*the dog*) (*chased the*) (*ball*). In spontaneous speech only a very fluent speaker consistently follows the pauses specified by the phrase structure of the sentence. Most of us in searching for the appropriate word with which to express our thoughts frequently pause in the middle of phrases; we may hesitate after the article while groping for the right word or pause between an adjective and the noun it modifies (Maclay and Osgood, 1967). There is evidence, however, that despite such fumbling, our listener tends to hear the pauses in the proper place. In an experiment

Fig. **11-5 Tree diagrams representing the phrase structure of two sentences**   The phrase-marking shows how the words are related to one another and what role each plays in the sentence.

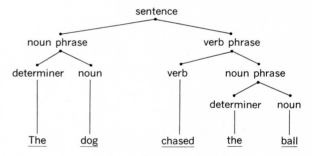

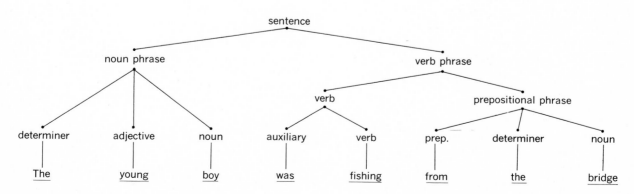

in which a click sounded at various times while a sentence was being uttered, the click tended to be perceived at the boundaries of phrases rather than at the point where the disruption actually occurred (Fodor and Bever, 1965). A subsequent study showed that the clicks were not simply displaced to positions where there were pauses; rather, they were displaced only to those pauses that marked the boundary of phrases (Garrett, Bever, and Fodor, 1966).

Phrase-markers provide structure for the sentence, and experiments have shown that material with a definite structure is easier to learn. For example, nonsense syllables are easier to learn when they appear in structured sentences than when they do not. The structured sequence *The yigs wur vumly rixing hum in jegest miv* is easier to learn than *The yig wur vum rix hum in jeg miv,* despite the fact that the first sentence is longer, and both are nonsense. The difference in learning these two sequences disappears when the syllables are presented one at a time by means of a memory drum so that they are not perceived as a sentence (Epstein, 1961).

Deep structure and surface structure

Language is essentially a system that relates sound to meaning. The same meaning can be expressed by different patterns of sound. The sentences *John read the book* and *The book was read by John* share the same meaning expressed by different sound patterns. Conversely, a single sound pattern can have more than one meaning. The sentence *They are eating apples* can be interpreted as stating that some people are eating apples or that those apples are good for eating (see Figure 11-6). Examples of this sort have led to the distinction between the *surface structure* and the

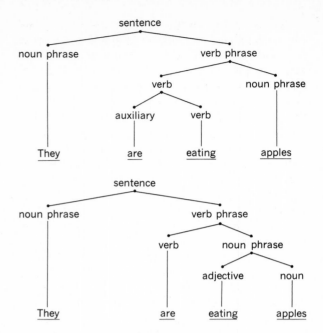

Fig. **11-6 An ambiguous sentence** Two phrase structures for the ambiguous sentence "They are eating apples." (After Neisser, 1967)

deep structure of a sentence. Linguists use the concept of deep structure to refer to the intended meaning of a sentence—the thought behind it. The surface structure is the actual sound sequence—the production of the sentence. Theoretically, by applying certain linguistic rules the deep structure is transformed into the surface structure. The system of rules that links the deep structure to the surface structure constitutes the *grammar* of the language. For the linguist, grammar is the system of rules that enables an arbitrary string of sounds or written symbols to mean something.

Consideration of the sentences given below will help to clarify the need for a distinction between deep and surface structure (McNeill, 1970).

Sentences	Paraphrases	Nonparaphrases
1. They are buying glasses.	- - - - - -	- - - - - -
2. They are drinking glasses.	They are glasses to use for drinking.	They are glasses that drink.
3. They are drinking companions.	They are companions that drink.	They are companions to use for drinking.

The sentences on the left all have the same superficial form. They start with the pronoun *they*, followed by *are*, followed by a verb, followed by a plural noun. But sentence 1 differs from sentences 2 and 3 in several respects. The pauses occur in different places. For sentence 1 we would say *(They) (are buying) (glasses)*; for sentences 2 and 3, *(They) (are) (drinking glasses)* and *(They) (are) (drinking companions)*. A second difference is that the articles occur in different places. For sentence 1 we would say *They are buying the glasses,* but not *They are the buying glasses.* For sentences 2 and 3, on the other hand, we would say *They are the drinking glasses* and *They are the drinking companions.* In essence, sentence 1 has a different phrase, or surface, structure than sentences 2 and 3.

Sentences 2 and 3 have pauses in the same place and take articles in the same place. In brief, they have the same surface structure. But it is clear that their meaning is quite different. The paraphrases and nonparaphrases of these two sentences point up this difference. Sentence 2 means *They are glasses to use for drinking,* whereas sentence 3 means *They are companions that drink.* Exchanging the form of the paraphrase between sentences 2 and 3 results in nonparaphrases. Sentence 2 does not mean *They are glasses that drink,* and sentence 3 does not mean *They are companions to use for drinking.* Despite the similar surface structure of these two sentences, they differ in deep structure.

It is assumed that the deep structure is transformed into the surface structure by a series of rules. These *transformational rules,* which are too complicated to present here, specify the steps by which the thought is related to the actual sentence. A simple declarative sentence (*The boy fed the dog*) is assumed to be closely related to its deep structure, having undergone fewer transformations than a passive sentence (*The dog was fed by the boy*) or other more complex sentences such as negatives.

Since the deep structure is not manifest in speech, it can be studied only indirectly. One experiment used immediate memory span to study the operation of deep structure. The experimenters assumed that in order to store sentences in memory, we must reduce the surface structure of the sentence to its deep structure. The deep structure is stored in memory along with additional information concerning the specific transformations needed to generate the surface sentence. Thus, a complex sentence involving several transformations would take up more room in memory than a simple declarative sentence. An ingenious method was used to test this hypothesis. It is based on the idea that an irregular-shaped object can be measured by placing it in a full container of water and noting how much water overflows. In this experiment the "water" was a series of unrelated words that the subject had to learn in addition to a sentence. By noting how many of the words "overflowed," that is, were not remembered, it was possible to determine how much space in memory the sentence required. For example, on one trial the subject might be required to memorize *The girl was hit by the ball . . . house, man, blanket, rain, shirt, blue.* The subject was then asked to first recall the sentence and then as many words as he could. The number of words recalled was assumed to provide an inverse measure of the space in memory occupied by the sentence. When this number was tabulated for all trials on which the sentence was recalled correctly, it was found that the simplest type of sentence (active declarative) produced less interference with the recall of the words than any of the more complex types (passive sentences, negatives, questions, and sentences containing clauses). In fact, the degree of interference with recall of the unrelated words was a direct function of the number of transformations required to derive the sentence from its deep structure. The length of the sentence had less influence on recall of the extra words than its deep structure (Savin and Perchonek, 1965).

This brief description of the structure of language is enough to indicate the enormity of the task confronting a child as he learns to speak his native tongue. He must learn not only the proper pronunciation of words but also their meaning and the multitudinous ways they may be combined into sentences to express thoughts. How the human organism acquires and uses language has received a great deal of attention in recent years from both psychologists and linguists.

Development of language

The development of speech follows a fairly regular course. Most children begin to babble at about six months, say their first word at about a year, combine words at anywhere from eighteen to twenty-four months, and by the age of four and a half years have mastered the basic grammar of adult speech. The regularity of this development makes it clear that language depends very much upon maturation. But we know that learning also plays a vital role. Deaf children who hear no language never acquire any unless specially trained. The development of language depends upon both learning and maturation; neither alone is sufficient.

Babbling and initial words

During the first months of life vocalization is very limited, but at about six months infants begin to produce an immense variety of sounds in increasingly complex combinations. This repetition of the syllables resembling those used in adult speech is called *babbling*. During the early babbling stage infants are able to produce all the sounds that form the basis of any language, including German gutterals and French trills. Experiments have shown that the babbling of a Chinese baby cannot be distinguished from that of a Russian or English infant during this period (Atkinson, MacWhinney, and Stoel, 1970). By about nine months the range of babbled sounds narrows, and the infant begins to concentrate on those sounds that will appear in his first words. It is as if the child suddenly stopped experimenting with sounds and started concentrating on those syllables that are to form the initial words.

Regardless of the child's native language, the first words consist of a front consonant, *p, m, b,* or *t* (produced with the tongue in the front of the mouth), and a back vowel, *e* or *a* (produced with the tongue in the back). This undoubtedly is the reason why the words for *mama* and *papa* are so similar in many languages. This is also why English children say *tut* before *cut;* Swedish children say *tata* before *kata;* and Japanese children say *ta*

before *ka* (McNeill, 1970). Interestingly enough, back consonants such as *k* and *g*, which the child cannot yet use properly in words, may appear correctly in vocal play. There seems to be a difference between spontaneously producing a sound and producing it voluntarily. A child who uses only *p, m,* and *a* in speech will at the same time use many other sounds in nonspeech (Jakobson, 1968).

Words and meaning

To produce a word sound is one thing, but a second step is required before the word has meaning—before it stands as a symbol for something else. How do children go from sound production to the association of that sound with a particular object or activity?

Long before he is able to speak the child has learned to recognize and to identify many features of his environment. Certain faces, toys, foods, and sounds are recognized as familiar. When a word is paired with one of these familiar objects or experiences, as when the mother repeats *doll* every time she hands the child his favorite doll, an association is established between the word and the object. An example that is more readily observable in the child's behavior is the parent's saying "no" and simultaneously slapping the child's hand when he reaches for a forbidden object. The hand-withdrawal response, which was originally elicited by the slap, is soon elicited by the word alone. An observer would say that the child had learned the meaning of the word "no."

Operant conditioning also plays a role in language development. The child's vocalizations may be "shaped" by reinforcement in much the same way as an animal's behavior can be shaped in an operant-conditioning situation; he is reinforced when he makes sounds similar to those his parents use in their language and not reinforced when he makes other sounds. When the child produces a sound that approximates a word, the reinforcement he receives is usually strong and immediate —judging from the delight most parents express when their baby says his first word! And we can observe many instances during the child's daily activity when verbal responses are reinforced. Sometimes a sound produced at random by the child is sufficient to cause the parent to provide an object that satisfies some need of the child. For example, the random sound "bahta" is close enough to *bottle* that the parent may think the child is asking for his bottle and hurry to provide it. Such a sequence repeated several times increases the probability that "bahta" or something similar will be produced by the child when hungry. Also, the child's tendency to imitate words produced by adults speeds up the process of vocabulary learning.

Development of grammar

Associating vocal responses with presented stimuli is only a small part of the total process of learning a language. After the child has acquired a modest vocabulary he must begin the task of learning to put these words together in sentences. Eventually he must comprehend long and complicated sentences, many of which he has never heard before, and must produce phrases and sentences of his own, using proper grammatical sequences. This is a vastly more complicated problem than learning to use single words, and it seems unlikely that grammatical learning can be accounted for by the operant conditioning of word sequences. There are too many ways in which words can be combined into sentences for each combination to be learned through a process of conditioning. It seems more likely that what the child learns are *rules* of generating acceptable sequences of words. Even as adults we may not be able to formulate these rules, but we know when an utterance is or is not correct. We know, for example, that the utterance "ran handsome rapidly boys" is not a sentence because the words do not follow the adjective-noun-verb-adverb sequence characteristic of English sentences. We recognize this sequence as unacceptable, not because we have never heard it before, but because it does not match the rules we employ for generating sentences.

Another reason to doubt that simple learning principles can account for the child's acquisition of grammatical sequence lies in the fact that many of the child's earliest grammatical constructions are not imitations of adult sentences. In their spontaneous speech two year olds will say things like "allgone shoe" and "go car Daddy," which undoubtedly they have never heard an adult say. And when a child imitates his parents' speech, he does not mimic the entire phrase; he leaves out prepositions, articles, suffixes, prefixes, and auxiliary words as illustrated in the samples below.

Parent says	*Child repeats*
Where is Daddy's coat	Where Daddy coat
John will be unhappy	John unhappy
He is going out	He go out

Speech at this stage of development (at about two years) has been termed *telegraphic speech.* The child preserves the order of the parent's speech but leaves out the less important words or word parts.

Experts looking at samples of children's speech during the period when they are first forming two- or three-word sentences of this sort have concluded that the child is using an initial grammar of his own. And he is trying to fit what he hears into his own grammar. The two-word sentences given below are samples taken from recordings of the speech of a child between the ages of nineteen and twenty-two months (Braine, 1963).

allgone shoe	my coat
allgone milk	my sock
allgone watch	my mommy
see boy	do it
see sock	push it
see hot	buzz it

It is apparent that the words in these samples can be grouped into two classes. One class consists of a small group of words, called *pivot* words, that appear frequently in the child's speech. Words in the *pivot class* never occur alone or with one another but always in combination with words from the *open class.* Open words form a larger group that appears less frequently in the child's speech. Open words may stand alone or in combination with pivot words in two-word sentences.

From the first birthday to the age of about a

year and a half children utter only single words. Some of these words later become pivot words and appear only in combination, whereas others become open words and appear both in combination and alone. The pivot words seem to indicate the acquisition of a basic concept. In the above example, *my* appears to refer to the concept of possessions—*my mommy, my sock,* and so on. *Allgone* seems to indicate a concept of disappearance.

Open words increase rapidly in number while pivot words do not, indicating that the child finds it easier to acquire words that denote tangible objects than more abstract words. Table 11-1 lists pivot and open words obtained from studying the speech records of several different children. Note that pivot words represent many parts of speech—nouns, pronouns, adjectives, verbs, and adverbs—while open words tend to be nouns almost exclusively, although other parts of speech do occur. A word that one child uses as a pivot

TABLE 11-1 PIVOT AND OPEN WORDS FOR THREE CHILDREN					
BRAINE STUDY		BROWN & BELLUGI STUDY		MILLER & ERVIN STUDY	
PIVOT	OPEN	PIVOT	OPEN	PIVOT	OPEN
allgone byebye big more pretty my see night-night hi	boy sock boat fan milk plane shoe vitamins hot Mommy Daddy ⋮	my that two a the big green poor wet dirty fresh pretty	Adam Becky boot coat coffee knee man Mommy nut sock stool tinkertoy ⋮	this that	arm baby dolly's pretty yellow come doed ⋮
				the a	other baby dolly's pretty yellow ⋮
				here there	arm baby dolly's pretty yellow ⋮

Source: McNeill (1970).

The table summarizes the speech of three children and is based upon three separate studies (Braine, 1963; Brown and Bellugi, 1964; Miller and Ervin, 1964). The pivot classes are given in their entirety (left column of each array), but because of lack of space, only a portion of the open words are listed (right column). Each of these children characteristically formed a sentence by taking a word from the left-hand column and following it by a word from the right-hand column. Pivot words are not always the first in a sentence; although first-position pivot words are more common, most children have a smaller class of pivot words that appear only in the second position. The table lists only first-position pivot words. The separate braces on the pivot words in the Miller and Ervin study indicate that for this child not all pivot words occurred with all open words.

word may be classed as an open word for another child (for example, *pretty* occurs in both classes), but a given child uses a particular word in one class or the other, not both.

An example of a child's experimenting with one pivot word in combination with a variety of open words is found in the following excerpt from a recording taken while the child was alone, lying in his crib prior to falling asleep (Weir, 1962).

go for glasses	go throw
go for them	go for blouse
go to the top	go for shoes

Starting from this simple grammar of combining pivot and open words, children progress rapidly to more complicated sentences until by the age of four and a half they have mastered the basic grammar used by adults. They are, of course, aided in this development by feedback from the parents. Recordings of parent-child interactions show that parents repeat a great deal (as much as 30 percent) of what children say. But instead of verbatim repetition the parent tends to *expand* upon the child's utterances, retaining the message but putting it in correct grammatical form. For example, the child says "turn round," and the adult responds "Yes, it is turning around." In response to an expanded sentence the child frequently repeats his own sentence but in a slightly more complex form, as in the following sequence:

CHILD—Baby highchair
MOTHER—Baby is in the highchair.
CHILD—Baby in highchair

The child compares his sentences with the parent's and modifies his own accordingly.

Although many of his early speech forms are learned through imitation of adults, it is clear that as the child matures in his language development he seeks a system of grammatical rules. Some of the earliest verbs the child acquires have an irregular past tense (*come-came, run-ran, take-took*). These are verbs heard frequently in both the present and past tense, so the child has ample opportunity to learn both forms. Initially a child will use the past tense correctly; he will say "Mommy came home" or "Daddy took the book." Later when he begins to acquire regular verbs and learns the rule that past tenses are formed by adding *-ed,* he will regularize the irregular verbs. He will say "Mommy comed home" or "Mommy camed home" and "Daddy tooked the book" or "Daddy taked the book." Verb forms that he practiced a great deal are replaced by forms with which he had little practice. The child appears to be striving for a general rule. Eventually he learns that verbs such as *come* and *take* are exceptions to the past-tense rule, and he returns to his initial correct form, saying "Mommy came home" and "Daddy took the book." The same sort of learning procedure occurs with other exceptions to grammatical rules, such as the plural formation of *man;* the sequence followed by the child is *men, mans, men.* Children acquire general rules in learning a language and only through time and experience learn to modify these rules to accommodate exceptions.

In summary, it appears that language acquisition depends upon both learning specific word-meaning associations (stimulus-response associations) and developing general rules that permit one to understand and generate an infinite variety of sentences. The individual may not be able to formulate these rules explicitly, but he knows whether an utterance he is producing or hearing is correct.

[continued on page 286]

There is no doubt that some animals can communicate with one another. Many animals have "distress cries" that signal the approach of danger. By a sequence of "dance movements" honeybees can communicate to their hive mates the direction and distance of food sources. When food is close by, the dance pattern is circular. More remote food sources are indicated by a dance in the form of a figure eight; the more rapid the dance, the farther away the food source (von Frisch, 1955). But communication is not the same as language. A single item of information can be communicated either verbally or nonverbally. Language, by using a system of arbitrary and conventional symbols, can convey an infinite variety of messages. It is this capacity that sets man apart from the lower animals.

Psychologists have long been intrigued with the possibility of teaching language to an animal, and several unsuccessful attempts have been made. Nearly forty years ago a psychologist and his wife raised a female chimpanzee named Gua along with their own son and compared the two developmentally. Although Gua showed considerable comprehension of English, responding appropriately to some seventy commands, she never did learn to speak (Kellogg and Kellogg, 1933). A subsequent attempt, which focused more specifically on language training, was made by another couple, both psychologists. They adopted an infant chimpanzee, Vicki, and gave her intensive speech training, actually shaping her lips in an attempt to get her to produce various sounds. After three years Vicki could repeat only three sound patterns (*Mama, Papa,* and *cup*) that were recognizable approximations to English words (Hayes, 1951).

On the assumption that these earlier efforts failed because the chimpanzee's vocal apparatus is not well adapted to the production of human speech, a more recent attempt has been made to teach a chimpanzee *American Sign Language*—a language used by deaf persons in this country and Canada (Gardner and Gardner, 1969). Since chimpanzees are very facile with their fingers, this approach seemed more promising than trying to teach vocal speech. Training was begun with Washoe, a female chimpanzee, when she was one year old and continued to age four at the time of the report. She lived in a completely equipped house trailer with access to children's toys and play equipment as well as extensive play areas. She heard no spoken words. Those with whom Washoe came in contact communicated with her and with each other while in her presence by means of sign language. At the age of four years Washoe could use about eighty-five signs appropriately. Some of the signs and the context in which they occurred may be seen in Table 11-2.

At first signs were taught by shaping procedures (p. 201); the Gardners waited for Washoe to make a response that could be shaped into the sign they wished her to acquire. For example, when Washoe wanted to get through a door she would hold up both hands and pound on the door with her palms or knuckles. This is the beginning position for the "open" sign. By waiting for Washoe to place her hands on the door and then lift them, the Gardners were able to shape a good approximation of the "open" sign. Later it became apparent that Washoe could learn signs if her hands were formed into the proper position for a sign and then guided through the desired movement. This was a much faster procedure than waiting for a spontaneous approximation to occur at the proper moment.

Washoe was clearly able to generalize a sign from one situation to another. For example, she first learned the sign for "more" in connection with "more tickling," an activity of which she was extremely fond. The sign for "more" soon generalized to other situations such as the desire for second helpings of a food she liked (more dessert, more milk, more grapefruit juice) and then to the request that activities be continued (more swing, more write). When shown pictures in a book of objects she knew and asked "What's this?" Washoe proved able to give the appropriate sign. But she had not progressed to the stage where she herself asked the questions. Most human two year olds show a keen interest in having objects identified, and are continually asking, "What's that?" Washoe at the age of four did not show this type of behavior.

Washoe combined a number of signs in sequences that seem similar to the two- and three-word sentences of a two-year-old child. Examples are sign sequences that translated into English would mean *Hurry gimme toothbrush, Listen dog* (at the sound of barking), *You drink, Roger Washoe tickle,* and *Come hug-love sorry sorry* (as appeasement for some wrongdoing). However, at the time of this report Washoe did not use these signs in a consistent order. She was just as apt to sign *Drink you* as *You drink.* In other words, she did not make use of syntax. Two-year-old children, on the other hand, use the proper noun-verb order fairly consistently. But it should be pointed out that word order is less strict in sign language than in English. The possibility still remains that Washoe may develop some syntactic capacity at a later age (Brown, 1970).

Even though we may not feel safe in considering Washoe's present signing skill to be language, her ability exceeds any previously reported efforts to establish a two-way communication system between an animal and a human. And it seems likely that enough has been learned from this first project about the most effective training procedures that future efforts may be even more successful. For example, a chimpanzee raised by deaf mutes might progress more rapidly; Washoe's companions were facile in sign language, but it was not their primary language.

TABLE 11-2   GESTURE-LANGUAGE SIGNS USED BY A CHIMPANZEE

MEANING OF SIGN	DESCRIPTION	CONTEXT
Come-gimme	Beckoning motion, with wrist or knuckles as pivot.	Sign made to persons or animals, also for objects out of reach. Often combined: "come tickle," "gimme sweet," etc.
More	Fingertips are brought together, usually overhead. (Correct ASL form: tips of the tapered hand touch repeatedly.)	When asking for continuation or repetition of activities such as swinging or tickling, for second helpings of food, etc. Also used to ask for repetition of some performance, such as a somersault.
Sweet	Index or index and second fingers touch tip of wagging tongue. (Correct ASL form: extended index and second fingers touch lower lip or tongue.)	For dessert; used spontaneously at end of meal. Also, when asking for candy.
Open	Flat hands are placed side by side, palms down, then drawn apart while rotated to palms up.	At door of house, room, car, refrigerator, or cupboard; with containers such as jars; and with faucets.
Hurry	Open hand is shaken at the wrist. (Correct ASL form: index and second fingers extended side by side as hand is shaken, but open hand is acceptable.)	Often follows signs such as "come-gimme," "out," "open," and "go," particularly if there is a delay before Washoe is obeyed. Also, used while watching her meal being prepared.
Hear-listen	Index finger touches ear.	For loud or strange sounds: bells, car horns, sonic booms, etc. Also, for asking someone to hold a watch to her ear.
Hurt	Extended index fingers are jabbed toward each other. Can be used to indicate location of pain.	To indicate cuts and bruises on herself or on others. Can be elicited by red stains on a person's skin or by tears in clothing.
Sorry	Fisted hand clasps and unclasps at shoulder. (Correct ASL form: fisted hand is rubbed over heart with circular motion.)	After biting someone, or when someone has been hurt in another way (not necessarily by Washoe). When told to apologize for mischief.
Flower	Tip of index finger touches one or both nostrils. (Correct ASL form: tips of tapered hand touch first one nostril, then the other.)	For flowers.
Dog	Repeated slapping on thigh.	For dogs and for barking.
Smell	Palm is held before nose and moved slightly upward several times.	For scented objects: tobacco, perfume, sage, etc.
Cat	Thumb and index finger grasp cheek hair near side of mouth and are drawn outward (representing cat's whiskers).	For cats.

Source: Gardner and Gardner (1969).

These are only a few of the signs used by Washoe, a female chimpanzee, at four years of age. ASL stands for American Sign Language.

Language in children's thinking

There is a close correspondence between the child's ability to use language and his ability to deal with concepts and relationships. This correspondence is illustrated by an experiment (Kuenne, 1946) in which preschool children were taught to select the smaller of a pair of squares, each mounted on the lid of a box. If the child chose the smaller square, he found the box open and an attractive toy inside. If he mistakenly chose the larger square, he found the box locked. The child began by learning to choose a 6-inch square in preference to an 8-inch one. When he had learned to choose the 6-inch square regularly, he was ready for the crucial tests with smaller squares.

He was now confronted with two test pairs, all pairs being smaller than the original ones. Of these smaller pairs, one (known as the "near pair") was close to the original squares in size (4.5 inches and 6 inches), the other (known as the "remote pair") was much smaller (1.4 and 1.9 inches). If the child had learned to "transpose," that is, to choose the smaller square regardless of absolute size, he should succeed in choosing the smaller square for both the near and the remote pairs. The results are plotted in Figure 11-7. Although all children did well on the near pair, they showed a striking increase in success with age on the remote pair.

The reason that the older children did better with the remote pair was quite clearly related to their use of language. If a child could say the equivalent of "The smaller one is always right," he could succeed with the remote pair. Of the children who failed to express in words the principle of correct choice during initial learning, none transposed the correct response on the test with the remote pair; of the children who stated the correct solution in words, either spontaneously or upon questioning, 73 percent successfully transposed what they had learned.

Of course, the older children were more developed as problem-solvers, regardless of whether they relied upon language; the younger children were able to use language to some extent, but not well enough to serve as a tool for thinking in the transposition. We can recognize that language and thought are related, without making the assumption that they are identical. Studies comparing the performances of deaf-mute and hearing children indicate that although language may facilitate the thought processes necessary for solving problems of relationships and concept formation, it is by no means essential for the development of such cognitive abilities (Robertson and Youniss, 1969).

Fig. 11-7 **Language and the perception of relationships** The older children, who were better able to state a test relationship in the form "The smaller one is always right," were able to transpose what they had learned from one pair to another remote pair, while the younger children could transpose the correct response only to pairs close in size to those used in training. (After Kuenne, 1946)

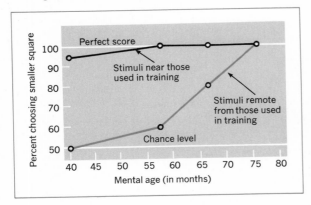

Linguistic-relativity hypothesis

Most of us assume that reality, as we know it, exists independently of the ways in which we talk about it. We believe, for example, that any idea expressed in one language can be translated into another language. This statement seems so obvious that to question it is rather startling. But a student of American Indian languages (Whorf, 1956) found such direct translation often impossible: one of the languages he studied makes no clear distinction between nouns and verbs; another blurs the distinctions of past, present, and future; a third uses the same name for the colors gray and brown.

These differences led Whorf to two conclusions:

1. The world is conceived very differently by those whose languages are of completely unlike structure.

2. The structure of the language is a cause of these different ways of conceiving the world.

Whorf's thesis (known as the *linguistic-relativity hypothesis* because it proposes that thought is relative to the language in which it is conducted) has been the subject of active debate among psychologists. Most of them accept a correspondence between the language and the ways of conceiving the world, but they tend to turn things around and try to show that the experiences significant to the people affect the way things are expressed in language. Thus Eskimos have different words for different kinds of snow that we would scarcely be able to tell apart, and the Hanunóo of the Philippine Islands have names for ninety-two varieties of rice. For us, the important part of Whorf's conjecture is that there is a close correspondence between language and thinking.

Experimenters interested in his theory have tested it in a study of two groups of Navajo children. Both groups lived on a reservation, but one spoke only English and the other only Navajo. A special characteristic of the Navajo language is that certain verbs of handling—the Navajo equivalents of *to pick up, to drop, to hold in the hand,* and so on—require special forms depending upon the nature of the object being handled. There are eleven different forms, one for round spherical objects, one for round thin objects, one for long flexible objects, and so forth. Even the very young Navajo-speaking children knew and used these forms correctly. These children were compared to English-speaking Navajos of the same age, with respect to how often they used shape, form, or material as a basis for sorting objects, rather than color. The objects given them were those that are usually sorted by young children on the basis of color. The Navajo-speaking children tended to sort on the basis of form at significantly younger ages than the English-speaking children. The fact that the Navajo language required attention to shapes, forms, and materials of objects presumably made the Navajo-speaking child pay more attention to this aspect of his environment (Carroll, 1964).[1]

Information-processing models of thinking

Man achieves his most complex use of language and concepts when he is engaged in the task of solving a problem. Whether the problem is as simple as multiplying nine times eighty-two or as difficult as proving a theorem in mathematics, the thought processes are not easy to analyze. None of the traditional theories that attempt to explain thinking in terms of associations or stimulus-response connections have proved adequate to the task. We saw that language acquisition involves more than associating strings of words. So too, there is more to solving a problem than simply following a chain of stimuli and responses from some initial cue to an eventual solution. When faced with a problem we often sort through and reorganize a great deal of information according to various rules and procedures in order to arrive at a solution; the information processed may have been stored in memory or may have been immediately available in the environment. The nature of this problem-solving activity has many similarities to the way information is processed by a high-speed computer. These similarities have led to some interesting efforts to formulate models of human thinking based on the methods and procedures developed for programing and organizing computer systems.

Today computers are able to handle easily many tasks previously performed only by human beings. We are all familiar with these developments.

[1]For a critical review of this study and a more extensive discussion of the linguistic-relativity hypothesis, see Miller and McNeill (1969).

Computers balance bank accounts, figure payrolls, prepare tax returns, control manufacturing plants, translate foreign-language material, play reasonably good games of chess, and so forth. In fact, many of the tasks that twenty years ago we would have all agreed required thinking can now be done by computers. Does this mean that computers can indeed "think"? An immediate answer in the negative—that they can do only what they have been programed to do—is too glib. Perhaps a human thinker can do only what he has been programed to do also, either by inheritance or training. It is clear that a wide continuum of intellectual behavior describes human organisms; it is an open question just how far out on this continuum we can push the computer.

Computer programs and flow charts

Before examining the role of computers as a tool for studying cognitive processes, it will be useful to describe briefly the basic features of a computer program. The computer cannot figure out how to solve a problem by itself; it is helpless until it has been given a detailed set of instructions. These instructions make up what is called the *computer program*. To write a program it is first necessary to analyze the problem to be solved and to break it down into its component parts. One of the best ways to do this is to construct a *flow chart*, which is like the diagram of a football play that a coach might draw on a blackboard. It shows component parts of the problem just as the coach's diagram indicates each player's assignment. The flow chart also shows how the various parts are to be fitted together. Once the problem has been mapped out in a flow chart, each part of the chart must be broken down into detailed instructions telling the computer how to handle each operation. One part of a flow chart might require a hundred or more individual steps in the program.

The flow chart illustrated in Figure 11-8 deals with a very simple information-processing problem, but it illustrates the main points. The problem depicted in the flow chart is to find the distribution of word lengths for a passage of English text. The input to the program is the text material, which

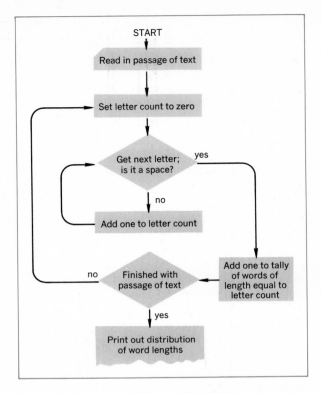

Fig. **11-8 Flow chart** This chart illustrates a program for tallying distribution of word lengths. The output of this program is the count of the number of words in the text that have a length of one letter, a length of two letters, three letters, and so on. (After Green, 1963)

has been punched on cards with numerical codes for the letters and space with all other punctuation ignored. The boxes in the flow chart represent work to be done, and the diamonds, decisions to be made. This flow chart by itself is not very impressive, but when many of them are cascaded one onto another into a hierarchy of operations the computer can indeed perform in a truly intelligent fashion.[2]

The flow chart of a computer program is a convenient way of picturing the flow of information through a system. The human organism can be

[2] For an example of a more elaborate flow chart, see Figure 10-4 (p. 252), which describes the sequence of instructions and decisions involved in teaching a college-level course under computer control.

conceptualized as an information-processing system, and it is quite natural sometimes to use flow charts as models of psychological processes. Models based on flow charts have come to be called information-processing models.[3] Many psychologists feel that information-processing models are well suited for theorizing about psychological phenomena, particularly about complex cognitive processes.

Simulation models

When information-processing systems are used to mirror the cognitive activity of human beings, they are called *simulation models*. The first significant attempt to simulate complex cognitive processes was made by Newell and Simon (1956), who developed an information-processing model to prove theorems in symbolic logic. Their program, which was dubbed the *Logic Theorist,* did not try to prove theorems by a brute-force technique of searching through all possible sequences of logical operations until one was found that yielded a proof. Rather, the approach taken in the Logic Theorist was to incorporate *heuristic* methods of the type used by human beings for proving theorems. A *heuristic* is a strategy, trick, simplification, gimmick, or any other procedure that drastically limits the search for solution in difficult problems. Heuristics do not guarantee that a solution will be found, but when they do work, they greatly reduce the search time required to obtain a solution. Human thinking obviously makes use of heuristic procedures. A good chess player solves his problem heuristically; he could not possibly see the consequences of every possible move (see Figure 11-9). In solving a geometrical problem we often add a line here or there, hoping that by forming a new diagram we may perceive relations that were previously not evident. This new construction may help, but there are no guarantees implied.

The use of heuristic procedures by human subjects is not well understood, but there can be little doubt that they play an important role in most

[3]Information-processing models for memory were discussed in Chapter 9, p. 240.

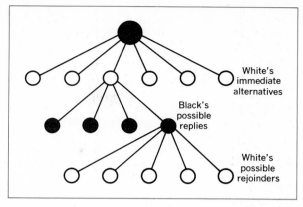

Fig. 11-9 Exhaustive vs. heuristic search One method of problem-solving in chess and related games is to enumerate exhaustively all possible sequences of moves, and then select one that is guaranteed to lead to a win. Part of the "tree of possibilities" for a chess game is illustrated in this figure: the complete tree would follow each branch out to a conclusion, and the end of each branch would be labeled win for white, win for black, or draw. The white player would then inspect the complete tree and select a move that would lead eventually to checkmate of black's king no matter how black played. In principle, this enumerative approach to chess could be programed on a computer and would make the computer an unbeatable opponent. In actual practice, however, such an approach is not feasible, for it has been estimated that there are 10^{120} (give or take a few trillion) different paths through a complete chess tree. If this procedure of exhaustive search were employed it is unlikely that a single game could be completed within a lifetime, even if the enumeration were carried out at the speed of the fastest computer now in existence. Instead, to develop a chess-playing computer that simulates human players we must program it to behave intelligently—to make use of such heuristics as "try to control the center of the board," "protect your king." It must search the problem tree in a selective fashion, exploring paths of the tree that look promising and ignoring those that do not. (After Feigenbaum and Feldman, 1963)

problem-solving tasks. Several examples of heuristics particularly relevant to human thinking are worth describing. One of these is the heuristic of "working backwards": we begin with the result to be proved and then attempt to work backwards step by step to that which is initially given. Another is the "make-a-plan" heuristic: we think of another problem that is similar to the one we are trying to solve but to which the solution is already known; this method of solution is then used as a plan for solving the more difficult problem. A third heuristic is the "means-end" procedure: here we compare

The ability to simulate complex cognitive processes is a major accomplishment in itself. But what is more significant is that information-processing models developed for quite different problems (for example, a model to prove theorems in geometry versus a model to describe neurotic behavior) turn out to have many component processes in common. This commonality of processes among models suggests that a general theory of complex cognitive processes may not be too far away. Simon and Newell (1964) were the first to isolate some of the components common to many information-processing models and pull them together into a single model, which they dubbed the General Problem-Solver (GPS). They propose that we should be able to combine the special information of any particular task (chess playing, theorem proving, music composition) with GPS and come up with a composite program that can solve the task, using strategies and tactics of the type employed by human beings.

The GPS simulates in a formal manner what the individual does when he attacks a problem. The programs that have to be written to instruct a computer to carry out the essential steps are very complex and can be characterized here only in the barest outline. The actual program for GPS is built around two basic processes that follow each other

the current state of affairs with that which we wish to obtain, find a difference between the two states, seek an operation that will reduce the difference, and repeat the operation until we obtain the desired effect.

The Logic Theorist, with its various heuristic methods, is an extremely impressive computer model of human thinking. For example, it has been used to derive the fifty-two theorems in the second chapter of Whitehead and Russell's famous treatise, *Principia mathematica* (1925); whenever a theorem was proved, it was stored in memory and was available, together with the original axioms, for use in proving subsequent theorems. The Logic Theorist succeeded in giving adequate proofs for thirty-eight of the theorems, and some of the proofs were more elegant than those originally offered by Whitehead and Russell. Of course, the Logic Theorist was not programed to provide more rapid or "better" proofs than a human subject, but rather to simulate human behavior in an actual problem-solving task. When a computer can be programed to perform such a task and behaves in a way that is very much like a human being, then indeed progress is being made in understanding thought processes.

Since the development of the Logic Theorist many investigators have formulated simulation models for an array of complex behavioral processes. There are models for concept formation

(Gregg and Simon, 1967; Hunt, Marin, and Stone, 1966), for attitude change (Abelson, 1964), for verbal learning (Feigenbaum, 1970), for music composition (Reitman, 1965), for chess playing (Simon and Barenfeld, 1969), and even for neurotic personality processes (Colby and Enea, 1967)—to name a few. These exciting developments are of great importance in unraveling the problems of human thinking. But the development of these models is clearly a two-way street, for one has to know something about how creative problem-solving goes on in order to program it on a computer. Because the computer will do only what it is instructed to do, the steps have to be clearly and completely specified in the computer program. If the psychologist who charts the computer program has made any errors in his interpretation of the steps involved in problem-solving, the program will not succeed or at least will not display outputs that accurately simulate the behavior of human subjects. The computer serves to check the adequacy of the theoretical notions that the psychologist believes will account for the psychological process under study. The chief advantage that the computer has over a human theorist is its perfect memory and its attention to all details of what it is programed to do.

The development of information-processing models for psychological phenomena is still in an early stage, but the results have been encouraging.

in repeated cycles until the problem is solved, or until it is abandoned as too difficult or insoluble. The first process, part of what is called the *problem-solving organization,* is to set subgoals that might be appropriate to the solution of the problem. These subgoals are then evaluated and the one that looks promising is selected for exploration. Note that this is a kind of "executive," or "decision-making," function, including both a search and an evaluation phase. A subgoal, for example, might be the solution of a simplified version of the more general problem. Once the executive routine selects a subgoal, the process known as the *means-end analysis* applies relevant heuristics to reach the subgoal. This requires that the information-processing mechanism begin with data that are given and follow permissible transformations as in ordinary problem-solving. Because the heuristic approach does not guarantee a solution, if the initially selected approach does not succeed, the executive routine then searches for other subgoals that appear more productive.

The approach to complex cognitive processes exemplified by GPS is quite promising. If it turns out that information-processing models based on only a few basic methods of symbolic representation and a small number of elementary information processes can simulate complex human behavior, then we have truly advanced our understanding.

There is now substantial evidence that we can explain much of human thinking in terms of a few basic processes, arranged and ordered into an appropriate hierarchy yielding outputs that appear incredibly complex. The evidence suggests that the human information-processing system is primarily serial in its operation: it can process only a few symbols at a time, and the symbols being processed must be held in a limited short-term memory (see p. 238) the content of which can be rapidly reordered and changed. The major limitations on the subject's capacities to employ efficient strategies arise from the very small capacity of the short-term memory and from the relatively long time needed to transfer information from short-term to long-term memory. What is not well understood and will require much research is the way the human system generates internal symbols from stimulus inputs, and the nature of these symbols (Simon, 1969).

Summary

1. Thinking is behavior that uses *symbols* as "representations" of objects and events. It thus can go beyond perceptual solution of problems, or solution through manipulation, by having reference to events not present—to remembered, absent, or imagined things.

2. A symbol *stands for* something else. Some symbols are concrete objects, such as a stop sign; because *words* are especially powerful symbols, language is an important agent in the thinking process. A symbol conveys *meaning;* but the precise relation between the symbol and the object it stands for (that is, its meaning) is a subject on which psychologists are not agreed.

3. A useful distinction can be made between *denotative* meanings, which are fixed and specific, and *connotative* meanings, which express evaluation or preference. One attempt to measure connotations is by means of the *semantic differential.*

4. When a symbol stands for a class of objects or events with common properties, we say that it refers to a *concept.* Studies of *concept formation* show that object concepts are usually attained more easily than abstract concepts, such as numbers.

5. Language provides a major source of symbols used in thinking. The structure of language can be analyzed at several levels: *phonemes* are the basic units of sound; *morphemes* are the basic units of meaning; and *phrases* are the units from which sentences are constructed. Analysis in terms of *phrase structure* helps us to understand the meaning of a simple declarative sentence, but more complex sentences have usually undergone one or more *transformations* in their relationship to the *deep structure*, or underlying meaning of the sentence.

6. Both classical and operant conditioning appear to play a role in the acquisition of word meaning. However, grammatical learning does not involve simple stimulus-response associations; rather it requires the acquisition of *rules* for generating acceptable word sequences. The first such rule employed by the child specifies the use of *pivot* and *open* words in combination. Further grammatical development is aided by the adult's expansion of the child's utterances; imitation of parental speech is not exact but is filtered through the child's own grammatical system. Language acquisition is the opposite of concept formation in that general rules are learned first and then the specific exceptions to them.

7. Language and thought are intimately related. Thus children are able to solve some kinds of transposition problems only when they are old enough to state the solution in words. Even man's way of conceiving the world is reflected in the language forms he uses.

8. Information-processing models of thinking utilize *flow charts* that comprise the program (set of instructions) delivered to an electronic computer to *simulate* the processes of human problem-solving. *Heuristic* methods (such as the means-end analysis) are valuable aids in reducing the search time required to solve a problem. The *General Problem-Solver* incorporates heuristic methods common to a number of information-processing models in an attempt to devise a general theory of complex cognitive processes.

Suggestions for further reading

Concept formation is dealt with in Bourne, *Human concept behavior* (1966); in Hunt, *Concept learning: An information processing problem* (1962); in Klausmeier and Harris (eds.), *Analysis of concept learning* (1966); and in Trabasso and Bower, *Attention in learning* (1968).

A very readable introduction to the psychology of language is provided by Deese, *Psycholinguistics* (1970). An excellent survey of the developmental aspects of language may be found in McNeill, *The acquisition of language: The study of developmental psycholinguistics* (1970). Useful references on theory and research are Jakobovits and Miron (eds.), *Readings in the psychology of language* (1967), Dixon and Horton (eds.), *Verbal behavior and general behavior theory* (1968), and Smith and Miller (eds.), *The genesis of language: A psycholinguistic approach* (1966). The transformational theory of grammar is expounded in Chomsky, *Language and mind* (1968).

Information-processing models of thinking are discussed in Feigenbaum and Feldman (eds.), *Computers and thought* (1963); in Newell and Simon, *Human problem solving* (1971); and in Simon, *The science of the artificial* (1969). Also see Voss (ed.), *Approaches to thought* (1969), for a varied and interesting set of papers on thinking. *Digital computers in research* (1963) by Green and *Real-time computers: Technique and applications in the psychological sciences* (1968) by Uttal present various uses of computers in psychological research.

physiological background of motivation

ALTHOUGH ORGANISMS ARE OCCASIONALLY quiescent, as in sleep or hibernation, it is much more characteristic of them to be active. In order to understand the active organism—why it does what it does when it does it—we search for motives, for springs of action. By a *motive* we mean something that incites the organism to action or that sustains and gives direction to action once the organism has been aroused. A dog buries a bone, a child practices on the piano, a task force sends a man to the moon. When we ask why these actions take place, we are inquiring about motives.

Motivated behavior has two main aspects: the *activating,* or *energizing,* aspect and the *directional* aspect. By activation we mean the change that

occurs between sleeping and waking, between being relaxed and being tense, between "taking it easy" and putting forth effort. Motivational activation produces a state of readiness for behavior, as in the horse's change from standing quietly in the stall to his champing at the bit when ready for the race. The same act engaged in by an activated organism will be done more vigorously than by an unaroused one. In addition to producing a state of readiness for behavior, an activated motive also tends to set off behavior in a particular direction. The hungry animal is ready to run to food and to eat, the thirsty one to drink, the one in pain to escape the painful stimulus.

Is *all* behavior motivated? The answer is not easy, for even such reflex behaviors as the heartbeat and digestion serve purposes in the life of the organism and are responsive to various kinds of motivational activation. Simple reflex behavior is not usually thought of as motivated, although there is no easy rule by which it is excluded, but all more complex behavior, especially all learned behavior, is clearly responsive to motivational activation and control.

The most dramatic human motives are revealed in daring and heroic action: when determined explorers penetrate new lands and outer space, when one person sacrifices his life to save another, when someone withstands the pains of torture rather than renounce an ideal. If we began our psychological study of motivation by trying to account for such noble human motives, we would soon find our tools inadequate to the task. So we start much more modestly by studying need-satisfying behavior, as represented by the familiar motives of hunger and thirst. Man never outgrows these basic biological needs, for he must have food and water to survive. When we understand these simpler, more elemental motives, we may hope eventually to understand more about the bolder, more complex motives that characterize man at his best; there may, indeed, be some important bridges between them.

In this chapter we shall primarily consider motives for which the bodily needs are obvious, which are commonly called *organic* or *physiological* motives. Much of the behavior of the newborn baby can be explained on a physiological basis. He is primarily occupied with satisfaction of the needs for food, water, sleep, excretion of wastes, and avoidance of pain and discomfort. These are all motives that man shares with the lower animals; we shall be concerned here primarily with this common biological inheritance.

In the next chapter we shall examine human motivation more directly, not on the assumption that there is any sharp break between motives with a physiological basis and other human motives, but because man is a social animal capable of planning and foresight, and therefore has motivational controls that are distinctively his own.

Physiological needs as determiners of behavior

A great many words describe motivation: needs, urges, impulses, desires, goals. They all refer in some way to the forces that energize behavior and give it direction. Although the vocabulary of the psychology of motivation has not yet been firmly established, it is convenient to distinguish between *needs* and *drives*.

Needs and drives

If a rat that has been deprived of food for several hours is placed in a checkerboard maze, such as the one illustrated in Figure 12-1, it will be active. We may keep track of its movements and find how many squares it covers. A well-fed rat placed in the same maze may move about a little, but it will cover less ground than the hungry rat. We may say that a food-deprived rat is an *active* rat. If the same rat is placed in a maze consisting of several alleys, one of which leads to food, it will run about until it happens to reach the food. Then it will eat. We may say now that a food-deprived rat is also a *hungry* rat. After eating, the rat is no longer restless. If returned to its cage, it is likely to curl up and go to sleep. When the rat is hungry again, its activity cycle will begin again.

How shall we talk scientifically about the behavior of the rat just described? We refer to the food-deprived state as a state of *need*. The organism needs food, and when the rat has not eaten for a while, chemical changes in its blood indicate its need. The need for food is physiological, not psychological, but a state of physiological need has psychological consequences. We call the psychological consequences of a need a *drive*. Thus the food-need in the rat leads, through processes that we shall investigate, to the hunger drive.

While need and drive are parallel, they are not

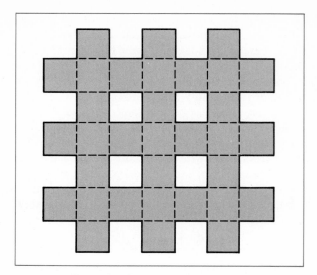

Fig. **12-1 Checkerboard maze** Differences in amount of exploratory behavior of hungry and well-fed rats can be recorded by counting the number of squares entered. Even though no food is present, the hungry animals are more active than the well-fed ones. (After Dashiell, 1925)

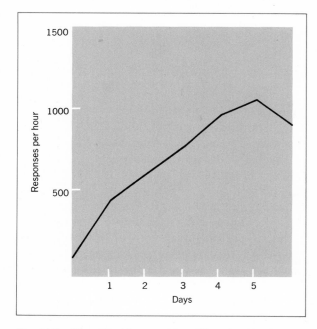

Fig. **12-2 Strength of hunger drive** When food is withheld, the rate of responding to the bar that previously delivered food increases each day, up to a maximum on the fifth day, indicating a progressive increase in drive as the need for food increases. Later, as the rat becomes weakened by starvation, the rate of response falls off. (After Heron and Skinner, 1937)

the same. Drive does not necessarily get stronger as need gets stronger. A starved organism may be so weakened by its great need that drive is weakened (Figure 12-2). Men who have fasted for a long time report that their hunger pangs (a subjective representation of hunger drive) come and go, but, of course, their need for food persists.

Typical deprivation drives based on physiological needs are hunger, thirst, and the drive to avoid suffocation. Other physiological drives (sex, maternal activity, pain avoidance) are somewhat differently related to deprivation. However, each of the needs, as it becomes sufficiently intense owing to deprivation, leads to a corresponding drive.

Measuring drives

A good deal of ingenuity has been used in finding ways to measure drives, since psychologists often want to know the "drive level" in order to relate it to other behavior, such as learning. We may consider four such methods: measures of general activity level, the rate of performing learned acts, the obstruction method, and the choice method.

1. Measures of general activity level. On the assumption that heightened drive leads to restlessness, restless behavior should increase as drive increases. Thus the speed of running in an activity cage (Figure 12-3) can be directly related to the number of hours of food deprivation. Another form of activity measurement is provided by suspending the animal's cage on springs with markers, so that the amount of restless activity is recorded.

These measures, while useful, have to be handled with some sophistication. For example, the cage activity of unfed rats is not greater than that of well-fed rats *unless* some external stimulation such as a disturbing noise occurs, in which case the differences become marked (Campbell and Sheffield, 1953). In measuring drive level we are really more concerned with the *internal conditions* of arousal, but under appropriate circumstances the overt activity serves as a useful indicator of drive.

Lafayette Instrument Co.

Fig. **12-3** **Activity measurement** The distance that the rat runs in the activity cage is recorded by a revolving drum. The longer the rat is without food, the more it runs.

2. Rate of performing learned acts. If a rat has learned to press a bar in order to receive food pellets but the pellets come only occasionally, the rat will press the bar more rapidly when hungry. Thus the rate of bar-pressing may be used as a measure of drive. Alternate drive measures are the delay of starting a run down an alley to a food box (latency of response) or the running speed itself. Care must be taken not to depend upon one measure only; for example, it may be found that rate of bar-pressing and amount of water ingested are not equivalent measures of the thirst drive (Miller, 1961).

3. Overcoming an obstruction. Drive strength may be assessed by observing how much punishment the organism will take in order to satisfy the drive. One method of measuring this behavior utilizes an *obstruction box* that has a grid floor through which the animal may receive a shock. The aroused animal is placed at the starting point in the box and allowed to run across the uncharged grid to a chamber in which the goal-object (food, water) is placed. On succeeding trials the shock is turned on and a record is kept of the number of crossings that the animal will make in a given twenty-minute period.

4. The choice method. Occasionally more than one drive is active at a time. In the case of two simultaneously aroused drives, the relative strengths of the drives may be determined by permitting the animal to choose one goal-object if he turns in one direction, another goal-object if he turns in the other direction.

Of the four methods, those most used today are the first two, in one or another variation. The first method relies on the general restlessness associated with heightened drive; the second depends upon the intensification of a well-learned behavior under the pressure of an appropriate drive.

Hunger drive

Studies of hunger permit us to understand some of the components of motivation. The need for food arises from the depletion of food substances in the blood. This condition leads to restless activity in animals and, in man, to the awareness of a craving for food. The need to replenish depleted food substances causes an increase in stomach contractions. These stomach contractions produce internal stimuli that are part of the aroused state: they make the organism active and are the source of hunger pangs.

A person who has gone without food for some hours does not feel hungry all the time. The aching or gnawing feelings described as hunger pangs occur irregularly. In experiments designed to discover the basis for these pangs, the food-deprived subject swallowed a rubber balloon, which was then inflated until it was firm against the walls of the stomach. A small tube from the balloon was connected to a recording instrument, so that a pointer moved whenever the walls of the stomach contracted (see Figure 12-4). The subject, who could not see the pointer, was given a telegraph

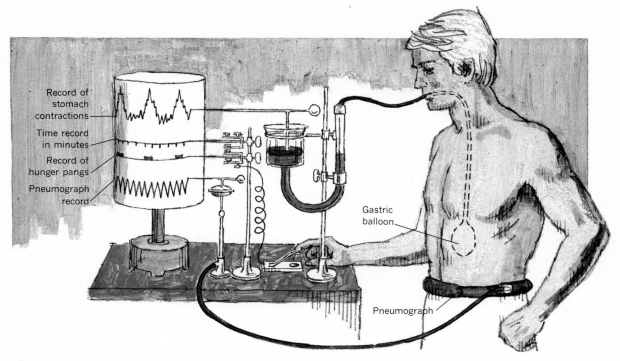

Record of
stomach
contractions

Time record
in minutes

Record of
hunger pangs

Pneumograph
record

Gastric
balloon

Pneumograph

Fig. **12-4 Hunger pangs and stomach contractions** The reported hunger pangs correspond closely
to the periods when stomach contractions are at their maximum. These observations led, however,
to an incomplete explanation of hunger. (The pneumograph provides a record of breathing, but is
incidental to the main purpose of measuring stomach movements.) (After Cannon, 1934)

key to press whenever he felt the pangs of hunger.
It was found that his pressing of the key was
almost simultaneous with the contractions of his
stomach (Cannon, 1934). It would seem from this
experiment that the hunger drive may be identified
with stimuli from the contracting stomach.

The explanation is not so simple, however, for
hunger can occur in the absence of stomach contractions. For example, a man whose stomach had
been removed surgically and whose esophagus was
then connected directly to his intestine reported
periodic desires for food much the same as those
of persons with stomachs (Hoelzel, 1927). And rats
whose stomachs were removed for experimental
purposes showed hunger behavior like that of normal rats, except that they tended to show it more
frequently. The more frequent hunger undoubtedly was due to the reduced food-storage capacity
(Tsang, 1938).

As we have said, hunger stirs a rat to activity.
If we assume that its hunger is caused by stomach
contractions, we must also assume that its activity
is the result of sensory messages from the stomach
to the brain; however, when the sensory nerves
from the stomach to the brain are cut, a rat still
exhibits hunger behavior (Morgan and Morgan,
1940).

There is now evidence that indicates that the
chemical state of the body influences the hunger
drive in ways other than by stomach contractions.
The complexity of hunger is further indicated by
the presence not only of a general hunger drive
but of specific hungers, that is, drives toward specific food incentives. The interpretation of the sensation of hunger as depending upon *local* sources
of stimulation (stomach contractions) has now
given way, under new evidence, to its interpretation according to *central* sources, that is, to

brain processes, chiefly in the hypothalamus, stimulated by chemicals in the blood.

Specific hungers. A child who is not hungry for spinach may still be hungry for ice cream. Foods differ in their attractiveness to different people. Differences in food preferences are sometimes owing to cultivated tastes. They may, however, arise from specific bodily needs. A diet that is deficient in some essentials causes special drives. Experiments with animals have shown that such specific drives are satisfied only by the foods appropriate to them.

Rats on a fat-free diet, when offered a choice among fat, sugar, and wheat, exhibit a marked preference for fat. Similarly, rats deprived of either sugar or wheat will prefer the food of which they have been deprived. Other experiments have shown that rats have specific hungers for sugar, fat, protein, thiamine, riboflavin, salt, phosphorus, sodium, and calcium (see Figure 12-5).

Still other experiments have shown that barnyard animals (pigs, dairy cows, chickens) as well as laboratory animals will commonly select a well-balanced diet if given a wide range of foods from which to choose. The results of these experiments indicate that animals demand in their food something more than the requisite number of calories; they hunger for the necessary chemical constituents of a balanced diet. It is not clear how specific hungers are regulated, but it is assumed that the needed foods taste better to the animal or child choosing from a variety of foods. The influence of taste on choosing is indicated by the fact that rats with their taste nerves cut failed to select a balanced diet (Richter, 1943).

A later set of experiments provides a related but somewhat different interpretation. Rats fed a diet deficient in thiamine (or in calcium or magnesium) appear to develop an *aversion* to the deficient diet and avidly accept a novel diet, even though it is also deficient. Later the new diet, if deficient, becomes aversive. Once a satisfactory diet has been accepted, the old diet remains aversive, even though it has been supplemented with the missing element (Rozin, 1967). Thus the acceptance of a diet is guided not so much by detection of a needed food component as by rejection of a generally deficient diet. This is not, however, the whole story; in the case of sodium, which is more readily detected by taste (as in common salt), sodium-deficient rats appear to have a specific unlearned preference for a sodium-rich diet (Rodgers, 1967).

Whatever may be the origin of appetite and food

Fig. **12-5 Self-selection of diet** This apparatus is used in studies in which rats are allowed to select their own diet from 15 to 18 different substances. Under these conditions, rats select a healthful, nutritious diet.

Dr. Curt Richter

preference, it is evident from ordinary observation that the preferences can be distorted by learning. The deficiency disease beriberi is found among peoples whose diet consists largely of polished rice, which some people have learned to prefer. The disease does not occur if whole-grain rice is substituted for polished rice. Animal experiments have also shown that preference can be established for poor diets, so that the animal may continue for some time to choose the poor food to which it has become accustomed, even though a more balanced food is accessible. We need neither carry "naturalness" too far nor be alarmed by the harmful results of learning. Dietitians can provide diets for both animals and human beings that are more nutritious than those naturally selected, and organisms can learn to like these as well as poorer diets.

Thirst drive

When the tissues of the mouth and throat are relatively dry, we are aware of being thirsty. This is the interpretation of thirst based on local stimulation. But the craving for water can be satisfied only in part through stimulating salivation by chewing gum, wetting the mouth, or anesthetizing the skin of mouth and throat. Just as stomach contractions provide only one component of the hunger drive, so dryness in the mouth and throat provides only one component of the thirst drive. Experiments with dogs confirm that water intake is regulated by the amount of water that the body needs, not merely by the dryness of the mouth.

In one of these experiments dogs whose normal daily intake of water had been computed were placed on a schedule limiting the amount of water they were given, so that the water deficit could be known and systematically varied. When later tested, the dogs showed an accurate "ability to estimate" the amount of water needed to make up the deficit; that is, they drank an amount of water equivalent to the amount of which they had been deprived (Adolph, 1939).

In another experiment, water equal to the deficit was placed directly in the dog's stomach either through a surgical opening or by means of a tube. Thus the water entered the stomach without affecting the dryness of the mouth and throat tissues.

If allowed to drink before the water had been assimilated into its system, the dog drank as much as it would have if no water had been artificially placed in its stomach. If, however, a fifteen-minute wait was introduced so that the water could be assimilated, the dog did not drink at all; its thirst had been relieved without any direct wetting of the mouth and throat tissues (Adolph, 1941).

How can we explain results such as these? There must be some regulator within the nervous system that acts to control the thirst drive much as a thermostat regulates the temperature of a room. Experimenters have located a region in or near the hypothalamus where such regulation may occur. The first experiments testing this theory used goats, but the results have since been confirmed with other animals. If a slight amount of salt solution is injected into the third ventricle (a fluid-filled cavity inside the brain, in the region of the hypothalamus), the goat drinks an excessive amount of water. Injection of pure water does not lead to such drinking (Andersson, 1953). The conclusion is that there must be some "brain center," sensitive to the body's need for liquid, that controls thirst. The speculation naturally arises that there may be such "centers" for other drives.

Sex as a drive

The male mammal can live out his life without sexual activity; he is not in pain because of being deprived of sex, and his health does not suffer. His sexual motivation is very much incentive-related rather than need-related: the odor of a female in heat or, in some animals, changes in coloring or size of the genital areas attract the male and lead to the remainder of the sexual cycle.

In many species there is no special cycle of sexual activity for the male, so that he is hormonally prepared for mating at any time, except, perhaps, when depleted by too much sexual activity. In some males there is a particular time for mating. In the Virginia deer, for example, there is a fall rutting season, and prior to this the male gonads grow in size.

The cycle of sexual receptivity in female animals, known as the *estrus cycle,* demonstrates the influence of sex hormones upon sex drive. The estrus

CRITICAL
DISCUSSION

**Local versus
central
determiners
of hunger
and thirst**

In the discussion of hunger and thirst drives, attention was called to both local and central sources for the activated drive. By "local sources" we mean, for hunger, sources near the stomach, as in stomach contractions, and, for thirst, sources near the mouth and throat, such as dryness of tissues. By "central sources" we mean portions of the brain that monitor chemical substances in the blood.

Rosenzweig (1962) has given an illuminating history, beginning with the ancient Greeks, of preferences for one or the other of these interpretations. Until quite recently the local theories have been the most widely accepted, despite a great deal of contradictory evidence that has been available for a century. The preference for the local theories illustrates a kind of "sociology of science" whereby one position is favored over another because of prevailing common-sense views, the testimony of authorities, and an occasional dramatic experiment, all of which overshadow equally good observations made on the other side.

The testimony of authorities from the time of Plato, Aristotle, and Galen, through that of Erasmus Darwin (Charles's grandfather), was on the side of local theories, and the first modern experimental work also favored this position. In the period from 1824 to 1833, William Beaumont, an army surgeon, studied a man who as a result of gunshot had a fistula in his stomach, so that the activity of his stomach could be observed. Beaumont reported that when he placed food directly through the aperture the motions of the stomach subsided and the hunger also ceased immediately. This was the beginning of the kinds of observations later made impressive by the experiments of Carlson and Cannon (see Figure 12-4). Thus it seemed well established that the stomach was the source of the sensations of hunger.

Actually this theory had been questioned for many years. Adults questioned by Schiff (1867) as to where they felt hunger failed to localize it in the stomach (only two of some thirty designating the stomach region at all). A number of experiments with animals were also critical of the local hypothesis, but it prevailed until more modern methods of brain study have now shown very clearly that a large portion of hunger and thirst behavior, as reflected in eating and drinking, is indeed controlled by the brain, particularly in the region of the hypothalamus.

cycle in the rat is between four and five days in length. Every fourth or fifth day of her life the mature female rat is in the receptive state known as *estrus,* or, as we say colloquially, she is *in heat.* The sexually aroused state in the female rat leads to tension and restless activity similar to that of the hunger and thirst drives. An illustration of the increase in the rate of a female rat's running in an activity cage during estrus is given in Figure 12-6. At the height of estrus the female rat is sexually receptive as well as physically active; when placed with a male rat, she actively seeks copulation by presenting herself appropriately.

Sexual receptivity and appropriate mating behavior can be made to appear (or reappear) in female rats through the injection of ovarian hormones. If young female rats receive injections of ovarian hormones, they develop mature mating patterns well in advance of the time when such

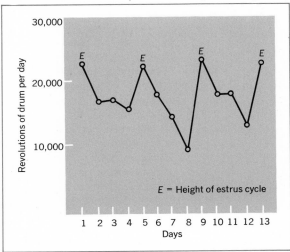

Fig. **12-6 Estrus cycle and activity**   Specimen record showing the effect of the estrus cycle in the female rat. Activity hits its maximum near the peak of estrus. (After Wang, 1923)

patterns would normally appear. Mature female rats whose sexual activity has ceased after removal of the ovaries will again engage in normal sexual behavior if treated with ovarian hormones. Mating patterns will appear whether the ovaries were removed before or after sexual maturity had been reached.

Immature male rats engage in incomplete sexual behavior while they are still incapable of complete copulation. In this they differ from young female rats, which do not indulge in sexual behavior until they are sexually mature. Castration does not completely abolish mating behavior in the male; this persistence of sexual behavior of the castrated adult male contrasts with the immediate cessation of sexual responsiveness in the female after loss of the ovaries (Beach, 1944).

These studies suffice to indicate the important role played by hormones in the sexual behavior of lower animals (although the conduct of the castrated adult male rat gives a hint of controls other than hormones). Among higher animals, including primates and man, hormonal control in sexual behavior is less important (Beach, 1956). The results of castration in the human male and ovarian removal in the female are variable. In a high proportion of women whose ovaries have been surgically removed, sexual desire and capacity are little changed. Castration of the male may result in gradual diminution of sexual interest, but

The complex behaviors of various animal species—the nest-building of birds, swarming of bees, migration of birds and fishes, mating rituals, caring for the young—have defied explanation on any simple drive-incentive basis. The word "instinct" was widely used in the past to refer to such unlearned, patterned, goal-directed behavior characteristic of a species. The word was often used in reference to human behavior as well—a mother's love illustrating a parental instinct, warfare an aggressive instinct, social behavior a gregarious or herd instinct.

The presence or absence of instincts in man was a source of intense controversy in the 1920s. The argument became part of a larger controversy over the relative contributions of heredity and environment to development. Those who believed in instincts attributed the major developmental influence to heredity. Those who did not believe in them won the victory because the believers failed to agree with one another on either the number or the kinds of instincts man possessed. Because of man's prolonged infancy and the great importance of learning in all that he does, the concept of instinct has not proved helpful in studying or understanding human behavior.

The problems raised by the study of instincts in animals other than man have taken on renewed interest under the influence of a group of European zoologists who call themselves "ethologists" (Tinbergen, 1961; Thorpe, 1963; Hinde, 1966; Lorenz, 1965). Their studies have called attention to study of organisms in their natural environments.

Imprinting, one of their concepts, is a kind of learning that capitalizes on an inherited tendency appearing when the time is ripe. The clearest example is given by the tendency of a young duckling to start following its mother shortly after it is hatched, and then to follow only this particular female duck. Incubator-hatched ducklings can be imprinted upon artificial models, both inanimate and human. For example, mallard ducklings exposed to a moving model for ten minutes between twelve and seventeen hours after hatching will continue to treat the model as though it were the "mother" and remain with it against the attraction of live mallard ducks (Figure 12-7). Once imprinting has occurred, the response of following will be elicited only by the imprinted object (Hess, 1959).

Another concept developed by the ethologists is that of a *releaser,* a particular environmental stimulus that sets off a kind of behavior characteristic of a species. Thus a spot on the mother's beak "releases" a pecking response in some young gulls, causing the mother to regurgitate the food that the infant will eat. The swollen abdomen of the female of a species of small fish (the three-spined stickleback) initiates courtship behavior by

sex drive and the capacity for sexual intercourse may persist undiminished in the human male for several decades.

Maternal drive

A mother rat is strongly motivated to care for her newborn offspring. She will return them to the nest if they are placed outside it. If she is separated from them, she will overcome barriers and suffer pain in order to reach them.

The physiological states that activate this maternal behavior are complex. The hormone *prolactin,* associated with milk secretion, is one influence; if it is injected into virgin female rats or even into males, they begin to build nests and take care of young rats as a mother does. Nest-building among rats appears to be regulated in part by temperature. The hormonal condition may reduce the body temperature, so that the mother rat builds a nest not so much because of the needs of her young as to make herself comfortable.

The human mother shares with the lower animals the bodily changes associated with pregnancy and lactation as well as some aspects of maternal drive. But her care of children differs from culture to culture and is largely regulated by learning. It is a general rule that human motives can never be fully explained on the basis of physiological influences alone.

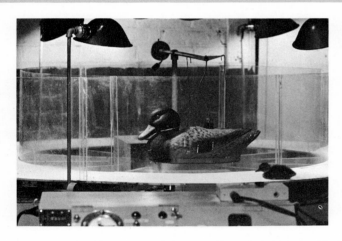

Fig. **12-7 Imprinting in ducklings** The newly hatched duckling learns to follow the model duck around a circular track, and later follows this model in preference to a live duck of its own species.

Dr. Eckhard H. Hess

the male. Owl-like figures initiate mobbing behavior—a kind of feigned attack—by some birds for which the owl is a natural enemy. The highly specific nature of some releasers shows how some motivated behavior is under control of the *environment* and not merely under the control of internal drives.

Because the concept of instinct has continued to lead to controversy, the ethologists have adopted instead the more neutral expression *species-specific behavior.* The difficulty with "instinct" is that it tends to be used as an explanation for what is found, when in fact it is a mere label for species-specific behavior. The homing instinct is given as the explanation for the return of the homing pigeon, but this tells us no more than that it came home. The label is not entirely inappropriate, because not all pigeons have this tendency, but the tendency for the label to become an explanation has led to the abandonment of the term "instinct" in most discussions of behavior of this kind. The *explanation* of "instinctive" behavior turns out to be very complex and depends upon breaking up the total instinctive behavior into its component parts. For example, there is now good evidence that both bees and birds use the sun in "navigation"; this partially explains the success of bees in foraging and of birds in their migrations, but it does not tell the whole story of other features of foraging and migrating (von Frisch, 1955; Matthews, 1968).

Pain as a drive

The drive to avoid pain arises from the organism's need to escape damage through tissue injury and is created by the discomfort and intolerability of the painful state. It illustrates the fact that physiological drives are aversive, that they are states from which the organism is led to escape. Just as the hunger drive leads to escape from hunger pangs and the thirst drive leads to escape from a parched throat, so the pain-avoidance drive leads to whatever behavioral sequence will reduce the organism's discomfort—running off a charged grid, taking off a shoe that pinches, placing an ice pack on a feverish brow, escaping to a safe place.

Pain differs from hunger and thirst in that it is not a result of deprivation, but is based on a perpetual state of readiness that is inactive until a painful (noxious) stimulus is encountered. Thus pain is *episodic,* while other drives tend to be *cyclical,* depending as they do upon the body's metabolism.

Other drives with physiological bases

Many other conditions serve as drives. We have a drive to avoid extremes of temperature, a drive to avoid suffocation, a drive against accumulating waste products in the body, a drive against excessive fatigue and exhaustion. Note that these operate as subordinate pain-avoidance drives; all are aversive states.

Sometimes the physiological basis of a drive is acquired. Drug addiction provides an example—a person who habitually takes morphine originally had no need for the drug. Continued use creates an imperative need for it, and the addict becomes driven by his craving. Deprived of the drug, he becomes restless and develops symptoms of acute illness that are relieved only by the drug.

The need-drive-incentive formulation

Thus far we have talked about the drives that goad the organism into activity, but we have touched only lightly on the rest of the motivated behavior sequence. The full pattern of goal-directed activity, as formulated in terms of need, drive, and incentive, moves from the drive to the goal in a number of steps:

1. The condition of *need* is established either through deprivation or through noxious stimulation (need for sustenance; need to avoid damage to the tissues).

2. The need comes to be represented as an active, directed state of behavior known as *drive* and characterized by tension, energy, and (usually) goal-directedness.

3. The first phase of the motivated behavior sequence, initiated and sustained by drive, is *preparatory activity,* such as going to the place where food or water can be found. This activity, particularly if undertaken by an experienced animal, shows marks of being *goal-directed* or *goal-seeking.*

4. The preparatory activity, if successful, leads the organism to an environmental object called a *positive incentive,* that is, an object that can typically reduce the drive through satisfying the conditions of need. When we bait a trap we place a positive incentive in it. The words "lure," "reward," "goal-object," and "reinforcement"[1] all refer to positive incentives. Food as an incentive satisfies the hunger drive; water as an incentive satisfies the thirst drive. In the case of the pain drive, the positive incentive is anything that brings relief.

5. The incentive arouses *goal-activity* or *consummatory behavior.* The animal eats the food, drinks the water, or jumps from the charged grid. The reduction of drive through consummatory behavior ends the motivated behavior sequence.

Positive incentives

A positive incentive is considered first as something that can satisfy a drive condition, but incen-

[1]"Reinforcement" is a technical word for "incentive," used in connection with learning theory (Chapter 8).

tives have other characteristics as well. Limiting incentives to their drive-reducing properties places too much importance upon need satisfaction and avoidance of discomfort. A full definition of a *positive incentive* must recognize two possible roles:

1. A positive incentive may be an object or circumstance that can reduce a drive through satisfying a need, as food can satisfy hunger.

2. A positive incentive may be incapable of satisfying a physiological need but may direct behavior toward itself for a variety of other reasons. Thus a sweet-tasting substance, such as saccharin, may satisfy an appetite, even though it has no nutritive value. Good music as a positive incentive attracts behavior toward itself, but the behavior does not satisfy a physiological need.

Complexity of the drive-incentive relationship

In the uncomplicated form of the drive-incentive pattern, the drive initiates activity of a preparatory sort, leading the organism eventually to the incentive. The incentive then reduces the drive, and the organism is less tense and restless.

We have already encountered a few complications. Experience with incentives may lead to changes in their attractiveness and to changes in drive arousal (as in specific acquired food preferences or in drug addiction). Changes occur also in the preparatory activity: with practice the random activity of the hungry animal becomes learned goal-seeking activity, as when the animal looks for the food where it was before. In other words, there is an interrelatedness among drive, preparatory activity, incentive, and goal-activity, so that the whole cycle of behavior becomes modified as the organism engages repeatedly in a motivated sequence. Three illustrations of such modifications follow.

Positive incentives may enhance drives. A person who is not especially hungry may have his hunger drive aroused by seeing pastries in a bakery window or by smelling the odor of freshly baked bread. The incentive (fresh bakery goods) can activate the hunger as well as reduce it.

An experiment with chickens illustrates this point. A hen that has not eaten for twenty-four hours will eat more from a larger pile of grain than from a smaller pile; in this case the *total amount* of incentive enhances drive. If the remainder of the pile is brushed away as soon as it has stopped eating, the hen will start again when a new pile of grain is placed before it. With some hens this process was repeated as often as eight times, and each time the hens would eat from the new pile. They ate as much as 67 percent more from the new piles than they had eaten up to the first point of ceasing to eat. Here *renewal* of incentive reactivated the drive (Bayer, 1929; Katz, 1937).

Drive-incentive relationships may become channelized. The well-fed child who has his eye on a candy bar is not hungry for a piece of bread and butter. Only the candy bar will do. Rats that have learned to run a maze for bran mash will make errors again if sunflower seeds are substituted, though they can learn to run the maze as well with sunflower seeds as the incentive (Elliott, 1928). Apparently when they have learned to work for one incentive, they do not work as well when another incentive is substituted. This kind of limitation of the drive-incentive pairing is known as *channelization* (Miller, 1959).

Various drive-incentive relationships may be interrelated. Logan (1964) studied the cycle of eating, drinking, and sleeping behavior of rats that could choose their own periods of eating, drinking, and sleeping, but supplies of food and water were occasionally restricted. For example, if their intake of water was limited, they ate less, as though they regulated the food consumed by the amount that could be "washed down" or digested. Hunger drive, at least as shown by behavior, had to come into some sort of equilibrium with the availability of water. The periods of eating and drinking also had cyclical qualities, so that eating and drinking did not necessarily occur when deprivation was greatest, particularly if the deprivation coincided with a sleep cycle. These findings are not in themselves surprising, but they warn against too strict adherence to a simple need-drive-incentive formula, even when dealing with such activities as eating and drinking.

As we have noted, the theory of need-drive-incentive based upon deprivation and aversive stimulation (hunger, thirst, pain) can with a little forcing be made to fit other obviously physiological motives, such as sexual and maternal ones. Some motives, which appear to be basic ones because they are found among young organisms in many species, fit the ordinary conceptions of needs and drives even less well. We shall therefore simply use the more neutral term *motive* in describing them. They include such motives as *activity, manipulation,* and *investigation.*

Activity as a motive

It is the nature of animals to be in active interchange with the environment, and to some extent this activity has a tonic effect apart from the specific needs that are being served. We noted in Chapter 3 that development of the organism proceeds normally only if it has sufficient stimulation; evidently the need for stimulation has its own biological basis. Impressed by the urge animals have to be active, Woodworth (1958) proposed a *behavior-primacy* theory of motivation, which is opposed to the *need-primacy* theory considered above. Through this point of view we can more readily account for play (in animals as well as in children), for curiosity, and for strenuous kinds of adventure that serve only slightly to satisfy the needs of the body. A related position has been taken by White (1959), who believes organisms are motivated by a desire for *competence,* that is, a desire for effective functioning.

It is possible to set up experiments to test whether activity serves as a motive with some of the characteristics of a drive. Hill (1956) did this by limiting the activity of rats and then seeing whether the opportunity to be active had incentive properties in testing situations. He found that animals would learn certain tasks in order to be rewarded by the opportunity to be active, thus appearing to enjoy activity for its own sake.

The manipulation motive

Activity readily takes the form of manipulation. We give babies rattles and other toys because we know that they like to hold them, shake them, pull them. We are aware that monkeys do this sort of

Fig. **12-8 Manipulation motive** The monkey takes the latches apart, even though there is no "reward" except that deriving from the manipulation itself.

University of Wisconsin Regional Primate Research Center

thing; in fact the word "monkey" serves as a verb to describe casual manipulation for whatever satisfaction it brings. That monkeys do indeed like to "monkey" is illustrated by a number of experiments. If various mechanical devices are placed in the monkey's cage (Figure 12-8), the monkey will begin to take them apart, becoming more skilled with practice, without any evident reward other than the satisfaction of some sort of manipulation drive (Harlow, Harlow, and Meyer, 1950). If it is fed each time that it takes the puzzle apart, the behavior changes: the interest in manipulation is reduced in favor of finding in the puzzle a means to food. It appears, therefore, that manipulation is a motive in its own right.

Investigation as a motive

In a number of experiments in which a monkey had the opportunity to open a window and see what was going on outside, that opportunity operated as a positive incentive (Butler, 1953). It seems then that animals can be motivated by curiosity. The growing interest in such behavior has resulted in a number of experiments, which may be subdivided into those dealing with locomotor exploration and investigatory responses.

Locomotor exploration. Locomotor exploration refers to the tendency of animals to run about when in a new place, investigating and inspecting the environment—like a cat in a new house. Hungry laboratory rats, well trained through eighty trials to select an arm of a Y-shaped maze for food, selected a new arm on the eighty-first trial when this opportunity for exploration was first opened to them (Thiessen and McGaugh, 1958). When the rear walls of otherwise empty goal boxes at the end of a runway contained either familiar or novel visual figures, rats spent more time in the goal box exploring the novel figures than they did with the familiar ones (Berlyne and Slater, 1957). That this may be a variety of complexity-seeking, rather than novelty alone, is shown in later experiments reported by Walker (1964), in which rats spent more time in rooms with greater complexity than in more monotonous ones, regardless of familiarity.

Infants in their early months do not of course run about, but in their visual explorations they too seem attracted by complexity. When shown the patterns of Figure 12-9, they most frequently looked first at the patterns on the right (Berlyne, 1966).

Investigatory responses. Berlyne (1966) calls investigatory responses those that involve some sort of manipulation that changes the unfamiliar object: picking it up, tearing it apart, and so on. This differs from the manipulation motive in that its aim is to gain new information.

Piaget has made a number of observations bearing on investigatory responses early in life. Within the first few months of life the human infant learns to pull a string to activate a hanging rattle—a form of manipulation that must be considered merely entertaining. Between five and seven months the infant will remove a cloth covering his face, anticipating the peekaboo game. At eight to ten months the infant will begin to look for things behind or beneath other things. By eleven months he will "experiment" with things, varying the response each time (Piaget, 1952). Inquisitive behavior is a dependable characteristic of the growing child.

Fig. **12-9 Complexity and curiosity** Three- to nine-month-old infants looked first at the right-hand figures, presumably because they were more complex. (After Berlyne, 1966)

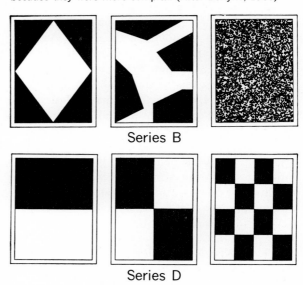

Series B

Series D

Appetites and aversions: alternatives to need, drive, and incentive

At the time of the height of acceptance of the need-drive-incentive formulation of motivation some years ago, many other theories seemed translatable in its terms. Hull based his learning theory on the notion that learning took place when an incentive reduced a drive (Hull, 1943). Motivation was given a general biological basis by those who believed that in reducing drive the incentive returned the organism to a more homeostatic state (Chapter 2, p. 34). Activity was found to be manipulable by depriving the animal of food or water or by subjecting it to pain. That aspect of psychoanalytic theory which stated that much behavior is motivated to escape anxiety and guilt had a similar biological basis.

With this basis in observed relationships securely established, there were many speculations about how other motives were derived from the basic drives. The infant's attachment to his mother, for example, was attributed to her being the source of food and thus a token for satisfaction, like any other reward-object. Her absence would arouse a tension state, or anxious state, which would be relieved when she returned. Actually, many doubts were later thrown upon this plausible derivation of the need-drive-incentive theory, as we noted earlier (Chapter 3, pp. 68–69).

Criticisms of the theory had been made all along, but they began to mount in the 1950s. A strong attack by Harlow (1953) on the deprivation theory of drive came at a time when many others had begun to express their doubts and turn their attention to such motives as activity, manipulation, and curiosity, which did not fit the need-drive-incentive pattern. Even Hull, who had done so much to popularize the theory, began to see that too little attention had been paid to the motivational significance of the incentive, and too much to the condition of drive. He added a concept of incentive motivation to that of drive, giving incentive a role beyond that of reducing drive (Hull, 1952). This was carried forward by his follower, Spence (1956), who believed drive and incentive motivation could be added together, thus making what happens in the presence of the incentive (or in anticipation of it) a component of drive. Even those who continued to uphold the need-drive-incentive formula began to pay much more attention to the incentive.

Deprivation and aversive drives do exist and are highly motivating, but we need to find some way of talking about those motives that do not fit into the drive pattern. One way to begin is by creating a category of *negative incentives*. In the theory of deprivation and noxious drives, all incentives are positive; that is, they are sought in order to reduce the drive through satisfying the need or through eliminating the noxious stimulation. We already noted (p. 305) that some positive incentives do not reduce any readily definable drive; they are defined as directing behavior toward themselves. We may define a *negative incentive* as any object or circumstance that when perceived or anticipated directs behavior *away* from itself. Note that by this definition a source of pain (which is a source of *drive* in the need-drive-incentive formulation) may serve as a *negative incentive* when it is perceived as an object to be avoided. This distinction permits us to study the differences in motivational effect between promised reward and threatened punishment, treating reward as a positive incentive and punishment as a negative incentive.

When we distinguish between positive and negative incentives we are at the same time pointing out a fundamental dichotomy in motivated behavior. A positive incentive is one for which the organism has an *appetite,* such as tasty food; a negative incentive is one for which the organism has an *aversion,* such as a repugnant odor.

Appetite and pleasure-seeking

The need to satisfy hunger is based upon the chemistry of the body, but the appetite for a particular food depends upon the chemistry of the food. The two are related in that appetite is increased by hunger, even though a hungry person may have no appetite for a food that is extremely distasteful for him. Some Chinese, for example, are said to find cheese so distasteful that they may starve before eating it. Appetite thus calls attention to the quality of the positive incentive; an appetizing food is something sought, not merely something accepted to relieve hunger pangs.

Support for an interpretation that certain goal-activity may be pleasurable apart from conditions of need has been given by experiments utilizing electrical stimulation of parts of the central nervous system.[2] Electrodes were planted in the brains of rats, and a healing period was allowed until the rats appeared to be suffering no discomfort. Shocks could then be administered through these electrodes to specific portions of the brain. A bar placed in the rat's cage permitted the rat to control the current, so that when it pressed the bar the current was turned on. When certain centers of the brain were stimulated, particularly those lying deep in the midline between the two hemispheres, the rats gave appetitive responses to the current; that is, they positively sought the stimulation through repeated bar-pressing. When the stimulating devices were disconnected, the bar-pressing no longer produced excitation, and bar-pressing ceased (Olds and Milner, 1954; Olds, 1956).

The most plausible interpretation of these results is that the electrical stimulation produces in the rat a state equivalent to what we would call "pleasure." An interpretation in terms of satisfaction through drive reduction is not plausible.

Aversion and pain avoidance

Similar experiments have investigated aversive centers in the brain. When the electrodes are placed in such centers, the rat will press the bar or perform other learned acts in order to *turn off* the current (Delgado, Roberts, and Miller, 1954). These experiments, though fully as important as the others, seem less striking because we are familiar with headaches and might assume that an electric shock to the rat's brain has some sort of painful consequence.

When pain is a continuing state of annoyance, it has all the properties of a drive, producing ten-

[2] See earlier references in Chapter 8, pp. 207–08.

sion, activity, and a search for relief. Thus headaches or stomach aches act as drives but not as incentives. A negative incentive is different: it is something to be avoided because of the pain that it *might* cause. If the negative incentive were not always perceived or anticipated, it would have no effect; moreover, the incentive exists in the environment, and not (as a drive) within the organism.

Environmental objects may have at once appetitive and aversive qualities. The bitter medicine that cures an ailment is at once desirable and forbidding. Mixed incentives lead to a conflict between the desire to approach and the desire to avoid. We shall return in a later chapter (Chapter 19) to a consideration of motivational conflicts and their handling.

Appetites, aversions, and perceived incentives

Because incentives may be positive, negative, or mixed, their relationships to behavior can be understood only if they are more fully specified. The following outline summarizes the relationships of perceived incentives to the enhancement of goal-related behavior.

1. Appetitive behavior (approach behavior) is enhanced by the appearance of a positive incentive and by the withdrawal of a negative incentive. A house-to-house salesman enters a house because he hopes to make a sale (positive incentive), but he hesitates to enter when there is a barking dog unless the dog is on a leash (withdrawal of negative incentive).

2. Aversive behavior (avoidance behavior) is enhanced by the appearance of a negative incentive and by the withdrawal of a positive incentive. The attentive eye of the teacher (negative incentive) may inhibit the whispering schoolchild; the lack of ice cream in the freezer (withdrawal of positive incentive) may inhibit the tendency to make a midnight trip to the kitchen.

3. Conflict behavior is induced by a forced choice among incentives, either positive or negative, or by confrontation by an incentive that has

at once positive and negative characteristics. A choice between two bitter pills or between two attractive desserts can be conflictual, as is the choice of being pained by the dentist or of enduring the pain of the toothache.

These relationships are what we would expect from our familiarity with rewards and punishments. Satisfactions can come from either a reward or relief from threatened punishment; annoyance can come from either punishment or withheld reward.

Learned appetites and aversions

Whatever inventory of basic drives and motives we accept, motivation in both animals and man cannot be completely described in terms of a few primary drives or motives alone. So much learning takes place, in addition to species-specific behavior, that actual behavior is bound to be complexly motivated in ways highly dependent upon specific circumstances.

Many experiments have shown that originally neutral objects may acquire incentive value. A simple illustration is money, which acquires its incentive value because of the things it can buy. Something of the same sort occurs with animals, as shown in *token-learning* experiments conducted with chimpanzees (Cowles, 1937). Chimpanzees were taught to work for poker chips as incentives rather than for food. The chimpanzee could later use the poker chip to obtain food from a vending machine called a "Chimp-o-mat" (Figure 12-10). After learning about tokens, the animal would work as hard for a poker chip as for the food itself,

Yerkes Regional Primate Research Center

Fig. **12-10** **The Chimp-o-mat** Poker chips that can be used to obtain food have acquired incentive value.

occasionally saving up a few poker chips before converting them into the food reward.

Notice that the drive—hunger—has remained the same, but something other than food has acquired incentive value. There is little doubt that the number of things that can come to serve as both positive and negative incentives becomes greatly increased by satisfactions and dissatisfactions experienced in the past.

The learning of appetites and aversions for particular foods has already been indicated. In man the things that are sought, appreciated, and preferred are so diverse that a separate chapter is devoted to human motivation.

Summary

1. Behavior is in part regulated by *drives* that are the consequences of *needs*. Among the deprivation drives are hunger and thirst. Pain as a noxious drive is a special case: it typically indicates a danger to the organism, so it is related to the need for protection or safety.

2. Some evidence favors *local* theories of the origin of hunger and thirst drives (hunger related to stomach contractions, thirst to dryness of the mouth and throat), but more recent experimentation increasingly favors *central* theories, that is, control of drive by centers in the brain (chiefly in the hypothalamus) sensitive to chemical changes in the blood.

3. The need-drive-incentive formulation is that as a result of *need* the total motivated behavior sequence moves from *drive* through *preparatory activity* to *goal-activity*, which takes place when a *positive incentive* is encountered. The effect of the goal-activity is usually to reduce the drive through satisfying the need, thus producing a more relaxed state.

4. *Positive incentives* are environmental objects or circumstances that act upon motivated behavior as follows: (a) some positive incentives bring an end to the motivated behavior sequence by reducing the drive through satisfying the need; (b) other positive incentives when perceived or anticipated lead the motivated organism toward themselves and further goal-activity, regardless of whether they satisfy a need.

5. Perceived incentives may serve to arouse or intensify drives rather than satisfy them. Through learning, a drive-incentive relationship may become channelized, so that drive behavior is no longer motivated when the incentive is changed. In free environments need, drive, and incentive are very complexly interrelated.

6. Some basic motives (basic in the sense that they are found widely in the animal world and early in the life of human infants) are without clearly specified physiological correlates. Among these are *activity, manipulation,* and *investigation* motives. Investigation, or curiosity, motives may be subdivided into locomotor exploration and investigatory responses.

7. Increased dissatisfaction with the need-drive-incentive formulation has focused more attention on the influence of incentives—a *positive incentive* being one that the motivated organism tends to approach, a *negative incentive* one that it tends to avoid or withdraw from.

8. *Appetites* and *aversions* parallel the distinction between positive and negative incentives. Appetitive behavior is associated with pleasure; experiments on electrical self-stimulation of the brain suggest that certain centers in the brain, when stimulated, give experiences corresponding to a pleasurable state. There are also centers in the brain that self-stimulation experiments show give painful experiences and result in aversive behavior.

9. The possibility exists that complex motives may be derived from a few basic drives. Acquired incentives are readily demonstrated, as in the token-learning experiments. Many appetites and aversions may be acquired through learning.

Suggestions for further reading

Some short summaries on motivation, taking similar positions to those of this chapter, are Fuller, *Motivation: A biological perspective* (1962), and Murray, *Motivation and emotion* (1964).

More extensive accounts can be found in a number of advanced books on motivation, of which the following are representative: Atkinson, *An introduction to motivation* (1964); Cofer and Appley, *Motivation: Theory and research* (1964).

For collections of readings on motivation, dealing with topics similar to those of this chapter, see Haber, *Current research in motivation* (1966), and Teevan and Birney, *Theories of motivation in learning* (1964a).

human motivation

WHY MEN BEHAVE AS THEY DO HAS intrigued thinkers from earliest times; much of the thematic material in literature, art, and drama is concerned with goal-striving, ambition, jealousy, heroism, sacrifice, love, hostility—all intensely motivated human behavior. The variety and richness of these themes makes it difficult to formulate a simple and orderly theory of human motivation that will be adequate to the subject matter. In this chapter some of the difficulties of formulating a motivational theory will be noted. Then a few of the major theories that have attempted to give some order to what we know will be considered. Representative motives will be discussed to illustrate each of the theories, but no attempt will be made to give a scientific inventory of the totality of human motivated behavior.

Everyday experiences teach us a good deal about motivated behavior. We are aware of those who set high goals and then work strenuously to reach them. Athletic competition provides ready examples, with broken records and Olympic gold medals serving as signs of success. But many nonathletes, too, set difficult goals and work hard to reach them: artists, musicians, scientists, businessmen. At the other extreme we find those who are apathetic and seem unable to make the effort to plan ahead or to compete enough in daily activities to sustain a participative role in society. We find still others who give up lives of ease and security to face hardships in order to serve the needy in far-off places. People obviously differ widely in the activities that they find most satisfying and in the energy that they invest in the activities they choose.

Motivational dispositions and motivational arousal

Not all motives that can incite an organism to action are operative at the same time. A student who spends long hours studying during the week because of his motivation to do well on his examinations may be seen yelling excitedly at the Saturday afternoon football game for quite a different motive. He carries many possibilities of motivated action within him, even when they are not being expressed. These possibilities are called *motivational dispositions* because they are persistent tendencies to express particular motives when the conditions are appropriate.

To the extent that it is universal (the tendency to eat when hungry, to drink when thirsty) the motivational disposition can be inferred from the behavior, but even such basic motives as hunger and thirst show large individual differences in behavior. For instance, in the satisfaction of hunger drives we distinguish between the voracious eater and the one with a moderate appetite. Moreover, at any one time the voracious eater may be well fed and not ready to eat more, while the person with a moderate appetite may be very hungry indeed. This example calls attention to two important points: (1) people differ in the strengths of their motivational dispositions, and (2) at any one time the relevant behavior may not correspond to the strengths of the persisting dispositions.

Motivational dispositions become evident in behavior when the conditions are appropriate: for example, when a state of need is created through deprivation, or when an incentive stirs the organism to action. Hence, in addition to disposition, we are interested in *motivational arousal*. If we were able to equate the conditions of arousal for two people, then the one who engaged most strongly in the motivated activity would be said to be the one with the stronger disposition.

To illustrate how behavior is affected jointly by motivational dispositions and conditions of arousal, we may consider a study by French (1958). By means of a test she devised she selected two groups of subjects, 128 found to be high in achievement motivation but low in affiliative motivation, and 128 high in affiliative motivation but low in achievement motivation. Those with achievement motivation tend to work toward some standard of excellence; those with affiliative motivation work in such a way as to belong to and be accepted by a certain group. The enduring nature of these dispositions was tested by setting a task for the

Fig. 13-1 Effect of appropriate motivation on performance For each of the groups, arousal of the appropriate motive (through achievement feedback or affiliation feedback) leads to superior performance. (Data from French, 1958)

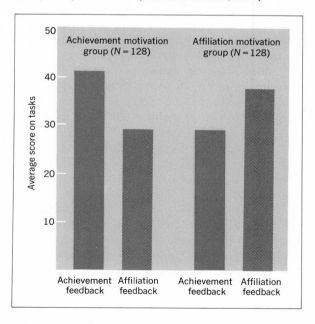

subjects and at various times providing conditions of motivational arousal appropriate to one disposition or the other. Of course, conditions appropriate to the arousal of one disposition would not be appropriate to the arousal of the other.

The task consisted of assembling a story from phrases or short sentences printed on separate cards. The subjects had to get the information from others in order to complete the story but were not permitted to show one another their cards. The members of each group worked in teams of four. The experimenter periodically interrupted the task to record scores and to give a progress report, or "feedback," telling each team member how he was doing. One kind of feedback aroused achievement motivation by emphasizing how well the team was completing the task: "This team is working very efficiently." The other feedback aroused affiliative tendencies by emphasizing the feeling of belonging: "This team works very well together." The results were in the direction predicted (see Figure 13-1): the group performance of those with high achievement dispositions was better when achievement feedback capitalized on these tendencies, and the group performance of those with high affiliative tendencies was better when these tendencies were aroused through feedback. Thus when conditions of arousal favor those with a given motivational disposition, their performance of the required task is superior to those lacking (or lower) in this motivational disposition.

This experiment emphasizes the interaction between the enduring motivational disposition and the corresponding aroused motive. Motivational dispositions persist and may be thought of as enduring personality characteristics, while aroused motives affect only the present ongoing behavior.

Difficulties of a theory of motivation

The relation of motives to behavior

There is a tendency to infer motives directly from behavior, on the plausible assumption that all behavior is motivated. In this manner a classification of behavior becomes converted into a classification of motives—nest-building motive, mothering motive, fighting motive, and so on. This approach errs in failing to distinguish between the *goal* that the behavior serves, and the *activity* that leads to this goal (sometimes described as the *instrumental activity* because it is "instrumental" to goal achievement). Thus hunting is distinguished from target-practice, even though both involve aiming and shooting of firearms, because the shooting serves different purposes or reaches different goals. The disparity between instrumental activity and goals establishes the need for extreme caution in inferring motivation from behavior. A person may eat an unappetizing food not because he is hungry but because he does not wish to offend his hostess; he may pass up a dessert at a cafeteria because he is on a diet rather than because it is unappetizing. Actual behavior is often the result of a resolution or compromise between conflicting goals.

There are several types of discrepancy between instrumental behavior and goals.

1. The same goal may be reached by different kinds of behavior. Sometimes these differences are culturally determined, as when affection is expressed by rubbing noses rather than by kissing. Circumstances may make opposite kinds of behavior serve the same goals. Cooperating with neighbors might secure some benefits for a resident in a community, while competing with them might secure other benefits. The goal of self-interest can thus be served sometimes through cooperation and sometimes through competition.

2. Different goals may be reached by the same instrumental behavior. Thus one person might take up guitar-playing to please a parent, the other to annoy a parent.

3. Any single set of instrumental activities may serve several goals at once. A scientist at work in

his laboratory may be motivated by a yearning to search for truth, by a desire for fame, and by the necessity of increasing his earning power to support his family. The principle of multiple determination of behavior makes difficult the description of the motives active at a given time.

Difficulties in making an inventory of motives

The above considerations indicate that an inventory of behavior will not be an inventory of the goals that such behavior serves. Even so, there is a strong temptation to develop classificatory schemes that will provide a list of human motivational dispositions closely related to human behavior in all its variety. This is coherent with the tendency within any science to sort out its objects of investigation as a starting point (animal, vegetable, mineral; solid, liquid, gas; bird, beast, fish; cirrus, cumulus, and other clouds). Very often the science in its advanced stages abandons the earlier sorting, but the classification has at least helped to define the subject matter of the science. Present lists of human motives have the status of a preliminary sorting—they have not been agreed upon as appropriate final categories.

In one of the most influential lists, Murray (1938) sets forth twelve "viscerogenic needs" (corresponding to the physiological needs discussed in Chapter 12) and twenty-eight "psychogenic needs" (Table 13-1). Such a long list helps us to see the kinds of behaviors that a complete theory of human motivation will have to comprehend. It is of course possible that the number of basic motives will be reduced in some orderly manner.

More than an inventory of human behavior, Murray's list shows signs of reflectiveness about goal-seeking and goal conflicts, making it not only plausible but useful as a reminder of the many facets of human motivation. Many writers on motivation have indeed made use of portions of the Murray list as they proceeded to study the need for achievement, or affiliation, or nurturance, or succorance. But the list is not formally accepted, as is a botanical taxonomy or the periodic table of the elements. That it is not accepted owes in part to a lack of clarity in the list regarding the status of different "needs"—the failure to specify, for example, whether "contrariness" is really in itself a goal to be served, or merely an instrumental strategy to serve some other needs, such as a need for recognition. Is there any chance that some other list of this kind will eventually be accepted?

There are some principles according to which such a list could be made a firmer part of science. The scientific procedure would be to identify a fairly large list of observable instrumental activities as goal-related behaviors, and then to collect evidence for these behaviors from a large number of people. Statistical methods could then be applied to determine how the observed behaviors cluster together.[1] If some persons are consistently high on behaviors A, B, C, and D, and others high on E, F, G, and H, we would be able to classify A, B, C, and D as one "dispositional cluster," and E, F, G, and H as another. Presumably, if such a study were conducted on a sufficiently large scale and with enough care, the list of motivational dispositions could be reduced to a reasonably basic list. Actually the methods available (chiefly factor analysis) are not fully satisfactory for the task, but, in principle, such a simplification could take place. Studies of this kind have been made, but instead of beginning with a larger number of needs than Murray's, an effort was made to shorten the list initially, so that the basic dispositions that emerged were of necessity from the Murray list (Frenkel-Brunswik, 1942; Edwards, 1954). Because motivational dispositions are thought to be persistent characteristics of persons, their appraisal merges into personality study (Chapter 18).

[1]One such method, factor analysis, is discussed in Chapter 15.

Is a universally accepted list of human motivational dispositions possible?

TABLE 13-1 A LIST OF PSYCHOGENIC NEEDS

A. Needs associated chiefly with inanimate objects
   1. **Acquisition:** the need to gain possessions and property.
   2. **Conservation:** the need to collect, repair, clean, and preserve things.
   3. **Orderliness:** the need to arrange, organize, put away objects, to be tidy and clean; to be precise.
   4. **Retention:** the need to retain possession of things; to hoard; to be frugal, economical, and miserly.
   5. **Construction:** the need to organize and build.

B. Needs expressing ambition, will power, desire for accomplishment, and prestige
   6. **Superiority:** the need to excel, a composite of achievement and recognition.
   7. **Achievement:** the need to overcome obstacles, to exercise power, to strive to do something difficult as well and as quickly as possible.
   8. **Recognition:** the need to excite praise and commendation; to command respect.
   9. **Exhibition:** the need for self-dramatization; to excite, amuse, stir, shock, thrill others.
  10. **Inviolacy:** the need to remain inviolate, to prevent a depreciation of self-respect, to preserve one's "good name."
  11. **Avoidance of inferiority:** the need to avoid failure, shame, humiliation, ridicule.
  12. **Defensiveness:** the need to defend oneself against blame or belittlement; to justify one's actions.
  13. **Counteraction:** the need to overcome defeat by striving again and retaliating.

C. Needs having to do with human power exerted, resisted, or yielded to
  14. **Dominance:** the need to influence or control others.
  15. **Deference:** the need to admire and willingly follow a superior; to serve gladly.
  16. **Similance:** the need to imitate or emulate others; to agree and believe.
  17. **Autonomy:** the need to resist influence, to strive for independence.
  18. **Contrariness:** the need to act differently from others, to be unique, to take the opposite side.

D. Needs having to do with injuring others or oneself
  19. **Aggression:** the need to assault or injure another; to belittle, harm, or maliciously ridicule a person.
  20. **Abasement:** the need to comply and accept punishment; self-depreciation.
  21. **Avoidance of blame:** the need to avoid blame, ostracism, or punishment by inhibiting unconventional impulses; to be well behaved and obey the law.

E. Needs having to do with affection between people
  22. **Affiliation:** the need to form friendships and associations.
  23. **Rejection:** the need to be discriminating; to snub, ignore, or exclude another.
  24. **Nurturance:** the need to nourish, aid, or protect another.
  25. **Succorance:** the need to seek aid, protection, or sympathy; to be dependent.

F. Additional socially relevant needs
  26. **Play:** the need to relax, amuse oneself, seek diversion and entertainment.
  27. **Cognizance:** the need to explore, ask questions, satisfy curiosity.
  28. **Exposition:** the need to point and demonstrate; to give information, explain, interpret, lecture.

Source: Murray and others (1938).

The psychogenic needs are distinguished from viscerogenic, or physiological, ones. In the listing, changes of wording have been made to avoid some of the neologisms coined by Murray.

Some approaches to a theory of human motivation

The nature and origins of differences in motivational dispositions, the circumstances of arousal, both internal and environmental, and the type of behavior that results, are all matters for theoretical discussion. No consensus on motivational theory has yet been reached in contemporary psychology; some even argue that the concept of motive is so unclear that it should be dispensed with altogether. But as the concept is probably here to stay, we may examine three theories as representative of the efforts to deal with its perplexing problems.

The three approaches to be discussed are *psychoanalytic theory, behavior theory,* and *cognitive theory.* Freud's theory, with its emphasis upon the two basic motives of sex and aggression, grew out of his interpretation of irrational, neurotic behavior, which he extended to account for much of our normal, socially acceptable behavior. Behavior theory takes as its starting point the need-drive-incentive interpretation and then shows how adult human motivation may be derived from a few motives in childhood through a process of learning. Finally, cognitive theory focuses attention upon man's awareness of what is going on, his deliberate tendency to anticipate the future, to plan, to take risks. The theories are not as far apart as this brief description indicates, but it helps to see them first as somewhat different before noting where they overlap.

The psychoanalytic theory of motivation

Psychoanalysis, apart from its purposes in treating neurotic disorders, is best known as a psychology of human motivation. It was, in fact, one of the first modern psychological theories of human motivation, beginning with Freud's *Interpretation of dreams* in 1900. Because psychoanalysis has evolved gradually over time, a complete exposition of it would require a lengthy discussion of its numerous changes. For our purposes a broad outline of the theory will suffice.

The two basic drives that Freud treated were *sex* and *aggression.* He was not unaware of physiological needs, or of the role of fear, but these two seemed to be the most powerful of human motives as they were presented to him in his study of disturbed people. Before discussing these two motives, we should review Freud's *conception* of motivation, which is as important to his theory as the particular motives he emphasized.

Freud believed that forerunners of sex and aggression are found early in the child's life: sex is expressed in the pleasure derived from stimulating the sensitive zones of the body; and aggression, in biting or hitting. When parental prohibitions soon place taboos on both sex and aggression, their free expression becomes, in Freudian terms, *repressed,* so that instead of finding full conscious expression they remain active as *unconscious motives.* Sex undergoes more severe repression than aggressive behavior, but the expression of either motive may make the child anxious because of the negative attitudes of his parents. Unconscious motives then find expression in disguised form. The theory of *unconscious motivation* is one of the cornerstones of the psychoanalytic theory.

Behavior from which unconscious motives are inferred

Literary men have long recognized the existence of some unconscious controls over human conduct, but it remained for Freud to call to public attention the powerful role of unconscious motives in human behavior. He pointed to several forms of behavior through which unconscious motives are expressed:

1. The dreamer often expresses in his dreams wishes of which he is unaware.
2. Unconscious mannerisms and slips of speech "let the cat out of the bag" and reveal hidden motives.
3. Symptoms of illness (especially the symptoms of neurotic illnesses) often can be shown to serve the unconscious needs of the person.

Following Freud's lead, most psychologists now accept the existence of unconscious motives (or at least unclear motives), although they differ from one another in their ways of talking about them. Sometimes a person is aware of certain motives in himself but is unaware of how important they are. He may know that he works hard and likes to succeed, but he may not realize how overweening his ambition is and how incapable he is of accepting defeat. Thus a motive need not be completely unconscious to have undergone some unconscious distortion.

Calling attention to the impulsive, unconscious aspects of human motivation need not lead to pessimism about human nature. On the contrary, the only hope of rational control of conduct lies in our facing the unconscious springs of action. It is a triumph of rationality that we have been able to discover how much of our behavior is irrational. If we are to behave reasonably, we must be ready to unmask our own unreasonableness.

The possibility that Freud was right, or at least hit on important partial truths, makes theorizing about unconscious motives a significant contribution to the explanation of human motives.

Sex

The fundamental social institution, the family, is based upon a sexual union in which, under ideal conditions, an enduring relationship of affection binds the parents together and gives them a feeling of security. As a physiological drive, sexual behavior may lead to sexual pleasure and the release of tension, but as a social motive it leads also to abiding personal attachments. In most cultures the sexual partner is highly prized, and jealousy of rivals becomes motivationally important. The social aspects of sex provide a clear illustration of a motive with a physiological basis in the sex drive, yet with a central role in the evolution of acquired social behavior.

The theory of unconscious motivation asserts that sexual motivation has many ramifications that are not directly sexual. Earlier Freudian theory found sexual motivation underlying nearly all of human behavior, but later psychoanalysts have tended to reduce the emphasis upon the pervasiveness of the sex drive by paying more attention to what they call the *ego*—the part of the person that copes realistically with the environment in all its aspects.

The means by which suppression of sexual expression leads to symbolic derivatives of sexual interest was illustrated in some experiments by Clark (1952; see also Clark and Sensibar, 1956). Clark studied the stories written by male college students as they viewed some pictures of neutral content after having been sexually aroused by

viewing pictures of attractive nude females. The experiment was carried out under two conditions: in the classroom and at a party when the students were under the influence of alcohol. The results may be summarized as follows:

1. Direct arousal under classroom conditions did *not* increase the *overt sexual imagery* appearing in the stories. This suggests that whatever sexual fantasies were aroused under these conditions led to some anxiety and hence to suppression.
2. Direct arousal under classroom conditions *did* increase the *indirect* or *symbolic* expression of sex, thus conforming to the above conjecture that sexual fantasy was indeed aroused.
3. Direct arousal under the alcoholic condition *did* increase the *overt sexual imagery* in the stories, indicating less anxiety and suppression under the influence of alcohol.
4. Direct arousal under the alcoholic condition did *not* increase the *indirect* or *symbolic* expression of sex. The direct expression eliminated the need for resort to disguised representation.

This is a very brief specimen of the theory of unconscious motivation, but it illustrates the main point that suppressed[1] motives find indirect, symbolic, or disguised expression. More illustrations will be given later, particularly in the discussion of defense mechanisms with which the person deceives himself and others in order to deny or transform his motives (Chapter 19).

Aggression

The problem of human cruelty is a baffling one, but the history of human behavior abounds with instances of man's imposition of suffering upon other men. The fact that man's potential aggressiveness has an evolutionary basis may explain why he is capable of cruel and destructive behavior, but it does not necessarily *justify* his aggressiveness.

[1]Strictly speaking, a distinction should be made between *suppression,* in which the motive is still capable of appearing in awareness, even though its expression is denied, and *repression,* in which the motive is no longer accessible to awareness. For purposes of illustrating the processes, however, suppression, with its symbolic derivatives, shows at a surface level what repression is inferred to do at a deeper level.

Within recent years several books have reached a wide audience with the general message that aggression is so deeply entrenched in the evolutionary line from which man is descended that it is almost inevitable that man should find his tendencies toward aggression very difficult, if not impossible, to bring under control. Although each of the authors expresses some caveats that give man a chance to control his violence and cruelty, the overall impression created by these books is a pessimistic one.

Lorenz (1966), one of the European ethologists whose work has been mentioned in connection with the controversy over instincts (p. 302), shows how widespread aggression is, but he also points out the limitations on aggression, as when one dog (or wolf) assumes the helpless position of lying down with neck exposed to the aggressor; under this admission of defeat, the aggressor does not attack. (Perhaps here is an evolutionary justification for nonresistance.)

Ardrey (1966) is not a professional biologist, but he interviewed many leading authorities and found *territoriality* to be a major source of aggressive behavior. Many species of birds and other animals stake out their own territory, which they defend by driving off any intruder. Ardrey believes that this defense of the homeland is the evolutionary source of man's fighting. The defensive activity readily becomes offensive warfare through symbolic extension of the concept of defense, a familiar enough tendency in the pronouncements of modern heads of state who are justifying their military activities.

Koestler (1967), a popular writer widely acquainted with biological, physiological, and psychological literature, has decided that man is an evolutionary anomaly, combining the vegetative nervous system of more primitive forms (an "alligator brain"), the emotions of more evolved forms (a "horse brain"), and a brain capable of rational problem-solving (man's "higher cortex"). The trouble is that these "brains" do not get along well together; when emotions are aroused, the rational part of man is inhibited or debased to serve his emotions. Koestler's solution, scarcely an optimistic one, is that we must wait for the biochemists to produce a pill that will integrate these three parts of man's regulatory apparatus; it is hoped that the biochemists will do this before man destroys himself.

There is doubtless plenty of reason for gloom about man's ability to control his tendencies to aggression, but the picture is not all bleak. Some specific forms of aggressive behavior, such as piracy at sea and the widespread use of torture to produce religious conformity, have essentially disappeared; at one time, these behaviors must have seemed inevitable. Perhaps man's destructiveness in other areas can also be brought under control.

A suggestion, deriving from Freud and widely accepted by others, is that aggression is one of the consequences of frustration (Dollard and others, 1939). Sears and others (1953) studied the relationship between feeding frustration and severity of weaning in early infancy and aggressive activity in the preschool years. Because the correlation was not found to be significant these authors suggest that the learning involved in true hostile aggression (making another person experience pain) develops slowly. The kinds of aggression shown by the infant are mere obstacle-removing activities, often violent or strenuous but not really oriented toward a goal response of inflicting pain upon another. If this suggestion is correct, the true motive for aggression develops late and is not directly correlated with the experiences of early infancy.

Punishment of aggression also has its consequences. A parent who punishes a child excessively tends to set up in the child some sort of wish to punish in return. This tendency is clearly revealed in the doll play of children grouped according to the punitiveness of their mothers (Figure 13-2). The more punitive the mother, the more aggressive are the acts shown in doll play.

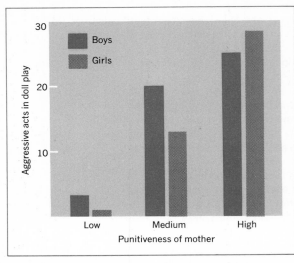

Fig. **13-2 Punishment and aggression** The more punitive the mother, the more the aggression revealed by the son or daughter in doll play. (After Sears and others, 1953)

In addition to being moved to aggression by frustration, children *imitate* aggression displayed by adult models (Bandura, Ross, and Ross, 1963; Figure 13-3). When a child observes aggressive behavior in a parent, physical attack as a form of behavior is thereby justified somehow. Furthermore, aggressive behavior may be effective in obtaining reinforcement: the child gets what he wants by taking it away from another child, or gains leadership through successful fighting.

For boys there is a continuity between the early expression of aggression and its later expression (Sears, 1961). For girls, who may have been permitted to express unladylike aggression in the early years, social pressures produce anxiety about aggression as they grow older, and may reduce its expression.

Aggression can take many forms: angry physical attacks, verbal insults, and even self-punishment.

Fig. **13-3 Children's imitation of adult aggression** Nursery school children observed a motion picture in which an adult expressed various forms of aggressive behavior toward a clown figure. After watching the film both boys and girls behaved aggressively toward the clown figure, using many of the detailed acts of aggression that the adult had displayed, including lifting and throwing, striking with a hammer, and kicking.

Dr. Albert Bandura

There is also the form called *prosocial aggression,* in which right and order are strongly defended by means of aggression against the one who violates prohibitions. We have to be careful in the case of aggression to distinguish between aggression as a means to an end and aggression as a motive in its own right. That is, does a person have some sort of *need* to inflict pain on another person, in the same way that he has, perhaps, a need for affection? Freud was one of the first to accept the interpretation that aggression was a fundamental human tendency; as already indicated, he ranked it as one of the two basic human drives.

However the aggression comes about, some children and some adults develop strong tendencies to injure themselves or others. The extreme forms have been given names: *sadism,* for the extreme motive to pain others; *masochism,* for the

extreme motive to inflict pain upon oneself. In some forms of sadism and masochism the satisfaction to the aggressive person appears to be sexual in nature, illustrating how the strands from different motivational dispositions may become intertwined.

Violence and destructiveness have become major problems of contemporary society, not only the sanctioned violence of warfare but the unsanctioned violence in cities and on college and university campuses throughout the world. These social expressions of aggressiveness go beyond the familiar aggressive acts of individual criminals and add new dimensions to persisting problems of public order. A need to understand what lies behind motives to aggression is one of the crucial problems facing psychology, and society at large.

Behavior theory: the concept of behavior systems

Behavior theory emphasizes stimulus-response relationships and learning (habit formation) in accounting for the development of behavior and its present manifestations. We shall follow here a developmental scheme of behavior theory as set forth by Whiting and Child (1953).

They proposed that we can classify adult behavior appropriately into a few *behavior systems,* each system consisting of a set of habits or customs motivated by a common innate or early acquired motive and leading to common satisfactions. They selected five behavior systems for consideration: the oral, anal, and sexual systems, dependency, and aggression. The first three systems are developed from motives with evident physiological bases (hunger, elimination, and sex); the other two (dependency and aggression) are assumed to be developed from motives acquired universally in early childhood as a result of the infant's helplessness, on the one hand, and inevitable frustrations, on the other. The debt to psychoanalytic theory is evident in the choice of these systems. Psychoanalysis makes much of orality and anality as significant features of development, and sex and

aggression are its emphasized drives. Dependency also reflects the psychoanalytic interest in the infant's attachment to his mother.

The following steps are implied in the behavior-system approach to human motivation:

1. The motive that defines a behavior system can be identified in early childhood.

2. The methods of "socializing" the motive can be identified and studied. Each culture rewards the "approved" methods of satisfying the motive and punishes the attempts to satisfy the motive in other ways. Diverse methods of child training, whether they differ from one culture to another or within the culture, produce differentiated social behavior within the particular behavior system under study.

3. The "causal" connections between the early manifestations of the motive and social behavior of adult life can be studied to find out whether the later practices are to some extent continuous with and predictable from the early experiences. We expect to find some general theme common to behavior within the selected system, and also variations on it. The variations among cultures will

depend in part upon the differences in socialization practices within those cultures, but even within a culture variations may be caused by differences in individual experiences.

Behavior related to the hunger drive

As an illustration of the behavior-system approach we may consider the complex outcome of the hunger drive, based initially on the helpless infant's need for nutrients.

The hunger drive leads to all manner of food-related behavior, as Table 13-2 shows. Obviously the behavior of the people engaged in the activities suggested in the right-hand column involves a good deal more than the drive for food: it includes the complex motivations of farmers and entrepreneurs; chefs, grocers, and night-club operators; priests, policemen, and doctors. In other words, as social behavior proliferates we can trace some aspects of it back to a common source, but we must also be reminded that such food-related behavior is not motivated by the hunger drive alone.

Behavior related to the dependency motive

The early dependency of the infant upon the adults who care for him can be interpreted as providing a foundation for various sorts of affiliative behavior later. Such behavior is motivated at least in part by the support that comes from the presence of other people, from ordinary companionship and friendship in childhood to enduring adult friendships, group memberships, and the closely knit loyalty and devotion within marriage and the family.

As representative studies within the dependency behavior system we will consider two investigations, one of young children and one of college students under conditions of experimental arousal.

Sources of dependent behavior in young children. Although, as noted earlier, children form early attachments to persons other than the mother, the mother's special role in feeding and handling may make her relationship of special importance in the development of the dependency motive. In an attempt to test this assumption, preschool children were studied (Sears and others, 1953). First an attempt was made to determine their present disposition to show dependent behavior. Teachers rated their dependency, and research workers derived dependency scores based on observing the reactions of the children (1) to other children and to the teacher in the nursery

TABLE 13-2   SOCIAL BEHAVIOR RELATED TO THE HUNGER DRIVE

BASIC ORGANIC BACKGROUND	PRIMARY DRIVE	EARLY DRIVE DIFFERENTIATION	SOCIAL BEHAVIOR, CUSTOMS, AND INSTITUTIONS RELATED TO THESE MOTIVES
Infant's helplessness and need for nutrients →	Hunger drive →	Food-related behavior ("oral drive") →	1. **Food production and conservation** (Hunting, fishing, agricultural crops, dairying, etc.; drying, salting, canning, storage, refrigeration) 2. **Meal preparation and social eating** (Food preparation and cooking, staple foods and varied menus, appetites and aversions, eating habits, table manners, etc.) 3. **Food ceremonies little related to satisfying hunger** (Fasts, food taboos, food sacrifices to the gods, Communion) 4. **Other symbolic and nonfood consequences of deriving satisfaction through the mouth** (Alcoholism and drug addiction; chewing gum and tobacco; smoking; oral interpretation of illness) 5. **Resistance to overeating** (Dieting, neurotic loss of appetite)

school, and (2) under controlled conditions in which the child played with dolls representing his family. A single dependency score was arrived at that best characterized the child at the nursery school age.

These same children received separate ratings on infancy experiences, based upon interviews with their mothers. Scales were designed to rate *nurturance* (the mother's care in feeding) and *frustration* (the infant's helplessness in the face of insoluble problems). The feeding practices of mothers who used the self-demand schedule were scored as high nurturance; those based on rigidly scheduled feeding were rated as low nurturance. The abruptness and harshness of weaning determined the score on feeding frustration. The resulting correlations between infant experiences and later dependent behavior are given in Table 13-3.

Contrary to initial expectations, the most carefully nurtured children (those on the self-demand schedule) showed *less* dependent behavior than those whose nurturance was strictly scheduled. Apparently feeding *frustration* is the variable that results in later dependent behavior, if we interpret rigid scheduling as well as severe weaning as being frustrating.

The investigators of the foregoing experiment gave an explanation of their findings along the following lines. In order to survive at all, the infant must have his basic needs met. Hence *all* infants have their hunger drives satisfied in a social context, and they all develop a normal amount of dependency motive. If the mother's behavior in scheduling or weaning produces frustration, something happens in addition to the normal hunger drive satisfaction. That is, the mother comforts or caresses the troubled infant, so that she provides other satisfactions to encourage dependency. In any case, the infant who has experienced a great deal of feeding frustration with accompanying feelings of helplessness is the one who later turns to others for support.

Affiliative behavior in young adults when anxiety is aroused. If we accept the above interpretation of the origin of dependency behavior in early life, we may assume that under anxiety-producing conditions the dependency drive will manifest itself (in some socially approved form) in adult life as well. An experiment by Schachter (1959) tested this assumption.

Schachter showed to some university women who reported for an experiment a forbidding-looking apparatus that they were made to believe could deliver severe electric shocks; these subjects constituted a high-anxiety group. Another group, similarly reporting for an experiment, was shown nothing threatening and was assured that the experimental procedures were mild and nonpainful; this group was thus characterized by low anxiety. When the subjects in both groups were given the choice of waiting for their turn alone or waiting with others, a larger proportion of the threatened group preferred to wait with others (Table 13-4). The general interpretation is that the more threatened, or anxious, subjects turned to company because affiliative needs were aroused. (In the end, of course, neither group had to undergo any painful experiences.)

Another analysis of the behavior in the same experiment showed that some individuals, under threat of pain, were more eager to have company than others. When the data from only children and first-born children were considered separately from that of later-born ones, it was found that the only and first-born children showed higher tendencies toward affiliation in this situation. Schachter inter-

TABLE 13-3   CORRELATIONS BETWEEN INFANCY EXPERIENCES AND PRESCHOOL DEPENDENT BEHAVIOR

| INFANCY EXPERIENCES | CORRELATIONS WITH TOTAL DEPENDENCY MEASURES* | |
	GIRLS	BOYS
Self-demand feeding	− .38	− .08
Weaning severity	.54	.40

*With the number of children (*N*) between 18 and 21 in the different comparisons, correlations must reach at least .35 to approach significance.

Source: Sears and others (1953).

The data are coherent with the interpretation that feeding frustration enhances dependency.

TABLE 13-4 RELATIONSHIP BETWEEN ANXIETY
AND THE AFFILIATIVE TENDENCY AMONG
COLLEGE WOMEN

EXPERIMENTAL MANIPULATION	WAITING CONDITIONS CHOSEN			
	TOGETHER	DON'T CARE	ALONE	TOTAL
High anxiety	20	9	3	32
Low anxiety	10	18	2	30

Source: Schachter (1959).

The anxious subjects were more eager to wait in the company of others when faced with a threatening situation.

prets this result to mean that the first-born child probably experienced more adult responsiveness to his uneasiness in early childhood than later-born children, whom parents may have taken more for granted.

Schachter's interpretation of the way in which parents rewarded dependency in first-born and later-born children is conjectural, but it is coherent with the origins of dependency motive as described in the earlier study of young children. The above study indicates that adult affiliative behavior may have a historical connection with early childhood experiences related to dependency. Furthermore, it shows that the motivational disposition becomes more evident when aroused by threat, so that those who do very well alone under ordinary circumstances will seek companionship when their anxieties are raised.

These illustrations of attempts to bring dependent or affiliative tendencies under experimental observation do not, of course, exhaust the kinds of things men do in seeking companionship of other people or in participating in group life. But they do indicate that it is possible to make measurements even in such a complex field and obtain the kinds of results that will eventually add up to a science of human motives.

Cognitive theory of motivation

Many aspects of individual motivation are represented in awareness. To the extent that an individual makes clear plans, is guided by his expectations and the risks involved, and moves steadfastly toward his goals, he is motivated according to his *cognitions* (a word with the root meaning of "to know"), and it is possible to formulate a theory of human motivation in these terms.

Goals, purposes, and plans

When an individual knows what he wants, knows the effort that will be required to overcome obstacles along the way, and knows what satisfaction the end state will bring, he can formulate his goal. If there are risks, he is prepared to face them. Behavior that is directed toward such a goal is clearly *purposeful*. The student who enters college to train himself to become an engineer knows in general what the profession of engineering is and what courses he must pursue in order to achieve his goal. Mathematics may be an obstacle

for him, but he attempts to learn it, even though he risks failing.

There is no doubt that an individual can make *plans* and carry them out. He knows where he wants to be at a particular time and what he wants to do there, and he arranges things so that he gets there. Discounting unforeseeable circumstances there is a high probability that whatever his plan is it will materialize. A person of "strong will" is one who can adopt a plan and commit himself so firmly to it that he will resist distractions and will be resourceful in finding ways to continue toward the intended goal. A person of "weak will" is one who is unable to stick to a plan, no matter how clearly he may be able to formulate it; he gives up easily in the face of obstacles or distractions. People differ in their capacities to formulate and fulfill plans just as they differ in their capacities to solve intellectual problems or to perform acts of skill.

Plans are of various kinds and lengths: they include not only the long-term seeking of certain goals but also *stop-plans* to avoid fatigue or danger. A stop-plan, for example, is not taking too many cups of coffee before retiring, or determining to leave a card game in order to have enough sleep. The more a person is able to formulate plans, even short-term ones, and carry them out, the greater sense of self-control he develops.

Level of aspiration

Goal-setting has been studied in experiments on the *level of aspiration.* In these experiments level of aspiration refers to a fairly immediate goal, that is, something almost within reach. The goal-setting in the experiments parallels what the high jumper does when he sets the bar between the posts. Where he sets it is his momentary goal, a measure of his level of aspiration. He expects to succeed, but he sets it high enough that he might fail. He would take no satisfaction in setting it so low that he could jump successfully every time.

Studies of aspiration level illustrate cognitive-type motivation because the individual becomes involved in a task, estimates his own level of achievement, sets his goals, and experiences success or failure. The first experiment concerned with aspiration problems revealed that the person's feeling of success or failure depends upon the difficulty of the task (Hoppe, 1930). As shown in Figure 13-4, a task may be "much too easy." Then the person experiences no sense of success, even though he accomplishes the task. A person who can play chess is not satisfied to win at dominoes. Or a task may be "much too difficult." Because he has no *ego involvement,* a person who makes no pretense of knowing Russian grammar will not have a sense of failure if he is unable to answer questions about it; he does not expect himself to know the answers. Success and failure experiences come in the in-between range: between the point at which success is highly probable, but failure possible, and that at which failure is highly probable, but success possible. This is the range in which the high jumper in the example will set his bar.

Other experiments on level of aspiration have been concerned with the effect of group standards on individual behavior. In one experiment, college

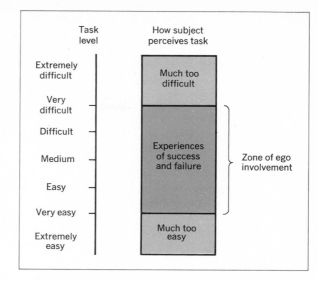

Fig. 13-4 **Level of aspiration** The subject tends to set his own goal (level of aspiration) within the zone of ego involvement, in which he can experience success or failure. (After Hoppe, 1930)

students worked together in small groups (usually consisting of four students). The task consisted of simple arithmetic problems, the score being the time required to complete a page. Public announcement of the finishing times was made, so that each student knew what the others were doing. Each student recorded privately his level of aspiration, that is, the score he expected to make on the next test. It was found that these private expectations were modified by the group performances: those who had scores above the group average tended to lower their estimates; those with scores below the group average tended to expect a gain (Hilgard, Sait, and Magaret, 1940).

In another experiment with college students shifts in aspiration level were studied when (1) the student knew only his own previous scores, and (2) he was told that his score was above or below that of one of three reference groups: high school, college, and graduate students. The results are shown in Figure 13-5. If the score was below that of the low-prestige group (high school students), the aspiration level increased most; if it was above that of the high-prestige group (graduate students), aspiration level decreased most (Festinger, 1942).

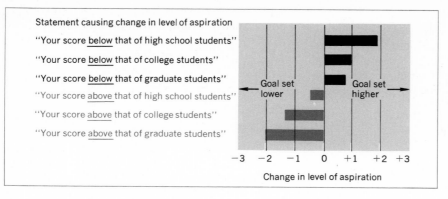

Statement causing change in level of aspiration

"Your score <u>below</u> that of high school students"

"Your score <u>below</u> that of college students"

"Your score <u>below</u> that of graduate students"

"Your score <u>above</u> that of high school students"

"Your score <u>above</u> that of college students"

"Your score <u>above</u> that of graduate students"

Goal set lower ← → Goal set higher

−3 −2 −1 0 +1 +2 +3

Change in level of aspiration

Fig. 13-5 Effect of prestige of reference groups on level of aspiration If his score is interpreted as below that of a group to which the individual feels superior he is spurred to increase his level of aspiration; if his score is interpreted as above that of a group thought superior to him he may lower his level of aspiration. (After Festinger, 1942)

Individual goal-setting is thus modified by prestige-seeking, self-protection, and other motives that reflect the settings in which behavior occurs.

The level of aspiration experiments provided the background for a later series of experiments on achievement motivation.

Achievement motivation

Man is a doer. Observers have long identified some sort of achievement motive, whether in the form of an "instinct of workmanship" or in the desire to master nature or to be a leader of men. Achievement motivation, as defined in the experiments reported here, refers to a tendency to define one's goals according to some standard of excellence in the product or performance attained.

McClelland and his associates (1953) developed a method by which fantasy productions are used for measuring achievement motivation. This method reflects the influence of the theory of unconscious motivation, for the assumption is made that if there is a strong motivational disposition toward achievement it will be revealed in fantasy without the subject's knowing that he is telling something about himself. The following account illustrates the method.

The experimenter showed male college students three pictures and instructed them to spend five minutes writing a brief story about each. The pictures suggested a work situation (two men working at a machine), a study situation (a boy seated at a desk with a book in front of him), and a fa-

ther-son situation. The stories centered around the following four questions printed on the answer sheet:

"What is happening?"
"What has led up to this situation?"
"What is being thought?"
"What will happen?"

The stories were examined for notions emphasizing the importance of achievement, of getting things done, of success. Subjects who wrote into their stories many such ideas were scored as having a high motive for achievement, those with few such ideas a low one.

Following this test the experimenter asked the subjects to work on a twenty-minute scrambled-words test, in which they had to rearrange an anagram such as WTSE into a meaningful word such as WEST. Results for those classified as high or low in achievement motive are given in Figure 13-6. Similar results were found for problems in addition: output was higher for those who were attributed with having a strong achievement motivation. Evidently the results in the test of fantasy did measure a motive having to do with success in laboratory tests.

Later studies of achievement-oriented behavior began to note a complication that had appeared in earlier studies of level of aspiration: some individuals appeared to be motivated by *pleasure in success* and others by *fear of failure*. It had been found much earlier that children with a history of success tended to set realistic goals that they had

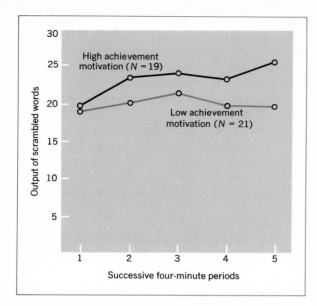

Fig. **13-6 Achievement motivation and performance** Those
with high achievement motivation continued to improve in the
performance of their task; those with low achievement motivation remained at about their initial levels. (After Lowell,
1950; McClelland, 1955)

a chance of reaching and enjoying, while children
with histories of failures either set goals very low,
so as to avoid the repeated experience of defeat,
or very high, so that they would not feel degraded
by failure (Sears, 1940).

It appears, then, that people whose fantasy
scores show them to be imagining success are
generally those who have realistic confidence in
themselves, while those whose fantasy scores show
low achievement motivation are those who are
anxious about failure. Raphelson (1957) tested
achievement motivation through the use of the
storytelling cards, but he also measured the same
subjects for (1) their test anxiety, by way of a
specially designed questionnaire, answered verbally, and (2) a physiological correlate of anxiety,
the galvanic skin response (GSR). He found under
achievement-oriented conditions a correlation of
− .43 between achievement motivation and anxiety, whether measured by the verbal test of anxiety
or by the GSR measure. The more testlike and
competitive a situation is, the better the high-
achievement subjects do, while those in the low-

achievement and high-anxiety category do less well
under such pressure (Moulton and others, 1958).
A low score on achievement motivation, therefore,
may not necessarily reflect a lack of desire for
success but rather a fear of failure, with the result
that the subject does not risk setting his sights too
high.

The achievement theme—a prominent one in
Western culture—appears to be inculcated early in
life. Mothers of boys with high achievement motivation tend to make more demands for achievement of their sons, and at an earlier age, than do
mothers of boys with low achievement motivation
(Winterbottom, 1958). In another experiment nine-
to eleven-year-old boys were put to work at
achievement tasks under some handicap (for example, building towers with blocks while blindfolded and permitted to use only one hand). They
were watched by their parents, and the investigators noted how much the parents tried to
help. The parents of the more highly motivated
boys set higher goals for their sons than the parents
of the less motivated boys, and they proved also
to be warmer and more appreciative. The mothers
of the highly motivated boys, more than their
fathers, broke in with hints to improve their
productions and urged them on (Rosen and
D'Andrade, 1959).

A formulation of cognitive motivational theory

One way of looking at a cognitive theory of
motivation is to regard it as a theory of preferential
choice or of decision-making. That is, the decision
to engage in a given activity in preference to alternatives, and how deeply to become involved in it,
is made on the basis of cognitive considerations.
J. W. Atkinson (1964) proposed an interpretation
of achievement motivation based upon an inter-
relation among conjectures concerning success
motivation, on one hand, and fear of failure, on
the other. The first conjecture is that the suc-
cess-oriented subject should work hardest at a task
of intermediate difficulty, when the outcome has
a 50/50 chance of success or failure. This is true
because a task of very high probability of success
has low incentive value, while a task of low proba-

bility of success discourages effort even though its incentive value is high. The second conjecture is that the anxiety-ridden subject (who has fear of failure) will show the reverse reaction; his anxiety will be highest at the 50/50 point, so he will avoid tasks of intermediate difficulty, preferring those that are very easy or very hard. If he fails on the hard task, no one will blame him; on the easy task he is almost sure to succeed. A further assumption is that achievement (success) tendencies and anxiety (fear of failure) interact and produce behavior representing a compromise between them.

In one experiment designed to test these predictions (Atkinson and Litwin, 1960), male college students participated in a ring-toss game in which the subject was given the choice of making his shots at any distance from 1 to 15 feet from the peg. It was presumed that some middle distance (corresponding roughly to the 50/50 likelihood of success as predicted by the theory) would be most preferred by those with high achievement motivation and low anxiety. In descending order those expected to choose the middle distance were: high-achievement plus low-anxiety subjects, high-achievement plus high-anxiety subjects, low-achievement plus low-anxiety subjects, and, finally, low-achievement plus high-anxiety subjects. The

experiment assumes of course that adequate measures of achievement motivation and test anxiety were obtained and that achievement motivation was indeed aroused in the ring-toss game. The arousal motive was enhanced by having other subjects standing around and by giving the goading instruction "See how good you are at this." The results were as predicted (Figure 13-7): the high-achievement plus low test-anxiety subjects selected an intermediate task in 77 percent of their choices, while the low-achievement plus high test-anxiety subjects selected this range in only 31 percent of their shots. The performance of the other groups fell in between.

The studies of achievement motivation and fear of failure indicate the usefulness of a cognitive theory in the analysis of motivation.

The motivational theories selected for discussion (psychoanalytic theory, behavior theory, and cognitive theory) represent selections from among current efforts to find some orderly way in which to deal with human motivation. Each has sufficient success to its credit to make it of value. The overlaps have been noted; each theory, for example, has its developmental aspects. In behavior theory this development is usually described according to

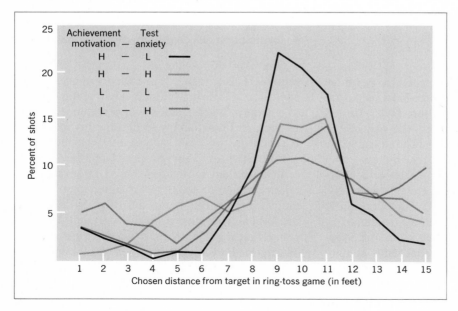

Fig. **13-7 Performance according to varying degrees of achievement motivation and anxiety** Those high in achievement motivation and low in test anxiety (fear of failure) (solid black line) preferred the task of intermediate difficulty as predicted. For those low in achievement motivation and high in anxiety (gray line) the middle-range choices are fewer and there are more choices near the extremes of difficulty (positions near and far from the target). (After Atkinson and Litwin, 1960)

a specific learning theory, while in the psychoanalytic theory more emphasis is upon a maturational theory of stages (as we saw in Chapter 3). Cognitive theory also looks for childhood influences upon the development of motivational dispositions.

The unconscious plays a role in each of the theories. In behavioral theory the unconscious is usually associated with habits that operate outside the system of verbal behavior. In psychoanalysis the concept of some sort of active unconscious is a central feature of the theory. And in cognitive theory unconscious influences affect the fantasy behavior that is widely used in the measurement of motivation. No one of the theories has gained universal acceptance among psychologists as a satisfactory account of the complexity of human motivation.

Self-reference in human motivation

Most experimental studies of motivation are concerned with specific, isolated fragments of behavior, as in the choices between two alternatives or in the behavior elicited under specific conditions of arousal. A difficulty with such studies is that they do not come to grips with the organization of motives in the individual and with the *hierarchical* nature of motives. Some things are more important to the person than others, and some activities are engaged in merely because they contribute to long-range goals. When we attempt to deal with motivational hierarchies, we often find that they depend upon the individual's perception of himself, his expectations, his confidence, his ideals. Many motives can be understood in relation to some sort of self-image: self-assertion, self-debasement, the desire for power or for recognition.

Self-consistency and the reduction of cognitive dissonance

We like to think that our attitudes, beliefs, and related behavior form a consistent pattern. Incongruity that is detected results in a sense of imbalance or dissonance, which we then seek to correct. The motivating effects of the need to correct incongruity, imbalance, or dissonance have been the subject of several theories.

We may select for consideration the theory proposed by Festinger (1957), which treats *cognitive dissonance* and its reduction. The kind of disagreement or disharmony with which Festinger has been chiefly concerned is that which occurs after a decision has been made—after an individual is committed to a course of action. Under such circumstances there is often a lack of harmony between what he does and what he believes, and there is pressure to change either his behavior or his beliefs. For example, if a regular smoker reads about the relationship between smoking and lung cancer, the habitual action and the new information are dissonant. If the decision is made to continue smoking, the dissonance will be reduced by disbelieving the information about the relationship between smoking and lung cancer; if the decision is made to give up smoking, the information on the linkage between smoking and lung cancer will be accepted. The fact that this information also affected the decision is not important here. As Festinger and others (1964) have shown, the weighing of alternatives is realistic prior to the decision, but after the decision the pressure is great to bring belief and action into balance. The results plotted in Figure 13-8 support this interpretation. (These results were obtained before the case for a linkage between lung cancer and smoking was as well established as it is now.)

The dissonance theory goes on to make some unobvious predictions: for example, in some cases failure of expectations may strengthen belief rather than destroy it. This was illustrated by the study of a religious cult that expected to be saved from a prophesied disastrous flood by the intervention of a heavenly being. The theory predicted that when the long-awaited day arrived and the prophecy failed (no flood), those who had the

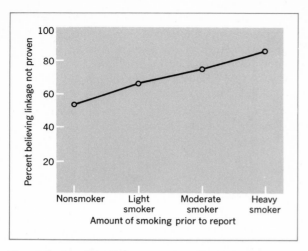

Fig. 13-8 Cognitive dissonance reduced by change in belief
This figure illustrates the belief in lack of linkage between smoking and lung cancer on the part of those who smoke. The heavy smoker remains consistent by denying more often than others that there is any link between smoking and lung cancer. (Data from Minneapolis *Sunday Tribune*, March 21, 1954, as reported by Festinger, 1957)

social support of other believers would proselyte for their beliefs with new enthusiasm, whereas those who had to face the crisis in faith alone would have their faith weakened. These predicted results did indeed occur: the rationalization for the group of disappointed believers who faced failure together was that God had postponed his vengeance because of their faith (Festinger, Riecken, and Schachter, 1956).

Motives toward self-actualization

The tendency to be consistent is but one aspect of how self-perception influences motivation. Earlier illustrations of human motivation might also be reinterpreted in these terms. For example, the success motivation and the avoidance of failure are also concerned with how a person sees himself. White (1959) interprets many motives concerned with curiosity and the desire for knowledge and achievement as though they are all concerned with one's sense of *competence* as a person who effectively relates to the environment. In another sense, the person wants to develop his potential to the fullest, to be as complete a person as he can.

For such a pervasive type of motive the expression *self-actualization* was coined, originally by Carl Jung, one of Freud's followers who later developed a system of his own. By self-actualization he meant the development of full individuality, with all parts of the personality somehow in harmony. This term and closely related ones (productive orientation, creative becoming) have been used by many psychologists who criticize contemporary motivational theory as being too narrow, concerned with short episodes of choice and behavior rather than with the more profound and pervasive aspects of individual hopes and aspirations. The term has been widely used by Maslow, and the following discussion will be based on his conjectures and experiments (Maslow, 1968).

In addition to his general motivational hierarchy (from lower to higher: physiological needs, safety needs, belongingness and love needs, esteem needs, and the need for self-actualization), Maslow distinguishes between the lower and the higher motives in this hierarchy as *deficiency motives* (D-motives) and *being motives* (B-motives). In general, the lower motives are aroused through deficiency; they are urgent determiners of behavior when their satisfaction is lacking. The higher motives (B-motives) come into play chiefly when the D-motives have been cared for. For man to function at his highest level his survival needs and normal social requirements must first be satisfied.

In order to give some empirical support to his position, Maslow sought people who appeared to him to be *self-actualizing persons,* so that he might study them. The selection of these persons did not follow the ordinary methods of choosing a sample and then sorting those within it according to scores on some kind of test. Instead, a great many people were reviewed, of whom a few were selected as best representing what Maslow had in mind as self-actualizers (Maslow, 1970). In a study of a college population, those selected as self-actualizers turned out to be the healthiest 1 percent of the students—that is, they were not characterized by neurotic or psychotic trends and they had full use of their talents, capacities, and potentialities. Eminent historical figures selected by Maslow as self-actualizers included such persons as Abraham

Lincoln, Thomas Jefferson, Albert Einstein, Eleanor Roosevelt, and William James. After an impressionistic study of self-actualizers, Maslow arrived at a kind of composite picture of such a person. His characterization included fifteen items such as the following: efficient perception of reality and comfortable relations with it, acceptance of self and others, spontaneity and continued freshness of appreciation, sense of humor, creativeness, resistance to enculturation (while not especially unconventional, they are relatively independent of their culture).

These qualities are admirable, but it takes a good deal of analysis to see how they come about. Some empirical studies of narrower focus do support many of Maslow's ideas. For example, Kaplan and Singer (1963) report that people who score high on a dogmatism scale (who would be classified as non-self-actualizers because of their inflexibility) are less perceptive in some respects than others; laboratory measures show a correlation of −.61 between dogmatism and sensory acuity. This would support Maslow's notion that self-actualizers are more efficient in the perception of reality. In another study a personality-orientation inventory

was developed based essentially on the characteristics of self-actualizers; results of this were then correlated with a personality inventory scoring both neurotic and extravert-introvert tendencies (Knapp, 1965). The results showed a negative correlation between the personality orientation in the direction of self-actualization and the neuroticism scores, which would support Maslow's contention that he was describing mentally healthy people.

In looking for some other aspects of self-actualizers, Maslow (1959) turned his attention to what he called *peak experiences*. A peak experience is one of happiness and fulfillment. In his terms it is an experience of *being*, which means for him a temporary, nonstriving, non-self-centered, purposeless, self-validating end experience—a state of perfection and goal attainment. After asking some 190 college students to describe any experience that came near to being a peak experience, he attempted to categorize what they said. He came up with a list of values found in such experiences—"B-values," as he called them. They include wholeness, perfection, aliveness, uniqueness, effortlessness, self-sufficiency, and the standard values of beauty, goodness, and truth.

CRITICAL DISCUSSION

Self-actualization and existentialism

There is a robust, optimistic flavor to the concept of self-actualization, which is often reflected in the writings of those who take positions similar to that of Maslow. Rogers says, for example, "It has been my experience that persons have a basically positive orientation [Rogers, 1961, p. 26]."

Existentialism, the closely related view that has emerged from the writings of philosophers, theologians, and humanists, tends to take a somewhat more pessimistic position, or at least a position more oriented toward the tragic in life. Consider, for example, what the theologian Paul Tillich says in *The courage to be* (1952). According to him the three great anxieties that all men must face are those of fate and death, emptiness and meaninglessness, and guilt and condemnation. His thesis is that it takes courage to overcome the despair that all reflective men share. One finds little of this negative view in Maslow or Rogers.

The views of all those mentioned are concerned with man at his most reflective, as well as with man at his moral best. Psychologists have paid little attention to the fact that great literature tends to be tragic and that somehow the basic human problems are reflected in these tragic themes. Self-actualization and other theories of self-fulfillment need to be rounded out by a recognition that many individuals face tragedy in life through no failures of their own. For an understanding of some of the inherent weaknesses in the optimistic "positive thinking" emphases so frequently found in America, a useful review is that of Meyer (1965).

As a result of the study of peak experiences, Maslow has modified his conception of the self-actualizer. It appears now that nearly everyone may at some time have had a peak experience, during which he was, for a time, a self-actualizer. The consistent self-actualizers that Maslow sought earlier differ only in that they have these satisfying peak experiences more frequently, intensely, and perfectly.

Summary

1. The complexity of human motivation is evident when we think of the number of persistent *motivational dispositions,* which differ from one man to another. These dispositions may be quiescent or become manifested in behavior under conditions of appropriate *motivational arousal.*

2. A given type of arousal, say, of achievement motive, will be more effective for those whose motivational dispositions include high achievement motivation, while another type of arousal may be more effective for those with another high motivational disposition, such as affiliative tendencies.

3. *Overt behavior,* while motivated and hence expressive of motives, cannot be used to infer motives directly, because the same behavior may serve different goals. The difficulties in inferring motives directly from behavior lead to arbitrariness in the listing of human motives, although such lists may be useful in a preliminary way by calling attention to the range of motivated behavior in which man engages.

4. Three theories of human motivation were used in this chapter to illustrate the nature of such theories: *psychoanalytic theory, behavior theory,* and *cognitive theory.*

5. The psychoanalytic theory of Freud emphasizes two basic drives: *sex* and *aggression.* These motives arise in infancy, but their free expression is forbidden by parents, and *repression* occurs. A repressed tendency remains active, however, as an *unconscious motive* and finds expression in indirect or symbolic ways.

6. Behavior theory as proposed by Whiting and Child makes the assumption that a few basic motives acquired in early infancy proliferate into *behavior systems* in later life, in which many kinds of behavior are influenced by a common motive. The mechanism of development is assumed to be that of learning and habit formation. Two such basic motives are *hunger,* with its derivatives in all sorts of food-related behavior, and *dependency,* with its derivatives in all kinds of behavior involving attachment to and affiliation with other people.

7. The cognitive theory of motivation accepts the essential findings of the other theories and combines with them an interest in resourcefulness, goal-setting, and decision-making in which the subject is often aware of the risks involved and controls his behavior accordingly. Two sets of experiments illustrate the cognitive theory: one is on *level of aspiration,* in which goal-setting is determined in part by difficulty level, the involvement of the person in the task, and prior experiences of success and failure. The second set concerns *achievement motivation;* that is, behavior directed toward successful performance according to a standard of excellence.

8. When motives are studied in relation to their organization within the individual, we often find some sort of *self-reference* in the motive, having to do with the way the individual sees himself, what he hopes to become, what values he holds. One aspect of this pattern is the desire of the person to see himself as *consistent,* so he is uneasy when he detects a lack of consistency between what he believes and what he does, or between two belief systems. This discordance is called *cognitive dissonance,* and it has motivational power in causing the individual to make some changes in belief or behavior in order to reduce the dissonance.

9. A broad approach to self-reference in motivation is by way of the conception of *self-actualization.* Maslow introduced the concept of a hierarchy of motives, with deficiency motives (D-motives) lower in the hierarchy and being motives (B-motives) higher. As proposed by Maslow, the self-actualizing tendency has full play only when the lower motives are satisfied. These conceptions concerning self-reference challenge current experimentation on human motivation chiefly by asserting that present approaches to motivation are too fragmentary and do not represent man at his best.

Suggestions for further reading

The most general coverage of human motivation and the most complete bibliography are found in Cofer and Appley, *Motivation: Theory and research* (1964). Shorter treatments can be found in Murray, *Motivation and emotion* (1964), and in two collections of readings, Birney and Teevan (eds.), *Measuring human motivation* (1962), and Teevan and Birney (eds.), *Theories of motivation in personality and social psychology* (1964b). For childhood origins of motives, see Berkowitz, *The development of motives and values in the child* (1964).

Because of the current concern over violence, studies of aggression are particularly timely. Among these (in addition to the popular books referred to in the text) are Carthy and Ebling (eds.), *The natural history of aggression* (1964), Berkowitz (ed.), *Roots of aggression* (1969), and Daniels, Gilula, and Ochberg (eds.), *Violence and the struggle for existence* (1970).

Achievement motivation continues to be one of the more widely studied human motives. Among the recent books are Atkinson and Feather (eds.), *A theory of achievement motivation* (1966), and Heckhausen, *The anatomy of achievement motivation* (1967). On fear of failure as one aspect of achievement motivation, see Birney, Burdick, and Teevan, *Fear of failure* (1969). Achievement motivation in relation to the economic activity of entrepreneurs is considered in McClelland, *The achieving society* (1961), and in McClelland and Winter, *Motivating economic achievement* (1969).

A number of experiments relating dissonance reduction to motivation may be found in Zimbardo, *The cognitive control of motivation* (1968).

For Maslow's views, see his *Toward a psychology of being* (1968) and the references found therein.

affect
and
emotion

LIFE WITHOUT EMOTION WOULD BE DRAB. IF
there were no joys and sorrows, no hopes and
dismays, no triumphs or failures, human
experience would lose its warmth and color.

Man likes to have pleasurable states endure and
does things to make them recur; man also prefers
to have unpleasant, painful, or annoying states end
promptly and does what he can to avoid them. But
is this a sufficient statement of the relation between
emotion and motivation? We need to look more
closely into pleasant and disturbing affective states
to see how they are related to goal-directed behavior.

When we call attention to the pleasantness or
unpleasantness of experiences, we are referring to
their *affective tone.* At a time when psychologists
were more given to making fine introspective distinctions than they are today, they called the mild
affective states *feelings* and reserved the term *emotion* for the more profound and stirred-up states
suggested by such words as terror, grief, rage, or
exultation. But the characterization of "stirred-up"
is not enough to distinguish between emotions and
other states, for the body is stirred up when we
play tennis or swim; it is really the *intensity*
of the affective toning that makes the state emotional. A full-fledged emotion will be reflected in
characteristic behavior and diffuse changes in body
physiology—the kinds of behavior that permit us
to detect emotions in others or in animals. There
may be, however, many intermediate states between the very mild experiences of pleasantness

and unpleasantness and the violent, intense emotions: less-defined states of excitement or quiescence, of appreciation of beauty or dislike of ugliness. We shall therefore not attempt to pinpoint where on this scale "emotions" begin, but instead we will be concerned with a variety of affective states.

Virtually all psychologists who have classified emotions divide them into those that are *pleasant* (joy, love) and those that are *unpleasant* (anger, sadness)—a classification that suggests the primacy of acceptance and rejection, of approach and avoidance as the very basis of emotion. Further classification according to intensity is provided by many of our emotional terms. Word pairs such as anger-rage, fear-horror, pain-agony, sadness-grief convey differences of intensity. By treating at once the whole family of experiences from mild satisfactions and annoyances at one end of the scale through weak emotional states up to the most

intense emotions at the other end, we emphasize the continuities among these affective states.

In an experiment to see how our language reflects differences in emotional intensity, Plutchik (1962) presented some lists of emotional words to college students, asking them to rate the intensity of emotion that the word signified, using a scale from 1 to 11, with 1 being low and 11 very intense. Representative of his results are the ratings found for six classes, or "dimensions," of emotional experience (Table 14-1). Note that at quite a high level (rated between 9 and 10 on the 11-point scale) are *rage, ecstasy, astonishment, terror, grief,* and *loathing,* while terms in corresponding dimensions rated at a lower level (below 9 on the 11-point scale) are *anger, joy, surprise, fear, sorrow,* and *disgust.*

Once we recognize the gradation from less intense to more intense experiences, the traditional distinction between feeling and emotion loses its

TABLE 14-1 JUDGED INTENSITY OF EMOTIONAL SYNONYMS						
RATED INTENSITY	I	II	III	IV	V	VI
10	—Rage	—Ecstasy		—Terror / —Panic		
9	—Anger		—Astonishment / —Amazement		—Grief	—Loathing
8		—Joy		—Fear		—Disgust
7		—Happiness	—Surprise		—Sorrow	
6				—Apprehension	—Dejection	
5	—Annoyance	—Pleasure			—Gloominess	—Dislike

Source: Modified from Plutchik (1962).

In each column the synonym high in the column was rated as a more intense experience than one lower in the column.

force. In discussing the emotional aspects of behavior and experience, we shall include all our affectively toned activity regardless of intensity. In summary, we shall define as an *affective state* the condition of the organism during emotionally toned experience, regardless of whether the emotional toning is mild or intense and whether the motor accompaniments are slight or conspicuous.

Physiology of emotion

The symptoms of fear reported by fliers on missions in the Second World War (Table 14-2) well illustrate the complexity of the bodily processes in an emotional state. The symptoms at the top of the list, the ones most frequently mentioned, are the milder ones (pounding heart, tense muscles), while the less frequent symptoms, near the bottom of the list, are more severe (confusion, faintness, loss of memory, nausea).

The symptoms of emotion, especially of intense emotion, include profound changes throughout the body that are regulated in a complex way by the central nervous system, by both divisions of the autonomic system, and by the endocrine glands.

Brain mechanisms in emotion

In intense emotion (but in milder affective states as well) a complex patterning of brain processes occurs. The central nervous system, controlling the striate muscles, is responsible for frowning, grimacing, muscular tension, moaning, whining, purring, snarling. The autonomic system and the endocrine glands control the flow of epinephrine (also known as adrenalin), the acceleration of the heart, and other visceral responses that are part of the total emotional response pattern. The tears in laughter and weeping are controlled by the autonomic system, the vocal and facial muscles by the central nervous system, and the changes in breathing by both systems.

How are these patterned states regulated? Many theories and much fragmentary evidence are available, but we need to know a great deal more before we fully understand the physiological patterning of emotional expression. There is evidence that the hypothalamus plays a central role in the organization and activation of many types of emotional and motivational behavior. For example, the hypothalamus exerts control over the pattern

TABLE 14-2 SYMPTOMS OF FEAR IN COMBAT FLYING			
"DURING COMBAT MISSIONS DID YOU FEEL"	"OFTEN"	"SOMETIMES"	TOTAL
A pounding heart and rapid pulse	30%	56%	89%
That your muscles were very tense	30	53	83
Easily irritated, angry, or "sore"	22	58	80
Dryness of the throat or mouth	30	50	80
"Nervous perspiration" or "cold sweat"	26	53	79
"Butterflies" in the stomach	23	53	76
Sense of unreality, that this couldn't be happening to you	20	49	69
Need to urinate very frequently	25	40	65
Trembling	11	53	64
Confused or rattled	3	50	53
Weak or faint	4	37	41
Right after a mission, unable to remember details of what happened	5	34	39
Sick to the stomach	5	33	38
Unable to concentrate	3	32	35
That you have wet or soiled your pants	1	4	5

Source: Based on reports of 1985 flying officers and 2519 enlisted fliers of the Second World War. After Shaffer (1947).

described as "rage." A restricted surgical lesion in part of the hypothalamus may make a cat that formerly welcomed friendly petting and caressing turn savagely upon the person who tries to handle it in a gentle manner. Other portions of the old brain appear to participate in affective responses as well; much of the gray matter at the base of the brain, called the *limbic system,* is involved. The reticular activating system, as a general arousal mechanism, has a role. It should be noted, however, that none of these systems has exclusively affective functions; they participate in a wide range of behavior. As we shall see presently, the attempt to define or classify emotions according to the bodily responses has not proved successful.

Classifying emotions and distinguishing among them

The most familiar emotions are those that occur with great intensity and hence are readily identified: fear, anger, pain, grief, great joy. But when we examine the rich vocabulary of emotion in our common language, we note how incomplete this list is. How about envy, jealousy, disgust, sexual love, mother love, esthetic pleasure, uneasiness, comfort? The more subtle the affective experience, the more difficult it is to name it and specify it.

Physiological differentiation. Because strong emotions have been associated with violent and widespread disturbances in the body, there has long been an attempt to differentiate emotions on the basis of bodily responses. If the face always flushed in anger and always blanched in fear, this would be a convenient way to describe the differences between anger and fear. Unfortunately, it is not easy to find such consistent differences, although there has been some limited success in showing a difference for these two kinds of experience.

Ax (1953) attached various devices to his subjects so that he could simultaneously record seven different physiological indicators of emotional response (pulse rate, heart stroke, breathing rate, face temperature, hand temperature, galvanic skin response, and muscle action currents above the eyes).

He then frightened his subjects on some occasions and angered them on others. In doing this, he made clever use of the technicians in his laboratory, whose clumsiness with the instruments invoked fear and whose temperamental remarks induced anger; the emotional arousal obtained was more natural than is usually the case in laboratory experiments. Each of the subjects was angered once and frightened once (about half in one order, half in the reverse) and then questioned about the reality of the emotion as it was experienced.

The experimenter developed fourteen indexes or scores, based on the seven physiological indicators, to use in describing the emotional responses of the subjects. Half of these were common to both fear and anger. But the other half showed significant differences in the degree to which they were displayed in anger and in fear (Figure 14-1). The differences more prominent in fear correspond to the action of epinephrine; those more prominent in anger correspond to the action of both epinephrine and norepinephrine (see p. 27).

These findings on the differences between fear and anger are supported by studies of the adrenal medullas of wild animals. Rabbits, which depend for survival on the ability to run away quickly (as in fear), show a predominance of epinephrine; lions and other aggressive animals (whose responses resemble behavior in anger) show a relatively high amount of norepinephrine (Funkenstein, 1955).

This type of research has been extended to include chemical studies of the blood (Funkenstein, King, and Drolette, 1957). Under experimental circumstances designed to arouse anger, some subjects openly expressed their anger, others felt angry but turned the anger inward upon themselves, still others became severely anxious. The open expression of anger and the anxiety reaction were associated with the secretion of norepinephrine in the blood; the controlled, inward-directed anger was associated with the secretion of epinephrine.

While these experiments showed some slight differences between responses interpreted as fear and anger, even anger did not turn out to have

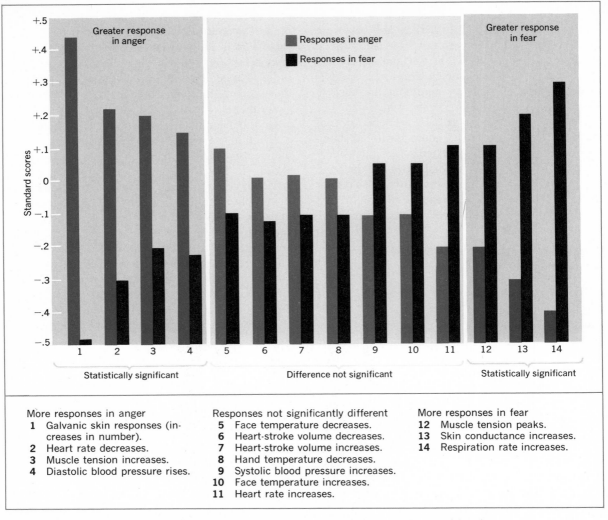

Fig. **14-1 Differential reactions in anger and fear** The chart plots changes from the normal (zero) level for 14 physiological indicators all simultaneously recorded. The indicators below are numbered to correspond to the numbers at the base of the chart. (After Ax, 1953)

just one set of indicators; its physiological pattern depended upon how open or inward the expression of anger was. It is apparent that for more subtle degrees of affective response, physiological differentiation will not prove very satisfactory.

Other kinds of evidence bear this out. For one thing, the patterns of response may be quite consistent within the individual but differ sharply from one person to another. The consistent patterns of

bodily responses an individual might exhibit under a variety of conditions are illustrated in a study conducted by Schnore (1959). The subjects were required to do a number of tasks under varying degrees of motivational arousal (presumably having different affective accompaniments). A record was kept of certain physiological indicators. The results for two subjects are shown in Figure 14-2. The patterns of the indicators are remarkably

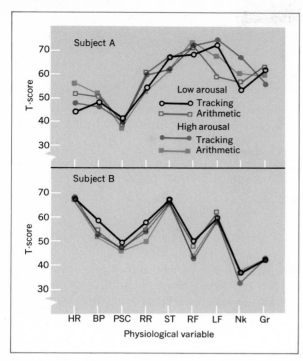

Fig. 14-2 **Consistency of patterns for physiological activity levels** Subjects A and B did two tasks (tracking and arithmetic), each under two levels of arousal (low and high). The consistency of their response patterns is charted on the graph. (After Schnore, 1959) The various physiological indicators are noted along the baseline, as follows:

HR heart rate
BP blood pressure
PSC palmar skin conductance
RR respiration rate

ST skin temperature
RF tension in right forearm
LF tension in left forearm
Nk tension in neck
Gr strength of grip

constant for each of the subjects, but very different from one subject to the other.

Role of situational determinants in defining emotion. When subjects are asked to describe their emotions, they usually begin by telling about the arousing circumstances, that is, what angered them, what pleased them, what frightened them. Then they go on to describe some of their bodily reactions (palpitations of the heart, dry throat, and so on); they may add something about mental confusion or other difficulties in dealing with the situation; and they usually tell what the episode led them to do (Fraisse, 1968). They do not define the

emotion by a simple "introspective" description of their psychological states.

A number of years ago Cantril and Hunt (1932) injected epinephrine into adult subjects and questioned them about their emotions resulting from the symptoms that the drug produced (trembling, increased breathing, disturbed pulse and heartbeat). Several of the subjects gave responses such as: "I feel as if afraid or angry, but I am not afraid or angry." One of them said: "I feel that during the whole reaction I should be readily subject to any kind of emotional suggestion." The physiological state alone was insufficient to define the emotion.

Thirty years later Schachter and Singer (1962) extended the experiment by injecting the drug and manipulating the environmental conditions in such a way as to test some conjectures about the way in which emotions become labeled. They proposed that, in man at least, an emotional state depends both upon the state of physiological arousal and upon a cognition appropriate to this state of arousal; the cognition determines what label will be assigned to the emotion. More specifically, they formulated and tested the following three propositions:

1. If a person is in a physiological state for which he has no immediate explanation, he will label this state according to the environmental circumstances determining his cognitions.

2. If the person has an appropriate explanation for his state ("I feel this way because I just received a drug injection"), then the environmental circumstances will have less influence on the label he assigns because he has no need for a further evaluative label.

3. Even given the same environmental circumstances that led to assigning an emotional label appropriate to the subject's cognitions when he was physiologically aroused, no such emotional label will be assigned when he is not aroused.

In order to test the adequacy of these propositions, epinephrine was administered to the following three groups of subjects: (1) epinephrine-informed subjects, who were told what physiological changes to expect after the drug was injected (accelerated heartbeat, involuntary tremor of hands, arms, or legs); (2) epinephrine-ignorant subjects, who received no information about expected symptoms; (3) epinephrine-misinformed subjects, who were told to expect the wrong symptoms (numbness, itching, headache). Finally a placebo group was treated with a neutral saline solution that would not produce any physiological arousal; they received the same instructions as the epinephrine-ignorant group. The conjecture is that the more ambiguous the physiological state, the greater the likelihood that its emotional labeling will be assigned according to the environmental context. The unaroused placebo group has little physiological disturbance to require an emotional label. The other conditions, all aroused conditions but each with different amounts of ambiguity regarding the physiological symptoms, should be subject to the increasing influence of context upon emotional labeling, in the order of the groups listed above. This follows because the physiological symptoms are fully explained in the first group, unaccounted for in the second, and completely puzzling in the third.

To test the cognitive influences, two opposite cognitions were created by the use of a "stooge"—a trained companion subject who had presumably been given the same drug and who supposedly was participating in the experiment under the same circumstances as the untrained subjects. This trained subject acted either "euphoric," that is, playfully doodling, making paper airplanes, playing "basketball" by throwing wads of paper into the wastebasket (and encouraging his partner to join him), or "angry," that is, complaining about the experiment, resenting a questionnaire that he and his partner had to fill out, and so on. The prediction was that the subject most confused about his physiological arousal would interpret his mood according to that of the companion, and would feel euphoric in the one instance and angry in the other. A subject given the placebo, with no physiological arousal, should show relatively little emotion.

The conditions and the experimental predictions are summarized in Table 14-3. The results based

TABLE 14-3   PHYSIOLOGICAL AROUSAL AND COGNITIVE INFLUENCE UPON THE LABELS ASSIGNED EMOTIONAL STATES

AROUSAL CONDITION	EMOTIONAL STATE REPORTED	
	EUPHORIA COGNITION	ANGER COGNITION
Placebo	Little euphoria	Little anger
Epinephrine-informed	Little euphoria	Little anger
Epinephrine-ignorant	More euphoria	More anger
Epinephrine-misinformed	Much euphoria	*not tested*

Source: Schachter and Singer (1962).

both on the observed behavior of the subjects and on their self-reports were essentially in agreement with the conjectures, although they were somewhat more pronounced for the euphoria condition than for the anger condition. The experiment has recently been repeated, but with the use of hypnosis to control the cognitive condition (Zimbardo and others, 1970). The results were not exactly those reported by Schachter and Singer. They found that an aroused condition, without environmental justification, was considered to be unpleasant.

In a somewhat related experiment Valins (1967) was able to show that subjects used the perception of their physiological responses (heart rate) to interpret how emotional a stimulus was, rather than conforming to the expectation that their emotional perception would control their heartbeat. This experiment used the ingenious method of having a subject listen to the supposed recording of his heartbeat as he viewed some seminude photographs of young women. Actually the subject was listening to a randomly assigned heart recording. Those pictures that were associated with a more pronounced heart reaction were judged to be the most emotionally arousing by the subjects. A control group, which knew that the heart responses were irrelevant, did not permit the recordings to affect their judgments of the pictures' emotional arousal.

The foregoing discussion indicates that attempts to formulate theories of emotion on the basis of physiological responses alone are likely to be unsuccessful. There have been several historically important theories, however, and a number of contemporary attempts to formulate an interpretation of emotion.

Darwin's theory

Charles Darwin, having proposed that man's behavior was the evolutionary product of a long ancestry, tested his evolutionary theory in the field of emotions by studying the emotional expressions of animals and men. He proposed three principles (Darwin, 1872):

1. *The principle of associated habits.* If teeth are bared in fighting, bared teeth become the expression of anger; if protruding lips are used in discharging substances from the mouth, similar movements are used in expressing disgust.

2. *The principle of antithesis.* If a crouching movement prepares the organism for attack or for defense against aggression, then its opposite—a defenseless, fawning response as a gesture of friendliness or welcome—signals the opposite emotion. Thus, in man, extending the hand in welcome (the opposite of a fighting posture) or removing the glove (a residue of the mailed fist) are gestures that illustrate this Darwinian principle.

3. *The principle of direct action of the nervous system.* Darwin saw that some responses, such as writhing in pain, had little meaning other than being an intense and widespread physiological response, what today would be called arousal or activation.

The evolutionary principle is still an important one in interpreting emotion. It may account, in part, for the prevailing view that there is something very primitive about emotion, including its control by older parts of the brain.

The James-Lange theory

The *James-Lange theory,* a classic theory of emotions named after the two men who originated it in the 1880s, stressed the importance in felt emotion of the repercussion of the bodily responses. William James stated this in the form of seeming paradoxes that put the cart before the horse: "We are afraid because we run." "We are angry because we strike." What gives the theory some plausibility is that our awareness of bodily states not only involves a judgment of the situation evolving the emotion (for example, perceiving it as dangerous or frightening) but also involves what today we call a *feedback* from the bodily responses released in emotion. Thus when we stumble on the stairs, we automatically grasp the handrail before we have time to recognize our emotional state; our felt emotion, after the crisis is over, includes the perception of a pounding heart and exaggerated breathing. Because this recognition comes after the bodily responses, the theory has some plausibility; at the same time, in view of the fact that recognition comes after the circumstances have already been judged (as dangerous, and so on), it is doubtful that the felt bodily responses are entirely responsible for the quality differentiating one emotion from another.

Activation theory

Because they have not been successful in making fine distinctions among the various emotions, theorists have turned their attention to the general state of excitement characteristic of strong emotion, rather than to differentiation of one state from another on a physiological basis. This shift is consonant not only with Darwin's third principle (direct action of the nervous system) but also with the experiments that show surrounding circumstances to be important in distinguishing one state from another. Such a viewpoint may be called an *activation theory* (Lindsley, 1951; Malmo, 1959; Duffy, 1962). According to this theory, the main dimension of emotion is that of arousal (as by the reticular system), from quiescent sleep at one extreme to diffuse excitement at the other. Under excitement, energy gets mobilized for action, so that it becomes difficult to distinguish between motivation and emotion.

Perceptual-motivational theories

Arnold (1960) is one of those who has stressed the role of perception in emotion. She rightly points out that the tears brought on by a letter bearing bad news must be based on some kind of judgment of the content of the letter. Revising the James-Lange theory, she recognizes the following sequence of events in emotion:

perception → appraisal → emotion → expression and action

She considers the emotion (as the middle term in this series) to be a general tendency to approach or continue situations judged as pleasant and to avoid or terminate situations judged as unpleasant. For her, emotion is intimately tied to motivation.

Leeper (1965), also proposing a perceptual-motivational theory of emotion, argues that the motivational and emotional significance of the widespread bodily changes in emotion arises only because these changes affect the organization of cortical processes: the cortical processes, by way of their perceptual or representational functions, are the truly motivational processes. His complete argument is that (1) it is a mistake to emphasize the disruptive emotions, because affective processes range from mild to intense, and may be pleasant or unpleasant; (2) emotions are motives; and (3) emotional processes, along with other motives, have important perceptual aspects. Activation is not the only function of emotions; Leeper, in agreement with Arnold, believes that emotions also give direction to behavior.

Perhaps one reason for the unsatisfactory state of theories of emotion is that the more precise theories attempt to account for limited aspects of what is a very broad and complex field, and that the more general theories attempt to cover the whole range but get caught in the complexity of human motivation as it is related to emotion.

Emotional development

Emotional expression, like other complex behavior, develops through both maturation and learning. The infant is born with the capacity to cry, and the capacity to laugh comes through maturation. However, some aspects of his emotional behavior are acquired. As the child grows older, he learns to cry for a purpose—to gain parental attention or sympathy—and he learns to withhold his tears sometimes when he feels like crying. He learns, too, that there are times when it is proper to laugh and times when laughter is frowned upon. The child has to learn not only the occasions for emotion, but how to control emotional expression according to the patterns considered proper in his culture. He may laugh and cry softly or loudly, with or without restraint. He learns to distinguish among a pleasant smile, a gentle laugh, and a loud guffaw.

Unlearned aspects of emotional arousal and expression

The newborn infant has a very limited repertoire of emotional responsiveness. Most contemporary students of infant behavior agree that at birth the only distinguishable emotion is excitement. Aside from this emotion there is only quiescence, probably not an emotional state at all. The state of excitement (crying, straining, thrashing about) appears to the observer to be an emotionally unpleasant one. The resting or quiet state of the newborn child is emotionally neutral, without the positive qualities of the later cheerful, cooing, delighted state. If, in the beginning, the one emotional state is a rather unpleasant departure from quiescence, how does emotional responsiveness develop?

We may recall from the Schachter and Singer study (p. 340) that the adult's labeling of an emotion depends very much upon the environmental context, which provides cognitive cues for the chosen label. We cannot expect this cognitive process to occur in the young infant; behavior in the early months—smiling and laughing, crying, yelling, thrashing about—is no doubt more a reflection of the infant's internal state of arousal. The adult is likely to name these states as pleasure, fear, or rage, but in the infant they represent fairly direct responses to environmental stimulation (caressing, restricting movements, and so on) and to internal states. The child gradually comes to recognize the different emotional states and learns the words with which to label them. This development has both maturational and learning aspects, as in connection with a child's reaction to strangers (see Figure 14-3).

That the process of differentiation of emotional responsiveness through maturation goes on beyond early infancy is supported by a study of emotional expression in a ten-year-old child, deaf and blind from birth. This child had had no opportunity to learn the expression of emotions from other children; her only observations came through touch. Yet under conditions that would tend to provoke fear, anger, or pleasure, her facial expressions of crying or laughter and her accompanying postures and gestures all accorded very well with the typical descriptions of emotional behavior (Goodenough, 1932). It appears that characteristic forms of emotion as well as many of the actions that indicate emotion to us are essentially inborn and develop without any special opportunities for learning. The same is true of many of the occasions for emotion. Animals, as well as men, show fear when confronted by novel, unusual, or unexpected situations. Anger tends to be provoked, as we shall see, by any restraint against the free running of a motivated sequence of behavior.

Learned emotional responsiveness

The occasions that arouse emotion and the forms of emotional expression appear to have inborn aspects but also may be modified by learning.

Alone, but calm and attentive.

Apprehension and screaming at approach of stranger.

Stranger turns away; screaming subsides.

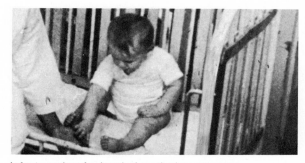
Infant reaches for hand of motionless stranger.

Fig. **14-3 Fear of strangers** At about eight months, the child's ability to discriminate among people leads to increasing uneasiness with strangers.

Learning the occasions for emotion. As indicated above, there are some innately frightening stimuli (sudden loud sounds, the appearance of strange stimuli), but the *occasions* on which we are frightened change as we grow older. Though we may not have to learn how to be afraid, we learn what to be afraid of—dangers that are perceived to be dangerous as the result of experience. As the infant grows he learns to distinguish between what is familiar, and therefore "safe," and what is unfamiliar, and therefore perhaps "dangerous" or "threatening."

In the course of giving psychological tests to a number of infants during their first year of life, Bayley (1932) noted the occasions on which the infants cried. As the infants grew older the causes of crying shifted, as shown in Figure 14-4. Strangeness of places and persons produces the largest increase in relative frequency of crying as the child gets older. A possible interpretation is that the older the child is, the better he is able to discriminate between the familiar and the strange, and hence the more often he reacts to strangeness by crying.

An experiment was designed by Hebb (1946) to study the kinds of objects that provoked fear in

Fig. **14-4** **Infants' reasons for crying change with age** The relative amount of crying to be attributed to strangeness increases as contrasted with other causes of crying—fatigue after testing and reaction to specific test. (After Bayley, 1932)

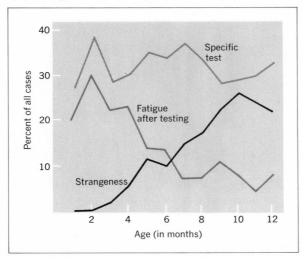

chimpanzees born and reared in captivity so that the history of their previous experience with objects would be known. These chimpanzees tended to show fear of many strange objects that they saw for the first time: a skull, a painted wax snake, a disembodied chimpanzee head. They showed marked fear of strangers and were disturbed by slight changes in the clothing of familiar attendants.

Learning may influence emotions in other ways. One explanation of the manner in which emotions become associated with new objects or occasions is through *conditioning*. For example, a song heard during an unhappy experience may always thereafter arouse in the hearer an emotion of unhappiness.

A famous experiment in which a child learned to fear a white rat serves as the prototype of emotional conditioning (Watson and Rayner, 1920). When shown a white rat the infant boy Albert reached for it and showed no signs of fear. While he was paying attention to the rat, he was suddenly frightened by a loud sound. Thereafter he was afraid of the rat. The originally neutral rat became a "conditioned stimulus" to fear. Albert then also showed fear of his mother's fur neckpiece and of other soft and furry objects. He showed no such fear of rubber balls or blocks, which were entirely un-ratlike in appearance.

It is supposed that many irrational fears are acquired in this relatively automatic way. Because lightning precedes thunderbolts, the child comes to fear the lightning as much as the thunder, although the loud sound of the thunder is the primary reason for fright. But many children (and adults) experience fear when they are aware of impending danger; their fear of lightning is probably less related to its association with thunderclaps than to the real danger of being struck by lightning. One must be careful not to explain too much by conditioning; fear of real danger is rational and arises, in part at least, through understanding.

Ordinary observation shows many learned occasions for emotions. In the American culture, for example, men seldom weep, whether the occasion be a wedding, a funeral, or failure to pass an examination in college, although American women commonly weep on such occasions. Frenchmen weep much more freely than American men. Sending a loved one off on a trip may be the cause for weeping by the whole French family. How to weep is not learned, but when and where to weep are.

Learning how to express emotion. Laughing and weeping have large unlearned aspects, as other emotions do. This does not prevent many modifications in emotional expression. Anger, for example, may be expressed by fighting, by using abusive language, or by leaving the room. Leaving the room is not an expression of emotion that is known at birth, and certainly the abusive language has to be learned.

Studies of emotional expression in different cultures demonstrate impressively how much expression is developed by learning. One psychologist reviewed several Chinese novels in order to determine how a Chinese writer portrayed various human emotions. Many of the bodily changes in emotion (flushing, paling, cold perspiration, trembling, goose pimples) are used as symptoms of emotion in Chinese fiction much as they are in Western writing. He found, however, that the Chinese have many other and quite different ways of expressing emotion. The following quotations from Chinese novels would surely be misinterpreted by an American reader unfamiliar with the Chinese (Klineberg, 1938):

"Her eyes grew round and opened wide."
(She became angry.)
"They stretched out their tongues."
(They showed signs of surprise.)
"He clapped his hands."
(He was worried or disappointed.)
"He scratched his ears and cheeks."
(He was happy.)

Such evidence indicates that cultures teach conventionalized or stereotyped forms of expression, which become a kind of "language of emotion" recognized by others within the culture. Skilled actors are able to convey to their audiences any intended emotion by using facial expression, tone of voice, and gesture according to the patterns the audience recognizes. In simulating emotion those of us who are less skilled actors can convey our intent by exaggerating the conventional expressions: gritting our teeth and clenching our fists to indicate anger, turning down the corners of our mouth to look sad, raising our eyebrows to express doubt or disapproval.

Emotion and motivation

No arguments are needed to establish the close relationship between emotion and motivation. Think of the stirring scenes in the theater or in literature, in which emotions provoke men to violent or desperate action and in which resolute, heroic, or shameful actions are accompanied by an intensification of emotion. These scenes, reflecting as they do what transpires in real life, suggest that emotion acts both as a *motive* and as an *accompaniment to motivated action*. The triangle theme of love and jealousy is at once a story of motivation and of emotion. Sex is not only a powerful motive; it is a source of vivid emotional experience as well. The emotional experience itself may become a goal for which behavior is undertaken.

The motivational significance of fear, anxiety, and jealousy

Emotional states are aroused states. An unpleasant emotional state corresponds to the tension state in aroused drive, and the organism seeks to terminate it. If frightened, the organism tries to escape exactly as it attempts to escape from pain. The person who fears high places will learn to avoid such places or, if he finds himself at a height, will be restless until he gets away. Reduction of the tension aroused in unpleasant emotion is equivalent to the reduction of drive tension. Actually, in this situation emotion *is* drive. The interpretation of emotion as drive is illustrated by the following study of fear built upon pain.

Fear. Miller (1948a) conducted an experiment in which he placed rats one at a time in the left compartment of the box shown in Figure 14-5. Each rat received an electric shock in the closed compartment, with no means of escape. Each reacted to the shock with signs of pain and fright—jumping about, squealing, defecating. After a few repetitions of shock in this compartment, each rat became emotionally agitated when placed in the compartment, even though shock was no longer administered. They had all acquired a conditioned fear of the compartment.

Next the rats learned to use a trap door as a means of escape into the second compartment, in which they had never received a shock. For several hundred trials, whenever a conditioned rat was placed in compartment A, it went through the trap door to compartment B, even though it no longer received shocks in compartment A. When the trap door was locked and a second escape device substituted, the rat learned to use the new device as a means of escape.

Fig. **14-5 Apparatus used in studying fear as an acquired drive** The apparatus contains two compartments: one that is white with a grid as a floor, and the other black with a smooth solid floor. The compartments are separated by a door that can be opened by the rat's moving a wheel above the right-hand half of the door. Because the rat has been shocked in the white compartment, it is tense and agitated there, and learns to use the wheel that permits it to go to the "safety" of the black compartment. It continues to do this for many trials after the shocks in the white compartment have ceased. (After Miller, 1948a)

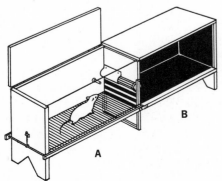

This experiment shows not only that the rats acquired a fear of the compartment in which they were shocked, but that the fear became an acquired drive. The animals were driven to go from the compartment in which they were tense and agitated to that in which they were more relaxed and comfortable. The "safe" compartment served as an incentive to relieve the fear. Thus aroused fear and the impulse toward fear reduction are not unlike aroused hunger and the impulse to reduce hunger pangs. Many psychologists believe that such acquired fears and related states of anxiety and apprehension account for much human motivation.

Once a fear is acquired, it leads to strong avoidance of those situations in which the feared object or event is likely to appear. Fear motivates the organism both to escape from the feared object and to avoid contact with it. Extreme or pathological fears, known as *phobias*, greatly affect the conduct of those who suffer from them. The fears may be of such things as high places, closed spaces, open spaces, animals, dirt, diseases—almost anything can become the object of a phobia. A striking case history of a phobia was given by William Ellery Leonard in his autobiography, *The locomotive god.* His fear of a locomotive, based on a childhood incident, led to fear of leaving home, until he virtually imprisoned himself. He dared go only a short distance away. Fear was a powerful motive greatly affecting his movements, and hence the very course of his life.

Anxiety. Anxiety is a state closely related to fear and, like fear, has motivational consequences. Because the vocabulary of emotion comes from the language of ordinary life and of literature, it lacks scientific precision. *Anxiety* is a word from this vocabulary, and psychologists are not consistent in the way they use it. Perhaps the most common meaning for psychologists is *vague fear.* Ordinary fear always has an object, but anxiety is fear with only a vague object or with no object at all.

Anxiety, like fear, is unpleasant, a tension state from which we yearn to escape. Hence anxiety, too, can be considered a drive. An individual is often made to conform to social expectations by threats to his security; that is, the threats make

Although the definition of anxiety as a vague fear, as in "free-floating" anxiety, covers many instances, several other conjectures have found some support.

A second use of anxiety restricts it to a more specific kind of vague fear—the *fear of insecurity*. According to the concept on which this use is based, anxiety is social in its origin, beginning in infancy, when the child is dependent upon the adults who care for him. Deprivation, neglect, and loss of affection arouse feelings of insecurity that the infant comes to fear. This fear of insecurity is considered the basic anxiety, and it is always associated with other people. What is feared is isolation and lack of affectionate responses from others. This meaning of anxiety is distinguished from fear in that *things* can cause fear but only *people* can cause insecurity (Sullivan, 1949).

Anxiety is used in a third way to mean *concern over our own conduct,* that is, feelings of guilt. We are uneasy about forbidden impulses or past misdemeanors. We fear that if they come to light, our guilt will be uncovered. Children, for example, learn to show love and respect for their parents, yet they are often resentful of parental authority; fear of blurting out their hidden resentments may be a source of anxiety. The adolescent may fear to reveal his intensified interest in sex. Fear of being afraid or of showing fear may give rise to anxiety, especially if the accepted code (as in some military groups) is to appear fearless. Concern about our own feelings is undoubtedly one important form that anxiety takes.

Modern existentialists, concerned with man's concept of himself, identify other aspects of anxiety but describe them in such half-mystical ways that it is difficult to incorporate their findings in science. Anxiety in this usage is said to arise in part because of the contemplation of the inevitability of death and in part because of a sense of man's unrealized possibilities. These views derive from Søren Kierkegaard (1813–55), an early existentialist philosopher (Kierkegaard, 1844; tr. by Lowrie, 1944). While Kierkegaard's translator uses the word "dread," the word "anxiety" can be substituted for it (May, 1950; Tillich, 1952).

---

him anxious if he does not conform. If he breaks the law, he may be punished by a fine or by imprisonment. Society hopes that the punishment will not only control his conduct in the future but also stand as a warning to others, intensifying their anxieties if they violate the code. Not all nonconformity is serious enough to require punishment, but the nonconformer may find himself teased or ridiculed. Because ridicule sets him apart and makes him feel ostracized, it arouses anxiety about his status and puts pressure upon him to behave like those about him.

Jealousy. Jealousy, a special form of anxiety based on insecurity, involves *fear of loss of affection to a rival.* That it has strong drive properties is evident enough from the frequent occurrence of the triangle theme in dramatic literature. The husband who is jealous of another man believes that

the man is stealing his wife's affection; even if there is no rival, the jealous husband guards his wife lest one appear. The reactions of the jealous person may be violent. He may attack a genuine rival, or if there is only the fear of a rival, he may go to great pains to protect and keep informed about the loved one whose faithfulness he is afraid of losing.

Emotions such as jealousy and envy are distinguished more by their motivational aspects than by the states of arousal that accompany them. A careful effort to distinguish between envy and jealousy as *states* that could be described introspectively or according to bodily responses has led to failure (Ankles, 1939). As *motives,* however, useful distinctions can be made between jealousy as fear of a rival and envy as wishing for something possessed by another. For example, a person may *envy* another person for his car without bearing any ill will toward that person. But in jealousy, attitudes toward the rival are always hostile. These illustrations point up the importance of considering emotions as motives and not merely as stirred-up states of the organism.

The motivational significance of anger and frustration

The earlier discussion of aggression (Chapter 13) might as well have been a discussion of anger, for anger is commonly the instigator of aggressive behavior, or its accompaniment. It is hard, and perhaps futile, to decide which is the emotion and which the motive.

Anger. The primary occasion for anger is the thwarting of goal-seeking activity. Hence anger may be the by-product of any interrupted motivational sequence. The motivational sequence need not be observable in overt activity: an insult produces anger because it is a threat to maintaining self-esteem (Geen, 1968). Although anger may in turn acquire drive properties and lead to retaliatory action against the person or object held responsible for the thwarting, anger *begins* as an emotional accompaniment of some other motivational sequence.

TABLE 14-4 REPORTS BY COLLEGE WOMEN ON IMPULSES STIRRED UP BY ANGER

IMPULSES FOLLOWING ANGER	NUMBER OF REPORTS
To make a verbal retort	53
To do physical injury to offender (slap, pinch, shake, strike, choke, push, step on, scratch, shoot, beat, throw out of window, kill, tear to pieces, throw something at, spank)	40
To injure inanimate objects	20
To run away, leave the room	12
To cry, scream, swear	10
Total reports	135
Number reporting	51

Source: Gates (1926).

In one experiment college women kept records of the occasions on which they experienced anger or extreme irritation and of the impulses that resulted. The annoyances that produced anger or extreme irritation included such matters as unjust accusations and insults, contradictions, scoldings, loss of a fountain pen, breaking of glasses. The impulses to which the anger or irritation led are given in Table 14-4.

Once aroused, anger starts sequences of retaliatory action. To this extent anger functions as a motivator.

Frustration. Any interference with goal-seeking activity has widespread consequences, many of which are emotional.[1] Angry, aggressive action is one of these consequences. However, even in situations with relatively mild deprivation of goal-expectations, frustration appears to be a motivating factor. This has been the inference from a number of experiments by Amsel (1967).

Experiments in frustration often utilize a two-section runway: after receiving a reward in a box at the end of the first section, the animal runs on to a reward in the second. If, after learning this sequence, food is omitted in the first reward box, the animal runs more rapidly to the second. The interpretation is that the frustration through non-reward has increased the motivation. Additional experiments, such as those of Wagner (1963), show that the frustration acts like an aversive drive-stimulus (for example, mild punishment) and can be conditioned just as fear was conditioned in Miller's fear experiment (p. 346). Thus we have evidence for the motivating effect of a mild frustration, with its accompanying affective states (in man) of disappointment or anger.

Laughter and weeping in the context of motivation

Psychologists appear to be preoccupied with unpleasant emotions—fear, anger, rage, pain—while the emotions of joy and laughter tend to be somewhat neglected. As weeping is not entirely an

[1]Some of these consequences, important for mental health and personal adjustment, will be dealt with in Chapter 19.

unpleasant act and is closely related to laughter, we shall consider both of these responses.

Laughter. The child who jumps up and down in joyous laughter at the announcement that he is going to the circus illustrates an emotional accompaniment of motivation. The laughter here is not an end in itself, for laughter as a goal has not been substituted for the desire to go to the circus. While psychologists are by no means in agreement as to all the occasions for laughter, two aspects about them are commonly recognized.

First, most occasions arousing laughter are *social*. One investigator found that in 223 situations in which preschool children laughed, 209 (or 94 percent) of the laughing episodes occurred in the presence of a second person (Kenderdine, 1931). Another investigator, studying 240 college students, found their laughter attributed to social situations in 98 percent of the instances (Young, 1937). Even the physiological response to tickling has a large social component. The child does not laugh when he tries to tickle himself; he laughs only when someone else tickles him (Leuba, 1941).

Second, most occasions for laughter have in them an *element of surprise*. Tickling—one of the most primitive and universal sources of laughter—usually has in it such an element: the tickling is generally threatened before it begins, but the moment of beginning is uncertain. Children's games that call forth laughter, such as "peekaboo," have both social and surprise elements.

The preliminary stages of the laughter-provoking sequences are usually tension-producing, so that the laughter comes as an expression of relief. One of the motivational aspects of laughter is this relief from certain tension-producing situations in the presence of other people. The excitement of mild tension is not damaging, the social

attention is welcome, and the resolution through laughter provides a happy ending. Adults as well as children seek such sequences of events; under these circumstances laughter becomes a goal. It is these sequences that produce laughter in plays, movies, and stories, and on radio and television; their popularity sufficiently attests to their appeal.

Weeping. Laughter and tears are often closely associated, and although we associate laughter with joy and tears with sadness, there are also tears of joy. The writer Arthur Koestler has noted the failure of psychology textbooks to treat weeping, and he has attempted to supply this lack by an analysis of his own. He notes five kinds of situations in which weeping accompanies motivated behavior (Koestler, 1965):

1. *Raptness.* Listening to an organ in a cathedral, looking at a majestic landscape from a mountaintop, watching an infant hesitatingly return a smile—instances such as these may be touching and may provoke tears.

2. *Mourning.* When nothing can be done, on the occasion of loss one "gives in to grief."

3. *Relief.* A mother's reaction to her son's returning from war may be one of joyful relief, yet she may weep, perhaps saying "How silly of me to cry."

4. *Sympathy.* Sharing another's sorrow or joy may bring forth tears.

5. *Self-pity.* A little boy who is attacked by bullies may cry, not so much out of helplessness as out of impotent rage.

These illustrations show how some emotions provide a kind of commentary on ongoing motivated behavior. The weeping is neither a motive nor a goal, but is a sign that something motivationally important is occurring.

Affective states as adaptive and disruptive

What is the role of emotions in civilized life? Do they help organisms to survive or are they chiefly sources of disturbance and maladjustment?

When we consider this question, we first have to inquire about the intensity of the affective experience.

Intensity of emotion and adaptive significance

Affective responses vary from the mildest satisfaction (or dissatisfaction) to the most complete panic (or joy). One consequence of mild emotion is a moderate increase in normal physiological functioning, possibly due to a slight increase in general tension. We know that a moderate increase in tension aids learning. This principle has been demonstrated in experiments in which the subject had to squeeze a dynamometer while memorizing. The subject memorized the material best while under mild tension, when neither too relaxed nor under too much strain (Courts, 1939). If mild emotion produces similar tensions, it may also aid learning. A second consequence of mild emotion, provided it is relevant to a task, is to make the task more important and meaningful. Without affective coloring, activity becomes dull and meaningless and takes on a monotonous tone. Therefore, a mild affective state, generated by interest in a task, has a tonic influence.

Intense emotions, ranging from the unpleasant states of anger, fear, and grief to the pleasant ones of love and joy, play a more ambiguous role. When intense emotions are free to run their course, they do no harm and may increase one's zest for living. Excitement may be followed by relaxation, fear by relief, despair by satisfaction. But situations may arise in which intense emotions cannot run their course. Then worry, anxiety, and heightened tension develop and interfere with smooth performance. In the experiments on the role of tension in memorizing, it was found that there was an optimum point beyond which tension interfered with memorization.

A similar experiment was conducted by Yerkes and Dodson (1908) with mice, chicks, kittens, and men. The subjects were given tasks requiring a discrimination between two levels of brightness; if the wrong one of the two was chosen, the subject received an electric shock. The tasks were of three levels of difficulty, and the shocks of three levels of intensity. It was found that high levels of shock controlled the easiest task very well, but very weak shocks were more effective with the most difficult

task. These results are intuitively reasonable: if the anxiety level is too high over the possibility of receiving a shock, the discriminative processes of the subject are interfered with. The more finely tuned these perceptual processes have to be, the more they are subject to interference by disrupting affects. A moderate level of anxiety facilitates learning at all levels of difficulty.

This experiment has produced a generalization that serves well as a model for the relation between affective intensity and adaptive behavior. The generalization, called the *Yerkes-Dodson Law,* can be stated as follows:

> *The optimum level of aversive stimulation in the control of learning is at some moderate intensity, lower and higher values being less effective; the optimum level decreases as task complexity increases.*

Emotionality and enduring emotional states

Some individuals react more strongly to mild emotional stimuli than others do; we consider such people "emotional." This means that there are emotional dispositions just as there are motivational dispositions, persisting through time and ready to be activated on appropriate occasions. Moreover, just as some motivational arousal is episodic—such as the withdrawal of a hand from a hot stove—so some emotional shocks are episodic, such as a sudden shock of surprise. But aversive states may endure (chronic anxiety instead of sudden fear), and affective states characteristically outlast the immediate situations that provoke them.

Temperament. The word *temperament* has long been used to describe differences in emotionality; we say of one person that he is even-tempered, of another that he is quick to "fly off the handle." Such terms describe emotionality, that is, the readiness to experience and to express emotional responses of various kinds.[2]

[2]Because persisting individual differences of this kind are considered to be aspects of personality, further discussion of temperament appears in Chapter 17.

What should be called an emotion is in part a matter of definition. In this chapter we have emphasized the continuity between mild affective states and the more intense ones, and in the section on the facing page we have treated emotions as occasionally adaptive, occasionally disruptive. Even the disruption may, of course, have adaptive significance under some circumstances, but it is recognized that there may be evolutionary residues in the behavior not appropriate to the conditions of modern civilized life.

Some experts on emotion, taking a different position, limit emotion to those states that are by their nature disorganizing. Young (1961) states: "An emotion is here defined as an acutely disturbed affective state [p. 355]." He recognizes the gradation of affective states but limits emotions to the "acutely disturbed" ones. Fraisse (1968) is so insistent on the loss of control under emotion that he denies that pleasure is an emotion, even sexual pleasure "in so far as the sexual act takes place normally [p. 123]." Joy may become an emotion, but only "when its intensity causes us to lose control of our reactions [p. 124]."

There are two main objections to limiting emotions as Young and Fraisse have done. In the first place, by limiting the definition to a consequence not peculiar to the state itself (for disruption can occur for reasons other than emotion), the definition is not as clear as it at first seems to be. Second, the imposition of this limitation sets aside legitimate empirical questions. For example, what are the psychological consequences of sexual pleasure? This question is not answered by eliminating sexual emotion from study merely because the sex act is not disruptive. That sex is a powerful motive with rich affective connotations is not easily ignored by saying "let's not count it."

Even relatively mild affective states, such as the anxiety states aroused in a psychotherapeutic interview, can show detectable effects in the form of flustered or confused speech (Mahl, 1963)—a form of disorganization that might classify such states as emotional under the definitions of Young and Fraisse. Still, these effects would only be discovered through experimentation in emotions in which the investigator did not feel the need to produce violent disruption.

Psychology must be prepared to deal with the subtle as well as intense effects; a sharp limitation of emotions to responses above some arbitrary point on a scale of disruption seems unwise.

Mood. A state of emotional reactivity that continues through a limited period of time is called a *mood*. Mood is like temperament, but it is not as enduring. Only a person who is characteristically cheerful has a cheerful temperament; anyone, even a characteristically grouchy person, may for a short time be in a cheerful mood. Either temperament or mood will prepare the individual to experience emotion congruent with it. For example, events otherwise more or less neutral become affectively colored according to the prevailing mood. If a person is in a happy mood he may see minor setbacks as amusing challenges and take them in his stride; if he is in a troubled mood he may see them as occasions for anger or despair.

Moods sometimes represent the aftereffects of an emotional shock, as when a person remains somewhat depressed for a time after having received bad news. The mood may linger on, even if the emotion has already been overtly expressed; occasionally the mood continues as a state of tension because the feelings were not freely expressed when the occasion for them arose. Both internal conditions and external events may determine moods. A study of the time of day when children are most likely to show anger revealed that the peak of irascibility was just before meals and just before retiring. Hunger and sleepiness undoubtedly had some influence in arousing the irritable mood (Goodenough, 1931).

Psychosomatic disorders. Medical men today are aware of a group of illnesses that they call *psychosomatic disorders.* Although the symptoms themselves are "somatic," that is, symptoms of damage or disturbance in bodily organs or tissues, the circumstances that give rise to these symptoms appear to lie in the emotional life of the person. Prominent among these psychosomatic illnesses are ulcerative disorders of the digestive tract. It is supposed that ulcers of the stomach may be caused by the changes in muscular tension and in blood distribution in the walls of the stomach resulting from often-repeated or long-continued emotional states. Excessive digestive secretions, which are stimulated by intense emotion, may have chemical effects accentuating the damage. Although the details concerning these effects are still somewhat in question, the association of various organic ailments with prolonged emotional states of certain kinds appears now to be well established.

We have seen, then, that emotional intensity affects the role of emotion in furthering or hindering man's adaptation to his environment. Mild emotions are tonic; intense emotions, sometimes disruptive. More enduring emotional states, as in temperament and mood, may also make adjustment to life's demands easy or difficult and may occasionally lead to actual illness.

Emotional suppression and release

If some features of emotional behavior are adaptive and other features disruptive, we need a hygiene of emotions so that people can enjoy emotional expression without suffering the damage caused by emotional excesses. The hygiene of emotions largely involves the question of emotional control. Does maturity consist primarily of suppressing emotional expression so that life can be conducted more rationally? Or is emotional expression a kind of safety valve essential to healthy living?

Civilization requires us to suppress much overt emotional expression. To be civilized is to be moderate in behavior, not to "lose one's head." We consider imperturbability a virtue. While we admire emotional sensitivity in the form of social warmth and tenderness, we think it should be exercised with restraint. We conventionally tend to admire temperance over free indulgence.

Psychologists doubt the desirability of a general suppression of emotional expression. Some emotional control is no doubt essential for adults as well as for children, but two qualifications concerning the *amount* of control should be kept in mind. (1) Emotional suppression is not always successful; instead of being eliminated, the emotion may express itself in distorted form or in illness. (2) The beneficial results of appropriate emotional release can sometimes be demonstrated.

Many of the physiological aspects of emotional expression—say, muscular tension or blushing—are not under voluntary control. Hence voluntary suppression may not completely suppress, much less always succeed in eliminating, the emotional state. Sometimes, however, the suppression goes on so long and so successfully that one is no longer consciously aware of any need to suppress. Under such circumstances the emotion is said to be repressed. (We will return to the problems of repression and suppression in Chapter 19.) But even repressed emotions are not lost; by appropriate means it is possible to find signs that they are still active.

It is not healthful to deny expression to emotional impulses that are genuine and natural. Although free play should not be given to each and every impulse, emotional control is possible without need for emotional denial. When a person can experience emotionally charged impulses without anxiety and guilt and can achieve a proper balance between expression and control, he is then emotionally healthy. He finds it possible to accept his emotional impulses as natural and to handle their expression in socially acceptable ways.

It is easy to make generalizations about emotional expression and emotional control, but the generalizations are often difficult to apply. For one thing, their application may depend upon circumstances peculiar to a culture or subculture (for example, how would they apply to a Buddhist monk?). For another, in applying them to oneself, one encounters tendencies to self-deception that make self-regulation of emotion particularly difficult. We shall return to these topics in Chapters 19-21.

Summary

1. Affective states range from the *mild* feelings of pleasantness and unpleasantness that accompany virtually all behavior to the *more intense* states usually identified as emotions. The more intense states can also be classified into those that are pleasant (joy, love) and those that are unpleasant (anger, fear, grief).

2. Emotional states as experienced in ordinary life are complex, and little is to be gained by trying to distinguish sharply among them. Studies of the bodily processes in emotion show that widespread changes are common to all intense emotions, although some physiological differentiation has proved possible. For example, one study showed responses in *fear* to be those predictable from the action of epinephrine; those in *anger* predictable from the action of epinephrine combined with norepinephrine. Still, there is much overlap and a good deal of individual idiosyncrasy in physiological patterns of response. The whole matter of distinguishing among emotional states is further complicated by the large role played by situational determinants; the same state of arousal may be given one emotional label under some circumstances, another under other circumstances.

3. Among the theories of emotion and emotional expression are (a) *Darwin's evolutionary theory,* with its three principles of associated habits, antithesis, and direct action of the nervous system; (b) the *James-Lange theory,* which states that the quality of the emotion is determined by the feedback from the bodily responses; (c) the *activation theory,* which stresses the arousal aspects of emotion, permitting the differentiation of emotions to be made on grounds other than differences in physiological responses; and, finally, (d) *perceptual-motivational theories,* which subordinate the physiological responses to the cognitive processes of judging a situation, and to the motivational processes of doing something about it, perhaps by means of approach or avoidance.

4. Many of the *occasions* that elicit emotion and many of the *forms of emotional expression* appear to be inborn, or to develop through maturation with a minimum of contribution through learning. Evidence is provided by the similarities of expression of emotion in deaf-blind children to that in physically normal children. Learning is involved, however, in determining the occasions upon which emotions can be safely expressed and in shaping the form of expression to conform to patterns approved within the culture.

5. There is an intimate relationship between motivation and emotion. Sometimes, as in cases of fear and frustration, the emotion acts very much the same as an aversive drive and is related to learning according to the drive-reduction formulation. Emotional experiences may also be sought as goals, as when one goes to a comedy for a good laugh. In some cases, emotions may be thought of as accompaniments of motivated behavior, as in triumphant joy, which in itself is neither a drive nor a goal but may indeed be relevant to the choice of instrumental activities serving other ends.

6. Emotions may be both useful and harmful. They may serve the purposes of smooth adjustment and problem-solving, but they may also interfere with those purposes. *Intensity* is an important factor: *mild* emotional states are generally tonic and helpful; *strong* emotional states are often debilitating and disruptive. The *Yerkes-Dodson Law* expresses the role of intensity, adding that the more difficult the task, the more the disruption by aversive affect.

7. The study of emotion is incomplete without recognizing individual differences in emotionality. Enduring differences in the disposition to experience emotions of certain kinds are classified as differences in *temperament*. More temporary tendencies to be disposed toward certain kinds of emotion are known as *moods*. Long-continuing emotional states, particularly conflictual ones, may result in the bodily symptoms of *psychosomatic illness*.

8. Modern civilization may have gone too far in seeking to suppress emotional expression. For one thing, the effort to be rid of emotion through suppression or repression is relatively unsuccessful, as shown by the signs of residual emotional effects. Emotional control need not mean emotional denial. It is possible to accept emotions as normal and natural, while directing emotional expression into channels that are socially acceptable.

Suggestions for further reading

The following accounts, all relatively brief, give a good introduction to contemporary thinking about emotion: Mandler, "Emotion," in *New directions in psychology* (1962); Murray, *Motivation and emotion* (1964); Plutchik, *The emotions: Facts, theories, and a new model* (1962).

An interesting multiple-author book on human emotional expression is that edited by Knapp, *Expression of the emotions in man* (1963). For an appraisal of theories of emotion, and evidence from biobehavioral studies, see Glass (ed.), *Neurophysiology and emotion* (1967).

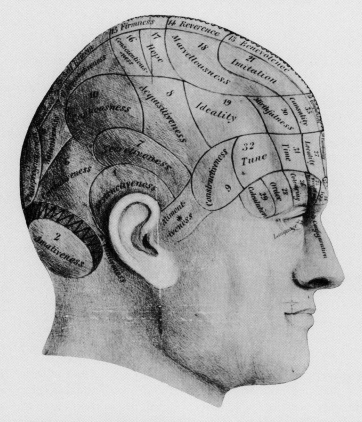

ability testing and intelligence

THE STUDY OF GROWTH, MOTIVATION, AND learning indicates that one man will differ from another not only because he inherits individual characteristics but also because he experiences his culture through home, school, and community in unique ways, thereby acquiring habits, attitudes, and understandings that are distinctively his own. We are now interested in the individual as a unique person, the product of all these influences. We wish to know in what ways men differ, the extent of their differences, and how to judge the differences.

This is not a task of idle curiosity, for our society requires individuals to be appraised, classified, and given responsibilities on the assumptions that they differ and that their differences will suit them better for one social role than for another. We decide by examination who should be admitted to college and who should be granted scholarship aid. Within a college we try to assess individual differences in order to help students choose their majors or their vocational objectives. In industry and government adults are tested in order to place them in the jobs best suited to them.

This chapter deals with *ability testing*—the study of individual differences in knowledge and skills and in aptitudes and achievements.

What a person can do now and what he might do if he were trained are not the same. For example, John is an excellent premedical student who someday will be a fine physician, but we would not ask him to remove an appendix before he had completed his medical training. James is a young trainee who someday will be a good pilot, but we do not trust him with an airplane before he has learned to fly. This distinction between a *capacity to learn* and an *accomplished skill* is important in our appraisal devices. Tests designed to measure capacities, that is, to *predict* what one can accomplish with training, are known as *aptitude tests*. Tests that tell what one can do now are *achievement tests*. Intelligence tests that predict how well you will do in college are aptitude tests; examinations given at the end of the term to see how much you have learned are achievement tests. Both are ability tests.

Testing aptitudes and achievements

Aptitude tests, by definition, predict performances not yet attained. But the *items*—the units of which a test is composed—must consist of samples of achievements, that is, of what can be accomplished *now*. How, then, is it possible to construct anything but achievement tests? This difficulty does not constitute an impasse, because it is possible to construct the tests from performances other than those being predicted. For example, one of the abilities contributing to success in typing is good spelling. Because spelling can be tested before one has had experience with typewriters, the typing *aptitude* tests may include a spelling test—even though from another point of view the spelling test is an achievement test. The distinction between an aptitude test and an achievement test is not based on the content of the items, but upon the *purposes* of the two kinds of tests.

Aptitude tests

Aptitude tests are sometimes classified according to the breadth or generality of the abilities they predict. Tests of abilities used in a wide range of performances, the best known being those testing *general intelligence,* are treated more fully later in this chapter. A number of tests measure *mechanical aptitude,* because these aptitudes are required in work done either by hand or with mechanical devices.

Many tests are given to discover *special apti-* *tudes.* For example, tests of *musical aptitude* measure discrimination of pitch, rhythm, and other aspects of musical sensitivity that might be predictive of musical performance with training. Another such test measures *clerical aptitude;* a test in simple number-checking proves predictive of an individual's later achievement as an office clerk. Many aptitude tests have been constructed for the purpose of predicting success in specific jobs or vocations. Since the beginning of the Second World War the armed forces have devised tests to select pilots, radio technicians, submarine crews, and other specialists for the various skilled jobs within the services.

In attempting to measure aptitude it is usually necessary to use a number of different tests in combination. We used the illustration of present ability in spelling as a test for predicting typing ability. But spelling is not the only ingredient in typing skill; a thorough assessment of typing aptitude must also include tests of finger dexterity and other skills. A combination of tests used for prediction is known as a *test battery*. A well-planned battery is composed only of tests that aid in the final prediction. Scores from the individual tests are *weighted* in such a way as to get the best possible prediction; that is, scores on the tests that predict well count more in the prediction than scores on the tests that do not predict well. For instance, if a finger-dexterity test predicts typing success better than a spelling test, scores in finger dexterity will be weighted more heavily than scores in spelling.

Achievement tests

Although achievement tests are most commonly used in school and civil service examinations, they are also used to assess what has been learned in preparation for the practice of a specialty, such as law, medicine, or accounting. The consequences of all these achievement tests are highly important to the person who takes them. If he succeeds, he will receive a degree or a license to practice or an opportunity to enter a desired career. If he fails, many paths may be blocked for him; if the tests are in any way inappropriate, their use may lead to social injustice. It is crucial that examinations be well conceived so that they measure what they are intended to measure and their scores represent fairly the relative abilities of the candidate who takes the tests.

Psychologists have been led to take an interest in the development of achievement tests for two reasons. First, there is much demand for tests, especially in education and civil service. Second, *achievement tests furnish a standard on which aptitude tests are based.* To prepare and try out an aptitude test for typing, we first need a standard of good typing against which to measure the aptitude. Otherwise we have no way of checking predictions. If professors assigned college grades whimsically instead of on the basis of the student's achievement in the course, it would be futile to try to predict grades from an aptitude battery. Thus, achievement tests furnish one standard, or *criterion,* for the prediction of aptitudes. With improved achievement examinations, predictions can be made more efficiently. Of course, other criteria, such as success in a job, can be used. Then the measure of success serves as a measure of achievement.

Reliability and validity

Test scores must be trustworthy if they are to be used for scientific purposes. In terms used by psychologists, this means that they must meet two requirements: *reliability* and *validity.*

Test scores are *reliable* when they are dependable and reproducible, and when they measure *consistently* whatever they measure. Tests that are confusing, misleading, or tricky may mean different things to different subjects, or even different things to the same subject at different times. Tests may also be too short to be reliable, or scoring may be too subjective. If a test is inconsistent in its results when measurements are repeated or when it is scored by two people, it is unreliable. A simple analogy is a rubber yardstick; if we didn't know how much it stretched each time we made a measurement, the results would be unreliable, no matter how carefully we had marked the measurement. We need stable and consistent tests if we are to use the results with confidence.

In order to evaluate reliability, we must secure two independent scores for the same individual from the same test—by treating halves of the test separately, by repeating the test, by giving it in two forms, or by deriving some sort of statistical measure equivalent to having two such scores. We can then compare the first and second set of scores. If the same relative score levels are preserved on the two scores, the test is reliable. Some departures from identity of score are to be expected, owing to errors of measurement and sampling errors, so that a measure of *degree of relationship* between the two sets of scores is needed. This relationship is provided by the *coefficient of correlation,* already familiar to us as a measure of degree of correspondence between two sets of scores. The coefficient of correlation between the two sets of scores, adjusted according to statistical conventions, is in this case a *reliability coefficient.* Well-constructed psychological tests of ability usually have reliability coefficients of $r = .90$ or above.

Tests are *valid* when they measure what they are intended to measure. A college examination in economics full of trick questions might turn out to be a test of student intelligence rather than of the economics that was to have been learned in the course. Such an examination might be reliable, but it would not be a valid test of achievement for the course. A test of sense of humor, for example, might be made up of jokes that were hard to catch unless one were both very bright and very well-read. Hence it might turn out to be a *reliable* test of something (intelligence? educational achievement?) but still not be *valid* as a test of sense of humor.

To measure validity, we must also have two scores for each person. One of these is the test score, the reliability of which we have just been discussing. The other is some measure of what the test is supposed to be measuring. This measure is called a *criterion.* Suppose that a test is designed to predict success in learning to receive telegraphic code. To determine whether the test is valid, it is given to a group of men beginning to study code. After he has been trained to receive coded messages, each man is tested on the number of words per minute he can receive. This later measure furnishes an additional set of scores, which can serve as a criterion. Now we can obtain a coefficient of correlation between the early test scores and the scores on the criterion. This correlation coefficient is known as a *validity coefficient,* and it tells something about how valuable a given test is for a given purpose. The higher the coefficient, the better the prediction that can be made from an aptitude test.

High validity coefficients are desirable if test scores are to be used to help an individual with such an important decision as vocational choice. But even relatively low validity coefficients may prove useful when large numbers of people are tested. For example, a battery of tests used for the selection of air-crew specialists in the Second World War proved effective in predicting job success, even though some of the validity coefficients were of very moderate size. Illustrative validity coefficients from this battery are shown in Table 15-1. Although no single test showed a validity above .49, the "composite" score derived from the battery of tests correlated .64 with the criterion.

Test scores as a basis for prediction

With high enough reliability and validity coefficients we know that we have satisfactory tests, but the problem of using the tests in prediction still remains. The method of prediction most easily understood is the one based on *critical scores.* By this method, a critical point on the scale of scores is selected after experience with the tests. Only those candidates with scores above the critical

TABLE 15-1 VALIDITY COEFFICIENTS FOR PREDICTION OF SUCCESS IN PILOT TRAINING	
TESTS AMONG THOSE IN CLASSIFICATION BATTERY	VALIDITY FOR COMPLETED PILOT TRAINING (N = 1275) VALIDITY COEFFICIENT*
Printed tests with highest validity coefficients	
General information	.49
Instrument comprehension	.46
Mechanical principles	.42
Dial and table reading	.40
Spatial orientation II	.38
Apparatus tests with highest validity coefficients	
Complex coordination	.42
Discrimination reaction time	.41
Rudder control	.36
Two-hand pursuit	.35
Rotary pursuit	.31
Pilot stanine (a composite score)	.64

*In the group studies, pilot selection was not based upon test scores, because the success of the tests was still under study. Because the criterion was simply that of passing or failing in pilot training, a special kind of correlation coefficient (called biserial r) was computed; the usual r requires scaled values for both variables.

Source: DuBois (1947).

point are accepted—for training, for admission to college, or for whatever purpose the testing may serve.

The pilot-selection program of the Air Force illustrates this use of critical scores. The composite scores (called stanines) gave each candidate a pilot-prediction rating from 1 to 9. Figure 15-1 shows that during the experimental period those with low stanines were eliminated much more frequently than those with high stanines. After experience with the tests, the examiners eliminated those with low stanines from further training. For example, a candidate had to receive a stanine score of 5 or better to be accepted for pilot training. Thus a stanine of 5 became a critical score. Had this critical score been adopted before carrying all the candidates represented in Figure 15-1 through

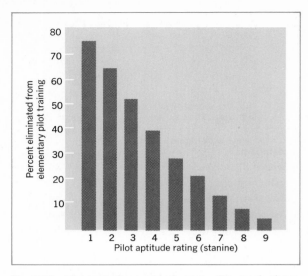

Fig. 15-1 The basis for a critical score The graph shows the percentage of failures in pilot training at each stanine level. At one point the Air Force established a stanine score of 5 as a requirement for further pilot training. (After DuBois, 1947)

their training, only 17 percent of those accepted would have failed to complete training. Those dropped would have been the group of low scorers, of whom 44 percent failed elementary pilot training.

The critical score is but one way in which to use data of this kind for prediction. The data of Figure 15-1, expressed in correlational terms, represent a correlation between stanine and completion of training of $r = .51$ for the total group of 166, 507 trainees. Advanced statistical methods can be used to estimate from the size of a validity coefficient just how successful predictions may be.

Another method of using predictive information is according to an *expectancy table* based on earlier established relationships between the predictor and the predicted. One such table for using high-school rank to predict college grades is shown in Table 15-2. Note that high-school rank, even though in itself it is an achievement, is here being used as an indicator of *aptitude* for college achievement.

	CHANCES IN 100 OF A FRESHMAN'S RECEIVING AN AVERAGE GRADE OF:		
HIGH-SCHOOL CENTILE RANK	D OR HIGHER	C OR HIGHER	B OR HIGHER
80–100	97	70	15
60–79	92	46	—*
40–59	88	29	1
20–39	75	—*	—*

TABLE 15-2 PREDICTION OF FRESHMAN COLLEGE GRADES ON BASIS OF HIGH-SCHOOL RANK

*Less than 1 chance in 100.

Source: Berdie (1969). The data are for freshmen entering the College of Education at the University of Minnesota.

Using his high-school rank, the student (and his adviser) can better predict his achievement as a college freshman, in terms of his chances in 100 of attaining a particular average grade.

Tests of general intelligence

Intelligence tests are designed to measure the abilities that distinguish the bright from the dull. Because these distinctions are significant for school and vocational success and for social adjustment generally, the intelligence test is an important tool of psychology. In our study of individuality we will do well to scrutinize carefully the nature of intelligence tests and their findings.

Alfred Binet (1857–1911), a French psychologist, invented the intelligence test as we now know it. In 1904 the French government asked him to devise a test to detect those children who were too dull to profit from ordinary schooling. In collaboration with Theodore Simon (1873–1961), another French psychologist, Binet published a scale in 1905, which he revised in 1908 and again in 1911. These Binet scales are the direct predecessors of contemporary intelligence tests.

Binet's method: a mental-age scale

Binet assumed that a dull child was like a normal child but retarded in his mental growth; he reasoned that the dull child would perform on tests like a normal child of younger age. Binet decided to scale intelligence as the kind of change that ordinarily comes with growing older. Accordingly, he devised a scale of units of *mental age*. Average mental-age (M.A.) scores correspond to *chronological age* (C.A.), that is, to the age determined from the date of birth. A bright child's M.A. is above his C.A.; a retarded child has a M.A. below his C.A. The mental-age scale is easily interpreted by teachers and others who deal with children differing in mental ability.

Item selection

Because the intelligence test is designed to measure brightness rather than the results of special training, it must consist of items that do not assume any specific preparation. In other words, the intelligence test is designed to be an *aptitude* test rather than an *achievement* test, and it must be constructed accordingly.

There are two chief ways to find items on which success is uninfluenced by special training. One way is to choose *novel items* with which an untaught child has as good a chance to succeed as one who has been taught at home or in school. Figure 15-2 illustrates novel items. In this particular case the child is asked to choose figures that are alike; the assumption is that the designs are unfamiliar to all children. The second way is to choose *familiar items,* so that all those for whom the test is designed will be presumed to have had the requisite prior experience to deal with the items. The following problem provides an example of a supposedly familiar item:

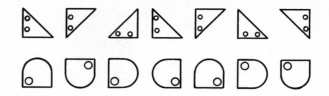

Fig. **15-2** **Novel items used in intelligence tests** The following instructions accompany the test: "Here are some cards for you to mark. In each row mark every card that is like the first card in the row." (After Thurstone and Thurstone, 1941)

Mark F if the sentence is foolish; mark S if it is sensible.

S F Mrs. Smith has had no children, and I understand that the same was true of her mother.[1]

This item is "fair" only for children who know the English language, who can read, and who understand all the words in the sentence. For such children, detection of the fallacy in the statement becomes a valid test of intellectual ability.

Many of the items on an intelligence test of the Binet type are of the second sort, requiring the assumption of general familiarity. A vocabulary test, for example, appears in almost all the scales. Familiarity with the standard language of the test is necessarily assumed.

The intelligence test is in some respects a crude instrument, for its assumptions can never be strictly met. The language environment of one home is never exactly that of another, the reading matter available to the subjects differs, and the stress upon cognitive goals varies. Even the novel items depend upon perceptual discriminations that may be acquired in one culture or subculture and not in another. Despite the difficulties, items can be chosen that work reasonably well. The items included in contemporary intelligence tests are those that have survived in practice after many others have been tried and found defective. Whatever success intelligence tests have achieved is related, however, to socially defined goals, so that emphasis is placed upon achievement in schools as defined within a particular culture.

[1] Thurstone and Thurstone (1941).

As indicated, items for an intelligence test are often selected on the assumption that the substance is equally familiar to all those being tested. This assumption is impossible to satisfy, because of the way environments differ.

Serious efforts have been made to construct tests that will be less dependent on the child's specific culture than are the more familiar tests of the Binet type. Among these efforts are the tests constructed by Cattell (1949), called a "culture-free" test, and by Davis and Eells (1953), called a "culture-fair" test. Both attempt to provide tests that will not penalize the child from a lower-class home and reward the middle-class or upper-class child.

Consider the following item:

Pick out ONE WORD that does not belong with the others.

cello   harp   drum   violin   guitar

This item was used by Eells and others (1951) to illustrate how experience can determine vocabulary. Eighty-five percent of the children from homes of high socioeconomic status chose "drum," the intended correct answer, while only 45 percent of the children from homes of low socioeconomic status answered with this word. The low-status children most commonly answered "cello," the word on the list least likely to be familiar to them and hence thought to be the word that did not belong. Children from homes of high socioeconomic status are more likely to be acquainted with cellos or at least to have heard the word than children from poorer homes.

Many other items in this study showed class differences for which the effects of differing experience would be hard to demonstrate. For example, the following item was also answered correctly more often by those from homes of higher socioeconomic status than by those from homes of lower status.

Find the THREE THINGS which are alike in each list.

store   banana   basket   apple   seed   plum

This item requires the child taking the test to note that banana, apple, and plum are fruits and that store, basket, and seed are nonfruits. It is hard to believe that nine- and ten-year-old children, even from underpriviledged homes, would be unacquainted with the six words or with the fruits, although we know little at present about the effects of severe environmental restriction upon the ability to categorize. Such an item may be "culture-fair," even though it shows class differences in its answer; the classes may actually differ in cognitive performance as measured by items that are "fair."

Although high hopes were expressed for culture-fair tests by those who developed them, the subsequent results have not been encouraging. In some cases class differences in scores have been reduced, but for the most part the class differences found with these tests are very similar to the differences found with the more usual tests. Moreover, as predictors of scholastic achievement the newer tests are inferior to the more conventional ones because of a recognized middle-class bias in the schools. Hence, with all their difficulties, the ordinary Binet-type tests serve their predictive purposes as well as or better than these substitute tests.

Item testing

It is not enough to look at an item and to decide that it requires intelligence to answer it successfully. Some "tricky" or "clever" items, which would appear to put the test-taker on his mettle, turn out to be poor because of the successes or failures that occur through guessing. More pedestrian items, such as matters of common information, sometimes turn out to be most useful. These are "fair" items if all have had a chance to learn the answers.

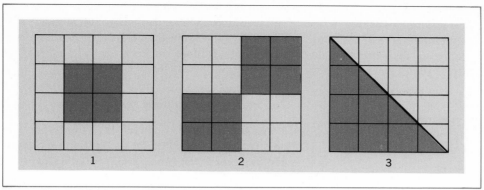

Fig. 15-3 **Block designs used with rural Nigerian children** The third design proved very difficult for 8-year-old children to copy if presented as a drawing to be copied with blocks, but it was much easier when the design to be copied was itself made with blocks. Once having done it this way, the children could copy with their blocks other designs from drawings. (After D'Andrade, 1967)

Because performance on a nonverbal test appears to be less subject to the influence of the cultural environment than performance on a verbal test, there is a temptation to assign the differences in performance between racial groups to innate differences. But caution is needed, for performance tests have been found to be subject to practice effects (Vernon, 1969). Black children in the United States, as well as in Africa, often score more poorly on some types of nonverbal performance tests (see p. 366) than on verbal tests, for which their handicaps might be expected to be greater. Studies of black children in a rural village in Nigeria bear this out.

The Kohs block test is an item in the Wechsler Intelligence Scale for Children. The test consists of sixteen painted blocks, each cube having two sides painted red, two white, and two divided diagonally into red and white. The child is shown the drawing of a design and asked to arrange the blocks to form the same design. When rural eight-year-old Nigerian children were shown the designs pictured in Figure 15-3, they succeeded very well with the first figure, moderately well with the second, but very poorly with the third, only six of thirty-one arranging the blocks correctly. The average result would yield an I.Q. of 80 by American white norms. However, when the instructor made his design with blocks, rather than with a drawing, the children learned promptly to match the design with their blocks. Having done this, they could match other drawings with blocks, as the original test required. The investigator concluded that these children were not inferior to American white children in this performance once they had ''caught on'' to what was expected in an otherwise alien situation. In the villages where these children are raised there is almost total lack of familiarity with pictorial representation. Even adults are baffled by maps, building designs, or (in some cases) the contents of ordinary photographs (D'Andrade, 1967).

Matters taken for granted in one culture cannot be taken for granted in another; this warning applies to deprived subcultures in more advanced countries as well.

How did Binet and those who came after him know when they had hit upon a good item? One method of testing an item is to study the *changes in proportions of children answering it correctly at different ages.* Unless older children are more suc-

cessful than younger ones in answering the item, the item is unsatisfactory in a test based on the concept of mental growth.

A second method of testing an item is to find out whether the results for it *correspond to the results on the test as a whole.* This can be done by correlating success and failure on the item with the score made on the remaining items. If all items measure something in common, then every single item ought to contribute a score that correlates with the total score.

These two requirements for an acceptable item (increase in percentage passing with age and correlation with total score) reflect both validity and reliability. The first of these requirements is an indirect way of guaranteeing validity, being based on the inference that what we mean by intelligence should distinguish an older child from a younger one, while the second requirement is a guarantee of reliability through internal consistency of the measures.

By choosing items that meet these requirements and by arranging them in a convenient form for the person giving the test, one obtains a self-consistent and useful test of intelligence.

Contemporary Binet tests

The tests originally developed by Alfred Binet underwent several revisions in this country, the first by Goddard in 1911. For many years the best-known and most widely used revision was that made by Terman at Stanford University in 1916, commonly referred to as the Stanford-Binet. The test was later revised by Terman and Merrill in 1937 and again in 1960.

In the Binet tests, an item is age-graded at the level at which a substantial majority of the children pass it. The present Stanford-Binet has six items of varied content assigned to each year, each item when passed earning a score of two months of mental age.

The procedure for testing is first to establish the child's *basal mental age,* the mental-age level at which he passes all items. Two months of mental age are then added for each item he passes at higher age levels. Consider, for example, the child who passes all items at the mental-age level of six years. If he then passes two items at the seven-year level, four months are added to his mental age; if he passes an additional item at the eight-year level, two more months are added. The earned

mental age for this particular child will be six years and six months, whatever his chronological age. The test allows for some unevenness in development, so that two children can earn the same mental age by passing different items on the test.

The intelligence quotient (I.Q.)

Terman adopted a convenient index of brightness that was suggested by the German psychologist William Stern (1871–1938). This index is the *intelligence quotient,* commonly known by its initials I.Q. It expresses intelligence as a ratio of the mental age to the chronological age:

$$\text{I.Q.} = 100 \, \frac{\text{Mental age (M.A.)}}{\text{Chronological age (C.A.)}}$$

The 100 is used as a multiplier to remove the decimal point and to make the I.Q. have a value of 100 when M.A. equals C.A. It is evident that if the M.A. lags behind the C.A., the resulting I.Q. will be less than 100; if the M.A. is above the C.A., the I.Q. will be above 100. Thus the brightness scale has about the same meaning from one age to another.

How is the I.Q. to be interpreted? The distribu-

Fig. **15-4   A normal distribution curve of I.Q.'s**   Distribution of I.Q.'s for 2904 children and youths, ages 2 to 18. This is the group upon which the Revised Stanford-Binet was standardized. (After Terman and Merrill, 1937)

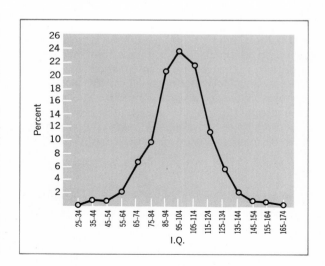

TABLE 15-3 INTERPRETATION OF INTELLIGENCE QUOTIENTS ON THE STANFORD-BINET

I.Q.	VERBAL DESCRIPTION	PERCENT FALLING IN EACH GROUP (AMONG 2904 SUBJECTS, AGES 2 TO 18)
140 and above	Very superior	1
120–139	Superior	11
110–119	High average	18
90–109	Average	46
80–89	Low average	15
70–79	Borderline	6
Below 70	Mentally retarded or defective	3
		100

Source: Merrill (1938).

tion of I.Q.'s follows the form of curve found for many differences among individuals, such as differences in height; this is the bell-shaped "normal" distribution curve shown in Figure 15-4. In this curve most cases cluster around a midvalue, tapering off to a few at both extremes. The adjectives commonly used to describe the various I.Q. levels are given in Table 15-3, along with the proportions of an early standardization sample that fell at each point.

In their 1960 revision of the earlier Stanford-Binet the authors introduced a method of computing the I.Q. from tables. The meaning of an I.Q. remains essentially the same as before, but the tables permit corrections to allow the I.Q. at any age to be interpreted somewhat more exactly. It is now arranged so that for each age the I.Q. averages 100 and has a standard deviation of 16. The I.Q. is thus a kind of *standard score,* with a fixed mean and standard deviation.[2] This type of I.Q. is known as a *deviation* I.Q., and was earlier used in the Wechsler Adult Intelligence Scale, to be considered in the next section.

A modern I.Q. is merely a test score adjusted

[2] The concepts of standard deviation and standard score are explained in the Appendix.

for the age of the person being tested. It is therefore no longer a "quotient" at all, but the expression I.Q. persists because of its familiarity and convenience.

Tests with more than one scale

Tests following the pattern originated by Binet use a great assortment of items to test intelligence, and a pass or a fail on one kind of item is scored the same as a pass or a fail on another item. But those who are skilled in the use and scoring of the tests learn much more from them than appears in the final I.Q. They may note special strengths and weaknesses; tests of vocabulary, for example, may be passed at a higher level than tests of manipulating form boards. These observations lead to the conjecture that what is being measured is not one simple ability but a composite of abilities,

One way to obtain information on specific kinds of abilities, rather than a single mental-age score, is to separate the items into more than one group and to score the groups separately. The Wechsler Adult Intelligence Scale and the Wechsler Intelligence Scale for Children use items similar to those in the familiar Binet tests, but they divide the total test into two parts according to the content of the items, resulting in two scales—a *verbal* scale and

TABLE 15-4 TESTS COMPRISING THE WECHSLER ADULT INTELLIGENCE SCALE AND THE WECHSLER INTELLIGENCE SCALE FOR CHILDREN

VERBAL	PERFORMANCE
Information	Digit symbol*
Comprehension	Picture completion
Arithmetic	Block design
Similarities	Picture arrangement
Digit span†	Object assembly
Vocabulary	Coding‡
	Mazes§

*Adult scale only.
†Adult scale; alternate test for children.
‡Scale for children only.
§Alternate test for children.
Source: Wechsler (1949, 1958).

Fig. **15-5 An intelligence test requiring nonverbal performance** An item in the Wechsler object assembly test.

a *performance* scale. A *performance* item is one that requires manipulation or arrangement of blocks, beads, pictures, or other materials in which both stimuli and responses are nonverbal. The separate scaling of the items within one test is convenient for diagnostic purposes.

The tests comprising the two scales are listed in Table 15-4. The names of the tests in most cases suggest their content, though some of them require a word of explanation. The *digit span* test calls for the subject to recite back to the tester a series of numerical digits, such as 7-5-8-3-6, that he repeats aloud in a forward direction; other series have to be repeated in a backward direction. The score depends upon the length of the series that the subject gets correct. The *digit symbol* test requires following a code in which marks of various shapes are paired with numerals to which they correspond. The subject then fills in blank squares to pair many randomly arranged numerals with corresponding shapes according to the code provided. The *object assembly* test calls for putting together parts to complete a figure, such as a manikin, human profile, hand, or elephant (Figure 15-5).

In general, the full scale (verbal and performance) and the verbal scale of the Wechsler Scale yield scores corresponding closely to the scores of the Stanford-Binet. In one study of young adults (Wechsler, 1955), the following correlations were obtained between scores on the Stanford-Binet and the Wechsler Adult Intelligence Scale: with the full scale, .85; with the verbal scale, .86; with the performance scale, .69. The verbal scale of the Wechsler correlated .77 with its performance scale.

Factor-analyzed tests

Statistical methods have been devised to give much more precise information about the abilities underlying intelligence. These methods are collectively known as *factor analysis*. As a tool of test construction and interpretation, factor analysis is still in a developmental stage, even though the first steps were taken (by Charles Spearman) as early as 1904, before the Binet-Simon test appeared. There have been many developments in factor analysis since that time; the most widely used procedures stem from the work of L. L. Thurstone (1947) on *multiple factor analysis*.[3]

[3] These methods are far too intricate to describe in any detail here, but, as we shall see, it is possible to gain some understanding of what they try to do even though the details are unfamiliar.

Theory of intelligence as a composite

Mathematical methods in science are most successful when they are used in relation to theory; there must be a "fit" between the kind of mathematics and the way the theory creates order or lawfulness in empirical data. Factor analysis is a useful tool in the theory that interprets intellectual ability as a composite. The essential part of the theory asserts that there are different aspects or dimensions of intelligence according to which people vary, so that, for example, one person may be better in language abilities, another in the abilities underlying mathematical computation. Those who accept this essential theory may disagree as to how the components are organized. The originator of factor analysis, Spearman, thought a general factor (called *g*) was common to all the components, so that a person could be called generally bright or generally dull. The use of a single index, such as I.Q., seems to imply such a general intellectual level. But he went on to state that special abilities (called *s*'s) produced individual variation around the general level. His method was primarily designed to measure the prominence of the *g*-factor.

Later investigators have proposed various models for relating general and specialized abilities; thus Burt (1949) and Vernon (1950a) developed *hierarchical models,* with the most general abilities at the top of the hierarchy, then major group factors at another level, and finally the most specific factors (many in number) at the lowest level. Others, including Guilford (1967), doubt the evidence for any general factor; the positive intercorrelations among tests designed to measure special factors can be accounted for on other grounds, such as overlap in some of the psychological processes involved. They point out that whenever there are zero correlations between tests, as there are in some instances, the *g*-factor is denied.

The foregoing discussion indicates the kind of theoretical problems that call for precise methods of data collection and analysis if any independently established theory of intelligence is to be achieved. In order to understand later discussions about test scores that have been correlated and factor analyzed, it is necessary to have some familiarity with factor analysis.

The method of factor analysis and the meaning of factors

What are the data that enter into factor analysis, and what are the major steps in the analysis? The data are simply scores on a variety of tests, which are often designed to illustrate a variety of psychological contents or processes. Each of a large number of individuals obtains a score for each of a number of tests. All these scores for many individuals can then be intercorrelated. That is, we know how the scores of many individuals on Test 1 relate to their scores on Test 2, and so on. These intercorrelations yield a table of correlations known as a *correlation matrix* (Table 15-5). If the table contains a number of statistically significant correlations and a number of near-zero correlations it is apparent that some tests measure similar abilities of one kind and others similar abilities of other kinds. The purpose of factor analysis is to be more precise about these underlying abilities.

Factor analysis then uses mathematical methods

TABLE 15-5   CORRELATION MATRIX FOR NINE APTITUDE TESTS

TESTS	2	3	4	5	6	7	8	9
1	.38	.55	.06	−.04	.05	.07	.05	.09
2		.36	.40	.28	.40	.11	.15	.13
3			.10	.01	.18	.13	.12	.10
4				.32	.60	.04	.06	.13
5					.35	.08	.13	.11
6						.01	.06	.07
7							.45	.32
8								.32

Source: Guilford (1967).

The three outlined clusters of correlations indicate that these are groups of tests with something in common not shared by other tests. The inadequacy of making such a judgment from a table of correlations of this kind is shown by noting the additional correlations of Test 2 with Tests 4, 5, and 6, not included in the outlined clusters. We rely on factor analysis to tell us more precisely what underlies these correlations. See Table 15-6.

TABLE 15-6   FACTOR MATRIX FOR NINE APTITUDE
TESTS AND THREE FACTORS

TESTS	FACTORS		
	I	II	III
1	.75	−.01	.08
2	.44	.48	.16
3	.72	.07	.15
4	.08	.76	.08
5	−.01	.49	−.01
6	.16	.73	.02
7	−.03	.04	.64
8	.02	.05	.66
9	−.01	.10	.47

Source: Guilford (1967).

The outlined factor loadings show which tests are most highly correlated with each of the underlying factors. The clusters are the same as those found in Table 15-5, but now given greater precision. The problem of Test 2 remains, because it is loaded almost equally on Factor I and Factor II. It is obviously not a "factor pure" test.

(assisted by high-speed computers) to compute the correlation of each of the tests with a few factors. Such correlations between test scores and factors are known as *factor loadings;* if a test correlates .05 on Factor I, .10 on Factor II, and .70 on Factor III, it is most heavily "loaded" on Factor III. For example, the nine tests yielding the correlation

matrix of Table 15-5 yield the *factor matrix* of Table 15-6.

Having found the three factors that account for the intercorrelations of the nine tests, the factors can be interpreted by studying the content of the tests most highly weighted on each factor. The factor analysis itself is strictly a mathematical process, but the naming of the factors depends upon a psychological analysis.

The factors comprising intelligence

What are the results of the use of factor analysis in describing the components of intelligence? Two major sets of investigations, those of Thurstone and of Guilford, tell us where we now stand.

Thurstone's primary abilities. Thurstone set out to find a few clusters of abilities that make up the composite tested by Binet-type intelligence tests. He wished to find a method of grouping items that would be more reliable than earlier item-sorting, as in the verbal and performance scales of Wechsler and the verbal and mathematical subtests of the Scholastic Aptitude test. He turned to factor analysis and developed a battery of tests for Primary Mental Abilities (Thurstone, 1938).

Thurstone's method was to give a large number of tests to the same children. As many as sixty tests

---

CRITICAL DISCUSSION

Some problems within factor analysis

Factor analysis has great logical appeal; it is an elegant tool for dealing with many problems that require the analysis of complex data. Unfortunately, factor analysis is not quite as straightforward as the simplified exposition in the text implies. For one thing, alternative methods of factor analysis yield slightly different results. For another, the precision with which the factors are determined is still in question.

It is desirable to specify factors in such a way that tests correlating higher on one factor than on another, and vice versa, should have factor scores that are in as great contrast as possible. There are two methods of converting factor scores in order to maximize the separation among factors. Each method obtains differing results, but both utilize a mathematical process called *rotation of axes*. Such a conception requires a geometrical interpretation of factors: a factor is represented by an axis in space, permitting the plotting of tests according to their factor loadings. In one method, the axes are rotated so that a relationship is found by which a maximum correlation on one factor will lead to a minimum one on another. Such a rotation procedure was used in arriving at Table 15.6. This method, yielding maximum contrast, is called *orthogonal rotation* (because, as

were used (Thurstone and Thurstone, 1941). Each test was composed of items very much alike, so that the test content was easily described. One test was for verbal comprehension, another for arithmetical computations, and so on. After intercorrelating the scores of all the tests, the investigators abstracted factors by the methods previously described. Then those items were retained that best represented each of the discovered factors.

After a number of studies of this kind, Thurstone identified seven factors as the *primary abilities* revealed by the items on intelligence tests. These seven are:

1. *Verbal comprehension* (V). Vocabulary tests represent this factor.
2. *Word fluency* (W). This factor calls for the ability to think of words rapidly, as in solving anagrams or in thinking of words that rhyme.
3. *Number* (N). Simple arithmetic tests, especially those calling for computations, represent this factor.
4. *Space* (S). Tests of this factor deal with visual form relationships, as in drawing a design from memory.
5. *Memory* (M). This ability is found in tests requiring that pairs of items be recalled.
6. *Perceptual speed* (P). This factor calls for the grasping of visual details and of the similarities and differences between pictured objects. (Tests for P are omitted from some forms of the Primary Mental Abilities batteries.)

7. *Reasoning* (R). Tests for this ability call for finding a general rule on the basis of presented instances, as in determining how a number series is constructed after being presented with only a portion of that series.

Once the several factors have been identified, it is possible to construct tests that are truly diagnostic for each factor. A test profile for the individual will indicate how well he performs on tests that demand each of the several abilities.

Thurstone's method and his results gave hope that there might indeed be a small number of *primary abilities* discoverable by factor analysis, that it might be possible to break intelligence down into its fundamental elements. This hope has not been realized, for two reasons: the so-called primary abilities turn out not to be independent, and the number of factors can be multiplied by an appropriate choice of items out of which to construct the tests.

Are primary abilities tests more efficient predictive instruments than the earlier general intelligence tests? At present, both are equally successful. But the possibility of gaining more fundamental information on patterns of ability through tests of

represented geometrically, the axes are at right angles to each other). Another method maximizes correlations with factors but does not seek as much contrast among factors. This is called *oblique rotation*. In this case the axes are not at right angles, and a maximum correlation with one of the factors still permits a moderate correlation with other factors. The issues surrounding the appropriateness of one method above the other are complex and as yet unsettled; some investigators, such as Guilford (1967), prefer to use orthogonal rotation only, while others, such as Cattell (1952), prefer oblique rotation. As a consequence, some of their theoretical interpretations of test results differ.

Alternatives to factor analysis attempt to account for complexly related data in ways other than correlation with underlying factors. The name for these alternative methods is *multiple regression analysis;* together multiple regression analysis and factor analysis are called methods of *multivariate analysis* (Cattell, 1966).

The complexity and sophistication of these methods is one reason that advanced training in the behavioral sciences is heavily dependent upon a good mathematical background.

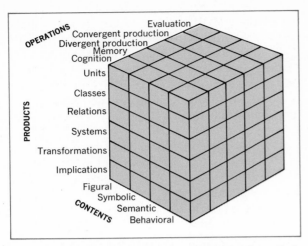

Fig. 15-6 Cubical model of the structure of intellect Each of the small cubes in the solid represents a primary ability to be specified by factor analysis. (After Guilford, 1967)

known factor structure is so great that tests constructed with the aid of factor analysis have become more and more widely used.

Guilford's structure-of-intellect model.

The work of Guilford tends to multiply factors rather than to reduce their number. In a model of intellectual ability that he has been developing over a number of years, he proposes the domain of intelligence as shown graphically in Figure 15-6. The three edges of the cube illustrate five kinds of operations, six kinds of products, and four kinds of contents, resulting in 120 (5 × 6 × 4) "cells" defining specific intellectual factors. This is a conceptual scheme, but Guilford and his associates have carried on a vast amount of empirical work in designing tests that, through factor analysis, can be shown to fit the specifications for many of the 120 predicted factors. Evidence for the factors has gradually accumulated, so that 77 cells of the model have been empirically demonstrated (Guilford, 1967). Guilford believes that the prospect is for *more* than the 120 abilities hypothesized.

One reason for the larger number of factors in Guilford's model than in Thurstone's is that Guilford has broadened the concept of intellect beyond that of the familiar I.Q. tests. The conventional intelligence test determined how well the child could respond "in accordance with truth and fact." This is known as *convergent production;* the information leads to one "correct" answer. One of Guilford's chief concepts is *divergent production,* which is more creative; it is concerned with "possible" answers, not merely a single correct one. Tests for divergent thinking include such items as: "What uses can you think of for a brick?" The child who gives the most varied answers ("heat to keep your bed warm," "as a weapon," "to hold the shelves of a bookcase") is the one who scores highest on divergent thinking. This kind of thinking has been neglected in the standard intelligence test, and Guilford rightly thinks it belongs within the total intellectual domain. Some illustrations of "creativity" items, lacking in most intelligence tests, are presented in Table 15-7.

Experiments comparing results on intelligence tests of the usual sorts and on tests designed to measure divergent thinking have tended to yield relationships such as those indicated in Figure 15-7. That is, highly creative persons tend frequently to be highly intelligent, but high intelli-

Fig. 15-7 Divergent production as related to I.Q. More high scores for divergent production are associated with high I.Q. than with low I.Q., but there are many moderately high scores on divergent thinking among those with average I.Q.'s, and a high I.Q. is no guarantee of a high score on divergent thinking. (After Guilford, 1967)

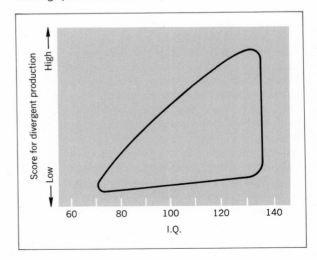

TABLE 15-7	EXAMPLES OF ITEMS USED IN TESTS OF CREATIVITY

1. Ingenuity (Flanagan, 1963)

    a. A very rare wind storm destroyed the transmission tower of a television station in a small town. The station was located in a town in a flat prairie with no tall buildings. Its former 300-foot tower enabled it to serve a large farming community, and the management wanted to restore service while a new tower was being erected. The problem was temporarily solved by using a _____.

    b. As part of a manufacturing process, the inside lip of a deep cup-shaped casting is machine threaded. The company found that metal chips produced by the threading operation were difficult to remove from the bottom of the casting without scratching the sides. A design engineer was able to solve this problem by having the operation performed _____.

2. Unusual uses (Guilford, 1954a)

    Name as many uses as you can think of for:
        a. a toothpick   b. a brick   c. a paper clip

3. Consequences (Guilford, 1954a)

    Imagine all of the things that might possibly happen if all national and local laws were suddenly abolished.

4. Fable endings (Getzels and Jackson, 1962)

    Write three endings for the following fable: a moralistic, a humorous, and a sad ending.

THE MISCHIEVOUS DOG

    A rascally dog used to run quietly to the heels of every passerby and bite them without warning. So his master was obliged to tie a bell around the cur's neck that he might give notice wherever he went. This the dog thought very fine indeed, and he went about tinkling it in pride all over town. But an old hound said . . . .

5. Product improvement (Torrance, 1966)

    The subject is presented with a series of objects such as children's toys or instruments used in his particular occupation and asked to make suggestions for their improvement.

6. Pattern meanings (Wallach and Kogan, 1965a)

    The subject is shown a series of patterns of geometric forms (like the samples shown below) and asked to imagine all the things each pattern could be.

  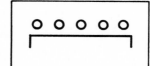

7. Remote associations (Mednick, 1962)

    Find a fourth word which is associated with each of these three words:
        a. rat—blue—cottage   b. out—dog—cat   c. wheel—electric—high   d. surprise—line—birthday

8. Word association (Getzels and Jackson, 1962)

    Write as many meanings as you can for each of the following words:
        a. duck   b. sack   c. pitch   d. fair

gence (as measured by conventional tests) is no guarantee of creativity (Getzels and Jackson, 1962; Yamamoto and Chimbidis, 1966).

It does not appear now that there will be agreement on the number and nature of primary abilities as a result of factor analysis, but this does not mean that factor analysis has been useless. It is a technical aid in the purification of tests, making known their factor structure. Also it permits us to obtain answers to a number of pertinent questions about ability, such as the change in ability patterns with increasing age.

The Binet test was developed on the principle that whatever processes influence intelligence test performance grow with the years, so that a mental-age score remains appropriate at least through childhood; the I.Q. was based on the presumption that the mental age for a bright child would grow more rapidly than for a dull one, so that some degree of constancy would be found for the ratio of M.A. to C.A. Both of these conjectures were found to be approximately true (Figure 15-8), although later work has made it necessary to supply a number of qualifications.

Relative stability of the I.Q. during the school years

If I.Q.'s remain consistent through the years, there will be a high positive correlation between scores on successive I.Q. tests. Such correlations are indeed positive (Table 15-8), but there are also changes with the years, as shown by a gradual decline in the size of the correlations as the tests are separated more and more in time.

Fig. **15-8 Consistency of mental age differences** Two groups of boys were selected at age five, one scoring high on intelligence tests, one average. The superior group gained in mental age more rapidly than the average one, thus approximating a constant I.Q. difference between the groups as they grew older. (After Baldwin and Stecher, 1922)

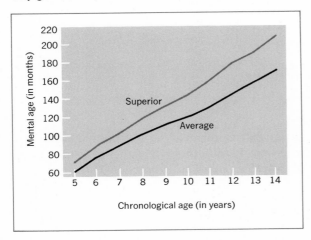

TABLE **15-8**	INTER-AGE STANFORD-BINET CORRELATIONS				
AGE	4	6	8	10	12
3	.83	.73	.60	.54	.46
5		.87	.79	.70	.62
7			.91	.82	.73
9				.90	.81
11					.90

Source: Sontag, Baker, and Nelson (1958).

Table entries give correlations between I.Q.'s obtained for the same individuals at different ages. Data based on 50 cases. Note that correlations tend to fall as years between testing increase.

Growth of intelligence in childhood and youth

The mental-age tests are so scored that if they are properly standardized an average growth curve will be a straight line; average M.A. will equal average C.A. at all ages. Hence some other method must be used to scale actual growth in units that are not forced to correspond to age. Scores on Thurstone's primary abilities tests have been used for this purpose; although there are some differences in the rate at which the separate abilities grow, the gain is generally rapid in childhood and slows in the teens (Figure 15-9).

Smooth group curves and positive correlations on successive tests mask the differences that may be found for individual children. Some show generally increasing I.Q.'s over the years, but the I.Q. of others decreases (Figure 15-10).

Efforts to relate changes in I.Q. of individual children to events happening in their environment have not proved satisfactory, although some relationships have been noted. For example, those children whose I.Q.'s increased during the early years (between ages three and six) were less emotionally dependent upon their parents than those whose I.Q.'s failed to increase (Sontag, Baker, and Nelson, 1958). In later years (up to age ten) the changes in I.Q. appeared most closely related to

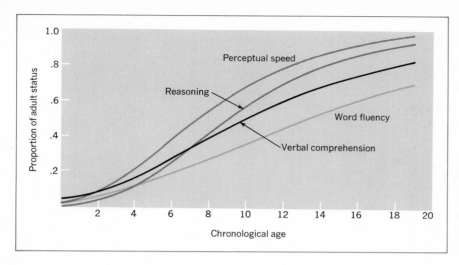

Fig. **15-9 Growth of four primary abilities** The scale adopted is that of 1.0 for adult status. Thus 80 percent of adult status is achieved for perceptual speed at age 12, for reasoning at age 14, for verbal comprehension at age 18, and for word fluency later than 20. (After Thurstone, 1955)

high achievement motivation (see Chapter 13, p. 326). Of course, from these relationships alone it is not possible to infer whether the rising intelligence produced school successes that enhanced achievement motivation, or whether a rise in I.Q. was the result of achievement motivation that was enhanced independently.

Intelligence in later life

The slowing of the growth in the processes measured by intelligence tests in the late teens, as shown in Figure 15-9, leads us to expect a peak in the early adult years and a decline thereafter. This decline is generally found when scores in the later years are compared with averages for the early adult years (Figure 15-11).

The study resulting in the scores plotted in Figures 15-11 and 15-12 was conducted in such a way that a comparison could be made between cross-sectional and longitudinal scores. Cross-sectional scores are obtained by sampling the different ages at one point in time. For this purpose, quotas of 25 men and 25 women were selected for each five-year interval from twenty to seventy years from a larger population of 18,000 members of a prepaid medical plan. Longitudinal scores require that the same individual be tested more than once. In this study the subjects tested earlier who could be located were tested again

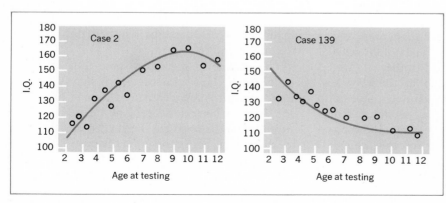

Fig. **15-10 Progressively changing I.Q.'s on repeated tests in individual cases** Note that for Case 2 the initial I.Q. was about 115 at age two and a half, but the last five tests were in the range of 150 to 170. The opposite trend was found for Case 139. With early tests in the range of 130 to 150, the final test scores were in the range of 110 to 120. (After Sontag, Baker, and Nelson, 1958)

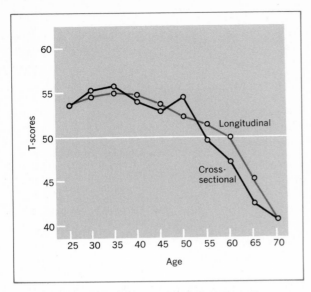

Fig. **15-11 Age changes in intellectual ability** The scores are based on a composite of five primary abilities tests, and weight heavily a speeded test such as word fluency. Both longitudinal and cross-sectional methods indicate that the height of ability appears at age 35 and declines fairly rapidly after age 50. T-scores are in units of the standard deviation, with mean of 50 and standard deviation of 10 (see the Appendix). The average of 50 is based on a sample of 1000 adult subjects. (After Schaie and Strother, 1968)

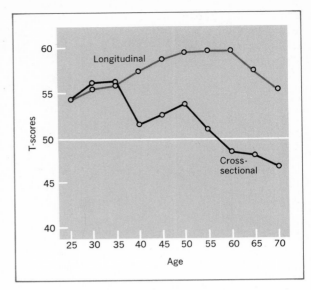

Fig. **15-12 Age changes in educational aptitude** The index is constructed by combining verbal meaning and reasoning scores, both of which do not contain any highly speeded measures. Here the cross-sectional and longitudinal methods yield strikingly different results: the cross-sectional data show a peak at age 35, but the longitudinal data postpone the peak to age 60. In both cases the decline with age is much less sharp than in Figure 15-11. (After Schaie and Strother, 1968)

seven years later. By using the changes in the scores of individuals of different ages over this seven-year period, the total longitudinal changes could be inferred without actually studying the same individuals for fifty years. In Figure 15-11 the two methods yielded essentially similar age changes (Schaie and Strother, 1968).

Earlier investigators had found that tests with strict time limits, thus requiring speed, were less favorable to the older subject than nonspeeded tests of information calling for general knowledge or understanding. Schaie and Strother confirmed these findings but also added to them by discovering that the longitudinal estimates gave quite different results from the cross-sectional scores (Figure 15-12). The cross-sectional method showed the familiar peak at age thirty-five, but the longitudinal method delayed the peak until age sixty.

How is this difference between the cross-sectional and longitudinal data to be explained?

The difference is coherent with the assumption that by these measures the population is performing better on nonspeeded tests as the years go by; a cross-sectional measure thus confounds individual age changes in intelligence test scores with average changes that depend upon the year in which a person was born—later-born doing better on the average than earlier-born. This assumption is supported by analyses that showed a large gain in intelligence test scores between the First and Second World Wars.

The decline in scores on some tests of intelligence in the later years does not signify that the mature adult is less competent to play his role in life. He may be accumulating new experiences less rapidly than he once did, but he has not forgotten all that he has accumulated in the past. If we think of *wisdom* as an accumulation from past experience and of *intelligence* as the ability to apply that experience to problems in the present, we may see how an older person may in some cases be more competent than a brighter younger person who lacks his experience. Intelligence tests weight items demanding cleverness, alertness, and adaptability to novel situations. They do not weight as strongly the background of experience that permits the older person to meet wisely the familiar situations in his own life and work.

The extremes of intelligence

The mentally subnormal

Intelligence tests were developed initially to identify those children least likely to profit from ordinary schooling. There is no sharp break between the subnormal and the normal, and many borderline cases exist. Furthermore, the classification of a child as retarded tells us very little about him. There are many kinds and degrees of retardation; because retarded children are not alike, calling them by a common name such as "feeble-minded" is misleading.

The prevalence of subnormality. The classification of a child as mentally subnormal or retarded depends primarily upon social competence. An intelligence test is not needed, for a child can be classified according to what he can do. Any classification runs into difficulty with borderline cases.

The distinction between dull normal and subnormal depends upon an interpretation of "marginal social success under favorable conditions." The farm hand who was unable to finish school but lives his own life as a hired man on the farm is economically independent and is normal in his environment, even though he may be recognizably dull; the same man might find it difficult to live successfully in the city. Thus the distinction between dull normal and subnormal rests upon the complexity of the social conditions under which independence must be maintained. By social criteria, an individual might change his classification just in moving from one place to another, even though his tested intelligence does not change.

The importance of social demands in determining retardation is illustrated by the ages at which retardation is most readily detected. Surveys of the number of retarded children at each age

---

The mentally subnormal child suffers a number of handicaps, but he is able to overcome many of them and live a useful and satisfying life. One of the most difficult handicaps to overcome is simply the stigma of being classified as subnormal. The terms that society uses sooner or later become terms with negative connotations. Such terms as "half-wit" and "simpleton," familiar to an earlier generation, were replaced by the then less offensive term "feeble-minded," but this too has come to have unfavorable connotations. The classification of the retarded into a less deficient group (moron), intermediate group (imbecile), and severely deficient group (idiot) has also outlived its usefulness, as the descriptive words have become terms of reproach.

The modern approach recognizes that there are mentally subnormal children with a variety of handicaps and avoids general terms of classification. Descriptive expressions, such as more severely defective, less severely retarded, trainable, or educable, have come into use to avoid the stigma of harsh labels. One main distinction, supported by the World Health Organization and encouraged by the National Association for Retarded Children, has been made between the individual who is organically damaged, classified as "mentally defective," and the individual whose problems lie in a learning disability, classified as "mentally retarded."

CRITICAL
DISCUSSION

Some rejected labels for the subnormal

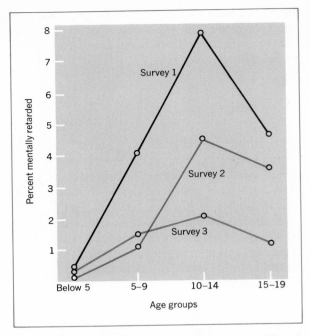

Fig. **15-13 Incidence of mental retardation** Three different surveys disagree on the total incidence, but agree in finding a larger proportion of children classified as retarded in the 10- to 14-year-old bracket. There is no reason for measured intelligence to show such changes with age; hence social criteria must be entering. (After Masland, Sarason, and Gladwin, 1958)

show that the highest percentage of retardation is found between the ages of ten and fourteen, when the competitive demands of academic performance become emphasized in judging retardation (Figure 15-13). There is no other reasonable explanation of this kind of change in the proportion of retarded individuals with age.

Because of these uncertainties regarding what

constitutes retardation, it is hard to make an accurate assessment of the prevalence of mental subnormality. It is usually asserted that about 1 or 2 percent of the population can be classified as subnormal, but, as indicated in Table 15-9, the potentially retarded may constitute as much as 3 percent of the population (Masland, Sarason, and Gladwin, 1958).

Causes of subnormality. A useful distinction is now made between the mentally retarded child and the mentally defective child. A child belongs to the *mentally retarded* group if he is essentially sound physically and if there is no history of disease or injury that might have caused intellectual impairment. He suffers from a general deficiency rather than an identifiable specific defect. Such a child often has a history of retardation in the family, so the possibility of inherited mental weakness is not ruled out. A child is classified as belonging to the *mentally defective* group if his mental impairment is caused by brain injury, disease, or accidents of development that preclude normal intellectual growth. The causes may occur during fetal life, childhood, or even adult life. Such individuals may appear in any family or socioeconomic group, regardless of family history of retardation.

Now and then we come upon a child who is apparently subnormal but actually is not. He reacts emotionally to his environment by withdrawal and negativism, so that his learning of language is delayed and his test performances are poor. Only a skilled test administrator can discover through the patterning of his test scores that the test result is misleading. Such a child can be aided by psychotherapy.

Treatment of the subnormal. From time to time dramatic reports appear of remarkable achievements in raising the I.Q. scores of subnormal children. Headlines in newspapers and articles in magazines raise hopes of countless parents who have retarded children. This publicity is unfortunately misleading because the overall evidence we have today is not encouraging. It gives little promise of dramatic improvement in the mentally sub-

TABLE 15-9 ESTIMATED PREVALENCE OF RETARDATION IN THE TOTAL POPULATION	
Potentially retarded, educable (ultimate M.A. under 12)	3.0%
Moderately severe retardation, trainable (ultimate M.A. from 4 to 7)	0.3
Most severely retarded, helpless (ultimate M.A. under 4)	0.1
Source: Masland, Sarason, and Gladwin (1958).	

normal, although this does not mean that the retarded or defective child cannot be helped.[4]

A great deal can be done for the subnormal child. He can be taught social habits; he can learn vocational skills appropriate to his intellectual level; in some instances he may learn to take his place in the community outside an institution. Social aid for the mentally subnormal must not be confused, however, with raising the I.Q. In many subnormal individuals a small increase in I.Q. comes with better social adjustment, but there is little reason to expect striking changes as a result of bettered environment (Kirk, 1958).

Many persons of low intelligence get along satisfactorily in the community. Several follow-up studies have been made of children whose I.Q.'s during school age rated them as mentally retarded. The investigators all found that a substantial proportion of these individuals were able to maintain themselves vocationally in the community when they became adults.

The mentally gifted

At the other end of the scale from the mentally retarded and defective are those who are intellectually gifted. With the development of intelligence tests it has become possible to select for study large groups of superior children and then to follow their careers. One of the best known of these studies, started by Terman and his associates in 1921, followed the progress of over 1500 gifted children from their early school years through the middle years of adult life. A forty-year follow-up has been published (Oden, 1968).

The group was chosen on the basis of I.Q.'s of 140 or above. About 10 or 11 out of every 1000 children in the public schools have I.Q.'s that high; less than 1 out of every 1000 has an I.Q. above 160.

Terman's gifted children were better than aver-

[4] The child who has special problems because he is socially disadvantaged, and who may be underachieving in school, can be helped. The disadvantaged child may be backward in school but should not for that reason be classified as mentally subnormal. With help there is usually an increase in measured I.Q. (Miller, 1970).

age physical specimens. They averaged more than an inch taller than others of the same age in elementary school. Their birth weights were above normal. They talked early and walked early. When the tests started, seven out of eight were in grades ahead of their age group in school; none was below grade level. They read an unusually large number and variety of books, but reading did not interfere with their superiority in leadership and social adaptability.

These characteristics of the gifted children contradict the notion that the very bright child is a weakling and a social misfit. The evidence is all to the contrary. Superior intelligence in Terman's subjects was associated with good health, social adaptability, and leadership.

Gifted children as young adults. The extent to which early promise was fulfilled by the gifted children of Terman's group can be estimated from their performances in early adult life. Although the group on the whole gave a superior account of itself, not all the subjects had a history of success. Some failed in college, some were vocational misfits, some ran afoul of the law. But the less successful differed little in their adult intelligence test scores from the more successful. The comparative scores are given in Table 15-10. The average I.Q. difference between the most and least successful is only six points. The slight difference in intellec-

TABLE 15-10   ADULT INTELLIGENCE OF SUCCESSFUL AND UNSUCCESSFUL MEN AMONG A GROUP WITH HIGH I.Q.'S AS CHILDREN

GROUP	MEAN SCORE ON CONCEPT MASTERY TEST	ESTIMATED EQUIVALENT I.Q. AS ADULTS
A Most success as adults (N = 79)	112	139
B Intermediate success (N = 322)	99	134
C Least success as adults (N = 116)	94	133

Source: Terman and Oden (1947).

The main point is that the differences in success were very little reflected in differences in I.Q. as adults.

tual level as measured cannot account for the differences in achievement. We must conclude that nonintellectual qualities are very important in success.

What does "successful" and "unsuccessful" mean in these comparisons? The subjects whose test scores are reported in Table 15-10 were classified into three success groups: A, the most successful; B, the intermediately successful; and C, the least successful. The criterion of success was primarily "the extent to which a subject made use of his intellectual ability." Listing in such books as *Who's who in America* or *American men of science,* representation in literary or scholarly publications, holding responsible managerial positions, outstanding achievement in any intellectual or professional calling—all entered into the judgments. Earned income was taken into account but was given relatively little weight in grouping the subjects.

Although the A and C groups did not differ very much in I.Q., a study of their records showed that they differed in many other respects—chiefly in general social adjustment and in achievement motivation. These are personality and motivational traits rather than intellectual ones.

A later follow-up (Terman and Oden, 1959) showed that the distinctive abilities of Terman's gifted subjects were becoming more fully recognized as they grew older. The 1955 edition of *American men of science* listed seventy men and seven women, whereas the 1944 edition had listed only nineteen of the men and none of the women. Listings in *Who's who* grew from five in 1946 to thirty-three in 1958. It takes time to achieve recognition, and this group, chosen in childhood, eventually gave a good account of itself.

It is of interest to know whether these intellectually able people have passed on their abilities to the next generation. Tests given to 1571 of their offspring (among a total of 2600 children produced) showed an average I.Q. of 133, although, as expected, the scores ranged from mentally subnormal to above 200 (Oden, 1968).

Present status of ability tests

Among the various tests of ability, we have chosen to consider the intelligence test in greatest detail. Despite its limitations, the intelligence test provides what is perhaps the most useful quantitative tool that psychology has developed. The usefulness of such tests will continue, provided they are kept in perspective and neither overvalued as telling more about a person than they actually measure nor undervalued because of their obvious defects. In the discussion that follows we shall try to view them in the perspective of other ability measures, and in relation to the social consequences of their use.

Some emerging concepts: fluid and crystallized intelligence

Despite the long interest in intelligence and its measurement, many unsolved problems remain, and new conceptions are frequently being offered, such as the structure-of-intellect model discussed earlier (p. 370).

Cattell (1963) suggests that there is a distinction between *fluid* and *crystallized* intelligence; this suggestion is supported by later work (Horn and Cattell, 1967). Fluid intelligence is analytic and is said not to be much influenced by prior learning; it is therefore likely to have a high hereditary component. Crystallized intelligence, on the other hand, depends very much upon prior habits and is therefore subject to the influence of schooling and other cultural opportunities.

The blurred distinction between aptitude tests and achievement tests

We pointed out earlier that aptitudes have to be assessed on the basis of prior achievements. It is a mistake to assign aptitude to innate potential and achievement entirely to training; both are complex results of innate potential, generalized experience with the environment, and specific training. Thus a scholastic aptitude test (the preferred name for an intelligence test that predicts school or college grades) includes learned material, although it does not demand that the student have taken a particular course in, say, mathematics or foreign language; an achievement test in a particular subject does presuppose acquaintance with a particular body of material.

A useful illustration of the blurred distinction between the two types of tests is the National Merit Scholarship Qualifying Test (NMSQT), given annually to about 800,000 high school students in the United States. This test is given to all students regardless of the school subjects they have studied, but it is still a test of *educational development,* not of aptitude alone; it is a measure of both the contribution of the student's aptitude and the effectiveness of his schooling. The success of the test in predicting success in college is quite high. For example, the first group of 520 Merit Scholarship recipients entered college in 1956. For those on whom records were available in 1965 (94 percent of the original group), it was found that 96 percent had graduated from college, and advanced degrees had been obtained by more than half of the men and by 40 percent of the women. (Stalnaker, 1965). In terms of our definition of aptitude testing as designed for prediction, the NMSQT reveals aptitude for college work, but of course various achievement tests and high school grades also predict college success.

For practical purposes of prediction, the fact that test content reflects both individual potential and the results of good schooling is immaterial. From the point of view of understanding the nature of intelligence it does matter, however, whether or not effective schooling actually raises intellectual potential.

Public attacks on testing

Early in the 1960s a number of attacks were made upon psychological testing (Black, 1963; Gross, 1962; Hoffman, 1962). These attacks were based on several objections, such as the invasion of privacy, the secrecy surrounding test scores, the types of talent selected by tests, and the unfairness of the tests to minority groups. These are all problems that have to be taken seriously by psychologists and others using tests.

Because a test is personal, it is not necessarily an invasion of privacy. When the purpose of the test is benign, when it is used to help the individual to plan his life and to avoid failure, it is no different, in principle, from the physical examination required for participation in athletics; the child with a heart ailment should not be advised to go out for long-distance running.

The secrecy surrounding test scores arose through the fear that parents might give too much credence to tests indicating their child to be somewhat handicapped, whereas the psychologist would prefer to give repeated tests and to make all sorts of allowances. This generally good reason for withholding scores has backfired somewhat, however, because it has made the test scores appear to be more important than they are. The best that they do is predict school grades, and there should be no more damage in one's knowing that he has a low I.Q. than in knowing he is doing poorly in school. Results of attitude studies show that children who were given their test scores more often than not raised their estimates of their own intelligence (Brim, 1965). In other words, the child has many indicators, beyond intelligence test scores, that he is brighter or duller than the other children. The National Merit Scholarship Corporation gives full disclosure of its scores, with apparently beneficial results.

Any prejudicial treatment of individuals because of the types of talent selected by tests would indeed be a serious matter if school and college admissions were based on intelligence tests alone. There is a good deal of pressure within the psychological profession itself to place more emphasis on creativity and nonintellectual factors in academic selection (Getzels and Jackson, 1962; Gough, 1965). Psychologists know that the intelligence test is a limited predictor of success (as the study of gifted persons showed, p. 377), but they do not therefore condemn it as useless.

The fairness of the tests to underprivileged and

minority groups is a complex problem to which psychologists have devoted considerable study (Deutsch and others, 1964). A point often overlooked is that ability tests provide objective criteria and, when properly used, may overcome some of the discrimination practiced against minority groups, thus increasing the opportunities of members of minority groups. This follows because the tests measure ability rather than social status. In some recent comparisons of white and black adult respondents, controlled for social class, it was found that lower-class blacks indeed favored the use of tests in job selection and promotion more than did the white respondents (Brim, 1965).

Summary

1. Individuals differ in all sorts of ways, and any one of these differences may affect how well they succeed in their work and in society.

2. The psychologist uses ability testing to study individual differences. *Aptitude tests* attempt to predict the success in some kind of performance not yet attained, as in judging how much an individual will profit by training before training is undertaken. *Achievement tests* measure present attainment, or what the subject has learned after the completion of training. Both tests can use similar items. The difference between them lies in their purposes.

3. In order to make predictions from tests, tests must meet certain specifications. Studies of *reliability* tell us whether the test scores are self-consistent. Studies of *validity* tell us how well the tests measure what they are supposed to measure—how well they predict according to an acceptable criterion.

4. When tests meet these specifications, they can be applied in schools, in industry, in civil service, or in the armed forces. The pilot-selection program of the U. S. Army Air Forces during the Second World War illustrates the nature of a *test battery* and how the results of tests are used in prediction.

5. The simplest application of the results of studies in prediction is the *critical score*, which is set so that those who score below this point are disqualified, while those above it are accepted or permitted to continue. A correlation coefficient between the test and some *criterion* can also be used in prediction. An *expectancy table* provides another method.

6. The first successful intelligence tests were developed by Alfred Binet in France in 1905. We owe to him the concept of *mental age*, according to which we regard dull children as slow in their development, their responses being like those of children younger in age. Conversely, bright children are advanced beyond their years. This concept has been followed in later revisions of Binet's scales, of which the most widely used has been the Stanford-Binet.

7. Terman, who was responsible for the Stanford-Binet, introduced the *intelligence quotient* (I.Q.) as an index of mental development. The I.Q. originally expressed intelligence as a ratio of mental age (M.A.) to chronological age (C.A.). The *deviation* I.Q. adopted in the most recent Stanford-Binet adjusts the obtained I.Q.'s so that at each chronological age they have a mean of 100 and a standard deviation of 16. Hence a contemporary I.Q. is no longer a ratio, but a score adjusted for the age of the person being tested.

8. Efforts to improve the diagnostic value of intelligence tests have taken two chief forms. One is to divide the items of the test into more than one scale. This attempt is illustrated by the verbal and performance scales of the Wechsler Adult Intelligence Scale and the Wechsler Intelligence Scale for Children. The second method is to arrange subtests according to the findings of *factor analysis*. The individual tests can then represent the factors found to determine the test intercorrelations. One factor-based test battery, the tests for Primary Mental Abilities developed by Thurstone, has proved to be a promising tool of research and prediction. However, Guilford has shown that there may be many more factors than Thurstone found; his structure-of-intellect model proposes 120 factors.

9. Guilford has broadened the concept of intelligence beyond that of the conventional I.Q. test. One of the distinctions he made is that between *divergent production* (creative thinking) and *convergent production* (logical solution to find the one correct answer). The usual I.Q. test does not stress divergent production, so the correlation between I.Q. and creativity is low. In general, those with high creativity commonly have high I.Q.'s, but a high I.Q. is no guarantee of creativity.

10. Among groups of children selected as brighter and less bright by tests when they are young (say, at age five), the differences in mental age persist; the relative constancy of the I.Q. is shown by high correlations between successive tests. This constancy is only relative, for the correlations tend to fall with greater time between tests, and some children show large changes in I.Q. between tests. Scores on the various primary abilities tests reach 80 percent of adult values at ages varying from twelve to beyond twenty.

11. By using deviation I.Q.'s, the Wechsler Adult Intelligence Scale makes it possible to apply the concept of intelligence quotient to adults, and to interpret such an I.Q. approximately as it is interpreted earlier in life. When intelligence test scores are not adjusted in this way, it is found that verbal intelligence reaches its peak at the age level of twenty-five through thirty-four, performance intelligence somewhat earlier. The decline in intelligence test scores with age is misleading when based on cross-sectional studies; with longitudinal studies, speeded tests show rapid decline, but nonspeeded tests of verbal meaning and reasoning, for instance, show no such decline until the sixties.

12. The extremes of intelligence are represented by the *mentally subnormal*, at one end of the scale, and the *intellectually gifted*, at the other. A final decision that a child is or is not subnormal depends upon social criteria as well as intelligence test scores; for example, of two children with the same score one may be classed as subnormal, the other as normal. The subnormal are classified as *mentally retarded* or *mentally defective*. Mental retardation is a deficiency present from birth, with no obvious brain damage. Mental defectiveness results from illness, injury, or a physical defect. Subnormal children can learn; thus many of them can do socially useful work under supervision or even achieve a measure of social independence. The fact that the impairment in intelligence level persists throughout life means only that this condition imposes a special responsibility upon society to make provision for adequate care and training.

13. As a group the mentally gifted show superior attainments throughout childhood and adult life. Their histories belie the notion that highly intelligent people are maladjusted in some way. Superior intelligence is in itself no assurance of success; some gifted children are misfits in adult life even though their intelligence scores remain high.

14. Public attacks upon testing are based on such objections as invasion of privacy, secrecy surrounding test scores, types of talent selected by tests, and unfairness of the tests to disadvantaged and minority groups. Psychologists have incomplete answers to these criticisms, but they do recognize that ability testing carries with it social responsibility.

Suggestions for further reading

For general reviews of individual differences and psychological testing, see Anastasi, *Psychological testing* (3rd ed., 1968), and Cronbach, *Essentials of psychological testing* (3rd ed., 1970). Among the books that specifically treat the problems of intelligence testing are Guilford, *The nature of human intelligence* (1967), Butcher, *Human intelligence* (1968), and Vernon, *Intelligence and cultural environment* (1969).

behavior genetics 16

MODERN GENETICS, THE SCIENCE of heredity, shows how the physical characteristics of offspring derive from characteristics of the parents. Behavior genetics is a newer branch of genetics, concerned with the hereditary correlates of behavior rather than of physical structure. An interesting question is whether anything is added to the knowledge of genetics by studying behavior, for surely behavior (if its potentials are inherited) must depend upon physical structures and their related physiological and biological processes. That is, if intelligence depends in part upon inheritance, it is because the brighter person inherits a nervous system that is better adapted to intelligent behavior than the one inherited by the less bright person. This sounds logical enough, but inherited structure is not observed directly; what is observed, even in such features as size and coloration, reflects the interaction of heredity and environment. Thus a rat's ability to run a maze may be as useful an indicator of heredity as the weight of its brain. The inheritance of correlates of behavior can be studied, just as the inheritance of physical structure can be studied.

There is no point in arguing an extreme view that all that matters is heredity, or all that matters is environment. A little reflection will point immediately to an interaction, for an organism cannot grow at all without the sustenance that the environment provides. There may be a hereditary component to height, but the actually attained height will depend upon the variety and adequacy of the diet; so, too, a behavioral characteristic such as intelligence may have hereditary correlates, but the intellectual level actually attained will depend upon various kinds of stimulation during growth. To try to decide between heredity and environment, or even to divide up their influences for an individual, is to create pseudoproblems. Rather, we wish to learn what we can of the limitations imposed by heredity on the individual potential, and the range of change that can be produced by favorable and unfavorable environments.

Phenotypes and genotypes

While heredity generally produces resemblances between parents and offspring, the science of genetics teaches us to search beneath superficial resemblances; in fact, certain *lacks* of resemblance between parents and offspring give us our chief clues to the mechanism of heredity. For example, the fact that the offspring of black guinea pigs are in the proportion of three black to one white illustrates a fundamental principle of heredity; the fact that half the sons of some parents who see colors normally may be colorblind illustrates another principle. To understand these illustrations we have to distinguish between the *phenotype,* the characteristics that an individual manifests (as in the parent with normal color vision), and the *genotype,* the genetic characteristics that an individual inherits, carries, and may or may not display (as in a mother who may transmit color blindness to her sons).

Chromosomes and genes

The hereditary units that an individual has received from his parents and that he will transmit to his offspring are carried by microscopic particles, known as *chromosomes,* found within each cell of the body. A chromosome is composed of many individual determiners of heredity called *genes.* Each body cell in man has 46 chromosomes. At conception the human being receives 23 chromosomes from the father's sperm and 23 chromosomes from the mother's ovum. These 46 chromosomes form 23 pairs, which are duplicated in every cell of the body as the individual develops (Figure 16-1). It was thought at first that man had 24 pairs of chromosomes, but the lower number is now established as typical, although there are some abnormal cases (Tjio and Levan, 1956).

Genes also occur in pairs—one gene of each pair comes from the sperm chromosomes and one gene from the ovum chromosomes. We have no exact way of counting the genes, for unlike the chromosomes they do not show up under the microscope as separate particles. The total number of genes in each human chromosome is on the order of 1000, and perhaps higher. Because the numbers of genes and chromosomes are so high, it is extremely unlikely that two human beings would have the same heredity, even with the same parents. One exception is identical (monozygotic) twins, who, having developed from the same egg, have the same chromosomes and genes.

An important attribute of the gene is *dominance* or *recessiveness.* If both members of a gene pair are dominant, the individual will manifest the trait determined by the genes. If one is dominant and the other recessive, he will show the form of the trait expressive of the dominant gene, but he will also carry the recessive gene, which may be expressed in a different way as a trait in his offspring. A recessive form of the trait will be expressed only if both genes are recessive (blue eyes, for example, since brown eyes are dominant).

One pair of chromosomes that is of particular interest is the pair associated with the sex of the individual and with the genes of certain traits that

Fig. 16-1 **Chromosomes** A photo of the 46 human chromosomes; based on skin tissue, male (enlarged 1500 times actual size). Chromosome pictures such as this permit the study of genetic abnormalities of some types, such as XXY and XYY. (See Critical Discussion.)

Dr. J. H. Tjio

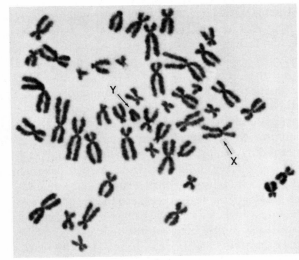

A number of deviations from normal human development can now be traced to chromosomal abnormalities. A male difficulty, known as *Klinefelter's syndrome,* is one in which the male genitals fail to develop normally. A test of skin tissue cells in normal males yields a result known as chromatin negative, but cases of Klinefelter's syndrome are chromatin positive, as in normal females. This sexual ambiguity in development is associated with an *extra* sex chromosome; the person has two X-chromosomes *and* a Y-chromosome, thus of a type XXY, with 47 chromosomes altogether (Jacobs and Strong, 1959).

A related difficulty in the female, a condition known as *Turner's syndrome* is characterized by lack of development of secondary sex characteristics at the age when pubertal changes are expected. Those suffering from this anomaly are sterile and usually small in stature, averaging under 5 feet tall. One of the X-chromosomes is missing, so that there are only 45 chromosomes instead of 46; the type is XO instead of the normal XX. An interesting psychological accompaniment of Turner's syndrome is a deficiency in one of the Primary Mental Ability factors, visual space-form perception (Shaffer, 1962; Money, 1963). Here is possible genetic evidence for linking this ability to sex (see p. 394).

Another type of anomaly is based on a reduplication of the Y-chromosome, yielding a male of type XYY. Some males with this genetic composition appear to be unusually aggressive, and a few cases have been discovered among those guilty of crimes of violence. The significance of this abnormality has therefore been the occasion for a good deal of discussion. The present conclusion is that no special stigmatization should be assigned to those having this chromosomal structure. Aggressive behavior has to be modified in these cases as it does in any other aggressive individual, and the behavior is not itself inevitable.

are "sex-linked." These pairs are made up of X- and Y-chromosomes, with the normal female having two X-chromosomes in the pair and the normal male one X-chromosome and one Y-chromosome (see Figure 16-1). The female inherits one X-chromosome from the mother, one from the father; the male inherits his X-chromosome from his mother, his Y-chromosome from his father. The X-chromosome may carry either dominant or recessive genes; the Y-chromosome carries a few genes dominant for sexual characteristics but is not known to carry recessive genes.[1] Thus a recessive characteristic in the male like color blindness comes about only when the male inherits a recessive color-blindness gene from his mother. Females are less often colorblind, because to be so they would have to have both a colorblind father and a mother who was either colorblind or carried a recessive gene for color blindness. In this manner the X-chromosomes and Y-chromosomes have helped to unravel some of the puzzling problems of human hereditary traits.

Other advances in human cytogenetics have made possible the discovery of a chromosomal basis for some developmental difficulties. One such condition is a form of mental subnormality known as mongolism. It turns out that the mongoloid individual has an extra small chromosome, probably one of his chromosomes reduplicated (Lejeune, Gautier, and Turpin, 1959).

Biochemical genetics

Within the past few years the mechanism of heredity has come to be much better understood through biochemical research. A complex substance known as DNA (*deoxyribonucleic acid*) has been found to be the material basis for gene action, and considerable ingenuity has been exercised in deciding how the genetic "code" succeeds in directing the development of the organism (Crick, 1962). The DNA must be quite stable and yet capable of duplicating itself in all the cells of the

[1] The whole question of traits specifically linked to the Y-chromosome, other than maleness, is a matter of uncertainty.

body; this appears to be the case, making possible not only the development of the organism but the transmission of its hereditary characteristics to succeeding generations. The DNA somehow directs the formation of amino acids that in turn form the proteins that are at the base of the cellular processes from which the organism is eventually constructed and by which it is controlled. The process of protein formation uses another nucleic acid, RNA (*ribonucleic acid*), which exists in several forms, of which *messenger* RNA and *transfer* RNA describe the different functions. Messenger RNA is synthesized in the nucleus of the cell by DNA and then leaves the nucleus. The transfer RNA "recognizes" the code of the messenger RNA and combines with amino acids in a sequence dictated by the messenger RNA, thus forming the protein chains. The messenger RNA is used up in the process; the transfer RNA becomes detached from the amino acids after it has served its purpose in lining them up according to the prescribed code.

Population genetics

The basic characteristics of a population of animals or human beings depend upon the genes extant in that population. Because of various selective factors that occur through inbreeding (the death of the unfit, and the like), over long periods of time there is a "drift" in the genes available, with the result that various intermarrying human groups form different blood groups, although all human beings share the same basic blood types. The study of the gene distribution throughout groups of individuals that mate with one another, and the consequences of this distribution, is known as *population genetics*.

The principles that have been developed in connection with population genetics have an important consequence for the study of human genetics: since evidence can be obtained simultaneously on the characteristics of parents and children, a single scientist can carry out his study in a lifetime, without needing to gather family histories over several generations. The application of this method to the study of psychological inheritance has thus far

been slight, but eventually more ways may be found to use the method.

The study of population genetics resulted in the discovery of a curious kind of taste deficiency in about 30 percent of the population. A substance with the chemical name of phenyl-thio-carbamide (PTC) tastes very bitter to 70 percent of the population when taken into the mouth at low concentrations. It is insipid or tasteless to the rest.

Since taste is not a characteristic by which people choose their mates, there is probably no selective factor affecting gene distribution. If this is so, the genetic determiners for PTC tasting should be distributed at random through the population. That is, in any one hundred people tested from a given intermarrying population, the proportion of tasters to nontasters will be relatively constant. Because the ratio is constant, it is possible to predict the taste deficiencies of the offspring of marriages of tasters and nontasters, according to the principles of genetic determination. The prediction is based on the assumption that tasting is a simple trait, determined by one gene pair, and that tasting is dominant and nontasting is recessive. Since all nontasters are assumed to be pure recessives (having two recessive genes), all the children of two nontasters should be nontasters. When both parents carry a dominant and a recessive gene, the offspring, according to the Mendelian ratio, should be in the proportion of 3 tasters to 1 nontaster. Whenever one parent is pure dominant, all children should be tasters. The results of a study of the inheritance of taste deficiency are given in Table 16-1. The data show how successful the

TABLE 16-1 INHERITANCE OF TASTE DEFICIENCY TO PHENYL-THIO-CARBAMIDE		
MATINGS OF PARENTS	CHILDREN WITH TASTE DEFICIENCY	
	PREDICTED	OBSERVED
Taster × taster (N = 425)*	12.4%	12.3%
Taster × nontaster (N = 289)	35.4	36.6
Nontaster × nontaster (N = 86)	100.00	97.9

*N = number of families tested.
Source: Snyder (1932).

prediction is: the phenotypes occur in the proportions expected from the inferred genotypes.

Most psychological characteristics do not lend themselves to as straightforward a study as that of taste deficiency. The greater complexity is in part due to the fact that some psychological characteristics enter into the choice of mates, and hence a random distribution of genetic determiners cannot be assumed. In addition, few psychological characteristics are likely to be determined by single gene pairs.

Heredity in animal behavior

Animal-breeding experiments tell us something about the influence of heredity on behavior. Some strains of mice, for example, go into convulsions when they are exposed to high-pitched sounds, while others do not. When these strains were crossed, the susceptibility to seizures appeared to follow genetic rules, as though the seizures were inherited as a dominant trait (Witt and Hall, 1949). Later studies, however, using various strains of mice, showed the matter to be more complex, although the hereditary basis is not challenged (Schlesinger, Elston, and Boggan, 1966). Wildness and tameness in rats are hereditary. According to some authorities, change in a single gene pair will convert a wild strain into a tame one (Keeler and King, 1942).

Fig. **16-2** **Inheritance of maze learning in rats** Mean error scores of "bright" and "dull" rats selectively bred for performance on the Hebb-Williams maze. (After Thompson, 1954)

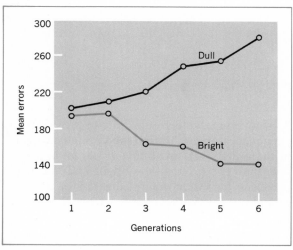

Maze learning in rats. Several experiments have been directed to a study of the inheritance of learning ability in rats. By mating those that did poorly in maze learning with others that did poorly, a "dull" strain was produced; by mating those that did well with others that did well, a "bright" strain was produced (Tryon, 1940; 1963). Other experimenters have also succeeded in a separation of bright and dull strains within a few generations (Figure 16-2). The descendants of Tryon's maze-bright and maze-dull strains were tested many years later: the descendants of the maze-bright rats were still superior to those of the maze-dull rats in the learning of several different mazes (Rosenzweig, 1969).

Phototaxis in fruit flies. Satisfactory experiments from the point of view of genetics have also been performed with the fruit fly, Drosophila. The behavior selected for study was phototaxis, the tendency to be attracted to a source of light. By mating those showing a strong tendency with others showing a strong tendency, and those showing a weak tendency with others showing a weak tendency, a segregation of types was attempted (Hirsch and Boudreau, 1958). The results over successive generations led to the same kind of separation of strains as was found in the rat (Figure 16-3). The use of the fruit fly has two advantages over use of the rat for this kind of experiment: (1) it takes far less time to breed successive generations, and (2) the detailed mapping of genes and chromosomes has been carried out more successfully with the fruit fly, so that a genetic interpretation of the behavioral findings can be more precise.

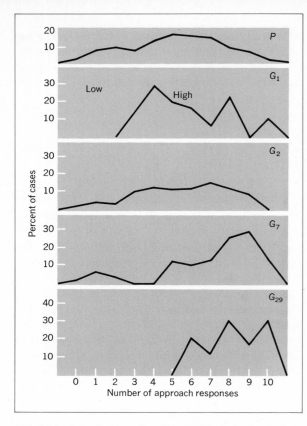

Fig. 16-3 Selective breeding for phototaxis in the fruit fly
With ten opportunities to make approach responses to light, the offspring of parents selected for a high number of approaches average much higher in successive generations than the offspring of those selected for a low number of approaches. The vertical axis shows the percentage of cases yielding each number of approaches. The original parent generation (P) is shown with the first (G_1), second (G_2), seventh (G_7), and twenty-ninth (G_{29}) offspring generations. (After Hirsch and Boudreau, 1958)

Other evidence. Maze learning in rats and phototaxis in fruit flies are but two illustrations of many animal experiments concerned with the hereditary correlates of behavior (Fuller and Thompson, 1960). The dog has served as a subject in a number of these studies. James (1941) found Basset hounds to be lethargic and German shepherds excitable; when he bred the two kinds together, the offspring were found to be somewhere in between. Later studies (for example, Scott and Fuller, 1965) have shown other differences in emotionality among well-established dog breeds, as well as differences in trainability. These differences may be considered essentially hereditary, although environment is certainly a contributing factor.

The carefully controlled breeding experiments carried out with animals are not possible with human beings for a number of obvious reasons. The geneticist cannot make marriages to suit his convenience. Even if marriages could be planned, the long life span of human beings would make it difficult to follow several generations except by going back to old records, which are often incomplete. These difficulties do not, however, prevent our obtaining satisfactory evidence that the human inheritance of some characteristics does in fact follow the genetic principles established by the study of other animals. The evidence is fairly satisfactory for eye color, hair color, and many body features. It is much harder to evaluate evidence regarding the inheritance of psychological characteristics.

Heredity in human intelligence and mental illness

The rules of genetics, as presented above, are stated in terms of unitary traits determined by single gene pairs, but actually most traits for which the determiners are known do not fit so simple a description. Traits that vary along a dimension, as height does in man, tend to be determined by more than one gene. If there were only one pair, we would have one height for dominant men and one height for recessive men, just as the tasters and nontasters form two separable groups. Intelligence varies, as height does, on a scale from subnormality to genius, without the sharp break that would let us classify men into two groups—the bright and the stupid. Hence to the extent that intelligence (or any other complex trait) may be inherited, we would expect it to be contributed to by a number of genes.

Man's inheritance of a psychological characteristic has been most thoroughly investigated in the field of intelligence. Moreover, the heredity-environment relations in this area are very complex indeed. Much of the remainder of this chapter will therefore be devoted to evidence concerning the hereditary and environmental correlates of intelligence.

The role of heredity and environment in intelligence

To study the possibility of hereditary correlates of a complex trait, we may begin by examining *resemblances* between parents and offspring or of offspring to one another. A convenient index of resemblance is the familiar coefficient of correlation. We turn now to some studies that use the coefficient of correlation to determine evidence for the role of heredity in intelligence.

Parents and children. If parents contribute to the intelligence of their children through heredity, we would expect a correlation between the intelligence of parents and children. The earlier in the child's life this correlation is found, the more evidence it will give for heredity; after the child has lived in a home for several years, the influence of environment cannot be ruled out. But the discovery of a correlation early in life depends upon whether intelligence can be measured early.

Although a number of scales have been prepared for measuring the psychological development of infants, we now know that these scales do not adequately predict the scores a child will later make on intelligence tests. At least up to the age of two, the child's I.Q. at age six can be better predicted from the educational level of his parents than from his test scores as an infant (Bayley, 1940a; 1940b). Part of the reason for the low correlations between early and later tests lies in the shift in test content. Tests of infants are necessarily nonverbal, whereas verbal tests become very important later. Not until the child becomes verbal (beginning at the age of two, so far as test results indicate) is the tested I.Q. predictive of later I.Q. This instability of scores during the first years prevents us from obtaining an early estimate of intelligence free of environmental influence.

If we wait until the school years, when the I.Q. can be satisfactorily measured, we find a positive correlation between the parents' and the child's I.Q. With a large parent-child sample (428 father-child scores and 534 mother-child scores) the score of either parent alone correlated .49 with that of the school-age offspring (Conrad and Jones, 1940). This correlation is about the same size as that obtained between parent and child for a physical characteristic such as height and gives some indication of hereditary influence, although, of course, environment has now become a factor.

Foster parents. One way to isolate the influences of inheritance and environment is to study children raised by foster parents. A great many children are placed for adoption each year. Because adoptions are handled by social agencies, tests are usually given and records are kept so that the opportunity for follow-up studies is good.

Two main questions require answers:

1. Does the ultimate I.Q. of children adopted within the first few months of life correlate more highly with that of their *biological* parents or with that of their *foster* parents? Does the I.Q. of foster children also correspond to the educational and occupational levels of their *foster* parents?
2. Does the generally favorable atmosphere of homes into which children are adopted raise the general *mean level* of intelligence, regardless of whether the correlation changes?

The answer to the first of these questions is that the correlation is higher with the *biological* parents than with the *foster* parents (Table 16-2). Other studies commonly find some correlation with the foster parents, but not as high as that with biological parents. This small correlation with foster parents is to be expected as a result of selective placement, for the children of more intelligent parents tend to be placed with more intelligent foster parents (Honzik, 1957). This evidence favors the interpretation that there is a hereditary component to intelligence.

As for the second question, it has been found that placement in a good home tends to raise the

TABLE 16-2	RESEMBLANCES IN INTELLIGENCE OF FOSTER CHILDREN TO THEIR BIOLOGICAL AND FOSTER PARENTS*	
	NUMBER OF CASES	COEFFICIENT OF CORRELATION (r)
Biological parents, with whom child has not lived		
Mother's I.Q. and child's I.Q.	63	.44
Mother's education and child's I.Q.	92	.32
Father's education and child's I.Q.†	60	.40
Foster parents, with whom child has lived at least 10 years		
Mother's education and child's I.Q.	100	.02
Father's education and child's I.Q.	100	.00

* All children were placed for adoption before the age of 6 months. Children's I.Q.'s used in correlations were obtained at ages 10–18 (mean age, 13).
† Not given in the report, but computed from the data given there. The biological father's education was unknown for the other 40 cases in the sample of 100.

Source: Skodak and Skeels (1949).

I.Q. of the adopted child beyond the I.Q. that would be predicted from the biological-parent I.Q. (Skodak and Skeels, 1949). Here is evidence for an environmental influence. When there has been very severe early deprivation, improvement in a child's I.Q. as a result of being placed in a good home may be permanent. Skeels (1966) followed into adult life some individuals who had been studied much earlier (Skeels and Dye, 1939). As deprived orphanage children these individuals had I.Q.'s averaging 64 at nineteen months; through special attention they were prepared for adoption (see Chapter 3, p. 61) and placed in good homes between the ages of two and three. Their I.Q.'s improved to a mean level of 96 at age six. As adults they lived as normal average citizens in their communities, and their children had tested I.Q.'s averaging 105. Those in a control group, who were not placed for adoption at an early age, showed retardation throughout life. The intellec-

tual status of the biological parents should be ascertained in order to know whether the original retardation was definitely below the child's potential, and hence whether the stimulating environment had done more than correct an early environmental deficiency. There is no doubt that intelligence is affected by both hereditary and environmental factors; the issue that is much debated is their relative importance.

Twin studies. Study of the effects of heredity and environment on man is greatly furthered by the study of *monozygotic* (MZ) *twins,* who are genetically identical, having been developed from the same ovum.[2] Consider, for example, family resemblances in height (Table 16-3). Ordinary brothers and sisters (known as *siblings*) show a moderate degree of resemblance, as represented by a correlation of $r = .60$. *Dizygotic* (DZ) *twins,* who develop from separate ova, are no more alike genetically than ordinary siblings; they need not be of the same sex nor do they necessarily resemble each other. It is possible that the effects of a common intra-uterine environment and common diet and treatment after birth might make DZ twins slightly more alike than ordinary siblings, but the greater similarity, if any, is not fully proved by the correlation of $r = .64$. The highest degree of similarity is found for MZ twins ($r = .93$).

What can correlation coefficients tell us about heredity and intelligence? Again the study of twins provides us with the most illuminating data (Table

TABLE 16-3	RESEMBLANCE IN HEIGHT OF CHILDREN OF THE SAME PARENTS	
PAIRS OF CHILDREN	NUMBER OF PAIRS	COEFFICIENT OF CORRELATION (r)
Ordinary siblings (like-sexed)	52	.60
Dizygotic (DZ) twins (like-sexed)	52	.64
Monozygotic (MZ) twins	50	.93

Source: Newman, Freeman, and Holzinger (1937).

[2] They are of the same sex, except in rare cases in which one is male (XY) and the other a Turner-syndrome female (XO).

TABLE 16-4	RESEMBLANCE IN I.Q.'S OF CHILDREN OF THE SAME PARENTS	
PAIRS OF CHILDREN	NUMBER OF PAIRS	COEFFICIENT OF CORRELATION (r)
Ordinary siblings*	384	.53
Dizygotic (DZ) twins†	482	.63
Monozygotic (MZ) twins†	687	.87

*Source: McNemar (1942).
†Source: Nichols (1965).

TABLE 16-5	CORRELATIONS BETWEEN INTELLIGENCE TEST SCORES OF MZ TWINS REARED APART	
TEST	NUMBER OF PAIRS	COEFFICIENT OF CORRELATION (r)
Stanford-Binet*	19	.77
Vocabulary and Progressive Matrices†	37	.77
Stanford-Binet (English form)‡	53	.86

*Source: Newman, Freeman, and Holzinger (1937).
†Source: Shields (1962).
‡Source: Burt (1966).

16-4). We find the resemblances follow the same order as those for height: ordinary siblings are least alike, dizygotic twins more alike but close to siblings, and monozygotic twins most alike. The differences in correlation between MZ and DZ twin pairs have by now been shown in numerous studies done around the world. Erlenmeyer-Kimling and Jarvik (1963) found fourteen studies yielding an average correlation of .87 in intellectual resemblance between MZ twins and eleven studies yielding an average correlation of .53 for DZ twins.

Monozygotic twins reared apart. The most interesting cases for the study of the role of inheritance are those of MZ twins reared apart, particularly if it can be assumed that the environments differ in a random fashion. Were that the case, the correlation between the twin pairs would give a direct estimate of the *heritability*.[3]

After diligent searches, three different investigators were able to locate and test a number of MZ twins reared apart. The resulting correlations are given in Table 16-5. Using these figures, with some corrections introduced for test unreliability, Jensen (1969) has estimated heritability of intelligence to be .80, meaning that 80 percent of the variance in intrafamilial I.Q. results from variance

[3] *Heritability* is defined as the proportion of phenotype variance in a population owing to variance in genotypes; variance is the square of the standard deviation (see the Appendix). This rather technical definition is stated to avoid an assertion that a given person's intelligence is determined to such-and-such a percent by his heredity. Such percents apply to populations of phenotypes and genotypes, not to individuals, and under quite specific conditions. Hence they cannot be generalized from one environment to another, or from one generation to the next.

in the genotypes. Jensen's estimate is a confirmation of findings (with some variations in the precise estimate) holding for forty years (Burks, 1928).

When computations are made in the way that Burks and Jensen made them, results tend to turn out as indicated above. There are, however, serious constraints upon the interpretation of such findings, because they depend upon (1) the particular populations studied (for example, whites in the early twentieth century), (2) the nature of the intelligence tests used, and (3) the types of statistical assumptions involved.

That environment makes some contribution is, of course, indicated by the twin studies as well as by the adoption studies. In each of the studies the correlation obtained between the intelligence test scores of twins reared apart was lower than that found for the scores of the twins reared together. In the Newman, Freeman, and Holzinger (1937) study the greatest difference in scores between pairs was found for the four pairs whose members had been reared in the most contrasting environments.

At this point a word of caution is in order. Studies of the kind cited leave no doubt that heredity plays a sizable role in intelligence, but any effort to assign an exact proportion to the contribution of heredity and environment to the I.Q. of a single individual is scientifically futile and socially misleading. Modern behavior geneticists agree with this statement. One geneticist, in summarizing a symposium concerned with these topics, concludes:

Heated controversies have flared up from time to time among psychologists over the interpretation of data on heredity and environment, particularly some of the data from studies of foster homes and twins that have just been reviewed. It turns out, in retrospect, that one source of disagreement arose through a failure to see that for a given body of data, interpretations based on *correlation coefficients* might lead to one result, whereas interpretations based on *mean scores* might lead to another. As a general rule, correlation coefficients lead to results favoring the hereditary role (as based on variances inferred from these correlations), while mean scores favor the environmental role. Those engaged in the debate have in the past tended to emphasize the kinds of data that supported their own perferences.

That correlations and means consider different aspects of the data is clear from a comparison of two early foster-child studies, one by Burks (1928), the other by Leahy (1935). The results from the studies, considering correlations only, were alike; both showed lower correlations in intelligence between foster parents and children than between biological parents and children. Results for means differed, however. The Burks foster children had ultimate I.Q.'s below those of the biological children, while the Leahy foster children had ultimate I.Q.'s equal to those of the biological children. Hence studies agreeing on correlations need not agree on means. The differences are not haphazard; the point is that a full understanding of the data requires a consideration of both correlations and means.

While the difference between correlational results and mean results is at first puzzling, another example takes away some of the mystery. Consider the heights of children as related to the heights of parents. Within the last several decades there has been a remarkable increase of height, owing to improved diet and control of disease, so that children now tend to be taller than their parents. If one were to argue that height is a matter of environment, he could point to the increase in the stature of Italians in New York City over their counterparts in Italy, the increase in height of the Japanese since the Second World War, as well as the gradual increase in height of American college students. If, however, one were to argue that height is a matter of heredity, he would use correlation coefficients to show that taller parents still have taller children than shorter parents do, and that the present correlation between parent and child height is the same as it was a century ago.

The point needs repeated emphasis: if attention is paid to correlation coefficients, weight will be given to heredity, while if attention is paid to changes in mean scores, weight will be given to environment.

The problem of whether a certain behavioral character is determined by genes or by the environment, or even of partitioning of the variance into genetic and environmental variance, is therefore misleading from the point of view of understanding behavior. Rather, the question, particularly with respect to human psychology, is how genetic individuality, which is a demonstrated fact, will express itself under the influence of diverse social and environmental conditions [Caspari, 1967, p. 275].

Heredity and mental illness

Because as we shall see later (Chapter 20), mental illness is a social problem of great magnitude, a number of studies have been undertaken to determine the hereditary component in such illness. Particular attention has been given to a prevalent mental illness known as *schizophrenia* (see p. 473).

Here again the studies of twins have proved

to be illuminating. If one member of a twin pair is diagnosed as schizophrenic, what are the chances that his twin will also be schizophrenic? If there is a hereditary component to the illness, it will be expected that among MZ twins the chances will be much higher than among DZ twins. A number of studies, summarized in Table 16-6, have found this to be the case.

The concordance percentages—the percent of pairs in which the second twin is diagnosed schizophrenic when one twin is so diagnosed—vary from zero to 88 in the studies reported. But eight of the twelve studies show a concordance above 50 percent for MZ pairs, while none of the studies shows a rate this high for DZ pairs. All the studies in which the comparison is possible show a higher rate for the MZ pairs. A subordinate finding worth noting is that in six of the seven studies in which the comparison is possible, like-sexed DZ twins show a higher concordance than opposite-sexed

ones. This suggests an environmental contribution.

The conclusion to be drawn from these studies is that a genetic factor does operate in some types of schizophrenia. This conclusion is shared by those who retain their belief that family interaction is an important environmental influence in bringing out the genetic potential for schizophrenia (Rosenthal, 1968).

As in the case of intelligence, there are a number of complicating factors. For example, most of the studies referred to in Table 16-6 have found higher concordance rates among the more severely disturbed patients. Even those concordant in diagnosis often exhibit very different symptoms. Perhaps most instructive of all is the study of those MZ twin pairs in which one twin is schizophrenic, the other not. One possibility is that some types of schizophrenia are inherited and others are not (Rosenthal, 1959). Another possibility is that some kind of unusual stress, perhaps even prior to birth,

TABLE 16-6   SUMMARY OF STUDIES OF SCHIZOPHRENIA IN TWINS

INVESTIGATOR	COUNTRY	CONCORDANCE		
		MZ TWINS	DZ TWINS (SAME SEX)	DZ TWINS (OPPOSITE SEX)
		PERCENT	PERCENT	PERCENT
Kallmann (1956, 1946)				
Preadolescent	USA	88 (N = 17)	23 (N = 35*)	—
Adult	USA	69 (N = 174)	11 (N = 296)	6 (N = 221)
Slater (1953)				
First sample	UK	65 (N = 26)	11 (N = 35)	0 (N = 36)
Second sample	UK	64 (N = 11)	17 (N = 23)	11 (N = 18)
Essen-Möller (1941)	Sweden	64 (N = 11)	15 (N = 27)	—
Rosanoff (1934)	USA	61 (N = 41)	13 (N = 53)	6 (N = 48)
Inouye (1961)	Japan	60 (N = 55)	18 (N = 11)	0 (N = 6)
Luxenburger (1928)	Germany	58 (N = 19)	0 (N = 13)	0 (N = 20)
Gottesman and Shields (1966)	UK	42 (N = 24)	9 (N = 33)	—
Harvald and Hauge (1965)	Denmark	29 (N = 7)	6 (N = 31)	4 (N = 28)
Kringlen† (1964)	Norway	25 (N = 8)	17 (N = 12)	—
Tienari† (1963)	Finland	0 (N = 16)	—	—

*Dizygotic pairs not broken down by type, and include opposite-sexed pairs.
†Male subjects only.

Source: Gottesman and Shields (1966). Citations of the studies mentioned can be found in this source.

Concordant pairs are those in which both members are schizophrenic. Highest concordance is for MZ twins, next for DZ same-sex twins, and lowest for DZ opposite-sexed twins.

may have encouraged schizophrenic symptoms in one member of the pair, even though the other (with equal potential for schizophrenia) did not develop these symptoms. It has been found, for example, that the member of a MZ twin pair who develops schizophrenia is likely to be smaller at birth, to have some signs of neurological defect, and to have more disturbances of sleep and motility than the nonaffected twin (Pollin and Stabenau, 1968).

New approaches to the study of heredity

Evidence gathered over many years indicates that there is a genetic background for differences in intelligence and for differences in susceptibility to schizophrenia. Minor differences in the studies are to be expected. It is equally evident that environment is important. It would be as unwise to discount the environment in studies of behavioral differences as to discount nutrition in studies of height and weight, even though genetic factors can be demonstrated in both cases.

Future studies will go beyond a futile search for proportionate variance from heredity and environment toward far more specific investigation of the actual genetic transmission involved. One example may serve to show the kind of information that might arise. As pointed out earlier (p. 385), Turner-syndrome females, who have a deficient X-chromosome, have normal I.Q.'s but perform poorly on special tests, particularly visual space-form perception. This perception deficiency may be linked to sex, because the genetic deficiency is sex-linked. Stafford (1961) reported that on a test of spatial visualization, father-daughter and mother-son correlations were .31, but the father-son correlation was an insignificant .02. Because a daughter receives one X-chromosome from her father, and a son receives his only X-chromosome from his mother, these correlations are understandable if this ability is linked to the X-chromosome. Thus two lines of evidence lead to the same genetic conclusion, one that is quite different from any analyses based on ordinary intelligence tests.

Many other lines of inquiry concerning behavior genetics are open. Most heritability measures for intelligence have been based upon standard I.Q. tests; because the tests of divergent thinking (see Chapter 15, pp. 370–71) correlate only slightly with I.Q., studies of the heritability of such abilities are needed. In one such study, based on MZ and DZ twins, the results show a lack of any significant genetic factor (Vandenberg, 1967). Because these abilities are important in creative activity, the results, if substantiated, might well change some of the emphasis upon hereditary correlates of cognitive abilities. In the course of the same investigation a number of primary abilities tests were also studied, and earlier studies were reviewed. In some tests (verbal, word fluency, and spatial scores) MZ twins tend to be more alike than DZ twins, thus indicating a hereditary correlate. In the other tests, the results are somewhat variable; several of the studies provide little evidence of hereditary correlates for reasoning and memory scores.

A concern for the genetic quality of the population is a scientifically justified one. It is desirable to preserve diversity in the gene pool because we know little about future demands on human beings. Individuals are bound to differ, but society requires differentiated roles, and it is well that some individuals fit one role more readily than others. The more that we know about these differences—how they can be capitalized on to the benefit of the individual and society—the better will be the quality of life. The discovery of genetic differences does not mean that we are headed for a labeling of individuals for life according to inborn characteristics; it means, rather, that the methods we use for changing behavior will be more appropriate to the individual differences with which we begin.

Summary

1. The methods of the science of genetics are proving to be as applicable to behavior as to physical structure. The same distinctions are needed between the *phenotype* (the expressed characteristic) and the *genotype* (the underlying hereditary determiners that will be transmitted to the offspring) as are made when physical characteristics are under consideration. The *chromosomes* and *genes* are responsible for the role of heredity in behavior, just as they are for inherited structures.

2. Because some genes are *dominant*, some *recessive*, and some *sex-linked*, various statistical predictions can be made about the traits of the offspring of particular kinds of matings. When these studies are conducted on whole populations, the methods become those of *population genetics*, an approach likely to prove important in the study of the role of heredity in human behavior.

3. Important new knowledge is being revealed through *biochemical genetics*, which studies how genetic information is coded in DNA molecules and converted into proteins by way of RNA.

4. Selective-breeding experiments with animals have resulted in convincing evidence that many forms of behavior have genetic correlates. Illustrations include maze learning in rats, phototaxis in fruit flies, and temperament in dogs.

5. Because selective breeding is unacceptable for human studies and because many human characteristics are complexly determined, we are led to depend upon studies of *resemblance* between parent and offspring.

6. Studies of parent-child resemblance in intelligence are limited because the I.Q. of a child cannot be determined accurately before the age of two, when the influence of the home environment is already considerable. At later ages, parent-child resemblances in intelligence correlate in much the way as resemblances in height.

7. The study of foster children provides an opportunity to isolate the effect of home environment on intelligence. Such studies lead to these conclusions: (a) the *correlation* between the biological parents' intelligence and the child's intelligence remains higher than that between the foster parents' intelligence and the child's, even though the child moves into the adopted home within the first few months of life; (b) *mean scores* indicate that intelligence develops within the favorable environment of the foster homes to a level above that predicted from the biological mother's intelligence and, on the average, to a level corresponding closely to that of children born into homes with the same characteristics as the foster homes.

8. In studies of sibling resemblances twins provide much useful information because there are two types of twins (*monozygotic* and *dizygotic*) with unlike degrees of genetic similarity. Studies based on the correlations between the intelligence test scores of ordinary siblings, dizygotic twins, and monozygotic twins (including monozygotic twins reared apart) lead to the conclusion that both heredity and environment are important as correlates of individual differences in intelligence.

9. Studies of *schizophrenia* in dizygotic and monozygotic twins have found so much more correspondence for monozygotic twin pairs that a strong hereditary background is plausible. However, complexities in the relationship are shown by studies of monozygotic twins of which only one is schizophrenic.

10. Interaction between heredity and environment is the rule, even for traits known to have strong hereditary components. This interaction leads to much of the controversy surrounding such a problem as the role of heredity in intelligence.

Suggestions for further reading

For a general introduction to genetics, see Lerner, *Heredity, evolution, and society* (1968).

There are now a number of books on behavior genetics, of which the following are representative: Fuller and Thompson, *Behavior genetics* (1960); Hirsch (ed.), *Behavior genetic analysis* (1967); Manosevitz, Lindzey, and Thiessen (eds.), *Behavioral genetics: Method and research* (1969); Spuhler (ed.), *Genetic diversity and human behavior* (1967); Vandenberg (ed.), *Methods and goals in human behavior genetics* (1965). These are general summaries of a large literature dealing with experimental studies with animals and (chiefly) with correlational studies with human subjects.

For those who wish to delve into the controversial literature, the most heated discussions are those concerned with race differences. A book with a balanced position is that edited by Mead and others, *Science and the concept of race* (1968). A controversial article by Jensen in the *Harvard educational review*, "How much can we boost I.Q. and scholastic achievement?" (1969), led to a number of replies and criticisms in a later issue of the same journal: Kagan and others, "Discussion: How much can we boost the I.Q. and scholastic achievement?" (1969). A carefully reasoned discussion of the issues by two geneticists, Bodmer and Cavalli-Sforza, appears in an article in *Scientific American* entitled "Intelligence and race" (1970). They present an analysis of both the psychological and genetic data and conclude that definite answers to the question of genetic contributions to race differences in intelligence cannot be given yet.

theories of personality

PERSONALITY IS ONE OF THE MOST FAMILIAR concepts in psychology; at the same time it is one of the most difficult. All of us use the term in our everyday conversation, but most of us would be hard put to provide an accurate statement of its meaning. The psychologist, for whom the concept of personality is of central importance, cannot escape the need to attempt a precise statement.

Personality is in some respects a shorthand statement describing an individual biography. To describe an individual completely we would have to know all about his development throughout life, his successes and failures, his joys and sorrows, how he managed various crises. This is the task con-

fronting the author of a biography: to put the chronological facts in order and to characterize the subject of his biography in a meaningful way, so that he stands out as an individual, strictly himself, yet understandable because of the way in which he faced situations typical of those we all encounter. We learn something about his individual style, the persistence of his motivational patterns, and thus come to know him.

The scientific student of personality is not a biographer in this sense, yet his task of understanding individuality overlaps with that of the biographer. He sets himself an additional task, however—the prediction of behavior that has not yet occurred. Except for some biographies of political candidates, in which the biographer tries to show what kind of president or other official the man is likely to make, the biographer generally subordinates prediction to an understanding of a life already lived.

Personality, as studied by the psychologist, may be defined as the characteristics and ways of behaving that determine a person's unique adjustments to the environment. The fact that a man eats, sleeps, and works does not define his personality; his personality is defined by what he eats, how he sleeps, and what is distinctive about his work patterns. Hence individuality and uniqueness are essential to the definition. What a man does in a given environmental context because of the kind of person he is, beyond the predictions that can be made from the context alone, is a reflection of his personality, however it is defined.

Students of personality stress in particular those personal characteristics that affect an individual's ability to get along with other people and with himself. These characteristics are important in the individual's personal adjustment, in his maintenance of self-respect. Any description of the individual personality must take into account appearance, abilities, motives, emotional reactivity, and the residues from earlier experiences that have shaped the person as we find him. The term "personality" is thus widely inclusive, but it is not synonymous with all of psychology, because it refers specifically to the given individual as he differs from other men.

The shaping of personality

The broad outlines of personality formation are clear enough. We have already noted the importance of heredity, maturation, training in infancy, social motives acquired through learning, and ways of perceiving. What we are attempting now is a kind of summary of these many factors in development and socialization *as they have shaped the particular individual before us* and as they affect our understanding of him. The individual before us now is an end product of his potentialities as they have been realized in the course of growing up. Our task is to understand the patterning of the consequences of experience that gives the individual his uniqueness.

Inborn potential

In surveying the origin of the personality we can begin with the infant's potentialities as established by his specific heredity and by whatever influences impinged upon him prior to birth. One infant does not start on equal terms with another. One may be born sturdy, another weak. One may be lively and responsive, another more placid. Parents respond differently to babies with these differing characteristics; in this way a reciprocal process starts that may exaggerate the characteristics present from birth (Bell, 1960).

The problem of separating the hereditary and acquired components of personality is even more difficult than the similar task for intelligence (discussed in Chapter 16), partly because the measurement devices are less satisfactory.[1] Even so, it appears from studies of twins that there may be some tendency to inherit characteristics to respond in certain ways to personality tests such as the Minnesota Multiphasic Personality Inventory (MMPI).[2] Gottesman (1963) studied the scores of thirty-four pairs of monozygotic (MZ) twins and thirty-four pairs of dizygotic (DZ) same-sex twins, all of high school age. He found sufficiently greater similarity between MZ pairs to indicate a possible hereditary component for scales measuring a tendency to depression, psychopathic deviation, and social introversion. These results are subject to the uncertainties of all such studies, but the possibility of hereditary influence is certainly not ruled out.

[1]The problems of personality measurement are discussed in Chapter 18.
[2]For further discussion of the MMPI, see pp. 429–31.

Even the inheritance of a particular kind of body configuration may have an influence upon personality. The general significance of body type for personality is not widely accepted, but some residual influence can scarcely be denied. As Lindzey (1967) points out:

> Even the most dedicated and competitive 145-pound tackle cannot aspire realistically to play first-string tackle for a Big Ten university, nor is it likely that the 260-pound tackle could ever compete successfully in a marathon race or as an effective jockey. . . . Height, strength, weight, and comparable dimensions place direct and unmistakable limits upon what responses the individual can hope to make adaptively in a given environmental setting [p. 230].

The best-known system of body-typing is that of Sheldon, which classifies individuals according to three components. The *endomorphic* component refers to the prominence of the intestines and other visceral organs. The obese individual fits in this category; his paunch indicates excess viscera as well as fat. The *mesomorphic* component refers to bone and muscle. The athlete is predominantly mesomorphic, having wide shoulders, narrow hips, and rippling muscles. The *ectomorphic* component is based upon delicacy of skin, fine hair, and a sensitive nervous system. The ectomorphic person is tall, thin, stoop-shouldered; no one would confuse him with a mesomorph or an endomorph. There are few "pure" types, but all men can be rated on each of the components (Sheldon, Stevens, and Tucker, 1940; Sheldon, 1954).

Although many claims have been made for the relation between body type and characteristics of personality, with some supporting evidence from studies of delinquents (Glueck and Glueck, 1950) and children (Walker, 1962), on the whole the high correlations originally proposed have not held up. There is abundant evidence for the inheritance of physical differences, and some effects upon behavior cannot be doubted.

The potentialities with which a person is born are developed through maturation and learning as he grows up. Although all experiences are individual, we may distinguish between two broad classes: the *common experiences* shared by most individuals growing up in a given culture and the *unique* or *individual experiences,* not predictable from the roles that the culture assigns us.

Experiences common to the culture

The process of growing up includes learning to behave in ways expected by our society. We usually accept group values without much reflection and without awareness that peoples of other cultures may not share these values. If our culture values cleanliness, promptness, and hard work, we try to be clean, prompt, and industrious. We tend to admire people who exhibit these qualities, unless we are in some way alienated from the culture and thus protest against its values.

Conspicuous among the influences of the culture upon a person are the *roles* that it assigns to him. He is born into some of these: for example, the boy is born into a masculine sex role and the girl into a feminine sex role. The demands of these roles vary from culture to culture, as we learned earlier (Chapter 3), but it is considered "natural" in any culture for boys and girls to have predictable differences in personality merely because they belong to one or the other sex.

Some roles are of our own choosing but are also patterned by the culture. Occupation is a conspicuous role of this kind. Occupational training requires more than the learning of technical skills associated with the job; to be successful and comfortable in an occupation or profession, one must also behave as others do in that occupation and be prepared to accept the status that his occupation brings. Sometimes the occupation has its visible sign: the doctor's white coat is not unlike the military uniform, as both are signs of a social role. Occupations may develop special attitudes and speech forms as well as special types of dress. The counterman at the soda fountain not only dons a white jacket but also uses a special vocabulary that enables him to communicate swiftly and efficiently with his co-workers. An expression such as "combo wheat, hold the mayo" cannot be defined from the dictionary, but it is perfectly clear in its context.

Because adult behavior largely conforms to social roles, to some extent it is predictable. We know what behavior to expect of people at a formal tea or reception, or at a football rally or a national political convention. At a college reunion a naturally dignified and reserved man may act like his fellows, calling each by his first name, sharing the mood of open friendliness. When the reunion is over, he becomes again his usual reserved self.

The suggestion has been made that each culture develops a somewhat characteristic personality structure; one culture may be typically more aggressive or more passive than another. Individuals within any culture then represent this typical personality, with some individual departures from the average tendency. This theory fits in with popular notions of "national character," whereby Italians, for example, differ characteristically from Germans or Irishmen. But caution is needed lest the basic truths be exaggerated (Inkeles and Levinson, 1969).

Even though cultural pressures impose some personality similarities, individual personality is not completely predictable from a knowledge of the culture in which a person is raised, for three reasons: (1) the cultural impacts upon the person are not actually uniform, because they come to him by way of particular people—parents and others— who are not all alike in their values and practices; (2) the individual has some kinds of experiences that are distinctively his own; and (3) the individual, because of the kind of person he is, redefines the roles he is required to fit into.

Unique experiences

Each person reacts in his own way to the social pressures upon him. As Allport effectively put it: "The same fire that melts the butter hardens the egg [Allport, 1937, p. 102]."

Personal differences in response may result from the biological equipment of the individual. As we noted earlier, no two individuals (except monozygotic twins) have identical hereditary characteristics. In addition to differences in size and intelligence, individuals may inherit all kinds of subtle differences in sensitivity, reactivity, and endurance, which bear upon ultimate personality development. When an individual is notably different (for example, born with a club foot, a defacing birthmark, or a hearing defect), we expect him to face problems that are out of the ordinary; but every individual, if we could only know everything about his inheritance, would appear "notably different" in his own way.

The biological potentialities of a child are soon socialized under the influence of significant persons, such as his parents and his brothers and sisters. These significant persons transmit the culture in the precise form in which it makes its impact upon the individual. They impose social roles and provide the models that show how the roles are played. They reward or punish primitive impulses: for example, they give food to satisfy hunger and use force to prevent biting. They approve and disapprove the child's social behavior.

As the child comes to seek approval and to avoid disapproval, he becomes capable of hindsight and foresight and begins to see himself as a responsible agent. He develops a *conscience* whereby he judges his own conduct according to ideals he has acquired.

Not all parents (or parent substitutes) are equally successful in the process of cultural transmission. Some are incapable of providing the affection that the child needs in order to grow up a secure person. Others have themselves so resisted adopting conventional social roles that they do a poor job of transmitting the roles to the new generation.

A child always shows the influences of his parents, though he need not resemble them. The contrasting possibilities of these influences are well described by two brothers in Sinclair Lewis' novel *Work of art*. Each of them ascribes his personality to his home surroundings.

> My father [said Oral] was a sloppy, lazy, booze-hoisting old bum, and my mother didn't know much besides cooking, and she was too busy to give me much attention, and the kids I knew were a bunch of foul-mouthed loafers that used to hang around the hoboes up near the water tank, and I never had a chance to get any formal schooling, and I got thrown on my own as just a brat. So naturally I've become a sort of vagabond that can't be bored by thinking about his "debts" to a lot of little shopkeeping lice, and I suppose I'm inclined to be lazy, and not too

scrupulous about the dames and the liquor. But my early rearing did have one swell result. Brought up so unconventionally, I'll always be an Anti-Puritan. I'll never deny the joys of the flesh and the sanctity of Beauty.

My father [said Myron] was pretty easy-going and always did like drinking and swapping stories with the boys, and my mother was hard-driven taking care of us, and I heard a lot of filth from the hoboes up near the water tank. Maybe just sort of as a reaction I've become almost too much of a crank about paying debts, and fussing over my work, and being scared of liquor and women. But my rearing did have one swell result. Just by way of contrast, it made me a good, sound, old-fashioned New England Puritan.[3]

Beyond his unique biological inheritance and the specific ways in which the culture is transmitted to him, the individual is shaped by particular experiences. An illness with a long convalescence may provide satisfactions in being cared for and waited upon that profoundly affect the personality structure. Death of a parent may disrupt the usual identifications. Unusual successes or failures, accidents, opportunities for heroism, winning a contest, moving to another part of the country—countless such experiences are relevant for development but are not predictable from the culture, although of course their effects are partly determined by the culture.

Major approaches to understanding personality

Theories of personality are attempts to account in an orderly way for personality as we find it, and to describe that personality in ways suitable for both understanding and prediction. A successful theory must weave together the various strands descriptive of individuality in such a manner as to demonstrate some inner *consistency* over time, as well as some *generality,* so that predictions can be made of behavior likely to occur in a variety of contexts. There are many theories—partly because personality is so loosely defined that all theories do not deal with the same subject matter, partly because the facts upon which a generally acceptable theory must be based are not yet well enough known. Recently many personality theorists have turned away from general theories to specific ones having to do with more limited domains of personal characteristics and behavior. We shall first examine some representatives of the broad theories of *traits, types,* and *psychoanalysis,* and then consider the *theory of behavioral specificity,* which is highly critical of these approaches.

Trait theory

According to a theory of traits, one can describe a personality by its position on a number of *scales* or *dimensions,* each of which represents a trait. We may rate the person on a scale of intelligence as indicating one personality trait, on a scale of emotional sensitivity as another trait, on a scale of ascendance-submission as a third. A mere listing of specific traits descriptive of a person is not enough to provide a coherent science of personality; some sort of order must be established out of the countless ways in which a person can be characterized by traits. To illustrate how an ordering is attempted, we shall consider the proposals of Cattell.

[3]Lewis (1934), as quoted by Allport (1937), p. 102.

Cattell's theory of surface and source traits

A theory of traits without some sort of ordering principle simply provides a description of a person's position on a number of scales. If we could arrive at a *short* list of the main *common traits,* then we could characterize a person according to a *trait profile,* or *psychograph* (Figure 17-1). The problem is to obtain a short list that is not arbitrary.

Many investigators have attempted this, but we will study the work of Cattell because it represents a prodigious amount of data collection and analysis. In gathering his data, Cattell has used behavior observations and ratings, laboratory

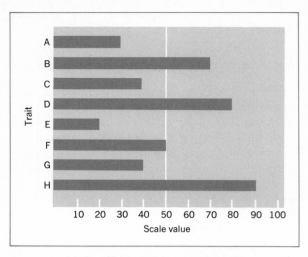

Fig. 17-1 Trait profile (hypothetical) If a standard set of common traits (such as A through H) could be agreed upon as giving a satisfactory characterization of a person, then an individual trait profile, such as the one shown here, would be as characteristic of the person as his fingerprints, provided the traits were stable and could be satisfactorily appraised.

studies, and inventories, and has worked with many different populations and age groups.

Allport and Odbert (1936) listed 17,953 English words used to distinguish the behavior of one person from another. Cattell began his research with this list of trait names, adding the terms that psychologists have coined in their researches. By eliminating overlap of meanings, he came out with 171 personality variables describing the whole "personality sphere" (Cattell, 1946). Although some traits, such as ability, can be thought of as having positions along a scale ranging from zero to a high value, most personality variables can be expressed as polar opposites, with the zero point lying between them (for example, cheerful vs. gloomy). Cattell prefers such paired terms whenever possible.

If many such variables are used to describe the same group of individuals, the variables can be correlated to find out which are closely related and which are distinct. Two main techniques of examining the interrelationships exist, leading to a distinction that Cattell makes between *surface traits* and *source traits.*

Surface traits are found by studying the *clusters*

of the actually obtained correlations. For example, all traits that intercorrelate .60 or higher can arbitrarily be assumed to be a manifestation of one cluster, or surface trait. Thus it is found that ratings for people judged on the three trait pairs of thoughtful vs. unreflective, wise vs. foolish, and austere vs. profligate tend to fall in similar positions on all three scales (at least to the extent of a correlation of .60); hence these three pairs are clustered together into the surface trait of disciplined thoughtfulness vs. foolishness. This and a few other surface traits are listed in Table 17-1. They are called *surface traits* because their similarity lies on the "surface" (that is, it is evident in the raw ratings), without requiring any transformation or process of inference to point to some less obvious underlying uniformity.

Source traits are found by *factor analysis,* a more refined mathematical technique than *cluster analysis.* Factor analysis will show that traits correlating highly with one another belong together, but it may also assign to one factor some traits that correlate less highly with one another, and by

TABLE 17-1 ILLUSTRATIVE SURFACE TRAITS
Integrity, altruism vs. dishonesty, undependability
Honest vs. dishonest
Loyal vs. fickle
Fair-minded vs. partial
Disciplined thoughtfulness vs. foolishness
Thoughtful vs. unreflective
Wise vs. foolish
Austere vs. profligate
Heartiness vs. shyness
Sociable (forward) vs. shy
Sociable (gregarious) vs. seclusive
Intrusive vs. reserved
Thrift, tidiness, obstinacy vs. lability, curiosity, intuition
Habit-bound vs. labile
Thrifty vs. careless of property
Pedantic, tidy vs. disorderly
Source: Cattell (1950).

The traits clustered together have all correlated at least r = .60 with one another in at least four investigations conducted with adults. The specific traits listed are examples from longer lists, and some liberties have been taken in shortening trait names as stated by Cattell.

TABLE 17-2   ILLUSTRATIVE SOURCE TRAITS
Affectothymia vs. sizothymia
Good-natured vs. critical, grasping
Attentive to people vs. cool, aloof
Trustful vs. suspicious
Ego strength vs. emotionality and neuroticism
Mature vs. unable to tolerate frustration
Realistic about problems vs. evasive, avoids decisions
Absence of neurotic fatigue vs. neurotically fatigued
Dominance vs. submissiveness
Self-assertive, confident vs. submissive, unsure
Boastful, conceited vs. modest, retiring
Aggressive, pugnacious vs. complaisant
Surgency vs. desurgency
Cheerful, joyous vs. depressed, pessimistic
Sociable, responsive vs. seclusive, retiring
Energetic vs. subdued, languid
Source: Cattell (1965).

A source trait is identified through factor analysis, and is said to determine the variability in measured surface traits. The examples are selected from a longer list.

assigning appropriate numerical loadings it will tell the extent to which each of the traits also reflects other factors. The traits that belong together as a result of factor analysis are called *source traits,* on the assumption that they represent a deeper unity than that revealed through surface traits. The measured traits provide scores from which the factor-analyzed source traits are derived. These source traits presumably stand for basic aspects of the personality not revealed through any clustering of surface traits. Some of the chief source traits reported by Cattell are given in Table 17-2.

The ideal is to find the few main source traits that turn up in a number of separate investigations. If these source traits can be identified, tests can be constructed to measure them; by using the known factor loadings, these test scores can then be weighted for any kind of personality assessment or prediction that may be desired. As we shall see later (Chapter 18, p. 431), Cattell has indeed constructed a test that is designed to assess sixteen source traits.

Cattell and his co-workers have produced and stimulated a great deal of research bearing upon such basic problems as anxiety and its physiological correlates, and such practical issues as educational prediction, delinquency, and occupational success. Owing to some unresolved problems in the use of factor analysis as a model, the ultimate aim of achieving an agreed-upon list of source traits to characterize personality has not been realized.

Evaluation of trait theory

How might we evaluate the success of trait theory in providing a parsimonious and useful description of personality?

1. The trait approach is a straightforward one, lending itself readily to experimentation. By breaking down the total field of personality into more manageable items, the consistencies and generalities can be readily subjected to study. Hence methods of trait appraisal are legitimate and merit additional careful investigation. There are some interesting theoretical problems as to how traits should be considered. For example, should they be considered motivational (as in the need for achievement), emotional (as in the expression of anxiety), attitudinal (as in prejudice)? Merely choosing a trait approach does not answer these questions.

2. The piecemeal nature of traits means that something is needed to describe their organization within the individual. The trait profile that emerges from a set of rated traits is not an adequate description of a personality, even though it may be a true one. When behavior is broken down into traits, we have no way of knowing how the traits fit into a hierarchical order in the goal-seeking behavior of the individual. A person characterized by the trait of compulsiveness may occupy himself merely with useless repetitive rituals, causing interference with the exercise of other traits, or he may show dogged determination to stay with a productive task, and thus take advantage of other traits. One method of meeting this objection to the trait profile is to consider the overall characteristics of the profile. The proposed method, known as *profile analysis,* consists of appraising trait patterns, stressing interrelationships and hierarchical organ-

ization as well as individual traits (Meehl, 1950).

3. There is some objection to assigning traits to an individual as though they assert something fundamental about the way he is, causing him to do what he does. Another way of looking at the matter is to consider the trait as an assertion of the individual's capability of behaving in certain ways under certain environmental provocations; thus he is capable of aggression under some circumstances and of nurturant behavior under others (Wallace, 1966). In their study of aggressive boys, for example, Bandura and Walters (1963) found that all boys were not aggressive under all provocations. The boys had to be known well before it could be predicted when they would express aggression and when they would inhibit it.

Some sort of interactive theory is needed to replace a pure "trait" theory. That is, the "trait" has to be appraised according to a range of situational circumstances in which the disposition or capability to act in a certain way tends to be called into play; when these circumstances are known, practices of trait modification are likely to be suggested also.

Type theory

Theories of *personality types* are ancient in origin and they persist today, despite repeated rejections of type classifications by psychologists. The reasons for the prevalence of these theories are not hard to find. Classification into *kinds* is the beginning of most sciences—kinds of rocks, kinds of clouds, kinds of plants and animals. Why not kinds of personalities? Furthermore, type theories build upon the common observation that the personalities of at least *some* people revolve about a dominant characteristic, such as ambition, pride, adventure, bodily comfort. Thus it might be possible to classify all people into a few types if we could arrive at a short list of these central *themes* or *styles of life* that characterize some individuals so well.

Most of the historical objections to type theories were objections to a kind of pigeonholing, which made the types distinct and independent. Those who held these objections often claimed that a type theory would require a bimodal or multimodal distribution of traits, with a peak for each of the separate types. Modern type theories (including the body-type theory of Sheldon, mentioned earlier) do not take the position that types are so distinct. They maintain that a limited number of components can be found along dimensions that vary continuously, as most psychological characteristics are found to do; it is the *combinations* of these components, at specified values, that differentiate the major "types." As an illustration of a contemporary type theory that has stimulated a great deal of research and has gained a moderate amount of support, we shall examine the position of Eysenck.

Eysenck's two-dimensional theory

Eysenck has proposed that many important aspects of personality can be understood through a combination of two dimensions: stable-unstable (sometimes called normal-neurotic) and introverted-extraverted. If one divides these dimensions at the midpoint of the distributions (half the subjects being higher or lower on each of the dimensions), four personality types emerge:

Stable-Extravert	Unstable-Extravert
Stable-Introvert	Unstable-Introvert

Before proceeding to characterize these types, something may be said about the component dimensions.

The terms "extraversion" and "introversion," while not originated by him, owe their popularity to Carl J. Jung (1875–1961), a prominent Swiss psychologist who was originally a follower of Freud but later developed his own system of analytic psychology. The introvert tends to withdraw into himself, especially in times of emotional stress or conflict. Characteristics of introversion include shyness and a preference for working alone. The introvert may take to the speaking platform, as in the leading of a religious movement, but even then he is impelled from within. The extravert, by contrast, when under stress tends to lose himself among people. He is likely to be very sociable, a "hail fellow well met." He tends to choose occupations such as sales or promotional work, in which he deals with people rather than with things. He is likely to be conventional, well-dressed, outgoing. It is not difficult to find among our acquaintances a "typical" introvert or a "typical" extravert. This gives such a classification plausibility and accounts for its popular appeal (Jung, 1923).

The other dimension, stability-instability, simply means that at the stable end are people whose emotions are controlled and not easily aroused, who are generally calm, even-tempered, and reliable; at the other end are those who are "moody, touchy, anxious, restless" (Eysenck and Rachman, 1965).

When these dimensions are combined, the resulting four types are very similar to those of one of the oldest of type classifications, that of temperament, going back to the ancient Greeks. The four types—*sanguine, phlegmatic, melancholic,* and *choleric*—were based on the prominence of one of four "body fluids": the sanguine person, generally warm-hearted and pleasant, had a prominence of blood; the qualities of the phlegmatic person, listless and slow, were attributed to phlegm; the melancholic person, suffering from depression and sadness, had too much black bile; the choleric person, easily angered and quick to react, was influenced by his yellow bile. The modern counterpart of this theory would assign such functions to hormones.

Remaining on the psychological level and disregarding the underlying endocrinology, Eysenck has stated the relationship of his theory to the ancient Greek temperaments and to modern trait theories by means of the graphic device depicted in Figure 17-2. Eysenck's method relies upon factor analysis to define the major axes and to permit him to construct a personality inventory that will then yield appropriate measures. The tests and measurement methods are described in Chapter 18 (pp. 431–32).

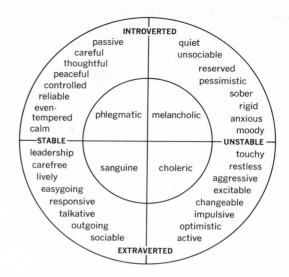

Fig. 17-2 Eysenck's dimensions related to temperaments and traits The inner ring shows the four temperaments of the Greeks; the outer ring represents the location of various traits studied by factor-analytic methods in relation to the two principal axes of Eysenck. (After Eysenck and Eysenck, 1963)

How Eysenck's classification is used may be illustrated by the differences between the problems and conduct of unstable introverts and unstable extraverts (Figure 17-3). The problems of unstable introverts tend to be personal, while unstable extraverts tend more to get into trouble because of delinquent behavior.

Evaluation of type theory

A satisfactory type theory is not impossible. It may be that we shall eventually isolate men into personality types as distinctive as blood types. There are no logical barriers against such theories. The fact is, however, that present theories, including Eysenck's, have not produced the evidence needed to gain widespread support (Vernon, 1964). Even if the evidence were more satisfactory than it is now, two dangers in type theory would remain.

1. *The type description tends to assert too much about the individual.* As soon as a person is tagged according to a type theory, the assumption is that a great many assertions can safely be made about

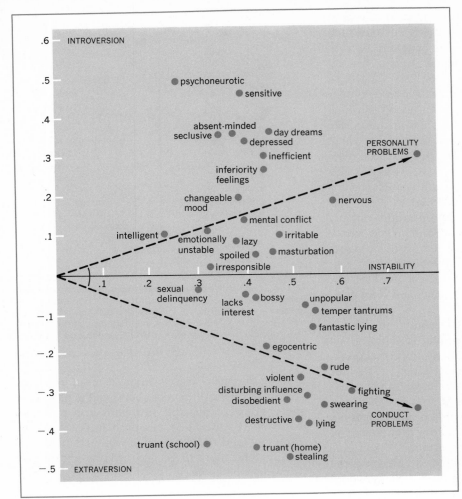

Fig. **17-3 Characteristics and problems of unstable introverts and extraverts** The unstable introverts (in the upper half of the diagram) are characterized by personality problems, such as depression, nervousness, inferiority feelings; the unstable extraverts (in the lower half of the diagram) show more conduct problems, such as stealing, truancy, lying, fighting. (Note that the "stable" half of the diagram has been omitted.) (After Eysenck, 1960)

him; that is, he is expected to have all the characteristics belonging to that type. But the determiners of individual personality are too numerous, and they combine into something both too rich and too unusual to be described by a single general term.

The danger is that of assigning the person to a *stereotype*. We all too readily come to believe that Italians are volatile, Scots thrifty, Swedes stolid. Such stereotypes ignore the individual differences among members of a group. A stereotype is, to be sure, a faulty type classification, but even a better type classification easily lends itself to abuse.

2. *The type description tends to hold to out-moded conceptions of personality and especially neglects cultural influences.* Students of the development of the individual are aware of the enormous importance of childhood experiences and later opportunities in shaping personality. Type theories are generally sponsored by those who regard human characteristics as chiefly the result of biological inheritance. That is why many type theories refer to body form or body chemistry. The body is an important locus of personality, but personality is also interpersonal, that is, dependent upon relations to other people. When one understands the richness and diversity of cultural influences, he loses faith in type theories.

Psychoanalytic theory

In seeking the enduring aspects of personality, we are led to characterize them according to traits or types that have come about as a result of developmental history. Another way of looking at personality takes into account various dispositions that are currently in unstable equilibrium, with the result that present behavior represents the interplay of these dispositions, often in conflict. Theories of *personality dynamics*—the theories concerned with these present conflicts—are inevitably *interactive* rather than developmental. This causes something of a problem, because many personality theories that are from one viewpoint developmental are from another viewpoint psychodynamic. This is certainly true of psychoanalysis, which has provided much of the theoretical background for current dynamic theories.

Developmental aspects of psychoanalytic theory

Psychoanalytic theory has both a developmental and an interactive aspect: it is concerned both with the course of development from earliest childhood and with the motivational conflicts and crises that occur at any given time. At this point we shall be concerned primarily with the developmental aspects of the theory, returning later to the interactive (dynamic) aspects. Psychoanalysis, as we noted earlier (Chapter 3, pp. 65–66), stresses a continuity in growth. Beginning in earliest childhood a shaping process goes on that results in a relatively enduring personality structure, one that changes slowly and is therefore characteristic of the mature individual at any given time. The steps, as we noted, could be defined either as those of psychosexual development (oral, anal, phallic, latent, genital), or as those of psychosocial development, each with a developmental crisis to be surmounted until identity is eventually achieved.

The fact that earlier modes of dealing with crises may persist in the present is emphasized in the psychoanalytic concept of *fixation,* which refers to arrested development. An individual may in some sense have remained immature by being fixated, or caught, at one stage of development, so that there are excessive manifestations of that stage in his adult behavior. Such arrested development is partial only; in other respects the person may be more fully grown up. Fixations lead to forms of personality structure associated with the stage at which the person is fixated. One form of personality structure that has been widely studied, the compulsive personality, may serve to illustrate the psychoanalytic interpretation.

The *compulsive* personality is characterized by excessive cleanliness, orderliness, obstinacy, and stinginess. In extreme cases, behavior becomes repetitive and ritualistic. Originally, psychoanalysts believed that this personality structure arose through excessive cleanliness training in the period of early infancy and therefore called it the "anal" character, referring to the developmental stage in which it presumably arose. In this view, if the crises associated with the anal stage are not successfully resolved, there will be residual fixations, or excessive residues from this stage, operating in adult behavior. Later investigators have questioned this oversimplification of the origin of such a personality pattern. They point out that the same parents who are excessive in cleanliness training are likely to make excessive demands for conformity, punctuality, and so on, beyond early infancy, and that the compulsive personality structure may very well come about through such continued childhood training.

The existence of the compulsive personality (the anal type, in psychoanalytic theory) received at least partial confirmation in one experiment in which men living together in college fraternities rated one another on three traits. The ratings were made on a seven-point scale, and a pooled rating was obtained for each of the men on the traits of stinginess, obstinacy, and orderliness. The reliabilities of these averaged ratings were found to be satisfactory, and they could therefore be interpreted like test scores.

The test of the theory that the three traits form

a pattern rests upon a correspondence among the traits. The correlations between trait ratings turned out as follows:

Stinginess and orderliness	.39
Stinginess and obstinacy	.37
Obstinacy and orderliness	.36

The correlations, while low, are all positive and in the expected direction. The results are all the more interesting in light of the fact that we consider orderliness a desirable trait, but both stinginess and obstinacy undesirable (Sears, 1936; 1943).[4]

Many other experiments also tend to yield results that give some support to the psychoanalytic theory. The oral personality, for example, should contrast with the anal personality, because it is based upon residual conflicts from a different stage of development. An experiment was designed to separate those who were more "oral" from those more "anal," and then to predict some experimental consequences (Noblin, Timmons, and Kael, 1966). College students responded to the Blacky Test, a series of pictures of puppies experiencing various developmental conflicts. After the students were classified as more "oral" or "anal" on the basis of these responses, they took part in a learning experiment. Orals, who are supposed to seek gratification, increased responses to positive verbal reinforcement and decreased responses to negative reinforcement. Anals, who are supposed to be somewhat obstinate and resistant to outside pressure, responded in the opposite way.

The results of these experiments support the psychoanalytic theory, but they are too weak to separate individuals into classes similar to "types." In any case, psychoanalytic types are not types of the sort that the theories of body type propose, because they presumably result from the impact of experiences in childhood, and are subject to remedial treatment.

[4]It may be noted that one of Cattell's surface traits includes thrift, tidiness, and obstinacy (Table 17-1). In theory, one might expect these to be a source trait because of the supposed common origin of these diverse manifestations.

Dynamic aspects of psychoanalytic theory

As one way of approaching the problems of conflicting tendencies within the individual, Freud (1927) introduced the concepts of the *id, ego,* and *superego.* Each of these portions of the personality has its own developmental history, but we are here concerned with the interactions that take place at any one time in the developing personality.

The *id* is the depository of the innate instinctual drives (sex and aggression). If unbridled, the id would always seek immediate gratification of primitive, irrational, pleasure-seeking impulses. The id is manifested at an early stage of development, but it is not outgrown; we are all our lives to some extent creatures of impulse, and it is this irrational, impulsive part of ourselves that is used to infer the id as part of the structure of the adult personality.

Classic psychoanalytic theory recognizes the *ego* as developing later out of the id, but modern ego theory within psychoanalysis postulates a primitive ego alongside a primitive id. In any case, the more fully developed ego, as the part of the personality responsible for controlling behavior in socially approved ways, comes into play later in life. The desire for immediate pleasure must be held in check; a long route may be necessary before the pleasure can be obtained in a proper manner. With maturity, the ego rules the id, but there are conflicts between them, and occasionally the id has its way. In dreams, for example, when the ego is relaxed, wish-fulfillment (an id function) may hold sway, and rational controls may be abdicated. The ego represents our ordinary social self, going about the work of the world, being as realistic and rational as possible; it causes us to act in ways congenial with other people and to accept the prescribed social roles. If the id is in the service of the "pleasure principle" (implying immediate gratification), the ego is subservient to the "reality principle" (implying postponed gratification).

The third part of the personality, the *superego,* develops out of the ego's experiences with social reality and the rules laid down by parents. The inferred superego is most nearly synonymous with *conscience.* It keeps us working according to an ideal of the self arising in early childhood, an ideal formed especially as a consequence of parental prohibitions.

From the point of view of a dynamic interpretation of personality, the key concept here is that these three inferred parts of the personality are often at odds: the ego postpones the gratifications that the id wants right away, and the superego wars with both the id and the ego because they often fall short of the moral code that it represents. There is some danger in thinking of these inferred parts of the personality as three warring persons within the individual, but the threefold classification, if not overemphasized, usefully calls attention to discordant trends commonly found within the same person.

The bearing of these concepts on personality theory is that the balance of id, ego, and superego processes differs from one individual to another. How one approaches a problematic situation may be a way not only of coping with the environmental problem but perhaps of trying to solve a personal problem at the same time. We shall discuss defense mechanisms in problem-solving, and other forms of coping, in Chapter 19.

Evaluation of psychoanalytic personality theory

According to psychoanalysis, underlying motives for behavior undergo some kinds of symbolic distortion before they appear in conduct. Thus the anal character is not confined to problems of the bowels and anus (as perhaps in constipation or hemorrhoids) but supposedly finds expression in cleanliness, greediness, and obstinacy, connected only by inference with the source. This indirect and inferential character of psychoanalytic explanations makes it difficult to assemble evidence that is entirely convincing, although considerable ingenuity has been shown, and many of the principles receive at least some support (Hilgard, 1968b).

The prediction of behavior is particularly difficult from a theory of this kind because of the possibility that opposite consequences in behavior may have identical deeper meanings. Psychoanalysis tends to be in disfavor among present-day students of personality, but their dissatisfaction is commonly with its efficacy as a therapy rather than with the possibility of learning something from many of the personality characteristics that it has brought to the fore.

The theory of behavioral specificity

The personality theories thus far considered all assume some consistency within personality, so that a person can be characterized according to his enduring traits, or type, or developmental history and psychodynamic structure. Each of these positions has come under attack by a group of social behavior theorists who insist that behavior is much more specific to situations than the prevailing theories of personality indicate. They maintain that very little can be said about persistent individual differences in personality.

The term *social behavior theory* (or the equivalent, *social learning theory*) has come to mean an integration of learning theory in its broadest sense (including classical and operant conditioning, modeling, cognitive learning) with problems of personal and social behavior (Bandura and Walters, 1963; Bandura, 1969). The social behavior theorists have shifted interest away from a search for consistency and generality in personality to a study of the malleability of behavior and procedures for changing behavior. Any consistency of behavior over time that may be noted (such as the persistence of psychotic behavior of a patient in a mental hospital) is not used to support claims for an inherent continuity of personality but rather to deplore the weakness of the interventions that were made, thus—in the illustration above—continuing the psychotic behavior rather than changing it.

Prediction within specificity theory

There is obviously some consistency in behavior, for it led to the formulation of personality theories in the first place. How does a theory that insists upon the specificity of behavior to situations (rather than consistency in different situations), account for actually observed consistencies? The following four points, paraphrased from Mischel (1968, pp. 281–301), reveal how these theorists view consistencies:

1. Behavior stability rests primarily upon the *consequences* of behavior remaining stable, and the *evoking conditions* remaining in the future similar to what they were in the past.

2. One basis for behavior stability is *environmental stability,* not only of the physical environment, but of the social environment as well. Society tends to set up rules and sanctions that are relatively constant. Many people lead so routine a life that if you know the time of day and where they are you can fairly well predict what they are doing.

3. Another basis for behavior stability is *"constructed" stability,* that is, expectations about others and the self that have been so labeled ("mental patient," "alcoholic," "ex-convict") that they are likely to endure and produce uniformity in conduct. This kind of stability may be undesirable, in that it works against potential for change.

4. Behavior learned under the strong influence of intermittent reinforcement gets fixed well enough to persist in the face of variable outcomes and is likely to be retained with "considerable tenacity."

These points are sufficient to account for some stability in behavior, even though such behavior is conceived as highly dependent upon stimulus conditions. If such stability is in fact the rule, why don't the ordinary measures of personality show more predictive power?

There is an apparent paradox here. The theories that expect *more* consistency predict less well than the theories that expect *less* consistency, precisely because the more general theories are less clear about a satisfactory basis for prediction. A specificity theory looks for identifiable variables that are likely to control later behavior. Two examples will illustrate what is meant.

Suppose one wishes to predict the success of psychotherapy. A more general personality theory might say that a compulsive patient is harder to treat than an anxious one, or a character disorder is harder to treat than a phobia. The social behavior theorists hold that such general statements are not very helpful. If we know something *specific* about behavior prior to attempted behavior change, we may be able to make some predictions. For example, it has been found that the more fears a person has before coming for a treatment in which fears are gradually removed by a desensitization technique (to be described in Chapter 21), the *less* will be the success in removing them. This inverse relationship implies a negative correlation, which in this study turned out to be $r = -.58$ between fears reported at pretesting and the number of fears overcome in treatment (Lang and Lazovik, 1963).

As a second example, we may consider the influence of a child's environment on intelligence test scores. Ordinarily, correlations of .20 to .40 are found when general measures of socioeconomic status are correlated with intelligence test results. The specificity theorists claim that a socioeconomic index is too general; it does not tell us enough about the influences upon the child. When a much more careful (and specific) measurement was made of the intellectual environment of the home, a correlation of .69 was obtained between this measure and tested intelligence (Wolf, 1966).

The emphasis placed by the social behavior theorists upon specificity has the advantage of repeatedly reminding those who would understand personality that we are really trying to understand behavior—and behavior is always related to the context in which it occurs.

Evaluation of specificity theory

The specificity theory, as proposed by the social behaviorists, represents a vehement attack upon those who would support other viewpoints toward personality, because all the other viewpoints stress some generality of traits or other dimensions of personality. Those who have come under attack find it difficult to believe that they have been as wrong as the social behavior theorists imply. New theories often get attention by being somewhat extreme; they then gradually become attenuated. What considerations suggest that this will happen to the specificity theory?

Some possible reservations about the specificity theory, which may lead to a modification of it, are the following:

1. Genetic or congenital aspects of behavior no doubt provide some basis for generality of personality beyond what the specificity doctrine proposes. The tendency for the social behavior theorists to be environmentalists is surely influenced in part by their historical affiliation with behaviorism, which has typically been environmentalist. Although the social behaviorists do not deny congenital influences, they show little interest in them.

2. The social behavior theorists maintain a specificity doctrine against opposing evidence for generality by making a distinction between the personality domain and the cognitive domain. They claim that the relative stability of intelligence test scores is not critical of their theory, because intelligence falls in the cognitive domain. This is a doubtful distinction, however; cognitive factors cannot be sharply divorced from personality ones. Many behaviors that are clearly within the personality domain show substantial correlations with measured intelligence. These include anxiety, need for approval, postponement of gratification, and cognitive style. Because cognitive aspects are indeed central to a conception of the total personality (and function in social discrimination, sense of humor, and self-perception), the cognitive domain cannot be sharply distinguished from the personality domain. If not distinguished, then any generality in cognitive aspects is critical of the specificity theory of personality.

The recurring specificity problem

The issue of behavior specificity arose in similar form many years ago. In a series of studies on character, Hartshorne and May (1928) found that some character traits, such as deceitfulness, were situation-specific, because when children were tempted to cheat they might cheat in the classroom but not on the playground, or they might cheat a bus driver but not a friend. The low correlations of one deceit score with another supported their view.

Their studies evoked a redefinition by Allport and Vernon (1933) of what kinds of traits should be measured and correlated. They pointed out that some types of behavior might be *congruent* even though they were not *consistent,* so that one kind of measure would produce a high correlation, another a low correlation. For example, if a person is asked to walk as if he is just out for a stroll, he may adopt a leisurely pace; the same person, asked to walk as if he must meet an appointment, may markedly hasten his pace. A study of his walking in various situations will indicate little correlation, for he sometimes walks fast and sometimes slowly. If, however, a change-of-pace is studied, his behavior in changing from leisure to purposive action may be very characteristic of him. Thus change-of-pace (from purposeful walking to leisurely strolling; from writing large to writing small) may indicate congruency of personality style, while the pace itself may not. Allport and Vernon's position, although making a good logical point, when tested did not yield correlations between congruencies substantially higher than the Hartshorne and May measures of consistency. Hence the controversial issue was not really resolved.

By now far more data have accumulated, so that the possibility exists for a more lasting resolution of the issues. Modern social behavior theory has revived the Hartshorne-May specificity position. The fact that an issue once raised and widely discussed, should remain an issue for so many years, poses an interesting question for the historian of science, because one would expect active research to move toward agreement.

3. High consistencies over the years have been reported in tests other than those of intelligence, such as in the Strong Vocational Interest Test, which is clearly in the personality domain. The social behavior theorists tend to reject self-report tests, holding that they are consistent in terms of verbal habits rather than owing to the fact that personality is consistent. But the Strong test scores have been validated by external criteria, such as occupational success as related to expressed interests (Strong, 1955). It is difficult to see how a specificity doctrine can account for all the generality of this test; for example, consistencies have been found to begin at the junior high school level, when there has been relatively little contact with the range of occupations.

Such considerations suggest that preoccupation with behavior change has led those promoting specificity theory either to overlook or to underplay some demonstrated stabilities. Although their view is somewhat extreme, it is valuable because it is optimistic: it looks toward changing undesirable or crippling behavior.

Experimental approaches to personality

The last few years have seen a substantial increase in experimental approaches to personality. These studies, which tend to be directed toward selected aspects of interpersonal behavior, have supplemented the earlier study of personality, which relied heavily upon personality ratings or measurements.

Instead of trying to characterize a personality as a whole, finding its unique structure, and describing it according to a theoretical model, the investigator who decides in favor of an experimental approach is more likely to ask far more specific questions: What is the effect of anxiety on learning? What are the circumstances that lead to aggression? How do successes and failures modify self-esteem? The answers to these questions clearly lie within the realm of the psychology of personality, even though they are somewhat piecemeal and do not ultimately give a clear picture of a total individual.

Experiments dealing with child development, motivation, and emotion are relevant to an understanding of personality, particularly if the contexts in which behavior is studied are important for the functioning of the person as a social being. Many such studies have been described in earlier chapters. In this chapter we have discussed other studies of this type: for example, the experimental demonstration of differences in responses to reinforcement of those selected as "oral" or "anal" (p. 408).

Many fairly specific personality variables have been related to various types of behavior through experiment. Among these variables are the need for approval, the need for achievement, manifest anxiety, ego strength, risk-taking, delayed gratification, aggression, and cognitive styles. Any "trait" might be treated experimentally, but the investigator usually hopes that he has chosen some aspect of personality with significant generality. In line with the social behavior viewpoint, however, he tests this generality against environmental contexts in order to determine what ranges of behavior result. To illustrate this approach, two variables of personality have been selected: the need for approval and delay of gratification.

The need for approval

The investigations reported here arose out of some findings from personality test literature. It was discovered that those describing themselves in personality inventories often tended to reply in a socially desirable direction, that is, in a direction that would generally be approved, even though the responses might not be entirely descriptive of their actual behavior (Edwards, 1957). Using this finding as a point of departure, Crowne and Marlowe (1964) argued that such desirable responding constituted meaningful goal-directed behavior, and individual differences in this respect might be related to other forms of approval-seeking actions. They proceeded to test this hypothesis in the laboratory.

First they constructed a scale to determine the extent to which the subjects sought to reply in socially approved ways; then they sorted the subjects into groups high and low in these social-desirability scores, and, by implication, high and low in need for social approval. They found that those high in their inferred need for social approval, by contrast with those lower on the scale, (1) showed more conforming behavior under social pressure in the laboratory, (2) modified their verbal behavior more through verbal reinforcement, (3) were less likely to express aggression in a situation provocative of anger, and (4) were more cautious in setting goals in a risk-taking situation.

How Crowne and Marlowe moved from personality measurement to tests of experimental hypotheses may be illustrated by one of the several experiments they conducted. In a verbal-conditioning experiment the experimenter gave a "verbal reinforcement" (in the form of a "Mm-hmm") to the subject whenever he said a plural noun. Under these circumstances, those more susceptible to the reinforcement procedures increase the proportion of plural nouns in their conversation, even though they are unaware of doing so. Crowne and Marlowe predicted that those high in need for approval would be susceptible to the reinforcement of the experimenter and would increase the number of plural nouns, while those low in need for approval would not be influenced by the experimenter. As Figure 17-4 illustrates, this is what they found.

The overall results of these studies led to an interpretation of high need for approval as reflecting low self-esteem. Low self-esteem was manifested in many ways: for example, those with high need for approval were unable to behave in autonomous, self-assertive ways, and they avoided talking introspectively about themselves. Thus a single personality characteristic that was assessed by a pencil-and-paper inventory proved diagnostic of a variety of behaviors that could be studied under experimental conditions. The testing method and laboratory method were usefully combined.

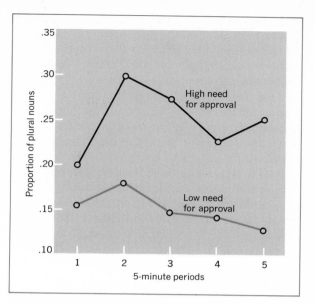

Fig. 17-4 **Need for approval and verbal conditioning** Those with high need for approval, as measured by their responses on the social-desirability scale, yielded more plural nouns under conditions in which the experimenter reinforced them by saying "Mm-hmm" and nodding his head. (After Crowne and Marlowe, 1964)

Delay of gratification

A central distinction in psychoanalytic theory is that between primary- and secondary-process thinking. Primary process, the more primitive, is said to be under the control of pleasure-seeking; it insists upon immediate gratification of impulse. Secondary process is characterized by social controls that delay gratification; the stronger the subject's ego, the more likely he is to delay when social requirements call for such a delay. In the end his needs are satisfied, so that pleasure is not denied, but a planned delay has intervened. This kind of distinction suggests a possible direct test of a personality variable: ability to postpone gratification.

This variable has been frequently studied in a behavioral setting. Children readily express their preferences between getting a small notebook now versus a large one in a week, or a small magnifying glass now versus a larger one later, or 15 cents now versus 30 cents in three weeks. In one of the experiments the achievement motivations and re-

EXPERIMENTAL APPROACHES TO PERSONALITY **413**

ward preferences of sixth-grade children were assessed by a story-telling procedure (p. 326). In a second session they engaged in a target-practice game in which they recorded their own scores, under strong temptation to cheat in order to achieve a score high enough to obtain a reward. Those children with high achievement motives and less willingness to wait for rewards tended to cheat more and sooner—a result the experimenters had predicted (Mischel and Gilligan, 1964).

Relationships that have been demonstrated for those choosing to wait for rewards are higher social-responsibility scores, higher achievement concerns, higher intelligence, and an increase in preference for delay with increasing age. These results do not mean that the capacity to delay reward is an unchangeable aspect of personality. The manipulation of certain cognitive and learning conditions can produce great changes, thus giving support to social behavior theory (Mischel, 1966).

Evaluation of experimental studies of personality

The experimental studies of personality, which have proliferated during the last few years, have given us a great deal of empirical evidence bearing upon important problems, but they have done little to answer some of the larger questions about what, if anything, can serve as the touchstones for describing individuality. Surely there are some organizing principles, some hierarchical structures within potentials or habit systems, that make one man stand out from another in his ability to shape his environment as well as adjust to it. The emphasis within social behavior theory upon change, and the specificities of situational determinants so often stressed in the experimental studies, lead to the impression that men are, after all, essentially alike, except for their individual encounters with the environment. It is the function of a psychology of individuality, however, to discover what persistent differences there may be, and how well these predict later behavior.

Many of the problems being experimentally investigated—including anxiety, aggression, defensiveness—originated with those who were able to think of personality in the large sense, as Freud did. Perhaps we are again in need of those who can think about personality in broad terms, with less emphasis upon the specific.

Personality integration and the concept of the self

One of the concepts that serves to bring the various components of personality back together again into some sort of coherent pattern is the concept of the self. On empirical grounds, the concept of a unified person is strengthened from the outside by the fact that the locus of the person is a single body, and from the inside by the fact that memories are continuous and belong to the "same" person.

Actually, the personality is not so highly unified. The fact of tensions and conflict within the person has long been recognized; the tensions among the id, ego, and superego were anticipated by the struggles of body, mind, and spirit emphasized within the Hebraic-Christian traditional beliefs. Modern role theory indicates that a person may play several roles at once and may vacillate between roles. The concept of *dissociation* is used to state the fact that there are sometimes split-off aspects of personality functioning, as found normally in dreams. Cases of multiple personality illustrate in dramatic ways the problems involved.

Multiple personality

An extreme case testing the notion of personality unity is that in which several "personalities" exist at once in the same person, so that the individual at some times behaves in accordance with one integrated behavior pattern, at other times in accordance with another. To the classic cases in personality literature (Prince, 1906; Franz, 1933), there has been added the case of Eve White, with her alternate personalities known as Eve Black and Jane (Thigpen and Cleckley, 1954, 1957; Lancaster, 1958).

Eve White was a serious-minded and conscientious young mother who went to a therapist for treatment of severe headaches. In the midst of one of her interviews, in which she reported with considerable agitation that she had occasionally been hearing hallucinatory "voices," she suddenly underwent a striking personality change and became a youthful, buoyant, flirtatious personality who called herself Eve Black. The personality Eve Black was completely aware of the thoughts and activities of Eve White, but Eve White did not even suspect Eve Black's existence, until they became "acquainted" in the therapist's office. Later a third personality emerged, a more mature one who called herself Jane.

The major differences between Eve White and Eve Black have been summarized as follows:[5]

EVE WHITE	EVE BLACK
Demure, retiring, in some respects almost saintly.	Obviously a party girl. Shrewd, childishly vain, and egocentric.
Face suggests a quiet sweetness; the expression in repose is predominantly one of contained sadness.	Face is pixie-like; eyes dance with mischief as if Puck peered through the pupils.
Voice always softly modulated, always influenced by a specifically feminine restraint.	Voice a little coarsened, "discultured," with echoes or implications of mirth or teasing.
An industrious and able worker; also a competent housekeeper and a skillful cook. Not colorful or glamorous. Limited in spontaneity.	A devotee of pranks. Her repeated irresponsibilities have cruel results on others. More heedless and unthinking, however, than deeply malicious.

The Eve White and Eve Black personalities had apparently been coexisting since early childhood, when Eve Black would get Eve White into trouble, only to withdraw leaving Eve White to suffer more

[5] Quoted, with some abbreviation, from Thigpen and Cleckley (1954), pp. 141–42.

extreme punishment because she denied what Eve Black has caused her, unknowingly, to do. Some of these childhood incidents were substantiated by interviews with her parents. Recently Eve Black had gone on a clothes-buying spree and had then hidden the clothes at home. When the irate husband reprimanded Eve White, she could only deny that she had purchased the clothes; she escaped her husband's further anger by her eagerness to take the clothes back to the store in order to replenish their bank account.

The distinctiveness of the personalities of Eve White and Eve Black showed up on personality tests (see Chapter 18), on electroencephalograms, and in handwriting studies by experts. A "blind analysis" made from the case material by other workers (Osgood and Luria, 1954) by means of the semantic differential method (pp. 272–73) also distinguished between personalities and gave some cues as to the variety of roles and role conflicts involved. It is fairly evident that Eve White's primary identification was with her mother, who had trouble with her husband when Eve was young, just as Eve was later having trouble with her husband. Eve Black's identification appears to have been with her father. Those who studied the case find no good explanation for Jane. A possibility is that she represents the grandmother with whom Eve lived after her mother was separated from her father and went to earn a living in a distant city. The extreme disparity of childhood *identifications* seems to have prevented the achievement of a single *identity* for Eve's various aspects.

What can we learn from this case? First, we should hesitate to make any effort to correlate personality strictly with the body, for here we have the quite discordant possibilities of an Eve White and an Eve Black in the same physique. Second, we see that the recognizable unity of an individual personality is based solely upon its behavioral characteristics, for with the same body and the same physical and social history, personalities as different, yet as individually consistent, as Eve White and Eve Black emerge. Third, what we find dramatized here is also true to a lesser extent of the normal person: the typical personality integrates a number of strands that at different times and under different circumstances may cause us to behave in ways that seem very different, and yet reflect certain basic personality needs. The unity of personality is at best precarious.

The concept of identity

The unity of the self is not automatically given; one possibility is that it is an achievement. Erikson (1968) has described the process of achieving adult personality integration as *identity formation*. What are the steps through which the final adult identity comes about?

An important series of steps results in the *identifications* of the child with significant people in his environment—with mother and father, with a brother or a sister, with a favorite neighbor or teacher. As long as these separate identifications remain, the personality is made up of parts, often not self-consistent. To be at once like a mother and a father, an older brother and a favored music teacher, is to be torn into a variety of roles—to experience what Erikson calls *role diffusion*. Such role diffusion, unless outgrown, may result in serious personality disturbance.

Role diffusion is normally characteristic of early adolescence, when the youth has not yet "found himself" (not yet achieved identity), when he is both dependent and independent, loyal and defiant, daring and timid. He must master these divergent trends, give up being a carbon copy of other people (his identifications), and become himself (achieve identity).

The processes by which identity is finally achieved are various, but they all imply some experimentation with various experiences and roles. The adolescent characteristically seeks a range of subjective experiences, examines a number of philosophies of life (whether religious or political ideologies or both), commits himself temporarily (seriously or playfully) to occupational and other choices. Most societies allow a certain amount of freedom during the transition from childhood to adulthood, a period Erikson describes as a kind of *moratorium* (literally, a delayed period during which debts do not have to be paid; in this case, a period during which the adolescent does

not have to assume full social obligations). If all goes well, the young adult emerges from that period prepared to make life-long commitments. He has then achieved identity.

Self-esteem

A widespread dissatisfaction with contemporary life in our industrialized technological society has led many people to return to the ancient question, Who am I? Various practices, including drug usage and meditation (as noted in Chapter 7), arise in this context.

The origins of self-esteem in early childhood have been studied by Coopersmith (1967). He found that parents who set firm limits for the child's behavior, but did so in an atmosphere of warmth, concern, and mutual respect, raised children who at the ages of ten to twelve were high in self-esteem; that is, they were self-confident, assertive, optimistic, and relatively free of anxiety.

Low self-esteem has been found to be related to many types of behavior, such as social persuasibility (Janis and Field, 1959) and reaction to failure (Solley and Stagner, 1956). Solley and Stagner found that subjects low in self-esteem, when subjected to failure on laboratory tasks, took a longer time than high self-esteem subjects to complete later tasks. Cohen (1959) found that when two people work together in such a manner as to produce reciprocal influence, who influences whom depends in part upon their relative self-esteem. Those with high self-esteem recognize that they make more attempts than those with low self-esteem to influence the other person (Figure 17-5).

The picture a person has of himself affects the choices he makes, choices of a major in college, of a vocation, of whether to be conventional or defiant of convention, to be daring or to "play it safe." Many defiant social protests arise out of circumstances in which a person's self-esteem is lowered or threatened—when he is rejected by others because of color or status, when he cannot find a job, when he is conscripted into a war of which he disapproves. His self-esteem is enhanced when he has a sense of alternatives, a confidence that he can cope on his own terms with the prob-

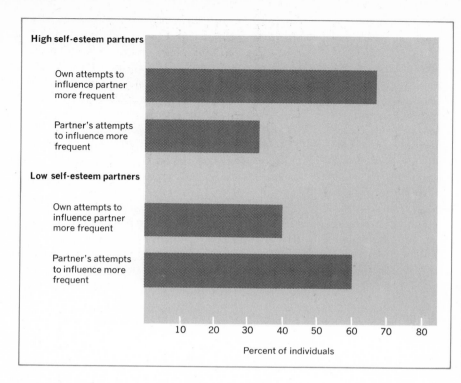

High self-esteem partners

Own attempts to influence partner more frequent

Partner's attempts to influence more frequent

Low self-esteem partners

Own attempts to influence partner more frequent

Partner's attempts to influence more frequent

10 20 30 40 50 60 70 80

Percent of individuals

Fig. 17-5 Self-esteem and attempts to influence a partner Those high in self-esteem recognize that they have tried more often to influence a partner than the partner has tried to influence them; the opposite is true for those lower in self-esteem. (Data from Cohen, 1959)

lems that he faces. To some extent self-esteem is a function of self-perception; what we mean by high self-esteem is a favorable self-perception.

Self-perception

A newborn child makes no distinction between himself and things outside himself. Self-perception is an achievement that comes through growth and experience. In time the child learns that his fingers are attached to his body as his clothes are not; he learns that there are people who treat him in special ways and whom he can influence. He learns to stand off and take a look at himself, to see his behavior in relation to others. The result is the complex awareness of self. Four aspects of self-awareness are worth noting.

Perceiving the self as an agent. We feel responsible for our acts; we pride ourselves on our achievements and blame ourselves for our failures. This feeling of responsibility implies an active "someone" who does things, an actor behind the activity. Because we tend to think primarily in concrete terms, we often identify this agent with our bodies. The body enters self-awareness because it is sensitive (the pains of your body are your pains) and because it is able to do things (it is *you* who play tennis). Threats to your body are threats to *you.* But you and your body are not quite one and the same; in one sense the body belongs to you, and as an agent you make use of it. The feeling of effort—that you have to force your body to do what you wish it to do—gives a subjective basis for the distinction between your body and you. One source of self-awareness is, then, the feeling of the self as in control of the body, as something that receives impressions and manages the body's affairs.

Perceiving the self as continuous. To the external observer the continuity of the bodily organism suffices to make John the same person today that he was yesterday. But to John himself his identity is maintained by his memories—continuous memories dated in his personal past. Multiple personalities (as in the Eve White case) persist only because some of the memories are not available.

Perceiving the self in relation to other people. Just as the personality structure is largely the result of interpersonal relations, of social interaction with other people, so, too, self-perception is importantly influenced by others. That is, our self-perceptions are formed largely by the acceptances and rejections of other people, although we may in self-defense deny what they see in us.

Perceiving the self as the embodiment of values and goals. Consider what is meant by ambition, jealousy, vanity, prestige, shame, guilt. Self-regard looms large in all of these. Detach them from a perception of the self, and the words have no meaning for the individual. A system of values and attitudes is built up around situations that are goal-directed, that can stir up feelings of self-enhancement or self-degradation. An *ideal self* (the self one would wish to become) is developed, and a person judges his actual conduct against this ideal. The ideal and the judgments combine to give self-perception a central place in social motivation. The self is assuredly of primary value to us. Because we perceive the self as something of value, its successes and failures are important to us.

Self-perception and self-evaluation are likely to take an increasingly greater place in the psychology of personality. The individual as a planner and decision-maker, who knows what he is about and how he feels, is too important to ignore.

Summary

1. *Personality,* as studied by the psychologist, may be defined as the characteristic ways of behaving that determine an individual's unique adjustments to his environment.

2. Personality is shaped by *inborn potential* as modifed by experiences *common to the culture,* such as the various roles the individual is called upon to play, and by the *unique experiences* that affect him as an individual.

3. The major theoretical approaches to an understanding of personality include *trait theory, type theory, psychoanalytic theory,* and the *specificity theory* of the social behavior theorists.

4. Cattell's distinction between *surface traits* and *source traits* serves as an illustration of trait theory. Surface traits are grouped together by combining those traits that correlate highly with one another according to the raw ratings (a method known as *cluster analysis*); source traits are arrived at through *factor analysis,* which uses a more complex mathematical model. It is hoped that a limited number of source traits might someday suffice to be used in the satisfactory appraisal of personality as a whole.

5. Eysenck's two-dimensional model of personality (*stable-unstable; extravert-introvert*), an illustration of type theory, is a modern version of the ancient Greek classification of temperaments into the four types of *sanguine, choleric, phlegmatic,* and *melancholic.* Some promising results have been found in predicting behavior in the laboratory on the basis of tests for these dimensions, but it is doubtful that the whole range of personality can be comprehended in this simplified manner.

6. Psychoanalytic theory infers some underlying structure of personality that affects behavior in indirect ways. Psychoanalysis as a *developmental theory* proposes that some kinds of personality or character types (such as oral or anal) come about through *fixation* (arrested development) at one or another of the psychosexual stages. Some experimental support can be found for the resulting contrasting patterns of behavior.

7. Psychoanalysis as a *dynamic theory* infers an *id, ego,* and a *superego* as persistent features of the personality that enter into conflict and are continuously interacting. The id is irrational and impulsive, seeking immediate gratification; the ego postpones gratification, so that gratification can be achieved realistically and in socially approved ways; the superego (conscience) imposes a moral code.

8. *Social behavior theorists* are critical of all the foregoing theories, believing that they are too broad and do not sufficiently recognize the importance of the context in which behavior occurs; they propose a *behavioral specificity theory* as an alternative. The social behavior theorist uses learning principles from the psychological laboratory and demonstrates how widespread the possibilities of behavior change are. The low correlations that are found between traits, their lack of consistency and generality, are explained on the grounds of variations in stimulus conditions. Of course, some stability is produced by environmental regularities, social custom, and the persistence of behavior labels used by the self or by others. The social behavior theorist combines his negative attitudes toward existing theories of personality with great optimism for behavior change in desirable directions.

9. *Experimental approaches* to the study of personality can be illustrated by studies of the relationship between the approval motive and such behavior as verbal conditioning, and by experimental studies of a child's preference for immediate gratification through a small reward versus postponing gratification for a larger one. In general, experimental studies select limited personality domains and then observe how people sorted according to the selected variable behave under a variety of conditions. Thus the studies yield the specific kinds of information that the social behavior theorists desire, although they may or may not support the specificity doctrine when the traits are tested in many situations for generality. The chief criticism is that the studies provide a piecemeal picture of the person and do not yield a conception of the personality as a whole.

10. The concept of the self provides a possible approach to the study of *personality integration.* The self is perceived as an agent, as being continuous, as being influenced by relations with other people, and as the embodiment of goals and values. Experiments dealing with self-esteem and self-perception help to elucidate the significance of the self as experienced by the person under study.

Suggestions for further reading

General books on personality include Hall and Lindzey, *Theories of personality* (2nd ed., 1970), with its accompanying book of readings, Lindzey and Hall (eds.), *Theories of personality: Primary sources and research* (1965), and Mischel, *Introduction to personality* (1971).

A number of Cattell's books describe his researches and his orientation; a useful one is *The scientific analysis of personality* (1965). Guilford, *Personality* (1959), gives an excellent review of personality dimensions, especially those arrived at by factor analysis, which allows his summaries to be compared with those of Cattell.

Eysenck's type theory is propounded and illustrated in his books *The structure of human personality* (1960) and *The biological basis of personality* (1967).

For psychoanalytic theories of personality, Blum, *Psychodynamics: The science of unconscious mental forces* (1966), is a paperback source. See also Janis (ed.), *Personality: Dynamics, development, and assessment* (1969).

The social behavior viewpoint is presented by Mischel, *Personality and assessment* (1968), Peterson, *The clinical study of social behavior* (1968), and Bandura, *Principles of behavior modification* (1969). See also Mischel, *Introduction to personality* (1971).

A review series is devoted to the experimental study of personality: Maher (ed.), *Progress in experimental personality research,* with annual volumes beginning in 1964. Specimen studies are reproduced in Millon (ed.), *Approaches to personality* (1968), and in Sarason (ed.), *Contemporary research in personality* (2nd ed., 1969).

Problems of the concept of the self have been reviewed by Wylie, *The self concept* (1961), and by Gordon and Gergen (eds.), *The self in social interaction* (1968).

18

personality assessment

WHATEVER ONE'S THEORY of personality, a person has become what he is through his innate potential, his acquired habits, his interactions with the environment of things and other people. What we can expect him to do on various occasions is at least moderately predictable, provided we know him well; it is on the basis of such predictions that we are able to characterize his personality. An informal type of characterization, of course, goes on all the time; the problem for a science of personality is to move from informal appraisals of a person to some sort of formal assessment.

The informal occasions for appraising personality are so familiar that they need little discussion. As we select our friends, size up customers or competitors, choose candidates for political office, select marriage partners, we not only form impressions of people but try to predict what may be consistent in their behavior in the future.

Judgments of other people are often greatly influenced by first impressions, but these are subject to many kinds of error. The observer may be influenced by *hearsay* and read into the person traits that someone has said he exhibits, or he may produce a *halo effect* through finding some one characteristic that he likes or dislikes, and then assigning this characteristic to other features of the person's behavior. He may use a *stereotype* based on the characteristics believed to be universal in the group to which the person belongs. Then, too, the person being judged may behave in such a manner as to create a false first impression: he may come from a background that makes him so differ-ent from the observer that he is hard to under-stand; he may be putting his "best foot forward"; or he may even be making a deliberate effort to deceive by assuming a temporary role that is not really characteristic of him.

These informal processes are themselves subject to study, but the psychology of personality is primarily concerned with more formal appraisal.

Occasions for formal assessments of personality

The settings in which formal personality assess-ment goes on are much the same as those in which intelligence and other abilities are measured: (1) educational settings, in which decisions regarding educational placement or vocational choice are made; (2) clinical settings, in which procedures are undertaken to relieve suffering and to produce appropriate behavior change; (3) business and industry, in which personnel problems of all kinds arise; (4) legal settings, in which the prisoner who has violated the legal code is judged as an indi-vidual, in the hope of rehabilitating him; and (5) research settings, in which the investigator un-dertakes to improve the processes of appraisal while at the same time learning more about per-sonality and its organization.

Special problems arise in connection with these settings, because the individual who is being ap-praised is often not in a situation in which he feels comfortable about offering the self-disclosures that are called for. This is less true of course on those occasions when he seeks assistance, as in visits to the school guidance counselor or to the clinician, when he is aware of a personal problem. The difficulties of assessment are heightened when the judgments of others affect the outcome, as when the person being judged is to be employed for a job, or granted parole, or perhaps committed to an institution for the mentally ill.

The appraiser of personality encounters ethical and technical problems. The ethical problem con-cerns the invasion of privacy incurred by study-ing deeply into a personality, if the person being studied does not give his informed consent. In our culture privacy is considered a fundamental right, not to be lightly abused (see Chapter 23, pp. 552-55). The technical problem arises because of the strong tendencies of some individuals to fal-sify responses under pressure to behave in so-cially approved ways.

These issues are more troublesome in personality appraisal than in other areas of psychology, such as intelligence. Although some invasion of privacy may be found in intelligence testing, the main use of the tests is to predict school success, which is in any case a matter of public knowledge. Because there are no such public criteria for personality, some see personality tests as invading privacy more than ability measures. The technical problems are also less severe for intelligence measurement be-cause the intelligence test is designed to reveal behavior at its best, and the pressure to respond in socially approved ways is not a limitation on the test. A personality measure seeks to find char-acteristic or probable behavior, not behavior at its best; an alcoholic's characteristic use of alcohol is the pertinent behavior in his personality, but he knows that when his personality is under study it would be better to act as if he did not drink.

The importance of personality appraisal is evi-dent from the number of settings in which such appraisal is called for; the difficulties of that task, described above, enable us to understand why personality appraisal still has a long way to go. We will turn now to those aspects of the individual that can be assessed in evaluating his personality.

Personality characteristics subject to assessment

The present personality is of course a product of its development, but it is appraised or characterized by the way it is now expressed in behavior. The present personality can be *understood* according to its developmental history, but it is *assessed* according to present behavior in varied environmental contexts.

Behavior samples versus inferred traits or dispositions

When we assert something about an individual's personality we mean to say that when given the opportunity he will behave in a certain way: when given an assignment he will complete it on time, when engaged in a quarrel he will be likely to start a fistfight, on a political issue he will take the liberal side. We are making a probabilistic kind of prediction that he will show some consistency in what he does and that this consistency will cover a fairly wide range of behaviors. These issues of consistency have entered into the formulation of personality theories, as we have seen (Chapter 17). If many behavior samples would show these consistencies, we could assign appropriate dispositional or trait names and state that the individual reveals in his behavior a trait of planfulness, or combativeness, or political liberalism. The danger of such labels is that, in stressing consistency and generality, they may lose contact with their origins in observed behavior. When cautiously used, however, some sort of trait or dispositional statement serves to summarize whatever predictable uniformity exists.

The prevalence of "type" theories throughout history shows that there is a strong desire to define a person's "essence," to discover the way he "really is." The more modern approach recognizes that although personality is unique, it is not necessarily highly unified; it is now considered preferable to make assertions about particular aspects of behavior than about the personality as a whole. Even so, it is desirable to achieve some sort of ordering of the information about how a person behaves. One way of going about this is to list some categories or modalities of traits that are subject to assessment.

Allport (1960) listed ten kinds of units used in describing personality, ranging from "ideational schemes" to unconscious motives. Guilford (1959) proposed seven "modalities of traits," indicating that the kind of trait we see depends upon the direction from which we view personality (Figure 18-1). Many terms in their lists overlap, but the lack of agreement shows that some arbitrariness enters.

A short list of important descriptive aspects of personality would include: morphology and physiology; intellectual and other abilities; motivational dispositions and needs; expressive and stylistic traits; and interests, values, and social attitudes. A brief statement on each of these will help define what characteristics are subject to personality assessment.

Fig. **18-1 Different aspects of personality** In this diagram, personality is shown as an integrated whole, which can be viewed from different directions: from one direction we see one kind of trait, from another we see another kind of trait. (After Guilford, 1959)

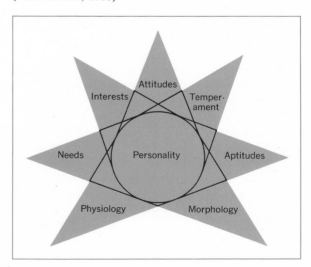

Morphology and physiology

A person's physical endowments of bodily size, strength, agility, and appearance are aspects of his personality; they influence the manner in which other people react to him, and these reactions, in turn, shape his image of himself as worthy or unworthy. Precise measurements are implied in those theories that stress body types (Chapter 17, p. 399), but other theories call attention to the body also. For example, we noted earlier in the discussion of adolescence that early or late development had an influence on the developing personality (pp. 86–87). Hence the first characteristic of the person subject to measurement and relevant to behavior is *morphology,* the conformation of his body.

The body is a complex and finely tuned machine; its activity depends upon internal conditions of metabolism, energy utilization, and the balance of competing systems. Hence body *physiology* is also important in personality assessment. Individuals can be characterized as being of high or low physiological reactivity on such measures as changes in pulse pressure, heart rate, or galvanic skin response, under circumstances in which they are subjected to stress. But as there is a high degree of specificity of response, various physiological measures of stress do not correlate highly with one another (Lacey, 1967).

Despite the high degree of idiosyncrasy in physiological responding, the *physiological* responses to stress can be shown to be important in experiments bearing on the *psychological* responses to stress. For example, in a fairly complex type of experiment subjects were grouped according to those characterized by achievement motivation or by affiliation motivation (see pp. 313–14) and those characterized by high physiological reactivity or low reactivity. A laboratory task was arranged to arouse stress relevant to the characteristic motivational disposition. In a scrambled-word task, for instance, the words for the achievement group were words like "fail," "poorest," "teacher," while for the affiliation group they were words like "mother," "company," "lonely." As Figure 18-2 shows, only the high physiological reactivity group

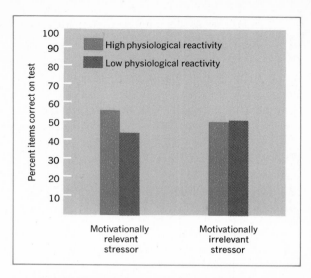

Fig. **18-2 Physiological reactivity in interaction with the motivational relevance of a stressful task** When the stressful task was motivationally relevant, those with high physiological reactivity did significantly better on the task than those with low physiological reactivity; when the task was irrelevant the degree of physiological reactivity did not matter. (Results on two tasks are averaged; $N = 10$ in each of the four groups.) (Data from Vogel, Raymond, and Lazarus, 1959)

showed a superior performance on the stressful task that was motivationally relevant; the less reactive group showed an inferior performance (Vogel, Raymond, and Lazarus, 1959).

Even though the reported experiment yielded positive results, it should be noted that not very much could have been predicted from the physiological reactivity alone. Thus, while physiological measures are seen to be appropriate, we do not know from an experiment of this kind how useful such measures would be for saying anything about an individual (beyond the fact that a person with high physiological reactivity will probably perform well on a motivationally relevant task). This is why personality assessment requires something more than knowledge that a particular characteristic is pertinent to behavior.

Intellectual and other abilities

Personality covers the whole field of individual differences, and it is important to bear in mind that behaviors relating to intelligence are also a part of personality, even though for convenience we may sometimes distinguish between "intelligence tests" and "personality tests." A developed sense of humor requires a quick appreciation of literary allusions; the detection of similarities and incongruities depends upon a high order of intelligence. Other abilities, such as the skills involved in musical performance, are also relevant to personality. It is evident that personality and abilities are intertwined in many ways.

Motivational dispositions and needs

To the extent that motivational dispositions or needs are characteristic of the person over time, they are features of his personality. We have already described attempts to assess individuals according to their achievement motives or their affiliative motives (Chapter 13, pp. 326–27). Other motivational dispositions, such as those listed among Murray's needs (Chapter 13, Table 13-1), have served in the description of individual personalities. Some of the motives implied may be unconscious. In any case, motives and needs constitute a category of personality-relevant determiners of behavior.

Expressive and stylistic traits

Very often when we characterize a person we tell something about his style: polite, talkative, consistent, hesitant, sociable, critical. There are a great many such "personality traits" that seem somewhat independent of time and place; that is, they will be expressed at home and at the office, in social groups and in professional meetings. The assessment of these expressive and stylistic traits is a significant task for the student of personality.

Some special forms of stylistic traits much studied over the years go by the general name of *cognitive styles*. Calling cognitive style a trait means that there are not only individual differences in the manner of perceiving the world, but that these differences show both some constancy and some generality. Various paired terms have been used to describe cognitive styles; examples are *levelers*

versus *sharpeners* (that is, those who tend to smooth out differences and detect similarities, as against those who magnify the differences), or *repressors* versus *sensitizers* (those who tend to deny their problems, as against those who show a tendency to exaggerate them).

One of the most carefully explored dimensions of cognitive style has been that called *field dependence* versus *field independence*. The descriptive names derive from the tendency for some people to be influenced more than others by the context (field) in which a perceptual judgment has to be made. One such judgment is the perception of verticality of a rod presented against a frame that can be rotated so that its sides are not actually vertical (the Rod-and-Frame Test). When the frame is rotated from the vertical, some subjects distort the position of the rod according to the position of the frame (they are field dependent), while others are little influenced by the position of the frame (they are field independent). Another test calls for detecting figures embedded in a background (Hidden Figures Test). Those who most readily detect the hidden figures are more field independent.

Field dependence and independence turn out to be quite stable, with retest correlations for the Rod-and-Frame Test reported to be from .62 to .92 over a span of fourteen years (Witkin, Goodenough, and Karp, 1967). The personality characteristics revealed by these tests also relate to other aspects of behavior—for example, to creative test performance (Spotts and Mackler, 1967) and to aspects of self-control (Willoughby, 1967).

Interests, values, and social attitudes

Personality is in part reflected in the kinds of things one likes to do, what one enjoys, what one appreciates. *Interests* are usually defined according to objects or activities; that is, one may be interested in stamps or coins or old motor cars, in chemistry, biology, international affairs, reading, music, or sports. The list of potential interests is practically limitless, but a sampling of these interests can clearly tell us something about the person who has them.

Measures of interest have proved to be particularly important in vocational guidance. For a person to enjoy a given occupation or profession he must like the things that people in that vocation do and the conditions under which they work (alone or in company, sedentary or active, safe or risky). One of the successful measures, known as the Strong Vocational Interest Blank, calls for replies of likes and dislikes for a great many items; by comparing the answers of the person taking the test with answers of those who have engaged successfully in the occupation, a score is obtained of the "match" between the person's expressed interests and those of people in various occupations. A high match indicates a likelihood that the individual will be comfortable in that occupation, provided he has the requisite ability and obtains the necessary training. The relative permanence of such interests, and their relationship to stability in vocational choice, have been amply demonstrated (Strong, 1955; Campbell, 1966).

Values are related to interests in that they tend to place some sorts of involvement higher on a scale of preference than other sorts; when one says he prefers classical music to popular music he is telling something about his values as well as about his interests. When men are classified according to their dominant values, larger classes of activities are usually specified than in the case of interests. The *scale of values* (Allport, Vernon, and Lindzey, 1960) attempts to measure the extent to which one's values can be classified as theoretical, economic, esthetic, social, political, or religious.

A person necessarily adopts *attitudes* toward features of his culture. He is likely to be either more conservative or more liberal in politics; he may have strong feelings for or against racial equality, or academic freedom, or birth control. Expressed in personality terms, these attitudes toward particular features of life reveal such characteristics as authoritarianism, equalitarianism, or dogmatism. The problems of attitudes and opinions will be treated in greater detail in Chapter 22.

The variety of aspects subject to appraisal sets a task of a large order for the designer of instruments used in the formal assessment of personality. If he is to provide a reasonably complete inventory of the behavioral tendencies in which one individual differs from another, he must cover a wide range of topics, and he must find some way in which to assess or measure the appropriate characteristics covered within each topic.

Interviews and rating scales

The method of naturalistic or field observation is widely employed in science, particularly when the complexity of the phenomena defy simple classification. The method is familiar in biology, geology, meteorology, and in the social sciences, especially anthropology. It is not surprising that as we try to understand personality we move from the informal observations of everyday life to methods of observation closely related to these: to the interview, which replaces casual conversation with more structured and purposeful conversation, and to the rating scale, which provides a more formal record of impressions.

The interview: transition between informal and formal methods

The interview is a conversation with a purpose: to determine whether a student should be admitted to an advanced class, whether a job applicant should be employed, whether a person who threatens suicide should be placed in protective custody, or to determine, in general, how best to help someone in trouble. To the extent that the interview is *diagnostic* (that is, probing at the root of trouble, or sizing up the individual in the light of a decision to be made) it is used as a device for personality appraisal; to the extent that it is *prognostic* (estimating whether the individual will succeed in college, violate parole, be relieved of his symptoms of disturbance) it attempts to predict personality-relevant behavior.

The many skills that the interviewer may bring to his task depend upon the purpose of the interview and the theory under which he is operating. In addition to clinical interviews (discussed later in Chapter 21) there are interviews for educational and vocational guidance, public opinion interviews, and many others.

The interview may be *unstructured,* in which case the person interviewed determines very largely what is discussed, although the interviewer through the skilled use of supplementary questions may elicit pertinent examples or in other ways make the interview more informative. Or the interview may be *structured,* in which case it follows a stan-dard pattern, much like a printed questionnaire, assuring that all relevant topics are touched upon and clear answers given. The unstructured interview is more likely to be used in the repeated interviews of a clinical or counseling relationship, whereas the structured interview is more likely to be used in a research program in which compara-ble data are needed from a number of respondents.

Because the interview is so widely used, increasing attention is being given to the interviewing process (Matarazzo, 1965). The behavior of the interviewer markedly affects what the person interviewed does; for example, a simple head nod at the right moment by the interviewer may greatly increase the amount of talking on the part of his client, and a similar increase can be produced by his saying "Mm-hmm" in response to the client's comments (Figure 18-3). Increases in the amount of talking do not in themselves guarantee that such an interview is more revealing than one with less conversation, but on the whole (provided the talk is not merely repetitive) a person who talks more freely gives the interviewer more information and thus a firmer basis on which to make judgments.

Rating scales

Many situations require making personality judgments. The employer selects his employee; the jury decides the responsibility of the accused; the scholarship committee decides which students deserve aid; each of us decides whose friendship to cultivate. A rating scale is a device by which a rater can record his judgment of another person according to the traits defined by the scale. The preferred form of rating scale is that known as the *graphic rating scale,* an example of which is shown in Figure 18-4. Each trait is represented by a segmented line; one end indicates one extreme of the trait to be rated, and the other end represents the opposite extreme. The rater places a check mark at an appropriate place on the scale to represent the degree to which the subject possesses the trait.

The rater must understand the scale; he must be sufficiently acquainted with the person rated so that he can make useful judgments of him; and

Fig. **18-3** **Effects of interviewer on person interviewed** The results shown are based on interviews with twenty young normal applicants for positions as policemen or firemen. In the control condition (before and after the special treatment of the experimental condition) the interviewer was careful to avoid nodding his head in response to the applicant's replies. When, in the experimental condition, the interviewer responded with head nods, the subject lengthened his replies to the interviewer's questions. The same results were found in another experiment, in which the interviewer responded to the applicant with verbal reinforcement ("Mm-hmm"). (Data from Matarazzo, 1965)

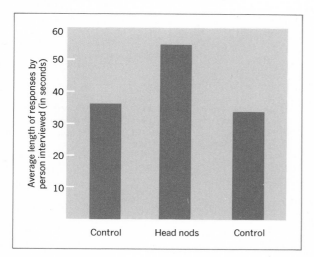

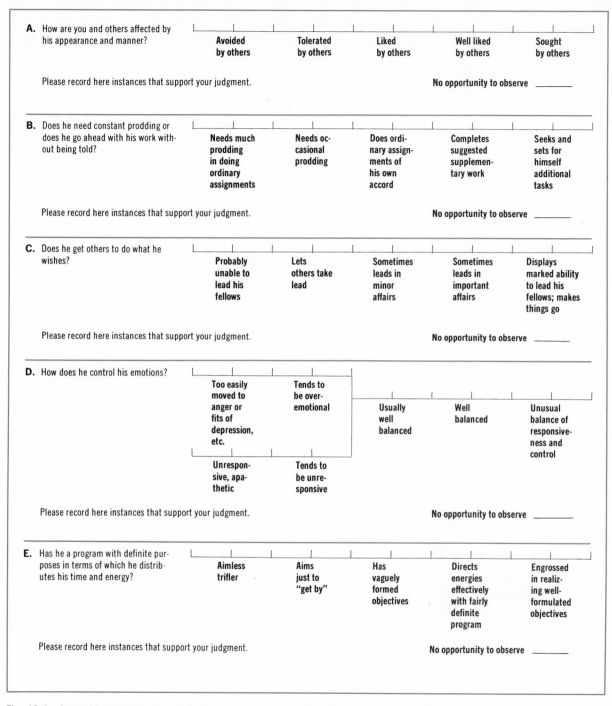

A. How are you and others affected by his appearance and manner?

| Avoided by others | Tolerated by others | Liked by others | Well liked by others | Sought by others |

Please record here instances that support your judgment.   No opportunity to observe _____

B. Does he need constant prodding or does he go ahead with his work without being told?

| Needs much prodding in doing ordinary assignments | Needs occasional prodding | Does ordinary assignments of his own accord | Completes suggested supplementary work | Seeks and sets for himself additional tasks |

Please record here instances that support your judgment.   No opportunity to observe _____

C. Does he get others to do what he wishes?

| Probably unable to lead his fellows | Lets others take lead | Sometimes leads in minor affairs | Sometimes leads in important affairs | Displays marked ability to lead his fellows; makes things go |

Please record here instances that support your judgment.   No opportunity to observe _____

D. How does he control his emotions?

| Too easily moved to anger or fits of depression, etc. | Tends to be over-emotional | | | |
| Unresponsive, apathetic | Tends to be unresponsive | Usually well balanced | Well balanced | Unusual balance of responsiveness and control |

Please record here instances that support your judgment.   No opportunity to observe _____

E. Has he a program with definite purposes in terms of which he distributes his time and energy?

| Aimless trifler | Aims just to "get by" | Has vaguely formed objectives | Directs energies effectively with fairly definite program | Engrossed in realizing well-formulated objectives |

Please record here instances that support your judgment.   No opportunity to observe _____

Fig. **18-4 A graphic rating scale**   A scale such as this one helps the judge to be specific about the basis for each of his judgments. (American Council on Education; after Fryer and Henry, 1950)

he must avoid the *halo effect* and other common errors in rating. (The halo effect is the tendency to rate a person high on all traits because he makes a very good impression on one or two or, conversely, to rate him low throughout because he makes a poor impression on one or two traits.) When used with proper care, the rating scale is a very helpful device for recording judgments of other people.

Personality inventories

The desire to develop more objective personality tests arose in part through the success of the intelligence test. The pencil-and-paper intelligence test served rather well in the assessment of intellectual abilities; it consisted, as we have learned, essentially of a number of questions the answers of which could be scored, and a sum of correct answers secured. The higher the number of correct answers, the more intelligent the responder. Those who began constructing objective personality tests used this same model and came up with a number of questions having answers that could be scored and added up to obtain a measure of "neuroticism," or "ascendancy-submission," or "introversion-extraversion." Some of the rules of test construction are the same: the scores must be *reliable* (self-consistent) and they must be *valid* (measuring what they are supposed to measure).

Beyond this, the parallels between intelligence and personality tests are not so close. Thus an item such as "Do you usually keep your shoes shined?" may be answered truthfully, but the test designer may intend a positive answer to indicate either neatness or compulsiveness. Which one of these intended meanings it has is not self-evident. Furthermore, the person can choose to answer the item either way, depending upon how he interprets "usually," and what impression he wishes to make. In the intelligence test the difficulty of the item limits the possibility of "correct" answers, but this is not the case for personality-type items, for there is no one "correct" answer. Hence the validation of personality inventories requires approaches more subtle than those needed for intelligence measurement. The difficulties are so great that these inventories have not, in fact, proved as satisfactory as intelligence tests for the purposes intended.

A personality inventory may be designed to measure a single trait or dimension of personality. Thus we have tests of ascendance-submission and tests of introversion-extraversion. Or the test may provide an overall estimate of personal adjustment in an attempt to distinguish between those who are adjusted and those who are neurotic. When a test seeks to measure several aspects of personality at once, it may come out with a *profile* of scores rather than a single score.

Several strategies have been adopted to meet some of the difficulties inherent in constructing personality inventories. The strategy of *empirical construction* makes use of the responses of reference groups of individuals who show the characteristics that are being appraised; another strategy is *factor analysis* of a large number of items, with an ultimate purification of the test to provide an appraisal of the main factors that emerge; a third is *design according to theory, with experimental validation;* and a fourth is a *correction for response style.* Of course, it is possible to use two or more of these strategies in combination, but it is convenient to consider them separately here. They can be illustrated by well-known tests that have used them.

Empirical construction: the Minnesota Multiphasic Personality Inventory

The Minnesota Multiphasic Personality Inventory (MMPI) is a self-rating instrument designed to detect pathological trends within the personality through comparison of the test-taker's responses with those of patients having known kinds of personality disorders. The test is arranged in the form of 495 statements that the person checks as true or not true for him; he leaves blank those on which he "cannot say," but is requested to leave as few blanks as possible. Some of the items are

I have never done anything dangerous for the thrill of it.
I daydream very little.
My mother or father often made me obey even when I thought it was unreasonable.
At times my thoughts have raced ahead faster than I could speak them.

Responses are scored according to the correspondence between the answers given by the subject and those given by patients with different kinds of psychological disturbances. The result is a profile of ten scores.

It may be noted that the kinds of items included are both "obvious" and "subtle." An affirmative reply to a statement such as "I sometimes think I am losing my mind" is an obvious admission of

trouble; reply to a statement such as "I like to read newspaper editorials" has no self-evident personality indications. In general, there appear to be few advantages to the more subtle questions; direct self-ratings often seem as satisfactory as those derived from complex scales (Peterson, 1968).

The number of items on the MMPI is so large and the range of questions asked so great that it is possible to construct scales that reflect many dimensions of personality other than those for which the test was originally intended. At least one hundred such scales have been constructed since the original scales were devised (Butcher, 1969).

Although the scales were derived from comparison groups suffering from personality disorders often severe enough to require hospitalization, the scales have been widely used in the study of other populations. One of these studies, illustrated in Figure 18-5, compares the scores of delinquents

Fig. **18-5 Personality profiles of delinquents and nondelinquents** The delinquents show three unusually high scores: on the psychopathic deviation, schizophrenia, and hypomania scales. Psychopathic deviation refers to the disregard of rules expected to characterize the delinquent; the schizophrenia scale, applied to the normally adjusted person, refers to negative or odd behavior, lack of social grace; hypomania refers to expansive behavior, not bound by custom. The scores on the scale of patterns of interest of the opposite sex are lower for delinquents than for nondelinquents, suggesting an excessively masculine type of response on the part of the delinquents. (Data from Hathaway and Monachesi, 1963)

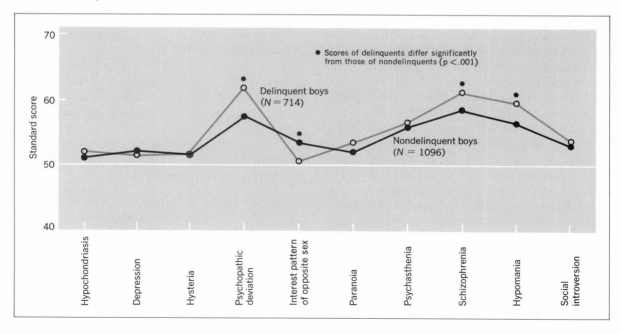

and nondelinquents (Hathaway and Monachesi, 1963). Recognizable group differences do result from comparison of these scores, but they are frequently not of great enough magnitude to be useful in individual cases. The MMPI is most useful for separating the less severely disturbed neurotic from the more severely disturbed psychotic patient. Even in this case, however, it was found that a group of 861 inventories, half from neurotic patients and half from psychotic patients, yielded at best a 69 percent correct classification. In other words, nearly one-third of the patients would be misclassified on the basis of MMPI scores (Goldberg, 1969).

The MMPI illustrates the strategy of validation according to criterion groups. A number of other tests have used this method, including the Strong Vocational Interest Blank (see p. 426) and the California Psychological Inventory (CPI) (Gough, 1957).

Construction through factor analysis: Cattell's 16 PF Questionnaire

We noted in the preceding chapter how Cattell distinguished between surface traits and source traits (pp. 401–03). It was his hope that by taking a very large number of trait ratings and measurements and then analyzing them by factor-analytic methods, he could come out with a picture representative of the whole personality sphere. An individual would be characterized according to his standing with respect to the most fundamental source traits.

Cattell's 16 PF (personality factors) scales illustrate this approach. The questionnaire that he constructed represents an enormous amount of work in locating the main source traits, selecting items to best represent them, and then assembling them into a short and usable test (Cattell and Ebel, 1964). It yields scores on sixteen relatively independent personality characteristics (source traits) such as dominance, emotional stability, radicalism, and will control. In principle the test has certain advantages over the MMPI in that it is less arbitrarily related to pathology; it is the result of a wide search for the most significant characteristics

of a personality. Unfortunately, the individual scales as subtests sample too little information to be reliable, so that the test is not in fact very useful in giving a description of a single subject's personality.

The 16 PF test is but one of a number of tests constructed by factor-analytic methods. Another one, based on a very large pool of items, is the Edwards Personality Inventory (Edwards, 1966).[1] Factor analysis was used in the course of the test's construction, but the final fifty-three scales are not, strictly speaking, representative of that many factors. The test has the advantage, for research purposes, that each of its items is used in only one of the scales. It also avoids items that some people find offensive (questions on religion, politics, family, health, bodily functions). It remains to be seen whether its wide range of items will make it more advantageous than the other tests.

Design according to theory, with experimental validation: the Eysenck Personality Inventory

The Eysenck Personality Inventory (EPI) is constructed on the basis of a theory of personality (Eysenck and Eysenck, 1963). The theory, discussed in Chapter 17 (see pp. 404–05), makes the assumption that there are two main dimensions of personality, the stable-unstable dimension and the introverted-extraverted dimension. The Eysenck inventory can be administered quite easily and contains only fifty-seven questions, many of which are like those on the MMPI. The questions have been selected to give reliable and statistically independent measures of the stable-unstable and introverted-extraverted dimensions. Eysenck's validation of the test comes not only from factor analysis but also from the correspondence between the test results and behavior observed in laboratory studies; for example, the test scores are used to predict the rate of acquiring a new response as a function of the cognitive complexity and anxiety-arousing features of the learning situation. To the extent that actual behavior can be predicted from

[1]This inventory is to be distinguished from an earlier one by the same author, the *Edwards Personal Preference Schedule* (EPPS), described later in this chapter (p. 432).

a pencil-and-paper test, more confidence resides in the value of the test.

A test based upon theory has the advantage over the tests previously described in that the theory provides a basis for selecting test items.

Correction for response style: the Edwards Personal Preference Schedule

One of the difficulties that haunts the self-descriptive kind of personality inventory is the tendency for the person taking the test to present himself in a favorable light by responding in a manner that he believes to be socially desirable. This "social desirability" variable has been a source of ambiguity in many personality tests (Edwards, 1957).[2]

Edwards (1954) constructed a test to minimize the influence of the social-desirability variable by arranging his items as forced choices between statements judged to be equally desirable (or undesirable). Thus the subject taking the test must choose either A or B of an item such as the following:

A I like to be successful in things undertaken.
B I like to form new friendships.

Both are socially acceptable statements, but one stresses achievement and the other stresses affiliation. Some items require a choice between unfavorable statements:

A I feel depressed when I fail at something.
B I am nervous when talking before a group.

The choices between A and B made by persons for whom the items are essentially inapplicable ought to be about 50/50, because the items are equally desirable or undesirable so far as they could be made so.

The forced-choice method has a disadvantage in that it gives only the *relative* preferences for one

---

[2]Social desirability is but one of the kinds of response styles that bias personality tests. For a useful review, see Wiggins (1968). Block (1965) provides a defense of the MMPI as having content significance beyond stylistic features of response. See earlier discussion of approval motive (Chapter 17, pp. 412–13).

pattern of motive over another; it does not reveal the *absolute* level of that motive. That is, a relatively listless person might come out with a ranking of his motives similar to that of a highly energetic person; unless their hierarchies differed, there would be no way to distinguish their general arousal levels. However, if it is assumed that each person is strongly motivated in some direction, then a motive that is chosen consistently against others must fairly well characterize his motivational system.

Edwards chose his items to represent the content of fifteen basic motivational dispositions or needs, as set forth by Murray (1938) (see Chapter 13, p. 316). These include such needs as abasement, achievement, dominance, aggression, and autonomy. The inventory consists of 225 items presented in pairs; it contains thirty statements bearing upon each of the fifteen needs. The emphasis is not on psychopathology, as in the MMPI, but rather on motives found among all members of a normal population.

Which is the preferred strategy?

It might be supposed that one of the four strategies discussed above would work out so much better than the others that it would eventually win out, becoming the accepted method for constructing personality inventories. The difficulty is that the success of any one of the strategies has been sufficient to keep its proponents busy at improving their tests by using that strategy, and the success of no one of the strategies has been great enough for it to command general acceptance.

When the various stylistic problems first became apparent, it was feared that they contributed more to the scores on personality inventories than did the actual content of the items. Since then, however, ingenious methods have been devised to separate out the effects of stylistic influences and content influences; the results show that content is indeed effective in predicting independent criteria such as peer ratings, popularity, academic achievement, academic interest, and conformity to social norms (Hase and Goldberg, 1967).

People experienced in the judging of other persons can often take advantage of slight clues and specific individual experiences that are missed by objective tests standardized on groups of people. Their judgments, which can be called *clinical,* are the alternatives to predictive scores arrived at by methods that can be called *statistical.* How does the issue stand between the relative successes of clinical and statistical predictions?

A careful review by Meehl (1954), who has had abundant clinical and statistical experience, is informative. He examined a series of studies that provided competent clinicians with information of a type that could also be expressed in statistical formulas. With the same type of information available for judgment, in all but one of the studies the statistical predictions based on the formula were equal to or superior to the predictions made by the clinicians. In most cases if the clinician supplemented the statistical predictions by corrections made on the basis of his clinical intuitions, the prediction was weakened rather than improved.

This support for tests (which produce scores that can be entered into formulas) must not be taken as an indictment of the clinical method, and was not so intended by Meehl, who pointed out that many times a usable formula is not available (Meehl, 1957). Holt (1958), in a reply and supplement to Meehl, pointed out that the clinicians were sometimes denied information and forced to guess in situations in which the statistical evidence was available, such as the relation between high school and college grades. The discussion has been continued by Gough (1962) and Sawyer (1966).

In view of the tendency to be biased in favor of personal judgment (as in the desire to interview job applicants or candidates for admission to a college, rather than to rely on records), it is worth noting how fallible human judgment is when it comes to making predictions in fairly complex situations. One illustration, differing in substance from the kinds of studies reviewed by Meehl but leading to similar conclusions, is given by a study of the prediction of football game outcomes made by coaches as compared with a purely statistical prediction of the outcomes based on past team performances. The coaches were given the predictions, and asked to correct them on the basis of their knowledge of supplementary factors, such as injuries, home games, traditional rivalries, and so on. The corrections of the coaches almost invariably made the predictions less accurate than if reliance was on the formula alone (Harris, 1963).

It would be foolish to interpret studies showing the limitations of clinical prediction as denying the validity of the face-to-face relationships of the clinic. The purpose of the clinician is not so much to make predictions as to produce changes in desirable directions. As long as progress is made, it does not matter that a number of false leads (or false predictions) have had to be rejected in the course of clinical treatment.

Projective tests

Personality inventories strive for objectivity, in that they are readily scored and can be evaluated for reliability and validity. But their fixed structure, which allows the respondent little or no opportunity to refine or qualify his answers, has been partially responsible for their very limited success. Some investigators have therefore been led to adopt a far less structured type of test, called a *projective test.* It is so named because the subject through freer answers puts more of himself into his responses, and so is said to *project* his personality through them, as the movie camera projects the image on the screen. This kind of test calls for an imaginative production, through which the individual is free to build his own world and to make himself the central figure in whatever drama he chooses to construct; in this free play he may reveal unconscious tendencies—tendencies of which he is not fully aware. Two examples of projective tests will be discussed here: the *Thematic Apperception Test* and the *Rorschach Inkblot Test.*

Thematic Apperception Test

One kind of projective test consists of a series of pictures about which the subject tells stories. The subject usually becomes absorbed in the imaginative productions he is building around each picture and says things about the characters in the stories that really apply to himself. The name of this test, Thematic Apperception Test (TAT), is intended to describe the fact that the test reveals basic "themes" that recur in the imaginative productions of a person. *Apperception* means a readiness to perceive in certain ways, based on prior individual experience. Hence the test name implies that a subject interprets an ambiguous stimulus according to his individual readiness to perceive in a certain way, and that he elaborates the stories in terms of preferred plots or themes that reflect his fantasies.

When confronted with a picture similar to that in Figure 18-6, a 21-year-old patient told the following story.

> She has prepared this room for someone's arrival and is opening the door for a last general look over the room. She is probably expecting her son home. She tries to place everything as it was when he left. She seems like a very tyrannical character. She led her son's life for him and is going to take over again as soon as he gets back. This is merely the beginning of her rule, and the son is definitely cowed by this overbearing attitude of hers and will slip back into her well ordered way of life. He will go through life plodding down the tracks she has laid down for him. All this represents her complete domination of his life until she dies [Arnold, 1949, p. 100].

Although the original picture shows only a woman standing in an open door, the subject's readiness to respond with something about his relationship to his mother led to this story of a

Fig. **18-6 A picture similar to one used in the Thematic Apperception Test** The pictures usually have elements of ambiguity in them, so that the subject can "read into" them something from his own experience or fantasy.

woman's domination of her son. The clinician whose patient told this story reports that facts obtained later confirmed the interpretation that the story reflected the subject's own problems.

In taking the TAT, the subject tells stories about twenty pictures. If particular problems are preoccupying him, they may show up in a number of the stories. Special scoring keys have been devised in order to make the test useful for specific purposes. For instance, the test can be used to measure achievement motivation (reported earlier, p. 326) and aggression (Megargee and Cook, 1967). Appropriately used, the test can supplement other measures in the prediction of academic performance (Harrison, 1965).

Rorschach Inkblot Test

The Rorschach Inkblot Test consists of a series of cards, each displaying a rather complex inkblot (Rorschach, 1942; first published in 1921). If ink is spilled on a piece of paper that is then creased down the middle, a bilaterally symmetrical blot like that shown in Figure 18-7 will result. From many such designs, a few standard ones were selected to make up the Rorschach Test. The experienced tester knows something about the responses to be expected from each.

The subject simply tells what he sees on the card.

He may see several different things on a single card, or he may see the same ambiguous shape as representing several figures at once. The test capitalizes on the familiar tendency to see imaginary faces, animals, battle scenes, or fairyland figures in cloud formations.

The subject's responses to the inkblot are in some ways more revealing than his replies to a personality inventory. He is much less self-conscious about these responses than when replying to direct questions about himself in a personality questionnaire. What appear to him to be matter-of-fact responses to what he sees in the blots may be revealing of unconscious aspects of his personality. The TAT has a similar advantage over the personality inventory, but even in it the characters of the stories are often recognizable to the subject. The Rorschach is the more subtle of these tests.

Although subtle, and felt to be useful by some clinical psychologists, most of the efforts to obtain demonstrations of validity have been damaging to the test's reputation (Cronbach, 1970). A systematic effort to improve the test has been made by Holtzman and others (1961), who have developed

Fig. **18-7 An inkblot test** This inkblot is similar to the standardized blots used in the Rorschach or Holtzman series. The subject is asked to tell what he sees in the blot. He may look at it from any angle he wishes.

many new inkblots, with variations among them based on data from research on Rorschach's original blots. Their test, consisting of forty-five inkblot cards, yields interesting interrelationships with other personality measures, such as the MMPI (Moseley, Duffey, and Sherman, 1963).

Behavioral observation

A dissatisfaction with any partial approach to the measurement of personality has led to a number of studies in which very extensive observations were made of the actual behavior of those being appraised. Subjects under study were assigned special field tasks to perform, such as building a shelter or bridging a stream in a group effort. While under observation for many hours in "naturalistic" settings, their behavior was recorded and analyzed. This kind of observation procedure came to be called *assessment,* a familiar term used in this more specialized sense by the Office of Strategic Services during the Second World War, when such methods were used to select candidates for very important and hazardous missions (OSS Assessment Staff, 1948).

The major studies that have used behavioral

observation are not altogether encouraging in their results. The most successful study was one of candidates for the British civil service, in which there had been a careful job analysis. Among the tasks assigned the candidates during a three-day "house party" were civil service paperwork, committee tasks, and group discussions; the future occupational duties of the candidates were clearly related to these tasks. Correlations with later job performances were in the range from .50 to .65 (Vernon, 1950b).

In summarizing the behavioral-observation procedures that have shown most promise of success in prediction, Cronbach (1970) mentions three:

1. Ratings by peers of the candidate being assessed often appear to be as useful as those of

CRITICAL
DISCUSSION

Improving the
validity of
personality
measures

Personality measures of all kinds (clinical predictions, objective tests, projective tests) have the annoying tendency to yield correlations of about .30 with the criterion behavior. Hence, with samples of sufficient size, *something* significant is being measured, but the predictive significance is quite low and its usefulness in individual cases is slight. This is annoying because the correlations have been high enough to spur investigators on to make some kind of improvement in their measures, but, even after years of effort, little gain has been made. What is worse is that correlations of this size can be found with very simple measures. For example, one of the highest predictive correlations—an $r = .61$ with the likelihood that a patient would be readmitted to a mental hospital after discharge—was found by measuring the thickness of the patient's file in the hospital; the thicker the file, the more likely that the patient would return (Lasky and others, 1959). This simply means, of course, that past behavior is a good predictor of future behavior—a fact long known to credit agencies such as Dun and Bradstreet. Hence tests with low validities, even if correlations are statistically significant, may be adding nothing to self-report or quite simple, direct measures of past behavior.

One possibility, favored by Mischel (1968) and Peterson (1968), is that we are simply on the wrong track: personality is so modifiable in specific situations that our low correlations are merely facts of life, not failures of measurement.

Others believe that we can still improve validity by making better use of available knowledge and making sharper distinctions than are now made. For example, a distinction between a motivational disposition and an aroused motive (see pp. 313–14) becomes

trained psychologists, probably because the peer may know more about the job requirements than the psychologist.

2. Observations made on performance tests very similar to the criterion task about which predic-

tions are being made have considerable validity.

3. The most important criterion for valid assessment is that the assessors have a clear understanding of the psychological requirements of the criterion task.

The status of personality assessment

Our review of personality appraisal, especially the personality inventories, projective tests, and behavioral observations, has indicated that all these methods lead to about the same conclusions: results come out above the chance level, showing that something significant is being measured. When adopted for experimental purposes, any of the methods has some success. But for the purposes of giving an adequate characterization of the individual and predicting his behavior in a real-life situation, none of the methods prove very satisfactory.

The ultimate criterion for evaluating any assessment procedure must be its ability to predict actual

behavior. When this is tried, it is usually found that personality is much less consistent than previously believed. Verbal habits and self-descriptions are indeed persistent, but they often fail to tell us very much about the actual behavior in specific situations. A new emphasis on behavior in specific situations, and the circumstances under which behavior is modified, has led to a rather negative attitude toward personality testing (Mischel, 1968; Peterson, 1968). This attack may have been carried a bit far (see p. 411), but it serves as a warning that new and imaginative approaches will be needed if significant gains are to be made in personality appraisal.

important in personality appraisal. A tendency to become anxious readily, as measured, say, by the Manifest Anxiety Scale, does not mean that the person is anxious now; personality assessments must distinguish between more permanent dispositions and present aroused states (Johnson and Spielberger, 1968).

There is increasing evidence that the *additive assumption* in personality inventories may be faulty. It works reasonably well in an intelligence test to add up the number of correct answers, because the more correct (for items graded in difficulty), the more intelligent the person is. But this concept need not hold for personality measurement; personality is doubtless organized in a more nearly hierarchical pattern, with some items more important for the individual than others.

The additive assumption has been questioned as a result of some efforts to measure personality characteristics predictive of hypnotic susceptibility (J. R. Hilgard, 1970). It was found that subjects who ranked very high on only *one* of several characteristics related to hypnotic susceptibility scored as high on the criterion of hypnosis as those who ranked fairly high on *all* the characteristics. This led to the suggestion of *alternative* predictors, as contrasted with *additive* predictors. The possibility exists that this distinction may hold in the prediction of personality functioning in other areas.

The conventional methods of personality assessment have yielded about all that can be expected of them. While slight gains are being made, they are at such great cost of time and effort that there is little point in going further along this line. Bold new thinking is required, which hopefully a new generation of workers will provide.

Summary

1. Informal appraisal of personality goes on all the time; more *formal appraisal* is necessary when decisions are to be made regarding educational or vocational plans, employment, treatment of the emotionally maladjusted or the criminal offender. Both ethical and technical difficulties arise in such appraisals.

2. Personality can be assessed according to behavior samples of various kinds. The characteristics subject to appraisal in the prediction of behavior include (a) *morphology and physiology,* (b) *intellectual and other abilities,* (c) *motivational dispositions and needs,* (d) *expressive and stylistic traits,* and (e) *interests, values, and social attitudes.*

3. In the transition from informal to formal methods of personality assessment, note is taken of the *interview* as an arranged conversation and of *rating scales* as devices for making judgments more systematic.

4. Objective personality tests, modeled somewhat after intelligence tests, take the form of *personality inventories* containing many items descriptive of the personality. These are constructed according to several strategies, each of which may be illustrated by one or more of the existing inventories.

    a. *Empirical construction,* using the responses from comparison groups in determining the scales, is illustrated by the Minnesota Multiphasic Personality Inventory (MMPI).

    b. *Construction through factor analysis* is illustrated by Cattell's 16 PF Questionnaire, using sixteen categories chosen according to the results of factor analysis.

c. A test *designed according to a theory of personality organization* is represented by the Eysenck Personality Inventory (EPI), which uses two dimensions only: stability-instability and extraversion-introversion.

d. A test using forced choice *to correct for response style* is the Edwards Personal Preference Schedule (EPPS), based on Murray's theory of needs.

When the various strategies of inventory construction are compared, little advantage is found for one strategy over another. The results for each are better than chance, but none is satisfactory for describing an individual personality.

5. Another kind of personality appraisal device is preferred by some to the objective personality inventory. This is the less structured *projective test,* which is intended to reveal deeper, more unconscious aspects of personality. Examples are the story-telling picture test, known as the Thematic Apperception Test (TAT), and the Rorschach Inkblot Test. Like the objective personality test, these tests are found to have limited usefulness, although their ability to predict behavior at better than a chance level indicates they are measuring some relevant personality dimensions.

6. Because in the end personality is inferred from behavior, and because personality measures are used to predict behavior, *direct observation of behavior* under controlled conditions offers promise as a means of assessing personality. Efforts have been made to arrange behavioral settings (house parties, group tasks, simulated office practices) in which skilled observers record their judgments of the participating individuals. The results have been only moderately successful thus far.

Suggestions for further reading

Cronbach, *Essentials of psychological testing* (3rd ed., 1970) has a number of chapters on personality appraisal. Other books devoted to personality appraisal include Mischel, *Personality and assessment* (1968); Semeonoff, *Personality assessment* (1966), a paperbound book that includes readings from the major theorists and test constructors; and Vernon, *Personality assessment: A critical survey* (1964). Holt has prepared a thoughtful discussion of the problems of assessment in his section called "Assessing personality" in Janis (ed.), *Personality: Dynamics, development, and assessment* (1969). A readable short paperback is Cohen, *Personality assessment* (1969).

The MMPI is probably the most carefully researched of the personality inventories. A recent book, which can serve as a guide to this topic, is Butcher, *MMPI: Research development and clinical applications* (1969). Cattell continues to turn out numerous books on his work; the one specifically on the 16 PF Questionnaire is Cattell and Ebel, *Handbook for the Sixteen Personality Factor Questionnaire* (1964). Eysenck is also a prolific writer; the EPI is described in Eysenck and Eysenck, *Eysenck Personality Inventory* (1963). In *The social desirability variable in personality assessment and research* (1957) Edwards states why he designed the EPPS as he did. His more recent test, the Edwards Personality Inventory (unfortunately, a second test with the initials EPI), is based in part upon the EPPS, but does not use the forced-choice technique (*Edwards Personality Inventory Manual,* 1966).

There are numerous review volumes on projective tests. Harrison reviews several hundred investigations using the TAT in Wolman, *Handbook of clinical psychology* (1965). On various projective tests a useful source is Rabin, *Projective techniques in personality assessment* (1968b), which includes material on Holtzman's inkblot technique, an advance over the standard Rorschach.

The extensive use of behavioral observation began with the assessment procedures of the Office of Strategic Services (OSS) during the Second World War, discussed in the book, OSS Assessment Staff, *Assessment of men* (1948). Later adaptations of the method can be found reviewed in the books by Cronbach and by Vernon mentioned above.

CONFLICT, ADJUSTMENT, AND MENTAL HEALTH

conflict and adjustment

NO MATTER HOW RESOURCEFUL WE MAY BE in coping with our problems, the circumstances of life inevitably involve stress. Our motives are not always easily satisfied; there are obstacles to be overcome, choices to be made, and delays to be tolerated. Each of us tends to develop characteristic ways of responding when our attempts to reach a desired goal are blocked. The nature of these response patterns to frustrating situations determines, to a large extent, the adequacy of our adjustment to life.

Types of conflict

In any individual there are always many motives active at a given time, and the goals to which they lead may be mutually exclusive. When two motives conflict, the satisfaction of one leads to the frustration or blocking of the other. Often a student cannot be an outstanding college athlete and still earn the grades needed to enter graduate school. Even when only one motive is involved, there may be various ways of approaching the goal, and conflict arises at the point where the paths to the goal diverge. For example, one can get an education at any one of a number of colleges, but choosing which one to enter presents a conflict situation. Even though the goal will eventually be reached, progress toward it is disrupted by the necessity for making a choice.

One way of viewing conflict situations is to classify them into the following three categories: *approach-approach, avoidance-avoidance,* and *approach-avoidance.* These are defined, respectively, as requiring a choice between two positive incentives, between two negative incentives, or between two aspects of an incentive at once positive and negative. The conflicts of real life often involve more than two alternatives; classifying the conflicts according to two alternatives is convenient but does not, of course, tell the whole story.

Approach-approach conflict

When a person has two or more desirable but mutually exclusive goals, he is temporarily torn between them. Two interesting classes may be scheduled for the same period; two attractive jobs may become available at the same time; a menu may offer a choice among equally attractive entrees. When such acceptable alternatives occur (all positive incentives), the choice is usually made promptly after a brief period of vacillation. Sometimes, however, if the decision is important and the two goals have equally strong appeal, an approach-approach conflict can be a difficult one. This is especially true for children. If a youngster has to make a choice between a racing bicycle and a completely equipped camping tent for his birthday, he may spend a long period in uncomfortable vacillation before making his decision. In this case the conflict has an avoidant as well as an approach component: choosing the bicycle causes anxiety about losing the tent. This more complex situation has been called *double approach-avoidance* conflict.

Avoidance-avoidance conflict

Given a choice between two unattractive alternatives (both incentives negative), there is a strong tendency to escape the dilemma by doing something else. The child who is told to eat his spinach or go right to bed may play with his fork or stare out the window. If he is forced to choose, he takes longer to decide and vacillates more than he would in choosing between two attractive alternatives.

The difference in the choice behavior called forth by approach-approach and avoidance-avoidance conflicts depends upon changes in the attractiveness (or repugnance) of the goal as it is approached. The nearer one gets to a positive incentive, the stronger the approach reactions; the nearer one gets to a negative incentive, the stronger the avoidance reactions. When there are two attractive goal-objects (an approach-approach conflict), starting toward one of them increases the tendency to go toward it, at the same time reducing the tendency to go to the other, so that a return to the state of indecision is unlikely. When there are two unattractive goal-objects (an avoidance-avoidance conflict), starting toward one of them increases the desire to withdraw and tends to force the individual back into indecision and vacillation. The spinach becomes more repugnant when it is on the fork than when it is on the plate, but the thought of bed keeps the child at the table.

Approach-avoidance conflict

Many incentives are at once desirable and undesirable, both positive and negative. Candy is delicious, but also fattening. Going off for a weekend of skiing is fun, but the consequences of lost study time can be anxiety producing. The attitude toward a goal at once wanted and not wanted, liked and disliked, is called an *ambivalent* attitude. Ambivalent attitudes are very common: the child runs away from home to escape parental domination, only to come running back to receive parental protection; his attitude toward his parents is ambivalent. Another child enjoys school but looks forward to vacation. The approach-avoidance conflict is one of the most important for us to understand, for many of the conflicts of ordinary life are of this sort.

A person confronted by a goal-object that is at once attractive and dangerous vacillates in his approach. The dangers seem less real when the

Fig. **19-1 A case of ambivalence** The girl wants both to approach the duck and to back away from it. Such an approach-avoidance conflict results in a great amount of vacillation; the attractiveness of the object keeps the child in the region of conflict, but fear is enhanced as she gets closer.

goal is at a distance, so that the inviting character of the incentive leads to approach reactions. But the sense of danger increases as the goal is approached, so that nearer to the incentive one has a tendency to withdraw (Figure 19-1). This simultaneous tendency "to" and "from" leads to vacillation at some point near enough to the goal for one to be aware of the dangers but distant enough to be safe from them. When a shy adolescent boy is about to call a girl for a date, he is drawn to the telephone by the possibility of success, but his anxiety about possible rebuff mounts as he approaches. As a result he may make several false starts before he either carries through his plan or abandons it.

This type of conflict is illustrated by an experiment in which hungry rats were taught to run the length of an alley to obtain food at a point made distinctive by the presence of a light; this training established approach reactions. Then the rats were given a brief electric shock while eating. The shock added avoidance tendencies to the approach tendencies and hence produced an approach-avoidance conflict, or ambivalence toward the food.

To test the resulting conflict behavior, the rats were placed at the start of the maze. The characteristic behavior corresponded to that predicted: the rat started in the direction of the food but came to a stop before reaching it. The place of stopping could be controlled by modifying the strength of either hunger or shock (Miller, 1959).

The behavior of the rats in this experiment can be better understood by using the concept of *gradients* of approach and avoidance. By a gradient we mean a change in the response strength as a function of the distance from the goal-object. The pull of a magnet upon a piece of iron is an analogous gradient. The pull (or strength of the gradient) increases as the distance between the piece of iron and the magnet is shortened.

Brown (1948) devised a method for determining gradients, as follows. The rats wore a light harness so that the experimenter could restrain them briefly along the route to the food (Figure 19-2). When they were restrained, the amount of pull on the harness could be recorded in grams, thus providing a measure of the approach tendency at that point. When restrained near the goal, the rats pulled harder than when restrained farther from the goal. This increase in pull is shown in Figure 19-3 (left) by the slight rise in the line representing the gradient of approach between the far and the near test.

Other rats received a brief electric shock at the end of the alley. When placed at that end of the alley without shock, they tended to run away from the place where the shock had been received.

Fig. **19-2 Measuring approach and avoidance gradients** The harness permits measurement of the amount of pull exerted by the rat, thereby yielding the results plotted in Figure 19-3.

Dr. Neal E. Miller

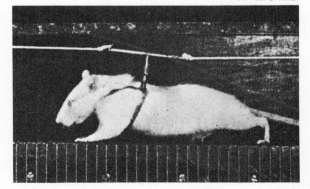

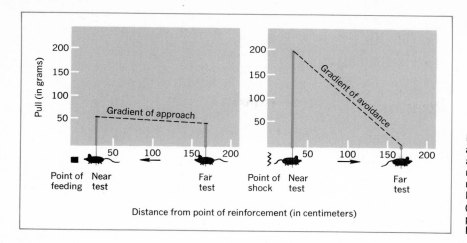

Fig. **19-3 Gradients of approach and avoidance** The strength of approach and avoidance is measured by the pull on the restraining harness on the rat. Note that the avoidance gradient (right) is steeper than the approach gradient (left). (After Brown, 1948)

When restrained nearer to the place of shock, the rats pulled away from the place of shock much harder than when restrained farther away from it. The difference between the test near shock and that far from shock is shown in the gradient of avoidance in Figure 19-3 (right). Note also that the slope of the two lines differs: the line for avoidance is much steeper than the one for approach.

How do the results of this experiment on gradients of approach and avoidance help us understand the results of the experiment on ambivalence? If we examine the two plotted gradients, the one for approach represents a pull on the harness to the left, the one for avoidance represents a pull on the harness to the right. When a rat has been fed and shocked at the same point, both gradients are set up at once. If we imagine the two gradients superimposed, they would cross at a point somewhere between 100 and 150 centimeters from the goal. At this point the two opposing tendencies would exactly balance. If the lines represented the true reaction tendencies, the rat in the experiment on ambivalence would be expected to stop at the point where the lines cross, and this is approximately what happened. This point of intersection can be moved either to the right or to the left by changing the strengths of either the approach or the avoidance tendencies. The effect of increasing the shock is to raise the avoidance gradient, thus placing the point of intersection farther from the place of shock. These predictions were made from

the experiment on gradients and later were confirmed in the experiment on ambivalence.

The two foregoing sets of experiments, taken together, illustrate several principles important in the understanding of ambivalent behavior.

1. The tendency to approach a positive incentive is stronger the nearer the subject is to it.

2. The tendency to go away from a negative incentive is stronger the nearer the subject is to it.

3. The strength of avoidance increases more rapidly with proximity than does that of approach. In other words, the avoidance gradient is steeper than the approach gradient.

4. The strength of the tendency to approach or to avoid varies with the strength of the drive upon which it is based. Increased drive tends to raise the height of the entire gradient of approach or avoidance (Miller, 1959).

For human beings the practical consequences of conflicts of the approach-avoidance type are great. As we shall see in the next chapter, enduring approach-avoidance conflicts form the basis for serious behavior problems. The third principle helps explain how a person is drawn back into an old conflict situation by his own tendencies. He follows the pull, because at a distance the positive aspects seem more inviting than the negative ones seem forbidding. For example, the swimmer who wants to show off as a diver is led by his positive wishes to climb to the high platform. As he climbs, however, he begins to realize that it is a long way to the water. His fears mount, and he may suffer the humiliation of climbing down again. He need not have placed himself in the conflict, but at a distance the desire to dive took precedence over the fear. Such conflicts are characteristic of ambivalence. They are not resolved smoothly: even though the conflict situation is avoidable, the approach tendencies draw the individual back into the zone where the avoidance tendencies begin to mount. Everyone knows of couples who go steady, break up, make up again, only to break up once more. Away from each other, their mutual attraction takes precedence because negative feelings are reduced; close to each other, the negative feelings drive them apart. To an outsider it appears irrational that people who get along so poorly attempt reconciliation. Once the ambivalence of their attitudes is recognized, however, their attempts at reconciliation become understandable, even if not reasonable.

Some complications result from the fact that the gradients of real life are usually multiple. A conflict over the use of alcohol usually involves more than a choice between the amount of liking for the taste of alcohol and the amount of dislike for the after-effects; it can be affected by religious scruples, the desire to forget troubles, loss of self-control, search for companionship, escape from responsibility. Sometimes an approach-avoidance conflict is resolved by refusing to select either alternative or in some way evading the choice.

In our society the approach-avoidance conflicts that are most pervasive and difficult to resolve generally take place in the following areas:

1. *Independence versus dependence.* We may in times of stress want to resort to the dependency that is characteristic of childhood, to have someone take care of us and solve our problems for us. But we are taught that the ability to stand on our own two feet and assume responsibilities is a mark of maturity.

2. *Cooperation versus competition.* In American life much emphasis is placed on competition and success. Competition begins in early childhood among siblings, continues through school and college, and culminates in business and professional rivalry. At the same time we are urged to cooperate and help our fellow men. The concept of "team spirit" is as American as the success story. Such contradictory expectations constitute potential conflict.

3. *Impulse expression versus moral standards.* All societies have to place some degree of regulation upon impulse control. We noted in Chapter 3 that much of childhood learning involves imposing cultural restrictions upon innate impulses. Sex and aggression are two areas in which our impulses most frequently conflict with moral standards, and violation of these standards may generate strong feelings of guilt.

These three areas constitute the greatest potential for serious conflict. As we shall see in the next chapter, failure to find a workable compromise may lead to severe psychological problems.

Frustration

A continuing or unresolved motivational conflict is a source of frustration. We have used the term *frustration* several times in our discussion thus far but have not provided a definition. Because the word has developed several different connotations in everyday speech, it is important that we clarify its meaning before going on to consider its consequences.

Whenever a person's progress toward a desired goal is blocked, delayed, or otherwise interferred with, we say he encounters frustration. The word "frustration" has sometimes been used to refer to an emotional state instead of to an event. That is, as a consequence of blocked goal-seeking a person becomes confused, baffled, and annoyed; if we were to ask him how he feels he would probably say he felt angry and frustrated. He is thus equating frustration with an unpleasant emotional state.

In this book, however, we shall hold to the meaning of frustration as the *thwarting circumstances,* rather than their consequences.

The various types of conflict provide a major source of human frustration. But there are other barriers to the satisfaction of drives. The physical environment presents such obstacles as icy weather, rugged mountains, and arid deserts. The social environment presents obstacles through the restrictions imposed by other people and the customs of social living. Offspring are thwarted by parental denials, disapprovals, and postponements: Larry must share his tricycle with his sister; John's father will not let him have the car for a date; and Jane's parents insist that she is not old enough to live in an apartment away from home. The list is endless.

Deficiencies in the environment prevent need-satisfaction quite as effectively as obstacles. A drought can be as frustrating to a farmer as a flood. Many of the deficiencies found to be frustrating are those within the individual himself. Some people are handicapped by blindness, deafness, or paralysis. Not everyone who wants to can become a distinguished painter or can pass the examination necessary to become a physician or lawyer. If someone sets his goals beyond his ability, then frustration because of his own deficiencies will be the inevitable result.

Immediate consequences of frustration

Frustration—whether it is the result of obstacles, deficiencies, or conflict—has both immediate and remote consequences. When blocked in his goal-seeking, the individual may react immediately or he may develop attitudes toward uncertainty or risk-taking that have more enduring consequences. We shall turn first to a consideration of some of the immediate consequences of frustration. These consequences might equally well be called *symptoms* or *signs* of frustration.

A classic experiment on the effects of frustration in young children illustrates several of its immediate consequences (Barker, Dembo, and Lewin, 1941). The subjects were children of nursery school and kindergarten age. The experiment will be described in the present tense, as though we were observing it.

The children come one at a time into a room that contains several toys, parts of which are missing—a chair without a table, an ironing board with no iron, a telephone receiver without a transmitter, a boat and other water toys but no water. There are also papers and crayons. Most of the children set about playing eagerly and happily. They make up for the missing parts imaginatively. They use paper as water on which to sail a boat, or they use their fist for a telephone transmitter.

On the second day of observation we see a group of children who behave quite differently. Although they appear to be in the same general physical condition as the first group and their clothes show that they come from similar social and economic backgrounds, they seem unable to play constructively, unable to fit the toys into meaningful and satisfying activities. They play roughly with the toys, occasionally jumping on one and breaking it. If they draw with the crayons, they scribble like younger children. They whine and nag at the adult who is present. One of them lies on the floor, stares at the ceiling, and recites nursery rhymes, paying no attention to anyone else.

What accounts for the differences in behavior of these two sets of youngsters? Is the second group suffering from some sort of emotional disturbance? Have some of these children been mistreated at home? Actually, the children in this second group are the same as those in the first group; they are simply in a later stage of the experiment. They are showing the symptoms of frustration, which has been deliberately created in the following way.

After playing happily with the half-toys, as described earlier, the children were given an added experience. An opaque screen was removed, allowing them to see that they were in a larger room containing not only the half-toys but other toys that were much more elaborate and attractive. This part of the room contained a table for the chair, a dial and bell for the telephone, a pond of real water for the boat. When we see the unhappy children in the later stage of the experiment, they are separated by a wire screen from the more desirable toys. They are denied the "whole" toys and can use only the "part" ones. They are frustrated.

Why was the half-toy situation satisfying the first time and frustrating the second? The answer is easy to find. Goal-seeking behavior was satisfied the first time, as the children played happily with the available toys; in the second stage they knew of the existence of the more attractive and satisfying toys, and so a new goal had been set up. The first day the goal was attainable; the second day it was not. To play now with the half-toys is to be stopped short of a richer experience, and hence is frustrating.

This experiment illustrates a number of the immediate consequences of frustration. In discussing some of these consequences, we shall refer to additional details of the experiment and draw illustrations from related experiments and from the frustrating experiences of everyday life.

Restlessness and tension

In the toy experiment one of the first evidences of frustration shown by the children was an excess of movement: fidgeting about and generally restless behavior. This restlessness was associated with many actions indicating unhappiness: whimpering, sighing, complaining. Unhappy actions were recorded for less than 20 percent of the children in the free-play situation but for over 80 percent in the frustrating situation.

An increase in tension and in the level of excitement also occurs when adults are blocked and thwarted. They blush or tremble or clench their fists. Children under tension fall back upon thumb-sucking and nail-biting; adults also turn to nail-biting, as well as to smoking and gum-chewing, as outlets for their restlessness and tensions.

Aggression and destructiveness

Closely related to increased tension and restless movements are the rage states that lead to destructiveness and hostile attacks. In the toy experiment, kicking, knocking, breaking, and destroying were greatly increased following frustration. Only a few children did any kicking or knocking in the original free-play situation, but the majority did so in frustration.

Direct aggression. Frustration often leads to aggression against the individual or object that is the source of the frustration. In ordinary play situations, when one small child takes a toy from another child, the second is likely to attack the first in an attempt to regain the toy. For many adults the aggression may be verbal rather than physical: the victim of a slighting remark usually replies in kind. The anger engendered when one is blocked tends to find expression in some kind of direct attack.

Because the obstacle or barrier was the source of the blocking in the toy experiment, the children's first attempt at problem-solving was to get by the barrier or remove it. Aggression of this kind need not be hostile; it may be a learned way of solving a problem. When the obstacle is another person, the first tendency is to attack that person, treating him as a barrier. But this may not be the only form of aggression in response to frustration.

Displaced aggression. Frequently the frustrated individual cannot satisfactorily express his aggression against the source of the frustration. Sometimes the source is vague and intangible. Then he does not know what to attack, yet he feels angry and seeks *something* to attack. At other times the person responsible for the frustration is so powerful that to attack him would be dangerous. When circumstances block direct attack on the cause of frustration, aggression may be "displaced." Displaced aggression is an aggressive action against an innocent person or object rather than against the actual cause of the frustration. The man who is bawled out by his supervisor may come home and take out his unexpressed resentment on his wife or children. The tongue-lashing Bill gives his roommate may be related to the poor grade Bill received on the midterm quiz. The child who is not getting along well with his playmates may pull the tail of his cat.

The practice of "scapegoating" is an example of displaced aggression. An innocent victim is blamed for one's troubles and becomes the object of aggression. Prejudice against minority groups has a large element of displaced aggression, or scapegoating. The fact that for the period from 1882 to 1930 the price of cotton in certain regions of the South was negatively correlated with the number of lynchings in the same regions (the lower the price of cotton, the higher the number of lynchings) suggests that the mechanism of dis-

CRITICAL
DISCUSSION

Physiological basis of aggression

Aggression is frequently the result of frustrating circumstances, but an explanation of aggression based solely on environmental influences is incomplete. Recent research indicates the importance of internal factors in the instigation of aggression. Rage and attack responses can be elicited in normally peaceful animals by mild electrical stimulation of a specific region of the hypothalamus. When a cat's hypothalamus is stimulated via implanted electrodes, the animal hisses, its hair bristles, its pupils dilate, and it will strike out at a rat or other objects placed in its cage. Even more startling is evidence indicating that an innate "killing response" can be elicited in some animals by stimulation of a slightly different region of the hypothalamus. When this region is stimulated in a cat, the animal does not respond with the above rage pattern but instead will coldly stalk a rat and kill it.

Killing in many animals is an expression of a highly specific pattern of behavior. When a wild rat encounters a mouse, the rat will pounce on its back and kill it with a hard bite through the neck that severs the spinal cord. Many laboratory-bred rats appear to have no such instinct; they will live peacefully in the same cage with mice without harming them. But electrical stimulation of a specific region of the lateral hypothalamus will cause a rat that has never killed or witnessed killing by other rats to pounce upon its mouse cage-mate and kill it with the same response pattern exhibited by wild rats. It is as if the stimulation triggered an innate killing response that had until this time remained dormant. Recent experiments point to specific neurochemicals that mediate this response. When *carbachol* (a drug known to facilitate nerve conduction) is injected by means of tiny tubes into the lateral hypothalamus, rats that have never killed before will pounce upon a mouse and kill it. Other substances such as salt solution or amphetamine have no such effect; carbachol introduced into other regions of the hypothalamus is similarly ineffective (Smith, King, and Hoebel, 1970).

Hypothesizing that a reaction elicited chemically could also be restrained by chemical means, the investigators repeated the experiment with rats known to be killers, rats that normally killed a mouse within two minutes after it was introduced into the cage. This time the drug used was one known to inhibit nerve conduction, and it was injected into the same area of the hypothalamus. More than 80 percent of the rats so treated showed no killing response for up to an hour; they would approach and sniff at the mouse but made no attempt to attack or kill it. After the drug wore off, these animals reverted to their killing behavior.

This research is intriguing but leaves many questions unanswered. We do not know why some laboratory rats are born pacifists, while most of their kin are born killers, nor how killing behavior relates to other forms of aggression. Investigators are now concerned with discovering how other parts of the brain are connected with the killing center in the hypothalamus. Of even greater interest is the possibility that eventually aggressive behavior in man may be controlled by chemical means.

Dr. N. E. Miller

Fig. **19-4 Displaced aggression** When the rat that has been the object of aggression is not present, the attacking rat displaces its aggression toward the doll (Miller, 1948b).

placed aggression may have been involved. The greater the economic frustration, the greater the likelihood that aggression would be displaced against the blacks, a group serving as a scapegoat, since they were not responsible for the price of cotton.

Displaced aggression can be demonstrated experimentally. One rat can be taught to strike another by being rewarded for such aggression. When it strikes the other rat, the electric current that has been building up in the grid on which it stands is turned off, and the attacking rat escapes the shock. When another rat is no longer present, the trained rat directs its aggressive behavior toward the "innocent bystander," a rubber doll that the rat had previously ignored (Figure 19-4). Thus aggression is transferred from an inaccessible to an accessible object (Miller, 1948b).

Apathy

One of the factors complicating the study of human behavior is the tendency for different individuals to respond to similar situations in a variety of ways. Thus, although a common response to frustration is active aggression, another response is its opposite—apathy, indifference, withdrawal (in the toy experiment, the child who lay on the floor staring at the ceiling). We do not know why one person reacts with aggression and another with apathy to the same frustrating situation, but it seems likely that learning is an important factor; reactions to frustration can be learned in much the

same manner as other habits. The child who strikes out angrily when frustrated and finds that his need is then satisfied (either through his own efforts or because a parent rushes to placate him) will probably resort to the same behavior the next time his motives are thwarted. The child whose aggressive outbursts are never successful, who finds he has no power to satisfy his needs by means of his own behavior, may well resort to apathy and withdrawal when confronted with a frustrating situation.

When resistance is futile, the frustrated person may become sullen and detached instead of angry and defiant. Studies of inmates in concentration or prisoner-of-war camps indicate that apathy may be the "normal" reaction to extremely frustrating situations of long duration from which there is no hope of escape. Bettelheim (1943) has described the behavior of prisoners exposed to the incredibly inhuman conditions of the Nazi concentration camps at Dachau and Buchenwald. He observed that many of the prisoners developed an attitude of detachment and extreme indifference in the face of continual deprivation, torture, and threats of death. Reports by American servicemen who were confined in Korean prisoner-of-war camps indicate a similar phenomenon. A large number of these men were interviewed and given psychological tests immediately following their repatriation. Almost all of them at some time during their imprisonment experienced a reaction characterized by listlessness, indifference to the immediate situation, lack of emotional expression, and complete absorption within themselves. Since these men could respond appropriately and rationally when spoken to and since the content of their speech and their behavior did not suggest depression or psychosis, the reaction seems best described as apathy. The most severe of such "apathy reactions" frequently resulted in death. Two remedies seemed capable of saving the man close to death; getting him on his feet and doing something, no matter how trivial, and getting him interested in some current or future problem. It was usually the efforts and support of a friend that helped the individual to snap out of a state of apathy (Strassman, Thaler, and Schein, 1956).

Fantasy

When problems become too much for us, we sometimes seek the "solution" of escape into a dream world, a solution through *fantasy* rather than on a realistic level. This was the solution of the child who lay on the floor reciting nursery rhymes in the toy experiment and of other children in the experiment who in imagination crossed the barrier by talking about the whole toys on the other side. One girl fished through the wire, imagining the floor on the other side to be the pond that was actually out of reach.

Unrealistic solutions are not limited to children. The pin-up girls in the soldiers' barracks symbolize a fantasy life that goes on when normal social life with women is frustrated. Experiments have also shown that men on a starvation diet lose their interest in women and instead hang on their walls pictures of prepared food cut from magazines (Guetzkow and Bowman, 1946).

As we shall see in the next chapter, severe and continuous frustration may produce such complete escape into fantasy that the individual loses his ability to distinguish between his fantasy world and the real one.

Stereotypy

Another consequence of frustration is *stereotypy* in behavior, that is, a tendency to exhibit blind, repetitive, fixated behavior. Ordinary problem-solving requires flexibility, striking out in new directions when the original path to the goal is blocked. When repeated frustration baffles a person, some of his flexibility appears to be lost, and he stupidly makes the same effort again and again, though experience has shown its futility.

For example, a white rat can be taught to jump to one of a pair of stimulus cards attached to windows, by so arranging the cards that the rat finds food behind the positive card but is punished if it jumps to the negative card. The positive card may be one with a black circle on a white background, the negative one a white circle on a black background. The cards are so arranged that the rat knocks over the positive card when it hits it, thus opening the window that gives access to a platform where there is a food reward. If the rat jumps against the negative card, the card does not give way. Instead, the rat bumps against the card and falls into a net. By varying the positions of the cards, the experimenter can teach the rat to select the positive one and to jump consistently to it.

This discrimination experiment is converted into a frustration experiment by making the problem insoluble. That is, each of the two cards leads half the time to reward (positive reinforcement) and half the time to punishment (negative reinforcement), regardless of its position on the left or the right. Hence, whatever choice the animal makes is "correct" only half the time. The result is that the rat, forced to jump, tends to form a stereotyped habit of jumping regularly to one side, either to the right or to the left, no longer paying attention to which card is exposed. The rat is still rewarded half the time and punished half the time after having adopted this stereotyped habit.

Once the stereotyped habit has been adopted, it is very resistant to change, so much so that it has been called an "abnormal fixation." For example, if the rat that has come to jump regularly to the right is now punished on every jump, it may continue to jump to the right for as many as 200 trials, even though the left window remains open as an easy and safe alternative (Figure 19-5). The behavior is so stereotyped that psychologically the alternative no longer exists for the rat (Maier, 1949).

More recent experiments have shown that stere-

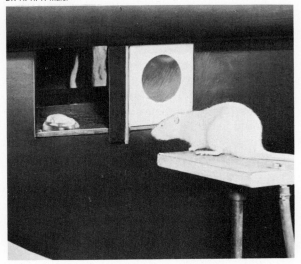

Fig. **19-5 Stereotypy** Shown here is the apparatus used in Maier's experiment on stereotypy. Top: The left window is open, the food exposed, and the frustrated rat seems to pay attention to it. Bottom: The rat's jump remains fixated; that is, despite the open window the rat continues to jump to the right and to bump its nose and fall into the net below.

otyped behavior occurs in the presence of conflict even though the problem is soluble. Two groups of rats were trained to press one of two identical levers to obtain a food reward. The correct response was always rewarded by food, but the con-

sequences of an incorrect response varied. The rats in one group received punishment, a mild electric shock every time they pressed the wrong lever; they may be called the "food versus shock" group. The second group received *both* food and shock for an incorrect response ("food versus food-and-shock" group). The groups performed equally well on this learning task. On the next day the problem was reversed so that the initially correct bar became incorrect and vice versa. This reversal procedure continued for twenty-five days; each day consisted of ten warm-up trials on the bar that had been correct on the previous day followed by fifty reversal trials. The food versus shock group quickly learned to reverse their choice from day to day; in fact the speed with which they accomplished the reversal improved as the experiment continued. The food versus food-and-shock group did not reverse their choice at all; they fixated on one lever and continued to choose it regardless of whether it was the correct bar on a particular day. In the presence of conflict (receiving both food and shock for an incorrect response) the animals tended to fixate on a single response whether or not it led to shock (Karsh, 1970).

The fact that these animals did learn to avoid the punished bar during the initial learning task indicates that the shock was aversive enough to be avoided. Moreover, animals that never received shock but were rewarded with food regardless of which bar they pressed did not develop the degree of fixation shown by the conflict group. These animals continued to choose both levers (see Figure 19-6).

Further studies must be made before we know just what analogies are permissible between human behavior and these experimental results. It is quite possible that some forms of persistent behavior, such as thumb-sucking in young children or stuttering, have become fixated because punishment and repeated frustration in efforts to get rid of them have intensified the undesirable responses. The persistence of difficulties in arithmetic and reading among bright children may be explained in part as a consequence of errors similarly stereotyped by early frustration.

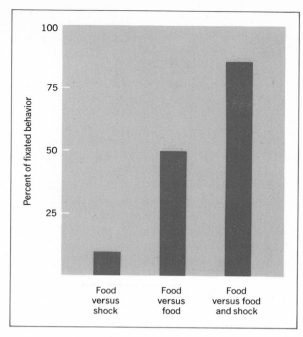

Fig. 19-6 Fixated responses to conflict Rats that received food for pressing the correct bar and both food and shock for pressing the incorrect bar (food versus food-and-shock group) showed a high degree of fixated behavior when the position of the correct bar was reversed from day to day; that is, they continued to press the same bar day after day, regardless of whether it was correct or incorrect. Rats that received food for a correct response and shock alone for an incorrect response (food versus shock group) exhibited virtually no stereotyped behavior. A control group that received food alone for whichever response they made (food versus food) showed an intermediate degree of fixated responding (Karsh, 1970).

Regression

Regression is defined as a return to more primitive modes of behavior, that is, to modes of behavior characterizing a younger age. There are two interpretations of regression. One is that in the midst of insecurity the individual attempts to return to a period of past security. The older child seeks the love and affection bestowed upon him in childhood by behaving again as he did when younger: crying, seeking parental caresses, and so on. This type of regression is called *retrogressive behavior,* a return to behavior once engaged in.

The second interpretation of regression is that the childish behavior following frustration is simply a more primitive kind of behavior, not actually a return to earlier behavior. This kind of regression, in contrast to retrogression, is called *primitivation.* Thus the adult accustomed to the restraints of civilized behavior may become so upset by frustration as to lose control and start a fistfight, even though he did no fistfighting as a child.

Both forms of regression may, of course, occur together. In the toy experiment discussed earlier, regression was shown through decrease in the constructiveness of play. We consider that this decreased constructiveness is a form of primitivation rather than retrogression, because we do not ask whether the child returns to a mode of play characteristic of *him* at an earlier age. Without careful case studies we have no way of being sure, however, that the behavior was not in fact retrogressive. It is a safe conjecture that it was in some instances. By means of a rating scale, each child's play in both the free and the frustrating situation was appraised as to its degree of constructiveness, that is (1) according to its likeness to the well-thought-out and systematic play of older children, or (2) according to its similarity to the fragmentary play of younger children. As a consequence of frustration the play tended to deteriorate. Drawing became scribbling; instead of pretending to iron clothes on the ironing board, children would knock the board down. In this experiment the total loss in maturity shown amounted to 17.3 months of mental age; that is, the play of these children became like that of children about a year and a half younger.

The immediate consequences of frustration—the evidence that a person has been thwarted—are themselves ways of fighting the frustration. They are not merely signs of trouble but are also attempts at solution. If the solution is successful, the obstacles are overcome, the needs met, the conflicts resolved, and the frustrating episode is ended. However, some personal problems endure for a long time. They have continuing histories, and ways of dealing with them become habitual. These ways become so typical of the person that they help reveal what he is like. When we say that a person is aggressive or retiring, that he stands up for his rights, that he lets himself get pushed around, that he lives in a dream world, that he has a suspicious nature, we are talking about ways in which he habitually meets frustration.

Defense mechanisms

The immediate reactions to frustration (restlessness, destructiveness, apathy, fantasy, stereotypy, regression) illustrate general techniques that children adopt in order to solve their problems. These attempts at solution may become habitual; even in children as young as nursery school age individual differences in ways of coping with problems may be observed. In adults these habitual ways of meeting repeated or continuing conflict and frustration are highly individual and complex, but a few modes of adjustment occur so frequently that they have been sorted out and given names. They are called *defense mechanisms* because they protect the individual's self-esteem and defend him against excessive anxiety when faced with continuing frustrations.

When the fox in Aesop's fable rejected the grapes that he could not reach "because they were sour," he illustrated a defense mechanism known as rationalization. He escaped acknowledging his inability to reach the grapes by asserting that he did not really want them. In the following discussion we shall consider a number of other mechanisms, such as projection, in which we falsely attribute to others the undesirable traits that we possess, and repression, in which we conveniently forget what might otherwise be troublesome. Because nearly all these mechanisms distort reality in one way or another, we may well consider what purposes they serve.

The purposes of defense mechanisms are twofold: they seek *to maintain or enhance self-esteem,* and they seek *to escape or defend against anxiety.* The goal of seeing ourselves as commendable, admirable, and strong makes us enhance our self-respect as best we can, partly by denying any memory, impulse, or action that might be interpreted as self-belittling or self-degrading and partly by taking credit for whatever appears fine and noble in our behavior. The goal of reducing anxiety is a closely related one, for a good deal of anxiety has to do with security or status. In any case, a state of anxiety is unpleasant; we seek to avoid such states and to reduce them if they arise.

All defense mechanisms have in common the quality of *self-deception,* which may be evident in two chief forms—*denial* and *disguise.*

The clearest evidence for *denial* of impulses, memories, or actions that might cause us anxiety comes through *amnesia,* a state in which memory is temporarily lost. As noted earlier (p. 235), the observation that such memories may be recovered supports the interpretation that they are not "lost" but merely hidden by repressive mechanisms. The fact that the lost memories tend to be personal supports the interpretation that the repression in amnesia is often motivated by anxiety or guilt.

Disguise is the second form of self-deception. Whenever impulses are falsified, as in rationalization, or whenever traits are inappropriately assigned, as in projection, the person's true motives are being masked. We shall consider other disguises in the mechanisms known as reaction-formation and substitution.

Three precautions should be kept in mind during the discussion of individual defense mechanisms.

1. Defense mechanisms are psychological constructs inferred from observations of the way people behave. They are useful ways of summarizing what we think is going on when we observe behavior. But although some of the mechanisms are supported by experimental evidence, others have little scientific verification.

2. Labeling a person's behavior (for example, as displaced aggression, rationalization, or substi-

tution) may provide useful descriptive information, but it is not an explanation of the behavior. A full explanation requires understanding the needs that cause the person to rely on defense mechanisms in dealing with his problems.

3. All the mechanisms are to be found in the everyday behavior of normal people. Used in moderation, they increase satisfaction in living and are therefore helpful modes of adjustment. It is only when the mechanisms become the dominant modes of problem-solving that they indicate personality maladjustment.

Rationalization

Each of us wishes to act reasonably and on the basis of acceptable motives. If we act impulsively, or for motives that we do not wish to acknowledge even to ourselves, we often interpret what we have done in such a way that we seem to have behaved rationally. Assigning logical reasons or plausible excuses for what we do impulsively is known as *rationalization*. Rationalization does not mean "to act rationally"; it means to so justify conduct according to personally desirable motives that we *seem* to have acted rationally.

In the search for the "good" reason rather than the "true" reason for what we do, a number of excuses can be put forth. These excuses are usually plausible, and the circumstances they justify may be true ones; they simply do not tell the whole story. A few illustrations may serve to show how common rationalization is.

1. Liking or disliking as an excuse: The girl who was not invited to the dance said she would not have gone if asked because she did not like some of the people involved.

2. Blaming other people and circumstances as an excuse: "Mother failed to wake me." "My tools were dull." (Note that in true rationalization as distinguished from deliberate falsifying, the actual situation would be that the mother *had* failed to do the waking or that the tools *had* been dull. But the mother may have expected her child to set the alarm clock as usual, and sharpening the tools may have been the responsibility of the user.)

3. Necessity as an excuse: "I bought this new model because the old car would have had a lot of expensive repairs coming up before next summer."

While the foregoing examples show the person fooling himself instead of others, the excuses are of the sort that a person might consciously use to put himself in a favorable light with others. We therefore need a more convincing illustration to show us that rationalization may be used when the person is completely unenlightened about the reason for his conduct—when, in other words, rationalization is unconsciously motivated. Such an illustration is provided by the results of experiments on posthypnotic suggestion.

A subject under hypnosis is told that when he wakes from the trance he will watch the pocket of the hypnotist. When the hypnotist removes a handkerchief from the pocket, the subject will raise the window. The subject is told that he will not remember the hypnotist's telling him to do this. Aroused from the trance, the subject feels a little drowsy, but presently circulates among the people in the room and carries on a normal conversation, all the while furtively watching the hypnotist's pocket. When the hypnotist in a casual manner removes his handkerchief, the subject feels an impulse to open the window; he takes a step in that direction, but hesitates. Unconsciously he mobilizes his wishes to be a reasonable person; so, seeking for a reason for his impulse to open the window, he says, "Isn't it a little stuffy in here?" Having found the needed excuse, he opens the window and feels more comfortable (Hilgard, 1965).

Projection

All of us have undesirable traits or qualities that we do not acknowledge even to ourselves. One unconscious mechanism that protects us from acknowledging them is called *projection*. In projection we protect ourselves from recognizing our own undesirable qualities by assigning them in exaggerated amount to other people; our own tendencies are thereby justified. We remove the stigma from our bad qualities by minimizing them in ourselves and by exaggerating them in others. Suppose you have a tendency to be critical of or unkind to other people, but would dislike yourself if you recognized this tendency. If you are convinced that those around you are cruel or unkind, then any harsh treatment you give them is not based upon *your* bad qualities. You are simply giving them what they deserve. If you can assure yourself that everybody else cheats in college examinations, your unacknowledged tendency to take some academic shortcuts is not so bad. Projection is really a form of rationalization, but the tendency to projection is so pervasive in our culture that it merits discussion in its own right.

Two experiments highlight the pervasiveness of projection. The first deals with a group of university students, all members of fraternities. The members of each fraternity were asked to rate the other members on four undesirable traits: stinginess, obstinacy, disorderliness, and bashfulness. The first three of these are strongly disapproved-of traits, while the fourth is mildly disapproved of. Each student also was asked to rate himself on each of these traits.

Some members obviously possessed one or another of the traits to a high degree. Among these, some, as shown by their self-ratings, were aware of their traits; others were unaware of them. Those students who possessed an undesirable trait to a high degree and yet were unaware of possessing it tended to assign this trait to others to a greater extent than did the rest of the students. The correlations on which these interpretations are based were all low, but they were consistently in the direction that would be expected if they were interpreted as indicating a projection mechanism (Sears, 1936).

The second experiment in projection used as subjects graduate students with whom the judges in the experiment were well acquainted. The most striking finding of this study was a tendency on the part of the students to go so far in self-ratings as to convert bad traits to their opposites. The person who said of himself that he was "sincere under all conditions" was rated by the judges as lacking in sincerity. This subject, of course, found

others full of sham and insincerity as compared with himself (Frenkel-Brunswik, 1939).

Reaction-formation

A person can often conceal a motive from himself by giving strong expression to its opposite. We have seen this tendency, called *reaction-formation*, in the foregoing experiment on projection, in which some self-appraisals were completely the reverse of fact. The mother of an unwanted child may feel guilty about not welcoming her child, and so become overindulgent and overprotective of the child in order to assure the child of her love and also, perhaps, to assure herself that she is a good mother.

One mother who wished to do everything for her daughter could not understand why the child was so unappreciative. At great sacrifice she had the daughter take expensive piano lessons. She sat beside the little girl to assist her in the daily practice sessions. While she thought she was being extremely kind to her child, she was actually demanding and, in fact, hostile. She was unaware of her own hostility, but, when confronted with it, she admitted that as a child she had hated piano lessons. Under the conscious guise of being kind, she was unconsciously being cruel to her daughter. The daughter, vaguely sensing what was going on, developed the symptoms that brought her to a child-guidance clinic.

There is always the possibility that reaction-formation is active among those who engage in "anti" activities, such as censoring pornographic literature or preventing cruelty to animals. The censoring individual may actually be fascinated by such literature. He wages a campaign against it in order to fight its fascination for him and to convince others of his "purity." Among the ardent antivivisectionists there undoubtedly are some who fear their own tendency toward cruelty so deeply that they become sentimental about protecting animals from the implied cruelty of others.

The existence of reaction-formation in some people does not mean that motives can never be taken at their face values. Not all reformers are moved to action by veiled or hidden impulses. Real abuses need to be corrected: if a polluted water supply is spreading disease, rational men seek to get rid of the source of trouble. It would be foolhardy to say that those who take responsibility for correcting such an abuse are illustrating reaction-formation against their own unconscious desires to poison someone.

Dissociation

In the normal course of events, actions, feelings, and thoughts belong together. If you realize that someone is hurting you, you feel angry and strike back; your thought, your anger, and your muscular actions are all part of one harmonious whole. But such a unity of thinking, feeling, and doing is easily disrupted by the conflicts that early training produces. Then *dissociation,* or a splitting of the total activity, occurs. Although dissociation takes many forms, we shall consider here only two of its manifestations: *compulsive movements* and *excessive theorizing.*

Compulsive movements, actions that the person feels compelled to repeat over and over again, show the splitting off of movement from the feelings appropriate to it. For some people such compulsive movements are very important: one person avoids the lines on the sidewalk, another touches the telephone poles as he walks by them, a third counts things. Folklore gives us a hint of what sort of impulse may be dissociated: "Step on a crack and you'll break your mother's back." Why, then, avoid cracks? When you avoid cracks, you avoid the impulse to injure someone. Your self-esteem is maintained because, through dissociation, your hostile impulses or fears are concealed (Figure 19-7).

Compulsive routines are carried out quite automatically and usually with little emotion, thus belying the depth of feeling that motivates them. But the compulsive person may display excessive emotion when, for any reason, his ritualized behavior is interrupted. He thus shows, indirectly, that the behavior is actually strongly motivated. Why is the behavior strongly motivated? In the first place, the ritualistic activity stands for some-

LINES AND SQUARES

Whenever I walk in a London street,
I'm ever so careful to watch my feet;
*   And I keep in the squares,*
*   And the masses of bears,*
Who wait at the corners all ready to eat
The sillies who tread on the lines of the street,
*   Go back to their lairs,*
*   And I say to them, "Bears,*
*   Just look how I'm walking*
*   in all of the squares!"*

Fig. **19-7 Compulsive behavior as a defense** Compulsive behavior in both children and adults reduces anxiety by a magical, ritualistic protection against a worry or fear. The true basis for the anxiety is often unacknowledged, as indeed it is in the Milne poem. The child's fears are not really "the bears who wait at the corners." (From *When we were very young,* by A. A. Milne)

thing else, not recognized by the person himself. A twitching arm may substitute for the act of hitting in anger; blinking eyes may symbolize a wish to look at some forbidden scene, and at the same time express a conflict about looking; avoiding cracks may symbolize avoiding temptation. In the second place, carrying out the ritual, without emotion, unconsciously assures the person that the dangerous or forbidden act for which the movement stands will not be carried out, and possible guilt is successfully warded off. We will see this defense mechanism carried to the extreme when we discuss obsessive-compulsive neurosis in the next chapter.

Excessive theorizing is another form of dissociation, in which talking or thinking about something becomes a substitute for action, and the person thereby avoids the feelings of self-depreciation that might otherwise result from the incapacity for action. A young psychologist, for example, found participation in group discussion very difficult. He then became interested in the theory of group discussion, took a notebook along to record what people did in discussion groups, and so protected himself from feeling inadequate as a group member. Adolescents, alarmed by the emotions accompanying newly intensified sexual impulses, sometimes go through a period when they scorn all emotions and try to make everything as impersonal, abstract, and theoretical as possible.

Repression

We are now prepared to see how each defense mechanism is a method of protecting a person from full awareness of impulses that he (perhaps unconsciously) would prefer to deny. If the impulse is denied entirely, the mechanism of *repression* is illustrated.

Repression must be distinguished from suppression. The process of suppression is one of deliberate self-control—keeping impulses, tendencies, or wishes in check and perhaps holding them privately while denying them publicly. In such an instance, the person is aware of a suppressed impulse. In the mechanism of repression, the person himself is unaware of whatever it is that is repressed.

Repression, if completely successful, results in a total forgetting—a total absence of awareness of the personally unacceptable motive and a total absence of behavior resulting from such a motive. Usually, however, repression is not completely successful, and impulses find indirect expression.

Many of the defense mechanisms already discussed serve repression, as they protect the individual from awareness of his partially repressed impulses.

Cases of *amnesia* illustrate some aspects of repression. In one case, a man was found wandering the streets, not knowing his name or where he had come from. Study by means of hypnosis and other techniques made it possible to reconstruct his history and to restore most of his memory. Following domestic difficulties he had gone on a drunken spree completely out of keeping with his earlier social behavior, and he had subsequently suffered deep remorse. His amnesia was motivated, first of all, by the desire to exclude from memory the embarrassing experiences that had occurred during his spree. He succeeded in forgetting all the events associated with the spree that might remind him of it. In this way amnesia spread, and he completely lost his sense of personal identity. When his memories returned, he could recall events before the drinking episode as well as subsequent happenings, but the deeper repression of the period of which he was most ashamed successfully protected him from recalling its disagreeable events.

As we saw earlier (Chapter 9, p. 236), experimental studies of memory have demonstrated some of the typical characteristics of repression. These studies, taken in conjunction with clinical observations of the sort described above, have contributed to our knowledge of the dynamics of motivated forgetting.

Substitution

The last defense mechanism to be considered is the one that best succeeds in fulfilling its function, that is, solving a person's problems and reducing his tensions without exposing to him (or to others) motives or tendencies of which he or his culture disapproves. This is the mechanism of *substitution,* whereby approved goals are substituted for unapproved ones, and activities that have possibilities of success are entered upon instead of activities that are doomed to failure. Substitution can be divided into two forms: *sublimation* and *com-*

pensation. Both are incompletely understood, but the behavior patterns to which they refer are familiar and important.

Sublimation is the process whereby socially unacceptable motives find expression in socially acceptable form. The desire for sexual gratification, if frustrated, may be sublimated in the writing of poetry or in painting. Hostile impulses may find socially acceptable expression in the development of boxing or wrestling skills. It seems unlikely that sublimation actually eliminates the frustrated impulses, but substitute activities do help to reduce tension whenever a basic drive is thwarted. For example, the activities of mothering, being mothered, or seeking companionship may help reduce the tension associated with unsatisfied sexual needs.

Compensation is a strenuous effort to make up for failure or weakness in one activity through excelling in either a different or an allied activity. The boy who fails at sports may compensate for the failure by excessive study in order to gain recognition in the classroom. Here, a completely different activity substitutes for the athletic ineffectiveness.

A special form of compensation, known as *overcompensation,* comes from an attempt to deny a weakness by trying to excel where one is weakest. The weakness thus acts as a goad to superior performance. Such overcompensation was stressed by Alfred Adler (1870–1937), one of the early psychoanalysts who broke with Freud and set up his own system of individual psychology. Illustrations are not hard to find. Several power-driven dictators in recent history have been men of short stature, who may have suffered a sense of physical powerlessness for which they overcompensated by a struggle for political might. Mussolini, Hitler, and Stalin were short, as was Napoleon before them. Theodore Roosevelt, a frail boy with weak eyes, took up boxing at Harvard and later led the Rough Riders during the Spanish-American War. Overcompensation is an energetic and effective (though not necessarily admirable) way of meeting weakness.

CRITICAL DISCUSSION

Defensive versus coping behavior

Our discussion has tended to emphasize the negative aspects of defense mechanisms. But some experts feel that not enough attention has been paid to the manner in which healthy, effective people handle their frustrations and conflicts. The behaviors we have been describing as defenses against anxiety can also be viewed as distorted adaptations of effective ways of coping with conflicts; that is, they are potentially adaptive processes that have gone astray.

Most mechanisms have a positive or *coping* aspect as well as a defensive aspect. Denial, the refusal to face painful thoughts or feelings, is a form of selective awareness or attention. Its positive aspect is *concentration,* the ability to temporarily set aside painful thoughts in order to stick to the task at hand. Projection is an exaggerated and erroneous sensitivity to another person's unexpressed feelings or thoughts. A positive form of sensitivity would be *empathy,* the ability to appreciate how another person feels. Table 19-1 lists some basic processes, or mechanisms, each followed by its defensive aspect and its coping aspect. For any given conflict situation an individual might use one or more of these mechanisms in its defensive form, its coping form, or a combination of both. One estimate of a person's mental health would be based on the extent to which he habitually uses these mechanisms in a coping manner rather than in a defensive manner.

In a study designed to investigate the usefulness of this formulation of defensive and coping behavior a large group of men and women were rated (on the basis of extensive

TABLE 19-1 MECHANISMS AND THEIR MANIFESTATIONS

MECHANISM	AS A DEFENSE	AS A METHOD OF COPING
Discrimination: ability to separate idea from feeling, idea from idea, feeling from feeling.	**Dissociation:** keeps apart ideas that emotionally belong together or severs ideas from their appropriate emotion.	**Objectivity:** separates ideas from feelings to achieve a rational evaluation or judgment when necessary.
Means-end symbolization: ability to analyze experience, to anticipate outcomes, to entertain alternative choices.	**Rationalization:** offers apparently plausible explanation for behavior to conceal nature of underlying impulse.	**Logical analysis:** analyzes carefully the causal aspects of situations.
Selective awareness: ability to focus attention.	**Denial:** refuses to face painful thoughts or feelings.	**Concentration:** temporarily sets aside painful thoughts in order to stick to task at hand.
Sensitivity: apprehension of another's unexpressed feelings or ideas.	**Projection:** unrealistically attributes an objectionable tendency of his own to another person instead of recognizing it as part of himself.	**Empathy:** puts himself in the other person's place and appreciates how the other fellow feels.
Time reversal: ability to recapture feelings and ideas from the past.	**Regression:** resorts to age-inappropriate behavior to avoid responsibility or demands from others and to allow self-indulgence.	**Playfulness:** utilizes feelings and ideas from the past to add to his solution of problems and enjoyment of life.
Impulse diversion: ability to modify aim or object of an impulse.	**Displacement:** temporarily and unsuccessfully represses unacceptable impulses. May displace to an inappropriate object.	**Substitution:** finds alternate channels that are socially acceptable and satisfying for expression of primitive impulses.
Impulse restraint: ability to control an impulse by inhibiting expression.	**Repression:** totally inhibits feelings or ideas. Repressed material revealed only symbolically, as in dreams.	**Suppression:** holds impulses in abeyance until the proper time and place with the proper objects.

Source: Adapted with modifications from Kroeber (1963).

interviews) as to the type of mechanisms they characteristically used in response to conflict and the degree to which they utilized the coping or defensive form. An attempt was then made to predict from these ratings the individual's behavior on the Rorschach Inkblot Test (p. 434). An elaborate set of hypotheses was developed that specified how each of the mechanisms would be reflected in a specific Rorschach score. For example, use of the defense mechanism of dissociation should be positively related to a tendency to give part responses to inkblot areas that are commonly seen as wholes. A sufficient number of hypotheses were verified to suggest that this might be a fruitful model for describing human conflict behavior (Kroeber, 1963).

Defense mechanisms and adjustment

Man is capable of rational problem-solving; that is, he can face a problem squarely, weigh the alternatives according to their probable consequences, and take action guided by the results of deliberation. Our knowledge of the defense mechanisms tells us, however, that much behavior that appears to be activated by conscious reasoning is in fact directed by unconscious motives.

Limitations upon direct problem-solving

It is possible to attack and solve a personal problem as we do any other kind of problem—such as one in mathematics or science—by asking clear questions, assembling evidence, judging the possible consequences, and trying to verify in practice what we have concluded from the evidence. But there are two chief reasons why we are often not able to solve our personal problems in this straightforward, rational manner.

1. A person's motives or emotions may be so strongly involved that they distort the evidence or the problem itself, so that the person is incapable of direct problem-solving. The self-deceptive mechanisms that we have been considering tend to set up such obstacles. For example, the engineering or premedical student who finds himself failing cannot admit to himself that he is not bright enough to pursue certain courses at the college of his choice; he must therefore find a rationalization instead of solving his academic problem. If he gets sick, he converts an academic problem into a health problem; if he becomes a subject for disciplinary action, he converts an intellectual problem into a moral one. When defense mechanisms hold sway, the person himself sets up obstacles that stand in the way of a rational solution to his problems.

2. Sometimes there are too many unknowns in the equation. The world in which we live is not sufficiently orderly to permit fully rational problem-solving. A man has to take risks based on his best estimates against the uncertainty of the future; but while the estimate of probabilities is the most rational solution it may not satisfy the person, so he may relieve his anxiety by adopting a superstitious or fatalistic solution.

Because of these limitations—both internal and external—upon purely reasonable conduct, man is often tempted to fall back on irrational mechanisms.

How defense mechanisms may contribute to satisfactory adjustment

How successfully can a person use defense mechanisms to avoid or reduce anxiety and to maintain self-esteem? If defense mechanisms were not partially successful, they would not persist as they do. They may provide a protective armor while we are learning more mature and realistic ways of solving our problems. When we no longer need the defenses, their importance fades, and we increasingly face our problems according to the demands of the total situation. The defense mechanisms thus help toward satisfactory adjustment in several ways.

1. *They give us time to solve problems that might otherwise overwhelm us.* Being able to rationalize failures that would otherwise cause us to despair, or to find partial justification for conduct that would otherwise make us despise ourselves, sustains us until we can work out better solutions to our conflicts. These defense mechanisms provide palliatives comparable to those drugs that reduce symptoms without curing disease. Some of the antihistamines, for example, get rid of the sneezing and itching and tearing of the hayfever victim until he takes the pollen tests and allergy shots that will get at the cause of the hayfever. The temporary relief helps him to live more comfortably until he is cured. Ultimately, of course, he wants to find a cure so that he will no longer need the drugs. So, too, one should no longer need his defense mechanisms if he attains realistic ways of solving his personal problems.

2. *The mechanisms may permit experimentation with new roles and hence teach new modes of adjustment.* Even when we adopt new roles for faulty reasons, as in reaction-formation, or when we misjudge people, as in projection, we expose ourselves to corrective experiences from which we may learn social techniques. We may judge someone to be unkind, but as we discover his genuine acts of kindness we may learn to correct our error in judgment. What begins as self-deception may provide occasions for modifying the self.

3. *Rationalization, by starting a search for reasons, may lead to rational conduct in the future.* The tendency to justify behavior that we have found satisfying may lead to false reasons, but it may also lead to a more careful analysis of cause-and-effect relationships. If the latter occurs, a present rationalization may become a future reason.

4. *Behavior illustrative of a mechanism may be socially useful and even creative.* Romantic poetry or art, even though it is produced as a substitute for, or sublimation of, unfulfilled desires, may still be valuable art. So, too, compulsive tendencies may lead to concentrated effort on a task. The person who works hard toward well-defined objectives because of an excessive need for achievement may, in fact, achieve a great deal. Thus the defense mechanisms may get us over rough spots and give a motivational lift leading to better adjustment.

Why defense mechanisms may fail to provide satisfactory adjustment

Nearly all the statements just made about the usefulness of defense mechanisms can also be reversed to point up their failures. The person who depends upon defense mechanisms for protection may never be forced to learn more mature ways of behaving; the roles adopted through the mechanisms may remain unrealistic, leading to withdrawal from social contacts rather than to improved relationships with people; rationalizations may take the form of useless rituals or wasteful compulsions instead of creative effort.

Even when behavior based on defense mechanisms is socially useful, it may not prove completely satisfying to the individual as long as the motives underlying the behavior remain. Actions based on such defense mechanisms never reach their goals; the drive continues, and the resulting behavior is not fully tension-reducing.

Summary

1. When two motives conflict, the satisfaction of one leads to the blocking of the other. *Conflicts* are of three major types: *approach-approach, avoidance-avoidance,* and *approach-avoidance.* Behavior in a conflict situation can be understood according to four principles: the gradient of approach, the gradient of avoidance, the greater steepness of the avoidance gradient, and the heightening of the gradients with increased motivation.

2. *Frustration* arises whenever ongoing, goal-seeking activity is obstructed. The chief sources of frustration are motivational conflicts produced by obstacles (the opposition furnished by things or people) and deficiences in the environment or in the person himself.

3. Some of the immediate consequences of frustrations are *restlessness* and *tension, destructiveness* and *aggression, apathy, fantasy, stereotypy,* and *regression.* They show us how important it is to understand the behavior of individuals when their goal-seeking behavior is blocked.

4. The *defense mechanisms* represent habitual efforts to meet more enduring conflicts. Among the defense mechanisms found in everyday behavior are

rationalization, projection, reaction-formation, dissociation, repression, and *substitution.* The defense mechanisms have two purposes in common: to protect the individual against excessive anxiety and to maintain his self-esteem. They serve these purposes and effect tension reduction by means of self-deception—denial of impulses and disguise of motives.

5. Many personal problems can be solved rationally, that is, by taking into account the evidence, the alternatives, and the consequences of each of the alternatives. But clear, logical choice is difficult for two reasons: (a) the person's own emotions and prejudices often get in the way of such a choice; and (b) the future is always uncertain, so that there are always unknowns and risks that have to be taken. Here defense mechanisms often enter. When defense mechanisms are employed in moderation and do not exclude more realistic solutions of problems, they may increase a person's sense of well-being and so serve a useful purpose, sometimes protecting him until he can reach a realistic solution.

Suggestions for further reading

The experimental analysis of conflict has been formulated by Miller in a chapter entitled "Liberalization of basic S-R concepts: Extensions to conflict behavior, motivation, and social learning" in Koch, *Psychology: A study of a science,* vol. II (1959). A more recent survey of this work may be found in Maher, *Principles of psychopathology* (1966). Research on conflict behavior is included in Haber (ed.), *Current research in motivation* (1966), and in Cofer and Appley, *Motivation* (1964).

Frustration as a source of aggressive behavior is discussed in Berkowitz, *Aggression* (1962), and Buss, *The psychology of aggression* (1961). See also Lawson, *Frustration: The development of a scientific concept* (1965), and Yates, *Frustration and conflict* (1965).

The classic account of defense mechanisms is Anna Freud, *The ego and the mechanisms of defense* (1937). A discussion of the many mechanisms that have been proposed is given by Coleman and Broen, *Abnormal psychology and modern life* (4th ed., 1971), and Lazarus, *Psychological stress and the coping process* (1966). An interesting treatment of conflict and defense mechanisms may be found in Janis (ed.), *Personality: Dynamics, development, and assessment* (1969).

behavior disorders 20

ALL PEOPLE ARE OCCASIONALLY PLACED UNDER conditions of stress and conflict that cause them to experience strong feelings of anxiety. Some of us, by virtue of our biological make-up, the techniques we have developed to handle conflict, and the amount of support provided by our environment, are better able to withstand stress than others. But there is no such thing as an ideally adjusted person; we all resort to self-deception and mechanisms of defense at times. Nor is there complete agreement as to what characteristics would describe a hypothetical, ideally adjusted person. As we shall see later, the concept of adjustment and normality depends to some extent upon the cultural and social group to which the individual belongs.

It is possible, however, to conceive of a continuum of adjustment with positive, highly adaptive behavior at one end and complete helplessness and self-defeating behavior at the other. Most of us would fall somewhere between the middle and the well-adjusted end of the continuum. Below the middle are those individuals who experience such severe conflicts that their attempts to cope with the resulting anxiety seriously interfere with their ability to meet the problems of everyday life, although they can usually hold down a job and get along to some extent with their family and friends;

such people are called *neurotic*. At the extreme end of the continuum below the middle are those individuals who are so burdened with conflicts and who have resorted to such radical methods of defense that they are helpless to deal with reality and may be dangerous to themselves and to others; such people are called *psychotic*.

Thus, psychosis, neurosis, and normal adjustment may be regarded as varying degrees along a continuum of mental health, with no sharp dividing line separating any of the three. In this chapter we will discuss first some of the characteristics considered to be indicative of "good adjustment" or "mental health" in our Western culture, and then go on to discuss the various forms of behavior disorder, including neurosis and psychosis. The characteristics indicative of adjustment do not sharply distinguish between the mentally healthy and the mentally ill, but instead represent traits that the well-adjusted person possesses to a greater degree.

Adjustment

The well-adjusted person experiences conflicts, but he is not unduly distressed by them. He attacks his problems in a realistic manner; he accepts the inevitable; he understands and accepts his own shortcomings and the shortcomings of those with whom he must deal. The maladjusted person, by contrast, is unduly disturbed by his conflicts. He often tries to solve his problems by denying reality. He commonly tends to take issue with other people over matters that cannot be helped, or he may withdraw from other people so that mutually satisfactory solutions are impossible.

The well-adjusted person need not be a social conformist. It is true that adjustment through conforming may, and often does, result in less conflict than protesting against the status quo. A person who lives comfortably under the rules of the group with which he associates is saved some of the problems that confront the social reformer. But a reformer can be as well adjusted as a conformer. The reformer may have a vision of the good society that he seeks, he may associate with others who agree with him, and he may accept on a realistic basis the clashes with those who disagree.

Productivity

A mentally healthy or well-adjusted person is also a productive person. That is, he has a quality of spontaneity in work and in social relations that we recognize as creative, as using his potentialities and powers. He is able to use his endowments, whether meager or ample, in productive activity. A well-adjusted person has zest for living; he does not have to drive himself to meet the demands of the day but enters into activities with enthusiasm. A chronic lack of energy and a readiness to fatigue are common symptoms of psychological tension and unresolved conflicts.

It is sometimes argued that people who suffer from unresolved conflicts turn to creative work precisely because of their suffering. Artists such as Van Gogh and Gauguin were artistically productive but emotionally disturbed, and one wonders if achieving mental health would have robbed them of creative power. The question is debatable, but it is clear from their lives that these artists achieved their artistic products at the cost of great pain to themselves, their families, and their friends. Although a few people somehow turn their troubles to advantage, many others are unable to use their creative abilities because of the conflicts that inhibit their productivity.

Ability to form affectionate relationships

The well-adjusted person is able to form satisfying relationships with other people. He is sensitive to their needs and feelings, does not make excessive demands for the gratification of his own needs, and is able to both give and receive affection. Often the mentally ill person is so lacking in self-esteem and so concerned with protecting his own security that he becomes extremely self-centered; he is preoccupied with his own feelings and strivings and can only seek affection, without being able to reciprocate.

Self-knowledge and acceptance

The well-adjusted person has some awareness of his own motives and feelings. Although no one fully understands why he feels or behaves as he does toward certain people and situations, the mentally healthy person has considerably more self-awareness than one who is mentally ill. He is not trying to hide important feelings and motives from himself. He appraises fairly accurately his abilities and liabilities and does not grossly over-estimate or underestimate what he is capable of doing. For this reason he does not try to achieve totally unrealistic goals and in turn feel guilty when he fails; nor, on the other hand, does he shy away from tasks of which he is capable because he lacks confidence in his ability. In addition to being aware of his own impulses the well-adjusted individual has a certain confidence that he can control and direct his own behavior. He does not feel that he is the helpless victim of external forces.

We have listed only some of the traits that the well-adjusted individual possesses to a greater degree than the maladjusted one. Other experts, particularly those from a country whose culture is quite different from ours, might emphasize different characteristics. Our discussion of disordered behavior may give some clues as to factors that predispose one toward good adjustment by noting conditions that lead to maladjustment. At the end of the next chapter we will discuss some of the practices that can enhance mental health.

Abnormal behavior

Concept of abnormality

Before discussing the types of behavior that are classed as abnormal, it is worth considering what we mean by "abnormal." Even within psychology the terms "abnormal" and "normal" are not used consistently. One definition is based on *statistical frequency*. Many characteristics of people, such as height, weight, and intelligence, take on a range of values when measured over a large population. Most people fall within the middle range of height, with a few who are abnormally tall or abnormally short. "Abnormal" by this definition is that which is statistically infrequent or deviant from the norm. But such a definition would also classify as abnormal the person who is extremely intelligent or extremely happy. Obviously, in defining behavior that is maladjustive we consider more than statistical frequency.

The *society* in which we live classifies certain behavior as abnormal according to its *standards.* Usually, but not always, such behavior is also statistically infrequent within that group. But behavior that is considered normal or well adjusted by one society may be considered abnormal by another. Among the Tchambuli, a New Guinea tribe, the men are shy and subservient, and they engage in what we might consider feminine activities, such as cooking and weaving. The women are the dominant sex: they choose their mates and manage the affairs of the tribe. In our society such subservient behavior on the part of men would be considered an indication of insecurity and weakness. Among some American Indian tribes there is nothing unusual about "hearing voices" when no one is actually talking, or "seeing visions," but most people would consider such behavior abnormal. Even among white Americans the different social classes hold divergent views as to what is considered abnormal or deviant sexual behavior. In his classic survey, *Sexual behavior in the human male,* Kinsey reported that among the working class masturbation as a sexual outlet was viewed as abnormal and a form of perversion; middle-class, college-educated men considered such behavior acceptable, although not necessarily commendable.

A third, and perhaps most important, means of defining maladjusted behavior is according to *degree of impairment*. If a person is so immobilized by conflict and anxiety that he cannot meet his everyday responsibilities, or if his behavior threatens harm to himself or someone else, he is considered to be behaving abnormally.

In most instances all three types of definition—statistical, social, and behavioral impairment—are used in diagnosing maladjustment.

The normal person's quota of symptoms

Before we consider the symptoms of disordered behavior it might be well to reemphasize the point that there is no sharp distinction between adequate adjustment and mental illness. A person well within the range of normal physical health is seldom entirely free of the symptoms of sickness. How many people have no cavities, no skin blemishes, or no colds? Yet most people are healthy. Similarly, a person well within the range of normal mental health may have occasional outbursts of temper, may get a headache after an unpleasant argument, may become nauseated because of an emotional crisis, or may become suspicious that someone is talking about him. As we go on to consider some of the symptoms of disordered behavior, it is well to acknowledge that each of us has his quota of symptoms, and that to be free of mental illness does not require us to be symptom-free.[1]

Neuroses

The less severe forms of behavior disorder, troublesome enough to call for expert help and occasionally requiring hospitalization, are called *neuroses*.[2] These disturbances are often merely extreme and enduring forms of normal defense mechanisms used in an attempt to resolve a persistent conflict. We noted in the preceding chapter that conflicts of the approach-avoidance type are usually the most difficult to resolve satisfactorily, particularly if they stem from two equally strong motives. As one need becomes stronger and is about to be gratified, the opposing need, which is in danger of being frustrated, increases in strength, and a state of vacillation ensues. Such unresolved conflicts result in feelings of anxiety, tension, and helplessness. And if a realistic solution cannot be achieved, the individual either remains in a state of severe anxiety or resorts to one or more of the defense mechanisms in an attempt to reduce anxiety. In the neurotic individual this defense is seldom satisfactory for two reasons: it usually alleviates only a small part of the total anxiety; and it interferes with the person's daily functioning, thereby creating further problems.

The chief symptom of neurosis, then, is *anxiety*. Often the anxiety is obvious. The individual appears strained and tense; his increased tension may result in such symptoms as indigestion, diarrhea, loss of appetite, and insomnia. Sometimes the anxiety is not really apparent, but we judge from the person's maladaptive behavior that he is defending against anxiety by the extreme use of one or more defense mechanisms.

We cannot attempt to cover all the various types of neurotic behavior, but we will briefly describe four of the more common reactions. These are *anxiety reactions, obsessive-compulsive reactions, phobic reactions,* and *conversion reactions.* Traditionally, neurotic disorders have been classified according to symptoms rather than type of conflict. Such a classification is not completely satisfactory, however, because frequently a neurotic has symptoms of more than one reaction type.

[1]A person with any doubts about the severity of his symptoms should not hesitate to seek professional psychological help.

[2]Plural form of *neurosis.* The terms "psychoneurosis" and "neurosis" are used interchangeably as are "psychoneurotic" and "neurotic."

Anxiety reactions

Although we have said that anxiety is the predominant characteristic of neurosis, in many of the neurotic reactions it is concealed by other symptoms. In *anxiety reactions,* however, it is very much in the open. The typical anxiety neurotic lives each day with a level of tension much greater than that of the normal individual. This chronic state of apprehension is often punctuated by *acute anxiety attacks* that may occur as often as several times a day or as infrequently as once a month. During acute attacks the individual has an overwhelming feeling that something dreadful is about to happen; this feeling is usually accompanied by such physiological symptoms as heart palpitations, rapid breathing, perspiration, muscle tension, faintness, and nausea. These physiological symptoms result from excitation of the sympathetic division of the autonomic nervous system (see p. 43) and are the same symptoms that one may experience when extremely frightened.[3]

The anxiety neurotic usually has no idea why he is frightened. His anxiety is sometimes termed "free-floating," because it is not associated with a particular stimulus or object but occurs in a wide variety of situations. It is less a function of external stimulus events than of feelings and conflicts within the individual. Anxiety that is evoked by specific situations (for example, speaking before a group or going out on a blind date) is called "bound" anxiety because it is bound to a specific situation. Bound anxiety is less incapacitating than free-floating anxiety, but it sometimes can be troublesome enough to be classed as neurotic.

Most anxiety reactions lie between the very diffuse, free-floating anxiety and highly specific fears. The mother who worries constantly about her child's safety is afraid of a number of possible accidents. A person who fears for his bodily safety is afraid of any one of a number of different possible mishaps. The general anxiety is diffuse, but at any point in time it may be specific (Levitt, 1967).

Most of us have experienced feelings of anxiety and tension in the face of threatening or stressful situations. Such feelings are normal reactions to stress; they are considered neurotic only when they become habitual ways of responding to situations that most people can handle with little difficulty. In most cases the anxiety neurotic is a person who has strong feelings of inadequacy and inferiority yet at the same time maintains unrealistically high standards of achievement and feels guilty when he fails to live up to them. No matter how successful he may be he cannot relax; he still feels apprehensive about his ability to meet the demands of the future. Any sudden stress in his life situation may precipitate an acute anxiety attack—the threatened loss of professional or social goals, the loss of a parent or other person upon whom he felt dependent, and the threatened breakthrough of unacceptable and dangerous impulses are all factors that may lead to an acute anxiety attack. The following is a case study of a person for whom the threatened breakthrough of hostile feelings was sufficient to trigger anxiety attacks.

An eighteen-year-old male student developed severe anxiety attacks just before he went out on dates. Analysis revealed that he came from a very insecure home in which he was very much attached to an anxious, frustrated, and insecure mother. He was not particularly attractive and had considerable difficulty getting dates, particularly with the girls of his choice. The girl he had been recently dating, for example, would not make any arrangements to go out until after 6:00 P.M. of the same day after her chances for a more preferable date seemed remote. This had increased his already strong feelings of inferiority and insecurity, and had led to the development of intense hostility toward the opposite sex which was mostly on an unconscious level.

The symptoms of this repressed hostility, however, came out in obsessive thoughts on the part of the patient of choking the girl to death each time they were out together. As he put it, "When we are alone in the car, I can't get my mind off her nice white throat and what it would be like to choke her to death." At first he put these thoughts out of his mind, but they returned on subsequent nights with increas-

[3]Several organic conditions, such as overactivity of the thyroid gland, heart disease, hypoglycemia, and some endocrine disorders, can produce the same symptoms as an anxiety attack. It is always wise to rule out such possibilities by taking a thorough medical examination before assuming that the symptoms are of psychological origin.

ing persistency. Then, to complicate the matter, he experienced his first acute anxiety attack. It occurred in his car on the way over to pick up his date and lasted only a few minutes, but the patient was panic stricken and thought that he was going to die. After that he experienced several additional attacks, strangely enough under the same conditions.

The relationship of the repressed hostility to the patient's obsessive thoughts and to the development of anxiety is quite obvious in this case. However, it was not at all obvious to him. He was at a complete loss to explain both his obsessive thoughts and the anxiety attacks [Coleman, 1964, p. 198].

Obsessive-compulsive reactions

Next to anxiety reactions, *obsessive-compulsive reactions* are the most frequent of the neurotic disorders. Obsessive-compulsive reactions occur in three major forms: obsessive thoughts—those that recur persistently, often unwelcome and disturbing; compulsive acts—irresistible urges to repeat a certain stereotyped or ritualistic act; obsessive thoughts with compulsive acts—for example, thoughts of lurking disease germs combined with the compulsion of excessive hand-washing. All of us at times have persistently recurring thoughts ("Did I leave the gas turned on?") and urges toward ritualistic behavior (knocking on wood after boasting). But for the obsessive-compulsive neurotic these obsessive thoughts and compulsive urges occupy so much time that they seriously interfere with his daily life. He recognizes the irrationality of his thoughts and behavior but is unable to control them. Often the attempt to stop produces anxiety.

Obsessive thoughts cover a wide variety of topics, but most frequently they deal with aggressive or sexual impulses—the person has persistently recurring thoughts of pushing his mother down the stairs, drowning his infant son in the bathtub, throwing himself in front of a speeding car, walking naked down a church aisle, raping little children. The possibility of these thoughts being carried out is virtually nil, but the individual feels no control over them, cannot understand why they persist, and fears not only that he will perform the act but that he is becoming insane.

Compulsive acts are frequently designed to counteract such unacceptable impulses (impulses of which the individual may or may not be aware). For example, a person who feels guilty about masturbation or other sexual behavior he views as sinful may feel compelled to wash his hands many times a day, thereby cleansing himself of immoral thoughts or behavior. A mother who has feelings of hostility and resentment toward her children may find herself continually compelled to check on their safety. Coleman (1964) cites the case of a woman whose repressed hostile feelings toward her daughter resulted in a compulsive urge to make the sign of the cross and repeat, "God protect my dearly beloved little daughter." The behavior seemed senseless to the woman, who had no idea why she felt the compulsion.

Elaborate and time-consuming routines control the daily activities of many obsessive-compulsives (for example, washing and dressing in a specified order, stirring coffee exactly ten times, arranging food in a set number of piles on the plate and consuming the piles in a certain order). This type of ritualistic behavior seems designed to serve two purposes: to establish order in a world that is confusing and threatening, and to guard against unacceptable impulses (if one is continually busy and thinking of something else, there is less opportunity for improper thoughts or actions). Even when the dangerous impulses do enter consciousness they are dissociated from their normal emotion and appear in the form of obsessive thoughts that, although disturbing, are not felt by the individual to be really a part of himself. For example, the college student who had difficulty getting dates was upset by his thought of choking his dates but would have been considerably more disturbed had he realized the extent of his hostile feelings and destructive impulses toward females.

Phobic reactions

Phobic reactions are excessive fears of certain kinds of situations in the absence of real danger, or fears that are totally out of proportion to the amount of danger that a situation may involve. The person usually realizes that his fear is irrational but still feels anxiety (ranging from mild feelings of uneasiness to an acute anxiety attack), which is relieved only by avoiding the phobic situation. The list of objects or situations that can evoke phobic reactions is endless; some of the more common are fear of closed places (*claustrophobia*), fear of high places (*acrophobia*), fear of crowds (*ocholophobia*), fear of animals (*zoophobia*), and fear of the dark (*nyctophobia*). A scientific name can be constructed for any irrational fear simply by prefixing the word "phobia" with the Greek word for the object feared, and some of the earlier literature on phobias is replete with impressive diagnoses.

Most of us have some minor irrational fears, but in phobic reactions the fears are so intense as to interfere with the person's daily living. Examples would be the person whose fear of closed places is intense enough to prevent him from traversing narrow hallways or entering small rooms, even though his daily activities require him to do so, or the individual whose fear of crowds prevents him from attending movies or walking down congested sidewalks. Occasionally a person may have one specific phobia and yet be quite normal in every other respect. But often a phobic individual shows other symptoms of neurotic disorder, such as tenseness and feelings of inadequacy.

How do phobic reactions develop? When a person shows fear of something that he knows is harmless, we assume that the phobic object is associated with (or symbolizes) something else that is dangerous. Some phobic reactions are simply conditioned fear reactions. We saw in Chapter 14 (p. 344) how the boy Albert was conditioned to fear a white rat when the appearance of the rat was paired with a noxious stimulus. This conditioned fear response then generalized to other furry objects. If in adult life Albert showed strong fear reactions to his wife's mink coat and had no awareness of the source of this fear (because he had forgotten the conditioning experience of his childhood), we would say he had a phobic reaction. Some phobic reactions can be similarly traced to a traumatic childhood experience. Cameron and Magaret (1951) cite the case of a man who feared red skies at evening. After extensive analysis he

was helped to recall that as a boy he had been terrified by the red flames of a tenement fire in which he erroneously thought his mother was being burned to death. The red sky of the sunset symbolized the red flames he feared would destroy his mother, upon whom he was very dependent. Frequently, as in this case, the fear is displaced by means of stimulus generalization from the originally feared object to another object or idea, so that the person is unaware of the source of his anxiety.

Phobic reactions of a more pervasive nature may develop as a means of defending the individual from repressed impulses (usually aggressive or sexual) that he feels may become dangerous. A woman who had a phobic fear of walking down the street unless someone else was with her was found to be actually fearful of her own sexual feelings toward men (feelings that her strict upbringing had convinced her were sinful). By avoiding situations in which she might encounter men alone, she avoided the possibility of losing control of her sexual impulses. In one sense, phobias have an advantage over anxiety states or obsessive-compulsive reactions. In phobic reactions the fear is directed toward a specific object, and the person can reduce anxiety by avoiding the object. The obsessive-compulsive and the anxiety neurotic have no such easy way out.

Conversion reactions

In *conversion reactions*[4] physical symptoms appear without any underlying organic cause. The symptoms may be (1) sensory—loss of sensation in some part of the body, blindness, or deafness; (2) motor—paralysis of a limb or entire side of the body, muscular tremors or tics, speech disturbances, and occasional convulsions or "fits" similar to epileptic convulsions; (3) visceral—including such symptoms as coughing or sneezing spells, persistent hiccuping, choking sensations, lump in the throat, and a variety of vague aches or pains. The presumption is that anxiety has been reduced or dispelled by being "converted" into symptoms

[4]Formerly called hysteria or conversion hysteria.

that serve unconscious purposes of the patient. For example, if, through conversion reactions, a soldier's legs become paralyzed, he is protected from acknowledging his fear of battle, which would be belittling to him; he is likely to be sent away from the battlefront, so that the occasion for his fear will be removed. Discharged from the army, he will probably recover the normal use of his legs, for he has no organic injury.

It should be emphasized that the person with a conversion reaction is not faking; his disorder is quite real to him, and it usually is easy to distinguish him from a malingerer. In fact, in the case of a sensory symptom of loss of pain sensitivity (analgesia) in some part of the body, the patient reports no pain when stuck with a pin. (This situation is similar to that of a hypnotized subject who, under instructions that he will feel no pain, shows none when his skin is deeply pierced by a needle.) Even though real, the disorder may be selective: a pilot whose conversion reaction of night blindness prevents him from flying at night may be able to drive a car; a person whose symptom is total blindness may be able to see well enough to dodge an object thrown at him; a person reacting with deafness may be able to hear instructions shouted in an emergency.

As in the case of the soldier with paralyzed legs, almost every conversion reaction can be traced to an attempt to avoid or solve a problem by means of illness. Most of us have at times pleaded illness to avoid some particularly unpleasant situation. The neurotic carries this tendency to the extreme when faced with a serious conflict, so that he cannot function adequately in his daily life. In addition to avoiding the problem, the conversion symptom provides the secondary gain of eliciting sympathy and support from relatives and friends.

It is interesting to note that the more dramatic types of reactions, such as sudden paralysis or being struck blind or deaf, are becoming increasingly rare in civilian life, although they are still relatively common among servicemen during wartime. It may be that with the increasing medical sophistication of our population such dramatic afflictions are no longer viewed as medically feasible, and patients seem to be developing instead vague aches and pains that are more difficult to distinguish from organic disorders.

Concluding comments on neurotic reactions

We have discussed four types of neurotic reactions. As mentioned before, the symptoms frequently overlap, and it is not always clear how to categorize a particular patient. The college student who had difficulty dating (p. 468) could be classified as exhibiting an anxiety reaction or an obsessive-compulsive reaction, depending upon which symptoms seemed the most predominant. Actually he was using obsessive thoughts as a defense against anxiety, but this defense was not very successful, and the anxiety was breaking through in the form of acute panic reactions. The four neurotic reactions could be placed on a continuum according to the degree of observable anxiety. The person with an anxiety reaction exhibits the greatest amount of anxiety; indeed, he has no successful defense against it. The phobic individual comes next with his intense fear of one particular situation. The obsessive-compulsive shows less manifest anxiety than the phobic individual. And the person with a conversion reaction shows the least amount of anxiety, presumably because his tension has been diverted into physical symptoms.

We have stressed the fact that neurotic reactions are exaggerated forms of normal defense mechanisms; neurotic symptoms are responses that the individual has learned to use to defend himself against anxiety and to increase his feelings of security. Because these responses may be fairly successful in reducing anxiety initially, they are reinforced and strengthened. Under conditions of increased stress, however, the individual redoubles his defensive efforts so that they reach maladaptive proportions and are only partially successful in reducing anxiety. He is thus stuck with a pattern of responding that not only fails to relieve his anxiety but creates additional adjustment problems for him.

Since feelings of inadequacy and anxiety underlie all the neurotic reactions, we may well ask what determines the particular symptoms an individual develops. Why is one person plagued by obsessive thoughts while another develops paralysis of the arm in response to a conflict situation? We do not know the complete answer. The most plausible explanation is that neurotic symptoms are extreme forms of the reaction patterns a child learns in his early life through interaction with the important people in his environment. Often such reaction patterns are appropriate in the situation in which they were learned but are maladaptive when applied to situations in later life. For example, the parent who rewards the child with excessive fussing and attention when he is sick and who encourages him to stay home from school when there is the slightest sign of illness may predispose the youngster to retreat into illness whenever he encounters a difficult situation in later life. We can see how a person with this type of background might develop a conversion reaction when faced with a crisis situation. Or the parents who place great emphasis upon correct and proper behavior and instill feelings of guilt whenever the child deviates from their standards may be predisposing the child to an obsessive-compulsive reaction in adult life. Although such hypotheses are plausible, they cannot be verified until intensive studies have been made of the family relationships of children who later became neurotic.

Psychoses

The person with a *psychotic disorder* (*psychosis,* plural *psychoses*) is more severely disturbed than one with a neurotic disorder. His personality is disorganized, and his normal social functioning is greatly impaired. Although in the past it was generally believed that neuroses and psychoses were two distinctly different kinds of disorders, many experts today believe that there is a continuity from normality through neurosis and psychosis, the differences being largely a matter of severity of the symptoms. Perhaps one of the chief distinctions is that while the neurotic is trying desperately to cope with his anxiety in order to function in the world, the psychotic has to some extent given up the struggle and *lost contact with reality*. He may withdraw into his own fantasy world and fail to respond to things going on around him. Or he may respond with exaggerated emotions and actions that are inappropriate to the situation. Frequently his thought processes are disturbed to the extent that he experiences delusions (false beliefs) or hallucinations (sense experiences occurring in the absence of appropriate external stimuli, such as imagining voices talking to him in abusive language). For these reasons the psychotic individual is more likely to require hospitalization and protective care than the neurotic.

It is customary to distinguish between two general categories of psychoses: *organic* and *functional*. *Organic psychoses* refer to psychotic symptoms that are the result of a known physiological cause. *Functional psychoses* are disorders of psychological origin without any demonstrable physiological cause. (This distinction will be considered in more detail later in the chapter.) We will limit our discussion here primarily to the functional psychoses, since they are of greatest interest to the psychologist. Two of the most prevalent functional psychoses are *manic-depressive reactions* and *schizophrenic reactions*.

Manic-depressive reactions

The *manic-depressive reactions* are characterized by recurrent and exaggerated deviations of mood from normal to either the *manic phase* (strong excitement and elation) or the *depressive phase* (extreme fatigue, despondency, and sadness). A few patients exhibit the whole cycle, but most vary between the normal mood state and one of the extreme phases, depression being the most common.

In the milder form of the manic phase (*hypomania*) the patient shows great energy and enthusiasm. He talks continually, has unbounded confidence in his ability, rushes from one activity to another with little need of sleep, and makes grandiose plans with little attention to their practicality (but seldom puts these plans into action or completes them if he does). His behavior is similar in some respects to an individual who is mildly intoxicated.

In the more severe form of mania (*hypermania*) the patient behaves more like the popular notion of the raving maniac. He may be continually pacing about, singing, shouting obscene phrases, screaming. He is confused and disoriented and may experience hallucinations and delusions. Some hypermanic patients abandon all moral inhibitions and may exhibit unrestrained sexual behavior or violent assaultive behavior. The intense excitement of the hypermanic state can be reduced by the use of sedatives and hydrotherapy, so the visitor to a neuropsychiatric ward seldom sees the violent ravings and uncontrolled behavior that were more commonly seen thirty years ago.

In the depressed phase the patient's behavior is essentially the opposite of what we have described in the manic phase. Instead of being overactive the individual's mental and physical activity is much slower than normal. Instead of feeling overconfident and boastful, his self-esteem is at its lowest ebb. He feels dejected and discouraged; life seems hopeless and not worth living. Feelings of worthlessness and guilt predominate, and it is not infrequent that patients in this condition will attempt suicide. In the most intense state of depression the patient is bedridden and indifferent to all that goes on around him. He refuses to speak or to eat, and he has to be fed intravenously and completely cared for by others.

As we have said, most patients experience either mania or depression with periodic recovery to more normal behavior, but some develop a cycle of alternating between manic and depressed phases. It is not clear what factors initiate the switch from one phase to the other, but despite the extreme dissimilarity of manic and depressive behavior, many experts conclude that they are psychologically related. They propose that the elation and energetic activity of the manic phase are a defense against underlying feelings of inadequacy and worthlessness, which break through in the depres-

sive phase. Such a reaction is not unlike that of a normal person who tries to escape from the anxiety of a stressful situation by throwing himself into a full round of gay and busy activities in an attempt to forget about his problems. Unlike some forms of psychosis, manic-depressive psychosis does not result in progressive degeneration of social behavior and mental ability. Between psychotic episodes the individual may function quite normally.

There is much we do not know about the etiology of manic-depressive psychoses. The fact that this type of reaction occurs much more frequently among the offspring of manic-depressives than in the general population suggests that there may be a genetic predisposition to the disorder. Studies of individuals with depressive reactions indicate that two main psychological factors are involved: (1) high standards of achievement and feelings of extreme guilt and worthlessness when these standards are not attained, and (2) a rigid conscience that prohibits the outward expression of hostility so that the anger experienced in the face of frustration is turned inward against the self. Usually some crisis in the individual's life situation precipitates the disorder: the death of a loved one, failure in marriage, a severe setback in work (Bunny, 1968).

Schizophrenic reactions

Schizophrenia is by far the most common of the psychotic disorders. It has been estimated that 50 percent of all neuropsychiatric hospital beds are occupied by patients diagnosed as schizophrenic. The word *schizophrenic* is derived from the Greek words *schizin* ("to split") and *phren* ("mind"). The split does not refer to multiple personalities as in the case of Eve White (see p. 415) or as in the famous fictional account of Dr. Jekyll and Mr. Hyde, but rather to a splitting of the thought processes from the emotions; one of the symptoms of schizophrenia is a blunting or dulling of emotional expression or the display of an emotion that is inappropriate to the situation or the thought being expressed. The symptoms of schizophrenia are many and varied, so much so that some experts believe that the term is currently being used to cover more than one type of disorder. The primary symptoms, however, can be summarized under the following headings (although not every schizophrenic will show all of the symptoms):

1. *Disturbances of affect.* The schizophrenic does not show emotion in a normal way. He usually appears dull and apathetic or he may display inappropriate emotions, for example, speaking of tragic events without any display of emotion or while actually smiling.

2. *Withdrawal from active interchange with the realistic environment.* The schizophrenic loses interest in the people and events around him. In extreme cases the patient may remain silent and immobile for days (in what is called a *catatonic stupor*) and may have to be cared for as an infant.

3. *Autism.* Withdrawal from reality is usually accompanied by absorption in an inner fantasy life. This state of self-absorption is known as *autism* (from the Greek *autos*, meaning "self"). Inappropriate emotional behavior can sometimes be explained by the fact that the schizophrenic may be reacting to what is going on in his private world rather than to external events. The schizophrenic may be so enmeshed in his fantasy world that he is disoriented in time and space; that is, he does not know what day or month it is or where he is.

4. *Delusions and hallucinations.* The most common delusions experienced by the schizophrenic are the beliefs that external forces are trying to control his thoughts and actions (delusions of influence) or that certain people or groups are persecuting him (delusions of persecution). Auditory hallucinations are much more common than visual ones—the schizophrenic frequently hears voices. When persecutory delusions or hallucinations are predominant the person is called *paranoid.* He may become suspicious of his friends and relatives, fear that they are poisoning him, complain that he is being watched, followed, and talked about. Paranoid delusions can be understood as extreme forms of the defense mechanism of projection. Rather than face the anxiety generated by recognition of his own hostile impulses, the paranoid schizophrenic projects his hostility onto others; it is they who are unjustly trying to harm him.

5. *"Bizarre" behavior.* The schizophrenic's behavior may include peculiar gestures, movements, and repetitive acts that make no sense to the observer but are usually closely related to the schizophrenic's fantasy world.

6. *Disturbances of thought.* The schizophrenic's speech is frequently incoherent and disconnected. He makes associations that seem senseless to the observer and may even coin new words to express his peculiar thoughts. When the disorder is long-standing there is progressive deterioration of intellectual ability as measured by standard intelligence tests.

In most cases these symptoms do not develop overnight. They are the result of a gradual process of increasingly unsatisfactory interpersonal relationships and withdrawal from social contacts. The following case history illustrates this gradual process.

A. J. was always extremely shy and as a small child would run away and hide when visitors came to the house. He had one or two boy friends but as a teen-ager he never associated with girls and did not enjoy school parties or social functions. He had few interests and did not engage in sports. His school record was mediocre, and he left high school at the end of his sophomore year. The principal felt that he "could have done better" and remarked about his "queer" and seclusive behavior. Shortly before leaving school his shyness increased considerably. He expressed fears that he was different from other boys and complained that the other children called him names. He became untidy, refusing to wash or wear clean clothes.

After leaving school A. J. worked at a number of odd jobs but was irregular in performing his duties and never held any one job longer than a few weeks. He finally became unemployable and stayed home, becoming more and more seclusive and withdrawn from community and family life. He would sit with his head bowed most of the time, refused to eat with the family, and when visitors came would hide under the bed. He further neglected his appearance, refusing to bathe or get a hair cut. He occasionally made "strange" remarks and frequently covered his face with his hands because he felt he looked "funny."

The psychiatrist who interviewed the boy when he was brought to a local mental hygiene clinic at the age of 17 noted frequent grimacing and silly and inappropriate smiling but found that he was correctly oriented in terms of time and place and could answer questions coherently in a flat tone of voice. He complained of having recurring thoughts but denied any hallucinations or delusions. He expressed a wish for help so that he could go back to work.

A. J. was admitted to the state neuropsychiatric hospital with a diagnosis of schizophrenia. Testing with the Welchsler Adult Intelligence Scale showed that he had average intelligence (full scale I.Q. 96) but indicated the beginnings of some intellectual impairment. The results of the Rorschach test reinforced the schizophrenic diagnosis [Rabin, 1947, pp. 23–30].

Attempts to classify schizophrenic reactions

Traditionally the schizophrenic reactions have been classified into nine different types based on the predominant clinical symptoms. But this system of classification has not proved to be satisfactory, because the symptoms overlap from one category to the next, and the diagnosis for a single patient may change from one type to another during the course of his illness. More recently a two-dimensional classification has been proposed, based not on the schizophrenic's present symptoms, but on his premorbid (pre-illness) adjustment and the prognosis for recovery. A *process schizophrenic* has a history of long-term, progressive deterioration in adjustment with little chance of recovery. A *reactive schizophrenic* has had a fairly adequate premorbid social development, the illness being precipitated by some sudden stress, such as the death of a loved one or loss of his job; the prognosis for recovery is good. A number of rating scales have been developed that attempt to evaluate the patient's premorbid personality and the nature of the onset of illness and to classify him accordingly. Some of these scales have shown good ability to predict a patient's speed of recovery. But it appears that there is no clear-cut dichotomy between the two groups; rather, there is a continuum of personality organization from the most process to the most reactive schizophrenic (Higgins and Peterson, 1966).

Once a classification has been made according to one set of criteria, the next step is to examine the groups so classified in order to determine additional variables that distinguish between them. It is hoped that such a procedure will add to our knowledge about etiological factors and types of treatment. Initially some experts thought that the two groups might be distinguished on a neurological basis. They hypothesized that process schizophrenia, which starts comparatively early in life, might be caused by some sort of brain damage or deficit; consequently, process schizophrenics might respond on certain tests in a manner similar to patients with diagnosed brain damage, while the reactive schizophrenics would not. Such studies have generally had negative results. So far little empirical evidence supports the notion that process schizophrenia has an organic etiology and reactive does not (Buss, 1966). However, it has been possible to differentiate between process and reactive schizophrenics on some physiological and psychological measures. For example, reactive schizophrenics are more responsive physiologically (in terms of blood pressure response to a chemical stimulant) than process schizophrenics and more responsive emotionally to anxiety-producing stimuli (Stephens, Astrup, and Mangrum, 1967). These results support the conclusion that the withdrawal of the process schizophrenic is of long duration,

TABLE 20-1 ADOLESCENT PEER INTERACTION AND LENGTH OF HOSPITALIZATION AS AN ADULT SCHIZOPHRENIC			
	NUMBER OF CASES IN EACH INTERACTION CATEGORY		
LENGTH OF HOSPITALIZATION	HIGH INTER-ACTION	MEDIUM INTER-ACTION	LOW INTER-ACTION
Short term (6 months)	8	2	1
Relapsing (at least 2 separate admissions and total hospitalization 1–3 years)	1	4	6
Long term (3 years or more)	0	2	9

Source: Modified from Pitt and Hage (1964).

Adult hospitalized schizophrenics were categorized (on the basis of intensive interviews) as to amount of weekly interaction they had with their peers during mid-adolescence (ages 15–17). Clearly, those schizophrenics who withdraw from social interaction earlier in life are likely to remain hospitalized longer. This result lends support to the distinction between slow-onset (process) schizophrenia and crisis-onset (reactive) schizophrenia.

while the withdrawal of the reactive schizophrenic is in response to more recent environmental stress. The fact that the severity of the schizophrenic disorder (as measured by length of hospitalization) is positively correlated with the degree of withdrawal from interpersonal contacts during adolescence is indicated in Table 20-1.

Organic and functional illness

The neuroses and psychoses described in the preceding sections are classified as "psychogenic" or "functional," meaning that there is no identifiable organic change in the brain or nervous system associated with them. There are in addition to these reactions many kinds of mental disturbance associated with known organic changes in the brain or nervous system—with alcoholism, acute infections, syphilis, tumors, head injuries, epilepsy, and cerebral arteriosclerosis (hardening of the arteries). Usually the individual has shown normal adjustment prior to the disease or injury, and his subsequent peculiarities in behavior are attributed to damage of the nervous system.

The distinction between functional and organic disorders is not completely clear-cut, however. An already unstable individual might become psychotic following a brain injury, while a better-adjusted person might show little change in behavior. In the case of cerebral arteriosclerosis in an elderly person, for example, there appears to be little correlation between the degree of cerebral damage and the severity of the mental symptoms. One patient with extensive damage may show only mild intellectual impairment, whereas another with less damage may show signs of mental confusion, uncontrolled emotional outbursts, and such a lack of responsible behavior that he requires hospitalization. It is apparent that factors other than the actual physiological damage (such as the individual's pre-illness personality and the amount of stress to which he is subjected in his present environment) influence the person's reaction to his illness.

It also seems probable that some of the psychotic cases now classed as functional will ultimately be traced to physiological variables. General paresis, a disorder characterized by progressive deterioration of behavior and mental ability, was once classed as functional. Early in the 1900s it was discovered that this disorder resulted from destruction of brain tissue by the syphilis spirochete. Although only about 5 percent of untreated syphilitics develop paresis, those that do, show a wide variety of mental symptoms like those associated with functional psychoses.

When an illness is called functional or psychogenic, we do not mean that there are no changes in the nervous system associated with it. There may indeed be some hereditary basis for susceptibility to the particular disturbance. We imply, however, that the changes are of the kind that take place in learning and habit formation, rather than the kind associated with bacterial infection or neural damage. If the changes are of the functional variety, the disorder is more likely to be reversible—more susceptible to cure through a process of reeducation—than is an organically based disorder.

Moreover, functional psychological illness may be associated with organic physical change in parts of the body other than the nervous system. These are the illnesses commonly called *psychosomatic*. A dramatic illustration is provided by experiments with monkeys in which duodenal ulcers and other gastrointestinal disturbances were induced through a conditioning procedure (Brady and others, 1958). In one arrangement, monkeys participated in the experiment in pairs, each monkey being confined in a restraining device (Figure 20-1). An electric shock was delivered at intervals. One of the monkeys (whimsically called the "executive" monkey) had a lever that could be used to turn off or prevent the shock. When the "executive" pressed the lever, the shock was turned off for *both* monkeys. Thus both monkeys suffered identical shocks; if their physiological damage were due to

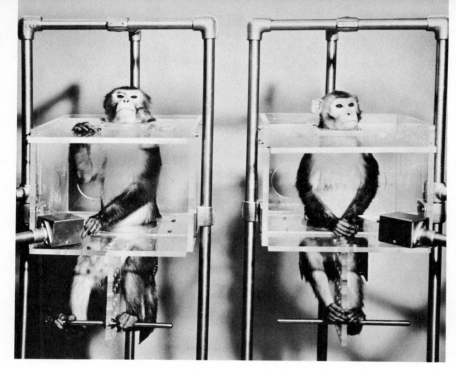

Fig. **20-1 Ulcers in executive monkeys** Both animals receive brief electric shocks at 20-second intervals. The one at the left (the "executive") has learned to press its lever, which is able to prevent shocks to both animals provided it is pressed at least once every 20 seconds; the lever for the monkey at the right is a dummy. Although both monkeys receive the same number of shocks, only the "executive" monkey develops the ulcers (Brady, 1958).

Medical Audio Visual Dept., Walter Reed Army Inst. of Research

shocks, it would affect both equally. What happened was that only the "executive" monkey developed the ulcers; apparently the constant alertness required to turn off or prevent the shock produced a continuing state of tension that resulted in the ulcers. The helpless monkey, which could only take the shocks as they came, was somehow less reactive and less disturbed.

While the functional origin of symptoms in neurotic reactions has been rather firmly established, the causative factors in the psychotic reactions are still the subject of intensive investigation.

Research on the causes of schizophrenia

Arguments over organic versus functional causes of behavior disorders currently center around schizophrenia. The fact that schizophrenia is at present classified as a functional psychosis does not mean that it will necessarily remain in that category. Research on schizophrenia can be classified into three groups, each having a different point of view about cause.

Research on heredity

As noted in Chapter 16, there is good evidence in favor of a hereditary factor in schizophrenia (see p. 393). If a schizophrenic has a monozygotic twin, the probability is 46 percent that his twin will also become schizophrenic. Even if the twin is not diagnosed schizophrenic there is a high probability that he will be abnormal in certain respects; a review of a number of studies suggests that only about 13 percent of the monozygotic twins of schizophrenics can be regarded as normal or nearly normal (Heston, 1970).

The presence of schizophrenic-like disabilities among the relatives of schizophrenics is so striking that the term *schizoid* has been coined to refer to those who resemble the schizophrenic in many traits but whose pathology is not severe enough to warrant the diagnosis of schizophrenia. The characteristics included under this still ill-defined label are many: social isolation, suspiciousness,

TABLE 20-2 PERCENTAGES OF FIRST-DEGREE RELATIVES FOUND TO BE SCHIZOPHRENIC OR SCHIZOID			
RELATIONSHIP	SCHIZOPHRENIA	SCHIZOID	TOTAL: SCHIZOID AND SCHIZOPHRENIC
RELATIVES OF SCHIZOPHRENICS			
Children (N = 1000)	16.4%	32.6%	49.0%
Siblings (N = 1191)	14.3	31.5	45.8
Parents (N = 2741)	9.2	34.8	44.0
BOTH PARENTS SCHIZOPHRENIC			
Children (N = 171)	33.9	32.2	66.1

Source: Heston (1970), summarizing other studies.

The incidence of schizophrenia and schizophrenic-like disabilities among relatives of schizophrenics provides evidence of familial influences, both genetic and environmental.

extreme anxiety in social situations, rigidity of thinking, and blunting of affect are some of the more prevalent features. When the presence of both schizophrenia and schizoidia in families is studied (on the assumption that they are manifestations of the same disorder), the evidence in favor of a genetic basis is even more striking. Table 20-2 shows the incidence of schizophrenia and schizoidia among the immediate relatives of schizophrenics. Note that the child of a schizophrenic has a 49 percent chance of being either schizophrenic or schizoid; if both parents are schizophrenic the probability increases to 66 percent. These proportions are close to those that would be expected were the disorder the result of a dominant gene.

It can be argued, of course, that the clustering of schizophrenia and schizoidia in families may result solely from environmental factors. The schizophrenic parent may transmit the disorder to his offspring by means of faulty child-rearing practices rather than faulty genes. And two schizophrenic parents would surely provide a more abnormal environment than one. A study of children born to schizophrenic mothers and raised in foster homes, however, provides additional support for the genetic hypothesis. These children were permanently separated from their parents shortly after birth. They were assessed in adulthood, by means of interviews and records of their past history, and compared with a control group born to normal parents and reared in foster homes. The incidence of schizophrenia and schizoidia was much higher among those individuals whose biological mothers were schizophrenic (Heston, 1970).

Although strong evidence favors a hereditary factor in the etiology of schizophrenia, we have no clear idea of how this susceptibility is transmitted. And even given an inherited predisposition, it is apparent that environmental factors play a major role. The fact that the monozygotic twin of a schizophrenic is as likely to be schizoid as schizophrenic points up the influence of environment.

Research on functional causation

Those promoting a functional theory believe that early child-care practices and interpersonal relationships in the home are the crucial variables in schizophrenia. They have looked for factors in the parent-child relationship (particularly the relationship with the mother) that would account for the social withdrawal, poor reality contact, and insecurity characteristic of the schizophrenic. Numerous studies in which the parents of schizophrenics were interviewed or patients were questioned about their early home life have had conflicting results. Mothers have been found to be both overprotective and rejecting, neglectful and overly involved with their offspring, too restrictive and too permissive. Fathers of schizophrenics have tended to be characterized as weak and ineffectual, or aloof and uninvolved with their children.

There are major difficulties with studies that attempt to relate early child-care practices with the development of schizophrenia. Most of them fail to provide a control group of parents whose children did not become schizophrenic. Hence, it is not clear whether the behavior of the parents of schizophrenics does actually differ from that of other parents. In those few studies that do have adequate controls it is difficult to determine whether the parents' attitudes caused the schizophrenia or whether the child was deviant to begin with and the parents' behavior was in response to this abnormality. The tendency for the mother to be over-controlling, for example, may be a reaction to deviance in her child. When mothers of schizophrenic, brain-injured, and retarded children were questioned about their child-rearing practices, all three groups were found to be more possessive and over-controlling than mothers of normal children (Klebanoff, 1959). This finding suggests that mothers tend to develop similar attitudes when confronted by abnormal behavior regardless of the nature of the behavior. Hence, maternal attitudes toward preschizophrenic children may be an effect and not a cause of the disorder.

Other investigators have focused not on specific patterns of child rearing but on the nature of communication within the family. They hypothesize that the tendency of the schizophrenic to retreat into fantasy and his difficulty in distinguishing real events from fantasied events and hallucinations stem from a family in which he was forced to accept confusing messages. The mother, for example, may say that she loves the child but communicates hostility by her behavior toward him. In order for the child to maintain a relationship with his mother, he must learn to falsely interpret his own feelings about her behavior (he cannot accept the possibility that she does not love him) and falsely interpret the message she is communicating. Such a situation would predispose the individual to distortions of reality.

Still other studies indicate that the disruption of the home by the death of one or both parents occurs more frequently in the background of schizophrenics than in that of normal individuals (Hilgard and Newman, 1961). Also more prevalent in the schizophrenic's background are home environments in which there is intense conflict, with both parents trying to dominate and devalue the other and to win the child to his side, or else a very skewed marital relationship, in which the more disturbed parent dominates the family (Lidz and others, 1965).

Research efforts over the past forty years have failed to reveal any single pattern of family interaction that leads to schizophrenia. Instead, it appears that stressful childhoods of various kinds may contribute to the disorder.

Research on biochemical factors

It may be that as a result of a hereditary defect, prenatal deficiency, or some other factor schizophrenics metabolize products that cause their mental symptoms. Some investigators have therefore searched for products in the blood or urine that differentiate schizophrenics from other persons.

To be fully meaningful the biochemical studies should provide the answers to the following questions. (1) If the kinds of chemical products found excessively in schizophrenics' blood or urine are injected into a normal person, will he develop symptoms resembling those of schizophrenia? (2) If known chemical antidotes to those products are injected, will the symptoms of schizophrenics be alleviated? While a clear answer cannot be given to these questions, partial evidence is encouraging to those who believe in a chemical basis for the symptoms. The drug LSD-25, if injected, produces hallucinatory symptoms in a normal person that somewhat resemble those in schizophrenics. Drugs known to be antagonistic to LSD-25 sometimes have ameliorative effects in schizophrenia. The drugs are marketed under many names, two of which are the so-called tranquilizers chlorpromazine and reserpine. The results of research are not yet sufficiently established to provide a chemical explanation of schizophrenia. For a critique of such studies, see Kety (1960).

All the developments we have discussed are promising, all are controversial, and no two are mutually exclusive. It is highly probable that there is a hereditary component to schizophrenia; most likely it takes the form of an inherited defect in the metabolism of certain chemical transmitters involved in neural activity, which predisposes the individual to a schizophrenic reaction when under stress. But it seems unlikely that heredity alone can account for schizophrenia. The situation may be similar to the case of allergies; there is an inherited predisposition to allergic sensitivities but certain environmental events are necessary to trigger the reaction. The controversial issue is whether schizophrenia can result from faulty learning in childhood in the absence of an inherited predisposition. Those who advocate an extreme hereditary viewpoint maintain that all schizophrenics have an inherited predisposition that will eventually lead to the disorder regardless of the nature of the early family environment. A stressful childhood will lead to an early and more severe illness (corresponding to process schizophrenia). Those raised in a favor-able family situation will not develop the disorder until they encounter stress later in life. Their illness will be less severe and more easily reversible (reactive schizophrenia). Research workers who emphasize the role of the environment point to the variety and complexity of schizophrenia symptoms as evidence that we are dealing not with a single disorder but with a group of disorders, which have some symptoms in common. Consequently, there may be a number of etiological agents. In some cases inherited physiological or biochemical weaknesses are primarily responsible for the schizophrenic symptoms, while in others environmental factors play the major role. This conception is also related to the process-reactive distinction, process schizophrenia presumably referring to those cases with a hereditary basis.

Psychopathic personality

The term *psychopathic personality* (also known as *antisocial personality*) refers to basically unsocialized individuals who are repeatedly in conflict with society. The psychopathic reaction differs from neurotic and psychotic reactions in that it is manifested by a life-long pattern of socially deviant behavior, rather than mental or emotional symptoms, and the individual experiences little, if any, anxiety or distress. The disorder is a serious one that seems peculiarly resistant to treatment.

Characteristics of the psychopathic personality

The chief characteristic of the psychopath is a lack of moral development, or conscience, and an inability to abide by the laws and customs of his society. His behavior is determined almost entirely by his own needs, and he is largely oblivious to the needs of others. He behaves impulsively, seeks immediate gratification of his desires, and cannot tolerate frustration. Whereas the average child realizes by the age of two that there are some restrictions in his environment and that at times he must postpone his pleasures in consideration of his parents' needs, the psychopath seldom learns to consider any but his own desires. It is this need for immediate gratification with no thought for the consequences that frequently puts him in conflict with the law. Seldom is his crime a premeditated one. He behaves on impulse; indeed, his life seems to be a series of erratic and impulsive acts with no long-range goals or purposes in view.

Unlike the neurotic, the psychopathic personality shows few, if any, signs of anxiety or guilt. In fact, several studies have indicated that he is at ease in situations that would make the average person tense and apprehensive. In a study by Lippert and Senter (1966) measurements of GSR were taken on two groups of adolescent delinquents selected from the detention unit of a juvenile court: one group had been diagnosed psychopathic reaction and the other "adjustment reaction of adolescence." The measurements were taken from each subject during successive periods of rest, auditory and visual stimulation, and stress.

During the stress period dummy electrodes were attached to the subject's leg, and he was told that in ten minutes he would be given a very strong but not harmful shock. (A large clock was visible so that the subject knew precisely when the shock was supposed to occur; no shock was actually administered.) The results showed no difference between the two groups in GSR measures during rest or in response to auditory or visual stimulation. However, during the ten minutes of shock anticipation the nonpsychopathic group showed significantly more tension than the psychopathic group, and, at the moment when the clock indicated shock was due, most of the nonpsychopathic delinquents showed an abrupt drop in skin resistance (indicating a sharp increase in anxiety); *none* of the psychopaths showed this reaction. These results support the clinical impression that the psychopathic individual has little anxiety concerning future discomforts or punishments. If this is the case, his impulsive acts become more understandable, since he is not deterred by fear of the consequences.

Often, the psychopath on first meeting appears to be an intelligent, pleasant, and well-mannered individual who gives the impression of frankness and honesty. It soon becomes apparent, however, that he feels no guilt concerning his antisocial acts (no matter how appalling) and has no compunctions about lying, which he does skillfully and convincingly. Unlike the nonpsychopathic delinquent, who may rebel against society but who still adheres to the code of his "gang," the psychopath seems to have few values—neither those of society nor of a gang—and he feels no alliance or loyalty to anyone but himself. Although superficially he may appear friendly, the psychopath is usually a lone wolf who is incapable of forming a close relationship with another person. These two characteristics, guiltlessness and lovelessness, are so outstanding that they are considered the distinguishing features in the diagnosis of psychopathic personality disorder (McCord and McCord, 1964).

In the same way that neurotic reactions were described as being exaggerated forms of normal defense mechanisms, the characteristics of the psychopath can be found in a much milder degree among normal persons. We all vary in our ability to postpone gratifications of our impulses, in the strictness of our conscience and feelings of guilt when we break social codes, and in our ability to be concerned with the welfare of other people. There is no sharp dichotomy between the normal individual and the psychopath. Individuals could be placed along a continuum in terms of the characteristics we have described; the psychopaths would be those persons who fell at the extreme end of the continuum.

Causative factors in psychopathic personality

What factors contribute to the development of the psychopathic personality? We might expect such individuals to come from homes in which they received no discipline or training in moral behavior. But the answer is not that simple. Although some psychopaths do come from slum neighborhoods where antisocial behavior may actually be reinforced and where adult criminals may serve as models for personality development, many more come from "good" homes and their parents are prominent and respected members of the community.

Many theorists believe that the development of a mature conscience depends upon an affectionate relationship with an adult during the early childhood years. The normal child internalizes his parents' values (which generally reflect the values of his society) because he wants to be like them and because he fears the loss of their love if he does not behave in accordance with their values. When a child receives no love from either of his parents, he does not fear its loss. Because he does not identify with the rejecting parents he does not internalize their rules. Wrongdoing consists not of breaking rules, only of getting caught and punished; he experiences little or no anxiety or guilt. Such a person is classified as a psychopath. While this theory of the origin of psychopathic behavior has some plausibility, confirmation awaits further research.

What should our laws be with regard to treatment of a mentally disturbed person who commits a criminal act? This is a question that is of great concern to social scientists, members of the legal profession, and to anyone who works with criminal offenders. The psychopath can be one of the most dangerous types of criminals; nevertheless, by legal definition he is not insane and, consequently, cannot be committed to a neuropsychiatric hospital for treatment.

The idea that a person is not responsible for an act that is due to a mental disorder was first introduced into law in 1724, when an English court maintained that a man was irresponsible if "he doth not know what he is doing, no more than . . . a wild beast." Contemporary standards of legal responsibility, however, are based on the M'Naghten decision of 1843. M'Naghten, a Scotsman, suffered the paranoid delusion that he was being persecuted by the English prime minister, Sir Robert Peel. In an attempt to kill Peel he mistakenly shot Peel's secretary. All involved in the trial were convinced by M'Naghten's senseless ramblings that he was insane. He was judged not responsible by reasons of insanity and sent to a mental hospital, where he remained until his death. The reigning monarch at the time, Queen Victoria, was not pleased by the verdict—apparently feeling that political assassinations should not be taken lightly—and called upon the House of Lords to review the decision. The decision was upheld and the rules were put into writing regarding the legal definition of insanity. The M'Naghten Rules state that a defendant may be found "not guilty" by reasons of insanity only if he were so severely disturbed at the time of his act that he did not know what he was doing or, if he did know, did not know that it was wrong.

The distinction of knowing right from wrong has been the basis of decisions on legal insanity up to the present time. Many psychologists and psychiatrists who are called upon for expert testimony in such trials feel that the M'Naghten Rules are much too narrow. Frequently individuals who are clearly psychotic can still respond correctly when asked if a particular act is morally right or wrong. And a kleptomaniac knows that it is wrong to steal, but his compulsion to do so is so intense that such knowledge does not deter him. A few states, recognizing this situation, have added to their statutes the doctrine of "irresistible impulse"; in such states a defendant may be declared legally insane, even

Prevalence of mental disorders

Severe mental illness is an important social problem. At any given moment approximately 750,000 patients are being cared for in the mental hospitals of the United States, and they occupy more than half of all hospital beds.[5] This means that more people are presently hospitalized for mental illness than for cancer, heart disease, tuberculosis, and all other diseases combined. Estimates indicate that one out of every ten babies born today will be hospitalized for mental illness

at some time during his life. If these statistics sound too depressing, we should hasten to add that half the patients admitted to mental hospitals are eventually discharged as improved or recovered, most of these within the first year of entering the hospital. The percentage is higher for patients in well-staffed hospitals that use modern treatment methods.

The approximate distribution of mental hospital admissions according to type of disorder is shown in Figure 20-2. The most prevalent diagnosis is schizophrenic reaction; about 25 percent of first admissions to public mental hospitals are individuals classed as having one of the schizophrenic

[5]This somewhat astonishing figure results from the fact that many mental patients are hospitalized for several months or even years, while general medical patients require an average hospitalization of only two weeks.

if he knew what he was doing and knew right from wrong, if the jury decides he was driven to his crime by a compulsion too strong to be resisted.

A more reasonable legal definition of insanity was adopted by the U. S. Court of Appeals for the Second Circuit in 1966. The definition of criminal responsibility had been proposed by the American Law Institute after a careful ten-year study. It is: "A person is not responsible for criminal conduct if at the time of such conduct as a result of mental disease or defect he lacks substantial capacity either to appreciate the wrongfulness of his conduct or to conform his conduct to the requirements of the law." The word "substantial" suggests that "any" incapacity is not enough to avoid criminal responsibility, but "total" incapacity is not required either. The word "appreciate" rather than "know" implies that intellectual awareness of right or wrong is not enough; the person must have some understanding of the moral or legal consequences of his behavior before he can be held criminally responsible. This new rule is mandatory in all federal courts in New York, Connecticut, and Vermont. But it is expected that the lower courts in these states will also follow the rule, and it is to be hoped that other state and federal courts will adopt it also.

The problem of legal responsibility in the case of mentally disordered individuals is indeed complex. A revolutionary approach toward criminal law has been proposed by Glueck (1962). His proposal would separate two functions of the law: determination of guilt and imposition of the sentence. The jury hearing a criminal case in which the defendant's sanity is in question would be asked only to determine whether the defendant is guilty of the crime with which he is charged. If he is convicted, the determination of treatment would be made by a tribunal of criminologists, psychologists, and psychiatrists who would evaluate the nature and causes of his behavior and decide whether the needs of society and the individual's chances for rehabilitation would be best served by treating him in a neuropsychiatric hospital or punishing him in a prison. The convicted individual's progress could be evaluated periodically and a decision made as to when he had made a sufficiently satisfactory adjustment so that he could be released. This procedure would be superior to a system under which the judge must prescribe at the time of sentencing the length of time the individual should be hospitalized.

disorders. Because the schizophrenic patients tend to be young and their death rate is comparatively low, those who are not discharged accumulate over the years to make up half the resident population of mental hospitals. Older persons suffering from senile disorders related to cerebral arteriosclerosis and other physiological conditions of aging constitute 24 percent of first admissions; since their death rate is relatively high they make up only about 14 percent of the resident hospital population.

The admission rate for neuroses is low because many neurotics are treated as outpatients and therefore are not entered on hospital records. For this reason, and because the disorder is not clearly defined and merges with the normal, the prevalence of neuroses in the general population is hard to estimate. The existing data suggest that neurotic disorders are far more prevalent than one might expect. Two community studies, one in New York City and another in a small town in Nova Scotia, give some measure of the extent of symptoms of disturbed mental health. The New York study estimates that 30 percent of the population have clinical symptoms sufficient to disturb their everyday lives. That this high figure is not due solely to the strains of urban life is indicated by the figure of 32 percent for the small town (Srole and others, 1962; Leighton and others, 1963).

Community surveys have begun to provide some interesting information concerning the distribution of the various disorders in different socioeconomic groups, although the reasons for the differences are

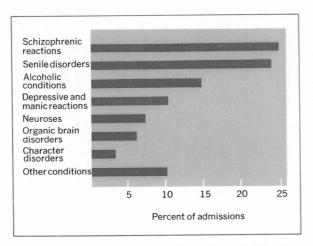

Fig. **20-2** **First admissions to U. S. public mental hospitals in 1969** In this figure senile disorders refer to cerebral arteriosclerosis and other physiological conditions of aging; organic brain disorders refer to infection, injury, epilepsy, and so on. (Data from the U. S. Public Health Service)

differences in child-rearing practices that may predispose the children to different kinds of defense mechanisms, and (3) the devastating effect of poverty, which engenders a feeling of helplessness and a desire to withdraw from the harshness of reality. Much more information is needed before we can evaluate the contribution of these and other factors to the higher incidence of psychoses among the lower class.

The question has often been asked whether the conditions of modern life have increased the amount of mental illness. This is an extremely difficult, if not impossible, question to answer. Although mental-hospital admission rates have increased more rapidly than the increase in population within the past eighty years, the difference can be largely explained by increased hospital facilities, a more enlightened attitude toward mental illness, and a major increase in the number of senile patients being cared for in hospitals. Careful

not at all clear. Several studies have found that the neuroses are more prevalent in the upper and middle classes, whereas a disproportionate number of psychotic reactions occur in the lower class. In the New York study, which covered all ranges of socioeconomic status, the incidence of psychotic disorders was found to be 13 percent in the lowest socioeconomic group, as compared with 3.6 percent in the upper class (Srole and others, 1962). A study in New Haven, Connecticut, found similar results and noted that even among the neurotics there were class differences in types of symptoms. The upper-class neurotics tended to report more subjective emotional discomfort—anxiety, dissatisfaction, and unhappiness with themselves—while the lower-class neurotics tended to show more somatic symptoms and unhappiness and friction with other people. Neurotics in the middle class were characterized by both sorts of symptoms (Hollingshead and Redlich, 1958; Myers and Bean, 1968).

A number of hypotheses have been offered to explain the class differences in incidence of psychoses. These include (1) movement downward in class status as the individual becomes more seriously disturbed and less able to hold a job, (2) class

Fig. **20-3** **Patients in mental hospitals** This figure compares the number of patients in mental hospitals with the total population (age 15 and over) of the United States from 1900 to 1970. The black curve measures the total population in units of 10 million. The color curve measures the number of hospitalized mental patients per 100,000 persons in the population. Note that the number of patients increased more rapidly than the population until the 1950s, and then dropped off. (Data from the U. S. Department of Health, Education, and Welfare)

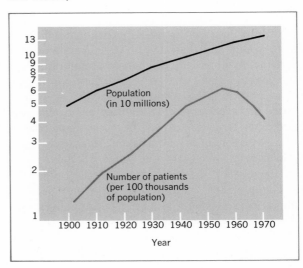

consideration of these and other facts has led most experts to conclude that there was little if any increase in severe mental illness between the years 1885 and 1940. During the Second World War there was a noticeable increase in mental-hospital admission rates for males of service age. This increase could be explained by (1) increased facilities provided by the Veterans Administration Hospitals, (2) the possibility that induction examinations identified as mentally ill some individuals who would otherwise have gone undetected, and (3) the possibility that war conditions and separation from home actually increased the severity and frequency of mental disorders (Pugh and Mac-Mahon, 1962).

Since 1955 we have seen for the first time a significant decline in the number of patients in mental hospitals. Despite an increasing population there were 158,000 fewer patients in United States mental hospitals in 1968 than there were in 1955, and the decline appears to be continuing (see Figure 20-3). This encouraging trend can be attributed in part to improved techniques of treatment, including the use of tranquilizing drugs, which will be discussed in the next chapter.

Summary

1. We can think of a continuum of adjustment ranging from the well-adjusted individual—who is characterized by productivity, zest for life, ability to relate warmly to other people, and acceptance of his own motives and feelings—through the maladjusted *neurotic* and the more seriously disturbed *psychotic*. The diagnosis of abnormal behavior is based on statistical frequency, social values, and degree of impairment.

2. *Neurotic reactions,* characterized by anxiety, are usually extreme forms of normal defense mechanisms used in an unsuccessful attempt to resolve persistent conflicts. These include *anxiety reaction, obsessive-compulsive reaction, phobic reaction,* and *conversion reaction.*

3. *Psychotic reactions* reflect a more serious disintegration of behavior, disturbance of thought processes, and a weakened contact with reality. Two common *functional psychoses* (those with no clear organic basis) are *manic-depressive reaction,* characterized by exaggerated periodic deviations in mood, and *schizophrenic reaction,* which may include such symptoms as withdrawal, autism, delusions, hallucinations, and dulled or inappropriate affect. There are also mental disorders associated with definite *organic* causes (alcoholism, physical disease, and injury) and *psychosomatic* illnesses, in which physiological changes (such as ulcers) accompany psychological conditions.

4. Research on the causative factors in schizophrenia has been concerned with evidence for a hereditary predisposition to the disorder, pathology of the schizophrenic's early home life, and the possibility that biochemical defects may cause schizophrenic symptoms.

5. Individuals classified as *psychopathic personalities* are impulsive, concerned only with their own needs, unable to form close relationships, free from anxiety or guilt, and frequently in trouble with the law. Severe rejection by both parents during childhood is postulated as the factor responsible for failure to develop a mature conscience.

6. Mental disorders constitute a serious social problem. It is estimated that one out of every ten babies born today will spend some time in a mental hospital; community studies have shown that as many as 30 percent of the population have clinical symptoms of personality disturbance sufficient to interfere with their daily efficiency. Severity of mental disorder is inversely related to socioeconomic status: three times as many lower-class people are diagnosed psychotic as compared with those in the upper classes.

Suggestions for further reading

For general discussions of mental disorders, see such textbooks in psychiatry as Redlich and Freedman, *The theory and practice of psychiatry* (1966), and those in abnormal psychology, such as Coleman and Broen, *Abnormal psychology and modern life* (4th ed., 1971), White, *The abnormal personality* (3rd ed., 1964), and London and Rosenhan (eds.), *Foundations of abnormal psychology* (1968). Two books that emphasize an experimental approach to psychopathology are Buss, *Psychopathology* (1966), and Maher, *Principles of psychopathology: An experimental approach* (1966). An excellent text stressing a sociopsychological approach to behavior disorders is Ullmann and Krasner, *A psychological approach to abnormal behavior* (1969).

Problems of adjustment, especially as faced by college students, are treated in Lindgren, *Psychology of personal development* (1964), and Sawrey and Telford, *Psychology of adjustment* (3rd ed., 1971).

A comprehensive review of research and theory on schizophrenia is provided by Jackson, *The etiology of schizophrenia* (1960), and Rosenthal and Kety (eds.), *The transmission of schizophrenia* (1968).

psychotherapy and related techniques

THE LAST CHAPTER DESCRIBED VARIOUS TYPES of behavior disorders. We shall now go on to discuss the kinds of therapeutic techniques that are being used to treat these disorders. These techniques can be divided into two major classes: *somatotherapy,* which attempts to change the patient's behavior by physiological methods (drugs, shock treatment, or psychosurgery); and *psychotherapy,* which attempts to bring about behavior change through psychological methods, most frequently processes of communication between the patient and another person called the *psychotherapist.* We shall mention the somatotherapies only briefly and devote most of our discussion to various psychotherapies. Before we do so, however, it is enlightening to consider briefly the history of treatment of the mentally ill.

Historical background

Man's attitude toward and treatment of mental illness has varied throughout the ages as a function of his attitude toward himself and the world around him. The early Chinese, Egyptians, and Hebrews considered disordered behavior to be caused by demons or evil spirits that had taken possession of the body. The treatment then was to exorcise the demons by such techniques as prayer, incantation, magic, and the use of purgatives concocted from herbs. In the event that such treatment brought no improvement, more extreme measures were taken to ensure that the body would be an unpleasant dwelling place for the evil spirit; flogging, starving, burning, even stoning to death were not infrequent forms of treatment. The Old Testament makes a number of references to demonology. In Leviticus (20:28) it is stated that "A man also or woman that hath a familiar spirit, or that is a wizard, shall surely be put to death: they shall stone them with their stones: their blood shall be upon them." Although in most cases possession was thought to be by evil spirits, instances in which the behavior was of a mystical or religious nature were believed to result from possession by a good or holy spirit. Such people were therefore respected and worshiped. During this period treatment of the mentally ill was in the hands of the priests, who had the power to perform the exorcism.

The first progress in the understanding of mental disorders came with the Greek physician Hippocrates (c. 460–377 B.C.). Hippocrates rejected the idea of demonology and maintained that mental disorders were the result of a disturbance in the balance of body fluids. He and the Greek and Roman physicians who followed him argued for a more humane treatment of the mentally ill. Instead of the primitive methods of exorcism they stressed the importance of pleasant surroundings, exercise, proper diet, massage, soothing baths, and some less desirable methods such as bleeding, purging, and mechanical restraints. Although there were no institutions as such for the mentally ill, many were cared for with great kindness by physicians in temples dedicated to the Greek and Roman gods.

Such progress did not last, however. The Middle Ages saw a growing revival of primitive superstition and demonology. The mentally ill were thought to be in league with Satan and to possess supernatural powers by which they could cause floods, pestilence, and all sorts of injuries to others. In the belief that by treating an insane person cruelly one was punishing the devil inside him, those living in medieval times justified such measures as beating, starving, and branding with hot

The Bettmann Archive

Fig. 21-1 Early methods for treating the mentally ill
An early method of treatment called for the branding of the patient's head with hot irons to bring him to his senses.

As late as the early nineteenth century, English asylums used rotating devices of this sort, in which the patients were whirled around at high speeds.

The Bettmann Archive

irons (see Figure 21-1). This type of cruelty reached its culmination with the witchcraft trials that sentenced to death thousands of people (many of them mentally ill) during the fifteenth through the seventeenth centuries.

Early asylums

To cope with the mentally ill who roamed the streets in the latter part of the Middle Ages, asylums were created. These were not treatment centers but simply prisons; the inmates were chained in dark and filthy cells and treated more like animals than human beings. It was not until 1792, when Philippe Pinel was put in charge of an asylum in Paris, that some improvement was made in the treatment of these unfortunate people. Pinel was allowed, as an experiment, to remove the chains from the inmates. Much to the amazement of the skeptics who thought he was mad to unchain such "animals," Pinel's experiment was a success. With release from restraint, placement in clean and sunny rooms instead of dungeons, and kind treatment, many who had been considered hopelessly mad for years improved sufficiently to leave the asylum.

The turn of this century brought great forward strides in medicine and psychology. The discovery of the syphilis spirochete in 1905 demonstrated that there was a physical cause for the mental disorder general paresis and encouraged those physicians who held that mental illness was organic in origin. The work of Sigmund Freud and his followers laid the groundwork for an understanding of mental illness as a function of environmental factors. And Pavlov demonstrated in his laboratory experiments on conditioning that a state similar to an acute neurosis could be produced in animals by requiring them to make discriminations beyond their capacities.

Despite these scientific advances the general public in the early 1900s still had no understanding of mental illness and viewed mental hospitals and their inmates as objects of fear and horror. The education of the public in the principles of mental health was begun through the efforts of Clifford Beers. As a young man Beers developed a manic-depressive psychosis and was hospitalized for three years in several private and state hospitals. Although chains and other methods of torture had long since disappeared, the straightjacket was still widely used to restrain excited patients; lack of adequate funds made the average state mental hospital—with its overcrowded wards, poor food, unsympathetic and frequently sadistic attendants—a far from pleasant place to live. After his recovery Beers published his experiences in a now famous book entitled *A mind that found itself* (1908). This book did much to arouse public interest. Beers worked ceaselessly in an effort to educate the public in an understanding of mental illness and helped to organize the National Committee for Mental Hygiene. In 1950 this organization joined with two related groups to form what is now the National Association for Mental Health. The mental-hygiene movement played an invaluable role in educating the public and in stimulating the organization of child-guidance clinics and community mental-health clinics, which could aid in the prevention as well as the treatment of mental disorders.

Modern treatment facilities

In the past twenty-five years a great improvement in treatment facilities for the mentally disturbed has taken place. The neuropsychiatric hospitals established by the Veterans Administration after the Second World War were generally superior to the average state-supported hospital and served as an impetus for the improvement of state hospitals. Although some state hospitals are still primarily custodial institutions where inmates lead an idle and futile existence in run-down, overcrowded wards, most mental hospitals today are attractive, well-kept, and busy places, where trained personnel guide the patients through a wide range of activities. Each patient's daily schedule is planned to meet his particular needs and may include time with his individual therapist, in group psychotherapy, or in occupational therapy designed to teach skills as well as provide relaxation. Treatment may also include physical recreation to help relieve tensions, and educational therapy to prepare the patient for a job upon release from the hospital. Patients who are well enough may work part-time in the various hospital departments as patient-employees, thereby earning some money and feeling that they are contributing to the welfare of the hospital community.

In the past mental hospitals have been fairly isolated institutions located away from the major cities, but the current trend is toward building hospitals near universities and medical schools in more populated areas. In this way the latest research developments and various specialists on the university or medical school faculty are accessible to the hospital staff. Many mental hospitals serve as training centers for interns in psychiatry, psychology, and psychiatric social work as well as for students in psychiatric nursing and occupational and physical therapy. In addition, some mental hospitals carry on large-scale research projects of their own. Locating mental hospitals in or near the cities also makes the task of gradually integrating the patient back into community life much easier.

Another current trend is to provide treatment centers for the mentally ill in general medical hospitals. At present, more patients are treated in psychiatric wards of general hospitals than are admitted to state or federal mental hospitals. Outpatient and mental-health clinics also serve an extremely important function. A number of general and neuropsychiatric hospitals maintain outpatient clinics where discharged patients may be seen for follow-up treatment. Mental-health clinics supported by federal, state, and county funds now service almost every community, as do a number of private clinics. They play a crucial role in preventing serious mental illness by treating emotionally disturbed individuals before their condition becomes acute enough to require hospitalization.

Because current methods of treatment have proved far from satisfactory in ameliorating established behavior disorders, early detection and prevention become all the more important. To this end greater emphasis is being placed on psychological services in the early school years. Studies have shown that children identified as having emotional problems in the elementary-school grades do not outgrow such problems as a matter of development, but instead function even more ineffectively by the time that they enter high school.

Since, as we have seen, the incidence of psychosis is highest among the lower classes, another current emphasis is on "community mental health," which involves practical attempts to alleviate the environment of the poor and to help them cope with the problems of everyday existence.

Professions involved in psychotherapy

A professional team composed of a psychiatrist, clinical psychologist, and psychiatric social worker may work together on a given case or they may function independently. A *psychiatrist* is a physician whose experience covers cases both in mental hospitals and in outpatient clinics. He takes medical responsibility for the patient in addition to any psychotherapeutic role he may play. A *psychoanalyst* is a specialist within psychiatry who uses methods and theories derived from those of Sigmund Freud. A psychoanalyst is today almost always a psychiatrist,[1] but a psychiatrist is most often not a psychoanalyst.

A *clinical psychologist* has had graduate training in psychology, has usually earned his Ph.D., and has served special internships in the fields of testing and diagnosis, psychotherapy, and research. He tends mainly to administer and interpret psychological tests and to conduct psychotherapy. He is also active in research.

A *psychiatric social worker* usually has earned his M.A. at a graduate school of social work, and has special training in interviewing in the home and in carrying treatment procedures into the home and community. Because of this special training, the social worker is likely to be called upon to collect information about the home and to interview relatives, in addition to participating in the therapeutic procedures with the patient.

In mental hospitals a fourth professional person

[1] There are a few "lay" psychoanalysts, that is, analysts without an M.D. degree

joins the team: the *psychiatric nurse.* Psychiatric nursing is a specialty within the nursing profession and calls for special training in the handling of mental patients—both those severely disturbed and those on the way to recovery.

In our discussion of psychotherapeutic techniques we will not specify the profession to which the psychotherapist belongs; the assumption is that he is a trained and competent member of any one of these professions.

The techniques of psychotherapy

The term *psychotherapy* embraces a wide variety of techniques, all of which have the goal of helping the emotionally disturbed individual modify his behavior so that he can make a more satisfactory adjustment to his environment. As we shall see, some psychotherapists believe that modification of behavior is dependent upon the patient's understanding of his unconscious motives and conflicts, while others feel that patients can learn more adaptive ways of coping with their problems without necessarily exploring factors in the past that have led to the development of the problems. Despite differences in techniques, all methods of psychotherapy have certain basic features in common. They involve communication between two individuals, the patient and the therapist, in which the patient is encouraged to express freely his most intimate fears, emotions, and experiences without fear of being judged or condemned by the therapist. The therapist, in turn, while being sympathetic and understanding of the patient's problems, does not become emotionally involved (as would a friend or relative) but maintains an objectivity that enables him to view the patient's difficulties more clearly.

The techniques of psychotherapy have been used most successfully with the milder forms of mental disorder, the neuroses, although some therapists have reported success with psychotics. The neurotic is usually aware that he has problems, is anxious for help, and is able to communicate with the therapist. The psychotic, on the other hand, is frequently so involved in his fantasy world and so unaware of reality that it is extremely difficult to communicate with him. The process of establishing contact (developing what is called *rapport*) with the psychotic is a lengthy one, which must be undertaken before psychotherapy can begin. Fortu-

nately, some new drugs being used with psychotic patients make them more amenable to treatment by psychotherapy.

Psychoanalysis

The psychotherapeutic technique with which the average layman is most familiar is psychoanalysis, a method of treatment based on the concepts of Sigmund Freud. Psychoanalysis is not a large profession; in 1970 there were some 1250 active members of the American Psychoanalytic Association, the recognized organization for fully accredited psychoanalysts in this country. But the influence of psychoanalysis is much more pervasive than the small number of practitioners would suggest.

Along with a method of treatment, Freud proposed a body of psychological theory that has, in one form or another, influenced much of modern thinking—in literature as well as in psychology, medicine, and social science. We shall be concerned chiefly with the nature of psychoanalytic therapy, but it should be kept in mind that the observations made within this technique represent the basic data upon which Freud's theories rest.

Free association. The psychoanalyst ordinarily sees a patient for fifty-minute visits several times a week for periods of from one to several years. Psychoanalytic therapy, in its original form, is thus not only intensive but extensive. In the introductory sessions the patient gives a description of his symptoms. He recounts relevant facts from his personal biography. He is then prepared to enter upon *free association,* one of the foundations of the psychoanalytic method. The purpose of free association is to bring to awareness and to put into words thoughts and feelings of which the patient is unaware or that ordinarily go unacknowledged if they come to awareness.

In free association the patient is taught the "basic rule" that he is to say everything that enters his mind, without selection, without editing. This rule is a very difficult one to follow. The patient's lifetime has been spent in learning self-control, in learning to hold his tongue, in learning to think before speaking. Even the patient who tries conscientiously to follow the rule finds that he fails to tell many things. Some passing thoughts seem to be too unimportant to mention, some too stupid, others too indiscreet.

Suppose, for example, that a person's freedom is being hampered by the presence in his household of an invalid for whose care he is responsible. Under such circumstances he may unconsciously wish for the relief that death of the invalid might bring. But he would disapprove of such a death wish because it would be a violation of his loyalty to the sick person. Actually, a death wish of this kind may be very near to awareness, but the habits of a lifetime make the patient deny the wish even to himself. He may show in his fantasies or in other ways a preoccupation with death; possibly he hums tunes that are played at funerals. By acknowledging these fleeting thoughts instead of repressing them, he becomes aware, first of all, of previously unrecognized ideas and feelings close to awareness. With practice, he gradually brings to consciousness ideas and feelings that have been deeply repressed.

A person unconsciously represses or resists the recall of certain thoughts and feelings because he fears that to acknowledge them will threaten or degrade him. This *resistance* must be overcome before the patient can associate freely; one of the tasks of the therapist is to aid him in overcoming his resistances. Sometimes a patient has a free flow of associations until he comes to something that blocks him. Then his mind seems to go blank, and he can think of nothing to say. This blankness is judged to be resistance to the recall of something effectively repressed. Sometimes, after a particularly revealing session, the patient may forget his next appointment, another indication of resistance to revealing what is hidden. Because resistances are unconscious, they mean that the patient is unable to cooperate fully even though he consciously wishes to do so.

Interpretation. The psychoanalyst attempts to overcome the patient's resistance and to lead him to fuller self-understanding through *interpretation*. The interpretation is likely to take two forms. First, the analyst calls the attention of the patient to his resistances. The patient often learns something about himself when he discovers that a train of associations is suddenly blocked, that he forgets his appointment, that he wants to change the subject, and so on. Second, the analyst may privately deduce the general nature of what lies behind the patient's statements and by imparting a hint may facilitate further associations. The patient may say something that seems trivial to him and half apologize for its unimportance. Here the analyst may point out that what seems trivial may in fact allude to something important. This hint may lead, if the interpretation is appropriately timed, to significant associations. It should be noted that the analyst is careful not to suggest *just what it is* that is important to the patient; this the patient must discover for himself.

The analyst gives somewhat different interpretations in the early and late stages of analysis. Early in the analysis he is likely to give interpretations that help the patient to understand resistance. He may encourage free association by pointing out the importance of the seemingly trivial or by noting connections in the patient's associations between thoughts that at first seemed totally unrelated. But, as the analysis moves on, the analyst gives more complex interpretations of the content of the patient's associations.

Transference. Any psychotherapeutic relationship is social, involving as it does an interaction between the patient and therapist. In psychoanalytical treatment the attitudes of the patient toward the analyst become important in determining his progress. Sooner or later in analysis the patient develops strong emotional responses to the psychoanalyst, perhaps admiring him greatly in one session but despising him in the next. This tendency of the patient to make the therapist the object of emotional response is known as *transference,* and the interpretation of transference, although a controversial topic, is one of the foundations of psychoanalytic therapy. According to the theory, the patient sees the therapist as possessing attitudes and attributes like those of his parents or those of his brothers and sisters, even though the therapist may be very unlike any of the people for whom he substitutes.

To cite one example: A young woman being treated by a woman psychoanalyst remarked one day as she entered the analyst's office, "I'm glad you're not wearing those lace collars you wore the last several times I was here. I don't like them on you." During the hour, the analyst was able to point out that she had not in fact worn any lace collars. During the preceding sessions the patient had assigned to the analyst the role of the patient's mother and had falsely pictured the analyst as dressing as the patient's mother had dressed when the patient was a child undergoing the emotionally disturbing experiences being discussed with the analyst. The patient, while surprised, accepted the interpretation and thereby gained understanding of transference.

Transference is not always manifested in false perceptions; often the patient simply expresses feelings toward the analyst that he had felt toward figures important earlier in his life. On the basis of these expressed feelings, the analyst is able to interpret the nature of the impulses that have been displaced in his direction. For example, a patient who has always admired an older brother detects something in the analyst's attitude that reminds him of the brother. An angry attack upon the analyst may lead to the uncovering of hostile feelings toward his brother that the patient heretofore had never acknowledged. By studying how the patient feels toward him, the analyst helps the patient to better understand his conduct in relation to others.

Abreaction, insight, and working through. The course of improvement during psychoanalytic therapy is commonly attributed to three main experiences: *abreaction,* gradual *insight* into one's difficulties, and the patient's repeated *working through* of his conflicts and his reactions to them.

A patient experiences *abreaction* when he freely expresses a repressed emotion or relives an intense emotional experience. The process is also called "catharsis," as though it were a kind of emotional cleansing. Such free expression may bring some relief, but by itself it does not eliminate the causes of conflict.

A patient has *insight* when he understands the roots of the conflict. Sometimes insight comes upon the recovery of the memory of a repressed experience, but the popular notion that a psychoanalytic cure typically results from the sudden recall of a single dramatic episode is mistaken. The patient's troubles seldom have a single source, and insight comes through a gradual increase in self-knowledge. Insight and abreaction must work together: the patient must understand his feelings and feel what he understands. The reorientation is never simply intellectual.

As analysis progresses the patient goes through a lengthy process of reeducation known as *working through.* By examining, in the consultation room's supportive atmosphere, the same conflicts over and over again as they have appeared in a variety of situations during his life, the patient learns to face rather than to deny reality and to react in more mature and effective ways. By working through, the patient becomes strong enough to face the threat of the original conflict situation and to react to it without undue anxiety.

The end result claimed for a successful psychoanalysis is a deep-seated modification of the personality that makes it possible for the patient to cope with his problems on a realistic basis, without the recurrence of the symptoms that brought him to treatment, and that will lead to a more comfortable and richer life.

Psychoanalysis is a lengthy process and generally very expensive. It is most successful with individuals who are highly motivated to solve their problems and who can verbalize their feelings with some degree of ease.

Client-centered psychotherapy

Client-centered or *nondirective* psychotherapy is a method of treatment developed by Carl Rogers and his associates (Rogers, 1961; 1967) that in some respects is markedly different from psychoanalysis. It is *client-centered* because its purpose is to have the client or patient arrive at the insights and make the decisions rather than the therapist. It is *nondirective* because the therapist does not try to direct the patient's attention to specific topics (such as his relationship with his wife or his early childhood experiences) but leaves the topics to be discussed up to the patient. Unlike psychoanalysis, client-centered therapy does not attempt to relate the patient's problems to experiences in his early history. It is concerned with the patient's *present* attitudes and behavior; for this reason the client-centered therapist does not believe it necessary to obtain a case history or to spend the initial interviews gathering biographical material.

Client-centered therapy can be described rather simply, but in practice it requires great skill and is much more subtle than it first appears. The therapist begins by structuring the interview, by explaining the terms of agreement between him and the client: the responsibility for working out his problems is the client's; he is free to leave at any time, and to choose whether or not to return; the relationship is a private and confidential one; the client is free to speak of intimate matters without fear of reproof or of having the information revealed to others. Once the interview is structured, the client does most of the talking. Usually he has a good deal to "get off his chest." The therapist is a patient but alert listener. When the client stops, as though expecting the therapist to say something, the therapist usually acknowledges and accepts the feelings the client has been expressing. For example, if the client has been telling about how he is nagged by his mother, the therapist may say: "You feel that your mother tries to control you." His object is to *clarify* the feelings the client has been expressing, not to judge them or to elaborate on them.

What usually happens is that the client begins with a rather low evaluation of himself, but in the course of facing up to his problems and bringing his own resources to bear on them he becomes more positive. For example, one reported case began with statements such as the following:

> Everything is wrong with me. I feel abnormal. I don't do even the ordinary things of life. I'm sure I will fail on anything I undertake. I'm inferior. When I try to imitate successful people, I'm only acting. I can't go on like this [case reported by Snyder and others, 1947].

By the time of her final interview she expressed the following attitudes, contrasting strikingly with those of the first interview:

> I am taking a new course of my own choosing. I am really changing. I have always tried to live up to others' standards that were beyond my abilities. I've come to realize that I'm not so bright, but I can get along anyway. I no longer think so much about myself. I'm much more comfortable with people. I'm getting a feeling of success out of my job. I don't feel quite steady yet, and would like to feel that I can come for more help if I need it.

To determine whether this kind of progress is typical, experimenters have carefully analyzed recorded interviews. When the client's statements are classified and plotted, the course of therapy turns out to be fairly predictable. For example, in the early interviews the client spends a good deal of time talking about his difficulties, stating his problem, describing his symptoms. In the course of therapy he increasingly makes statements showing that he understands the implications for his personality of the topics being discussed. By classifying all the client's remarks as either problem restatements or statements of understanding and insight, one can see the progressive increase in insight as therapy proceeds (Figure 21-2).

What does the therapist do to bring about these changes? First of all, he creates an atmosphere in which the client feels his own worth and significance. The atmosphere arises not as a consequence of technique but out of the therapist's conviction that every person has the capacity to deal constructively with his psychological situation and with those aspects of his life that can come into conscious awareness.

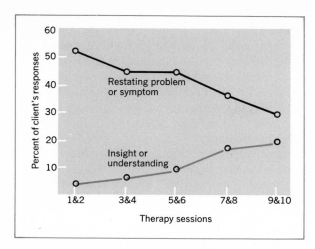

Fig. 21-2 Changes during client-centered therapy Recital of the problem on the part of the client gradually gives way during the course of therapy to increased frequency of statements indicating understanding. (Data from Seeman, 1949)

In accepting this viewpoint the therapist is not merely a passive listener; if he were, the client might feel that the therapist was not interested in him. The therapist listens intently and tries to show in what he says that he can see things as the client sees them. When he originated client-centered therapy, Rogers laid great emphasis upon having the therapist try to clarify the feelings expressed by the client. Rogers now believes that method to be too intellectualistic; currently he places the emphasis upon the therapist's trying to adopt the client's own frame of reference, upon his trying to see the problems as the client sees them, but without becoming emotionally involved in them. To have therapeutic value, the change in the client must be a change in feeling, a change in attitude—not merely a change in intellectual understanding.

For Rogers the most important element of a therapeutic relationship is a therapist who is a "genuine or self-congruent person," that is, one who is not playing a role or operating behind a professional front but is open and honest in his relationship with the patient. People tend not to reveal themselves to those who seem to be saying things they do not feel and who are not completely genuine in their relationship with others.

A great deal has been learned from those who advocate and practice client-centered therapy. It is difficult to know with certainty what its range of usefulness is and wherein its limitations lie. It does appear that this method (as is true of psychoanalysis) can function successfully only with individuals who are fairly verbal and motivated to discuss their problems. With persons who do not voluntarily seek help, such as prisoners and juvenile delinquents, and with psychotics who are too withdrawn to be able to discuss their feelings, more directive methods are usually necessary. The techniques of client-centered therapy have been used successfully, however, in counseling with neurotic patients, in play therapy with children, and in group therapy.

Behavior therapy

A more recent approach to psychotherapy attempts to apply the principles of learning discussed in Chapter 8 to the treatment of neurotic (and in some instances psychotic) disorders. If maladaptive behavior is learned, then by employing some of the techniques developed in experimental work on learning, we should be able to substitute new and more appropriate responses for the maladaptive ones. Psychotherapy based on this approach has been given various names; the one currently favored is *behavior therapy,* so named because it is concerned with modifying the *behavior* of the patient rather than developing insight or resolving unconscious conflicts (Wolpe and Lazarus, 1966; Ullmann and Krasner, 1969; Bandura, 1969).

One of the techniques frequently used is based on the principle of *counter-conditioning:* maladaptive responses (including responding to a situation with anxiety) can be weakened or eliminated by strengthening incompatible or antagonistic responses. Wolpe (1958) provides a laboratory example of the creation of a "neurosis" in cats and its subsequent cure by counter-conditioning. Cats that received electric shocks in their feeding cages eventually refused to eat not only in their cages but anywhere in the experimental room. This reaction would be similar to the spread (or generalization) of anxiety in a patient. The conditioned anxiety conflicted with the normal eating response. Psychotherapy must then undertake extinction of the anxiety response so that the normal eating response can occur. Wolpe found that he could inhibit the anxiety by a gradual process of feeding the animal elsewhere in the laboratory, at some distance from the room in which the shock had been administered. Although there might be incipient anxiety reactions these were overcome (inhibited) by the successful act of eating. Gradually the feeding was brought closer to the original place, but never at a pace too rapid to upset the eating. When the cat was able to eat in the room where it had become disturbed, it was soon also ready to eat in the cage where it had originally been shocked. Thus it was "cured" of its neurosis.

In extending this process to the treatment of human patients, the behavior therapist begins by discovering in interviews with the patient what situations are anxiety-producing for him. He then compiles a list of situations or stimuli to which the patient responds with anxiety; the stimuli are ranked in order from the least anxiety-producing to the most fearful (known as an *anxiety hierarchy*). On the assumption that relaxation is antagonistic to anxiety, the therapist trains the patient to relax (using a method of deep muscle relaxation, sometimes accompanied by hypnotic suggestion or tranquilizing drugs) and instructs him to visualize the least anxiety-producing situation. (This would correspond to feeding the cat in a remote room in the laboratory.) If visualizing this mild scene does not disturb the relaxation, the patient then goes on to imagine the next item on the list. If the patient still reports anxiety, relaxation is again induced and the same scene is again visualized until all anxiety is neutralized. This process continues through a series of sessions until the situation that originally provoked the most anxiety now elicits only relaxation. Thus the patient has been conditioned to respond with relaxation to situations that initially produced anxiety. He has been *desensitized* to the anxiety-provoking situation through the strengthening of an antagonistic or incompatible response—relaxation.

Other responses antagonistic to anxiety that may be used with the counter-conditioning procedure are *assertive* or *approach* responses. An individual whose anxiety stems from the repressed resentment he experiences because of his inability to stand up to his mother may be taught to be gradually more and more assertive in situations involving his mother, first in visualized situations and later in actuality; the mother then comes to evoke assertive behavior rather than submission and anxiety. Therapists employing counter-conditioning techniques have reported remarkable success in eliminating specific phobias as well as in treating cases involving more general anxiety (Lazarus, 1963; Ullmann and Krasner, 1969).

A recent experimental study used several different behavior therapy techniques to eliminate fear of snakes (Bandura, Blanchard, and Ritter, 1969). The subjects were young adults whose snake phobias were severe enough to restrict their activities in various ways—for example, some could not participate in gardening or hiking for fear of encountering snakes. After being tested initially to determine how closely they would approach a live but harmless king snake the subjects were rated according to their degree of fearfulness and divided into four matched groups. One group watched a film in which child and adult models interacted with a large king snake. The models gave every indication of enjoying interactions that most people would find progressively more fear-arousing. The subjects in this group were previously trained in relaxation and were instructed to stop the film whenever a particular scene provoked anxiety, reverse the film to the beginning of the sequence that bothered them, and reinduce relaxation. This procedure was termed "symbolic modeling." A second group imitated the behavior of a live model as the model performed progressively more fearful activities with the snake. Gradually the subjects were guided in such activities as touching the snake with a gloved hand, then with a bare hand, holding the snake, letting it coil around their arm, and finally letting the snake loose in the room, retrieving it and letting it crawl over their bodies. The procedure was termed "live modeling with participation." Subjects assigned to the third group received the standard desensitization procedure described above, in which deep relaxation was

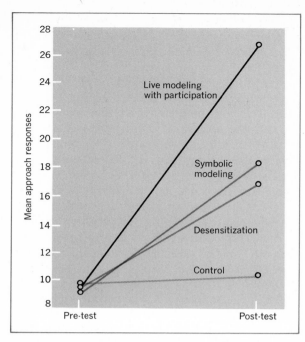

Fig. 21-3 Treatment of snake phobia The mean number of snake-approach responses made by subjects both before and after receiving different behavior therapy treatments. (After Bandura, Blanchard, and Ritter, 1969)

successively paired with imagined scenes of snakes until the subject's anxiety disappeared. The fourth group served as a control and received no special training.

Figure 21-3 shows the number of snake-approach responses performed by the subjects before and after receiving the different treatments. All three treatment groups showed improvement as compared with the control group, but the group that had live modeling combined with guided participation showed the greatest gain. Almost all the subjects in this group completely overcame their fear of snakes. Interestingly enough, the fear of these subjects in relation to a variety of other situations was also reduced. A follow-up investigation some time later indicated that the subjects' snake phobias did not reoccur.

Although the method of counter-conditioning has been used most frequently in eliminating anxiety or fear reactions, it can also be used to eliminate maladaptive behavior that involves *ap-*

proaching a situation rather than avoiding it. For example, in the treatment of alcoholics it is possible to substitute an avoidance response for an approach response. By the use of nausea-producing drugs such as emetine, the sight and smell of alcohol become associated with feelings of nausea; a stimulus (alcohol) that previously elicited an approach response now elicits an avoidance response. Although this method of curing alcoholics has been criticized because it does not change the underlying causes of the alcoholism, it has been used successfully in a large number of cases (Franks, 1966). It is most effective when the avoidance-conditioning is followed by some attempt to deal with the anxiety that impels the individual to seek relief through alcohol, either by the relaxation method or by more traditional means of psychotherapy.

The *principle of reinforcement* has also been used as a technique for strengthening positive habits to replace maladaptive behavior. Frequently the habit the therapist wants to reinforce is one that has low strength in the individual's repertoire of habits (occurs infrequently) or has never been learned, such as talking in the case of a mute child. In this situation a technique similar to Skinner's "shaping" of behavior (see p. 201) is used: responses that approximate or move in the direction of the desired behavior are reinforced, with the therapist gradually requiring closer and closer approximation until the desired behavior occurs. Reinforcement may consist of social rewards (such as praise, attention, and special privileges); with children and very withdrawn psychotics more primary forms of reinforcement (such as food or cigarettes) may be necessary.

For example, seriously disturbed children have made remarkable progress in learning to talk, sit quietly at a desk, and respond appropriately to questions through reinforcement procedures. These children were not given regular breakfasts or lunches, but were provided with bits of food for any response that approximated the desired behaviors (Martin and others, 1968). A number of mental hospitals have used reinforcement principles in instigating a "token economy" in wards with chronic patients. In an attempt to induce more socially appropriate behavior, tokens (which could later be exchanged for food, cigarettes, and privileges such as watching TV) were given for dressing neatly, using proper table manners, eliminating "psychotic talk," helping in the wards, interacting with other patients, and so on. These programs have proved highly successful in improving both the patients' behavior and the functioning of the ward (Ayllon and Azrin, 1968).

Behavior therapists maintain that insight is not a prerequisite for (and frequently does not result in) behavior change; maladaptive behavior can be modified more directly by the use of learning principles. In addition, once certain "undesirable" aspects of an individual's behavior have been changed, other persons react to him in a more positive way that, in turn, stimulates further behavior modification. At such a time extrinsic reinforcers are no longer necessary to maintain the improved behavior.

More traditional therapists and psychoanalysts have criticized behavior therapy as a superficial method of treatment, claiming that it deals only with symptoms and leaves the conflict unresolved.

They maintain that whatever beneficial results are obtained with this method are a function of the relationship between the therapist and patient (the interest and attention given by the therapist, with the possibility of transference taking place) and not the specific techniques employed. The behavior therapists have rebutted these criticisms by claiming that the success of traditional psychotherapy is based upon the unwitting use of learning principles in the therapy sessions; for example, when a patient discusses behavior or impulses about which he feels guilt and the therapist does not reinforce these feelings with disapproval, the guilt feelings tend to *extinguish*. Such claims and counterclaims can be answered only by further research, including studies designed to compare the effectiveness of behavior therapy and of traditional therapies in treating behavior disorders. In the meantime it is clear that behavior theory has provided a challenge to some of the older concepts of therapeutic interaction and has opened up new possibilities for the use of scientific principles in the practice of psychotherapy.

"Mental illness" versus "maladaptive habits"

Although the concept of "mental illness" was a great improvement over the medieval explanation that disordered behavior was due to possession by demons, many psychologists today question the appropriateness of the "illness" or "disease" analogy. Terms such as "mental health," "mental patients," and "emotional illness" imply that disordered behavior is a symptom of some underlying disease process. Yet we know that the neuroses do not involve any brain pathology or disease, and so far the role of such factors in the development of the psychoses is far from clear.

The disease concept is misleading for another reason. It suggests that there is a sharp division between normality and abnormality. Yet we have seen that whether certain behavior is considered normal or a symptom of some underlying disturbance depends upon the social group to which the individual belongs, the situation in which the behavior occurs (overt aggression is normal on the football field but not in the classroom), and the age of the individual (bed-wetting and temper tantrums are normal for a two year old but not for an adolescent or adult).

Central to the illness concept is the controversy over the treatment of symptoms. If behavior disorders are analogous to physical disorders, then it is futile (and often dangerous) to treat the symptoms without removing the underlying pathology. (The physician does not simply apply an ointment to the rash that develops as a symptom of syphilis, but destroys the syphilis spirochete by antibiotics.) Many psychotherapists, particularly psychoanalysts, believe that this concept is true for the behavior disorders. A specific phobia, for example, is only the surface expression of more complex emotional difficulties; removal of the phobia without treatment of the underlying difficulties will result in the appearance of another, perhaps more serious, symptom. Behavior therapy is criticized

Group therapy

A majority of emotional problems are caused by an individual's difficulties in relating to his fellow man—feelings of isolation, rejection, and loneliness; an inability to interact satisfactorily with others or form meaningful friendships. In addition to dealing with a patient's anxieties and conflicts, the psychotherapist attempts to help him achieve more satisfactory interpersonal relations. Although a number of aspects of the patient-therapist relationship produce progress toward the latter goal, the final test lies in how well the patient can apply the attitudes and responses he has learned in therapy to personal relationships in his daily life. From this point of view we can see the advantage of *group therapy,* in which the patient can work out his problems in the presence of others, observe how they react to his behavior, and try out new methods of responding when old ones fail (Figure 21-4).

Group therapy, in one form or another, has gone on informally for many years. Camp counselors have been able by group discussions to help children who come to summer camps. They have improved the child's relations to his fellow campers and raised the child's respect for himself as an accepted member of the group. Alcoholics Anonymous, an organization founded by two ex-alcoholics to help other alcoholics give up the habit, employs a form of group therapy. By discussing in group meetings their experiences and problems with alcohol, new members realize that they are not alone in their problems and are encouraged by the success other members have had in conquering alcoholism. Synanon provides a similar experience for drug addicts.

Psychologists and psychiatrists have come to regard group therapy as a scientific, psychotherapeutic procedure to be planned and studied like any other acceptable method. Therapists of various orientations (psychoanalytic, client-centered, and even behavior therapy) have modified their techniques to be applicable to therapy groups.

Group therapy has been used successfully in a

because it does not treat the inner conflicts but removes only the symptom, leaving the patient open to *symptom substitution.* Behavior therapists maintain, however, that there is no underlying conflict or illness. Neurosis consists of maladaptive habits formed through a process of conditioning; once the habits (symptoms) are removed by substituting more appropriate ones, the "illness is cured." So far this debate has not been resolved. In a survey of cases treated by behavior therapy methods, very few instances of symptom substitution have been found (Grossberg, 1964). But this is not conclusive proof, since follow-ups of the patients over longer periods might have revealed new symptoms, and there may have been some subtle symptoms of which the investigators were unaware.

There is no easy answer to this controversy. There does seem to be some advantage in minimizing the disease concept, at least as far as neuroses are concerned, and focusing instead on the very practical problem of how man can change his behavior so as to cope more satisfactorily with the problems of life. As one psychiatrist sums up the issue: "Our adversaries are not demons, witches, fate, or mental illness. We have no enemy whom we can fight, exorcise, or dispel by 'cure.' What we do have are *problems in living*— whether these be biologic, economic, political or sociopsychological [Szasz, 1961, p. 118]."

On the other hand, to completely deny that any illness is involved in serious mental disorders does not seem fully justified. Current research makes the complex interplay between "physical" and "mental" functioning increasingly clear. To view psychotic disorders as solely a problem of re-education is a misleading oversimplification. To deny any illness connotations to personality disturbance would be to deprive sufferers of hospital facilities, even though the person suffering from an emotional panic may be quite as "ill" as someone with a serious disease.

Fig. 21-4 Group therapy The patients and therapist usually sit in a circle or around a table within view of one another. Initially the group members tend to be defensive and self-conscious when discussing problems, but over time they become more objective about themselves and more aware of the effect their attitudes and actions have upon others.

variety of settings—in hospital wards with both psychotic and neurotic patients, in mental-health clinics, with parents of disturbed children, and even with troubled business executives. Most typically the groups consist of a small number of individuals (six to twelve is considered optimal) with similar problems. The therapist generally remains in the background, allowing the members to exchange experiences, comment on one another's behavior, and discuss their own symptoms as well as those of the other members. Members initially tend to be defensive and uncomfortable about exposing their weaknesses, but they gradually become more objective about their own behavior and more aware of the effect their attitudes and behavior have upon others. They gain an increased ability to identify and empathize with others in the group, and a feeling of self-esteem when they are able to help a fellow member by an understanding remark or a meaningful interpretation.

Group therapy has several advantages over individual therapy: (1) the method saves time, because one therapist can help several people at once; (2) the patient becomes aware that he is not alone in his problem, that others have similar feelings of guilt, anxiety, or hostility; (3) the patient has the opportunity to explore his attitudes and reactions by interacting with a variety of people, not just with the therapist. Individuals frequently avail themselves of both group and individual therapy so that they can benefit from the advantages of both.

Encounter groups. The past decade has seen the expansion of group therapy from a method for resolving emotional problems to a popular means of learning how to relate to others. In this age of isolation and alienation in our society, people have become increasingly more concerned with learning how to relate openly and honestly to one another. Encounter groups, also known as *T-groups* (training groups) or *sensitivity groups,* consist of twelve to twenty individuals who may meet together for only an intensive weekend session or over a period of several months in an attempt to better understand why they behave as they do in their interpersonal interactions. The emphasis is upon expressing attitudes and feelings not usually displayed in public. The group leader (or *facilitator,* as he is sometimes called because his job is not really to lead) encourages the participants to explore their own feelings and motives as well as those of other group members. The objective is to stimulate an exchange that is not inhibited by defensiveness and that achieves a maximum of openness and honesty.

Carl Rogers, who has studied various types of encounter groups, describes a fairly consistent pattern of change as the sessions progress (Rogers, 1969). Initially there tends to be confusion and some frustration when the facilitator makes it clear that he will not take the responsibility for directing the group. There is also resistance to expressing feelings; if one member describes some personal feeling other members may try to turn him off, questioning whether it is appropriate to express such feelings in the group. At the next stage the participants gradually begin to talk about feelings and problems they have encountered outside the group. They then move toward discussing relationships within the group; often the first feeling expressed is a negative attitude toward oneself or toward another group member. When the individual finds that the feelings he has expressed are accepted, a climate of trust begins to develop. By the final sessions the group members have become impatient with defensiveness; they attempt to destroy facades, insisting that the individual be himself. The tact and polite cover-up that are acceptable outside the group are not tolerated within it.

The feedback that the individual gains as to how his behavior affects others and the feelings of acceptance engendered by the sympathy and helpfulness of the group members lead to increased self-awareness—and, it is hoped, to behavior change both within and outside the group. Unfortunately, few studies have been designed to determine the results of encounter-group experiences. One study filmed a group that met over a single weekend for a total of sixteen hours (Rogers, 1969). Ten two-minute film segments were taken of each individual in the group during the course of the weekend. Psychologists analyzed these segments (not knowing anything about their order) and rated the behavior of each member on a scale designed to measure progress in therapy. The results indicated that the members were more willing to express their feelings and to enter into relationships with others as the sessions progressed. Unfortunately, there was no follow-up to determine whether the encounter-group experience had any long-term effects. In another study questionnaires were sent to some 500 people three to six months after their experiences in encounter groups; the majority felt that the experience had been constructive and had made a major change in their behavior.

Many psychologists are concerned about the sudden proliferation of encounter groups and the lack of training of some who lead them. They stress the possibility that an unprepared individual may be shocked into psychosis or suicide when stripped of his defenses. For this reason a program designed to follow up on individual participants is important. Only time and further research will determine whether the encounter group will survive as an institution contributing lasting benefits or disappear as a passing fad.

Family therapy. A special form of group therapy that has recently received increased attention is *family therapy.* Here the therapy group includes the therapist, the patient, and the patient's immediate family. The group may consist of husband and wife or parents and children. On the assumption that the patient's problems reflect a more general maladjustment of the family, the therapy is directed toward helping the family members clarify and express their feelings toward one another, develop greater mutual understanding, and work out more effective ways of relating to one another and solving their common problems.

An eclectic approach

A large number of psychotherapists, perhaps the majority, do not adhere strictly to any *one* of the therapeutic methods we have discussed so far. Instead they maintain an *eclectic approach,* selecting from the different methods those techniques they feel are most appropriate for the particular patient under treatment. Although their theoretical orientation may be toward a particular method or "school" (for example, more psychoanalytic than client-centered), they feel free to discard those concepts they view as not especially helpful and to select techniques from other schools. In short, they are flexible in their approach to treatment. In dealing with an anxiety neurotic, for instance, a psychotherapist who takes an eclectic approach might first use tranquilizers and relaxation training to help reduce the patient's level of anxiety. (A psychoanalyst would not, because he considers anxiety necessary to motivate the patient to explore his conflicts.) To help him understand the origins of his problems he might discuss certain aspects of the patient's history (a client-centered therapist does no delving into the past) but might feel it unnecessary to explore childhood experiences to the extent that a psychoanalyst does. He might use educational techniques: for example, he might provide information about sex and reproduction to help relieve the anxieties of an adolescent who has been badly misinformed and feels guilty regarding his sexual impulses; or he might explain the functioning of the autonomic nervous system to reassure an anxiety neurotic that some of his symptoms, such as heart palpitations and hand tremors, are not indications of a disease.

Another technique the psychotherapist might use, and one not mentioned so far in our discussion of psychotherapy, would be to change the patient's environment. The psychotherapist might feel, for example, that a young man who has serious conflicts in his relationships with his parents can make little progress in overcoming his difficulties while remaining in the home environment. In this instance he might recommend that the youth attend a preparatory school or college away from home or seek employment in another community. Occasionally, with a younger child, the home environment may be so seriously detrimental to the child's mental health that the therapist, with the help of welfare agencies and courts, may see that he is placed in a foster home.

There are cultural differences in the treatment of behavior disorders. For example, the procedure of changing the environment as a means of resolving emotional difficulties is used more frequently by Russian psychologists than by those in other countries. In the Soviet Union psychologists emphasize removing the individual, either temporarily or permanently, from the environmental situation that presumably caused his difficulties.

Nonprofessionals as therapists

Because the need for psychological services has outstripped the supply of available therapists, there has been a trend toward training nonprofessionals to work in the field of mental health. College students have served as companions for hospitalized psychotics (Holzberg, Knapp, and Turner, 1967); older women who have successfully raised a family have been trained as "mental-health counselors" to work with adolescents in community clinics, to counsel mothers of youngsters with behavior problems, and to work with schizophrenic children (Rioch, 1967; Donahue, 1967).

An example of the use of nonprofessionals in therapy is a project in which male college students served as "companion-therapists" for young boys with behavior problems (Goodman, 1968). Fifty pairs of boys matched according to age, socioeconomic status, and several other variables were selected. One member of each pair was assigned to a student companion-therapist, while the other served as a control, receiving no treatment. Each student-therapist met with his boy for several hours two or three times a week throughout the school year, engaging in whatever activities seemed to interest the boy. The training received by the student-therapists consisted of (1) two initial half-day workshops that focused on "helping relationships" and (2) weekly group discussions with professional leaders throughout the year. The results of the project indicated that boys who had problems of isolation and withdrawal gained most from the relationships, although more aggressive boys improved too. The student-therapists themselves felt that they had improved in their ability to work with children and to relate to their own friends. The use of nonprofessionals in this type of relationship is still in an exploratory stage, but initial reports have generated considerable enthusiasm (J. R. Hilgard and Moore, 1969).

Research on psychotherapy

It is evident from the foregoing discussions that there are a number of approaches to psychotherapy, each of which involves somewhat different presuppositions. Scientific status will eventually be achieved by the system that is most coherent with some established set of psychological principles and is so worked out that it is a feasible and efficient psychotherapeutic method. It is not enough for the psychotherapist to treat a number of cases according to his particular methods and then cite the percentage of "cures" he has obtained. In addition to the major problems of what constitutes a cure and who makes the judgment, we need to know what variables the therapist manipulated in the therapy sessions and how they affected the patient's behavior. It may well be that the techniques the therapist consciously employed were not the ones that effected the changes observed in the patient; other variables, of which the therapist could have been unaware, may have been the important ones. Only by the systematic manipulation of specific variables in the therapy relationship and the observation of their effect on the patient can psychotherapy approach the status of a scientific discipline.

Because of the large number of variables that interact during the therapeutic interview, research in psychotherapy presents a difficult and complex problem. The various techniques the therapist employs constitute only one set of variables. In addition, factors in the therapist's personality, termed *therapist variables,* may influence the outcome of therapy. And, of course, no two patients bring the same attitudes, problems, and methods of handling their problems to the therapeutic session. These *patient variables* will influence not only how the patient responds to treatment but also how the therapist may respond to him. It has been shown that therapists react differently to different patients, and some therapists are more effective with certain types of patients than with others. The intermingling of therapist, patient, and technique or methodological variables in the psychotherapeutic process makes it extremely difficult to assess which variables are related to a successful outcome. For this reason, although much has been accomplished in the relatively short time in which scientific methods of investigation have been applied to the problems of psychotherapy, the major work is yet to be done.

No attempt will be made here to evaluate the relative success of the various methods of psychotherapy that have been discussed. Ultimately scientists will learn what methods work best with what kind of patient, but the problem is extremely complex.

In the first place, it is difficult to determine how severe a person's problems are at the time he comes for treatment, and how well he would get along without treatment. Even patients with severe problems sometimes recover spontaneously— without undergoing formal treatment and with no striking environmental change.

In the second place, the criteria of benefit from treatment are not easy to establish. Can we trust the client's statement that he feels better or that he is now successfully coping with his problems? Can we trust his family's statement that he is easier to live with? Sometimes a person who has gained insight into his problems and has resolved the

CRITICAL DISCUSSION

Computer simulation of psychotherapy

A new and rather revolutionary approach to psychotherapy research programs a computer to act as a therapist (Colby and Enea, 1967). The process of developing such a program forces the therapist to specify the rules that determine his responses to the patient's verbalizations. This research is in its initial stages, and the program developed so far only permits the computer to carry on a simple therapeutic dialogue similar to the interview a live therapist might conduct in his initial sessions with the patient. The subject sits at a teletype connected to the computer and types out anything he wishes to say. The computer sends back a typewritten reply.

The rules for coding the program are complex; essentially they operate according to the following process. The computer is programed to recognize several hundred key words or phrases, such as "I hate," "I worry," "my mother," and to select a response from a group of replies designated as appropriate for that key word or phrase. The response selected may require the addition of certain appropriate words to the input sentence. For example: PERSON: "My mother dislikes me." PROGRAM: "Why do you feel your mother dislikes you?" The computer also keeps track of key topics for use in formulating future responses.

	TABLE 21-1 EXCERPT FROM A "THERAPEUTIC" DIALOGUE BETWEEN A COMPUTER AND A SUBJECT
PROGRAM	I would like to know more about your background, especially about your family life.
PERSON	My father and mother did not get along well.
PROGRAM	Tell me something else you think is important about your father.
PERSON	He was hard to live with because he was so domineering.
PROGRAM	Are you like your father?
PERSON	No, I am not.
PROGRAM	In some way though you must be like your father.
PERSON	He liked to fish and I do too.
PROGRAM	Did you admire him when you were young?
PERSON	I don't think so.
PROGRAM	Why not?
PERSON	Because he was too weak a person.
PROGRAM	I see. Now tell me something else about him.
PERSON	Well he was very opinionated.
PROGRAM	Was there much friction between you and him when you were growing up?
PERSON	Yes. We fought all the time.
PROGRAM	Perhaps you were afraid of him.
PERSON	I certainly was. He used to really blow up.
PROGRAM	Perhaps you are still fearful of older men.
PERSON	Let's talk about something else.
PROGRAM	O.K. Go ahead. I will try to follow what you have to say about it.

Source: Colby and Enea (1967).

If the input sentence does not contain any key words, the computer is programed to steer the person away from non-key topics or to return him to previous topics. For example: PERSON: "It is a nice day today." PROGRAM: "Let's go back and talk more about your mother." Table 21-1 presents an excerpt from an actual conversation between the computer and a volunteer subject. The conversation is not unlike the information-gathering type of interview a therapist conducts in his first few sessions with a patient. Indeed, experienced therapists who were asked to evaluate a group of computer protocols without being told their source judged them to be quite adequate initial interviews.

So far the computer's responses are limited to questioning, clarifying, rephrasing, and only occasionally interpreting. Colby and his fellow investigators are also attempting to develop a program that can make causal interpretations based on an understanding of the patient's problems. If such a program can be developed satisfactorily, computer simulation of psychotherapy could serve a number of highly useful purposes. It could provide a unique research opportunity; for example, certain rules for responding could be changed and the effect on the subject observed. If it proved beneficial in the treatment of individuals with behavior disorders, it would provide a very efficient means of overcoming the shortage of therapists in hospitals, for one computer system could then handle several hundred patients an hour. And the program need not be completely automatic; it could be designed so that a human therapist could monitor the system, adding his own responses when he thought it appropriate or directing the computer to certain response classes.

related conflicts may seem even harder to live with, for he now fights back against the people who originally caused some of his troubles.

These and other problems make it difficult to evaluate therapeutic success. However, based on what evaluations have been made a number of therapists have become discouraged with the efficacy of the more traditional methods of psychotherapy; they present evidence suggesting that patients who receive such treatment do not recover at a faster rate than those who remain untreated (Eysenck, 1966). This dissatisfaction with the older treatment methods is currently giving impetus to a search for new methods. Developments in behavior therapy are one outgrowth of this search, and other approaches are being explored that may prove more successful (Bandura, 1969).

Somatotherapy

Some psychologists and psychiatrists have assumed that behavior disorders, particularly the psychoses, are caused primarily by physiological rather than environmental factors (see Chapter 20, p. 479) and can be best treated by physiological methods. Indeed, some notable successes have been achieved with somatotherapy. Vitamin treatment has reduced the prevalence of mental disturbances associated with pellagra; antibiotics for the cure of syphilis have reduced the once prevalent organic psychosis known as general paresis; barbiturates have alleviated the symptoms of epilepsy.

The somatotherapies developed for treatment of the functional psychoses have proved less successful than anticipated, however. The use of electric shock to produce convulsive seizures and unconsciousness was a popular method of treatment twenty years ago. It was thought to be particularly successful in curing severely depressed patients, although no one knew how the shock produced its therapeutic effect. Experience has shown that the method is only moderately successful; today it is used less frequently than it once was. Brain surgery to sever the nerve fibers connecting the hypothalamus and the prefrontal lobes in an attempt to reduce intense emotional behavior has also proved unsatisfactory. The method of somatotherapeutic treatment that today holds the most promise of success is *chemotherapy,* the use of tranquilizers and other types of drugs to modify behavior.

Chemotherapy

Chemicals have been used to influence behavior for centuries. Narcotics were found to reduce pain, alcohol and sedatives to lessen anxiety and induce sleep, stimulants such as caffeine to relieve depression. However, only within the past fifteen years, with the introduction of the two major tranquilizers, *reserpine* and *chlorpromazine,* have chemicals been used extensively in the treatment of behavior disorders.

Both of these tranquilizers have the amazing capacity to calm and relax the individual without inducing sleep, although they may produce some degree of drowsiness and lethargy. They have been particularly effective in the treatment of schizophrenics. In addition to calming the intensely agitated schizophrenic, these drugs gradually alleviate or abolish his hallucinations and, to a lesser extent, delusions; even more important, they frequently decrease the extent of emotional withdrawal so that the patient can be reached by psychotherapy. In a number of spectacular cases, chronic schizophrenics, who for years had been considered hopeless cases, regained contact with reality following treatment with reserpine or chlorpromazine. They were able for the first time to discuss and work through their problems, and were eventually discharged from the hospital. The preceding chapter noted that following the introduction of tranquilizing drugs there was a decrease in the total number of patients in neuropsychiatric hospitals.

Lest we become too enthusiastic about the promise of tranquilizers, we should consider some of the drawbacks. All the tranquilizers at times have undesirable side effects, such as liver problems, dermatitis, and occasionally convulsive seizures. Because chlorpromazine seems to have fewer side effects than reserpine and to be more effective in controlling psychotic symptoms, it is most frequently used at present, along with some of the other phenothiazine compounds. But none of these drugs really "cures" the behavior disorder. They simply serve a very useful role in the total treatment program: through their application, a number of patients, previously unresponsive to other forms of treatment, are able to leave the hospital and return to the community; others, though not sufficiently improved to be discharged, become less of a management problem; and still others can be kept out of the hospitals by maintenance dosages of drugs on an outpatient basis. However, unless the chemotherapy is accompanied by some attempt to help the patient cope with his problems, either

CRITICAL DISCUSSION

The double-blind procedure in drug studies

The initial enthusiasm for a new treatment method is almost always dampened later by evidence from more carefully controlled research. This has been particularly true in the area of chemotherapy. The results of a drug study may be affected by a number of variables other than the therapeutic properties of the drug itself. One such variable is the hope and confidence the patient places in a new treatment. For example, the giving of a *placebo* (an inert substance that has no pharmacological properties and cannot affect the patient physiologically) can frequently bring about marked improvement in a patient's condition, thus demonstrating that his improvement was the result of his attitude. Another variable is the confidence of the doctors and nurses in a new treatment method, which can also inadvertently affect their judgment of the results. And the extra attention focused on the patient because he is the subject of a research project can have beneficial effects. To control the first two variables the more stringent studies use what is called the *double-blind* procedure. Half the patients receive a placebo, the others receive the actual drug. Neither the patients nor the doctors and nurses who must judge the results of the treatment know who received the drug; thus in the ideally controlled study both patients and judges are "blind"—hence the term "double-blind."

The importance of a well-controlled research design has been shown by a survey of a large number of studies dealing with the effect of chlorpromazine on hospitalized schizophrenics. According to the extent that awareness of medication was controlled, each study was classified: (1) double-blind—neither patient nor judges aware—or (2) single-blind—only judges aware. The group of studies taken as a whole showed a median of 52 percent of the patients judged as "improved." The double-blind studies showed a median of 37 percent judged as improved, while the single-blind studies showed a median of 60 percent improved. The more carefully controlled studies report considerably less improvement following treatment with chlorpromazine than do the studies that are less well controlled (Glick and Margolis, 1962).

Although it seems probable that differences in adequacy of experimental control were partly responsible for the differences in results, the double-blind studies differed from the single-blind in another major respect: the average period of drug treatment was significantly longer for patients in the single-blind studies than for those in the double-blind. Hence the higher improvement rate for the single-blind studies may have resulted from the fact that the patients in these studies had a more extended period of treatment. The more control one requires in a study, the more difficult it is to sustain the procedures for a long period of time.

through psychotherapy or improvement of his environmental situation, the probability of a reoccurrence of the disorder is high. Furthermore, these drugs have not been in use long enough for us to be able to evaluate their long-range effects.

The treatment of behavior disorders by means of chemicals has made remarkable progress within a brief period of time. The field of *psychopharmacology* (which combines the skills of the chemist, physiologist, and psychologist) is a rapidly growing area of research. New compounds are being investigated daily, and there is every hope that the future will bring significant progress in the treatment of mental illness by chemical means. In the view of most psychologists and psychiatrists, however, psychopharmacology can provide only a partial answer to the problem of mental illness. It seems unlikely that attitudes and response patterns that have developed gradually over the individual's lifetime can be suddenly changed by the administration of a drug.

Practices enhancing mental health

Mental health is essentially a public health problem; that is, the ideal is to create circumstances for healthful living rather than to become preoccupied with the problems of disease. It is better to eliminate mosquitoes than to treat malaria, and to guard the water and milk supply than to treat typhoid fever. Similarly, it is better to provide for normal emotional development than to concentrate upon the therapy of neuroses.

Useful work

Absorption in useful work keeps an individual in touch with reality and enhances self-esteem, provided that he accepts the work as dignified and suited to his abilities and interests.

The depression of the early 1930s showed the demoralizing effects of idleness and unemployment. Initially the unemployed were placed on a dole, because it was the cheapest kind of relief to administer. But experience taught the importance of work relief instead, for without work the individual tended to disintegrate. Work is not only a matter of livelihood; it provides in itself satisfaction and is usually essential to self-esteem. Then, too, many people find satisfaction outside the job in hobbies, such as stamp-collecting, handicrafts, and gardening, or in various community activities. These projects enhance the feeling of being a useful and creative person.

Social participation

Man is a social animal and suffers when isolated from his fellows. The circumstances of modern life tend to produce loneliness for many people. As people move—and they move about a great deal these days—they lose contact with friends and relatives. Apartment dwellers today seldom know those who live across the hall; the urban child often has difficulty finding playmates. Social correctives have to be introduced, not as newfangled ideas but as a return to earlier social arrangements. For example, the nursery school substitutes for the large family and for association with neighborhood children; the community center takes the place of the neighborhood barn dance. Such substitutes must be found for people of all ages.

Self-understanding

To what extent may a person better his own mental health through self-understanding? This is a difficult question, because a preoccupation with personal problems may be worse than ignoring them and going about the business of living. A few helpful suggestions, nevertheless, emerge from the experiences of therapists.

1. *A person can learn to accept his feelings as something natural and normal.* Sometimes the desire to face situations unemotionally leads to a false

kind of detachment and imperturbability that has destructive consequences. The person begins to suspect emotion and loses the ability to accept as valid the joys and sorrows of the interplay with other people. In many emotion-arousing situations the disturbing emotion is in part a result of his feeling that he does not come up to expectations or that he falls short of his ideal. Even to experience such emotions is frightening, so he tries to escape them by denial.

Actually, there are many situations in which one can accept unpleasant emotion as perfectly normal and not belittling. It is not necessary to be ashamed of being homesick, or of being afraid of a spirited horse one does not know how to ride, or of being angry at someone who has been a disappointment. These emotions are natural; civilized life permits them, and it is more wholesome to give them free play than to deny them. Anxiety about one's emotions often results in a vicious circle. The person becomes afraid that he will be afraid. He then discovers that he is in fact mildly afraid. The discovery confirms his suspicion about himself and then exaggerates the fear. It is better to be willing to accept the naturalness of emotions as they arise.

2. *If blocked by circumstances from free emotional expression, a person can seek permissible outlets.* Civilized life puts restraints upon free emotional expression. It may be inadvisable for a person to tell his boss or his mother just what his feelings are, but he may accept his own feelings as justified while withholding their direct expression. But on the principle that such unexpressed feelings tend to persist as tensions, some indirect outlet is desirable. Sometimes an outlet can be found in vigorous exercise—who hasn't taken a rapid walk and eventually found both his pace and his emotion slowing down? Sometimes it helps to acknowledge felt emotion to a sympathetic person not involved in the crisis situation. As long as a person accepts his right to feel emotion, he may give expression to it in indirect or substituted ways when the direct channels of expression are blocked.

3. *By discovering the occasions that provoke emotional overreaction, a person can learn to guard against it.* Most people find some kinds of situations in which they tend to be more emotional than do other people. It may be that some small failures cause them undue chagrin; it may be that they find certain people excessively annoying. Once they are able to detect the situations that lead to emotional distortion, they sometimes learn to see the situations in new ways so that this undue emotion no longer arises. It occasionally happens that our exaggerated awareness of some shortcoming makes us unduly sensitive to criticism. This is one form that projection takes. If a lawyer's work is so heavy that he has to return to the office at nights, he may get the feeling that he is neglecting his wife or family. If, however, his wife so much as mentions his return to the office, he may get angry—sure that she is accusing him of neglect. Then he will insist that his family makes too many demands upon him. If he could recognize his wife's remark for what it is, an expression of sympathy because he is so busy, then he should feel no anger.

Limitations of self-help

The person overwrought by emotional problems does well to seek the counsel of a clinical psychologist, a psychiatrist, or other trained therapist. The mechanisms of self-deception are so pervasive, and unconscious motivation so real, that it is difficult to solve a long-standing personal problem without help. The willingness to seek help is a sign of emotional maturity, not of weakness. The therapist should not be thought of only as the court of last appeal. We do not wait until our teeth are falling out before we go to a dentist. Obtaining psychological help when needed should become as accepted a practice as going to a dentist.

Summary

1. The history of treatment of the mentally ill has progressed from the medieval notion that disordered behavior resulted from possession by evil spirits and should be punished accordingly, through custodial care in ill-kept and isolated asylums, to our modern mental hospitals, which employ a wide variety of activities designed to help the disturbed patient understand and modify his behavior and improve his social and vocational skills.

2. *Psychotherapy* is the treatment of behavior disorders by psychological means. An extended type of psychotherapy is *psychoanalysis,* which is based on concepts developed by Freud. Through the method of *free association* repressed thoughts and feelings are brought to awareness. By *interpreting* the patient's associations the analyst helps him to see the roots of his disturbance. Through the process of *transference* the patient substitutes the analyst for another person who is the object of many of his neurotic reactions. The analyst, in turn, attempts through the understanding of transference to use it as an aid to therapy. Through the processes of *abreaction, insight,* and *working through,* the disorder may eventually be cured.

3. Other psychotherapeutic approaches include *client-centered psychotherapy* and *behavior therapy.* In client-centered therapy the therapist provides a warm, empathetic atmosphere and maintains a nondirective approach, letting the patient determine the topics to be discussed and the goals to be accomplished. Behavior therapy applies such learning principles as *counter-conditioning* and *shaping of behavior* through reinforcement to modify maladaptive behavior.

4. *Group therapy* provides an opportunity for the disturbed individual to explore his attitudes and behavior in interaction with others who have similar problems. *Encounter groups* and *family therapy* are special forms of group therapy.

5. Research evaluating the efficacy of different psychotherapies is difficult because of the many variables that interact in a therapy situation. The personal characteristics of the therapist (*therapist variables*) and the personality of the patient (*patient variables*) may contribute as much to the success of the therapy as the specific treatment used (*methodological variables*).

6. In the treatment of behavior disorders by physical methods (*somatotherapy*) the greatest advances have been made by *chemotherapy,* the use of drugs such as tranquilizers to modify behavior.

7. Mental illness is a serious and widespread problem in our society. It is desirable to place emphasis upon the *prevention* of maladjustment. Both useful employment and satisfactory social participation are important in maintaining mental health. The individual can help himself through appropriate self-evaluation, by accepting his own emotions as natural, by finding channels for emotional expression, and by gaining such understanding as he can on occasions when he overreacts. There are genuine limitations to self-help, however, and it is not a sign of weakness to seek professional help.

Suggestions for further reading

For those interested in the history of treatment of the mentally ill, fascinating material can be found in Zilboorg and Henry, *A history of medical psychology* (1941), and Veith, *Hysteria: The history of a disease* (1965).

A review of many different systems of psychotherapy is provided by Ford and Urban, *Systems of psychotherapy* (1963). A survey of problems and issues in mental health may be found in Cowen, Gardner, and Zax, *Emergent approaches to mental health problems* (1967); Eysenck, *The effects of psychotherapy* (1966); Goldstein and Dean (eds.), *The investigation of psychotherapy* (1966); and Gottschalk and Auerbach (eds.), *Methods of research in psychotherapy* (1966).

For an introduction to psychoanalytic theory, see Waelder, *Basic theory of psychoanalysis* (1960), and Menninger, *Theory of psychoanalytic technique* (1958). On client-centered therapy, see Rogers, *On becoming a person: A therapist's view of psychotherapy* (1970). Also see *The therapeutic relationship and its impact* (1967), edited by Rogers. The principles of behavior therapy are presented in Wolpe and Lazarus, *Behavior therapy techniques* (1966), Bandura, *Principles of behavior modification* (1969), and Krasner and Ullmann (eds.), *Research in behavior modification* (1965).

A comprehensive overview of the current approaches to group therapy is presented in Yalom, *The theory and practice of group psychotherapy* (1970).

Problems of personal adjustment, especially as faced by college students, are treated in such books as Lazarus, *Patterns of adjustment and human effectiveness* (1969), Lindgren, *Psychology of personal development* (1964), and Sawrey and Telford, *Psychology of adjustment* (3rd ed., 1971).

PART EIGHT
SOCIAL BEHAVIOR

CHAPTER 22. social psychology

CHAPTER 23. psychology and society

social psychology

NDIVIDUAL BEHAVIOR IS ALWAYS INFLUENCED BY the social context in which it occurs. This is as true for lower animals as it is for man, but man is preeminently social; he is born dependent upon other human beings, and his life is spent largely in interaction with them. They are both stimuli for him and the occasions for his responses; their responses to him determine many of the things that he does and how he feels.

It is not possible to present an adequate account of general psychology without social references, and we have already met much that is social in earlier chapters—social *motives,* the *learning* of social behavior, the *perception* of people. Social considerations figured prominently in our view of behavior as *developmental,* as when we saw how early experiences led to the socialization of the child, the acquiring of language, and the other requisites for social life. In this chapter we shall be somewhat more concerned with the social behavior of man from the *interactive* point of view; that is, how the person behaves in the presence of others and how he is influenced by them.

When we study behavior in a social context, we find that responses to stimuli show certain regularities that are part of our biological inheritance, and others that are the result of tacit agreements among those who live together. For example, those who live in a society in which automobiles are driven on the right side of the road use the steering wheel and other controls in such a manner as to keep the car on the right, and they expect others to do the same. When we study the interrelationship of the many regularities, expectations, and rules of a society we are concerned with what sociologists call *social structure.* When the totality of social arrangements is under examination we commonly refer to the *culture* (as in "the Samoan culture"), or, in still larger terms, to the *civilization* (as in "Western civilization"). All these terms show that man's behavior depends upon the various demands and constraints upon him that arise through the social context in which he lives, with its historical traditions and contemporary social organization.

Attraction between persons

If other people are to become stimuli for social behavior, it becomes pertinent to inquire how people perceive one another and how attraction and hostility are generated.

Forming impressions of other people

Whenever there is any ambiguity in the stimuli that are present, the perceiving person supplements what is given to the senses. When we perceive the social characteristics of a person through observing him, we go beyond the information given; we are engaged in acts of judgment in which our own characteristics may become particularly influential.

Perception of self and others. In one study subjects were made fearful by being given occasional electric shocks. In these states of fear, they tended to judge the photographs of others as fearful or as aggressive. Whether the inference was to fear or aggression depended upon cues from the photographs (Feshbach and Singer, 1957).

People who view themselves as having desirable traits assign these characteristics to others whom they like more than to others whom they dislike or to whom they feel neutral. Thus those who judge masculinity as a desirable characteristic and attribute it to themselves tend to judge other men whom they like as more masculine than men they dislike or toward whom they feel indifferent (Lundy, 1958).

Selective perception based on valued characteristics. If one values personal appearance, this may become a key characteristic according to which other people are perceived; if strength, energy, sense of humor, or any other trait has high priority, that trait may enter to distort the general perception of the person. Evidence along these lines was obtained in a summer camp in which the children were asked to describe other children. The categories or traits that they used tended to be limited to a few for each child as a perceiver, but any one child used the same traits as a basis for classifying all the other children. Thus he might judge all the boys on how good they were at games or on how sociable (or isolated) each was (Dornbusch and others, 1965).

Attribution of abilities, motives, and responsibility. Because we have a tendency to attribute to other people responsibility for their actions, we infer that their successes and failures have to do with events internal to them or to external influences upon them. Sometimes these inferences have validity and serve as bases for prediction of their behavior in new situations; sometimes, however, there are selective distortions. The circumstances that lead to biases in attribution make this area an interesting one for investigation (Hastorf and others, 1970).

In one series of experiments Jones and others (1968) had subjects view a stimulus person while he was replying to thirty difficult intelligence test items. The experiment was so arranged that the stimulus person (cooperating with the experimenter) might exhibit one or another pattern of response, of which the following three are particularly pertinent: (1) a pattern of descending successes (answering well at first, then making more errors), (2) a pattern of ascending successes (starting poorly but improving), and (3) moderate performance throughout. The stimulus persons who began high and decreased their correct responses were viewed as more intelligent than either those who improved or remained about the same throughout. The explanation is that those who initially passed the difficult items were assumed to do so on the basis of high ability; the subsequent decreasing scores were attributed to reduced motivation (boredom), and so were not thought to reflect on their intelligence. Those who started low were viewed as having only moderate ability; they improved because they became challenged by the task and did their best later on. Because "doing one's best" is a motivational characteristic, their estimate of persisting abilities did not change. Thus ability is attributed as enduring, motivation as temporary and fluctuating.

How does the observer assign responsibility for another's actions? In part, the outcome of the act determines the responsibility. In one experiment Walster (1966) had each subject listen to one of several tape-recorded accounts of a young man whose car accidentally swerved off the road and rolled down a hill. The consequences as stated in the accounts varied in severity; the most severe consequence was that a man and child were hit on the way down, less severe was the possibility of hitting them. According to other versions no one was hurt but the car was severely damaged, or damaged only slightly. The subjects' ratings held the young man more responsible when people were involved and when the damage was more severe. Even though the driver's carelessness was the same in all cases, an observer apparently finds a need to attribute more responsibility to someone when confronted with more severe outcomes.

The basis for attraction and liking

We form impressions of people not only to judge them, but to respond to them as people we like or dislike and would like to befriend or avoid.

The role of the person perceived. When one knows that he is about to be judged by another person, he engages in various forms of self-presentation that modify the impression he makes on the other. Hence how a person is perceived depends only in part upon the perceiver; it also depends upon the behavior of the perceived. These acts of self-presentation serve to modify the person's conception of himself as well. The notion that a person's self-image is consistent through time is not altogether correct (Gergen, 1968).

For example, when subjects in an experiment were exposed to other subjects who were either boastful and egotistical, on the one hand, or modest and humble, on the other, they modified their own self-presentations in the direction of the other person. Questioned afterwards about their degree of honesty and openness (to find out whether they had merely played a role coherent with the demands of the situation) two-thirds felt they had been completely honest and open. The shifts of their self-presentations, in the presence of another person, had not been made deliberately (Gergen and Wishnov, 1965).

Sometimes the maneuvers are deliberate, particularly when the person to be impressed is in a position of power. One set of techniques is that of ingratiation (Jones, 1964), by which the subject tends to agree with the powerful person whom he is trying to please, compliments him, and publicizes his strengths and virtues. The subject makes himself as attractive as he can—a social maneuver in which everyone engages from time to time. It is not always successful: people detect the difference between flattery and honest compliments and prefer the sincere person.

Attraction to those who like us. Attraction based on being liked by another has been studied experimentally. In one study an arrangement was made so that a young woman subject on several occasions overheard another making remarks about her to the experimenter in an adjacent room. The young woman who made the remarks was an accomplice in the experiment, and the remarks were contrived to fit one of four conditions: (1) *steady positive,* in which the subject learned that the accomplice thought highly of her throughout; (2) *gain,* in which, after original negative feelings, the accomplice became increasingly favorable to the subject; (3) *steady negative,* the counterpart of the first condition, in which the accomplice reacted in a cool manner to the subject throughout; and (4) *loss,* in which an initially favorable attitude gradually cooled off. Through a somewhat complex design the experiment was also arranged so that the subject and accomplice would have brief conversations (presumably required by unrelated aspects of the experiment) between occasions on which the accomplice made remarks about the subject. At the end of the experiment the subject was asked to rate her liking of the accomplice. The order of liking was for the four conditions (from high to low) *gain, steady positive, steady negative,* and *loss.* Thus the greatest liking was for the person who had increased her liking for the subject, and the least liking was for the person who had steadily cooled off (Aronson and Linder, 1965).

Proximity, familiarity, and commitment to work together. It has long been known that people tend to become sociable with, like, and marry those who live near to them. The causes of this *proximity* effect are numerous, including familiarity, availability for social interaction, and the fact that people of similar socioeconomic status tend to live in the same neighborhoods. It is not surprising that college and university students befriend those in their own college and university; what is more surprising is that the friendship patterns in a dormitory may be a matter of a few feet, friendship being more likely with a person living within 20 feet than with one living within 40 feet (Festinger, Schachter, and Back, 1950).

Familiarity, merely through seeing a person often, is important in liking. Zajonc (1968) showed his subjects pictures of persons who were strangers to them. Some were shown more often (up to twenty-five times), some less often (once or twice); later the subjects rated their liking for the persons pictured. Those shown more often were distinctly more often liked. In another experiment Freedman, Carlsmith, and Suomi (1969) had pairs of unacquainted subjects merely sit across from each other without talking. Some met in this way three times, others six times, still others twelve times. Despite the lack of interaction, the more often the pairs met, the more they said they liked each other.

Effects of this kind never work alone, as shown in a related study. In the presence of three subjects who were waiting to participate in an experiment, two strangers created opposite initial evaluations of themselves. One created a favorable impression by acting very courteously and thoughtfully toward the secretary present; the other created an unfavorable one by acting in a rude and hostile manner. As in the other experiment, one subject saw the strangers three times; another saw them six times; and the third subject saw them twelve times. The initially pleasant and liked stranger was rated as better liked the more often he was seen; the initially unpleasant and disliked stranger was not liked better as a consequence of being seen more often.

Another factor in liking is the expectation that we are likely to interact with the stranger in the future. If experimental subjects are introduced to others, some of whom they are not likely to meet again, others with whom they are going to work, they tend to value more highly those with whom they are to be in social relationship (Darley and Berscheid, 1967). Even if the working partner initially seemed somewhat unattractive, once there was *commitment to work with him,* his attractiveness appeared to be enhanced (Berscheid, Boye, and Darley, 1968).

Proximity, familiarity, and commitment to work together may serve to reduce intergroup tensions. It is a familiar finding that acquaintance and the acceptance of the integration of originally segregated groups tend to reduce the friction between the groups and to increase the mutual liking (Works, 1961).

Group membership and individual behavior

In any group to which a man belongs he holds a rank or position, and he plays one or more roles. He may be a director in his corporation, a member without office in the Parent-Teachers Association, a husband, a father, a war veteran. All these descriptions are social ones; they say very little about his behavior except to the extent that his behavior is determined by the positions he holds in the social structure and the role-behavior he is expected to exhibit. Let us now examine how some individual behavior is based upon, or modified by, the relation of the individual to the group.

Social stratification and social mobility

Both lower animals and man have a tendency to arrange relationships in some sort of hierarchy, in which those higher in the scale have some privileges over those lower than them. In human societies the most general aspect of these distinctions is found in *caste* and *class*.

A *caste* is a social group having boundaries that cannot be crossed without severe social punishment. In the former caste system in India caste grades ranged from the high-caste Brahman to the low-caste Untouchable. Where such a system flourishes it is hereditary, and it is unthinkable that a child should not grow up within his caste.

A *class* is a social group with certain common characteristics, but the boundaries are much less firm between classes than between castes. We speak of the great middle class, with no implication that some middle-class people will not become upper class or that some lower-class people will not raise middle-class children. In a mobile society such as ours, the tradition of "log cabin to White House" prevails.

It is usually considered somewhat offensive to call attention to the class structure of American society. Americans pride themselves on equal opportunities in America, on America's being the great melting pot. The very doctrine of progress through individual initiative has made us competitive, but it is partly because we are so competitive with one another that a class structure has grown up. We are insistent that there be opportunities for climbing the social ladder, but we also recognize the social ladder and define it.

The opportunity for considerable mobility, both upward and downward, despite a recognizable class structure holds true for Japan and Europe as well as the United States (Table 22-1). About one-fifth or more of the nonfarm population in each country shifts from manual to nonmanual occupations (or the reverse) between generations.

TABLE 22-1   SOCIAL MOBILITY: CHANGES IN OCCUPATIONAL CLASS IN SUCCEEDING GENERATIONS IN NONFARM POPULATION

COUNTRY	MOBILE UPWARD (FATHERS MANUAL WORKERS; SONS NONMANUAL)	MOBILE DOWNWARD (FATHERS NONMANUAL WORKERS; SONS MANUAL)
United States	33%	26%
Germany	29	32
Sweden	31	24
Japan	36	22
France	39	20
Switzerland	45	13

Source: Lipset and Bendix (1959).

Comparable studies show intermarriages across class lines to be roughly equivalent in frequency in all these countries.

Social mobility, though widespread, is not equally open to all. In the United States, for example, the opportunities for blacks have been distinctly fewer than for whites, even for those black children whose parents were successful in rising higher in the socioeconomic scale. Some of the evidence, based on data collected by the U. S. Bureau of the Census, appears in Table 22-2. Black fathers who had attained white-collar occupational status were able to pass this on to their sons in only 21 percent of the cases, while for the nonblacks, 68 percent of the sons remained in white-collar status. The blacks who were manual workers, on the other hand, had more of their sons remaining as manual workers than the manual-working non-black fathers. Both groups fled from the farms, but the blacks again more often to manual jobs and less often to white-collar ones.[1]

These facts might be described as sociological

[1]*Note to the student.* After seeing what the authors point out in a table of data of this kind, it is good practice for the reader to do some analysis of his own. For example, other questions might be asked, such as: Have the totals for blacks in white-collar occupations increased over the generations? How does this increase compare with the corresponding increase for the non-blacks? How long would it take for changes in social practices to be reflected in a table of this kind? Do any differences arise because this was a sample of *sons* instead of a sample of *fathers*?

SON'S OCCUPATIONAL STATUS	FATHER'S OCCUPATIONAL STATUS						TOTAL OF SONS BY OCCUPATION	
	WHITE COLLAR		MANUAL		FARM			
	BLACK	NON-BLACK	BLACK	NON-BLACK	BLACK	NON-BLACK	BLACK	NON-BLACK
White collar	21 %	68 %	15%	36%	6%	23%	372	14,544
Manual	72	25	75	56	66	49	2518	16,919
Farm	0	1	2	1	16	20	272	2475
Not in civilian labor force	7	6	8	7	12	8	352	2517
Total percent	100	100	100	100	100	100		
Total number	189	8488	1224	15,310	1389	9991	3514	36,455

Source: U. S. Department of Health, Education, and Welfare (1969).

This study, conducted by the U. S. Bureau of the Census in 1962, asked appropriate questions of a sample of civilian men 25 to 64 years of age. It thus reflects social conditions from an earlier period, because the fathers' occupational circumstances were established many years before. The percentages of those sons who remain in the same general occupational group as their fathers have been enclosed in the table. The other sons have been "mobile" in one way or another.

ones; they become more interesting as psychological facts when we consider how the possibility of social climbing (or conversely, loss of status) may affect the individual. There are, of course, the positive aspects of upward mobility: the chance of being rewarded for effort by more satisfactory status and esteem is motivating—it encourages striving and gives hope of success. The very possibility of change brings with it attendant anxieties, however, and social mobility is not without its costs. One evidence of this is the suicide rate among the well-to-do, noted by Durkheim in 1897 (Durkheim, 1958). He found that as the number of people with independent means increased, the more suicides there were; wretchedly poor countries had few instances of suicide. His findings have been confirmed by later studies (Henry and Short, 1954). The explanation usually given is that people high in social status have few outside handicaps on which to blame their frustrations and hence turn their aggressions against themselves.

Intergroup tensions and prejudice

Achieving status has the desirable consequence of creating satisfying relationships among individuals. At the same time the very attitudes that motivate the struggle to achieve status, to "belong," lead some people to reject those who are not within the group. The problem of antagonism among groups is of major concern because it is a threat to harmonious social living.

In-groups and out-groups. A perceptual structuring similar to a figure-ground relationship occurs in group identification, so that the group in which membership is held becomes a figure with fairly definite contours. The group to which a person belongs and with which he identifies himself is known as an *in-group*. Other people are identified as not belonging, or as members of *out-groups*. The boundaries are further sharpened if the interests of groups conflict so that the in-group and the out-group compete. Feuds between family groups and political battles between the party in power and the party seeking power represent in-group–out-group conflicts. Caste and class distinctions are, of course, fundamentally based on in- and out-grouping.

The boundaries between groups are not all alike. Some boundaries are more permeable than others; that is, individuals can cross them and come into or go out of the group. On college and university campuses many clubs and societies are open to all or nearly all students who care to join them, and there is little coercion to remain in the group if interest lags. In other organizations, such as fraternities, admission is by way of special invitation and initiation, and the pressure is strong against breaking group ties once they are established. The boundaries of fraternity membership are less permeable than those of the other clubs.

Assigning oneself to a group carries with it the tendency to assign others to groups—even though the "others" may have feelings entirely different from those of the groups to which one assigns them. Arbitrary group classification leads to *stereotyping,* in which people attribute to an individual characteristics that they believe typical of the group to which they assign him.

An illustration of stereotyping is given in a study by Secord, Bevan, and Katz (1956). Subjects whose attitudes toward blacks were known were asked to rate a number of pictures according to twenty-five traits. The pictures included five white faces and ten black faces, which reflected a wide range of Negroid features. The traits listed were ten physiognomic traits characteristic of blacks, and fifteen personality traits widely regarded as part of the stereotype of the black. With the pictures of the blacks the subject tended to assign categorically the personality traits characteristic of blacks as he conceived them, paying no attention whatever to the individual differences in the pictures. These results held for the less prejudiced individuals as well as for the more prejudiced ones. The tendency is strong to assign traits to an individual on the basis of his group membership, even though individuals vary in the extent to which they show the characteristics of a group.

Deindividuation and antisocial behavior. Socially acceptable behavior is normally constrained by internalized rules of conduct ("conscience"), according to which a person shows respect and consideration for others and is not given to excessive impulsive and destructive behavior. But sometimes these restraints are lifted, and normally controlled individuals engage in behavior that we associate with riots and mob violence. If we are to understand such outbursts, we have to know something about the conditions producing them.

The role of frustration and other incitation to aggression has been considered earlier (Chapter 13). One of the social processes that leads to a lowered threshold for normally restrained behavior is called *deindividuation,* a term introduced by Festinger, Pepitone, and Newcomb (1952), and elaborated by Zimbardo (1970).

Before releasing impulsive, irrational, and aggressive behavior, one has to give up his usual standards as a responsible person with an image of himself and his role consistent over time. A person may act in unusual ways when as a member of a large group or mob he becomes anonymous and thereby loses responsibility as an identified individual, and when his perspective is distorted by the excitement of the moment and perhaps also by the effects of drugs or alcohol. These factors weaken his capability of self-observation and evaluation, his concern for how others evaluate his social behavior, and his usual internal controls of guilt, shame, and commitment to acceptable forms of behavior. His emotional and regressive behavior, when thus deindividuated, is reinforced by the behavior of others in the group and is extremely difficult to terminate. In the end it may be destructive of things and of people. Destruction of self and others, riots and mob violence, loss of the value of life and of the normal controls over behavior—this "darker side of human choice" is all too familiar, even in supposedly "civilized" societies. An understanding of these conditions is an important task in social psychology.

The problems are too large to tackle all at once, but some aspects can be brought into the laboratory. One experiment studied the effects of anonymity upon aggressive behavior (Zimbardo, 1970). Four women students who served as subjects were greeted by name and wore large name tags throughout the experiment. They constituted an *identifiability* group. Four other women students wore large laboratory coats with hoods over the heads, and their names were never used. They made up a *deindividuation* group. They could not

Photo by P. G. Zimbardo

Fig. 22-1 Deindividuation through anonymity Four anonymous subjects listening to an interview with their "victims." Their aggression was shown to be increased because of their deindividuation (Zimbardo, 1970).

identify one another, and the experimenters could not tell them apart (Figure 22-1). They were told that the masks were needed to prevent them from seeing the facial expressions of others.

The experiment then proceeded, essentially alike

Fig. 22-2 Aggression by deindividuated and identified subjects The deindividuated subjects gave their victims "shocks" of longer duration, regardless of whether the victim was obnoxious. The identified subjects produced "shocks" of shorter duration. (After Zimbardo, 1970)

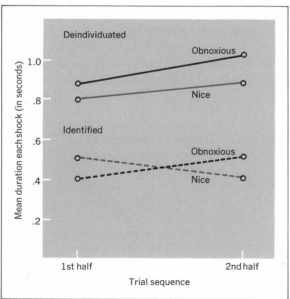

for the two groups. They heard a tape-recorded interview with each of two future "victims," whom they were going to "shock" at a later time. One of the "victims" came across in the interview as a nice, accepting, altruistic, sweet girl. The other came across as obnoxious, self-centered, conceited, and critical. After hearing the interviews each subject was placed in a booth and told to "shock" the "victim" visible in another room by pressing a key (the details of the rationalization for shocking and the arrangements need not concern us here). The "victim," actually a collaborator in the experiment, was taught to react appropriately when a light showed the key depressed, although no shock was actually presented.

The hypothesis was that the deindividuated subjects would deliver shocks of longer duration than the identified ones. This proved to be the case (Figure 22-2). The deindividuated subjects showed greater aggression against both the obnoxious and the nice victims, and there was some tendency for the aggression to increase over time.

Scapegoating. The notion of a "scapegoat" derives from an ancient practice reported in the Old Testament. Periodically the sins of a tribe were transferred with appropriate ceremonies to a goat, which was then driven off into the wilderness. The innocent goat was made to suffer for the sins of the people.

The practice of finding a victim upon whom to place the blame for our troubles and hence to make the object of our aggressions is a familiar one. The child may retaliate against a pet when frustrated by parents or playmates; Hitler threw the blame for Germany's plight on the Jews; farmers blame politicians for hard times connected with crop failures; industrialists blame labor unions for rising prices; labor unions blame capitalists for causing depressions.

The victim of displaced aggression may be chosen on the basis of difference: the aggressor usually finds it easier to assail someone who differs from him. An experiment was designed to see if this would hold in a laboratory setting (Freedman and Doob, 1968). After taking personality tests, three subjects privately received results indicating that they deviated from the rest; three other subjects were told that they were about average for the group. Each subject was then led to perceive the group as consisting, in addition to himself, of four nondeviant subjects and one deviant subject, although he did not know which was which, except by code letter. When in a later portion of the experiment the subject was asked to select by code letter other members of the group to receive either rewards or shocks, he tended to choose on the basis of similarity and difference from himself; that is, he rewarded those like himself and shocked those who were not (Table 22-3). Thus, even though the victim was not known, the deviant was chosen as the target for aggression by the nondeviant and was protected by the other deviant in the group.

How do group phenomena enter into the selection of objects for scapegoating? In an analysis of scapegoating, Allport (1944) pointed out the following characteristics that make some people easy victims.

1. Members of the group to receive the aggression must be easily identifiable. The dark skin color of blacks makes them much more vulnerable to attack than if they looked more like whites. A perceptible difference is enough to favor the separation of figure and ground, and to serve as a reminder of the possibility of difference between in-group and out-group. Sometimes identifiability is enforced, as when Hitler required Jews to wear special insignia.

TABLE 22-3   SIMILARITY AND DIFFERENCE
AS BASES OF CHOICE

THOSE CHOOSING	AVERAGE RANK OF DEVIANT AMONG CHOICES*	
	TO BE REWARDED	TO BE SHOCKED
Deviants	1.27	2.82
Nondeviants	2.18	1.09

* Among four choices, 1 = first choice, 4 = last choice.
Source: Freedman and Doob (1968).

The table indicates that deviants preferred to reward deviants and not to shock them, while nondeviants preferred to shock the deviants and not to reward them.

2. Members of the out-group must be accessible. The mechanism of aggression displacement requires that we substitute an accessible target for an inaccessible one (see p. 448). When Hitler had to find an enemy to attack before Germany rearmed, he turned to the Jews within Germany. In times of economic hardship in the early South the preferred targets of blame might have been northern industrialists, but it was easier to give vent to feeling against the blacks, who were accessible, than against the absent industrialists.

3. Those selected as scapegoats must be unable to retaliate. If aggression is in danger of punishment, the aggressor swerves away and finds a victim who is unable to strike back. In an authoritarian situation—that is, one in which there is a strong leader—the leader may be responsible for much of the frustration of group members. But since the leader is in a protected and powerful position, the aggression is taken out on some lesser individual or individuals.

4. The scapegoats usually will have been scapegoats before. People and nations manage to justify their aggressions self-righteously. The current inciting incident is often too trivial or the responsibility of the scapegoat too remote to justify the extent of the aggression except on the basis of previous antagonism. An insignificant incident is often the excuse for new aggression, because an undercurrent of hostility has persisted from the past. The Turk may attack the Armenian in his midst or the Japanese the Korean, partly because they have attacked these people before.

If a community wants to protect a group habitually chosen as scapegoats, it must invoke the usual sanctions that protect individual liberty as well as counteract the four conditions outlined above. The correctives are not easy to apply. Racial characteristics that make some members of a group identifiable cannot be erased. But habits of dress and gesture that make ethnic groups different from others can be modified so that the minority group conforms more nearly to the practices of the dominant group, with a consequent reduction in social distance. Ideally, tolerance of difference should be encouraged.

The accessibility of the target groups is lessened when segregation is lessened. Rioting against black minorities in the North has occurred almost exclusively in cities in which a high degree of segregation exists, where a mob can find a black community to attack. In the more recent rioting by blacks, the existence of an unfavored black area in the midst of a surrounding white community has a similar effect when retaliation is incited. Group boundary phenomena are enhanced when the boundaries are visible geographically.

Racial prejudice. By "racial prejudice" we mean expressions of disapproval toward members of given ethnic groups, whether racial in a biological sense or merely in the sense of their cultural or national origins. Such prejudices in America are commonly expressed against blacks, Jews, Orientals, Italians, Mexicans, Puerto Ricans, and other groups considered "foreign," even though, like the American Indians, they are frequently as native as the groups showing the prejudice.

Three methods of attacking the problem of race prejudice are possible. One is to try to improve the mental health of children as they grow up so that they do not need to indulge in scapegoating in order to maintain status or to excuse their inadequacies. The second is to reduce social supports given to prejudice by community arrangements, such as segregation in residence, in schools, or in jobs. And, finally, it is possible to reduce the teaching of prejudice that goes on subtly through the stereotypes of comic strips, TV programs, and motion pictures.

The problem will not be fully solved until adults become aware of the degree to which they pass on to their children their own attitudes, often without intended malice. The unintentional transmission of prejudice through casual remarks, anecdotes, and innuendoes probably accounts for more prejudice than do the direct efforts of individuals and agencies promoting hatred.

Conformity and compliance behavior

A *social norm* of conduct is a type of social behavior the regularity of which can be understood only in reference to the group to which the person belongs. Eating when hungry does not represent a social norm, but holding the knife and fork in a certain way while eating does. Obviously behavior in groups runs more smoothly when people observe the expected norms—in this way they come to appointments at the time agreed upon, stop their cars for red lights, remain appropriately quiet during concerts, and so on. Although this is all fairly obvious, it is equally evident that some people are nonconformists and do not like to accept the general norms of conduct. As we shall see, a good deal of social pressure favors compliance, and we turn now to some experimental studies of how social influence is exerted.

Conformity to social influences. How much pressure does a group put upon its members to conform to the ideas of the majority? We all know the appeal of the expression, "When in Rome, do as the Romans do." Conformity is not only an effective way to get along, it is also for most people a congenial way. The question remains whether group pressures operate in ways beyond mere congeniality in order to influence a person's judgment.

In an experiment designed to study the effect of majority opinion, even when it is contrary to fact, small groups of subjects observed a standard straight line and then judged which of three other lines equaled it in length. One of the other lines was longer, one shorter, one equal to the standard; the differences were great enough so that threshold judgments were not involved. All but one member of each group had been instructed to agree upon a wrong answer for a majority of the trials. The experimental subject was thus pitted against a majority, and his problem was whether to report what he would have reported had he been alone, and hence to disagree with the majority, or to doubt his own judgment and agree. Many subjects refused to change and continued to hold to their independent appraisals. But a substantial number yielded under pressure from the others' apparent judgments. The amount of yielding depended upon (1) the clarity of conditions (lack of clarity led to conformity to majority opinion), (2) individual differences, and (3) the size and unanimity of the

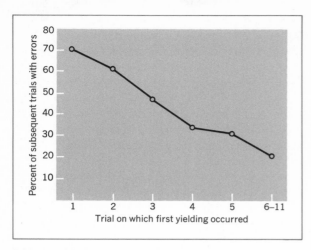

Fig. **22-3 Yielding under group pressure** Those who yield early tend to continue to yield, thus making many errors of judgment on the later trials. (After Asch, 1956)

opposition. With the opposition of only one other person there was very little yielding; with two against one the amount of yielding became pronounced; and a majority of three in a group of six or seven was nearly as effective as larger majorities against the lone dissenter.

The importance of some factor within the individual is suggested by the ease of yielding. Those who yielded early in the experiment showed greater willingness to conform than those who yielded late (Figure 22-3). Questioning of the subjects showed that for the most part they respected the genuineness of the judgments expressed by the majority and had great doubt about their own judgments when they disagreed with the majority. However, some of them merely conformed to the pressure of the majority without rejecting their initial beliefs (Asch, 1956).

The experiment showed that the mere assertion of contrary opinion, without any effort to persuade, may lead susceptible individuals to agree with the majority even on a factual matter on which individual judgment would lead to opposite conclusions. It should be noted, however, that a single ally weakens the effect of the contrary position.

Circumstances favoring compliance. A great deal of social behavior is regulated by group norms to which the group members are expected to comply. Thus closely knit groups come to share common attitudes and opinions on many topics. When a member is assimilated into a group, his perceptions tend to change to conform to the group norms. Studies have shown that the more strongly a member is attracted to a group, the more he tends to conform to the group norms (Kelley and Volkart, 1952). Moreover, a member who is not fully acceptable to a group tends to be more sensitive to majority group opinion than fully accepted members, who are freer to deviate and to hold opinions of their own (Jackson and Saltzstein, 1958).

A person's behavior in any situation is often heavily influenced by what someone else has just done. For example, Helson, Blake, and Mouton (1958) found that they could increase the number of signatures on a petition by strengthening the request to sign and by emphasizing the reaction of others (for example, by manipulating the number of signatures already on the petition when it was circulated).

Social conformity and independence of judgment are both essential to the smooth running of social life and to progress. The foregoing studies admittedly deal with small-scale social processes, but they are relevant to social behavior of broader significance.

Individual and group risk-taking. A whole series of experiments has shown that subjects who have discussed risk-taking behavior together are willing to take more risks than they were prior to the discussion. This change to greater willingness to take risks has come to be known as the *risky-shift*. In these experiments the investigator typically presents the subjects with a set of "life dilemma" problems, and then provides a series of choices, the subject indicating the risks considered acceptable in the solution of each problem. For example, if a man now comfortably employed is invited to join a new company, at a higher salary, but the future of the company is uncertain, what odds will he require for the success of the company in order to join it? One in 10? 5 in 10? 9 in 10? Or if he is about to marry, but a marriage counselor informs him and his fiancée that there is serious doubt that the marriage will work out, what odds will he consider acceptable in order to go ahead with the marriage? The content of the items seems to matter very little (provided they involve real risks), and a consensus in the group discussion does not appear to be necessary in order for the participants to be willing to accept greater risks after the group discussion (Wallach and Kogan, 1965b).

A number of explanations have been offered for the risky-shift, and experiments have been devised to test them. For example, it was thought that perhaps high-risk takers are more verbal and hence more influential in the discussions, but this turns out not to be the case (Wallach, Kogan, and Burt, 1968). The fact that discussion brings more information into the decision process may be a partial explanation; Bateson (1966) found that when subjects who did not participate in group discussions were asked to give further study to the "choice dilemma" problems, they also raised their willingness to take risks, suggesting that internal dialogue has some of the effects of group discussion. Two considerations seem important: first, that there is some sharing of responsibility when the decision is made on the basis of group discussion, so that the personal risk does not seem quite so great; and, second, that there is often a socially desirable outcome from assuming some risk—a fact that the group discussion may well bring out.

Attitudes and opinions

In ordinary social interchange the attitudes, preferences, and prejudices that sway people affect the satisfactions of living together. In a political democracy, sensitive to the wishes of the people, the molding and expression of public opinion are essential to the political process. In an international situation in which the sensitivities of peoples are easily injured and antagonisms aroused, the understanding of attitudes and opinions may mean the difference between war and peace. Attitudes and opinions—who holds them and how they change—are topics for serious study.

Attitudes

A precise definition of attitude is difficult because attitudes overlap with other kinds of psychological preparation for response. The following definition will become clearer when placed in the context of the studies presented below: an *attitude* represents both an *orientation* toward or away from some object, concept, or situation and a *readiness to respond* in a predetermined manner to these or *related* objects, concepts, or situations. Both orientation and readiness to respond have emotional, motivational, and intellectual aspects, and they may in part be unconscious ("I do not like thee, Dr. Fell, the reason why I cannot tell. . . .").

Because attitudes are so interwoven with affective and highly motivated experiences, they become important personality characteristics. On the other hand, attitudes as components of personality cannot be separated from the objects or events in the social context to which they refer. Thus a "conforming" person is not necessarily socially conservative; a member of a left-wing group may have conforming tendencies that make him go along with his group. An extended study of ten men by Smith, Bruner, and White (1956) showed a good deal of correspondence between their individual life histories and their attitudes toward Russia, but the relationships were by no means one-to-one. It was clear, however, that their attitudes toward Russia were dictated only in part by the facts as they saw them; the attitudes were also expressions of aspects of the individual personalities. For example, men who were more likely to blame others than themselves when things went wrong in their personal lives were also more likely to place the burden of blame on Russia for the worsening of United States-Soviet relations.

A number of methods have been devised to measure attitudes. These commonly consist of a number of statements on some topic on which people are divided, such as attitudes toward labor unions, the church, political radicalism or conservatism, women's rights, and so on. The statements can cover the range of attitudes. For example, the following statement is extremely favorable to labor unions: "All industrial workers should belong to unions." The following is extremely unfavorable: "Labor unions should be forbidden by law." There are many in-between possibilities: "Labor leaders do not represent the wishes of the rank-and-file members." The person whose attitudes are being studied fills out a questionnaire by expressing agreement or disagreement with each of a number of such statements; he then receives a "score" for the degree to which his attitudes are favorable or unfavorable on the topic. The scales have proved useful in discovering the attitudes of various parts of the population on important issues, and in studies of attitude change.

Opinions

Attitudes blend into opinions, and there is no sharp difference between them. We may attempt, however, to hold to a difference proposed by Hovland, Janis, and Kelley (1953). An attitude, as indicated earlier, represents an orientation or preference and may be in part unconscious. An *opinion,* according to the above authors, always involves some kind of *expectation* or *prediction* (not merely a preference), and it can always be put into words. The subject may avoid putting his opinions into words, or what he says may not express his true opinion, but according to this definition an opinion is always *capable* of being verbalized.

No matter how we separate attitudes and opinions by definition, they are closely related. If you hate a person (expressing an *attitude* of hatred), you are likely to expect bad behavior of him (expressing an *opinion* about his behavior). If he behaves better than predicted (thus changing your *opinion*), you may like him better (thus changing your *attitude*).

Opinion surveys. The public opinion survey first attracted national interest with the presidential election of 1936. Using the "straw-vote" technique then in vogue, the *Literary digest* incorrectly predicted the election of Landon over Roosevelt, while

the better-designed polls, of which the Gallup poll is the best known, predicted Roosevelt's reelection. The success of the public opinion polls brought them into prominence.

The public opinion survey is not to be identified only with the election poll, for many surveys have purposes other than predicting election outcomes. But because newspaper and magazine polls grew out of the election-prediction polls, the public opinion "ballot" tended at first to be modeled largely after an election ballot. People were asked to state what side of an issue they were on, and the percentage of answers was then reported.

We now know that the simple "yes-no" answer to a question about a public issue is likely to be very misleading. For one thing, the form of the question may produce a great variation in the number answering one way or the other. Here are two questions asked of a sample of the public early in 1945:[2]

> After the war would you like to see the United States join some kind of world organization, or would you like to see us stay out? (National Opinion Research Center, January, 1945)

Join	64%
Stay out	26
Undecided	10
	100%

> Do you think the United States should join a world organization with police power to maintain world peace? (American Institute of Public Opinion, April, 1945)

Yes	81%
No	11
No opinion	8
	100%

There is no reason to suppose that the difference between 64 percent and 81 percent is a reflection of any change in international attitudes between January and April. The phrase "to maintain world peace" in the second question no doubt raised the percentage of affirmative answers.

One of the chief difficulties with the opinion

[2]Quoted by Cartwright (1946), p. 28.

ballot is that it is hard to know how firmly the respondent holds his convictions, a problem met also in attitude scaling. The answers to "yes-no" questions may be given as casually as they sometimes are to the questions in a college "true-false" examination. The vagueness or firmness of answers is partly dependent upon the extent to which public opinion has crystallized on an issue. Often people are asked to give opinions about highly technical matters, such as the influence of atomic energy on the future of civilization. In response to such questions there is often a high percentage of "No opinion." Interpretations of the opinions that are offered must be made with extreme caution.

Even though the ballot form is used, many refinements in questioning are possible. One device is to use a number of *fixed alternatives* instead of

The problem of sampling

A properly conducted public opinion survey is like any other scientific investigation: it has to be carefully designed in order to yield unambiguous results. We have considered some of the pitfalls in the form of the poll question. It is important that we know how the respondent interprets our questions, how thoughtful and informed his opinion is, with what conviction he states his answer, and what he intends by it. It is also important that we ask our questions of the right people. The selection of those whose replies we seek constitutes the problem of *sampling*. We have made great advances in selecting samples, but our sampling methods are still not foolproof.

The logic of sampling is simple. Ideally, once we have defined the total group to be sampled (for example, registered voters, males of draft age, owners of motor vehicles), we should so design the sample that each person in the group has an equal (or known) chance of being represented. If we could give every person in the country a number chosen at random, and then make our sample by drawing, say, every thousandth person, we would have a simple random sample. The cost of doing this would, of course, be prohibitive, so methods have to be devised to achieve a compromise that lies near this ideal.

Any method that requires the interviewer to choose those to be interviewed introduces bias. For instance, he gets more interviews by talking with people standing on street corners or by calling on people usually at home. But as a result he may get too many unemployed men on street corners or too many mothers with small babies at home. To correct such biases, a method known as *area sampling* has been developed. By this method, whether applied on a national or local basis, interview assignments are usually made according to residence units. The interviewer has no choice; he is told exactly where to go and whom to interview. No substitutions are allowed, for the person hard to reach may be the very one needed to assure the representativeness of the sample. Not all desired respondents will be reached, but with this method their number can be ascertained, and something about them can be known from the neighborhoods in which they live.

Area sampling is really a variation of the broader method of *probability sampling*, in which the probability that any one member of the population is included in the sample is determined in advance so that sampling statistics can be accurately applied. There are other ways of obtaining the specific assignments required by probability sampling. In a wartime study of small manufacturing plants, for example, a representative sample was drawn from the social security files, and assignments were made by name and address of the plant.

Surprising accuracy can be achieved with small samples if they are carefully designed. The confidence limits of the results can be determined by appropriate statistical formulas, so that the degree of accuracy can be known in advance and the sample size determined in accordance with the accuracy needed for the purposes at hand.

a mere "yes-no" reply. A printed card with four or more possible replies is handed to the person being interviewed, and he is asked to select the one that most nearly represents his own opinion. Another device is that of the "filter" question, used to determine what question should be asked next. The following illustration[3] shows how a stereotyped reply can be broken down by asking a second question of those who answer in a conventional manner:

Do you believe in freedom of speech?

Yes	97%
No	1
Don't know	2
	100%

If "Yes," do you believe in it to the extent of allowing Fascists and Communists to hold meetings and express their views in this community?

Yes	23%
No	72
No opinion	5
	100%

Because answers depend upon the context in which the questions are asked as well as upon both the form and the wording of the question, a single percentage can never be interpreted unambiguously. Successive polls repeating identical questions do indicate trends, however, and these are often very revealing.

The alternative to the ballot form of question is that known as the *free-answer* or *open* question, that is, a question to which the respondent must reply in his own words. This method requires somewhat more skilled interviewers (who must record answers as nearly verbatim as possible) and makes statistical analysis more difficult, but it has genuine advantages. For one thing, the free answer provides a better understanding of how the respondent interpreted the question. It also makes possible an understanding of the meaning of the reply. "Yes-no" answers often conceal meaning.

Many public opinion surveys now make use of both free-answer and fixed-alternative questions.

[3]American Institute of Public Opinion, November, 1940. Quoted by Cantril (1944), p. 22.

The study of voting behavior. Not only has the study of elections served well as a testing ground for public opinion measurement but the substance of such study has social psychological importance because of the importance of the problem and the precision of the data. Elections are significant in a democracy, the issues and candidates are widely publicized, and accurate records are kept. The initial interest in studying voting behavior—the prediction of election results—has come to be supplemented by many other interests related to the sources of political affiliation, such as the effects of income, education, and social class upon loyalty to a party, or the nature of those who switch allegiance.

The fact that a poll result does not agree perfectly with the election result does not necessarily detract from the usefulness of the poll as a method of studying voting behavior. A poll reflects voting behavior at a given time; since elections are held at another point in time, the results may have been influenced in the meantime by several factors beyond the pollster's control. One of these factors is that voters change their minds. Even though they answer honestly about how they plan to vote, they may hear a speech or have a talk with friends and

Fig. **22-4 Unpredictability of late deciders** Within two elections it was found that the decisions of those who made up their minds late could not be predicted as well from their partisan attitudes as the decisions of those who made up their minds early. This is interpreted as due to conflict. (After Campbell and others, 1960)

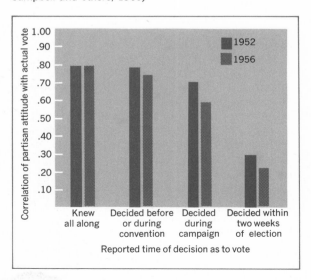

ultimately decide to vote differently. Then, too, not all of those interviewed will vote, so that the interview sample may not represent the voting sample. In states that discourage voting by blacks, a representative sample of blacks and whites would not be a good election sample. Bad weather may affect the farm and urban votes differently, since farmers find it harder than city residents to get to election booths.

The actual process by which a voter decides how to vote and the issues that may influence him vary from election to election. Some voters have no trouble at all making up their minds how they will vote: their party affiliations, their social class or economic group interests, their liking for the party's candidate—all are in harmony. But other voters are in conflict: they like the candidate, but do not like the party's policies; they like the domestic policy, but are out of sympathy with the foreign policy. They then have trouble making up

their minds and often decide late. In the elections of both 1952 and 1956, partisan attitudes readily predicted how those who decided early would vote, but they did not predict for the late deciders, as shown in Figure 22-4 (Campbell and others, 1960).

The purpose of public opinion surveys in an election year is not simply to predict an outcome. This should be clear from the election of 1968, in which Nixon's overwhelming victory over Humphrey was easily reflected in the preelection polls. The election had many uncertainties, however, and the study of its antecedents and of the patterns of voting behavior turns out to be informative.

The first important factor was the decline of President Johnson's popularity after his sweeping victory over Goldwater in 1964. Despite his high popularity at the time of election and the generally widespread support for his domestic policies, the escalation of the war in Vietnam (which Goldwater

Fig. 22-5   Declining popularity of President Johnson as related to the war in Vietnam   Note that the handling of the presidency (color line) is judged very largely according to the handling of the situation in Vietnam (black line). (After Appleton, 1968)

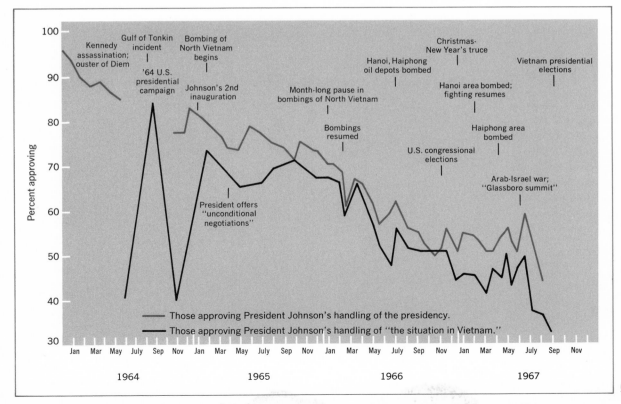

had favored) diminished Johnson's popularity as a president as the war events became increasingly unpopular (Figure 22-5). The consequence of President Johnson's withdrawal as a candidate for reelection was a wide division within the Democratic party; McCarthy, Robert Kennedy, and McGovern emerged to challenge the expected nominee, Humphrey. Kennedy's assassination added another uncertainty. Still another complicating factor—doubtless the most unusual feature of the election—was the third-party movement of Wallace, which might have thrown the presidential contest into the House of Representatives.

The shift of votes from one party to another—40 percent of Nixon's votes coming from those who had supported Johnson in 1964—oddly enough does not reflect a shift in party identifications. The overall proportion of citizens who are self-proclaimed Democrats, Independents, and Republicans has scarcely changed over twenty years (Converse and others, 1969). All this means is that party identification does not override other salient issues.

If party is not overriding, what is?—in part, the current issues; in part, the personal popularity of candidates. After the election was over, when pushing for one candidate over another would have no influence upon outcomes, a national sample of voters was asked to rate twelve political figures on a "feeling thermometer" running from zero (cold) to 100° (warm), with a response of 50° representing an indifferent point. The results for the national sample are given in Table 22-4. The table has to be interpreted with some caution. Robert Kennedy's ratings may be exaggerated because of his martyr status. It is clear that Humphrey suffered from his tie to Johnson: their ratings are very similar throughout. The dissatisfaction over Vietnam—among whites—hurt Johnson and Humphrey, but this issue was not salient for the blacks; for them civil rights issues were more important.

TABLE 22-4 POST-ELECTION RATINGS OF MAJOR 1968 POLITICAL FIGURES BY A NATIONAL SAMPLE					
	MEAN RATING ON SCALE (MAXIMUM = 100)				
	NON-SOUTH		SOUTH		
PRESIDENTIAL POSSIBILITIES	WHITE RESPONDENTS	BLACK RESPONDENTS	WHITE RESPONDENTS	BLACK RESPONDENTS	ALL RESPONDENTS
Robert Kennedy	70	92	60	89	69
Richard Nixon	67	53	67	57	66
Hubert Humphrey	61	85	53	84	61
Lyndon Johnson	56	81	54	82	58
Eugene McCarthy	56	59	50	54	55
Nelson Rockefeller	54	61	51	53	54
Ronald Reagan	50	43	50	42	49
George Romney	50	48	46	50	49
George Wallace	28	9	48	13	31
VICE-PRESIDENTIAL NOMINEES					
Edmund Muskie	62	71	55	69	61
Spiro Agnew	51	38	53	42	50
Curtis LeMay	34	21	44	23	35
Source: Converse and others (1969).					

The table illustrates how opinion surveys are useful in ways beyond the prediction of election results. Notable are the high ratings of Robert Kennedy, the close tie of Humphrey's ratings to those of Johnson, the preference of the blacks for the Democratic nominees over the Republican ones.

This is not the place to go into further detail regarding the interpretation of a particular election; the purpose in presenting the data has been merely to show how the measuring of opinions through the survey method may enhance our understanding of social processes.

Changing attitudes and opinions

Although the foregoing account could not avoid some mention of how attitudes and opinions are formed and changed, let us now look more specifically at the ways such changes come about.

Consistency in attitude change

In addition to knowing what attitudes people hold, psychologists are interested in how these attitudes change. We shall study later some of the attempts to alter what people believe by using persuasive communications (pp. 531–35), but at this point it is appropriate to discuss a theory that has preoccupied many social psychologists over the last decade. This theory, in most general terms, states that a person likes his beliefs and his behavior to be consistent, and if he finds them inconsistent he maneuvers in one way or another to reduce the discrepancy—by altering his beliefs, by changing his behavior, or both. Brown (1965) calls this a *consistency* theory. There are three closely related variants of the theory: *balance, congruity,* and *cognitive dissonance.*

The *balance model* has several forms. It was originally proposed by Heider (1946, 1958), again on the assumption that we like consistency between what we believe and how we (and others) behave. To illustrate Heider's theory let us consider one person perceiving two others, and perceiving some sort of relationship between them. If he likes them both, he expects them to like each other; if he likes one and not the other, he expects them to dislike each other. A *balanced state* is one in which the perceived relationships are harmonious and internally consistent. For example, if A likes B, and A also likes C, then A's perception will be in balance if he finds that B and C also like each other; but his perception will be imbalanced if he notes that B and C dislike each other. The tendency is to perceive balanced states; imbalance motivates change in the direction of cognitive balancing. Thus if a good friend A dislikes your acquaintance B, you may cool off toward B in order to preserve balance.

The *congruity* theory (Osgood and Tannenbaum, 1955) assumes that we can scale our attitudes toward people and proposals along a scale from very positive ($+3$) to very negative (-3). It differs from the balance theory, in that it adds quantities by which changes can be measured. We suffer no sense of incongruity when a liked person likes what we like or when a disliked person approves something we dislike. Conversely, there is incongruity when a liked person dislikes something we like or a disliked person likes something we like. Where there is incongruity, the theory proposes that something will be done to restore equilibrium. The amount and direction of movement will depend, according to the theory, on the amount of polarization, that is, on how extreme our views are either about the person or about the proposition. Thus if our state senator, whom we admire, comes out in support of farm subsidies, which we do not favor, we are likely to change our views on farm subsidies if we are great admirers of the senator. If, however, we are only moderate supporters of the senator and feel very strongly about the issue at hand, the discrepancy will lead to a less favorable attitude toward the senator. The theory has been moderately successful in describing the shifts in attitude that do indeed occur in cases of incongruity (Tannenbaum and Gengel, 1966; Tannenbaum, 1967).

The third of the consistency theories, that of *cognitive dissonance,* was originated by Festinger (1957), as earlier noted (Chapter 13, p. 329). This theory focuses attention on the aftereffects of decision-making; it is at this point that any discrepancy between what was believed and what was done might be reduced. A good clothing salesman knows that it is wise to keep on selling after the deal is closed: "I am glad you chose that one, because I was hoping all along you would choose it. It is such a fine value, looks so good on you." The purchaser may have had a momentary fear that he made a wrong choice or that he paid too much, and he needs the reassurance that will reduce his cognitive dissonance. There is of course conflict prior to choice, but at that stage, according to Festinger, the person is more open to a realistic appraisal of alternatives. It is after he has committed himself that his dissonance is most felt, and he then begins to alter his cognitions in such a way as to reduce the dissonance. This is the mechanism whereby the belief in the association between tobacco smoking and lung cancer depended upon the subject's decision to smoke or not to smoke (see Chapter 13, p. 330).

CRITICAL DISCUSSION

Controversial aspects of dissonance theory

The theory of cognitive dissonance has led not only to a substantial amount of research but to a great deal of theorizing pro and con. The predecision stage is usually somewhat conflictual because alternatives are being weighed, but the postdecision phase is also conflictual because something has been given up or rejected in favor of something else. Festinger's dissonance theory is concerned with the postdecision phase, with a person's maneuvers to justify the decision to himself, to reduce regret, and to see his own beliefs and actions as consistent.

The first source of argument concerns the relative importance of the pre- and post-decision phases. According to Janis (1959, 1968), the conflicts are already present in the predecision phase, and the postdecision behavior emphasized by Festinger can be understood only in relation to the total behavior, including the incentives involved; somewhat related interpretations are offered by Elms (1967) and Rosenberg (1968). Festinger, in a series of experiments, defended the importance of the post- versus the predecision phase (Festinger and others, 1964).

A second source of argument pertains to the paradoxical prediction that greater change of belief will be found in forced compliance situations when the compliance is accompanied by a *small* reward rather than a *large* reward. Ordinary reinforcement theory would predict that the more rewarded behavior would be the more strengthened. The reasoning behind the contention of dissonance theory that greater change of belief will be produced by small rewards (or bribes) is not easy to state briefly, but its subjective interpretation is as follows. When offered a very large bribe to make a statement contrary to your belief, you are willing to make the statement for the money, without really altering your belief. If you are persuaded to modify your belief for a very small amount of money, you would feel ashamed to "sell out" so cheaply; hence you justify the change on its own merits (not on the basis of the bribe), and such a justified change is more permanent. This is considered paradoxical because we generally expect larger rewards to have larger effects. Early experiments on dissonance with human subjects (Festinger and Carlsmith, 1959), and analogous experiments with white rats (Lawrence and Festinger, 1962), supported the predictions from dissonance theory.

Not all experiments have supported the original dissonance contentions, however. One experimenter and his collaborators have conducted over a dozen studies without finding the expected dissonance effect (Collins, 1969). This has led to a search for the specific circumstances under which the dissonance effects will hold. A promising theory holds that only when the subject is genuinely free to make choices will dissonance arise, and the smaller rewards will prove effective; when the tasks are assigned without any freedom of choice, the larger rewards will be more effective in producing an attitude change (Linder, Cooper, and Jones, 1967).

The three consistency theories (congruity, balance, and cognitive dissonance) represent some of the most significant theorizing within the field of attitude change. That they predict many of the same findings is encouraging; that there are some disagreements among them is to be expected in scientific research.

The mass media as channels of influence

How are people influenced to change their attitudes, opinions, and beliefs? The answer is found in part through ordinary learning experiences and through the rewards and punishments the individual receives from his culture. Attempts to influence people in large numbers come mainly by way of the *mass media* of communication: through the spoken word over the radio; through the printed word in newspapers, books, and magazines; and audiovisually through motion pictures and television. Many studies are concerned with the type and size of audience reached by the mass media and with their influence upon such audiences. Only a few selected examples can be given here.

The newspaper is not as important as it once was because of other sources of news reports, but it has many features (in addition to news coverage) that make it a significant part of the daily lives of a great many people. A seventeen-day newspaper strike in New York City provided the occasion for a study of what "missing the newspaper" meant to its readers (Berelson, 1954). People felt that they were less certain as to what was going on in the world, and they reported missing the satisfaction provided by the act of reading, without primary concern in some cases for the content being read. The paper was a source of security, providing an indirect social contact and a feeling of intimacy with important people and serving satisfying "ritualistic" values.

The increasing influence of radio and television has emphasized certain requisites of candidates for political office; those who are "cosmetic" personalities come across most favorably to the TV viewer, and those who are wealthy enough to afford air time are able to reach more voters.

The importance of TV in the lives of contemporary schoolchildren is brought out strikingly in some studies by Schramm and others (1961). Of a sample of 508 fifth- and sixth-grade children in San Francisco, 74 percent viewed TV every day, with an average viewing time of two and a half hours, about the same amount of time spent daily in free play. Very little of the viewing was of educational programs.

A large-scale study in England of TV viewing by children (Himmelweit, Oppenheim, and Vince, 1958) showed that viewing was negatively correlated with intelligence; the higher a child's intelligence, the less time he spent before the TV screen. Children can learn from TV, but there appears to be no net gain, because TV replaces other experiences, such as reading. Television does not appear to lead to action; when a model for making something was shown on television few children in the study then proceeded to make it.

The importance of TV as an influential medium cannot be doubted, even though the specifics of its influence are not yet fully understood. For example, the question of whether the prevalence of pictured violence on TV has served to legitimize violent action is currently being widely debated.

The effectiveness of communications

One approach to the study of communication effectiveness is through controlled experiments that permit changes of the communicator, the message, and the audience to be influenced.

Credibility of the source. Whether or not an opinion will be changed by a communication depends in part upon the confidence the listener has in the speaker. In one experiment three groups of high school students, who had been invited to a studio, were addressed on juvenile delinquency by a guest speaker who favored extreme leniency in the treatment of delinquents. The speaker was introduced to each group in a different way:

POSITIVE: As an authority; a judge of a juvenile court.
NEUTRAL: As an unidentified member of the studio audience.

NEGATIVE: As a member of the studio audience who had been a delinquent and was now out on bail, having been charged with dope peddling.

The audience's opinions on leniency of treatment of juvenile offenders that resulted from the talk varied according to the order of credibility of the speaker, the "positive" speaker having most effect, the "negative" speaker least. The differences between the group who heard the positive speaker and those who heard the negative were highly significant statistically (Kelman and Hovland, 1953).

A retest three weeks later revealed an important finding: those exposed to the communication from the negative source showed more opinion change in the direction of the content of the communication than they had immediately after the communication, while those exposed to the positive source showed a reduced effect after three weeks (Figure 22-6). The communicator and the message apparently became dissociated, and the people remembered what was said without thinking about who said it.

The prestige effect of the communicator can be

Fig. **22-6 Effect of credibility of speaker upon opinion change** The high-prestige speaker caused more immediate changes in opinions than did the other two. After three weeks, however, the results were quite different. The three-weeks effect for the neutral source is inferred from the report. (After Kelman and Hovland, 1953)

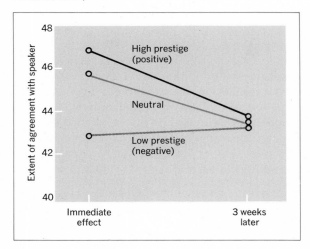

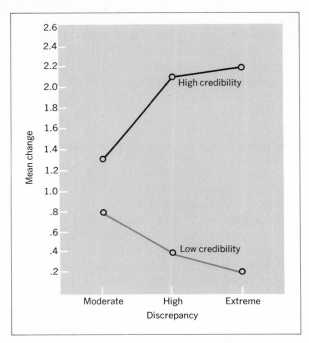

Fig. **22-7 Communicator credibility and change in self-ratings** Note that when the communicator of personality-test information has high credibility, the self-rating is changed to correspond to his message, and the change is greater the more his message disagrees with the original self-rating. For the communicator of low credibility, some change also occurs, but the amount of change is small, and is *less* when the discrepancy is greater between the communicator's message and the self-rating. (After Bergin, 1962)

demonstrated to affect self-appraisal as well as attitudes toward other people or events (Bergin, 1962). Ratings of masculinity, based on personality-test scores interpreted in a setting of authority for the communicator, produced great changes in self-ratings, while corresponding ratings, given in a setting that did not evoke confidence, produced little change in self-ratings (Figure 22-7).

Effects of fear arousal. The appeal to fear is familiar in persuasive communications, whether in lectures on health, in religious revivals, or in political campaigns. Experimental results have been somewhat contradictory. An early experiment showed fear-appeals to be unsuccessful in changing behavior (Janis and Feshbach, 1953) and was supported by a few later experiments, but most of the later experiments had the opposite result, supporting the effectiveness of appeals to fear (Leventhal and Singer, 1966). The experiments have dealt with a great many issues, such as following hygienic practices to prevent tooth decay, giving up smoking because of the threat of cancer, receiving injections to protect against tetanus, and using seat belts to prevent injury in automobile accidents.

McGuire (1969) has proposed that at low levels of initial anxiety, fear arousal will make the subject more receptive to the message and will thus enhance opinion change; however, at high levels of initial anxiety, further fear arousal would mobilize defenses and thus produce a resistance to change.

Effects of commitment. Salesmen have long known that if they can get the prospective customer to do something, such as accept a free sample, the chance of getting him to do something else, such as purchase the product, is more likely. An experiment performed in a nonlaboratory context provided evidence. The experimenters called on housewives, explaining that they were working for the Committee for Safe Driving. They asked each housewife to sign a petition urging the senators from California to support legislation to encourage safe driving. Most of the women agreed and signed the petition. Several weeks later different experimenters called on the women who had signed the petitions and upon other women in similar neighborhoods who had not been reached before. This time they asked the women for permission to place in their front yards a large unattractive sign that said "Drive Carefully." The women who had not been contacted in connection with the petition thought this was an encroachment: only 17 percent of them agreed to post the sign. Those who had responded earlier to the petition request acceded to the further request in a much greater proportion: 55 percent of them agreed to have the sign placed in their front yards (Freedman and Fraser, 1966).

The initial response provides a kind of commitment to an implied position; in the foregoing experiment it was a commitment to support safe driving. In general, prior commitment produces a tendency to resist a change in attitude. In an ex-

TABLE 22-5	COMMITMENT AND RESISTANCE TO CONFORMITY	
DEGREE OF COMMITMENT (IN DECREASING ORDER)	CONFORMITY
Public announcement	6%
Private, permanent writing	6
Private, temporary writing*	16
No commitment	25

*A "magic pad" was used, so that raising the plastic sheet erased the record of choice.

Source: Deutsch and Gerard (1955).

periment modeled after Asch's on group influences (p. 521), Deutsch and Gerard (1955) gave subjects the task of deciding which of two lines was longer. They were given the choice of stating their decisions publicly or writing them down on either a regular pad or a temporary "magic pad." These methods of response represented three degrees of commitment. The conforming responses, which involved a change in original beliefs on the basis of group pressure, were inversely proportional to the amount of commitment (Table 22-5). Another experiment showed that once an individual had conformed to social pressure, later conformity on a different problem was increased, as though he had committed himself to follow the group (Allen and Crutchfield, 1963).

Coercive persuasion and immunization to change

Although much of the experimentation on the effectiveness of communications may play into the hands of advertisers, propagandists, and others interested in influencing people's opinions and beliefs, there is also a scientific problem in determining the circumstances under which resistance to persuasion can be taught. The need for such determinations was felt when fears of successful "brainwashing" began to arise.

Brainwashing. The term "brainwashing" was introduced by Hunter (1951) as a translation of a Chinese term meaning "cleansing of the mind," which was used in reference to ridding the Chinese of old beliefs in order to become reeducated for life in a Communist state. The word has come to be applied to various efforts to change the outlook of prisoners, both military and civilian, through various persuasive techniques used while the authorities have control over the lives of the prisoners. The expression "coercive persuasion" is favored by Schein and others (1961).

The possibility of controlling men's minds came strongly to public attention during the purge trials of the Soviet Union in the late 1930s, in which former leaders in the Communist movement publicly confessed their "crimes" before they were executed. The confessions seemed so out of character that the Western world assumed that some special psychological methods (or perhaps drugs) had been used to produce the confessions. Later examination of the evidence (Leites and Bernaut, 1954) showed that a complex set of historical and situational as well as psychological factors were involved. Smith (1954), finding some parallels in English treason trials in the sixteenth century, considered the confessions of the Russian prisoners to be some strange means of proving that the regime was more important than their own lives. The Russians traditionally isolated the prisoner from others and, through repeated interrogation, extracted a confession from him.

The Chinese methods tend to be quite different, with the objective being to make the individual a useful member of the Communist community rather than to liquidate him. Detailed information on Chinese methods of "thought reforms" have come through two main sets of interviews—the first, with American war prisoners who were returned from Chinese prisons during the exchange of prisoners after the Korean fighting ended in 1953 (Lifton, 1954; Schein, 1956); the second, with civilian Westerners—doctors, missionaries, students, and businessmen—who were returned from Chinese prisons to Hong Kong (Lifton, 1956). In the exchange of military prisoners it was found that a few Americans had collaborated with the Chinese Communists, and twenty-one refused repatriation; in view of the great number of Chinese and North Korean prisoners who refused repatriation, the twenty-one Americans did not represent significant validation of the Chinese indoctrination methods. The civilians who had been prisoners of the Chinese actually proved in some ways more interesting, because among them were those who showed definite signs of change as a result of their experiences.

The aim of the Chinese prison "reform" was to obtain a confession of past transgressions, and then to produce "conversion" to Communist ideals and programs. This took place in three major steps— "unfreezing" (to begin to doubt one's past standards to the point of wishing to change), "changing" (to begin to see merit in the Communist position and to imitate others who have accepted it), and "refreezing" (consolidating the new position in order to find it congenial) (Schein and others, 1961).

A number of theories have been proposed to account psychologically for the changes that take place under these circumstances. Some theories consider physiological stress along with the psychology of learning. One of these, for example, shows how "debility, dependency, and dread" could be used, according to what we know about learning, to produce the kinds of changes found (Farber and others, 1957). Other theories suggest that psychoanalytic mechanisms can account for the change, especially various aspects of guilt, dependency, identification, and identity struggles (Moloney, 1955). Still others make use of the concepts familiar in the social psychology of attitude change (Kelman, 1958). Although it is possible to interpret the results in these ways, it is widely conceded that those responsible for the indoctrination programs in the prisons of China were probably little influenced by any academic theory, basing their methods much more on such Confucian concepts as "sincerity," "self-cultivation," and "harmony," combined with the practices and theories of Marxist-Leninist doctrine (Lifton, 1961).

Immunization against persuasion. The circumstances under which coercive persuasion takes place may be so extreme that suggestions for defying it have to go beyond the psychological studies of persuasibility. For example, as in the case of the captured crew of the U. S. Naval vessel Pueblo, some officers gave false confessions in order to prevent torture of crew members; these officers were not "brainwashed" and did not come out of the experience with views different from those with which they went in. There is little evidence that any current techniques of extreme coercion have produced fundamental changes in outlook, except with a very small number of individuals who were in some sense ready for the changes.

For the milder forms of persuasion constantly with us enough knowledge is available from experimentation to tell us something about the processes that protect against undue influence. Such protection comes from a heightened self-esteem ("a strong ego") built upon success experiences; a training in critical abilities (specific to the issues involved); a commitment that permits holding fast to a chosen position (although, as noted earlier, a "foot-in-the-door" commitment may make it easier to adopt a more extreme position). Finally, if a particular issue is imbedded in a larger set of beliefs related to positively valued goals, it is resistant to change.

One experimental approach to inducing resistance to persuasion has been called the *inoculation approach* (McGuire, 1969; Tannenbaum, 1967). It works particularly well in relation to *cultural truisms,* statements so widely believed that they are seldom doubted. Examples are: "It's good to brush your teeth three times a day"; "Mental illness is not contagious"; "The effects of penicillin have been, almost without exception, of great benefit to mankind"; "Everyone should get a yearly chest X-ray to detect any signs of TB at an early stage."

The analogy suggested by the term "inoculation approach" is that of a germ-free environment, so that the possibility of illness is not considered: a "truism" corresponds to a germ-free ideological environment. Just as natives in a germ-free environment are very susceptible to disease (for exam-

ple, the American Indians suffered severely from the white man's smallpox and other diseases), so, too, these universally and uncritically held beliefs are readily shattered by arguments against them. The inoculation approach holds that small doses of counterarguments, like small quantities of germs, may immunize against a more drastic attempt at change. Experimenters have studied four kinds of "inoculation": (1) building up positive arguments to support the already accepted belief before attempts at attitude change are made; (2) presenting counterarguments along with their immediate refutation; (3) presenting the counterargument without refuting it; (4) merely forewarning that an attack is to come. While there have been many subtle variations, the general results of these approaches can be summarized as follows (McGuire, 1969):

1. A weakened form of counterargument (a mention of the argument and then a refutation of it) is more effective in producing resistance to attitude change than supportive arguments. This is true even if the argument used in the later attack differs from that used in the inoculation.

2. Mentioning the argument without refuting it may be *more* effective than preparing a defense through refutation.

3. A mere forewarning that the attack is to come, without mention of the arguments, produces equivalent resistance to influence, especially on issues in which there is high personal involvement (Freedman and Sears, 1965; Apsler and Sears, 1968).

These results have in common an alerting of the subject to the fact that his position is vulnerable to attack, thus permitting him to prepare his own defense; when the attack comes, he is ready and is less influenced by it. Presentation of supporting arguments, without counterarguments, fails in effectiveness because it lacks the threats that arouse defense.

Summary

1. Because life is lived among other people, we form *impressions* of people, and these impressions serve in part as a basis for our liking or disliking them. Perceptions of other people are influenced by how a person perceives himself, by the specific characteristics he values highly. Some distortions occur in the attribution of abilities, motives, and responsibility, because abilities are viewed as stable, motives as fluctuating, and responsibility is assigned in part on the basis of severity of outcome of the person's behavior.

2. Among the bases for *attraction* and *liking* are the role of the person perceived (how he presents himself and behaves toward us): we are attracted to those who like us. Proximity, familiarity, and commitment to work together also influence liking.

3. Social behavior in man is influenced by physical and social environments. *Social norms* represent expected regularities in conduct and tacit agreements about how to behave. The broadest aspects of arrangements for group living are referred to as the *culture* or the *civilization* of which the individual is a part.

4. Social stratification occurs according to *caste* or *class*. The caste system has boundaries that cannot be crossed (for example, by way of intermarriage), while the class system permits such crossing. Moving across class lines is called *social mobility*. The opportunity for upward mobility is motivating because it provides the hope of improved status, but it also has the attendant cost of anxiety. One extreme expression of this is the increased suicide rate among the well-to-do.

5. Intergroup tensions arise in part because of boundaries between *in-groups* and *out-groups*. Sometimes rioting and mob behavior can be accounted for on the basis of circumstances leading to *deindividuation,* in which the usual social restraints are weakened, and impulsive, aggressive, and regressive tendencies are released. Racial prejudice is an illustration of the ways in which *stereotyping* and *scapegoating* operate.

6. Individual behavior tends to be influenced by the group of which the individual is a member. What someone else has already done may determine what the individual does. This is also shown in *risk-taking,* when the willingness to take risks tends to increase after group discussion.

7. An *attitude* can be described as an *orientation* favorable or unfavorable to some object, concept, or situation, and a *readiness to respond* in some predetermined manner to these or related objects, concepts, or events.

8. *Opinions* deal with *expectations* or *predictions* about the consequences of a certain course of action. Attitudes may in some cases be unconscious, but opinions are always conscious and can be put into words.

9. Two ways of conducting public opinion surveys are by means of *fixed-alternative* questions and *free-answer* questions. The free-answer questions have the advantage of revealing how the respondent interprets the question and what he intends by his answer, but the difficulties of interviewing and interpreting are increased.

10. The study of voting behavior is now aimed at understanding characteristics of the voter and considerations affecting his choices, with the prediction of election outcomes a secondary matter. The effects of party loyalty versus personal popularity of a candidate and the salience of particular issues, among other topics, are open to study.

11. Attitude and opinion changes have led to several theories based on the notion that a person prefers to have his attitudes, beliefs, and behavior internally consistent. When they are found inconsistent, he tends to shift one or another of these in order to bring them more nearly into balance. Three related theories emphasizing *cognitive consistency* are the *balance* theory of Heider, the *congruity* theory of Osgood and Tannenbaum, and the *dissonance* theory of Festinger.

12. The *mass media* (newspapers and magazines, motion pictures, radio, television) affect the attitudes, opinions, and beliefs of a large audience. Television is currently being studied for its more specific role in educating the young.

13. Laboratory studies of the effectiveness of communication have dealt with a number of topics, among them the credibility of the communicator, the effects of fear arousal, and the effects of commitment.

14. *Coercive persuasion* ("brainwashing") refers to the efforts to convert the thinking of prisoners (both military and civilian) to a point of view favorable to the regime of the captors by means of coercive techniques. These techniques include environmental control (physical or social), deprivation, reward, and confession. The steps of change can be described as *unfreezing* of familiar attitudes, beliefs, and values, *changing* these attitudes, beliefs, and values, and then *refreezing,* or consolidating, the new position.

15. *Immunization against persuasion* has been studied particularly in relation to beliefs so universally held that they are extremely vulnerable to attack ("cultural truisms"). Supporting arguments to the position already held are not as effective in producing resistance to an attack as are small doses of counterarguments, whether or not the counterarguments are refuted. In addition, those who hold uncriticized beliefs will apparently build their own defenses if they are simply warned that an attack on the beliefs is to come.

Suggestions for further reading

For a general orientation to social psychology, recent textbooks include Jones and Gerard, *Foundations of social psychology* (1967), Collins, *Social psychology* (1970), Freedman, Carlsmith, and Sears, *Social psychology* (1970), and Sherif and Sherif, *Social psychology* (1969). Mills (ed.), *Experimental social psychology* (1969), Proshansky and Seidenberg (eds.), *Basic studies in social psychology* (1965), and Steiner and Fishbein (eds.), *Current studies in social psychology* (1965), provide a well-selected collection of studies. For special topics, Lindzey and Aronson (eds.), *Handbook of social psychology* (rev. ed., 5 vols., 1968–69), is a good resource. On forming impressions of people, see Hastorf, Polefka, and Schneider, *Person perception* (1970).

Interpersonal behavior is dealt with more fully in Cartwright and Zander (eds.), *Group dynamics* (3rd ed., 1968), and Bennis and others (eds.), *Interpersonal dynamics* (rev. ed., 1968). On prejudice, see Allport, *The nature of prejudice* (1954), and Pettigrew, *A profile of the American Negro* (1964).

Attitudes and attitude change are treated in an excellent review by McGuire in the Lindzey and Aronson *Handbook,* vol. III. For a recent treatment of attitude scales, see Shaw and Wright, *Scales for the measurement of attitudes* (1967). A useful source is Kiesler, Collins, and Miller, *Attitude change* (1969). For a lively account, which brings the student actively into the role of critic and interpreter of research, see Zimbardo and Ebbesen, *Influencing attitudes and changing behavior* (1969).

The consistency theories are reviewed in an authoritative manner in the eighty-four original chapters by sixty-three contributors found in Abelson and others (eds.), *Theories of cognitive consistency: A sourcebook* (1968).

On survey research a useful book is Glock, *Survey research in the social sciences* (1967). Voting behavior is treated in Campbell and others, *The American voter* (1960).

Two books on "brainwashing" are Lifton, *Thought reform and the psychology of totalism* (1961), and Schein and others, *Coercive persuasion* (1961). See also Biderman and Zimmer (eds.), *The manipulation of human behavior* (1961).

psychology and society

THE SCIENCES OF MAN BEAR UPON TWO MAJOR problems: first, how to plan so that mankind may survive; second, how to enhance the quality of life for surviving mankind. Both are perennial problems, but they arise today in new forms because accelerated technology has created new problems and because modern knowledge has made possible new solutions.

The impact of sheer numbers and quantities is now beginning to be felt severely. We are confronted with population increases of a size that could only have been conjectured in Malthus' time, with the consumption of natural resources proceeding at a rate undreamed of a few years ago, and with the creation of waste products in such quantity that scientists fear we are approaching the environment's maximum capacity to assimilate waste (National Academy of Sciences, 1969). We are moving from a frontier mentality, in which conquering nature was the ideal, to a conception of "Spaceship Earth" as a limited area in which to accomplish man's purposes without exhausting its resources.

Basic and applied psychology

Events of recent years have led to some disparagement of science as the handmaiden of a technology that, originally designed to serve man, is now tending to bring about the destruction of cherished values (such as joy in unspoiled nature) and is threatening life itself through the power of the weapons of war that it has created. On the one hand, science is accused of being an ivory-tower enterprise, not concerned with real life. On the other hand, it is thought to be all too practical, for its very objectivity and lack of concern with values have accelerated trends that many deplore. Where does psychology fit into this picture of contemporary science?

Types of research

To answer this question, it is first necessary to take a look at the distinctions made within scientific research among basic research, applied research, and development. We may illustrate these different types of research within psychology by considering the various ways in which research in the psychology of learning relates to instruction and education in the broad sense. Table 23-1 shows that at least seven types of research are involved, quite apart from detailed differences in the topics of study.

The first three of these (Types 1, 2, and 3) are classified as basic research, because the motives of the investigator are those of the pure scientist: to seek understanding, to find relationships that link events together in a way that is comprehensible. A prime motive is to satisfy curiosity, along with an esthetic desire to find order and simple relationships in what at first seem to be complex and confusing phenomena. Relevance to the task of the teacher may indeed be there, but the research is not motivated by the desire to find anything applicable to teaching.

The next three types of research (Types 4, 5, and 6) comprise the steps that together are called research and development (often abbreviated R & D); they are applied research in the sense that they attempt to develop something usable in instruction. In common with R & D in the biological and physical sciences (in medicine and engineering, for example), R & D in psychology may involve invention as well as research. A console for a language laboratory and an arrangement of electric typewriters and display screens for computer-assisted instruction are inventions that require ingenuity and design ability; as such, they are not derivable from experiments of Types 1, 2, and

3 (Schwitzgebel, 1970). The development step (Type 6) often requires innovation in packaging, so that machines and methods can be widely used by the non-expert.

The last type of research (Type 7) is somewhat discontinuous from the other steps, but it is perhaps the most important of all. It views any kind of instruction that goes on as part of a larger process in which questions of goals of learning, the nature of the social group in which learning takes place, and other such questions must be answered before the adoption of specific learning materials and methods. At this stage many considerations beyond the laws of learning enter into the research plan, and research workers from several disciplines are likely to be involved.

Although Table 23-1 refers to learning and educational practices, a corresponding table could be constructed for any field of psychological research, such as child psychology or social psychology. Developmental steps must always take place before science serves practice. In addition, there are always larger contextual questions of what purposes are to be served, what is desirable, and what will improve the quality of life.

One misconception to be avoided is that the different types of research are sequential steps—that basic science comes first, and that applied science cannot go ahead when there are no results from basic science to apply. The whole history of science contradicts this concept: research is carried on simultaneously at all levels, and complex feedbacks take place all along the line. Sometimes basic science contributes to applied science, and sometimes applied science contributes new insights to basic science.

The need for professional services

The utilization of science for problem-solving engages the efforts of professional workers (physicians, engineers, personnel officers, managers) as well as scientific researchers. Thus one might enlarge the responsibilities represented in Table 23-1 to include, in addition to basic research, applied research, and development (including policy and planning), a set of responsibilities that might be

TABLE 23-1 TYPES OF RESEARCH RELATING THE PSYCHOLOGY OF LEARNING TO EDUCATIONAL PRACTICES

TYPES OF RESEARCH	RELATION TO EDUCATIONAL PRACTICES	ILLUSTRATIVE RESEARCH
A. Basic science research in learning		
Type 1	Not directly relevant to school practices: neither to the learners taught nor to the skills learned	Animal maze learning; eyelid conditioning; influence of drugs on memory
Type 2	Partially relevant to school practices: either to children as learners or to acquisition of desirable cognitive skills	Human verbal learning; concept formation; tracking eye movements in reading
Type 3	Relevant to school practices: to children as learners and to practice on school subject matters	Mathematics learning by school-age children; prior perceptual training in learning to read
B. Technological research and development bearing upon instruction		
Type 4	Relevant because taught by special teacher in simulated classroom	Computer-assisted instruction; modified alphabets for teaching initial reading; language laboratory
Type 5	Relevant because proposals tried out in "normal" classroom with regular students and teacher	Results of Type 4 in later stages of research
Type 6	Materials available for wide adoption	Planning of manuals and textbooks; planning of in-service teacher training
C. Policy research bearing upon innovations in curriculum and practices		
Type 7	Experimental or demonstration schools showing what can succeed; "schools without walls"	Head Start program; educational TV outside the school; nongraded schools; involvement of parents and older children in instruction

Source: Modified from Hilgard and Bower (1966).

The types of research numbered from 1 through 6 represent an increasing degree of relevance to school practices; that is, the types with higher numbers are more helpful in assisting the teacher to instruct children effectively. Type 7 is not on quite the same dimension because it is concerned with the goals of education as well as with educational practices: Why study spelling separately from its use in writing and reading? Why go to a formal school? Should all schooling have some vocational goals? The types are not sequential; all these kinds of research go on simultaneously.

called *professional services.* For example, following research aimed at understanding the problem of juvenile delinquency, and following the design of programs for prevention and treatment, professional workers have to be trained for doing the actual work of the programs. These workers may be clinical psychologists, social workers, or parole officers. The responsibilities of science to society are not fulfilled until the services that scientists recommend are provided.

We are now ready to ask the question: Is there at present some imbalance in psychology among the various types of research, development, and professional services? There is no easy answer. Within the academic world those who work on the more abstract and theoretical problems defined as basic research still enjoy some advantage in prestige. But psychology is flexible, and patterns are changing. The following statements conclude a recent survey of psychology by a national panel:

> Psychology is a field that is easily susceptible to change. It has not suffered the rigidity of many other disciplines; it has accommodated itself to the changes in views and values of its members. In its early days, psychologists developed a substantial base of laboratory and experimental work that has increased the rigor and objectivity of the work of all psychologists. During the past thirty years it added an emphasis on the application of psychology to the problems of individuals. We believe that during the next generation psychology will change again. We are willing to predict that the new area of emphasis will relate to the problems of groups and societies. We not only accept this new direction but welcome it and call upon our fellow psychologists and our supporters to assist in accelerating it [Clark and Miller, 1970, p. 140].

Contemporary social problems

Many topics that have long been part of psychology's interests bear upon social problems: child rearing, education, mental health, satisfaction in work, prejudice and its reduction, conflict and its resolution. What is new today is the attempt to see these problems in a much larger social context, with concern not only for explaining what occurs but for devising policy proposals to meet the problems on a national scale. In this larger effort psychologists should not work alone but with other scientists whose fields are related to the problems that must be faced.

Social problems have always existed, but events of recent years have brought a number of them into sharper focus, in part through protest movements of various sorts. In this connection we may list such current problems as environmental pollution, overpopulation, poverty, inequality of educational opportunity, deterioration in the inner city, public order and safety of life and property, the sense of alienation from responsible participation in political life, racial prejudice, segregation in schools and communities, unequal treatment of the sexes, war and other forms of international conflict. Any such listing reminds us that the behavioral sciences have a long way to go in suggesting ways in which the quality of life can be improved and in providing information that will permit appropriate steps to be taken.

If any one of the social problems mentioned above were to be selected for review, a large body of behavioral and social science research would be found related to it. However, some steps will often be missing between the availability of research data and effective use of the data.

Educational problems provide a ready example. Educational psychologists have been active in applied research for many years, yet many practices in the schools do not conform to their standards. For example, psychologists have long been aware of individual differences and the need for individualized instruction. Yet, even today, there is a good deal of lock step in the schools. This type of discrepancy follows in part because psychologists do not control the schools, and innovations in education require social changes that the communities, school boards, parents, and teachers must bring about.

A responsible approach to educational reform must deal with the social processes as well as with psychological principles. The universities provide an illustration of this: a desire for a curriculum relevant to today's problems started a movement in the 1960s for "free universities" in which the students themselves introduced subject matters and teaching methods that the universities had proved too inflexible to provide. Other forms of student protest, calling for more participation in the management of universities, have had a greater effect upon teaching methods than recent advances in the psychology of learning.

Health practices provide many illustrations of the difference between having scientific knowledge available and using it beneficially. The anti-cigarette campaign, based upon the demonstrated relationship between heavy cigarette-smoking and lung cancer, is a case in point. An effective social science must deal with the motivations that lead to smoking, and not only with the health factors.

Problems of violence have taken on alarming proportions of late: people have become concerned not only with public safety, as on neighborhood streets at night, but with mob destruction of property and the occasional brutal police reprisals. The nature of aggression and its arousal have been topics of study for a long time in the social sciences, but procedures for bringing violence under control have been given less scientific attention. This is not to say that useful information is lacking. What is lacking are effective measures for testing plausible scientific conjectures in practical situations (Daniels, Gilula, and Ochberg, 1970; Zimbardo, 1970).

Social problems can come to public attention one at a time, but they are obviously all interrelated. A relatively new task for psychologists and other behavioral scientists is the need to step back from their practice of dealing with piecemeal problems, so that they might see social problems in their larger setting. One occasion for this new outlook has been the growing alarm over population increases, destruction of resources, and pollution and waste. This alarm has led in turn to an inquiry into man-environment interactions, the concern of *ecology*. Until recently, social scientists, apart from their interest in population growth, were relatively unconcerned with problems of the environment. Currently their interest takes several forms.

1. Social problems arise not only from the pressure of numbers of people on the food supply, but also from their pressures on one another as they increasingly migrate to urban centers (Figure 23-1).

One answer, of course, is to reduce the rate at which the population is growing. Even the small

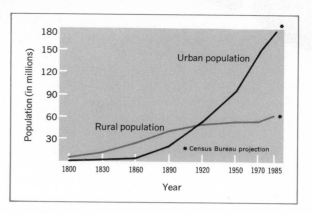

Fig. **23-1 Population growth in the United States** Cities in the United States are growing at a pace that far outstrips the growth of the rural population. By the end of the century, 80 million more Americans will live in or around cities than do now. But the rapid urbanization is not confined to the United States or even to the industrialized countries. Most urban growth is taking place in the developing areas of Asia, Africa, and Latin America, those areas least able to cope with it. (Data from the U. S. Bureau of the Census)

rate of growth in the United States, 1 percent a year, means a doubling of the population in seventy years. The growth rate can change only through increasing the death rate or decreasing the birth rate. The values of civilized men favor the latter alternative—a reduction in fertility, that is, a reduction in the number of live births in a population in a given period of time. But this is clearly a psychological problem, because having children (or preventing conception) must rest upon decisions of individuals within their physical and social environments. Among the factors known to affect the number of children born are education, religion, the work status of women, urban or rural residence, and size of the parental family. Of psychological importance is the meaning of the child to the parent, or why parents want children. In the decade of the 1960s psychologists became more actively interested in these problems than they had been before (Fawcett, 1970).

Problems of crowding and space requirements are of concern to psychologists. Although in the past psychologists had shown some interest in how patterns of living arrangements affect sociability (Festinger, Schachter, and Back, 1950), it is only recently that they have become interested in how the problem of personal space affects designs for living (Sommer, 1969).

2. Some kinds of environmental change proposed by experts are rejected by members of a community because small groups of citizens object to the changes and political leaders are indifferent to them. Why such innovations are adopted or resisted is of interest to behavorial scientists. One illustration of the resistance to innovation is the fluoridation of water, designed to reduce tooth decay. Experts are in substantial agreement that fluoridation of water is beneficial, but of the local referendums that have been held, some 60 percent have failed to support fluoridation (Crain, Katz, and Rosenthal, 1969).

3. It will take vast funds to improve the environment, but many kinds of public expenditures compete for the scarce resources provided by the citizen's taxes. It is cheaper to dispose of untreated sewage than to treat it, cheaper to strip-mine coal than to use other methods that will preserve the landscape, cheaper to emit fumes from an automobile than to redesign the engine to use other fuels. Social scientists are able to discover what people want, and what they are willing to pay for. Economists do this for goods that compete in the market, but other behavioral scientists are needed to work with them in estimating how much people value clean air, or escape from noise, and how much they enjoy a trip to the country or a national park. These are matters of attitude and value, which go beyond the usual technological estimates in terms of energy consumed or the economic estimates in terms of money.

4. The restoration of a more satisfying and livable environment will *not* be a "return to nature." Hence an important problem for the psychologist is to find an appropriate balance between making the environment suitable to man, and changing man so that he may be content in a new environment. The hands of the clock will not turn back, but we can still be sensitive to ecology as the biologist perceives it.

. . .we must be careful about equating "biological" with "natural." A forest may be a phenomenon of nature; a farm certainly is not. The very species upon which man depends for his food—his corn and his cattle—are artifacts of his ingenuity. A plowed field is no more part of nature than an asphalted street—no more and no less [Simon, 1969, p. 3].

The kind of science needed to relate man to the new technologically created environment is a science of *synthesis* and *design* rather than one of *analysis* and *explanation,* the traditional form of basic science. Such a new orientation of science requires that it be concerned with policy decisions: How are public attitudes formed and how do they find expression, what institutions within (or outside of) government can take effective action, how feasible are recommended changes in terms of costs and present technology, and how much time remains before conditions are no longer reversible? Such questions call for answers from social scientists in collaboration with engineers and others.

We have used environmental problems as merely one illustration of what confronts science today as it becomes alert to the problems of society on a large scale.[1] Let us now turn to the problem-solving methods that are available.

[1] Awareness of environmental problems in the United States increased following the appearance of *Silent spring* by Rachel Carson in 1962. The title of the book was derived from the issue of the possible destruction of bird life through the careless and excessive use of pesticides. Public attention gradually became aroused, until the Congress of the United States enacted legislation, which President Nixon signed in January 1970, establishing a Council on Environmental Quality in the Executive Office of the President. Nixon sent the first report of this council, entitled *Environmental quality,* to the Congress in August 1970.

Large-scale methods applicable to social problems

In the physical sciences the distinction is sometimes made between "little science" and "big science," a distinction that rests largely upon the amount of money required to sustain the science.

For example, a modern observatory is necessary for studying astronomy, and a modern accelerator for studying high-energy physics—these "big sciences" require vast sums. The scientist who works in his laboratory with the simpler devices of a less technologically advanced science requires much smaller amounts. The distinction has been less used in the social sciences; for the most part they have been content to operate on a small scale as "little sciences." But it is pertinent to note that the need for large-scale research, with attendant large-scale costs, is beginning to emerge in the social sciences. Some large expenditures have already taken place: hundreds of millions of dollars are expended on the production of the Decennial Census, which in its modern form gathers huge quantities of data rather than simply making a head count. These data are then used as a resource for social scientists, just as observations through a large telescope become resources for astronomers. Except for survey research and some aspects of computer-assisted research, behavioral scientists have not tended to work on a large scale. There are signs that they will have to expand the comprehensiveness (and costs) of their research if they are to meet the demands being placed upon them to contribute to the solution of public problems.

Social indicators

If psychology and the other behavioral sciences are to take responsible positions with respect to the management of social problems, they need to work from a base of firm data, assessing these problems on a broad scale—national and international. Individual scholars have long expressed such interests, but they have lacked the finances to work on the scale required. Consequently, large national efforts are now being recommended to improve the data base and to construct *social indicators.*

Social indicators would be analogous to economic indicators, which include the index of consumer prices, the rate of unemployment, and estimates of the gross national product. These economic indicators, as interpreted by the Council of Economic Advisers, provide guidelines for the President in his report to Congress, and are taken seriously in the formulation and management of monetary and fiscal (taxation) policies. Social indicators would be a series of indicators in the social aspects of life, such as health, education, recrea-

tion, and public safety, that would serve to guide policy in these areas.

In order to see where psychology is likely to fit into the formulation of social indicators, it is desirable to take a look at the areas in which indicators might be used and the kinds that might be developed. Many indicators already exist in the form of statistics on health, education, housing, and crime, but these are not always organized in such a manner as to make them most useful for describing changes in the quality of life.

In 1966 Biderman made an analysis to see to what extent the national goals stated in 1960 by a President's Commission were reflected in available data. After searching for data from official government sources to serve as indicators of the progress made, he found that indicators were available for only 48 of 81 stated goals, leaving 33 goals (41 percent) unrepresented by data (Table 23-2). A pertinent question for psychologists is: How many of these goals require some sort of psychological data? An examination of the goal areas shows that psychological factors loom large in most areas, less perhaps in economics and agriculture, but tangentially related even there.

Another listing of possible social indicators is found in a government publication entitled *Toward a social report* (U.S. Department of Health, Education, and Welfare, 1969). The seven major headings of that report, with a brief characterization of each, will clarify the scope of social indicators.

1. *Health and illness.* The major indicators are increases in life expectancy and the expectancy of a healthy life during the later years, with attention to differences by race, sex, and place of residence. Related problems are the availability of health services and their costs. Psychology has a clear role to play because of its concern for health, especially mental health.

2. *Social mobility.* Social mobility refers to the opportunity to improve one's status (see Chapter 22, pp. 516–17). The opportunity is not yet equal by race. And although educational opportunities are open to all, they are more available to those whose parents have had more education. Full equality of opportunity has not been achieved. Indicators are required to support such assertions

TABLE 23-2   AVAILABILITY OF INDICATORS RELEVANT TO GOALS FORMULATED BY PRESIDENT'S COMMISSION

GOAL AREA	NUMBER OF SPECIFIC GOALS	GOALS TO WHICH SOME INDICATOR RELEVANT	GOALS TO WHICH NO INDICATOR RELEVANT
The individual	6	3	3
Equality	3	2	1
Democratic process	11	5	6
Education	5	5	0
Arts and sciences	8	2	6
Democratic economy	9	5	4
Economic growth	9	9	0
Technological change	5	1	4
Agriculture	5	4	1
Living conditions	10	2	8
Health and welfare	10	10	0
Total	81	48	33

Source: Biderman (1966). The goals are from *President's Commission on national goals* (1960). The indicators reviewed were those in *Statistical abstract of the United States* and *Historical statistics of the United States.*

Statistical data are needed to determine how well national goals are realized. According to this survey, such data were lacking for 33 of the 81 recognized national goals.

and to detect improvements, if they come about. Psychology's interest in education and its interest in individual differences make problems of social mobility pertinent.

3. *The physical environment.* Some environmental issues have already been discussed (see pp. 543–44). Indicators are needed to show how well we are handling water and air pollution, how adequate housing is, and how public transportation is functioning. As psychologists become interested in man's relationship to space and overcrowding, and his desire for privacy and escape from noise, they will become increasingly involved with environmental problems.

4. *Income and poverty.* Although America claims to have the highest standard of living in the world, it is well known that our affluence is not equally distributed. Rising income levels have reduced the number classified as being below the poverty line from about 40 million in 1960 to 26 million in 1967, but income distribution has not changed appreciably and the problems of poverty have certainly not been solved. Among the programs devised to meet the problems of the poor

are the public assistance programs that give aid to the aged or disabled or unemployed, and that provide for a minimum wage and job training. Currently under study are several income maintenance programs, such as a guaranteed annual wage, or a negative income tax for those whose earnings fall below a minimum. Psychologists are required to determine the motivational consequences of the several alternative solutions.

5. *Public order and safety.* The Federal Bureau of Investigation's index of major crimes per 100,000 population increased at an average rate of 8.7 percent per year between 1958 and 1967. This increase is a sign of an unhealthy society, and the reduction of crime, with the attendant reduction of the fear of being victimized, become major tasks. As a first step, crime reporting can be greatly improved; types of crime, and types of victim, are not well reflected in the statistics available at present, because many victims do not report what happened to them. Many assaultive attacks occur within the family or within neighborhoods, where the difficulties are resolved locally or are hushed up; for example, parents often make restitution for

juvenile thefts to avoid a police record. Psychology's interest in antisocial behavior and aggression gives it responsibilities in the area of public order.

6. *Learning, science, and art.* The quality of life is presumably enriched by educational opportunities, the advances in science, and the satisfactions provided by the arts. But are cultural tastes being degraded by some forms of mass entertainment, such as that reflected in many television programs? We need to know what is happening. These are difficult fields in which to make appropriate measurements; as indicators are developed, psychologists will certainly be called upon for assistance in interpreting them.

7. *Participation and alienation.* A representative democracy attempts to achieve a favorable balance between individualism and a sense of community. The first is furthered by a sense of freedom and self-determination, the second by a feeling of effective participation. If either of these breaks down, the individual feels alienated and becomes apathetic or angry. How well is contemporary society serving our people? The violent conflicts on the streets and campuses provide evidence of strong disruptive forces. The problems are both psychological and political; the behavioral and social sciences should attempt to bring about an understanding of the issues and seek a resolution of the tensions in accordance with the shared values of our society. The task of social indicators is to assess the satisfactions and dissatisfactions and to find their root causes, so that, on the basis of adequate information, remedies can be proposed that reach these causes and do not merely treat superficial manifestations of discontent.

As behavioral scientists are called upon to recommend and develop appropriate indicators they will find that much of their previous experience with survey research, test construction, and attitude study will be relevant to the task, but problems will emerge because of the scale of the work and because of the importance likely to be given indicators. Various economic indicators already carry heavy weight, as when the consumer price index enters into union wage contracts, or farm prices determine subsidies to farmers. Certain noneconomic indicators now carry some weight, as when

the number of cases of influenza or German measles determines the innoculations that are recommended, or when the level of air pollutants restricts incineration, or when water level in the reservoirs restricts lawn-watering. Because social indicators will undoubtedly be weighted much more heavily in the future, they must be designed now with great care.

The assessment of social problems should be made on a continuing basis at least annually so that we might know the extent to which we are meeting our national goals in areas affecting the general goodness and vitality of our society. Thus the social indicators should reflect changes indicating whether literacy is being improved, infant mortality reduced, highway safety advanced, pollution cleared up, and extreme poverty eliminated. The purpose would be twofold: to indicate desirable changes and to sound warnings when such changes are not being made or when undesirable changes are being foreshadowed.

Social indicators would of course have to be interpreted. Once they are in good order, some sort of annual report to the nation, prepared either by private agencies or by the government, would serve to highlight the gains and the losses. Eventually, a Council of Social Advisers might be formed to translate the recommendations into proposals for government policy.[2]

Program evaluation

Social indicators cannot reflect all the facets of the quality of life, and they cannot fulfill all the promises expected of them, particularly in the evaluation of specific ameliorative programs, such as those designed to improve education, to enhance mental health, or to upgrade the job capabilities of the hard-core unemployed. These remedial programs are usually not of sufficient scale to be reflected well in national indicators, or they may be carried out in an uneven way, so that while effective in some places they are ineffective in others.

[2] These issues are discussed in a report on the behavioral and social sciences prepared by a special committee of the National Academy of Sciences/Social Science Research Council in 1969.

Moreover, the complexities of society are such that there are multiple causal factors for most changes, and only careful analysis can isolate the effects of a single innovative program upon social life. Because general social indicators are not likely to be precise enough for the crucial early stages of program evaluation, behavioral scientists are faced with the large task of preparing such evalutions. For instance, we are obviously interested in a promising development such as computer-assisted instruction (CAI) in reading. The first steps in evaluation will consist of studying the effectiveness of such instruction in a few schools or a few communities. Only after positive evaluations emerge would a widespread adoption of CAI be recommended. Eventually a CAI program on a national level might be expected to influence a social indicator reflecting the distribution of literacy, but not before the program was in use for a number of years.

Social indicators may not immediately reflect the effect of individual programs, but they do reflect changes over time when programs are strikingly effective. Hospital statistics readily show that hospitalization for paresis, a form of cerebral syphilis, was drastically reduced when syphilis became controlled by drugs. The fluoridation of water (and toothpaste) can make a detectable difference in the number of cavities, although experimental comparisons rather than general indicators are needed to decide whether the change owes to the water or the toothpaste.

It is important to be reminded that social invention is as possible as other forms of invention. A program for the more efficient use of home instruction through television may depend as much upon someone's imaginative use of the medium as upon scientific research. When a new program is essentially an innovative invention, science can be useful in its evaluation. Thus the parole system was not invented by social scientists, but studies of its effectiveness rest upon their investigations.

Forecasting the future

If scientific knowledge is to be a guide to policies bearing upon the future, it should be able to tell us something about a number of possible futures and the directions in which alternative policies will lead. We should leave options open for future generations, because we cannot predict with any assurance what people will want in the years ahead. Thus the kind of forecasting under consideration here is not a form of prophecy that implies inevitability.

One reason for making forecasts is to set in operation policies that will prevent undesirable features from coming about. Thus the consequences of the rapidly expanding population may be forecast, in the hope that birth control methods will be adopted in time to prevent the dire consequences of mass starvation. The amount of pollution of rivers and lakes may be projected, in the hope that the devastating consequences of present-day trends will eventually be reversed by better sewage disposal systems and other methods.

Much of psychology has been concerned with making predictions about individual behavior: the likelihood that a child will be able to do satisfactory work in school, that a patient with given symptoms of disturbance can be helped, that certain treatments of criminal offenders will lead to rehabilitation. Some predictions have been in the social sphere, such as the effects of school or residential desegregation. Fewer of the predictions have concerned large-scale social processes, such as violence in the cities or international conflict, although isolated cases can be cited of studies directed toward almost any social problem. We will be concerned here not so much with specific problems as with the methods by which the future course of socially important events can be predicted. Two main methods will be considered: *trend analysis* and *expert judgment*.

Trend analysis. Although the causes of social phenomena are very complex, the interaction of many causes may produce considerable uniformity in large-scale events. For instance, highway accidents have innumerable causes (defects in highway engineering, excessive speeds, bad weather, poorly trained drivers, drivers excessively fatigued or under the influence of alcohol, automobiles in poor condition, disregard of seat belts, and so on), but it is possible to predict with a fair degree of accuracy how many persons will be killed over a holiday weekend on the basis of the number killed in the preceding years.

As another example, the total number of doctoral degrees conferred by American universities each year since 1880 yields a relatively uniform curve of growth, despite all the changes brought about by new universities and new fields of knowledge. As Figure 23-2 shows, the growth follows an essentially uniform exponential (logarithmic) pattern with time. The points that fall outside the shaded area in the figure represent the low production of degrees during the two world wars, but

Fig. **23-2 Production of doctorates** Because the vertical axis (number of degrees) is plotted exponentially, and the horizontal axis (years) is plotted arithmetically, this is a semi-logarithmic plot. The long-term trend lies well within the shaded area, except for the years of the First and Second World Wars. The unfilled dots represent projections. (After National Science Board, 1969b)

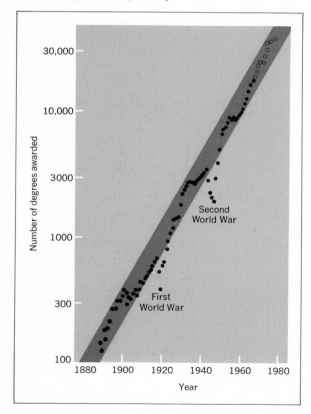

later degree production makes up for lost time and degrees again follow the trend line. Large errors in forecasting would occur over the short range because of the many perturbations, but over the long range the trend is unmistakable, permitting the future estimates shown in the figure.

Trends often have breaks in them, so that they present a scalloped appearance when plotted. For example, the American involvement in the war in Southeast Asia has shown two such scallops, one prior to the election of 1964, the other after it (Figure 23-3). The close correspondence between increases in the number of military personnel in the field and the number of casualties indicates the kinds of consistencies found when large numbers are involved. The dotted portion of the curves represents predictions made from the trends prior to mid-1968; it was predicted that results would fall on the dotted lines. The actual data are plotted to show how close the predictions came.

Data on a large scale can often be forecasted moderately well, even though the future depends upon discoveries, inventions, or choices not yet predictable in detail.

Expert judgment. Trend analysis alone cannot take into account current events that have not yet affected the trend. An example from contemporary debate illustrates the possibilities. There is a race going on between population expansion and the expansion of the food supply. Plotting both trends provides an intersection point in the very near future at which time population will so outrun the food supply that mass starvation will be imminent (Ehrlich and Ehrlich, 1970). But corrections have to be made in the trends according to what is to be expected from the new technologies of population control and food production.

An example of the kind of change that is physically possible (but psychologically unlikely) is a widespread change in the habits of food consumption. A large portion of the caloric value of perhaps half the food produced is wasted in one way or another. One major source of waste is the conversion of grain to meat by feeding it to animals. The world's food supply could be enormously increased if men ate the grain themselves—if, in other words,

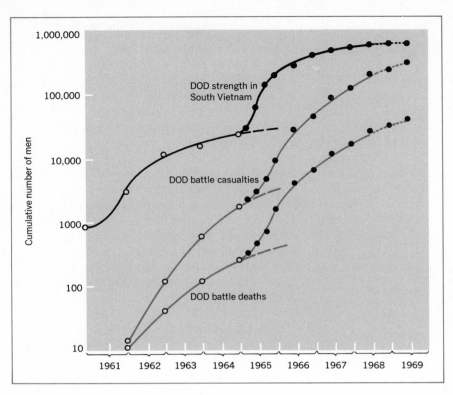

Fig. **23-3 Trends in the Vietnam War** The dotted portions from mid-1968 to mid-1969 represent projections from data available in mid-1968. The plotted points for late 1968 and mid-1969 are actual data, to indicate the extent to which they conform to the projected trend. DOD refers to Department of Defense, including Army, Navy, Air Force, and Marine Corps. (After Voevodsky, 1969, as updated by Dr. Voevodsky)

they reduced their meat eating. Modern chemistry could provide the amino-acid supplements to make the grain diet fully adequate.

Expert judges are often able to supplement trend analysis through their knowledge of basic science advances that have not yet led to practical consequences, or through their sensitivity to side effects or interactions that have not yet entered into current statistics. The use of expert judgment adds an oracular aspect to forecasting, which, in deference to the ancient and celebrated oracle of Apollo at Delphi, is known as the *Delphi method* (Helmer, 1966). The Delphi method is a formal procedure for pooling the judgments of experts about events likely to take place in the years ahead that are not fully reflected in available trend analyses. In estimating the number of doctoral degrees in psychology to be produced in the 1970s, for example, experts would take into account such facts as the effect of the draft, the reduction in federal expend-

itures for fellowships and research assistantships in the post-1967 period, the number of bachelor's degrees granted (from which the doctoral students must come), the current interest in social problems, and anything else that might affect a choice.

Forecasting by a combination of trend analysis and the Delphi method has inherent paradoxes within it, especially when short-range and long-range predictions are compared. Usually short-range predictions are best, because trends can be projected quite well for a few months ahead. In some cases, however, short-range effects (such as stock market fluctuations, natural calamities, election upsets) have important immediate consequences that cannot be predicted. As in the case of degree production (Figure 23-2), the long-range prediction may be better than the short-range one because of basic underlying regularities that influence the long-range trends.

Whether the predictions are short-term or

long-term, discontinuities are commonly caused by new inventions or technologies. In time, new trends become established following such breaks with the past. Consider, for example, the long-range changes that took place when the automobile replaced the horse, and the changes now still taking place as the airplane has replaced the train. We must make some effort to anticipate these inventions and technologies if we are to prepare for future discontinuities. Hence there is interest in making predictions of when plastic organs will be transplanted into human beings, when thermonuclear power will be controlled for domestic use, when molecular engineering will correct genetic defects, when chemical control of aging will be achieved. Such science-fiction fantasies have within them a degree of possibility, but their predictions are much less secure than those that merely adjust trend analysis.

A step beyond the Delphi method is the *cross-impact matrix* method (Gordon and Hayward, 1968). Forecasted events are not independent, but necessarily interact; the concept of "cross-impact" calls attention to this interaction. Suppose, for example, we want to make predictions about the operation of weather forecasting in 1980. Then we need to know: (1) What is likely to be the state of the art of weather forecasting by extensions of present methods of meteorology? (2) What is likely to be the influence of new technologies based upon the use of satellites, computer simulation, and more massive world data? (3) What are the chances that artificial control of the weather will be achieved through cloud-seeding or other methods? (4) What political obstacles will stand in the way of adopting available methods? When studied in their interaction, independent Delphi estimates for each of these questions produce a more likely overall estimate of what kind of weather forecasting will be done in 1980.

Because in predicting the future of society man has an appreciable opportunity to *create* it as well, those concerned with outlining possible futures may engage in *scenario writing,* a current method of formulating prescriptive Utopias, or, occasionally, anti-Utopias (Manuel, 1967; Hillegas, 1967).

University arrangements for the study of social problems

Most of those who have reported on the problems of making behavioral science research relate more directly to the solution of social problems (National Academy of Sciences/Social Science Research Council, 1969; National Science Board, 1969a) have asserted that the departmental structure of universities, built around disciplinary specialties, is unfavorable to such research and application. They have recommended the establishment of multidisciplinary institutes inside or outside of universities, or a school of applied behavioral science modeled after a school of engineering or a school of medicine. These suggestions are not idle predictions of a distant future: many new units that fit such descriptions are coming into being, with local variations.

There is, however, a great deal of resistance to change within universities and in some cases psychology departments have found it more feasible to retain their departmental structure while extending their teaching and research into community psychology, or into specialties concerned with public affairs. Because psychology covers a broad spectrum, from the biological to the social sciences, and because psychology departments have usually been congenial to both basic and applied research, many of them find it easier to extend their own degree programs than to establish new degree-granting schools within their universities. These programs usually include seminars taught by scholars from other departments (Brayfield, 1969).

The foregoing account of social indicators, program evaluation, and forecasting of the future suggests kinds of topics that are not ordinarily taught within psychology departments. Those who believe that psychologists must join with economists, engineers, architects, and others, if they are to train students to serve the public more effectively, also believe that the broadening of the psychology department's own program will not suffice for what is needed. The opportunities for design and social invention are open in the development of new arrangements for teaching and research within universities.

The problem of objectivity and human values

Objectivity lies at the center of the scientific attitude. As repeatedly pointed out in earlier chapters, the scientific aim is to make research findings public, unbiased, and repeatable by competently trained people. The best guardians of the integrity of any one scientist are other scientists, who repeat his work, criticize it, verify it, and demonstrate its limitations. Science rests its claim to objectivity on its public information-seeking and information-testing method.

But a science concerned with the solving of human problems soon encounters issues of value. The basic scientist can perhaps detach himself from the question of how his research is to be used, but the applied scientist is called upon to design instruments that serve ends. Whenever a means-end relationship exists, value preferences are involved. Should science be used to serve this end? Are the by-products desirable or undesirable? Words such as "should" or "ought" or "desirable" or "undesirable" indicate that relative values are being judged.

Respect for privacy

The development of the behavioral sciences requires a great deal of knowledge about people. The U. S. Census asks questions, the federal Monthly Survey of the Labor Force asks questions, and, as social indicators are developed, more questions will be asked of more people. How do these questions affect the right of privacy, one of our democratic values? With modern computer technology it will be possible to assemble information about individuals from their income tax returns, social security records, and other forms, keyed to their social security numbers. Unless foolproof guarantees are provided, privacy is threatened.

The Census has a remarkable record in providing statistical information without exposing identity. Other forms of record-keeping, both governmental and private, must observe similar cautions. Some of the most severe intrusions into privacy come from nongovernmental sources; credit bureaus, for example, may report private information quite freely to business firms requesting it.

Fortunately, many government officials and behavioral scientists are alert to the problem of privacy. Under the auspices of the Office of Science and Technology, Executive Office of the President (1967), a special committee headed by a psychologist and including several other psychologists issued a report on privacy and behavioral research. Their suggestions, slightly paraphrased, are:

1. Participation in behavioral investigations should be voluntary and based on informed consent to the extent that this is consistent with the objectives of the research.

2. It is fully consistent with the protection of privacy that, in the absence of full information, consent is based on trust in the qualified investigator and the integrity of the institution under whose auspices the research is conducted.

3. The preservation of confidentiality, once consent has been obtained or institutional justification for the research is received, is the responsibility of the investigator [National Academy of Sciences/Social Science Research Council, 1969, p. 130].

Behavioral scientists recognize the benefits of having public policy guided by accurate information about the welfare of its citizens, but there are limitations on the amount of information that can be obtained without posing a threat to freedom. It is better that some information be sacrificed than that freedom be curtailed (Westin, 1967; Kelman, 1968).

Respect for individual choice

A person does not feel free unless he can make choices, unless he has a sense of alternatives. Subtle coercion of choice is another threat of the behavioral sciences as behavioral control techniques become more powerful. Consider the effect of obedience training upon a dog. The animal appears to love its master and to do what is called for with a minimum of coercion once the training has been successfully completed. But would a citizen care to be trained to his role, so that he is comfortable in it, under such a regimen? In some sense, child-rearing practices utilize corresponding techniques. The child is socialized to eat three meals a day, to obey his parents and teachers, to respect the law. He is supposed to internalize these behaviors so that he is happy and comfortable in conforming; if he does not conform he is "defiant" or "delinquent." Here is a real dilemma: it is necessary to socialize in order for society to run smoothly, for a society in which everyone gave way to his unbridled impulses would only lead to anarchy. Under these circumstances how can sufficient freedom be preserved within the bounds of a necessary conformity?

In the abstract this problem is nearly insoluble, but in its concrete forms it often does not prove so difficult. For example, an individual has no choice about which side of the highway to drive on, but by acceding to the social choice (to drive on the right, in the United States), the driver has more freedom in the smooth-running traffic than if he had to fight every inch of the way. Some balancing of individual duty with individual rights is worked out in all successful societies.

How can the individual be protected from exploitation? The best answer is through education and knowledge, through teaching him his rights and how to appraise the consequences of his acts, and helping him to exert as much control as possible from within, so that he might treat others with respect and kindness in reciprocation for such behavior from them. Society always has a residual threat of coercion by force for those who lack self-control, but when things are running well this social coercion should withdraw into the background. The society with the largest number of police is not the safest; the fewer the police required to maintain order, the safer the society.

The issues before the behavioral scientists as their techniques become more powerful require continued review and debate. Taking opposite sides in a debate in print, Skinner viewed behavior control as necessary and essentially benign, while Rogers viewed it as a threat to individual freedom (Rogers and Skinner, 1956). Siding more with Rogers than with Skinner, but recognizing some basis for both of their arguments, Kelman (1968) proposed that the individual therapist should use his professional skills and the therapeutic relationship to increase the client's range of choices and ability to choose; the applied psychologist should inform those who are the target of a proposed change (such as the workers in a manufacturing plant) so that they may have some choices about features of the planned change.

Whose values will prevail?

Many policy decisions are made according to some hierarchy of values but values, being relative, are often in dispute. The behavioral scientist concerned with the formulation of policy manages to attain objectivity in the face of this dilemma in several ways.

In the first place, to be *value-neutral* does not require one to be unconcerned with values. It is possible to make an objective and value-neutral study of the consequences when groups of people hold different values. Values can themselves be studied objectively. Thus the amount of church loyalty among those who subscribe to different religions can be studied independent of the scientist's own religious preferences.

Second, many values are *widely shared*, so the scientist is able to work within that framework of values. A physician who cures a disease is assuming that health is better than illness; this value is so widely shared that his objectivity is not in question, even though some people might see the disease as God's punishment for sin, and something with which man should not meddle.

Solving the value problem by working within values on which there is consensus is much more difficult than it might seem. Offhand we think of life as preferable to death, health to illness, cleanliness to filth, freedom to slavery, and so on; we do, in fact, carry on many of our programs with such values taken for granted. But even some of our best-established values are contradicted by others. The value placed upon life is countered by the value placed upon taking up arms in defense of the nation and taking the lives of the enemy as necessary. Equality is another generally accepted value, but the areas in which equality is to be served are limited by other values, such as the respect for private property and the right to pass it on to heirs. These value issues are eventually resolved by negotiation and compromise, as are many other complex issues.

Third, in the case of values that are not widely shared, or that differ greatly from one segment of the society to another, the task of the behavioral scientist is much more difficult but not impossible.

Some societies, including American society, can tolerate a considerable diversity in values, out of respect for cultural pluralism. The separation of church and state in the United States, allowing religious freedom, is one indication of permissiveness in regard to cultural diversity. The social problem that arises can be stated as a question: How much diversity of values is permissible without disrupting the common good? Despite the doctrine of religious freedom, the United States Government felt that the Mormons had gone too

CRITICAL
DISCUSSION

The revolt against objectivity and rationality

The very advantages of a developed behavioral science—objectivity and reliance upon the analysis of complex information as a background for policy—are being attacked by some persons who believe that such an approach leads to dehumanization. An extreme form of this viewpoint is found in Roszak's *The making of a counter culture* (1969), in which he makes a general protest against technological civilization, combined with an attack on what is called "the myth of objective consciousness," an expression meant to cast aspersion on the scientific expertise that supports industrial society. He asserts that social scientists, by gaining assent to their objective methods, certify themselves (falsely) as experts on human experience and force the humanistic nonexpert (by their standards) to yield to their guidance. This is the power of "the myth of objective consciousness" that he finds distasteful.

The protest against "objective consciousness" is said to be part of the platform of some of the youth in American colleges and universities who are protesting against contemporary society and its values, particularly those who are exploring modes of nonintellective consciousness through consciousness-expanding drugs or mystical experiences (see Chapter 7). Their alternative to the dominant technological culture gives a higher value to purely personal experiences.

Holding less extreme views, though similarly critical of objectivity, the humanistic psychologists have urged a study of man that emphasizes subjectivity.

> The revival of humanistic psychology means that scientific attention is once again being directed toward the primacy of the subjective (not to the exclusion of attention to the objective and to behavior, by any means, however). Thus the more fundamental concerns of a psychology of the human experience will once again be explored [Bugental, 1967, p. 7].

These are significant rumblings in the intellectual life of our day. As yet they have little influence at the center of leading behavioral science departments, but their impact will gradually be felt in producing a greater sensitization to human values as the sciences of man progress.

One might reasonably argue that there is a higher morality in the rationality of conventional science than in the subjectivity of the counterscience: *the scientific method produces a means of consensus through negotiating differences on the basis of established information.* If subjectivity is to produce consensus, it becomes merely a struggle for power, because one man's personal beliefs are as valid as another's: the stronger man eventually forces his beliefs upon the weaker.

far in permitting polygamy. Libel and sedition laws set some limits on the doctrines of freedom of speech and freedom of the press. Problems of censorship of reputedly salacious literature arise at the borderlines of permissible values. One task of the social scientist is to study the effects of diversity upon the quality of life of the nation as a whole and to make recommendations bearing upon the restriction of this diversity.

In areas in which a *consensus on values* proves to be essential, whether at community or national levels, an additional task before the social scientist is to investigate how such a consensus can be reached in order for effective social action to be planned and undertaken.

The behavioral or social scientist need not be a threat to the public just because he works in value-laden areas. The fear that the behavioral scientist will usurp power and then distort the human values that social processes serve led the Dean of the John F. Kennedy School of Government at Harvard to write:

> The maturity of a science may be measured not only by its power but by its discrimination in knowing

the limits of its power. And if this is so, the layman does not need to worry lest the social sciences, as they become more scientific, will be more likely to usurp political authority. On the contrary, they will stop short of trying to solve completely our major political problems not because they are unlike the natural sciences but to the extent that they are like them [Price, 1965, p. 111].

Characteristic professional values also protect the public from abuse by behavioral scientists—such values as explicitness in the statement of value assumptions and objectivity in the recording and presentation of data, including the presentation of data that may refute the scientist's favorite hypotheses. Many value commitments go beyond the technical requirements of the field of inquiry. The behavioral scientist tends to accept, for example, certain higher-level values that are not forced upon him by his discipline, such as respect for human life, respect for privacy, the ethical equality of all men (despite differences in their descriptive characteristics), and a commitment to policies that will allow future generations choices of their own.

Psychology and the problems of society

The topics studied by psychologists—individual development, perception, motivation, learning, social behavior, deviancy—inevitably bear upon social issues, but the kinds of specialization that are required for the advancement of basic science often produce a gap between research results and the solution of pressing problems. As mentioned earlier, the preoccupation of the basic scientist with analysis and explanation is not sufficient to lead to policy recommendations, for such recommendations require both the synthesis of findings from a variety of fields (not all within psychology or the behavioral sciences) and creative or inventive activity in designing ways and means for achieving desirable ends.

Social effectiveness as a new frontier for psychology

The relation of man to man has always been important, but it is especially important in this time of rapid social change, conflicting values, generation gaps, and anti-Establishment protests. Social psychologists have taken increasingly to the laboratory in order to break down their conceptions into experimentable form, but they must, at the same time, move out into the community and accept some relationship to social managers. This concern has been expressed for psychologists generally by the psychology panel of the Behavioral and Social Sciences Survey:

Means and methods of interaction between social managers and psychological scientists can be institutionalized more efficiently than are our current practices. We should begin to search for such an institutional solution by initiating, for example, a study of how and where such a match is succeeding most imaginatively and competently, with the expectation that the most effective methods might be adopted elsewhere. Even a cursory consideration of the problem indicates that new career patterns are needed to provide scientific training and experience in applying psychology along with managerial skills; individuals with such experience exist, but the relatively low prestige accorded them by the community of academic psychologists suggests that their contribution is not properly appreciated and that their number is unlikely to grow commensurate with our need for their services [Clark and Miller, 1970, p. 10].

Psychology and other social sciences are similar to all sciences in having sources of information and methods that bear upon the making of policy. But they have the advantage over the other scientific fields in that their methods are appropriate to the study of policy formation itself (Bauer and Gergen, 1968). By making both research and training increasingly pertinent to social problems, a more responsible and effective policy science is bound to emerge, to the eventual benefit of all mankind.

Some specific suggestions

Because the issues that must be debated as psychology becomes more pertinent to the solution of social problems have not been resolved in the literature of psychology, this section (and, indeed, much of this chapter) departs from the expository nature of the book to provide a series of suggestions that may serve as a basis for discussion. To be sure, recognition has been accorded the issues by the American Psychological Association (Korten, Cook, and Lacey, 1970; Reiff, 1970).

In the course of making psychology more relevant, the following considerations apply:

1. *Basic research must not be disparaged or neglected.* Basic research, in the spirit of pure science, continues to explore the unknown and to provide new methods and theories, the results serving as

the lifeblood of the science. The desire to move to the solution of pressing problems must not override these sources of new knowledge.

2. *All levels of research must share in the research effort.* But another consideration is that those who work in the various areas of basic, applied, development, and policy research must share equally in the research effort and the prestige rewards. Many believe that there has been an imbalance, with so much prestige assigned to basic research that it has been permitted to become somewhat trivial, a scientific game in which researchers write their articles for one another with little concern for broader implications. Such research is not necessarily good science. The point is that good science can be practiced in either basic or applied areas, and should be recognized as such.

3. *In facing social problems psychologists cannot go it alone.* Social problems with strong psychological components are not simply psychological problems. The psychologist who works with others on social problems must be a problem-solver first and a psychologist second. This is one reason for the suggestion that new arrangements be made for training and research in our universities, outside of the existing departmental structuring of the disciplines (see p. 551).

4. *Psychologists, and behavioral scientists generally, must be careful not to promise too much.* Societal problems are very complex, and the by-products of change are often unpredictable from present knowledge. Social scientists often have to recognize the limitations of present knowledge rather than deplore the fact that their wisdom is not being used. An attack upon the usefulness of social science was made by a social scientist who was at the time of writing also a close presidential adviser (Moynihan, 1969; 1970). His main points were (1) that the selection of members of the social science professions was too "elitist," so that the members were not representative of the people they were to serve; (2) that social scientists were over-optimistic regarding their role in policy-making (an area in which some of their recommendations were indeed more harmful than helpful); and (3) that perhaps social scientists should confine themselves to the evaluation of social programs initiated by

others. While the arguments are somewhat extreme, they have substance, and the general position is sound that psychologists and other behavioral scientists must prepare themselves carefully for their new roles, and must not expect to be able to make wise applications of present knowledge merely because policy-makers are willing to listen to them.

5. *The services of applied psychology must not be merely technological.* One way to avoid attempting too much is simply to serve the goals that others set. Thus a psychologist in industry may aid in fitting the worker to the job, without asking anything about the industry, or he may help to gain acceptance of a new product through market research, without asking whether the product ought to be marketed. Such "value-indifferent" roles can be served competently, and where the values are widely shared (as, for example, in education and health), the technological service may be of aid in the solution of social problems. Hence this role, like that of basic science, is not to be disparaged, but it is incomplete. Beyond mere technological services (constructing and deriving norms for tests, making better instrument displays for the human operator, preparing programs for instruction) lies the whole area of design in relation to social goals— innovative practices, social arrangements for participative management, and priority determination. This area is called social problem-solving or policy science and can be distinguished from the purely technological area, although it is possible that they will overlap.

6. *Policy proposals must steer a negotiated course between Utopian ideals and realistic possibilities.* Discourse over values and goals should go forward, but it must be carried on in a context of facts and theories if the social sciences are to remain true to their status as sciences.

The President's National Goals Research Staff in its first report (1970) stressed the goal of balanced growth. This sounds harmless enough, but in fact it runs counter to the long-prevailing American ideal of "the bigger the better." If we approached some sort of equilibrium in population, the use of resources, and the production of energy, many changes would be implied. Among these are profound changes in attitudes—and attitude change is one of the favorite topics of social psychology. Hence, in one way or another, psychologists ought to be brought into the debate over restraints upon growth.

Utopianism suggests a picture of an ideal society toward which policy should be directed—perhaps an egalitarian society in which democratic values are fully embodied in practice, in which the relationships between man and nature are balanced so that options are left open for future societies, in which nations live together in peace, in which the conditions allowing for human diversity are met, so that happiness can be widespread. Psychologists have not engaged in such thinking to any great extent, although one attempt was made by Skinner (1948) to describe in fictional form a community called Walden Two, based upon psychologically sound practices. *Walden Two* has been controversial, but it succeeded in stimulating much public discussion, and even some attempts to establish small communities based upon its principles. Some aspects of Utopian thinking are highly desirable in the consideration of social goals, but other kinds of thinking must consider the immediate steps that have some chance of succeeding.

7. *Psychological research, in conjunction with that of other behavioral sciences, must be large in scale and wide in scope.* It is clear that if large social problems are to be considered, the data-gathering and analysis must be made pertinent to them; the problems cannot be studied piecemeal if reliable inferences are to be drawn from adequate data. The data must not only be large-scale but cumulative, so that changes in society can be detected in advance of crisis. One analysis by a psychologist calls our society an "unprepared society," because we have not been ready for events that could have been foreseen (Michael, 1968).

Because of the rapidity of modern communications and travel, the long-distance effectiveness of nuclear weapons, and the general interdependence of all men, the scope of scientific inquiry must be wide enough to detect unpredictable effects throughout the world. This type of inquiry will require new forms of international cooperation, some of which have already been initiated through international scientific societies and the United Nations Educational, Scientific and Cultural Organization (UNESCO). That psychologists are aware of the problems of large scope is shown by their inquiries into problems of international conflict and international understanding (de Rivera, 1968; Stagner, 1967).

Only an informed group of scientists, with a responsible attitude toward the relevance and application of their results, and an understanding relationship with those who make and administer policy decisions, can be expected to contribute effectively to social policies leading to the gradual amelioration of social ills and the creation of a better society.

Summary

1. The new phase of technological development in our society is causing strain as population expands and the per-capita use of energy exhausts natural resources while polluting the environment. Behavioral scientists, joining with other scientists and technologists, have an opportunity to provide research and services bearing upon the improvement of the quality of life.

2. In considering psychology's role in relation to the problems of society, one should distinguish between the *basic* and *applied* aspects of psychology. There are many gradations from the most basic research that has little relevance for practical problems, through basic research with higher potential for relevance, to work that is planned to be of service, consisting of several steps from applied research through development, culminating in professional services designed to carry out adopted policies. The order is not simply from basic to applied; complex feedbacks occur all along the line, with applied research contributing to the solution of basic problems, just as basic research contributes to the solution of practical problems.

3. In facing the opportunity for social-problem solving, behavioral scientists are finding it necessary to increase the scope of their research to include the development of *social indicators,* to engage in *program evaluation,* and to participate in *forecasting the future* and planning for it.

4. In order to detect the emergence of social problems, and to assess trends both beneficial and harmful to the quality of life, behavioral scientists have been recommending the development of improved *social indicators,* analogous to the economic indicators widely depended upon today. Social indicators can be developed in such areas as health, education, the physical environment, income and poverty, public order and safety, recreation, participation and alienation. The survey and testing methods with which psychologists are familiar should make it possible for them to join with others in this task.

5. Social indicators should reflect the cumulative effects of various social programs, but specific programs have to be evaluated by methods designed specifically for them. Even though the programs are neither invented nor initiated by behavioral scientists, they may make a contribution through *program evaluation* methods, which determine how well the program has done what it set out to do.

6. In recommending solutions to public problems, behavioral scientists can engage in *forecasting the future* on sounder bases than those used in the past. The two main methods are (a) the direct *projection of trends,* based upon the collection of appropriate data in time series, and (b) the use of *expert judgment* to assess those factors, including probable developments within science, that will modify trends. This method is known as the *Delphi method. The cross-impact matrix method,* a refinement of the Delphi method, synthesizes the projections made by a number of experts to take into account the interdependencies of their predictions. The purpose in forecasting is not to predict what is actually going to occur, but to project possible futures, which present action may modify, and to assure that options are left open for future generations.

7. As behavioral scientists move into the sensitive areas of social policy, in which conflicts of interest arise and political power is involved, they must face the questions of human values and social goals without sacrificing the objectivity of scientific research. Some issues are the *protection of privacy* and *freedom of choice,* particularly as methods of control over behavior become more powerful.

8. An increasing desire is being manifested to make psychology more pertinent to the problems of society. Some suggestions for discussion include the desirability of not sacrificing basic science for socially relevant research, but rather allowing all areas of research to share equally in the research effort and supplement one another; not trying to deal with social problems as though they could be solved by psychology alone; not promising too much, because social problems are complex and behavioral science knowledge is often inadequate; keeping in mind long-range goals and purposes but dealing realistically with feasible immediate steps; enlarging both the scale and the scope of research to make it commensurate with the problems that are being faced.

Suggestions for further reading

Several reports initiated by national agencies relate psychology and the other behavioral sciences to problems of policy. These include one from the National Academy of Sciences, *The behavioral sciences and the federal government* (1968), and a somewhat more general one under the auspices of both the National Academy of Sciences and the Social Science Research Council, *The behavioral and social sciences: Outlook and needs* (1969). A special panel report on psychology has come out under the same auspices: Clark and Miller (eds.), *Psychology* (1970). In addition, there is a report from a special commission of the National Science Board of the National Science Foundation—*Knowledge into action: Improving the nation's use of the social sciences* (1969a). For a history of the social sciences in relation to the American government, see Lyons, *The uneasy partnership: Social sciences and the federal government in the 20th century* (1969).

Among those who report on the behavioral sciences and the environment are Garnsey and Hibbs (eds.), *Social sciences and the environment* (1967), Sommer, *Personal space* (1969), and Proshansky, Ittleson, and Rivlin (eds.), *Environmental psychology* (1970). For a broad assessment of environmental problems, see Council on Environmental Quality, *Environmental quality* (1970). A collection of articles that focuses on seven major social problems is found in Korten, Cook, and Lacey (eds.), *Psychology and the problems of society* (1970). On population problems, see Fawcett, *Psychology and population* (1970).

Introductions to the literature on social indicators include Bauer (ed.), *Social indicators* (1966); U.S. Department of Health, Education, and Welfare, *Toward a social report* (1969); Sheldon and Moore (eds.), *Indicators of social change* (1968).

The study of the future is leading to a burgeoning literature, including Kahn and Wiener, *The year 2000* (1967), Bell (ed.), *Toward the year 2000* (1968), and Wallia (ed.), *Toward century 21* (1970). A useful introduction to rigorous future-casting (the Delphi technique) is Helmer, *Social technology* (1966). The National Goals Research Staff of the Executive Office of the President issued its first report on July 4, 1970, under the title *Toward balanced growth: Quantity with quality.* This provides a background for policies directed toward the future.

The need for objectivity in science generally and in the social sciences is discussed in Scheffler, *Science and subjectivity* (1967), and in Myrdal, *Objectivity in social research* (1969). The special problems of social science and human values are treated in Kelman, *A time to speak: On human values and social research* (1968), Westin, *Privacy and freedom* (1967), and Denzin (ed.), *The values of social science* (1970). On the ethics of controlling behavior, see London, *Behavioral control* (1969). A general source, with extensive bibliographies, is Baier and Rescher (eds.), *Values and the future: The impact of technological change on American values* (1969).

There are many ways in which to keep alert to the frontiers of psychology. The most convenient scholarly source is the *Annual review of psychology,* consisting of critical reviews of the current literature, with extensive bibliographies. A popular source is the magazine *Psychology today,* which gives much of its attention to the excitement in the growing areas of psychology.

statistical methods and measurement | APPENDIX

MUCH OF THE WORK OF PSYCHOLOGISTS, like that of other scientists, calls for making measurements either in the laboratory or under field conditions. This work may involve measuring eye movements of infants when first exposed to a novel stimulus, recording the galvanic skin response of people under extreme stress, counting the number of trials required to condition a monkey with a prefrontal lobotomy, determining achievement test scores for students using computer-assisted instruction, or counting the number of patients who show improvement following a particular type of psychotherapy. In all these examples the *measurement operation* yields numbers, and the psychologist has the problem of interpreting them and arriving at some general conclusions. Basic to this task is *statistics*—the discipline that deals with collecting and handling numerical data and with making inferences from such data. The purpose of this Appen-

dix is to review certain statistical methods that play an important role in psychology.

The Appendix is written on the assumption that the problems of statistics are essentially problems of logic, that is, problems of clear thinking about data, and that an introductory acquaintance with statistics is *not* beyond the scope of anyone who understands enough algebra to use plus and minus signs and to substitute numbers for letters in equations.

Even an introductory acquaintance with statistics, however, requires practice in applying what has been learned. The treatment that follows states the essential relationships first in words and then with simple numerical examples that require little computation. These examples use a minimum of data, artificially selected to make the operations clear even to the student who is mathematically unskilled. Because of the scantiness and artificiality of the data, these specimen computations violate an important principle in the use of statistics, namely, that a formula should be used only with appropriate data. But this violation can be justified here, because our purpose is to provide examples that are easy to master so the process can be understood.

Descriptive statistics

Statistics serves, first of all, to provide a short-hand description of large amounts of data. Suppose that we want to study the college entrance examination scores of 5000 students, recorded on cards in the registrar's office. These scores are the raw data. Thumbing through the cards, we will get some impressions of the students' scores, but it will be impossible to keep all of them in mind. So we make some kind of summary of the data, possibly averaging all the scores or finding the highest and lowest scores. These statistical summaries make it easier to remember and think about the data. Such simplified or summarizing statements are called *descriptive statistics*.

Frequency distributions

Items of raw data become comprehensible when they are ranked in numerical order or grouped in a *frequency distribution*. To group these items of data, we must first divide the scale along which they are measured into intervals and then count the number of cases that fall into each interval. An interval in which scores are grouped is called a *class interval* and represents a portion of the measurement scale. The decision of how many class intervals the data are to be grouped into is not fixed by any rules, but based upon the judgment of the investigator. It will depend to some extent upon what he intends to do with the grouped data, but also upon the range of values to be covered and the actual number of scores to be grouped.

Table 1 provides a sample of raw data, representing college entrance examination scores for fifteen students. The scores are listed in the order in which the students were tested (the first student tested had a score of 84, the second 61, and so

TABLE 1	RAW SCORES	
84	75	91
61	75	67
72	87	79
75	79	83
77	51	69

College entrance examination scores for 15 students, listed in the order in which they were tested.

TABLE 2	FREQUENCY DISTRIBUTION
CLASS INTERVAL	NUMBER OF PERSONS IN CLASS
50–59	1
60–69	3
70–79	7
80–89	3
90–99	1

Scores of Table 1 accumulated with class intervals of 10.

on). Table 2 shows these data in a frequency distribution for which the class interval has been set at 10. One student has a score that falls in the interval from 50–59, three scores fall in the interval from 60–69, and so forth. Note that most scores are in the interval from 70–79, and that none are below the 50–59 interval or above the 90–99 interval.

A frequency distribution can often be better understood in a graphic presentation. The most widely used graph form is the *frequency histogram;* an example is shown in the left panel of Figure 1. Histograms are constructed by drawing bars, the bases of which are given by the class intervals and the heights of which are determined by the corresponding class frequencies. An alternative way of

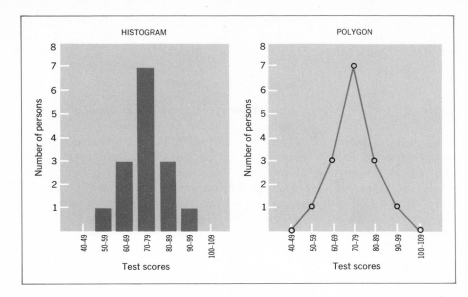

Fig. 1 **Frequency diagrams**
The data plotted are those from
Table 2. A frequency histogram
is on the left, and a frequency
polygon on the right.

presenting frequency distributions in graph form is to use a *frequency polygon,* an example of which is shown in the right panel of Figure 1. Frequency polygons are constructed by plotting the class frequencies at the center of the class interval and connecting by straight lines the points thus obtained. In order to complete the picture one extra class is usually added at each end of the distribution, and since these classes have zero frequencies, both ends of the figure will come down to the horizontal axis. The frequency polygon gives the same information as the frequency histogram, but by means of lines rather than bars.

In practice one would want far more cases than those plotted in Figure 1, but all our illustrations use a minimum of data so that the reader can easily check the steps in tabulating and plotting.

Measures of central tendency

A *measure of central tendency* is simply some representative point on our scale, a central point with scores scattering on either side. Three such measures are in common use: the *mean,* the *median,* and the *mode.*

The *mean* is the familiar arithmetic average obtained by adding the scores and dividing by the number of scores. The sum of the raw scores of Table 1 is 1125. Divide this by 15 (the number of students' scores), and the mean turns out to be 75.

The *median* is the score of the middle case, obtained by arranging the scores in order and then counting in to the middle from either end. When the 15 scores in Table 1 are placed in order from highest to lowest, the eighth from either end turns out to be 75. If the number of cases is even, one may simply average the two cases on either side of the middle. For instance, with 10 cases, the median can be taken as the arithmetic average of the fifth and sixth cases.

The *mode* is the most frequent score in a given distribution. In Table 1 the most frequent score is 75; hence the mode of the distribution is 75.

In a *symmetrical distribution,* in which the scores distribute evenly on either side of the middle (as in Figure 1), the mean, median, and mode all fall together. This is not true for distributions that are *skewed,* that is, unbalanced. Suppose we were analyzing the starting times of a morning train. The train is usually on time in leaving; occasionally it starts late, but it never starts early. For a train with a scheduled starting time of 8:00 A.M., one week's record might be:

M	8:00	Mean starting time:	8:07
Tu	8:04	Median starting time:	8:02
W	8:02	Modal starting time:	8:00
Th	8:19		
F	8:22		
Sat	8:00		
Sun	8:00		

The distribution of starting times in this example is skewed because of the two late departures; they raise the mean departure time but do not have much effect on either the median or the mode. Skewed distributions are either "skewed left" or "skewed right," according to the direction in which the *tail* of the distribution falls—the direction of the most extreme scores (see Figure 2). The skew in our train example is toward the late departure, and so is skewed right.

Skewness is important because unless it is understood the differences between the median and mean may sometimes prove misleading. Suppose that two political parties are arguing about the prosperity of the country. It is quite possible (though not common) for the mean and median incomes to move in opposite directions. Suppose, for example, that a round of wage increases was combined with a reduction in extremely high incomes. The median income might go up while the mean went down. The party wanting to show that incomes were getting higher would choose the median; the one that wishes to show that incomes were getting lower would choose the mean.

The mean is the most widely used of the meas-

ures of central tendency but, as we will see later, there are times when the mode or median is more appropriate.

Measures of variation

Usually more information is needed about a distribution than can be obtained from a measure of central tendency. For example, we need a measure to tell us whether scores cluster closely around their average or whether they scatter widely. A measure of the spread, or dispersion, of scores around the average is called a *measure of variation.*

Measures of variation are useful in at least two ways. First, they tell us how representative the average is. If the variation is small, we know that individual cases are close to it. If the variation is large, we can make use of the mean as a representative value with less assurance. Suppose, for example, that clothing is being designed for a group of people without the benefit of precise measurements. Knowing their average size would be helpful; but it would be very important to also know the spread of sizes. The second measure provides a "yardstick" by which we can decide on how much variability there is among the sizes.

To illustrate, consider the data in Figure 3, which shows frequency distributions of entrance examination scores for two classes of thirty students. Both classes have the same mean of 75, but they exhibit clearly different degrees of variation. All the students of Class I have scores clustered close to the

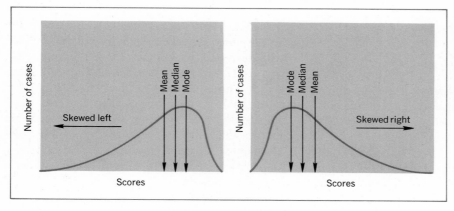

Fig. **2 Skewed distribution curves** Note that skewed distributions are named by the direction in which the tail falls. Also note that the mean, median, and mode are not identical for a skewed distribution; the median commonly falls between the mode and the mean.

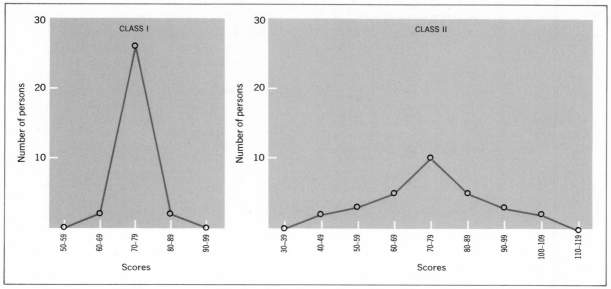

Fig. 3 Distributions differing in variation It is easy to see that the scores for Class I cluster closer to the mean than those for Class II, even though the means of the two classes are identical (75). For Class I all the scores fall between 60 and 89, with the large majority of them in the interval from 70 through 79; for Class II the scores are distributed fairly uniformly over a wide range from 40 through 109. This difference in variability between the two distributions can be measured using the standard deviation, which would be much smaller for Class I than for Class II.

mean, whereas the scores of Class II are spread over a wide range. Some measure is required to specify more exactly how these two distributions differ. Two measures of variation frequently used by psychologists are the *range* and the *standard deviation*.

In order to simplify our example for ease in arithmetic computation, let us suppose that five students from each of these classes seek entrance to college, and their entrance examination scores are as follows:

Student scores from Class I:
73, 74, 75, 76, 77 (mean = 75)
Student scores from Class II:
60, 65, 75, 85, 90 (mean = 75)

Let us now compute the measures of variation for these two small samples, one from Class I, the other from Class II.

The *range* is the spread between the highest and the lowest score. The range for the five students from Class I is 4 (from 73 to 77); for those from Class II it is 30 (from 60 to 90).

The range is very easy to compute, but the *standard deviation* is more frequently used because it has certain properties that make it the preferred measure. One such property is that it is an extremely sensitive measure of variation because it takes account of every score, not just extreme values as does the range. The standard deviation, which we will abbreviate with the lower-case Greek letter *sigma* (σ), measures how far the scores making up a distribution depart from that distribution's mean.[1] The deviation, *d*, of each score from the mean is computed and squared; then the average

[1] For this introductory treatment we shall use *sigma* (σ) throughout. However, in scientific literature the lower-case letter *s* is used to denote the standard deviation of a sample, whereas σ is used for the standard deviation of the population. Moreover, in computing the standard deviation of a sample, *s*, the sum of d^2 is divided by $N - 1$ rather than N. For reasonably large samples, however, the actual value of the standard deviation is little affected whether we divide by $N - 1$ or N. To simplify this presentation we will not distinguish between the standard deviation of a sample and that of a population, but instead will use the same formula to compute both. For a more detailed discussion of this point, see Mc-Nemar (1969).

of these squared values is obtained. The standard deviation is the square root of this average. Written as a formula

$$\sigma = \sqrt{\frac{\text{Sum of } d^2}{N}}$$

Specimen computation of the standard deviation. The scores for the samples from the two classes are arranged in Table 3 for separate computation of the standard deviation. The first step involves subtracting the mean from each score (the mean is 75 for both classes). This operation yields positive d values for scores above the mean, and negative ones for scores below the mean. The minus signs disappear when the d's are squared in the next column. The squared deviations are then added and divided by N, the number of cases in the sample; in our example $N = 5$. Taking the square root of this average yields the standard deviation. In this example the two standard deviations tell much the same story as the ranges, although they are not equivalent.

TABLE 3	COMPUTATION OF STANDARD DEVIATION					
CLASS I SCORES (MEAN = 75)			CLASS II SCORES (MEAN = 75)			
	d (DEVIATION FROM MEAN)	d^2 (DEVIATION SQUARED)		d (DEVIATION FROM MEAN)	d^2 (DEVIATION SQUARED)	
77 − 75 =	2	4	90 − 75 =	15	225	
76 − 75 =	1	1	85 − 75 =	10	100	
75 − 75 =	0	0	75 − 75 =	0	0	
74 − 75 =	−1	1	65 − 75 =	−10	100	
73 − 75 =	−2	4	60 − 75 =	−15	225	
		10			650	
Sum of d^2 = 10			Sum of d^2 = 650			
Mean of $d^2 = \frac{10}{5} = 2.0$			Mean of $d^2 = \frac{650}{5} = 130$			
Standard deviation (σ) = $\sqrt{2.0} = 1.4$			Standard deviation (σ) = $\sqrt{130} = 11.4$			

Statistical inference

Now that we have become familiar with statistics as ways of describing data, we are ready to turn to the processes of interpretation, to the making of inferences from data.

Populations and samples

First it is necessary to distinguish between a *population* and a *sample* drawn from that population. The U. S. Census Bureau attempts to describe the whole population by obtaining descriptive material on age, marital status, and so on, from everyone in the country. The word "population" is appropriate to the Census, because it represents *all* the people living in the United States.

The word "population" in statistics is not limited to people or animals or things. The population may be all the temperatures registered on a thermometer during the last decade, all the words in the English language, or all of any other specified supply of data.[2] Often we do not have access to the total population, and so we try to represent it by a sample drawn in a *random* (unbiased) fashion. We may ask some questions of a random fraction of the people, as the U. S. Census Bureau

[2]Sometimes the supply of data (the total population) is not so easily specified, as when we sample a subject's speed of reaction by taking 100 measurements among all those he might possibly yield if we continued the experiment endlessly. As long as the total supply of data is many times that of the sample—whether finite (all college students studying Latin) or indeterminate (all possible reaction times)—statistical theory can be used in treating the results.

has done as part of recent censuses; we may derive average temperatures by reading the thermometer at specified times, without taking a continuous record; we may estimate the words in the encyclopedia by counting the words on a random number of pages. These illustrations all represent the selection of a *sample* from a larger population. If any of these processes are repeated, we will come out with slightly different results, owing to the fact that a sample does not fully represent the whole population and hence has within it *errors of sampling*. This is where statistical considerations enter.

A sample of data is collected from a population in order to make inferences about that population. A sample of census data may be examined to see whether the population is getting older or whether the trend of migration to the suburbs is continuing. Similarly, experimental results are studied to find out what effects experimental manipulations have had upon behavior—whether the threshold for pitch is affected by loudness, whether child-rearing practices have detectable effects later in life. In order to make *statistical inferences* we have to evaluate carefully the relationships revealed by our sample of data. These inferences are always made under circumstances in which there is some degree of uncertainty because of sampling errors. If the statistical tests indicate that the magnitude of the effect found in the sample is fairly large relative to the estimate of the sampling error, then we can have confidence that the effect that was observed in the sample also holds for the population at large.

Thus, statistical inference deals with the problem of making an inference or judgment about some feature of a population based solely on information obtained from a sample of that population. As an introduction to statistical inference let us first consider the normal distribution and its use in interpreting standard deviations. Then we shall turn to problems of sampling errors and the significance of differences.

The normal distribution

When large amounts of data are collected, tabulated, and plotted on a graph, they often fall into a symmetrical distribution of roughly bell shape, known as the *normal distribution* and plotted as the *normal curve*. Most cases fall near the mean, thus giving the high point of the bell, and the bell tapers off sharply at very high and very low scores. This form of curve is of special interest because it also arises when the outcome of a process is based on a large number of *chance* events all occurring independently.

What do we mean by "chance" events? We mean only that the causal factors are complex and numerous, yielding results of the sort found when we toss dice or spin a roulette wheel. The demonstration device displayed in Figure 4 illustrates how

Fig. **4 A device to demonstrate a chance distribution** To observe chance factor at work one first holds the board upside-down until all the steel balls fall into the reservoir. Then he turns the board over and holds it vertically until the balls fall into the nine columns at the bottom (as shown in figure). The precise number of balls falling into each column will vary from one demonstration to the next. On the average, however, the heights of the columns of balls approximate a normal distribution, with the greatest height in the center column and gradually decreasing heights in the outer columns. (Hexstat Probability Demonstrator, Harcourt Brace Jovanovich, Inc.)

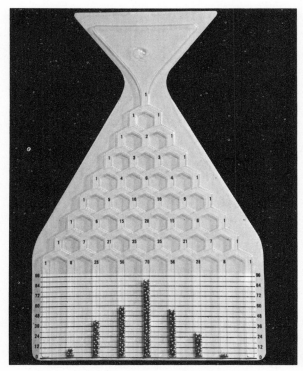

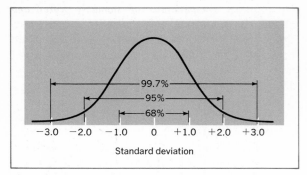

Fig. **5** **The normal curve** The normal distribution curve can be constructed provided the mean and standard deviation are known. For all practical purposes the area under the curve below -3σ and above $+3\sigma$ is negligible.

	TABLE **4** AREA UNDER NORMAL CURVE AS PROPORTION OF TOTAL AREA		
STANDARD DEVIATION	(1) AREA TO THE LEFT OF THIS VALUE	(2) AREA TO THE RIGHT OF THIS VALUE	(3) AREA BETWEEN THIS VALUE AND MEAN
-3.0σ	.001	.999	.499
-2.5σ	.006	.994	.494
-2.0σ	.023	.977	.477
-1.5σ	.067	.933	.433
-1.0σ	.159	.841	.341
-0.5σ	.309	.691	.191
0.0σ	.500	.500	.000
$+0.5\sigma$	.691	.309	.191
$+1.0\sigma$	.841	.159	.341
$+1.5\sigma$	.933	.067	.433
$+2.0\sigma$	.977	.023	.477
$+2.5\sigma$	.994	.006	.494
$+3.0\sigma$	.999	.001	.499

a sequence of chance events gives rise to a normal distribution. The chance factor of whether a steel ball will fall left or right each time it encounters a point where the channel branches results in a symmetrical distribution; more balls fall straight down the middle, but an occasional one reaches the end compartments. This is a useful way of visualizing what is meant by a chance distribution closely approximating the "normal" curve.

The normal curve (Figure 5) can be defined mathematically to represent the idealized distribution approximated by the device shown in Figure 4. It gives the likelihood that cases within a normally distributed population will depart from the mean by any stated amount. Roughly two-thirds of the cases (68 percent) will tend to fall between plus and minus one standard deviation of the mean ($\pm 1\sigma$); 95 percent of the cases within plus and minus 2σ; and virtually all cases (99.7 percent) within plus and minus 3σ. Thus, if we understand the properties of the normal curve, we can interpret any statistic expressed in units of the standard deviation, provided the cases upon which the statistic is based are normally distributed. The percentages shown in Figure 5 represent the *percentage of the area* lying under the curve between the indicated scale values, with the total area representing the whole population. A more detailed listing of areas under portions of the normal curve is given in Table 4.

Using Table 4, let us trace where the 68-percent and 95-percent values of Figure 5 come from. We find from column 3 of Table 4 that between -1σ and the mean there lies .341 of the total area, and between $+1\sigma$ and the mean also lies .341 of the area. Adding these, we get .682, which has been expressed in Figure 5 as 68 percent. Similarly, we can find the area between -2σ and $+2\sigma$ to be $2 \times .477 = .954$, which has been expressed as 95 percent.

We shall have two uses for these percentages in the Appendix. One of them is in connection with the interpretation of standard scores, to which we turn next. The other is in connection with tests of the significance of the differences between means and other statistical measures. Both of these uses make the important assumption that the scores being considered are sampled from a normal distribution. It is fortunate that a great many frequency distributions do fit the normal curve or come very close to it, so that this basic assumption usually does not lead to difficulties.

Scaling of data

In order to interpret a score we often want to know whether it is high or low in relation to other scores. If a person takes a driver's test and finds that he needs 0.500 seconds to put his foot on the brake after a danger signal, how can he tell whether his performance is fast or slow? If he gets a 60 on a physics examination, does he pass the course? To answer questions of this kind we have to derive some sort of *scale* against which the scores can be compared.

Ranked data. By placing scores in rank order from high to low we derive one kind of scale. An individual score is interpreted by telling where it ranks among the group of scores. For example, the graduates of West Point know where they stand in their class—perhaps 35th or 125th among a class of 400.

Standard scores. The standard deviation is a very convenient unit for scaling, because we know how to interpret how far away 1σ or 2σ is from the mean (Table 4). A score based on some multiple of the standard deviation is known as a *standard score*. Many scales used in psychological measurement are based on the principle of standard scores, with modifications often being made to eliminate negative signs and decimals. Some of these scales derived from standard scores are given in Table 5.

Specimen computations of standard scores and transformation to arbitrary scales. Table 1 presented college entrance scores for fifteen students. Without more information we do not know whether these are representative of the population of all college applicants. Let us assume, however, that on this examination the population mean is 75 and its standard deviation is 10.

What then is the *standard score* for a student who made 90 on the examination? We must express how far this score lies above the mean in multiples of the standard deviation.

$$\text{Standard score for grade of } 90 = \frac{90 - 75}{10}$$
$$= \frac{15}{10} = 1.5\sigma$$

As a second example consider a student with a score of 53.

$$\text{Standard score for grade of } 53 = \frac{53 - 75}{10}$$
$$= \frac{-22}{10} = -2.2\sigma$$

In this case the minus sign tells us that the student is below the mean, and by 2.2 standard deviations. Thus the sign of the standard score ($+$ or $-$) indicates whether the score is above or below the mean, and its value indicates how far in standard deviations. Suppose we wish to compare the first standard score

	STANDARD SCORE	GRADUATE RECORD EXAMINATION	ARMY GENERAL CLASSIFICATION TEST	NAVY GENERAL CLASSIFICATION TEST	AIR FORCE STANINE *
	-3σ	200	40	20	—
	-2σ	300	60	30	1
	-1σ	400	80	40	3
	0σ	500	100	50	5
	$+1\sigma$	600	120	60	7
	$+2\sigma$	700	140	70	9
	$+3\sigma$	800	160	80	—
Mean	0	500	100	50	5
Standard deviation	1.0	100	20	10	2

TABLE 5   SOME REPRESENTATIVE SCALES DERIVED FROM STANDARD SCORES

*The word "stanine" was coined by the Air Force to refer to a scale with scores ranging from 1 to 9, known originally as "standard nine," a type of standard score with a mean of 5 and a standard deviation of 2.

computed above to a score on the scale used in the Navy General Classification Test, as shown in Table 5. This scale has a mean of 50 and a standard deviation of 10. Therefore the standard score of 1.5σ becomes $50 + (10 \times 1.5) = 50 + 15 = 65$.

Using column 1 of Table 4, we find beside the value for a standard score of $+ 1.5\sigma$ the number .933. This means that 93 percent of the scores of a normal distribution will lie *below* a person whose standard score is $+1.5\sigma$. Thus a score of 65 on the Navy General Classification Test, 650 on a Graduate Record Examination, or 8 on the Air Force Stanine (all equivalent as standard scores) is above that achieved by 93 percent of those on whom the test was calibrated. Scores representing any other multiple of the standard deviation can be similarly interpreted.

How representative is a mean?

When we ask about the representativeness of a mean, we are really implying two questions. First, what are the *errors of measurement?* Second, what are the *errors of sampling?* Two people measuring the same length with a rule or timing an event with a stopwatch may not get exactly the same results. These differences are errors of measurement, which usually can be assumed to be small if care is taken in making the measurement. The second kind of error, the sampling error, interests us now. Suppose we were to select two random samples from the same population, make the necessary measurements, and compute the mean for each sample. What differences between the first and the second mean could be expected by chance?

Successive random samples drawn from the same population will have different means, forming a distribution of *sample means* around the *true mean* of the population. These sample means are themselves numbers for which one can compute their own standard deviations. We call this standard deviation the *standard error of the mean,* or σ_M, and can make an estimate of it on the basis of the following formula:

$$\sigma_M = \frac{\sigma}{\sqrt{N}}$$

where σ is the standard deviation for the sample and N is the number of cases from which each sample mean is computed.

According to the formula, the size of the standard error of the mean decreases with increase in the sample size; thus, a mean based on a large sample is more trustworthy (more likely to be close to the actual population mean) than one based on a smaller sample. Common sense would lead us to expect this. Computations of the standard error of the mean permit us to make clear assertions about the degree of uncertainty in our computed mean. The more cases in the sample, the more uncertainty has been reduced.

Specimen computation of the standard error of the mean. In order to estimate the standard error of the mean, we need the number of cases in the sample and the standard deviation of the sample. Suppose we take the mean and standard deviation computed in Table 3 for Class II but assume that the sample was larger. The sample mean is 75, and the standard deviation is 11.4. Let us assume sample sizes of 25, 100, and 900 cases; the standard errors of the mean would be, respectively:

$$N = 25: \quad \sigma_M = \frac{11.4}{\sqrt{25}}$$
$$= \frac{11.4}{5} = 2.28$$

$$N = 100: \quad \sigma_M = \frac{11.4}{\sqrt{100}}$$
$$= \frac{11.4}{10} = 1.14$$

$$N = 900: \quad \sigma_M = \frac{11.4}{\sqrt{900}}$$
$$= \frac{11.4}{30} = 0.38$$

Now we may ask, how much variation can be expected among means if we draw samples of 25, 100, and 900? We know from Table 4 that 68 percent of the cases in a normal distribution lie between -1σ and $+1\sigma$ of the mean. The sample mean of 75 is the best estimate of the population mean. We know the size of σ_M, so we may infer that the probability is .68 that the population mean lies between the following limits:

$N = 25:$ 75 ± 2.28, or between 72.72 and 77.28

$N = 100:$ 75 ± 1.14, or between 73.86 and 76.14

$N = 900:$ 75 ± 0.38, or between 74.62 and 75.38

Thus, on the basis of sample data it is possible to specify the probability that the mean for the entire population will lie in a certain interval. Note from the above computations that the estimated interval decreases as the size of the sample increases. The larger the sample, the more precise is the estimate of the true population mean.

Significance of a difference between sample means

Many psychological experiments collect data on two groups of subjects, one group exposed to certain specified experimental conditions and the other serving as a control. The question then is whether there is a difference in the mean performance of the two groups, and if such a difference is observed, whether it holds for the population from which these groups of subjects are a sample. Basically, we are asking whether a difference between two sample means reflects a true difference, or whether this difference is simply the result of sampling error.

As an example, let us consider scores on a reading test for a sample of first-grade boys, compared with the scores for a sample of first-grade girls. The boys score lower than the girls, as far as mean performances are concerned; but there is a great deal of overlap, some boys doing extremely well and some girls doing very poorly. Hence, we cannot accept the obtained difference in means without making a test of its *statistical significance*. Only then can we decide whether the observed differences in sample means reflect true differences in the population, or arose because of sampling error. The difference could be due to sampling error if by sheer luck we happened to get some of the brighter girls and some of the duller boys in the samples.

As a second example, suppose that in an experiment to determine whether right-handed men are stronger than left-handed men the results shown in the first table (next column) had been obtained. Our sample of·five right-handed men averaged eight kilograms stronger than our sample of five left-handed men. What can be inferred about left-handed and right-handed men in general? Can we argue from the sample data that right-handed men are stronger than left-handed men? Obviously not, for the averages derived from most of the

STRENGTH OF GRIP IN KILOGRAMS, RIGHT-HANDED MEN	STRENGTH OF GRIP IN KILOGRAMS, LEFT-HANDED MEN
40	40
45	45
50	50
55	55
100	60
Sum 290	Sum 250
Mean 58	Mean 50

right-handed men would not differ from averages derived from the left-handed men; the one very deviant case (score of 100) tells us we are dealing with an uncertain situation.

Suppose that, instead, the results had been those shown in the second table.

STRENGTH OF GRIP IN KILOGRAMS, RIGHT-HANDED MEN	STRENGTH OF GRIP IN KILOGRAMS, LEFT-HANDED MEN
56	48
57	49
58	50
59	51
60	52
Sum 290	Sum 250
Mean 58	Mean 50

Again the same mean difference of eight kilograms is found, but we are now inclined to have greater confidence in the results, because the left-handed men scored consistently lower than the right-handed men. What we ask of statistics is that it provide a precise way of taking into account the reliability of the mean differences, so that we do not have to depend solely on intuition that one difference is more reliable than another.

The above examples suggest that the significance of a difference will depend both upon the size of the obtained difference and upon the variability of the means being compared. We shall find below that from the standard error of the means we can compute a *standard error of the difference between two means* (σ_{D_M}). We can then evaluate the obtained difference by using a *critical ratio*, which is the ratio of the obtained difference between the means (D_M) to the standard error of the difference between the means:

$$\text{Critical ratio} = \frac{D_M}{\sigma_{D_M}}$$

This ratio helps us to evaluate the significance of the difference between the two means.[3] As a rule of thumb, a critical ratio should be 2.0 or larger in order for the difference between means to be accepted as significant. Throughout this book statements that the difference between means is "statistically significant" mean that the critical ratio is at least that large.

Why is a critical ratio of 2.0 selected as statistically significant? Simply because a value this large or larger can occur by chance only 5 in 100 times. Where do we get the 5 in 100? We can treat the critical ratio as a standard score, for it is merely the difference between two means, expressed as a multiple of its standard error. Referring to column 2 in Table 4, we note that the likelihood of a standard deviation as high as or higher than +2.0 occurring by chance is .023. Because the chance of deviating in the opposite direction is also .023, the total probability is .046. This means that 46 times in 1000, or about 5 in 100, a critical ratio as large as 2.0 would be found by chance if the population means were identical.

The rule of thumb that says a critical ratio should be at least 2.0 is just that—an arbitrary but convenient rule that defines the "5-percent level of significance." Following this rule we will make less than 5 errors in 100 decisions by concluding on the basis of sample data that a difference in means exists when in fact there is none. The 5-percent level need not always be used; a higher or lower level of significance may be appropriate in certain experiments depending upon how willing we are to make an occasional error in inference.

Specimen computation of the critical ratio. The computation of the critical ratio calls for finding the *standard error of the difference between two means,* which is given by the following formula:

$$\sigma_{D_M} = \sqrt{(\sigma_{M_1})^2 + (\sigma_{M_2})^2}$$

In this formula, σ_{M_1} and σ_{M_2} are the standard errors of the two means being compared.

As an illustration, suppose we wanted to compare reading achievement test scores for first-grade boys and girls in the United States. A random sample of boys and girls would be identified and given the test. Suppose for the boys the mean score was 70 with .40 as the standard error of the mean, and for the girls a mean of 72 and a standard error of .30. We want to decide, on the basis of these samples, whether there is a real difference between boys and girls in the population as a whole. The sample data suggest that girls are better than boys, but can we infer that this would have been the case if we had tested all the girls and all the boys in the United States? The critical ratio helps us make this decision.

$$\sigma_{D_M} = \sqrt{(\sigma_{M_1})^2 + (\sigma_{M_2})^2}$$
$$= \sqrt{.16 + .09} = \sqrt{.25}$$
$$= .5$$

$$\text{Critical ratio} = \frac{D_M}{\sigma_{D_M}} = \frac{72 - 70}{.5} = \frac{2.0}{.5} = 4.0$$

Because the critical ratio is well above 2.0, we may assert that the observed mean difference is statistically significant at the 5-percent level. Thus we conclude that there is a reliable difference between boys and girls in performance on the reading test.

The coefficient of correlation and its interpretation

Correlation refers to the concomitant variation of paired measures, so that when one member of the pair rises, so does the other, or (in negative correlation) as one rises, the other falls. Correlation is often used in psychology. Suppose that a test is designed to predict success in college. If it is a good test, high scores on it will be related to high performance in college, and low scores will be related to poorer performance. The *coefficient of*

[3]Care must be taken in interpreting a critical ratio when the computations are based on small samples. With small samples the ratio should be interpreted as a *t*-test (see p. 19), but for large samples *t* and the critical ratio are equivalent. For an explanation of this see McNemar (1969).

correlation gives us a way of stating more precisely the degree of relationship.[4]

Product-moment correlation (*r*)

The most frequently used method of determining the coefficient of correlation is the *product-moment method,* which yields the index conventionally designated *r*. The product-moment coefficient *r* varies between perfect positive correlation (*r* = +1.00) and perfect negative correlation (*r* = −1.00). Lack of relationship is designated *r* = .00.

The formula for computing the product-moment correlation is

$$ r = \frac{\text{Sum}\ (dx)(dy)}{N\sigma_x\sigma_y} $$

Here one of the paired measures has been labeled the *x*-score and the other the *y*-score. The *dx* and *dy* refer to the deviations of each score from its mean, *N* is the number of paired measures, and σ_x and σ_y are the standard deviations of the *x*-scores and the *y*-scores.

The computation of the coefficient of correlation requires the determination of the sum of the products of the deviation of each of the two scores (*x* and *y*) from its respective mean, that is, the sum of the (*dx*) (*dy*) products for all of the subjects entering into the correlation. This sum, in addition to the computed standard deviations for the *x*-scores and *y*-scores, can then be entered into the formula.

Specimen computation of product-moment correlation. Suppose that we had the following pairs of scores, the first being a score on a college entrance

NAMES OF STUDENTS	ENTRANCE TEST (*x*)	FRESHMAN GRADES (*y*)
Adam	71	39
Bill	67	27
Charles	65	33
David	63	30
Edward	59	21

[4] This topic was discussed in Chapter 1 (pp. 18–20). The reader may find it helpful to review that material.

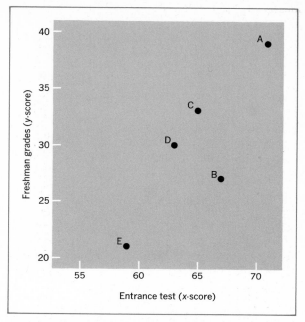

Fig. **6 Scatter diagram for hypothetical data** Each point represents the *x*- and *y*-scores for a particular student. The letters appended to the points identify the students in the data table (A = Adam, B = Bill, etc.).

test (to be labeled arbitrarily as the *x*-score) and the second being freshman grades (the *y*-score). Figure 6 shows a *scatter diagram* of these data. Each point simultaneously represents the *x*-score and *y*-score for a given subject; for example, the uppermost right-hand point is for Adam (labeled A). Looking at these data, we can easily detect that there is some positive correlation between the *x*-scores and the *y*-scores. Adam makes the highest score on the entrance test and also the highest freshman grades; Edward makes the lowest score on both. The others are a little irregular, so we know that the correlation is not perfect; hence *r* is less than 1.00.

We shall compute the correlation to illustrate the method, though no researcher would consent, in practice, to determining a correlation with so few cases. The details are given in Table 6. Following the procedure outlined in Table 3, we compute the standard deviation of the *x*-scores and then the standard deviation of the *y*-scores; it is 4 for the *x*-scores, and 6 for the *y*-scores. Next we compute the (*dx*) (*dy*) products for each subject and total the five cases. Entering these results in our equation yields an *r* of +.85.

TABLE 6 COMPUTATION OF A PRODUCT-MOMENT CORRELATION					
SUBJECT	ENTRANCE TEST (x-score)	FRESHMAN GRADES (y-score)	(dx)	(dy)	(dx)(dy)
Adam	71	39	6	9	+54
Bill	67	27	2	−3	−6
Charles	65	33	0	3	0
David	63	30	−2	0	0
Edward	59	21	−6	−9	+54
Sum	325	150	0	0	+102
Mean	65	30			

$$\sigma_x = 4 \qquad \sigma_y = 6 \qquad r = \frac{\text{Sum } (dx)(dy)}{N\sigma_x\sigma_y} = \frac{+102}{5 \times 4 \times 6} = +.85$$

Rank correlation (ρ)

When computers or desk calculators are not available and computations must be done by hand, a simpler method for determining correlations makes use of ranked scores. The resulting correlation is not an exact equivalent of r, but rather it is an estimate of r. The coefficient obtained by the rank method is designated by the lower-case Greek letter *rho* (ρ). The formula for the rank-correlation coefficient is

$$\rho = 1 - \frac{6(\text{Sum } D^2)}{N(N^2 - 1)}$$

where D is the difference in ranks for the scores of any one subject, and N is the number of subjects whose scores are being correlated.

Specimen computation of rank-correlation coefficient. We shall use the same data employed in the preceding example. All the details are given in Table 7. The procedure is to rank both sets of scores from highest to lowest, obtain the differences in ranks for each subject on the two tests, square and sum the differences, and enter them into the formula. The value of ρ for our example turns out to be $+.70$. As indicated above, ρ may be viewed as an estimate of r. The fact that in our example the values of r and ρ are not closer together is due to the small number of cases ($N = 5$). When reasonably large samples are taken, ρ and r will closely approximate each other.

When is a coefficient of correlation significant?

A coefficient of correlation, like other statistical measures, has a standard error. That is, if a second sample were taken from a particular population, the correlation computed from it would not be exactly the same as that obtained from the first sample. The *standard error of r* (denoted as σ_r) can be used to determine whether an r based on a sample of data is significantly different from zero. The formula for computing the standard error of r is

$$\sigma_r = \frac{1}{\sqrt{N - 1}}$$

TABLE 7 COMPUTATION OF A RANK-CORRELATION COEFFICIENT						
SUBJECT	ENTRANCE TEST	FRESHMAN GRADES	RANK, ENTRANCE TEST	RANK, FRESHMAN GRADES	DIFFERENCE IN RANK (D)	SQUARED DIFFERENCE (D²)
Adam	71	39	1	1	0	0
Bill	67	27	2	4	−2	4
Charles	65	33	3	2	+1	1
David	63	30	4	3	+1	1
Edward	59	21	5	5	0	0
					Sum D² =	6

$$\rho = 1 - \frac{6(\text{Sum } D^2)}{N(N^2 - 1)} = 1 - \frac{6 \times 6}{5 \times 24} = 1 - \frac{36}{120} = +.70$$

where N is the number of pairs entering into the correlation.

If r is divided by σ_r, we get a critical ratio that can be interpreted just like the critical ratios discussed before. If the value of r/σ_r is greater than 2.0, we may be fairly confident that the "true" value of r for the population as a whole is significantly greater than zero; stated otherwise, that there is a real correlation between the scores in the population from which the sample was drawn.

Interpreting a correlation coefficient

It is not always enough to know that a correlation is significantly greater than zero. Sometimes we want to make use of correlations in prediction. For example, if we know from past experience that a certain entrance test correlates with freshman grades, we can predict the freshman grades for beginning college students who have taken the test. If the correlation were perfect, we would predict their grades without error. But r is usually less than 1.00, so we will make some errors in prediction; the closer r is to zero, the greater the sizes of the errors in prediction.

While we cannot go into the technical problems of predicting freshman grades from entrance examinations or of making other similar predictions, we can consider the meanings of correlation coefficients of different sizes. It is evident that with a correlation of zero between x and y, knowledge of x will not help to predict y. If weight is unrelated to intelligence, it does us no good to know weight when we are trying to predict intelligence. At the other extreme, a perfect correlation would mean 100 percent predictive efficiency—knowing x we can predict y. What of intermediate values of r?

Because correlation coefficients vary from between zero and ± 1.00, there is a temptation to interpret the correlation as a percent, which would imply that a correlation of .50 is twice as large as one of .25. This is not correct; a more appropriate interpretation is based on the square of the correlation. The squared correlation (r^2) multiplied by 100 provides an estimate of the percentage of the variance that the distribution of x-scores and y-scores have in common. If $r = .50$, then $100 \times$

$(.50)^2$ or 25 percent of the variation of the y's is accounted for by differences in x; similarly, if $r = .40$, 16 percent of the variation of the y's is accounted for by the relation with x. In the sense of "percentage of variance accounted for" we can say that a correlation of $r = .70$ is twice as strong as a correlation of $r = .50$, and that a correlation of $r = .50$ is twenty-five times as strong as a correlation of $r = .10$.

Some appreciation of the meaning of correlations of various sizes can be gained by examining the scatter diagrams in Figure 7. Each dot represents the score of two tests for the same individual. If the correlation is $+1.00$, then all the points in the scatter diagram fall on a straight line. When the correlation is zero, the points in the scatter diagram are uniformly distributed and do not line up in any particular direction.

In the preceding discussion we did not emphasize the sign of the correlation coefficient, since this has no bearing on the strength of a relationship. The only distinction between a correlation of $r = +.70$ and $r = -.70$ is that for the former increases in x are accompanied by increases in y, and for the latter increases in x are accompanied by decreases in y.

Cautions on the use of correlation coefficients

While the correlation coefficient is one of the most widely used statistics in psychology, it is also one of the most widely misused procedures. First, those who use it sometimes overlook the fact that r measures only the strength of a linear (straight-line) relationship between x and y. Second, they often fail to recognize that r does not necessarily imply a cause-and-effect relation between x and y.

Correlation measures linear relationships. If r is calculated for the data plotted in Figure 8, a value close to zero will be obtained, but this does not mean that the two variables are not related. The curve of Figure 8 provides an excellent fit even though a straight line does not; knowing the value of x we could predict very precisely what y would be by plotting it on the curve. Let us therefore emphasize that the correlation coefficient measures

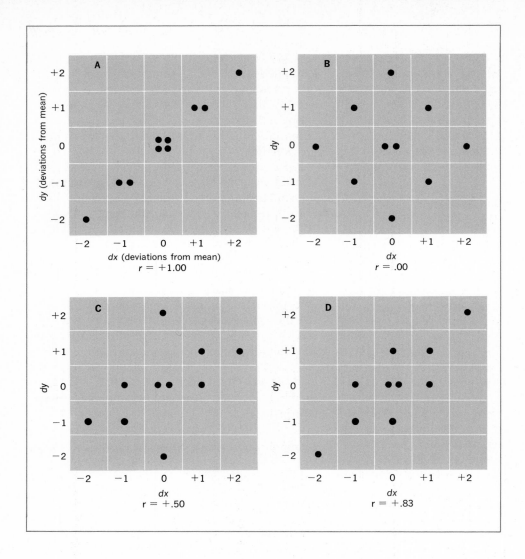

Fig. **7** **Scatter diagrams illustrating correlations of various sizes** Each dot represents one individual's score on two tests, *x* and *y*. In A all cases fall on the diagonal and the correlation is perfect (*r* = +1.00); if we know a subject's score on *x*, we know that it will be the same on *y*. In B the correlation is zero; knowing a subject's score on *x*, we cannot predict whether it will be at, above, or below the mean on *y*. For example, of the four subjects who score at the mean of *x* (*dx* = 0), one makes a very high score on *y* (*dy* = +2), one a very low score (*dy* = −2), and two remain average. In both C and D there is a diagonal trend to the scores, so that a high score on *x* is associated with a high score on *y*, and a low score on *x* with a low score on *y*, but the relation is imperfect. The interested student will discover that it is possible to check the value of the correlations by using the formulas given in the text for the coefficient of correlation (p. 573). The computation has been very much simplified by presenting the scores in the deviation form that permits entering them directly into the formulas. (The fact that the axes do not have conventional scales does not change the interpretation. For example, if we assigned the values 1 through 5 to the left-hand and bottom coordinates and then computed *r* for these new values, the correlation coefficients would be the same.)

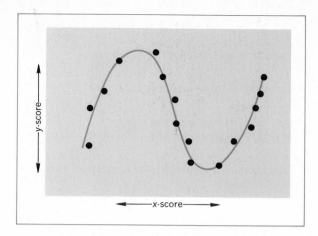

Fig. 8 Hypothetical scatter diagram An illustration in which data would be poorly accounted for by a straight line but are well accounted for by the s-shaped curve. Application of the correlation coefficient to these data would be inappropriate.

only the strength of a linear (straight-line) relationship between two variables. If there is reason to believe that a *nonlinear* relation holds, then other statistical procedures need to be used.

Correlation does not yield cause. When two sets of scores are correlated, we may suspect that they have some causal factors in common, but we cannot conclude that one of them causes the other (see Chapter 1, p. 18).

Correlations sometimes appear paradoxical. For example, the correlation between study time and college grades has been found to be slightly negative (about $-.10$). If a causal interpretation were assumed, one might suppose that the best way to raise grades would be to stop studying. The negative correlation arises because some students have advantages over others in grade-making (possibly because of native ability or better college preparation), so that often those who study the hardest are those who have difficulty earning passing grades.

This example provides sufficient warning against giving a causal interpretation to a coefficient of correlation. It is possible, however, that when two variables are correlated one may be the cause of the other. The search for causes is a logical one, and correlations can help by providing leads to experiments that can verify cause-and-effect relations.

Statistics in psychology

Statistical methods are becoming increasingly important in all sciences, but particularly so in psychology because of the complexity and variability of the phenomena it studies.

The earliest demand upon statistics was made when psychologists began to use psychophysical methods for *threshold measurement*. A weight that is slightly heavier than another is not always judged as heavier, even though the judgment "heavier" is made more frequently than judgments of "lighter." Hence the threshold requires a statistical definition.

The most widespread use of statistical methods came in connection with the development of intelligence tests and related research on *individual differences*. More recently statistical considerations have entered increasingly into the *design of experiments* in all branches of psychology. While some statistical considerations have long been important

(such as in computing the significance of differences between performances of experimental and control groups), newer methods permit the economical treatment of a number of variables at once. These methods not only save in the time and costs of experimentation but yield information that earlier experimental comparisons could not.

Another field, that of *attitude and opinion surveys* (of which election polls are one illustration), relies heavily upon sampling methods to determine how many and which people to interview. The results must meet acceptable statistical standards if they are to be appropriately interpreted.

Modern computational aids, including high-speed computers and automatic test-scoring machines, permit the rapid handling of masses of data. The procedures of modern psychology, as we know them, would be impossible without these developments.

Summary

1. *Statistics* is the science that deals with the collection and handling of numerical data and with inferences made from such data.

2. *Descriptive statistics* provides a shorthand summary of large numbers of observations.

3. *Measures of central tendency* include the *mean,* the *median,* and the *mode.* Because of its mathematical properties, the mean (the ordinary arithmetic average) is the most favored of these measures.

4. *Measures of variation* include the *range* and the *standard deviation.* The standard deviation, although fairly complex, is the most useful measure.

5. *Statistical inference* deals with the problem of making an inference or judgment about some feature of a population when the inference must be based solely upon information obtained from a sample of the population. The accuracy of such inferences depends upon two factors: the size of the sample and the faithfulness with which the sample represents the population. *Random-sampling* procedures are most frequently used in order to ensure a representative sample.

6. In the *scaling* of data, raw scores may be converted into *ranks* or *standard scores.* Standard scores have many advantages and are widely used; they are based on distance from the mean expressed as multiples of the standard deviation.

7. It is possible to compute a *standard error of the difference between two means* from the *standard error* of each mean. The *critical ratio* expresses the obtained difference between two means in multiples of the standard error of the difference between the means. If the critical ratio is 2.0 or above, we have confidence that a true difference between the means exists, and is not likely to be the result of chance factors.

8. The *coefficient of correlation* is a convenient method for expressing the degree of relationship between two variables. The *product-moment correlation* is the one favored in psychological research. A convenient approximation is provided by the *rank-correlation coefficient.*

9. Statistics plays an important role in all branches of psychology. It is especially important in research on *individual differences,* in the *design of experiments,* and in *attitude and opinion surveys.*

Suggestions for further reading

A number of textbooks on statistics are available to students of psychology, of which Hays, *Statistics for psychologists* (1963), McNemar, *Psychological statistics* (4th ed., 1969), and McCall, *Fundamental statistics for psychology* (1970), are excellent examples. For aid in computation, Bruning and Kintz, *Computational handbook of statistics* (1968), is a useful resource. The role of statistics in the design of psychological experiments is explained in Winer, *Statistical principles in experimental design* (1962), and Edwards, *Experimental design in psychological research* (3rd ed., 1968).

glossary

The glossary defines technical words appearing in the text and some common words when they are used in psychology with special meanings. No attempt is made to give the range of variations of meaning beyond those used in the text. For fuller definitions and other shades of meaning, consult any standard dictionary of psychology, such as English and English, *A comprehensive dictionary of psychological and psychoanalytical terms* (1958).

ability. Demonstrable knowledge or skill. Ability includes aptitude and achievement (cf. *aptitude, achievement*).

abnormal fixation. A stereotyped habit very resistant to change (cf. *stereotypy*).

abreaction. In psychoanalysis, the process of reducing emotional tension by reliving (in speech or action or both) the experience that caused the tension (syn. *catharsis*).

absolute threshold. The intensity or frequency at which a stimulus becomes effective or ceases to become effective, as measured under experimental conditions (cf. *threshold, difference threshold*).

achievement. Acquired ability, e.g., school attainment in spelling (cf. *aptitude*).

achievement motive. The social motive to accomplish something of value or importance, to meet standards of excellence in what one does.

achromatic colors. Black, white, and gray (cf. *chromatic colors*).

acquiescence. A biasing variable in personality inventories, leading some subjects to reply more frequently in the affirmative, regardless of the content of the test item (cf. *social desirability variable*).

acquisition. The stage during which a new response is learned and gradually strengthened.

adaptive behavior. Behavior that brings the organism into adjustment with its variable environment (cf. *behavior*).

additive mixture. The mixture of lights; two spotlights focused on the same spot yield additive mixture; colored sectors of paper rotated on a color wheel also yield additive mixture (cf. *subtractive mixture*).

adolescence. In human beings, the period from puberty to maturity, roughly the early teens to the early twenties (cf. *puberty, pubescence*).

adrenal gland. One of a pair of endocrine glands located above the kidneys. The medulla of the gland secretes the hormones epinephrine and norepinephrine. The cortex of the gland secretes a number of hormones, collectively called the adrenocortical hormones, which include cortisone (cf. *endocrine gland*).

adrenalin. Cf. *epinephrine*.

affective experience. An emotional experience, whether pleasant or unpleasant, mild or intense (cf. *emotional state*).

afferent nerve. A bundle of nerve fibers transmitting impulses into the central nervous system from the periphery. Receptors connect directly with afferent nerves (usually synonymous with *sensory nerve;* cf. *efferent nerve*).

affiliative motive. In man, the tendency to depend upon another person or persons, to associate with them, to form friendships or other attachments (syn. *dependency motive*).

afterimage. The sensory experience that remains when a stimulus is withdrawn. Usually refers to visual experience, e.g., the negative afterimage of a picture, or the train of colored images that results after staring at the sun.

age-mates. Other children of the same age with whom a child associates and from whom he commonly derives some of his standards (syn. *peer group*).

aggression. (1) Destructive activity of any sort. (2) Activity undertaken in order to do harm to another person either through actual physical injury or through some kind of belittling or malicious ridicule (this is the usual text usage).

agoraphobia. Fear of open places (cf. *phobic reaction*).

algorithm. A fixed routine for finding a mathematical solution, an exact procedure, as in extracting a square root. A computer commonly uses algorithmic methods, but may use other methods (cf. *heuristic method*).

ambivalence. Simultaneous liking and disliking of an object or person; the conflict caused by an incentive that is at once positive and negative (cf. *conflict*).

amnesia. The partial or total loss of memory for past experiences. The memories lost in amnesia have not been completely destroyed, for the forgotten events may again be remembered without relearning when the person recovers from his amnesia (cf. *repression*).

amphetamines. Central nervous system stimulants that produce restlessness, irritability, anxiety, and rapid heart rate. Dexedrine sulfate ("speed") and methamphetamine ("meth") are two types of amphetamines.

anal stage. The second stage according to the psychoanalytic theory of psychosexual development, following the oral stage. The sources of gratification and conflict have to do with the expulsion and retention of feces (cf. *psychosexual development*).

androgen. The collective name for male sex hormones, of which testosterone, secreted by the testes, is best known (cf. *sex glands, estrogen*).

antagonistic muscles. Muscles arranged in pairs, so that when one contracts, the other stretches, e.g., the biceps and triceps muscles of the upper arm (cf. *reciprocal innervation*).

anthropology. The science that studies chiefly nonliterate ("primitive") societies. Its main divisions are archaeology (the study of the physical monuments and remains from earlier civilizations), physical anthropology (concerned with the anatomical differences among men and their evolutionary origins), linguistic anthropology, and social anthropology (concerned with social institutions and behavior) (cf. *behavioral sciences*).

anticipation method. A method of rote memorization, appropriate to either serial memorization or paired-associate learning, in which the subject learns to respond to a stimulus item with the response item next to appear in the aperture of the memory drum. The method permits the scoring of successes and failures throughout memorization.

antisocial personality. Cf. *psychopathic personality*.

anxiety. A state of apprehension or uneasiness, related to fear. The object of anxiety (e.g., a vague danger or foreboding) is ordinarily less specific than the object of fear (e.g., a vicious animal).

anxiety reaction. A form of neurotic reaction characterized by a diffuse dread, often accompanied by tenseness, palpitation, sweating, nausea (cf. *neurotic reaction*).

apathy. Listlessness, indifference; one of the consequences of frustration (cf. *frustration*).

aphasia. Impairment or loss of ability to articulate words or to comprehend speech.

appetitive behavior. Seeking behavior (cf. *aversive behavior*).

aptitude. The capacity to learn, e.g., typing aptitude prior to practice on a typewriter. Aptitude tests are designed to predict the outcome of training, hence to predict future ability on the basis of present ability (cf. *achievement*).

area sampling. A method used in making surveys of attitudes and opinions, the respondents being selected according to their place of residence; one form of probability sampling (cf. *quota control, probability sampling*).

aroused motive. A motive that is inferred from behavior actually occurring (cf. *motivational disposition*).

artificial intelligence. The performance by a computer of tasks that have hitherto required the application of human intelligence.

association areas. Portions of the cerebral hemispheres other than the projection areas. Because their function is unknown, the assumption is made that these areas serve some sort of integrative ("association") function (cf. *intrinsic cortex*).

association psychology. A pre-experimental psychology, whose basic explanatory principle was the association of ideas (cf. *faculty psychology*).

asymptote. The stable level to which a variable tends over the course of time; e.g., in learning, the final response strength after an extended period of acquisition. The asymptote is the point at which the learning curve levels out.

attention. The focusing of perception leading to heightened awareness of a limited range of stimuli.

attitude. An orientation toward or away from some object, concept, or situation; a readiness to respond in a predetermined manner to the object, concept, or situation (cf. *attitude scale, opinion, prejudice*).

attitude scale. A scale for the quantitative appraisal of attitudes.

authoritarian personality. A personality syndrome said to be common to those whose attitudes are authoritarian instead of democratic. The syndrome is characterized by highly conventional behavior, concern over sex, superstitiousness, destructiveness, and cynicism.

autistic thinking. A form of associative thinking, controlled more by the thinker's needs or desires than by reality; wishful thinking (cf. *daydreaming, rationalization*).

autism. Absorption in fantasy to the exclusion of interest in reality; a symptom of schizophrenia.

autokinetic effect. The apparent movement of a stationary spot of light when viewed in a totally dark room.

autonomic nervous system. A system of nerve cells and nerve fibers regulating smooth muscle and glandular activities. While the system is closely integrated with the brain and spinal cord, it has some cell bodies and synapses lying outside the brain and spinal cord (syn. *vegetative nervous system;* cf. *parasympathetic division, sympathetic division*).

average. Cf. *measure of central tendency*.

aversive behavior. Avoidance behavior (cf. *appetitive behavior*).

avoidance learning. A form of learning controlled by the threat of punishment. The learning is motivated by the anxiety raised by the threat and the reduction of anxiety when the punishment is avoided (cf. *escape learning*).

axon. That portion of a neuron that transmits impulses to other neurons (cf. *neuron, dendrite*).

basal mental age. In individual tests of the Binet type, the highest age level at which, and below which, all tests are passed (cf. *mental age*).

basilar membrane. A membrane of the ear within the coils of the cochlea, supporting the organ of Corti. Movements of the basilar membrane stimulate the hair cells of the organ of Corti, producing the neural effects of auditory stimulation (cf. *cochlea, organ of Corti*).

behavior. Those activities of an organism that can be observed by another organism or by an experimenter's instruments. Included within behavior are verbal reports made about subjective, conscious experiences (cf. *conscious processes, mental activity*).

behavior therapy. A method of psychotherapy based on learning principles. It uses such techniques as counter-conditioning, reinforcement, and shaping to modify behavior.

behavioral sciences. The sciences concerned in one way or another with the behavior of man and lower organisms; especially social anthropology, psychology, and sociology, but including some aspects of biology, economics, political science, history, philosophy, and other fields of study (cf. *anthropology, psychology, sociology*).

behavioral specificity theory. The assumption, proposed by social behavior theorists, that behavior is specific to the situation in which it occurs; opposed to the notion of personality traits or types (cf. *social behavior theory, type theory, trait theory*).

behaviorism. A school or system of psychology associated with the name of John B. Watson; it defined psychology as the study of behavior and limited the data of psychology to observable activities. In its classical form it was more restrictive than the contemporary objective (behavioral) viewpoint in psychology (cf. *school of psychology*).

bimodal distribution. A frequency distribution with two points at which there are a high number of cases, hence two modes (cf. *mode*).

binocular cues. Cf. *distance cues.*

binocular disparity. Cf. *retinal disparity.*

blood pressure. The pressure of the blood against the walls of the blood vessels. Changes in blood pressure following stimulation serve as one indicator of emotion (cf. *emotional indicator*).

blood volume. The volume of the blood in a bodily member (e.g., hand, finger) due to dilation or constriction of blood vessels. Changes in volume serve as one indicator of emotion (cf. *emotional indicator*).

body-sense area. A projection area of the cerebral cortex lying behind the central fissure. Electrical stimulation of the area commonly results in the report of sensory experiences, e.g., "It feels as though I am moving my finger" (syn. *somesthetic area;* cf. *motor area*).

brain stem. The structures lying near the core of the brain; essentially all of the brain with the exception of the cerebral cortex and the cerebellum and their dependent parts.

brainwashing. Cf. *coercive persuasion.*

branching program. A teaching program often implemented by a computer in which the student's path through the instructional materials varies as a function of his performance. The student may branch rapidly through the material if his responses are generally correct, or go off to remedial loops if he encounters difficulties (cf. *linear program*).

brightness. The dimension of color that describes its nearness in brilliance to white (as contrasted with black). A bright color reflects more light than a dark one (cf. *hue, saturation*).

brightness constancy. The tendency to see a familiar object as of the same brightness, regardless of light and shadow that change its stimulus properties (cf. *color constancy, object constancy*).

Broca's speech area. A portion of the left cerebral hemisphere said to control motor speech.

CAI. A common abbreviation for computer-assisted instruction, i.e., instruction carried out under computer control.

cardiac muscle. A special kind of muscle found only in the heart (cf. *smooth muscle, striate muscle*).

case history. A biography obtained for scientific purposes; the material is sometimes supplied by interview, sometimes collected over the years.

caste. Social stratification in which boundaries are sharply defined and not to be crossed (cf. *class*).

castration. Surgical removal of the gonads; in the male, removal of the testes; in the female, removal of the ovaries.

center. A place within the nervous system where impulses in activated neurons can produce impulses in other neurons across synapses. A center contains numerous cell bodies of neurons; while most centers are within the brain and spinal cord, some lie outside (syn. *central processes;* cf. *ganglion*).

central fissure. A fissure of each cerebral hemisphere that separates the frontal and parietal lobes (syn. *fissure of Rolando*).

central nervous system. In vertebrates, the brain and spinal cord,

as distinct from the nerve trunks and their peripheral connections (cf. *autonomic nervous system*).

centralist position. A theoretical position held by certain psychologists who believe that thinking can best be explained as processes going on inside the brain or nervous system, with muscular movements as mere accompaniments or facilitators of the central processes (cf. *peripheralist position*).

cerebral cortex. The surface layer of the cerebral hemispheres in higher animals, including man. It is commonly called gray matter because its many cell bodies give it a gray appearance in cross section, in contrast with the nerve fibers that make up the white matter.

cerebral hemispheres. Two large masses of nerve cells and fibers constituting the bulk of the brain in man and other higher animals. The hemispheres are separated by a deep fissure, but connected by a broad band of fibers, the corpus callosum (syn. *cerebrum;* cf. *cerebral cortex*).

cerebrum. Cf. *cerebral hemispheres.*

chemical integration. Bodily organization for harmonious or unified action through chemical substances transmitted via the bodily fluids, especially the hormones (cf. *hormones, mechanical integration, neural integration*).

chemotherapy. The use of drugs in the treatment of mental disorders (cf. *somatotherapy*).

chlorpromazine. Cf. *tranquilizer.*

chromatic colors. All colors other than black, white, and gray, e.g., red, yellow, blue (cf. *achromatic colors*).

chromosome. Small particles found in pairs in all the cells of the body, carrying the genetic determiners (genes) that are transmitted from parent to offspring. A human cell has 46 chromosomes, arranged in 23 pairs, one member of each pair deriving from the mother, one from the father (cf. *gene*).

chronological age (C.A.). Age from birth; calendar age (cf. *mental age*).

clairvoyance. A form of extrasensory perception in which the perceiver is said to identify a stimulus that is influencing neither his own sense organs nor those of another person (cf. *extrasensory perception, telepathy, precognition*).

class. A level of social stratification, e.g., upper, middle, and lower class, but without the rigid boundaries characterizing caste, so that mobility between classes is possible (cf. *caste*).

class interval. In statistics, a small section of a scale according to which scores of a frequency distribution are grouped, e.g., heights grouped into class intervals of a half inch (cf. *frequency distribution*).

classical conditioning. Conditioned-response experiments conforming to the pattern of Pavlov's experiment. The main feature is that the originally neutral conditioned stimulus, through repeated pairing with the unconditioned one, acquires the response originally given to the unconditioned stimulus (syn. *stimulus substitution;* cf. *operant conditioning*).

claustrophobia. Fear of closed places (cf. *phobic reaction*).

client. A synonym for *patient,* the term used by counselors who wish to avoid the medical connotations of the patient-physician relationship (cf. *client-centered therapy*).

client-centered therapy. A method of psychotherapy designed to let the client learn to take responsibility for his own actions and to use his own resourcefulness in solving his problems (syn. *nondirective counseling*).

clinical psychologist. A psychologist, usually with a Ph.D. degree, whose training includes hospital and clinic experience. His techniques include testing, diagnosis, interviewing, psychotherapy, and conducting research (cf. *counseling psychologist, psychiatrist*).

cluster analysis. An analysis of trait (or item) intercorrelations, based on grouping together those traits (or items) that show similar patterns of inter-item correlation. The method is more superficial than factor analysis, for which it sometimes substitutes (cf. *factor analysis, surface trait*).

cochlea. The portion of the inner ear containing the receptors for hearing (cf. *basilar membrane, organ of Corti*).

coefficient of correlation. A numerical index used to indicate the degree of correspondence between two sets of paired measurements. The most common kind is the product-moment coefficient designated by *r*.

coercive persuasion. Influencing the thought patterns of prisoners whose lives are completely under the control of those seeking to influence them, thereby permitting kinds of influence not ordinarily possible (syn. *brainwashing*).

cognitive dissonance. The condition in which one has beliefs or knowledge that disagree with each other or with behavioral tendencies; when such cognitive dissonance arises, the subject is motivated to reduce the dissonance through changes in behavior or cognition (Festinger) (cf. *consistency theory*).

cognitive theory. A point of view contrasted with stimulus-response (S-R) theory, more concerned with "knowing" and "perceiving" than with "movement-responses" (cf. *stimulus-response psychology*).

color blindness. Defective discrimination of chromatic colors (cf. *monochromatism, dichromatism, red-green color blindness*).

color circle. An arrangement of chromatic colors around the circumference of a circle in the order in which they appear in the spectrum, but with the addition of nonspectral reds and purples. The colors are so arranged that those opposite each other are complementaries in additive mixture.

color constancy. The tendency to see a familiar object as of the same color, regardless of changes in illumination on it that alter its stimulus properties (cf. *object constancy*).

color-mixing primaries. Three hues chosen to produce the total range of hues by their additive mixture. A spectral red, green, and blue are usually selected (cf. *psychological primaries*).

comparative psychology. The study of the behavior of lower organisms in their interrelationships with one another and with man.

compensation. A form of defense mechanism by which one attempts to cover up or balance failure in, or lack of talent for, one activity by a strenuous effort to excel in either a different or an allied activity (cf. *substitution, sublimation, overcompensation*).

complementary hues. Two hues that in additive mixture yield either a gray or an unsaturated color of the hue of the stronger component.

compulsive movements. Repetitive actions that a person feels driven to make and that he is unable to resist; ritualistic behavior; a form of dissociation (cf. *dissociation*).

compulsive personality. A personality syndrome characterized by cleanliness, orderliness, and obstinacy. In the extreme, behavior becomes repetitive and ritualistic (syn. *anal character*).

concept. The properties or relationships common to a class of objects or ideas. Concepts may be of concrete things, e.g., the concept "poodle" referring to a given variety of dog, or of abstract ideas, e.g., equality, justice, number, implying relationships common to many different kinds of objects or ideas.

concurrent validity. Validity determined by the internal consistency of the parts of a test, all scores obtained at the same testing (cf. *construct validity, predictive validity*).

conditioned emotion. An emotional response acquired by conditioning, i.e., one aroused by a stimulus that did not originally evoke it (cf. *conditioning*).

conditioned response. The learned or acquired response to a conditioned stimulus, i.e., to a stimulus that did not evoke the response originally (cf. *classical conditioning, unconditioned response*).

conditioning. The process by which conditioned responses are learned (cf. *classical conditioning, operant conditioning*).

cone. In the eye, a specialized cell of the retina found predominantly in the fovea and more sparsely throughout the retina. The cones mediate both chromatic and achromatic sensations (cf. *retina, rod, fovea*).

confidence limits. In statistics, upper and lower limits derived from a sample, used in making inferences about a population; e.g., from the mean of a sample and its standard error one can determine limits which permit a statement that the probability is 95 in 100 that the population mean falls within these limits (cf. *statistical inference, statistical significance*).

conflict. The simultaneous presence of opposing or mutually exclusive impulses, desires, or tendencies.

connotative meaning. The suggestions and emotional meanings of a word or symbol, beyond its denotative meaning. Thus naked and nude both refer to an unclothed body (denotative meaning), but they have somewhat different connotations (cf. *denotative meaning, semantic differential*).

conscience. An internal recognition of standards of right and wrong by which the individual judges his own conduct (cf. *superego*).

conscious processes. Events such as perceptions, afterimages, private thoughts, and dreams, of which only the person himself is aware. They are accessible to others through verbal report or by way of inference from other behavior (syn. *experience, awareness;* cf. *unconscious processes*).

consistency theory. The theory that a person wants his beliefs and his behavior to be consistent, and if he finds them inconsistent maneuvers to reduce the discrepancy, by altering his beliefs or changing his behavior, or both. Variants of the theory are balance theory, congruity theory, and cognitive dissonance (cf. *cognitive dissonance*).

consolidation theory. The assumption that changes in the nervous system produced by learning are time dependent, and particularly vulnerable to obliteration during this consolidation period.

construct validity. Validity determined by a process of inference more complex than that involved in predicting a specific criterion. The inference is usually in hypothetical form; e.g., if this is a good measure of achievement motivation, it should relate to scores on a learning task, even though that task is not itself a measure of achievement motivation (cf. *concurrent validity, predictive validity*).

control group. In an experimental design contrasting two groups, that group not given the treatment whose effect is under study (cf. *experimental group*).

consummatory behavior. Cf. *goal activity.*

controlled association. The process in word-association experiments in which the subject is instructed to give a specific kind of associated word, e.g., one opposite to that of the stimulus word (cf. *free association*).

convergent production. In tests of intellect, producing a specified "correct" response in accordance with truth and fact (cf. *divergent production*).

conversion reaction. A form of neurotic reaction in which the symptoms are paralysis of the limbs, insensitive areas of the body (anesthesias), uncontrolled emotional outbursts, or related bodily symptoms. The presumption is that anxiety has been "converted" into a tangible symptom (syn. *hysteria;* cf. *neurotic reaction*).

coping. A method of direct problem-solving in dealing with personal problems, contrasted with defense mechanisms (q.v.).

corpus callosum. A large band of fibers (white matter) connecting the two cerebral hemispheres.

correlation. Cf. *coefficient of correlation.*

counseling psychologist. A trained psychologist, usually with a Ph.D. or Ed.D. degree, dealing with personal problems not classified as illness, such as academic, social, or vocational problems of students. His skills are similar to those of the clinical psychologist, but his work is usually in a nonmedical setting (cf. *clinical psychologist*).

counter-conditioning. The replacement of a particular response to a stimulus by the establishment of another (usually incompatible) response.

criterion. (1) A set of scores or other records against which the success of a predictive test is verified. (2) A standard selected as the goal to be achieved in a learning task, e.g., the number of runs through a maze to be made without error as an indication that the maze has been mastered.

critical flicker frequency. If the rate of alternation between light and dark phases of stimuli is increased, there comes a point at which flicker disappears and a steady light is perceived; this fusion rate is known as the critical flicker frequency (syn. *critical fusion frequency*).

critical period. A stage in development during which the organism is optimally ready to learn certain response patterns. It is closely related to the concept of maturational readiness.

critical ratio. A mean, mean difference, or coefficient of correlation, divided by its standard error. Used in tests of significance (cf. *statistical significance, t-test*).

critical scores. Scores based on experience with tests used for a given purpose, so that persons scoring below the critical level are rejected as unlikely to succeed; e.g., a critical score on a scholastic aptitude test for college students is one below which no candidate is accepted for admission.

cross-impact matrix method. A method of predicting possible future events by synthesizing the predictions made by a number of experts to take into account their interdependencies; a refinement of the Delphi method (cf. *trend analysis, Delphi method*).

cue-dependent forgetting. The proposition that forgetting is not due to the loss of information in memory, but rather that the retrieval cues necessary to locate the information in memory are lacking. Information not recalled at one time may become accessible later when appropriate retrieval cues become available (cf. *trace-dependent forgetting*).

cues to distance. Cf. *distance cues.*

culture-fair test. A type of intelligence test that has been so constructed as to minimize bias due to the differing experiences of children raised in a rural rather than an urban culture or in a lower-class rather than in a middle-class or upper-class culture (syn. *culture-free test*).

cybernetics. The study of regulatory mechanisms, such as thermostats and governors. One of the several models used in theory construction (cf. *model*).

dark adaptation. The increased sensitivity to light when the subject has been continuously in the dark or under conditions of reduced illumination (cf. *light adaptation*).

daydreaming. Reverie; free play of thought or imagination. Because of self-reference, usually a form of autistic thinking (cf. *autistic thinking*).

decibel. A unit for measuring sound intensity, which has a logarithmic relation to the amplitude.

deep structure. A term used in linguistics and psychology to refer to the intended meaning of a sentence (cf. *surface structure*).

defense mechanism. An adjustment made, often unconsciously, either through action or the avoidance of action in order to escape recognition by oneself of personal qualities or motives that might lower self-esteem or heighten anxiety (cf. *rational problem-solving*).

deindividuation. The process whereby social restraints are weakened and impulsive, aggressive, and regressive tendencies released as the person loses his individual identity, usually as the result of being part of a large group or having his identity concealed in some way, as by a mask.

delayed-response experiment. An experiment used with both animals and man as a test of memory. The subject observes the experimenter place an incentive under one of two or more containers. Then a shield is placed between the subject and the containers for a period of delay before the subject chooses the proper container. Accuracy of his choice tests his memory for the placing of the incentive.

Delphi method. A procedure for pooling the judgments of experts about new events that are likely to occur in the future in an effort to improve predictions based on trend analyses (cf. *trend analysis, cross-impact matrix method*).

delusion. False beliefs characteristic of some forms of psychotic disorder. They often take the form of delusions of grandeur or delusions of persecution (cf. *paranoid schizophrenia*).

dendrite. The specialized portion of the neuron that (together with the cell body) receives impulses from other neurons (cf. *axon*).

denial. Cf. *self-deception.*

denotative meaning. The primary meaning of a symbol, something specific to which the symbol refers or points; e.g., my street address is denotative; whether or not I live in a desirable neighborhood is a connotative meaning secondary to the address itself (cf. *connotative meaning*).

deoxyribonucleic acid (DNA). Large molecules found in the cell nucleus and primarily responsible for genetic inheritance. These molecules manufacture various forms of RNA, which are thought by some to be the chemical basis of memory (cf. *ribonucleic acid*).

dependency motive. A motive based on the need to be taken care of by someone, to gain support through affiliation (syn. *affiliative motive*).

dependent variable. The variable whose measured changes are attributed to (or correspond to) changes in the independent variable. In psychological experiments, the dependent variable is often a response to a measured stimulus (cf. *independent variable*).

depth perception. The perception of the distance of an object from the observer or the distance from front to back of a solid object (cf. *distance cues*).

descriptive statistics. Simplifying or summarizing statements about measurements made on a population. Strictly speaking, descriptive statistics should apply solely to populations, rather than to samples, but the term is used loosely for summarizing statements about samples when they are treated as populations (cf. *statistical inference*).

developmental explanation. An explanation of behavior that stresses the historical roots of present activity, focusing on accumulating experience as the individual grows and learns (cf. *interactive explanation*).

developmental psychologist. A psychologist whose research interest lies in studying the changes that occur as a function of the growth and development of the organism, in particular the relationship between early and later behavior.

deviation I.Q. An intelligence quotient (I.Q.) computed as a standard score with a mean of 100 and a standard deviation of 15 (Wechsler) or 16 (Stanford-Binet), to correspond approximately to traditional intelligence quotient (cf. *intelligence quotient*).

dichromatism. Color blindness in which either the red-green or the blue-yellow system is lacking. The red-green form is relatively common; the blue-yellow form is the rarest of all forms of color blindness (cf. *monochromatism, red-green color blindness*).

difference equation. An equation used in probabilistic treatments of learning to express the change in probability of response from one trial to the next (syn. *linear operator*).

difference threshold. The minimum difference between a pair of stimuli that can be perceived under experimental conditions (cf. *threshold, absolute threshold, just noticeable-difference*).

digital computer. A computer that performs mathematical and logical operations with information, numerical or otherwise, represented in digital form.

dimension. A scale from one extreme to another along which orderly variations occur, e.g., pitch as a dimension of tone, brightness as a dimension of light, length as a size dimension, the degree of favorableness as a dimension of attitude (cf. *scale*).

direct aggression. Aggression against the person or object producing frustration (cf. *aggression, displaced aggression*).

discrimination. (1) In perception, the detection of differences between two stimuli. (2) In conditioning, the differential response to the positive (reinforced) stimulus and to the negative (nonreinforced) stimulus (cf. *generalization*). (3) In social psychology, prejudicial treatment, as in racial discrimination.

discriminative stimulus. A stimulus that becomes an occasion for an operant response, e.g., the knock that leads one to open the door. The stimulus does not elicit the operant response in the same sense that stimulus elicits respondent behavior (cf. *operant behavior*).

disguise. Cf. *self-deception*.

displaced aggression. Aggression against a person or object other than that which was (or is) the source of frustration (cf. *direct aggression*).

displacement. In psychoanalysis, the substitution of one object for another as a source of gratification.

dissociation. A defense mechanism in which there is splitting of aspects of behavior or experience that normally would occur together. Thus dissociated movements occur without their appropriate emotional accompaniments, or dissociated thoughts occur without appropriate action (cf. *compulsive movements, defense mechanism, multiple personality*).

dissonance. (1) In music, an inharmonious combination of sounds; contrasted with consonance. (2) In social psychology, Festinger's term for a perceived inconsistency between one's own attitudes and one's behavior (cf. *cognitive dissonance*).

distance cues. (1) In vision, the monocular cues according to which the distance of objects is perceived—such as superposition of objects, perspective, light and shadow, and relative movement—and the binocular cues used in stereoscopic vision (cf. *stereoscopic vision*). (2) In audition, the corresponding cues governing perception of distance and direction, such as intensity and time differences of sound reaching the two ears (cf. *stereophonic hearing*).

divergent production. In tests of intellect (or creativity), producing one or more "possible" answers rather than a single "correct" one (cf. *convergent production*).

dizygotic twins. Twins developed from separate eggs. They are no more alike genetically than ordinary brothers and sisters and can be of the same or different sexes (syn. *fraternal twins;* cf. *monozygotic twins*).

DNA. Cf. *deoxyribonucleic acid*.

dominance. The higher status position when social rank is organized according to a dominance-submission hierarchy; commonly found in human societies and in certain animal groups.

dominant gene. A member of a gene pair, which, if present, determines that the individual will show the trait controlled by the gene, regardless of whether the other member of the pair is the same or different, that is, recessive (cf. *recessive gene*).

double blind. An experimental design, often used in drug research, in which neither the investigator nor the patients know which subjects are in the treatment and which in the nontreatment condition until the experiment has been completed.

drive. (1) An aroused condition of the organism based upon deprivation or noxious stimulation, including tissue needs, drug or hormonal conditions, and specified internal or external stimuli, as in pain (text usage). (2) Loosely, any motive (cf. *motive*).

drive-reduction principle. The principle that a motivated sequence of behavior can be best explained as moving from an aversive state of heightened tension (i.e., drive) to a goal state in which the drive is reduced. The goal of the sequence, in other words, is drive reduction.

dualism. The assumption that psychic (mental) and physical (body; brain) phenomena are both real but fundamentally different in nature.

duct gland. A gland, such as the tear gland or salivary gland, that secretes its product on the surface of the body or into the body cavities but not directly into the blood stream (cf. *endocrine gland*).

dynamometer. An instrument used in measuring strength of grip.

eardrum. The membrane at the inner end of the auditory canal, leading to the middle ear (cf. *middle ear*).

ectomorphic component. The third of the three components of physique in Sheldon's type theory. It comprises delicacy of skin, fine hair, and ultrasensitive nervous system (cf. *endomorphic component, mesomorphic component, type theory*).

educational psychologist. A psychologist whose research interest lies in the application of psychological principles to the education of children and adults in schools (cf. *school psychologist*).

EEG. Cf. *electroencephalogram.*

effector. A bodily organ activated by motor nerves; a muscle or gland (cf. *receptor*).

efferent nerve. A bundle of nerve fibers transmitting impulses from the central nervous system in the direction of the peripheral organs. Efferent nerve tracts commonly end in muscles or glands (usually synonymous with *motor nerve;* cf. *afferent nerve*).

ego. In Freud's tripartite division of the personality, that part corresponding most nearly to the perceived self, the controlling self that holds back the impulsiveness of the id in the effort to delay gratification until it can be found in socially approved ways (cf. *id, superego*).

ego involvement. Commitment to and absorption in a task so that success in it becomes important to self-esteem and failure leads to chagrin (cf. *level of aspiration*).

ego theory. The theory in psychoanalysis that stresses functions of the ego, as against almost exclusive preoccupation with libido (cf. *ego, libido theory*).

eidetic imagery. The ability to retain visual images of pictures that are almost photographic in clarity. Such images can be described in far greater detail than would be possible from memory alone.

electroconvulsive shock therapy. A form of shock treatment for mental illness in which high-voltage current is passed briefly through the head, producing temporary unconsciousness and convulsions, with the intention of alleviating depression or other symptoms (cf. *shock therapy*).

electroencephalogram (EEG). A record obtained by attaching electrodes to the scalp (or occasionally to the exposed brain) and amplifying the spontaneous electrical activity of the brain. The EEG is useful in studying some forms of mental disturbance (e.g., epilepsy) and in research on brain function.

emergency reactions. The physiological accompaniments of intense emotional excitement interpreted (by Cannon and others) as a method of preparing the organism to meet emergencies.

emotional indicator. A sign or symptom of the activity going on in an emotional state. Physiological indicators that can be continuously recorded are commonly selected for experimental purposes.

emotional state. The condition of the organism during affectively toned experience, whether mild or intense (cf. *affective experience*).

empiricism. The view that behavior is learned as a result of experience (cf. *nativism*).

encounter group. A group of individuals who meet together in an attempt to understand and improve their interpersonal communications and interactions. They may or may not have a leader who has professional training.

endocrine gland. A ductless gland, or gland of internal secretion, that discharges its products directly into the blood stream. The hormones secreted by the endocrine glands are important chemical integrators of bodily activity (cf. *duct gland, hormones*).

endomorphic component. The first of three components of physique in Sheldon's type theory. It comprises prominence of intestines and other visceral organs, including a prominent abdomen, as in the obese individual (cf. *mesomorphic component, ectomorphic component, type theory*).

envy. The emotional and motivational consequence of rivalry with another person, based on some desired characteristic or possession of that person (cf. *jealousy*).

epinephrine. One of the hormones secreted by the adrenal medulla, active in emotional excitement (syn. *adrenalin;* cf. *norepinephrine*).

equilibratory senses. The senses that give discrimination of the position of the body in space and of the movement of the body as a whole (cf. *kinesthesis, semicircular canals, vestibular sacs*).

errors of measurement. That part of the variation in a distribution of scores, or in statistics derived from them, attributable to the fallibility of the measuring instrument, errors in observation, etc. (cf. *sampling errors*).

escape learning. A form of learning controlled by actual painful stimulation. Escape from the punishment brings an end to the unpleasant or painful situation and is therefore rewarding (cf. *avoidance learning*).

ESP. Cf. *estrasensory perception.*

estrogen. The collective name for female sex hormones secreted within the ovary (syn. *ovarian hormones;* cf. *sex glands, androgen*).

estrus. The sexually receptive state in female mammals. It is a cyclical state, related to menstruation in the primates and man (syn. *heat;* cf. *menstruation*).

ethologist. One of a group of zoologists and naturalists particularly interested in kinds of behavior that are specific to a species. More of their work has been on insects, birds, and fishes than on mammals (cf. *instinct*).

evoked potential. An electrical discharge in some part of the nervous system produced by stimulation elsewhere. The measured potential is commonly based upon response averaging by a computer.

existentialism. A philosophical viewpoint emphasizing that man is not a ready-made machine, but rather that he has the freedom to make vital choices and to assume responsibility for his own existence. It emphasizes subjective experience as a sufficient criterion of truth.

existential therapy. Derived from the existentialist philosophical belief that each individual has to choose his values and decide the meaning of his life. The therapist tries to achieve an authentic, spontaneous relationship with the patient in order to help him discover his free will and make his choices.

expectation. An anticipation or prediction of future events based on past experience and present stimuli (cf. *sign learning*).

expectation-value theory. A theory of motivation and decision-making that accounts for choices on the basis of values (or utility) and the risks involved, e.g., the probability that such values will be attained.

experimental design. A plan for collecting and treating the data of a proposed experiment. The design is evolved after preliminary exploration, with the aims of economy, precision, and control, so that appropriate inferences and decisions can be made from the data.

experimental group. In an experimental design contrasting two groups, that group of subjects given the treatment whose effect is under investigation (cf. *control group*).

experimental psychologist. A psychologist whose research interest is in the laboratory study of general psychological principles as revealed in the behavior of lower organisms and man.

explicit movements. Movements easily observed and measured; overt movements (cf. *implicit movements*).

exploratory behavior. Behavior leading to inferences concerning the curiosity motive (cf. *investigatory response, locomotor response, orienting reflex*).

extinction. (1) The experimental procedure, following either classical or operant conditioning, of presenting the conditioned stimulus without the usual reinforcement. (2) The reduction in response that results from this procedure (cf. *reinforcement*).

extrasensory perception (ESP). A controversial category of experience consisting of perception not mediated by sense-organ stimulation (cf. *clairvoyance, precognition, telepathy, psychokinesis*).

extravert. One of the psychological types proposed by Jung. The extravert is more preoccupied with social life and the external world than with his inward experience (cf. *introvert, type theory*).

extrinsic motivation. The motivational control of behavior through the possibility of reward or punishment external to whatever satisfactions or annoyances reside in the behavior itself, e.g., working for a prize rather than the satisfactions in the task (cf. *intrinsic motivation*).

factor analysis. A statistical method used in test construction and in interpreting scores from batteries of tests. The method enables the investigator to compute the minimum number of determiners (factors) required to account for the intercorrelations among the scores on the tests making up the battery.

faculty psychology. A pre-experimental psychology that viewed the mind as composed of a number of separate powers or faculties, including intellect, feeling, will, and many others (cf. *association psychology*).

family therapy. Psychotherapy with the family members as a group rather than treatment of the patient alone (cf. *group therapy*).

fantasy. Daydreaming, "wool gathering," imagination; sometimes a consequence of frustration. It is used as a personality indicator in projective tests (cf. *projective tests*).

feedback. The returning to a control center of the information regarding events under its control; in psychology, the sensory return from the periphery used in the control of movement and analogous processes (cf. *cybernetics*).

feeling tone. The pleasantness or unpleasantness of an affective experience (cf. *affective experience*).

field observation. Observation of events as they occur in nature, without experimental control of behavior; e.g., studying the nest-building of birds or observing the sleeping postures of a newborn human infant (syn. *naturalistic observation*).

field properties. In Gestalt psychology, the properties of organized wholes that influence the interpretation or action of the parts. The term derives by analogy to fields of force in physics (cf. *Gestalt psychology*).

field theory. That form of Gestalt psychology associated particularly with Kurt Lewin (cf. *Gestalt psychology*).

figure-ground perception. Perceiving a pattern as foreground against a background. Patterns are commonly perceived this way even when the stimuli are ambiguous and the foreground-background relationships are reversible.

fixation. In psychoanalysis, arrested development through failure to pass beyond one of the earlier stages or to change the objects of attachment (e.g., fixated at the oral stage, or fixated upon the mother).

fixed-alternative question. A question asked on a test, an examination, or a survey, requiring the answer to be selected from alternatives provided by the questioner (syn. *multiple-choice question;* cf. *free-answer question*).

flow chart. A diagrammatic representation of the sequence of choices and actions in an activity.

forebrain. The portion of the brain evolved from the foremost of the three enlargements of the neural tube, consisting of the cerebrum, thalamus, hypothalamus, and related structures (cf. *hindbrain, midbrain*).

formal discipline. An older interpretation of transfer of learning, justifying the study of a subject not for its own sake but for the training it supposedly gives the mental faculties, e.g., studying Latin not to learn Latin but to improve judgment and reasoning (cf. *faculty psychology, transfer of learning*).

fovea. In the eye, a small area in the central part of the retina, packed with cones; in daylight, the most sensitive part of the retina for detail vision and color vision (cf. *retina, cone*).

fraternal twins. Cf. *dizygotic twins.*

free-answer question. A question asked on an examination or in a survey, requiring a reply in the form of a comment, sentence, or longer discourse (syn. *open question;* cf. *fixed-alternative question*).

free association. (1) The form of word-association experiment in which the subject gives any word he thinks of in response to the stimulus word (cf. *controlled association*). (2) In psychoanalysis, the effort to report without modification everything that comes into awareness.

frequency distribution. A set of scores assembled according to size and grouped into class intervals (cf. *class interval, normal distribution*).

frequency theory. A theory of hearing that assumes that neural impulses arising in the organ of Corti are activated by the basilar membrane of the ear in accordance with the frequency of its vibration rather than with the place of movement (cf. *place theory, traveling wave theory, volley theory*).

frontal lobe. A portion of each cerebral hemisphere, in front of the central fissure (cf. *occipital lobe, parietal lobe, temporal lobe*).

frustration. (1) As an event, the thwarting circumstances that block or interfere with goal-directed activity. (This is the usage in the text.) (2) As a state, the annoyance, confusion, or anger engendered by being thwarted, disappointed, defeated.

functional autonomy. The theory that motives may become independent of their origins, e.g., the miser may come to value money for its own sake rather than for the motive-satisfying things that originally gave it reinforcing value.

functional psychosis. A psychotic disorder of psychogenic origin without clearly defined structural change (cf. *organic psychosis*).

functionalism. Cf. *stimulus-response psychology.*

galvanic skin response (GSR). Changes in electrical conductivity of, or activity in, the skin, detected by a sensitive galvanometer. The reactions are commonly used as an emotional indicator (cf. *emotional indicator*).

ganglion (pl. *ganglia*). A collection of nerve cell bodies and synapses, constituting a center lying outside the brain and spinal cord, as in the sympathetic ganglia (cf. *center*).

gastrointestinal motility. Movements of parts of the digestive tract caused by contraction of smooth muscle; one form of emotional indicator (cf. *emotional indicator*).

gene. The unit of hereditary transmission, localized within the chromosomes. Each chromosome contains many genes. Genes are typically in pairs, one member of the pair being found in the chromosome from the father, the other in the corresponding chromosome from the mother (cf. *chromosome, dominant gene, recessive gene*).

generalization. (1) In concept formation, problem-solving, and transfer of learning, the detection by the learner of a characteristic or principle common to a class of objects, events, or problems. (2) In conditioning, the principle that once a conditioned response has been established to a given stimulus, similar stimuli will also evoke that response (cf. *gradient of generalization, discrimination*).

general aptitude. The aptitude for acquiring proficiency in many activities rather than in a special set of activities. An intelligence test is designed to measure general aptitude; a typing test is designed to measure special aptitude (cf. *special aptitude*).

general factor. (1) A general ability underlying test scores, especially in tests of intelligence, as distinct from special abilities unique to each test (Spearman). (2) A general ability with which each of the primary factors correlates (Thurstone) (cf. *factor analysis*).

genetics. That branch of biology concerned with heredity and the means by which hereditary characteristics are transmitted (cf. *population genetics*).

genital stage. In classical psychoanalysis, the final stage of psychosexual development, culminating in sexual union with a member of the opposite sex (cf. *psychosexual development*).

genotype. In genetics, the characteristics that an individual has inherited and will transmit to his descendants, whether or not he manifests these characteristics (cf. *phenotype*).

Gestalt psychology. A system of psychological theory emphasizing pattern, organization, wholes, and field properties. It permits a form of introspection known as phenomenology (cf. *behaviorism, field properties, phenomenology*).

glia cells. Supporting cells (not neurons) composing a substantial portion of brain tissue; recent speculation suggests that they may play a role in the storage of memory.

goal. (1) An end state or condition toward which the motivated behavior sequence is directed and by which the sequence is completed. (2) Loosely, the incentive (cf. *incentive*).

goal activity. The activity in the presence of the incentive that reduces the drive or in other ways completes the motivated sequence of behavior (syn. *consummatory behavior;* cf. *preparatory activity*).

gradient. (1) Any regular change correlated with a change in some dimension such as distance; often plotted as a curve (cf. *gradient of texture*). (2) A change in the tendency to respond in relation to a systematic change in distance, time interval, or other dimension of stimulation (cf. *gradient of approach, gradient of avoidance, gradient of generalization*).

gradient of approach. The increase in the strength of the tendency to move toward a positive incentive the nearer the subject is to the incentive (cf. *gradient of avoidance*).

gradient of avoidance. The increase in the strength of the tendency to withdraw from a negative incentive the nearer the subject is to the incentive (cf. *gradient of approach*).

gradient of generalization. The orderly decrease in strength of the generalized conditioned response with decreasing similarity of the stimuli used in testing to the original stimulus used in conditioning; often plotted as a curve (cf. *gradient, generalization*).

gradient of texture. If a surface is perceived visually as having substantial texture (hard, soft, smooth, rough, etc.) and if the texture has a noticeable grain, it becomes finer as the surface recedes from the viewing person, producing a gradient of texture that is important in judgments of slant and of distance (cf. *distance cues*).

grammar. The system of rules that links the deep structure of a sentence to its surface structure (cf. *surface structure, deep structure*).

graphic rating scale. One of several kinds of scales used when one person rates another. The rater records his judgment by placing a mark at some point along a printed line, one end of which indicates the lowest degree of the trait, and the other, the highest degree (cf. *rating scale*).

group test. A test administered to several people at once by a single tester. A college examination is usually a group test (cf. *individual test*).

group therapy. A group discussion or other group activity with a therapeutic purpose participated in by more than one client or patient at a time (cf. *psychotherapy*).

GSR. Cf. *galvanic skin response.*

habit. A learned stimulus-response sequence (cf. *conditioned response, sensorimotor task*).

hallucination. A sense experience in the absence of appropriate external stimuli; a misinterpretation of imaginary experiences as actual perceptions (cf. *illusion, schizophrenic reaction*).

halo effect. The tendency to rate an individual improperly as high or low on a wide range of traits because we have prior information that he is high or low on one or a few of these traits.

hedonism. The theory that man seeks pleasure and avoids pain; an extreme form of the theory (in philosophy) is that pleasure or happiness is the highest good.

hertz (Hz). The wave frequency of a sound source measured in cycles per second.

heterosexuality. Interest in or attachment to a member of the opposite sex; the normal adult outcome of psychosexual development.

heuristic method. A nonrigorous method for discovering the correct solution to a problem through obtaining approximations to the correct answer, through using analogies and other methods of search, without the painstaking exploration of all possibilities. Computing machines can be programed to use such methods (cf. *algorithm*).

hindbrain. The portion of the brain evolved from the final one of the three enlargements of the primitive neural tube, consisting of the cerebellum, the medulla, and related structures (cf. *forebrain, midbrain*).

homeostasis. An optimal level of organic function, maintained by regulatory mechanisms known as homeostatic mechanisms, e.g., the mechanisms maintaining a uniform body temperature (cf. *homeostat*).

homeostat. A particular portion of the brain that regulates the equilibrium point of some bodily system, analogous to the regulation of temperature by a thermostat (cf. *homeostasis*).

homosexuality. (1) The adoption in adult life of the cultural role appropriate to a member of the opposite sex. (2) Engaging in sexual relations with a member of the same sex.

hormones. The internal secretions of the endocrine glands that are distributed via the blood stream and affect behavior (cf. *chemical integration, endocrine gland*).

hue. The dimension of color from which the major color names are derived (red, yellow, green, etc.), corresponding to wavelength of light (cf. *brightness, saturation*).

human factors research. An applied science participated in jointly by engineers and psychologists, concerned with the design of equipment and the arrangement of work conditions to provide the most effective combination of man and machine (syn. *applied experimental psychology, biomechanics, human engineering*).

hunger drive. A drive based on food deprivation (cf. *drive, hunger pangs, specific hunger*).

hunger pangs. The twinges of pain experienced during stomach contractions.

hypnotic trance. The dreamlike state of heightened suggestibility induced in a subject by a hypnotist (cf. *post-hypnotic suggestion*).

hypnotism. The process of inducing the hypnotic trance (syn. *hypnosis*).

hypothalamus. One of the structures at the base of the brain, portions of which are significant in sleep and in emotional and motivational behavior.

hypothetical construct. One form of inferred intermediate mechanism. The construct is conceived of as having properties of its own, other than those specifically required for the explanation, e.g., the memory trace, which is inferred to explain the retention curve, is assumed to have electrochemical properties, localization in the nervous system, etc. (cf. *intervening variable*).

Hz. Cf. *hertz.*

id. In Freud's tripartite division of the personality, that part reflecting unorganized, instinctual impulses. If unbridled, it seeks immediate gratification of primitive needs (cf. *ego, superego*).

identical twins. Cf. *monozygotic twins.*

identification. (1) The normal process of acquiring appropriate social roles in childhood through copying, in part unconsciously, the behavior of significant adults, e.g., the child's identification with his like-sexed parent (cf. *imitation*). (2) Close affiliation with others of like interest, e.g., identifying with a group.

identification figures. Adult models (especially parents) copied, partly unconsciously, by the child (cf. *identification*).

identity formation. The process of achieving adult personality integration, as an outgrowth of earlier identifications and other influences (cf. *identification, role diffusion*).

illusion. In perception, a misinterpretation of the relationships among presented stimuli, so that what is perceived does not correspond to physical reality; especially, but not exclusively, an optical or visual illusion (cf. *delusion, hallucination*).

imitation. Behavior that is modeled upon or copies that of another (cf. *identification*).

immediate memory span. The number of items (digits, letters, words, etc.) that can be repeated after a single presentation.

implicit movements. Movements that can be detected only with sensitive measuring instruments; covert movements (cf. *explicit movements*).

imprinting. A term used by ethologists for a species-specific type of learning that occurs within a limited period of time early in the life of the organism and is relatively unmodifiable thereafter; e.g., young ducklings learn to follow one adult female (usually the mother) within 11 to 18 hours after birth. But whatever object they are given to follow at this time they will thereafter continue to follow (cf. *ethologist*).

incentive. (1) A tangible goal object that provides the stimuli that lead to goal activity. (2) Loosely, any goal (cf. *goal*).

independent variable. The variable under experimental control with which the changes studied in the experiment are correlated. In psychological experiments, the independent variable is often a stimulus, responses to which are the dependent variables under investigation (cf. *dependent variable*).

individual differences. Relatively persistent unlikenesses in structure or behavior between persons or members of the same species.

individual test. A test designed to be administered to one person at a time. Binet intelligence tests are individual tests (cf. *group test*).

infancy. The period of helplessness and dependency in man and other organisms; in man, roughly the first two years (cf. *childhood, adolescence*).

information-processing model. A model based on assumptions regarding the flow of information through a system; usually best realized by a computer program.

in-group. A group to which a person belongs and with which he identifies himself (cf. *out-group*).

inner ear. The internal portion of the ear containing, in addition to the cochlea, the vestibular sacs and the semicircular canals (cf. *cochlea, semicircular canals, vestibular sacs*).

insight. (1) In problem-solving experiments, the perception of relationships leading to solution. Such a solution can be repeated promptly when the problem is again confronted. (2) In psychotherapy, the discovery by the subject of dynamic connections between earlier and later events, so that he comes to recognize the roots of his conflicts.

instinct. The name given to unlearned, patterned, goal-directed behavior, which is species-specific, as illustrated by nest-building in birds or by the migration of salmon.

insulin. The hormone secreted by the pancreas (cf. *hormones, insulin shock*).

insulin shock. A state of coma resulting from reduced blood sugar when insulin is present in excessive amounts. Insulin shock is used as one form of shock therapy in treating mental illness (cf. *shock therapy*).

integration. The organization of parts into a harmoniously operating whole, as in the expression "integrated personality" (cf. *chemical integration, mechanical integration, neural integration*).

intelligence. (1) That which a properly standardized intelligence test measures. (2) According to Binet, the characteristics of an individual's thought processes that enable him to take and maintain a direction without becoming distracted, to adapt means to ends, and to criticize his own attempts at problem solution (cf. *mental age*).

intelligence quotient (I.Q.). A scale unit used in reporting intelligence test scores, based on the ratio between mental age and chronological age. The decimal point is omitted, so that the average I.Q. for children of any one chronological age is set at 100 (cf. *chronological age, mental age, deviation I.Q.*).

intensity. One of the dimensions of sensory experience; a quantitative measure of strength or degree, e.g., a bright light has a high intensity, a soft tone a low intensity. A change in intensity is distinguished from a change in quality, which is a change in kind (cf. *dimension, quality, quantity*).

interactive explanation. An explanation of behavior that deals with the arousal and control of behavior in the present, according to stimuli that are currently responded to, motives that are active, and possibilities of response that are open; nonhistorical explanation (cf. *developmental explanation*).

interest. A persisting tendency to pay attention to and enjoy some activity or content, especially a vocational interest.

intermittent reinforcement. Cf. *partial reinforcement.*

interpretation. In psychoanalysis, the analyst's calling attention to the patient's resistances in order to facilitate the flow of associations; also his explanation of symbols, as in dream interpretation (cf. *resistance*).

intervening variable. A process inferred to occur between stimulus and response, thus accounting for one response rather than another to the same stimulus. The intervening variable may be inferred without further specification, or it may be given concrete properties and become an object of investigation.

interview. A conversation between an investigator (the interviewer) and a subject (the respondent) used for gathering pertinent data either for the subject's benefit (as in the psychotherapeutic interview) or for information-gathering (as in a sample survey).

intracerebral processes. Inferred processes in the brain used to account for response classes including perceptions, images, and thoughts that are incompletely specified in terms of movement (cf. *intervening variable*).

intrinsic cortex. Term used by Pribram for the so-called association areas, on the assumption that they have integrative functions in handling complex activities but that this handling does not necessarily involve learned associative links (cf. *association areas*).

intrinsic motivation. Motivation in which the action and the ends served by the action are organically or inherently related, as distinct from action motivated by promise of reward or threat of punishment, e.g., assembling a model airplane in order to fly it, composing a sonnet to give expression to a mood (cf. *extrinsic motivation*).

introspection. (1) A specified form of introspection (trained introspection) describing mental content only, without the intrusion of meanings or interpretations. (2) Any form of reporting on subjective (conscious) events or experiences (cf. *phenomenology*).

introvert. One of the psychological types proposed by Jung, referring to the individual who, especially in time of emotional stress, tends to withdraw into himself and to avoid other people (cf. *extravert, type theory*).

investigatory response. The form of exploratory behavior that involves the manipulation of an unfamiliar object, picking it up, tearing it apart, etc. (Berlyne) (cf. *exploratory behavior, locomotor exploration*).

item. Any single unit of test or experimental materials, e.g., a single question in a test composed of many questions or a single nonsense syllable in a list of syllables to be memorized (cf. *test, test battery*).

James-Lange theory. A classical theory of emotion, named for the two men who independently proposed it. The theory states that the stimulus first leads to motor responses, and then the awareness of these responses constitutes the experience of emotion.

jealousy. A special form of anxiety arising from fear of loss of a loved one's affection to a rival, with both emotional and motivational consequences (cf. *envy*).

j.n.d. Cf. *just noticeable difference.*

just noticeable difference (j.n.d.). A barely perceptible physical change in a stimulus; a measure of the difference threshold. The term is used also as a unit for scaling the steps of sensation corresponding to increase in the magnitude of stimulation (cf. *difference threshold*).

kinesthesis. The muscle, tendon, and joint senses, yielding discrimination of position and movement of parts of the body (cf. *equilibratory senses*).

latency. (1) A measure of response, referring to the delay between the occurrence of the stimulus and the onset of the response. (2) In psychoanalysis, a period in middle childhood, roughly the years from six to twelve, when both sexual and aggressive impulses are said to be in a somewhat subdued state, so that the child's attention is directed outward, and his curiosity about the environment makes him ready to learn (cf. *psychosexual development*).

latent content. The underlying significance of a dream, e.g., the motives or wishes being expressed by it, as interpreted from the manifest content (cf. *interpretation, manifest content*).

latent-learning experiment. A type of experiment in which opportunity for learning spatial relationships is given under conditions of inappropriate drive or absent incentive; e.g., a rat is permitted to explore a maze without food in the goal box. The learning is later tested under changed drive-incentive conditions. The experiment, when successful, is used to support the sign learning theory (cf. *sign learning*).

lateral fissure. A deep fissure at the side of each cerebral hemisphere, below which lies the temporal lobe (syn. *fissure of Sylvius*).

law of effect. Thorndike's principle that the consequences of an activity determine whether or not it will be learned. In its later forms stress was placed on the influence of reward. Hence learning under the law of effect is virtually synonymous with operant conditioning (q.v.).

learning. A relatively permanent change in behavior that occurs as the result of practice. Behavior changes due to maturation or temporary conditions of the organism (e.g., fatigue, the influence of drugs, adaptation) are not included.

learning curve. A graph plotting the course of learning, in which the vertical axis (ordinate) plots a measure of proficiency (amount per unit time, time per unit amount, errors made, etc.), while the horizontal axis (abscissa) represents some measure of practice (trials, time, etc.).

learning set. A case in which an animal's rate of learning gradually improves over a series of problems of the same general type; in essence, the phenomenon of learning to learn.

level of aspiration. A goal that the individual sets as something he expects to achieve or strives to achieve. Reaching the goal is interpreted by him as success, falling short as failure (cf. *achievement motive*).

libido theory. The theory within psychoanalysis that human development and motivation are best understood by studying the manifestations of the libido—the energy of the sexual instinct—which throughout life becomes attached to new objects and expressed through various types of motivated behavior (cf. *ego theory*).

lie detector. An apparatus using one or more of the emotional indicators in order to determine guilt of a subject through his emotional responses while answering questions in a false or unintentionally revealing manner (cf. *emotional indicator*).

light adaptation. The decreased sensitivity of the eye to light when the subject has been continuously exposed to high levels of illumination (cf. *dark adaptation*).

limbic system. A set of structures in and around the midbrain, forming a functional unit regulating motivational-emotional types of behavior, such as waking and sleeping, excitement and quiescence, feeding, and mating.

linear operator. Cf. *difference equation.*

linear program. A teaching program in which the student progresses along a fixed track from one instructional frame to the next. After responding to a frame he moves to the next frame regardless of whether his answer is correct (cf. *branching program*).

linguistics. The investigation of problems of language; linguistics has also been a branch of anthropology, but psychologists have been participating increasingly in studies of language (syn. *psycholinguistics*).

localized functions. Behavior controlled by known areas of the brain; e.g., vision is localized in the occipital lobes (cf. *projection area*).

location constancy. The tendency to perceive the place at which a resting object is located as remaining the same even though the relationship to the observer has changed (cf. *object constancy*).

locomotor exploration. That form of exploratory behavior that consists of running about, inspecting the environment (Berlyne) (cf. *exploratory behavior, investigatory response*).

longitudinal study. A research method that studies an individual through time, taking measurements at periodic intervals.

long-term memory (LTM). The relatively permanent component of the memory system, as opposed to short-term memory (q.v.).

loudness. An intensity dimension of hearing correlated with the amplitude of the sound waves that constitute the stimulus. Greater amplitudes yield greater loudnesses (cf. *pitch, timbre*).

LSD-25. Cf. *lysergic acid derivatives.*

LTM. Cf. *long-term memory.*

lysergic acid derivatives. Chemical substances derived from lysergic acid, the most important of which is LSD-25. When taken by a normal person, it produces symptoms similar in some respects to those of the schizophrenic reaction (cf. *schizophrenic reaction*).

manic-depressive reaction. A psychotic reaction characterized by mood swings from the normal in the direction either of excitement and elation (manic phase) or of fatigue, despondency, and sadness (depressive phase). Many patients do not show the whole cycle.

manifest content. The remembered content of a dream, the characters and their actions, as distinguished from the inferred latent content (cf. *latent content*).

marijuana. The dried leaves of the hemp plant; also known as hashish, "pot," or "grass." Intake may enhance sensory experiences and produce a state of euphoria.

masochism. A pathological desire to inflict pain upon oneself or to suffer pain at the hands of others (cf. *sadism*).

mass media. The instruments of communication that reach large numbers of people simultaneously, including the press, radio, television, and motion pictures.

massed practice. Practice in which trials are continuous or closely spaced (cf. *spaced practice*).

maternal drive. The drive, particularly in animals, induced in the female through bearing and nursing young, leading to nest-building, retrieving, and other forms of care (cf. *drive*).

mathematical model. A model of a phenomenon formulated in mathematical terms (cf. *model*).

maturation. Growth processes in the individual that result in orderly changes in behavior, whose timing and patterning are relatively independent of exercise or experience though they may require a normal environment (cf. *training*).

maze. A device commonly used in the study of animal and human learning, consisting of a correct path and blind alleys.

mean. The arithmetical average; the sum of all scores divided by their number (cf. *measure of central tendency*).

mean deviation. The average amount by which each score departs from the mean of all the scores (cf. *measure of variation*).

measure of central tendency. A value representative of a frequency distribution, around which other values are dispersed, e.g., the mean, median, or mode of a distribution of scores (syn. *average*).

measure of response. A quantitative index of response strength, such as amplitude, latency, probability, and rate of response.

measure of variation. A measure of the dispersion or spread of scores in a frequency distribution, e.g., the range, the mean deviation, the standard deviation (q.v.).

mechanical integration. Bodily organization for harmonious action through the mechanical arrangements of bones, joints, and muscles (cf. *chemical integration, neural integration*).

median. The score of the middle case when cases are arranged in order of size of score (cf. *measure of central tendency*).

membership group. A social group to which an individual belongs (cf. *reference group*).

memory drum. A mechanical device used to present verbal materials in rote-learning experiments.

memory trace. The inferred change in the nervous system that persists between the time that something is learned and the time that it is recalled.

menarche. The first menstrual period, indicative of sexual maturation in a girl (cf. *menstruation*).

menstruation. The approximately monthly discharge from the uterus (cf. *menarche*).

mental activity. The kinds of processes, whether in observed behavior, subjective experience, or inferences from these, used as indications of mentality (cf. *behavior*).

mental age (M.A.). A scale unit proposed by Binet for use in intelligence testing. If an intelligence test is properly standardized, a representative group of children of age six should earn an average mental age of six, those of age seven, a mental age of seven, etc. A child whose M.A. is above his chronological age (C.A.) is advanced; one whose M.A. lags behind is retarded (cf. *chronological age, intelligence quotient*).

mental health. Absence of mental illness; more positively, a state characterized by adjustment, a productive orientation, and zest (cf. *mental illness*).

mental illness. Emotional, motivational, and social maladjustment severe enough to interfere with the ordinary conduct of life (cf. *mental health, neurotic reaction, psychotic disorder*).

mentally defective. A descriptive term applied to a mentally subnormal individual whose deficiency is based on some sort of brain damage or organic defect (cf. *mentally retarded*).

mentally gifted. An individual with an unusually high level of intelligence, commonly an I.Q. of 140 or above.

mentally retarded. A mentally subnormal individual whose problems lie in a learning disability with no evident organic damage (cf. *mentally defective*).

mentally subnormal. An individual whose intelligence is below that necessary for adjustment to ordinary schooling; the more intelligent among the subnormal are classified as *educable* in special classes, the next level as *trainable,* while the lowest group classifies as more severely retarded (syn., but now obsolete, *feeble-minded;* cf. **mentally defective, mentally retarded**).

mesomorphic component. The second of three components of physique in Sheldon's type theory. Refers to the prominence of bone and muscle, as in the typical athlete (cf. **endomorphic component, ectomorphic component, type theory**).

midbrain. The second of the three enlargements of the neural tube, upon which later structures of the brain have evolved. The midbrain in the fish consists chiefly of the optic lobes ("eye brain"); in man this portion has not been greatly increased in relative size, the most pronounced evolutionary changes having taken place in the forebrain (cf. **forebrain, hindbrain**).

middle ear. The portion of the ear containing the hammer, anvil, and stirrup bones, which connect the eardrum to the oval window of the inner ear.

mirror drawing. A laboratory learning task in which the skill under study is that of tracing the contour of a star or other figure while viewing it in a mirror.

mnemonics. A system for improving memory often involving a set of symbols that can substitute for the material to be remembered. For example, in attempting to remember a number sequence one may translate the sequence into letters of the alphabet that in turn approximate words that are easily remembered.

modality. A separate sense or sensory department, e.g., vision, audition. Experiences within a single modality can be arranged along continuous dimensions, with intermediate values. There is no simple way of moving across from one modality to another, e.g., to find the experience lying midway between a given odor and a given color.

mode. The most frequent score in a distribution, or the class interval in which the greatest number of cases fall (cf. **measure of central tendency**).

model. Miniature systems are often constructed according to a logical, mathematical, or physical model. That is, the principles according to which data are organized and made understandable parallel those of the model; e.g., the piano keyboard is a model for understanding the basilar membrane; the speed-regulating governor is a model for the feedback principle of cybernetics.

monochromatism. Total color blindness, the visual system being achromatic. A rare disorder (cf. **dichromatism**).

monocular cues. Cf. **distance cues.**

monozygotic twins. Twins developed from a single egg. They are always of the same sex and commonly much alike in appearance, although some characteristics may be in mirror-image, e.g., one right-handed, the other left-handed (syn. *identical twins;* cf. **dizygotic twins**).

mood. A state of emotional susceptibility, enduring for some minutes or hours, in which most of the person's emotional responses tend to be similar, e.g., cheerful mood, morose mood (cf. **temperament**).

morpheme. The smallest meaningful unit in the structure of a language, whether a word, base, or affix; examples—*man, strange, ing, pro* (cf. **phoneme**).

motivated forgetting. The theory that forgetting can be explained according to the motives of the learner (cf. **repression**).

motivation. A general term referring to the regulation of need-satisfying and goal-seeking behavior (cf. **motive**).

motivational disposition. A persistent tendency to the arousal of a specific motive; the tendency exists even though the motive is not being expressed. Most classifications of motives refer to motivational dispositions (cf. **aroused motive**).

motivational sequence. A sequence of behavior that begins with a motive, continues in preparatory or goal-directed activity, and ends in goal activity in the presence of an incentive.

motive. Any condition of the organism that affects its readiness to start upon or continue in a sequence of behavior (cf. **motivational sequence, physiological motive, social motive**).

motor area. A projection area in the brain lying in front of the central fissure. Electrical stimulation commonly results in motor responses (cf. **body-sense area**).

multimodal distribution. A distribution curve with more than one mode (cf. **mode**).

multiple personality. An extreme form of dissociation in which the individual's personality is split into separate personalities often alternating with each other. The memories of one of the split-off personalities commonly are not accessible to the other (cf. **dissociation**).

multiple-response learning. The acquiring of patterns or sequences of responses in mastering a task, e.g., in learning a skill or memorizing a poem (cf. **sensorimotor task, rote memorization**).

muscle. The effectors through which motion is produced. Muscles are of three types: smooth muscle, striate muscle, and cardiac muscle (q.v.).

muscle tone. A state of slight contraction that keeps muscle in a readiness to respond. A tense person may have an exaggeration of muscle tone (syn. *muscle tonus*).

myelin. The fatty sheath surrounding certain nerve fibers known as myelinated fibers. Impulses travel faster and with less energy expenditure in myelinated fibers than in unmyelinated fibers.

narcissism. Self-love; in psychoanalytic theory, the normal expression of pregenital development (cf. **pregenital stages**).

nativism. The view that behavior is innately determined (cf. **empiricism.**).

naturalistic observation. Cf. **field observation.**

nature-nurture issue. The problem of determining the relative importance of the hereditary component (nature) and the result of up-bringing in the particular environment (nurture) upon mature ability; such a determination is especially important in relation to intelligence.

need. A physical state involving any lack or deficit within the organism. (cf. **motive, drive**).

negative incentive. An object or circumstance away from which behavior is directed when the object or circumstance is perceived or anticipated (cf. **positive incentive**).

negativism. A type of defiant behavior in which there is active refusal to carry out requests. Common in early childhood but met occasionally at all ages (syn. *negativistic behavior*).

nerve cell. Cf. **neuron.**

nerve net. A nervous system characteristic of lower organisms, in which impulses are transmitted in all directions from the point of stimulation (cf. **synaptic nervous system**).

neural integration. Bodily organization for harmonious or unified action through the brain and nervous system (cf. **chemical integration, mechanical integration**).

neural quantum theory. A theory of psychophysical phenomena that views the sensory system as a discrete, step-wise process.

neuron. The nerve cell; the unit of a synaptic nervous system.

Man's brain contains billions of neurons (cf. *polarized synaptic transmission*).

neurosis. Cf. *neurotic reaction.*

neurotic reaction. A form of maladjustment in which the individual is unable to cope with his anxieties and conflicts and develops abnormal symptoms. The disturbance is not so severe as to produce a profound personality derangement, as with the psychotic reactions (syn. *psychoneurosis, neurosis;* cf. *anxiety reaction, conversion reaction, phobic reaction, obsessive-compulsive reaction*).

nonliterate society. A society or culture without written records, formerly called a primitive society (cf. *anthropology*).

nonparametric statistics. Statistics computed without the assumption of an underlying distribution of known form. The formulas of nonparametric statistics commonly make use of ranked data, as in rank-difference correlation (syn. *distribution-free statistics*).

nonsense syllable. An item used in rote memorization experiments, usually consisting of two consonants with a vowel between, e.g., PUV, GEB. The combination of letters must not form a word in familiar languages.

noradrenalin. Cf. *norepinephrine.*

norepinephrine. One of the hormones secreted by the adrenal medulla. Its action is in some, but not all respects, similar to that of epinephrine (syn. *noradrenalin;* cf. *epinephrine*).

norm. An average, common, or standard performance under specified conditions, e.g., the average achievement test score of nine-year-old children or the average birth weight of male children (cf. *test standardization*).

normal curve. The plotted form of the normal distribution (q.v.).

normal distribution. The standard symmetrical bell-shaped frequency distribution, whose properties are commonly used in making statistical inferences from measures derived from samples (cf. *normal curve*).

null hypothesis. A statistical hypothesis that any difference observed among treatment conditions occurs by chance and does not reflect a true difference. Rejection of the null hypothesis means that we believe the treatment conditions are actually having an effect.

nystagmus. Involuntary eye movements characterized by slow and quick phases in opposite directions; one of the consequences of bodily rotation.

object achievement. Perceiving an object as enduring and permanent, e.g., when the subject recognizes the object he now sees as the same object he saw before (cf. *object constancy*).

object constancy. The tendency to see objects as relatively unchanged under widely altered conditions of illumination, distance, and position (cf. *color constancy, location constancy, shape constancy, size constancy*).

object size. The size of an object as determined from measurement at its surface. When size constancy holds, the observer perceives a distant object as being near its object size (cf. *perspective size, size constancy*).

objective science. A science whose data are open to observation by any competent observer, as in the physical and biological sciences. Behaviorism sought to eliminate subjectivity from psychology, hence to make it an objective science (cf. *subjective science*).

objective scoring. Scoring done according to a code so that all competent scorers arrive at the same score for the same test, e.g., the scoring of fixed-alternative (multiple-choice) questions (cf. *subjective scoring*).

obsessive-compulsive reaction. A neurotic reaction taking one of three forms: (1) recurrent thoughts, often disturbing and unwelcome (obsessions); (2) irresistible urges to repeat stereotyped or ritualistic acts (compulsions); (3) both of these in combination (cf. *neurotic reaction*).

occipital lobe. A portion of the cerebral hemisphere, behind the parietal and temporal lobes (cf. *frontal lobe, parietal lobe, temporal lobe*).

occupational therapy. A form of help to a patient suffering from personality maladjustment or mental illness, whereby he is kept busy in constructive work.

Oedipal stage. In psychoanalysis, an alternative designation of the phallic stage of psychosexual development, because it is at this stage that the Oedipus complex arises (cf. *psychosexual development, Oedipus complex*).

Oedipus complex. In psychoanalytic theory, sexual attachment to the parent of the opposite sex, originating as the normal culmination of the infantile period of development.

open words. In the development of children's language, words that occur less frequently than pivot words and may stand alone or in combination with pivot words to form two-word sentences (cf. *pivot words*).

operant behavior. Behavior defined by the stimulus to which it leads rather than by the stimulus that elicits it; e.g., behavior leading to reward (syn. *emitted behavior, or instrumental behavior;* cf. *respondent behavior, voluntary action*).

operant conditioning. The strengthening of an operant response by presenting a reinforcing stimulus if, and only if, the response occurs (syn. *instrumental conditioning, reward learning;* cf. *classical conditioning*).

opinion. A judgment or belief involving an expectation or prediction about behavior or events (cf. *attitude*).

opponent-process theory. The theory that human color vision depends upon three pairs of opposing processes: white-black, yellow-blue, and red-green.

oral behavior. Behavior deriving from the infant's need to suck or, more generally, to be fed through the mouth.

oral stage. In psychoanalysis, the first of the stages of psychosexual development, in which pleasure is derived from the lips and mouth, as in sucking at the mother's breast (cf. *psychosexual development*).

organ of Corti. In the ear, the actual receptor for hearing, lying on the basilar membrane in the cochlea and containing the hair cells where the fibers of the auditory nerve originate (cf. *basilar membrane, cochlea*).

organic motive. Cf. *physiological motive.*

organic psychosis. A psychotic disorder caused by disease, injury, drugs, or other definable structural change (cf. *functional psychosis, psychotic disorder*).

organism. In biology, any form of plant or animal life. In psychology, the word is used to refer to the living individual animal, whether human or subhuman.

orienting reflex. (1) A nonspecific response to change in stimulation involving depression of cortical alpha rhythm, galvanic skin response, pupillary dilation, and complex vasomotor responses (a term introduced by Russian psychologists). (2) Head or body movements that orient the organism's receptors to those parts of the environment in which stimulus changes are occurring.

otoliths. "Ear stones" (cf. *vestibular sacs*).

out-group. Persons outside the in-group, especially if they belong to a group with which the in-group is in conflict (cf. *in-group*).

ovarian hormones. Cf. *estrogen.*

overcompensation. A form of compensation in which extreme effort is made to overcome feelings of weakness or inferiority by excelling where one is weakest. Thus a sickly youngster may try to become an athlete or a professional dancer (cf. *compensation*).

overlearning. Any learning beyond bare mastery.

overtone. A higher frequency tone, a multiple of the fundamental frequency, which occurs when a tone is sounded by a musical instrument (cf. *timbre*).

pain drive. The drive aroused by noxious stimulation, revealed by agitated behavior or behavior directed toward removing or escaping from the painful stimulus (cf. *drive*).

paired-associate learning. The learning of stimulus-response pairs, as in the acquisition of a foreign language vocabulary. When the first member of a pair (the stimulus) is presented, the subject's task is to give the second member (the response).

pancreas. A bodily organ situated near the stomach. As a duct gland it secretes pancreatic juice into the intestines, but some specialized cells function as an endocrine gland, secreting the hormone insulin into the blood stream (cf. *endocrine gland*).

parameter. Any of the constants in a function that defines the form of the curve. It ordinarily differs when experimental conditions or subjects are changed.

paranoid schizophrenia. A schizophrenic reaction in which the patient has delusions of persecution (cf. *schizophrenic reaction*).

parasympathetic division. A division of the autonomic nervous system, nerve fibers of which originate in the cranial and sacral portions of the spinal cord. Active in relaxed or quiescent states of the body, and to some extent antagonistic to the sympathetic division (q.v.).

parathyroid glands. Endocrine glands adjacent to the thyroid gland in the neck, whose hormones regulate calcium metabolism, thus maintaining the normal excitability of the nervous system. Parathyroid inadequacy leads to tetany (cf. *endocrine gland, tetany*).

parietal lobe. A portion of the cerebral hemisphere, behind the central fissure and between the frontal and occipital lobes (cf. *frontal lobe, occipital lobe, temporal lobe*).

partial reinforcement. Reinforcing a given response only some proportion of the times it occurs (syn. *intermittent reinforcement*).

passive decay. A theory of forgetting that implies that the memory trace fades with disuse (cf. *memory trace*).

percentile scale. Cf. *centile scale.*

perception. The process of becoming aware of objects, qualities, or relations by way of the sense organs. While sensory content is always present in perception, what is perceived is influenced by set and prior experience, so that perception is more than a passive registration of stimuli impinging on the sense organs.

perceptual patterning. The tendency to perceive stimuli according to principles such as proximity, similarity, continuity, and closure. Emphasized by Gestalt psychologists (cf. *figure-ground perception*).

performance. Overt behavior, as distinguished from knowledge or information not translated into action. The distinction is important in theories of learning.

peripheralist position. A view held by some psychologists that all thinking goes on in action (in speech or other movements) (cf. *centralist position*).

personality. The individual characteristics and ways of behaving that, in their organization or patterning, account for an individual's unique adjustments to his total environment (syn. *individuality*).

personality assessment. (1) Generally, appraisal of personality by any method. (2) More specifically, personality appraisal through complex observations and judgments, usually based in part upon behavior in contrived social situations.

personality dynamics. Theories of personality that stress personality dynamics are concerned with the interactive aspects of behavior (as in conflict resolution), with value hierarchies, with the permeability of boundaries between differentiated aspects of personality, etc. Contrasted with developmental theories, though not incompatible with them (cf. *interactive explanation*).

personality inventory. An inventory for self-appraisal, consisting of many statements or questions about personal characteristics and behavior that the person judges to apply or not to apply to him (cf. *projective test*).

personality structure. The inferred unifying pattern underlying individual ways of behaving, giving consistency to otherwise contradictory traits and meaning to otherwise inexplicable mannerisms and eccentricities.

perspective size. The size of an object according to the geometry of perspective, i.e., its size diminishes directly in proportion to its distance (cf. *object size, size constancy*).

phallic stage. In psychoanalysis, that stage of psychosexual development in which gratification is associated with sex organ stimulation and the sexual attachment is to the parent of the opposite sex (cf. *Oedipal stage, psychosexual development*).

phenomenology. Naive report on conscious experience, as by a child, as contrasted with trained introspection; the study of unanalyzed experience (cf. *Gestalt psychology*).

phenotype. In genetics, the characteristics that are displayed by the individual organism, e.g., eye color, intelligence, as distinct from those traits that he may carry genetically but not display (cf. *genotype*).

phi phenomenon. Stroboscopic motion in its simpler form. Commonly produced by successively turning on and off two separated stationary light sources; as the first is turned off and the second turned on, the subject perceives a spot of light moving from the position of the first to that of the second (cf. *stroboscopic motion*).

phobic reaction. Excessive fear in the absence of real danger (cf. *agoraphobia, claustrophobia, neurotic reaction*).

phoneme. The smallest unit in the sound system of a language; it serves to distinguish utterances from one another (cf. *morpheme*).

phrase structure. The analysis of a sentence in terms of its component phrases, e.g., noun phrase, verb phrase, article (cf. *deep structure, surface structure*).

physical sciences. Those sciences, such as astronomy, chemistry, mineralogy, and physics, dealing chiefly with laws and relationships derived from study of the inanimate world, rather that with laws and relationships peculiar to living things.

physiological motive. A motive based upon an evident bodily need, such as the need for food or water (syn. *organic motive;* cf. *social motive*).

physiological psychology. That branch of experimental psychology concerned with the relationship between physiological functions and behavior.

physiology. That branch of biology concerned primarily with the functioning of organ systems within the body.

pilomotor response. The response of muscles in the skin in which the hairs stand on end, giving a roughened appearance to the skin known as "goose flesh" or "goose pimples." May result either from cold or as part of an emotional state (cf. *emotional indicator*).

pitch. A qualitative dimension of hearing correlated with the frequency of the sound waves that constitute the stimulus. Higher frequencies yield higher pitches (cf. *loudness, timbre*).

pituitary gland. An endocrine gland located centrally in the head. It consists of two parts, the anterior pituitary and the posterior pituitary. The anterior pituitary is the more important part because of its regulation of growth and of other endocrine glands. One of its hormones, ACTH (adrenocorticotropic hormone), has become medically important (syn. *hypophysis;* cf. *endocrine gland*).

pivot words. In the development of children's language, words the child uses frequently to combine with open words to form two-word sentences (cf. *open words*).

place-learning experiment. A variety of animal maze experiments designed to test whether what is learned is the location of the goal in space rather than the movements required to reach the goal (cf. *sign learning*).

place theory. A theory of hearing that associates pitch with the place on the basilar membrane where activation occurs (cf. *frequency theory, traveling wave theory, volley theory*).

placebo. An inert substance used in place of an active drug; given to the control group in an experimental test.

plateau. In a learning curve a period of no improvement, preceded and followed by improvement (cf. *learning curve*).

polarized synaptic transmission. The transmission of nervous impulses across synapses in one direction only (from axon to dendrite or cell body); characteristic of higher nervous systems, beyond the stage of the nerve net.

population. The total universe of all possible cases from which a sample is selected. The usual statistical formulas for making inferences from samples apply when the population is appreciably larger than the sample, e.g., five to ten times larger than the sample (cf. *sample*).

population genetics. That branch of genetics concerned with the distribution of genetic determiners throughout the population (cf. *genetics*).

positive incentive. An object or circumstance toward which behavior is directed when the object or circumstance is perceived or anticipated (cf. *negative incentive*).

post-hypnotic suggestion. A suggestion made to a hypnotized subject that he will perform in a prescribed way after coming out of the trance. The activity is usually carried out without the subject's awareness of its origin in a specific suggestion (cf. *hypnotism*).

precognition. A claimed form of extrasensory perception in which a future event is perceived (cf. *extrasensory perception, clairvoyance, telepathy*).

predictive validity. Validity determined by how well a test predicts a criterion (cf. *concurrent validity, construct validity*).

pregenital stages. In psychoanalysis, the oral, anal, and phallic stages of psychosexual development (cf. *psychosexual development*).

prejudice. An attitude that is firmly fixed, not open to free and rational discussion, and resistant to change (cf. *attitude*).

preparatory activity. Goal-directed or goal-seeking activity aroused by a drive or by external stimuli when the drive is active.

preparatory set. Cf. *set.*

primary abilities. The abilities, discovered by factor analysis, that underlie intelligence test performance (cf. *factor analysis*).

primary colors. Cf. *color-mixing primaries, psychological primaries.*

primary sex characteristics. The structural or physiological characteristics that make possible sexual union and reproduction (cf. *secondary sex characteristics*).

primitive society. Cf. *nonliterate society.*

proactive inhibition. The interference of earlier learning with the learning and recall of new material (cf. *retroactive inhibition, transfer of learning*).

probability sampling. A general method of sampling, applicable to attitude and opinion surveys, in which the probability that any one member of the population will be included in the sample is known. The actual selection of cases is random so that inferences based on sampling statistics can be made (cf. *area sampling*).

probability value. A probability statement associated with a statistical inference, e.g., "The probability is .05 that a difference of this size between the sample means would have occurred even though the population means were the same" (cf. *statistical inference, statistical significance*).

product-moment correlation. Cf. *coefficient of correlation.*

program. (1) A plan for the solution of a problem; often used interchangeably with "routine" to specify the precise sequence of instructions enabling a computer to solve a problem. (2) In connection with teaching, a set of materials arranged in sequences of units, called frames, so that learning can proceed with a minimum of error. The program can be presented in book form as well as in a form suitable for use with a teaching machine (cf. *teaching machine*).

projection. A defense mechanism by which a person protects himself from awareness of his own undesirable traits by attributing those traits excessively to others (cf. *defense mechanism*).

projection area. A place in the cerebral cortex where a function is localized; e.g., the visual projection area is in the occipital lobes.

projective test. A personality test in which the subject reveals ("projects") himself through his imaginative productions. The projective test gives much freer possibilities of response than the fixed-alternative personality inventory. Examples of projective tests are the Rorschach Test (ink blots to be interpreted) and the Thematic Apperception Test (pictures that elicit stories) (cf. *personality inventory*).

prolactin. A pituitary hormone associated with the secretion of milk (cf. *hormones*).

psi. The special ability said to be possessed by the subject who performs successfully in experiments on extrasensory perception and psychokinesis (cf. *extrasensory perception, psychokinesis*).

psychedelic drugs. An alternate name for "consciousness-expanding" drugs (cf. *psychotomimetic drugs, LSD-25*).

psychiatric nurse. A nurse specially trained to deal with patients suffering from mental disorders.

psychiatric social worker. A social worker trained to work with patients and their families on problems of mental health and illness, usually in close relationship with psychiatrists and clinical psychologists (cf. *psychiatrist, clinical psychologist*).

psychiatrist. A medical doctor specializing in the treatment and prevention of mental disorders both mild and severe (cf. *psychoanalyst, clinical psychologist*).

psychiatry. A branch of medicine concerned with mental health and mental illness (cf. *psychiatrist, psychoanalyst*).

psychoactive drugs. Drugs that affect man's behavior and consciousness (cf. *tranquilizers, psychedelic drugs, psychotomimetic drugs, LSD-25*).

psychoanalysis. (1) The method developed by Freud and extended by his followers for treating neuroses. (2) The system of psychological theory growing out of experiences with the psychoanalytic method.

psychoanalyst. A psychotherapist, now usually trained as a psychiatrist, who uses methods related to those originally proposed by Freud for treating neuroses and other mental disorders (cf. *psychiatrist, clinical psychologist*).

psychodrama. A form of spontaneous play acting used in psychotherapy.

psychogenic. Caused by psychological factors (e.g., emotional conflict, faulty habits) rather than by disease, injury, or other somatic cause; functional rather than organic.

psychograph. Cf. *trait profile*.

psychokinesis (PK). A claimed form of mental operation said to affect a material body or an energy system without any evidence of more usual contact or energy transfer, e.g., affecting the number that comes up in the throw of dice by a machine through wishing for that number (cf. *extrasensory perception*).

psychological primaries. Hues that appear to be pure, i.e., not composed of other hues. Most authorities choose a particular red, yellow, green, and blue. (The red-green and blue-yellow pairs chosen in this way are not complementary colors.) (cf. *color-mixing primaries*).

psychology. The science that studies behavior and mental activity (cf. *behavior, mental activity*).

psychopathic personality. A type of character disorder marked by impulsivity, inability to abide by the customs and laws of society, and lack of anxiety or guilt regarding behavior (syn. *antisocial personality*).

psychopharmacology. The study of the effects of drugs on behavior.

psychophysical function. A curve relating the likelihood of a response to the intensity of the presented stimulus.

psychophysical methods. Experimental and statistical methods for determining absolute thresholds, difference thresholds, and scale values for stimuli that can be arranged along a physical continuum (cf. *threshold*).

psychophysics. A name used by Fechner for the science of the relationship between mental processes and the physical world. Now usually restricted to the study of the sensory consequences of controlled physical stimulation (cf. *psychophysical methods*).

psychosexual development. In psychoanalysis, the theory that development takes place through stages (oral, anal, phallic, latent, genital), each stage characterized by a zone of pleasurable stimulation and appropriate objects of sexual attachment, culminating in normal heterosexual mating (cf. *oral stage, anal stage, phallic stage, latency, genital stage, psychosocial crises*).

psychosocial crises. A modification by Erikson of the psychoanalytic theory of psychosexual development, giving more attention to the social and environmental problems associated with the various stages of development, and adding some adult stages beyond genital maturing (cf. *psychosexual development*).

psychosomatic disorders. Ailments with organic symptoms attributable to emotional or other psychological causes.

psychotherapy. Treatment of personality maladjustment or mental illness by psychological means, usually, but not exclusively, through personal consultation (cf. *somatotherapy*).

psychotic disorder. Mental illness in which the patient shows severe change or disorganization of personality, often accompanied by depression, delusions, hallucinations; commonly requires hospitalization (syn. *psychosis,* pl. *psychoses;* cf. *functional psychosis, organic psychosis*).

psychotomimetic drugs. Drugs that produce psychotic symptoms (cf. *LSD-25*).

puberty. The climax of pubescence, marked by menstruation in girls and the appearance of live sperm cells in the urine of boys (cf. *pubescence, adolescence*).

pubescence. A period of about two years prior to puberty during which the secondary sex characteristics appear and sex functioning begins to mature. Pubescence culminates in puberty (cf. *puberty, adolescence*).

public opinion. Widely shared beliefs, including common plans for action, chiefly in respect to problems of governmental policy (cf. *attitude, opinion*).

punctiform distribution. The arrangement of sensitive areas of the skin; a distribution of sensitive spots with insensitive areas between them.

punishment. A negative incentive, capable of producing pain or annoyance (cf. *reward*).

pupillary response. The constriction or dilation of the pupil of the eye, brought about either by changes in illumination or as an emotional accompaniment (cf. *emotional indicator*).

purpose. A goal that can be stated in words and toward which action is directed (cf. *unconscious motive*).

pursuit learning. A laboratory task in which the subject learns to keep the point of a hinged stylus in contact with a small metal target mounted on a rotating turntable.

quality. A characteristic denoting differences in kind, rather than differences in intensity or amount; e.g., a light and a sound differ in quality; red and blue, and the notes A and B♭, differ in quality (cf. *quantity*).

quantity. Amount or intensity (cf. *quality*).

quota control. A sampling method used in attitude and opinion surveys, in which the interviewer is instructed to select respondents with certain defined characteristics, e.g., of stated age, sex, economic level (cf. *area sampling*).

range. The variation of scores in a frequency distribution from the lowest to the highest. A value that grows larger as the number of cases increases, hence to be used with extreme caution (cf. *measure of variation*).

rank correlation (ρ). A correlation computed from ranked data. The coefficient is designated by the small Greek letter rho (ρ) to distinguish it from the product-moment correlation (r), of which it is an approximation (cf. *coefficient of correlation*).

rapid eye movements (REMs). Eye movements that usually occur during dreaming and that can be measured by attaching small electrodes laterally to and above the subject's eye. These register changes in electrical activity associated with movements of the eyeball in its socket.

rapport. (1) A comfortable relationship between the subject and the tester, ensuring cooperation in replying to test questions. (2) A similar relationship between therapist and patient. (3) A special relationship of hypnotic subject to hypnotist.

rating scale. A device by which a rater can record his judgment of another person (or of himself) on the traits defined by the scale (cf. *graphic rating scale*).

rational problem-solving. Arriving at a solution by sound reasoning on the basis of the best available evidence; realistic problem-solving (cf. *defense mechanism*).

rationalization. A defense mechanism in which self-esteem is maintained by assigning plausible and acceptable reasons for conduct entered upon impulsively or for less acceptable reasons (cf. *defense mechanism*).

reaction-formation. A defense mechanism in which a subject denies a disapproved motive through giving strong expression to its opposite (cf. *defense mechanism*).

reaction time. The time between the presentation of a stimulus and the occurrence of a response (cf. *latency*).

recall. The form of remembering in which the subject demonstrates retention by repeating what was earlier learned, e.g., demonstrating recall of a poem by reciting it (cf. *recognition, redintegrative memory, relearning*).

receiver-operating-characteristic curve (ROC curve). The function relating the probability of hits and false alarms for a fixed signal level in a detection task. Factors influencing response bias may cause hits and false alarms to vary, but their variation is constrained to the ROC curve (cf. *signal detection task*).

receptor. A specialized portion of the body sensitive to particular kinds of stimuli and connected with sensory nerves, e.g., the retina of the eye. Used more loosely, the organ containing these sensitive portions, e.g., the eye or the ear (cf. *effector*).

recessive gene. A member of a gene pair that determines the characteristic trait or appearance of the individual only if the other member of the pair is recessive. If the other member of the pair is dominant, the effect of the recessive gene is masked (cf. *dominant gene*).

reciprocal inhibition. (1) The relationship between muscles that are controlled through reciprocal innervation (Sherrington). (2) A variety of psychotherapy in which symptoms are decreased through presenting their occasion under circumstances in which response is inhibited (Wolpe).

reciprocal innervation. A form of neural integration in which one of a pair of antagonistic muscles is actively inhibited when the other member of the pair contracts (cf. *antagonistic muscles*).

recognition. That form of remembering indicated by a feeling of familiarity when something previously encountered is again perceived (cf. *recall, redintegrative memory, relearning*).

recurrent inhibition. A process whereby some receptors in the visual system when stimulated by nerve impulses inhibit the firing of other visual receptors, thus making the visual system responsive to changes in illumination.

red-green color blindness. The commonest form of color blindness, a variety of dichromatism. In the two sub-varieties, red-blindness and green-blindness, both red and green vision are lacking, but achromatic bands are seen at different parts of the spectrum (cf. *color blindness, dichromatism*).

redintegrative memory. Remembering the whole of an earlier experience on the basis of partial cues; recollection of events in the personal history of the subject, with their attendant circumstances (cf. *recall, recognition, relearning*).

reduction screen. A screen containing a small aperture so that a restricted area of a surface can be viewed through it. With a reduction screen, brightness constancy and other constancies tend to be lessened (cf. *object constancy*).

reference group. The group with which an individual compares himself when he makes self-estimates of status. Most people have several reference groups. A reference group may or may not be a membership group (cf. *membership group*).

reflex action. A relatively simple response largely under the control of a specific stimulus, occurring rather mechanically, such as the pupillary response to light or the knee-jerk from a tap on the tendon below the knee. Other examples of reflex action

are sneezing, perspiring, and the beating of the heart (cf. *respondent behavior*).

refractory phase. The period of temporary inactivity in a neuron after it has once fired.

regression. A return to more primitive or infantile modes of response, either (1) retrogression to behavior engaged in when younger, or (2) primitivism, i.e., more infantile or childlike behavior, but not necessarily that which occurred in the individual's earlier life.

rehearsal buffer. The array of information that is undergoing rehearsal and consequently being continuously regenerated in short-term memory. The process facilitates the short-term recall of information and its transfer to long-term memory.

reinforcement. (1) In classical conditioning, the experimental procedure of following the conditioned stimulus by the unconditioned stimulus. (2) In operant conditioning, the analogous procedure of following the occurrence of the operant response by the reinforcing stimulus. (3) The process that increases the strength of conditioning as a result of these arrangements (cf. *classical conditioning, operant conditioning, extinction*).

reinforcing stimulus. (1) In classical conditioning, the unconditioned stimulus. (2) In operant conditioning, the stimulus that reinforces the operant (typically, a reward).

relearning. That form of remembering in which the subject demonstrates memory for something previously learned through the saving in time or trials required for learning the material again (cf. *recall, recognition, redintegrative memory*).

releaser. A term used by ethologists for a stimulus that sets off a cycle of instinctive behavior (cf. *ethologist, instinct*).

reliability. The self-consistency of a test as a measuring instrument. Reliability is measured by a coefficient of correlation between scores on two halves of a test, alternate forms of the test, or retests with the same test, a high correlation signifying high consistency of scores for the population tested (cf. *validity*).

REMs. Cf. *rapid eye movements.*

reminiscence. In psychology, a term for the occasional rise in a curve of retention before it falls, e.g., when under some circumstances more may be retained after an interval than immediately upon completion of learning (cf. *retention curve*).

repression. (1) A defense mechanism in which an impulse or memory that might provoke feelings of guilt is denied by its disappearance from awareness (cf. *defense mechanism, suppression*). (2) A theory of forgetting (cf. *motivated forgetting*).

reserpine. Cf. *tranquilizer.*

resistance. In psychoanalysis, a blocking of free association; a psychological barrier against bringing unconscious impulses to the level of awareness. Resistance is part of the process of maintaining repression (cf. *repression, interpretation*).

respiration rate. The rate of breathing. When respiration rate is used in the study of emotion, an additional measure is commonly used, known as the inspiration-expiration ratio. This is computed as a ratio between the time spent in inspiration and the time spent in expiration (I/E) (cf. *emotional indicator*).

respondent. (1) One who responds; used chiefly to refer to those interviewed in public opinion surveys. (2) A class of responses (cf. *respondent behavior*).

respondent behavior. A type of behavior corresponding to reflex action, in that it is largely under the control of, and predictable from, the stimulus (syn. *elicited behavior;* cf. *operant behavior*).

response. (1) The behavioral result of stimulation in the form of a movement or glandular secretion. (2) Sometimes, any activity of the organism, including central responses (such as an image or fantasy), regardless of whether the stimulus is identified and whether identifiable movements occur. (3) Products of the organism's activity, such as words typed per minute.

retention curve. A curve plotted with some measure of remembering on the vertical axis and the elapsed time since learning on the horizontal axis. The curve tends to fall rapidly at first, then more slowly, though this is not invariable (cf. *reminiscence*).

reticular formation. A system of ill-defined nerve paths and connections within the brain stem, lying outside the well-defined nerve pathways, and important as an arousal mechanism.

retina. The portion of the eye sensitive to light, containing the rods and the cones (cf. *rod, cone*).

retinal disparity. The fact that an object projects slightly different images on the two retinas due to the different positions of the right and left eyes (syn. *binocular disparity*).

retroactive inhibition. (1) The interference in recall of something earlier learned by something subsequently learned. (2) The theory of forgetting which proposes that much, or most, forgetting is due to the interference by new learning with the recall of the old (cf. *proactive inhibition, transfer of learning*).

retrograde amnesia. The inability to recall events that occurred during a period of time immediately prior to a shock or functional disturbance, although the memory for earlier events remains relatively unimpaired.

retrogression. Cf. *regression*.

reward. A positive incentive capable of arousing pleasure or satisfying a drive; a reinforcing stimulus (cf. *punishment*).

rhodopsin. A light-sensitive substance contained in the rods of the eye (syn. *visual purple*).

ribonucleic acid (RNA). Complex molecules that control cellular functions; theorized by some to be the chemical mediator of memory.

risky-shift. The tendency for those who have engaged in group discussion about certain issues to be willing to take greater risks than they were prior to the discussion.

RNA. Cf. *ribonucleic acid*.

ROC. Cf. *receiver-operating-characteristic curve*.

rod. In the eye, an element of the retina mediating achromatic sensation only; particularly important in peripheral vision and night vision (cf. *retina, cone*).

role. By analogy with an actor's role, the kind of behavior expected of an individual because of his place within social arrangements, e.g., the male role, the mother's role, the lawyer's role. Any one person fulfills or adopts numerous roles on varied occasions.

role diffusion. A stage of development said by Erikson to characterize many adolescents (and others) in which various identifications with others have not been harmonized and integrated (cf. *identification, identity formation*).

role playing. A method for teaching principles affecting interpersonal relations by having the subject assume a part in a spontaneous play, whether in psychotherapy or in leadership training (cf. *psychodrama*).

rote memorization. Verbatim learning, as in learning a poem "by heart" (cf. *paired-associate learning, serial memorization*).

saccule. Cf. *vestibular sacs*.

sadism. A pathological motive that leads to inflicting pain upon another person (cf. *masochism*).

salivary secretion. Secretion of the salivary glands, elicited by food or chemical substance in the mouth or by conditioned stimuli,

or occurring as an emotional accompaniment (cf. *emotional indicator*).

sample. A selection of scores from a total set of scores known as the "population." If selection is random, an unbiased sample results; if selection is nonrandom, the sample is biased and unrepresentative (cf. *population*).

sampling errors. The variation in a distribution of scores, or of statistics derived from them, to be attributed to the fact that measurements are made on a variable sample from a larger population. Thus sampling errors persist even though all measurements are accurate (cf. *errors of measurement, sample*).

saturation. The dimension of color that describes its purity; if highly saturated it appears to be pure hue and free of gray, but if of low saturation it appears to have a great deal of gray mixed with it (cf. *brightness, hue*).

scale. A set of ascending or descending values used to designate a position or an interval along a dimension. Thus a ruler may have a scale in inches, a test a scale in I.Q. units (cf. *interval scale, ordinal scale, ratio scale*).

scaling. Converting raw data into types of scores more readily interpreted, e.g., into ranks, centiles, standard scores (cf. *attitude scale*).

scapegoating. A form of displaced aggression in which an innocent but helpless victim is blamed or punished as the source of the scapegoater's frustration (cf. *displaced aggression*).

schedule of reinforcement. A well-defined procedure for reinforcing a given response only some proportion of the time it occurs (cf. *partial reinforcement*).

schizophrenic reaction. A functional psychotic disorder in which there is a lack of harmony or split between aspects of personality functioning, especially between emotion and behavior. Symptoms may include autism, hallucinations, and delusions (syn. *schizophrenia,* formerly *dementia praecox;* cf. *psychotic disorder*).

school of psychology. An all-embracing system designed to encompass the data of psychology according to a limited set of principles and procedures. Such schools are not as prominent today as they once were (syn. *system of psychology;* cf. *behaviorism, Gestalt psychology, psychoanalysis, S-R psychology*).

school psychologist. A professional psychologist employed by a school or school system, with responsibility for testing, guidance, research, etc. (cf. *educational psychologist*).

secondary reinforcer. A stimulus that has become reinforcing through prior association with a reinforcing stimulus (cf. *reinforcing stimulus*).

secondary sex characteristics. The physical features distinguishing the mature male from the mature female, apart from the reproductive organs. In man, the deeper voice of the male and the growth of the beard are illustrative (cf. *primary sex characteristics*).

second-order conditioning. Conditioning in which what was previously the conditioned stimulus now serves as the unconditioned or reinforcing stimulus (cf. *secondary reinforcer*).

selectivity. The perceptual response to parts of incoming stimuli and the ignoring of others (cf. *attention*).

self. The subject's personality as perceived by the subject (cf. *personality*).

self-consciousness. A form of heightened self-awareness when an individual is especially concerned about reactions of others to him.

self-deception. Behavior the motives of which are unconscious or inadequately perceived by the person himself because of (1) denial of the true motives, or (2) disguise of these motives (cf. *defense mechanism*).

self-demand schedule. A flexible arrangement for feeding in which the time an infant is fed is determined according to his behavior. It replaces a four-hour or other rigid schedule (syn. *self-schedule, demand schedule*).

self-perception. The individual's awareness of himself; differs from self-consciousness because it may take the form of objective self-appraisal (cf. *self-consciousness*).

self-recitation. In memorization, the method of spending some fraction of the study time in attempted recall.

semantic differential. A method developed by Osgood for using rating scales and factor analysis in studying the connotative meanings of words (cf. *connotative meaning*).

semicircular canals. Three curved tubular canals, in three planes, which form part of the labyrinth of the inner ear and are concerned with equilibrium and motion.

sensorimotor task. A multiple-response task in which muscular movement is prominent, e.g., riding a bicycle, playing a piano. Laboratory sensorimotor tasks include mazes, mirror drawing, pursuit learning, etc. (cf. *multiple-response learning*).

sensory adaptation. The reduction in sensitivity that occurs with prolonged stimulation and the increase in sensitivity that occurs with lack of stimulation; most noted in vision, smell, taste, and temperature sensitivity (cf. *dark adaptation, light adaptation*).

septal area. A portion of the brain deep in the central part, between the lateral ventricles, which when stimulated electrically (in the rat, at least) appears to yield a state akin to pleasure.

serial memorization. That form of rote memorization in which a list of items, or a passage of prose or poetry, is learned in sequence from beginning to end, so that each item or word is a cue to the one that follows it (cf. *paired-associate learning*).

serial position effect. The difficulty in memorization and recall resulting from position of items within a list to be learned and remembered. The point of maximum difficulty is just after the middle of the list.

set. (1) A preparatory adjustment or readiness for a particular kind of action or experience, usually as a result of instructions, e.g., the set to respond with a word opposite in meaning to the stimulus word in an experiment on controlled association. (2) A habitual tendency to respond in a particular manner.

sex gland. As duct glands, the sex glands are active in mating behavior, but as endocrine glands their hormones affect secondary sex characteristics as well as maintaining functional sexual activity. The male hormones are known as androgens, the female hormones as estrogens (syn. *gonads;* cf. *endocrine gland*).

sex-linked trait. A trait determined by a gene transmitted with the same chromosomes that determine sex, e.g., red-green color blindness (cf. *X-chromosome, Y-chromosome*).

sex-role behavior. Behavior that a society considers appropriate for the individual because of his sex.

shape constancy. The tendency to see a familiar object as of the same shape regardless of the viewing angle (cf. *object constancy*).

shaping of behavior. Modifying operant behavior by reinforcing only those variations in response that deviate in a direction desired by the experimenter; the whole population of responses thus reinforced then drifts in the desired direction (Skinner) (syn. *method of approximations*).

shock therapy. A form of treatment of mental illness, especially in the relief of depression (cf. *electroconvulsive shock therapy, insulin shock*).

short-term memory (STM). The assumption that certain components of the memory system have limited capacity and will maintain information for only a brief period of time. The precise definition varies somewhat from theory to theory (cf. *long-term memory*).

sibling. A brother or a sister.

sibling rivalry. Jealousy between siblings, often based on their competition for parental affection.

signal detection task. A procedure whereby the subject must judge on each trial whether or not a weak signal was embedded in a noise background. Saying "yes" when a signal was presented is called a hit and saying "yes" when the signal was not presented is called a false alarm (cf. *receiver-operating-characteristic curve*).

signal detectability theory. A theory of the sensory and decision processes involved in psychophysical judgments, with special reference to the problem of detecting weak signals in noise (cf. *signal detection task*).

sign learning. An acquired expectation that one stimulus (the sign) will be followed by another (the significate) provided a familiar behavior route is followed. This interpretation of learning, by Tolman, is considered by him an alternative to the interpretation of learning as habit formation (cf. *latent-learning experiment, place-learning experiment*).

simulation. The representation of the essential elements of some phenomenon, system, or environment to facilitate its study (often by or involving an automatic computer).

sine wave. A cyclical wave that when plotted corresponds to the plot of the trigonometric sine function. The sound waves of pure tones yield this function when plotted.

size constancy. The tendency to see a familiar object as of its actual size regardless of its distance (cf. *object constancy*).

skewed distribution. A frequency distribution that is not symmetrical. It is named for the direction in which the tail lies; e.g., if there are many small incomes and a few large ones, the distribution is skewed in the direction of the large incomes (cf. *frequency distribution, symmetrical distribution*).

smooth muscle. The type of muscle found in the digestive organs, blood vessels, and other internal organs. Controlled via the autonomic nervous system (cf. *cardiac muscle, striate muscle*).

social behavior theory. The application of learning theory to the problems of personal and social behavior (syn. *social learning theory*).

social desirability variable. A biasing variable in personality inventories, leading some subjects to reply in the direction of socially approved responses, regardless of whether their answers are descriptive of themselves (cf. *acquiescence*).

social learning theory. Cf. *social behavior theory*.

social motive. A motive serving group life, involving particularly interactions with other organisms of the same species (cf. *survival motive*).

social psychologist. A psychologist whose research interest lies in the behavior of the individual as he influences and is influenced by other individuals in a social environment (cf. *anthropologist, sociologist*).

socialization. The shaping of individual characteristics and behavior through the training that the social environment provides.

sociogram. A social map or diagram showing interactions, usually of mutual attraction or antagonism, among group members (cf. *sociometry*).

sociology. The behavioral or social science dealing with group life and social organization in literate societies (cf. *behavioral sciences*).

sociometry. A method of social mapping to indicate relationships of attraction and rejection among members of a social group. Each member expresses his choices for or against other members. The social map is constructed from the data provided by these choices (cf. *sociogram*).

somatotherapy. Treatment of personality maladjustment or mental illness by drugs, electric shock, surgery, or other methods directly affecting bodily processes (cf. *psychotherapy, chemotherapy*).

source trait. A trait derived by the method of factor analysis; all traits loaded heavily on a common factor belong together (Cattell) (cf. *surface trait*).

spaced practice. An arrangement of learning trials in which there is a time interval between trials, as opposed to immediately consecutive trials (syn. *distributed practice;* cf. *massed practice*).

spastic paralysis. A condition of excessive isotonic muscular contraction, commonly due to a brain injury at birth (syn. *cerebral palsy*).

special aptitude. The degree of aptitude to learn a specific activity, e.g., musical aptitude, clerical aptitude (cf. *general aptitude*).

specific hunger. Hunger for a specific food incentive, such as a craving for sweets (cf. *hunger drive*).

split-brain preparation. A deep vertical incision through the corpus callosum in an animal's brain that separates most of the two hemispheres. It is used to study the bilateral transfer of training (cf. *corpus callosum*).

spontaneous recovery. The return in strength of a conditioned response after a lapse of time following extinction (cf. *extinction*).

S-R psychology. Cf. *stimulus-response psychology.*

standard deviation. The square root of the mean of the squares of the amount by which each case departs from the mean of all the cases (syn. *root mean square deviation;* cf. *measure of variation, standard error, standard score*).

standard error. The standard deviation of the sampling distribution of a mean and of certain other derived statistics. It can be interpreted as any other standard deviation (cf. *standard deviation*).

standard error of estimate. The standard error of the differences between predicted values and true values of some measure; used, for example, in interpreting a coefficient of correlation.

standard score. (1) A score that has been converted to a scale of measurement with a mean of zero and a standard deviation of 1.0, based on a distribution of scores used in calibration. (2) A score based on standard scores but converted to another scale for convenience, e.g., with a mean of 50 and a standard deviation of 10.

stanine score. A U. S. Air Force type of standard score (originally, "standard nine"), with a mean of five and standard deviation of two. Scores range from one through nine (cf. *standard score*).

statistical inference. A statement about a population or populations based on statistical measures derived from samples (cf. *descriptive statistics*).

statistical significance. The trustworthiness of an obtained statistical measure as a statement about reality, e.g., the probability that the population mean falls within the limits determined from a sample. The expression refers to the reliability of the statistical finding and not to its importance (cf. *confidence limits, critical ratio, probability value*).

statistician. An applied mathematician; in psychology, one especially trained in the statistical tools useful in test construction and the interpretation of test data and in the design of experiments.

stereophonic hearing. The binaural perception of the distance and direction of a sound source owing to the difference in reception by the two ears.

stereoscopic vision. (1) The binocular perception of depth and distance of an object owing to the overlapping fields of the two eyes. (2) The equivalent effect when slightly unlike pictures are presented individually to each eye in a stereoscope (cf. *distance cues*).

stereotype. A biased generalization, usually about a social or national group, according to which individuals are falsely assigned traits they do not possess. Thus a person may have a stereotyped conception of the Italians or Scots that distorts his perception of any individual Italian or Scot.

stereotypy. The continued repetition of behavior that appears to serve no realistic purpose and may, in fact, be punished: inflexible behavior, which may be a consequence of frustration (cf. *frustration*).

steroids. Complex chemical substances, some of which are prominent in the secretions of the adrenal cortex and may be related to some forms of mental illness (cf. *adrenal gland*).

stimulus (pl. **stimuli**). (1) Some specific physical energy impinging upon a receptor sensitive to that kind of energy. (2) Any objectively describable situation or event (whether outside or inside the organism) that is the occasion for an organism's response (cf. *response*).

stimulus-response psychology. A psychological view that all behavior is in response to stimuli and that the appropriate tasks of psychological science are those identifying stimuli, the responses correlated with them, and the processes intervening between stimulus and response. There are several varieties of stimulus-response (S-R) theory, depending on the kind of intervening processes inferred (cf. *intervening variables*).

stimulus-sampling theory. A theory of behavior with primary emphasis on learning and related phenomena. The effective stimulus is viewed as a sample of stimulus elements from a potentially larger set; the state of conditioning of the sampled elements determines the response, and the learning that occurs following a reinforcement is specific to the sampled stimulus elements.

stimulus substitution. Cf. *classical conditioning.*

STM. Cf. *short-term memory.*

striate area. Cf. *visual area.*

striate muscle. Striped muscle; the characteristic muscles controlling the skeleton, as in the arms and legs. Activated by cerebro-spinal nervous system (cf. *cardiac muscle, smooth muscle*).

stroboscopic motion. An illusion of motion resulting from the successive presentation of discrete stimulus patterns arranged in a progression corresponding to movement, e.g., motion pictures (cf. *phi phenomenon*).

subjective science. A science limited to self-observation, so that its data are not public. Psychology based solely on introspection is subjective in that its raw data are limited to the observations of the subject on his own conscious processes. However, the report of these experiences provides objective data, so that introspection does not have to be excluded from objective psychology (cf. *objective science*).

subjective scoring. Test scoring requiring complex judgments by the scorer, as in the grading of essay examinations (cf. *objective scoring*).

sublimation. A form of the defense mechanism of substitution, whereby socially unacceptable motives find expression in socially acceptable forms; most commonly applied to the sublimation of sexual desires (cf. *substitution, compensation*).

submission. Cf. *dominance.*

substitution. A defense mechanism whereby the person maintains self-esteem by substituting approved goals for unapproved ones and activities that can be carried out successfully for activities doomed to failure (cf. *sublimation, compensation, overcompensation*).

subtractive mixture. Color mixture in which absorption occurs, so that results differ from additive mixture obtained by rotating colors on a color wheel or by mixing projected lights. Subtractive mixture occurs when transparent colored filters are placed one in front of the other, and when pigments are mixed (cf. *additive mixture*).

superego. In Freud's tripartite division of the personality, that part corresponding most nearly to conscience, controlling through moral scruples rather than by way of social expediency. The superego is said to be an uncompromising and punishing conscience (cf. *id, ego*).

suppression. A process of self-control in which impulses, tendencies to action, wishes to perform disapproved acts, etc., are in awareness, but not overtly revealed (cf. *repression*).

surface structure. In linguistics the sound sequence of a sentence (cf. *deep structure*).

surface trait. A trait derived by the method of cluster analysis; all traits that intercorrelate above some predicted value (e.g., above $r = .60$) can be considered to have something in common (Cattell) (cf. *source trait*).

survey method. A method of obtaining information by questioning a large sample of people (cf. *test method, experimental method, field observation*).

survival motive. A motive closely related to maintaining the life of the organism in its environment; thus motives related to bodily needs for food, water, air, moderate temperatures, etc. (cf. *social motive*).

symmetrical distribution. A frequency distribution in which cases fall equally in the class intervals on either side of the middle; hence the mean, median, and mode fall together (cf. *frequency distribution, skewed distribution*).

sympathetic division. A division of the autonomic nervous system, characterized by a chain of ganglia on either side of the spinal cord, with nerve fibers originating in the thoracic and lumbar portions of the spinal cord. Active in emotional excitement and to some extent antagonistic to the parasympathetic division (q.v.).

synapse. Cf. *synaptic nervous system.*

synaptic nervous system. A nervous system characteristic of all higher organisms, in which nerve cells are distinct and conduction is polarized, that is, occurs only in one direction across the junction between nerve cells called a synapse (cf. *nerve net*).

taboo. Something strongly prohibited or banned within a culture, usually with severe penalties for violation.

tachistoscope. An instrument for the brief exposure of words, symbols, pictures, or other visually presented material; sometimes called a T-scope.

taste deficiency. A trait used in the study of population genetics. Nontasting of certain substances, such as phenyl-thio-carbamide, is a recessive characteristic in man, while tasting is a dominant characteristic (cf. *dominant gene, recessive gene, population genetics*).

teaching machine. A device to provide self-instruction by means of a program proceeding in steps following each other at a rate determined by the learner; the machine is arranged to provide knowledge about the correctness or incorrectness of each reply (cf. *programing*).

telepathy. The claimed form of extrasensory perception in which what is perceived depends upon thought transference from one person to another (cf. *extrasensory perception, clairvoyance, precognition*).

temperament. That aspect of personality revealed in the tendency to experience moods or mood changes in characteristic ways; general level of reactivity and energy (cf. *mood*).

temporal lobe. A portion of the cerebral hemisphere, at the side below the lateral fissure and in front of the occipital lobe (cf. *frontal lobe, occipital lobe, parietal lobe*).

test. A collection of items (questions, tasks, etc.) so arranged that replies or performances can be scored and the scores used in appraising individual differences (cf. *item, test battery*).

test battery. A collection of tests whose composite scores are used to appraise individual differences (cf. *item, test*).

test method. A method of psychological investigation. Its advantages are that it allows the psychologist to collect large quantities of useful data from many people, with a minimum of disturbance of their routines of existence and with a minimum of laboratory equipment (cf. *test, experimental method*).

test profile. A chart plotting scores from a number of tests given to the same individual (or group of individuals) in parallel rows on a common scale, with the scores connected by lines, so that high and low scores can be readily perceived (cf. *trait profile*).

test standardization. The establishment of norms for interpreting scores by giving a test to a representative population and by making appropriate studies of its reliability and validity (cf. *norm, reliability, validity*).

tetany. A physiologically disturbed state of the organism marked by widespread intermittent muscular contractions and muscular pain; may be caused by calcium deficiency as a consequence of defective parathyroid secretion (cf. *parathyroid glands*).

theory. A set of assumptions (axioms) advanced to explain existing data and predict new events; usually applicable to a wide array of phenomena and experimental situations.

thinking. Behavior carried on in terms of ideas (representational or symbolic processes); ideational problem-solving as distinguished from solution through overt manipulation.

threshold. The transitional point at which an increasing stimulus or an increasing difference not previously perceived becomes perceptible (or at which a decreasing stimulus or previously perceived difference becomes imperceptible). The value obtained depends in part upon the methods used in determining it (cf. *absolute threshold, difference threshold, psychophysical methods*).

thyroid gland. An endocrine gland located in the neck, whose hormone thyroxin is important in determining metabolic rate (cf. *endocrine gland*).

thyroxin. The hormone of the thyroid gland (cf. *thyroid gland*).

timbre. The quality distinguishing a tone of a given pitch sounded by one instrument from that sounded by another. The differences are due to overtones and other impurities (cf. **overtone**).

tip-of-the-tongue phenomenon. The experience of failing to recall a word or name when we are quite certain we know it.

T-maze. An apparatus in which an animal is presented with two alternative paths, one of which leads to a goal box. It is usually used with rats and lower organisms (cf. **maze**).

token learning. An arrangement within operant conditioning in which a token (e.g., a poker chip) as a secondary reinforcer can be exchanged for a primary reinforcing stimulus (e.g., food).

trace-dependent forgetting. The proposition that information stored in memory decays over time; the rate of decay may depend on both the elapsed time and the intervening activity (cf. **cue-dependent forgetting**).

trained introspection. Cf. **introspection**.

training. Learning that is guided by another individual, such as a parent or teacher, or, as in self-training, learning that is deliberately undertaken to shape behavior in particular directions (cf. **maturation**).

trait. A persisting characteristic or dimension of personality according to which individuals can be rated or measured (cf. **trait profile, type theory**).

trait profile. A chart plotting the ratings of a number of traits of the same individual on a common scale in parallel rows, so that the pattern of traits can be visually perceived (syn. *psychograph;* (cf. **trait, test profile**).

trait theory. The theory that human personality is most profitably characterized by the scores that an individual makes on a number of scales, each of which represents a trait or dimension of his personality (cf. **type theory**).

tranquilizer. A drug such as chlorpromazine or reserpine used to reduce anxiety and relieve depression; hence useful in the therapy of mental disorders.

transfer of learning. The effect of prior learning on present learning. If learning a new task is facilitated, transfer is positive; if the new learning is interfered with, transfer is negative (cf. **formal discipline, proactive inhibition, retroactive inhibition**).

transfer through principles. A theory of transfer of learning that proposes that new learning is facilitated by detecting the applicability of principles or generalizations discovered in prior learning (cf. **transfer of learning**).

transference. In psychoanalysis, the patient's unconsciously making the therapist the object of emotional response, thus transferring to him responses appropriate to other persons important in the life history of the patient.

traveling wave theory. A modification by Békésy of the place theory of hearing. The theory states that when a sound of given frequency enters the ear, a wave travels along the basilar membrane and displaces it a maximum amount at a certain point, the point depending on its frequency (cf. **basilar membrane, frequency theory, place theory, volley theory**).

trend analysis. A method of forecasting the future based on past events, e.g., predicting the number of people that will be killed in automobile accidents this year on the basis of the number killed in previous years and the expected increase in the number of drivers (cf. **Delphi method, cross-impact matrix method**).

trial-and-error learning. An expression characterizing multiple-response learning, in which the proper response is selected out of varied behavior through the influence of reward and punishment. Variously described as approximation and correction, fumble and success, etc. (cf. **multiple-response learning, operant conditioning**).

trichromatism. Normal color vision, based on the classification of color vision according to three color systems: black-white, blue-yellow, and red-green. The normal eye sees all three; the colorblind eye is defective in one or two of the three systems (cf. **dichromatism, monochromatism**).

t-test. A preferred measure for interpreting the significance of differences with small samples; for large samples, equivalent to critical ratio (cf. **critical ratio, statistical significance**).

type theory. The theory that human subjects can profitably be classified into a small number of classes or types, each class or type having characteristics in common that set its members apart from other classes or types (cf. **trait theory**).

unconditioned response. The response given originally to the unconditioned stimulus used as the basis for establishing a conditioned response to a previously neutral stimulus (cf. **conditioned response**).

unconscious motive. A motive of which the subject is unaware, or aware of in distorted form. Because there is no sharp dividing line between conscious and unconscious, many motives have both conscious and unconscious aspects.

unconscious processes. (1) Processes, such as wishes or fears, that might be conscious but of which the subject is unaware. (2) Less commonly, physiological processes of the body (circulation, metabolism, etc.) that go on outside of awareness (cf. **conscious processes**).

utricle. Cf. **vestibular sacs**.

validity. The predictive significance of a test for its intended purposes. Validity can be measured by a coefficient of correlation between scores on the test and the scores that the test seeks to predict, i.e., scores on some criterion (cf. **criterion, reliability**).

variable. One of the conditions measured or controlled in an experiment (cf. **dependent variable, independent variable**).

variance. The square of a standard deviation.

variation. Cf. **measure of variation**.

verbal report. A statement in words by a subject; often an account of his subjective, conscious experiences, thus making them accessible for study (cf. **behavior**).

vestibular sacs. Two sacs in the labyrinth of the inner ear, called the saccule and utricle, which contain the otoliths ("ear stones"). Pressure of the otoliths on the hair cells in the gelatinous material of the utricle and saccule gives us the sense of upright position or departure from it (cf. **equilibratory senses**).

visual area. A projection area lying in the occipital lobe. In man, partial damage to this area produces blindness in portions of the visual field corresponding to the amount and location of the damage (syn. *striate area*).

visual field. The total visual stimuli acting upon the eye when it is directed toward a fixation point.

visual purple. Cf. **rhodopsin**.

volley theory. A modified frequency theory of hearing proposed by Wever and Bray suggesting that the frequency of the stimulus may be represented in bundles of fibers in the auditory nerve responding somewhat independently, so that the frequency is represented by the composite volley, even though no single fiber carries impulses at that rate (cf. **frequency theory, place theory, traveling wave theory**).

voluntary action. Self-initiated action (cf. **operant behavior**).

Weber's law. A law stating that the difference threshold is proportional to the stimulus magnitude at which it is measured. It is known to be accurate only over limited stimulus ranges (cf. **difference threshold**).

weighted items. If one item (or a single test in a battery of tests) has been found to predict better than another, it is assigned a higher weight, so that it will influence a composite score more than the item (or test) of lower predictive value.

whole learning. Learning a multiple-response task as a unit, e.g., memorizing a long poem from beginning to end without separate practice of the parts (cf. *part learning*).

word-association experiment. An experiment designed for studying associative processes in which the subject responds to a stimulus word by saying as promptly as possible the first word that he thinks of (cf. *free association, controlled association*).

working through. In psychoanalytic therapy, the process of re-education by having the patient face the same conflicts over and over again in the consultation room, until he can independently face and master the conflicts in ordinary life.

X-chromosome. A chromosome that, if paired with another X-chromosome, determines that the individual will be a female. If it is combined with a Y-chromosome, the individual will be a male. The X-chromosome transmits sex-linked traits (cf. *chromosome, sex-linked trait, Y-chromosome*).

Y-chromosome. The chromosome that, combined with an X-chromosome, determines maleness (cf. *chromosome, sex-linked trait, X-chromosome*).

Young-Helmholtz theory. A theory of color perceptions that postulates three basic color receptors, a "red" receptor, a "green" receptor, and a "blue" receptor.

references
and index
to authors
of works cited

The numbers in **bold face** following each reference give the text pages on which the paper or book is cited. Citations in the text are made by author and date of publication.

AARONSON, B., and OSMOND, H. (eds.) (1970) *Psychedelics: The uses and implications of hallucinogenic drugs.* Garden City, N.Y.: Doubleday.—**182**

ABELSON, P. H. (1968) LSD and marijuana. *Science,* 159:1189.—**182**

ABELSON, R. P. (1964) Mathematical models for the distribution of attitudes under controversy. In Frederiksen, N., and Gulliksen, H. (eds.) *Contributions to mathematical psychology.* N.Y.: Holt, Rinehart and Winston, 41–160.—**290**

ABELSON, R. P., ARONSON, E., MCGUIRE, W. J., NEWCOMB, T. M., ROSENBERG, M. J., and TANNENBAUM, P. H. (eds.) (1968) *Theories of cognitive consistency: A sourcebook.* Chicago: Rand McNally.—**538**

ADAMS, J. (1967) *Human memory.* N.Y.: McGraw-Hill.—**245**

ADAMS, J. F. (1968) *Understanding adolescence.* Boston: Allyn and Bacon.—**104**

ADELSON, J., *see* Douvan and Adelson (1966).

ADOLPH, E. F. (1939) Measurements of water drinking in dogs. *American Journal of Physiology,* 125:75–86.—**300**

ADOLPH, E. F. (1941) The internal environment and behavior: Water content. *American Journal of Psychiatry,* 97:1365–73.—**300**

AGNEW, H. W., JR., *see* Williams, Agnew, and Webb (1964).

ALLEN, V. L., and CRUTCHFIELD, R. S. (1963) Generalization of experimentally reinforced conformity. *Journal of Abnormal and Social Psychology,* 67:326–33.—**533**

ALLPORT, F. H. (1955) *Theories of perception and the concept of structure.* N.Y.: Wiley.—**161**

ALLPORT, G. W. (1937) *Personality.* N.Y.: Holt.—**400, 401**

ALLPORT, G. W. (1944) *ABC's of scapegoating.* Chicago: Central Y.M.C.A. College.—**520**

ALLPORT, G. W. (1954) *The nature of prejudice.* Reading, Mass.: Addison-Wesley.—**537**

ALLPORT, G. W. (1960) *Personality and social encounter.* Boston: Beacon Press.—**423**

ALLPORT, G. W., and ODBERT, H. S. (1936) Trait-names: A psycholexical study. *Psychological Monographs,* 47, No. 211.—**402**

ALLPORT, G. W., and VERNON, P. E. (1933) *Studies in expressive movement.* N.Y.: Macmillan.—**411**

ALLPORT, G. W., VERNON, P. E., and LINDZEY, G. (1960) *A study of values: A scale for measuring the dominant interests in personality* (3rd ed.). Boston: Houghton Mifflin.—**426**

ALTUS, W. C. (1966) Birth order and its sequelae. *Science,* 151:44–49.—**76**

AMERICAN PSYCHOLOGICAL ASSOCIATION (1970) *A career in psychology.* Washington, D.C.: American Psychological Association.—**23**

AMMONS, R. B. (1960) Reactions in a projective doll-play interview of white males two to six years of age to differences in skin color and facial features. *Journal of Genetic Psychology,* 76:323–41.—**77**

AMSEL, A. (1958) The role of frustrative nonreward in noncontinuous reward situations. *Psychological Bulletin,* 55:102–19.—**348**

AMSEL, A. (1967) Partial reinforcement effects on vigor and persistence. In Spence, K. W., and Spence, J. T. (eds.). *The psychology of learning and motivation,* vol. I. N.Y.: Academic Press, 1–65.—**348**

ANAND, B., *see* Wenger, Bagchi, and Anand (1961).

ANASTASI, A. (1968) *Psychological testing* (3rd ed.). N.Y.: Macmillan.—**382**

ANDERSEN, M. L., *see* Sarbin and Andersen (1967).

ANDERSON, W. L., *see* Sachs and Anderson (1967).

ANDERSSON, B. (1953) The effect of injections and hypertonic solutions in parts of the hypothalamus of goats. *Acta Physiologica Scandinavica,* 28:188–201.—**300**

ANKLES, T. M. (1939) *A study of jealousy as differentiated from envy.* Boston: Bruce Humphries.—**347**

APPLETON, S. (1968) *United States foreign policy.* Boston: Little, Brown.—**527**

APPLEY, M. H., *see* Cofer and Appley (1964).

APSLER, R., and SEARS, D. O. (1968) Warning, personal involvement, and attitude change. *Journal of Personality and Social Psychology,* 9:162–66.—**535**

ARAKAKI, K., *see* Kobasigawa, Arakaki, and Awiguni (1966).

ARCHER, E. J., *see* Bourne and Archer (1956).

ARDREY, R. (1966) *The territorial imperative.* N.Y.: Atheneum.—**319**

ARKIN, A. M., HASTEY, J. M., and REISER, M. F. (1966) Post-hypnotically stimulated sleeptalking. *Journal of Nervous and Mental Disease,* 142:293–309.—**171**

ARNOLD, M. (1949) A demonstrational analysis of the TAT in a clinical setting. *Journal of Abnormal and Social Psychology,* 44:97–111.—**434**

ARNOLD, M. (1960) *Emotion and personality* (2 vols.). N.Y.: Columbia Univ. Press.—**342**

ARONSON, E., *see* Abelson, Aronson, McGuire, Newcomb, Rosenberg, and Tannenbaum (eds.) (1968); Lindzey and Aronson (1968–69).

ARONSON, E., and LINDER, D. (1965) Gain and loss of esteem as determinants of interpersonal attractiveness. *Journal of Experimental Social Psychology,* 1:156–71.—**515**

ASCH, S. E. (1956) Studies of independence and submission to group pressure: I. A minority of one against a unanimous majority. *Psychological Monographs,* 70, No. 416.—**522**

ASCHOFF, J. (1965) Circadian rhythm in man. *Science,* 148:1427.—**166**

ASTRUP, C., *see* Stephens, Astrup, and Mangrum (1967).

ATKINSON, J. W. (1964) *An introduction to motivation.* Princeton, N.J.: Van Nostrand.—**311, 327**

ATKINSON, J. W., *see* McClelland, Atkinson, Clark, and Lowell (1953); Moulton, Raphelson, Kristofferson, and Atkinson (1958).

ATKINSON, J. W., and FEATHER, N. T. (eds.) (1966) *A theory of achievement motivation.* N.Y.: Wiley.—**333**

ATKINSON, J. W., and LITWIN, G. H. (1960) Achievement motive and test anxiety conceived as motive to approach success and motive to avoid failure. *Journal of Abnormal and Social Psychology,* 60:52–63.—**328**

ATKINSON, K., MACWHINNEY, B., and STOEL, C. (1970) An experiment on recognition of babbling. *Papers and reports on child language development.* Stanford, Calif.: Stanford Univ. Press.—**71, 280**

ATKINSON, R. C. (1957) A stochastic model for rote serial learning. *Psychometrika,* 22:87–95.—**212**

ATKINSON, R. C. (1968) Computerized instruction and the learning process. *American Psychologist,* 23:225–39.—**250**

ATKINSON, R. C., *see* Hopkins and Atkinson (1968).

ATKINSON, R. C., BOWER, G. H., and CROTHERS, E. J. (1965) *An introduction to mathematical learning theory.* N.Y.: Wiley.—**215, 224**

ATKINSON, R. C., and ESTES, W. K. (1963) Stimulus sampling theory. In Luce, R. D., Bush, R. R., and Galanter, E. (eds.) *Handbook of mathematical psychology,* vol. II. N.Y.: Wiley, 121–268.—**220**

ATKINSON, R. C., and PAULSON, J. A. (1971) An approach to the psychology of instruction. *Psychological Bulletin,* in press.—**254**

ATKINSON, R. C., and SHIFFRIN, R. M. (1968) Human memory: A proposed system and its control processes. In Spence, K. W., and Spence, J. T. (eds.) *The psychology of learning and motivation,* vol. II. N.Y.: Academic Press.—**238**

ATKINSON, R. C., and WICKENS, T. D. (1971) Human memory and the concept of reinforcement. In Glaser, R. (ed.) *The nature of reinforcement.* Columbus, Ohio: Merrill. —**238**

ATKINSON, R. C., and WILSON, H. A. (eds.) (1969) *Computer-assisted instruction.* N.Y.: Academic Press.—**249, 270**

AUERBACH, A. H., *see* Gottschalk and Auerbach (1966).

AWIGUNI, A., *see* Kobasigawa, Arakaki, and Awiguni (1966).

AX, A. F. (1953) The physiological differentiation between fear and anger in humans. *Psychosomatic Medicine,* 15:433–42.—**337, 338**

AYLLON, T., and AZRIN, N. H. (1968) *The token economy: A motivational system for therapy and rehabilitation.* N.Y.: Appleton-Century-Crofts.—**498**

AZRIN, N. H., *see* Ayllon and Azrin (1968).

BABICH, F. R., *see* Jacobson, Babich, Bubash, and Jacobson (1965).

BACK, K., *see* Festinger, Schachter, and Back (1950).

BAER, D., *see* Rosenfeld and Baer (1969).

BAER, P. E., and FUHRER, M. J. (1968) Cognitive processes during differential trace and delayed conditioning of the G.S.R. *Journal of Experimental Psychology,* 78:81–88.—**195**

BAGCHI, B., *see* Wenger and Bagchi (1961); Wenger, Bagchi, and Anand (1961).

BAIER, K., and RESCHER, N. (eds.) (1969) *Values and the future: The impact of technological change on American values.* N.Y.: Free Press.—**560**

BAKER, C. T., *see* Sontag, Baker, and Nelson (1958).

BALDWIN, A. L. (1967) *Theories of child development.* N.Y.: Wiley.—**81**

BALDWIN, B. T., and STECHER, L. I. (1922) Mental growth curves of normal and superior children. *University of Iowa Studies in Child Welfare,* 2, No. 1.—**372**

BALL, E. S., *see* Bossard and Ball (1955).

BANDURA, A. (1969) *Principles of behavior modification.* N.Y.: Holt, Rinehart and Winston.—**409, 420, 495, 505, 510**

BANDURA, A., BLANCHARD, E. B., and RITTER, B. (1969) The relative efficacy of desensitization and modeling approaches for inducing behavioral, affective, and attitudinal changes. *Journal of Personality and Social Psychology,* 13:173–99.—**496, 497**

BANDURA, A., and MCDONALD, F. (1963) The influence of social reinforcement and the behavior of models in shaping children's moral judgment. *Journal of Abnormal and Social Psychology,* 67:274–81.—**79**

BANDURA, A., and WALTERS, R. H. (1963) *Social learning and personality development.* N.Y.: Holt, Rinehart and Winston.—**73, 404, 409**

BANUAZIZI, A., *see* Miller and Banuazizi (1968).

BARBER, T. X. (1969) *Hypnosis: A scientific approach.* N.Y.: Van Nostrand Reinhold. —**177, 185**

BARENFELD, M., *see* Simon and Barenfeld (1969).

BARKER, C. H., *see* Schein, Schneier, and Barker (1961).

BARKER, R. G., and BARKER, L. S. (1963) Sixty-five and over. In Williams, R. H., Tibbitts, C., and Donahue, W. (eds.) *Processes of aging,* vol. I. N.Y.: Atherton Press, 246–72.—**95**

BARKER, R. G., DEMBO, T., and LEWIN, K. (1941) Frustration and regression: An experiment with young children. *University of Iowa Studies in Child Welfare,* 18, No. 386.—**447**

BARRON, J. N., *see* Kelsey and Barron (1958).

BARRY, W. A. (1970) Marriage research and conflict: An integrative review. *Psychological Bulletin,* 73:41–54.—**98**

BATEMAN, F., *see* Soal and Bateman (1954).

BATESON, N. (1966) Familiarization, group discussion, and risk taking. *Journal of Experimental Social Psychology,* 2:119–29. —**523**

BAUER, J. A., JR., *see* Held and Bauer (1967).

BAUER, R. A. (ed.) (1966) *Social indicators.* Cambridge, Mass.: M.I.T. Press.—**559**

BAUER, R. A., and GERGEN, K. J. (eds.) (1968) *The study of policy formation.* N.Y.: Free Press.—**556**

BAYER, E. (1929) Beiträge zur Zweikomponententheorie des Hungers. *Zeitschrift für Psychologie,* 112:1–54.—**305**

BAYLEY, N. (1932) A study of the crying of infants during mental and physical tests. *Journal of Genetic Psychology,* 40:306–29. —**344**

BAYLEY, N. (1940a) Mental growth in young children. *39th Yearbook, Part II, National Society for the Study of Education.* Chicago: Univ. of Chicago Press.—**389**

BAYLEY, N. (1940b) Factors influencing the growth of intelligence in young children. *39th Yearbook, Part II, National Society for the Study of Education.* Chicago: Univ. of Chicago Press.—**389**

BEACH, F. A. (1944) Relative effects of androgen upon the mating behavior of male rats subjected to pre-brain injury or castration. *Journal of Experimental Zoology,* 97:249–85.—**302**

BEACH, F. A. (1956) Characteristics of masculine "sex drive." *Nebraska symposium on motivation.* Lincoln, Nebr.: Univ. of Nebraska Press, 4:1–32.—**302**

BEAN, L. L., *see* Myers and Bean (1968).

BEAR, R. M., *see* Hess and Bear (eds.) (1968).

BECK, W. S., *see* Simpson and Beck (1965), (1969).

BECKER, W. C., PETERSON, D. R., HELLMER, L. A., SHOEMAKER, D. J., and QUAY, H. C. (1962) Factors in parental behavior and personality as related to problem behavior in children. *Journal of Consulting Psychology,* 33:509–35.—**73**

BEERS, C. W. (1908) *A mind that found itself.* N.Y.: Doubleday.—**489**

BEIDLER, L. M. (1961) Mechanisms of gustatory and olfactory receptor stimulation. In Rosenblith, W. A. (ed.) *Sensory communication.* N.Y.: Wiley.—**130**

BÉKÉSY, G. V. (1960) *Experiments in hearing.* N.Y.: McGraw-Hill.—**134**

BÉKÉSY, G. V. (1967) *Sensory inhibition.* Princeton, N.J.: Princeton Univ. Press.— **134**

BELL, D. (ed.) (1968) *Toward the year 2000.* Boston: Houghton Mifflin.—**559**

BELL, R. Q. (1960) Relations between behavior manifestations in the human neonate. *Child Development,* 31:463–77.—**398**

BELLUGI, U., *see* Brown and Bellugi (1964).

BENDIX, R., *see* Lipsit and Bendix (1959).

BENNETT, E. L., *see* Rosenzweig and Bennett (1970).

BENNIS, W. G., SCHEIN, E. H., BERLEW, D. E., and STEELE, F. I. (eds.) (1968) *Interpersonal dynamics* (rev. ed.). Homewood, Ill.: Dorsey Press.—**537**

BENZINGER, T. H. (1961) The human thermostat. *Scientific American,* 204:134–47.— **35, 36**

BERDIE, R. F. (1969) The uses of evaluation in guidance. In Tyler, R. W. (ed.) *Educational evaluation: New roles, new means.* 68th Yearbook, Part II, National Society for the Study of Education. Chicago: Univ. of Chicago Press, 51–80.—**360**

BERELSON, B. (1954) What "missing the newspaper" means. In Schramm, W. (ed.) *The process and effects of mass communication.* Urbana, Ill.: Univ. of Illinois Press, 36–47.—**531**

BERGER, R. J. (1963) Experimental modification of dream content by meaningful verbal stimuli. *British Journal of Psychiatry,* 109:722–40.—**171**

BERGIN, A. E. (1962) The effect of dissonant persuasive communications upon changes in self-referring attitudes. *Journal of Personality,* 30:423–38.—**532**

BERKOWITZ, L. (1962) *Aggression: A social psychological analysis.* N.Y.: McGraw-Hill.—**463**

BERKOWITZ, L. (1964) *The development of motives and values in the child.* N.Y.: Basic Books.—**333**

BERKOWITZ, L. (ed.) (1969) *Roots of aggression.* N.Y.: Atherton Press.—**333**

BERLEW, D. E., *see* Bennis, Schein, Berlew, and Steele (1968).

BERLYNE, D. E. (1966) Curiosity and exploration. *Science,* 153:25–33.—**307**

BERLYNE, D. E., and SLATER, J. (1957) Perceptual curiosity, exploratory behavior and maze learning. *Journal of Comparative and Physiological Psychology,* 50:228–32.—**307**

BERNAUT, E., *see* Leites and Bernaut (1954).

BERSCHEID, E., *see* Darley and Berscheid (1967).

BERSCHEID, E., BOYE, D., and DARLEY, J. M. (1968) Effect of forced association upon voluntary choice to associate. *Journal of Personality and Social Psychology,* 8:13–19.—**515**

BETTELHEIM, B. (1943) Individual and mass behavior in extreme situations. *Journal of Abnormal and Social Psychology,* 38:417–52.—**450**

BEVAN, W., *see* Helson and Bevan (1967); Secord, Bevan, and Katz (1956).

BEVER, T. G., *see* Fodor and Bever (1965); Garrett, Bever, and Fodor (1966).

BIDERMAN, A. D. (1966) Social indicators and goals. In Bauer, R. A. (ed.) *Social indicators.* Cambridge, Mass.: M.I.T. Press, 68–153.—**545, 546**

BIDERMAN, A. D., and ZIMMER, H. (eds.) (1961) *The manipulation of human behavior.* N.Y.: Wiley.—**538**

BIRNEY, R. C., *see* Teevan and Birney (1964a); Teevan and Birney (1964b).

BIRNEY, R. C., BURDICK, H., and TEEVAN, R. C. (1969) *Fear of failure.* N.Y.: Van Nostrand Reinhold.—**333**

BIRNEY, R. C., and TEEVAN, R. C. (eds.) (1962) *Measuring human motivation.* Princeton, N.J.: Van Nostrand.—**333**

BLACK, H. (1963) *They shall not pass.* N.Y.: Morrow.—**379**

BLAKE, R. R., *see* Helson, Blake, and Mouton (1958).

BLAKESLEE, P., *see* Gunter, Feigenson, and Blakeslee (1965).

BLANCHARD, E. B., *see* Bandura, Blanchard, and Ritter (1969).

BLOCK, J. (1965) *The challenge of response sets: Unconfounding meaning, acquiescence, and social desirability in the MMPI.* N.Y.: Appleton-Century-Crofts.—**432**

BLOCK, J. H., HAAN, N., and SMITH, M. B. (1968) Activism and apathy in contemporary adolescents. In Adams, J. F. (ed.) *Understanding adolescence.* Boston: Allyn and Bacon, 198–231.—**92**

BLOOD, R. O., and WOLFE, D. M. (1968) Husbands and wives. In Bell, R. (ed.) *Studies in marriage and the family.* N.Y.: Crowell.—**98**

BLUM, G. S. (1966) *Psychodynamics: The science of unconscious mental forces.* Belmont, Calif.: Wadsworth.—**420**

BLUM, R. H., and Associates (1969) *Drugs: Vol. I. Society and drugs; Vol. II. Students and drugs.* San Francisco, Calif.: Jossey-Bass.—**185**

BODMER, W. F., and CAVALLI-SFORZA, L. L. (1970) Intelligence and race. *Scientific American,* 223:19–29.—**396**

BOGGAN, W., *see* Schlesinger, Elston, and Boggan (1966).

BOREN, J. J., *see* Brodie, Malis, Moreno, and Boren (1960).

BORING, E. G. (1950) *A history of experimental psychology* (2nd ed.). N.Y.: Appleton-Century-Crofts.—**22**

BORING, E. G., *see* Herrnstein and Boring (1965).

BOSSARD, J. H. S., and BALL, E. S. (1955) Personality roles in the large family. *Child Development,* 26:71–78.—**76**

BOTWINICK, J., and THOMPSON, L. (1968) Age difference in reaction: An artifact? *Gerontologist,* 8:25–28.—**99**

BOUDREAU, J. C., *see* Hirsch and Boudreau (1958).

BOULTER, L. R., *see* Endler, Boulter, and Osser (eds.) (1968).

BOURNE, L. E., JR. (1966) *Human conceptual behavior.* Boston: Allyn and Bacon.—**292**

BOURNE, L. E., JR., and ARCHER, E. J. (1956) Time continuously on target as a function of distribution of practice. *Journal of Experimental Psychology,* 51:25–33.—**211**

BOUTERLINE-YOUNG, H., *see* Mussen and Bouterline-Young (1968).

BOWER, G. H. (1966) A descriptive theory of human memory. In Kimble, D. P. (ed.) *Learning, remembering, and forgetting,* vol. II. N.Y.: New York Academy of Science.—**138, 151, 213**

BOWER, G. H. (1970a) Analysis of a mnemonic device. *American Scientist,* 58:496–510.—**242**

BOWER, G. H. (1970b) Organizational factors in memory. *Journal of Cognitive Psychology,* 1:18–46.—**243, 260**

BOWER, G. H., *see* Atkinson, Bower, and Crothers (1965); Hilgard and Bower (1966); Trabasso and Bower (1968).

BOWLBY, J. A. (1960) Separation anxiety. *International Journal of Psychoanalysis,* 41:89–113.—**70**

BOWMAN, P. H., *see* Guetzkow and Bowman (1946).

BOYE, D., *see* Berscheid, Boye, and Darley (1968).

BRADY, J. V., PORTER, R. W., CONRAD, D. G., and MASON, J. W. (1958) Avoidance behavior and the development of gastroduodenal ulcers. *Journal of the Experimental Analysis of Behavior,* 1:69–73.—**476, 477**

BRAINE, M. D. S. (1963) The ontogeny of English phrase structure: The first phrase. *Language,* 39:1–13.—**281, 282**

BRAYFIELD, A. H. (1969) Developmental planning for a graduate program in psychology. *American Psychologist,* 24:669–74.—**551**

BRELAND, K., and BRELAND, M. (1966) *Animal behavior.* N.Y.: Macmillan.—**202**

BRELAND, M., *see* Breland and Breland (1966).

BRIER, R., *see* Rhine and Brier (1968).

BRIM, O. G., JR. (1965) American attitudes toward intelligence tests. *American Psychologist,* 20:125–30.—**379–80**

BRITTAIN, C. V. (1968) An exploration of the bases of peer-compliance and parent-compliance in adolescence. *Adolescence,* 2:445–58.—**90**

BROADBENT, D. E. (1963) Flow of information within the organism. *Journal of Verbal Learning and Verbal Behavior,* 4:34–39.—**238**

BROCK, T., *see* Greenwald, Brock, and Ostrum (eds.) (1968).

BRODIE, D. A., MALIS, J. L., MORENO, O. M., and BOREN, J. J. (1960) Nonreversibility of appetitive characteristics of intracranial stimulation. *American Journal of Physiology,* 199:707–09.—**209**

BROEN, W. E., *see* Coleman and Broen (1971).

BROWN, J. F., and VOTH, A. C. (1937) The path of seen movement as a function of the vector field. *American Journal of Psychology,* 49:543–63.—**146**

BROWN, J. S. (1948) Gradients of approach and avoidance responses and their relation to motivation. *Journal of Comparative and Physiological Psychology,* 41:450–65.—**444, 445**

BROWN, R. (1962) Models of attitude change. In Brown, R., and others *New directions in psychology.* N.Y.: Holt, Rinehart and Winston, 1–85.—**329**

BROWN, R. (1965) *Social psychology.* N.Y.: Free Press.—**529**

BROWN, R. (1970) The first sentences of child and chimpanzee. In Brown, R., and others *Psycholinguistics: Selected papers.* N.Y.: Free Press, 208–31.—**285**

BROWN, R., and BELLUGI, U. (1964) Three processes in the child's acquisition of syntax. *Harvard Educational Review,* 34:133–51.—**282**

BROWN, R., and HILDUM, D. C. (1956) Expectancy and the identification of syllables. *Language,* 32:411–19.—**277**

BROWN, R. W., and MCNEILL, D. (1966) The "tip-of-the-tongue" phenomenon. *Journal of Verbal Learning and Verbal Behavior,* 5:325–37.—**230**

BRUNER, J. S. (1966) *Toward a theory of instruction.* Cambridge, Mass.: The Belknap Press of Harvard Univ. Press.—**270**

BRUNER, J. S., and GOODMAN, C. C. (1947) Value and need as organizing factors in perception. *Journal of Abnormal and Social Psychology,* 42:33–44.—**156**

BRUNING, J. L., and KINTZ, B. L. (1968) *Computational handbook of statistics.* Chicago: Scott, Foresman.—**578**

BRYAN, W. L., and HARTER, N. (1897) Studies in the physiology and psychology of the telegraphic language. *Psychological Review,* 4:27–53.—**210**

BUBASH, S., *see* Jacobson, Babich, Bubash, and Jacobson (1965).

self-esteem for social influence. In Hovland, C. I., and Janis, I. J. (eds.) *Personality and persuasibility,* vol. II. New Haven, Conn.: Yale Univ. Press, 102–18.—**416, 417**

COHEN, J. (1969) *Personality assessment.* Chicago: Rand McNally.—**438**

COLBY, K. M., and ENEA, H. (1967) Heuristic methods for computer understanding of natural language in the context-restricted on-line dialogue. *Mathematical Biosciences,* 1:1–25.—**290, 503, 504**

COLEMAN, J. C. (1964) *Abnormal Psychology in modern life* (3rd ed.). Chicago: Scott, Foresman.—**463, 469**

COLEMAN, J. C., and BROEN, W. E. (1971) *Abnormal Psychology and modern life* (4th ed.). Chicago: Scott, Foresman.—**486**

COLLINS, B. E. (1969) The effect of monetary inducements on the amount of attitude change induced by forced compliance. In Elmo, A. (ed.) *Role playing, reward, and attitude change.* N.Y.: Van Nostrand Reinhold.—**530**

COLLINS, B. E. (1970) *Social psychology.* Reading, Mass.: Addison-Wesley.—**537**

COLLINS, B. E., *see* Kiesler, Collins, and Miller (1969).

CONGER, J. J., *see* Mussen, Conger, and Kagan (1969); Sawrey, Conger, and Turrell (1956).

CONRAD, D. G., *see* Brady, Porter, Conrad, and Mason (1958).

CONRAD, H. S., and JONES, H. E. (1940) A second study of familial resemblance in intelligence. *39th Yearbook, Part II, National Society for the Study of Education.* Chicago: Univ. of Chicago Press.—**389**

CONVERSE, P. E., *see* Campbell, Converse, Miller, and Stokes (1960).

CONVERSE, P. E., MILLER, W. E., RUSK, J. G., and WOLFE, A. G. (1969) Continuity and change in American politics: Parties and issues in the 1968 elections. *American Political Science Review,* 63:1083–105.—**528**

COOK, P. E., *see* Megargee and Cook (1967).

COOK, S. W., *see* Korten, Cook, and Lacey (1970).

COOMBS, C. H., DAWES, R. M., and TVERSKY, A. (1970) *Mathematical psychology: An elementary introduction.* Englewood Cliffs, N.J.: Prentice-Hall.—**224**

COOPER, J., *see* Linder, Cooper, and Jones (1967).

COOPER, L. M., *see* Hoskovec and Cooper (1967).

COOPERSMITH, S. (1967) *The antecedents of self-esteem.* San Francisco, Calif.: Freeman.—**72, 416**

COPPOCK, H. W., and CHAMBERS, R. M. (1954) Reinforcement of position preference by automatic injection of glucose. *Journal of Comparative and Physiological Psychology,* 47:355–57.—**207**

CORNELISON, A. R., *see* Lidz, Fleck, and Cornelison (1965).

CORNSWEET, T. N. (1969) Information processing in human visual systems. *Stanford*

Research Institute Journal, Feature Issue No. 5, 16–27.—**122, 123**

COSTA, L. D., *see* Vaughan, Costa, Gilden, and Schimmel (1965).

COUNCIL ON ENVIRONMENTAL QUALITY (1970) *Environmental quality.* Washington, D.C.: Superintendent of Documents.—**559**

COURTS, F. A. (1939) Relations between experimentally induced muscular tension and memorization. *Journal of Experimental Psychology,* 25:235–56.—**350**

COWEN, E. L., GARDNER, E. A., and ZAX, M. (1967) *Emergent approaches to mental health problems.* N.Y.: Appleton-Century-Crofts.—**510**

COWLES, J. T. (1937) Food-tokens as incentives for learning by chimpanzees. *Comparative Psychology Monographs,* 14, No. 71.—**310**

CRAIGHILL, P. G., *see* Sarason, Mandler, and Craighill (1952).

CRAIN, R. L., KATZ, E., and ROSENTHAL, D. B. (1969) *The politics of community conflict: The fluoridation decision.* Indianapolis, Ind.: Bobbs-Merrill.—**544**

CRICK, F. H. C. (1962) The genetic code. *Scientific American,* 207:66–74.—**385**

CRONBACH, L. J. (1970) *Essentials of psychological testing* (3rd ed.). N.Y.: Harper and Row.—**382, 435, 438**

CROTHERS, E. J., *see* Atkinson, Bower, and Crothers (1965).

CROTHERS, E. J., and SUPPES, P. C. (1967) *Experiments in second language learning.* N.Y.: Academic Press.—**213**

CROWNE, D. P., and MARLOWE, D. (1964) *The approval motive.* N.Y.: Wiley.—**412, 413**

CRUTCHFIELD, R. S., *see* Allen and Crutchfield (1963).

CUMMINGS, E., DEAN, L. R., NEWELL, D. S., and MCCAFFREY, I. (1960) Disengagement—A tentative theory of aging. *Sociometry,* 22:23–35.—**102**

DALLENBACH, K. M., *see* Jenkins and Dallenbach (1924); Minami and Dallenbach (1946).

D'ANDRADE, R. C. (1967) *Report on some testing and training procedures at Bassawa Primary School, Zaria, Nigeria.* Unpublished manuscript.—**363**

D'ANDRADE, R. C., *see* Rosen and D'Andrade (1959).

DANIELS, D. N., GILULA, M. F., and OCHBERG, F. M. (eds.) (1970) *Violence and the struggle for existence.* Boston: Little, Brown.—**333, 543**

DARLEY, J. M., *see* Berscheid, Boye, and Darley (1968).

DARLEY, J. M., and BERSCHEID, E. (1967) Increased liking caused by anticipation of personal contact. *Human Relations,* 20:29–40.—**515**

DARWIN, C. (1872) *The expression of emotions in man and animals.* N.Y.: Philosophical Library, 1955.—**341**

DASHIELL, J. F. (1925) A quantitative demonstration of animal drive. *Journal of Comparative Psychology,* 5:205–08.—**296**

DAVENPORT, J. W., CHAMOVE, A. S., and

HARLOW, H. F. (1970) The semi-automatic Wisconsin general test apparatus. *Behavioral Research Methods and Instrumentation,* 2:135–38.—**258**

DAVERT, E., *see* Morgan, Davert, and Hilgard (1970).

DAVIES, J. T. (1962) The mechanism of olfaction. In *Biological receptor mechanisms.* 16th Symp. Exptl. Biol., Univ. Birmingham, England, Sept. 1962. Cambridge: Cambridge Univ. Press.—**129**

DAVIS, A., *see* Eells, Davis, Havighurst, Herrick, and Tyler (1951).

DAVIS, A., and EELLS, K. (1953) *Davis-Eells games.* Yonkers, N.Y.: World Book.—**362**

DAWES, R. N., *see* Coombs, Dawes, and Tversky (1970).

DEAN, L. R., *see* Cummings, Dean, Newell, and McCaffrey (1960).

DEAN, S. J., *see* Goldstein and Dean (1966).

DE COURSEY, P. J. (1960) Phase control of activity in a rodent. *Cold Spring Harbor Symposia on Quantitative Biology,* 25:49–55.—**167**

DEESE, J. E. (1970) *Psycholinguistics.* Boston: Allyn and Bacon.—**292**

DEESE, J. E., and HULSE, S. (1967) *Psychology of learning* (3rd ed.). N.Y.: McGraw-Hill.—**224, 246, 270**

DEIKMAN, A. J. (1963) Experimental meditation. *Journal of Nervous and Mental Disease,* 136:329–73.—**179**

DELGADO, J. M. R., ROBERTS, W. W., and MILLER, N. E. (1954) Learning motivated by electrical stimulation of the brain. *American Journal of Physiology,* 179:587–93.—**209, 309**

DE LUCIA, L. A. (1963) The toy preference test: A measure of sex-role identification. *Child Development,* 34:107–17.—**74**

DEMBER, W. N. (1960) *The psychology of perception.* N.Y.: Holt, Rinehart and Winston.—**161**

DEMBO, T., *see* Barker, Dembo, and Lewin (1941).

DEMENT, W. (1960) The effect of dream deprivation. *Science,* 131:1705–07.—**172**

DEMENT, W. (1965) An essay on dreams: The role of physiology in understanding their nature. In Barron, F., and others *New directions in psychology,* vol. II. N.Y.: Holt, Rinehart and Winston, 135–257.—**169**

DEMENT, W. (1967) Discussion. In Kety, S. S., Evarts, E. V., and Williams, H. L. (eds.) *Sleep and altered states of consciousness.* Baltimore, Md.: Williams and Wilkins, 502–04.—**170**

DEMENT, W., and KLEITMAN, N. (1957) The relation of eye movements during sleep to dream activity: An objective method for the study of dreaming. *Journal of Experimental Psychology,* 53:339–46.—**168**

DENNIS, W. (1954a) Bibliographies of eminent scientists. *Scientific Monthly,* 79:180–83.—**101**

DENNIS, W. (1954b) Predicting scientific productivity in later decades from records of earlier decades. *Journal of Gerontology,* 9:465–67.—**101**

DENNIS, W. (1955) Variations in productivity

among creative workers. *Scientific Monthly,* 80:277–78.—**101**

DENZIN, N. K. (ed.) (1970) *The values of social science.* Chicago: Aldine.—**560**

DE RIVERA, J. H. (1968) *The psychological dimensions of foreign policy.* Columbus, Ohio: Merrill.—**558**

DEUTSCH, M., FISHMAN, J. A., KOGAN, N., NORTH, R., and WHITMAN, M. (1964) Guidelines for testing minority group children. *Journal of Social Issues,* 22:127–45.—**380**

DEUTSCH, M., and GERARD, H. B. (1955) A study of normative and informational social influences upon individual judgment. *Journal of Abnormal and Social Psychology,* 51:629–36.—**533**

DE VALOIS, R. L., and JACOBS, G. H. (1968) Primate color vision. *Science,* 162:533–40. —**121**

DINITZ, S., *see* Lively, Dinitz, and Reckless (1962).

DISTLER, L., *see* Mussen and Distler (1960).

DIXON, T. R., and HORTON, D. L. (eds.) (1968) *Verbal behavior and general behavior theory.* Englewood Cliffs, N.J.: Prentice-Hall.— **224, 292**

DOANE, B. K., MAHATOO, W., HERON, W., and SCOTT, T. H. (1959) Changes in perceptual function after isolation. *Canadian Journal of Psychology,* 13:210–19.—**48**

DODDS, J. B., *see* Frankenburg and Dodds (1967).

DODSON, J. D., *see* Yerkes and Dodson (1908).

DOLLARD, J., and others (1939) *Frustration and aggression.* New Haven, Conn.: Yale Univ. Press.—**319**

DONAHUE, G. (1967) A school district program for schizophrenic children. In Cowen, E., Gardner, E., and Zax, M. (eds.) *Emergent approaches to mental health problems.* N.Y.: Appleton-Century-Crofts, 369–86.—**502**

DONAHUE, W., *see* Williams, Tibbitts, and Donahue (1953).

DOOB, A. N., *see* Freedman and Doob (1968).

DORNBUSCH, S. M., HASTORF, A. H., RICHARDSON, S. A., MUZZY, R. E., and VREELAND, R. S. (1965) The perceiver and the perceived: Their relative influence on the categories of interpersonal cognition. *Journal of Personality and Social Psychology,* 1:434–40.—**513**

DOUVAN, E., and ADELSON, J. (1966) *The adolescent experience.* N.Y.: Wiley.—**89, 104**

DOWLING, J. E. (1966) Night blindness. *Scientific American,* 215:78–84.—**117**

DROLETTE, M. E., *see* Funkenstein, King, and Drolette (1957).

DU BOIS, P. H. (ed.) (1947) The classification program. *AAF Aviation Psychology Program Research Report,* No. 2.—**359, 360**

DUFFEY, R. F., *see* Moseley, Duffey, and Sherman (1963).

DUFFY, E. (1962) *Activation and behavior.* N.Y.: Wiley.—**341**

DURKHEIM, E. (1958) *Suicide* (original date, 1897). N.Y.: Free Press.—**517**

DYE, A. B., *see* Skeels and Dye (1939).

EBBESON, E. B., *see* Zimbardo and Ebbeson (1969).

EBBINGHAUS, H. (1885) *Memory* (Trans. by H. A. Ruger and C. E. Bussenius). N.Y.: Teachers College (1913).—**211, 228**

EBBINGHAUS, H. (1964) *Memory* (original date, 1885). N.Y.: Dover.—**245**

EBEL, H. W., *see* Cattell and Ebel (1964).

EBLING, F. J., *see* Carthy and Ebling (1964).

ECCLES, J. C. (1958) The physiology of imagination. *Scientific American,* 199:135–46.—**38**

EDWARDS, A. L. (1954) *Edwards Personal Preference Schedule* (*Manual*). N.Y.: Psychological Corporation.—**315, 432**

EDWARDS, A. L. (1957) *The social desirability variable in personality assessment and research.* N.Y.: Dryden.—**412, 432, 438**

EDWARDS, A. L. (1966) *Edwards Personality Inventory, Manual.* Chicago: Science Research Associates.—**431, 438**

EDWARDS, A. L. (1968) *Experimental design in psychological research* (3rd ed.). N.Y.: Holt, Rinehart and Winston.—**578**

EELLS, K., *see* Davis and Eells (1953).

EELLS, K., DAVIS, A., HAVIGHURST, R. J., HERRICK, V. E., and TYLER, R. W. (1951) *Intelligence and cultural differences.* Chicago: Univ. of Chicago Press.—**362**

EHRLICH, A. H., *see* Ehrlich and Ehrlich (1970).

EHRLICH, P. R., and EHRLICH, A. H. (1970) *Populations, resources, environment: Issues in human ecology.* San Francisco, Calif.: Freeman.—**549**

ELKIND, E., and FLAVELL, J. H. (eds.) (1969) *Studies in cognitive development: Essays in honor of Jean Piaget.* N.Y.: Oxford Univ. Press.—**81**

ELLIOTT, M. H. (1928) The effect of change of reward on the maze performance of rats. *University of California Publications in Psychology,* 4:19–30.—**305**

ELLIS, H. (1965) *The transfer of learning.* N.Y.: Macmillan.—**270**

ELMS, A. C. (1967) Role playing, incentive, and dissonance. *Psychological Bulletin,* 68:132–48.—**530**

ELSTON, R. C., *see* Schlesinger, Elston, and Boggan (1966).

EMERSON, P. E., *see* Schaffer and Emerson (1964).

EMMONS, W. W., and SIMON, C. W. (1956) The non-recall of material presented during sleep. *American Journal of Psychology,* 69:76–81.—**171**

ENDLER, N., BOULTER, L. R., and OSSER, H. (eds.) (1968) *Contemporary issues in developmental psychology.* N.Y.: Holt, Rinehart and Winston.—**81**

ENEA, H., *see* Colby and Enea (1967).

EPSTEIN, W. (1961) The influence of syntactical structure on learning. *American Journal of Psychology,* 74:80–85.—**278**

ERIKSEN, C. W. (ed.) (1962) *Behavior and awareness.* Durham, N.C.: Duke Univ. Press.—**185**

ERIKSON, E. H. (1954) The dream specimen of psychoanalysis. *Journal of the American Psychoanalytic Association,* 2:5–56.—**172**

ERIKSON, E. H. (1963) *Childhood and society* (2nd ed.). N.Y.: Norton.—**55, 65, 66**

ERIKSON, E. H. (1968) *Identity, youth, and crisis.* N.Y.: Norton.—**416**

ERLENMEYER-KIMLING, L., and JARVIK, L. F. (1963) Genetics and intelligence: A review. *Science,* 142:1477–79.—**391**

ERON, L. D., WALDER, L. O., TOGIO, R., and LEFKOWITZ, M. M. (1963) Social class, parental punishment for aggression, and child aggression. *Child Development,* 34:849–67.—**72**

ERVIN, S., *see* Miller and Ervin (1964).

ESTES, W. K. (1949) A study of motivating conditions necessary for secondary reinforcement. *Journal of Experimental Psychology,* 39:306–10.—**201**

ESTES, W. K. (1950) Toward a statistical theory of learning. *Psychological Review,* 57:94–107.—**220**

ESTES, W. K. (1959) The statistical approach to learning theory. In Koch, S. (ed.) *Psychology: A study of a science,* vol. II. N.Y.: McGraw-Hill, 380–491.—**220**

ESTES, W. K. (1960) Learning theory and the new "mental chemistry." *Psychological Review,* 67:207–23.—**213**

ESTES,, W. K. (1964) All-or-none processes in learning and retention. *American Psychologist,* 19:16–25.—**215**

ESTES, W. K. (1970) *Learning theory and mental development.* N.Y.: Academic Press. —**224, 264**

ESTES, W. K., *see* Atkinson and Estes (1963); Neimark and Estes (1967).

ESTES, W. K., and BURKE, C. J. (1953) A theory of stimulus variability in learning. *Psychological Review,* 60:276–86.—**220**

ESTES, W. K., and SUPPES, P. C. (1959) Foundations of linear models. In Bush, R. R., and Estes, W. K. (eds.) *Studies in mathematical learning theory.* Stanford, Calif.: Stanford Univ. Press, 137–79.—**220**

EVANS, F. J., *see* Cobb, Evans, Gustafson, O'Connell, Orne, and Shor (1965).

EYSENCK, H. J. (1960) *The structure of human personality.* N.Y.: Macmillan.—**406, 419**

EYSENCK, H. J. (1966) *The effects of psychotherapy.* N.Y.: International Science Press. —**505, 510**

EYSENCK, H. J. (1967) *The biological basis of personality.* Springfield, Ill.: Thomas.—**419**

EYSENCK, H. J., and EYSENCK, S. B. G. (1963) *The Eysenck Personality Inventory.* San Diego, Calif.: Educational and Industrial Testing Service; London: Univ. of London Press.—**405, 431, 438**

EYSENCK, H. J., and RACHMAN, S. (1965) *The causes and cures of neurosis.* San Diego, Calif.: Knapp; London: Routledge and Kegan Paul.—**405**

EYSENCK, S. B. G., *see* Eysenck and Eysenck (1963).

FARBER, I. E., HARLOW, H. F., and WEST, L. J. (1957) Brainwashing, conditioning, and DDD. *Sociometry,* 20:271–85.—**534**

FAWCETT, J. T. (1970) *Psychology and population.* N.Y.: Population Council.—**559**

FEATHER, N. T., *see* Atkinson and Feather (1966).

FECHNER, G. (1860) *Elements of psychophysics* (Trans. by H. E. Adler). N.Y.: Holt, Rinehart and Winston, 1966.—**109**

FEIGENBAUM, E. A. (1970) Information processing and memory. In Norman, D. A. (ed.) *Models of human memory.* N.Y.: Academic Press, 451–68.—**290**

FEIGENBAUM, E. A., and FELDMAN, J. (eds.) (1963) *Computers and thought.* N.Y.: McGraw-Hill.—**289, 292**

FEIGENSON, L., *see* Gunter, Feigenson, and Blakeslee (1965).

FELDMAN, J., *see* Feigenbaum and Feldman (1963).

FESHBACH, S., *see* Janis and Feshbach (1953).

FESHBACH, S., and SINGER, R. D. (1957) The effects of fear arousal and suppression of fear upon social perception. *Journal of Abnormal and Social Psychology,* 63:381–85.—**513**

FESTINGER, L. (1942) Wish, expectation, and group standards as affecting level of aspiration. *Journal of Abnormal and Social Psychology,* 37:184–200.—**325, 326**

FESTINGER, L. (1957) *A theory of cognitive dissonance.* Evanston, Ill.: Row, Peterson.—**329, 330, 529**

FESTINGER, L., *see* Lawrence and Festinger (1962).

FESTINGER, L., and CANNON, L. K. (1965) Information about spatial location based on knowledge about efference. *Psychological Review,* 72:373–84.—**141**

FESTINGER, L., and CARLSMITH, J. M. (1959) Cognitive consequences of forced compliance. *Journal of Abnormal and Social Psychology,* 58:203–10.—**530**

FESTINGER, L., PEPITONE, A., and NEWCOMB, T. M. (1952) Some consequences of deindividuation in a group. *Journal of Abnormal and Social Psychology,* 47:382–89.—**518**

FESTINGER, L., RIECKEN, H. W., and SCHACHTER, S. (1956) *When prophecy fails.* Minneapolis: Univ. of Minnesota Press.—**330**

FESTINGER, L., SCHACHTER, S., and BACK, K. (1950) *Social pressures in informal groups: A study of human factors in housing.* N.Y.: Harper and Row.—**515, 545**

FESTINGER, L., and others (1964) *Conflict, decision, and dissonance.* Stanford, Calif.: Stanford Univ. Press.—**329, 530**

FIELD, P. B., *see* Janis and Field (1959).

FISHBEIN, M., *see* Steiner and Fishbein (1965).

FISHER, C., GRASS, J., and ZUCH, J. (1965) A cycle of penile erection synchronous with dreaming (REM) sleep. *Archives of General Psychiatry,* 12:29–45.—**172**

FISHMAN, J. A., *see* Deutsch, Fishman, Kogan, North, and Whitman (1964).

FLANAGAN, J. C. (1963) The definition and measurement of ingenuity. In Taylor, C. W., and Barron, F. (eds.) *Scientific creativity: Its recognition and development.* N.Y.: Wiley.—**371**

FLAVELL, J. H., *see* Elkind and Flavell (eds.) (1969).

FLECK, S., *see* Lidz, Fleck, and Cornelison (1965).

FLEXNER, L. (1967) Dissection of memory in mice with antibiotics. *Proceedings of the American Philosophical Society,* 111:343–46.—**232**

FODOR, J. A., *see* Garrett, Bever, and Fodor (1966).

FODOR, J. A., and BEVER, T. G. (1965) The psychological reality of linguistic segments. *Journal of Verbal Learning and Verbal Behavior,* 4:414–20.—**278**

FORD, D. N., and URBAN, H. B. (1963) *Systems of psychotherapy.* N.Y.: Wiley.—**510**

FORGUS, R. H. (1966) *Perception: The basic process in cognitive development.* N.Y.: McGraw-Hill.—**134, 161**

FORWALD, H. (1961) A PK experiment with die faces as targets. *Journal of Parapsychology,* 25:1–12.—**156**

FOULKES, D., *see* Monroe, Rechtschaffen, Foulkes, and Jensen (1965).

FRAISSE, P. (1968) The emotions. In Nuttin, J., Fraisse, P., and Meili, R. *Motivation, emotion, and personality.* N.Y.: Basic Books, 102–91.—**339, 351**

FRANKENBURG, W. K., and DODDS, J. B. (1967) The Denver developmental screening test. *Journal of Pediatrics,* 71:181–91.—**57**

FRANKIE, G., *see* Hetherington and Frankie (1967).

FRANKS, C. M. (1966) Conditioning and conditioned aversion therapies in the treatment of the alcoholic. *International Journal of the Addictions,* 1:61–98.—**497**

FRANZ, S. I. (1933) *Persons one and three.* N.Y.: McGraw-Hill.—**414**

FRASER, S. C., *see* Freedman and Fraser (1966).

FREEDMAN, D. X., *see* Redlich and Freedman (1966).

FREEDMAN, J. L., CARLSMITH, J. M., and SEARS, D. O. (1970) *Social psychology.* Englewood Cliffs, N.J.: Prentice-Hall.—**537**

FREEDMAN, J. L., CARLSMITH, J. M., and SUOMI, S. (1967) The effect of familiarity on liking. Unpublished paper cited by Freedman, Carlsmith, and Sears (1970), 72.—**515**

FREEDMAN, J. L., and DOOB, A. N. (1968) *Deviancy.* N.Y.: Academic Press.—**519, 520**

FREEDMAN, J. L., and FRASER, S. C. (1966) Compliance without pressure: The foot-in-the-door technique. *Journal of Personality and Social Psychology,* 4:195–202.—**533**

FREEDMAN, J. L., and SEARS, D. O. (1965) Selective exposure. In Berkowitz, L. (ed.) *Advances in experimental social psychology,* vol. II. N.Y.: Academic Press.—**535**

FREEDMAN, M., *see* Webster, Freedman, and Heist (1962).

FREEMAN, F. N., *see* Newman, Freeman, and Holzinger (1937).

FRENCH, E. G. (1958) Effects of the interaction of motivation and feedback on performance. In Atkinson, J. W. (ed.) *Motives in fantasy, action, and society.* Princeton, N.J.: Van Nostrand, 400–08.—**313**

FRENCH, G. M., and HARLOW, H. F. (1962) Variability of delayed-reaction performance in normal and brain-damaged rhesus monkeys. *Journal of Neurophysiology,* 25:585–99.—**42**

FRENCH, T. M., and FROMM, E. (1963) *Dream interpretation: A new approach.* N.Y.: Basic Books.—**172**

FRENKEL-BRUNSWIK, E. (1939) Mechanisms of self-deception. *Journal of Social Psychology,* 10:409–20.—**456**

FRENKEL-BRUNSWIK, E. (1942) Motivation and behavior. *Genetic Psychology Monographs,* 26:121–265.—**315**

FREUD, A. (1937) *The ego and the mechanisms of defense.* London: Hogarth Press.—**463**

FREUD, S. (1900) *The interpretation of dreams.* (standard ed., 1953), vols. IV, V. London: Hogarth Press.—**171, 317**

FREUD, S. (1927) *The ego and the id.* London: Hogarth Press.—**408**

FREUD, S. (1933) *New introductory lectures on psychoanalysis.* N.Y.: Norton.—**7, 72**

FRIED, R. K., and SMITH, E. E. (1962) Post-menarcheal growth patterns. *Journal of Pediatrics,* 61:562–65.—**84**

FROMM, E., *see* French and Fromm (1963).

FRYER, D. H., and HENRY, E. R. (eds.) (1950) *Handbook of applied psychology* (2 vols.). N.Y.: Rinehart.—**428**

FUHRER, M. J., *see* Baer and Fuhrer (1968).

FULLER, J. L. (1962) *Motivation, a biological perspective.* N.Y.: Random House.—**311**

FULLER, J. L., *see* Scott and Fuller (1965)

FULLER, J. L., and THOMPSON, W. R. (1960) *Behavior genetics.* N.Y.: Wiley.—**388, 396**

FUNKENSTEIN, D. H. (1955) The physiology of fear and anger. *Scientific American,* 192:74–80.—**337**

FUNKENSTEIN, D. H., KING, S. H., and DROLETTE, M. E. (1957) *Mastery of stress.* Cambridge, Mass.: Harvard Univ. Press.—**337**

GAGNÉ, R. M. (1970) *The conditions of learning* (2nd ed.). N.Y.: Holt, Rinehart and Winston.—**261, 270**

GALANTER, E. (1962) Contemporary psychophysics. In Brown, R., and others (eds.) *New directions in psychology.* N.Y.: Holt, Rinehart and Winston, 89–156.—**108**

GALANTER, E., *see* Luce, Bush, and Galanter (1963), (1965); Miller, Galanter, and Pribram (1960).

GARDNER, B. T., and GARDNER, R. A. (1969) Two-way communication with an infant chimpanzee. In Schrier, A., and Stollnitz, F. (eds.) *Behavior of non-human primates,* vol. III. N.Y.: Academic Press.—**284, 285**

GARDNER, E. A., *see* Cowen, Gardner, and Zax (1967).

GARDNER, R. A., *see* Gardner and Gardner (1969).

GARNSEY, M. E., and HIBBS, J. R. (eds.) (1967) *Social sciences and the environment.* Boulder, Colo.: Univ. of Colorado Press.—**559**

GARRETT, M., BEVER, T., and FODOR, J. A. (1966) The active use of grammar in speech perception. *Perception and Psychophysics*, 1:30–32.—**278**

GATES, A. I. (1917) Recitation as a factor in memorizing. *Archives of Psychology*, No. 40.—**243, 244**

GATES, G. S. (1926) An observational study of anger. *Journal of Experimental Psychology*, 9:325–36.—**348**

GAUTIER, M., *see* Lejeune, Gautier, and Turpin (1959).

GEEN, R. G. (1968) Effects of frustration, attack, and prior training in aggressiveness upon aggressive behavior. *Journal of Personality and Social Psychology*, 9:316–21. —**348**

GENGEL, R. W., *see* Tannenbaum and Gengel (1966).

GERARD, H. B., *see* Deutsch and Gerard (1955).

GERGEN, K. J. (1968) Personal consistency and the presentation of self. In Gordon, C., and Gergen, K. J. (eds.) *The self in social interaction*, vol. I. N.Y.: Wiley, 299–308.—**514**

GERGEN, K. J., *see* Bauer and Gergen (1968); Gordon and Gergen (1968).

GERGEN, K. J., and WISHNOW, B. (1965) Others' self-evaluations and interaction anticipation as determinants of self-presentation. *Journal of Personality and Social Psychology*, 2:348–58.—**514**

GETZELS, J. W., and JACKSON, P. W. (1962) *Creativity and intelligence: Explorations with gifted students.* N.Y.: Wiley.—**371, 379**

GIBSON, E. J. (1969) *Principles of perceptual learning and development.* N.Y.: Appleton-Century-Crofts.—**161**

GIBSON, E. J., and WALK, R. D. (1956) The effect of prolonged exposure to visually presented patterns on learning to discriminate them. *Journal of Comparative and Physiological Psychology*, 49:239–42.—**17**

GIBSON, E. J., and WALK, R. D. (1960) The "visual cliff." *Scientific American*, 202:64–71.—**151, 152**

GILDEN, L., *see* Vaughan, Costa, Gilden, and Schimmel (1965).

GILLIGAN, C., *see* Mischel and Gilligan (1964).

GILULA, M. F., *see* Daniels, Gilula, and Ochberg (1970).

GIRDEN, E. (1962) A review of psychokinesis. *Psychological Bulletin*, 59:353–88.—**159**

GLADWIN, T., *see* Masland, Sarason, and Gladwin (1958).

GLASER, R. (ed.) (1971) *The nature of reinforcement.* Columbus, Ohio: Merrill.—**224**

GLASER, R., *see* Taber, Glaser, and Schaefer (1965).

GLASS, D. C. (ed.) (1967) *Neurophysiology and emotion.* N.Y.: Rockefeller Univ. Press.—**354**

GLICH, B. S., and MARGOLIS, R. (1962) A study on the influence of experimental design on clinical outcome in drug research. *American Journal of Psychiatry*, 118:1087–96.—**506**

GLOCK, C. Y. (ed.) (1967) *Survey research in the social sciences.* N.Y.: Russell Sage Foundation.—**538**

GLUCKSBERG, S., and KING, J. (1967) Motivated forgetting mediated by implicit verbal chaining: A laboratory analog of repression. *Science*, 158:517–19.—**236**

GLUECK, E. T., *see* Glueck and Glueck (1950), (1964).

GLUECK, S. (1962) *Law and psychiatry.* Baltimore, Md.: Johns Hopkins Press.—**483**

GLUECK, S., and GLUECK, E. T. (1950) *Unraveling juvenile delinquency.* Cambridge, Mass.: Harvard Univ. Press.—**399**

GLUECK, S., and GLUECK, E. T. (1964) Potential juvenile delinquents can be identified: What next? *British Journal of Criminology*, 4:215–26.—**91**

GOETHALS, G. R., *see* Jones, Rock, Shaver, Goethals, and Ward (1968).

GOLDBERG, L. R. (1969) The search for configural relationships in personality assessment: The diagnosis of psychosis vs. neurosis from the MMPI. *Multivariate Behavioral Research*, 4:523–36.—**431**

GOLDBERG, L. R., *see* Hase and Goldberg (1967).

GOLDSTEIN, A. P., and DEAN, S. J. (eds.) (1966) *The investigation of psychotherapy.* N.Y.: Wiley.—**510**

GOLDSTEIN, K., and SHEERER, M. (1941) Abstract and concrete behavior: An experimental study with special tests. *Psychological Monographs*, 53, No. 239.—**276**

GOLUB, A. M., MASIARZ, F. R., VILLARS, T., and MCCONNELL, J. V. (1970) Incubation effects in behavior induction in rats. *Science*, 168:392–95.—**233**

GOODE, E. (ed.) (1969) *Marijuana.* N.Y.: Atherton Press.—**185**

GOODENOUGH, D. R., *see* Lewis, Goodenough, Shapiro, and Sleser (1966); Rechtschaffen, Goodenough, and Shapiro (1962); Witkin, Goodenough, and Karp (1967).

GOODENOUGH, D. R., SHAPIRO, A., HOLDEN, M., and STEINSCHRIBER, L. (1959) A comparison of dreamers and nondreamers: Eye movements, electroencephalograms and the recall of dreams. *Journal of Abnormal and Social Psychology*, 59:295–302.—**170**

GOODENOUGH, F. (1931) Anger in young children. *University of Minnesota Institute of Child Welfare Monograph Series*, No. 9.—**351**

GOODENOUGH, F. (1932) Expression of the emotions in a blind-deaf child. *Journal of Abnormal and Social Psychology*, 27:328–33.—**343**

GOODMAN, C. C., *see* Bruner and Goodman (1947).

GOODNOW, V. V., *see* Williams, Lubin, and Goodnow (1959).

GORDON, C., and GERGEN, K. J. (eds.) (1968) *The self in social interaction*, vol. I. N.Y.: Wiley.—**420**

GORDON, T. J., and HAYWARD, H. (1968) Initial experiments with the cross-impact matrix method of forecasting. *Futures*, 1:100–17.—**551**

GOSLIN, D. A. (ed.) (1969) *Handbook of socialization: Theory and research.* Chicago: Rand McNally.—**81**

GOTTESMAN, I. I. (1963) Heritability of personality: A demonstration. *Psychological Monographs*, 77, Whole No. 572.—**398**

GOTTESMAN, I. I., and SHIELDS, J. (1966) Contributions of twin studies to perspectives on schizophrenia. In Maher, B. A. (ed.) *Progress in experimental personality research.* N.Y.: Academic Press, 1–84.—**393**

GOTTSCHALK, L. A., and AUERBACH, A. H. (eds.) (1966) *Methods of research in psychotherapy.* N.Y.: Appleton-Century-Crofts. —**510**

GOUGH, H. G. (1957) *California Psychological Inventory.* Palo Alto, Calif.: Consulting Psychologists Press.—**431**

GOUGH, H. G. (1962) Clinical versus statistical prediction in psychology. In Postman, L. (ed.) *Psychology in the making.* N.Y.: Knopf, 526–84.—**433**

GOUGH, H, G. (1965) Misplaced emphasis in admissions. *Journal of College Student Personnel*, 6:130–35.—**379**

GRAHAM, C. H. (ed.) (1965) *Vision and visual perception.* N.Y.: Wiley.—**134, 161**

GRAHAM, C. H., *see* Hsia and Graham (1965).

GREEN, B. F. (1963) *Digital computers in research.* N.Y.: McGraw-Hill.—**288, 292**

GREEN, D. M., and SWETS, J. A. (1966) *Signal detection theory and psychophysics.* N.Y.: Wiley.—**111, 134**

GREENO, J. G., *see* Restle and Greeno (1970).

GREENWALD, A. G., BROCK, T. C., and OSTRUM, T. M. (eds.) (1968) *Psychological foundations of attitudes.* N.Y.: Academic Press.—**537**

GREGG, L., and SIMON, H. A. (1967) Process models and stochastic theories of simple concept formation. *Journal of Mathematical Psychology*, 4:246–76.—**290**

GREGORY, R. L. (1966) *Eye and brain: The psychology of seeing.* N.Y.: McGraw-Hill. —**134, 143, 161**

GRIFFIN, G. A., *see* Mitchell, Harlow, Griffin, and Moller (1967).

GRINDER, R. E. (ed.) (1963) *Studies in adolescence.* N.Y.: Macmillan.—**104**

GROSS, J., *see* Fisher, Gross, and Zuch (1965).

GROSS, M. L. (1962) *The brain watchers.* N.Y.: Random House.—**379**

GROSSBERG, J. M. (1964) Behavior therapy: A review. *Psychological Bulletin*, 62:73–85. —**499**

GROSSMAN, S. P. (1967) *A textbook of physiological psychology.* N.Y.: Wiley.—**51**

GUETZKOW, H., and BOWMAN, P. H. (1946) *Men and hunger.* Elgin, Ill.: Brethren Publishing House.—**451**

GUILFORD, J. P. (1954) A factor analytic study across the domains of reasoning, creativity, and evaluation I: Hypothesis and description of tests. *Reports from the psychology laboratory.* Los Angeles, Calif.: Univ. of Southern California.—**371**

GUILFORD, J. P. (1959) *Personality.* N.Y.: McGraw-Hill.—**419, 423**

GUILFORD, J. P. (1967) *The nature of human*

intelligence. N.Y.: McGraw-Hill.—**367, 368, 369, 370, 382**

GUNTER, R., FEIGENSON, L., and BLAKESLEE, P. (1965) Color vision in the cebus monkey. *Journal of Comparative and Physiological Psychology,* 60:107–13.—**274**

GUSTAFSON, L. A., *see* Cobb, Evans, Gustafson, O'Connell, Orne, and Shor (1965).

GUTHRIE, E. R. (1952) *The psychology of learning* (rev. ed.) N.Y.: Harper and Row.—**207**

HABER, R. N. (ed.) (1966) *Current research in motivation.* N.Y.: Holt, Rinehart and Winston.—**134, 311, 463**

HABER, R. N. (ed.) (1968) *Contemporary theory and research in visual perception.* N.Y.: Holt, Rinehart and Winston.—**161**

HABER, R. N. (1969a) Eidetic images. *Scientific American,* 220:36–55.—**229**

HABER, R. N. (ed.) (1969b) *Information-processing approaches to visual perception.* N.Y.: Holt, Rinehart and Winston.—**161**

HAGE, J., *see* Pitt and Hage (1964).

HALL, C. S. (1953) *The meaning of dreams.* N.Y.: Harper and Row.—**172**

HALL, C. S., *see* Lindzey and Hall (1965); Witt and Hall (1949).

HALL, C. S., and LINDZEY, G. (eds.) (1970) *Theories of personality* (2nd ed.). N.Y.: Wiley.—**419**

HAMILTON, M., *see* Pond, Ryle, and Hamilton (1963).

HANSEL, C. E. M. (1966) *ESP: A scientific evaluation.* N.Y.: Scribners.—**161**

HARDING, J. S., *see* Leighton, Harding, Macklin, Macmillan, and Leighton (1963).

HARLOW, H. F. (1949) The formation of learning sets. *Psychological Review,* 56:51–65.—**257, 259**

HARLOW, H. F. (1953) Mice, monkeys, men, and motives. *Psychological Review,* 60:23–32.—**308**

HARLOW, H. F., *see* Davenport, Chamove, and Harlow (1970); Farber, Harlow, and West (1957); French and Harlow (1962); Mitchell, Harlow, Griffin, and Moller (1967).

HARLOW, H. F., and HARLOW, M. K. (1966) Learning to love. *American Scientist,* 54:244–72.—**69**

HARLOW, H. F., HARLOW, M. K., and MEYER, D. R. (1950) Learning motivated by a manipulation drive. *Journal of Experimental Psychology,* 40:228–34.—**307**

HARLOW, H. F., and SUOMI, S. J. (1970) Nature of love—simplified. *American Psychologist,* 25:161–68.—**69**

HARLOW, M. K., *see* Harlow and Harlow (1966); Harlow, Harlow, and Meyer (1950).

HARRIS, C. S., *see* Rock and Harris (1967).

HARRIS, C. W., *see* Klausmeier and Harris (1966).

HARRIS, F. R., JOHNSTON, M. K., KELLEY, C. S., and WOLF, M. M. (1965) Effects of positive social reinforcement on regressed crawling of a nursery school child. In Ullmann, L., and Krasner, L. (eds.) *Case studies in behavior modification.* N.Y.: Holt, Rinehart and Winston, 313–19.—**204**

HARRIS, I. D. (1961) *Emotional blocks to learning.* N.Y.: Free Press.—**270**

HARRIS, J. G., JR. (1963) Judgmental versus mathematical prediction: An investigation by analogy of the clinical versus statistical controversy. *Behavioral Sciences,* 8:324–35.—**433**

HARRISON, R. (1965) Thematic apperceptive methods. In Wolman, B. B. (ed.) *Handbook of clinical psychology.* N.Y.: McGraw-Hill, 562–620.—**434, 438**

HARTSHORNE, H., and MAY, M. A. (1928) *Studies in the nature of character.* Vol. I: *Studies in deceit.* N.Y.: Macmillan.—**411**

HASE, H. D., and GOLDBERG, L. R. (1967) Comparative validity of different strategies of constructing personality inventories. *Psychological Bulletin,* 67:231–48.—**432**

HASTEY, J. M., *see* Arkin, Hastey, and Reiser (1966).

HASTORF, A. H., *see* Dornbusch, Hastorf, Richardson, Muzzy, and Vreeland (1965).

HASTORF, A. H., SCHNEIDER, D. J., and POLEFKA, J. (1970) *Person perception.* Reading, Mass.: Addison-Wesley.—**513, 537**

HATHAWAY, S. R., and MONACHESI, E. D. (eds.) (1963) *Analyzing and predicting juvenile delinquency with the MMPI.* Minneapolis: Univ. of Minnesota Press.—**430, 431**

HAVIGHURST, R. J. (1957) The social competence of middle-aged people. *Genetic Psychology Monographs,* 59:297–375.—**102**

HAVIGHURST, R. J., *see* Eells, Davis, Havighurst, Herrick, and Tyler (1951).

HAYES, C. (1951) *The ape in our house.* N.Y.: Harper and Row.—**284**

HAYS, W. L. (1963) *Statistics for psychologists.* N.Y.: Holt, Rinehart and Winston.—**578**

HAYWARD, H., *see* Gordon and Hayward (1968).

HEATH, R. G. (1964) *The role of pleasure in behavior.* N.Y.: Hoeber.—**209**

HEBB, D. O. (1946) On the nature of fear. *Psychological Review,* 53:259–76.—**344**

HECKHAUSEN, H. (1967) *The anatomy of achievement motivation.* N.Y.: Academic Press.—**333**

HEIDBREDER, E. (1947) The attainment of concepts: III. The problem. *Journal of Psychology,* 24:93–138.—**275**

HEIDER, F. (1946) Attitudes and cognitive organization. *Journal of Psychology,* 21:107–12.—**529**

HEIDER, F. (1958) *The psychology of interpersonal relations.* N.Y.: Wiley.—**529**

HEIST, P., *see* Webster, Freedman, and Heist (1962).

HELD, R. (1965) Plasticity in sensory-motor systems. *Scientific American,* 213:84–94.—**140**

HELD, R., and BAUER, J. A., JR. (1967) Visually guided reaching in infant monkeys after restricted rearing. *Science,* 155:718–20.—**141**

HELLMER, L. A., *see* Becker, Peterson, Hellmer, Shoemaker, and Quay (1962).

HELMER, O. (1966) *Social technology.* N.Y.: Basic Books.—**550, 559**

HELSON, H., and BEVAN, W. (eds.) (1967) *Contemporary approaches to psychology.* Princeton, N.J.: Van Nostrand.—**23**

HELSON, H., BLAKE, R. R., and MOUTON, J. S. (1958) Petition-signing as adjustment to situational and personal factors. *Journal of Social Psychology,* 48:3–10.—**522**

HENDRICKSON, G., and SCHROEDER, W. H. (1941) Transfer of training in learning to hit a submerged target. *Journal of Educational Psychology,* 32:205–13.—**259**

HENRY, A. F., and SHORT, J. F. (1954) *Suicide and homicide: Some economic, sociological, and psychological aspects of aggression.* N.Y.: Free Press.—**517**

HENRY, E. R., *see* Fryer and Henry (1950).

HENRY, G. W., *see* Zilboorg and Henry (1941).

HERNÁNDEZ-PEÓN, R. (1961) Reticular mechanisms of sensory control. In Rosenblith, W. A. (ed.) *Sensory communication.* N.Y.: Wiley, 497–520.—**156**

HERNÁNDEZ-PEÓN, R., SCHERRER, H., and JOUVET, M. (1956) Modification of electric activity in the cochlear nucleus during "attention" in unanesthetized cats. *Science,* 123:331–32.—**155, 156**

HERON, W., *see* Doane, Mahatoo, Heron, and Scott (1959).

HERON, W. T., and SKINNER, B. F. (1937) Changes in hunger during starvation. *Psychological Record,* 1:51–60.—**296**

HERRICK, V. E., *see* Eells, Davis, Havighurst, Herrick, and Tyler (1951).

HERRNSTEIN, R. J., and BORING, E. G. (1965) *A source book in the history of psychology.* Cambridge, Mass.: Harvard Univ. Press.—**22**

HERRON, E. W., *see* Holtzman, Thorpe, Swartz, and Herron (1961).

HERZ, M., *see* McGaugh and Herz (1970).

HESS, E. H. (1959) Imprinting. *Science,* 130:133–41.—**302**

HESS, E. H., and POLT, J. M. (1960) Pupil size as related to the interest value of visual stimuli. *Science,* 132:349–50.—**113**

HESS, R. D., and BEAR, R. M. (eds.) (1968) *Early education: Current theory, research, and action.* Chicago: Aldine.—**81**

HESTON, L. (1970) The genetics of schizophrenia and schizoid disease. *Science,* 167:249–56.—**477, 478**

HETHERINGTON, E. M., and FRANKIE, G. (1967) Effects of parental dominance, warmth, and conflict on imitation in children. *Journal of Personality and Social Psychology,* 6:119–25.—**75**

HIBBS, J. R., *see* Garnsey and Hibbs (1967).

HIGGINS, J., and PETERSON, J. C. (1966) Concept of process-reactive schizophrenia: A critique. *Psychological Bulletin,* 66:201–06.—**475**

HILDUM, P. C., *see* Brown and Hildum (1956).

HILGARD, E. R. (1961) Hypnosis and experimental psychodynamics. In Brosen, H. (ed.) *Lectures on experimental psychiatry.* Pittsburgh: Univ. of Pittsburgh Press.—**19**

HILGARD, E. R. (ed.) (1964) *Theories of learning and instruction.* 63rd Yearbook, Part I, National Society for the Study of Education. Chicago: Univ. of Chicago Press.—**270**

HILGARD, E. R. (1965) *Hypnotic susceptibility.*

N.Y.: Harcourt Brace Jovanovich.—**175, 455**

HILGARD, E. R. (1968a) *The experience of hypnosis.* N.Y.: Harcourt Brace Jovanovich.—**185**

HILGARD, E. R. (1968b) Psychoanalysis: Experimental studies. In *International Encyclopedia of the Social Sciences,* vol. XIII. N.Y.: Macmillan and Free Press, 37–45. —**409**

HILGARD, E. R. (1969) Pain as a puzzle for psychology and physiology. *American Psychologist,* 24:103–13.—**14**

HILGARD, E. R., *see* Morgan, Davert, and Hilgard (1970); Weitzenhoffer and Hilgard (1959).

HILGARD, E. R., and BOWER, G. (1966) *Theories of learning* (3rd ed.). N.Y.: Appleton-Century-Crofts.—**224, 270, 541**

HILGARD, E. R., SAIT, E. M., and MAGARET, G. A. (1940) Level of aspiration as affected by relative standing in an experimental social group. *Journal of Experimental Psychology,* 27:411–21.—**325**

HILGARD, E. R., and TART, C. T. (1966) Responsiveness to suggestions following waking and imagination instructions and following induction of hypnosis. *Journal of Abnormal Psychology,* 71:196–208.—**173**

HILGARD, E. R., WEITZENHOFFER, A. M., LANDES, J., and MOORE, R. K. (1961) The distribution of susceptibility to hypnosis in a student population: A study using the Stanford Hypnotic Susceptibility Scale. *Psychological Monographs,* 75, No. 512.—**174**

HILGARD, J. R. (1970) *Personality and hypnosis: A study of imaginative involvement.* Chicago: Univ. of Chicago Press.—**75, 176, 185, 437**

HILGARD, J. R., and MOORE, U. S. (1969) Affiliative therapy with young adolescents. *Journal of Child Psychiatry,* 8:577–605.—**502**

HILGARD, J. R., and NEWMAN, M. F. (1961) Evidence for functional genesis in mental illness: Schizophrenia, depressive psychoses, and psychoneuroses. *Journal of Nervous and Mental Disease,* 132:3–16.—**479**

HILL, W. F. (1956) Activity as an autonomous drive. *Journal of Comparative and Physiological Psychology,* 49:15–19.—**306**

HILLEGAS, M. R. (1967) *The future as nightmare: H. G. Wells and the Anti-Utopians.* London: Oxford Univ. Press.—**551**

HIMMELWEIT, H. T., APPENHEIM, A. N., and VINCE, P. (1958) *Television and the child.* N.Y.: Oxford Univ. Press.—**531**

HINDE, R. A. (1966) *Animal behavior: A synthesis of ethology and comparative psychology.* N.Y.: McGraw-Hill.—**302**

HIRSCH, J. (ed.) (1967) *Behavior genetic analysis.* N.Y.: McGraw-Hill.—**396**

HIRSCH, J., and BOUDREAU, J. C. (1958) Studies in experimental behavior genetics: I. The heritability of phototaxis in a population of *Drosophila melanogaster. Journal of Comparative and Physiological Psychology,* 51:647–51.—**387**

HOCHBERG, J. (1964) *Perception.* Englewood Cliffs, N.J.: Prentice-Hall.—**161**

HOEBEL, B., *see* Smith, King, and Hoebel (1970).

HOELZEL, F. (1927) Central factors in hunger. *American Journal of Physiology,* 82:665–71. —**298**

HOFFMAN, B. (1962) *The tyranny of testing.* N.Y.: Crowell-Collier.—**379**

HOLDEN, M., *see* Goodenough, Shapiro, Holden, and Steinschriber (1959).

HOLLINGSHEAD, A. B., and REDLICH, F. C. (1958) *Social class and mental illness: A community study.* N.Y.: Wiley.—**484**

HOLLISTER, L. E., *see* Sjoberg and Hollister (1965).

HOLT, R. R. (1958) Clinical and statistical prediction: A reformulation and some new data. *Journal of Abnormal and Social Psychology,* 56:1–12.—**433**

HOLTZMAN, W. H., THORPE, J. S., SEVORTZ, J. D., and HERRON, E. W. (1961) *Inkblot perception and personality.* Austin, Tex.: Univ. of Texas Press.—**435**

HOLZBERG, J. D., KNAPP, R., and TURNER, J. (1967) College students as companions to the mentally ill. In Cowen, E., Gardner, E., and Zax, M. (eds.) *Emergent approaches to mental health problems.* N.Y.: Appleton-Century-Crofts, 91–109.—**502**

HOLZINGER, K. H., *see* Newman, Freeman, and Holzinger (1937).

HONIG, W. K. (ed.) (1966) *Operant behavior: Areas of research and application.* N.Y.: Appleton-Century-Crofts.—**224**

HONZIK, C. H., *see* Tolman and Honzik (1930).

HONZIK, M. P. (1957) Developmental studies of parent-child resemblance in intelligence. *Child Development,* 28:215–28.—**389**

HOPKINS, R. H., and ATKINSON, R. C. (1968) First-letter cues in the retrieval of proper names from long-term memory. *Psychological Reports,* 23:851–66.—**230**

HOPPE, F. (1930) Erfolg und Misserfolg. *Psychologische Forschung,* 14:1–62.—**325**

HORN, G. (1965) Physiological and psychological aspects of selective perception. In Lehrman, D. S. (ed.) *Advances in the study of behavior,* vol. I. N.Y.: Academic Press.—**156**

HORN, J. L., and CATTELL, R. B. (1967) Age differences in fluid and crystallized intelligence. *Acta Psychologica,* 26:107–29.—**378**

HORROCKS, J. E. (1969) *The psychology of adolescence* (3rd ed.). Boston: Houghton Mifflin.—**104**

HORTON, D. L., *see* Dixon and Horton (1968).

HOSKOVEC, J., and COOPER, L. M. (1967) Comparison of recent experimental trends concerning sleep learning in the U.S.A. and the Soviet Union. *Activitas Nervosa* (Prague), 9:93–96.—**171**

HOVLAND, C. I. (1937) The generalization of conditioned responses: I. The sensory generalization of conditioned responses with varying frequencies of tone. *Journal of General Psychology,* 17:125–48.—**194**

HOVLAND, C. I., *see* Kelman and Hovland (1953).

HOVLAND, C. I., JANIS, I. L., and KELLEY, H. H. (1953) *Communication and persuasion.* New Haven, Conn.: Yale Univ. Press.—**524**

HSIA, Y., and GRAHAM, C. H. (1965) Color blindness. In Graham, C. H. (ed.) *Vision and visual perception.* N.Y.: Wiley, 395–413.—**119**

HUBEL, D. H., and WIESEL, T. N. (1965) Receptive fields and functional architecture in two non-striate visual areas (18 and 19) of the cat. *Journal of Neurophysiology,* 28:229–89.—**41, 152**

HUDSPETH, W. J., MCGAUGH, J. L., and THOMPSON, C. W. (1964) Aversive and amnesic effects of electroconvulsive shock. *Journal of Comparative and Physiological Psychology,* 57:61–64.—**241**

HULL, C. L. (1943) *Principles of behavior.* N.Y.: Appleton-Century-Crofts.—**433**

HULL, C. L. (1952) *A behavior system.* New Haven, Conn.: Yale Univ. Press.—**308**

HULSE, S., *see* Deese and Hulse (1967).

HUMPHREY, E. M., and ZANGWILL, O. L. (1952) Dysphasia in left-handed patients with unilateral brain lesions. *Journal of Neurology, Neurosurgery, and Psychiatry,* 15:184–92.—**42**

HUNT, E. B. (1962) *Concept learning: An information processing problem.* N.Y.: Wiley. —**292**

HUNT, E. B., MARIN, J., and STONE, P. J. (1966) *Experiments in induction.* N.Y.: Academic Press.—**290**

HUNT, W. A., *see* Cantril and Hunt (1932).

HUNTER, E. (1951) *Brainwashing in Red China.* N.Y.: Vanguard.—**533**

HUNTER, I. M. L. (1964) *Memory* (rev. ed.). Middlesex, England: Penguin Books.—**246**

HYDÉN, H. (1967) Biochemical and molecular aspects of learning and memory. *Proceedings of the American Philosophical Society,* 111:347–51.—**233**

HYDÉN, H. (1969) Biochemical aspects of learning and memory. In Pribram, K. (ed.) *On the biology of learning.* N.Y.: Harcourt Brace Jovanovich.—**232**

INHELDER, B., *see* Piaget and Inhelder (1941).

INKELES, A., and LEVINSON, D. J. (1969) National character: The study of modal personality and sociocultural systems. In Lindzey, G., and Aronson, E. (eds.) *Handbook of social psychology* (2nd ed.), vol. IV. Reading, Mass.: Addison-Wesley, 418–506. —**400**

ITTLESON, W. H., *see* Proshansky, Ittleson, and Rivlin (1970).

JACKSON, C. M. (1928) Some aspects of form and growth. In Robbins, W. J., and others *Growth.* New Haven, Conn.: Yale Univ. Press.—**87**

JACKSON, D. D. (ed.) (1960) *The etiology of schizophrenia.* N.Y.: Basic Books.—**486**

JACKSON, D. D., *see* Lederer and Jackson (1968).

JACKSON, J. M., and SALTZSTEIN, H. D. (1958) The effect of person-group relationships on conformity processes. *Journal of Abnormal and Social Psychology,* 57:17–24.—**522**

JACKSON, P. W., *see* Getzels and Jackson (1962).

JACOBS, G. H., *see* DeValois and Jacobs (1968).

JACOBS, P. A., and STRONG, J. A. (1959) A case of human intersexuality having a possibly XXY sex-determining mechanism. *Nature* (London), 183:302.—**385**

JACOBSON, A., *see* Jacobson, Babich, Bubash, and Jacobson (1965).

JACOBSON, A., and KALES, A. (1967) Somnambulism: All-night EEG and related studies. In Kety, S. S., Evarts, E. V., and Williams, H. L. (eds.) *Sleep and altered states of consciousness.* Baltimore, Md.: Williams and Wilkins, 424–48.—**171**

JACOBSON, A. L., BABICH, F. R., BUBASH, S., and JACOBSON, A. (1965) Differential approach tendencies produced by injection of ribonucleic acid from trained rats. *Science,* 150:636–37.—**233**

JACOBSON, H. (1952) Conflict of attitudes toward the roles of the husband and wife in marriage. *American Sociological Review,* 17:146–50.—**98**

JAKOBOVITS, L. A., and MIRON, M. S. (eds.) (1967) *Readings in the psychology of language.* Englewood Cliffs, N.J.: Prentice-Hall.—**292**

JAKOBSON, R. (1968) *Child language, aphasia, and general sound laws* (Trans. by A. Keiler). The Hague, Netherlands: Mouton.—**280**

JAMES, W. (1902) *The varieties of religious experience.* N.Y.: Longmans, Green.—**165**

JAMES, W. T. (1941) Morphological form and its relation to behavior. In Stockard, C. R. (ed.) *The genetic and endocrinic basis for differences in form and behavior.* Philadelphia: Wistar Institute, 525–643.—**388**

JANIS, I. L. (1959) Motivational factors in the resolution of decisional conflicts. *Nebraska symposium on motivation.* Lincoln, Nebr.: Univ. of Nebraska Press, 7:198–231.—**530**

JANIS, I. L. (1968) Attitude change via role playing. In Abelson, R. P., and others (eds.) *Theories of cognitive consistency.* Chicago: Rand McNally, 810–18.—**530**

JANIS, I. L. (ed.) (1969) *Personality: Dynamics, development, and assessment.* N.Y.: Harcourt Brace Jovanovich.—**81, 420, 438, 463**

JANIS, I. L., *see* Hovland, Janis, and Kelley (1953).

JANIS, I. L., and FESHBACH, S. (1953) Effects of fear-arousing communications. *Journal of Abnormal and Social Psychology,* 48:78–92.—**532**

JANIS, I. L., and FIELD, P. B. (1959) Sex differences and personality factors related to persuasibility. In Hovland, C. I., and Janis, I. L. (eds.) *Personality and persuasibility.* New Haven, Conn.: Yale Univ. Press, 55–68.—**416**

JARVIK, L. F., *see* Erlenmeyer-Kimling and Jarvik (1963).

JASTROW, J. (1935) *Wish and wisdom.* N.Y.: Appleton-Century-Crofts.—**158**

JENKINS, J. G., and DALLENBACH, K. M. (1924) Oblivescence during sleep and waking. *American Journal of Psychology,* 35:605–12.—**233, 234**

JENSEN, A. R. (1969) How much can we boost I.Q. and scholastic achievement? *Harvard Educational Review,* 39:1–123.—**391, 396**

JENSEN, J., *see* Monroe, Rechtschaffen, Foulkes, and Jensen (1965).

JOHNSON, D. T., and SPIELBERGER, C. D. (1968) The effects of relaxation training and the passage of time on measures of state- and trait-anxiety. *Journal of Clinical Psychology,* 24:20–23.—**437**

JOHNSON, J. I., *see* Welker, Johnson, and Pubols (1964).

JOHNSON, R. C., and MEDINNUS, G. R. (1969) *Child psychology: Behavior and development* (2nd ed.). N.Y.: Wiley.—**81**

JOHNSTON, M. K., *see* Harris, Johnston, Kelley, and Wolf (1965).

JONES, D. R. (1969) *Psychologists in mental health: 1966.* Washington, D.C.: National Institute of Mental Health, Public Health Service Publication, No. 1984.—**11**

JONES, E. E. (1964) *Ingratiation: A social psychological analysis.* N.Y.: Appleton-Century-Crofts.—**514**

JONES, E. E., *see* Linder, Cooper, and Jones (1967).

JONES, E. E., and GERARD, H. B. (1967) *Foundations of social psychology.* N.Y.: Wiley. —**533, 537**

JONES, E. E., ROCK, L., SHAVER, K. G., GOETHALS, G. R., and WARD, L. M. (1968) Pattern performance and ability attribution: An unexpected primacy effect. *Journal of Personality and Social Psychology,* 10:317–41.—**513**

JONES, H. E., *see* Conrad and Jones (1940).

JONES, M. C. (1957) The later careers of boys who were early- or late-maturing. *Child Development,* 93:87–111.—**86**

JONES, M. C., *see* Mussen and Jones (1957), (1958).

JOUVET, M., *see* Hernández-Peón, Scherrer, and Jouvet (1956).

JUNG, C. G. (1923) *Psychological types.* N.Y.: Harcourt Brace Jovanovich.—**405**

JUNG, J. (1968) *Verbal learning.* N.Y.: Holt, Rinehart and Winston.—**246**

KAEL, H., *see* Noblin, Timmons, and Kael (1966).

KAGAN, J. (1968) His struggle for identity. *Saturday Review,* Dec. 7, 80–88.—**72**

KAGAN, J., *see* Mussen, Conger, and Kagan (1969).

KAGAN, J., and MOSS, H. A. (1962) *Birth to maturity.* N.Y.: Wiley.—**78, 80**

KAGAN, J., and others (1969) Discussion: How much can we boost the I.Q. and scholastic achievement? *Harvard Educational Review,* 39:273–356.—**396**

KAHN, F. (1943) *Man in structure and function* (2 vols.). N.Y.: Knopf.—**149**

KAHN, H., and WIENER, H. J. (1967) *The year 2000.* N.Y.: Macmillan.—**559**

KALES, A. (1968) Effects of age on sleep patterns. *Annals of Internal Medicine,* 68:1085–86.—**169**

KALES, A. (ed.) (1969) *Sleep: Physiology and pathology.* Philadelphia: Lippincott.—**185**

KALES, A., *see* Jacobson and Kales (1967).

KAMIYA, J. (1961) Behavioral, subjective and physiological aspects of drowsiness and sleep. In Fiske, D. W., and Maddi, S. R. (eds.) *Functions of varied experience.* Homewood, Ill.: Dorsey Press.—**171**

KAMIYA, J., *see* Nowlis and Kamiya (1970); Stoyva and Kamiya (1968).

KAPLAN, M. F., and SINGER, E. (1963) Dogmatism and sensory alienation: An empirical investigation. *Journal of Consulting Psychology,* 27:486–91.—**331**

KARP, S. A., *see* Witkin, Goodenough, and Karp (1967).

KARSH, E. B. (1970) Fixation produced by conflict. *Science,* 168:873–75.—**452, 453**

KATZ, B., *see* Secord, Bevan, and Katz (1956).

KATZ, D. (1937) *Animals and men: Studies in comparative psychology.* N.Y.: Longmans, Green.—**305**

KATZ, E., *see* Crain, Katz, and Rosenthal (1969).

KAUFMAN, I. C., and ROSENBLUM, L. A. (1967) The reaction to separation in infant monkeys: Anaclitic depression and conservation-withdrawal. *Psychosomatic Medicine,* 29:648–75.—**70**

KEELER, C. E., and KING, H. D. (1942) Multiple effect of coat color genes in the Norway rat, with special reference to temperament and domestication. *Journal of Comparative Psychology,* 34:241–50.—**387**

KELLEY, C. S., *see* Harris, Johnston, Kelley, and Wolf (1965).

KELLEY, H. H., *see* Hovland, Janis, and Kelley (1953).

KELLEY, H. H., and VOLKART, E. H. (1952) The resistance to change of group-anchored attitudes. *American Sociological Review,* 17:453–65.—**522**

KELLOGG, L. A., *see* Kellogg and Kellogg (1933).

KELLOGG, W. N., and KELLOGG, L. A. (1933) *The ape and the child.* N.Y.: McGraw-Hill. —**284**

KELMAN, H. C. (1958) Compliance, identification, and internalization: Three processes of attitude change. *Conflict Resolution,* 2:51–60.—**534**

KELMAN, H. C. (1968) *A time to speak: On human values and social research.* San Francisco, Calif.: Jossey-Bass.—**552, 553, 560**

KELMAN, H. C., and HOVLAND, C. I. (1953) "Reinstatement" of the communicator in delayed measurement of opinion change. *Journal of Abnormal and Social Psychology,* 48:327–35.—**532**

KELSEY, D., and BARRON, J. N. (1958) Maintenance of posture by hypnotic suggestion in patient under-going plastic surgery. *British Medical Journal,* 5073:756–57.—**178**

KENDERDINE, M. (1931) Laughter in the preschool child. *Child Development,* 2:228–30. —**349**

KENISTON, K. (1966) Faces in the lecture room. *Yale Undergraduate,* 11:2–16.—**93**

KESSEN, M. L., *see* Miller and Kessen (1952).

KESSEN, W. (1965) *The child.* N.Y.: Wiley.—**81**

KETY, S. S. (1960) Recent biochemical theories of schizophrenia. In Jackson, D. D. (ed.) *The etiology of schizophrenia.* N.Y.: Basic Books, 120–45.—**479**

KETY, S. S., *see* Rosenthal and Kety (1968).

KIERKEGAARD, S. (1944) *The concept of dread.* (Trans. by W. Lowrie). Princeton, N.J.: Princeton Univ. Press.—**347**

KIESLER, C. A., COLLINS, B. E., and MILLER, N. (1969) *Attitude change.* N.Y.: Wiley.—**537**

KIMBLE, G. A. (1961) *Hilgard and Marquis' conditioning and learning* (2nd ed.). N.Y.: Appleton-Century-Crofts.—**224**

KIMBLE, G. A. (ed.) (1967) *Foundations of conditioning and learning.* N.Y.: Appleton-Century-Crofts.—**224**

KING, H. D., *see* Keeler and King (1942).

KING, J., *see* Glucksberg and King (1967).

KING, M., *see* Smith, King, and Hoebel (1970).

KING, S. H., *see* Funkenstein, King, and Drolette (1957).

KINSEY, A. C., POMEROY, W. B., and MARTIN, C. E. (1948) *Sexual behavior in the human male.* Philadelphia: Saunders.—**88**

KINTSCH, W. (1970) *Learning, memory, and conceptual processes.* N.Y.: Wiley.—**246**

KINTZ, B. L., *see* Bruning and Kintz (1968).

KIRK, S. A. (1958) *Early education for the mentally retarded.* Urbana, Ill.: Univ. of Illinois Press.—**377**

KLAUSMEIER, H. J., and HARRIS, C. W. (eds.) (1966) *Analyses of concept learning.* N.Y.: Academic Press.—**292**

KLEBANOFF, L. B. (1959) Parental attitudes of mothers of schizophrenics, brain-injured and retarded, and normal children. *American Journal of Orthopsychiatry,* 29:445–54.—**479**

KLEITMAN, N. (1939) *Sleep and wakefulness.* Chicago: Univ. of Chicago Press.—**166**

KLEITMAN, N. (1963) *Sleep and wakefulness* (2nd ed.). Chicago: Univ. of Chicago Press.—**166, 185**

KLEITMAN, N., *see* Dement and Kleitman (1957).

KLINEBERG, O. (1938) Emotional expression in Chinese literature. *Journal of Abnormal and Social Psychology,* 33:517–20.—**345**

KNAPP, P. H. (ed.) (1963) *Expression of the emotions in man.* N.Y.: International Universities Press.—**354**

KNAPP, R., *see* Holzberg, Knapp, and Turner (1967).

KNAPP, R. R. (1965) Relationship of a measure of self-actualization to neuroticism and extraversion. *Journal of Consulting Psychology,* 29:168–72.—**331**

KOBASIGAWA, A., ARAKAKI, K., and AWIGUNI, A. (1966) Avoidance of feminine toys by kindergarten boys: The effects of adult presence or absence, and an adult's attitudes toward sex-typing. *Japanese Journal of Psychology,* 37:96–103.—**74**

KOESTLER, A. (1965) *The act of creation.* N.Y.: Macmillan.—**349**

KOESTLER, A. (1967) *The ghost in the machine.* N.Y.: Macmillan.—**319**

KOGAN, N., *see* Deutsch, Fishman, Kogan, North, and Whitman (1964); Wallach and Kogan (1965); Wallach, Kogan, and Burt (1968).

KOHEN-RAZ, R. (1968) Mental and motor development of Kibbutz, institutionalized, and home-reared infants in Israel. *Child Development,* 39:489–504.—**71**

KOHLBERG, L. (1963) The development of children's orientations toward a moral order. I. Sequence in the development of moral thought. *Vita Humana,* 6:11–33.—**78, 79**

KOHLBERG, L. (1964) Development of moral character and moral ideology. In Hoffman, M. L., and Hoffman, L. W. (eds.) *Review of Child Development Research,* vol. I. N.Y.: Russell Sage Foundation, 383–431.—**79**

KOHLER, I. (1962) Experiments with goggles. *Scientific American,* 206:62–72.—**139**

KÖHLER, W. (1925) *The mentality of apes.* N.Y.: Harcourt Brace Jovanovich.—**217, 224**

KOOISTRA, W. H. (1963) Developmental trends in the attainment of conservation, transivity, and relativism in the thinking of children. Unpublished Ph.D. dissertation, Wayne State University.—**63**

KORTEN, F. F., COOK, S. W., and LACEY, J. I. (eds.) (1970) *Psychology and the problems of society.* Washington, D.C.: American Psychological Association.—**556, 559**

KRANTZ, D. L. (ed.) (1969) *Schools of psychology: A symposium.* N.Y.: Appleton-Century-Crofts.—**23**

KRASNER, L., *see* Ullmann and Krasner (1969).

KRASNER, L., and ULLMANN, L. P. (eds.) (1965) *Research in behavior modification.* N.Y.: Holt, Rinehart and Winston.—**510**

KRISTOFFERSON, A. B., *see* Moulton, Raphelson, Kristofferson, and Atkinson (1958).

KROEBER, T. C. (1963) The coping functions of the ego mechanisms. In White, R. W. (ed.) *The study of lives.* N.Y.: Atherton Press, 178–98.—**460**

KRUEGER, W. C. F. (1929) The effect of overlearning on retention. *Journal of Experimental Psychology,* 12:71–78.—**244**

KUENNE, M. R. (1946) Experimental investigation of the relation of language to transposition behavior in young children. *Journal of Experimental Psychology.* 36:471–90.—**286**

KULKA, A. M. (1968) Observations and data on mother-infant interaction. *Israel Annals of Psychiatry,* 6:70–83.—**67**

LACEY, J. I. (1967) Somatic response patterning and stress: Some revisions of activation theory. In Appley, M. H., and Trumbull, R. (eds.) *Psychological stress.* N.Y.: Appleton-Century-Crofts, 14–42.—**424**

LACEY, J. I., *see* Korten, Cook, and Lacey (1970).

LAMBERT, W. W., SOLOMON, R. L., and WATSON, P. D. (1949) Reinforcement and extinction as factors in size estimation. *Journal of Experimental Psychology,* 39:637–41.—**156**

LANCASTER, E. (1958) *The final face of Eve.* N.Y.: McGraw-Hill.—**415**

LANDAUER, T. K. (1967) *Readings in physiological psychology.* N.Y.: McGraw-Hill.—**51**

LANDAUER, T. K., and WHITING, J. W. M. (1964) Infantile stimulation and adult stature of human males. *American Anthropologist,* 66:1007–28.—**60**

LANDES, J., *see* Hilgard, Weitzenhoffer, Landes, and Moore (1961).

LANDIS, J. T. (1942) What is the happiest period of life? *School and Society,* 55:643–45.—**95, 96**

LANG, P. J., and LAZOVIK, A. D. (1963) Experimental desensitization of a phobia. *Journal of Abnormal and Social Psychology,* 58:170–80.—**410**

LANGNER, T. S., *see* Srole, Langner, Michael, Opler, and Rennie (1962).

LASKY, J. J., and others (1959) Post-hospital adjustment as predicted by psychiatric patients and their staffs. *Journal of Consulting Psychology,* 23:213–18.—**436**

LAWRENCE, D. H., and FESTINGER, L. (1962) *Deterrents and reinforcement: The psychology of insufficient reward.* Stanford, Calif.: Stanford Univ. Press.—**530**

LAWSON, R. (1965) *Frustration: The development of a scientific concept.* N.Y.: Macmillan.—**463**

LAZARUS, A. A. (1963) The results of behavior therapy in 126 cases of severe neurosis. *Behavioral Research Therapy,* 1:69–79.—**496**

LAZARUS, A. A., *see* Wolpe and Lazarus (1966).

LAZARUS, R. S. (1966) *Psychological stress and the coping process.* N.Y.: McGraw-Hill.—**463**

LAZARUS, R. S. (1969) *Patterns of adjustment and human effectiveness.* N.Y.: McGraw-Hill.—**510**

LAZARUS, R. S., *see* Vogel, Raymond, and Lazarus (1959).

LAZOVIK, A. D., *see* Lang and Lazovik (1963).

LEAHY, A. M. (1935) Nature-nurture and intelligence. *Genetic Psychology Monographs,* 17:235–308.—**392**

LEDERER, W. J., and JACKSON, D. D. (1968) *The mirages of marriage.* N.Y.: Norton.—**99**

LEEPER, R. W. (1965) Some needed developments in the motivational theory of emotions. *Nebraska Symposium on Motivation.* Lincoln, Nebr.: Univ. of Nebraska Press, 13:25–122.—**342**

LEFKOWITZ, M. M., *see* Eron, Walder, Togio, and Lefkowitz (1963).

LEHMAN, H. C. (1938) The most proficient years at sports and games. *Research Quarterly of the American Association for Health and Physical Education,* 9:3–19.—**99**

LEHMAN, H. C. (1953) *Age and achievement.* Princeton, N.J.: Princeton Univ. Press.—**100, 101**

LEIBOWITZ, H., *see* Parrish, Lundy, and Leibowitz (1968); Zeigler and Leibowitz (1957).

LEIGHTON, A. H., *see* Leighton, Harding, Macklin, Macmillan, and Leighton (1963).

LEIGHTON, D. C., HARDING, J. S., MACKLIN, D. B., MACMILLAN, A. M., and LEIGHTON, A. H. (1963) *The character of danger: Psychiatric symptoms in selected communities.* N.Y.: Basic Books.—**483**

LEITES, N., and BERNAUT, E. (1954) *Ritual of liquidation.* Glencoe, Ill.: Free Press.—**534**

LEJEUNE, L., GAUTIER, M., and TURPIN, R. (1959) Les chromosomes humains en culture de tissus. *Comptes Rendus,* Academy of Science, Paris, 248:262.—**385**

LERNER, I. M. (1968) *Heredity, evolution, and society.* San Francisco, Calif.: Freeman.—**396**

LEUBA, C. (1941) Tickling and laughter: Two genetic studies. *Journal of Genetic Psychology,* 58:201–09.—**349**

LEVAN, A., *see* Tjio and Levan (1956).

LEVENTHAL, H., and SINGER, R. P. (1966) Affect arousal and positioning of recommendations in persuasive communications. *Journal of Personality and Social Psychology,* 4:137–46.—**533**

LEVIN, H., *see* Sears, Maccoby, and Levin (1957).

LEVINE, S., and MULLINS, R. F., JR. (1966) Hormonal influences on brain organization in infant rats. *Science,* 152:1585–91.—**60**

LEVINSON, B., and REESE, H. W. (1963) Patterns of discrimination learning set in preschool children, fifth graders, college freshman, and the aged. *Final Report, Cooperative Research Project No. 1059,* U.S. Dept. of Health, Education, and Welfare.—**259**

LEVINSON, D. J., *see* Inkeles and Levinson (1969).

LEVITT, E. E. (1967) *The psychology of anxiety.* Indianapolis, Ind.: Bobbs-Merrill.—**468**

LEWIN, K., *see* Barker, Dembo, and Lewin (1941).

LEWIS, D. (1969) Sources of experimental amnesia. *Psychological Review,* 76:461–72.—**241**

LEWIS, H. B., GOODENOUGH, D. R., SHAPIRO, A., and SLESER, I. (1966) Individual differences in dream recall. *Journal of Abnormal Psychology,* 71:52–59.—**170**

LEWIS, S. (1934) *Work of art.* Garden City, N.Y.: Doubleday.—**401**

LIDZ, T., FLECK, S., and CORNELISON, A. R. (1965) *Schizophrenia and the family.* N.Y.: International Universities Press.—**479**

LIFTON, R. J. (1954) Home by ship: Reaction patterns of American prisoners of war repatriated from North Korea. *American Journal of Psychiatry,* 110:732–39.—**534**

LIFTON, R. J. (1956) "Thought reform" of Western civilians in Chinese Communist prisons. *Psychiatry,* 19:173–95.—**534**

LIFTON, R. J. (1961) *Thought reform and the psychology of totalism.* N.Y.: Norton.—**534, 538**

LINDER, D., *see* Aronson and Linder (1965).

LINDER, D. E., COOPER, J., and JONES, E. E. (1967) Decision freedom as a determinant of the role of incentive magnitude in attitude change. *Journal of Personality and Social Psychology,* 6:245–54.—**530**

LINDGREN, H. C. (1964) *Psychology of personal development.* N.Y.: American Book.—**486, 510**

LINDSLEY, D. B. (1951) Emotion. In Stevens, S. S. (ed.) *Handbook of experimental psychology.* N.Y.: Wiley, 473–516.—**341**

LINDZEY, G. (1967) Morphology and behavior. In Spuhler, J. N. (ed.) *Behavioral consequences of genetic differences in man.* Chicago: Aldine.—**399**

LINDZEY, G., *see* Allport, Vernon, and Lindzey (1960); Hall and Lindzey (1970); Manosevitz, Lindzey, and Thiessen (1969).

LINDZEY, G., and ARONSON, E. (eds.) (1968–69) *Handbook of social psychology* (rev. ed., 5 vols.). Reading, Mass.: Addison-Wesley.—**537**

LINDZEY, G., and HALL, C. S. (eds.) (1965) *Theories of personality: Primary sources and research.* N.Y.: Wiley.—**419**

LIPPERT, W. W., and SENTER, R. J. (1966) Electrodermal responses in the sociopath. *Psychonomic Science,* 4:25–26.—**480**

LIPSET, S. M., and BENDIX, R. (1959) *Social mobility in industrial society.* Berkeley, Calif.: Univ. of California Press.—**516**

LITWIN, G. H., *see* Atkinson and Litwin (1960).

LIVELY, E. L., DINITZ, S., and RECKLESS, W. C. (1962) Self-concept as a predictor of juvenile delinquency. *American Journal of Orthopsychiatry,* 32:159–69.—**91**

LOBBAN, M. C. (1965) Dissociation in human rhythmic functions. In Aschoff, J. (ed.) *Circadian clocks.* Amsterdam, Netherlands: North-Holland, 219–27.—**167**

LOEWENSTEIN, W. R. (1960) Biological transducers. *Scientific American,* 203:98–108.—**47**

LOGAN, F. A. (1964) The free behavior situation. *Nebraska Symposium on Motivation.* Lincoln, Nebr.: Univ. of Nebraska Press, 12:99–134.—**305**

LOGAN, F. A. (1970) *Fundamentals of learning and motivation.* Dubuque, Iowa: Brown.—**224**

LONDON, P. (1969) *Behavior control.* N.Y.: Harper and Row.—**560**

LONDON, P., and ROSENHAN, D. (eds.) (1968) *Foundations of abnormal psychology.* N.Y.: Holt, Rinehart and Winston.—**486**

LORENZ, K. (1965) *Evolution and modification of behavior.* Chicago: Univ. of Chicago Press.—**302**

LORENZ, K. (1966) *On aggression.* N.Y.: Harcourt Brace Jovanovich.—**319**

LORGE, I. (1930) Influence of regularly interpolated time intervals on subsequent learning. *Teachers College Contributions to Education,* No. 438.—**210**

LOURIE, R. S., *see* Chandler, Lourie, and Peters (1968).

LOWELL, E. L. (1950) A methodological study of projectively measured achievement motivation. Unpublished M.A. thesis, Wesleyan University.—**327**

LOWELL, E. L., *see* McClelland, Atkinson, Clark, and Lowell (1953).

LUBIN, A., *see* Williams, Lubin, and Goodnow (1959).

LUCE, G. G., and SEGAL, J. (1966) *Sleep.* N.Y.: Coward-McCann.—**185**

LUCE, R. D., BUSH, R. R., and GALANTER, E. (eds.) (1963), (1965) *Handbook of mathematical psychology,* vols. I, III. N.Y.: Wiley.—**134**

LUNDY, R. M. (1958) Self-perception regarding masculinity-femininity and descriptions of same and opposite sex sociometric choices. *Sociometry,* 21:238–46.—**513**

LUNDY, R. M., *see* Parrish, Lundy, and Leibowitz (1968).

LURIA, A. R. (1968) *The mind of a mnemonist.* N.Y.: Basic Books.—**242**

LURIA, Z., *see* Osgood and Luria (1954).

LYLE, J., *see* Schramm, Lyle, and Parker (1961).

LYONS, G. M. (1969) *The uneasy partnership: Social science and the federal government in the twentieth century.* N.Y.: Russell Sage Foundation.—**559**

MCCAFFREY, I., *see* Cummings, Dean, Newell, and McCaffrey (1960).

MCCALL, R. B. (1970) *Fundamental statistics for psychology.* N.Y.: Harcourt Brace Jovanovich.—**578**

MCCLELLAND, D. C. (ed.) (1955) *Studies in motivation.* N.Y.: Appleton-Century-Crofts.—**327**

MCCLELLAND, D. C. (1961) *The achieving society.* Princeton, N.J.: Van Nostrand.—**333**

MCCLELLAND, D. C., ATKINSON, J. W., CLARK, R. A., and LOWELL, E. L. (1953) *The achievement motive.* N.Y.: Appleton-Century-Crofts.—**326**

MCCLELLAND, D. C., and WINTER, D. G. (1969) *Motivating economic achievement.* N.Y.: Free Press.—**333**

MCCONNELL, J. V., *see* Golub, Masiarz, Villars, and McConnell (1970).

MCCONNELL, J. V., SHIGEHISA, T., and SALIVE, H. (1970) In Pribram, K. H., and Broadbent, D. E. (eds.) *Biology of memory.* N.Y.: Academic Press, 129–59.—**233**

MCCONNELL, R. A. (1968) ESP without cards. *The Science Teacher,* 35:29–33.—**158**

MCCONNELL, R. A. (1969) ESP and credibility in science. *American Psychologist,* 24:531–38.—**156, 161**

MCCONNELL, R. A., *see* Schmeidler and McConnell (1958).

MCCORD, J., *see* McCord and McCord (1964); McCord, McCord, and Zola (1959).

MCCORD, W., and MCCORD, J. (1964) *The psychopath: An essay on the criminal mind.* Princeton, N.J.: Van Nostrand.—**481**

MCCORD, W., MCCORD, J., and ZOLA, I. K. (1959) *Origins of crime.* N.Y.: Columbia Univ. Press.—**91**

MCDONALD, F., *see* Bandura and McDonald (1963).

MCGAUGH, J. L. (1970) Time-dependent processes in memory storage. In McGaugh, J. L., and Herz, M. J. (eds.) *Controversial issues in consolidation of the memory trace.* N.Y.: Atherton Press.—**241**

MCGAUGH, J. L., *see* Hudspeth, McGaugh,

and Thompson (1964); Thiessen and McGaugh (1958).

MCGAUGH, J. L., and HERZ, M. J. (eds.) (1970) *Controversial issues in consolidation of the memory trace.* N.Y.: Atherton Press.—**241, 246**

MCGUIRE, W. J. (1969) The nature of attitudes and attitude change. In Lindzey, G., and Aronson, E. (eds.) *Handbook of social psychology* (rev. ed.), 3:136–314.—**533, 535, 537**

MCGUIRE, W. J., *see* Abelson, Aronson, McGuire, Newcomb, Rosenberg, and Tannenbaum (eds.) (1968).

MACLEOD, R. B., and ROFF, M. F. (1936) An experiment in temporal disorientation. *Acta Psychologica,* 1:381–423.—**167**

MACMAHON, B., *see* Pugh and MacMahon (1962).

MCNEILL, D. (1970) *The acquisition of language: The study of developmental psycholinguistics.* N.Y.: Harper and Row.—**278, 280, 282, 292**

MCNEILL, D., *see* Brown and McNeill (1966); Miller and McNeill (1969).

MCNEMAR, Q. (1942) *The revision of the Stanford-Binet scale.* Boston. Houghton Mifflin.—**391**

MCNEMAR, Q. (1969) *Psychological statistics* (4th ed.). N.Y.: Wiley.—**565, 572, 578**

MACNICHOL, E. F., JR. (1964) Three-pigment color vision. *Scientific American,* 211:48–56.—**120**

MACWHINNEY, B., *see* Atkinson, MacWhinney, and Stoel (1970).

MAAS, H. (1963) The young adult adjustment of twenty wartime residential nursery children. *Child Welfare,* 42:57–72.—**70**

MACCOBY, E. E., *see* Sears, Maccoby, and Levin (1957).

MACKLER, B., *see* Spotts and Mackler (1967).

MACKLIN, D. B., *see* Leighton, Harding, Macklin, Macmillan, and Leighton (1963).

MACKWORTH, N. H. (1950) Researches in the measurement of human performances. *Medical Research Council Special Report Series,* No. 268. London: H. M. Stationery Office.—**164**

MACLAY, H., and OSGOOD, C. E. (1967) Hesitation phenomena in spontaneous English speech. In Jakobovits, L. A., and Miron, M. S. (eds.) *Readings in the psychology of language.* Englewood Cliffs, N.J.: Prentice-Hall, 305–24.—**277**

MACLAY, H., and WARE, E. E. (1961) Cross-cultural use of the semantic differential. *Behavioral Science,* 6:185–90.—**273**

MACMILLAN, A. M., *see* Leighton, Harding, Macklin, Macmillan, and Leighton (1963).

MADIGAN, S., *see* Tulving and Madigan (1970).

MADOW, L., and SNOW, L. H. (eds.) (1970) *The psychodynamic implications of the physiological studies on dreams.* Springfield, Ill.: Thomas.—**185**

MAGARET, A., *see* Cameron and Magaret (1951); Hilgard, Sait, and Magaret (1940).

MAHATOO, W., *see* Doane, Mahatoo, Heron, and Scott (1959).

MAHER, B. A. (ed.) (1964) *Progress in experimental personality research,* vol. I. N.Y.: Academic Press.—**420**

MAHER, B. A. (1966) *Principles of psychotherapy: An experimental approach.* N.Y.: McGraw-Hill.—**463, 486**

MAHL, G. F. (1963) The lexical and linguistic levels in the expression of the emotions. In Knapp, P. H. (ed.) *Expression of the emotions in man.* N.Y.: International Universities Press, 77–105.—**351**

MAIER, N. R. F. (1949) *Frustration: A study of behavior without a goal.* N.Y.: McGraw-Hill.—**451**

MALINOWSKI, B. (1929) *The sexual life of savages in northwestern Melanesia.* N.Y.: Liveright.—**88**

MALIS, J. L., *see* Brodie, Malis, Moreno, and Boren (1960).

MALMO, R. B. (1959) Activation: A neuropsychological dimension. *Psychological Review,* 66:367–86.—**341**

MANDLER, G. (1962) Emotion. In Brown, R., and others *New directions in psychology.* N.Y.: Holt, Rinehart and Winston, 269–343.—**354**

MANDLER, G. (1969) Words, lists and categories: An experimental view of organized memory. In Cowan, J. L. (ed.) *Thought and language.* Tucson, Ariz.: Univ. of Arizona Press.—**243**

MANDLER, G., *see* Sarason, Mandler, and Craighill (1952).

MANGRUM, J. C., *see* Stephens, Astrup, and Mangrum (1967).

MANOSEVITZ, M., LINDZEY, G., and THIESSEN, D. D. (eds.) (1969) *Behavioral genetics: Method and research.* N.Y.: Appleton-Century-Crofts.—**396**

MANUEL, F. E. (ed.) (1967) *Utopias and Utopian thought.* Boston: Beacon Press.—**551**

MARCUSE, F. L. (ed.) (1964) *Hypnosis throughout the world.* Springfield, Ill.: Thomas.—**177**

MARGOLIS, R., *see* Glick and Margolis (1962).

MARIN, J., *see* Hunt, Marin, and Stone (1966).

MARLOWE, D., *see* Crowne and Marlow (1964).

MARSHALL, G. D., *see* Zimbardo, Maslach, and Marshall (1970).

MARTIN, C. E., *see* Kinsey, Pomeroy, and Martin (1948).

MARTIN, E. (1965) Transfer of verbal paired associates. *Psychological Review,* 72:327–43.—**256**

MARTIN, M., BURKHOLDER, R., ROSENTHAL, T. L., THARP, R. G., and THORNE, G. L. (1968) Programming behavior change and reintegration into school milieux of extreme adolescent deviates. *Behavior Research and Therapy,* 6:371–83.—**497**

MASIARZ, F. R., *see* Golub, Masiarz, Villars, and McConnell (1970).

MASLACH, C., *see* Zimbardo, Maslach, and Marshall (1970).

MASLAND, R. L., SARASON, S. B., and GLADWYN, T. (1958) *Mental subnormality.* N.Y.: Basic Books.—**376**

MASLOW, A. H. (1959) Cognition of being in the peak experiences. *Journal of Genetic Psychology,* 94:43–66.—**165, 331**

MASLOW, A. H. (1968) *Toward a psychology of being* (2nd ed.). N.Y.: Van Nostrand Reinhold.—**330, 333**

MASLOW, A. H. (1970) *Motivation and personality* (2nd ed.). N.Y.: Harper and Row.—**330**

MASON, J. W., *see* Brady, Porter, Conrad, and Mason (1958).

MATARAZZO, J. D. (1965) The interview. In Wolman, B. B. (ed.) *Handbook of clinical psychology.* N.Y.: McGraw-Hill, 403–50.—**427**

MATTHEWS, G. V. T. (1968) *Bird navigation* (2nd ed.). London: Cambridge Univ. Press.—**303**

MAUPIN, E. W. (1965) Individual differences in response to a Zen meditation exercise. *Journal of Consulting Psychology,* 29:139–45.—**179, 180**

MAY, M. A., *see* Hartshorne and May (1928).

MAY, R. (1950) *The meaning of anxiety.* N.Y.: Ronald Press.—**347**

MEAD, M. (1935) *Sex and temperament in three primitive societies.* N.Y.: Morrow.—**88**

MEAD, M. (1949) *Male and female.* N.Y.: Morrow.—**97**

MEAD, M., and others (eds.) (1968) *Science and the concept of race.* N.Y.: Columbia Univ. Press.—**396**

MEDINNUS, G. R., *see* Johnson and Medinnus (1969).

MEDNICK, S. A. (1962) The associative basis of the creative process. *Psychological Review,* 69:220–32.—**371**

MEEHL, P. E. (1950) Configural scoring. *Journal of Consulting Psychology,* 14:165–71.—**404**

MEEHL, P. E. (1954) *Clinical vs. statistical prediction.* Minneapolis: Univ. of Minnesota Press.—**433**

MEEHL, P. E. (1957) When shall we use our heads instead of the formula? *Journal of Consulting Psychology,* 4:268–73.—**433**

MEGARGEE, E. I., and COOK, P. E. (1967) The relation of TAT and inkblot aggressive content scales with each other and with criteria of overt aggression in juvenile delinquents. *Journal of Projective Techniques and Personality Assessment,* 31:48–60.—**434**

MENNINGER, K. (1958) *Theory of psychoanalytic technique.* N.Y.: Basic Books.—**510**

MENZIES, R. (1937) Conditioned vasomotor responses in human subjects. *Journal of Psychology,* 4:75–120.—**194**

MERRILL, M. A. (1938) The significance of I.Q.'s on the revised Stanford-Binet scales. *Journal of Educational Psychology,* 26:641–51.—**365**

MERRILL, M. A., *see* Terman and Merrill (1937), (1960).

MEYER, D. (1965) *The positive thinkers: A study of the American quest for health, wealth and personal power from Mary Baker*

Eddy to Norman Vincent Peale. Garden City, N.Y.: Doubleday.—**184, 331**

MEYER, D. R., see Harlow, Harlow, and Meyer (1950).

MICHAEL, D. N. (1968) The unprepared society. N.Y.: Basic Books.—**557**

MICHAEL, S. T., see Srole, Langner, Michael, Opler, and Rennie (1962).

MILLER, G. A., see Clark and Miller (1970); Smith and Miller (1966).

MILLER, G. A., GALANTER, E., and PRIBRAM, K. H. (1960) Plans and the structure of behavior. N.Y.: Holt.—**163**

MILLER, G. A., and MCNEILL, D. V. (1969) Psycholinguistics. In Lindzey, G., and Aronson, E. (eds.) The handbook of social psychology (2nd ed.), vol. III. Reading, Mass.: Addison-Wesley, 666–794.—**287**

MILLER, J. M., MOODY, D. B., and STEBBINS, W. C. (1969) Evoked potentials and auditory reaction time in monkeys. Science, 163:592–94.—**41**

MILLER, J. O. (1970) Disadvantaged families: Despair to hope. In Korten, F. F., Cook, S. W., and Lacey, J. I. (eds.) Psychology and the problems of society. Washington, D.C.: American Psychological Association, 179–97.—**377**

MILLER, N., see Kiesler, Collins, and Miller (1969).

MILLER, N. E. (1948a) Fear as an acquired drive. Journal of Experimental Psychology, 38:89–101.—**346**

MILLER, N. E. (1948b) Theory and experiment relating psychoanalytic displacement to stimulus-response generalization. Journal of Abnormal and Social Psychology, 43:155–78.—**450**

MILLER, N. E. (1959) Liberalization of basic S-R concepts: Extensions to conflict behavior, motivation, and social learning. In Koch, S. (ed.) Psychology: A study of a science, vol. II. N.Y.: McGraw-Hill, 196–292.—**305, 444, 445, 463**

MILLER, N. E. (1961) Analytic studies of drive and reward. American Psychologist, 16:739–54.—**297**

MILLER, N. E. (1969) Learning of visceral and glandular responses. Science, 163:434–45.—**62, 202**

MILLER, N. E., see Delgado, Roberts, and Miller (1954).

MILLER, N. E., and BANUAZIZI, A. (1968) Instrumental learning by curarized rats of a specific visceral response, intestinal, or cardiac. Journal of Comparative and Physiological Psychology, 65:1–7.—**202, 203**

MILLER, N. E., and KESSEN, M. L. (1952) Reward effects of food via stomach fistula compared with those of food via mouth. Journal of Comparative and Physiological Psychology, 45:555–64.—**207**

MILLER, W. E., see Campbell, Converse, Miller, and Stokes (1960); Converse, Miller, Rusk, and Wolfe (1969).

MILLER, W., and ERVIN, S. (1964) The development of grammar in child language. In Bellugi, U., and Brown, R. (eds.) The acquisition of language. Monographs of the Society for Research in Child Development, 29:9–34.—**282**

MILLON, T. (ed.) (1968) Approaches to personality. N.Y.: Pitman.—**420**

MILLS, J. (ed.) (1969) Experimental social psychology. N.Y.: Macmillan.—**537**

MILNER, B. (1964) Some effects of frontal lobectomy in man. In Warren, J. M., and Akert, K. (eds.) The frontal granular cortex and behavior. N.Y.: McGraw-Hill, 313–34.—**42**

MILNER, P. M. (1966) Physiological psychology. N.Y.: Holt, Rinehart and Winston.—**36, 240**

MILNER, P. M., see Olds and Milner (1954).

MINAMI, H., and DALLENBACH, K. R. (1946) The effect of activity upon learning and retention in the cockroach. American Journal of Psychology, 59:1–58.—**234**

MIRON, M. S., see Jakobovits and Miron (1967).

MISCHEL, W. (1966) Theory and research on the antecedents of self-imposed delay of reward. In Maher, B. A. (ed.) Progress in experimental personality research, vol. III. N.Y.: Academic Press, 85–132.—**414**

MISCHEL, W. (1968) Personality and assessment. N.Y.: Wiley.—**410, 420, 436, 438**

MISCHEL, W. (1971) Introduction to personality. N.Y.: Holt, Rinehart and Winston.—**420**

MISCHEL, W., and GILLIGAN, C. (1964) Delay of gratification, motivation for the prohibited gratification, and responses to temptation. Journal of Abnormal and Social Psychology, 69:411–17.—**414**

MITCHELL, G. D., HARLOW, H. F., GRIFFIN, G. A., and MOLLER, G. W. (1967) Repeated maternal separation in the monkey. Psychonomic Science, 8:197–98.—**70**

MOLLER, G. W., see Mitchell, Harlow, Griffin, and Moller (1967).

MOLONEY, J. C. (1955) Psychic self-abandon and extortion of confession. International Journal of Psychoanalysis, 36:53–60.—**534**

MONACHESI, E. D., see Hathaway and Monachesi (1963).

MONEY, J. (1963) Cytogenetic and psychosexual incongruities with a note on space-form blindness. American Journal of Psychiatry, 119:820–27.—**385**

MONROE, L. J., RECHTSCHAFFEN, A., FOULKES, D., and JENSEN, J. (1965) The discriminability of REM and NREM reports. Journal of Personality and Social Psychology, 2:456–60.—**170**

MOODY, D. B., see Miller, Moody, and Stebbins (1969).

MOORE, R. K., see Hilgard, Weitzenhoffer, Landes, and Moore (1961).

MOORE, U. S., see Hilgard and Moore (1969).

MOORE, W. E., see Sheldon and Moore (1968).

MORENO, O. M., see Brodie, Malis, Moreno, and Boren (1960).

MORGAN, A. H., HILGARD, E. R., and DAVERT, E. (1970) The heritability of hypnotic susceptibility of twins: A preliminary report. Behavioral Genetics, 1:213–23.—**177**

MORGAN, C. M. (1937) The attitudes and adjustments of recipients of old age assistance in upstate and metropolitan New York. Archives of Psychology, 30, No. 214.—**96**

MORGAN, C. T. (1965) Physiological psychology (3rd ed.). N.Y.: McGraw-Hill.—**51**

MORGAN, C. T., and MORGAN, J. D. (1940) Studies in hunger: II. The relation of gastric denervation and dietary sugar to the effect of insulin upon food-intake in the rat. Journal of Genetic Psychology, 57:153–63.—**298**

MORGAN, J. D., see Morgan and Morgan (1940).

MORGULIS, S., see Yerkes and Morgulis (1909).

MORLAND, J. K. (1966) A comparison of race awareness in Northern and Southern children. American Journal of Orthopsychiatry, 36:22–31.—**77**

MORLOCK, H. C., see Williams, Morlock, and Morlock (1966).

MORLOCK, J. V., see Williams, Morlock, and Morlock (1966).

MORNINGSTAR, M., see Suppes and Morningstar (1969).

MOSELEY, E. C., DUFFEY, R. F., and SHERMAN, L. J. (1963) An extension of the construct validity of the Holtzman inkblot technique. Journal of Clinical Psychology, 19:186–92.—**435**

MOSS, H. A., see Kagan and Moss (1962).

MOULTON, R. W., RAPHELSON, A. C., KRISTOFFERSON, A. B., and ATKINSON, J. W. (1958) The achievement motive and perceptual sensitivity under two conditions of motive-arousal. In Atkinson, J. W. (ed.) Motives in fantasy, action, and society. Princeton, N.J.: Van Nostrand.—**327, 522**

MOUTON, J. S., see Helson, Blake, and Mouton (1958).

MOYNIHAN, D. P. (1969) Maximum feasible misunderstanding. N.Y.: Free Press.—**556**

MOYNIHAN, D. P. (1970) Eliteland. Psychology Today, September: 35–37; 66–70.—**556**

MUELLER, C. G. (1965) Sensory psychology. Englewood Cliffs, N.J.: Prentice-Hall.—**134**

MUELLER, C. G., and RUDOLPH, M. (1966) Light and vision. N.Y.: Time, Inc.—**134**

MULLINS, R. F., JR., see Levine and Mullins (1966).

MURDOCK, G. P. (1937) Comparative data on the division of labor by sex. Social Forces, 15:551–53.—**97**

MURPHY, G. (1949) Historical introduction to modern psychology (rev. ed.). N.Y.: Harcourt Brace Jovanovich.—**22**

MURRAY, E. J. (1964) Motivation and emotion. Englewood Cliffs, N.J.: Prentice-Hall.—**311, 333, 354**

MURRAY, H. A., and others (1938) Explorations in personality. N.Y.: Oxford Univ. Press.—**315, 316, 432**

MUSSEN, P. H. (1963) The psychological development of the child. Englewood Cliffs, N.J.: Prentice-Hall.—**81**

MUSSEN, P. H. (ed.) (1970) Carmichael's Manual of child psychology (3rd ed.), vols. I, II. N.Y.: Wiley.—**81, 104**

PARKER, E., *see* Schramm, Lyle, and Parker (1961).

PARRISH, M., LUNDY, R. M., and LEIBOWITZ, H. W. (1968) Hypnotic age-regression and magnitudes of the Ponzo and Poggendorff illusions. *Science,* 159:1375–76.—**145**

PAULSON, J. A., *see* Atkinson and Paulson (1970).

PAVLOV, I. P. (1927) *Conditioned reflexes.* N.Y.: Oxford Univ. Press.—**5, 192, 193, 224**

PENFIELD, W. (1969) Consciousness, memory, and man's conditioned reflexes. In Pribram, K. (ed.) *On the biology of learning.* N.Y.: Harcourt Brace Jovanovich. —**237**

PENFIELD, W., and RASMUSSEN, T. (1950) *The cerebral cortex of man.* N.Y.: Macmillan. —**41**

PENFIELD, W., and ROBERTS, L. (1959) *Speech and brain mechanisms.* Princeton, N.J.: Princeton Univ. Press.—**43**

PEPITONE, A., *see* Festinger, Pepitone, and Newcomb (1952).

PERCHONEK, E., *see* Savin and Perchonek (1965).

PETERS, A. D., *see* Chandler, Lourie, and Peters (1968).

PETERSON, D. R. (1968) *The clinical study of social behavior.* N.Y.: Appleton-Century-Crofts.—**430, 436**

PETERSON, D. R., *see* Becker, Peterson, Hellmer, Shoemaker, and Quay (1962).

PETERSON, J. C., *see* Higgins and Peterson (1966).

PETERSON, L. R., and PETERSON, M. J. (1959) Short-term retention of individual verbal items. *Journal of Experimental Psychology,* 30:93–113.—**238**

PETERSON, M. J., *see* Peterson and Peterson (1959).

PETTIGREW, T. F. (1964) *A profile of the American Negro.* Princeton, N.J.: Van Nostrand.—**537**

PFAFFMANN, C. (1964) Taste, its sensory and motivating properties. *American Scientist,* 52:187–206.—**130**

PIAGET, J. (1952) *The origins of intelligence in children.* N.Y.: International Universities Press.—**307**

PIAGET, J. (1970) Piaget's theory. In Mussen, P. H. (ed.) *Carmichael's Manual of child psychology,* vol. I. N.Y.: Wiley, 703–32.—**64**

PIAGET, J., and INHELDER, B. (1941) *Le développement des quantités chez l'enfant.* Neuchâtel, Switzerland: Delacheux et Niestle.—**63**

PITT, R., and HAGE, J. (1964) Patterns of peer interaction during adolescence as prognostic indicators in schizophrenia. *American Journal of Psychiatry,* 120:1089–96.—**475**

PLANT, W. T. (1968) Changes in ethnocentrism associated with a two-year college experience. *Journal of Genetic Psychology,* 92:189–97.—**94**

PLUTCHIK, R. (1962) *The emotions: Facts, theories, and a new model.* N.Y.: Random House.—**335, 354**

POLEFKA, J., *see* Hastorf, Schneider, and Polefka (1970).

POLLIN, W., and STABENAU, J. R. (1968) Biological, psychological, and historical differences in a series of monozygotic twins discordant for schizophrenia. In Rosenthal, D., and Kety, S. S. (eds.) *The transmission of schizophrenia.* N.Y.: Pergamon Press, 317–32.—**394**

POLT, J. M., *see* Hess and Polt (1960).

POLYAK, S. (1941) *The retina.* Chicago: Univ. of Chicago Press.—**113**

POMEROY, W. B., *see* Kinsey, Pomeroy, and Martin (1948).

POND, D. A., RYLE, A., and HAMILTON, M. (1963) Social factors and neurosis in a working-class population. *British Journal of Psychiatry,* 109:587–91.—**98**

PORTER, R. W., *see* Brady, Porter, Conrad, and Mason (1958).

POSTMAN, L. (1969) Experimental analysis of learning to learn. In Bower, G. H., and Spence, J. T. (eds.) *The psychology of learning and motivation.* N.Y.: Academic Press. —**234, 260**

PREMACK, D. (1971) Catching up with common sense or two sides of a generalization: Reinforcement and punishment. In Glaser, R. (ed.) *The nature of reinforcement.* Columbus, Ohio: Merrill.—**207**

PRESIDENT'S COMMISSION ON NATIONAL GOALS (1960) *Goals for Americans.* Englewood Cliffs, N.J.: Prentice-Hall.—**546**

PRESSEY, S. L. (1926) A simple apparatus which gives tests and scores—and teaches. *School and Society,* 23:373–76.—**248**

PRIBRAM, K. H. (1969a) The neurophysiology of remembering. *Scientific American,* 220:73–86.—**36, 42**

PRIBRAM, K. H. (ed.) (1969b) *On the biology of learning.* N.Y.: Harcourt Brace Jovanovich.—**51, 246**

PRIBRAM, K. H., *see* Miller, Galanter, and Pribram (1960).

PRICE, D. K. (1965) *The scientific estate.* Cambridge, Mass.: Belknap-Harvard.—**555**

PRINCE, M. (1906) *The dissociation of a personality.* N.Y.: Longmans, Green.—**414**

PRONKO, N. H., *see* Snyder and Pronko (1952).

PROSHANSKY, H. M., ITTLESON, W. H., and RIVLIN, L. G. (eds.) (1970) *Environmental psychology.* N.Y.: Holt, Rinehart and Winston.—**559**

PROSHANSKY, H. M., and SEIDENBERG, B. (eds.) (1965) *Basic studies in social psychology.* N.Y.: Holt, Rinehart, and Winston. —**537**

PUBOLS, B. H., *see* Welker, Johnson, and Pubols (1964).

PUGH, T. F., and MACMAHON, B. (1962) *Epidemiologic findings in United States mental hospital data.* Boston: Little, Brown.—**485**

QUAY, H. C., *see* Becker, Peterson, Hellmer, Shoemaker, and Quay (1962).

RABIN, A. I. (1947) A case history of a simple schizophrenic. In Burton, A., and Harris, R. E. (eds.) *Case histories in clinical and abnormal psychology.* N.Y.: Harper and Row.—**475**

RABIN, A. I. (1965) *Growing up in the Kibbutz.* N.Y.: Springer.—**71**

RABIN, A. I. (1968a) Some sex differences in the attitudes of Kibbutz adolescents. *The Israel Annals of Psychiatry,* 6:63–69.—**71**

RABIN, A. I. (ed.) (1968b) *Projective techniques in personality assessment.* N.Y.: Springer.—**439**

RABKIN, K., *see* Rabkin and Rabkin (1969).

RABKIN, Y., and RABKIN, K. (1969) Children of the Kibbutz. *Psychology Today,* 3:40–46. —**71**

RACHMAN, S., *see* Eysenck and Rachman (1965).

RADLER, D. H., *see* Remmers and Radler (1957).

RAND, A. (1964) *The virtue of selfishness.* N.Y.: New American Library.—**93**

RAPHELSON, A. C. (1957) The relationship between imaginative, direct, verbal, and physiological measures of anxiety in an achievement situation. *Journal of Abnormal and Social Psychology,* 54:13–18.—**327**

RAPHELSON, A. C., *see* Moulton, Raphelson, Kristofferson, and Atkinson (1958).

RASMUSSEN, T., *see* Penfield and Rasmussen (1950).

RATLIFF, F. (1965) *Mach bands: Quantitative studies on neural networks in the retina.* San Francisco, Calif.: Holden-Day.—**121**

RAYMOND, S., *see* Vogel, Raymond, and Lazarus (1959).

RAYNER, R., *see* Watson and Rayner (1920).

RECHTSCHAFFEN, A., *see* Monroe, Rechtschaffen, Foulkes, and Jensen (1965).

RECHTSCHAFFEN, A., GOODENOUGH, D. R., and SHAPIRO, A. (1962) Patterns of sleep talking. *Archives of General Psychiatry,* 7:418–26.—**171**

RECKLESS, W. C., *see* Lively, Dinitz, and Reckless (1962).

REDLICH, F. C., *see* Hollingshead and Redlich (1958).

REDLICH, F. C., and FREEDMAN, D. X. (1966) *The theory and practice of psychiatry.* N.Y.: Basic Books. —**486**

REESE, H. W., *see* Levinson and Reese (1963).

REIFF, R. (1970) Psychology and public policy. *Professional Psychology,* Summer: 315–24.—**556**

REIFF, R., and SCHEERER, M. (1959) *Memory and hypnotic age regression.* N.Y.: International Universities Press.—**226**

REISER, M. F., *see* Arkin, Hastey, and Reiser (1966).

REITMAN, W. R. (1965) *Cognition and thought.* N.Y.: Wiley.—**290, 292**

REMMERS, H. H., and RADLER, D. H. (1957) *The American teenager.* Indianapolis, Ind.: Bobbs-Merrill.—**89**

RENNIE, T. A. C., *see* Srole, Langner, Michael, Opler, and Rennie (1962).

RESCHER, N., *see* Baier and Rescher (1969).

RESTLE, F., and GREENO, J. G. (1970) *Introduction to mathematical psychology.* Reading, Mass.: Addison-Wesley.—**215, 224**

REYNOLDS, G. S. (1968) *A primer of operant conditioning.* Glenview, Ill.: Scott, Foresman.—**224**

RHINE, J. B. (1942) Evidence of precognition in the covariation of salience ratios. *Journal of Parapsychology,* 6:111–43.—**158**

RHINE, J. B., and BRIER, R. (1968) *Parapsychology today.* N.Y.: Citadel Press.—**156**

RICHARDSON, S. A., *see* Dornbusch, Hastorf, Richardson, Muzzy, and Vreeland (1965).

RICHTER, C. P. (1943) The self-selection of diets. In *Essays in biology.* Berkeley, Calif.: Univ. of California Press, 500–05.—**299**

RICHTER, C. P. (1965) *Biological clocks in medicine and psychiatry.* Springfield, Ill.: Thomas.—**185**

RIECKEN, H. W., *see* Festinger, Riecken, and Schachter (1956).

RIESEN, A. H. (1965) Effects of early deprivation of photic stimulation. In Osler, S., and Cooke, R. (eds.) *The biosocial basis of mental retardation.* Baltimore, Md.: Johns Hopkins Press.—**58, 151**

RIOCH, M. J. (1967) Pilot projects in training mental health counselors. In Cowen, E. L., Gardner, E. A., and Zax, M. (eds.) *Emergent approaches to mental health problems.* N.Y.: Appleton-Century-Crofts, 110–27. —**502**

RITTER, B., *see* Bandura, Blanchard, and Ritter (1969).

RIVLIN, L. G., *see* Proshansky, Ittleson, and Rivlin (1970).

ROBERTS, L., *see* Penfield and Roberts (1959).

ROBERTS, W. W., *see* Delgado, Roberts, and Miller (1954).

ROBERTSON, A., and YOUNISS, J. (1969) Anticipatory visual imagery in deaf and hearing children. *Child Development,* 40:123–35.—**286**

ROCK, I., and HARRIS, C. S. (1967) Vision and touch. *Scientific American,* 216:96–104.—**139**

ROCK, L., *see* Jones, Rock, Shaver, Goethals, and Ward (1968).

RODGERS, W. L. (1967) Specificity of specific hungers. *Journal of Comparative and Physiological Psychology,* 64:49–58.—**299**

ROFF, M. F., *see* MacLeod and Roff (1936).

ROGERS, C. R. (1961) *On becoming a person: A therapist's view of psychotherapy.* Boston: Houghton Mifflin.—**331, 494**

ROGERS, C. R. (ed.) (1967) *The therapeutic relationship and its impact: A study of psychotherapy with schizophrenics.* Madison, Wis.: Univ. of Wisconsin Press.—**494, 510**

ROGERS, C. R. (1969) The group comes of age. *Psychology Today,* 3:27–31.—**500, 501**

ROGERS, C. R. (1970) *On becoming a person: A therapist's view of psychotherapy.* Boston: Houghton Mifflin-Sentry Edition.—**510**

ROGERS, C. R., and SKINNER, B. F. (1956) Some issues concerning the control of human behavior: A symposium. *Science,* 124:1057–66.—**553**

RORSCHACH, H. (1942) *Psychodiagnostics.* Berne, Switzerland: Hans Huber.—**434**

ROSEN, B., and D'ANDRADE, R. C. (1959) The psychosocial origins of achievement motivation. *Sociometry,* 22:185–218.—**327**

ROSENBERG, M. (1965) *Society and the adolescent self-image.* Princeton, N.J.: Princeton Univ. Press.—**93, 94**

ROSENBERG, M. J. (1968) On reducing the inconsistency between consistency theories. In Abelson, R. P., and others (eds.) *Theories of cognitive consistency: A source-*

book. Chicago: Rand McNally, 827–33.—**530**

ROSENBERG, M. J., *see* Abelson, Aronson, McGuire, Newcomb, Rosenberg, and Tannenbaum (eds.) (1968).

ROSENBLUM, L., *see* Kaufman and Rosenblum (1967).

ROSENFELD, H., and BAER, D. (1969) Unnoticed verbal conditioning of an aware experimenter by a more aware subject: The double-agent effect. *Psychological Review,* 76:425–32.—**204**

ROSENHAN, D., *see* London and Rosenhan (1968).

ROSENTHAL, D. (1959) Some factors associated with concordance and discordance with respect to schizophrenia in monozygotic twins. *Journal of Nervous and Mental Disease,* 129:1–10.—**393**

ROSENTHAL, D. (1968) The heredity-environment issue in schizophrenia: Summary of the conference and present status of our knowledge. In Rosenthal, D., and Kety, S. S. (eds.) *The transmission of schizophrenia.* N.Y.: Pergamon Press, 413–27.—**393**

ROSENTHAL, D., and KETY, S. S. (eds.) (1968) *The transmission of schizophrenia.* N.Y.: Pergamon Press.—**486**

ROSENTHAL, D. B., *see* Crain, Katz, and Rosenthal (1969).

ROSENTHAL, R. A. (1966) *Experimenter effects in behavioral research.* N.Y.: Appleton-Century-Crofts.—**23**

ROSENTHAL, T. L., *see* Martin, Burkholder, Rosenthal, Tharp, and Thorne (1968).

ROSENZWEIG, M. R. (1962) The mechanisms of hunger and thirst. In Postman, L. (ed.) *Psychology in the making.* N.Y.: Knopf, 73–143.—**301**

ROSENZWEIG, M. R. (1969) Effects of heredity and environment on brain chemistry, brain anatomy, and learning ability in the rat. In Manosovitz, M., Lindzey, G., and Thiessen, D. D. (eds.) *Behavioral genetics.* N.Y.: Appleton-Century-Crofts, 256–70. —**387**

ROSENZWEIG, M. R., and BENNETT, E. L. (1970) Effects of differential environments on brain weights and enzyme activities in gerbils, rats, and mice. *Developmental Psychology,* in press.—**59**

ROSZAK, T. (1969) *The making of a counter culture.* Garden City, N.Y.: Doubleday.—**554**

ROZIN, P. (1967) Specific aversions as a component of specific hunger. *Journal of Comparative and Physiological Psychology,* 59:98–101.—**299**

RUBIN, R. T. (1969) Clinical aspects of marijuana and amphetamine use. *Annals of Internal Medicine,* 70:596–98.—**183**

RUDOLPH, M., *see* Mueller and Rudolph (1966).

RUMELHART, D. E., *see* Norman and Rumelhart (1970).

RUSK, J. G., *see* Converse, Miller, Rusk, and Wolfe (1969).

RUSSELL, B., *see* Whitehead and Russell (1925).

RUSSELL, W., and NATHAN, P. (1964) Traumatic amnesia. *Brain,* 69:280.—**241**

RUSSELL, W. A., and STORMS, L. H. (1955) Implicit verbal chaining in paired-associate learning. *Journal of Experimental Psychology,* 49:287–93.—**257**

RYLE, A., *see* Pond, Ryle, and Hamilton (1963).

SACHS, L. B., and ANDERSON, W. L. (1967) Modification of hypnotic susceptibility. *International Journal of Clinical and Experimental Hypnosis,* 15:172–80.—**175**

SACKETT, G. P. (1967) Some persistent effects of different rearing conditions on preadult social behavior of monkeys. *Journal of Comparative Physiological Psychology,* 64:363–65.—**69**

SAIT, E. M., *see* Hilgard, Sait, and Magaret (1940).

SALIVE, H., *see* McConnell, Shigehisa, and Salive (1970).

SALTZSTEIN, H. D., *see* Jackson and Saltzstein (1958).

SARASON, I. G. (1960) Empirical findings and theoretical problems in the use of anxiety scales. *Psychological Bulletin,* 57:403–15. —**267**

SARASON, I. G. (ed.) (1969) *Contemporary research in personality* (2nd ed.). N.Y.: Van Nostrand Reinhold.—**420**

SARASON, S. B., MANDLER, G., and CRAIGHILL, P. G. (1952) The effect of differential instructions on anxiety and learning. *Journal of Abnormal and Social Psychology,* 47:561–65.—**266, 267**

SARASON, S. B., *see* Masland, Sarason, and Gladwin (1958).

SARBIN, T. R. (1956) Physiological effects of hypnotic stimulation. In Dorcus, R. M. (ed.) *Hypnosis and its therapeutic applications.* N.Y.: McGraw-Hill, 4/1–4/57.—**173, 177**

SARBIN, T. R., and ANDERSEN, M. L. (1967) Role-theoretical analysis of hypnotic behavior. In Gordon, J. (ed.) *Handbook of clinical and experimental hypnosis.* N.Y.: Macmillan, 319–43.—**177**

SAVIN, H., and PERCHONEK, E. (1965) Grammatical structure and the immediate recall of English sentences. *Journal of Verbal Learning and Verbal Behavior,* 4:348–53.—**279**

SAWREY, J. M., and TELFORD, C. W. (1971) *Psychology of adjustment* (3rd ed.). Boston: Allyn and Bacon.—**486, 510**

SAWREY, W. L., CONGER, J. J., and TURRELL, E. S. (1956) An experimental investigation of the role of psychological factors in the production of gastric ulcers in rats. *Journal of Comparative and Physiological Psychology,* 49:457–61.—**193**

SAWYER, J. (1966) Measurement and prediction, clinical and statistical. *Psychological Bulletin,* 66:178–200.—**433**

SCHACHTER, S. (1959) *Psychology of affiliation.* Stanford, Calif.: Stanford Univ. Press. —**323, 324**

SCHACHTER, S., *see* Festinger, Riecken, and Schachter (1956); Festinger, Schachter, and Back (1950).

SCHACHTER, S., and SINGER, J. E. (1962) Cognitive, social and physiological determinants of emotional state. *Psychological Review,* 69:379–99 —**339, 340**

SCHAEFER, H., *see* Taber, Glaser, and Schaefer (1965).

SCHAFFER, H. R., and EMERSON, P. E. (1964) The development of social attachments in infancy. *Monographs of the Society for Research in Child Development,* 29, Serial No. 94.—**68**

SCHAIE, K. W., and STROTHER, C. R. (1968) A cross-sequential study of age changes in cognitive behavior. *Psychological Bulletin,* 70:671–80.—**374**

SCHEERER, M., *see* Goldstein and Scheerer (1941); Reiff and Scheerer (1959).

SCHEFFLER, I. (1967) *Science and subjectivity.* Indianapolis, Ind.: Bobbs-Merrill.—**560**

SCHEIN, E. H. (1956) The Chinese indoctrination program for prisoners of war. *Psychiatry,* 19:149–72.—**534**

SCHEIN, E. H., *see* Bennis, Schein, Berlew, and Steele (1968); Strassman, Thaler, and Schein (1956).

SCHEIN, E. H., SCHNEIER, I., and BARKER, C. H. (1961) *Coercive persuasion.* N.Y.: Norton. —**534, 538**

SCHERRER, H., see Hernández-Peón, Scherrer, and Jouvet (1956).

SCHIFF, L. F. (1966) Dynamic young fogies, rebels on the right. *Transaction,* 11:30–36. —**93**

SCHIFF, M. (1867) *Leçons sur la physiologie de la digestion,* vol. I. Florence and Turin, Italy: H. Loescher.—**301**

SCHIMMEL, H., *see* Vaughan, Costa, Gilden, and Schimmel (1965).

SCHLESINGER, K., ELSTON, R. C., and BOGGAN, W. (1966) The genetics of sound-induced seizure in inbred mice. *Genetics,* 54:95–103.—**387**

SCHMEIDLER, G. R., and MCCONNELL, R. A. (1958) *ESP and personality patterns.* New Haven, Conn.: Yale Univ. Press.—**158**

SCHNEIDER, D. J., *see* Hastorf, Schneider, and Polefka (1970).

SCHNEIER, I., *see* Schein, Schneier, and Barker (1961).

SCHNORE, M. M. (1959) Individual patterns of physiological activity as a function of task differences and degree of arousal. *Journal of Experimental Psychology,* 58:117–28.—**338, 339**

SCHRAMM, W., LYLE, J., and PARKER, E. (1961) *Television in the lives of our children.* Stanford, Calif.: Stanford Univ. Press.—**531**

SCHROEDER, W. H., *see* Hendrickson and Schroeder (1941).

SCHWITZGEBEL, R. L. (1970) Behavior instrumentation and social technology. *American Psychologist,* 25:117–28.—**540**

SCOTT, J. P. (1968) *Early experience and the organization of behavior.* Belmont, Calif.: Brooks-Cole.—**58**

SCOTT, J. P., and FULLER, J. L. (1965) *Genetics and the social behavior of the dog.* Chicago: Univ. of Chicago Press.—**388**

SCOTT, T. H., *see* Doane, Mahatoo, Heron, and Scott (1959).

SEARS, D. O., *see* Apsler and Sears (1968); Freedman, Carlsmith, and Sears (1970); Freedman and Sears (1965).

SEARS, P. S. (1940) Levels of aspiration in academically successful and unsuccessful children. *Journal of Abnormal and Social Psychology,* 35:498–536.—**327**

SEARS, P. S., *see* Sears, Whiting, Nowlis, and Sears (1953).

SEARS, R. R. (1936) Experimental studies of projection: I. Attribution of traits. *Journal of Social Psychology,* 7:151–63.—**408, 456**

SEARS, R. R. (1943) *Survey of objective studies of psychoanalytic concepts.* N.Y.: Social Science Research Council (Bulletin, No. 51).

SEARS, R. R. (1961) Relation of early socialization experiences to aggression in middle childhood. *Journal of Abnormal and Social Psychology,* 63:466–92.—**320**

SEARS, R. R., MACCOBY, E. E., and LEVIN, H. (1957) *Patterns of child rearing.* Evanston, Ill.: Row, Peterson.—**72, 73**

SEARS, R. R., WHITING, J. W. M., NOWLIS, V., and SEARS, P. S. (1953) Some child rearing antecedents of aggression and dependency in young children. *Genetic Psychology Monographs,* 47:135–234.—**319, 320, 322, 323**

SECORD, P. F., BEVAN, W., and KATZ, B. (1956) Perceptual accentuation and the Negro stereotype. *Journal of Abnormal and Social Psychology,* 53:78–83.—**518**

SEEMAN, J. (1949) A study of the process of nondirective therapy. *Journal of Consulting Psychology,* 13:157–68.—**495**

SEGAL, J., *see* Luce and Segal (1966).

SEIDENBERG, B., *see* Proshansky and Seidenberg (1965).

SELYE, H. (1956) *The stress of life.* N.Y.: McGraw-Hill.—**49**

SEMEONOFF, B. (ed.) (1966) *Personality assessment.* Baltimore, Md.: Penguin Books. —**438**

SENDEN, M. V. (1960) *Space and sight* (Trans. by P. Heath). N.Y.: Free Press.—**150**

SENSIBAR, M. R., *see* Clark and Sensibar (1956).

SENTER, R. J., *see* Lippert and Senter (1966).

SHAFFER, J. W. (1962) A specific cognitive defect observed in gonadal aplasia. *Journal of Clinical Psychology,* 18:403–06.—**385**

SHAFFER, L. F. (1947) Fear and courage in aerial combat. *Journal of Consulting Psychology,* 11:137–43.—**336**

SHAPIRO, A., *see* Goodenough, Shapiro, Holden, and Steinschriber (1959); Lewis, Goodenough, Shapiro, and Sleser (1966); Rechtschaffen, Goodenough, and Shapiro (1962).

SHAVER, K. G., *see* Jones, Rock, Shaver, Goethals, and Ward (1968).

SHEEHAN, M. R., *see* Woodworth and Sheehan (1964).

SHEER, D. (ed.) (1961) *Electrical stimulation of the brain.* Austin, Tex.: Hogg Foundation and Univ. of Texas Press.—**51**

SHEERER, M., *see* Reiff and Scheerer (1959).

SHEFFIELD, F. D. (1965) Relation between classical conditioning and instrumental learning. In Prokasy, W. F. (ed.) *Classical conditioning: A symposium.* N.Y.: Appleton-Century-Crofts, 302–22.—**207**

SHEFFIELD, F. D., *see* Campbell and Sheffield (1953).

SHELDON, E. B., and MOORE, W. E. (1968) *Indicators of social change.* N.Y.: Russell Sage Foundation.—**559**

SHELDON, W. H. (1954) *Atlas of men: A guide for somatotyping the adult male at all ages.* N.Y.: Harper and Row.—**399**

SHELDON, W. H., STEVENS, S. S., and TUCKER, W. B. (1940) *The varieties of human physique.* N.Y.: Harper and Row.—**399**

SHEPARD, R. N. (1967) Recognition memory for words, sentences, and pictures. *Journal of Verbal Learning and Verbal Behavior,* 6:156–63.—**227**

SHERIF, C. W., *see* Sherif and Sherif (1969).

SHERIF, M., and SHERIF, C. W. (1969) *Social psychology.* N.Y.: Harper and Row.—**537**

SHERMAN, L. J., *see* Moseley, Duffey, and Sherman (1963).

SHIELDS, J. (1962) *Monozygotic twins, brought up apart and brought up together.* London: Oxford Univ. Press.—**391**

SHIELDS, J., *see* Gottesman and Shields (1966).

SHIFFRIN, R. M., *see* Atkinson and Shiffrin (1968).

SHIGEHISA, T., *see* McConnell, Shigehisa, and Salive (1970).

SHOEMAKER, D. J., *see* Becker, Peterson, Hellmer, Shoemaker, and Quay (1962).

SHOR, R. E., *see* Cobb, Evans, Gustafson, O'Connell, Orne, and Shor (1965).

SHOR, R. E., and ORNE, M. T. (eds.) (1965) *The nature of hypnosis.* N.Y.: Holt, Rinehart and Winston.—**185**

SHOR, R. E., ORNE, M. T., and O'CONNELL, D. N. (1966) Psychological correlates of plateau hypnotizability in a special volunteer sample. *Journal of Personality and Social Psychology,* 3:80–95.—**175**

SHORT, J. F., *see* Henry and Short (1954).

SIDOWSKI, J. B. (ed.) (1966) *Experimental methods and instrumentation in psychology.* N.Y.: McGraw-Hill.—**23, 134**

SIGEL, I. E. (1964) The attainment of concepts. In Hoffman, M. L., and Hoffman, L. W. (eds.) *Review of child development research.* N.Y.: Russell Sage Foundation, 1:209–48.—**63**

SIMON, A. W., *see* Emmons and Simon (1956).

SIMON, H. A. (1969) *The sciences of the artificial.* Cambridge, Mass.: M.I.T. Press.— **291, 292, 544**

SIMON, H. A., *see* Gregg and Simon (1967); Newell and Simon (1956).

SIMON, H. A., and BARENFELD, M. (1969) Information-processing analysis of perceptual processes in problem solving. *Psychological Review,* 76:473–83.—**290**

SIMON, H. A., and NEWELL, A. (1964) Information processing in computer and man. *American Scientist,* 52:281–300.—**290**

SIMPSON, G. G., and BECK, W. S. (1965) *Life: An introduction to biology.* N.Y.: Harcourt Brace Jovanovich.—**29, 32**

SIMPSON, G. G., and BECK, W. S. (1969) *Life:*

An introduction to biology, Shorter ed. N.Y.: Harcourt Brace Jovanovich.—33

SINCLAIR, J., see Olds and Sinclair (1957).

SINGER, E., see Kaplan and Singer (1963).

SINGER, J. E., see Schachter and Singer (1962).

SINGER, J. L. (1966) Daydreaming: An introduction to the experimental study of inner experience. N.Y.: Random House.—185

SINGER, R. D., see Feshbach and Singer (1957).

SINGER, R. P., see Leventhal and Singer (1966).

SJOBERG, B. M., JR., and HOLLISTER, L. E. (1965) The effects of psychotomimetic drugs on primary suggestibility. Psychopharmacologia, 8:251–62.—183

SKEELS, H. M. (1966) Adult status of children with contrasting early life experiences: A follow-up study. Monographs of the Society for Research in Child Development, 31, Serial No. 105.—61, 390

SKEELS, H. M., see Skodak and Skeels (1949).

SKEELS, H. M., and DYE, H. B. (1939) A study of the effects of differential stimulation on mentally retarded children. Proceedings of the American Association for Mental Deficiency, 44:114–36.—61, 390

SKINNER, B. F. (1938) The behavior of organisms. N.Y.: Appleton-Century-Crofts.—198, 224

SKINNER, B. F. (1948) Walden Two. N.Y.: Macmillan.—557

SKINNER, B. F. (1954) The science of learning and the art of teaching. Harvard Educational Review, 24:86–97.—248

SKINNER, B. F. (1968) The technology of teaching. N.Y.: Appleton-Century-Crofts.—251, 270

SKINNER, B. F. (1969) Contingencies of reinforcement. N.Y.: Appleton-Century-Crofts.—5

SKINNER, B. F., see Heron and Skinner (1937); Rogers and Skinner (1956).

SKODAK, M., and SKEELS, H. M. (1949) A final follow-up of one hundred adopted children. Journal of Genetic Psychology, 75:3–19.—390

SLATER, J., see Berlyne and Slater (1957).

SLESER, I., see Lewis, Goodenough, Shapiro, and Sleser (1966).

SMEDSLUND, J. (1961) The acquisition of conservation of substance and weight in children. Scandinavian Journal of Psychology, 2:11–20, 71–84, 85–87, 153–55, 156–60, 203–10.—64

SMITH, D., KING, M., and HOEBEL, B. (1970) Lateral hypothalamic control of killing: Evidence for a cholinoceptive mechanism. Science, 167:900–01.—449

SMITH, E. E., see Fried and Smith (1962).

SMITH, F., and MILLER, G. A. (eds.) (1966) The genesis of language: A psycholinguistic approach. Cambridge, Mass.: M.I.T. Press.—292

SMITH, L. B. (1954) English treason trials and confessions in the sixteenth century. Journal of History of Ideas, 15:471–98.—534

SMITH, M. B. (1968) Morality and student protest. Psi Chi Invited Address, American Psychological Association, San Francisco, Calif.—92

SMITH, M. B., see Block, Haan, and Smith (1968).

SMITH, M. B., BRUNER, J. S., and WHITE, R. W. (1956) Opinions and personality. N.Y.: Wiley.—523

SNIDER, J. G., and OSGOOD, C. E. (eds.) (1969) Semantic differential technique. Chicago: Aldine.—272

SNOW, L. H., see Madow and Snow (1970).

SNYDER, F. W., and PRONKO, N. H. (1952) Vision with spatial inversion. Wichita, Kans.: McCormick-Armstrong.—139

SNYDER, L. H. (1932) Studies in human inheritance: IX. The inheritance of taste deficiency in man. Ohio Journal of Science, 32:436–40.—386

SNYDER, W. U., and others (1947) Casebook of nondirective counseling. Boston: Houghton Mifflin.—494

SOAL, S. G., and BATEMAN, F. (1954) Modern experiments in telepathy. New Haven, Conn.: Yale Univ. Press.—157, 159

SOKOLOV, E. N. (1963) Higher nervous functions: The orienting reflex. Annual Review of Physiology, 25:545–80.—155

SOLLEY, C. M., and STAGNER, R. (1956) Effects of magnitude of temporal barriers, type of goal, and perception of self. Journal of Experimental Psychology, 51:62–70.—416

SOLOMON, R. L., see Lambert, Solomon, and Watson (1949).

SOMMER, R. (1969) Personal space: The behavioral basis of design. Englewood Cliffs, N.J.: Prentice-Hall.—544, 559

SONTAG, L. W., BAKER, C. T., and NELSON, V. L. (1958) Mental growth and development: A longitudinal study. Monographs of the Society for Research in Child Development, 23, Serial No. 68.—372, 373

SPECHT, P. G., see Cameron, Specht, and Wendt (1967).

SPENCE, J. T., and SPENCE, K. W. (1966) The motivational components of manifest anxiety: Drive and drive stimuli. In Spielberger, C. D. (ed.) Anxiety and behavior. N.Y.: Academic Press, 291–326.—267

SPENCE, K. W. (1956) Behavior theory and conditioning. New Haven, Conn.: Yale Univ. Press.—262, 308

SPENCE, K. W., see Spence and Spence (1966).

SPERRY, R. W. (1961) Cerebral organization and behavior. Science, 133:1749–57.—260, 261

SPERRY, R. W. (1968) Hemisphere deconnection and unity in conscious awareness. American Psychologist, 23:723–33.—261

SPIELBERGER, C. D. (ed.) (1966) Anxiety and behavior. N.Y.: Academic Press.—267, 268, 270

SPIELBERGER, C. D., see Johnson and Spielberger (1968).

SPIES, G. (1965) Food versus intracranial self-stimulation reinforcement in food-deprived rats. Journal of Comparative Physiological Psychology, 60:153–57.—208

SPOTTS, J. V., and MACKLER, B. (1967) Relationships of field-dependent and field-independent cognitive styles to creative test performance. Perceptual and Motor Skills, 24:239–69.—425

SPUHLER, J. N. (ed.) (1967) Genetic diversity and human behavior. Chicago: Aldine.—396

SROLE, L., LANGNER, T. S., MICHAEL, S. T., OPLER, M. K., and RENNIE, T. A. C. (1962) Mental health in the metropolis: The Midtown Manhattan study. N.Y.: McGraw-Hill.—483, 484

STABENAU, J. R., see Pollin and Stabenau (1968).

STAFFORD, R. E. (1961) Sex differences in spatial visualization as evidence of sex-linked inheritance. Perceptual and Motor Skills, 13:428.—394

STAGNER, R. (1967) Psychological aspects of international conflict. Belmont, Calif.: Brooks-Cole.—558

STAGNER, R., see Solley and Stagner (1956).

STALNAKER, J. M. (1965) Psychological tests and public responsibility. American Psychologist, 20:131–35.—379

STANDISH, R. R., and CHAMPION, R. A. (1960) Task difficulty and drive in verbal learning. Journal of Experimental Psychology, 59:361–65.—267

STEBBINS, W. C., see Miller, Moody, and Stebbins (1969).

STECHER, L. I., see Baldwin and Stecher (1922).

STEINER, I. D., and FISHBEIN, M. (eds.) (1965) Current studies in social psychology. N.Y.: Holt, Rinehart and Winston.—537

STEINSCHRIBER, L., see Goodenough, Shapiro, Holden, and Steinschriber (1959).

STEPHENS, J. H., ASTRUP, C., and MANGRUM, J. C. (1967) Prognosis in schizophrenia. Archives of General Psychiatry, 16:693–98.—475

STEVENS, C. F. (1966) Neurophysiology: A primer. N.Y.: Wiley.—51

STEVENS, S. S. (1966) Metric for the social consensus. Science, 151:530–41.—109

STEVENS, S. S., and WARSHOFSKY, F. (1965) Sound and hearing. N.Y.: Time, Inc.—134

STEVENSON, H. W. (1967) Studies of racial awareness in young children. In Hartup, W. W., and Smothergill, N. L. (eds.) The young child. Washington, D. C.: National Association for the Education of Young Children, 206–13.—78

STOEL, C., see Atkinson, MacWhinney, and Stoel (1970).

STOKES, D. E., see Campbell, Converse, Miller, and Stokes (1960).

STONE, L. J., and CHURCH, J. (1968) Childhood and adolescence (2nd ed.). N.Y.: Random House.—81

STONE, P. J., see Hunt, Marin, and Stone (1966).

STORMS, L. H., see Russell and Storms (1955).

STOYVA, J., and KAMIYA, J. (1968) Electrophysiological studies of dreaming as the prototype of a new strategy in the study of consciousness. Psychological Review, 75:192–205.—9

STRASSMAN, H. D., THALER, M. B., and SCHEIN, E. H. (1956) A prisoner of war syndrome: Apathy as a reaction to severe stress. *American Journal of Psychiatry*, 112:998–1003.—**451**

STRATTON, G. M. (1897) Vision without inversion of the retinal image. *Psychological Review*, 4:341–60, 463–81.—**139**

STRONG, E. K., JR. (1955) *Vocational interests 18 years after college*. Minneapolis: Univ. of Minnesota Press.—**412, 426**

STRONG, J. A., *see* Jacobs and Strong (1959).

STROTHER, C. R., *see* Schaie and Strother (1968).

SULLIVAN, H. S. (1949) The theory of anxiety and the nature of psychotherapy. *Psychiatry*, 12:3–13.—**347**

SUOMI, S., *see* Freedman, Carlsmith, and Suomi (1967).

SUOMI, S. J., *see* Harlow and Suomi (1970).

SUPPES, P. C., *see* Crothers and Suppes (1967); Estes and Suppes (1959).

SUPPES, P. C., and MORNINGSTAR, M. (1969) Computer-assisted instruction. *Science*, 166:343–50.—**249, 250**

SUTCLIFFE, J. P. (1961) "Credulous" and "skeptical" views of hypnotic phenomena: Experiments on esthesia, hallucination, and delusion. *Journal of Abnormal and Social Psychology*, 62:189–200.—**176**

SWARTZ, J. D., *see* Holtzman, Thorpe, Swartz, and Herron (1961).

SWETS, J. A. (1964) *Signal detection and recognition by human observers*. N.Y.: Wiley.—**134**

SWETS, J. A., *see* Green and Swets (1966).

SZASZ, T. (1961) *The myth of mental illness: Foundations of a theory of personal conduct*. N.Y.: Harper and Row.—**499**

TABER, J., GLASER, R., and SCHAEFER, H. (1965) *Learning and programmed instruction*. Reading, Mass.: Addison-Wesley.—**270**

TAKAISHI, M., *see* Tanner, Whitehouse, and Takaishi (1966).

TANNENBAUM, P. H. (1967) The congruity principle revisited: Studies in the reduction, induction, and generalization of persuasion. In Berkowitz, L. (ed.) *Advances in experimental social psychology*, vol. III. N.Y.: Academic Press, 272–320.—**529, 535**

TANNENBAUM, P. H., *see* Abelson, Aronson, McGuire, Newcomb, Rosenberg, and Tannenbaum (eds.) (1968); Osgood and Tannenbaum (1955).

TANNENBAUM, P. H., and GENGEL, R. W., (1966). Generalization of attitude change through congruity principle relationships. *Journal of Personality and Social Psychology*, 3:299–304.—**529**

TANNER, J. M. (1970) Physical growth. In Mussen, P. H. (ed.) *Carmichael's Manual of child psychology* (3rd ed.), vol. I. N.Y.: Wiley, 77–155.—**84**

TANNER, J. M., WHITEHOUSE, R. H., and TAKAISHI, M. (1966) Standards from birth to maturity for height, weight, height velocity and weight velocity: British children 1965. *Archives of Diseases of Childhood*, 41:613–35.—**84, 85**

TART, C. T. (ed.) (1969) *Altered states of consciousness*. N.Y.: Wiley.—**185**

TART, C. T., *see* Hilgard and Tart (1966).

TEEVAN, R. C., *see* Birney, Burdick, and Teevan (1960); Birney and Teevan (1962).

TEEVAN, R. C., and BIRNEY, R. C. (eds.) (1964) *Theories of motivation in personality and social psychology*. Princeton, N.J.: Van Nostrand.—**311, 333**

TELFORD, C. W., *see* Sawrey and Telford (1971).

TERMAN, L. M., and MERRILL, M. A. (1937) *Measuring intelligence*. Boston: Houghton Mifflin.—**364**

TERMAN, L. M., and MERRILL, M. A. (1960) *Stanford-Binet intelligence scale: Manual for the third revision, form L-M*. Boston: Houghton Mifflin.—**364**

TERMAN, L. M., and ODEN, M. H. (1947) *The gifted child grows up*. Stanford, Calif.: Stanford Univ. Press.—**377, 378**

THALER, M. B., *see* Strassman, Thaler, and Schein (1956).

THARP, R. G., *see* Martin, Burkholder, Rosenthal, Tharp, and Thorne (1968).

THIESSEN, D. D., *see* Manosevitz, Lindzey, and Thiessen (1969).

THIESSEN, D. D., and MCGAUGH, J. L. (1958) Conflict and curiosity in the rat. Paper, Western Psychological Association, Monterey, Calif.—**307**

THIGPEN, C. H., and CLECKLEY, H. M. (1954) A case of multiple personality. *Journal of Abnormal and Social Psychology*, 49:135–51.—**415**

THIGPEN, C. H., and CLECKLEY, H. M. (1957) *The three faces of Eve*. N.Y.: McGraw-Hill. —**415**

THOMPSON, C. W., *see* Hudspeth, McGaugh, and Thompson (1964).

THOMPSON, L., *see* Botwinick and Thompson (1968).

THOMPSON, R. F. (1967) *Foundations of physiological psychology*. N.Y.: Harper and Row.—**31, 51, 128**

THOMPSON, W. R. (1954) The inheritance and development of intelligence. *Proceedings of the Association for Research on Nervous and Mental Disease*, 33:209–31.—**387**

THOMPSON, W. R., *see* Fuller and Thompson (1960).

THORNE, G. L., *see* Martin, Burkholder, Rosenthal, Tharp, and Thorne (1968).

THORPE, J. S., *see* Holtzman, Thorpe, Swartz, and Herron (1961).

THORPE, W. H. (1963) *Learning and instinct in animals* (2nd ed.). London: Methuen. —**302**

THURSTONE, L. L. (1938) Primary mental abilities. *Psychometric Monographs*, No. 1. Chicago: Univ. of Chicago Press.—**368**

THURSTONE, L. L. (1947) *Multiple-factor analysis*. Chicago: Univ. of Chicago Press. —**366**

THURSTONE, L. L. (1955) *The differential growth of mental abilities*. Chapel Hill, N.C.: Psychometric Laboratory, Univ. of North Carolina.—**373**

THURSTONE, L. L., and THURSTONE, T. G. (1941) Factorial studies of intelligence. *Psychometric Monographs*, No. 2. Chicago: Univ. of Chicago Press.—**361, 369**

THURSTONE, T. G., *see* Thurstone and Thurstone (1941).

TIBBITTS, C., *see* Williams, Tibbits, and Donahue (1963).

TILLICH, P. (1952) *The courage to be*. New Haven, Conn.: Yale Univ. Press.—**331, 347**

TIMMONS, E., *see* Noblin, Timmons, and Kael (1966).

TINBERGEN, N. (1961) *The herring gull's world* (rev. ed.). N.Y.: Basic Books.—**302**

TJIO, J. H., and LEVAN, A. (1956) The chromosome number of man. *Hereditas*, 42:1. —**384**

TOGIO, R., *see* Eron, Walder, Togio, and Lefkowitz (1963).

TOLMAN, E. C. (1932) *Purposive behavior in animals and men*. N.Y.: Appleton-Century-Crofts.—**224**

TOLMAN, E. C. (1948) Cognitive maps in rats and men. *Psychological Review*, 55:189–208.—**218**

TOLMAN, E. C., and HONZIK, C. H. (1930) Introduction and removal of reward, and maze performance in rats. *University of California Publications in Psychology*, 4:257–75.—**219, 220**

TORRANCE, E. P. (1966) *Torrance Tests of Creative Thinking*, Verbal Forms A and B. Princeton, N.J.: Personnel Press.—**371**

TRABASSO, T., and BOWER, G. H. (1968) *Attention in learning: Theory and research*. N.Y.: Wiley.—**292**

TRYON, R. C. (1940) Genetic differences in maze-learning ability in rats. *39th Yearbook, Part I, National Society for the Study of Education*. Chicago: Univ. of Chicago Press, 111–19.—**387**

TRYON, R. C. (1963) Experimental behavior genetics of maze learning and a sufficient polygenic theory. *American Psychologist*, 18:442.—**387**

TSANG, Y. C. (1938) Hunger motivation in gastrectomized rats. *Journal of Comparative Psychology*, 26:1–17.—**298**

TULVING, E., and MADIGAN, S. A. (1970) Memory and verbal learning. *Annual Review of Psychology*, 21:437–84.—**237**

TURIEL, E. (1966) An experimental test of the sequentiality of developmental stages in the child's moral judgments. *Journal of Personality and Social Psychology*, 3:611–18.—**79**

TURNBULL, C. M. (1961) Some observations regarding the experiences and behavior of the Ba Mbuti Pygmies. *American Journal of Psychology*, 74:304–08.—**139**

TURNER, J., *see* Holzberg, Knapp, and Turner (1967).

TURPIN, R., *see* Lejeune, Gautier, and Turpin (1959).

TURRELL, E. S., *see* Sawrey, Conger, and Turrell (1956).

TVERSKY, A., *see* Coombs, Dawes, and Tversky (1970).

TYLER, R. W., *see* Eells, Davis, Havighurst, Herrick, and Tyler (1951).

ULLMANN, L. P., *see* Krasner and Ullmann (1965).

ULLMANN, L. P., and KRASNER, L. (1969) *A*

psychological approach to abnormal behavior. Englewood Cliffs, N.J.: Prentice-Hall.—**486, 495, 496**

UNDERWOOD, B. J. (1957) Interference and forgetting. *Psychological Review,* 64:49–60.—**234, 235**

UNDERWOOD, B. J. (1961) Ten years of massed practice on distributed practice. *Psychological Review,* 68:229–47.—**262**

UNDERWOOD, B. J. (1966) *Experimental psychology* (2nd ed.). N.Y.: Appleton-Century-Crofts.—**23**

UNGERLEIDER, J. T. (1969) Treatment of hallucinogenic drug reactions. *Annals of Internal Medicine,* 70:598–600.—**183**

URBAN, H. B., *see* Ford and Urban (1963).

U.S. DEPT. OF HEALTH, EDUCATION, AND WELFARE (1969) *Toward a social report.* Washington, D.C.: U.S. Government Printing Office.—**517, 545, 559**

UTTAL, W. R. (1968) *Real-time computers: Technique and applications in the psychological sciences.* N.Y.: Harper and Row.—**292**

VALINS, S. (1967) Emotionality and information concerning internal reactions. *Journal of Personality and Social Psychology,* 6:458–63.—**340**

VANDENBERG, S. G. (ed.) (1965) *Methods and goals in human behavior genetics.* N.Y.: Academic Press.—**396**

VANDENBERG, S. G. (1967) Heredity factors in psychological variables in man, with special emphasis on cognition. In Spuhler, J. N. (ed.) *Genetic diversity and human behavior.* Chicago: Aldine, 99–133.—**394**

VAUGHAN, H. G., JR., COSTA, L. D., GILDEN, L., and SCHIMMEL, H. (1965) Identification of sensory and motor components of cerebral activity in simple reaction-time tasks. *Proceedings of the 73rd Annual Convention of the American Psychological Association,* 179–80.—**39**

VEITH, I. (1965) *Hysteria: The history of a disease.* Chicago: Univ. of Chicago Press.—**510**

VERNON, P. E. (1950a) *The structure of human abilities.* N.Y.: Wiley.—**367**

VERNON, P. E. (1950b) The validation of civil service selection board procedures. *Occupational Psychology,* 24:75–95.—**435**

VERNON, P. E. (1964) *Personality assessment: A critical survey.* London: Methuen.—**405, 438**

VERNON, P. E. (1969) *Intelligence and cultural environment.* London: Methuen.—**363, 382**

VERNON, P. E., *see* Allport and Vernon (1933); Allport, Vernon, and Lindzey (1960).

VERPLANCK, W. S. (1955) The control of the content of conversation: Reinforcement of statements of opinion. *Journal of Abnormal and Social Psychology,* 51:668–76.—**204**

VILLARS, T., *see* Golub, Masiarz, Villars, and McConnell (1970).

VINCE, P., *see* Himmelweit, Oppenheim, and Vince (1958).

VOEKS, V. (1970) *On becoming an educated person* (3rd ed.). Philadelphia: Saunders.—**270**

VOEVODSKY, J. (1969) Quantitative behavior of warring nations. *Journal of Psychology,* 72:269–92.—**550**

VOGEL, W., RAYMOND, S., and LAZARUS, R. S. (1959) Intrinsic motivation and psychological stress. *Journal of Abnormal and Social Psychology,* 58:225–33.—**424**

VOLKART, E. H., *see* Kelley and Volkart (1952).

VOLKOVA, V. D. (1953) On certain characteristics of conditioned reflexes to speech stimuli in children. *Fiziologicheskii Zhurnal S.S.S.R,* 39:540–48.—**195**

VON FRISCH, K. (1955) *The dancing bees.* N.Y.: Harcourt Brace Jovanovich.—**283, 303**

VOSS, J. F. (ed.) (1969) *Approaches to thought.* Columbus, Ohio: Merrill.—**292**

VOTH, A. C., *see* Brown and Voth (1937).

VREELAND, R. S., *see* Dornbusch, Hastorf, Richardson, Muzzy, and Vreeland (1965).

WAELDER, R. (1960) *Basic theory of psychoanalysis.* N.Y.: International Universities Press.—**510**

WAGNER, A. R. (1963) Conditioned frustration as a learned drive. *Journal of Experimental Psychology,* 66:142–48.—**348**

WALDER, L. O., *see* Eron, Walder, Togio, and Lefkowitz (1963).

WALK, R. D. (1968) Monocular compared to binocular depth perception in human infants. *Science,* 162:473–75.—**152**

WALK, R. D., *see* Gibson and Walk (1956), (1960).

WALKER, E. L. (1964) Psychological complexity as a basis for a theory of motivation and choice. *Nebraska Symposium on Motivation.* Lincoln, Nebr.: Univ. of Nebraska Press, 12:47–95.—**307**

WALKER, R. N. (1962) Body build and behavior in young children: I. Body build and nursery school teachers' ratings. *Monographs of the Society for Research in Child Development,* 27, Serial No. 84.—**399**

WALLACE, J. (1966) An abilities conception of personality: Some implications for personality measurement. *American Psychologist,* 21:132–38.—**404**

WALLACE, R. K. (1970) Physiological effects of transcendental meditation. *Science,* 167:1751–54.—**185**

WALLACH, M. A., and KOGAN, N. (1965a) *Modes of thinking in young children.* N.Y.: Holt, Rinehart and Winston.—**371**

WALLACH, M. A., and KOGAN, N. (1965b) The roles of information, discussion, and consensus in group risk-taking. *Journal of Experimental and Social Psychology,* 1:1–19.—**523**

WALLACH, M. A., KOGAN, N., and BURT, R. B. (1968) Are risk takers more persuasive than conservatives in group discussions? *Journal of Experimental and Social Psychology,* 4:76–88.—**523**

WALLIA, C. S. (ed.) (1970) *Toward century 21: Technology, society, and human values.* N.Y.: Basic Books.—**559**

WALLIN, P., *see* Burgess and Wallin (1953).

WALSTER, E. (1966) The assignment of responsibility for an accident. *Journal of Personality and Social Psychology,* 5:508–16.—**514**

WALTERS, R. H., *see* Bandura and Walters (1963).

WANG, G. H. (1923) The relation between "spontaneous" activity and oestrous cycle in the white rat. *Comparative Psychological Monographs,* 2, No. 6.—**301**

WAPNER, S., *see* Werner and Wapner (1952).

WARD, L. M., *see* Jones, Rock, Shaver, Goethals, and Ward (1968).

WARE, E. E., *see* Maclay and Ware (1961).

WARSHOFSKY, F., *see* Stevens and Warshofsky (1965).

WATSON, J. B. (1913) Psychology as the behaviorist views it. *Psychological Review,* 20:158–77.—**4**

WATSON, J. B., and RAYNER, R. (1920) Conditioned emotional reactions. *Journal of Experimental Psychology,* 3:1–14.—**344**

WATSON, P. D., *see* Lambert, Solomon, and Watson (1949).

WATSON, R. I. (1968) *The great psychologists: From Aristotle to Freud* (2nd ed.). Philadelphia: Lippincott.—**22**

WEATHERLY, D. (1964) Self-perceived rate of physical maturation and personality in late adolescence. *Child Development,* 35:1197–1210.—**86**

WEBB, E. (1961) Weber's law and consumer prices. *American Psychologist,* 63:450.—**109**

WEBB, W. B., *see* Williams, Agnew, and Webb (1964).

WEBSTER, H., FREEDMAN, M., and HEIST, P. (1962) Personality changes in college students. In Sanford, N. (ed.) *The American college.* N.Y.: Wiley.—**94**

WECHSLER, D. (1949) *Wechsler Intelligence Scale for Children.* N.Y.: Psychological Corp.—**365**

WECHSLER, D. (1955) *The Wechsler Adult Intelligence Scale Manual.* N.Y.: Psychological Corp.—**366**

WECHSLER, D. (1958) *The measurement and appraisal of adult intelligence.* (4th ed.). Baltimore: Williams and Wilkins.—**365**

WEIL, A. T., ZINBERG, N. E., and NELSEN, J. M. (1968) Clinical and psychological effects of marijuana in man. *Science,* 162:1234–42.—**182**

WEIR, R. H. (1962) *Language in the crib.* The Hague, Netherlands: Mouton.—**283**

WEITZENHOFFER, A. M., *see* Hilgard, Weitzenhoffer, Landes, and Moore (1961).

WEITZENHOFFER, A. M., and HILGARD, E. R. (1959) *Stanford Hypnotic Susceptibility Scales, Forms A and B.* Palo Alto, Calif.: Consulting Psychologists Press.—**174**

WELKER, W. I., JOHNSON, J. I., and PUBOLS, B. H. (1964) Some morphological and physiological characteristics of the somatic sensory system in raccoons. *American Zoologist,* 4:75–94.—**40**

WENDT, G. R., *see* Cameron, Specht, and Wendt (1967).

WENGER, M., and BAGCHI, B. (1961) Studies of autonomic function in practitioners of yoga in India. *Behavioral Science,* 6:312–23.—**180**

WENGER, M., BAGCHI, B., and ANAND, B. (1961) Experiments in India on "voluntary" control of the heart and pulse. *Circulation,* 24:1319–25.—**180**

WERNER, H., and WAPNER, S. (1952) Toward a general theory of perception. *Psychological Review,* 59:324–38.—**141**

WEST, L. J., *see* Farber, Harlow, and West (1957).

WESTIN, A. F. (1967) *Privacy and freedom.* N.Y.: Atheneum.—**552, 560**

WEVER, E. G. (1949) *Theory of hearing.* N.Y.: Wiley.—**128**

WHITE, B. L. (1969) Child development research: An edifice without a foundation. *Merrill-Palmer Quarterly of Behavior and Development,* 15:49–79.—**59, 60**

WHITE, R. W. (1959) Motivation reconsidered: The concept of competence. *Psychological Review,* 66:297–333.—**306, 330**

WHITE, R. W. (1964) *The abnormal personality* (3rd ed.). N.Y.: Ronald Press.—**486**

WHITE, R. W., *see* Smith, Bruner, and White (1956).

WHITEHEAD, A. N., and RUSSELL, B. (1925) *Principia mathematica* (2nd ed.). (original date, 1910–13). Cambridge, England: Cambridge Univ. Press.—**290**

WHITEHOUSE, R. H., *see* Tanner, Whitehouse, and Takaishi (1966).

WHITING, J. W. M., *see* Landauer and Whiting (1964); Sears, Whiting, Nowlis, and Sears (1953).

WHITING, J. W. M., and CHILD, I. L. (1953) *Child training and personality: A cross-cultural study.* New Haven, Conn.: Yale Univ. Press.—**321**

WHITMAN, M., *see* Deutsch, Fishman, Kogan, North, and Whitman (1964).

WHITTY, C. W. M., and ZANGWILL, O. L. (eds.) (1966) *Amnesia.* N.Y.: Appleton-Century-Crofts.—**246**

WHORF, B. L. (1956) *Language, thought, and reality* (Carroll, J. B. [ed.]). N.Y.: Wiley.—**286**

WICKENS, T. D., *see* Atkinson and Wickens (1971).

WIENER, H. J., *see* Kahn and Wiener (1967).

WIESEL, T. N., *see* Hubel and Wiesel (1965).

WIGGINS, J. S. (1968) Personality structure. *Annual Review of Psychology,* 19:293–330.—**432**

WILLIAMS, H. L. (1967) The problem of defining depth of sleep. In Kety, S. S., Evarts, E. V., and Williams, H. L. (eds.) *Sleep and altered states of consciousness.* Baltimore, Md.: Williams and Wilkins, 277–87.—**168**

WILLIAMS, H. L., LUBIN, A., and GOODNOW, J. J. (1959) Impaired performance with acute sleep loss. *Psychological Monographs,* 73, Whole No. 484.—**164**

WILLIAMS, H. L., MORLOCK, H. C., and MORLOCK, J. V. (1966) Instrumental behavior during sleep. *Psychophysiology,* 2:208–15.—**170**

WILLIAMS, R. H., TIBBITTS, C., and DONAHUE, W. (1963) *Processes of aging,* vol. I. N.Y.: Atherton Press.—**104**

WILLIAMS, R. L., AGNEW, H. W., JR., and WEBB, W. B. (1964) Sleep patterns in young adults: An EEG study. *EEG Clinical Neurophysiology,* 17:376–81.—**168**

WILLOUGHBY, R. H. (1967) Field-dependence and locus of control. *Perceptual and Motor Skills,* 24:671–72.—**425**

WILSON, H. A., *see* Atkinson and Wilson (1969).

WINER, B. J. (1962) *Statistical principles in experimental design.* N.Y.: McGraw-Hill.—**578**

WINTER, D. G., *see* McClelland and Winter (1969).

WINTERBOTTOM, M. R. (1958) The relation of need for achievement to learning experiences in independence and mastery. In Atkinson, J. W. (ed.) *Motives in fantasy, action, and society.* Princeton, N.J.: Van Nostrand, 453–78.—**327**

WISHNOW, B., *see* Gergen and Wishnow (1965).

WITKIN, H. A., GOODENOUGH, D. R., and KARP, S. A. (1967) Stability of cognitive style from childhood to young adulthood. *Journal of Personality and Social Psychology,* 7:291–300.—**425**

WITT, G. M., and HALL, C. S. (1949) The genetics of audiogenic seizures in the house mouse. *Journal of Comparative and Physiological Psychology,* 42:58–63.—**387**

WOLF, M. M., *see* Harris, Johnston, Kelley, and Wolf (1965).

WOLF, R. (1966) The measurement of environments. In Anastasi, A. (ed.) *Testing problems in perspective.* Washington, D.C.: American Council on Education, 491–503.—**410**

WOLFE, A. G., *see* Converse, Miller, Rusk, and Wolfe (1969).

WOLFE, D. M., *see* Blood and Wolfe (1968).

WOLFF, P. H. (1966) The causes, controls, and organization of behavior in the neonate. *Psychological Issues,* 5, Monograph 17.—**164**

WOLPE, J. (1958) *Psychotherapy by reciprocal inhibition.* Stanford, Calif.: Stanford Univ. Press.—**495**

WOLPE, J., and LAZARUS, A. A. (1966) *Behavior therapy techniques: A guide to the treatment of neuroses.* N.Y.: Pergamon Press.—**495, 510**

WOODWORTH, R. S. (1958) *Dynamics of behavior.* N.Y.: Holt.—**306**

WOODWORTH, R. S., and SHEEHAN, M. R. (1964) *Contemporary schools of psychology* (3rd ed.). N.Y.: Ronald Press.—**23**

WOOLDRIDGE, D. E. (1963) *The machinery of the brain.* N.Y.: McGraw-Hill.—**246**

WOOLDRIDGE, D. E. (1968) *Mechanical man: The physical basis of intelligent life.* N.Y.: McGraw-Hill.—**34**

WORKS, E. (1961) The prejudice-interaction hypothesis from the point of view of the Negro minority group. *American Journal of Sociology,* 67:47–52.—**515**

WRIGHT, R. H. (1964) Odor and molecular vibration: The far infrared spectra of some perfume chemicals. *Annals of the New York Academy of Science,* 116:552–58.—**129**

WYLIE, R. C. (1961) *The self concept.* Lincoln, Nebr.: Univ. of Nebraska Press.—**420**

YALOM, I. D. (1970) *The theory and practice of group psychotherapy.* N.Y.: Basic Books.—**510**

YAMAMOTO, K., and CHIMBIDIS, M. E. (1966) Achievement: Intelligence and creative thinking in fifth grade children: A correlational study. *Merrill-Palmer Quarterly,* 12:233–241.—**371**

YATES, A. J. (1965) *Frustration and conflict.* Princeton, N.J.: Van Nostrand.—**463**

YERKES, R. M., and DODSON, J. D. (1908) The relation of strength of stimulus to rapidity of habit-formation. *Journal of Comparative Neurology and Psychology,* 18:459–82.—**350**

YERKES, R. M., and MORGULIS, S. (1909) The method of Pavlov in animal psychology. *Psychological Bulletin,* 6:257–73.—**190**

YOUNG, P. T. (1937) Laughing and weeping, cheerfulness, and depression: A study of moods among college students. *Journal of Social Psychology,* 8:311–34.—**349**

YOUNG, P. T. (1961) *Motivation and emotion.* N.Y.: Wiley.—**351**

YOUNISS, J., *see* Robertson and Youniss (1969).

ZAJONC, R. B. (1968) Attitudinal effects of mere exposure. *Journal of Personality and Social Psychology,* 8 (Monograph Supplements 1–29).—**515**

ZANDER, A., *see* Cartwright and Zander (1968).

ZANGWILL, O. L., *see* Humphrey and Zangwill (1952); Witty and Zangwill (1966).

ZAX, M., *see* Cowen, Gardner, and Zax (1967).

ZEIGLER, H. P., and LEIBOWITZ, H. (1957) Apparent visual size as a function of distance for children and adults. *American Journal of Psychology,* 70:106–09.—**138**

ZILBOORG, G., and HENRY, G. W. (1941) *A history of medical psychology.* N.Y.: Norton.—**510**

ZIMBARDO, P. G. (1968) *The cognitive control of motivation.* Chicago: Scott, Foresman.—**333**

ZIMBARDO, P. G. (1970) The human choice: Individuation, reason, and order versus deindividuation, impulse, and chaos. *Nebraska Symposium on Motivation 1969,* 18:237–307.—**518, 519, 543**

ZIMBARDO, P. G., and EBBESEN, E. B. (1969) *Influencing attitudes and changing behavior.* Reading, Mass.: Addison-Wesley.—**537**

ZIMBARDO, P. G., MASLACH, C., and MARSHALL, G. D. (1970) *Hypnosis as a method for studying unexplained arousal.* Paper delivered at American Psychological Association Convention, Miami, Florida, September 1970.—**340**

ZIMMER, H., *see* Biderman and Zimmer (1961).

ZINBERG, N. E., *see* Weil, Zinberg, and Nelsen (1968).

ZOLA, I. K., *see* McCord, McCord, and Zola (1959).

ZUCH, J., *see* Fisher, Gross, and Zuck (1965).

Acknowledgments and Copyrights
continued from page iv

7-1 Weitzenhoffer, A. M., and Hilgard, E. R. *Stanford Hypnotic Susceptibility Scales, Forms A and B.* Stanford, Calif.: Stanford University Press, 1959.

9-1 Glucksberg, S., and King, J. Motivated forgetting mediated by implicit verbal chaining: A laboratory analog of repressions. *Science, 158,* 517–19, October 27, 1967. Copyright © 1967 by the American Association for the Advancement of Science. Used by permission of the publisher and the authors.

10-1 Russell, W. A., and Storms, L. H. Implicit verbal chaining in paired-associate learning. *Journal of Experimental Psychology, 49* (1955), 287–93. Copyright 1955 by the American Psychological Association, and reproduced by permission.

11-1 McNeill. The development of language. In P. Mussen (ed.), *Carmichael's handbook of child development.* New York: Wiley, 1970. **11-2** Gardner, B., and Gardner, R. Two-way communication with an infant chimpanzee. In A. Schrier and F. Stollnitz (eds.), *Behavior of nonhuman primates,* vol. III. New York: Academic Press, 1969. Copyright © 1969 by Academic Press.

13-1 From *Explorations in personality* by Henry A. Murray. Copyright 1938 by Oxford University Press, Inc.; renewed 1966 by Henry A. Murray. Reprinted by permission. **13-3** Adapted from Sears and others, Some child-rearing antecedents of aggression and dependency in young children. *Genetic Psychology Monographs,* 1953, *47,* 135–234. By permission of The Journal Press and the authors. **13-4** Drawn from Schachter, S., *Psychology of affiliation.* Stanford, Calif.: Stanford University Press, 1959.

15-2 Berdie, R. F. The uses of evaluation in guidance. In R. W. Tyler (ed.), *Educational evaluation: New roles, new means.* 68th Yearbook of the National Society for the Study of Education, Part II. Chicago: The University of Chicago Press, 1969. **15-3** Merrill, M. A. The significance of IQ's on the revised Stanford-Binet scales. *Journal of Educational Psychology, 29* (1938), 641–51. Copyright 1938 by the American Psychological Association, and reproduced by permission. **15-5, 15-6** From *The nature of human intelligence* by J. P. Guilford. Copyright © 1967 by McGraw-Hill, Inc. Used with permission of McGraw-Hill Book Company. **15-7** Flanagan, J. C. The definition and measurement of ingenuity. In C. W. Taylor and F. Barron (eds.), *Scientific creativity: Its recognition and development.* New York: Wiley, 1963. Guilford, J. P. A factor analytic study across the domains of reasoning, creativity, and evaluation I: Hypotheses and description of tests. *Reports from the Psychology Laboratory.* Los Angeles, Calif.: University of Southern California, 1954. Used by permission of the author. Getzels, J. W., and Jackson, P. W. *Creativity and intelligence:*

Explorations with gifted students. New York: Wiley, 1962. Torrance, E. Paul. *Torrance Tests of Creative Thinking,* Verbal Forms A and B, Personnel Press, Inc. Princeton, N. J., 1966. Wallach, M. A., and Kogan, N. *Modes of thinking in young children: A study of the creativity-intelligence distinction.* Copyright © 1965 by Holt, Rinehart and Winston, Inc. Reprinted by permission of Holt, Rinehart and Winston, Inc. Mednick, S. A., The associative bases of creative process. *Psychology Review, 69* (1962), 220–32. Copyright © 1962 by the American Psychological Association, and reproduced by permission. **15-8** Sontag, L. W., Baker, C. T., and Nelson, V. L. Mental growth and development: A longitudinal study. *Monographs of the Society for Research in Child Development,* 1958, *23* (Ser. no. 68), p. 28 (Adaptation of Table 8). Copyright © 1958 by The Society for Research in Child Development, Inc. Used by permission of the publisher and the authors. **15-9** From *Mental subnormality* by Richard L. Masland, Seymour B. Sarason, and Thomas Gladwin, Basic Books, Inc., Publishers, New York, 1958. **15-10** Drawn from Terman, L. M., and Oden, M. H., *The gifted child grows up.* Stanford, Calif.: Stanford University Press, 1947.

16-1 Snyder, L. H. Studies in human inheritance: IX. The inheritance of taste deficiency in man. *Ohio Journal of Science, 32* (1932), 436–40. **16-2** Adapted from Skodak, M., and Skeels, H. M., A final follow-up study of one hundred adopted children. *The Journal of Genetic Psychology,* 1949, *75,* 85–125. By permission of The Journal Press and Marie Skodak. **16-5** Newman, H. H., Freeman, F. N., and Holzinger, K. H. *Twins: A study of heredity and environment.* Chicago: The University of Chicago Press, 1937. Copyright 1937 by The University of Chicago. All rights reserved. **16-6** Gottesman, I. I., and Shields, J. Contributions of twin studies to perspectives on schizophrenia. In B. A. Maher (ed.), *Progress in experimental personality research.* New York: Academic Press, 1966. Copyright © 1966 by Academic Press.

17-1 From *Personality* by R. B. Cattell. Copyright 1950 by McGraw-Hill, Inc. Used with permission of McGraw-Hill Book Company. **17-2** Cattell, R. B. *The scientific analysis of personality.* Baltimore, Md.: Penguin Books, 1965 ($1.65).

19-1 Kroeber, T. C. The coping functions of the ego mechanisms. In R. W. White (ed.), *The study of lives.* Reprinted by permission of the publisher, Atherton Press, Inc. Copyright © 1968, Atherton Press, Inc., New York. All rights reserved.

20-1 Pitt, R., and Hage, J. Patterns of peer interaction during adolescence as prognostic indicators in schizophrenia. *The American Journal of Psychiatry,* 1964, Volume 120, pp. 1089–96. Copyright © 1964, the American Psychiatric Association. Used by permission of the publisher

and the authors. **20-2** Heston, L. L. The genetics of schizophrenic and schizoid disease. *Science, 167,* 249–56, January 16, 1970. Copyright © 1970 by the American Association for the Advancement of Science. Used by permission of the publisher and the author.

21-1 Colby, K. M., and Enea, H. Heuristic methods for computer understanding of natural language in context—restricted on-line dialogues. Originally appeared in *Mathematical Biosciences,* vol. 1, no. 1, published in 1967 by American Elsevier Publishing Company, Inc.

22-1 Lipset, S. M., and Bendix, R. *Social mobility in industrial society.* Berkeley, Calif.: University of California Press, 1959. Reprinted by permission of The Regents of the University of California. **22-3** Freedman, J. L., and Doob, A. N. *Deviancy: The psychology of being different.* New York: Academic Press, 1968. Copyright © 1968 by Academic Press. **22-5** Deutsch, M., and Gerard, H. G. A study of normative and informational social influence upon individual judgment. *Journal of Abnormal Social Psychology, 51* (1955), 629–36. Copyright 1955 by the American Psychological Association, and reproduced by permission.

23-1 Modified from Hilgard, E. R., and Bower, G. H. *Theories of learning,* 3rd ed. New York: Appleton-Century-Crofts, 1966, pp. 574–75. **23-2** Biderman, A. D., in R. A. Bauer (ed.), *Social indicators.* Cambridge, Mass.: The M.I.T. Press, 1966. Copyright by The American Academy of Arts and Sciences.

Figures

1-4 Hilgard, E. R., Pain as a puzzle for psychology and physiology. *American Psychologist, 24:*108. Copyright 1969 by the American Psychological Association, and used by permission. **1-6** Gibson, E. J., and Walk, R. D. The effect of prolonged exposure to visually presented patterns on learning to discriminate them. *Journal of Comparative and Physiological Psychology, 49:*239–42. Copyright 1956 by the American Psychological Association, and used by permission. **1-7** Hilgard, E. R. Hypnosis and experimental psychodynamics. In Brosen, H. (ed.), *Lectures on experimental psychiatry.* Pittsburgh, Pa.: University of Pittsburgh Press, 1961.

2-1 Simpson, G. G., and Beck, W. S. *Life: An introduction to biology,* Shorter Edition. Copyright 1957, 1965, 1969 by Harcourt Brace Jovanovich, Inc. and reproduced with their permission. **2-2** Simpson, G. G., and Beck, W. S. *Life: An introduction to biology,* 2nd ed. Copyright 1957, 1965 by Harcourt Brace Jovanovich, Inc. and reproduced with their permission. **2-6, 2-7** Simpson, G. G., and Beck, W. S. *Life: An introduction to biology,* Shorter Edition. Copyright 1957, 1965, 1969 by Harcourt Brace Jovanovich, Inc. and reproduced with their permission. **2-10** Adapted from The human thermostat by T. H. Benzinger. *204:*134–47.

Copyright © 1961 by Scientific American, Inc. All rights reserved. **2-12** Adapted from The physiology of imagination by J. C. Eccles. *199,* 135–46. Copyright © 1958 by Scientific American, Inc. All rights reserved. **2-13** Vaughn, A. G., Jr., Costa, L. D., Gilden, L., and Schimmel, H. Identification of sensory and motor components of cerebral activity in simple reaction-time tasks. Proceedings of the 73rd Annual Convention of the American Psychological Association, pp. 179–80. Copyright 1965 by the American Psychological Association, and used by permission. **2-15** Adapted from Penfield, W., and Rasmussen, T., *The cerebral cortex of man,* with permission of the Macmillan Company. Copyright 1950 by the Macmillan Company.

3-2 Frankenburg, W. K., and Dodds, J. B. The Denver development screening test. *Journal of Pediatrics* (1967), *71:*181–91. **3-6** Schaffer, H. R., and Emerson, P. E. The development of social attachments in infancy. *Monographs of the Society for Research in Child Development,* 1964, Vol. 29, No. 94. Copyright 1964 by The Society for Research in Child Development, Inc. **3-8** DeLucia, L. A. The toy preference test: A measure of sex-role identification. *Child Development,* 1963, *34:*107–17. Copyright 1963 by the Society for Research in Child Development, Inc. **3-9** Nisbett, R. E. Birth order and participation in dangerous sports. *Journal of Personality and Social Psychology, 8:*351–53. Copyright 1968 by the American Psychological Association, and used by permission. **3-10** Drawing based upon data from "Racial Identification and Preference in Negro Children" by Kenneth B. Clark and Mamie P. Clark, from *Readings in social psychology* edited by Theodore M. Newcomb and Eugene L. Hartley. Copyright 1947 by Holt, Rinehart and Winston, Inc. Used by permission of Holt, Rinehart and Winston, Inc. **3-11** Kohlberg, L. The development of children's orientations toward a moral order: I. Sequence in the development of moral thought. *Vita Humana* (1963), *6:*11–33 (Karger, Basel/New York). **3-12** Kagan, J., and Moss, H. A. *Birth to maturity.* New York: Wiley, 1962.

4-1 Osgood, C. E. The nature and measurement of meaning. *Psychological Bulletin, 49:* 197–237. Copyright 1952 by the American Psychological Association, and used by permission. **4-2** Tanner, J. M., Whitehouse, R. H., and Takaishi, M. Standards from birth to maturity for height, weight, height velocity and weight velocity: British Children, 1965, Part I. *Archives of Diseases of Childhood* (1966), *41:*467. **4-4** Jackson, C. M. Some aspects of form and growth. In Robbins, W. J., and others, *Growth.* New Haven, Conn.: Yale University Press, 1928. **4-6** Barker, R. B., and Barker, L. S. Sixty-five and over. In Williams, R. H., Tibbitts, C., and Donahue, W. (eds.), *Processes of aging,* Vol. I. Reprinted by permission of the publisher, Atherton Press, Inc. Copyright © 1963, Atherton Press, Inc., New York. All rights reserved. **4-7** Lehman, H. C. The most proficient years at sports and games. *Research Quarterly*

of the American Association for Health and Physical Education (1938), *9:*3–19. **4-8** Lehman, H. C. The age decrement in outstanding scientific creativity. *American Psychologist, 15:*128–34. Copyright 1960 by the American Psychological Association, and used by permission.

5-4 Hess, E. H., and Polt, J. M. Pupil size as related to the interest value of visual stimuli. *Science,* Vol. 32, pp. 349–50, August 5, 1960, a graph. Copyright 1960 by the American Association for the Advancement of Science. **5-5** Polyak, S. *The retina.* Chicago: University of Chicago Press. Copyright 1941 by The University of Chicago. All rights reserved. **5-15** Evans, R. M. *An introduction to color.* New York: Wiley, 1948. **5-16** Evans, R. M. *An introduction to color.* New York: Wiley, 1948. **5-18** Cornsweet, T. N. *Stanford Research Institute Journal.* 5 January 1969.

6-2 Zeigler, H. D., and Leibowitz, H. Apparent visual size as a function of distance. *American Journal of Psychology,* 1957, Vol. 70, 106–09. **6-3** Adapted from *Vision and touch* by I. Rock and C. S. Harris. *216,* 96–104. Copyright © 1967 by Scientific American, Inc. All rights reserved. **6-12** Brown, J. F., and Voth, A. C. The path of seen movement as a function of the vector field. *American Journal of Psychology* (1937), *49:*543–63. **6-15** Kahn, F. *Man in structure and function* (2 vols.) Adapted by permission of Alfred A. Knopf, Inc. Copyright 1943 by Fritz Kahn. **6-17** Hernández-Peón, R., Scherrer, H., and Jouvet, M. Modification of electric activity in the cochlear nucleus during "attention" in unanesthetized cats. *Science,* Vol. 123, pp. 331–32, Feb. 24, 1956.

7-1 Williams, H. L., Lubin, A., and Goodnow, J. J. Impaired performance with acute sleep loss. *Psychological Monographs,* 73, No. 14. Copyright 1959 by the American Psychological Association, and used by permission. **7-2** Kleitman, N. *Sleep and wakefulness,* 2nd ed. Copyright 1939, © 1963 by The University of Chicago. All rights reserved. **7-3** Kleitman, N. *Sleep and wakefulness.* Copyright 1939 by The University of Chicago. All rights reserved. **7-4** DeCoursey, P. J. Phase control of activity in a rodent. Cold Spring Harbor Symposia on Quantitative Biology, Vol. 25. Cold Spring Harbor, N.Y.: The Biological Laboratory, 1960. **7-5** Dement, W., and Kleitman, N. The relation of eye movements during sleep to dream activity: an objective method for the study of dreaming. *Journal of Experimental Psychology, 53:*339–46. Copyright 1957 by the American Psychological Association, and used by permission. **7-6** Williams, H. L. The problem of defining depth of sleep. In Kety, S. S., Evarts, E. V., and Williams, H. L. (eds.), *Sleep and altered states of consciousness.* Baltimore, Md.: Williams and Wilkins, 1967. **7-7** Kales, A. Effects of age on sleep patterns. *Annals of Internal Medicine* (1968), *68:*1085–86; data from Table 3, p. 1086. **7-8** Dement, W. Discussion. In Kety, S. S., Evarts, E. V., and Williams, H. L. (eds.), *Sleep and altered states of consciousness.* Baltimore,

Md.: Williams and Wilkins, 1967. **7-9** Hilgard, E. R., Weitzenhoffer, A. M., Landes, J., and Moore, R. K. The distribution of susceptibility to hypnosis in a student population: A study using the Stanford Hypnotic Susceptibility Scale. *Psychological Monographs,* 75, No. 512. Copyright 1961 by the American Psychological Association, and used by permission. **7-10** Hilgard, E. R. *Hypnotic susceptibility.* Copyright 1965 by Harcourt Brace Jovanovich and reproduced with their permission. **7-11** From Nash, H. *Alcohol and caffeine,* 1962. Courtesy of Charles C. Thomas, Publisher, Springfield, Illinois.

8-4, 8-5 Pavlov, I. P. Conditioned reflexes. Oxford: The Clarendon Press, 1927. **8-7** Hovland, C. I. The generalization of conditioned responses: I. The sensory generalization of conditioned responses with varying frequencies of tone. *Journal of General Psychology* (1937), *17:*123–48. **8-8** Fuhrer, M. J., and Baer, P. E. Differential classical conditioning: verbalization of stimulus contingencies. *Science,* Vol. 150, pp. 1479–81, December 10, 1965, a graph. Copyright 1965 by the American Association for the Advancement of Science. **8-9, 8-11** Skinner, B. F. *The behavior of organisms.* New York: Appleton-Century-Crofts, 1938. Reproduced by permission of Appleton-Century-Crofts, Educational Division, Meredith Corporation. **8-14** Miller, N. E., and Banuazizi, A. Instrumental learning by curarized rats of a specific visceral response, intestinal, or cardiac. *Journal of Comparative and Physiological Psychology, 65:*1–7. Copyright 1968 by the American Psychological Association and used by permission. **8-16** Clayton, K. N. T-maze choice-learning as a joint function of the reward magnitudes of the alternatives. *Journal of Comparative and Physiological Psychology, 58:*333–38. Copyright 1964 by the American Psychological Association, and used by permission. **8-18** Drawing based upon data from "Drives, Rewards, and the Brain" by James and Marianne Olds, from *New directions in psychology II* by Frank Barron, et al. Copyright © 1965 by Holt, Rinehart and Winston, Inc. Used by permission of Holt, Rinehart and Winston, Inc. **8-20** Lorge, I. Influence of regularly interpolated time intervals on subsequent learning. Teachers College Contributions to Education, No. 438. N.Y.: Teachers College Press, copyright 1930. Reprinted with permission of the publisher. **8-21** Bourne, L. E., Jr., and Archer, E. J. Time continuously on target as a function of distribution of practice. *Journal of Experimental Psychology, 51:*25–33. Copyright 1956 by the American Psychological Association, and used by permission. **8-23** Atkinson, R. C. A stochastic model for rote serial learning. *Psychometrika* (1957), *22:*87–95. **8-24** Crothers, E. J., and Suppes, P. C. *Experiments in second language learning.* Copyright © 1967, Academic Press, Inc. **8-29** Tolman, E. C., and Honzik, C. H. Introduction and removal of reward, and maze performance in rats. University of California Publication in Psychology, University of California Press, 1930, pp. 257–75. Reprinted by permission of The Regents of the University of California.

9-1 Ebbinghaus, H. *Memory* (Trans. by H. A. Ruger and C. E. Bussenius). N.Y.: Teachers College Press, copyright 1913. Reprinted with the permission of the publisher. 9-2 Jenkins, J. G., and Dallenbach, K. M. Oblivescence during sleep and waking. *American Journal of Psychology* (1924), *35:*605–12. 9-3 Underwood, B. J. Interference and forgetting. *Psychological Review, 64:*49–60. Copyright 1957 by the American Psychological Association, and used by permission. 9-4 Peterson, L. R., and Peterson, M. J. Short-term retention of individual verbal items. *Journal of Experimental Psychology, 58:*193–98. Copyright 1959 by the American Psychological Association, and used by permission. 9-6 Bower, G. H. Organizational factors in memory. *Journal of Cognitive Psychology* (1970), Vol. 1, in press. 9-8 Krueger, W. C. F. The effect of over-learning on retention. *Journal of Experimental Psychology, 12:*71–78. Copyright 1929 by the American Psychological Association, and used by permission.

10-3 From *Technology of teaching* by B. F. Skinner. Copyright © 1968. Reprinted by permission of the publishers, Appleton-Century-Crofts, Educational Division, Meredith Corporation. 10-4 By permission of the Director, Computer Assisted Instruction Laboratory, The Pennsylvania State University. 10-6 Harlow, H. F. The formation of learning sets. *Psychological Review, 56:*51–65. Copyright 1949 by the American Psychological Association, and used by permission. 10-7 Sperry, R. W. Cerebral organization and behavior. *Science,* Vol. 133, pp. 1749–57, June 2, 1961, a drawing. Copyright 1961 by the American Association for the Advancement of Science. 10-8 Spence, K. W., and Norris, E. B. Eyelid conditioning as a function of the inter-trial interval. *Journal of Experimental Psychology, 40:*716–20. Copyright 1946 by the American Psychological Association, and used by permission. 10-10 Sarason, S. B., Mandler, G., and Craighill, P. G. The effect of differential instructions on anxiety and learning. *Journal of Abnormal and Social Psychology, 47:*561–65. Copyright 1952 by the American Psychological Association, and used by permission. 10-11 Spielberger, D. C. The effects of manifest anxiety on the academic achievement of college students. *Mental Hygiene* (1962), *46:*420–26.

11-2 Maclay, H., and Ware, E. E. Cross-cultural use of the semantic differential. Reprinted from *Behavioral Science,* Volume 6, No. 3, 1961, by permission of James G. Miller, M.D., Ph.D., Editor. 11-4 Heidbreder, E. The attainment of concepts: III. The problem. *Journal of Psychology* (1947), *24:*93–138; adaptation of Table 1 and Figure 1. 11-6 Neisser, U. *Cognitive psychology.* N.Y.: Appleton-Century-Crofts, 1966. Reproduced by permission of Appleton-Century-Crofts, Educational Division, Meredith Corporation. 11-7 Kuenne, M. R. Experimental investigation of the relation of language to transposition behavior in young children. *Journal of Experimental Psychology, 36:*471–90. Copyright 1946 by the American Psychological Association, and used by permission. 11-8

Green, B. F. *Digital computers in research.* Copyright 1963 by McGraw-Hill, Inc. Used with permission of McGraw-Hill Book Company. 11-9 Feigenbaum, E. A., and Feldman, J. (eds.). *Computers and thought.* Copyright 1963 by McGraw-Hill, Inc. Used with permission of McGraw-Hill Book Company.

12-1 Dashiell, J. F. A quantitative demonstration of animal drive. *Journal of Comparative Psychology* (1925), *5:*205–08. 12-2 Heron, W. T., and Skinner, B. F. Changes in hunger during starvation. *Psychological Record* (1937), *1:*340–46. 12-4 Cannon, W. B. Hunger and thirst. In Murchison, C. (ed.), *Handbook of General Experimental Psychology.* Worchester, Mass.: Clark University Press, 1934. 12-9 Berlyne, D. E. Curiosity and exploration. *Science,* Vol. 153, pp. 25–33, July 1, 1966. Copyright 1966 by the American Association for the Advancement of Science.

13-1 From *Motives in fantasy, action, and society* by John W. Atkinson. Copyright © 1958, by Litton Educational Publishing, Inc., by permission of Van Nostrand Reinhold Company. 13-2 Sears, R. R., Whiting, J. W. M., Nowlis, V., and Sears, P. S. Some child rearing antecedents of aggression and dependency in young children. *Genetic Psychology Monographs* (1953), *47:*135–234; adaptation of Figure 10, p. 225. 13-4 Hoppe, F. Erfolg und Misserfolg. *Psychologisch Forschugen* (1930), *14:*1–62. 13-5 Festinger, L. Wish, expectation, and group standards as affecting level of aspiration. *Journal of Abnormal and Social Psychology, 37:*184–200. Copyright 1942 by the American Psychological Association, and used by permission. 13-6 Lowell, E. L. A methodological study of projectively measured achievement motivation. Unpublished M.A. thesis, Wesleyan University, 1950. And McClelland, D. C. (ed.). *Studies in motivation.* N.Y.: Appleton-Century-Crofts, 1955. Reproduced by permission of Appleton-Century-Crofts, Educational Division, Meredith Corporation. 13-7 Atkinson, J. W., and Litwin, G. H. Achievement motive and test anxiety conceived as motive to approach success and motive to avoid failure. *Journal of Abnormal and Social Psychology, 60:*52–63. Copyright 1960 by the American Psychological Association, and reproduced by permission.

14-1 Ax, A. F. The physiological differentiation between fear and anger in humans. *Psychosomatic Medicine* (1953), *15:*433–42. 14-2 Schnore, M. M. Individual patterns of physiological activity as a function of task differences and degree of arousal. *Journal of Experimental Psychology, 58:*122. Copyright 1959 by the American Psychological Association, and used by permission. 14-4 Bayley, N. A study of the crying of infants during mental and physical tests. *Journal of Genetic Psychology* (1932), *40:*306–29; adaptation of Figure 1. 14-5 Miller, N. E. Fear as an acquired drive. *Journal of Experimental Psychology, 38:*89–101. Copyright 1948 by the American Psychological Association, and used by permission.

15-2 Thurstone, L. L., and Thurstone, T. G. Factorial studies of intelligence. *Psychometric Monographs,* No. 2. Copyright 1941 The University of Chicago. All rights reserved. 15-4 Terman, L. M., and Merrill, M. A. *Measuring intelligence.* Boston: Houghton Mifflin, 1937. Adaptation of Figure 1, p. 37. 15-6, 15-7 Guilford, J. P. *The nature of human intelligence.* Copyright © 1967 by McGraw-Hill Book Company. 15-8 Baldwin, B. T., and Stecher, L. I. *Mental growth curves of normal and superior children.* University of Iowa Studies in Child Welfare, 2, No. 1, 1922. 15-9 Thurstone, L. L. *The differential growth of mental abilities.* Chapel Hill, N.C.: University of North Carolina Psychometric Laboratory, 1955. 15-10 Sontag, L. W., Baker, C. T., and Nelson, V. L. Mental growth and development: A longitudinal study. *Monographs of the Society for Research in Child Development,* 1958, Vol. 23, No. 68. Copyright 1958 by The Society for Research in Child Development, Inc. 15-11 Schaie, K. W., and Strother, C. R. A cross-sequential study of age changes in cognitive behavior. *Psychological Bulletin, 70:*677. Copyright 1968 by the American Psychological Association, and used by permission. 15-13 Adapted from Masland, R. L., Sarason, S. B., and Gladwyn, T. *Mental subnormality.* Basic Books, Inc., Publishers, New York, 1958.

16-2 Thompson, W. R. The inheritance and development of intelligence. *Proceedings of the Association for Research in Nervous and Mental Diseases* (1954), *33:*209–31. 16-3 Hirsch, J., and Boudreau, J. C. Studies in experimental behavior genetics: I. The heritability of phototaxis in a population of *Drosophila melanogaster. Journal of Comparative and Physiological Psychology, 51:*647–51. Copyright 1958 by the American Psychological Association, and used by permission.

17-2 Eysenck, H. J., and Eysenck, S. B. G. *The Eysenck Personality Inventory.* San Diego: Educational and Industrial Testing Service; London: University of London Press, 1963. 17-3 Eysenck, H. J. *The structure of human personality.* N.Y.: Macmillan, 1960; London: Methuen & Co. Ltd. 17-4 Crowne, D. P., and Marlow, D. *The approval motive.* N.Y.: Wiley, 1964. 17-5 Cohen, A. R. Some implications of self-esteem for social influence. In Hovland, C. I., and Janis, I. J. (eds.), *Personality and persuasibility,* Vol. 2. New Haven, Conn.: Yale University Press, 1959, pp. 102–18.

18-1 Guilford, J. P. *Personality.* Copyright 1959 by McGraw-Hill, Inc. Used with permission of McGraw-Hill Book Company. 18-2 Vogel, W., Raymond, S., and Lazarus, R. S. Intrinsic motivation and psychological stress. *Journal of Abnormal and Social Psychology, 58:*231. Copyright 1959 by the American Psychological Association, and used by permission. 18-3 Matarazzo, J. D. The interview. In Wolman, B. B. (ed.), *Handbook of clinical psychology.* Copyright 1965 by McGraw-Hill, Inc. Used with permission of McGraw-Hill Book Company.

18-5 Hathaway, S. R., and Monachesi, E. D. *Adolescent personality and behavior.* Minneapolis: University of Minnesota Press. © Copyright 1963 University of Minnesota.

19-3 Brown, J. S. Gradients of approach and avoidance responses and their relation to motivation. *Journal of Comparative and Physiological Psychology, 41:*450–65. Copyright 1948 by the American Psychological Association, and used by permission. **19-6** Karsh, E. B. Fixation produced by conflict. *Science* (1970), *168:* 873–75. Copyright 1970 by the American Association for the Advancement of Science. **19-7** From the book *When We Were Very Young* by A. A. Milne. Illustrated by E. H. Shepard. Copyright 1924 by E. P. Dutton & Co., Inc. Renewal 1952 by A. A. Milne. Published by E. P. Dutton & Co., Inc. and reprinted with their permission.

21-2 Seeman, J. A study of the process of non-directive therapy. *Journal of Consulting Psychology, 13:*157–68. Copyright 1949 by the American Psychological Association, and used by permission. **21-3** Bandura, A., Blanchard, E. B., and Ritter, B. The relative efficacy of desensitization and modeling approaches for inducing behavioral, affective, and attitudinal changes. *Journal of Personality and Social Psychology, 13:*173–99. Copyright 1969 by the American Psychological Association, and used by permission.

22-3 Asch, S. E. Studies of independence and submission to group pressure. I. A minority of one against a unanimous majority. *Psychological Monographs,* 70, No. 416. Copyright 1956 by the American Psychological Association, and used by permission. **22-4** Campbell, A., Converse, P. E., Miller, W. E., and Stokes, D. E. *The American voter.* N.Y.: Wiley, 1960. **22-5** Courtesy American Institute of Public Opinion. **22-6** Kelman, H. C., and Hovland, C. I. "Reinstatement" of the communicator in delayed measurement of opinion change. *Journal of Abnormal and Social Psychology, 48:*327–35. Copyright 1953 by the American Psychological Association, and used by permission. **22-7** Bergin, A. E. The effect of dissonant persuasive communications upon changes in self-referring attitudes. *Journal of Personality* (1962), *30:*423–38. By permission of Duke University Press.

index

Page numbers in *italics* refer to figures and tables.

446; consistency in changes of, 529–31; defined, 523; measurement of, 523–24; social, and personality assessment, 426; see also Opinions
Attraction between persons, 513–15
Attribution of responsibility, 513, 514
Audiometer, 14
Auditory area, of cerebral cortex, 41
Auditory canal, 126
Auditory nerve, 127, 128
Auditory sense, 108, 122–28, 136; see also Ear; Hearing; Sound waves
Autism, 474
Autokinetic effect, 145
Autonomic nervous system, 43–45, 44, 45, 112, 336, 468; parasympathetic division of, 202–03, 203; parasympathetic division of, 44, 44–45, 45, 112; sympathetic division of, 43–45, 44, 45, 112
Aversion: learned, 310; as negative incentive, 308; and pain avoidance, 309
Avoidance-avoidance conflict, 443
Awareness, see Consciousness
Axons, 29, 30, 30, 31, 32

Babbling, in infancy, 71, 280
Balance theory, of attitude change, 529, 531
Barbiturates, 505
Basal mental age, 364
Basic research, 540, 541, 542, 556
Basilar membrane, 127, 127, 128
Behavior, 3–5; abnormal, 466–67; affiliative, 323–24, 324; aggressive, see Aggression; antisocial, and deindividuation, 518–19, 519; appetitive, see Appetite; aversive, see Aversion; compliance, and conformity, 521–23, 522; consummatory, 304; coping versus defensive, 459–60; and dependency motive, 322–24, 323; and hunger, 322, 322; maze, 4, 205, 205–06, 207, 218, 219, 221, 295, 296, 387, 387, 388, 541; and motives, 314–15; negativistic, 73, 376; novelty in, 201; operant, see Operant conditioning; physiological needs as determiners of, 295–304; purposeful, 324; regressive, see Regression; respondent, 196; retrogressive, 453; shaping, 201, 201–04; species-specific, 303; stability in, 410; voting, 526, 526–29, 527, 528; see also Conditioning; Drive(s); Habit formation; Learning; Motivation (motives); Needs; Reinforcement
Behavior disorders, 464–86, 505; see also Mental illness; Psychotherapy
Behavior genetics, 383–96 passim; see also Heredity
Behavior systems, 321
Behavior theory, of human motivation, 317, 321–24
Behavior therapy, 495–99, 497
Behavioral and Social Sciences Survey, 555
Behavioral observation, 435–36
Behavioral sciences: family of, 9–10; and social problems, 545, 547, 548, 552, 553, 555, 556; survey method in, 12, 12 n.
Behavioral specificity, theory of, 401, 409–12
Behaviorism, 5, 20, 163
Being (B) motives (Maslow), 330
Beriberi, 300
Biceps, 25
Bilateral transfer, and cerebral hemispheres, 260–61

Binet scales, 361
Biobehavioral science, 7, 11
Biological clocks, 166–67
Bipolar cells, and rods and cones, 113, 113, 115, 120
"Black box," 8
Black children, 77, 78
Blind spot, 114, 114
Blue-yellow color blindness, 119
Body-mind problem, 9, 162
Body types, and personality, 399, 404, 424
Brain, 35, 37, 47; and alpha rhythm, 180; electrical stimulation of, 37, 38, 38, 39, 39, 40, 42, 43, 207–09, 208, 237; and emotion, 336–37; evolution of, 32–33, 37, 319; hierarchical organization of, 33–37; Koestler's view of, 319; role of, 7–8; study of, 37–38; surgery on, 5, 37, 505; tumor of, 37; visceral, 36; see also Cerebral cortex
Brain stem, 34, 156
Brain stimulation, and reinforcement, 207–09, 208
Brainwashing, 533–34
Branching teaching program, 250, 253
Breast-feeding, 67
Brightness constancy, 136
Brightness of color, 118, 125
British Medical Association, 177
Broca's speech area, 42
Buddhism, 178

Caffeine, effects of, 180, 181, 181, 505
CAI (computer-assisted instruction), 248–50, 249, 254, 541, 548; flow chart for, 252
California Psychological Inventory (CPI), 431
Carbachol, 449
Case histories, 16
Caste, defined, 516
Castration, results of, 302–03
Cat(s): auditory cortex of, 155, 155–56; counter-conditioning in, 495–96; hypothalamus of, 337, 449; and sensorimotor feedback, 140, 140–41; split-brain, 260–61, 261; visual cortex of, 152
Catatonic stupor, 474
Catch trials, and ROC curves, 110
Cell body, of neuron, 29, 30, 30, 32
Census, U.S., 545, 552, 566
Centers, nerve, 47
Central cerebral fissure, 39, 40
Central core, of brain, 34–36
Central nervous system, 35, 43, 46, 336
Cerebellum, 33, 34, 36
Cerebral cortex, 33, 34, 36, 38–43, 114, 155; association areas of, 42–43; auditory area of, 41; of horse, 33; localized functions of, 38, 40, 41; motor areas of, 38, 40, 41; projection areas of, 38, 40; sensory areas of, 38, 40, 41, 41; of shrew, 33; speech area of, 41–42; visual area of, 40–41; see also Brain
Cerebral hemispheres, 36, 38, 39, 40, 40, 42, 114, 115, 127; and bilateral transfer, 260–61
Cerebrum, 33, 34, 39, 41
Chance distribution, 567, 567, 568
Channelization, of drive-incentive relationships, 305
Chemotherapy, 505–07
Childhood (children): aggression in, 320, 320; black, and racial identification, 77, 77–78; and

correlation with adult behavior, 79, 80; dependent behavior in, 322–23, 323, 324; first-born, 76, 76; foster, I.Q. of, 389, 390, 390, 392; gifted, 377; identification in, process of, 73–80; I.Q. in, and intelligence of parents, 389, 390, 392; I.Q. in, stability of, 372, 372; in Kibbutz, 70–71; language in thinking of, 286; mentally subnormal, 361, 375–77, 376; negativistic behavior in, 73; and peers, 76, 90; personality development in early, 66–73, 68, 72, 73, 406; preoperational thought period in, 63, 63; self-esteem in, origins of, 416; self-perception in, 417; separation from parents in, effects of, 70–71; see also Adolescence; Parents
Chimpanzee(s): fear in, 344; field observations of, 15, 15; insight of, in problem-solving, 216, 216–17; sign language by, 284–85, 285; token-learning by, 310, 310; visual deprivation in, 150
Chimp-o-mat, 310, 310
China: brainwashing in, 534; emotional expression in, 345
Chlorpromazine, 183, 479, 505, 506
Choice, individual, respect for, 552–53
Choice point, in T-maze, 205
Chromatic colors, 114
Chromosomes, 384, 384, 385; abnormal numbers of, 385; X, 384, 385, 394; Y, 384, 385
Chronological age, and mental age, 361, 364, 372
Clairvoyance, 156, 157, 157, 159
Class, social, defined, 516
Class interval, in statistics, 562
Classical conditioning, 189–95, 190, 191, 192, 193, 194, 195, 202, 205; defined, 190; discrimination in, 195, 195; generalization in, 194, 194–95; laws of, 191–93; Pavlov's experiments in, 189–91, 190, 200; see also Reinforcement
Claustrophobia, 470
Clerical aptitude test, 357
Client-centered psychotherapy, 494–95, 495
Clinical prediction, 433
Clinical psychology, 11, 490
Clinics, mental-health, 490, 500
Cluster analysis, in trait theory of personality, 402
Cochlea, 127, 127, 128
Cockroach, experiment with, on retention, 234
Codeine, 183
Coding process, in transfer from STM to LTM, 240
Coefficient of correlation, 18, 19, 358, 359, 572–77, 573, 574, 576, 577; cautions on use of, 575, 577; in inheritance of intelligence, 390–91, 391; linear relationships measured by, 575, 577; versus mean scores, and data on heredity and environment, 392; and product-moment correlation, 573, 573, 574; understanding and interpreting, 19–20
Coercive persuasion, 533–35
Coffee, effects of, 181
Cognitive development: conservation concept in, 63–65, 64; stages in, 62–65, 63
Cognitive dissonance, 329–30, 330, 529–30, 531
Cognitive process, 189, 271; learning as, 216, 216–20, 219; simulation models for, 289–91; see also Concepts; Thought
Cognitive styles, 425
Cognitive theory of motivation, 317, 324–29
Cold, sensation of, 130, 131, 132

Secondary-process thinking, in psychoanalytic theory, 413
Secondary reinforcement, 200–01, 206
Secondary sex characteristics, 83
Self, ideal, 418
Self-actualization: and existentialism, 331; motives toward, 330–32
Self-deception, 454, 462, 464, 508
Self-esteem, 93, *93*, 413, 416–17, *417*, 454, 535
Self-perception, 417–18, 513
Self-pity, 349
Self-recitation, 243–44, *244*
Self-reference, in motivation, 329–32
Self-understanding, and mental health, 507–08
Semantic conditioning, 195
Semantic differential, 272, 273, *273*, 415
Semicircular canals, 132
Senses, 106; general characteristics of, 107–12
Sensitivity groups, 500–01
Sensitizers versus repressors, cognitive styles of, 425
Sensorimotor feedback, in perception, *140*, 140–41
Sensorimotor habits, 189
Sensorimotor period in infancy (Piaget), 63, *63*
Sensorimotor skills, 209–11
Sensory adaptation, 109, 112
Sensory areas, of cerebral cortex, 38, 40, 41, *41*
Sequential activities, and limbic system, 36
Serial memorization, 212
Sex, 337, 345; as drive, 300–03, 317, 318; in psychoanalytic theory, 317, 318; sublimation of, 459; and symbolization in dreams, 171
Sex characteristics, primary and secondary, 83
Sex glands, 26, *27*
Sex roles, 73–75, *74*, 80, 96–98, 399, 466
Shadow and light, perception of, 148–49, *149*
Shame, 418
Shape constancy, 136, 137
Sharpeners versus levelers, cognitive styles of, 425
Short-term memory (STM), 238, 239, *239*, 240, 291
Siblings: identification with, 76–77; resemblances between, 390, *390, 391, 391*; rivalry between, 77
Sign learning, 218–19
Signal detectability theory, 111
Significance, statistical, 18, 20, 158, 571, 572
Simulation models, for cognitive processes, 289–91
Simultaneous contrast, and complementary colors, 119
Sine wave, 123, *124*
Size constancy, 136, 137, *137*, 138
Skeleton, integration through, 25
Skewed distribution, 564, *564*
Skills, sensorimotor, 209–11
Skinner, B. F., *4*
Skinner box, 196, 197, *197*, 203, 264
Skin sensations, 130–33
Sleep, 165; in infancy, 165, *166*, 169, *169;* learning during, 170–71; NREM, 168, 169, 170, 171, 172; "paradoxical," 167; REM, 167, 168, 169, *169*, 170, 171, 172; rhythms of, 165, 166, *166;* stages of, 167–68, *168; see also* Dream(ing)
Sleeptalking, 171
Sleepwalking, 171
Smell, sense of, *108*, 129
Smooth muscles, 27, 43, 47
Social attitudes, and personality assessment, 426

Social behavior theory, 409, 410, 411, 414
Social conformity, 465, 521–23, *522, 533*
Social delinquency, 91
Social effectiveness, in psychology, 555–56
Social indicators, 545–47, *546*, 548, 552
Social mobility: social indicators for, 545–46; and social stratification, *516*, 516–17
Social norm of conduct, 521
Social participation, and mental health, 507
Social problems: contemporary, 542–44; large-scale methods applicable to, 544–51; and program evaluation, 547–48; and psychology, 555–58; and social indicators, 545–47, *546*, 548, 552; university arrangements for study of, 551
Social psychology, 11–12, 512–38; and formulation of social indicators, 545; and problems of society, 555–58
Social Science Research Council, 551, 552
Social sciences, *see* Behavioral sciences
Social stratification, and social mobility, *516*, 516–17
Social structure, 512
Social worker, psychiatric, 490
Socialization: early, 67–68; and language, 71–72
Sociology, 9, 10, 12 *n.*
Solar spectrum, 112, 117
Somatotherapy, 487, 505–07
Sorrow, 335, *335*, 349
Sound waves, 123, 124, *124*, 125, 127, 128
Source traits (Cattell), 402, 403, *403*
Soviet Union: brainwashing in, 534; child care in, 70; nursery schools in, 67; psychotherapy in, 502
Spaced practice, in learning skills, 210, 211
Spastic paralysis, 25
Species-specific behavior, 303
Specific nerve energies, doctrine of, 130
Specificity, behavioral, theory of, 401, 409–12
Spectrum, solar, 112, 117
Speech, telegraphic, 281
Speech area, of cerebral cortex, 41–42
Spermatozoa, 83, 86
Spinal cord, 33, *35*
Spontaneous recovery, of conditioned response, 193, *193*
Sports and games, productive years in, *99*, 99–101
Spreading effect, in vision, 119
Stability-instability dimension of personality, 404, 405
Standard deviation, 365, 365 *n.*, 565–66, *566, 568*, 569
Standard error: of coefficient of correlation, 574; of difference between two means, 571; of mean, 570
Standard scores, in statistics, 365, 365 *n., 569*, 569–70
Stanford-Binet Intelligence Test, 364, 365, *365*, 366
Stanford Hypnotic Susceptibility Scale, *174*
Stanine scores, 359, *359*, 360
Statistics, 466, 561–62; and coefficient of correlation, 572–77, *573, 574, 576, 577;* critical ratio in, 571–72, 575; descriptive, *562*, 562–66, *563, 564, 565, 566;* errors of measurement in, 570; errors of sampling in, 567; frequency distributions in, *562*, 562–63, *563;* inference in, 566–72; measures of central tendency in, 563–64; normal distribution in, *567*, 567–68, *568;* population in, 566; prediction in, 433; in psychology, 13, 18–19, *577;* sampling theory

in, 13, 525, 566, 567, 570; scaling of data in, 568–70, *569;* significance in, 18, 20, 158, 571, 572; skewed distributions in, 564, *564;* standard deviation in, 365, 365 *n.*, 565–66, *566, 568*, 569; standard scores in, 365, 365 *n., 569*, 569–70; symmetrical distributions in, 563, *563; t*-test in, 19, 572 *n.;* variation in, measures of, 564–66, *565*
Status, social, 516, 517
Stereoscopic vision, 147–48
Stereotypes, 406, 422, 518
Stereotypy, 451–52, *452*
Steroids, 27
Stimulation, early, and later development, 61–62
Stimuli, 5, 48, 107, 153; conditioned, 190, 194; determinants in selection of, 154; discriminative, 196; patterns of, 135; unconditioned, and reinforcement, 190, 191, 192; and vigilance, 164, *164*, 165
Stimulus-response psychology, 5, 20, 189
Stimulus sampling theory of learning, 220–23, *222*
Stimulus substitution, 190–91, 201; *see also* Classical conditioning
Stirrup, of ear, 127, *127*
STM (short-term memory), 238, 239, *239*, 240, 291
Stream of consciousness, 163
Stress, 48–49, 267, 424, 446, 464, 480–81; early, 60–61
Striate area, of cerebral cortex, 40
Striate muscles, 27, 43, 336
Stroboscopic motion, 145–46, *146*
Strong Vocational Interest Blank, 412, 426, 431
Student-therapists, 502
Sublimation, 458, 459, *460*
Subnormal intelligence, 361, 375–77, *376*
Substitution: as defense mechanism, 458–59; symptom, 499
Subtractive mixture of lights, 117
Suggestion: in hypnosis, 173, 175, *175*, 176, 177; and placebo, 181
Suicide, 96, 517
Superego, 408, 409, 414
Superposition of objects, as monocular cue to distance, 148
Suppression, 458, *460;* distinguished from repression, 318 *n.*, 458; and release, 352
Surface structure, of sentence, 278, 279
Surface traits (Cattell), 402, *402*
Surprise, 335, *335;* element of, in laughter, 349
Surveys, public opinion, 15, 524–29, *526, 527, 528, 577*
Symbolic logic, 289
Symbolization: as dream mechanism, 171; means-end, *460*
Symbols: and concepts, 272–76, *275;* and meaning, 271, 272–73, *273*
Symmetrical distribution, 563, *563*, 567
Sympathetic chains, 44
Sympathetic division, of autonomic nervous system, 43–45, *44, 45*, 112
Sympathy, and weeping, 349
Symptom substitution, 499
Synanon, 499
Synapses, 29, 43, 47; at cell body of neuron, *30;* excitatory, 32; inhibitory, 32; and nerves, 29–30; and transmission, 31–32
Syphilis, 476, 489, 505, 548

B 1 2
C 3
D 4
E 5
F 6
G 7
H 8
I 9
J 0